RON SHANDLER'S 2020

BASEBALL FORECASTER

AND ENCYCLOPEDIA OF FANALYTICS

TRIUMPH
BOOKS

Triumph Books and colophon are registered trademarks of Random House, Inc.

This book is available in quantity at special discounts for your group or organization. For further information, contact:

Triumph Books LLC
814 North Franklin Street
Chicago, Illinois 60610
(312) 337-0747
www.triumphbooks.com

Printed in U.S.A.
ISBN: 978-1-62937-744-5

Rotisserie League Baseball is a registered trademark of the Rotisserie League Baseball Association, Inc.

Statistics provided by Baseball Info Solutions

Cover design by Brent Hershey
Front cover photograph by Peter G. Aiken-USA TODAY Sports
Author photograph by Kevin Hurley

Ron Shandler's
BASEBALL FORECASTER

Editors
Ray Murphy
Brent Hershey

Associate Editors
Brandon Kruse
Ryan Bloomfield

• • • • • •

Tech/Data/Charts
Matt Cederholm
Mike Krebs

Graphic Design
Brent Hershey

Player Commentaries
Ryan Bloomfield
Brant Chesser
Alain de Leonardis
Arik Florimonte
Brent Hershey
Brandon Kruse
Ray Murphy
Stephen Nickrand
Kristopher Olson
Greg Pyron
Brian Rudd
Brian Slack
Paul Sporer
Jock Thompson
Rod Truesdell

Research and Articles
Ryan Bloomfield
Patrick Davitt
Arik Florimonte
Brad Kullman
Stephen Nickrand
Jeff Zimmerman

Prospects
Chris Blessing
Tom Mulhall

Injury Chart
Rick Wilton

Acknowledgments

Producing the *Baseball Forecaster* has been a team effort for a number of years now; the list of credits to the left is where the heavy lifting gets done. On behalf of Ron, Brent, and Ray, our most sincere thanks to each of those key contributors.

We are just as grateful to the rest of the BaseballHQ.com staff, who do the yeoman's work in populating the website with 12 months of incredible content: Dave Adler, Andy Andres, Matt Beagle, Dan Becker, Alex Beckey, Bob Berger, Derrick Boyd, Brian Brickley, Ed DeCaria, Doug Dennis, Matt Dodge, Alec Dopp, Jim Ferretti, Greg Fishwick, Neil FitzGerald, Rob Gordon, Rick Green, Phil Hertz, Ed Hubbard, Tom Kephart, Chris Lee, Dan Marcus, David Martin, Bill McKnight, Matthew Mougalian, Harold Nichols, Frank Noto, Josh Paley, Nick Richards, Peter Sheridan, Andy Smith, Tanner Smith, Skip Snow, Matthew St-Germain, Jeffrey Tomich, Michael Weddell and Mike Werner.

Thank you to all our industry colleagues, a truly impressive group. They are competitors, but they are also colleagues working to grow this industry, which is never more evident than at our annual First Pitch Arizona gathering each fall in Phoenix. See many of you in Florida!

Thank you to Chris Pirrone, Ryan Bonini, and the team at USA Today Sports Media Group.

Thank you for all the support from the folks at Triumph Books and Action Printing.

And of course, thank *you*, readers, for your interest in what we all have to say. Your kind words, support and (respectful) criticism move us forward on the fanalytic continuum more than you know. We are grateful for your readership.

•

From Brent Hershey Most large projects of any value require teamwork, and this volume is no different. The diversity of member strengths on the Forecaster team is what makes this book such a unique and comprehensive endeavor. Whether they assist in the guts of the player box construction, or pen the fantasy-specific research works, or craft the sharp and insightful player commentaries, the contributors are the stars here. Special thanks to Ryan and Brandon for some additional heavy editorial lifting, to Ron for big-picture wisdom, and of course to Ray, who reminds me daily that I could not ask for a better a leadership partner. Praise also is due to Lorie, Dillon and Eden, who remind me that family is the best team of all.

From Ray Murphy This one's for my father, who passed away this fall. As is so very common, he gave me my love of baseball. In my case, it wasn't just the game itself, but the stats as well. I have two memories: On July 10, 1980 (thank you, baseball-reference.com), eight-year-old me begged my dad to let me stay up to watch just the first inning of a Yankee game with him. Dad agreed, and the Yankees cooperated by scoring 10 runs in the top of the first. I got to stay up for an hour, and felt like I got away with murder.

Somewhere around that same time, I was looking at the back of Ron Guidry's baseball card. I showed the card to my Dad, and said something like "Wow, Guidry won 25 games in 1978. That's amazing!" He responded, "Yes, he was amazing that year, but not because he won 25 games. Here, take his hits and walks allowed, and add them together. See how that number is lower than his innings pitched? That's how you know a pitcher is awesome." Life lesson.

Thanks, Dad.

From Ron Shandler It is humbling to think that some of you have been on this journey from the earliest days, when this nerdy stat geek was printing out player analyses on an 8088 IBM clone with a 10 MG hard drive. The fact that you continue to rely on the Forecaster midway through its fourth decade is astounding. I am forever indebted to you all.

But I am just one guy, and this annual project would never happen without a team of folks who are smarter than me, taking the early germs of insight and creating these annual epiphanies. Led by the masters, Ray and Brent, and along with Brandon and Ryan, I'm proud to continue to have my name associated with this effort. Thanks, guys.

Finally, thank you to the support from my family of amazing women, from Michele in Virginia, to Justina in Los Angeles, to Darielle in New York City… and Sue here in Florida, whose big birthday dinner got to be immortalized in this year's edition. I love you all.

TABLE OF CONTENTS

Marketplaces

In October, I took my wife to a fancy seafood restaurant for her birthday. There are plenty of these in Florida, but we had not tried this place before and it had come highly recommended.

Scanning the menu, there was a scallops dish—I love scallops—and the description sounded mouth-watering: *"Sea scallops, bacon, corn, edamame, butternut squash, wild mushrooms, white truffle, lemon butter."* The cost was $35, which was a little steep, but I was willing to pay it for a gourmet meal at a high-end restaurant.

So, the dish came out and it was not what I expected. It had just two large scallops; all the other ingredients had been chopped up into tiny pieces and molded into a little mound. This was not worth $35, I thought. Maybe I'd pay $20 for this stingy offering, but for the price, it was a major disappointment.

Perhaps I could have done more research and known ahead of time what to expect. Then I suppose I could have chosen something else. But the restaurant sets the price and if they think someone will pay $35 for that dish, more power to them.

Funny, but as I sat at that dinner, I thought, "This is exactly how I felt after having paid $35 for Chris Sale last March." I had never previously owned him but he came highly recommended. Really, you could almost replace "scallops" with "Sale" in the above narrative and you wouldn't lose a thing.

Hmmm... let's try.

"Scanning the draft list, there was Chris Sale—I love Sale—and the description sounded mouth-watering: *"Elite pitcher, career low ERA and WHIP; career highs in fastball velocity, bacon, strikeout rate, butternut squash, RAR, WAR, lemon butter."* The cost was $35, which was a little steep, but I was willing to pay it for a gourmet skill set at a high-end part of the draft.

So, Sale came out and he was not what I expected. He was helpful in just two roto categories (Ks and WHIP); all the other roto stats had been chopped up into tiny pieces and never made it to the mound. This was not worth $35, I thought. Maybe I'd pay $20 for this stingy offering, but for the price, he was a major disappointment.

Perhaps I could have done more research and known ahead of time what to expect. Then I suppose I could have chosen someone else. But the marketplace sets the price and if they think someone will pay $35 for him, more power to them."

Okay, almost a perfect comp.

In the end, the marketplace was wrong on Sale. I didn't have to say $35 when the bidding stopped at $34, but that was the price that the marketplace had set. It is just like the restaurant determining that their 4.40 ERA-attempt at a scallops dish was worth $35. Perhaps others were fine paying it—obviously, someone was—but that didn't mean I had to buy into it.

And for all I knew, the market value of the Ahi Tuna Nicoise ($39) was wrong too. Certainly the Miso Glazed Sea Bass ($42)

had a lot to live up to. Heck, I'm willing to bet there would even be a question about the Scottish Salmon ($25).

There are two secrets of success in this game; here's the first:

We don't have to buy into anything the marketplace tells us.

Now let's talk about the Trout ($40).

The Deboning, uh… Dethroning of Trout

This is the year that Mike Trout falls from the top of the draft board.

It's tough to fathom. He has been the de facto top pick now for six straight years. He is coming off a typically Troutian season, even setting a new career high in home runs (okay, that was no great feat in 2019). But there are potentially better candidates now.

At least that is what the marketplace is saying.

Ironically, it's not like Trout has been the top earner over the course of his career anyway. Since 2012, he's earned the most roto dollars only once. Truth is, any player's position at the top of the Average Draft Position (ADP) rankings holds a good measure of randomness. It is less a statement of a high ceiling as it is a statement of a high floor. And in fact, Trout's floor has been very high. Since 2012, here were his earnings ranks:

Year	ADP	Earned
2012	228	1
2013	3	2
2014	1	4
2015	1	10
2016	1	3
2017	1	18
2018	1	10
2019	1	18

There have been a few recent challengers. Mookie Betts nearly unseated him in 2017. Jose Altuve actually out-earned Trout for four consecutive years—2014-2017—but could not steal the No. 1 ADP ranking in 2018. In the end, the top draft seed has always defaulted to the easy pick—Michael Nelson Trout.

And that is much of the issue—choosing Trout has always been a default decision. It was easy. It could not be challenged. It avoided mockery. Even this coming season, if you do draft Trout first, few will diss you.

But there are several legitimate challengers this year. Early drafts have seen the likes of Ronald Acuna, Christian Yelich and even Cody Bellinger making occasional appearances at No. 1. They are the trio that finished Nos. 3, 4 and 5 in roto earnings in 2019. Coincidence? No.

For those who believe pitchers deserve their due, there may not be a more legitimate candidate than Gerrit Cole. Why a pitcher? Justin Verlander and Cole were the players who finished Nos. 1 and 2 in earnings in 2019. Take a look at the first round earnings history in the Encyclopedia and you'll see that at least two pitchers have finished in the Top 5 in five of the last six seasons. Yet we never draft them that high.

Given Trout's decline in stolen base output and the scarcity and value of bags these days, you have to give extra consideration to

the fleet of foot. However, it is the negativity of recency bias that has been inflating the importance of his 11-SB output in 2019. As BaseballHQ's news director (and—full disclosure—Angels fan) Jock Thompson writes in Trout's player box: "Running game slowed by nagging groin/calf/foot injuries, but should rebound some." We project 18, which ain't nothing these days.

But speed is a skill of the young and Trout is not so young any more. At 27, he is an eight-year veteran. Acuna is 21. Bellinger is 23. Perhaps we have to resign ourselves to a changing of the guard.

Yelich is an interesting case at 27. His seven years of major league experience is nearly as long as Trout's but he's only put up superstar numbers for the past two.

Um, no… that's not exactly accurate. At mid-season 2018, Yelich had but 11 HRs and a .289 average. From July 1 forward he hit .357, and from August 1 forward he slammed 21 of his 25 second-half homers. This year, a broken kneecap cut short his season in early September.

So, if we are to do our bean-counting correctly, Christian Yelich has been a monster hitter for the equivalent of one full season, one month and a week.

That's not to take anything away from the caliber of monster numbers he put up. Well… maybe a little, since five months and one week of that tenure was during the juiciest power era in Major League history. And, um… if speed is a skill of the young, and Yelich is not as young as we'd like him to be, *aaand* there's that darn broken kneecap… maybe those bags are not as sustainable as we think. It appears that there is enough here to doubt the viability of Yelich as the Trout Dethroner.

Acuna is a better candidate anyway, right? His numbers are irrefutable—heck, he nearly went 40-40 last year! Okay, let's bullet-point the potential issues:

- It's been barely two seasons at this level. Can we trust that track record more than the seven years that Trout has given us?

- His poor second half contact rate (65%) highlights the potential vulnerability of his batting average. Can we give the No. 1 pick to someone whose BA might be closer to .250 than .300?

- In the second half, he got the green light nearly 40 percent of the time he reached base. Is that sustainable?

- Um, why did he fall short of 40-40? Hip injury, folks.

It appears that there is enough here to doubt the viability of Acuna as the Trout Dethroner.

As for Bellinger, after two monster seasons in the past three, we have to consider that "monsterability" is part of his profile. His consistent teens speed output is at least comparable to Trout at this point, with possibly higher power upside. But 2019 was his first full major league season at this level. His player commentary proclaims "2018 is the early career outlier," but "outlier" seems to be a premature label for a player with barely three years of experience.

Recency bias has its hooks in 2019, and while Bellinger's rookie year showed early signs of what was to come, there is a sedate $22 season mixed in that reminds us of the other possibility. Remember the Skills Ownership corollary: "Once a player displays a vulnerability, he owns that as well." It appears that there is enough here to doubt the viability of Bellinger as the Trout Dethroner.

Long time readers may be amused that I'm trying to build a case *for* Mike Trout. But actually, what I'm trying to build is *reasonable doubt for everyone*.

Let's take a look at what our projections engine spits out for this book:

Player	R$	AB	R	HR	RBI	SB	BA
Yelich,Christian	$43	552	104	43	102	23	.319
Betts,Mookie	$40	584	128	32	86	22	.309
Acuna,Ronald	$39	599	110	39	94	31	.275
Turner,Trea	$39	581	101	20	63	43	.289
Trout,Mike	$39	497	113	43	100	18	.299
Bellinger,Cody	$35	550	106	41	104	14	.287

If you consider this the definitive statement about how these players should be ranked, it's not. Projections can never be considered definitive. To wit:

Player	R$	AB	R	HR	RBI	SB	BA
Yelich,Christian	$43	552	104	43	102	23	.319
Trout,Mike	$39	497	113	43	100	18	.299

Yelich and Trout are ranked No. 1 and No. 5, respectively, separated by $4, but what are we really talking about here? Trout bests Yelich by nine runs, but the advantage is flipped in the other categories. HRs and RBIs are a wash. We've already determined that Yelich's knee makes SB too close to call. That leaves 20 points of batting average. If Yelich gets one less hit per month and Trout gets one more hit per month—"…*one extra flare, just one, a gork, a ground ball—a ground ball with eyes!—you get a dying quail, just one more dying quail…*"—then Trout wins that category.

Basically, $4 is way too close to call. Any of those six players above could finish first (and if I had to choose one, I'd still choose the field).

Trout in the Rotisserie Era

If we are, in fact, about to witness the Dethroning of Trout, we need to celebrate one specific aspect of the accomplishment that could potentially disappear.

While Trout returned the 18th best earnings among all players in 2017 and 2019, he has earned Top 15 value among all hitters for eight consecutive seasons. Take a look where that ranks during the Rotisserie Era (1980-):

Most Consecutive Seasons Earning Top 15 Value, Hitters

Barry Bonds	9
Mike Trout	8
Rickey Henderson	7
Alex Rodriguez	6
Miguel Cabrera	6
Albert Pujols	6
Ryan Braun	6
Eddie Murray	6

(From the Rotisserie Hall of Fame charts at RonShandler.com)

That's amazing company. Can Trout tie Barry Bonds in 2020? It's possible, but the one scarce commodity that has helped elevate him in the past is the one that eluded him in 2019. And that may be enough for Bonds to hang onto his crown.

So, is Trout still worthy of the top pick? The answer is actually quite simple…

It doesn't matter a whit. All of these players are worthy, as are a handful of others. The statistics are too volatile to project with enough precision for it to matter. We forget that Francisco Lindor was a carved-in-stone No. 4 pick last year before his spring training injury; he clearly has the goods too. A Colorockan with skills like Trevor Story could easily have a monster season. Throw 2020's Mr. Overhype, Yordan Alvarez, into the mix—and caution to the wind. If you want to get a little excited, check out Austin Meadows' player box in this book.

Any flavor of superstar could put up the numbers.

The current ADP leaders—Yelich, Acuna and Bellinger—are certainly worthy picks, but their elevation is steeped in a heavy brew of recency bias. It's pervasive; Blake Snell and Aaron Nola were among last year's overdrafted poster boys, as were players like Bryce Harper and Carlos Correa in the years before that. But 2019 does not equal 2020, so assuming this year's ADP trio goes chalk, don't agonize over who to take at pick 4, or 5, or 15… *just pick anyone!*

That's why there are so many anyones who could rise into the first round, especially if the baseballs stay as juicy or dragless as they were in 2019. All it takes is a handful of errant gusts of wind and a few weak-armed catchers to pad the counting stats for any number of players. It just doesn't make sense to obsess over the names, or the ADPs, or the idea that any player should be attached to any particular draft round or dollar value. Here's why:

The Evidence of Our Ineptitude

Research has shown that you can win a 15-team league from any position in the snake draft seeding. I have a personal preference for the wheel, because I'd rather have two shots at the top players during the part of the draft with the steepest talent decline. But it is still all based on the assumption that we can identify who those top players are in a given year, and that we can accurately rank all of them.

We can't.

No, seriously. We *really* can't.

Last spring, I ran a simple analysis for *The Athletic* in which I compared each player's 2018 ADP to his actual earnings. Not rocket science here. The results were beyond my wildest expectations of futility. But that was just one year, so I ran them again for 2019. It was slightly better, but still pretty much confirmed that 2018 was no fluke.

It's worthwhile to examine the data. Using the ADPs of a 15-team mixed league, I looked at each player, round by round, and tagged each one:

- PROFIT: Turned a profit on the round he was drafted in
- PAR: Earned back the exact value of the round he was drafted in
- LOSS: Took a 1-3 round loss on his draft round
- BUST: Took a 4-plus round loss on his draft round
- DISASTER: Returned earnings outside the top 750 players, essentially undraftable in a league with 50-man rosters. Disasters are subsets of Busts.

Let's assemble the results into groups of five rounds, and 10 rounds, so we can accumulate meaningful enough samples to review.

2018 Rds	Profit	Par	Loss	Bust	Dis
1-5	21%	8%	27%	44%	4%
6-10	24%	7%	24%	45%	4%
11-15	27%	3%	9%	61%	27%
16-20	37%	1%	8%	53%	25%
21-25	41%	1%	4%	53%	21%
26-30	40%	0%	0%	60%	35%
31-35	15%	0%	0%	85%	76%
36-40	15%	1%	0%	84%	79%
41-45	19%	3%	1%	77%	76%
46-50	28%	0%	3%	69%	68%
1-10	23%	7%	25%	45%	4%
11-20	32%	2%	9%	57%	26%
21-30	41%	1%	2%	57%	28%
31-40	15%	1%	0%	85%	77%
41-50	23%	1%	2%	73%	72%

2019 Rds	Profit	Par	Loss	Bust	Dis
1-5	20%	13%	21%	45%	4%
6-10	28%	8%	12%	52%	5%
11-15	35%	0%	5%	60%	15%
16-20	31%	3%	7%	60%	27%
21-25	37%	3%	4%	56%	39%
26-30	39%	4%	7%	51%	33%
31-35	35%	0%	1%	64%	49%
36-40	32%	0%	3%	65%	55%
41-45	37%	0%	3%	60%	57%
46-50	33%	0%	3%	64%	64%
1-10	24%	11%	17%	49%	5%
11-20	33%	1%	6%	60%	21%
21-30	38%	3%	5%	53%	36%
31-40	33%	0%	2%	65%	52%
41-50	35%	0%	3%	62%	61%

For starters, let's get something straight… there is no such thing as "Player-X is a Y-rounder." We had *virtually no ability* to identify exactly where a player should be drafted. Over the first five rounds, we got about 90 percent of them wrong. Over the rest of the draft, the right answers were blind dart throws.

Our percentage of profitable picks did increase as we progressed through the active draft rounds. We managed to touch 40 percent a few times in 2018, but fell short this past year. However, much of that is just probability at work; the deeper you get into a draft, the more room there is for picks to finish higher. But in most cases the draft round was random; the results were more of a "blind squirrel" or "monkeys with typewriters" phenomenon.

Still, in the quest for profitable picks, rounds 21-30 were the sweet spot. Yes, we fared best after the active part of the draft was mostly over.

Also revealing—and sobering—was the fact that, even as early as the first five rounds, nearly half of our picks are full-out busts.

If there was any sense at all that the marketplace knew what it was doing, it was focused in the first 10 rounds. Outside of Round 10, things went south in a hurry. The mere "losses" shifted sharply to full busts and the disaster rate more than quintupled. I have been a proponent of the 50-round Draft & Hold leagues, but when upwards of three quarters of the players selected outside of round 30 were undraftable disaster picks, then it is our aptitude in this format that is the real disaster. Squirrels and monkeys, indeed.

2018 Rds	Profit	Par	Loss	Bust	Dis
1-23	30%	4%	16%	50%	15%
24-50	24%	1%	1%	75%	64%

2019 Rds	Profit	Par	Loss	Bust	Dis
1-23	30%	5%	10%	55%	16%
24-50	35%	1%	3%	60%	51%

This is a helpful snapshot. As I wrote in *The Athletic*: This is "the split that matters. In the active roster draft, a third of our picks performed at par or better; two thirds performed worse than where we drafted them. Fully half of them could have been considered busts."

One more time—*every player we drafted had, at best, only a one-in-three chance of being a good pick.*

This is all snake draft research, but we only have slightly more control in auctions. The final price for any player is still contingent on market perception, influenced by the usual laundry list

of objective and subjective variables. In a snake draft, I might push up a personal fave a round or two before his ADP, but in an auction I can keep upping my bid to some unknown breaking point. And it still has little connection to reality. After all, the "value" of any player is just what the last bidder is willing to pay.

So… we can't trust the marketplace to give us any more than a rough idea of what a player's value is. And the percentage play is to assume that valuation is wrong.

A Decade of Decisive Data

This is a good subtitle for alliterative purposes, but the statistical environment has been decidedly *indecisive*. That environment is the natural habitat in which we play the game, and thus, is where the marketplace lives. But over the past few years, when we expected regression, a trend continued. When we expected a trend, there was regression. Each year has been an elusive, moving target.

In all this statistical chaos, I have been comforting myself with the notion that "a rising tide lifts all boats." No matter what has been going on, these challenges have been affecting everyone equally, more or less. But that's been scant consolation when one year is smooth sailing and the next is a Category 5 hurricane.

This is yet another reason why it's foolhardy to trust the marketplace. Why should we think that *it* has more insight than *you*?

It is helpful to see how big of an impact the environment has had on our ability to project performance.

Power

	Players with		
Year	Tot HR	20+	30+
2010	4613	77	18
2011	4552	68	23
2012	4934	79	27
2013	4661	70	14
2014	4186	57	11
2015	4909	64	20
2016	5610	111	35
2017	6105	118	41
2018	5585	100	27
2019	6776	130	58

One year ago, we were relieved to see some regression off of the skyrocketing power numbers. So our 2019 projections reflected some flattening of the trends. Instead, the number of players who hit 30 or more home runs more than doubled, setting new records. Thank you very much.

You may have gone into 2019 feeling secure with your post-regression power from Jose Abreu, Bryce Harper and Matt Olson, but your league's winner was whipping you into submission with Pete Alonso, Ketel Marte and Christian Vazquez… and at a fraction of the cost. Yes, a rising tide—yada, yada, yada—but you went into battle with a well-earned Destroyer; the winner went in with a Carrier that he didn't even know he owned.

The trends above show just enough volatility for us to consider some regression in 2020; regression is always the default, after all. But is that wise? Especially when the real culprit is here:

Year	HR/F%
2010	9.4%
2011	9.7%
2012	11.3%
2013	10.5%
2014	9.5%
2015	11.4%
2016	12.8%
2017	13.7%
2018	12.7%
2019	15.3%

With no significant changes in underlying skill, the record-setting rate at which fly balls went yard laid waste to any semblance of projective accuracy. As we watched all those half-swing pokes land in opposite field seats, we could only wonder if the old power benchmarks were gone.

Imagine! Alonso, Marte and Vazquez combined for 108 HRs and cost $8 *combined* in mixed leagues last March. Fight that! Still, some might think, "There are surprises every year." Sure, but rarely like 2019.

There were dozens of players (yes, dozens!) who had long-term established power levels yet posted home run totals at least 50 percent higher than anything they'd ever done. We can attribute some of the power surges to normal skills growth for players like Max Kepler, Eugenio Suarez and perhaps even Jorge Soler. But it's tougher to explain away players like Omar Narvaez, Danny Santana, Roberto Perez, Marte, Vazquez and others. These were players who once pined for anything close to double-digit power yet slammed over 20 or even 30 homers last year.

Many owners—like me—spent the season chasing home runs just to keep up. For those whose desperation somehow found players like Pedro Severino and Eric Sogard on their roster during the year, the news is not good. We're probably going to be doing that again in 2020, and quite possibly with a different group of unlikely players.

You have to think all the way back to 1987 to recall a time when there were so many outlier homerun totals. Established regulars like George Bell, Kent Hrbek, Wally Joyner and Wade Boggs reached career highs that year. But there were also a bunch of lesser names who became sudden sluggers, like Larry Sheets, Brook Jacoby, Dale Sveum and Matt Nokes. For those players, 1987 was their power pinnacle, a level that they never came remotely close to in any other year, before or after.

If only we could trust that a similar regression could be counted on for 2020. But we can't, because we don't know what baseball will show up in 2020…

- 2019 regular season ball
- 2019 post-season ball
- Pre-2015 All Star Break ball
- Some other ball

While we won't know for sure at draft time, research has shown that we will know pretty quickly once the season begins—as soon as two weeks in. So be prepared to act quickly come mid-April.

Stolen Bases

| | Players with | | |
Year	Tot SB	20+	30+
2010	2959	35	19
2011	3279	50	20
2012	3229	48	23
2013	2693	40	16
2014	2764	39	15
2015	2505	30	7
2016	2537	28	14
2017	2527	29	6
2018	2474	28	11
2019	2280	21	8

Less than a decade ago, there were nearly 1,000 more stolen bases and the leaderboard was populated with three times as many high-end speedsters. With the current paucity at the top, the popular thought is that high-end speed should go for premium prices. But the players who provided 30-plus SB last year also provided a wide range of earnings.

Fast guy	SB	R$
Christian Yelich	30	$40
Ronald Acuna	37	$39
Jonathan Villar	40	$31
Trea Turner	35	$28
Elvis Andrus	31	$21
*A. Mondesi	43	$20
*Mallex Smith	46	$14
*Jarrod Dyson	30	$7

Even the 13 players in the 20-29 SB range included these four roster drags:

Fast guy	SB	R$
*Dee Gordon	22	$6
Manuel Margot	20	$5
*D. Deshields	24	$4
*Billy Hamilton	22	-$2

The asterisked players hit fewer than 10 HRs last year. In today's game, you can't afford to have a dead spot in the home run category. Allowing that a full season of Mondesi should prove otherwise, there were still five other powerless 20-plus base-stealers whose roster-worthiness is questionable. It's tough when nearly 25 percent of players providing a desperately-needed skill in one category also inflict a severe burden on another category. Happy hunting.

Starting Pitching

| | Number of Pitchers with | | | | |
Year	200 IP	200 K	15 W	*10 W	*95mph FB
2010	50	15	24	93	50
2011	39	14	20	86	57
2012	31	13	27	84	61
2013	36	12	16	82	74
2014	34	13	25	83	76
2015	28	18	13	70	100
2016	15	12	23	70	107
2017	15	16	17	74	116
2018	13	18	19	59	130
2019	15	24	16	74	114

* includes relief pitchers

The splintering of innings among more and more pitchers has impacted our ability to build a staff that reaches acceptable productivity levels.

- A decade ago, each owner in a 15-team league could roster three 200-inning pitchers; now barely one.
- In 2019, almost all teams could roster a *second* 200-strikeout hurler after spending the past decade being hopeful of getting just one.
- A decade ago, you could count on rostering a half dozen pitchers who would get you 10 wins. Should 2018 scare us into wondering if we'll be able to roster more than three?

Call me naïve, but I wonder how more and more pitchers are suddenly able to increase a core skill like fastball velocity. For so long, we just assumed that human beings had physical limits. Back in 2006, Joel Zumaya's 100 mph fastball was viewed as a freak of nature; over the remaining four years of his career, he spent more days on the IL than on the mound. Wasn't that a sufficient cautionary tale to dissuade others from testing anatomical barriers? Apparently not—now everyone is doing it, and successfully! (Rising IL days be damned…)

More than twice as many pitchers are ticking 95 mph on radar guns as were a decade ago. I suppose it shouldn't be surprising; we have always revered extreme anything—power, speed, velocity. The obvious questions now: Where is the *real* limit? Is there a real limit? And how do we project it?

Relief Pitching

A more comprehensive version of the following chart appears in the Encyclopedia, but this extended timeline provides a better view of our bullpen investment trends. *Avg R$* represents the average purchase price for all pitchers drafted specifically for saves. *Failure %* is the percentage of saves sources drafted that did not return at least 50 percent of their purchase price.

Year	Avg R$	Failure %
2002	$22.00	29%
2003	$21.97	59%
2004	$19.78	38%
2005	$20.79	43%
2006	$17.80	33%
2007	$17.67	36%
2008	$17.78	31%
2009	$17.56	32%
2010	$16.96	25%
2011	$15.47	37%
2012	$15.28	66%
2013	$15.55	31%
2014	$15.54	39%
2015	$14.79	45%
2016	$13.30	58%
2017	$13.63	53%
2018	$13.22	63%
2019	$13.29	58%

Our risk tolerance for investing in saves has gotten more and more conservative over time, and rightly so. Who dares pay $20 for any reliever these days? When it comes to the failure rate, we have had those periodic bad years in the past (2003, 2012), but things have really gone south in the last four years.

In 2019, drafters spent $412 on 31 closer investments. Those 31 relievers returned just $130 in earnings. That is not an aberration. And yet we will go into 2020 knowing full well that each dollar we spend on saves might once again return just 31.5 cents. But ya gotta spend it on something, right? This spring, you should not be able to put all your pennies into Kirby Yates without the shadow of Edwin Diaz carved into your subconscious.

The distribution of saves has been changing recently as well, splintering among many more pitchers, especially over the last three years.

Number of pitchers with saves

Year	30+	20+	5+	1+
2010	14	29	48	125
2011	19	28	49	125
2012	15	27	49	141
2013	19	28	42	130
2014	17	25	49	134
2015	21	28	47	145
2016	16	22	53	148
2017	11	23	52	162
2018	11	20	59	165
2019	11	22	52	199

In basic terms, every owner in a 15-team league used to be able to draft at least one 30-save closer, and often two. Now, upwards of half the owners have to settle for a frontline closer whose saves total will top out in the 20s.

With bullpen usage continuing to evolve, it's very possible this situation will become even more muddled. Openers? Bulk men? Specialists? Closers? And now every arm on the mound has to face at least three batters. Consider what all these changes have been forcing us to do over the past two years:

- Separate starters from openers to preserve the chances of getting a Win.
- Identify who will be successful bulk men in hopes of vulturing Wins.
- Figure out if the pitchers in any of these new roles could morph into closers.
- Figure out if these roles will continue to be fluid or if a fixed structure will emerge.

In fact, if these roles remain fluid, starters workloads continue to decline and closer turnover continues to increase, all these roles may one day morph into a new, single role: Pitcher. Imagine the paradigm shift that might create in our leagues!

Playing time

Perhaps the least projectable elements of player performance are plate appearances and innings pitched.

The following is an accounting of roster attrition and gain, or what I like to call a Churn Chart. This represents the number of players who went on the IL each year, along with the number of players making their MLB debuts. It is not an exact one-to-one relationship, obviously—IL replacements are often players who already have MLB experience—but it gives us a sense of, well, the churn.

CHURN CHART — PLAYERS

Year	On IL	Debuts	% change
2010	393	203	
2011	422	239	+10.9%
2012	409	206	-6.9%
2013	442	230	+9.3%
2014	422	234	-2.4%
2015	454	255	+8.1%
2016	478	257	+3.7%
2017	533	262	+8.2%
2018	574	247	+3.2%
2019	563	261	+0.4%

The level of churn has now risen for five straight years. While not consistent, 2014 also represented a 10 percent increase over the prior four years. This is, roughly, a measure of the roster instability in our leagues. We are churning through more and more players to maintain an active roster.

In looking at the rising number of debuts, we have to remember that there is still a nearly fixed pool of plate appearances and innings in those 162 games each year. There are just more players claiming a piece of the pie, thereby driving down the amount of playing time that any one player can claim. The rising trend just makes it more and more difficult to manage our rosters. Project playing time? Ha!

There is good news on the horizon, however. The new MLB rule that expands each team's roster size to 26 while reducing September expansion to 28 will have an impact on these numbers. Analysts predict that the additional player on each team during the season will likely be another relief pitcher, which for the purposes of many fantasy formats will probably be irrelevant.

However, the number of debuts should drop because there will likely be fewer September call-ups. A slight offset to this could be an increased usage of the IL in September because teams may feel the limitation of only 28 players. Still, I expect the number of churned players to decline in 2020.

As a side benefit, this is particularly good news for fantasy owners in head-to-head leagues. We have forever bemoaned the irrelevance of the statistics in that all-important final week of the season, when the championship round takes place. The reduced roster churn could make the September playoffs somewhat more meaningful.

As a final benefit, the return to the 15-day IL for pitchers will also potentially cut down on the list's use for "nefarious" roster manipulation purposes. The IL data above shouts out the impact from the three years that the 10-day IL was used. With any luck, those plus-sized numbers will drop below 500 this coming season.

With all this uncertainty, it is no surprise that projecting performance is a challenge, and the marketplace has a tough time figuring out where any individual player fits. Imagine having to assemble 30 teams' worth of players into some type of ranking or valuation that even remotely reflects reality… Good luck.

But all hope is not lost.

An Answer

Here is the second secret of success in this game:

We don't need accurate projections. All we need are projections accurate enough to tell us when the marketplace is wrong.

That sounds like heresy coming from a book with this title. However, "accurate enough" is a bar that we can reasonably reach, and do quite well, thank you. Any other quest for "more accurate" has been proven to yield a level of incremental precision that is neither repeatable nor actionable. In truth, we really don't know what "more accurate" means anyway. (See: "Forecasting in Perspective" in the Encyclopedia.)

But "accurate enough?" Now, there's something!

The reason why "accurate enough" is, well… enough, is because our goal is not to get the best players—as if we could—but to stock our roster with the most profit. We find that profit by identifying errors in the marketplace using just enough sabermetric muscle to give us a sense of each player's general tendencies.

Lucky for you, this book is all about sabermetric muscle. We have been pioneers in deconstructing player performance for nearly three and a half decades, and this year we are adding a bunch of new tools to your analytic arsenal. They are all intended to provide a nuanced view of each player's skills without having to marry into rigid projections that infer something more than "accurate enough." Point #1 in the Consumer Advisory says it best.

But how can we assimilate all this information? Here's one way I suggest, using the tools in your very hands (or on your screen):

The **Mayberry Method** (MM) and **Total Control Drafting** (TCD) are processes that have been a part of this book's Encyclopedia for 10 years. They both embrace the whole concept of imprecision and "accurate enough." MM is an evaluative tool that provides a four-digit description of each player's skill set, plus three more characters that assess risk. Then TCD provides an approach that uses MM to build your roster.

TCD summarizes everything in two simple steps:

1: Create the optimal draft pool.

2: Get those players.

I'm not being flip; it's real.

Step 1: Create the optimal draft pool.

The purpose of this step is to narrow down the huge player population to a more manageable level. You don't want to be doing a market analysis on a thousand players when perhaps there are only 250 worth considering.

Here is where you employ the Mayberry Method to identify your best targets. The four-digit score rates, in order, power, speed, batting average and plate appearances (for pitchers—ERA, strikeouts, saves and innings) on a scale of 0 to 5. Higher numbers are better, so if you just target players whose skills are rated 3 or above, you can start weeding out the chaff.

Then, if you sort players by their MM groups, you can assemble pockets of like-skilled commodities. MM says that players within a group have comparable skills and could be considered

more-or-less interchangeable. Stats can be highly volatile, but skills less so. *This is your "accurate enough."*

Here is a sample group:

1445
Elvis Andrus
Lorenzo Cain
Ender Inciarte
Kevin Newman

This group contains moderately high average (4) full-time (5) speedsters (4) with little power (1). Our perception—and recent memory—of their respective stat lines might not let us see these players as comparable, but from a straight skills perspective, they are. Here's another group of like-skilled players:

4135
Pete Alonso
Matt Chapman
Edwin Encarnacion
Max Muncy
Kyle Schwarber

This is a group of full-time (5) power hitters (4) with decent batting average (3) and marginal speed (1). You might not perceive Pete Alonso as being comparable to any of the others, but a review of their underlying skills—and accounting for likely growth and regression—proves otherwise.

The Universal Draft Grid in the back of the book is very useful for this exercise. If you have the electronic edition of the book, especially the Mayberry scores in spreadsheet form, all the better.

Step 2: Get those players.

The marketplace is going to slap values on these players and try to rank them, because, well, everyone needs an ADP. But Mayberry says that the players in each of those groups have comparable underlying skills; if anything, they should be ranked nearly the same. But that's not what happens in real life.

Here's where you take control of your draft:

1445	ADP
Lorenzo Cain	105
Elvis Andrus	172
Kevin Newman	207
Ender Inciarte	312

4325	ADP
Pete Alonso	32
Max Muncy	86
Matt Chapman	96
Kyle Schwarber	109
Edwin Encarnacion	179

These ADPs are just rough estimates based on some early mock drafts last fall. But it doesn't matter because I could have used almost any numbers to represent the very fallible marketplace.

Most drafters will view these ADPs and perceive that the marketplace is telling them that Pete Alonso is the 32nd best player. No! All that "32" tells you is approximately when he would have to be drafted if you want to own him. It's the same as my $35 scallops dish, for good or bad. That's what it *costs*; it's not necessarily what it's *worth*. Only you can determine Alonso's worth to

your roster and whether that "32" is a draft round *cost* you are willing to pay.

The only use for ADPs (and Average Auction Values - AAVs) is to provide guideposts that tell you approximately how much players cost, not how good they will be.

The best part of these Mayberry groups is that they help reveal potential profit opportunities. The recency bias of Alonso's rookie season is going to inflate his asking price, so it's helpful to know there are players with comparable skills who you could roster later in the draft. Even pairing Mayberry with the projected dollar values in this book can provide insight. If the bidding on Elvis Andrus reaches his $27 book value, it is helpful to know that you can pass on that and target Kevin Newman's comparable skill set for perhaps $8 less.

That's how you build profit into your roster.

Formally defined, because it's important:

Cost: An assessment by the marketplace, expressed as an ADP or AAV

Worth: True value, expressed as end-of-season earnings or ranking, and estimated using MM

Together: A player's cost is not the same as what a player is worth, and the two often bear little resemblance to one another.

Projective accuracy is an afterthought. MM and TCD help us see the disconnects between skill and the marketplace. It also helps avoid the psychological pitfall of believing the marketplace is more important than it actually is.

> We don't need accurate projections. All we need are projections accurate enough to tell us when the marketplace is wrong.

That's it in a clamshell.

Admittedly, for me anyway, mastering the mental process of separating *cost* and *worth* has resulted in some significant fallout. I now find myself questioning everything I see, for everything I buy. On every menu, in every marketplace, everywhere. For instance, the complete cheat sheet of seafood AAVs looks like this:

Fish	R$
Lobster	$50
Sea Bass	$42
Grouper	$42
Ahi Tuna	$39
Scallops	$35
Halibut	$35
Bouillabaisse	$32
Swordfish	$29
Mahi-Mahi	$29
Snapper	$29
Shrimp	$27
Salmon	$25
Cod	$23

We already know that the Scallops will not return full value, which makes taking a chance on the more pricey seafood a bit more risky. As such, I can't comfortably consider the Lobster, or even the Sea Bass, which would force a Sharks & Scups strategy. I suppose I could spread the risk by going with the Swordfish or Mahi as my first pick, and hoping to get the Salmon later.

Then again, it might all depend on what the dayboat brings in this morning, or who the chef is tonight. These variables are going to affect my decisions no matter how high or low the environmental tide is.

Gauge the waters; check the weather. Or try a steakhouse instead.

• • •

Final Outs

This is the second year that I have had to write about important folks we've lost. I don't want to do this anymore.

On December 18, 2018, we lost fantasy baseball pioneer and Tout Warrior **Lawr Michaels**. This hobby started as a game driven by camaraderie and fun. As it evolved into a multi-billion dollar business, Lawr remained the heart of the industry, holding tight to the elements that made the game human. His creativesports.com website remains as a testament to his voice, designed to provide opportunities for new writers to hone their craft. This past year, Lawr was inducted posthumously into both industry Halls of Fame—the Fantasy Sports and Gaming Association (FSGA) and the Fantasy Sports Writers Association (FSWA).

On July 23, 2019, Rotisserie Founding Father **Glen Waggoner** passed away. If you ever wonder why this hobby exploded and didn't end up as just a boring parlor game, Glen was the reason. He took the rules crafted by Dan Okrent and gave them life in a little green book, published in 1984.

I had the honor of presenting him for his induction into the FSWA Hall of Fame back in 2012. An excerpt from that speech: "Glen took this set of complicated rules and made them fun. The writing was humorous, self-effacing—it engaged the reader and made us crave to have the same fun experience."

That was the key, to make us *crave* the experience. And we have.

On September 21, 2019, we lost BaseballHQ.com writer **Rob Carroll**. Rob was one of the nicest guys in this industry, with an intense love of our sport and its history. I hired him 10 years ago because he was an incredible writer, and he had composed player commentaries in this book for the past seven. Don't ever underestimate how difficult it is to write a player analysis in 70 words that is comprehensive, insightful and entertaining – Rob was one of our stars. This year's book is missing his voice.

Rest in peace, compadres.

Welcome to the 34th Edition

If you are new to the *Baseball Forecaster*, the sheer volume of information in this book may seem a bit daunting. We don't recommend you assessing its contents over a single commute to work, particularly if you drive. But do set aside some time this winter; instead of staring out the window, waiting for baseball to begin again, try immersing yourself in all the wisdom contained in this tome. There's a ton of it, and the payoff—Yoo-Hoo or otherwise—is worth it.

But where to begin?

The best place to start is with the Encyclopedia of Fanalytics, which provides the foundation concepts for everything else that appears in these pages. It's our research archive and collective memory, just as valuable for veterans as it is for rookies. Take a cursory read-through, lingering at any section that looks interesting. You'll keep coming back here frequently.

Then just jump in. Close your eyes, flip to a random page, and put your finger down anywhere. Oh, look—former #1 overall prospect (circa 2013) Jurickson Profar, who is no longer on the radar of any right-minded fantasy owner. But wait ... hidden behind that .218 BA is a .277 xBA, solid plate skills, improving pop and a second-half skills surge to die for. RandVar says he's a premium rebound candidate and one to consider for the end game. See, you've learned something already!

What's New in 2020?

Let's see ... where should we start? In fact, there's so much new in this year's version that we dedicate a whole page to the cutting-edge research that our team has been doing, much of it which we've incorporated into our player boxes. The full rundown is explained on page 11—for both veterans and rookies, it's required reading.

Also, answers to questions, such as: Can we use PQS to determine deserved wins? How does one churn hitters in weekly leagues? Are batter plate discipline metrics useful indicators of skills improvement? Do late free agent signings hamper performance? And much, much more.

Updates

The *Baseball Forecaster* page at BaseballHQ.com is at www.baseballhq.com/bf2020. This is your headquarters for all information and updates regarding this book. Here you will find links to the following:

Content Updates: In a project of this magnitude, there are occasionally items that need clarification or correction. You can find them here.

Free Projections Update: As a buyer of this book, you get one free 2020 projections update. This is a set of Excel spreadsheet files that will be posted on or about March 1, 2020. Remember to keep the book handy when you visit as the access codes are hidden within these pages.

Electronic book: The complete PDF version of the *Forecaster*—plus Excel versions of most key charts—is available free to those who bought the book directly through the BaseballHQ.com website. These files will be available in January 2020 for most of you; those who have an annual standing order should have received the PDF just before Thanksgiving. Contact us if you do not receive information via e-mail about access. Information about the e-book version can be found through the website.

If you purchased the book through an online vendor or bookstore, or would like these files earlier, you can purchase them from us for $9.95. Contact us at support@baseballhq.com for more information.

Beyond the Forecaster

The *Baseball Forecaster* is just the beginning. The following companion products and services are described in more detail in the back of the book.

BaseballHQ.com is our home website. It provides regular updates to everything in this book, including daily updated statistics and projections. A subscription to BHQ gets you more than 1,000 articles over the course of a year updated daily from spring training through the end of the regular season, customized tools, access to data going back over a decade, plus much more. For a free peek, sign up for our BaseballHQFriday newsletter at www.baseballhq.com/friday.

We take this show on the road twice a year via our *First Pitch Forums* weekend conferences. We just completed our 25th year of our Arizona Fall League symposium, *First Pitch Arizona*. It happens each October and it's the ultimate fantasy baseball getaway, where you can meet top industry analysts and network with fellow fantasy leaguers. This spring, we will present the inaugural *First Pitch Florida*—three days of baseball talk, spring training games, and the legendary LABR expert league drafts in St. Petersburg. Find out more about this great event on page 272 or at BaseballHQ.com

The 15th edition of the *Minor League Baseball Analyst* is the minor league companion to this book, with stat boxes for 900-plus prospects, essays on prospects, lists upon lists, and more. In an era where rookies matter, it is an essential resource. It is available in January.

RotoLab is the best draft software on the market and comes pre-loaded with our projections. Learn more at www.rotolab.com.

Even further beyond the Forecaster

Visit us on *Facebook* at www.facebook.com/baseballhq. "Like" the BaseballHQ page for updates, photos from events and links to other important stuff.

Follow us on *Twitter*. Site updates are tweeted from @BaseballHQ and many of our writers share their insights from their own personal accounts. We even have a list to follow: www.twitter.com/BaseballHQ/lists/hq-staff.

But back to baseball. Your winter comfort awaits.

—Brent Hershey and Ray Murphy

CONSUMER ADVISORY

AN IMPORTANT MESSAGE FOR FANTASY LEAGUERS
REGARDING PROPER USAGE OF THE *BASEBALL FORECASTER*

This document is provided in compliance with authorities to outline the prospective risks and hazards possible in the event that the Baseball Forecaster is used incorrectly. Please be aware of these potentially dangerous situations and avoid them. The publisher assumes no risk related to any financial loss or stress-induced illnesses caused by ignoring the items as described below.

1. The statistical projections in this book are intended as general guidelines, not as gospel. It is highly dangerous to use the projected statistics alone, and then live and die by them. That's like going to a ballgame, being given a choice of any seat in the park, and deliberately choosing the last row in the right field corner with an obstructed view. The projections are there, you can look at them, but there are so many better places to sit.

We have to publish those numbers, but they are stagnant, inert pieces of data. This book focuses on a live forecasting process that provides the tools so that you can understand the leading indicators and draw your own conclusions. If you at least attempt your own analyses of the data, and enhance them with the player commentaries, you can paint more robust, colorful pictures of the future.

In other words...

If you bought this book purely for the projected statistics and do not intend to spend at least some time learning about the process, then you might as well just buy an $8 magazine.

2. The player commentaries in this book are written by humans, just like you. These commentaries provide an overall evaluation of performance and likely future direction, but 70-word capsules cannot capture everything. Your greatest value will be to use these as a springboard to your own analysis of the data. Odds are, if you take the time, you'll find hidden indicators that we might have missed. Forecaster veterans say that this self-guided excursion is the best part of owning the book.

3. This book does not attempt to tackle playing time. Rather than making arbitrary decisions about how roles will shake out, the focus is on performance. The playing time projections presented here are merely to help you better evaluate each player's talent. Our online preseason projections update provides more current AB and IP expectations based on how roles are being assigned.

4. The dollar values in this book are intended solely for player-to-player comparisons. They are not driven by a finite pool of playing time—which is required for valuation systems to work properly—so they cannot be used for bid values to be used in your own draft.

There are two reasons for this:

a. The finite pool of players that will generate the finite pool of playing time will not be determined until much closer to Opening Day. And, if we are to be brutally honest, there is really no such thing as a finite pool of players.

b. Your particular league's construction will drive the values; a $10 player in a 10-team mixed league will not be the same as a $10 player in a 12-team NL-only league.

Note that book dollar values also cannot be compared to those published at BaseballHQ.com as the online values are generated by a more finite player pool.

5. Do not pass judgment on the effectiveness of this book based on the performance of a few individual players. The test, rather, is on the collective predictive value of the book's methods. Are players with better base skills more likely to produce good results than bad ones? Years of research suggest that the answer is "yes." Does that mean that every high skilled player will do well? No. But many more of them will perform well than will the average low-skilled player. You should always side with the better percentage plays, but recognize that there are factors we cannot predict. Good decisions that beget bad outcomes do not invalidate the methods.

6. If your copy of this book is not marked up and dog-eared by Draft Day, you probably did not get as much value out of it as you might have.

7. This edition of the Forecaster is not intended to provide absorbency for spills of more than 7.5 ounces.

8. This edition is not intended to provide stabilizing weight for more than 18 sheets of 20 lb. paper in winds of more than 45 mph.

9. The pages of this book are not recommended for avian waste collection. In independent laboratory studies, 87% of migratory water fowl refused to excrete on interior pages, even when coaxed.

10. This book, when rolled into a cylindrical shape, is not intended to be used as a weapon for any purpose, including but not limited to insect extermination, canine training or to influence bidding behavior at a fantasy draft.

Welcome to ... our new metrics!

The game is always in motion, as the players, team tactics (some above-board and some ... ahem, not so much) and measuring systems continue to get more advanced and sophisticated year after year.

One of our main goals in assembling the *Baseball Forecaster* is to always be abreast of these meta-level changes. Once we can accurately determine—often through the hard work of our research staff—how the new information affects our ability to project individual performance, we strive to incorporate them as a part of our toolbox. And then, by extension, they are a part of yours.

This year, we've made several significant changes to the player boxes that we feel better assist us all in providing a snapshot of that player's history, that subsequently contributes to projecting his performance for 2020. Walk along with us as we stroll through and point out the new gauges and tweaks we've made. Some of these might be different at first, but we feel all will have lasting impact on our projections process.

Batter boxes

Plate Appearances replace At-Bats

The first change is an easy one: the intent of the AB column was to capture playing time, but PA does a better job, giving a fuller representation of each time a batter steps into the box. *[Note: for stat lines that use minor-league stats, our minor-league PA calculation is just AB+BB. It doesn't include SF, HBP, Sac, etc.]*

Changing OPS and OPS vL/vR to OPS+

In this era where the league run-scoring environment is a moving target year-over-year, those environmental differences can make it hard to separate changes in individual player performance from league-wide changes. The answer to this problem is to use indexed stats. OPS+ is one such stat: it just takes OPS and divides it by the league average for each season. Thus, an OPS+ of 100 is league average; 110 is 10% above league average, 90 is 10% below average. The same is true for the platoon stats; vL+ and vR+ is OPS in those platoon situations, indexed against league average.

xHR and xHR/F

With balls flying out of parks more than ever, we needed another metric to quantify power skill. Enter xHR, the product of Arik Florimonte's research (found on page 65). In short, xHR takes the Statcast exit velocity (EV) and launch angle (LA) from all fly balls by a batter, and compares them to all fly balls hit with those EV and LA in MLB from 2015-19, to find out the chance that each fly ball should have been a HR. This gives us a total of "expected" HR for the batter, which we can compare to their actual HR total. We represent this data in two ways in the player box: as a raw xHR total (MLB numbers only), and as xHR/F, so you can compare to historical HR totals and historical HR/F rates. (For a compelling example of xHR in action, check out Yuli Gurriel's box on page 102.)

Focusing on BPX and removing BPV

Base Performance Value (BPV) and Base Performance Index (BPX) relate to each other just like OPS and OPS+ above. In the past several years, we have run BPV and BPX right next to each other in the boxes. In 2020, we've removed BPV in favor of BPX, which is simply BPV indexed to league average (again, 100 is league average). So now, rather seeing and benchmarking a raw BPV number yourself, BPX gives context to exactly how the player is performing in comparison to his peers in any given year—especially handy in these times of rapid change.

Pitcher boxes

xWHIP

How does a pitcher's hit rate (H%) affect WHIP? Arik Florimonte explored this question, and came up with a new Expected WHIP metric (xWHIP) that can provide a road map for predicting a pitcher's WHIP for the following season. All the details begin on page 66, but we found the work compelling enough to include in our pitcher's boxes this year.

Ball%

As Stephen Nickrand's research on page 67 shows, Ball% is a slightly better indicator of a pitcher's control than First Pitch Strike % (FpK%), which we had been using for the past several years. Ball% is simply the percentage of balls thrown vs. overall pitches, and so discrepancies between Ball% and Ctl can give us indications on how sustainable a pitcher's Ctl can be.

OPS+ vL and vR

We've removed the overall opposition OPS (oOPS) column from the pitcher box, but the vL and vR splits remain. As with the batters, we are now showing indexed values for these splits, which we are representing as vL+ and vR+. Again, figures of 100 represent league average.

xHR/F

Just like with the batters, we are using xHR to represent how many HR we would have expected a pitcher to give up, based on their exit velocity and launch angle data. For the pitchers, we display this in terms of xHR/F, as the HR rate is much more easily digested than the total of xHR or HR allowed. Again, see page 65 for the original research on xHR.

Focusing on BPX and removing BPV

As with batters above, we have moved to the indexed BPX to represent a pitcher's BPV. It also is just scaled against league average BPV for pitchers.

As with all in this book, we welcome your feedback on these changes. Our goal is to provide YOU the best fantasy baseball prep tool anywhere.

—Brent Hershey and Ray Murphy

For new readers...

Everything begins here. The information in the following pages represents the foundation that powers everything we do.

You'll learn about the underlying concepts for our unique mode of analysis. You'll find answers to long-asked questions, interesting insights into what makes players tick, and innovative applications for all this newfound knowledge.

This Encyclopedia is organized into several logical sections:

1. Fundamentals
2. Batters
3. Pitchers
4. Prospects
5. Gaming

Enough talking. Jump in.
Remember to breathe.

For veteran readers...

As we do in each edition, this year's ever-expanding Encyclopedia includes relevant research results we've published over the past year. We've added some of the essays from the Research Abstracts section in the 2019 *Forecaster* as well as some other essays from BaseballHQ.com.

And we continue to mold the content to best fit how fantasy leaguers use their information. Many readers consider this their fantasy information bible.

Okay, time to jump-start the analytical process for 2020. Remember to breathe—it's always good advice.

Abbreviations

Fundamentals

What is Fanalytics?

Fanalytics is the scientific approach to fantasy baseball analysis. A contraction of "fantasy" and "analytics," fanalytic gaming might be considered a mode of play that requires a more strategic and quantitative approach to player analysis and game decisions.

The three key elements of fanalytics are:

1. Performance analysis
2. Performance forecasting
3. Gaming analysis

For performance analysis, we tap into the vast knowledge of the sabermetric community. Founded by Bill James, this area of study provides objective and progressive new ways to assess skill. What we do in this book is called "component skills analysis." We break down performance into its component parts, then reverse-engineer it back into the traditional measures with which we are more familiar.

Our forecasting methodology is one part science and one part art. We start with a computer-generated baseline for each player. We then make subjective adjustments based on a variety of factors, such as discrepancies in skills indicators and historical guidelines gleaned from more than 25 years of research. We don't rely on a rigid model; our method forces us to get our hands dirty.

You might say that our brand of forecasting is more about finding logical journeys than blind destinations.

Gaming analysis is an integrated approach designed to help us win our fantasy leagues. It takes the knowledge gleaned from the first two elements and adds the strategic and tactical aspect of each specific fantasy game format.

Component Skills Analysis

Familiar gauges like HR and ERA have long been used to measure skill. In fact, these gauges only measure the outcome of an individual event, or series of events. They represent statistical output. They are "surface stats."

Raw skill is the talent beneath the stats. Players use these skills to create the individual events, or components, that are the building blocks of measures like HR and ERA. Our approach:

1. It's not about batting average; it's about seeing the ball and making contact. We target hitters based on elements such as their batting eye (walks to strikeouts ratio), how often they make contact and the type of contact they make. We then combine these components into an "expected batting average." By comparing each hitter's actual BA to how he should be performing, we can draw conclusions about the future.

2. It's not about home runs; it's about power. From the perspective of a round bat meeting a round ball, it may be only a fraction of an inch at the point of contact that makes the difference between a HR and a long foul ball. When a ball is hit safely, often it is only a few inches that separate a HR from a double. We tend to neglect these facts in our analyses, although the outcomes—the doubles, triples, long fly balls—may be no less a measure of that batter's raw power skill. We must incorporate all these components to paint a complete picture.

3. It's not about ERA; it's about getting the ball over the plate and keeping it in the park. Forget ERA. You want to draft pitchers who walk few batters (Control), strike out many (Dominance) and succeed at both in tandem (Command). You generally want pitchers who keep the ball on the ground (because home runs are bad), though some fly ball pitchers can succeed under the right conditions. All of this translates into an "expected ERA" that you can use to validate a pitcher's actual performance.

4. It's never about wins. For pitchers, winning ballgames is less about skill than it is about offensive support. As such, projecting wins is a very high-risk exercise and valuing hurlers based on their win history is dangerous. Target skill; wins will come.

5. It's not about saves; it's about opportunity first and skills second. While the highest-skilled pitchers have the best potential to succeed as closers, they still have to be given the ball with the game on the line in the 9th inning, and that is a decision left to others. Over the past 20 years, about 45% of relievers drafted for saves failed to hold the role for the entire season (that percentage is over 55% since 2016). The lesson: Don't take chances on draft day. There will always be saves in the free agent pool.

Accounting for "luck"

Luck has been used as a catch-all term to describe random chance. When we use the term here, we're talking about unexplained variances that shape the statistics. While these variances may be random, they are also often measurable and projectable. To get a better read on "luck," we use formulas that capture the external variability of the data.

Through our research and the work of others, we have learned that when raw skill is separated from statistical output, what's remaining is often unexplained variance. The aggregate totals of many of these variances, for all players, is often a constant. For instance, while a pitcher's ERA might fluctuate, the rate at which his opposition's batted balls fall for hits will tend towards 30%. Large variances can be expected to regress towards 30%.

Why is all this important? Analysts complain about the lack of predictability of many traditional statistical metrics. The reason they find it difficult is that they are trying to project performance using metrics that are loaded with external noise. Raw skills metrics follow better-defined trends during a player's career. Then, as we get a better handle on the variances—explained and unexplained—we can construct a complete picture of what a player's statistics really mean.

Baseball Forecasting

Forecasting in perspective

The crystal ball aura of "predicting the future" conceals the fact it is a process. We might define it as "the systematic process of determining likely end results." At its core, it's scientific.

However, the *outcomes* of forecasted events are what is most closely scrutinized, and are used to judge the success or failure of the forecast. That said, as long as the process is sound, the forecast has done the best job it can do. *In the end, forecasting is about analysis, not prophecy.*

Baseball performance forecasting is inherently a high-risk exercise with a very modest accuracy rate. This is because the

process involves not only statistics, but also unscientific elements, from random chance to human volatility. And even from within the statistical aspect there are multiple elements that need to be evaluated, from skill to playing time to a host of external variables.

Every system is comprised of the same core elements:

- Players will tend to perform within the framework of past history and/or trends.
- Skills will develop and decline according to age.
- Statistics will be shaped by a player's health, expected role and venue.

While all systems are built from these same elements, they also are constrained by the same limitations. We are all still trying to project a bunch of human beings, each one...

- with his own individual skill set
- with his own rate of growth and decline
- with his own ability to resist and recover from injury
- limited to opportunities determined by other people
- generating a group of statistics largely affected by external noise.

Research has shown that the best accuracy rate that can be attained by any system is about 70%. In fact, a simple system that uses three-year averages adjusted for age ("Marcel") can attain a success rate of 65%. This means all the advanced systems are fighting for occupation of the remaining 5%.

But there is a bigger question... *what exactly are we measuring?* When we search for accuracy, what does that mean? In fact, any quest for accuracy is going to run into a brick wall of paradoxes:

- If a slugging average projection is dead on, but the player hits 10 fewer HRs than expected (and likely, 20 more doubles), is that a success or a failure?
- If a projection of hits and walks allowed by a pitcher is on the mark, but the bullpen and defense implodes, and inflates his ERA by a run, is that a success or a failure?
- If the projection of a speedster's rate of stolen base success is perfect, but his team replaces the manager with one that doesn't run, and the player ends up with half as many SBs as expected, is that a success or a failure?
- If a batter is traded to a hitters' ballpark and all the touts project an increase in production, but he posts a statistical line exactly what would have been projected had he not been traded to that park, is that a success or a failure?
- If the projection for a bullpen closer's ERA, WHIP and peripheral numbers is perfect, but he saves 20 games instead of 40 because the GM decided to bring in a high-priced free agent at the trading deadline, is that a success or a failure?
- If a player is projected to hit .272 in 550 AB and only hits .249, is that a success or failure? Most will say "failure." But wait a minute! The real difference is only two hits per month. That shortfall of 23 points in batting average is because a fielder might have made a spectacular play, or a screaming liner might have been hit right at someone, or a long shot to the outfield might have been held up by the wind... once every 14 games. Does that constitute "failure"?

Even if we were to isolate a single statistic that measures "overall performance" and run our accuracy tests on it, the results will still be inconclusive.

According to OPS, these players are virtually identical:

BATTER	HR	RBI	SB	BA	OBA	SLG	OPS
Villar,J	24	73	40	.274	.339	.453	.792
Eaton,A	15	49	15	.279	.365	.428	.792
Calhoun,K	33	74	4	.232	.325	.467	.792

If I projected Villar-caliber stats and ended up with Kole Calhoun's numbers, I'd hardly call that an accurate projection, especially if my fantasy team was in dire need of stolen bases.

According to Roto dollars, these players are also dead-on:

BATTER	HR	RBI	Runs	SB	BA	R$
Brantley,M	22	90	88	3	.311	$20
Mondesi,A	9	62	58	43	.263	$20
Bell,J	37	116	94	0	.277	$20

It's not so simple for someone to claim they have accurate projections. And so, it is best to focus on the bigger picture, especially when it comes to winning at fantasy baseball.

More on this: "The Great Myths of Projective Accuracy"

http://www.baseballhq.com/great-myths-projective-accuracy

Baseball Forecaster's forecasting process

Our approach is to assemble component skills in such a way that they can be used to validate our observations, analyze their relevance and project a likely future direction.

In a perfect world, if a player's raw skills improve, then so should his surface stats. If his skills decline, then his stats should follow as well. But, sometimes a player's skill indicators increase while his surface stats decline. These variances may be due to a variety of factors.

Our forecasting process is based on the expectation that events tend to move towards universal order. Surface stats will eventually approach their skill levels. Unexplained variances will regress to a mean. And from this, we can identify players whose performance may potentially change.

For most of us, this process begins with the previous year's numbers. Last season provides us with a point of reference, so it's a natural way to begin the process of looking at the future. Component skills analysis allows us to validate those numbers. A batter with few HRs but elevated power metrics has a good probability of improving his future HR output. A pitcher whose ERA was poor while his pitching support metrics were solid might be a good bet for ERA improvement.

Of course, these leading indicators do not always follow the rules. There are more shades of grey than blacks and whites. When indicators are in conflict—for instance, a pitcher who is displaying both a rising strikeout rate and a rising walk rate—then we have to find ways to sort out what these indicators might be saying.

It is often helpful to look at leading indicators in a hierarchy. A rank of the most important pitching indicators might be: Command (k/bb), Dominance (k/9), Control (bb/9) and GB/FB rate. For batters, contact rate tops the list, followed by power, walk rate and speed.

Assimilating additional research

Once we've painted the statistical picture of a player's potential, we then use additional criteria and research results to help us add some color to the analysis. These other criteria include the player's health, age, changes in role, ballpark and a variety of other factors. We also use the research results described in the following pages. This research looks at things like traditional periods of peak performance and breakout profiles.

The final element of the process is assimilating the news into the forecast. This is the element that many fantasy leaguers tend to rely on most since it is the most accessible. However, it is also the element that provides the most noise. Players, management and the media have absolute control over what we are allowed to know. Factors such as hidden injuries, messy divorces and clubhouse unrest are routinely kept from us, while we are fed red herrings and media spam. *We will never know the entire truth.*

Quite often, all you are reading is just other people's opinions... a manager who believes that a player has what it takes to be a regular or a team physician whose diagnosis is that a player is healthy enough to play. These words from experts have some element of truth, but cannot be wholly relied upon to provide an accurate expectation of future events. As such, it is often helpful to develop an appropriate cynicism for what you read.

For instance, if a player is struggling for no apparent reason and there are denials about health issues, don't dismiss the possibility that an injury does exist. There are often motives for such news to be withheld from the public.

And so, as long as we do not know all the facts, we cannot dismiss the possibility that any one fact is true, no matter how often the media assures it, deplores it, or ignores it. Don't believe everything you read; use your own judgment. If your observations conflict with what is being reported, that's powerful insight that should not be ignored.

Also remember that nothing lasts forever in major league baseball. *Reality is fluid.* One decision begets a series of events that lead to other decisions. Any reported action can easily be reversed based on subsequent events. My favorite examples are announcements of a team's new bullpen closer. Those are about the shortest realities known to man.

We need the media to provide us with context for our analyses, and the real news they provide is valuable intelligence. But separating the news from the noise is difficult. In most cases, the only thing you can trust is how that player actually performs.

Embracing imprecision

Precision in baseball prognosticating is a fool's quest. There are far too many unexpected variables and noise that can render our projections useless. The truth is, the best we can ever hope for is to accurately forecast general tendencies and percentage plays.

However, even when you follow an 80% percentage play, for instance, you will still lose 20% of the time. That 20% is what skeptics use as justification to dismiss prognosticators; they conveniently ignore the more prevalent 80%. The paradox, of course, is that fantasy league titles are often won or lost by those exceptions. Still, long-term success dictates that you always chase

the 80% and accept the fact that you will be wrong 20% of the time. Or, whatever that percentage play happens to be.

For fantasy purposes, playing the percentages can take on an even less precise spin. The best projections are often the ones that are just far enough away from the field of expectation to alter decision-making. In other words, it doesn't matter if I project Player X to bat .320 and he only bats .295; it matters that I project .320 and everyone else projects .280. Those who follow my less-accurate projection will go the extra dollar to acquire him in their draft.

Or, perhaps we should evaluate the projections based upon their intrinsic value. For instance, coming into 2019, would it have been more important for me to tell you that J.D. Martinez was going to hit 35 HRs or that Josh Bell would hit 25 HRs (when all other touts predicted fewer)? By season's end, the Martinez projection would have been more accurate, but the Bell projection—even though it was off by 12 HRs—would have been far more valuable. The Bell projection might have persuaded you to go an extra buck on Draft Day, yielding far more profit.

And that has to be enough. Any tout who projects a player's statistics dead-on will have just been lucky with his dart throws that day.

Perpetuity

Forecasting is not an exercise that produces a single set of numbers. It is dynamic, cyclical and ongoing. Conditions are constantly changing and we must react to those changes by adjusting our expectations. A pre-season projection is just a snapshot in time. Once the first batter steps to the plate on Opening Day, that projection has become obsolete. Its value is merely to provide a starting point, a baseline for what is about to occur.

During the season, if a projection appears to have been invalidated by current performance, the process continues. It is then that we need to ask... What went wrong? What conditions have changed? In fact, has *anything* changed? We need to analyze the situation and revise our expectation, if necessary. This process must be ongoing.

When good projections go bad

All we can control is the process. We simply can't control outcomes. However, one thing we *can* do is analyze the misses to see *why* they occurred. This is always a valuable exercise each year. It puts a proper focus on the variables that were out of our control as well as providing perspective on those players with whom we might have done a better job.

In general, we can organize these forecasting misses into several categories. To demonstrate, here are all the players whose 2019 Rotisserie earnings varied from projections by at least $10.

The performances that exceeded expectation

Development beyond the growth trend: These are young players for whom we knew there was skill. Some of them were prized prospects in the past who have taken their time ascending the growth curve. Others were a surprise only because their performance spike arrived sooner than anyone anticipated... Ronald Acuna, Ozzie Albies, Pete Alonso, Yordan Alvarez, Josh Bell, Rafael Devers, Keston Hiura, Austin Meadows, Yoan Moncada, Bryan Reynolds, Fernando Tatis, Shane Bieber, Jack Flaherty, Lucas Giolito, Mike Soroka.

Skilled players who just had big years: We knew these guys were good too; we just didn't anticipate they'd be this good... Cody Bellinger, D.J. LeMahieu, Jeff McNeil, Ketel Marte, Marcus Semien, Gerrit Cole, Mike Minor, Justin Verlander.

Unexpected health: We knew these players had the goods; we just didn't know whether they'd be healthy or would stay healthy all year... Elvis Andrus, Jorge Soler, Charlie Morton, Hyun-Jin Ryu.

Unexpected playing time: These players had the skills—and may have even displayed them at some time in the past—but had questionable playing time potential coming into this season. Some benefited from another player's injury, a rookie who didn't pan out or leveraged a short streak into a regular gig... J.D. Davis, Hunter Dozier, Leury Garcia, Ramon Laureano, Danny Santana, Giovanny Urshela, Christian Walker.

Unexpected role: This category is reserved for players who played their way into, or backed into, a larger role than anticipated. For most, there was already some previously demonstrated skill... Liam Hendriks, Ian Kennedy, Emilio Pagan, Hansel Robles, Taylor Rogers, Brandon Workman, Ryan Yarbrough.

Unexpected discovery of the Fountain of Youth: These players should have been done, or nearly done, or at least headed down the far side of the bell curve. That's what the trends were pointing to. The trends were wrong... Howie Kendrick, Hunter Pence, Jake Odorizzi.

Surprise, yes, but not as good as it looked: These are players whose numbers were pretty, but unsupported by their skills metrics. Enjoy them now, but be wary of next year... Tim Anderson, Kevin Newman, Jorge Polanco, Christian Vasquez, Jonathan Villar, Domingo German, Sonny Gray, Lance Lynn, Jeff Samardzija.

Who the heck knows? Maybe there are reasonable explanations, but this year was so far off the charts for... Mitch Garver.

The performances that fell short of expectation

The DL denizens: These are players who got hurt, may not have returned fully healthy, or may have never been fully healthy (whether they'd admit it or not)... Miguel Andujar, Carlos Correa, Khris Davis, Mitch Haniger, Aaron Hicks, Aaron Judge, Andrew McCutchen, Daniel Murphy, Brandon Nimmo, David Peralta, AJ Pollock, Stephen Piscotty, Andrelton Simmons, Giancarlo Stanton, Mike Trout, Carlos Carrasco, Seranthony Dominguez, Corey Kluber, David Price, David Robertson, Chris Sale, Luis Severino, Blake Snell, Jameson Taillon, Blake Treinen.

Accelerated skills erosion: These are players who we knew were on the downside of their careers or had soft peripherals but who we did not think would plummet so quickly. In some cases, there were injuries involved, but all in all, 2019 might be the beginning of the end for... Miguel Cabrera, Lorenzo Cain, Robinson Cano, Matt Carpenter, Dee Gordon, Josh Harrison, Matt Kemp, Buster Posey, Joey Votto, Justin Upton, Jake Arrieta.

Inflated expectations: Here are players who we really should not have expected much more than what they produced. Some had short or spotty track records, others had soft peripherals

coming into 2019, and still others were inflated by media hype. Yes, for some of these, it was "What the heck was I thinking?" For others, we've almost come to expect players to ascend the growth curve faster these days. (You're 23 and you haven't broken out yet? What's the problem??) The bottom line is that player performance trends simply don't progress or regress in a straight line; still, the skills trends were intriguing enough to take a leap of faith. We were wrong... Andrew Benintendi, Scooter Gennett, Jose Peraza, Jose Ramirez, Trevor Bauer, Edwin Diaz, Kyle Freeland, Yusei Kikuchi, Miles Mikolas, Max Scherzer.

Unexpected loss of role: This category is reserved for players who ended up with a smaller role than expected, perhaps through a bad start, bad luck or bad timing... Wilmer Flores, Billy Hamilton, Jose Alvarado, Wade Davis, Craig Kimbrel, Jose Leclerc, Andrew Miller.

Surprise, yes, but not as bad as it looked: These are players whose numbers were ugly, but supported by better skills metrics. Diss them now, but keep an open mind for next year... Jose Altuve, Mookie Betts, Jake Bauers, Paul Goldschmidt, Rhys Hoskins, Aaron Nola.

Who the heck knows? Maybe any one of these players could have been slotted into another category, but they still remain head-scratchers... Jesus Aguilar, Manny Machado, Travis Shaw, Noah Syndergaard.

About fantasy baseball touts

As a group, there is a strong tendency for all pundits to provide numbers that are publicly palatable, often at the expense of potential accuracy. That's because committing to either end of the range of expectation poses a high risk. Few touts will put their credibility on the line like that, even though we all know that those outliers are inevitable. Among our projections, you will find no .350 hitters or 70-steal speedsters. *Someone* is going to post a sub-2.50 ERA next year, but damned if any of us will commit to that. So we take an easier road. We'll hedge our numbers or split the difference between two equally possible outcomes.

In the world of prognosticating, this is called the *comfort zone.* This represents the outer tolerances for the public acceptability of a set of numbers. In most circumstances, even if the evidence is outstanding, prognosticators will not stray from within the comfort zone.

As for this book, occasionally we do commit to outlying numbers when we feel the data support it. But on the whole, most of the numbers here can be nearly as cowardly as everyone else's. We get around this by providing "color" to the projections in the capsule commentaries, often listing UPside or DOWNside projections. That is where you will find the players whose projection has the best potential to stray beyond the limits of the comfort zone.

As analyst John Burnson once wrote: "The issue is not the success rate for one player, but the success rate for all players. No system is 100% reliable, and in trying to capture the outliers, you weaken the middle and thereby lose more predictive pull than you gain. At some level, everyone is an exception!"

Validating Performance

Performance validation criteria

The following is a set of support variables that helps determine whether a player's statistical output is an accurate reflection of his skills. From this we can validate or refute stats that vary from expectation, essentially asking, is this performance "fact or fluke?"

1. **Age:** Is the player at the stage of development when we might expect a change in performance?

2. **Health:** Is he coming off an injury, reconditioned and healthy for the first time in years, or a habitual resident of the injured list?

3. **Minor league performance:** Has he shown the potential for greater things at some level of the minors? Or does his minor league history show a poor skill set that might indicate a lower ceiling?

4. **Historical trends:** Have his skill levels over time been on an upswing or downswing?

5. **Component skills indicators:** Looking beyond batting averages and ERAs, what do his support ratios look like?

6. **Ballpark, team, league:** Pitchers going to Colorado will see their ERA spike. Pitchers going to Oakland will see their ERA improve.

7. **Team performance:** Has a player's performance been affected by overall team chemistry or the environment fostered by a winning or losing club?

8. **Batting stance, pitching style/mastery:** Has a change in performance been due to a mechanical adjustment?

9. **Usage pattern, lineup position, role:** Has a change in RBI opportunities been a result of moving further up or down in the batting order? Has pitching effectiveness been impacted by moving from the bullpen to the rotation?

10. **Coaching effects:** Has the coaching staff changed the way a player approaches his conditioning, or how he approaches the game itself?

11. **Off-season activity:** Has the player spent the winter frequenting workout rooms or banquet tables?

12. **Personal factors:** Has the player undergone a family crisis? Experienced spiritual rebirth? Given up red meat? Taken up testosterone?

Skills ownership

Once a player displays a skill, he owns it. That display could occur at any time—earlier in his career, back in the minors, or even in winter ball play. And while that skill may lie dormant after its initial display, the potential is always there for him to tap back into that skill at some point, barring injury or age. That dormant skill can reappear at any time given the right set of circumstances.

Caveats:

1. The initial display of skill must have occurred over an extended period of time. An isolated 1-hit shutout in Single-A ball amidst a 5.00 ERA season is not enough. The shorter the display of skill in the past, the more likely it can be attributed to random chance. The longer the display, the more likely that any reemergence is for real.

2. If a player has been suspected of using performance enhancing drugs at any time, all bets are off.

Corollaries:

1. Once a player displays a vulnerability or skills deficiency, he owns that as well. That vulnerability could be an old injury problem, an inability to hit breaking pitches, or just a tendency to go into prolonged slumps.

2. The probability of a player correcting a skills deficiency declines with each year that deficiency exists.

Contract year performance *(Tom Mullooly)*

There is a contention that players step up their game when they are playing for a contract. Research looked at contract year players and their performance during that year as compared to career levels. Of the batters and pitchers studied, 53% of the batters performed as if they were on a salary drive, while only 15% of the pitchers exhibited some level of contract year behavior.

How do players fare *after* signing a large contract (minimum $4M per year)? Research from 2005-2008 revealed that only 30% of pitchers and 22% of hitters exhibited an increase of more than 15% in BPV after signing a large deal either with their new team, or re-signing with the previous team. But nearly half of the pitchers (49%) and nearly half of the hitters (47%) saw a drop in BPV of more than 15% in the year after signing.

Risk Analysis

Risk management and reliability grades

Forecasts are constructed with the best data available, but there are factors that can impact the variability. One way we manage this risk is to assign each player Reliability Grades. The more certainty we see in a data set, the higher the reliability grades assigned to that player. The following variables are evaluated:

Health: Players with a history of staying healthy and off the IL are valuable to own. Unfortunately, while the ability to stay healthy can be considered skill, it is not very projectable. We can track the number of days spent on the injured list and draw rough conclusions. The grades in the player boxes also include an adjustment for older players, who have a higher likelihood of getting hurt. That is the only forward-looking element of the grade.

"A" level players would have accumulated fewer than 30 days on the major league IL over the past five years. "F" grades go to those who've spent more than 120 days on the IL. Recent IL stays are given a heavier weight in the calculation.

Playing Time and Experience (PT/Exp): The greater the pool of MLB history to draw from, the greater our ability to construct a viable forecast. Length of service—and consistent service—is important. So players who bounce up and down from the majors to the minors are higher risk players. And rookies are all high risk.

For batters, we simply track plate appearances. Major league PAs have greater weight than minor league PAs. "A" level players would have averaged at least 550 major league PAs per year over the past three years. "F" graded players averaged fewer than 250 major league PA per year.

For pitchers, workload can be a double-edged sword. On one hand, small IP samples are deceptive in providing a read on a

pitcher's true potential. Even a consistent 65-inning reliever can be considered higher risk since it would take just one bad outing to skew an entire season's work.

On the flipside, high workload levels also need to be monitored, especially in the formative years of a pitcher's career. Exceeding those levels elevates the risk of injury, burnout, or breakdown. So, tracking workload must be done within a range of innings. The grades capture this.

Consistency: Consistent performers are easier to project and garner higher reliability grades. Players that mix mediocrity with occasional flashes of brilliance or badness generate higher risk projections. Even those who exhibit a consistent upward or downward trend cannot be considered truly consistent as we do not know whether those trends will continue. Typically, they don't. *(See next: Using 3-year trends as leading indicators)*

"A" level players are those whose runs created per game level (xERA for pitchers) has fluctuated by less than half a run during each of the past three years. "F" grades go to those whose RC/G or xERA has fluctuated by two runs or more.

Remember that these grades have nothing to do with quality of performance; they strictly refer to confidence in our expectations. So a grade of AAA for a poor player only means that there is a high probability he will perform as poorly as we've projected.

Using 3-year trends as leading indicators *(Ed DeCaria)*

It is almost irresistibly tempting to look at three numbers moving in one direction and expect that the fourth will continue that progression. However, for both hitters and pitchers riding positive trends over any consecutive three-year period, not only do most players not continue their positive trend into a fourth year, their Year 4 performance usually regresses significantly. This is true for every metric tested (whether related to playing time, batting skills, pitching skills, running skills, luck indicators, or valuation). Negative trends show similar reversals, but tend to be more "sticky," meaning that rebounds are neither as frequent nor as strong as positive trend regressions.

Reliability and age

Peak batting reliability occurs at ages 29 and 30, followed by a minor decline for four years. So, to draft the most reliable batters, and maximize the odds of returning at least par value on your investments, you should target the age range of 28-34.

The most reliable age range for pitchers is 29-34. While we are forever looking for "sleepers" and hot prospects, it is very risky to draft any pitcher under 27 or over 35.

Evaluating Reliability *(Bill Macey)*

When you head into an upcoming auction or draft, consider the following with regard to risk and reliability:

- Reliability grades do help identify more stable investments: players with "B" grades in both Health and PT/Experience are more likely to return a higher percentage of their projected value.
- While top-end starting pitching may be more reliable than ever, the overall pool of pitchers is fraught with uncertainty and they represent a less reliable investment than batters.

- There does not appear to be a significant market premium for reliability, at least according to the criteria measured by BaseballHQ.com.
- There are only two types of players: risky and riskier. So while it may be worth going the extra buck for a more reliable player, be warned that even the most reliable player can falter—don't go overboard bidding up a AAA-rated player simply due to his Reliability grades.

Normal production variance *(Patrick Davitt)*

Even if we have a perfectly accurate understanding of a player's "normal" performance level, his actual performance can and does vary widely over any particular 150-game span—including the 150-game span we call "a season." A .300 career hitter can perform in a range of .250-.350, a 40-HR hitter from 30-50, and a 3.70/1.15 pitcher from 2.60/0.95 to 6.00/1.55. And all of these results must be considered "normal."

Health Analysis

Injury Primer *(James C. Ferretti, DO)*

You can gain a sizable advantage with a better understanding of both injuries and the corresponding medical terms. An overview of the human musculoskeletal system:

- *Bones:* The rigid support framework which is also a foundation for the other moving parts.
- *Cartilage:* Soft tissue that acts as a cushion and prevents wear—usually in areas where bones are close to each other.
- *Muscles:* Bundles of fibers that bend and stretch to perform work.
- *Tendons:* Bundles of (less bendy/stretchy) fibers that attach muscles to bones.
- *Ligaments:* Bundles of (even less bendy/stretchy) fibers that attach bones to other bones.

Some common ailments:

Fractures

A fracture is simply a break in a bone, which means it isn't able to act as a stabilizer or absorb/distribute forces. Time to heal and/or long-term effects? Usually 4-6 weeks, though sometimes longer, though once the new bone has matured, it's as good as new.

Strains/Sprains

These are tears of the fibers of muscles/tendons (strains) and ligaments (sprains). Most doctors categorize them on a Grade 1, 2, 3, scale, from less severe to most.

Time to heal and/or long-term effects? A rough estimate is 2-4 weeks for a Grade 1, 4-8 weeks for a Grade 2, and at least 8 weeks for a Grade 3. There can be long-term effects, notably that the repaired areas contain fibrous ("scar") tissue, which is neither as strong nor as flexible as the original tissue, and is more prone to re-injury.

Inflammation

Inflammation is an irritation of soft tissues, often from overuse or repetitive motion and the structures affected get "angry." Even if they occur for different reasons, inflammation and a Grade 1

strain can behave similarly—and both can keep a player out for weeks.

Long-term effects? Injury/pain can recur, or even worsen without adequate time to heal. (So, maybe your player coming back early isn't such good news after all.)

Let's examine a few widely-used injury terms used by MLB clubs and/or media outlets.

"No structural damage"

While it sounds reassuring, it's often misleading. When medical imagers unaffiliated with MLB clubs make an injury diagnosis, they might term it a fracture, dislocation, soft tissue tear, or inflammation; all of which are bad news. Or they may call it "normal," or "negative," which is good news. But rarely would they describe an injury in terms of "no structural damage," because it's not an actual diagnosis. Rather, it's a way of saying that whatever body part being imaged is intact, with no broken bone or soft tissue tear. This is not the same as a "normal" or "negative" diagnosis. When you hear "no structural damage", continue to keep a close eye on the situation.

"Day-to-Day"

Similarly, "day-to-day" sounds reassuring—but really doesn't tell you anything other than "We aren't sure," which can be far more worrisome.

"X-Rays are negative"

Imaging a player is usually prompted by sudden or increasing onset of pain. Most baseball injuries, though, are to soft tissue, which is never diagnosed with an X-ray alone. Unless there's suspicion of a broken bone or joint injury, an X-ray probably isn't going to tell you much. We often see writers and analysts use a "negative" X-ray report to justify that the injury is "not believed to be serious." Don't make that mistake—await the results of more definitive imaging/tests, like a CAT scan or MRI.

Conclusion

Every player injury and recovery process is unique and there is no shortage of information out there to sort through. But read between the lines and alter your approach if you must—both before you draft, and as you manage your in-season roster.

Injured list statistics

Year	#Players	3yr Avg	DL Days	3yr Avg
2010	393	408	22,911	25,783
2011	422	408	25,610	24,924
2012	409	408	30,408	27,038
2013	442	419	29,551	28,523
2014	422	424	25,839	28,599
2015	454	439	28,982	28,124
2016	478	451	31,329	28,717
2017	533	488	30,913	30,408
2018	574	528	34,284	32,175
2019	563	557	36,394	33,864

IL days as a leading indicator *(Bill Macey)*

Players who are injured in one year are likely to be injured in a subsequent year:

% IL batters in Year 1 who are also DL in year 2	38%
Under age 30	36%
Age 30 and older	41%
% IL batters in Year 1 and 2 who are also DL in year 3	54%
% IL pitchers in Year 1 who are also DL in year 2	43%
Under age 30	45%
Age 30 and older	41%
% IL pitchers in Yr 1 and 2 who are also DL in year 3	41%

Previously injured players also tend to spend a longer time on the IL. The average number of days on the IL was 51 days for batters and 73 days for pitchers. For the subset of these players who get hurt again the following year, the average number of days on the IL was 58 days for batters and 88 days for pitchers.

How a batter's age affects IL stays *(Jeff Zimmerman)*

Some players seem to get more than their fair share of injuries, but for those hitters with the "injury-prone" tag, it only takes one healthy season to make a difference. After breaking up hitters into three age groups (25 and younger; 26-29; 30 and older), a study examined length and frequency of IL stints. Among the findings:

1. If someone in the youngest group goes on the IL once, they aren't as likely to again the next season. The IL chance increase after two IL seasons is huge, however, going from 33% to 43%.

2. The best health is exhibited by the middle group. It seems this age is the sweet spot for avoiding hitter injuries. The hitters have shown they can hold up to a full season, but their bodies have not started to break down.

3. Not surprisingly, the oldest group takes longer to heal. The older player's IL-related stats hover above the league average, but the IL rate doesn't increase as a player racks up previous injuries.

As they age, a hitter's body breaks down more often and for longer periods of time, which may give them the appearance of being injury-prone. As a general overall rule, it's prudent to discount a hitter's injury history, especially those aged 26-29

Do overworked hitters wear down? *(Jeff Zimmerman)*

A study compared the first- and second-half statistics for batters who played the most games over the entire season from 2002-16. These players were continually run out on the field, and one figures that fatigue would show up in their statistics. But conversely, the numbers don't support the wear-down narrative. If anything, their output improves the more they play. Though this concept goes against conventional wisdom, it is true: If a hitter plays more, the more likely he is healthy and not wearing down.

Spring training spin *(Dave Adler)*

Spring training sound bites raise expectations among fantasy leaguers, but how much of that "news" is really "noise"? Thanks to a summary listed at RotoAuthority.com, we were able to compile the stats for 2009. Verdict: Noise.

BATTERS	No.	IMPROVED	DECLINED
Weight change	30	33%	30%
Fitness program	3	0%	67%
Eye surgery	6	50%	33%
Plans more SB	6	17%	33%
PITCHERS	**No.**	**IMPROVED**	**DECLINED**
Weight change	18	44%	44%
Fitness program	4	50%	50%
Eye surgery	2	0%	50%
New pitch	5	60%	40%

In-Season Analysis

April performance as a leading indicator

We isolated all players who earned at least $10 more or $10 less than we had projected in March. Then we looked at the April stats of these players to see if we could have picked out the $10 outliers after just one month.

	Identifiable in April
Earned $10+ more than projected	
BATTERS	39%
PITCHERS	44%
Earned -$10 less than projected	
BATTERS	56%
PITCHERS	74%

Nearly three out of every four pitchers who earned at least $10 less than projected also struggled in April. For all the other surprises—batters or pitchers—April was not a strong leading indicator. Another look:

	Pct.
Batters who finished +$25	45%
Pitchers who finished +$20	44%
Batters who finished under $0	60%
Pitchers who finished under -$5	78%

April surgers are less than a 50/50 proposition to maintain that level all season. Those who finished April at the bottom of the roto rankings were more likely to continue struggling, especially pitchers. In fact, of those pitchers who finished April with a value *under -$10*, 91% finished the season in the red. Holes are tough to dig out of.

The weight of early season numbers

Early season strugglers who surge later in the year often get little respect because they have to live with the weight of their early numbers all season long. Conversely, quick starters who fade late get far more accolades than they deserve.

For instance, take Paul DeJong's month-by-month batting average. The perception is that his .233 BA was within a reasonable range of variance of what we would have expected. Reality is not quite as optimistic. DeJong had a .350 mark on April 30, but that inflated his batting average for the rest of the year. From May 1 on—fully five months of the year—he batted only .204, and only .175 in September.

Month	BA	Cum BA
Mar-Apr	.350	.350
May	.200	.280
June	.218	.260
July	.205	.247
August	.233	.245
Sept-Oct	.175	.233

Courtship period

Any time a player is put into a new situation, he enters into a courtship period. This period might occur when a player switches leagues, or switches teams. It could be the first few games when a minor leaguer is called up. It could occur when a reliever moves into the rotation, or when a lead-off hitter is moved to another spot in the lineup. There is a team-wide courtship period when a manager is replaced. Any external situation that could affect a player's performance sets off a new decision point in evaluating that performance.

During this period, it is difficult to get a true read on how a player is going to ultimately perform. He is adjusting to the new situation. Things could be volatile during this time. For instance, a role change that doesn't work could spur other moves. A rookie hurler might buy himself a few extra starts with a solid debut, even if he has questionable skills.

It is best not to make a decision on a player who is going through a courtship period. Wait until his stats stabilize. Don't cut a struggling pitcher in his first few starts after a managerial change. Don't pick up a hitter who smacks a pair of HRs in his first game after having been traded. Unless, of course, talent and track record say otherwise.

Half-season fallacies

A popular exercise at the midpoint of each season is to analyze those players who are consistent first half to second half surgers or faders. There are several fallacies with this analytical approach.

1. Half-season consistency is rare. There are very few players who show consistent changes in performance from one half of the season to the other.

Research results from a three-year study conducted in the late-1990s: The test groups... batters with min. 300 AB full season, 150 AB first half, and pitchers with min. 100 IP full season, 50 IP first half. Of those groups (size noted):

3-year consistency in	BATTERS (98)	PITCHERS (42)
1 stat category	40%	57%
2 stat categories	18%	21%
3 stat categories	3%	5%

When the analysis was stretched to a fourth year, only 1% of all players showed consistency in even one category.

2. Analysts often use false indicators. Situational statistics provide us with tools that can be misused. Several sources offer up 3- and 5-year stats intended to paint a picture of a long-term performance. Some analysts look at a player's half-season swing over that multi-year period and conclude that he is demonstrating consistent performance.

The fallacy is that those multi-year scans may not show any consistency at all. They are not individual season performances but *aggregate* performances. A player whose 5-year batting average shows a 15-point rise in the 2nd half, for instance, may actually have experienced a BA decline in several of those years, a fact that might have been offset by a huge BA rise in one of the years.

3. It's arbitrary. The season's midpoint is an arbitrary delineator of performance swings. Some players are slow starters and might be more appropriately evaluated as pre-May 1 and

post-May 1. Others bring their game up a notch with a pennant chase and might see a performance swing with August 15 as the cut-off. Each player has his own individual tendency, if, in fact, one exists at all. There's nothing magical about mid-season as the break point, and certainly not over a multi-year period.

Half-season tendencies

Despite the above, it stands to reason logically that there might be some underlying tendencies on a more global scale, first half to second half. In fact, one would think that the player population as a whole might decline in performance as the season drones on. There are many variables that might contribute to a player wearing down—workload, weather, boredom—and the longer a player is on the field, the higher the likelihood that he is going to get hurt. A recent 5-year study uncovered the following tendencies:

Batting

Overall, batting skills held up pretty well, half to half. There was a 5% erosion of playing time, likely due, in part, to September roster expansion.

Power: First half power studs (20 HRs in 1H) saw a 10% drop-off in the second half. 34% of first half 20+ HR hitters hit 15 or fewer in the second half and only 27% were able to improve on their first half output.

Speed: Second half speed waned as well. About 26% of the 20+ SB speedsters stole *at least 10 fewer bases* in the second half. Only 26% increased their second half SB output at all.

Batting average: 60% of first half .300 hitters failed to hit .300 in the second half. Only 20% showed any second half improvement at all. As for 1H strugglers, managers tended to stick with their full-timers despite poor starts. Nearly one in five of the sub-.250 1H hitters managed to hit *more than* .300 in the second half.

Pitching

Overall, there was some slight erosion in innings and ERA despite marginal improvement in some peripherals.

ERA: For those who pitched at least 100 innings in the first half, ERAs rose an average of 0.40 runs in the 2H. Of those with first half ERAs less than 4.00, only 49% were able to maintain a sub-4.00 ERA in the second half.

Wins: Pitchers who won 18 or more games in a season tended to pitch *more* innings in the 2H and had slightly better peripherals.

Saves: Of those closers who saved 20 or more games in the first half, only 39% were able to post 20 or more saves in the 2H, and 26% posted fewer than 15 saves. Aggregate ERAs of these pitchers rose from 2.45 to 3.17, half to half.

In-season trends in hitting and pitching *(Bob Berger)*

A study of monthly trends in traditional statistical categories found:
- Batting average, HR/game and RBI/game rise from April through August, then fall in September/October.
- Stolen bases decline in July and August before rebounding in September.
- ERA worsens in July/August and improves in September.
- WHIP gets worse in July/August.
- K/9 rate improves all season.

The statement that hitters perform better in warmer weather seems to be true broadly.

Can we trust in-season sample size? *(Arik Florimonte)*

Using logs from 2010-17, we determined when current in-season data becomes more significant than previous historical data. For pitchers, we found the following:
- Year-to-year correlations for soft- and hard-contact rates were extremely small, and that using only a month of current-year data is better than using a pitcher's previous season.
- Pay some attention to the current year's Soft% and Hard%, but future outcomes are still largely noise and prone to regression.
- For the pitcher-influenced outcomes—K% and BB%, and GB% and FB%—we are better off waiting until June to rely on the year-to-date results than we are the previous season, but a combination of the two is even better.

For batters, we found the following:
- Batters' base skills are a little more stable than pitchers' from year-to-year. The prior-year results are a very good indicator of what to expect.
- Contrary to the results for pitchers, where the year-to-date results tended to dominate mid-way through the year, for batters the YTD results didn't outweigh the Prior Year until August.
- Projections based on prior years' skills should remain your fallback position, but keep moving the needle toward the current year's results as the year goes on.

Can in-season deficiencies in ratio categories be overcome? *(Patrick Davitt)*

Many fantasy players think that later in the season, we can't move the decimals (BA, ERA, WHIP) because with the majority of AB/IP in the books, the ratio's large denominators make it too hard. While it's true we can't move as much late as early, we can still gain points. We tested this idea at the two-thirds mark in the season. Using teams and stats in a 15-team mixed expert's league, we built tables to see how much an owner could gain—first just by dropping a poor performer, and then by replacing a poor performer with a good performer.

From a study of a 15-team mixed expert's league, we found that it's still possible to gain points in the ratio categories by replacing a poor performer with a good performer, even at the two-thirds mark of the season. (Obviously, stratification of league standings will vary.)

Batting Average

The BA test projected a team to finish with a .257 BA. With 190 remaining projected AB per batter, we found that by dropping a players and not replacing him:
- Drop a .245 hitter: Team BA .25730
- .235 hitter: .25756
- .225 hitter: .25783
- .215 hitter: .25810

The gains are amplified when the poor hitter is replaced with a high projected BA hitter. Dropping a .215 pBA hitter and adding a .305 guy jumps team pBA to .25927. Dropping a .245 and adding

a .265 still gains 57 baseline points. Again, depending on how close your league standings are, this matters.

ERA

Gains in pitching decimals can be greater because the denominator is smaller than BA. This study used a team with a 4.00 final pERA in 1,325 IP. Let's start again by just dropping a poor performer with 55 pIP:

- Dropping a 4.25 pERA pitcher, finished at 3.990
- 4.50 pitcher: 3.976
- 4.75 pitcher: 3.969
- 5.00 pitcher: 3.954
- 5.25 pitcher: 3.947
- 5.50 pitcher: 3.933

And now, by adding a low-pERA replacement: Dropping a 5.50 disaster for a 2.75 stud means a final pERA of 3.885, an improvement of .115.

Of course, much depends on how each category is stratified. But we can make late moves in the decimals.

Surprisingly Productive Years *(Ed DeCaria)*

Here's a skills-based method of finding productive in-season roster additions:

1. Consider all batters projected for 50% or less playing time, all starting pitchers projected for 10% or less of his team's innings pitched (about 140 IP), and all relief pitchers projected for less than 4% of his team's innings pitched (about 50 IP)

2. Using each player's projected skills—not stats—in the form of his Mayberry scores, include only batters whose sum of three Mayberry skills (power, speed, and hitting) was 7 or higher (8 or higher for mixed leagues). For pitchers, only consider players whose sum of two Mayberry skills (xERA and strikeout rate) was 4 or higher (5 or higher for mixed leagues). For relievers, we also counted Mayberry's saves potential score, so we included only relievers whose sum of three scores was 7 or higher (8 or higher for mixed leagues).

3. Examine the specific situation of each player that met our first two criteria and assign a realistic playing time upside given his skills and injury, consistency, and forecast risk, and that of the player(s) ahead of him on his team's depth chart.

4. Calculate a single number that measured their "projected skill" over their "potential playing time" to arrive at their "potential value."

   a. For hitters, take his Mayberry sum and multiply it by his potential playing time (pPT). Then rank batters by this metric and subtract the minimum value of the group from all players, so that the least valuable batter had a marginal score (mSCORE) of zero. Then use mSCORE to calculate each player's "share" of the total, and multiply that by the league's total wasted dollars (using a 65/35 batter/pitcher split) to determine each batter's potential value (pR$).

   b. Similarly for pitchers, take the Mayberry sum multiplied by potential innings percentage (pPT) and rank pitchers by this metric. Subtract the minimum value of the group from all pitchers, then use mSCORE to calculate each pitcher's "share" of the total, and multiply that by the league's total wasted dollars (using a 65/35 batter/pitcher split) to determine each pitcher's potential value (pR$).

Use these rankings to produce lists of players who are projected for far less than full playing time despite good or even great skills. A well-timed pick-up of any one of these players could be a boon to most teams' chances of winning their league. In 2019, this exercise identified Dylan Moore, Bo Bichette, Tommy La Stella and Keston Hiura among its top 10 hitters; and Caleb Smith and Anibal Sanchez on the pitching side. We will run the 2020 version shortly after Opening Day in 2020 at BaseballHQ.com.

Teams

Johnson Effect *(Bryan Johnson)*: Teams whose actual won/loss record exceeds or falls short of their statistically projected record in one season will tend to revert to the level of their projection in the following season.

Law of Competitive Balance *(Bill James)*: The level at which a team (or player) will address its problems is inversely related to its current level of success. Low performers will tend to make changes to improve; high performers will not. This law explains the existence of the Plexiglass and Whirlpool Principles.

Plexiglass Principle *(Bill James)*: If a player or team improves markedly in one season, it will likely decline in the next. The opposite is true but not as often (because a poor performer gets fewer opportunities to rebound).

Whirlpool Principle *(Bill James)*: All team and player performances are forcefully drawn to the center. For teams, that center is a .500 record. For players, it represents their career average level of performance.

Other Diamonds

The Fanalytic Fundamentals

1. This is not a game of accuracy or precision. It is a game of human beings and tendencies.

2. This is not a game of projections. It is a game of market value versus real value.

3. Draft skills, not stats. Draft skills, not roles.

4. A player's ability to post acceptable stats despite lousy support metrics will eventually run out.

5. Once you display a skill, you own it.

6. Virtually every player is vulnerable to a month of aberrant performance. Or a year.

7. Exercise excruciating patience.

Aging Axioms

1. Age is the only variable for which we can project a rising trend with 100% accuracy. (Or, age never regresses.)

2. The aging process slows down for those who maintain a firm grasp on the strike zone. Plate patience and pitching command can preserve any waning skill they have left.

3. Negatives tend to snowball as you age.

Steve Avery List
Players who hang onto MLB rosters for six years searching for a skill level they only had for three.

Bylaws of Badness
1. Some players are better than an open roster spot, but not by much.
2. Some players have bad years because they are unlucky. Others have *many* bad years because they are bad... and lucky.

Christie Brinkley Law of Statistical Analysis
Never get married to the model.

Employment Standards
1. If you are right-brain dominant, own a catcher's mitt and are under 40, you will always be gainfully employed.
2. Some teams believe that it is better to employ a player with any experience because it has to be better than the devil they don't know.
3. It's not so good to go *pffft* in a contract year.

Brad Fullmer List
Players whose leading indicators indicate upside potential, year after year, but consistently fail to reach that full potential. Players like Byron Buxton and Jon Gray are on the list right now.

Good Luck Truism
Good luck is rare and everyone has more of it than you do. That's the law.

The Gravity Principles
1. It is easier to be crappy than it is to be good.
2. All performance starts at zero, ends at zero and can drop to zero at any time.
3. The odds of a good performer slumping are far greater than the odds of a poor performer surging.
4. Once a player is in a slump, it takes several 3-for-5 days to get out of it. Once he is on a streak, it takes a single 0-for-4 day to begin the downward spiral. *Corollary:* Once a player is in a slump, not only does it take several 3-for-5 days to get out of it, but he also has to get his name back on the lineup card.
5. Eventually all performance comes down to earth. It may take a week, or a month, or may not happen until he's 45, but eventually it's going to happen.

Health Homilies
1. Staying healthy is a skill (and "IL Days" should be a Rotisserie category).
2. A $40 player can get hurt just as easily as a $5 player but is eight times tougher to replace.
3. Chronically injured players never suddenly get healthy.
4. There are two kinds of pitchers: those that are hurt and those that are not hurt... yet.
5. Players with back problems are always worth $10 less.
6. "Opting out of surgery" usually means it's coming anyway, just later.

The Health Hush
Players get hurt and potentially have a lot to lose, so there is an incentive for them to hide injuries. HIPAA laws restrict the disclosure of health information. Team doctors and trainers have been instructed not to talk with the media. So, when it comes to information on a player's health status, we're all pretty much in the dark.

The Livan Level
The point when a player's career Runs Above Replacement level has dropped so far below zero that he has effectively cancelled out any possible remaining future value. (Similarly, the Dontrelle Demarcation.)

The Momentum Maxims
1. A player will post a pattern of positive results until the day you add him to your roster.
2. Patterns of negative results are more likely to snowball than correct.
3. When an unstoppable force meets an immovable object, the wall always wins.

Noise
Irrelevant or meaningless pieces of information that can distort the results of an analysis. In news, this is opinion or rumor. In forecasting, this is random variance or irrelevant data. In ballparks, this is a screaming crowd cheering for a team down 12-3 with two outs and bases empty in the bottom of the ninth.

Paradoxes and Conundrums
1. Is a player's improvement in performance from one year to the next a point in a growth trend, an isolated outlier or a complete anomaly?
2. A player can play through an injury, post rotten numbers and put his job at risk... or... he can admit that he can't play through an injury, allow himself to be taken out of the lineup/rotation, and put his job at risk.
3. Did irregular playing time take its toll on the player's performance or did poor performance force a reduction in his playing time?
4. Is a player only in the game versus right-handers because he has a true skills deficiency versus left-handers? Or is his poor performance versus left-handers because he's never given a chance to face them?
5. The problem with stockpiling bench players in the hope that one pans out is that you end up evaluating performance using data sets that are too small to be reliable.
6. There are players who could give you 20 stolen bases if they got 400 AB. But if they got 400 AB, they would likely be on a bad team that wouldn't let them steal.

Paths to Retirement
1. **George Brett:** Get out while you're still putting up good numbers and the public perception of you is favorable. Like Chipper Jones, Mariano Rivera and David Ortiz.
2. **Steve Carlton:** Hang around the majors long enough for your numbers to become so wretched that people begin to forget your past successes. Current players who could be on a similar course include Robinson Cano, Ian Kisler and sadly, Miguel Cabrera.
3. **Johan Santana:** Stay on the disabled list for so long that nobody realizes you haven't officially retired until your

name shows up on a Hall of Fame ballot. Perhaps like Cliff Lee and Carl Crawford.

Process-Outcome Matrix *(Russo and Schoemaker)*

	Good Outcome	Bad Outcome
Good Process	Deserved Success	Bad Break
Bad Process	Dumb Luck	Poetic Justice

Quack!

An exclamation in response to the educated speculation that a player has used performance enhancing drugs. While it is rare to have absolute proof, there is often enough information to suggest that, "if it looks like a duck and quacks like a duck, then odds are it's a duck."

Situation Dependent

An event that is affected by the context of team, ballpark, or other outside variables.

RBI: You can't drive in runs if there is nobody on base.

Runs: You can't score a run if no one drives you in.

Wins: You can't win a game unless your offense scores runs, no matter how well you pitch.

Surface Stats

All those wonderful statistics we grew up with that those mean bean counters are telling us don't matter anymore. Home runs, RBIs, batting average, won-loss record. Let's go back to the 1960s and make baseball great again! [EDITOR: No.]

Tenets of Optimal Timing

1. If a second half fader had put up his second half stats in the first half and his first half stats in the second half, then he probably wouldn't even have had a second half.

2. Fast starters can often buy six months of playing time out of one month of productivity.

3. Poor 2nd halves don't get recognized until it's too late.

4. "Baseball is like this. Have one good year and you can fool them for five more, because for five more years they expect you to have another good one." — Frankie Frisch

The Three True Outcomes

1. Strikeouts
2. Walks
3. Home runs

The Three True Handicaps

1. Has power but can't make contact.
2. Has speed but can't hit safely.
3. Has potential but is too old.

Zombie

A player who is indestructible, continuing to get work, year-after-year, no matter how dead his skills metrics have become. Fringe guys like Sean Rodriguez and Tommy Milone fit the mold, but former stars like Jonathan Lucroy and Chris Davis are among the walking dead now too.

Batters

Batting Eye, Contact and Batting Average

Batting average (BA, or Avg)
This is where it starts. BA is a grand old nugget that has long outgrown its usefulness. We revere .300 hitting superstars and scoff at .250 hitters, yet the difference between the two is one hit every five games. BA is a poor evaluator of performance in that it neglects the offensive value of the base on balls and assumes that all hits are created equal.

Walk rate (bb%)
(BB / (AB + BB))
A measure of a batter's plate patience. BENCHMARKS: The best batters will have levels more than 10%. Those with poor plate patience will have levels of 5% or less.

On base average (OB)
(H + BB + HBP) / (AB + BB + HBP + Sac Flies)
Addressing a key deficiency with BA, OB gives value to events that get batters on base, but are not hits. An OB of .350 can be read as "this batter gets on base 35% of the time." When a run is scored, there is no distinction made as to how that runner reached base. So, two-thirds of the time—about how often a batter comes to the plate with the bases empty—a walk really is as good as a hit. BENCHMARKS: We know what a .300 hitter is, but what represents "good" for OB? That comparable level would likely be .340, with .290 representing the comparable level of futility.

Ground ball, line drive, fly ball percentages (G/L/F)
The percentage of all balls in play that are hit on the ground, as line drives and in the air. For batters, increased fly ball tendency may foretell a rise in power skills; increased line drive tendency may foretell an improvement in batting average. For a pitcher, the ability to keep the ball on the ground can contribute to his statistical output exceeding his demonstrated skill level.

*BIP Type	Total%	Out%
Ground ball	45%	72%
Line drive	20%	28%
Fly ball	35%	85%
TOTAL	*100%*	*69%*

*Data only includes fieldable balls and is net of HRs.

Line drives and luck *(Patrick Davitt)*
Given that each individual batter's hit rate sets its own baseline, and that line drives (LD) are the most productive type of batted ball, a study looked at the relationship between the two. Among the findings were that hit rates on LDs are much higher than on FBs or GBs, with individual batters consistently falling into the 72-73% range. Ninety-five percent of all batters fall between the range of 60%-86%; batters outside this range regress very quickly, often within the season.

Note that batters' BAs did not always follow their LD% up or down, because some of them enjoyed higher hit rates on other batted balls, improved their contact rates, or both. Still, it's justifiable to bet that players hitting the ball with authority but getting fewer hits than they should will correct over time.

Batting eye (Eye)
(Walks / Strikeouts)
A measure of a player's strike zone judgment. BENCHMARKS: The best hitters have Eye ratios more than 1.00 (indicating more walks than strikeouts) and are the most likely to be among a league's .300 hitters. Ratios less than 0.30 represent batters who likely also have lower BAs.

Batting eye as a leading indicator
There is a correlation between strike zone judgment and batting average but research shows that this is more descriptive than predictive.

However, we can create percentage plays for the different levels:

For Eye	Pct who bat	
Levels of	.300+	.250-
0.00 - 0.25	7%	39%
0.26 - 0.50	14%	26%
0.51 - 0.75	18%	17%
0.76 - 1.00	32%	14%
1.01 - 1.50	51%	9%
1.51 +	59%	4%

Any batter with an eye ratio more than 1.50 has about a 4% chance of hitting less than .250 over 500 at bats.

Of all .300 hitters, those with ratios of at least 1.00 have a 65% chance of repeating as .300 hitters. Those with ratios less than 1.00 have less than a 50% chance of repeating.

Only 4% of sub-.250 hitters with ratios less than 0.50 will mature into .300 hitters the following year.

In this study, only 37 batters hit .300-plus with a sub-0.50 eye ratio over at least 300 AB in a season. Of this group, 30% were able to accomplish this feat on a consistent basis. For the other 70%, this was a short-term aberration.

Contact rate (ct%)
((AB - K) / AB)
Measures a batter's ability to get wood on the ball and hit it into the field of play. BENCHMARKS: Those batters with the best contact skill will have levels of 80% or better. The hackers will have levels of 70% or less.

Contact rate as a leading indicator
The more often a batter makes contact with the ball, the higher the likelihood that he will hit safely.

	Batting Average				
Contact Rate	2015	2016	2017	2018	2019
0% - 60%	.194	.207	.206	.196	.179
61% - 65%	.217	.223	.226	.223	.223
66% - 70%	.236	.232	.244	.237	.241
71% - 75%	.254	.253	.248	.245	.252
76% - 80%	.257	.262	.268	.258	.264
81% - 85%	.268	.271	.270	.268	.277
Over 85%	.280	.282	.285	.277	.282

Contact rate and walk rate as leading indicators
A matrix of contact rates and walk rates can provide expectation benchmarks for a player's batting average:

	Walk rate (bb%)			
	0-5	**6-10**	**11-15**	**16+**
65-	.179	.195	.229	.237
66-75	.190	.248	.254	.272
76-85	.265	.267	.276	.283
86+	.269	.279	.301	.309

Contact rate (ct%) (left vertical label)

A contact rate of 65% or lower offers virtually no chance for a player to hit even .250, no matter how high a walk rate he has. The .300 hitters most often come from the group with a minimum 86% contact and 11% walk rate.

HCt and HctX *(Patrick Davitt)*

HCt= hard hit ball rate x contact rate
HctX= Player HCt divided by league average Hct, normalized to 100

The combination of making contact and hitting the ball hard might be the most important skills for a batter. HctX correlates very strongly with BA, and at higher BA levels often does so with high accuracy. Its success with HR was somewhat limited, probably due to GB/FB differences. **BENCHMARKS:** The average major-leaguer in a given year has a HctX of 100. Elite batters have an HctX of 135 or above; weakest batters have HctX of 55 or below.

Balls in play (BIP)

(AB – K)

The total number of batted balls that are hit fair, both hits and outs. An analysis of how these balls are hit—on the ground, in the air, hits, outs, etc.—can provide analytical insight, from player skill levels to the impact of luck on statistical output.

Batting average on balls in play *(Voros McCracken)*

(H – HR) / (AB – HR – K)

Or, BABIP. Also called hit rate (h%). The percent of balls hit into the field of play that fall for hits. **BENCHMARK:** Every hitter establishes his own individual hit rate that stabilizes over time. A batter whose seasonal hit rate varies significantly from the h% he has established over the preceding three seasons (variance of at least +/- 3%) is likely to improve or regress to his individual h% mean (with over-performer declines more likely and sharper than under-performer recoveries). Three-year h% levels strongly predict a player's h% the following year.

Pitches/Plate Appearance as a leading indicator for BA *(Paul Petera)*

The art of working the count has long been considered one of the more crucial aspects of good hitting. It is common knowledge that the more pitches seen, the greater opportunity he has to reach base safely.

P/PA	OBA	BA
4.00+	.360	.264
3.75-3.99	.347	.271
3.50-3.74	.334	.274
Under 3.50	.321	.276

Generally speaking, the more pitches seen, the lower the BA, but the higher the OBA. But what about the outliers, those players that bucked the trend in year #1?

	YEAR TWO	
	BA Improved	**BA Declined**
Low P/PA and Low BA	77%	23%
High P/PA and High BA	21%	79%

In these scenarios, there was a strong tendency for performance to normalize in year #2.

Expected batting average *(John Burnson)*

$xCT\% * [xH1\% + xH2\%]$

where

$xH1\% = GB\% \times [0.0004\ PX + 0.062\ ln(SX)]$
$+ LD\% \times [0.93 - 0.086\ ln(SX)]$
$+ FB\% \times 0.12$

and

$xH2\% = FB\% \times [0.0013\ PX - 0.0002\ SX - 0.057]$
$+ GB\% \times [0.0006\ PX]$

A hitter's expected batting average as calculated by multiplying the percentage of balls put in play (contact rate) by the chance that a ball in play falls for a hit. The likelihood that a ball in play falls for a hit is a product of the speed of the ball and distance it is hit (PX), the speed of the batter (SX), and distribution of ground balls, fly balls, and line drives. We further split it out by non-homerun hit rate (xH1%) and homerun hit rate (xH2%). **BENCHMARKS:** In general, xBA should approximate batting average fairly closely. Those hitters who have large variances between the two gauges are candidates for further analysis. **LIMITATION:** xBA tends to understate a batter's true value if he is an extreme ground ball hitter (G/F ratio over 3.0) with a low PX. These players are not inherently weak, but choose to take safe singles rather than swing for the fences.

Expected batting average variance

xBA – BA

The variance between a batter's BA and his xBA is a measure of over- or under-achievement. A positive variance indicates the potential for a batter's BA to rise. A negative variance indicates the potential for BA to decline. **BENCHMARK:** Discount variances that are less than 20 points. Any variance more than 30 points is regarded as a strong indicator of future change.

Power

Slugging average (Slg)

(Singles + (2 x Doubles) + (3 x Triples) + (4 x HR)) / AB

A measure of the total number of bases accumulated (or the minimum number of runners' bases advanced) per at bat. It is a misnomer; it is not a true measure of a batter's slugging ability because it includes singles. Slg also assumes that each type of hit has proportionately increasing value (i.e. a double is twice as valuable as a single, etc.) which is not true. For instance, with the bases loaded, a HR always scores four runs, a triple always scores three, but a double could score two or three and a single could score one, or two, or even three. **BENCHMARKS:** Top batters will have levels over .450. The bottom batters will have levels less than .350.

Fly ball tendency and power *(Mat Olkin)*

There is a proven connection between a hitter's ground ball/fly ball tendencies and his power production.

1. *Extreme ground ball hitters generally do not hit for much power.* It's almost impossible for a hitter with a ground/fly ratio over 1.80 to hit enough fly balls to produce even 25 HRs in a season. However, this does not mean that a low G/F ratio necessarily guarantees power production. Some players have no problem getting the ball into the air, but lack the strength to reach the fences consistently.

2. *Most batters' ground/fly ratios stay pretty steady over time.* Most year-to-year changes are small and random, as they are in any other statistical category. A large, sudden change in G/F, on the other hand, can signal a conscious change in plate approach. And so...

3. *If a player posts high G/F ratios in his first few years, he probably isn't ever going to hit for all that much power.*

4. *When a batter's power suddenly jumps, his G/F ratio often drops at the same time.*

5. *Every so often, a hitter's ratio will drop significantly even as his power production remains level. In these rare cases, impending power development is likely, since the two factors almost always follow each other.*

Home runs to fly ball rate (IIR/F)

The percent of fly balls that are hit for HRs.

HR/F rate as a leading indicator *(Joshua Randall)*

Each batter establishes an individual home run to fly ball rate that stabilizes over rolling three-year periods; those levels strongly predict the HR/F in the subsequent year. A batter who varies significantly from his HR/F is likely to regress toward his individual HR/F mean, with over-performance decline more likely and more severe than under-performance recovery.

Expected home runs to fly ball rate (xHR/F) *(Arik Florimonte)*

See full research on page 65.

Estimating HR rate for young hitters *(Matt Cederholm)*

Over time, hitters establish a baseline HR/F, but how do we measure the HR output of young hitters with little track record? Since power is a key indicator of HR output, we can look at typical HR/F for various levels of power, as measures by xPX:

	HR/F percentiles				
xPX	**10**	**25**	**50**	**75**	**90**
<=70	0.9%	2.0%	3.8%	5.5%	7.4%
71-80	3.3%	5.1%	6.4%	8.1%	10.0%
81-90	3.8%	5.4%	7.4%	9.0%	11.0%
91-100	4.7%	6.6%	8.9%	11.3%	13.0%
101-110	6.6%	8.3%	10.9%	13.0%	16.2%
111-120	7.4%	9.8%	11.9%	14.7%	17.1%
121-130	8.5%	10.9%	12.8%	15.5%	17.4%
131-140	9.7%	11.9%	14.6%	17.1%	20.4%
141-160	11.3%	13.1%	16.5%	19.2%	21.5%
161+	14.4%	16.5%	19.4%	22.0%	25.8%

To predict changes in HR output, just look at a player and project his HR as if his HR/F was at the median for his xPX level. For example, if a player with a 125 xPX exceeds a 12.8% HR/F, we would expect a decline in the following season. The greater the deviation from the mean, the greater the probability of an increase or decline.

Expected home runs (xHR) *(Arik Florimonte)*

A 2017 study created a model for expected home run rate given exit velocity (EV) and launch angle (LA) found in MLB's Statcast system. The model was applied to the entire database of batted balls over a two-year period to determine the likelihood that a particular batted ball "should" have been a home run, when adjusted for park effects. By comparing a hitter's actual home run total to deserved home runs (xHR) over a given year, we can estimate how much of that performance was earned or unearned, and adjust home run expectations for the following season.

Is fly ball carry a skill? *(Arik Florimonte)*

Using Statcast data from 2015-17, we determined that "Carry"—how much a fly ball travels compared to its projected distance based on Launch Angle and Exit Velocity—is a repeatable skill for batters. Specific findings from this study include:

- Carry is well-correlated from year-to-year, with Prior Year Carry explaining 47% of Current Year Carry.
- On average, a batter will retain two-thirds of his fly ball Carry from year-to-year.
- Batters with unlucky HR totals in Year 0 tend to see an improvement in Year 1. Of those with high Carry in Year 0, 88% saw improvement in the difference between HR/F and xHR/F (expected HR/F), and the average gain is +0.059 (including non-gainers).

We hope that as Statcast data accumulates, it will be possible to incorporate xHR with Carry into our models to further improve HR/F projections.

Hard-hit flies as a sustainable skill *(Patrick Davitt)*

A study of data from 2009-2011 found that we should seek batters with a high Hard-Hit Fly Ball percentage (HHFB%). Among the findings:

- Avoiding pop-ups and hitting HHFBs are sustainable core power skills.
- Consistent HHFB% performance marks batters with power potential.
- When looking for candidates to regress, we should look at individual past levels of HR/HHFB, perhaps using a three-year rolling average.

Linear weighted power (LWPwr)

((Doubles x .8) + (Triples x .8) + (HR x 1.4)) / (At bats- K) x 100

A variation of Pete Palmer's linear weights formula that considers only events that are measures of a batter's pure power. **BENCHMARKS:** Top sluggers typically top the 17 mark. Weak hitters will have a LWPwr level of less than 10.

Linear weighted power index (PX)

(Batter's LWPwr / League LWPwr) x 100

LWPwr is presented in this book in its normalized form to get a better read on a batter's accomplishment in each year. For instance, a 30-HR season today is much less of an accomplishment than 30 HRs hit in a lower offense year like 2014. **BENCHMARKS:** A level of 100 equals league average power skills. Any player with

a value more than 100 has above average power skills, and those more than 150 are the Slugging Elite.

Expected LW power index (xPX) *(Bill Macey)*
2.6 + 269*HHLD% + 724*HHFB%

Previous research has shown that hard-hit balls are more likely to result in hits and hard-hit fly balls are more likely to end up as HRs. As such, we can use hard-hit ball data to calculate an expected skills-based power index. This metric starts with hard-hit ball data, which measures a player's fundamental skill of making solid contact, and then places it on the same scale as PX (xPX). In the above formula, HHLD% is calculated as the number of hard hit-line drives divided by the total number of balls put in play. HHFB% is similarly calculated for fly balls. The variance between PX and xPX can be viewed as a leading indicator for other power metrics.

Pitches/Plate Appearance as a leading indicator for PX *(Paul Petera)*
Working the count has a positive effect on power.

P/PA	PX
4.00+	123
3.75-3.99	108
3.50-3.74	96
Under 3.50	84

As for the year #1 outliers:

	YEAR TWO	
	PX Improved	PX Declined
Low P/PA and High PX	11%	89%
High P/PA and Low PX	70%	30%

In these scenarios, there was a strong tendency for performance to normalize in year #2.

Doubles as a leading indicator for home runs *(Bill Macey)*
There is little support for the theory that hitting many doubles in year x leads to an increase in HR in year x+1. However, it was shown that batters with high doubles rates (2B/AB) also tend to hit more HR/AB than the league average; oddly, they are unable to sustain the high 2B/AB rate but do sustain their higher HR/AB rates. Batters with high 2B/AB rates and low HR/AB rates are more likely to see HR gains in the following year, but those rates will still typically trail the league average. And, batters who experience a surge in 2B/AB typically give back most of those gains in the following year without any corresponding gain in HR.

Opposite field home runs *(Ed DeCaria)*
Opposite field HRs serve as a strong indicator of overall home run power (AB/HR). Power hitters (smaller AB/HR rates) hit a far higher percentage of their HR to the opposite field or straight away (over 30%). Conversely, non-power hitters hit almost 90% of their home runs to their pull field.

	Performance in Y2-Y4 (% of Group)		
Y1 Trigger	<=30 AB/HR	5.5+ RC/G	$16+ R$
2+ OppHR	69%	46%	33%
<2 OppHR	29%	13%	12%

Players who hit just two or more OppHR in one season were 2-3 times as likely as those who hit zero or one OppHR to sustain strong AB/HR rates, RC/G levels, or R$ values over the following three seasons.

Y2-Y4 Breakout Performance			
(% Breakout by Group, Age <=26 Only)			
	AB/HR	RC/G	R$
Y1 Trigger	>35 to <=30	<4.5 to 5.5+	<$8 to $16+
2+ OppHR	32%	21%	30%
<2 OppHR	23%	12%	10%

Roughly one of every 3-4 batters age 26 or younger experiences a *sustained three-year breakout* in AB/HR, RC/G or R$ after a season in which they hit 2+ OppHR, far better odds than the one in 8-10 batters who experience a breakout without the 2+ OppHR trigger.

In fact, a 2015 Brad Kullman study that examined hard hit balls of all types (flies, liners, and grounders) by hitters with 100 or more plate appearances offered a broader conclusion. His research found that hitters who can effectively use the whole field are more productive in virtually every facet of hitting than those with an exclusively pull-oriented approach.

Home runs in bunches *(Patrick Davitt)*
A study from HR data from 2010-2012 showed that batters hit HRs in a random manner, with game-gaps between HRs that correspond roughly to their average days per HR. Thus, the theory that batters hit HRs in "bunches" is a fallacy. It appears pointless to try to "time the market" by predicting the beginning or end of a drought or a bunch, or by assuming the end of one presages the beginning of the other, despite what the ex-player in the broadcast booth tells you.

Power breakout profile
It is not easy to predict which batters will experience a power spike. We can categorize power breakouts to determine the likelihood of a player taking a step up or of a surprise performer repeating his feat. Possibilities:

- Increase in playing time
- History of power skills at some time in the past
- Redistribution of already demonstrated extra base hit power
- Normal skills growth
- Situational breakouts, particularly in hitter-friendly venues
- Increased fly ball tendency
- Use of illegal performance-enhancing substances
- Miscellaneous unexplained variables

Speed

Wasted talent on the base paths
We refer to some players as having "wasted talent," a high level skill that is negated by a deficiency in another skill. Among these types are players who have blazing speed that is negated by a sub-.300 on base average.

These players can have short-term value. However, their stolen base totals are tied so tightly to their "green light" that any change in managerial strategy could completely erase that value. A higher OB mitigates that downside; the good news is that plate patience can be taught.

In the past, there were always a handful of players who had at least 20 SBs with an OBP less than .300, putting their future SBs at risk. In 2019, only Adalberto Mondesi (43 SB, .291) and Billy Hamilton (22 SB, .289 OBP) fit this profile. Of course, last year saw only 21 players total with 20-plus SBs; back in 2011, there were 50!

Speed score *(Bill James)*

A measure of the various elements that comprise a runner's speed skills. Although this formula (a variation of James' original version) may be used as a leading indicator for stolen base output, SB attempts are controlled by managerial strategy which makes speed score somewhat less valuable.

Speed score is calculated as the mean value of the following four elements:

1. Stolen base efficiency = $(((SB + 3)/(SB + CS + 7)) - .4) \times 20$

2. Stolen base freq. = *Square root of $((SB + CS)/(Singles + BB))/.07$*

3. Triples rating = $(3B / (AB - HR - K))$ and the result assigned a value based on the following chart:

< 0.001	0	0.0105	6
0.001	1	0.013	7
0.0023	2	0.0158	8
0.0039	3	0.0189	9
0.0058	4	0.0223+	10
0.008	5		

4. Runs scored as a percentage of times on base = $(((R - HR) / (H + BB - HR)) - .1) / .04$

Speed score index (SX)

(Batter's speed score / League speed score) x 100

Normalized speed scores get a better read on a runner's accomplishment in context. A level of 100 equals league average speed skill. Values more than 100 indicate above average skill, more than 200 represent the Fleet of Feet Elite.

Statistically scouted speed (Spd) *(Ed DeCaria)*

$(104 + \{[(Runs-HR+10*age\_wt)/(RBI-HR+10)]/lg\_av*100\} / 5$
$+ \{[(3B+5*age\_wt)/(2B+3B+5)]/lg\_av*100\} / 5$
$+ \{[(SoftMedGBhits+25*age\_wt)/(SoftMedGB+25)]/lg\_av*100\} / 2$
$- \{[Weight (Lbs)/Height (In)^2 * 703]/lg\_av*100\}$

A skills-based gauge that measures speed without relying on stolen bases. Its components are:

- *(Runs – HR) / (RBI – HR)*: This metric aims to minimize the influence of extra base hit power and team run-scoring rates on perceived speed.

- *3B / (2B + 3B)*: No one can deny that triples are a fast runner's stat; dividing them by 2B+3B instead of all balls in play dampens the power aspect of extra base hits.

- *(Soft + Medium Ground Ball Hits) / (Soft + Medium Ground Balls)*: Faster runners are more likely than slower runners to beat out routine grounders. Hard hit balls are excluded from numerator and denominator.

- *Body Mass Index (BMI)*: Calculated as *Weight (lbs) / Height (in)2 * 703*. All other factors considered, leaner players run faster than heavier ones.

In this book, the formula is scaled as an index with a midpoint of 100.

Stolen base opportunity percent (SBO)

(SB + CS) / (BB + Singles)

A rough approximation of how often a baserunner attempts a stolen base. Provides a comparative measure for players on a given team and, as a team measure, the propensity of a manager to give a "green light" to his runners.

Stolen base success rate (SB%)

SB / (SB + CS)

The rate at which baserunners are successful in their stolen base attempts. BENCHMARK: It is generally accepted that an 80% rate is the minimum required for a runner to be providing value to his team.

Roto Speed (RSpd)

(Spd x (SBO + SB%))

An adjustment to the measure for raw speed that takes into account a runner's opportunities to steal and his success rate. This stat is intended to provide a more accurate predictive measure of stolen bases for the Mayberry Method.

Stolen base breakout profile *(Bob Berger)*

To find stolen base breakouts (first 30+ steal season in the majors), look for players that:

- are between 22-27 years old
- have 3-7 years of professional (minors and MLB) experience
- have previous steals at the MLB level
- have averaged 20+ SB in previous three seasons (majors and minors combined)
- have at least one professional season of 30+ SB

Overall Performance Analysis

On base plus slugging average (OPS)

A simple sum of the two gauges, it is considered one of the better evaluators of overall performance. OPS combines the two basic elements of offensive production—the ability to get on base (OB) and the ability to advance baserunners (Slg). BENCHMARKS: The game's top batters will have OPS levels more than .850. The worst batters will have levels less than .660.

Adjusted on base plus slugging average (OPS+)

OPS scaled to league average to account for year-to-year fluctuations in league-wide statistical performance. It's a snapshot of a player's overall skills compared to an average player; also used in platoon situations (vL+; vR+). BENCHMARK: A level of 100 means a player had a league-average OPS in that given season.

Base Performance Value (BPV)

(Walk rate - 5) x 2)
+ ((Contact rate - 75) x 4)
+ ((Power Index - 80) x 0.8)
+ ((Spd - 80) x 0.3)

A single value that describes a player's overall raw skill level. This formula combines the individual raw skills of batting eye, contact rate, power and speed.

Base Performance Index (BPX)

BPV scaled to league average to account for year-to-year fluctuations in league-wide statistical performance. It's a snapshot of a player's overall skills compared to an average player. BENCHMARK: A level of 100 means a player had a league-average BPV in that given season.

Linear weights *(Pete Palmer)*

((Singles x .46) + (Doubles x .8) + (Triples x 1.02)
+ (Home runs x 1.4) + (Walks x .33) + (Stolen Bases x .3)
- (Caught Stealing x .6) - ((At bats - Hits) x Normalizing Factor)

(Also referred to as Batting Runs.) Formula whose premise is that all events in baseball are linear; that is, the output (runs) is directly proportional to the input (offensive events). Each of these events is then weighted according to its relative value in producing runs. Positive events—hits, walks, stolen bases—have positive values. Negative events—outs, caught stealing—have negative values.

The normalizing factor, representing the value of an out, is an offset to the level of offense in a given year. It changes every season, growing larger in high offense years and smaller in low offense years. The value is about .26 and varies by league.

LW is not included in the player forecast boxes, but the LW concept is used with the linear weighted power gauge.

Runs above replacement (RAR)

An estimate of the number of runs a player contributes above a "replacement level" player. "Replacement" is defined as the level of performance at which another player can easily be found at little or no cost to a team. What constitutes replacement level is a topic that is hotly debated. There are a variety of formulas and rules of thumb used to determine this level for each position (replacement level for a catcher will be very different from replacement level for an outfielder). Our estimates appear below.

One of the major values of RAR for fantasy applications is that it can be used to assemble an integrated ranking of batters and pitchers for drafting purposes.

To calculate RAR for batters:
- Start with a batter's runs created per game (RC/G).
- Subtract his position's replacement level RC/G.
- Multiply by number of games played: (AB - H + CS) / 25.5.

Replacement levels used in this book:

POS	NL	AL
CA	3.52	3.38
1B	5.11	4.42
2B	4.27	4.08
3B	4.67	4.34
SS	3.82	4.10
LF	4.61	4.59
CF	4.24	4.04
RF	4.40	4.51
DH		4.51

RAR can also be used to calculate rough projected team won-loss records. *(Roger Miller)* Total the RAR levels for all the players on a team, divide by 10 and add to 53 wins.

Runs created *(Bill James)*

(H + BB − CS) x (Total bases + (.55 x SB)) / (AB + BB)

A formula that converts all offensive events into a total of runs scored. As calculated for individual teams, the result approximates a club's actual run total with great accuracy.

Runs created per game (RC/G)

Runs Created / ((AB - H + CS) / 25.5)

RC expressed on a per-game basis might be considered the hypothetical ERA compiled against a particular batter. Another way to look at it: A batter with a RC/G of 7.00 would be expected to score 7 runs per game if he were cloned nine times and faced an average pitcher in every at bat. Cloning batters is not a practice we recommend. BENCHMARKS: Few players surpass the level of a 10.00 RC/G, but any level more than 7.50 can still be considered very good. At the bottom are levels less than 3.00.

Plate Appearances as a leading indicator *(Patrick Davitt)*

While targeting players "age 26 with experience" as potential breakout candidates has become a commonly accepted concept, a study has found that cumulative plate appearances, especially during the first two years of a young player's career, can also have predictive value in assessing a coming spike in production. Three main conclusions:

- When projecting players, MLB experience is more important than age.
- Players who amass 800+ PAs in their first two seasons are highly likely to have double-digit Rotisserie dollar value in Year 3.
- Also target young players in the season where they attain 400 PAs, as they are twice as likely as other players to grow significantly in value.

When do hitters get platooned? *(Jeff Zimmerman)*

We created a talent baseline to determine when a hitter might get platooned by examining 24 actual platoon pairs from the 2017 season. We compared the more extreme hitter's projected OPS splits entering the year. Among the main findings:

- Normally, a spread of ~200 points of OPS is needed to start a platoon. In only two instances did a platoon happen with a projected split under 130 points.
- For most teams to implement a platoon, they need at least one player to have a projected platoon OPS around .030.
- The minimum projected OPS in which teams begin using platoons is around .590. A player could have a 200-point spread, but if the low projected OPS is over .700, teams aren't likely to add another player to make up the difference.

The simple rule of an ".800-.600 OPS spread" works great for an average platoon benchmark. Owners may want to relax the values to snare a few more players with a .775-.625 OPS spread, or an ".800-.600 OPS spread with shrinkage".

Skill-specific aging patterns for batters *(Ed DeCaria)*

Most published aging analyses are done using composite estimates of value such as OPS or linear weights. By contrast, fantasy

GMs are typically more concerned with category-specific player value (HR, SB, AVG, etc.). We can better forecast what matters most by analyzing peak age of individual baseball skills rather than overall player value.

For batters, recognized peak age for overall batting value is a player's late 20s. But individual skills do not peak uniformly at the same time:

Contact rate (ct%): Ascends modestly by about a half point of contact per year from age 22 to 26, then holds steady within a half point of peak until age 35, after which players lose a half point of contact per year.

Walk rate (bb%): Trends the opposite way with age compared to contact rate, as batters tend to peak at age 30 and largely remain there until they turn 38.

Stolen Base Opportunity (SBO): Typically, players maintain their SBO through age 27, but then reduce their attempts steadily in each remaining year of their careers.

Stolen base success rate (SB%): Aggressive runners (>14% SBO) tend to lose about 2 points per year as they age. However, less aggressive runners (<=14% SBO) actually improve their SB% by about 2 points per year until age 28, after which they reverse course and give back 1-2 pts every year as they age.

GB%/LD%/FB%: Both GB% and LD% peak at the start of a player's career and then decline as many hitters seemingly learn to elevate the ball more. But at about age 30, hitter GB% ascends toward a second late-career peak while LD% continues to plummet and FB% continues to rise through age 38.

Hit rate (h%): Declines linearly with age. This is a natural result of a loss of speed and change in batted ball trajectory.

Isolated Power (ISO): Typically peaks from age 24-26. Similarly, home runs per fly ball, opposite field HR %, and Hard Hit % all peak by age 25 and decline somewhat linearly from that point on.

Catchers and late-career performance spikes *(Ed Spaulding)*
Many catchers—particularly second line catchers—have their best seasons late in their careers. Some possible reasons why:

1. Catchers often get to the big leagues for defensive reasons and not their offensive skills. These skills take longer to develop.
2. The heavy emphasis on learning the catching/ defense/ pitching side of the game detracts from their time to learn about, and practice, hitting.
3. Injuries often curtail their ability to show offensive skills, though these injuries (typically jammed fingers, bruises on the arms, rib injuries from collisions) often don't lead to time on the disabled list.
4. The time spent behind the plate has to impact the ability to recognize, and eventually hit, all kinds of pitches.

Spring training Slg as leading indicator *(John Dewan)*
A hitter's spring training Slg .200 or more above his lifetime Slg is a leading indicator for a better than normal season.

Overall batting breakout profile *(Brandon Kruse)*
We define a breakout performance as one where a player posts a Roto value of $20+ after having never posted a value of $10. These criteria are used to validate an apparent breakout in the

current season but may also be used carefully to project a potential upcoming breakout:

- Age 27 or younger
- An increase in at least two of: h%, PX or Spd
- Minimum league average PX or Spd (100)
- Minimum contact rate of 75%
- Minimum xBA of .270

In-Season Analysis

Batting order facts *(Ed DeCaria)*
Eighty-eight percent of today's leadoff hitters bat leadoff again in their next game, 78% still bat leadoff 10 games later, and 68% still bat leadoff 50 games later. Despite this level of turnover after 50 games, leadoff hitters have the best chance of retaining their role over time. After leadoff, #3 and #4 hitters are the next most likely to retain their lineup slots.

On a season-to-season basis, leadoff hitters are again the most stable, with 69% of last year's primary leadoff hitters retaining the #1 slot next year.

Plate appearances decline linearly by lineup slot. Leadoff batters receive 10-12% more PAs than when batting lower in the lineup. AL #9 batters and NL #8 batters get 9-10% fewer PAs. These results mirror play-by-play data showing a 15-20 PA drop by lineup slot over a full season.

Walk rate is largely unaffected by lineup slot in the AL. Beware strong walk rates by NL #8 hitters, as much of this "skill" will disappear if ever moved from the #8 slot.

Batting order has no discernable effect on contact rate.

Hit rate slopes gently upward as hitters are slotted deeper in the lineup.

As expected, the #3-4-5 slots are ideal for non-HR RBIs, at the expense of #6 hitters. RBIs are worst for players in the #1-2 slots. Batting atop the order sharply increases the probability of scoring runs, especially in the NL.

The leadoff slot easily has the highest stolen base attempt rate. #4-5-6 hitters attempt steals more often when batting out of those slots than they do batting elsewhere. The NL #8 hitter is a SB attempt sink hole. A change in batting order from #8 to #1 in the NL could nearly double a player's SB output due to lineup slot alone.

DOMination and DISaster rates
Week-to-week consistency is measured using a batter's BPV compiled in each week. A player earns a DOMinant week if his BPV was greater or equal to 50 for that week. A player registers a DISaster if his BPV was less than 0 for that week. The percentage of Dominant weeks, DOM%, is simply calculated as the number of DOM weeks divided by the total number of weeks played.

Is week-to-week consistency a repeatable skill? *(Bill Macey)*
To test whether consistent performance is a repeatable skill for batters, we examined how closely related a player's DOM% was from year to year.

YR1 DOM%	AVG YR2 DOM%
< 35%	37%
35%–45%	40%
46%–55%	45%
56%+	56%

Quality/consistency score (QC)

(DOM% – (2 x DIS%)) x 2)

Using the DOM/DIS percentages, this score measures both the quality of performance as well as week–to–week consistency.

Projecting RBIs *(Patrick Davitt)*

Evaluating players in-season for RBI potential is a function of the interplay among four factors:

- Teammates' ability to reach base ahead of him and to run the bases efficiently
- His own ability to drive them in by hitting, especially XBH
- Number of Games Played
- Place in the batting order

3-4-5 Hitters:
(0.69 x GP x TOB) + (0.30 x ITB) + (0.275 x HR) – (.191 x GP)

6-7-8 Hitters:
(0.63 x GP x TOB) + (0.27 x ITB) + (0.250 x HR) – (.191 x GP)

9-1-2 Hitters:
(0.57 x GP x TOB) + (0.24 x ITB) + (0.225 x HR) – (.191 x GP)

...where GP = games played, TOB = team on-base pct. and ITB = individual total bases (ITB).

Apply this pRBI formula after 70 games played or so (to reduce the variation from small sample size) to find players more than 9 RBIs over or under their projected RBI. There could be a correction coming.

You should also consider other factors, like injury or trade (involving the player or a top-of-the-order speedster) or team SB philosophy and success rate.

Remember: the player himself has an impact on his TOB. When we first did this study, we excluded the player from his TOB and got better results. The formula overestimates projected RBI for players with high OBP who skew his teams' OBP but can't benefit in RBI from that effect.

Ten-Game hitting streaks as a leading indicator *(Bob Berger)*

Research of hitting streaks from 2011 and 2012 showed that a 10-game streak can reliably predict improved longer-term BA performance during the season. A player who has put together a hitting streak of at least 10 games will improve his BA for the remainder of the season about 60% of the time. This improvement can be significant, on average as much as .020 of BA.

What can foul balls tell us? *(Nick Trojanowski)*

Foul balls, because of their relatively meager influence on in-game outcomes, have been examined far less often than balls in play. Using 2008-17 data for every 500+ pitch season, we found that hitting and inducing foul balls is a skill, in that it's repeatable from year to year. Other findings:

1. Hitters who swing at more pitches, regardless of location, hit more foul balls, regardless of contact rate.
2. Pitchers who induce more swings at strikes allow more fouls, but pitchers who induce more chases do not.
3. Groundball pitchers tend to give up fewer foul balls than flyball pitchers.
4. For hitters, routinely fouling off pitches doesn't regularly lead to better outcomes, and in fact tends to make walks less likely.

Other Diamonds

It's a Busy World Shortcut

For marginal utility-type players, scan their PX and Spd history to see if there's anything to mine for. If you see triple digits anywhere, stop and look further. If not, move on.

Errant Gust of Wind

A unit of measure used to describe the difference between your home run projection and mine.

Mendoza Line

Named for Mario Mendoza, it represents the benchmark for batting futility. Usually refers to a .200 batting average, but can also be used for low levels of other statistical categories. Note that Mendoza's lifetime batting average was actually a much more robust .215.

Old Player Skills

Power, low batting average, no speed and usually good plate patience. Young players, often those with a larger frame, who possess these "old player skills" tend to decline faster than normal, often in their early 30s.

Esix Snead List

Players with excellent speed and sub-.300 on base averages who get a lot of practice running down the line to first base, and then back to the dugout. Also used as an adjective, as in "Esix-Sneadian."

Pitchers

Strikeouts and Walks

Fundamental skills

The contention that pitching performance is unreliable is a fallacy driven by the practice of attempting to project pitching stats using gauges that are poor evaluators of skill.

How can we better evaluate pitching skill? We can start with the statistical categories that are generally unaffected by external factors. These stats capture the outcome of an individual pitcher versus batter match-up without regard to supporting offense, defense or bullpen:

Walks Allowed, Strikeouts and Ground/Fly Balls

Even with only these stats to observe, there is a wealth of insight that these measures can provide.

Control rate (Ctl, bb/9), or opposition walks per game
BB allowed x 9 / IP
Measures how many walks a pitcher allows per game equivalent. **BENCHMARK:** The best pitchers will have bb/9 of 2.5 or less.

Ball% *(Stephen Nickrand)*
See full research on page 67.

Dominance rate (Dom, k/9), or opposition strikeouts/game
Strikeouts recorded x 9 / IP
Measures how many strikeouts a pitcher allows per game equivalent. **BENCHMARK:** The best pitchers will have k/9 levels of 9.0 or higher.

Command ratio (Cmd)
(Strikeouts / Walks)
A measure of a pitcher's ability to get the ball over the plate. There is no more fundamental a skill than this, and so it is used as a leading indicator to project future rises and falls in other gauges, such as ERA. **BENCHMARKS:** Baseball's best pitchers will have ratios in excess of 3.0. Pitchers with ratios less than 1.0—indicating that they walk more batters than they strike out—have virtually no potential for long-term success. If you make no other changes in your approach to drafting pitchers, limiting your focus to only pitchers with a command ratio of 2.5 or better will substantially improve your odds of success.

Command ratio as a leading indicator
The ability to get the ball over the plate—command of the strike zone—is one of the best leading indicators for future performance. Command ratio (K/BB) can be used to project potential in ERA as well as other skills gauges.

1. Research indicates that there is a high correlation between a pitcher's Cmd ratio and his ERA.

	Earned Run Average				
Command	2015	2016	2017	2018	2019
0.0 - 1.0	6.31	7.71	7.24	7.30	7.88
1.1 - 2.0	4.89	5.09	5.17	4.92	5.39
2.1 - 3.0	4.03	4.16	4.37	4.21	4.55
3.1 - 4.0	3.54	3.73	3.76	3.75	4.27
4.1 - 5.0	2.94	3.58	3.39	3.42	3.61
5.1+	3.18	2.79	2.88	3.01	3.04

We can create percentage plays for the different levels:

For Cmd	% with ERA of	
Levels of	3.50-	4.50+
0.0 - 1.0	2%	69%
1.1 - 2.0	7%	79%
2.1 - 3.0	20%	51%
3.1 - 4.0	22%	38%
4.1 - 5.0	42%	26%
5.1 +	69%	18%

2. A pitcher's Command in tandem with Dominance (strikeout rate) provides even greater predictive abilities.

	Earned Run Average	
Command	-8.0 Dom	8.0+ Dom
0.0-1.0	7.53	9.93
1.1-2.0	5.44	5.32
2.1-3.0	4.73	4.45
3.1-4.0	4.53	4.19
4.1-5.0	3.90	3.67
5.1+	3.75	2.95

The version of this chart in previous editions had a cut-off at the 5.6 Dom level, which used to be a roughly 50/50 split in terms how many pitchers fell on each side. To show how far we've shifted, We've set the cut-off at 8.0 and the split was still 37/63 in 2019. But the results remain: there is a lower ceiling for less dominant pitchers, even if they have pinpoint control. The extra dominance makes a difference, especially at the high end.

Swinging strike rate as leading indicator *(Stephen Nickrand)*
Swinging strike rate (SwK%) measures the percentage of total pitches against which a batter swings and misses. SwK% can help us validate and forecast a SP's Dominance (K/9) rate, which in turn allows us to identify surgers and faders with greater accuracy.

BENCHMARKS: SwK% baseline for all pitchers (SP and RP) is 11.5% in AL, 11.7% in NL; Expected Dom (xDom) can be estimated from SwK%; and a pitcher's individual SwK% does not regress to league norms.

The few starters per year who have a 12.0% or higher SwK% are near-locks to have a 9.0 Dom or greater. In contrast, starters with a 7.0% or lower SwK% have nearly no chance at posting even an average Dom. Finally, use an 9.5% SwK% as an acceptable threshold when searching for SP based on this metric; raise it to 10.5% to begin to find SwK% difference-makers.

Fastball velocity and Dominance rate *(Stephen Nickrand)*
It is intuitive that an increase in fastball velocity for starting pitchers leads to more strikeouts. But how much?

Research shows that the vast majority of SP with significant fastball velocity gains follow this three-step process:

1. They experience a significant Dom gain during the same season.
2. Most often, they give back those Dom gains during the following season.
3. They are likely to increase their Dom the following season, but the magnitude of the Dom increase usually is small.

By contrast, the vast majority of SP with significant fastball velocity losses are likely to experience a significant Dom decrease during the same season.

Those SP with significant fastball velocity losses from one season to the next are just as likely to experience a fastball velocity or Dom increase as they are to experience a fastball or Dom decrease, and the amounts of the increase/decrease are nearly identical.

How aging affects fastball velocity, swinging strikes and strikeout rate *(Ed DeCaria)*

On average, pitchers lose about 0.2 mph per season off their fastballs. Over time, this coincides with decreases in swinging strike rate (SwK%) and overall strikeout rate (K/PA)—the inevitable effects of aging. But one thing that pitchers can do to delay these effects is to throw more first pitch strikes.

Power/contact rating

(BB + K) / IP

Measures the level by which a pitcher allows balls to be put into play. In general, extreme power pitchers can be successful even with poor defensive teams. Power pitchers tend to have greater longevity in the game. Contact pitchers with poor defenses behind them are high risks to have poor W-L records and ERA. BENCHMARKS: A level of 1.13+ describes pure throwers. A level of .93 or less describes high contact pitchers.

Balls in Play

Balls in play (BIP)

(Batters faced – (BB + HBP + SAC)) + H – K

The total number of batted balls that are hit fair, both hits and outs. An analysis of how these balls are hit—on the ground, in the air, hits, outs, etc.—can provide analytical insight, from player skill levels to the impact of luck on statistical output.

Batting average on balls in play *(Voros McCracken)*

(H – HR) / (Batters faced – (BB + HBP + SAC)) + H – K – HR

Abbreviated as BABIP; also called hit rate (H%), this is the percent of balls hit into the field of play that fall for hits. In 2000, Voros McCracken published a study that concluded "there is little if any difference among major league pitchers in their ability to prevent hits on balls hit in the field of play." His assertion was that, while a Johan Santana would have a better ability to prevent a batter from getting wood on a ball, or perhaps keeping the ball in the park, once that ball was hit in the field of play, the probability of it falling for a hit was virtually no different than for any other pitcher.

Among the findings in his study were:

- There is little correlation between what a pitcher does one year in the stat and what he will do the next. This is not true with other significant stats (BB, K, HR).
- You can better predict a pitcher's hits per balls in play from the rate of the rest of the pitcher's team than from the pitcher's own rate.

This last point brings a team's defense into the picture. It begs the question, when a batter gets a hit, is it because the pitcher made a bad pitch, the batter took a good swing, or the defense was not positioned correctly?

BABIP as a leading indicator *(Voros McCracken)*

The league average is 30%, which is also the level that individual performances will regress to on a year to year basis. Any +/- variance of 3% or more can affect a pitcher's ERA.

Pitchers will often post hit rates per balls-in-play that are far off from the league average, but then revert to the mean the following year. As such, we can use that mean to project the direction of a pitcher's ERA.

Subsequent research has shown that ground ball or fly ball propensity has some impact on this rate.

Hit rate *(See Batting average on balls in play)*

Opposition batting average (OBA)

Hits allowed / (Batters faced – (BB + HBP + SAC))

The batting average achieved by opposing batters against a pitcher. BENCHMARKS: The best pitchers will have levels less than .235; the worst pitchers levels more than .280.

Opposition on base average (OOB)

(Hits allowed + BB) / ((Batters faced – (BB + HBP + SAC)) + Hits allowed + BB)

The on base average achieved by opposing batters against a pitcher. BENCHMARK: The best pitchers will have levels less than .290; the worst pitchers levels more than .350.

Walks plus hits divided by innings pitched (WHIP)

Essentially the same measure as opposition on base average, but used for Rotisserie purposes. BENCHMARKS: A WHIP of less than 1.15 is considered top level; more than 1.50 indicative of poor performance. Levels less than 1.00—allowing fewer runners than IP—represent extraordinary performance and are rarely maintained over time.

Expected walks plus hits divided by innings pitched (xWHIP) *(Arik Florimonte)*

See full research on page 66.

Ground ball, line drive, fly ball percentage (G/L/F)

The percentage of all balls-in-play that are hit on the ground, in the air and as line drives. For a pitcher, the ability to pitch to a ground ball or fly ball extreme can contribute to his statistical output exceeding his demonstrated skill level.

Ground ball tendency as a leading indicator *(John Burnson)*

Ground ball pitchers tend to give up fewer HRs than do fly ball pitchers. There is also evidence that GB pitchers have higher hit rates. In other words, a ground ball has a higher chance of being a hit than does a fly ball that is not out of the park.

GB pitchers have lower strikeout rates. We should be more forgiving of a low strikeout rate if it belongs to an extreme ground ball pitcher.

GB pitchers have a lower ERA but a higher WHIP than do fly ball pitchers. On balance, GB pitchers come out ahead, even when considering strikeouts, because a lower ERA also leads to more wins.

Groundball and strikeout tendencies as indicators
(Mike Dranchak)
Pitchers were assembled into 9 groups based on the following profiles (minimum 23 starts in 2005):

Profile	Ground Ball Rate
Ground Ball	higher than 47%
Neutral	42% to 47%
Fly Ball	less than 42%

Profile	Strikeout Rate (k/9)
Strikeout	higher than 6.6 k/9
Average	5.4 to 6.6 k/9
Soft-Tosser	less than 5.4 k/9

Findings: Pitchers with higher strikeout rates had better ERAs and WHIPs than pitchers with lower strikeout rates, regardless of ground ball profile. However, for pitchers with similar strikeout rates, those with higher ground ball rates had better ERAs and WHIPs than those with lower ground ball rates.

Pitchers with higher strikeout rates tended to strand more baserunners than those with lower K rates. Fly ball pitchers tended to strand fewer runners than their GB or neutral counterparts within their strikeout profile.

Ground ball pitchers (especially those who lacked high-dominance) yielded more home runs per fly ball than did fly ball pitchers. However, the ERA risk was mitigated by the fact that ground ball pitchers (by definition) gave up fewer fly balls to begin with.

Extreme GB/FB pitchers *(Patrick Davitt)*
Among pitchers with normal strikeout levels, extreme GB pitchers (>3–7% of all batters faced) have ERAs about 0.4 runs lower than normal-GB% pitchers but only slight WHIP advantages. Extreme FB% pitchers (32% FB) show no ERA benefits.

Among High-K (>=24% of BF), however, extreme GBers have ERAs about 0.5 runs lower than normal-GB pitchers, and WHIPs about five points lower. Extreme FB% pitchers have ERAs about 0.2 runs lower than normal-FB pitchers, and WHIPs about 10 points lower.

Revisiting fly balls *(Jason Collette)*
The increased emphasis on defensive positioning is often associated with infield shifting, but the same data also influences how outfielders are positioned. Some managers are positioning OFs more aggressively than just the customary few steps per a right- or left-handed swinging batter. Five of the top 10 defensive efficiency teams in 2013 —OAK, STL, MIA, LAA and KC—also had parks among the top 10 in HR suppression.

Before dismissing flyball pitchers as toxic assets, pay more attention to park factors and OF defensive talent. In particular, be a little more willing to roster fly ball pitchers who pitch both in front of good defensive OFs and in good pitchers' parks.

Line drive percentage as a leading indicator *(Seth Samuels)*
The percentage of balls-in-play that are line drives is beyond a pitcher's control. Line drives do the most damage; from 1994-2003, here were the expected hit rates and number of total bases per type of BIP.

	Type of BIP		
	GB	FB	LD
H%	26%	23%	56%
Total bases	0.29	0.57	0.80

Despite the damage done by LDs, pitchers do not have any innate skill to avoid them. There is little relationship between a pitcher's LD% one year and his rate the next year. All rates tend to regress towards a mean of 22.6%.

However, GB pitchers do have a slight ability to prevent LDs (21.7%) and extreme GB hurlers even moreso (18.5%). Extreme FB pitchers have a slight ability to prevent LDs (21.1%) as well.

Home run to fly ball rate (HR/F)
HR / FB
The percent of fly balls that are hit for home runs.

HR/F as a leading indicator *(John Burnson)*
McCracken's work focused on "balls in play," omitting home runs from the study. However, pitchers also do not have much control over the percentage of fly balls that turn into HR. Research shows that there is an underlying rate of HR as a percentage of fly balls of about 15%. A pitcher's HR/FB rate will vary each year but always tends to regress to that 15%. The element that pitchers do have control over is the number of fly balls they allow. That is the underlying skill or deficiency that controls their HR rate.

Expected home runs to fly ball rate (xHR/F) *(Arik Florimonte)*
See full research on page 65.

"Just Enough" home runs as a leading indicator *(Brian Slack)*
Using ESPN's Home Run Tracker data, we analyzed year-to-year consistency of "Just Enough" home runs (those that clear the fence by less than 10 vertical feet or land less than one fence height past the fence). For the 528 starting pitchers who logged enough innings to qualify for the ERA title in consecutive years from 2006 through 2016 season, research showed:

- The percentage of Just Enough home runs that a pitcher gives up gravitates towards league average (32%) the following year.
- There is only a tenuous connection between a pitcher's ability to limit the percentage of Just Enough home runs and a pitcher's HR/FB rate. So we should avoid the assumption that a pitcher with a high percentage of Just Enough home runs will necessarily improve his HR/FB rate (and presumably ERA) the following year, or vice versa.
- This means be careful not to over-draft a pitcher based solely on the idea of HR/FB improvement in the coming year. Conversely, one should not automatically avoid pitchers with perceived HR/FB downside.

Opposition home runs per game (hr/9)
(HR Allowed x 9 / IP)
Also, expected opposition HR rate = (FB x 0.10) x 9 / IP
Measures how many HR a pitcher allows per game equivalent. Since FB tend to go yard at about a 10% rate, we can also estimate this rate off of fly balls. **BENCHMARK:** The best pitchers will have hr/9 levels of less than 1.0.

Runs

Expected earned run average (xERA)

Gill and Reeve version: *(.575 x H [per 9 IP]) + (.94 x HR [per 9 IP]) + (.28 x BB [per 9 IP]) − (.01 x K [per 9 IP]) − Normalizing Factor*

John Burnson version (used in this book):
(xER x 9)/IP, where xER is defined as
xER% x (FB/10) + (1−xS%) x [0.3 x (BIP − FB/10) + BB]
where xER% = 0.96 − (0.0284 x (GB/FB))
and
xS% = (64.5 + (K/9 x 1.2) − (BB/9 x (BB/9 + 1)) / 20)
+ ((0.0012 x (GB%^2)) − (0.001 x GB%) - 2.4)

xERA represents the an equivalent of what a pitcher's real ERA might be, calculated solely with skills-based measures. It is not influenced by situation-dependent factors.

Expected ERA variance

xERA − ERA

The variance between a pitcher's ERA and his xERA is a measure of over or underachievement. A positive variance indicates the potential for a pitcher's ERA to rise. A negative variance indicates the potential for ERA improvement. **BENCHMARK:** Discount variances that are less than 0.50. Any variance more than 1.00 (one run per game) is regarded as a strong indicator of future change.

Projected xERA or projected ERA?

Which should we be using to forecast a pitcher's ERA? Projected xERA is more accurate for looking ahead on a purely skills basis. Projected ERA includes *situation-dependent* events—bullpen support, park factors, etc.—which are reflected better by ERA. The optimal approach is to use both gauges as *a range of expectation* for forecasting purposes.

Strand rate (S%)

(H + BB − ER) / (H + BB − HR)

Measures the percentage of allowed runners a pitcher strands (earned runs only), which incorporates both individual pitcher skill and bullpen effectiveness. **BENCHMARKS:** The most adept at stranding runners will have S% levels over 75%. Those with rates over 80% will have artificially low ERAs which will be prone to relapse. Levels below 65% will inflate ERA but have a high probability of regression.

Expected strand rate *(Michael Weddell)*

*73.935 + K/9 - 0.116 * (BB/9*(BB/9+1))*
*+ (0.0047 * GB%^2 - 0.3385 * GB%)*
+ (MAX(2,MIN(4,IP/G))/2-1)
+ (0.82 if left-handed)

This formula is based on three core skills: strikeouts per nine innings, walks per nine innings, and ground balls per balls in play, with adjustments for whether the pitcher is a starter or reliever (measured by IP/G), and his handedness.

Strand rate as a leading indicator *(Ed DeCaria)*

Strand rate often regresses/rebounds toward past rates (usually 69-74%), resulting in Year 2 ERA changes:

% of Pitchers with Year 2 Regression/Rebound			
Y1 S%	RP	SP	LR
<60%	100%	94%	94%
65	81%	74%	88%
70	53%	48%	65%
75	55%	85%	100%
80	80%	100%	100%
85	100%	100%	100%

Typical ERA Regression/Rebound in Year 2			
Y1 S%	RP	SP	LR
<60%	-2.54	-2.03	-2.79
65	-1.00	-0.64	-0.93
70	-0.10	-0.05	-0.44
75	0.24	0.54	0.75
80	1.15	1.36	2.29
85	1.71	2.21	n/a

Starting pitchers (SP) have a narrower range of strand rate outcomes than do relievers (RP) or swingmen/long relievers (LR). **Relief pitchers** with Y1 strand rates of <=67% or >=78% are likely to experience a +/- ERA regression in Y2. **Starters and swingmen/long relievers** with Y1 strand rates of <=65% or >=75% are likely to experience a +/- ERA regression in Y2. Pitchers with strand rates that deviate more than a few points off of their individual expected strand rates are likely to experience some degree of ERA regression in Y2. Over-performing (or "lucky") pitchers are more likely than underperforming (or "unlucky") pitchers to see such a correction.

Does it matter where runners are stranded? *(Nick Trojanowski)*

Leaving runners on base (S%) is more luck than skill, which holds true for stranding runners on a specific base as well. To confirm this, we created modified strand rates (mS%) for runners on first, second, and third base and found weak year-to-year correlations for all three. There isn't much evidence that stranding runners on a specific base is a skill, or that it's biased towards one type of pitcher (high-strikeout, high-groundball) or another.

Wins

Expected Wins (xW) *(Matt Cederholm)*

[(Team runs per game)^1.8]/[(Pitcher ERA)^1.8 + (Team runs per game)^1.8] x 0.72 x GS

Starting pitchers' win totals are often at odds with their ERA. Attempts to find a strictly skill-based analysis of this phenomenon haven't worked, but there is a powerful tool in the toolbox: Bill James' Pythagorean Theorem. While usually applied to team outcomes, recent research has shown that its validity holds up when applied to individual starting pitchers.

One key to applying the Pythagorean Theorem is factoring in no-decisions. Research shows that the average no-decision rate is 28% of starts, regardless of the type or quality of the pitcher or his team, with no correlation in ND% from one season to the next.

Overall, 70% of pitchers whose expected wins varied from actual wins showed regression in wins per start in the following year, making variation from Expected Wins a good leading indicator.

Projecting/chasing wins

There are five events that need to occur in order for a pitcher to post a single win...

1. He must pitch well, allowing few runs.
2. The offense must score enough runs.
3. The defense must successfully field all batted balls.
4. The bullpen must hold the lead.
5. The manager must leave the pitcher in for 5 innings, and not remove him if the team is still behind.

Of these five events, only one is within the control of the pitcher. As such, projecting or chasing wins based on skills alone can be an exercise in futility.

Home field advantage *(John Burnson)*

A 2006 study found that home starting pitchers get credited with a win in 38% of their outings. Visiting team starters are credited with a win in 33% of their outings.

Usage

Batters faced per game *(Craig Wright)*

((Batters faced – (BB + HBP + SAC)) + H + BB) / G

A measure of pitcher usage and one of the leading indicators for potential pitcher burnout.

Workload

Research suggests that there is a finite number of innings in a pitcher's arm. This number varies by pitcher, by development cycle, and by pitching style and repertoire. We can measure a pitcher's potential for future arm problems and/or reduced effectiveness (burnout):

Sharp increases in usage from one year to the next. Common wisdom has suggested that pitchers who significantly increase their workload from one year to the next are candidates for burnout symptoms. This has often been called the Verducci Effect, after writer Tom Verducci. BaseballHQ.com analyst Michael Weddell tested pitchers with sharp workload increases during the period 1988-2008 and found that no such effect exists.

Starters' overuse. Consistent "batters faced per game" (BF/G) levels of 28.0 or higher, combined with consistent seasonal IP totals of 200 or more may indicate burnout potential, especially with pitchers younger than 25. Within a season, a BF/G of more than 30.0 with a projected IP total of 200 may indicate a late season fade.

Relievers' overuse. Warning flags should be up for relievers who post in excess of 100 IP in a season, while averaging fewer than 2 IP per outing.

When focusing solely on minor league pitchers, research results are striking:

Stamina: Virtually every minor league pitcher who had a BF/G of 28.5 or more in one season experienced a drop-off in BF/G the following year. Many were unable to ever duplicate that previous level of durability.

Performance: Most pitchers experienced an associated drop-off in their BPVs in the years following the 28.5 BF/G season. Some were able to salvage their effectiveness later on by moving to the bullpen.

Effects of short-term workloads on relief pitcher value

(Arik Florimonte)

Using game logs from 2002-17, we studied the effects of recent workload on relief pitcher performance. After accounting for factors such as selection and usage bias—good pitchers get used on short rest more often—we discovered there is almost no measurable performance impact. Pitchers used heavily for several days, including the day before, show perhaps a 5-10% reduction in BPV.

Pitchers who have thrown often in the recent past are less likely to be used, which can significantly reduce their value, with a 36% reduction in saves and a 64% reduction in games pitched when "worn out".

In leagues with daily lineup changes, monitoring RP workloads can help owners decide to start rested closers of lesser quality, and therefore lower cost, over more expensive closers who may be worn out.

Protecting young pitchers *(Craig Wright)*

There is a link between some degree of eventual arm trouble and a history of heavy workloads in a pitcher's formative years. Some recommendations from this research:

Teenagers (A-ball): No 200 IP seasons and no BF/G over 28.5 in any 150 IP span. No starts on three days rest.

Ages 20-22: Average no more than 105 pitches per start with a single game ceiling of 130 pitches.

Ages 23-24: Average no more than 110 pitches per start with a single game ceiling of 140 pitches.

When possible, a young starter should be introduced to the majors in long relief before he goes into the rotation.

Overall Performance Analysis

Base Performance Value (BPV)

((Dominance Rate - 5.0) x 18)
+ ((4.0 - Walk Rate) x 27))
+ (Ground ball rate as a whole number - 40%)

A single value that describes a player's overall raw skill level. The formula combines the individual raw skills of dominance, control and the ability to keep the ball down in the zone, all characteristics that are unaffected by most external factors. In tandem with a pitcher's strand rate, it provides a more complete picture of the elements that contribute to ERA, and therefore serves as an accurate tool to project likely changes in ERA.

Base Performance Index (BPX)

BPV scaled to league average to account for year-to-year fluctuations in league-wide statistical performance. It's a snapshot of a player's overall skills compared to an average player. **BENCHMARK:** A level of 100 means a player had a league-average BPV in that given season.

Runs above replacement (RAR)

An estimate of the number of runs a player contributes above a "replacement level" player.

Batters create runs; pitchers save runs. But are batters and pitchers who have comparable RAR levels truly equal in value?

Pitchers might be considered to have higher value. Saving an additional run is more important than producing an additional run. A pitcher who throws a shutout is guaranteed to win that game, whereas no matter how many runs a batter produces, his team can still lose given poor pitching support.

To calculate RAR for pitchers:

1. Start with the replacement level league ERA.
2. Subtract the pitcher's ERA. (To calculate projected RAR, use the pitcher's xERA.)
3. Multiply by number of games played, calculated as plate appearances (IP x 4.34) divided by 38.
4. Multiply the resulting RAR level by 1.08 to account for the variance between earned runs and total runs.

Skill-specific aging patterns for pitchers *(Ed DeCaria)*

Baseball forecasters obsess over "peak age" of player performance because we must understand player ascent toward and decline from that peak to predict future value. Most published aging analyses are done using composite estimates of value such as OPS or linear weights. By contrast, fantasy GMs are typically more concerned with category-specific player value (K, ERA, WHIP, etc.). We can better forecast what matters most by analyzing peak age of individual baseball skills rather than overall player value.

For pitchers, prior research has shown that pitcher value peaks somewhere in the late 20s to early 30s. But how does aging affect each demonstrable pitching skill?

Strikeout rate (k/9): Declines fairly linearly beginning at age 25.

Walk rate (bb/9): Improves until age 25 and holds somewhat steady until age 29, at which point it begins to steadily worsen. Deteriorating k/9 and bb/9 rates result in inefficiency, as it requires far more pitches to get an out. For starting pitchers, this affects the ability to pitch deep into games.

Innings Pitched per game (IP/G): Among starters, it improves slightly until age 27, then tails off considerably with age, costing pitchers nearly one full IP/G by age 33 and one more by age 39.

Hit rate (H%): Among pitchers, H% appears to increase slowly but steadily as pitchers age, to the tune of .002-.003 points per year.

Strand rate (S%): Very similar to hit rate, except strand rate decreases with age rather than increasing. GB%/LD%/FB%: Line drives increase steadily from age 24 onward, and outfield flies increase beginning at age 31. Because 70%+ of line drives fall for hits, and 10%+ of fly balls become home runs, this spells trouble for aging pitchers.

Home runs per fly ball (HR/F): As each year passes, a higher percentage of a pitcher's fly balls become home runs allowed increases with age.

Catchers' effect on pitching *(Thomas Hanrahan)*

A typical catcher handles a pitching staff better after having been with a club for a few years. Research has shown that there is an improvement in team ERA of approximately 0.37 runs from a catcher's rookie season to his prime years with a club. Expect a pitcher's ERA to be higher than expected if he is throwing to a rookie backstop.

First productive season *(Michael Weddell)*

To find those starting pitchers who are about to post their first productive season in the majors (10 wins, 150 IP, ERA of 4.00 or less), look for:

- Pitchers entering their age 23-26 seasons, especially those about to pitch their age 25 season.
- Pitchers who already have good skills, shown by an xERA in the prior year of 4.25 or less.
- Pitchers coming off of at least a partial season in the majors without a major health problem.
- To the extent that one speculates on pitchers who are one skill away, look for pitchers who only need to improve their control (bb/9).

Overall pitching breakout profile *(Brandon Kruse)*

A breakout performance is defined here as one where a player posts a Rotisserie value of $20 or higher after having never achieved $10 previously. These criteria are primarily used to validate an apparent breakout in the current season but may also be used carefully to project a potential breakout for an upcoming season.

- Age 27 or younger
- Minimum 5.6 Dom, 2.0 Cmd, 1.1 hr/9 and 50 BPV
- Maximum 30% hit rate
- Minimum 71% strand rate
- Starters should have a H% no greater than the previous year; relievers should show improved command
- Maximum xERA of 4.00

Bounceback fallacy *(Patrick Davitt)*

It is conventional wisdom that a pitcher often follows a bad year (value decline of more than 50%) with a significant "bounceback" that offers profit opportunity for the canny owner. But research showed the owner is extremely unlikely to get a full bounceback, and in fact, is more likely to suffer a further decline or uselessly small recovery than even a partial bounceback. The safest bet is a $30+ pitcher who has a collapse—but even then, bid to only about half of the previous premium value.

Pitchers crossing leagues *(Bob Berger)*

The AL has higher league-wide ERA and lower K/9 when compared to the NL. Fantasy owners should consider adjusting their ERA, WHIP, and K/9 expectations for pitchers moving to the "other" league. Pitchers moving to the NL may perform better than expected based on their recent career trends; pitchers moving to the AL may perform worse than expected.

Closers

Saves

There are six events that need to occur in order for a relief pitcher to post a single save:

1. The starting pitcher and middle relievers must pitch well.
2. The offense must score enough runs.
3. It must be a reasonably close game.

4. The manager must put the pitcher in for a save opportunity.

5. The pitcher must pitch well and hold the lead.

6. The manager must let him finish the game.

Of these six events, only one is within the control of the relief pitcher. As such, projecting saves for a reliever has less to do with skills than opportunity. However, pitchers with excellent skills may create opportunity for themselves.

Saves conversion rate (Sv%)
Saves / Save Opportunities
The percentage of save opportunities that are successfully converted. BENCHMARK: We look for a minimum 80% for long-term success.

Leverage index (LI) (Tom Tango)
Leverage index measures the amount of swing in win probability indexed against an average value of 1.00. Thus, relievers who come into games in various situations create a composite score and if that average score is higher than 1.00, then their manager is showing enough confidence in them to try to win games with them. If the average score is below 1.00, then the manager is using them, but not showing nearly as much confidence that they can win games.

Saves chances and wins (Patrick Davitt)
Do good teams get more saves because they generate more wins, or do poor teams get more saves because more of their wins are by narrow margins. The "good-team" side is probably on firmer ground, though there are enough exceptions that we should be cautious about drawing broad inferences.

The 2014 study confirmed what Craig Neuman found years earlier: The argument "more wins leads to more saves" is generally correct. Over five studied seasons, the percentage of wins that were saved (Sv%W) was about 50%, and half of all team-seasons fell in the Sv%W range of 48%-56%. As a result, high-saves seasons were more common for high-win teams.

That wins-saves connection for individual team-seasons was much less solid, however, and we observed many outliers. Data for individual team-seasons showed wide ranges of both Sv%W and actual saves.

Finally, higher-win teams do indeed get more blowout wins, but while poorer teams had a higher percentage (73%) of close wins (three runs or fewer) than better teams (56%), good teams' higher number of wins meant they still had more close wins, more save opportunities and more saves, again with many outliers among individual team-seasons.

Origin of closers
History has long maintained that ace closers are not easily recognizable early on in their careers, so that every season does see its share of the unexpected. Ian Kennedy, Emilio Pagan, Luke Jackson, Brandon Workman, Hansel Robles...who would have thought it a year ago?

Accepted facts, all of which have some element of truth:

- You cannot find major league closers from pitchers who were closers in the minors.

- Closers begin their careers as starters.
- Closers are converted set-up men.
- Closers are pitchers who were unable to develop a third effective pitch.

More simply, closers are a product of circumstance.

Are the minor leagues a place to look at all?

From 1990-2004, there were 280 twenty-save seasons in Double-A and Triple-A. Over that period, only 13 pitchers ever saved 20 games in the majors and only five who ever posted more than one 20-save season: John Wetteland, Mark Wohlers, Ricky Bottalico, Braden Looper and Francisco Cordero.

More recent data is even more pessimistic:

Year	# with 20 Svs	MLB closers
2006	25	none
2007	22	none
2008	19	none
2009	17	none
2010	14	Craig Kimbrel
2011	16	none
2012	16	A.J. Ramos
2013	16	none
2014	12	none
2015	17	none

That's 177 twenty-save seasons and only two major league closers.

One of the reasons that minor league closers rarely become major league closers is because, in general, they do not get enough innings in the minors to sufficiently develop their arms into big-league caliber.

In fact, organizations do not look at minor league closing performance seriously, assigning that role to pitchers who they do not see as legitimate prospects. The average age of minor league closers over the past decade has been 27.5.

Elements of saves success
The task of finding future closing potential comes down to looking at two elements:

Talent: The raw skills to mow down hitters for short periods of time.

Opportunity: The more important element, yet the one that pitchers have no control over.

There are pitchers that have Talent, but not Opportunity. These pitchers are not given a chance to close for a variety of reasons (e.g. being blocked by a solid front-liner in the pen, being left-handed, etc.), but are good to own because they will not likely hurt your pitching staff. You just can't count on them for saves, at least not in the near term.

There are pitchers that have Opportunity, but not Talent. MLB managers decide who to give the ball to in the 9th inning based on their own perceptions about what skills are required to succeed, even if those perceived "skills" don't translate into acceptable metrics.

Those pitchers without the metrics may have some initial short-term success, but their long-term prognosis is poor and they are high risks to your roster. Classic examples of the short life span of these types of pitchers include Matt Karchner, Heath Slocumb, Ryan Kohlmeier, Dan Miceli, Joe Borowski and Danny

Kolb. More recent examples include Brandon Kintzler, Sam Dyson, Brad Ziegler and Jeanmar Gomez.

Closers' job retention *(Michael Weddell)*

Of pitchers with 20 or more saves in one year, only 67.5% of these closers earned 20 or more saves the following year. The variables that best predicted whether a closer would avoid this attrition:

- *Saves history:* Career saves was the most important factor.
- *Age:* Closers are most likely to keep their jobs at age 27. For long-time closers, their growing career saves totals more than offset the negative impact of their advanced ages. Older closers without a long history of racking up saves tend to be bad candidates for retaining their roles.
- *Performance:* Actual performance, measured by ERA+, was of only minor importance.
- *Being right-handed:* Increased the odds of retaining the closer's role by 9% over left-handers.

How well can we predict which closers will keep their jobs? Of the 10 best closers during 1989-2007, 90% saved at least 20 games during the following season. Of the 10 worst bets, only 20% saved at least 20 games the next year.

Closer volatility history

Year	Closers Drafted	Avg R$	Closers Failed	Failure %	New Sources
2010	28	$16.96	7	25%	13
2011	30	$15.47	11	37%	8
2012	29	$15.28	19	66%	18
2013	29	$15.55	9	31%	13
2014	28	$15.54	11	39%	15
2015	29	$14.79	13	45%	16
2016	33	$13.30	19	58%	17
2017	32	$13.63	17	53%	15
2018	27	$13.22	17	63%	20
2019	31	$13.29	18	58%	14

Drafted refers to the number of saves sources purchased in both LABR and Tout Wars experts leagues each year. These only include relievers drafted specifically for saves speculation. *Avg R$* refers to the average purchase price of these pitchers in the AL-only and NL-only leagues. *Failed* is the number (and percentage) of saves sources drafted that did not return at least 50% of their value that year. The failures include those that lost their value due to ineffectiveness, injury or managerial decision. *New Sources* are arms that were drafted for less than $10 (if drafted at all) but finished with at least 10 saves.

The 18 failed saves investments in 2019 were Cody Allen, Jose Alvarado, Matt Barnes, Brad Boxberger, Archie Bradley, Wade Davis, Edwin Diaz, Sean Doolittle, Mychal Givens, Jordan Hicks, Craig Kimbrel, Corey Knebel, Jose Leclerc, Trevor May, David Robertson, Pedro Strop, Blake Treinen and Arodys Vizcaino. Some of these "failures" amassed significant saves totals but their ERA/WHIP did not justify their draft investments.

The new sources in 2019 were Roenis Elias, Liam Hendriks, Greg Holland, Luke Jackson, Shawn Kelley, Ian Kennedy, Carlos Martinez, Mark Melancon, Hector Neris, Emilio Pagan, Blake Parker, Hansel Robles, Taylor Rogers and Brandon Workman.

Note that many of these were temporary assignments and were subsequently replaced as well.

Closers and multi-year performance *(Patrick Davitt)*

A team having an "established closer"—even a successful one—in a given year does not affect how many of that team's wins are saved in the next year. However, a top closer (40-plus saves) in a given year has a significantly greater chance to retain his role in the subsequent season.

Research of saves and wins data over several seasons found that the percentage of wins that are saved is consistently 50%-54%, irrespective of whether the saves were concentrated in the hands of a "top closer" or passed around to the dreaded "committee" of lesser closers. But it also found that about two-thirds of high-save closers reprised their roles the next season, while three-quarters of low-save closers did not. Moreover, closers who held the role for two or three straight seasons averaged 34 saves per season while closers new to the role averaged 27.

Other Relievers

Projecting holds *(Doug Dennis)*

Here are some general rules of thumb for identifying pitchers who might be in line to accumulate holds. The percentages represent the portion of 2003's top holds leaders who fell into the category noted.

1. Left-handed set-up men with excellent BPIs. (43%)
2. A "go-to" right-handed set-up man with excellent BPIs. This is the one set-up RHer that a manager turns to with a small lead in the 7th or 8th innings. These pitchers also tend to vulture wins. (43%, but 6 of the top 9)
3. Excellent BPIs, but not a firm role as the main LHed or RHed set-up man. Roles change during the season; cream rises to the top. Relievers projected to post great BPIs often overtake lesser set-up men in-season. (14%)

Reliever efficiency percent (REff%)

(Wins + Saves + Holds) / (Wins + Losses + SaveOpps + Holds)

This is a measure of how often a reliever contributes positively to the outcome of a game. A record of consistent, positive impact on game outcomes breeds managerial confidence, and that confidence could pave the way to save opportunities. For those pitchers suddenly thrust into a closer's role, this formula helps gauge their potential to succeed based on past successes in similar roles. **BENCHMARK:** Minimum of 80%.

Vulture

A pitcher, typically a middle reliever, who accumulates an unusually high number of wins by preying on other pitchers' misfortunes. More accurately, this is a pitcher typically brought into a game after a starting pitcher has put his team behind, and then pitches well enough and long enough to allow his offense to take the lead, thereby "vulturing" a win from the starter. This concept has been losing its relevance with the rising use of Openers. Today's "vulture" is the bulk inning relief pitcher who follows the one-inning Opener and does not have to pitch five innings to qualify for a Win.

In-Season Analysis

Pure Quality Starts

Pure Quality Starts (PQS) says that the smallest unit of measure should not be the "event" but instead be the "game." Within that game, we can accumulate all the strikeouts, hits and walks, and evaluate that outing as a whole. After all, when a pitcher takes the mound, he is either "on" or "off" his game; he is either dominant or struggling, or somewhere in between.

In PQS, we give a starting pitcher credit for exhibiting certain skills in each of his starts. Then by tracking his "PQS Score" over time, we can follow his progress. A starter earns one point for each of the following criteria:

1. *The pitcher must go more than 6 innings (record at least one out in the 7th). This measures stamina.*

2. *He must allow fewer hits than innings pitched. This measures hit prevention.*

3. *His number of strikeouts must equal to or more than 5. This measures dominance.*

4. *He must strike out at least three times as many batters as he walks (or have a minimum of three strikeouts if he hasn't walked a batter). This measures command.*

5. *He must not allow a home run. This measures his ability to keep the ball in the park.*

A perfect PQS score is 5. Any pitcher who averages 3 or more over the course of the season is probably performing admirably. The nice thing about PQS is it allows you to approach each start as more than an all-or-nothing event.

Note the absence of earned runs. No matter how many runs a pitcher allows, if he scores high on the PQS scale, he has hurled a good game in terms of his base skills. The number of runs allowed—a function of not only the pitcher's ability but that of his bullpen and defense—will tend to even out over time.

It doesn't matter if a few extra balls got through the infield, or the pitcher was given the hook in the fourth or sixth inning, or the bullpen was able to strand their inherited baserunners. When we look at performance in the aggregate, those events do matter, and will affect a pitcher's peripherals and ERA. But with PQS, the minutia is less relevant than the overall performance.

In the end, a dominating performance is a dominating performance, whether Max Scherzer hurls six innings of scoreless baseball or gives up two runs while striking out 12 in 7.2 IP. And a disaster is still a disaster, whether Dylan Bundy gets pulled in the second inning after allowing 7 runs, or gets a 6th inning hook after giving up 6 runs.

Skill versus consistency

Two pitchers have identical 4.50 ERAs and identical 3.0 PQS averages. Their PQS logs look like this:

```
PITCHER A:    3    3    3    3    3
PITCHER B:    5    0    5    0    5
```

Which pitcher would you rather have on your team? The risk-averse manager would choose Pitcher A as he represents the perfectly known commodity. Many fantasy leaguers might opt for Pitcher B because his occasional dominating starts show

that there is an upside. His Achilles Heel is inconsistency—he is unable to sustain that high level. Is there any hope for Pitcher B?

- If a pitcher's inconsistency is characterized by more poor starts than good starts, his upside is limited.
- Pitchers with extreme inconsistency rarely get a full season of starts.
- However, inconsistency is neither chronic nor fatal.

The outlook for Pitcher A is actually worse. Disaster avoidance might buy these pitchers more starts, but history shows that the lack of dominating outings is more telling of future potential. In short, consistent mediocrity is bad.

PQS DOMination and DISaster rates *(Gene McCaffrey)*

DOM% is the percentage of a starting pitcher's outings that rate as a PQS-4 or PQS-5. DIS% is the percentage that rate as a PQS-0 or PQS-1.

DOM/DIS percentages open up a new perspective, providing us with two separate scales of performance. In tandem, they measure consistency.

Quality/consistency score (QC)
(DOM% − (2 x DIS%)) x 2

Using PQS and DOM/DIS percentages, this score measures both the quality of performance as well as start-to-start consistency.

The predictive value of PQS *(Arik Florimonte)*

Using data from 2010-2015, research showed that PQS values can be used to project future starts. A pitcher who even threw only one PQS-DOM start had a slightly better chance of throwing another DOM in his subsequent start. For a pitcher who posts two, three, or even four PQS-DOMs in a row, the streak does portend better results to come. The longer the streak, the better the results.

Fantasy owners best positioned to take advantage are those who can frequently choose from multiple similar SP options, such as in a DFS league, or streaming in traditional leagues. In either case, make your evaluations as you normally would (e.g. talent first, then matchups, ballpark or by using BaseballHQ. com's Pitcher Matchups Tool)—and then give a value bump to the pitcher with the hot streak.

PQS correlation with Quality Starts *(Paul Petera)*

PQS	QS%
0	8%
1	18%
2	38%
3	63%
4	87%
5	99%

High pitch counts and PQS *(Paul Petera)*

A 2017 study found that high-scoring PQS starters who also ran up high pitch counts continued to thrive in their next start (and beyond). Taking three seasons of PQS and pitch-count data, starts were grouped by pitch count into five cohorts and averaged by PQS. The study then calculated the average PQS scores in the subsequent starts, and found that pitchers with higher pitch counts are safer bets to throw well in their next start (and beyond) than those who throw fewer pitches. Near-term fatigue or other

negative symptoms do not appear to be worthy of concern; so do not shy away from these pitchers solely for that reason.

In-season ERA/xERA variance as a leading indicator
(Matt Cederholm)

Pitchers with large first-half ERA/xERA variances will see regression towards their xERA in the second half, if they are allowed (and are able) to finish out the season. Starters have a stronger regression tendency than relievers, which we would expect to see given the larger sample size. In addition, there is substantial attrition among all types of pitchers, but those who are "unlucky" have a much higher rate.

An important corollary: While a pitcher underperforming his xERA is very likely to rebound in the second half, such regression hinges on his ability to hold onto his job long enough to see that regression come to fruition. Healthy veteran pitchers with an established role are more likely to experience the second half boost than a rookie starter trying to make his mark.

Pure Quality Relief *(Patrick Davitt)*

A system for evaluating reliever outings. The scoring :

1. Two points for the first out, and one point for each subsequent out, to a maximum of four points.
2. One point for having at least one strikeout for every four full outs (one K for 1-4 outs, two Ks for 5-8 outs, etc.).
3. One point for zero baserunners, minus one point for each baserunner, though allowing the pitcher one unpenalized runner for each three full outs (one baserunner for 3-5 outs, two for 6-8 outs, three for nine outs)
4. Minus one point for each earned run, though allowing one ER for 8– or 9-out appearances.
5. An automatic PQR-0 for allowing a home run.

Avoiding relief disasters *(Ed DeCaria)*

Relief disasters (defined as ER>=3 and IP<=3), occur in 5%+ of all appearances. The chance of a disaster exceeds 13% in any 7-day period. To minimize the odds of a disaster, we created a model that produced the following list of factors, in order of influence:

1. Strength of opposing offense
2. Park factor of home stadium
3. BB/9 over latest 31 days (more walks is bad)
4. Pitch count over previous 7 days (more pitches is bad)
5. Latest 31 Days ERA>xERA (recent bad luck continues)

Daily league owners who can slot relievers by individual game should also pay attention to days of rest: pitching on less rest than one is accustomed to increases disaster risk.

April ERA as a leading indicator *(Stephen Nickrand)*

A starting pitcher's April ERA can act as a leading indicator for how his ERA is likely to fare during the balance of the season. A study looked at extreme April ERA results to see what kind of in-season forecasting power they may have. From 2010-2012, 42 SP posted an ERA in April that was at least 2.00 ER better than their career ERA. The findings:

- Pitchers who come out of the gates quickly have an excellent chance at finishing the season with an ERA much better than their career ERA.
- While April ERA gems see their in-season ERA regresses towards their career ERA, their May-Sept ERA is still significantly better than their career ERA.
- Those who stumble out of the gates have a strong chance at posting an ERA worse than their career average, but their in-season ERA improves towards their career ERA.
- April ERA disasters tend to have a May-Sept ERA that closely resembles their career ERA.

Using K–BB% to find SP buying opportunities *(Arik Florimonte)*

Research showed that finding pitchers who have seen an uptick in k–bb% over the past 30 days is one way to search for mid-season replacements from the waiver wire. Using 2014-2016 player-seasons and filtering for starting pitchers with ≥ 100 IP, the k–bb% mean is about 13%. The overall MLB mean is approximately 12%, and the top 50 SP tend to be 14% or higher.
The findings:

- Last 30 days k–bb% is useful as a gauge of next 30 days performance.
- Pitchers on the upswing are more likely to climb into the elite ranks than other pitchers of similar YTD numbers; pitchers with a larger uptick show a greater likelihood.
- Last-30 k–bb% surgers could be good mid-season pickups if they are being overlooked by other owners in your league.

Second-half ERA reduction drivers *(Stephen Nickrand)*

It's easy to dismiss first-half-to-second-half improvement among starting pitchers as an unpredictable event. After all, the midpoint of the season is an arbitrary cutoff. Performance swings occur throughout the season.

A study of SP who experienced significant 1H-2H ERA improvement from 2010-2012 examined what indicators drove second-half ERA improvement. Among the findings for those 79 SP with a > 1.00 ERA 1H-2H reduction:

- 97% saw their WHIP decrease, with an average decrease of 0.26
- 97% saw their strand (S%) rate improve, with an average increase of 9%
- 87% saw their BABIP (H%) improve, with an average reduction of 5%
- 75% saw their control (bb/9) rate improve, with an average reduction of 0.8
- 70% saw their HR/9 rate improve, with an average decrease of 0.5
- 68% saw their swinging strike (SwK%) rate improve, with an average increase of 1.4%
- 68% saw their BPV improve, with an average increase of 37
- 67% saw their HR per fly ball rate (hr/f) improve, with an average decrease of 4%
- 53% saw their ground ball (GB%) rate improve, with an average increase of 5%
- 52% saw their dominance (k/9) rate improve, with an average increase of 1.3

These findings highlight the power of H% and S% regression as it relates to ERA and WHIP improvement. In fact, H% and S% are more often correlated with ERA improvement than are improved skills. They also suggest that improved control has a bigger impact on ERA reduction than does increased strikeouts.

Pitcher home/road splits *(Stephen Nickrand)*

One overlooked strategy in leagues that allow frequent transactions is to bench pitchers when they are on the road. Research reveals that several pitching stats and indicators are significantly and consistently worse on the road than at home.

Some home/road rules of thumb for SP:

- If you want to gain significant ground in ERA and WHIP, bench all your average or worse SP on the road.
- A pitcher's win percentage drops by 15% on the road, so don't bank on road starts as a means to catch up in wins.
- Control erodes by 10% on the road, so be especially careful with keeping wild SP in your active lineups when they are away from home.
- NL pitchers at home produce significantly more strikeouts than their AL counterparts and vs. all pitchers on the road.
- hr/9, groundball rate, hit rate, strand rate, and hr/f do not show significant home vs. road variances.

Other Diamonds

The Pitching Postulates

1. Never sign a soft-tosser to a long-term contract.
2. Right-brain dominance has a very long shelf life.
3. A fly ball pitcher who gives up many HRs is expected. A GB pitcher who gives up many HRs is making mistakes.
4. Never draft a contact fly ball pitcher who plays in a hitter's park.
5. Only bad teams ever have a need for an inning-eater.
6. Never chase wins.

Dontrelle Willis List

Pitchers with peripherals so horrible that you have to wonder how they can possibly draw a major league paycheck year after year.

Chaconian

Having the ability to post many saves despite sub-Mendoza peripherals and an ERA in the stratosphere.

ERA Benchmark

A half run of ERA over 200 innings comes out to just one earned run every four starts.

The Knuckleballers Rule

Knuckleballers don't follow no stinkin' rules.

Brad Lidge Lament

When a closer posts a 62% strand rate, he has nobody to blame but himself.

Vin Mazzaro Vindication

Occasional nightmares (2.1 innings, 14 ER) are just a part of the game.

PQS Benchmark

Generally, a single DISaster outing requires two DOMinant outings just to get back to par.

The Five Saves Certainties

1. On every team, there will be save opportunities and someone will get them. At a bare minimum, there will be at least 30 saves to go around, and not unlikely more than 45.

2. Any pitcher could end up being the chief beneficiary. Bullpen management is a fickle endeavor.

3. Relief pitchers are often the ones that require the most time at the start of the season to find a groove. The weather is cold, the schedule is sparse and their usage is erratic.

4. Despite the talk about "bullpens by committee," managers prefer a go-to guy. It makes their job easier.

5. As many as 50% of the saves in any year will come from pitchers who are unselected at the end of Draft Day.

Soft-tosser land

The place where feebler arms leave their fortunes in the hands of the defense, variable hit and strand rates, and park dimensions. It's a place where many live, but few survive.

Prospects

General

Minor league prospecting in perspective

In our perpetual quest to be the genius who uncovers the next Mike Trout when he's still in high school, there is an obsessive fascination with minor league prospects. That's not to say that prospecting is not important. The issue is perspective:

1. During the 10 year period of 1996 to 2005, only 8% of players selected in the first round of the Major League Baseball First Year Player Draft went on to become stars.

2. Some prospects are going to hit the ground running (Pete Alonso) and some are going to immediately struggle (Kyle Tucker), no matter what level of hype follows them.

3. Some prospects are going to start fast (since the league is unfamiliar with them) and then fade (as the league figures them out). Others will start slow (since they are unfamiliar with the opposition) and then improve (as they adjust to the competition). So if you make your free agent and roster decisions based on small early samples sizes, you are just as likely to be an idiot as a genius.

4. How any individual player will perform relative to his talent is largely unknown because there is a psychological element that is vastly unexplored. Some make the transition to the majors seamlessly, some not, completely regardless of how talented they are.

5. Still, talent is the best predictor of future success, so major league equivalent base performance indicators still have a valuable role in the process. As do scouting reports, carefully filtered.

6. Follow the player's path to the majors. Did he have to repeat certain levels? Was he allowed to stay at a level long enough to learn how to adjust to the level of competition? A player with only two great months at Double-A is a good bet to struggle if promoted directly to the majors because he was never fully tested at Double-A, let alone Triple-A.

7. Younger players holding their own against older competition is a good thing. Older players reaching their physical peak, regardless of their current address, can be a good thing too. The Christian Walkers and Mike Yazstremskis can have some very profitable years.

8. Remember team context. A prospect with superior potential often will not unseat a steady but unspectacular incumbent, especially one with a large contract.

9. Don't try to anticipate how a team is going to manage their talent, both at the major and minor league level. You might think it's time to promote Ryan Mountcastle and give him an everyday role. You are not running the Orioles.

10. Those who play in shallow, one-year leagues should have little cause to be looking at the minors at all. The risk versus reward is so skewed against you, and there is so much talent available with a track record, that taking a chance on an unproven commodity makes little sense.

11. Decide where your priorities really are. If your goal is to win, prospect analysis is just a *part* of the process, not the entire process.

Factors affecting minor league stats *(Terry Linhart)*

1. Often, there is an exaggerated emphasis on short-term performance in an environment that is supposed to focus on the long-term. Two poor outings don't mean a 21-year-old pitcher is washed up.

2. Ballpark dimensions and altitude create hitters parks and pitchers parks, but a factor rarely mentioned is that many parks in the lower minors are inconsistent in their field quality. Minor league clubs have limited resources to maintain field conditions, and this can artificially depress defensive statistics while inflating stats like batting average.

3. Some players' skills are so superior to the competition at their level that you can't get a true picture of what they're going to do from their stats alone.

4. Many pitchers are told to work on secondary pitches in unorthodox situations just to gain confidence in the pitch. The result is an artificially increased number of walks.

5. The #3, #4, and #5 pitchers in the lower minors are truly longshots to make the majors. They often possess only two pitches and are unable to disguise the off-speed offerings. Hitters can see inflated statistics in these leagues.

Minor league level versus age

When evaluating minor leaguers, look at the age of the prospect in relation to the median age of the league he is in:

Low level A	Between 19-20
Upper level A	Around 20
Double-A	21
Triple-A	22

These are the ideal ages for prospects at the particular level. If a prospect is younger than most and holds his own against older and more experienced players, elevate his status. If he is older than the median, reduce his status.

Triple-A experience as a leading indicator

The probability that a minor leaguer will immediately succeed in the majors can vary depending upon the level of Triple-A experience he has amassed at the time of call-up.

	BATTERS		PITCHERS	
	<1 Yr	Full	<1 Yr	Full
Performed well	57%	56%	16%	56%
Performed poorly	21%	38%	77%	33%
2nd half drop-off	21%	7%	6%	10%

The odds of a batter achieving immediate MLB success was slightly more than 50-50. More than 80% of all pitchers promoted with less than a full year at Triple-A struggled in their first year in the majors. Those pitchers with a year in Triple-A succeeded at a level equal to that of batters.

When do Top 100 prospects get promoted? *(Jeff Zimmerman)*

We created a simple procedure to determine if—and when—a player will make it to the majors in the season after being ranked in BaseballHQ.com's HQ100 prospect list (2010-17). We examined only the prospects who had not yet played in the majors, and found that the chances of a major league call-up for a healthy hitter or pitcher who last played in each level to be as follows:

- As a veteran in a foreign league: 100%
- In Triple-A: 90%
- In Double-A: 50%
- In A-ball: 20%
- Other: 0%

Additionally, to increase the odds of a call-up, take the (1) higher-ranked player; (2) the older player; and (3) the player on a contending team.

Major League Equivalency (MLE) *(Bill James)*

A formula that converts a player's minor or foreign league statistics into a comparable performance in the major leagues. These are not projections, but conversions of current performance. MLEs contain adjustments for the level of play in individual leagues and teams. They work best with Triple-A stats, not quite as well with Double-A stats, and hardly at all with the lower levels. Foreign conversions are still a work in process. James' original formula only addressed batting. Our research has devised conversion formulas for pitchers, however, their best use comes when looking at peripherals, not traditional stats.

Adjusting to the competition

All players must "adjust to the competition" at every level of professional play. Players often get off to fast or slow starts. During their second tour at that level is when we get to see whether the slow starters have caught up or whether the league has figured out the fast starters. That second half "adjustment" period is a good baseline for projecting the subsequent season, in the majors or minors.

Premature major league call-ups often negate the ability for us to accurately evaluate a player due to the lack of this adjustment period. For instance, a hotshot Double-A player might open the season in Triple-A. After putting up solid numbers for a month, he gets a call to the bigs, and struggles. The fact is, we do not have enough evidence that the player has mastered the Triple-A level. We don't know whether the rest of the league would have caught up to him during his second tour of the league. But now he's labeled as an underperformer in the bigs when in fact he has never truly proven his skills at the lower levels.

Bull Durham prospects

There is some potential talent in older players—age 26, 27 or higher—who, for many reasons (untimely injury, circumstance, bad luck, etc.), don't reach the majors until they have already been downgraded from prospect to suspect. Equating potential with age is an economic reality for major league clubs, but not necessarily a skills reality.

Skills growth and decline is universal, whether it occurs at the major league level or in the minors. So a high-skills journeyman in Triple-A is just as likely to peak at age 27 as a major leaguer of the same age. The question becomes one of opportunity—will the parent club see fit to reap the benefits of that peak performance?

Prospecting these players for your fantasy team is, admittedly, a high risk endeavor, though there are some criteria you can use. Look for a player who is/has:

- Optimally, age 27-28 for overall peak skills, age 30-31 for power skills, or age 28-31 for pitchers.
- At least two seasons of experience at Triple-A. Career Double-A players are generally not good picks.
- Solid base skills levels.
- Shallow organizational depth at their position.
- Notable winter league or spring training performance.

Players who meet these conditions are not typically draftable players, but worthwhile reserve or FAAB picks.

A Deep-league prospecting primer *(Jock Thompson)*

There's no substitute for having a philosophy, objective, and plan for your fantasy farm system. Here's a prospecting process checklist:

Commit to some prospecting time. Sounds intuitive, but some owners either don't have the time or won't take the time to learn about their league's available prospects.

Have a prospecting framework/philosophy. Such as TINSTAPP—there is no such thing as a pitching prospect. The non-linear rise and development of prospects can be frustrating in general, but much more so with pitchers. Unlike with hitters, you're usually safe in forgoing low-minors pitching, and are better off speculating on near-ready pitching names.

Have objectives. Upside vs. MLB proximity is an ongoing dilemma, but rebuilders will always need to take on some faraway high-ceiling flyers.

Devise a strategy and stick with it. You'll need an idea as to how you'll 1) acquire available talent; and 2) upgrade your roster deficiencies. Above all, play out the year. Your team will improve by making good free agent assessments all season—not by taking off in August and September.

Always account for defense. A plus glove is a real advantage in finding MLB opportunity. Versatility and athleticism are even better, and often feed multi-position eligibility.

Consider all the variables. Things like age, opportunity, organization, venue, and club positional needs should all be factors.

Exercise excruciating patience – with legit hitting prospects. Even the most highly-regarded prospects do not grow to the moon in linear fashion.

Speculate readily and be nimble with your in-season pitching moves. If you see something that looks more promising than what you have, grab it fast. If you don't, someone else will.

Pay attention and dig into in-season minor league developments. All of these lights can flicker on and turn into big edges if you can identify them. For example: a plus hit tool guy suddenly begins tapping into power, a pitcher makes in-season mechanical changes, a hitter makes across-the-board improvement following a position change.

Don't dismiss late bloomers with extended MLB opportunity. Like the more publicized names, plenty of lesser prospects have playable talent, and are just late figuring out how to unlock it.

Batters

MLE PX as a leading indicator *(Bill Macey)*

Looking at minor league performance (as MLE) in one year and the corresponding MLB performance the subsequent year:

	Year 1 MLE	Year 2 MLB
Observations	496	496
Median PX	95	96
Percent PX > 100	43%	46%

In addition, 53% of the players had a MLB PX in year 2 that exceeded their MLE PX in year 1. A slight bias towards improved performance in year 2 is consistent with general career trajectories.

Year 1 MLE PX	Year 2 MLB PX	Pct. Incr	Pct. MLB PX > 100
<= 50	61	70.3%	5.4%
51-75	85	69.6%	29.4%
76-100	93	55.2%	39.9%
101-125	111	47.4%	62.0%
126-150	119	32.1%	66.1%
> 150	142	28.6%	76.2%

Slicing the numbers by performance level, there is a good amount of regression to the mean.

Players rarely suddenly develop power at the MLB level if they didn't previously display that skill in the minors. However, the relatively large gap between the median MLE PX and MLB PX for these players, 125 to 110, confirms the notion that the best players continue to improve once they reach the major leagues.

MLE contact rate as a leading indicator *(Bill Macey)*

There is a strong positive correlation (0.63) between a player's MLE ct% in Year 1 and his actual ct% at the MLB level in Year 2.

MLE ct%	Year 1 MLE ct%	Year 2 MLB ct%
< 70%	69%	68%
70% - 74%	73%	72%
75% - 79%	77%	75%
80% - 84%	82%	77%
85% - 89%	87%	82%
90% +	91%	86%
TOTAL	**84%**	**79%**

There is very little difference between the median MLE BA in Year 1 and the median MLB BA in Year 2:

MLE ct%	Year 1 MLE BA	Year 2 MLB BA
< 70%	.230	.270
70% - 74%	.257	.248
75% - 79%	.248	.255
80% - 84%	.257	.255
85% - 89%	.266	.270
90% +	.282	.273
TOTAL	.261	.262

Excluding the <70% cohort (which was a tiny sample size), there is a positive relationship between MLE ct% and MLB BA.

Pitchers

Skills metrics as a leading indicator for pitching success

The percentage of hurlers that were good investments in the year that they were called up varied by the level of their historical minor league peripherals prior to that year.

Pitchers who had:	Fared well	Fared poorly
Good indicators	79%	21%
Marginal or poor indicators	18%	82%

The data used here were MLE levels from the previous two years, not the season in which they were called up. The significance? Solid current performance is what merits a call-up, but this is not a good indicator of short-term MLB success, because a) the performance data set is too small, typically just a few month's worth of statistics, and b) for those putting up good numbers at a new minor league level, there has typically not been enough time for the scouting reports to make their rounds.

Far East Baseball *(Tom Mulhall)*

Comparing MLB and Japanese Baseball

The Japanese major leagues are generally considered to be equivalent to Triple-A ball and the pitching possibly better. However, statistics are difficult to compare due to differences in the way the game is played in Japan.

1. While strong on fundamentals, Japanese baseball's guiding philosophy is risk avoidance. Runners rarely take extra bases, batters focus on making contact rather than driving the ball, and managers play for one run at a time. Bunts are more common. As a result, offenses score fewer runs per number of hits, and pitching stats tend to look better.

2. Stadiums in Japan usually have shorter fences. This should mean more HRs, but given #1 above, it is the American players who make up the majority of Japan's power elite. No power hitters have yet made an equivalent transition to MLB.

3. There are more artificial turf fields, which increases the number of ground ball singles. A few still use all dirt infields.

4. Though improving, the quality of umpiring is questionable. Fewer errors are called, possibly reflecting a cultural philosophy of low tolerance for mistakes and the desire to avoid publicly embarrassing a player.

5. Teams have smaller pitching staffs and use a six-man rotation. Starters usually pitch once a week, typically on the same day since Monday is an off-day for the entire league. Some starters will also occasionally pitch in relief between starts. Managers push for complete games, no matter what the score or situation. Because of the style of offense, higher pitch counts are common. Despite superior conditioning, Japanese pitchers tend to burn out early due to overuse.

6. The ball is smaller and lighter, and the strike zone is closer to the batter. A new ball was introduced in 2011 with lower-elasticity rubber surrounding the cork, which limited offense and inflated pitching stats. A more

hitter-friendly ball was used in 2013. But continue to exercise some skepticism when analyzing pitching stats.

7. If the score remains even after 12 innings, the game goes into the books as a tie.

8. There are fewer games in the Japanese schedule.

Japanese players as fantasy farm selections

When evaluating the potential of Japanese League prospects, the key is not to just identify the best Japanese players—the key is to identify impact players who have the desire and opportunity to sign with a MLB team. Opportunity is crucial, since players must have nine years of professional experience in order to qualify for international free agency, or hope that their team "posts" them early through a bidding process. With the success of players like Ichiro, Darvish and Ohtani, it is easy to overestimate the value of drafting these players. Still, for owners who are allowed to carry a large reserve or farm team at reduced salaries, these players could be a real windfall, especially if your competitors do not do their homework.

Korean players as fantasy farm selections

Korea also has a posting system which impedes free agency for seven professional seasons. Korean stadiums are notoriously hitter friendly. Jung-ho Kang had 40 HR the year before he joined the Pirates. When researching Korean players, note that the family name may be listed first, followed by the given name.

A list of Japanese and Korean League players who could jump to the majors appears in the Prospects section.

Other Diamonds

Age 26 Paradox

Age 26 is when a player begins to reach his peak skill, no matter what his address is. If circumstances have him celebrating that birthday in the majors, he is a breakout candidate. If circumstances have him celebrating that birthday in the minors, he is washed up.

A-Rod 10-Step Path to Stardom

Not all well-hyped prospects hit the ground running. More often they follow an alternative path:

1. Prospect puts up phenomenal minor league numbers.
2. The media machine gets oiled up.
3. Prospect gets called up, but struggles, Year 1.
4. Prospect gets demoted.
5. Prospect tears it up in the minors, Year 2.
6. Prospect gets called up, but struggles, Year 2.
7. Prospect gets demoted.
8. The media turns their backs. Fantasy leaguers reduce their expectations.
9. Prospect tears it up in the minors, Year 3. The public shrugs its collective shoulders.
10. Prospect is promoted in Year 3 and explodes. Some lucky fantasy leaguer lands a franchise player for under $5.

Some players that are currently stuck at one of the interim steps, and may or may not ever reach Step 10, include Kyle Tucker, Lewis Brinson and Corbin Burnes.

Bull Durham Gardening Tip

Late bloomers have fewer flowering seasons.

Developmental Dogmata

1. Defense is what gets a minor league prospect to the majors; offense is what keeps him there. *(Deric McKamey)*

2. The reason why rapidly promoted minor leaguers often fail is that they are never given the opportunity to master the skill of "adjusting to the competition."

3. Rookies who are promoted in-season often perform better than those that make the club out of spring training. Inferior March competition can inflate the latter group's perceived talent level.

4. Young players rarely lose their inherent skills. Pitchers may uncover weaknesses and the players may have difficulty adjusting. These are bumps along the growth curve, but they do not reflect a loss of skill.

5. Late bloomers have smaller windows of opportunity and much less chance for forgiveness.

6. The greatest risk in this game is to pay for performance that a player has never achieved.

7. Some outwardly talented prospects simply have a ceiling that's spelled "A-A-A."

Rule 5 Reminder

Don't ignore the Rule 5 draft lest you ignore the possibility of players like Jose Bautista, Delino Deshields, Odubel Herrera, Hector Rondon, Johan Santana, Joakim Soria, and Jayson Werth. All were Rule 5 draftees. The 2017 draft alone included such current players as Victor Reyes, Brad Keller and Elieser Hernandez.

Trout Inflation

The tendency for rookies to go for exorbitant draft prices following a year when there was a very good rookie crop.

Gaming

Standard Rules and Variations

Rotisserie Baseball was invented as an elegant confluence of baseball and economics. Whether by design or accident, the result has lasted for more than three decades. But what would Rotisserie and fantasy have been like if the Founding Fathers knew then what we know now about statistical analysis and game design? You can be sure things would be different.

The world has changed since the original game was introduced yet many leagues use the same rules today. New technologies have opened up opportunities to improve elements of the game that might have been limited by the capabilities of the 1980s. New analytical approaches have revealed areas where the original game falls short.

As such, there are good reasons to tinker and experiment; to find ways to enhance the experience.

Following are the basic elements of fantasy competition, those that provide opportunities for alternative rules and experimentation. This is by no means an exhaustive list, but at minimum provides some interesting food-for-thought.

Player pool

Standard: American League-only, National League-only or Mixed League.

AL/NL-only typically drafts 8-12 teams (pool penetration of 49% to 74%). Mixed leagues draft 10-18 teams (31% to 55% penetration), though 15 teams (46%) is a common number.

Drafting of reserve players will increase the penetration percentages. A 12-team AL/NL-only league adding six reserves onto 23-man rosters would draft 93% of the available pool of players on all teams' 25-man rosters.

The draft penetration level determines which fantasy management skills are most important to your league. The higher the penetration, the more important it is to draft a good team. The lower the penetration, the greater the availability of free agents and the more important in-season roster management becomes.

There is no generally-accepted optimal penetration level, but we have often suggested that 75% (including reserves) provides a good balance between the skills required for both draft prep and in-season management.

Alternative pools: There is a wide variety of options here. Certain leagues draft from within a small group of major league divisions or teams. Some competitions, like home run leagues, only draft batters.

Bottom-tier pool: Draft only players who posted a Rotisserie dollar value of $5 or less in the previous season. Intended as a test of an owner's ability to identify talent with upside. Best used as a pick-a-player contest with any number of teams participating.

Positional structure

Standard: 23 players. One at each defensive position (though three outfielders may be from any of LF, CF or RF), plus one additional catcher, one middle infielder (2B or SS), one corner infielder (1B or 3B), two additional outfielders and a utility player/designated hitter (which often can be a batter who qualifies anywhere). Nine pitchers, typically holding any starting or relief role.

Open: 25 players. One at each defensive position (plus DH), 5-man starting rotation and two relief pitchers. Nine additional players at any position, which may be a part of the active roster or constitute a reserve list.

40-man: Standard 23 plus 17 reserves. Used in many keeper and dynasty leagues.

Reapportioned: In recent years, new obstacles are being faced by 12-team AL/NL-only leagues thanks to changes in the real game. The 14/9 split between batters and pitchers no longer reflects how MLB teams structure their rosters. Of the 30 teams, each with 25-man rosters, not one contains 14 batters for any length of time. In fact, many spend a good part of the season with only 12 batters, which means teams often have more pitchers than hitters.

For fantasy purposes in AL/NL-only leagues, that leaves a disproportionate draft penetration into the batter and pitcher pools:

	BATTERS	PITCHERS
On all MLB rosters	195	180
Players drafted	168	108
Pct.	86%	60%

These drafts are depleting 26% more batters out of the pool than pitchers. Add in those leagues with reserve lists—perhaps an additional six players per team removing another 72 players—and post-draft free agent pools are very thin, especially on the batting side.

The impact is less in 15-team mixed leagues, though the FA pitching pool is still disproportionately deep.

	BATTERS	PITCHERS
On all rosters	381	369
Drafted	210	135
Pct.	55%	37%

One solution is to reapportion the number of batters and pitchers that are rostered. Adding one pitcher slot and eliminating one batter slot may be enough to provide better balance. The batting slot most often removed is the second catcher, since it is the position with the least depth.

Beginning in the 2012 season, the Tout Wars AL/NL-only experts leagues opted to eliminate one of the outfield slots and replace it with a "swingman" position. This position could be any batter or pitcher, depending upon the owner's needs at any given time during the season.

Selecting players

Standard: The three most prevalent methods for stocking fantasy rosters are:

Snake/Straight/Serpentine draft: Players are selected in order with seeds reversed in alternating rounds. This method has become the most popular due to its speed, ease of implementation and ease of automation.

In these drafts, the underlying assumption is that value can be ranked relative to a linear baseline. Pick #1 is better than pick #2, which is better than pick #3, and the difference between each pick

is assumed to be somewhat equivalent. While a faulty assumption, we must believe in it to assume a level playing field.

Auction: Players are sold to the highest bidder from a fixed budget, typically $260. Auctions provide the team owner with more control over which players will be on his team, but can take twice as long as snake drafts.

The baseline is $0 at the beginning of each player put up for bid. The final purchase price for each player is shaped by many wildly variable factors, from roster need to geographic location of the draft. A $30 player can mean different things to different drafters.

One option that can help reduce the time commitment of auctions is to force minimum bids at each hour mark. You could mandate $15 openers in hour #1; $10 openers in hour #2, etc.

Pick-a-player / Salary cap: Players are assigned fixed dollar values and owners assemble their roster within a fixed cap. This type of roster-stocking is an individual exercise which results in teams typically having some of the same players.

In these leagues, the "value" decision is taken out of the hands of the owners. Each player has a fixed value, pre-assigned based on past season performance and/or future expectation.

Stat categories

Standard: The standard statistical categories for Rotisserie leagues are:

4x4: HR, RBI, SB, BA, W, Sv, ERA, WHIP

5x5: HR, R, RBI, SB, BA, W, Sv, K, ERA, WHIP

6x6: Categories typically added are Holds and OPS.

7x7, etc.: Any number of categories may be added.

In general, the more categories you add, the more complicated it is to isolate individual performance and manage the categorical impact on your roster. There is also the danger of redundancy; with multiple categories measuring like stats, certain skills can get over-valued. For instance, home runs are double-counted when using the categories of both HR and slugging average. (Though note that HRs are actually already triple-counted in standard 5x5—HRs, runs, and RBIs)

If the goal is to have categories that create a more encompassing picture of player performance, it is actually possible to accomplish more with less:

Modified 4x4: HR, (R+RBI-HR), SB, OBA, (W+QS), (Sv+Hld), K, ERA

This provides a better balance between batting and pitching in that each has three counting categories and one ratio category. In fact, the balance is shown to be even more notable here:

	BATTING	PITCHING
Pure skill counting stat	HR	K
Ratio category	OBA	ERA
Dependent upon managerial decision	SB	(Sv+Hold)
Dependent upon team support	(R+RBI-HR)	(W+QS)
Alternative or addition to team support:		
Usage/stamina/health	Plate app	Innings

Replacing saves: The problem with the Saves statistic is that we have a scarce commodity that is centered on a small group of players, thereby creating inflated demand for those players. With the rising failure rate for closers these days, the incentive to pay

full value for the commodity decreases. The higher the risk, the lower the prices.

We can increase the value of the commodity by reducing the risk. We might do this by increasing the number of players that contribute to that category, thereby spreading the risk around. One way we can accomplish this is by changing the category to Saves + Holds.

Holds are not perfect, but the typical argument about them being random and arbitrary can apply to saves as well. In fact, many of the pitchers who record holds are far more skilled and valuable than closers; they are often called to the mound in much higher leverage situations (a fact backed up by a scan of each pitcher's Leverage Index).

Neither stat is perfect, but together they form a reasonable proxy for overall bullpen performance.

In tandem, they effectively double the player pool of draftable relievers while also flattening the values allotted to those pitchers. The more players around which we spread the risk, the more control we have in managing our pitching staffs.

Replacing wins: Using reasons similar to replacing Saves with Saves + Holds, some have argued for replacing the Wins statistic with W + QS (quality starts). This method of scoring gives value to a starting pitcher who pitches well, but fails to receive the win due to his team's poor offense or poor luck. However, with the decline in the average length of starts, the number of QS outings has dropped sharply. W+QS was a good idea a few years ago; less so now. A replacement stat gaining in popularity is Innings Pitched.

Keeping score

Standard: These are the most common scoring methods:

Rotisserie: Players are evaluated in several statistical categories. Totals of these statistics are ranked by team. The winner is the team with the highest cumulative ranking.

Points: Players receive points for events that they contribute to in each game. Points are totaled for each team and teams are then ranked.

Head-to-Head (H2H): Using Rotisserie or points scoring, teams are scheduled in daily or weekly matchups. The winner of each matchup is the team that finishes higher in more categories (Rotisserie) or scores the most points.

Free agent acquisition

Standard: Three methods are the most common for acquiring free agent players during the season.

First come first served: Free agents are awarded to the first owner who claims them.

Reverse order of standings: Access to the free agent pool is typically in a snake draft fashion with the last place team getting the first pick, and each successive team higher in the standings picking afterwards.

Free agent acquisition budget (FAAB): Teams are given a set budget at the beginning of the season (typically, $100 or $1000) from which they bid on free agents in a closed auction process.

Vickrey FAAB: Research has shown that more than 50% of FAAB dollars are lost via overbid on an annual basis. Given

that this is a scarce commodity, one would think that a system to better manage these dollars might be desirable. The Vickrey system conducts a closed auction in the same way as standard FAAB, but the price of the winning bid is set at the amount of the second highest bid, plus $1. In some cases, gross overbids (at least $10 over) are reduced to the second highest bid plus $5.

This method was designed by William Vickrey, a Professor of Economics at Columbia University. His theory was that this process reveals the true value of the commodity. For his work, Vickrey was awarded the Nobel Prize for Economics (and $1.2 million) in 1996.

The season

Standard: Leagues are played out during the course of the entire Major League Baseball season.

Split-season: Leagues are conducted from Opening Day through the All-Star break, then re-drafted to play from the All-Star break through the end of the season.

50-game split-season: Leagues are divided into three 50-game seasons with one-week break in between.

Monthly: Leagues are divided into six seasons or rolling four-week seasons.

The advantages of these shorter time frames:

- They can help to maintain interest. There would be fewer abandoned teams.
- There would be more shots at a title each year.
- Given that drafting is considered the most fun aspect of the game, these splits multiply the opportunities to participate in some type of draft. Leagues may choose to do complete re-drafts and treat the year as distinct mini-seasons. Or, leagues might allow teams to drop their five worst players and conduct a restocking draft at each break.

Daily games: Participants select a roster of players from one day's MLB schedule. Scoring is based on an aggregate points-based system rather than categories, with cash prizes awarded based on the day's results. The structure and distribution of that prize pool varies across different types of events, and those differences can affect roster construction strategies. Although scoring and prizes are based on one day's play, the season-long element of bankroll management provides a proxy for overall standings.

In terms of projecting outcomes, daily games are drastically different than full-season leagues. Playing time is one key element of any projection, and daily games offer near-100% accuracy in projecting playing time: you can check pre-game lineups to see exactly which players are in the lineup that night. The other key component of any projection is performance, but that is plagued by variance in daily competitions. Even if you roster a team full of the most advantageous matchups, even the best hitters can go 0-for-4 on a given night.

Snake Drafting

Snake draft first round history

The following tables record the comparison between pre-season projected player rankings (using Average Draft Position data from Mock Draft Central and National Fantasy Baseball

Championship) and actual end-of-season results. The 16-year success rate of identifying each season's top talent is only 33.75%. Even if we extend the study to the top two rounds, the hit rate is only around 50%.

2012	ADP		ACTUAL = 4
1	Matt Kemp	1	Mike Trout
2	Ryan Braun	2	Ryan Braun (2)
3	Albert Pujols	3	Miguel Cabrera (4)
4	Miguel Cabrera	4	Andrew McCutchen
5	Troy Tulowitzki	5	R.A. Dickey
6	Jose Bautista	6	Clayton Kershaw
7	Jacoby Ellsbury	7	Justin Verlander (8)
8	Justin Verlander	8	Josh Hamilton
9	Adrian Gonzalez	9	Fernando Rodney
10	Justin Upton	10	Adrian Beltre
11	Robinson Cano	11	Alex Rios
12	Joey Votto	12	David Price
13	Evan Longoria	13	Chase Headley
14	Carlos Gonzalez	14	Robinson Cano (11)
15	Prince Fielder	15	Edwin Encarnacion

2013	ADP		ACTUAL = 5
1	Ryan Braun	1	Miguel Cabrera (2)
2	Miguel Cabrera	2	Mike Trout (3)
3	Mike Trout	3	Clayton Kershaw (15)
4	Matt Kemp	4	Chris Davis
5	Andrew McCutchen	5	Paul Goldschmidt
6	Albert Pujols	6	Andrew McCutchen (5)
7	Robinson Cano	7	Adam Jones
8	Jose Bautista	8	Jacoby Ellsbury
9	Joey Votto	9	Max Scherzer
10	Carlos Gonzalez	10	Carlos Gomez
11	Buster Posey	11	Hunter Pence
12	Justin Upton	12	Robinson Cano (7)
13	Giancarlo Stanton	13	Alex Rios
14	Prince Fielder	14	Adrian Beltre
15	Clayton Kershaw	15	Matt Harvey

2014	ADP		ACTUAL = 4
1	Mike Trout	1	Jose Altuve
2	Miguel Cabrera	2	Clayton Kershaw (6)
3	Paul Goldschmidt	3	Michael Brantley
4	Andrew McCutchen	4	Mike Trout (1)
5	Carlos Gonzalez	5	Johnny Cueto
6	Clayton Kershaw	6	Felix Hernandez
7	Chris Davis	7	Victor Martinez
8	Ryan Braun	8	Jose Abreu
9	Adam Jones	9	Giancarlo Stanton
10	Bryce Harper	10	Andrew McCutchen (4)
11	Robinson Cano	11	Miguel Cabrera (2)
12	Hanley Ramirez	12	Carlos Gomez
13	Jacoby Ellsbury	13	Jose Bautista
14	Prince Fielder	14	Dee Gordon
15	Troy Tulowitzki	15	Anthony Rendon

2015	ADP		ACTUAL = 4
1	Mike Trout	1	Jake Arrieta
2	Andrew McCutchen	2	Zack Greinke
3	Clayton Kershaw	3	Clayton Kershaw (3)
4	Giancarlo Stanton	4	Paul Goldschmidt (5)
5	Paul Goldschmidt	5	A.J. Pollock
6	Miguel Cabrera	6	Dee Gordon
7	Jose Abreu	7	Bryce Harper
8	Carlos Gomez	8	Josh Donaldson
9	Jose Bautista	9	Jose Altuve (12)
10	Edwin Encarnacion	10	Mike Trout (1)
11	Felix Hernandez	11	Nolan Arenado
12	Jose Altuve	12	Manny Machado
13	Anthony Rizzo	13	Dallas Keuchel
14	Adam Jones	14	Max Scherzer
15	Troy Tulowitzki	15	Nelson Cruz

2016	ADP	ACTUAL = 7	
1	Mike Trout	1	Mookie Betts
2	Paul Goldschmidt	2	Jose Altuve (11)
3	Bryce Harper	3	Mike Trout (1)
4	Clayton Kershaw	4	Jonathan Villar
5	Josh Donaldson	5	Jean Segura
6	Carlos Correa	6	Max Scherzer (15)
7	Nolan Arenado	7	Paul Goldschmidt (2)
8	Manny Machado	8	Charlie Blackmon
9	Anthony Rizzo	9	Clayton Kershaw (4)
10	Giancarlo Stanton	10	Nolan Arenado (7)
11	Jose Altuve	11	Daniel Murphy
12	Kris Bryant	12	Kris Bryant (12)
13	Miguel Cabrera	13	Joey Votto
14	Andrew McCutchen	14	Jon Lester
15	Max Scherzer	15	Madison Bumgarner

2017	ADP	ACTUAL = 5	
1	Mike Trout	1	Charlie Blackmon
2	Mookie Betts	2	Jose Altuve (4)
3	Clayton Kershaw	3	Corey Kluber
4	Jose Altuve	4	Max Scherzer (12)
5	Kris Bryant	5	Paul Goldschmidt (7)
6	Nolan Arenado	6	Giancarlo Stanton
7	Paul Goldschmidt	7	Chris Sale
8	Manny Machado	8	Aaron Judge
9	Bryce Harper	9	Dee Gordon
10	Trea Turner	10	Clayton Kershaw (3)
11	Josh Donaldson	11	Nolan Arenado (6)
12	Max Scherzer	12	Jose Ramirez
13	Anthony Rizzo	13	Joey Votto
14	Madison Bumgarner	14	Marcell Ozuna
15	Carlos Correa	15	Elvis Andrus

2018	ADP	ACTUAL = 3*	
1	Mike Trout	1	Mookie Betts (7)
2	Jose Altuve	2	Christian Yelich
3	Nolan Arenado	3	J.D. Martinez
4	Trea Turner	4	Max Scherzer (11)
5	Clayton Kershaw	5	Jacob deGrom
6	Paul Goldschmidt	6	Jose Ramirez
7	Mookie Betts	7	Francisco Lindor
8	Giancarlo Stanton	8	Trevor Story
9	Charlie Blackmon	9	Justin Verlander
10	Bryce Harper	10	Mike Trout (1)
11	Max Scherzer	11	Blake Snell
12	Chris Sale	12	Javier Baez
13	Corey Kluber	13	Whit Merrifield
14	Carlos Correa	14	Aaron Nola
15	Kris Bryant	15	Manny Machado

*2018 represents the lowest first round hit rate in the 15 years. However, the next four players on the list would be:
16) Trea Turner (4); 17) Chris Sale (12); 18) Nolan Arenado (3); 19) Corey Kluber (13)

2019	ADP	ACTUAL = 4	
1	Mike Trout	1	Justin Verlander
2	Mookie Betts	2	Gerrit Cole
3	Jose Ramirez	3	Christian Yelich (6)
4	Max Scherzer	4	Ronald Acuna (8)
5	J.D. Martinez	5	Cody Bellinger
6	Christian Yelich	6	Rafael Devers
7	Nolan Arenado	7	Anthony Rendon
8	Ronald Acuna	8	Jacob deGrom (10)
9	Trea Turner	9	Jonathan Villar
10	Jacob deGrom	10	Trevor Story
11	Alex Bregman	11	Nolan Arenado (7)
12	Chris Sale	12	Ketel Marte
13	Francisco Lindor	13	D.J. LeMahieu
14	Aaron Judge	14	Zack Greinke
15	Jose Altuve	15	Xander Bogaerts

Similar to 2018, the next players on the 2019 list would be:
16) Alex Bregman (11); 17) Mookie Betts (2); 18) Mike Trout (1); 19) Trea Turner (9)

ADP attrition

Why is our success rate so low in identifying what should be the most easy-to-project players each year? We rank and draft players based on the expectation that those ranked higher will return greater value in terms of productivity and playing time, as well as being the safest investments. However, there are many variables affecting where players finish.

Earlier, it was shown that players spend an inordinate number of days on the disabled list. In fact, of the players projected to finish in the top 300, the number who were disabled, demoted or designated for assignment has been extreme:

Year	Pct. of top-ranked 300 players who lost PT
2010	44%
2011	49%
2012	45%
2013	51%
2014	53%
2015	47%
2016	47%
2017	58%
2018	60%
2019	59%

When you consider that well over half of each season's very best players had fewer at-bats or innings pitched than we projected, it shows how tough it is to rank players each year.

In addition, since 2004:

- Two-thirds of players finishing in the Top 15 were not in the Top 15 the previous year. There is a great deal of turnover in the first round, year-to-year.
- Of those who were first-timers, only 14% repeated in the first round the following year.
- Established superstars who finished in the Top 15 were no guarantee to repeat.

In past years, sudden stars like Jonathan Villar, Carlos Gonzalez, Curtis Granderson and Dustin Pedroia have failed to repeat. 2017's top two players—Charlie Blackmon and Jose Altuve—finished 2018 ranked 23rd and 39th, respectively. These are not bad finishes, mind you, and a high-priced player returning 60-75 percent of his draft investment is not a total bust. The issue is context. As talented as these players were, it's not just about skill; it's also about skill relative to the rest of a volatile player pool. The reasonable expectation from these early picks is a high floor rather than a high ceiling.

Importance of the early rounds *(Bill Macey)*

It's long been said that you can't win your league in the first round, but you can lose it there. An analysis of data from actual drafts reveals that this holds true—those who spend an early round pick on a player that severely under-performs expectations rarely win their league and seldom even finish in the top 3.

At the same time, drafting a player in the first round that actually returns first-round value is no guarantee of success. In fact, those that draft some of the best values still only win their league about a quarter of the time and finish in the top 3 less than half the time. Research also shows that drafting pitchers in the first round is a risky proposition. Even if the pitchers deliver first-round value, the opportunity cost of passing up on an elite batter makes you less likely to win your league.

How a strong draft contributes to a winning season *(Todd Zola)*
The standings correlation based on draft-to-final results ranges from 0.42 to 0.94, with the mean around 0.73. The top hitting counting stat drafted is home runs; the fewest is stolen bases. The top pitching counting stat drafted is saves; the fewest is wins. More hitting is acquired at the draft or auction than pitching. The in-season influx of stats is greatest in Mixed Leagues, suggesting that owners should practice patience with in-season free agents in AL/NL formats while being cautiously aggressive in Mixed formats.

Top teams almost always improve ratio categories from their drafted rosters, despite available free agents sporting poorer aggregate ratios. This is most apropos if favoring improving pitching staff as the year progresses, but it's easier said than done.

Being top-three in saves is far more important in Mixed leagues than in AL/NL. Most Mixed champions draft the majority of saves while AL/NL winners often acquire saves in season.

What is the best seed to draft from?
Most drafters like mid-round so they never have to wait too long for their next player. Some like the swing pick, suggesting that getting two players at 15 and 16 is better than a 1 and a 30. Many drafters assume that the swing pick means you'd be getting something like two $30 players instead of a $40 and $20.

Equivalent auction dollar values reveal the following facts about the first two snake draft rounds:

In an AL/NL-only league, the top seed would get a $44 player (at #1) and a $24 player (at #24) for a total of $68; the 12th seed would get two $29s (at #12 and #13) for $58.

In a mixed league, the top seed would get a $47 and a $24 ($71); the 15th seed would get two $28s ($56).

Since the talent level flattens out after the 2nd round, low seeds never get a chance to catch up:

$ difference between first player/last player selected

Round	12-team	15-team
1	$15	$19
2	$7	$8
3	$5	$4
4	$3	$3
5	$2	$2
6	$2	$1
7-17	$1	$1
18-23	$0	$0

The total value each seed accumulates at the end of the draft is hardly equitable:

Seed	Mixed	AL/NL-only
1	$266	$273
2	$264	$269
3	$263	$261
4	$262	$262
5	$259	$260
6	$261	$260
7	$260	$260
8	$261	$260
9	$261	$258
10	$257	$260
11	$257	$257
12	$258	$257
13	$254	
14	$255	
15	$256	

The counter-argument to this focuses on whether we can reasonably expect "accurate projections" at the top of the draft. Given the snake draft first round history, a case could be made that any seed might potentially do well. In fact, an argument can be made that the last seed is the best spot because it essentially provides two picks from the top 13 players (in a 12-team league) during the part of the draft with the steepest talent decline.

Using ADPs to determine when to select players *(Bill Macey)*
Although average draft position (ADP) data provides a good idea of where in the draft each player is selected, it can be misleading when trying to determine how early to target a player. This chart summarizes the percentage of players drafted within 15 picks of his ADP as well as the average standard deviation by grouping of players.

ADP Rank	% within 15 picks	Standard Deviation
1-25	100%	2.5
26-50	97%	6.1
51-100	87%	9.6
100-150	72%	14.0
150-200	61%	17.4
200-250	53%	20.9

As the draft progresses, the picks for each player become more widely dispersed and less clustered around the average. Most top 100 players will go within one round of their ADP-converted round. However, as you reach the mid-to-late rounds, there is much more uncertainty as to when a player will be selected. Pitchers have slightly smaller standard deviations than do batters (i.e. they tend to be drafted in a narrower range). This suggests that drafters may be more likely to reach for a batter than for a pitcher.

Using the ADP and corresponding standard deviation, we can to estimate the likelihood that a given player will be available at a certain draft pick. We estimate the predicted standard deviation for each player as follows:

Stdev = -0.42 + 0.42*(ADP - Earliest Pick)

(That the figure 0.42 appears twice is pure coincidence; the numbers are not equal past two decimal points.)

If we assume that the picks are normally distributed, we can use a player's ADP and estimated standard deviation to estimate the likelihood that the player is available with a certain pick (MS Excel formula):

=1-normdist(x,ADP,Standard Deviation,True)
where «x» represents the pick number to be evaluated.

We can use this information to prepare for a snake draft by determining how early we may need to reach in order to roster a player. Suppose you had the 8th pick in a 15-team league draft and your target was a player with an ADP of 128.9 and an earliest selection at pick 94. This would yield an estimated standard deviation of 14.2. You could have then entered these values into the formula above to estimate the likelihood that this player was still available at each of the following picks:

Likelihood	
Pick	Available
83	100%
98	99%
113	87%
128	53%
143	16%
158	2%

ADPs and scarcity *(Bill Macey)*

Most players are selected within a round or two of their ADP with tight clustering around the average. But every draft is unique and every pick in the draft seemingly affects the ordering of subsequent picks. In fact, deviations from "expected" sequences can sometimes start a chain reaction at that position. This is most often seen in runs at scarce positions such as the closer; once the first one goes, the next seems sure to closely follow.

Research also suggests that within each position, there is a correlation within tiers of players. The sooner players within a generally accepted tier are selected, the sooner other players within the same tier will be taken. However, once that tier is exhausted, draft order reverts to normal.

How can we use this information? If you notice a reach pick, you can expect that other drafters may follow suit. If your draft plan is to get a similar player within that tier, you'll need to adjust your picks accordingly.

Mapping ADPs to auction value *(Bill Macey)*

Reliable average auction values (AAV) are often tougher to come by than ADP data for snake drafts. However, we can estimate predicted auction prices as a function of ADP, arriving at the following equation:

$y = -9.8\ln(x) + 57.8$
where ln(x) is the natural log function, x represents the actual ADP, and y represents the predicted AAV.

This equation does an excellent job estimating auction prices ($r2=0.93$), though deviations are unavoidable. The asymptotic nature of the logarithmic function, however, causes the model to predict overly high prices for the top players. So be aware of that, and adjust.

The value of mock drafts *(Todd Zola)*

Most assume the purpose of a mock draft is to get to know the market value of the player pool. But even more important, mock drafting is general preparation for the environment and process, thereby allowing the drafter to completely focus on the draft when it counts. Mock drafting is more about fine-tuning your strategy than player value. Here are some tips to maximize your mock drafting experience.

1. Make sure you can seamlessly use an on-line drafting room, draft software or your own lists to track your draft or auction. The less time you spend looking, adding and adjusting names, the more time you can spend on thinking about what player is best for your team. This also gives you the opportunity to make sure your draft lists are complete, and assures all the players are listed at the correct position(s).

2. Alter the draft slots from which you mock. The flow of each mock will be different, but if you do a few mocks with an early initial pick, a few in the middle and a few with a late first pick, you may learn you prefer one of the spots more than the others. If you're in a league where you can choose your draft spot, this helps you decide where to select. Once you know your spot, a few mocks from that spot will help you decide how to deal with positional runs.

3. Use non-typical strategies and consider players you rarely target. We all have our favorite players. Intentionally passing on those players not only gives you an idea when others may draft them but it also forces you to research players you normally don't consider. The more players you have researched, the more prepared you'll be for any series of events that occurs during your real draft.

Draft preparation with a full-season mindset *(Matt Dodge)*

Each of the dimensions of your league setup—player pool, reserve list depth; type and frequency of transactions, scoring categories, etc.—should impact your draft day plan. But it may also be helpful to look at them in combination.

Sources of additional stats after draft day

League Player Pool

Reserve List	Mixed 15 team	AL- or NL-only 12 team
Short	free agents	trades, free agents
Long	free agents, trades	trades

Review the prior season's transactions for your league and analyze the successful teams' category contributions from trade acquisitions and free agent pickups. Trades are often necessary to add specific stats in AL/NL-only leagues as the player pool penetration is generally much deeper, and the size of a reserve roster further reduces the help possible from the free agent pool.

Draft strategies related to in-season player acquisition

Trade Activity

FA Pool	Low	High
Shallow	solid foundation (STR)	tradable commodoties surplus counting stats
Deep	gamble on upside (S&S)	ultimate flexibility

Trading activity is a function of multiple factors. Keeper leagues provide opportunities for owners to contend this year or play for next year. However, those increased opportunities are often controlled by rules to prevent "dump trading." Stratification of the standings in redraft leagues can cause lower ranked owners to lose interest, reducing the number of effective trading partners as the season goes on.

When deep rosters create a shallow free agent pool in a league with little trading, draft day success becomes paramount. In this case, a Spread the Risk strategy designed to accumulate at bats, innings, and saves is recommended. If the free agent pool is deep, the drafter can take more risks with a Stars and Scrubs approach, acquiring "lottery ticket" players with upside, knowing that replacements are readily available if the upside plays don't hit.

In leagues where trading is prevalent, a shallow free agent pool means you should acquire players on draft day with the intent of trading them. This could mean a traditional strategy of acquiring a category surplus (frequently saves and/or steals), and then trading them in-season to shore up other categories. In a keeper league, this includes grabbing a few bargains (to interest those who are rebuilding) or grabbing top performers to flip in trade (if you are already on "the two year plan").

Draft Day Considerations for In-season Roster Management

Reserve List Txn Freq	4 x 4 League Format	5 x 5 League Format
Daily	careful SP management batting platoons positional flexibility	RP (K, ERA, WHIP) batting platoons positional flexibility
Weekly	SP (2 start weeks) cover risky starters	SP (2 start weeks) cover risky starters

Owners must be careful with pitching, due to the negative impact potential of ERA and WHIP. Blindly streaming pitchers on a daily basis can be counter-productive, particularly in 4x4 leagues. In 5x5, the Strikeouts category can make a foundation of high Dom relievers a useful source of mitigation for the invariable starting pitching disappointments.

The degree that these recommendations can be implemented is also dependent on the depth of the reserve list. Those with more reserves can do more than those with fewer, obviously, but the key is deciding up front how you plan to use your reserves, and then tailoring your draft strategy toward that usage.

Draft-day cheat sheet *(Patrick Davitt)*

1. Know what players are available, right to the bottom of the pool.
2. Know what every player is worth in your league format.
3. Know why you think each player is worth what you think he's worth.
4. Identify players you believe you value differently from the other owners.
5. Know each player's risks.
6. Know your opponents' patterns.
7. For sure, know the league rules and its history, and what it takes to win.

Auction Value Analysis

Auction values (R$) in perspective

R$ is the dollar value placed on a player's statistical performance in a Rotisserie league, and designed to measure the impact that player has on the standings.

There are several methods to calculate a player's value from his projected (or actual) statistics.

One method is Standings Gain Points, described in the book, *How to Value Players for Rotisserie Baseball*, by Art McGee. SGP converts a player's statistics in each Rotisserie category into the number of points those stats will allow you to gain in the standings. These are then converted back into dollars.

Another popular method is the Percentage Valuation Method. In PVM, a least valuable, or replacement performance level is set for each category (in a given league size) and then values are calculated representing the incremental improvement from that base. A player is then awarded value in direct proportion to the level he contributes to each category.

As much as these methods serve to attach a firm number to projected performance, the winning bid for any player is still highly variable depending upon many factors:

- the salary cap limit
- the number of teams in the league
- each team's roster size
- the impact of any protected players
- each team's positional demands at the time of bidding
- the statistical category demands at the time of bidding
- external factors, e.g. media inflation or deflation of value

In other words, a $30 player is only a $30 player if someone in your draft pays $30 for him.

Roster slot valuation *(John Burnson)*

When you draft a player, what have you bought?

"You have bought the stats generated by this player."

No. You have bought the stats generated by his slot. Initially, the drafted player fills the slot, but he need not fill the slot for the season, and he need not contribute from Day One. If you trade the player during the season, then your bid on Draft Day paid for the stats of the original player plus the stats of the new player. If the player misses time due to injury or demotion, then you bought the stats of whoever fills the time while the drafted player is missing. At season's end, there will be more players providing positive value than there are roster slots.

Before the season, the number of players projected for positive value has to equal the total number of roster slots. However, the projected productivity should be adjusted by the potential to capture extra value in the slot. This is especially important for injury-rehab cases and late-season call-ups. For example, if we think that a player will miss half the season, then we would augment his projected stats with a half-year of stats from a replacement-level player at his position. Only then would we calculate prices. Essentially, we want to apportion $260 per team among the slots, not the players.

Average player value by draft round

Rd	AL/NL	Mxd
1	$34	$34
2	$26	$26
3	$23	$23
4	$20	$20
5	$18	$18
6	$17	$16
7	$16	$15
8	$15	$13
9	$13	$12
10	$12	$11
11	$11	$10
12	$10	$9
13	$9	$8
14	$8	$8
15	$7	$7

16	$6	$6
17	$5	$5
18	$4	$4
19	$3	$3
20	$2	$2
21	$1	$2
22	$1	$1
23	$1	$1

Benchmarks for auction players:

- All $30 players will go in the first round.
- All $20-plus players will go in the first four rounds.
- Double-digit value ends pretty much after Round 11.
- The $1 end game starts at about Round 21.

Dollar values: expected projective accuracy

There is a 65% chance that a player projected for a certain dollar value will finish the season with a value within plus-or-minus $5 of that projection. Therefore, if you value a player at $25, you only have about a 2-in-3 shot of him finishing between $20 and $30.

If you want to raise your odds to 80%, the range becomes +/- $9, so your $25 player has to finish somewhere between $16 and $34.

Dollar values by lineup position *(Michael Roy)*

How much value is derived from batting order position?

Pos	PA	R	RBI	R$
#1	747	107	72	$18.75
#2	728	102	84	$19.00
#3	715	95	100	$19.45
#4	698	93	104	$19.36
#5	682	86	94	$18.18
#6	665	85	82	$17.19
#7	645	81	80	$16.60
#8	623	78	80	$16.19
#9	600	78	73	$15.50

So, a batter moving from the bottom of the order to the clean-up spot, with no change in performance, would gain nearly $4 in value from runs and RBIs alone.

How likely is it that a $30 player will repeat? *(Matt Cederholm)*

From 2003-2008, there were 205 players who earned $30 or more (using single-league 5x5 values). Only 70 of them (34%) earned $30 or more in the next season.

In fact, the odds of repeating a $30 season aren't good. As seen below, the best odds during that period were 42%. And as we would expect, pitchers fare far worse than hitters.

	Total>$30	# Repeat	% Repeat
Hitters	167	64	38%
Pitchers	38	6	16%
Total	205	70	34%
*High-Reliability**			
Hitters	42	16	38%
Pitchers	7	0	0%
Total	49	16	33%
100+ BPV			
Hitters	60	25	42%
Pitchers	31	6	19%
Total	91	31	19%

	Total>$30	# Repeat	% Repeat
*High-Reliability and 100+ BPV**			
Hitters	12	5	42%
Pitchers	6	0	0%
Total	18	5	28%

*Reliability figures are from 2006-2008

For players with multiple seasons of $30 or more, the numbers get better. Players with consecutive $30 seasons, 2003-2008:

	Total>$30	# Repeat	% Repeat
Two Years	62	29	55%
Three+ Years	29	19	66%

Still, a player with two consecutive seasons at $30 in value is barely a 50/50 proposition. And three consecutive seasons is only a 2/3 shot. Small sample sizes aside, this does illustrate the nature of the beast. Even the most consistent, reliable players fail 1/3 of the time. Of course, this is true whether they are kept or drafted anew, so this alone shouldn't prevent you from keeping a player.

Predicting player value from year 1 performance *(Patrick Davitt)*

Year-1 (Y1, first season >=100AB) batter results predict some—but not all—subsequent-year performance. About half of all Y1 players have positive value. Players with higher Y1 value were likelier to get PT in subsequent seasons. Players with –$6 to –$10 in Y1 got more chances than players +$5 to –$5 and performed better. Batters with Y1 value of $16 or more are excellent bets to at least provide positive value in subsequent seasons, and those above $21 in Y1 value play in all subsequent seasons and return an average of $26. But even a $21 batter is only a 50-50 bet to do better in Y2.

How well do elite pitchers retain their value? *(Michael Weddell)*

An elite pitcher (one who earns at least $24 in a season) on average keeps 80% of his R$ value from year 1 to year 2. This compares to the baseline case of only 52%.

Historically, 36% of elite pitchers improve, returning a greater R$ in the second year than they did the first year. That is an impressive performance considering they already were at an elite level. 17% collapse, returning less than a third of their R$ in the second year. The remaining 47% experience a middling outcome, keeping more than a third but less than all of their R$ from one year to the next.

Valuing closers

Given the high risk associated with the closer's role, it is difficult to determine a fair draft value. Typically, those who have successfully held the role for several seasons will earn the highest draft price, but valuing less stable commodities is troublesome.

A rough rule of thumb is to start by paying $10 for the role alone. Any pitcher tagged the closer on draft day should merit at least $10. Those without a firm appointment may start at less than $10. Then add anywhere from $0 to $15 for support skills.

In this way, the top level talents will draw upwards of $20-$25. Those with moderate skill will draw $15-$20, and those with more questionable skill in the $10-$15 range.

Profiling the end game

What types of players are typically the most profitable in the end-game? First, our overall track record on $1 picks:

Avg Return	%Profitable	Avg Prof	Avg. Loss
$1.89	51%	$10.37	($7.17)

On aggregate, the hundreds of players drafted in the end-game earned $1.89 on our $1 investments. While they were profitable overall, only 51% of them actually turned a profit. Those that did cleared more than $10 on average. Those that didn't—the other 49%—lost about $7 apiece.

Pos	Pct.of tot	Avg Val	%Profit	Avg Prof	Avg Loss
CA	12%	($1.68)	41%	$7.11	($7.77)
CO	9%	$6.12	71%	$10.97	($3.80)
MI	9%	$3.59	53%	$10.33	($4.84)
OF	22%	$2.61	46%	$12.06	($5.90)
SP	29%	$1.96	52%	$8.19	($7.06)
RP	19%	$0.35	50%	$11.33	($10.10)

These results bear out the danger of leaving catchers to the end; only catchers returned negative value. Corner infielder returns say leaving a 1B or 3B open until late offers the best potential for positive return.

Age	Pct.of tot	Avg Val	%Profit	Avg Prof	Avg Loss
< 25	15%	($0.88)	33%	$8.25	($8.71)
25-29	48%	$2.59	56%	$11.10	($8.38)
30-35	28%	$2.06	44%	$10.39	($5.04)
35+	9%	$2.15	41%	$8.86	($5.67)

The practice of speculating on younger players—mostly rookies—in the end game was a washout. Part of the reason was that those that even made it to the end game were often the long-term or fringe type. Better prospects were typically drafted earlier.

	Pct.of tot	Avg Val	%Profit	Avg Prof	Avg Loss
Injury rehabs	20%	$3.63	36%	$15.07	($5.65)

One in five end-gamers were players coming back from injury. While only 36% of them were profitable, the healthy ones returned a healthy profit. The group's losses were small, likely because they weren't healthy enough to play.

Realistic expectations of $1 end-gamers *(Patrick Davitt)*

Many fantasy articles insist leagues are won or lost with $1 batters, because "that's where the profits are." But are they?

A 2011 analysis showed that when considering $1 players in deep leagues, managing $1 end-gamers should be more about minimizing losses than fishing for profit. In the cohort of batters projected $0 to -$5, 82% returned losses, based on a $1 bid Two-thirds of the projected $1 cohort returned losses. In addition, when considering $1 players, speculate on speed.

Advanced Draft Strategies

Stars & Scrubs v. Spread the Risk

Stars & Scrubs (S&S): A Rotisserie auction strategy in which a roster is anchored by a core of high priced stars and the remaining positions filled with low-cost players.

Spread the Risk (STR): An auction strategy in which available dollars are spread evenly among all roster slots.

Both approaches have benefits and risks. An experiment was conducted in 2004 whereby a league was stocked with four teams assembled as S&S, four as STR and four as a control group. Rosters were then frozen for the season.

The Stars & Scrubs teams won all three ratio categories. Those deep investments ensured stability in the categories that are typically most difficult to manage. On the batting side, however, S&S teams amassed the least amount of playing time, which in turn led to bottom-rung finishes in HRs, RBIs and Runs.

One of the arguments for the S&S approach is that it is easier to replace end-game losers (which, in turn, may help resolve the playing time issues). Not only is this true, but the results of this experiment show that replacing those bottom players is critical to success.

The Spread the Risk teams stockpiled playing time, which led to strong finishes in many counting stats, including clear victories in RBIs, wins and strikeouts. This is a key tenet in drafting philosophy; we often say that the team that compiles the most ABs will be among the top teams in RBI and Runs.

The danger is on the pitching side. More innings did yield more wins and Ks, but also destroyed ERA/WHIP.

So, what approach makes the most sense? **The optimal strategy might be to STR on offense and go S&S with your pitching staff.** STR buys more ABs, so you immediately position yourself well in four of the five batting categories. On pitching, it might be more advisable to roster a few core arms, though that immediately elevates your risk exposure. Admittedly, it's a balancing act, which is why we need to pay more attention to risk analysis.

The LIMA Plan

The LIMA Plan is a strategy for Rotisserie leagues (though the underlying concept can be used in other formats) that allows you to target high skills pitchers at very low cost, thereby freeing up dollars for offense. LIMA is an acronym for Low Investment Mound Aces, and also pays tribute to Jose Lima, a $1 pitcher whose 1998 breakout who exemplified the power of the strategy. In a $260 league:

1. Budget a maximum of $60 for your pitching staff.
2. Allot no more than $30 of that budget for acquiring saves.
3. Ignore ERA. Draft only pitchers with:
   - Command ratio (K/BB) of 2.5 or better.
   - Strikeout rate of 7.0 or better.
   - Expected home run rate of 1.0 or less.
4. Draft as few innings as your league rules will allow. This is intended to manage risk. For some game formats, this should be a secondary consideration.
5. Maximize your batting slots. Spend $200 on batters who have:
   - Contact rate of at least 80%
   - Walk rate of at least 10%
   - PX or Spd level of at least 100

Spend no more than $29 for any player and try to keep the $1 picks to a minimum.

The goal is to ace the batting categories and carefully pick your pitching staff so that it will finish in the upper third in ERA, WHIP and saves (and Ks in 5x5), and an upside of perhaps 9th in

wins. In a competitive league, that should be enough to win, and definitely enough to finish in the money. Worst case, you should have an excess of offense available that you can deal for pitching.

The strategy works because it better allocates resources. Fantasy leaguers who spend a lot for pitching are not only paying for expected performance, they are also paying for better defined roles—#1 and #2 rotation starters, ace closers, etc.—which are expected to translate into more IP, wins and saves. But roles are highly variable. A pitcher's role will usually come down to his skill and performance; if he doesn't perform, he'll lose the role.

The LIMA Plan says, let's invest in skill and let the roles fall where they may. In the long run, better skills should translate into more innings, wins and saves. And as it turns out, pitching skill costs less than pitching roles do.

In *snake draft leagues,* you may be able to delay drafting starting pitchers until Round 10. In *shallow mixed leagues,* the LIMA Plan may not be necessary; just focus on the support metrics. In *simulation leagues,* build your staff around those metrics.

Variations on the LIMA Plan

LIMA Extrema: Limit your total pitching budget to only $30, or less. This can be particularly effective in shallow leagues where LIMA-caliber starting pitcher free agents are plentiful during the season.

SANTANA Plan: Instead of spending $30 on saves, you spend it on a starting pitcher anchor. In 5x5 leagues, allocating those dollars to a high-end LIMA-caliber starting pitcher can work well as long as you pick the right anchor and can acquire saves during the season.

Total Control Drafting (TCD)

On Draft Day, we make every effort to control as many elements as possible. In reality, the players that end up on our teams are largely controlled by the other owners. Their bidding affects your ability to roster the players you want. In a snake draft, the other owners control your roster even more. We are really only able to get the players we want within the limitations set by others.

However, an optimal roster can be constructed from a fanalytic assessment of skill and risk combined with more assertive draft day demeanor.

Why this makes sense

1. Our obsession with projected player values is holding us back. If a player on your draft list is valued at $20 and you agonize when the bidding hits $23, odds are about two chances in three that he could really earn anywhere from $15 to $25. What this means is, in some cases, and within reason, you should just pay what it takes to get the players you want.

2. There is no such thing as a bargain. Most of us *don't* just pay what it takes because we are always on the lookout for players who go under value. But we really don't know which players will cost less than they will earn because prices are still driven by the draft table. The concept of "bargain" assumes that we even know what a player's true value is.

3. "Control" is there for the taking. Most owners are so focused on their own team that they really don't pay much attention to what you're doing. There are some exceptions, and bidding wars

do happen, but in general, other owners will not provide that much resistance.

How it's done

1. Create your optimal draft pool.

2. Get those players.

Start by identifying which players will be draftable based on the LIMA or Mayberry criteria. Then, at the draft, focus solely on your roster. When it's your bid opener, toss a player you need at about 50%-75% of your projected value. Bid aggressively and just pay what you need to pay. Of course, don't spend $40 for a player with $25 market value, but it's okay to exceed your projected value within reason.

From a tactical perspective, mix up the caliber of openers. Drop out early on some bids to prevent other owners from catching on to you.

In the end, it's okay to pay a slight premium to make sure you get the players with the highest potential to provide a good return on your investment. It's no different than the premium you might pay for a player with position flexibility or to get the last valuable shortstop. With TCD, you're just spending those extra dollars up front to ensure you are rostering your targets. As a side benefit, TCD almost assures that you don't leave money on the table.

Mayberry Method

The foundation of the Mayberry Method (MM) is the assertion that we really can't project player performance with the level of precision that advanced metrics and modeling systems would like us to believe.

MM is named after the fictional TV village where life was simpler. MM evaluates skill by embracing the imprecision of the forecasting process and projecting performance in broad strokes rather than with hard statistics.

MM reduces every player to a 7-character code. The format of the code is 5555 AAA, where the first four characters describe elements of a player's skill on a scale of 0 to 5. These skills are indexed to the league average so that players are evaluated within the context of the level of offense or pitching in a given year.

The three alpha characters are our reliability grades (Health, Experience and Consistency) on the standard A-to-F scale. The skills numerics are forward-looking; the alpha characters grade reliability based on past history.

Batting

The first character in the MM code measures a batter's power skills. It is assigned using the following table:

Power Index	MM
0 - 49	0
50 - 79	1
80 - 99	2
100 - 119	3
120 - 159	4
160+	5

The second character measures a batter's speed skills. RSpd takes our Statistically Scouted Speed metric (Spd) and adds the elements of opportunity and success rate, to construct the formula of RSpd = Spd x (SBO + SB%).

RSpd	MM
0 - 39	0
40 - 59	1
60 - 79	2
80 - 99	3
100 - 119	4
120+	5

The third character measures expected batting average.

xBA Index	MM
0-87	0
88-92	1
93-97	2
98-102	3
103-107	4
108+	5

The fourth character measures playing time.

Role	PA	MM
Potential full-timers	450+	5
Mid-timers	250-449	3
Fringe/bench	100-249	1
Non-factors	0-99	0

Pitching

The first character in the pitching MM code measures xERA, which captures a pitcher's overall ability and is a proxy for ERA, and even WHIP.

xERA Index	MM
0-80	0
81-90	1
91-100	2
101-110	3
111-120	4
121+	5

The second character measures strikeout ability.

K/9 Index	MM
0-76	0
77-88	1
89-100	2
101-112	3
113-124	4
125+	5

The third character measures saves potential.

Description	Saves est.	MM
No hope for saves; starting pitchers	0	0
Speculative closer	1-9	1
Closer in a pen with alternatives	10-24	2
Frontline closer with firm bullpen role	25+	3

The fourth character measures **playing time**.

Role	IP	MM
Potential #1-2 starters	180+	5
Potential #3-4 starters	130-179	3
#5 starters/swingmen	70-129	1
Relievers	0-69	0

Overall Mayberry Scores

The real value of Mayberry is to provide a skills profile on a player-by-player basis. I want to be able to see this…

Player A	4455 AAB
Player B	5245 BBD
Player C	5255 BAB
Player D	5155 BAF

…and make an objective, unbiased determination about these four players without being swayed by preconceived notions and baggage. But there is a calculation that provides a single, overall value for each player.

This is the calculation for the overall MM batting score:

MM Score =
(PX score + Spd score + xBA score + PA score) x PA score

An overall MM pitching score is calculated as:

MM Score =
((xERA score x 2) + K/9 score + Saves score + IP score) x (IP score + Saves score)

The highest score you can get for either is 100. That makes the result of the formula easy to assess.

BaseballHQ.com analyst Patrick Davitt did some great research about using Reliability Grades to adjust the Mayberry scores. His research showed that "higher-reliability players met their Mayberry targets more often than their lower-reliability counterparts, and players with all "D" or "F" reliability scores underperform Mayberry projections far more often. Those results can be reflected by multiplying a player's MM Score by each of three reliability bonuses or penalties:"

I've taken his work a minor step further and applied slightly different multipliers to each Reliability element.

	Health	Experience	Consistency
A	x 1.10	x 1.10	x 1.10
B	x 1.05	x 1.05	x 1.05
C	x 1.00	x 1.00	x 1.00
D	x 0.90	x 0.95	x 0.95
F	x 0.80	x 0.90	x 0.90

So, let's perform the overall calculations for Player A above, using these Reliability adjustments.

Player A: 4455 AAB
= (4+4+5+5) x 5
= 90 x 1.10 x 1.10 x 1.05
= 114.3

Portfolio3 Plan concepts

When it comes to profitability, all players are not created equal. Every player has a different role on your team by virtue of his skill set, dollar value/draft round, position and risk profile. When it comes to a strategy for how to approach a specific player, one size does not fit all.

We need some players to return fair value more than others. A $40/first round player going belly-up is going to hurt you far more than a $1/23rd round bust. End-gamers are easily replaceable.

We rely on some players for profit more than others. First-rounders do not provide the most profit potential; that comes from players further down the value rankings.

We can afford to weather more risk with some players than with others. Since high-priced early-rounders need to return at least fair value, we cannot afford to take on excessive risk. Our risk tolerance opens up with later-round/lower cost picks.

Players have different risk profiles based solely on what roster spot they are going to fill. Catchers are more injury prone. A closer's value is highly dependent on managerial decision. These types of players are high risk even if they have great skills. That needs to affect their draft price or draft round.

For some players, the promise of providing a scarce skill, or productivity at a scarce position, may trump risk. Not always, but sometimes. The determining factor is usually price.

Previously, we created a model that integrated these types of players into a roster planning tool, called the Portfolio3 Plan. However, over time, variables like baseball's changing statistical environment and the shifting MLB roster construction affected the utility of the model. The rigid player allocation framework of the tiers began to erode, and no fudging could retain the integrity of the model. So we have retired it. The Mayberry Method includes the relevant player evaluators that Portfolio3 used; you can rely on those to create your own roster plan that balances skill and risk.

Consistency in Head-to-Head leagues *(Dylan Hedges)*
Few things are as valuable to H2H league success as filling your roster with players who can produce a solid baseline of stats, week in and week out. In traditional leagues, while consistency is not as important—all we care about are aggregate numbers—filling your team with consistent players can make roster management easier.

Consistent batters have good plate discipline, walk rates and on base percentages. These are foundation skills. Those who add power to the mix are obviously more valuable, however, the ability to hit home runs consistently is rare.

Consistent pitchers demonstrate similar skills in each outing; if they also produce similar results, they are even more valuable.

We can track consistency but predicting it is difficult. Many fantasy leaguers try to predict a batter's hot or cold streaks, or individual pitcher starts, but that is typically a fool's errand. The best we can do is find players who demonstrate seasonal consistency; in-season, we must manage players and consistency tactically.

Building a consistent Head-to-Head team *(David Martin)*
Teams in head-to-head leagues need batters who are consistent. Focusing on certain metrics helps build consistency, which is the roster holy grail for H2H players. Our filters for such success are:
- Contact rate = minimum 80%
- xBA = minimum .280
- PX (or Spd) = minimum 120
- RC/G = minimum 5.00

Ratio insulation in Head-to-Head leagues *(David Martin)*
On a week-to-week basis, inequities are inherent in the head-to-head game. One way to eliminate your competitor's advantage in the pure numbers game is to build your team's pitching foundation around the ratio categories.

One should normally insulate at the end of a draft, once your hitters are in place. To obtain several ratio insulators, target pitchers that have:
- Cmd greater than 3.0
- Dom greater than 7.5
- xERA less than 3.30

While adopting this strategy may compromise wins, research has shown that wins come at a cost to ERA and WHIP. Roster space permitting, adding two to four insulators to your team will improve your team's weekly ERA and WHIP.

A Head-to-Head approach to the Mayberry Method *(David Martin)*
Though the Mayberry Method was designed for use in Rotisserie leagues, a skill set analysis about whether a player is head-to-head league material is built into each seven-digit Mayberry code. By "decoding" Mayberry and incorporating quality-consistency (QC) scores, one can assemble a team that has the characteristics of a successful H2H squad.

In reviewing the MM skills scores, we can correlate the power and contact skills as follows:
- PX > 4 or 5 = PX of 120 or higher
- xBA > 4 or 5 = xBA index of 103 or higher

Only full-time players will have an opportunity to produce the counting statistics required, so to create a top tier of players, we need to limit our search to those who earn a 5 for playing time. This top tier should be sorted by QC scores so that the more consistent players are ranked higher.

To create the second tier of players, lower the power index to 3, but keep all other skill requirements intact:

PWR	SPD	BA	PT	HLTH
3	N/A	4/5	5	A/B

The interplay between tiers is important; use Tier 2 in conjunction with Tier 1 and not simply after the top tier options are exhausted. For example, it might make sense to dip into Tier 2 if there is a player available with a higher QC score.

Additionally, while the H2H MM codes do not target players based on their speed skills, the second column of the MM codes contains this information. Though you are de-prioritizing the speed skill, you do not need to punt the steals category. You will typically find that the tiers nonetheless contain multiple players with a MM speed score of 3 or higher, so you can still be competitive in the steal category most weeks applying this approach.

Consistency in points leagues *(Bill Macey)*
Previous research has demonstrated that week-to-week statistical consistency is important for Rotisserie-based head-to-head play. But one can use the same foundation in points-based games. A study showed that not only do players with better skills post more overall points in this format, but that the format caters to consistent performances on a week-to-week basis, even after accounting for differences in total points scored and playing-time.

Therefore, when drafting your batters in points-based head-to-head leagues, ct% and bb% make excellent tiebreakers if you are having trouble deciding between two players with similarly projected point totals. Likewise, when rostering pitchers, favor those who tend not to give up home runs.

Daily Fantasy Baseball

Daily Fantasy Sports (DFS) is an offshoot of traditional fantasy sports. Many of the same analytic methods that are integral to seasonal fantasy baseball are just as relevant for DFS.

General Format

1. The overwhelming majority of DFS contests are pay-for-play where the winners are compensated a percentage of their entry fee, in accordance with the rules of that game.

2. DFS baseball contests are generally based on a single day's slate of games, or a subset of the day's games (i.e., all afternoon games or all evening games)

3. Most DFS formats are points-based salary cap games.

Most Popular Contests

1. Cash Games: Three variants (50/50, Multipliers, and Head-to-Head) all pay out a flat prize to a portion of the entries.

2. GPP (Guaranteed prize pool) Tournaments: The overall winner earns the largest prize and prizes scale downward.

3. Survivor: A survivor contest is a multiple-slate format where a portion of the entries survives to play the following day.

4. Qualifiers/Satellites: Tournaments where the prize(s) consist of entry tickets to a larger tournament.

DFS Analysis

1. Predicting single-day performance entails adjusting a baseline projection based on that day's match-up. This adjusted expectation is considered in context with a player's salary to determine his potential contributions relative to the other players.

2. Weighted on base average (wOBA) is a souped-up version of OBP, and is a favorite metric to help evaluate both hitters and pitchers. (For more useful DFS metrics, see next section)

3. Pitching: In DFS, innings and strikeouts are the two chief means of accruing points, so they need to be weighed heavily in pitching evaluation.

Tips for Players New to DFS

1. Start slow and be prepared to lose: While cogent analysis can increase your chances of winning, the variance associated with a single day's worth of outcomes doesn't assure success. Short-term losing streaks are inevitable, so start with low cost cash games before embarking on tournament play.

2. Minimize the number of sites you play: The DFS space is dominated by two sites but there are other options. At the beginning, stick to one or two. Once you're comfortable, consider expanding to others.

3. Bankroll management: The recommended means to manage your bankroll is to risk no more than 10% on a given day. Within that portion, the suggested ratio is 80% cash games to 20% GPP tournament action.

4. General Strategies

A. Cash Games: Conventional wisdom preaches to be conservative in cash games. Upper level starting pitchers make excellent cash game options. For hitters, it's best to spread your choices among several teams. In general, you're looking for players with a high floor rather than a high ceiling.

B: GPP Tournaments: In tournaments (with a larger number of entrants), a common ploy is to select a lesser priced, though risky, pitcher with a favorable match-up. It's also very common to overload—or stack—several batters from the same team, hoping that squad scores a bunch of runs.

5. Miscellaneous Tips

A. Pay extra attention to games threatened by weather, as well as players who are not a lock to be in the lineup.

B. Avoid playing head-to-head against strangers until you're comfortable and have enjoyed some success.

C. Stay disciplined. The worst thing you can do is eat up your bankroll quickly by entering into tournaments.

D. Most importantly, have fun. Obviously, you want to win, but hopefully you're also in it for the challenge of mastering the unique skills intrinsic to DFS.

Using BaseballHQ Tools in DFS

Here are some of the additional skill metrics to consider:

Cash Game Metrics

bb%: This simple indicator may receive only a quick glance when building lineups, but it is imperative in providing insight on a batter's underlying approach and plate discipline. Walks also equal points in all DFS scoring structures.

ct%: Another byproduct of good plate discipline, reflecting the percentage of balls put in play. Players with strong contact rates tend to provide a higher floor, and less chance of a negative score from a free swinger with a high strikeout rate.

xBA: Measures a hitter's BA by multiplying his contact rate by the chance that a ball in play falls for a hit. Hitters whose BA is far below their xBA may be "due" for some hits.

Tournament / GPP BPIs

PX / xPX: Home runs are the single greatest multi-point event. Using PX (power index) and xPX (expected power index) together can help identify underperformers who are due in the power category.

Choosing Pitchers in DFS

The criteria for choosing a pitcher(s) may be more narrow than for full-season league, but the skills focus should remain.

Major Considerations

• Overall skills. Look for the following minimums: 3.0 Ctl (bb/9), 9.0 Dom (k/9), 3.0 Cmd (k/bb), and max 1.0 HR/9.

• Home/Away. In 2019, MLB pitchers logged a 4.39 ERA, 9.0 Dom, 2.8 Cmd at home; 4.63 ERA, 8.8 Dom, 2.6 Cmd on the road.

• Is he pitching at Coors Field? (Even the best pitchers are a risky start there.)

Moderate Considerations

• Recent performance. Examine Ks and BBs over last 4-5 starts.

• Strength of opponent. Refer to opposing team's OPS for the season, as well as more recent performance.

Minor Considerations

• L/R issues. Does the pitcher/opponent have wide platoon splits?

• Park. Is the game at a hitter's/pitcher's/neutral park?

• Previous outings. Has he faced this team already this season? If so, how did he fare? (Skills; not just his ERA.)

You will hopefully be left with a tiered list of pitching options, ripe for comparing individual risk/reward level against their price point.

In-Season Analyses

The efficacy of streaming *(John Burnson)*

In leagues that allow weekly or daily transactions, many owners flit from hot player to hot player. But published dollar values don't capture this traffic—they assume that players are owned from April to October. For many leagues, this may be unrealistic.

We decided to calculate these "investor returns." For each week, we identified the top players by one statistic—BA for hitters, ERA for pitchers—and took the top 100 hitters and top 50 pitchers. We then said that, at the end of the week, the #1 player was picked up (or already owned) by 100% of teams, the #2 player was picked up or owned by 99% of teams, and so on, down to the 100th player, who was on 1% of teams. (For pitchers, we stepped by 2%.) Last, we tracked each player's performance in the next week, when ownership matters.

We ran this process anew for every week of the season, tabulating each player's "investor returns" along the way. If a player was owned by 100% of teams, then we awarded him 100% of his performance. If the player was owned by half the teams, we gave him half his performance. If he was owned by no one (that is, he was not among the top players in the prior week), his performance was ignored. A player's cumulative stats over the season was his investor return.

The results...

- 60% of pitchers had poorer investor returns, with an aggregate ERA 0.40 higher than their true ERA.
- 55% of batters had poorer investor returns, but with an aggregate batting average virtually identical to the true BA.

Sitting stars and starting scrubs *(Ed DeCaria)*

In setting your pitching rotation, conventional wisdom suggests sticking with trusted stars despite difficult matchups. But does this hold up? And can you carefully start inferior pitchers against weaker opponents? Here are the ERAs posted by varying skilled pitchers facing a range of different strength offenses:

	OPPOSING OFFENSE (RC/G)				
Pitcher (ERA)	5.25+	5.00	4.25	4.00	<4.00
3.00-	3.46	3.04	3.04	2.50	2.20
3.50	3.98	3.94	3.44	3.17	2.87
4.00	4.72	4.57	3.96	3.66	3.24
4.50	5.37	4.92	4.47	4.07	3.66
5.00+	6.02	5.41	5.15	4.94	4.42

Recommendations:

1. Never start below replacement-level pitchers.
2. Always start elite pitchers.
3. Other than that, never say never or always.

Playing matchups can pay off when the difference in opposing offense is severe.

Two-start pitcher weeks *(Ed DeCaria)*

A two-start pitcher is a prized possession. But those starts can mean two DOMinant outings, two DISasters, or anything else in between, as shown by these results:

PQS Pair	% Weeks	ERA	WHIP	Win/Wk	K/Wk
DOM-DOM	20%	2.53	1.02	1.1	12.0
DOM-AVG	28%	3.60	1.25	0.8	9.2
AVG-AVG	14%	4.44	1.45	0.7	6.8
DOM-DIS	15%	5.24	1.48	0.6	7.9
AVG-DIS	17%	6.58	1.74	0.5	5.7
DIS-DIS	6%	8.85	2.07	0.3	5.0

Weeks that include even one DISaster start produce terrible results. Unfortunately, avoiding such disasters is much easier in hindsight. But what is the actual impact of this decision on the stat categories?

ERA and WHIP: When the difference between opponents is extreme, inferior pitchers can be a better percentage play. This is true both for 1-start pitchers and 2-start pitchers, and for choosing inferior one-start pitchers over superior two-start pitchers.

Strikeouts per Week: Unlike the two rate stats, there is a massive shift in the balance of power between one-start and two-start pitchers in the strikeout category. Even stars with easy one-start matchups can only barely keep pace with two-start replacement-level arms in strikeouts per week.

Wins per week are also dominated by the two-start pitchers. Even the very worst two-start pitchers will earn a half of a win on average, which is the same rate as the very best one-start pitchers.

The bottom line: If strikeouts and wins are the strategic priority, use as many two-start weeks as the rules allow, even if it means using a replacement-level pitcher with two tough starts instead of a mid-level arm with a single easy start. But if ERA and/or WHIP management are the priority, two-start pitchers can be very powerful, as a single week might impact the standings by over 1.5 points in ERA/WHIP, positively or negatively.

Top 12 trading tips *(Fred Zinkie)*

We all need to make trades to win our leagues. And while every negotiation is unique, here are some quick tips that should make anyone more effective on the trade market.

1. Learn how the other owner wishes to communicate. Some owners prefer email, others like the league website, some prefer a Twitter DM, and texting is often a desirable option. And there are even some who still want a phone call. The easy way to figure this out is to send your initial contact in multiple ways. Generally, the other owner's preferred method is the one they use to send their initial reply.

2. All negotiations start with an offer. Don't beat around the bush—give the other owner something concrete to work with. You can start with your best deal or merely a respectable proposal, but you should get the ball rolling with a firm offer.

3. Check your ego at the door. You should enter trade talks with low expectations and a willingness to accept a different point of view. The other owner is not necessarily wrong when they disagree with your opinions on player values or what makes sense for their roster.

4. Be willing to unbalance your roster. Owners who draft a balanced team and then only seek out deals that maintain that balance are going to miss out on buying opportunities. To improve your roster—especially during the first half—you should be willing to have stretches with weak hitting, poor starting pitching, or a lack of saves. The goal is to acquire value.

5. Proofread. Always take the extra minute to proofread your communication and ensure your thoughts are clear. Beyond looking for typos, be sure that all players mentioned are the ones you intend to mention. Keep your initial communication to a couple sentences.

6. Be prompt. Trading can be inconvenient, but an active trader makes time when the opportunity arises. Don't get yourself fired or abandon your children in search of the perfect trade, but in general, you should be willing to work around your competitor's schedule.

7. Send multiple offers. Submitting multiple offers lets the other owner pick the proposal they like best. If you don't want to take the time to send multiple offers, you can at least mention that you would be willing to trade Player X, Y, or Z to get your desired return.

8. Be clear about all the players who interest you on the other team. An easy way to start negotiations is to mention all players who interest you on the other team. Again, this gives some control to the other owner, who can now tell you which players are most available.

9. The message board is your last resort. Trade messages can make you appear desperate. This is especially true when trying to unload a certain player. Like a house that sits on the market, the asking price on your player tends to drop once a couple days have passed.

10. Look for owners who may be desperate. Because most owners seek to achieve roster balance, you can find value by helping those who have an immediate need. And you can always help since you are the rare owner willing to unbalance their roster to obtain value. Look at the standings, as owners who are low in a roto category are likely to trade away value in order to address their weakness.

11. Look for owners who have a surplus. On the opposite end of the spectrum, owners can be willing to make deals when they have a surplus of a position or skill. Targeting the owner who is running away with the steals category could get you SB at a reasonable price.

12. Have the guts to trade away overachievers. This is one of the hardest tips to put into practice, but experience tells us that most players who have surprising stretches return to normal at some point. If it sometimes seems too good to be true, it probably is.

Six tips on category management *(Todd Zola)*

1. Disregard whether you are near the top or the bottom of a category; focus instead on the gaps directly above and below your squad.
2. Prorate the difference in stats between teams.
3. ERA tends to move towards WHIP.
4. As the season progresses, the number of AB/IF do not preclude a gain/loss in the ratio categories.
5. An opponent's point lost is your point gained.
6. *Most important!* Come crunch time, forget value, forget names, and forget reputation. It's all about stats and where you are situated within each category.

Other Diamonds

Cellar value
The dollar value at which a player cannot help but earn more than he costs. Always profit here.

Crickets
The sound heard when someone's opening draft bid on a player is also the only bid.

End-game wasteland
Home for players undraftable in the deepest of leagues, who stay in the free agent pool all year. It's the place where even crickets keep quiet when a name is called at the draft.

FAAB Forewarnings
1. Spend early and often.
2. Emptying your budget for one prime league-crosser is a tactic that should be reserved for the desperate.
3. If you chase two rabbits, you will lose them both.

Fantasy Economics 101
The market value for a player is based on the aura of past performance, not the promise of future potential. Your greatest advantage is to leverage the space between market value and real value.

Fantasy Economics 102
The variance between market value and real value is far more important than the absolute accuracy of any individual player projection.

Hope
A commodity that routinely goes for $5 over value at the draft table.

Seasonal Assessment Standard
If you still have reason to be reading the boxscores during the last weekend of the season, then your year has to be considered a success.

The Three Cardinal Rules for Winners
If you cherish this hobby, you will live by them or die by them...
1. Revel in your success; fame is fleeting.
2. Exercise excruciating humility.
3. 100% of winnings must be spent on significant others.

Re-Introducing: Expected Home Runs

by Arik Florimonte

Introduction

Good or back luck contributes an outsized amount to baseball outcomes in general, and batted ball outcomes in particular. Of perhaps the most interest is the binary outcome that causes the largest swing of all: the home run (HR).

Using batted ball data publicly available via MLB's Statcast, we can compare what actually happened to what usually happens, with a focus on HR outcomes. We can identify pitchers and batters who have benefited or struggled as a result of too many errant gusts of wind.

The Expected Home Run (xHR) made its Baseball Forecaster debut in 2018, then called "Deserved Home Runs". We are re-introducing it this year, as xHR and xHR/F (expected home run-per-flyball rate) will now appear in the player boxes.

Methodology

Using batted ball data from 2015-2019, we created a model for xHR given exit velocity (EV) and launch angle (LA). For each LA, we plot HR per batted ball by EV of that batted ball. We fit a logistic function to the data to create a formula that, for any combination of LA or EV, will output the likelihood of that batted ball becoming a home run: the Expected Home Run.

What do the numbers mean?

Expected HR is an average result for a combination of Launch Angle and Exit Velocity. However, there are other factors that can affect whether a batted ball becomes a home run or not. These include:

- Spray angle (direction of batted ball)
- Distance and height of fence in the batted ball direction
- Backspin or Topspin
- Hook or slice
- Wind velocity
- Temperature
- Humidity
- Variability in the baseball

The xHR metric ignores all of these. It is not a measure of whether a specific batted ball should have been a home run at that moment. Rather, it is a measure of how often, across all baseball conditions from 2015-2019, a ball struck in the way it was turned out to be a home run.

Players in a hitter's park may consistently have HR totals higher than xHR, while obviously the opposite is true for a pitcher's park. Batters who are better at imparting backspin, or who tend to pull the ball down the lines, may also have actual HR totals that exceed xHR.

We should therefore not draw any conclusions from just a few batted balls. Using xHR over a whole season does allow us to draw some conclusions.

How to use xHR

For pitchers, it is well-established that home run-per-flyball rate (HR/F) is not sticky from year to year and the best HR/F predictor for pitchers is league-average HR/F, which should then be adjusted to the pitcher's park. We tested whether knowing the prior year's xHR/F improved our model at all, and the amount of improvement was negligible.

Furthermore, other research at BaseballHQ.com has found the rate of hard contact allowed by a pitcher is very weakly correlated to the following year. Thus, if you notice a pitcher's xHR/F is high, it means that he was hit hard. It does not mean he will be hit hard again. In fact, unless he pitches in a bandbox, regression to league-average HR/F is still the best predictor.

For batters, HR/F does not, generally speaking, regress to league average. According to work done by Joshua Randall:

> *"Each batter establishes an individual home run to fly ball rate that stabilizes over rolling three-year periods; those levels strongly predict the HR/F in the subsequent year."*

We tested whether xHR can be used to predict a batter's HR/F. To do this, we first park-neutralized the HR that were hit (i.e. remove park effects), and then looked at the correlation between the input sample and the test sample.

As shown in the table below, we found that in smaller samples, xHR does a better job of assessing a batter's true HR ability than park-neutral HR/F does. That advantage seems to peak after about two months of data, where the correlation rises over 30%, from 0.23 to 0.29.

Input sample	Test sample	R^2 (xHR)	R^2 (park-neutral HR/F)
April	May	0.23	0.18
April-May	June	0.29	0.23
April-June	July	0.26	0.23
April-July	August	0.26	0.25
April-August	September	0.22	0.21
1st half	2nd half	0.59	0.52
Prior Year	Current Year	0.40	0.35
Prior 2 years	Current Year	0.43	0.43
Prior 3 years	Current Year	0.44	0.46

As the amount of data available increases, note that a batter's HR/F performance becomes more important. This is consistent with past studies showing that batted ball Carry is in part a skill of a batter.

Conclusion

For pitchers, HR/F should regress to the league average, and this is incorporated in most responsible projection systems. However, biases may linger against pitchers who have "proven" to have acute gopheritis, or in favor of pitchers who managed to avoid surrendering HR. This is another reminder to trust the math, and don't get suckered.

For batters, HR/F is a semi-stable ability of the individual. The better hitters will consistently exceed league average HR/F. When we have a small amount of data, xHR/F will paint a picture faster than HR/F will. After two seasons or more, a batter's HR/F track record is to be trusted more than his xHR/F.

Expected WHIP

by Arik Florimonte

Introduction

When a pitcher experiences good or bad luck with regard to hit rate (H%), our Expected ERA (xERA) metric takes this into account, along with a number of other factors, to determine what that pitcher's ERA should have been. But what about WHIP? Hit rate luck plays a part in both the numerator (hits) and denominator (outs). How much does it impact WHIP?

Methodology

We'll use pitcher seasons from 2002-2018 with 120+ innings pitched. We'll develop a mathematical model for xWHIP and then evaluate its usefulness in predicting regression and future performance.

The Equation

The details of the calculation can be found in the original published article on BaseballHQ.com. The end result is:

$$xWHIP = \frac{3 \cdot [bb\% + (1 - K\% - bb\% - HBP\%) \cdot xH\%]}{K\% + (1 - K\% - bb\% - HBP\%) \cdot [(1 - xH\%) + xDP\%]}$$

Where xH% depends on the pitcher's allowed G/F ratio, the league-average line drive and bunt rates, and the league-average hit rates on all batted ball types. xDP% is the league average of double plays per groundball, multiplied by the pitcher's expected ground ball rate. For K%, bb%, and HBP%, we use the pitcher's exhibited rates.

As expected, xH% appears in both the numerator and denominator. A high hit rate not only increases hits but decreases outs.

Testing Our New Metric

Our first test is to check whether WHIP and xWHIP agree within a season. When plotting WHIP against xWHIP, the slope of this line is 1.004 ± .018 and the intercept is -0.036 ± 0.024. The formula does what it is supposed to do.

Next, we check whether WHIP or xWHIP is better correlated year-to-year:

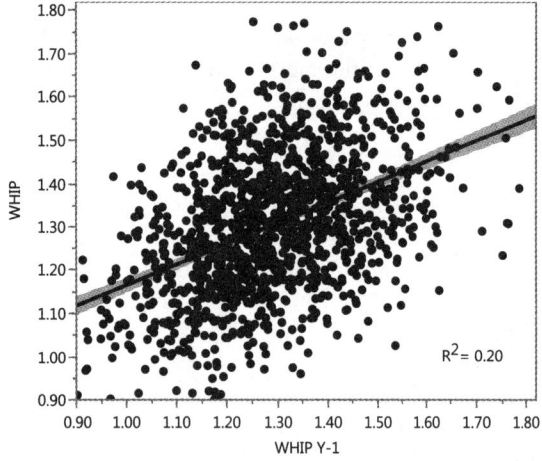

Finally, which is better at predicting the next season's WHIP? We already know this year's WHIP is 20% correlated to next year's. It turns out that this year's xWHIP is 29% correlated to next year's WHIP.

Outliers

The variation between WHIP and xWHIP in the prior year is also informative. Consider the WHIP change (current year minus prior year) plotted against the prior year WHIP minus xWHIP:

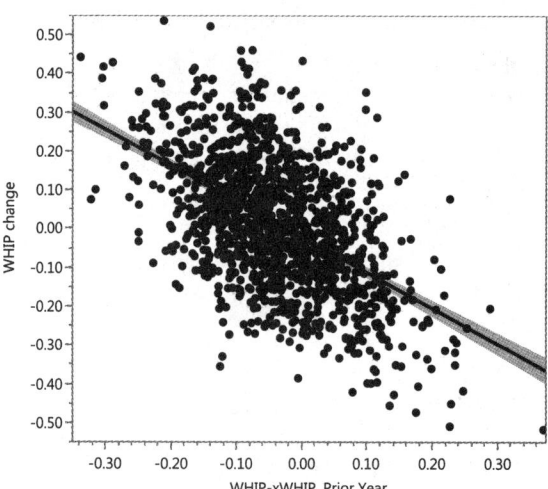

There is a pretty strong correlation. The linear fit has an equation of -0.02 - 0.92*(WHIP-xWHIP), with a R^2 value of 0.28. On average, pitchers give back over 90% of their prior year WHIP-xWHIP discrepancy.

Furthermore:

- Of the 196 pitchers whose WHIP was lower than xWHIP by one standard deviation or more, 82% saw their WHIP increase the following year; the mean change (for all 196) was +0.14.
- Of the 205 pitchers whose WHIP was higher than xWHIP by one standard deviation or more, 79% saw their WHIP decrease the following year; the mean change (for all 205) was -0.13.

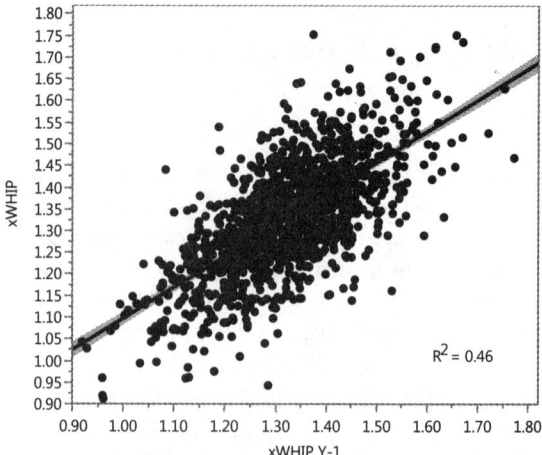

Projections

Many projection models rely on three years of data to project the following year's results. When we compare WHIP and xWHIP when we have three years of data available, xWHIP doesn't do appreciably better than WHIP at predicting the following year's outcome:

Using WHIP:

$$WHIP_{Y0} = 0.28 + 0.37*WHIP_{Y-1} + 0.27*WHIP_{Y-2} + 0.16*WHIP_{Y-3}$$
$$R^2 = .35$$

Using xWHIP:

$$WHIP_{Y0} = 0.09 + 0.55*xWHIP_{Y-1} + 0.28*xWHIP_{Y-2} + 0.09*xWHIP_{Y-3}$$
$$R^2 = .37$$

It turns out that the third year of WHIP allows it to "catch up" to xWHIP; xWHIP doesn't need that third year of data. Two years of xWHIP is just as good as three years of WHIP:

Using xWHIP:

$$WHIP_{Y0} = 0.15 + 0.59*xWHIP_{Y-1} + 0.29*xWHIP_{Y-2}$$
$$R^2 = .35$$

Similarly, one year of xWHIP ($R^2 = 0.29$) does just as well as two years of WHIP ($R^2 = 0.30$)

Conclusion

We set out to compute how hit rate would impact WHIP and create a new metric, xWHIP. We succeeded, with the following key takeaways:

- xWHIP is far better correlated to itself year to year ($R^2=0.46$) than WHIP ($R^2 = 0.20$).
- xWHIP is 50% better correlated to the following year's result than simple WHIP.
- We need fewer seasons of xWHIP than WHIP to predict the following year with the same accuracy.
- Pitchers whose WHIP-minus- xWHIP is more than one standard deviation from the mean will regress ~80% of the time, and heavily.

The Predictive Value of Linking Ball% with Control Rate

by Stephen Nickrand

Our prior research on swinging-strike rate (SwK%) and first-pitch strike rate (FpK%) confirmed that both have usefulness as a predictive tool for a pitcher's strikeout and walk rates, respectively. Can the same be said for the percentage of balls (Ball%) thrown by a pitcher?

Hypothesis

It seems intuitive that a pitcher who throws more balls as a percentage of total pitches will have a higher walk rate (Ctl, or BB/9) than his counterparts.

Let's also test the hypothesis that Ball% can be used as a measure to validate a SP's control, as well as predict future movements in control.

Method

We'll begin by taking an updated multi-season look at the relationship between a pitcher's walk rate with other stats and skills.

Then we'll look closely at Ball% to see how closely it correlates with strikeouts and walks, whether it has predictive value, and whether it is more likely to regress to a SP's own Ball% or the MLB norm.

As a reminder, correlations can range from -1.0 to +1.0. The strongest correlations are at the extremes; they get weaker as they get closer to zero:

+0.70 to +1.00	Strong positive relationship
+0.40 to +0.69	Moderate positive relationship
+0.20 to +0.39	Weak positive relationship
+0.19 to -0.19	No or negligible relationship
-0.20 to -0.39	Weak negative relationship
-0.40 to -0.69	Moderate negative relationship
-0.70 to -1.00	Strong negative relationship

Results

Below are the correlations between BB/9 and other indicators over the past ten seasons. The strongest correlations with BB/9 are ball/strike percentages, followed by WHIP, swing%, and FpK%:

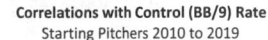

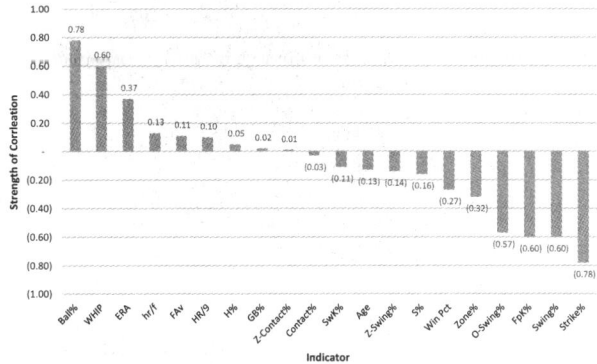

It does not come as a surprise to see that WHIP and ERA have strong negative correlations with BB/9, since walks directly impact WHIP and increase the risk of ERA blowups. Nor is it revealing that Strike% declines significantly as walks go up.

The above chart does show that Ball% and Strike% have the strongest correlation to a SP's control rate out of all indicators listed.

Historical Ball and Strike Percentages—Starting Pitchers

Let's establish some Ball% and Strike% baselines so that we know the marks typically shown by starting pitchers.

During the last ten seasons, the ball and strike percentages of starting pitchers have stayed extremely steady. Just under two-thirds of pitches thrown by starting pitchers are strikes (64%). A little more than one-third are balls (36%). There are no significant differences by league.

Over the last ten seasons, just over 60% of starting pitchers have produced a Ball% between 34% and 37%:

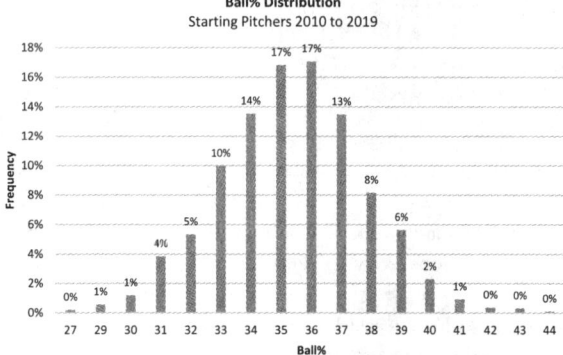

Ball% Stability

Does Ball% regress to league average, or do players set their own baselines?

Using a five-year sample of data from 2010 to 2015, there were 1,114 instances of SP with at least 40 innings pitched during a season.

Their average Ball% vs. MLB Ball% variance was +/-1.91%. By comparison, the average variance between a SP's Ball% and their own career Ball% was smaller: +/-1.71%.

This indicates that SP tend to set their own Ball% baselines more often than regressing to an overall norm. This makes sense, as we typically view balls, strikes, and walks as areas that are under a SP's control.

Predicting Control Rate from Ball% and Strike%

Using data over the last ten seasons, we can establish a SP's expected control rate (xCtl) using their Ball%. This table confirms the strong correlation between Ball% and Ctl:

Expected Control Rate by Percentile

Ball%	10th	25th	50th	75th	90th
<30%	0.8	1.0	1.3	1.4	1.9
31%	1.1	1.3	1.5	1.9	2.1
32%	1.2	1.6	1.8	2.1	2.3
33%	1.5	1.7	2.0	2.3	2.5
34%	1.7	2.0	2.3	2.6	2.9
35%	2.0	2.2	2.5	2.9	3.2
36%	2.1	2.4	2.8	3.2	3.4
37%	2.3	2.7	3.1	3.5	3.8
38%	2.6	3.0	3.3	3.8	4.2
39%	3.0	3.3	3.6	4.0	4.4
40%	3.2	3.5	4.0	4.5	4.9
41%	3.5	4.0	4.6	5.2	5.5
>42%	4.2	4.7	5.1	5.9	6.8

Ball% Outliers

From 2010 to 2014, 83 SP posted a control rate that was +/- 1.0 of their expected control rate (xCtl) based on their Ball%, using the 50th percentile of the above table as xCtl.

Of those, 35 SP had at least 40 IP as a starter during the following season.

In 29 of these 35 cases (83%), the SP's control rate in year two moved in the direction of his year one xCtl.

This indicates that SP with wide variances between Ctl and xCtl will overwhelmingly experience a correction in the direction of xCtl—as calculated by using Ball%—the following season.

Conclusions

- There are strong correlations between a SP's Ball% and Strike% and the number of walks he allows.
- Ball% provides the closest link to a pitcher's Ctl than any other indicator.
- There are weak correlations between a SP's Ball% and Strike% and the number of strikeouts he gets.
- Ball% more often regresses to a SP's career norm than it regresses to an MLB norm.
- SP with wide variances between Ctl and xCtl will overwhelmingly experience a correction in the direction of xCtl—as calculated by using Ball%—during the following season.

It Adds up: Churning Hitters in Weekly Leagues

by Ryan Bloomfield

Fantasy baseball is often referred to as a "season-long" game, but that's somewhat of a misnomer.

In weekly leagues, we're fielding roughly 27 different lineups throughout the year; even more so in leagues with mid-week changes. By thinking of each deadline as a "mini-season"—and strategically churning hitters based on each week's schedule—you can incrementally add counting stats that will have an impact over the course of a full season.

We'll cover some ways you can optimize weekly hitter lineups by racking up volume, leveraging platoon matchups, and preying on weak competition and favorable park factors.

A few quick disclaimers:

- Churning hitters should be limited to your last 1-2 active roster slots, as skills always trump matchups. So don't bench Mike Trout for Jordan Luplow just because Luplow faces four lefties next week.
- Your league size, and thus the quality of your free agent pool, should dictate how much you can churn on a weekly basis.

Number of games. The simplest way to increase counting stats over a full season is through sheer volume. In most weeks, there are several teams that play seven games, while others play just five. Using the average 5x5 output of 20 replacement-level hitters in 2019, we can see the potential gains made just by picking up two hitters that play two extra games each week:

League Size	Games	HR	SB	R	RBI
12-team mixed	54	+6	+2	+22	+22
15-team mixed	54	+6	+1.5	+19	+20

Go back and look at your final 2019 standings; how many points would you have gained with 6 more HR and 20 more R/RBI?

Platoon splits. Leveraging platoon hitters with uneven matchups for the week can further optimize your lineup, and not just in the counting stats.

In 2019, there were 57 hitters with a 150-point OPS edge against LHP over RHP (min. 300 PA). The difference in slash line splits for these players is shown below:

Split	AVG	OBP	SLG
vs. LHP	.319	.396	.587
vs. RHP	.246	.314	.422
vs. ALL	.265	.335	.464

And there were 49 hitters with the same 150-point difference, but against RHP over LHP:

Split	AVG	OBP	SLG
vs. RHP	.281	.362	.504
vs. LHP	.226	.301	.361
vs. ALL	.267	.345	.466

Of course, a hitter won't solely face LHP/RHP over an entire season, but these splits are worth exploiting in weeks when they have a platoon advantage (i.e. 4+ games vs. LHP, all 7 games vs. RHP, etc.).

Competition and Park factors. A common-sense suggestion, but in MLB's "tanking" environment (10 teams lost 90+ games in 2019), you can gain a FAAB edge when hitters face the Baltimore, Detroit, and Kansas City rotations of the world. Park factors are widely available and provide another avenue to boost hitting stats.

Think of your last two hitter spots as "churn-worthy" and use them to cycle through players with: 1) 6-7 games for the upcoming week, 2) favorable platoon splits, and/or 3) hitters facing weak pitching staffs in hitter-friendly parks. It takes work and persistence, but optimizing each week's lineup will yield a hidden counting-stat boost over the course of a full season.

Lucky/Unlucky Pitcher Wins

by Patrick Davitt

Four years ago, BaseballHQ.com analyst Matthew Cederholm invented a formula for Expected Wins (xW), identifying season-to-season outliers based largely on team-level run support (for more info, see the Encyclopedia entry on page 37). In 2019, we created a system to spot Wins outliers *in-season* using BHQ's Pure Quality Start (PQS) metric (a full explanation of PQS on page 42).

First, we used the PQS logs at BaseballHQ.com to find out how often non-"opener" starting pitchers got wins in 4,548 starts in 2019, using three PQS tiers:

PQS	Win
DOM (4-5)	61%
MED (2-3)	34%
DIS (0-1)	12%

The next step was to assess this season's starts, giving Deserved Wins (dW) in proportion to PQS outcomes. Finally, we ranked SP by Actual Wins minus dW—high positive totals indicate luck, high negative totals the opposite.

First, the 10 starters with the most wins above expected:

Pitcher	Tm	PQS (dW / W) DOM	DEC	DIS	Diff
Fried, Max	ATL	5 (3.0/ 5)	18 (6.2/10)	7 (0.8/ 2)	+7.0
Hudson, Dakota	STL	5 (3.0/ 4)	14 (4.8/ 8)	12 (1.4/ 4)	+6.8
German, Domingo	NYY	6 (3.6/ 6)	15 (5.2/ 8)	3 (0.4/ 2)	+6.8
Rodriguez, Eduardo	BOS	10 (6.1/ 8)	17 (5.8/ 9)	7 (0.8/ 2)	+6.3
Cole, Gerrit	HOU	14 (8.5/10)	15 (5.2/ 9)	4 (0.5/ 1)	+5.8
Senzatela, Antonio	COL	2 (1.2/ 1)	6 (2.1/ 5)	17 (2.0/ 5)	+5.7
Miley, Wade	HOU	4 (2.4/ 1)	12 (4.1/ 8)	16 (1.9/ 5)	+5.6
Paxton, James	NYY	9 (5.5/ 7)	9 (3.1/ 6)	9 (1.1/ 2)	+5.3
Anderson, Brett	OAK	0 (0.0/ 0)	18 (6.2/ 9)	13 (1.5/ 4)	+5.3
Fiers, Mike	OAK	5 (3.0/ 4)	16 (5.5/ 8)	12 (1.4/ 3)	+5.1

Most of these starters got more wins than expected from PQS-DOM starts, and all of them got more than expected in PQS-DEC and –DIS starts. In particular, Senzatela, Anderson, Miley, and Hudson each had four or more wins than expected in PQS-DIS starts.

Starters with the 10 most negative W-dW differences, possibly indicating bad luck:

Pitcher	Tm	PQS (dW / W) DOM	DEC	DIS	Diff
Darvish, Yu	CHC	10 (6.1/ 3)	15 (5.2/3)	5 (0.6/ 0)	-5.9
Mahle, Tyler	CIN	6 (3.6/ 1)	11 (3.8/2)	8 (0.9/ 0)	-5.3
Alcantara, Sandy	MIA	8 (4.8/ 4)	15 (5.2/2)	9 (1.1/ 0)	-5.1
Turnbull, Spencer	DET	2 (1.2/ 0)	16 (5.5/3)	10 (1.2/ 0)	-4.9
Zimmermann, Jordan	DET	3 (1.8/ 0)	8 (2.7/0)	12 (1.4/ 1)	-4.9
deGrom, Jacob	NYM	21 (12.7/10)	7 (2.4/1)	4 (0.5/ 0)	-4.6
Bumgarner, Madison	SF	12 (7.3/ 6)	16 (5.5/3)	5 (0.6/ 0)	-4.4
Boyd, Matt	DET	11 (6.7/ 3)	17 (5.8/6)	4 (0.5/ 0)	-4.0
Sale, Chris	BOS	8 (4.8/ 4)	13 (4.5/2)	4 (0.5/ 0)	-3.8
Thornton, Trent	TOR	6 (3.6/ 2)	11 (3.8/3)	12 (1.4/ 0)	-3.8

Every starter here came up short in PQS-DOM. For example, deGrom deserved 13 wins from his MLB-best 21 PQS-DOM starts, but got only 10. Nine of the 10 starters—all but Boyd—also missed dW in PQS-DEC. And in 73 combined PQS-DIS, which should have led to nine wins, Zimmermann got the only win.

None of this means that these pitchers are "due" to see more or fewer wins in 2020. Other factors affect wins. Eight of the "lucky" SP (but none of the "unlucky" ones) pitched for playoff teams. Use skills metrics to confirm interest (or lack) in pitchers whose primary source of interest (or lack) is wins.

Expected Dom and Swing Rates

by Arik Florimonte

Introduction

BaseballHQ.com and Baseball Forecaster readers are acquainted with expected Dom (xDom), which describes the relationship between swinging-strike rate (SwK) and Dom (or K/9). We'll examine whether additional swing and contact metrics can add to our understanding of xDom, and we'll also review several xDom models for the upcoming season.

Methodology

We'll use season totals for all pitchers from 2002-2018. For multiple-year comparisons, we'll weight the results by the harmonic mean of innings pitched over the seasons in question. The parameters we will consider are as follows:

- Dom (K/9)
- Ctl (BB/9)
- Fa% (fastball percentage)
- O-Swing% (% swings at pitches outside the zone)
- Z-Swing% (% swings at pitches inside the zone)
- Swing% (% of all pitches swung at)
- O-Contact% (% of swings outside the zone resulting in contact)
- Z-Contact% (% of swings inside the zone resulting in contact)
- Contact% (% of all swings resulting in contact)
- Zone% (% of pitches in the zone)
- FpK% (% of first pitches that are strikes)
- SwK (% of all pitches swung at and missed)

[Note: Contact includes foul balls]

The original work on swinging strikes at BaseballHQ.com used data from 2005-2008, and found that:

$$xDom = 335.93 \cdot e^{-4.9048 \cdot Contact\%}$$

That formula still holds up pretty well, with an R2 of 0.61. Using an updated data set, we'll revisit how Dom is related to each of SwK and Contact%:

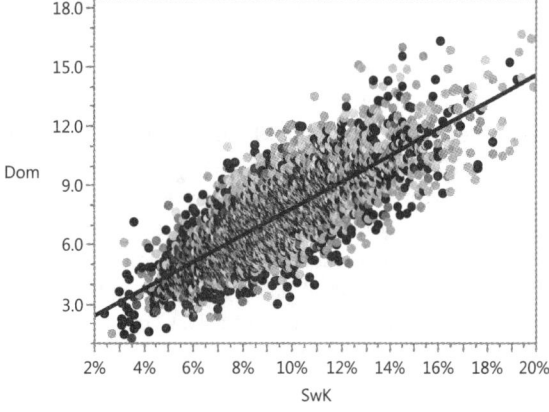

Each of these linear relationships is marginally better than the previous exponential, with SwK yielding an R^2 value of 0.63, and Contact% at 0.68.

Next, let's throw all our plate discipline metrics into a linear model and run a backward regression, removing the insignificant factors. We are left with a formula for Dom with an R^2 value of 0.74, a little bit better. Here is the formula with factors listed in order of significance:

$$xDom = 22.9 + 53.6 \cdot SwK - 15.9 \cdot Zswing\% - 12.3 \cdot ZContact\%$$

$$+2.17 \cdot Fa\% - 2.28 \cdot Zone\% + 1.59 \cdot OSwing\%$$

As a sanity check, we compare the new model to the SwK-only and Contact%-only models for each year and find that in every season from 2002-2018, the new model yields a higher R^2 value.

Behavior of outliers

Now that we have an updated xDom, what happens to pitchers when Dom exceeds xDom, and vice versa?

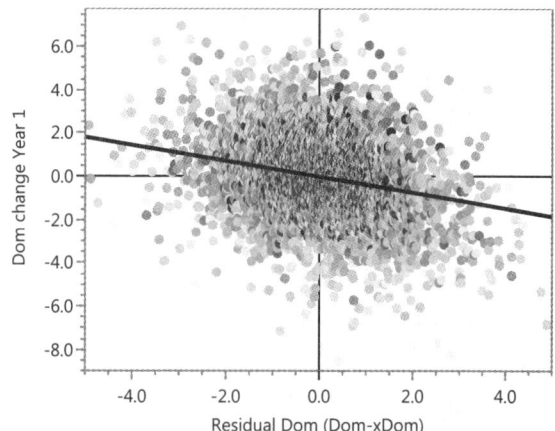

This line fit has an R^2 value of 0.06, so there is only a small tendency to regress. Still, on the end there are potentially some useful trends. Filtering only those with >100 IP (harmonic mean) over the two seasons:

- Pitchers whose Dom exceeds xDom by more than 1.5 K/9 (the upper 10%) will see their Dom drop by 0.7 ± 1.3 K/9, on average.

- Pitchers whose Dom falls short of xDom by more than 1.5 K/9 (the lower 10%) will see their Dom increase on average by 0.7 ± 1.1 K/9.
- Because of the weakness of the relationship, there is a large spread in individual outcomes.

So, while this seems like a good model for within a season, it isn't great predicting next year's Dom. Let's see if we can do better.

Next Year's Dom

Can we use xDom along with Dom in Year 0 to predict Dom in Year 1? For a baseline, Dom by itself is well-correlated with next year's Dom with R^2 of 0.52. If we also include xDom, we only get a little better, with an R^2 value of 0.53.

Many projection systems use three years of data to project the following year. So, we'll create one more model for next year's Dom for the cases when we have three years of history:

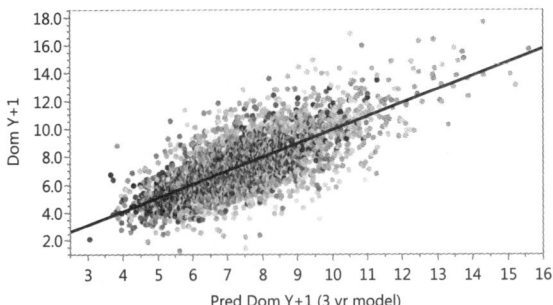

The formula is:

$$Dom_{Y1} = 1.51 + 0.49 \cdot Dom_{Y0} + 0.24 \cdot Dom_{Y-1} + 0.11 \cdot Dom_{Y-2}$$

$$-0.039 \cdot Age_{Y0} + 2.68 \cdot OSwing\%_{Y0}$$

This gives a somewhat improved R^2 value of 0.63.

Conclusions

For correlation with Dom within a season:

- We reviewed previous expected Dom formula, which used an exponential function of Contact%, and found that a linear fit now appears to work better.
- Using all available swing metrics, we can improve our model's correlation with this year's Dom.
- Using the improved xDom, the difference between xDom and Dom was found to be a weak predictor of Dom change in the following year.

For predicting next year's Dom:

- A model that makes use of a single year of additional swing metrics doesn't significantly improve the prediction of next year's Dom.
- With three years of Dom results, plus Age and last year's O-Swing%, we can do about 20% better than using one year of data.

Many prediction systems already make use of three years of data. The addition of the swing metrics, in this case, gives only marginal improvements. We conclude that a pitcher's Dom tells us 99% of what we need to know about their skill.

Are Batter Plate Discipline Metrics Useful Indicators of Skills Improvement?

by Arik Florimonte

Batter plate discipline metrics are often mentioned as providing evidence for a power breakout or improved plate skills. At BaseballHQ.com, we have long-established metrics such as PX, bb%, and ct% that are already quite reliable. Can we use plate discipline metrics to improve our understanding of a batter?

We considered three plate discipline metrics and examined whether they increased our understanding of a batter's plate skills (bb% and ct%) or power (PX):

- Chase%: percentage of swings at balls out of the zone
- ZSwing%: swings at pitches in the zone
- Contact%: percentage of swings that result in contact *(not to be confused with BHQ's ct%)*

Using data from 2009-2018, we first examined how well historical bb% and K% (i.e. 1- ct%), correlated with the next year's bb% and K%. Then, we examined whether Chase%, ZSwing%, or Contact% rates improved our predictions of the next year's results. Finally, we tested whether these metrics can improve our ability to project power.

To establish a baseline, we first found a formula for a batter's next year's bb% and K% given the three prior years of that metric. For simplicity, we excluded any batter-season that didn't have three prior years of data. We also excluded batters who saw fewer than 500 pitches in a season.

Starting with bb%, we re-ran a backward regression, incorporating the swing metrics, as well as K%. The impacts were tiny, so we experimented with using only one year of data. We found that that, too results in negligible improvement.

Next, we did the same for K%, adding the prior year's swing metrics to the backward regression and finding a new formula. As with walks, there was hardly any difference when compared to the baseline model. So we also examined just one season of data with and without the plate discipline metrics. Again, our results indicated very little improved accuracy.

To be succinct: plate discipline metrics do not add significant information about next year's walk and strikeout rates that we couldn't see by looking at previous year's walk and strikeout rates.

Lastly, we looked at power. We used PX to set a three-season baseline. Only Contact% looked like it had a chance to be useful. Re-run on a one-year input, the value of the constant increased, though it was balanced by a reduction in the sum of the linear weights of the prior PX results, and a negative contact% factor. That is, the higher the Contact%, the lower the PX. This jives with our notion of a hard-swinging slugger who doesn't care about whiffs. But, with such a small improvement in predictive value, contact rate's inclusion hardly seems worth it.

Swing metrics are well-correlated to results at the plate. Chase% is anti-correlated to walk rate, and Contact% is anti-correlated to both K% and PX. It is tempting to assume that means they add to our understanding of a batter's ability. However, when examined in the context of the other information we already have about a hitter, they add very little.

Keeper Leagues: Winning vs. Success

by Brad Kullman

We all know that "flags fly forever," but what does that really mean? In a 15-team keeper league, do we only have one successful "winner" and 14 "losers"? Sadly, that seems to be the prevailing attitude that has poisoned keeper leagues of all kinds. Even fans of all four major sports leagues (MLB, NBA, NFL, and NHL) increasingly urge their favorite teams to do a "full rebuild," intentionally tanking season(s) with inferior rosters, rather than to "fight the good fight" year after year.

For keeper leagues in which money is involved, generally the top three or four teams earn a monetary reward, so that provides at least some degree of incentive for teams in the top half to keep pushing through the dog days of August. Even leagues such as those, however, often leave teams at the bottom of the standings with no reason to remain engaged past Independence Day. Similar to their real-life brethren, in fact, they feel increasing pressure to pull the plug on a lost season by dumping high-priced non-keepers in exchange for prospective assets, no matter how dubious. "Anything is better than nothing", goes the thinking. And, of course, there's "nothing to play for in the current (lost) season," so let the fire sale begin!

There is a better way. Introducing Keeper League Competitor Rankings (KLCR). While the best team in any given season may be awarded the championship for that year, the best keeper league competitors are the ones who can successfully compete year in and year out, without the need to engage in a tanking-oriented "tear down and rebuild" in between. The true mark of keeper league success is the ability to keep building and reinforcing, even as one fights it out in the lead pack each season.

To compute this "success quotient," we count the number of teams in the league and award that many "competitor points" for the first-place team, reducing it by one for each place in the standings. In a 15-team league, for example, the owner who finishes in first is awarded 15 points. Second gets 14, third 13, etc., all the way down to last place, which receives one point. (A variation can be to award zero points to last place. After all, finishing above no one is not really much of an accomplishment. Finishing dead last should be something all owners desperately try to avoid.) Doing this every year and keeping a running total will reveal who is truly the most consistently successful keeper league competitor.

In a 15-team league, the owner who tanks and finishes last while he focuses on gathering assets to win the following season may well capture a championship, but he has only earned 16 (1+15) KLCR points. Meanwhile, the owner who finished third one year and fourth the next will receive a far superior 25 (13+12) KLCR points. Often times in a competitive league, a single-season championship is decided by a key injury or, even worse, a dump-trade. Finishing second (or even a close third or fourth) in a well-fought season is something we should all be proud of, even if we fall short of winning it all.

Of course, we can still celebrate the "winning" team, but conspicuous tabulations of your Keeper League's Competitor Ranking will give every owner a reason to compete from Opening Day through the final game. Even owners at the bottom of the standings suffering through a down season have reason to remain engaged, as they understand gaining a couple spots in the standings can be a boon to their overall KLCR standing. Every owner can enjoy the fun of competing and watching the standings every day of every season, which is really what it's all about.

Do Late Free Agent Signings Hamper Performance?

by Jeff Zimmerman

For this study, we looked at performance differences for free agents who: 1) signed in January or later, and 2) signed from 2005 (post-PED) to 2018. For hitters, we compared the average, median, and weighted plate-appearance OPS changes. For pitchers, we compared the median and weighted innings-pitched ERA changes.

Hitters

Here are the comparisons:

Month Signed	Change Weighting (OPS)	Full season	Mar/ April	May
January	Average	-.010	.015	.017
155 total	Median	-.018	.015	-.006
	Weight PA	-.008	-.013	.002
February	Average	-.028	-.038	-.012
93 total	Median	-.048	-.034	-.020
	Weight PA	-.028	-.032	.016
March/April	Average	-.016	-.056	-.014
29 total	Median	-.035	-.052	.042
	Weight PA	-.018	-.063	.022

It's no surprise to see the full-season values drop, as the average age of the free-agent hitters was 32.7 years old. These are old hitters whose age will weigh down their results. The most important values to focus on here are the March/April numbers. The later a hitter signs, the more they struggle in the season's first month. After the first month, the May results are mixed with some values heading up and others down.

To help remove some of the aging effects, we selected the hitters under 30 years of age. Because of the smaller sample, we grouped everyone who signed from February to April together:

Month Signed	Change Weighting (OPS)	Full season	Mar/ April	May
Feb/Mar/April	Average	.021	-.022	.046
15 total	Median	.029	-.034	.051
	Weight PA	.001	-.052	.053

The overall season drop was not as much, but they still struggled in April then came back in full force in May, erasing all the losses.

The one-month ramp-up could also come into play for hitters returning from injuries. Many times, an injury gets blamed for a hitter's poor return from the Injured List. Instead, the hitter may just need a month to get up to speed. While the hitter may have had some minor league games under his belt, few stay for the full 30-day rehab.

Pitchers

The following results don't follow the hitter's narrative. For pitchers, signing late doesn't matter.

Only starters remaining starters and relievers remaining relievers were examined because many older free agents transitioned from starter to reliever and their ERA improved:

Month Signed	Change Weighting (OPS)	Full season	Mar/ April	May
January	Median	-0.02	-0.23	-0.22
108 total	Weight IP	-0.11	-0.15	-0.42
February	Median	0.26	-0.63	-0.51
87 total	Weight IP	0.01	-0.35	-0.27
March/April	Median	-0.59	-0.25	-1.55
37 total	Weight IP	-0.03	0.02	-0.12

Those who signed in March or April saw more of an ERA drop than those who signed a month earlier, so the hitter narrative isn't extended to pitchers. By just looking at the May values, the median values are going down and the weighted innings values are going the other way. When values are all over the place like this, no conclusions can be drawn.

How Much Does Previous Total Production Matter?

by Jeff Zimmerman

Some owners will never draft an early hitter who has never previously put up numbers comparable to their projection. It seems like projections should take this inexperience into account, but still, others would like to see the player perform before buying in. Are these owners being paranoid, or is there something to their belief? It's time to find out.

First, some guidelines for comparing hitters:

1. We'll use BaseballHQ.com's 2010-2018 hitter projections (min. 100 PA).
2. For dollar values, we'll use the 15-team NFBC Standing Gains Points formula provided in The Process. No position scarcity will be added.
3. Any hitter with no previous MLB production will be removed.

Here are the projected vs. actual results:

Projected Range	Variable	Projected	Actual
>$30	Average	$34.1	$23.9
	Median	$32.6	$27.8
$20 to $30	Average	$23.9	$15.5
	Median	$23.5	$16.0
$10 to $20	Average	$14.3	$8.2
	Median	$13.8	$9.9
$0 to $10	Average	$4.8	$-0.6
	Median	$4.9	$-0.4

The underachievement, mainly from injuries, ranges from $5 to $8.

The previous season's dollar values were added to the projection to see if the overall results improve. Using linear regression, here are the final r-squares:

Value	Prev season	2-year average	2-year max	3-year average	3-year max
$0 to $10	.02	.01	.01	.01	.01
$10 to $20	.02	.02	.02	.20	.02
$20 to $30	.05	.04	.06	.04	.06
> $30	.18	.11	.04	.03	.04

Only two values stand out—the 'Previous season' and the 'Two-year average'. To test them, the four ranges were further divided. Here's just the previous season's data:

Proj	Prev Season	Avg Proj	Avg Result	Diff	Median Proj	Median Result	Diff
>$30	>$30	$34.6	$27.4	$7.2	$35.0	$28.3	$6.7
>$30	<$30	$33.2	$18.4	$14.8	$32.1	$19.2	$12.9
$20 to $30	>$30	$26.7	$21.4	$5.3	$26.7	$23.7	$3.0
$20 to $30	$20 to $30	$23.6	$15.2	$8.4	$23.5	$15.9	$7.5
$20 to $30	<$20	$22.9	$12.6	$10.3	$22.6	$15.0	$7.7
$10 to $20	>$20	$16.4	$10.2	$6.1	$17.2	$11.2	$6.0
$10 to $20	$10 to $20	$14.2	$9.4	$4.8	$13.8	$11.6	$2.2
$10 to $20	<$10	$13.2	$5.2	$8.0	$12.8	$6.0	$6.8
$0 to $10	>$10	$6.3	-$2.6	$8.9	$6.8	-$3.3	$10.1
$0 to $10	$0 to $10	$5.3	$0.5	$4.9	$5.5	$0.5	$4.9
$0 to $10	<$0	$3.8	-$0.7	$4.5	$3.4	-$0.5	$3.9

Start with the top dollar ranges. If a player previously had a matching or better season, they are more likely to meet their projections than those who didn't. Under $20, the advantage disappears.

Besides the previous season, here are the two previous seasons results:

Proj	Prev Season	Avg Proj	Avg Result	Diff	Median Proj	Median Result	Diff
>$30	>$30	$35.7	$28.2	$7.5	$35.4	$31.0	$4.5
>$30	<$30	$31.9	$18.1	$13.8	$31.5	$20.0	$11.5
$20 to $30	>$30	$26.9	$19.0	$7.9	$26.5	$16.5	$10.0
$20 to $30	$20 to $30	$24.2	$16.0	$8.2	$23.8	$16.0	$7.8
$20 to $30	<$20	$23.1	$14.4	$8.7	$22.6	$15.8	$6.8
$10 to $20	>$20	$17.3	$7.4	$9.9	$18.1	$6.9	$11.2
$10 to $20	$10 to $20	$14.5	$9.1	$5.4	$14.4	$10.7	$3.8
$10 to $20	<$10	$13.3	$7.5	$5.9	$12.8	$9.3	$3.5
$0 to $10	>$10	$6.0	-$2.1	$8.1	$6.8	-$0.1	$6.9
$0 to $10	$0 to $10	$5.6	-$0.2	$5.8	$5.6	-$0.2	$5.8
$0 to $10	<$0	$4.0	-$0.4	$4.4	$3.5	-$0.8	$4.4

The results are the same, as only the top two groups help predict better future results. After that, the difference between actual and projected results shrinks to nothing. Overall, previous production matters, but only for the top 20 or so hitters.

The following section contains player boxes for every batter who had significant playing time in 2019 and/or is expected to get fantasy roster-worthy plate appearances in 2020. You will find some prospects here, specifically the most impactful names who we project to play in 2020. For more complete prospect coverage, see our Prospects section.

Snapshot Section

The top band of each player box contains the following information:

Age as of Opening Day 2020.

Bats shows which side of the plate he bats from—(L)eft, (R)ight or (B)oth.

Positions: Up to three defensive positions are listed and represent those for which he appeared a minimum of 20 games in 2019.

Ht/Wt: Each batter's height and weight.

Reliability Grades analyze each batter's forecast risk, on an A-F scale. High grades go to those who have accumulated few disabled list days (Health), have a history of substantial and regular major league playing time (PT/Exp) and have displayed consistent performance over the past three years, using RC/G (Consist).

LIMA Plan Grade evaluates how well a batter would fit into a team using the LIMA Plan draft strategy. Best grades go to batters who have excellent base skills, are expected to see regular playing time, and are in the $10-$30 Rotisserie dollar range. Lowest grades will go to poor skills, few AB and values less than $5 or more than $30.

Random Variance Score (Rand Var) measures the impact random variance had on the batter's 2019 stats and the probability that his 2020 performance will exceed or fall short of 2019. The variables tracked are those prone to regression—h%, hr/f and xBA to BA variance. Players are rated on a scale of –5 to +5 with positive scores indicating rebounds and negative scores indicating corrections. Note that this score is computer-generated and the projections will override it on occasion.

Mayberry Method (MM) acknowledges the imprecision of the forecasting process by projecting player performance in broad strokes. The four digits of MM each represent a fantasy-relevant skill—power, speed, batting average and playing time (PA)—and are all on a scale of 0 to 5.

Commentaries for each batter provide a brief analysis of his skills and the potential impact on performance in 2020. MLB statistics are listed first for those who played only a portion of 2019 at the major league level. Note that these commentaries generally look at performance related issues only. Role and playing time expectations may impact these analyses, so you will have to adjust accordingly. Upside (UP) and downside (DN) statistical potential appears for some players; these are less grounded in hard data and more speculative of skills potential.

Player Stat Section

The past five years' statistics represent the total accumulated in the majors as well as in Triple-A, Double-A ball and various foreign leagues during each year. All non-major league stats have been converted to a major league equivalent (MLE) performance level. Minor league levels below Double-A are not included.

Nearly all baseball publications separate a player's statistical experiences in the major leagues from the minor leagues and outside leagues. While this may be appropriate for official record-keeping purposes, it is not an easy-to-analyze snapshot of a player's complete performance for a given year.

Bill James has proven that minor league statistics (converted to MLEs), at Double-A level or above, provide as accurate a record of a player's performance as major league statistics. Other researchers have also devised conversion factors for foreign leagues. Since these are adequate barometers, we include them in the pool of historical data for each year.

Team designations: An asterisk (*) appearing with a team name means that Triple-A and/or Double-A numbers are included in that year's stat line. Any stints of less than 20 AB are not included (to screen out most rehab appearances). A designation of "a/a" means the stats were accumulated at both AA and AAA levels that year. "for" represents a foreign or independent league. The designation "2TM" appears whenever a player was on more than one major league team, crossing leagues, in a season. "2AL" and "2NL" represent more than one team in the same league. Players who were cut during the season and finished 2019 as a free agent are designated as FAA (Free agent, AL) and FAN (Free agent, NL).

Stats: Descriptions of all the categories appear in the Encyclopedia.

- The leading decimal point has been suppressed on some categories to conserve space.
- Data for platoons (vL+, vR+), xHR and xHR/F, balls-in-play (G/L/F) and consistency (Wk#, DOM, DIS) are for major league performance only.
- Formulas that use BIP data, like xBA and xPX, only appear for years in which G/L/F data is available.

After the traditional five rotisserie stat categories, expected HR and expected BA are presented for comparision. On base average and slugging average appear next, and then OPS+, which is adjusted to league average, for both OPS itself, and OPS splits vs. left-handed and right-handed pitchers.

Batting eye and contact skill are measured with walk rate (bb%), contact rate (ct%). Eye is the ratio of walks to strikeouts.

Once the ball leaves the bat, it will either be a (G)round ball, (L)ine drive or (F)ly ball. Hit rate (h%), also referred to as batting average on balls-in-play (BABIP), measures how often a ball put into play results in a base hit. Hard contact index (HctX) measures the frequency of hard contact, compared to overall league levels. Looking at the ratio of fly balls is a good springboard to the Power

gauges. Linear weighted power index (PX) measures a batter's skill at hitting extra base hits as compared to overall league levels. xPX measures power by assessing how hard the ball is being hit (rather than the outcomes of those hits). And the ratio of home runs to fly balls shows the results of those hits. Expected home runs to fly balls give a sense of whether the player over or under-performed in the power department.

To assess speed, first look at on base average (does he get on base?), then Spd (is he fast enough to steal bases?), then SBO (how often is he attempting to steal bases?) and finally, SB% (when he attempts, what is his rate of success?).

In looking at consistency, we use weekly Base Performance Value (BPV) levels. Starting with the total number of weeks the batter accumulated stats (#Wk), the percentage of DOMinating weeks (BPV over 50) and DISaster weeks (BPV under 0) is shown. The larger the variance between DOM and DIS, the greater the consistency.

The final section includes two overall performance measures: runs above replacement (RAR) and base performance index (BPX, which is BPV indexed to each year's league average) and the Rotisserie value (R$).

2020 Projections

Forecasts are computed from a player's trends over the past five years. Adjustments were made for leading indicators and variances between skill and statistical output. After reviewing the leading indicators, you might opt to make further adjustments.

Although each year's numbers include all playing time at the Double-A level or above, the 2019 forecast only represents potential playing time at the major league level, and again is highly preliminary.

Note that the projected Rotisserie values in this book will not necessarily align with each player's historical actuals. Since we currently have no idea who is going to play third base for the Phillies, or whether Jo Adell is going to break camp with the Angels, it is impossible to create a finite pool of playing time, something which is required for valuation. So the projections are roughly based on a 12-team AL/NL league, and include an inflated number of plate appearances, league-wide. This serves to flatten the spread of values and depress individual player dollar

projections. In truth, a $25 player in this book might actually be worth $21, or $28. This level of precision is irrelevant in a process that is driven by market forces anyway. So, don't obsess over it.

Be aware of other sources that publish perfectly calibrated Rotisserie values over the winter. They are likely making arbitrary decisions as to where free agents are going to sign and who is going to land jobs in the spring. We do not make those leaps of faith here.

Bottom line… It is far too early to be making definitive projections for 2020, especially on playing time. Focus on the skill levels and trends, then consult BaseballHQ.com for playing time revisions as players change teams and roles become more defined. A free projections update will be available online in March.

Do-it-yourself analysis

Here are some data points you can look at in doing your own player analysis:

- Variance between vL+ and vR+ OPS+
- Growth or decline in walk rate (bb%)
- Growth or decline in contact rate (ct%)
- Growth or decline in G/L/F individually, or concurrent shifts
- Variance in 2019 hit rate (h%) to 2016-2018 three-year average
- Variance between Avg and xBA each year
- Variance between 2019 HR and 2019 xHR
- Growth or decline in HctX level
- Growth or decline in power index (PX) rate
- Variance between PX and xPX each year
- Variance in 2019 HR/F rate to 2016-2018 three-year average
- Variance in 2019 HR/F rate to 2019 xHR/F rate
- Growth or decline in statistically scouted speed (Spd) score
- Concurrent growth/decline of gauges like ct%, FB, PX, xPX, HR/F
- Concurrent growth/decline of gauges like OB, Spd, SBO, SB%
- Trends in DOM/DIS splits

Abreu,Jose

Age: 33 Bats: R Pos: 1B DH	Health	A	LIMA Plan	B	
Ht: 6' 3" Wt: 255	PT/Exp	A	Rand Var	-2	
	Consist	B	MM	3145	

Health returned, and with it, so did counting stats. To extent age is starting to show, signs are mostly faint (see ct%, HctX, xPX), though this is Year 2 of pedestrian vR+. Still, he should have another year at or near this level. Set ceiling at 2017 and bid accordingly.

Yr	Tm	PA	R	HR	RBI	SB	BA	xHR	xBA	OBP	SLG	OPS+	vL+	vR+	bb%	ct%	Eye	G	L	F	h%	HctX	PX	xPX	HR/F	xHR/F	Spd	SBO	SB%	#Wk	DOM	DIS	RAR	BPX	R$
15	CHW	668	88	30	101	0	290	26	276	347	502	118	91	124	6	77	0.28	47	21	32	33	115	136	116	20%	17%	81	0%	0%	26	54%	31%	18.2	149	$26
16	CHW	695	67	25	100	0	293	29	263	353	468	112	113	109	7	80	0.38	45	21	33	33	106	103	93	15%	17%	71	1%	0%	27	44%	33%	14.8	111	$22
17	CHW	670	94	33	102	3	302	30	293	352	552	121	136	114	5	81	0.30	45	18	37	33	132	135	122	18%	16%	98	2%	100%	27	59%	22%	25.3	221	$27
18	CHW	553	68	22	78	2	265	26	276	325	473	111	127	105	7	78	0.34	44	21	35	30	109	127	103	16%	19%	69	2%	100%	24	46%	25%	11.1	167	$16
19	CHW	693	85	33	123	2	284	37	273	330	503	111	132	103	5	76	0.24	46	22	32	33	107	117	104	21%	24%	72	3%	50%	28	50%	32%	14.3	119	$24
1st Half		346	41	19	60	2	268	22	271	309	508	109	124	105	5	75	0.23	45	20	35	30	100	129	117	22%	25%	69	6%	50%	15	47%	33%	1.4	141	$23
2nd Half		347	44	14	63	0	300	14	275	352	498	112	138	101	5	77	0.25	48	24	28	35	114	106	92	20%	20%	75	0%	0%	13	54%	31%	8.4	100	$26
20	**Proj**	**630**	**82**	**29**	**106**	**2**	**284**		**274**	**335**	**499**	**112**	**130**	**106**	**6**	**78**	**0.26**	**46**	**21**	**33**	**32**	**112**	**115**	**106**	**19%**		**78**	**2%**	**68%**				**20.0**	**123**	**$23**

Acuna,Ronald

Age: 22 Bats: R Pos: CF LF RF	Health	A	LIMA Plan	D+	
Ht: 6' 0" Wt: 180	PT/Exp	B	Rand Var	-1	
	Consist	A	MM	4535	

Monster season less about growth, more about full season of PA and added chances to run. That 2nd half SBO smells like an outlier and his mid-season drop in ct% suggests he's not infallible (yet). Late-season hip injury cost him chance at 40/40; but what's next? According to xHR and xBA, the bombs are more bankable than the BA.

Yr	Tm	PA	R	HR	RBI	SB	BA	xHR	xBA	OBP	SLG	OPS+	vL+	vR+	bb%	ct%	Eye	G	L	F	h%	HctX	PX	xPX	HR/F	xHR/F	Spd	SBO	SB%	#Wk	DOM	DIS	RAR	BPX	R$
15																																			
16																																			
17	a/a	478	66	16	62	29	306			358	468	111			8	73	0.30				39		94				107	35%	62%					55	$28
18	ATL *	586	86	27	67	20	276	31	252	344	499	117	138	122	9	71	0.36	42	18	39	34	117	139	140	21%	25%	140	19%	77%	21	52%	33%	26.7	197	$27
19	ATL	712	127	41	101	37	280	49	254	365	518	117	118	117	11	70	0.40	38	24	38	34	111	128	139	25%	30%	140	25%	80%	27	56%	19%	41.5	178	$42
1st Half		383	64	20	52	13	295	24	263	376	513	119	136	114	10	74	0.43	37	27	37	34	116	111	135	22%	26%	139	15%	81%	15	60%	20%	22.9	181	$38
2nd Half		329	63	21	49	24	261	25	245	353	523	115	97	120	12	65	0.39	40	21	39	33	106	150	145	29%	35%	135	37%	80%	12	50%	17%	16.6	170	$45
20	**Proj**	**665**	**110**	**39**	**94**	**31**	**275**		**255**	**354**	**523**	**118**	**121**	**116**	**10**	**70**	**0.37**	**40**	**21**	**38**	**33**	**113**	**135**	**141**	**24%**		**141**	**25%**	**74%**				**41.1**	**178**	**$39**

Adames,Willy

Age: 24 Bats: R Pos: SS	Health	A	LIMA Plan	B	
Ht: 6' 0" Wt: 205	PT/Exp	B	Rand Var	0	
	Consist	A	MM	3325	

On the surface, a growth year - in some small ways it was - but most of his support metrics were flat or declining. Platoon splits more pronounced. Plate patience continued its decline. Power flat. HR/F does support 20-HR output so that should maintain, or improve if he can work on his launch angle. Little sign of further upside right now, but it's early.

Yr	Tm	PA	R	HR	RBI	SB	BA	xHR	xBA	OBP	SLG	OPS+	vL+	vR+	bb%	ct%	Eye	G	L	F	h%	HctX	PX	xPX	HR/F	xHR/F	Spd	SBO	SB%	#Wk	DOM	DIS	RAR	BPX	R$
15																																			
16	aa	552	77	9	49	11	249			338	382	98			12	72	0.48				33		93				113	12%	63%					63	$11
17	aaa	568	69	9	58	10	258			339	383	97			11	71	0.42				35		84				109	10%	66%					21	$12
18	TAM *	591	74	13	63	9	268	10	212	335	386	100	94	108	9	68	0.32	52	18	30	37	87	77	89	17%	17%	162	10%	51%	17	24%	65%	3.5	7	$17
19	TAM	584	69	20	52	4	254	22	247	317	418	98	75	109	8	71	0.30	47	23	30	32	104	94	91	18%	19%	106	4%	67%	28	25%	39%	-10.6	33	$11
1st Half		306	35	10	26	3	253	11	247	319	412	98	65	113	8	71	0.31	48	23	29	32	105	90	83	18%	20%	111	6%	75%	15	27%	47%	-4.4	30	$10
2nd Half		278	34	10	26	1	256	11	245	314	425	97	85	104	8	71	0.29	45	23	32	32	102	98	100	17%	19%	102	3%	50%	13	23%	31%	-3.3	41	$12
20	**Proj**	**595**	**74**	**22**	**57**	**7**	**258**		**244**	**327**	**437**	**103**	**85**	**111**	**9**	**70**	**0.34**	**49**	**21**	**31**	**33**	**97**	**103**	**91**	**19%**		**127**	**8%**	**60%**				**10.7**	**26**	**$18**

Adams,Matt

Age: 31 Bats: L Pos: 1B	Health	C	LIMA Plan	D	
Ht: 6' 3" Wt: 245	PT/Exp	D	Rand Var	0	
	Consist	C	MM	4123	

Just one IL stint, but hard to find body part he didn't hurt (back, hip, ankle, shoulder x2, foot, knee), so PT proved elusive again. When he played, power was still there, but ct% fell through floor, particularly in 2nd half. It's time to give up the 400 PA dream, but these are still rosterable numbers, especially in deep leagues and for streaming.

Yr	Tm	PA	R	HR	RBI	SB	BA	xHR	xBA	OBP	SLG	OPS+	vL+	vR+	bb%	ct%	Eye	G	L	F	h%	HctX	PX	xPX	HR/F	xHR/F	Spd	SBO	SB%	#Wk	DOM	DIS	RAR	BPX	R$
15	STL	186	14	5	24	1	240	5	237	280	377	92	69	94	5	77	0.24	41	20	39	29	125	95	120	10%	10%	57	3%	100%	13	38%	31%	-9.2	32	$1
16	STL	327	37	16	54	0	249	16	252	309	471	106	111	103	8	73	0.31	32	20	48	29	108	142	159	15%	15%	70	2%	0%	25	40%	36%	-4.2	123	$7
17	2 NL	367	46	20	65	0	274	19	266	319	522	113	77	118	6	74	0.26	39	18	43	32	112	146	123	18%	17%	73	0%	0%	26	54%	38%	-0.2	148	$11
18	2 NL	337	42	21	57	0	239	19	259	309	477	109	86	111	8	76	0.37	35	21	45	25	110	132	141	20%	18%	61	0%	0%	25	44%	40%	-2.7	153	$9
19	WAS	333	42	20	56	0	226	21	235	276	465	98	88	101	6	63	0.17	31	24	45	29	84	147	148	23%	24%	64	0%	0%	25	24%	44%	-11.5	11	$6
1st Half		165	24	12	35	0	242	13	262	273	522	106	110	105	4	68	0.14	32	24	44	27	100	158	174	26%	28%	60	0%	0%	13	31%	31%	-1.6	104	$8
2nd Half		168	18	8	21	0	209	8	205	280	405	90	69	96	8	58	0.20	31	23	47	30	68	133	117	20%	20%	82	0%	0%	12	17%	58%	-7.7	-78	$3
20	**Proj**	**315**	**38**	**18**	**52**	**0**	**236**		**240**	**292**	**466**	**102**	**84**	**105**	**7**	**68**	**0.23**	**34**	**22**	**45**	**28**	**96**	**132**	**138**	**20%**		**67**	**0%**	**63%**				**-0.5**	**13**	**$9**

Adell,Jo

Age: 21 Bats: R Pos: LF	Health	A	LIMA Plan	C	
Ht: 6' 3" Wt: 215	PT/Exp	F	Rand Var	0	
	Consist	A	MM	3433	

Start to season delayed almost two months by ankle/hamstring injury, but still did enough to reach No. 2 on BaseballHQ.com's mid-season prospects list. Posted .943 OPS in 43 Double-A games; Triple-A proved stiffer challenge (64% ct%, 0 HR in 131 PA). More Triple-A time likely on tap, but it won't be long now.

Yr	Tm	PA	R	HR	RBI	SB	BA	xHR	xBA	OBP	SLG	OPS+	vL+	vR+	bb%	ct%	Eye	G	L	F	h%	HctX	PX	xPX	HR/F	xHR/F	Spd	SBO	SB%	#Wk	DOM	DIS	RAR	BPX	R$
15																																			
16																																			
17																																			
18	aa	68	13	2	6	2	225			285	402	95			8	63	0.23				32		146				104	15%	100%					60	-$1
19	a/a	303	40	7	25	6	257			315	415	97			8	67	0.25				36		110				97	8%	100%					11	$5
1st Half		81	15	3	11	4	383			436	633	143			9	81	0.50				44		141				98	17%	100%				13.5	319	$4
2nd Half		224	28	4	16	2	223			284	359	85			8	62	0.23				34		103				101	5%	100%				-6.1	-74	$6
20	**Proj**	**420**	**63**	**10**	**41**	**11**	**270**		**255**	**331**	**437**	**103**	**102**	**103**	**8**	**70**	**0.30**	**46**	**24**	**30**	**36**	**90**	**115**		**12%**		**97**	**11%**	**100%**				**8.0**	**72**	**$16**

Adrianza,Ehire

Age: 30 Bats: B Pos: 3B SS 1B	Health	D	LIMA Plan	D	
Ht: 6' 1" Wt: 195	PT/Exp	D	Rand Var	-1	
	Consist	A	MM	1221	

Before 2019, seemed to be making glacial progress towards fantasy relevance, but that has stopped. At his age, improved Eye, bb%, and ct% are not enough, and speed skill went untapped despite career-high OBP. There's still no power here, either. Does qualify at three positions, but you should be able to find someone better at any of them.

Yr	Tm	PA	R	HR	RBI	SB	BA	xHR	xBA	OBP	SLG	OPS+	vL+	vR+	bb%	ct%	Eye	G	L	F	h%	HctX	PX	xPX	HR/F	xHR/F	Spd	SBO	SB%	#Wk	DOM	DIS	RAR	BPX	R$
15	SF *	317	22	2	22	7	227	1	216	295	302	83	71	81	9	77	0.42	53	14	32	29	59	56	59	0%	3%	105	14%	69%	13	23%	54%	-7.3	8	$1
16	SF *	108	7	3	9	1	237	1	240	263	354	84	115	65	3	82	0.20	41	20	39	27	68	68	62	11%	5%	99	26%	14%	11	36%	36%	-6.7	57	-$1
17	MIN *	228	31	2	27	8	251	3	234	323	347	90	113	83	9	81	0.56	41	20	39	30	84	57	88	4%	5%	122	18%	78%	21	38%	29%	-4.4	82	$5
18	MIN	366	42	6	39	5	251	7	245	301	379	94	95	93	7	76	0.29	38	25	37	32	101	90	99	7%	8%	93	8%	83%	27	26%	44%	-1.8	57	$7
19	MIN	234	34	5	22	0	272	5	266	349	416	102	101	101	9	80	0.50	41	27	32	32	91	71	66	9%	9%	151	3%	0%	24	33%	54%	-2.3	156	$3
1st Half		133	22	4	13	0	277	4	274	376	420	106	127	98	11	82	0.70	42	28	30	31	94	64	74	14%	14%	133	0%	0%	14	29%	57%	1.1	163	$3
2nd Half		101	12	1	9	0	267	1	257	313	411	96	61	106	6	78	0.30	39	25	35	33	87	81	55	4%	4%	152	10%	0%	10	40%	50%	-2.4	133	$2
20	**Proj**	**175**	**23**	**3**	**18**	**1**	**259**		**251**	**321**	**389**	**96**	**96**	**95**	**8**	**79**	**0.39**	**40**	**24**	**35**	**31**	**89**	**72**	**75**	**7%**		**129**	**4%**	**48%**				**-2.0**	**58**	**$4**

Aguilar,Jesus

Age: 30 Bats: R Pos: 1B	Health	A	LIMA Plan	C	
Ht: 6' 3" Wt: 250	PT/Exp	C	Rand Var	0	
	Consist	D	MM	3023	

Late bloomer flopped in encore. Slow start slipped him into weak side of platoon; trade to TAM kept him there. Lack of discernible splits say he's not doomed to such a role—ct%, Eye actually improved, and there were some signs of life in his power skills, too, especially late. If role cooperates, he's a sneaky rebound candidate.

Yr	Tm	PA	R	HR	RBI	SB	BA	xHR	xBA	OBP	SLG	OPS+	vL+	vR+	bb%	ct%	Eye	G	L	F	h%	HctX	PX	xPX	HR/F	xHR/F	Spd	SBO	SB%	#Wk	DOM	DIS	RAR	BPX	R$
15	CLE *	569	48	16	81	0	244	0	281	296	394	96	80	112	7	75	0.29	42	33	25	30	215	107	171	0%	0%	57	0%	0%	4	0%	50%	-15.7	43	$9
16	CLE *	565	50	25	74	0	218	1	199	278	409	94	0	0	8	78	0.38	80	0	20	23	63	113	125	0%	100%	52	0%	0%	3	0%	33%	-18.3	100	$5
17	MIL	311	40	16	52	0	265	15	252	331	505	112	118	106	8	66	0.27	41	21	38	34	121	154	165	23%	21%	79	0%	0%	27	44%	48%	2.7	91	$8
18	MIL	566	80	35	108	0	274	33	269	352	539	123	129	120	10	71	0.41	35	24	41	32	115	163	158	24%	22%	45	0%	0%	28	57%	29%	31.1	167	$23
19	2 TM	366	39	12	50	0	236	14	230	325	389	95	91	97	12	74	0.53	42	20	38	28	107	83	106	13%	15%	71	0%	0%	28	25%	43%	-6.2	37	$4
1st Half		207	16	5	26	0	206	7	213	314	320	85	91	81	14	72	0.57	43	21	36	26	97	64	97	11%	15%	71	0%	0%	15	20%	47%	-10.5	-37	$0
2nd Half		159	23	7	24	0	273	7	252	340	475	107	92	118	10	77	0.47	41	19	40	31	120	105	117	16%	16%	78	0%	0%	13	31%	38%	2.3	137	$10
20	**Proj**	**385**	**48**	**18**	**62**	**0**	**255**		**248**	**331**	**463**	**107**	**104**	**108**	**10**	**73**	**0.42**	**39**	**21**	**39**	**30**	**114**	**114**	**135**	**19%**		**67**	**0%**	**0%**				**7.0**	**51**	**$12**

KRISTOPHER OLSON

Ahmed,Nick

Age: 30	Bats: R	Pos: SS	Health	C	LIMA Plan	B+
Ht: 6' 2"	Wt: 195		PT/Exp	B	Rand Var	0
			Consist	A	MM	2345

Elite defender set career highs across the board despite return of GB tendencies, diminished quality of contact, and ongoing struggles vR. On the plus side, plate skills took another nice step forward, while SB%/Spd keep a shred of hope alive for double-digit SB season. A solid late-round option as-is, with room for profit if h% ever cooperates.

Yr Tm	PA	R	HR	RBI	SB	BA	xHR	xBA	OBP	SLG	OPS+	vL+	vR+	bb%	ct%	Eye	G	L	F	h%	HctX	PX	xPX	HR/F	xHR/F	Spd	SBO	SB%	#Wk	DOM	DIS	RAR	BPX	R$
15 ARI	459	49	9	34	4	226	5	242	275	359	88	111	79	6	81	0.36	46	17	37	26	77	82	78	7%	4%	145	10%	44%	25	24%	28%	-8.3	127	$3
16 ARI	308	26	4	20	5	218	4	239	265	299	77	86	72	5	80	0.26	48	21	30	26	88	50	92	6%	6%	111	11%	71%	16	19%	50%	-18.5	9	$0
17 ARI	178	24	6	21	3	251	3	261	298	419	96	143	75	6	77	0.26	48	20	32	30	99	96	91	15%	7%	123	19%	43%	13	38%	46%	-3.3	103	$3
18 ARI	564	61	16	70	5	234	13	270	290	411	97	107	91	7	79	0.37	41	24	35	27	113	107	124	11%	9%	97	8%	56%	28	46%	29%	0.9	153	$11
19 ARI	625	79	19	82	8	254	19	273	316	437	100	122	92	8	80	0.46	48	20	32	29	104	95	99	13%	13%	123	7%	80%	28	36%	25%	0.0	185	$16
1st Half	332	42	7	35	5	258	8	267	308	416	97	121	87	7	79	0.37	49	20	31	31	92	88	75	9%	11%	118	7%	100%	15	27%	27%	-3.4	141	$14
2nd Half	293	37	12	47	3	248	11	279	324	461	104	125	97	10	81	0.58	48	19	33	27	118	104	127	17%	16%	127	8%	60%	13	46%	23%	0.2	244	$18
20 Proj	595	73	18	76	7	245		265	302	419	97	118	88	8	79	0.39	46	21	33	28	105	92	106	13%		122	10%	60%				0.8	132	$13

Alberto,Hanser

Age: 27	Bats: R	Pos: 2B 3B	Health	D	LIMA Plan	B+
Ht: 5' 11"	Wt: 215		PT/Exp	D	Rand Var	-5
			Consist	B	MM	1245

Rode defensive versatility and high-contact ways to near full-time AB, but warning signs abound. Aversion to walks keeps a lid on OBP, and anemic PX/xPX casts doubt on repeat of 2nd half HR output. When good fortune (43% h%) vL fades, shiny BA won't look as pretty. Let one of your leaguemates overpay.

Yr Tm	PA	R	HR	RBI	SB	BA	xHR	xBA	OBP	SLG	OPS+	vL+	vR+	bb%	ct%	Eye	G	L	F	h%	HctX	PX	xPX	HR/F	xHR/F	Spd	SBO	SB%	#Wk	DOM	DIS	RAR	BPX	R$
15 TEX *	422	46	3	30	5	262	0	249	279	353	88	42	82	2	87	0.18	51	16	33	30	62	58	41	0%	0%	128	12%	47%	12	8%	67%	-12.4	105	$6
16 TEX *	329	27	5	33	3	223	1	216	238	318	76	37	43	2	85	0.13	49	10	41	25	42	56	53	0%	6%	95	8%	53%	15	7%	80%	-22.6	51	$1
17																																		
18 TEX *	398	32	5	42	0	273	1	157	289	369	91	106	47	2	91	0.24	35	0	65	29	84	53	103	0%	7%	95	5%	0%	8	38%	38%	-6.0	133	$6
19 BAL	550	62	12	51	4	305	9	274	329	422	100	124	81	3	90	0.32	47	21	32	32	77	54	49	8%	6%	108	6%	50%	28	32%	21%	2.3	167	$15
1st Half	263	21	3	24	4	316	4	267	337	404	99	130	76	3	90	0.29	50	20	31	34	79	45	46	4%	6%	101	8%	67%	15	27%	27%	2.1	130	$12
2nd Half	287	41	9	27	0	296	6	280	322	438	100	119	86	3	91	0.35	44	22	34	30	75	63	52	11%	7%	114	3%	0%	13	38%	15%	1.7	204	$19
20 Proj	490	51	9	47	3	276		265	296	382	91	102	83	3	90	0.26	46	20	34	29	72	51	50	6%		110	4%	65%				-2.2	102	$13

Albies,Ozzie

Age: 23	Bats: B	Pos: 2B	Health	A	LIMA Plan	B+
Ht: 5' 8"	Wt: 165		PT/Exp	A	Rand Var	-1
			Consist	A	MM	3545

Stint near bottom of ATL order and underwhelming May (.239 BA, 1 HR, 1 SB) weren't enough to torpedo his stellar overall line. Hit rate correction vR, rebounding bb%, and surging hard-hit metrics provide renewed reason for excitement. Won't come cheap, but the best could be yet to come... UP: .300 BA, 25 SB

Yr Tm	PA	R	HR	RBI	SB	BA	xHR	xBA	OBP	SLG	OPS+	vL+	vR+	bb%	ct%	Eye	G	L	F	h%	HctX	PX	xPX	HR/F	xHR/F	Spd	SBO	SB%	#Wk	DOM	DIS	RAR	BPX	R$
15																																		
16 a/a	607	83	6	53	30	272			338	372	97			9	81	0.52				33		59				135	26%	69%					89	$23
17 ATL *	682	95	14	66	27	265	7	233	317	401	96	123	102	7	78	0.35	41	19	40	32	105	73	113	8%	10%	175	18%	90%	10	60%	20%	-8.0	118	$23
18 ATL	684	105	24	72	14	261	21	268	305	452	105	126	95	5	82	0.31	39	21	40	29	104	109	100	12%	10%	122	13%	82%	28	57%	18%	8.4	213	$24
19 ATL	702	102	24	86	15	295	26	285	352	500	113	143	104	8	83	0.48	38	25	37	33	121	103	114	12%	13%	132	11%	79%	28	46%	18%	32.0	259	$28
1st Half	365	51	13	46	6	281	15	270	342	465	108	136	99	8	82	0.50	40	22	38	31	120	89	121	13%	15%	135	9%	75%	15	47%	27%	8.6	222	$25
2nd Half	337	51	11	40	9	311	11	299	362	537	119	152	109	7	83	0.46	36	29	35	35	121	117	107	12%	12%	126	14%	82%	13	46%	8%	21.7	293	$31
20 Proj	686	101	25	76	19	285		276	340	489	112	136	102	7	82	0.45	38	23	38	31	112	102	108	12%		138	15%	80%				32.3	247	$31

Alfaro,Jorge

Age: 27	Bats: R	Pos: CA	Health	A	LIMA Plan	C
Ht: 6' 2"	Wt: 225		PT/Exp	C	Rand Var	-5
			Consist	A	MM	3215

Former prospect put together solid first season with new club, making small dent in ct% woes while riding sizeable BA/xBA gap for third straight year. Modest xPX impressive given low FB%, with xHR and xHR/F hinting at 20+ HR season on horizon. Even with some BA pullback, a useful power source from CA position.

Yr Tm	PA	R	HR	RBI	SB	BA	xHR	xBA	OBP	SLG	OPS+	vL+	vR+	bb%	ct%	Eye	G	L	F	h%	HctX	PX	xPX	HR/F	xHR/F	Spd	SBO	SB%	#Wk	DOM	DIS	RAR	BPX	R$
15 aa	197	17	4	16	2	222			251	369	87			4	66	0.11				32		124				100	9%	59%					3	$0
16 PHI *	437	51	12	50	2	236		226	267	373	87	45	38	4	69	0.13	63	13	25	32	0	95	-24	0%		92	5%	50%	3	0%	100%	-14.5	-31	$5
17 PHI *	452	41	11	51	1	239	5	200	267	365	85	66	139	4	62	0.10	53	16	31	36	61	92	68	22%	22%	108	2%	43%	9	22%	56%	-10.6	-112	$4
18 PHI	377	35	10	37	3	262	16	213	324	407	101	101	100	5	60	0.13	48	23	29	41	83	113	102	17%	27%	131	4%	100%	27	19%	63%	7.2	-60	$7
19 MIA	465	44	18	57	4	262	23	227	312	425	98	106	94	5	64	0.14	53	22	25	37	97	98	102	25%	32%	87	8%	50%	28	18%	61%	-1.3	-96	$10
1st Half	227	23	10	29	1	259	11	225	308	425	98	118	92	4	64	0.10	55	22	23	36	93	97	97	32%	35%	70	8%	25%	15	20%	53%	-0.3	-137	$8
2nd Half	238	21	8	28	3	265	12	229	315	425	98	97	98	6	65	0.18	51	22	28	37	101	99	108	20%	30%	108	7%	75%	13	15%	69%	3.6	-56	$12
20 Proj	455	44	20	52	4	246		230	301	434	99	94	100	5	63	0.13	51	21	28	34	87	117	98	27%		110	7%	62%				8.9	-85	$12

Allen,Greg

Age: 27	Bats: B	Pos: LF	Health	A	LIMA Plan	D
Ht: 6' 0"	Wt: 185		PT/Exp	D	Rand Var	+1
			Consist	B	MM	1511

4-27-.229 with 8 SB in 256 PA at CLE. Quality of contact suffered while OBP concerns continue to mount with second extended MLB look. Plus speed still intrigues, and 2nd half xBA/ct% rebound offers smidgen of hope. Still, looking more like 4th OF material at this point. Keep expectations low.

Yr Tm	PA	R	HR	RBI	SB	BA	xHR	xBA	OBP	SLG	OPS+	vL+	vR+	bb%	ct%	Eye	G	L	F	h%	HctX	PX	xPX	HR/F	xHR/F	Spd	SBO	SB%	#Wk	DOM	DIS	RAR	BPX	R$
15																																		
16 aa	161	21	3	11	6	269			342	398	101			10	82	0.60				32		76				122	28%	47%					131	$4
17 CLE *	315	37	3	25	18	240	1	223	288	329	83	172	46	6	78	0.32	58	8	35	30	102	61	31	11%	11%	108	28%	89%	6	17%	33%	-12.0	30	$8
18 CLE *	477	60	4	31	30	260	3	241	306	352	91	67	95	6	75	0.27	47	24	29	34	101	66	84	3%	5%	122	37%	73%	21	24%	52%	-4.7	13	$18
19 CLE *	470	59	8	40	16	231	5	238	276	350	83	55	97	6	76	0.26	49	19	32	29	82	65	54	7%	9%	159	25%	67%	22	23%	55%	-18.3	59	$10
1st Half	257	32	4	21	6	220	3	211	268	345	82	63	77	6	73	0.25	40	17	44	28	71	71	63	5%	14%	151	24%	52%	9	22%	67%	-11.9	33	$6
2nd Half	213	27	4	19	10	244	2	253	286	356	85	52	105	5	79	0.27	53	20	28	29	88	58	50	9%	6%	148	25%	83%	13	23%	46%	-5.0	70	$14
20 Proj	245	31	3	20	12	245		239	311	351	89	64	97	6	77	0.28	47	21	32	31	89	61	67	6%		139	30%	72%				-7.8	36	$9

Almora,Albert

Age: 26	Bats: R	Pos: CF	Health	A	LIMA Plan	D+
Ht: 6' 2"	Wt: 190		PT/Exp	C	Rand Var	+4
			Consist	C	MM	1343

12-32-.236 in 363 PA at CHC. Seemed poised for steady playing time in May (104 PA) before falling out of favor, eventual demotion. Defense and above-average ct% will likely keep him MLB-relevant, but too many GB, lack of underlying power, and absence of SB should keep him off fantasy radars until further notice.

Yr Tm	PA	R	HR	RBI	SB	BA	xHR	xBA	OBP	SLG	OPS+	vL+	vR+	bb%	ct%	Eye	G	L	F	h%	HctX	PX	xPX	HR/F	xHR/F	Spd	SBO	SB%	#Wk	DOM	DIS	RAR	BPX	R$
15 aa	431	56	5	37	7	248			294	361	91			6	87	0.51				27		74				108	12%	63%					149	$7
16 CHC *	444	50	6	47	8	268	2	280	288	383	91	112	97	3	84	0.17	43	28	29	31	96	72	92	12%	8%	113	12%	70%	12	42%	17%	-10.5	97	$10
17 CHC	323	39	8	46	1	298	6	273	338	445	105	119	94	6	82	0.36	49	21	30	34	98	85	69	11%	8%	111	1%	100%	27	33%	33%	3.7	133	$9
18 CHC	479	62	5	41	1	286	4	246	323	378	97	103	94	5	81	0.29	51	20	29	34	82	61	47	5%	4%	123	3%	25%	28	25%	39%	0.1	77	$11
19 CHC *	415	46	12	34	4	231	8	262	267	369	84	69	94	5	82	0.28	53	19	28	25	87	67	53	15%	10%	133	7%	63%	25	36%	40%	-12.3	122	$4
1st Half	248	27	7	24	2	252	5	262	291	396	92	75	99	5	84	0.33	55	15	30	27	89	70	49	12%	9%	123	4%	100%	15	47%	27%	-2.9	156	$6
2nd Half	167	19	5	10	2	200	3	268	236	330	75	60	84	4	78	0.21	49	27	24	22	83	63	63	25%	15%	141	13%	42%	10	20%	60%	-10.3	67	$1
20 Proj	350	39	9	29	3	253		266	288	388	91	88	92	5	82	0.27	50	22	28	29	88	70	60	12%		129	6%	57%				-1.4	55	$8

Alonso,Peter

Age: 25	Bats: R	Pos: 1B	Health	A	LIMA Plan	B
Ht: 6' 3"	Wt: 245		PT/Exp	C	Rand Var	+1
			Consist	D	MM	4135

Rookie slugger took home HR crown while carrying over MiLB patience flashed in 2018, and vs LHP/RHP alike. Be mindful of PX/xPX gap and ct%/xBA slippage in 2nd half. History says that 50-HR seasons regress sharply the following year—to the 30s, even 20s—so the percentage play will be to bid on less, hope for more. Fair warning.

Yr Tm	PA	R	HR	RBI	SB	BA	xHR	xBA	OBP	SLG	OPS+	vL+	vR+	bb%	ct%	Eye	G	L	F	h%	HctX	PX	xPX	HR/F	xHR/F	Spd	SBO	SB%	#Wk	DOM	DIS	RAR	BPX	R$
15																																		
16																																		
17 aa	47	7	2	5	0	290			322	543	116			5	82	0.27				31		138				114	0%	0%					252	$0
18 a/a	534	66	25	85	0	229			311	443	104			11	68	0.37				28		142				82	3%	0%					110	$12
19 NYM	693	103	53	120	1	260	49	272	358	583	125	123	125	10	69	0.39	41	18	41	28	101	176	153	31%	28%	90	1%	100%	28	68%	18%	24.5	252	$26
1st Half	355	54	28	64	1	278	26	289	372	627	133	159	125	11	71	0.40	40	19	41	30	111	188	169	31%	29%	95	1%	100%	15	80%	13%	23.4	315	$30
2nd Half	338	49	25	56	0	241	23	250	343	536	116	87	126	11	68	0.38	41	17	42	26	90	162	135	30%	27%	82	0%	0%	13	54%	23%	5.8	181	$21
20 Proj	630	92	43	101	0	255		253	354	539	120	113	122	11	69	0.39	41	18	41	29	98	160	149	27%		88	1%	53%				26.6	149	$24

BRIAN SLACK

Alonso,Yonder

Age: 33	Bats: L	Pos: DH 1B	Health A	LIMA Plan D	
Ht: 6' 1"	Wt: 230		PT/Exp B	Rand Var +4	
			Consist D	MM 2031	

10-37-.199 in 335 PA at CHW/COL. Hard contact and power tanked, leading him to be DFA in July. Surface numbers improved in 2nd half COL stint, but mediocre xPX, HctX say this was a mirage. Throughout, plate skills remained strong, suggesting average production going forward, if anyone gives him playing time.

Yr	Tm	PA	R	HR	RBI	SB	BA	xHR	xBA	OBP	SLG	OPS+	vL+	vR+	bb%	ct%	Eye	G	L	F	h%	HctX	PX	xPX	HR/F	xHR/F	Spd	SBO	SB%	#Wk	DOM	DIS	RAR	BPX	R$
15	SD	402	50	5	31	2	282	7	269	361	381	103	92	104	10	86	0.88	49	23	28	32	108	65	73	6%	8%	85	6%	29%	19	37%	11%	-7.4	124	$9
16	OAK	532	52	7	56	3	253	11	268	316	367	93	83	93	8	85	0.61	44	23	33	29	111	76	94	5%	8%	60	3%	75%	27	41%	30%	-19.2	103	$7
17	2 AL	521	72	28	67	2	266	25	265	365	501	116	90	119	13	74	0.58	34	23	43	30	108	135	124	19%	17%	66	1%	100%	27	44%	33%	5.5	155	$15
18	CLE	574	64	23	83	0	250	25	243	317	421	102	86	106	9	76	0.41	38	22	40	29	106	99	105	14%	16%	54	0%	0%	28	39%	39%	-8.5	67	$14
19	2 TM *	369	38	11	44	0	212	8	240	302	370	89	112	77	11	76	0.54	43	20	38	24	87	86	78	12%	10%	66	1%	0%	25	36%	48%	-18.4	67	$1
1st Half		251	23	7	27	0	178	6	221	275	301	77	116	66	12	76	0.55	43	19	38	20	84	64	73	11%	10%	68	2%	0%	14	29%	57%	-18.8	0	-$1
2nd Half		118	15	4	17	0	283	2	278	362	513	115	106	111	11	77	0.53	41	21	38	33	95	131	93	14%	10%	69	0%	0%	11	45%	36%	4.2	207	$5
20	**Proj**	**210**	**25**	**8**	**27**	**0**	**248**		**253**	**333**	**429**	**102**	**100**	**102**	**11**	**77**	**0.53**	**40**	**21**	**38**	**29**	**99**	**97**	**96**	**14%**		**70**	**1%**	**42%**				**0.5**	**86**	**$2**

Altuve,Jose

Age: 30	Bats: R	Pos: 2B	Health B	LIMA Plan D+	
Ht: 5' 6"	Wt: 165		PT/Exp A	Rand Var 0	
			Consist C	MM 3455	

31-74-.298 in 548 PA at HOU. Hamstring cost him 35 games in 1st half, likely diminished SBO. Swung harder and more often in monster 2nd half, yielding HctX- and xHR/F-backed surge, though xPX continues to warn of low power downside. Still-elite Spd plus GB profile boosts BA with plenty of infield hits. Remains a potential 5-category contributor.

Yr	Tm	PA	R	HR	RBI	SB	BA	xHR	xBA	OBP	SLG	OPS+	vL+	vR+	bb%	ct%	Eye	G	L	F	h%	HctX	PX	xPX	HR/F	xHR/F	Spd	SBO	SB%	#Wk	DOM	DIS	RAR	BPX	R$
15	HOU	689	86	15	66	38	313	12	281	353	459	113	134	102	5	89	0.49	47	18	35	33	103	89	92	7%	6%	135	29%	75%	27	67%	19%	27.2	219	$40
16	HOU	717	108	24	96	30	338	28	311	396	531	126	120	126	8	89	0.86	42	26	32	35	122	104	120	13%	15%	120	20%	75%	27	70%	15%	55.0	269	$46
17	HOU	662	112	24	81	32	346	23	299	410	547	128	129	126	9	86	0.69	47	20	33	37	98	106	87	15%	14%	132	19%	84%	27	63%	7%	63.4	264	$45
18	HOU	599	84	13	61	17	316	18	278	386	451	116	106	118	9	85	0.70	46	24	30	35	105	78	95	10%	13%	122	12%	81%	25	44%	8%	34.5	200	$27
19	HOU *	570	91	31	74	6	291	26	292	345	535	117	138	113	7	83	0.46	50	18	33	30	116	115	85	23%	20%	125	8%	55%	23	70%	9%	24.8	281	$23
1st Half		237	29	10	24	1	243	10	260	309	432	99	151	90	9	80	0.48	49	17	33	28	109	92	76	19%	19%	117	6%	33%	10	50%	20%	-2.0	181	$3
2nd Half		333	62	21	50	5	325	16	311	370	607	129	131	128	7	84	0.45	50	18	32	33	122	130	91	26%	20%	124	10%	63%	13	85%	0%	29.9	344	$37
20	**Proj**	**595**	**93**	**25**	**73**	**10**	**310**		**290**	**370**	**519**	**120**	**128**	**116**	**8**	**84**	**0.57**	**48**	**20**	**32**	**33**	**111**	**101**	**90**	**17%**		**130**	**8%**	**74%**				**42.9**	**245**	**$30**

Alvarez,Yordan

Age: 23	Bats: L	Pos: DH	Health A	LIMA Plan D+	
Ht: 6' 5"	Wt: 225		PT/Exp D	Rand Var 0	
			Consist F	MM 5145	

27-78-.313 in 369 PA at HOU. Phenom's destruction of MLB pitching fully supported by plate skills and elite HctX/xPX. Even scarier for the opposition: he mashed LHP and RHP alike. Struggles with curveball (43 ct%) the only chink in his armor, but will opposing pitchers be able to exploit that vulnerability? That might be the only obstacle to... UP: 50 HR

Yr	Tm	PA	R	HR	RBI	SB	BA	xHR	xBA	OBP	SLG	OPS+	vL+	vR+	bb%	ct%	Eye	G	L	F	h%	HctX	PX	xPX	HR/F	xHR/F	Spd	SBO	SB%	#Wk	DOM	DIS	RAR	BPX	R$
15																																			
16																																			
17																																			
18	a/a	369	51	17	60	5	261			328	469	110			9	70	0.33				32		136				83	8%	69%					110	$13
19	HOU *	610	95	44	130	1	305	27	295	396	632	137	135	144	13	71	0.53	38	25	37	35	126	182	155	33%	33%	70	2%	56%	17	71%	18%	55.8	293	$30
1st Half		310	49	24	73	1	298	5	300	381	628	135	182	142	12	73	0.50	27	30	43	33	138	175	208	37%	26%	85	3%	56%	4	100%	0%	25.3	307	$32
2nd Half		300	46	20	57	0	312	22	290	413	636	139	127	145	15	69	0.55	41	24	36	38	120	190	141	32%	35%	73	0%	0%	13	62%	23%	30.5	304	$27
20	**Proj**	**588**	**79**	**37**	**102**	**4**	**278**		**277**	**365**	**557**	**124**	**125**	**123**	**12**	**70**	**0.45**	**36**	**26**	**38**	**33**	**127**	**160**	**168**	**27%**		**70**	**4%**	**68%**				**35.8**	**179**	**$26**

Anderson,Brian

Age: 27	Bats: R	Pos: 3B RF	Health B	LIMA Plan B+	
Ht: 6' 3"	Wt: 185		PT/Exp B	Rand Var -2	
			Consist A	MM 3235	

Increased FB rate and hard contact fueled power growth before a fractured pinky ended his season in August. Shortened 2nd half helps to obscure a surge backed up by xHR, xPX, xBA, including intriguing FB rate and launch angle spikes. If he can carry it forward, the pieces are here to deliver... UP: 30 HR, .280 BA

Yr	Tm	PA	R	HR	RBI	SB	BA	xHR	xBA	OBP	SLG	OPS+	vL+	vR+	bb%	ct%	Eye	G	L	F	h%	HctX	PX	xPX	HR/F	xHR/F	Spd	SBO	SB%	#Wk	DOM	DIS	RAR	BPX	R$
15																																			
16	aa	333	34	7	36	0	216			292	315	83			10	78	0.48				26		59				95	0%	0%					23	$0
17	MIA *	567	77	18	80	1	246	2	273	317	418	99	72	104	9	72	0.38	49	28	23	31	87	105	83	0%	15%	119	2%	28%	6	17%	67%	-11.8	91	$10
18	MIA	670	87	11	65	2	273	19	252	357	400	105	104	104	9	78	0.48	52	20	29	33	110	82	78	8%	14%	125	3%	33%	27	48%	33%	4.9	120	$16
19	MIA	520	57	20	66	5	261	21	264	342	468	108	96	111	8	75	0.39	45	19	35	31	115	117	108	16%	17%	97	5%	83%	22	45%	27%	-1.2	156	$13
1st Half		348	33	11	38	4	255	13	259	339	428	102	75	112	9	76	0.44	49	20	31	30	114	96	94	15%	18%	101	6%	80%	15	47%	33%	-3.8	122	$14
2nd Half		172	24	9	28	1	275	9	273	349	549	118	146	111	7	73	0.29	39	18	43	32	117	160	136	18%	18%	103	3%	100%	7	43%	14%	5.0	252	$10
20	**Proj**	**560**	**71**	**21**	**73**	**3**	**268**		**260**	**345**	**462**	**109**	**107**	**108**	**9**	**75**	**0.38**	**45**	**20**	**35**	**32**	**109**	**110**	**99**	**15%**		**108**	**3%**	**66%**				**10.7**	**104**	**$18**

Anderson,Tim

Age: 27	Bats: R	Pos: SS	Health B	LIMA Plan D	
Ht: 6' 1"	Wt: 185		PT/Exp B	Rand Var -5	
			Consist C	MM 2535	

18-56-.335 with 17 SB in 518 PA at CHW. BA spike driven mainly by soaring h%, but excellent speed, GB tilt, and career-best ct% point to some sustainability—just not .300+. Was on MLB career-best SB pace until sprained ankle cost him July, killed SBO. Subpar xPX, HctX suggest shaky power footing; don't look for HR repeat. But UP: 30 SB

Yr	Tm	PA	R	HR	RBI	SB	BA	xHR	xBA	OBP	SLG	OPS+	vL+	vR+	bb%	ct%	Eye	G	L	F	h%	HctX	PX	xPX	HR/F	xHR/F	Spd	SBO	SB%	#Wk	DOM	DIS	RAR	BPX	R$
15	aa	536	70	5	41	43	287			318	389	99			4	75	0.18				38		69				145	42%	75%					24	$29
16	CHW *	685	89	12	46	19	279	11	248	300	407	96	108	96	3	72	0.11	54	21	25	37	94	86	86	12%	15%	176	17%	75%	18	28%	50%	-0.5	49	$22
17	CHW	602	72	17	56	15	257	16	248	277	403	91	108	83	2	72	0.08	52	19	28	33	83	89	69	14%	14%	144	14%	94%	27	15%	56%	-12.6	30	$15
18	CHW	606	77	20	64	26	240	17	248	281	406	95	110	89	5	74	0.20	47	20	33	29	82	104	83	14%	12%	123	30%	76%	27	41%	44%	-5.9	90	$21
19	CHW *	541	83	19	59	17	333	16	279	352	505	114	110	116	3	79	0.13	49	24	28	40	88	94	84	17%	15%	114	16%	77%	24	29%	38%	22.2	115	$28
1st Half		281	39	11	37	15	317	12	268	342	491	111	98	117	3	78	0.12	47	22	31	37	86	92	106	17%	18%	108	28%	79%	14	29%	43%	8.5	96	$32
2nd Half		260	44	8	22	2	351	4	291	371	520	117	126	116	3	79	0.15	50	26	23	42	90	96	57	17%	10%	124	4%	67%	10	30%	30%	16.3	141	$24
20	**Proj**	**595**	**82**	**18**	**57**	**20**	**289**		**262**	**315**	**445**	**102**	**108**	**99**	**3**	**76**	**0.15**	**49**	**22**	**28**	**35**	**87**	**88**	**78**	**14%**		**130**	**19%**	**78%**				**13.9**	**62**	**$27**

Andrus,Elvis

Age: 31	Bats: R	Pos: SS	Health C	LIMA Plan B	
Ht: 6' 0"	Wt: 200		PT/Exp A	Rand Var 0	
			Consist C	MM 1445	

Steals returned as he took full advantage of green light from new manager. And while overall 2nd half swoon is concerning on the surface, BA slide was h% fueled; xBA and xHR remained steady. xPX, xHR/F agree with tepid power output, so bank on value from SB and BA, but don't count on 20 HR coming back.

Yr	Tm	PA	R	HR	RBI	SB	BA	xHR	xBA	OBP	SLG	OPS+	vL+	vR+	bb%	ct%	Eye	G	L	F	h%	HctX	PX	xPX	HR/F	xHR/F	Spd	SBO	SB%	#Wk	DOM	DIS	RAR	BPX	R$
15	TEX	661	69	7	62	25	258	7	265	309	357	93	104	85	7	87	0.59	47	21	32	29	104	67	70	4%	4%	106	22%	74%	27	59%	15%	-10.3	132	$19
16	TEX	568	75	8	69	24	302	7	289	362	439	109	121	103	8	86	0.67	48	24	29	34	95	80	68	6%	6%	140	21%	75%	27	48%	7%	20.6	197	$26
17	TEX	689	100	20	88	25	297	17	289	337	471	108	112	105	6	84	0.38	49	20	32	33	104	97	80	12%	10%	115	22%	71%	27	52%	26%	18.0	188	$33
18	TEX *	454	54	6	33	5	243	8	252	294	348	89	101	90	7	83	0.43	50	19	31	28	104	63	59	6%	8%	132	9%	54%	19	42%	37%	-9.4	130	$6
19	TEX	648	81	12	72	31	275	14	272	313	393	94	95	93	5	84	0.35	51	21	28	31	112	60	72	8%	10%	119	25%	79%	28	50%	25%	-13.0	119	$26
1st Half		325	46	7	43	16	309	7	276	345	457	107	106	107	4	83	0.27	49	21	30	35	119	77	91	9%	9%	124	24%	84%	15	67%	13%	7.5	159	$32
2nd Half		323	35	5	29	15	240	7	268	282	328	80	87	77	6	85	0.44	53	22	25	27	105	44	54	8%	11%	107	26%	75%	13	31%	38%	-16.0	78	$21
20	**Proj**	**630**	**80**	**14**	**68**	**23**	**276**		**273**	**318**	**410**	**98**	**103**	**95**	**6**	**84**	**0.39**	**50**	**21**	**29**	**31**	**107**	**69**	**68**	**10%**		**122**	**20%**	**75%**				**7.4**	**149**	**$27**

Andujar,Miguel

Age: 25	Bats: R	Pos: DH	Health F	LIMA Plan B+	
Ht: 6' 0"	Wt: 215		PT/Exp D	Rand Var +5	
			Consist F	MM 3155	

Missed all but 13 games with a shoulder injury that required surgery in May. A lost year of development is bad, but hitters generally fully recover from labrum surgery when given enough time. Once healthy, ct%, HctX should enable a BA repeat, but demonstrated xPX and xHR warrant a merely league-average power projection.

Yr	Tm	PA	R	HR	RBI	SB	BA	xHR	xBA	OBP	SLG	OPS+	vL+	vR+	bb%	ct%	Eye	G	L	F	h%	HctX	PX	xPX	HR/F	xHR/F	Spd	SBO	SB%	#Wk	DOM	DIS	RAR	BPX	R$
15																																			
16	aa	302	27	2	40	2	255			305	343	88			7	84	0.44				30		57				90	4%	64%					66	$3
17	NYY *	516	62	18	81	6	306	0	284	343	492	112	177	211	5	84	0.36	57	14	29	34	97	104	81	0%	0%	72	7%	64%	5	40%	40%	16.9	161	$21
18	NYY	606	83	27	92	2	297	21	295	328	527	118	114	119	4	83	0.26	44	20	36	32	110	133	99	16%	12%	93	3%	67%	27	59%	19%	29.6	257	$25
19	NYY	49	1	0	1	0	128	1	115	143	128	36	0	47	2	77	0.09	49	8	43	17	86	0	65	0%	6%	92	0%	0%	5	20%	60%	-7.1	-219	-$5
1st Half		49	1	0	1	0	128	1	115	143	128	36	0	47	2	77	0.09	49	8	43	17	86	0	65	0%	6%	92	0%	0%	5	20%	60%	-7.5	-222	-$5
2nd Half																																			
20	**Proj**	**525**	**60**	**23**	**77**	**4**	**282**		**286**	**319**	**497**	**110**	**85**	**118**	**5**	**85**	**0.38**	**44**	**20**	**36**	**29**	**105**	**107**	**79**	**15%**		**70**	**5%**	**67%**				**13.4**	**206**	**$20**

ARIK FLORIMONTE

Aquino,Aristides

Age: 26	Bats: R	Pos: RF	Health	A	LIMA Plan B
Ht: 6' 4"	Wt: 220		PT/Exp	C	Rand Var 0
			Consist	D	MM 4215

19-47-.259 with 7 SB in 225 PA at CIN. Long-term power potential is intriguing, but he's not ready to be the next 50-HR young stud. Sizable gaps between PX/xPX, MLB HR/xHR; subpar hard contact; pitchers adjusted in Sept (.227 xBA, 96 xPX, 18% HR/F). Poor Eye and inconsistent SB history add to risk he'll be overvalued come draft day.

Yr	Tm	PA	R	HR	RBI	SB	BA	xHR	xBA	OBP	SLG	OPS+	vL+	vR+	bb%	ct%	Eye	G	L	F	h%	HctX	PX	xPX	HR/F	xHR/F	Spd	SBO	SB%	#Wk	DOM	DIS	RAR	BPX	R$
15																																			
16																																			
17	aa	501	56	19	58	9	215			281	408	92			8	65	0.26				29		125				119	13%	74%					42	$6
18	CIN *	435	41	18	46	3	216		234	270	403	93	0	0	7	68	0.23	44	20	36	27	0	123	-27	0%		100	11%	37%	1	0%	100%	-13.3	53	$5
19	CIN *	539	77	44	91	11	264	14	261	313	574	118	118	118	7	68	0.23	35	20	45	29	92	168	110	29%	21%	89	12%	91%	10	60%	30%	13.2	185	$24
1st Half		208	33	16	29	2	278		276	329	584	122			7	70	0.26				31		161		0%		112	6%	100%				9.1	222	$11
2nd Half		331	44	28	62	9	255	14	260	303	568	115	117	118	6	67	0.21	35	20	45	28	90	173	110	29%	21%	80	16%	88%	10	60%	30%	6.8	167	$33
20	**Proj**	**560**	**68**	**33**	**78**	**8**	**240**		**238**	**295**	**480**	**104**	**108**	**103**	**7**	**68**	**0.23**	**35**	**20**	**45**	**29**	**90**	**137**	**99**	**21%**		**98**	**11%**	**67%**				**1.6**	**69**	**$16**

Arcia,Orlando

Age: 25	Bats: R	Pos: SS	Health	A	LIMA Plan C+
Ht: 6' 0"	Wt: 165		PT/Exp	B	Rand Var +2
			Consist	B	MM 1325

HR rebound was nice, but low FB% and below-average HctX, xPX don't offer much future upside, and SBO/SB% declines show best source of value is heading in wrong direction. Without that, there's just no leading skill here to push R$ back to 2017 level. Glove should keep PA, meager counting stats tediously rolling alongzzzzz...

Yr	Tm	PA	R	HR	RBI	SB	BA	xHR	xBA	OBP	SLG	OPS+	vL+	vR+	bb%	ct%	Eye	G	L	F	h%	HctX	PX	xPX	HR/F	xHR/F	Spd	SBO	SB%	#Wk	DOM	DIS	RAR	BPX	R$
15	aa	540	67	7	63	23	296			332	432	107			5	85	0.36				34		90				105	24%	73%					149	$25
16	MIL *	641	64	11	56	19	228	2	250	272	349	84	114	75	6	78	0.27	54	17	29	28	80	74	59	9%	5%	152	21%	68%	10	40%	40%	-28.9	86	$10
17	MIL	548	56	15	53	14	277	10	259	324	407	98	83	101	7	80	0.36	52	20	29	32	98	70	78	13%	9%	138	15%	67%	26	31%	38%	0.5	100	$17
18	MIL *	458	43	4	35	8	244	4	232	280	325	84	83	78	5	76	0.21	56	19	25	31	71	58	54	5%	6%	121	13%	62%	25	16%	56%	-10.6	-7	$6
19	MIL	546	51	15	59	8	223	13	242	283	350	84	89	82	8	78	0.39	51	18	31	26	89	66	86	13%	11%	117	11%	62%	28	36%	46%	-23.6	63	$7
1st Half		304	33	11	36	4	237	9	254	299	399	93	88	95	8	78	0.41	52	18	30	27	88	81	86	17%	14%	127	10%	57%	15	40%	27%	-8.9	126	$11
2nd Half		242	18	4	23	4	204	4	224	263	287	73	91	66	8	78	0.38	51	18	31	24	91	45	87	7%	7%	107	12%	67%	13	31%	69%	-17.3	-11	$2
20	**Proj**	**525**	**50**	**11**	**51**	**9**	**237**		**240**	**288**	**346**	**85**	**92**	**83**	**7**	**78**	**0.33**	**53**	**18**	**29**	**28**	**85**	**59**	**74**	**10%**		**125**	**12%**	**62%**				**-12.9**	**-6**	**$11**

Arenado,Nolan

Age: 29	Bats: R	Pos: 3B	Health	A	LIMA Plan D+
Ht: 6' 2"	Wt: 215		PT/Exp	A	Rand Var -2
			Consist	A	MM 4255

Consistency of R$ is impressive, though you can find reasons he might slip below $30 in 2020: 1) xBA suggests .300+ BA could be tough to repeat; 2) lowest PX since rookie year; 3) largest gap between HR, xHR in last five seasons. Maybe it's nothing. But as a player nears 30, small flaws can become more significant.

Yr	Tm	PA	R	HR	RBI	SB	BA	xHR	xBA	OBP	SLG	OPS+	vL+	vR+	bb%	ct%	Eye	G	L	F	h%	HctX	PX	xPX	HR/F	xHR/F	Spd	SBO	SB%	#Wk	DOM	DIS	RAR	BPX	R$
15	COL	665	97	42	130	2	287	31	307	323	575	125	107	128	5	82	0.31	34	22	44	29	133	172	151	19%	14%	93	6%	29%	27	70%	15%	31.1	286	$32
16	COL	696	116	41	133	2	294	31	290	362	570	127	118	127	10	83	0.66	35	18	47	30	128	146	148	17%	13%	114	3%	40%	27	78%	11%	41.4	303	$32
17	COL	679	100	37	130	3	309	33	297	373	586	129	174	111	9	83	0.58	34	21	45	32	123	145	149	16%	15%	113	3%	60%	27	74%	7%	44.2	303	$32
18	COL	673	104	38	110	2	297	30	291	374	561	129	167	113	11	79	0.60	40	21	39	32	126	150	138	21%	16%	85	2%	50%	28	71%	11%	46.8	287	$31
19	COL	662	102	41	118	3	315	27	287	379	583	128	134	125	9	84	0.67	36	19	45	32	123	124	139	18%	12%	110	3%	60%	27	67%	11%	43.7	333	$32
1st Half		362	60	20	65	2	320	15	294	384	581	129	150	120	10	85	0.72	38	20	42	33	123	121	126	17%	13%	126	4%	50%	15	60%	7%	26.0	359	$36
2nd Half		300	42	21	53	1	308	12	278	373	586	127	116	131	10	83	0.61	33	18	48	31	123	127	154	19%	11%	83	1%	100%	12	75%	17%	20.8	289	$27
20	**Proj**	**665**	**102**	**38**	**115**	**3**	**298**		**281**	**366**	**556**	**124**	**140**	**117**	**10**	**82**	**0.62**	**36**	**20**	**44**	**31**	**125**	**124**	**143**	**18%**		**103**	**3%**	**57%**				**45.9**	**261**	**$33**

Arozarena,Randy

Age: 25	Bats: R	Pos: RF	Health	A	LIMA Plan C+
Ht: 5' 11"	Wt: 170		PT/Exp	D	Rand Var -5
			Consist	C	MM 2423

1-2-.300 with 2 SB in 23 PA at STL. Possibility of double-digit HR/SB combo—even with less than full-time PA—makes him worth watching this spring. That said, history of high GB% caps power potential, poor SB% could take a bite out of SBO. xBA, 2017-18 MLEs likely rule out another near-.300 BA. Be aware, but also be patient.

Yr	Tm	PA	R	HR	RBI	SB	BA	xHR	xBA	OBP	SLG	OPS+	vL+	vR+	bb%	ct%	Eye	G	L	F	h%	HctX	PX	xPX	HR/F	xHR/F	Spd	SBO	SB%	#Wk	DOM	DIS	RAR	BPX	R$
15																																			
16																																			
17	aa	187	30	3	8	7	236			332	352	92			13	78	0.67				29		73				127	21%	69%					115	$2
18	a/a	384	49	9	38	20	237			288	361	90			7	74	0.28				30		83				92	35%	69%					20	$12
19	STL *	395	56	13	45	16	299	1	260	354	481	111	152	112	8	77	0.37	56	13	31	36	100	100	42	20%	20%	136	30%	51%	6	33%	50%	12.8	170	$17
1st Half		184	21	5	21	8	291		250	345	451	106			8	76	0.35				36		90		0%		125	32%	54%				3.1	115	$11
2nd Half		211	35	8	24	8	306	1	267	362	508	115	150	112	8	77	0.39	56	13	31	36	100	108	42	20%	20%	138	29%	49%	6	33%	50%	8.7	207	$23
20	**Proj**	**350**	**50**	**10**	**37**	**13**	**269**		**244**	**329**	**426**	**102**	**101**	**101**	**8**	**76**	**0.38**	**44**	**19**	**37**	**33**	**100**	**89**		**11%**		**118**	**27%**	**59%**				**0.2**	**90**	**$15**

Arraez,Luis

Age: 23	Bats: L	Pos: 2B LF	Health	A	LIMA Plan B+
Ht: 5' 10"	Wt: 177		PT/Exp	F	Rand Var -2
			Consist	D	MM 0255

4-28-.334 in 366 PA at MIN. Highest ct%, 2nd-highest Eye among hitters with 300+ PA is a pretty good start to a career. xBA adds legitimacy to his efforts, and while he didn't hit for power vL (16 PX), 2.00 Eye in MLB says he's capable of holding his own. HR, SB totals likely to remain modest; full season of BA/OBP should drive value anyway.

Yr	Tm	PA	R	HR	RBI	SB	BA	xHR	xBA	OBP	SLG	OPS+	vL+	vR+	bb%	ct%	Eye	G	L	F	h%	HctX	PX	xPX	HR/F	xHR/F	Spd	SBO	SB%	#Wk	DOM	DIS	RAR	BPX	R$
15																																			
16																																			
17																																			
18	aa	189	21	2	13	2	277			317	337	91			6	91	0.63				30		35				100	3%	100%					113	$2
19	MIN *	600	77	4	48	6	333	5	298	398	418	108	91	118	10	92	1.29	41	29	29	36	110	46	73	5%	6%	108	5%	52%	18	61%	6%	20.6	211	$19
1st Half		301	33	1	25	5	348	0	323	416	414	111	134	135	11	93	1.60	35	38	27	37	133	37	103	7%	0%	114	8%	52%	6	67%	0%	13.0	211	$19
2nd Half		299	44	3	23	1	319	5	296	378	422	106	78	115	9	91	1.04	43	28	30	34	104	55	67	4%	7%	110	2%	50%	12	58%	8%	9.2	219	$19
20	**Proj**	**560**	**69**	**7**	**42**	**5**	**308**		**302**	**368**	**402**	**104**	**92**	**107**	**9**	**91**	**1.11**	**40**	**32**	**29**	**33**	**116**	**48**	**81**	**5%**		**106**	**5%**	**68%**				**19.0**	**158**	**$19**

Astudillo,Willians

Age: 28	Bats: R	Pos: CA	Health	C	LIMA Plan D+
Ht: 5' 9"	Wt: 225		PT/Exp	F	Rand Var -1
			Consist	A	MM 1051

4-21-.268 in 204 PA at MIN. Hit .327 with .344 xBA in 49 PA before May hamstring injury and oblique issue that cost him all of July. As we've seen in short bursts, ridiculous ct% gives him .300 BA upside; downside is that drops in HctX, LD%, or PX cause his value to crater. CA eligibility makes him worth a flyer.

Yr	Tm	PA	R	HR	RBI	SB	BA	xHR	xBA	OBP	SLG	OPS+	vL+	vR+	bb%	ct%	Eye	G	L	F	h%	HctX	PX	xPX	HR/F	xHR/F	Spd	SBO	SB%	#Wk	DOM	DIS	RAR	BPX	R$
15																																			
16	aa	327	23	3	28	1	235			246	283	72			2	96	0.37				24		24				86	3%	45%					97	$0
17	aaa	122	14	3	14	0	274			289	436	97			2	95	0.41				27		90				86	6%	0%					255	$1
18	MIN *	391	34	13	53	6	270	3	299	289	435	100	124	121	3	95	0.54	41	23	36	26	112	81	91	9%	9%	83	14%	55%	10	60%	10%	9.3	257	$11
19	MIN *	301	46	10	39	1	295	4	287	313	434	99	78	94	2	96	0.71	40	22	38	28	100	59	55	6%	6%	64	5%	24%	15	47%	27%	9.0	219	$8
1st Half		181	27	5	22	1	303	3	286	314	438	101	90	88	2	96	0.45	41	21	38	29	109	58	72	6%	6%	67	5%	38%	10	60%	20%	4.4	211	$9
2nd Half		121	19	4	17	0	281	0	287	309	424	97	52	108	4	96	1.09	39	22	39	26	80	59	15	5%	0%	76	4%	0%	5	20%	40%	1.4	241	$6
20	**Proj**	**245**	**31**	**6**	**31**	**1**	**286**		**284**	**316**	**410**	**98**	**86**	**101**	**3**	**96**	**0.67**	**40**	**22**	**38**	**28**	**100**	**57**	**60**	**7%**		**70**	**6%**	**39%**				**6.2**	**195**	**$8**

Bader,Harrison

Age: 26	Bats: R	Pos: CF	Health	A	LIMA Plan C+
Ht: 6' 0"	Wt: 195		PT/Exp	C	Rand Var +2
			Consist	B	MM 2505

12-39-.205 with 11 SB in 406 PA at STL. Regression in h%, LD% led to BA collapse. However, even in the ashes of a down year, there are positive signs in improved walk rate, massive growth in FB%/xPX. Lack of contact both hard and regular remains a concern, but if opportunity comes his way... UP: 20 HR, 20 SB... though with hard BA cap.

Yr	Tm	PA	R	HR	RBI	SB	BA	xHR	xBA	OBP	SLG	OPS+	vL+	vR+	bb%	ct%	Eye	G	L	F	h%	HctX	PX	xPX	HR/F	xHR/F	Spd	SBO	SB%	#Wk	DOM	DIS	RAR	BPX	R$
15																																			
16	a/a	494	57	15	47	11	242			287	393	92			6	71	0.21				31		97				112	24%	43%					20	$10
17	STL *	551	71	19	55	14	251	3	223	295	401	93	159	66	6	71	0.22	44	16	39	32	97	92	109	13%	13%	112	21%	57%	8	13%	50%	-19.6	15	$14
18	STL	427	61	12	37	15	264	11	234	334	422	105	123	95	7	67	0.25	40	27	33	36	93	111	95	14%	13%	147	19%	83%	27	30%	56%	5.6	57	$15
19	STL *	475	72	17	50	13	214	15	215	302	394	92	84	92	11	67	0.38	38	17	44	27	88	105	141	12%	15%	139	16%	82%	25	24%	48%	-4.5	63	$11
1st Half		214	24	6	19	4	206	7	212	324	372	93	89	94	12	68	0.41	35	19	46	27	89	98	144	11%	13%	134	16%	57%	14	29%	43%	-5.4	56	$0
2nd Half		261	48	11	31	9	220	8	218	305	411	94	78	91	11	66	0.36	42	16	43	28	88	111	137	13%	17%	132	16%	100%	11	18%	55%	-0.4	63	$19
20	**Proj**	**490**	**72**	**16**	**50**	**14**	**235**		**220**	**317**	**395**	**96**	**109**	**90**	**9**	**68**	**0.31**	**40**	**20**	**39**	**31**	**91**	**96**	**120**	**13%**		**142**	**18%**	**74%**				**1.1**	**17**	**$16**

BRANDON KRUSE

Baez,Javier

Age: 27 Bats: R Pos: SS | Ht: 6' 0" Wt: 190 | Health: A | PT/Exp: A | Consist: B | LIMA Plan: B | Rand Var: -1 | MM: 4445

Base-running regression the sole blemish in near-carbon copy of 2018...until fractured thumb shelved him in early Sept. Rock-solid hr/f, Spd, h% history all instructive, and he's young, athletic enough for more of the same over the near-term. Just don't expect more big SB value. Keeper league owners should watch those plate skills longer term.

Yr Tm	PA	R	HR	RBI	SB	BA	xHR	xBA	OBP	SLG	OPS+	vL+	vR+	bb%	ct%	Eye	G	L	F	h%	HctX	PX	xPX	HR/F	xHR/F	Spd	SBO	SB%	#Wk	DOM	DIS	RAR	BPX	R$
15 CHC *	377	41	11	51	14	287	1	248	325	443	107	149	85	5	69	0.18	37	31	31	39	103	117	121	6%	6%	116	21%	72%	6	33%	67%	13.1	46	$16
16 CHC	450	50	14	59	12	273	13	241	314	423	100	115	92	3	74	0.14	44	20	36	34	88	95	89	13%	12%	116	16%	80%	26	27%	38%	-2.1	49	$15
17 CHC	508	75	23	75	10	273	22	247	317	480	107	124	99	6	69	0.21	49	15	36	35	91	129	104	20%	19%	119	12%	77%	27	44%	41%	10.6	91	$19
18 CHC	645	101	34	111	21	290	37	283	326	554	122	130	119	4	72	0.17	46	22	32	35	96	163	110	24%	26%	155	25%	70%	28	61%	29%	41.5	260	$37
19 CHC	561	89	29	85	11	281	30	272	316	531	112	126	109	5	71	0.18	50	18	32	35	91	145	108	24%	25%	124	17%	61%	26	46%	35%	15.0	178	$24
1st Half	348	55	20	56	5	284	22	267	322	546	116	145	110	5	69	0.19	49	18	33	35	103	149	125	27%	29%	126	14%	50%	15	53%	33%	9.5	174	$29
2nd Half	213	34	9	29	6	276	8	279	305	507	107	104	109	4	73	0.16	52	18	30	34	73	137	83	20%	18%	119	22%	75%	11	36%	36%	2.7	174	$14
20 Proj	**630**	**97**	**30**	**97**	**16**	**281**		**266**	**315**	**513**	**112**	**123**	**108**	**5**	**71**	**0.17**	**48**	**19**	**32**	**35**	**90**	**134**	**104**	**21%**		**132**	**19%**	**70%**				**25.1**	**149**	**$29**

Barnes,Austin

Age: 30 Bats: R Pos: CA | Ht: 5' 10" Wt: 187 | Health: A | PT/Exp: D | Consist: F | LIMA Plan: D | Rand Var: +4 | MM: 1301

5-25-.203 in 235 PA at LA. Ct% failed to rebound; 2017 LD%, h%, power metrics and performance vR all now look like big outliers. Patience, age and health may offer opportunity, but they aren't enough. In an offensively-revitalized catcher universe, a second-stringer unless something changes. Mediocre two-year stretch leaves us skeptical.

Yr Tm	PA	R	HR	RBI	SB	BA	xHR	xBA	OBP	SLG	OPS+	vL+	vR+	bb%	ct%	Eye	G	L	F	h%	HctX	PX	xPX	HR/F	xHR/F	Spd	SBO	SB%	#Wk	DOM	DIS	RAR	BPX	R$
15 LA *	353	33	7	32	10	251	0	269	315	374	96	86	88	8	84	0.59	48	22	30	28	76	79	71	0%	0%	79	14%	80%	9	56%	33%	2.2	119	$8
16 LA *	403	47	5	31	13	231	0	187	297	337	86	107	40	9	80	0.46	32	9	59	28	70	70	89	0%	0%	121	19%	79%	9	11%	56%	-11.6	86	$6
17 LA	262	35	8	38	4	289	5	295	408	486	120	117	119	15	80	0.91	45	26	29	33	100	112	94	16%	10%	115	6%	80%	27	56%	26%	17.7	233	$8
18 LA	238	32	4	14	4	205	3	205	329	290	86	100	66	13	67	0.46	54	20	26	29	77	59	65	12%	9%	118	11%	57%	28	29%	64%	-4.3	-73	$1
19 LA *	337	40	9	36	4	201	4	223	277	352	83	75	87	9	72	0.38	41	17	42	25	84	89	85	8%	6%	107	8%	74%	23	30%	43%	-11.7	52	$2
1st Half	188	21	5	18	2	202	3	230	290	344	85	83	89	11	75	0.50	46	16	38	24	92	80	89	11%	7%	95	5%	100%	15	33%	40%	-3.8	67	$0
2nd Half	149	19	4	18	2	198	1	200	261	362	82	56	82	8	69	0.27	26	17	57	26	66	103	71	0%	5%	115	12%	56%	8	25%	50%	-4.6	33	$4
20 Proj	**210**	**27**	**4**	**21**	**3**	**219**		**224**	**317**	**351**	**90**	**94**	**86**	**11**	**72**	**0.45**	**42**	**19**	**38**	**28**	**80**	**79**	**76**	**9%**		**115**	**10%**	**71%**				**0.4**	**16**	**$4**

Barnhart,Tucker

Age: 29 Bats: B Pos: CA | Ht: 5' 11" Wt: 192 | Health: B | PT/Exp: C | Consist: B | LIMA Plan: D+ | Rand Var: 0 | MM: 1125

A tale of two half-seasons. Returned in late July following month-long IL stint (oblique); ct%, h% surges helped re-establish starter status. But xHR, xHR/F suggest some luck on the power front and when that gets taken away, there's not much left. It's an unexciting offensive profile.

Yr Tm	PA	R	HR	RBI	SB	BA	xHR	xBA	OBP	SLG	OPS+	vL+	vR+	bb%	ct%	Eye	G	L	F	h%	HctX	PX	xPX	HR/F	xHR/F	Spd	SBO	SB%	#Wk	DOM	DIS	RAR	BPX	R$
15 CIN	274	23	3	18	0	252	2	245	324	326	91	60	96	9	81	0.56	47	25	28	30	66	52	45	5%	4%	84	1%	0%	24	38%	33%	-2.0	35	$1
16 CIN	420	34	7	51	1	257	6	270	323	379	96	74	99	9	81	0.50	48	25	28	30	92	79	93	8%	7%	84	1%	100%	27	37%	30%	-2.1	89	$5
17 CIN	423	26	7	44	4	270	7	281	347	403	100	89	102	10	82	0.62	46	26	28	32	110	80	90	8%	8%	82	4%	100%	27	48%	33%	9.1	112	$7
18 CIN	522	50	10	46	0	248	9	254	328	372	97	104	94	10	79	0.56	45	24	31	29	112	75	81	9%	8%	88	3%	0%	28	32%	46%	6.3	87	$6
19 CIN	364	32	11	40	1	231	5	241	328	380	94	51	101	12	74	0.53	45	22	32	28	86	83	71	15%	7%	61	1%	100%	24	25%	54%	-2.2	22	$3
1st Half	187	18	5	18	0	191	3	228	290	315	81	69	83	12	69	0.46	46	25	29	24	90	72	86	15%	9%	86	0%	0%	13	15%	54%	-5.6	-48	-$2
2nd Half	177	14	6	22	1	273	2	255	367	448	108	38	122	12	79	0.64	45	20	35	31	81	94	57	14%	5%	57	2%	100%	11	36%	55%	7.6	122	$8
20 Proj	**455**	**39**	**9**	**48**	**1**	**248**		**249**	**333**	**371**	**95**	**73**	**99**	**11**	**78**	**0.55**	**46**	**23**	**31**	**30**	**95**	**70**	**75**	**10%**		**73**	**2%**	**61%**				**9.0**	**9**	**$8**

Barreto,Franklin

Age: 24 Bats: R Pos: 2B | Ht: 5' 10" Wt: 200 | Health: A | PT/Exp: C | Consist: B | LIMA Plan: D | Rand Var: 0 | MM: 4301

2-5-.123 in 58 PA at OAK. GB% spike fueled horrendous April-May (3 HR, 200+ PA) in AAA. June rebound led to July recall but then he vanished, courtesy of 23/1 K/BB. Pitch selection, ct% still glaring issues; once-promising power stroke needs an overhaul. Running game perked up, still has pedigree and time. But now a flyer with lots to prove.

Yr Tm	PA	R	HR	RBI	SB	BA	xHR	xBA	OBP	SLG	OPS+	vL+	vR+	bb%	ct%	Eye	G	L	F	h%	HctX	PX	xPX	HR/F	xHR/F	Spd	SBO	SB%	#Wk	DOM	DIS	RAR	BPX	R$
15																																		
16 a/a	510	57	9	47	26	268			313	390	96			6	80	0.32				32		76				105	36%	59%					74	$19
17 OAK *	567	62	13	51	14	256	2	196	291	394	92	39	98	5	67	0.15	29	21	50	36	92	88	125	11%	11%	160	19%	62%	8	13%	63%	-13.6	-6	$13
18 OAK *	389	55	19	54	4	231	5	201	296	449	103	95	107	8	60	0.23	35	9	56	33	90	163	159	21%	21%	117	8%	65%	14	21%	71%	2.9	80	$10
19 OAK *	463	75	16	56	13	240	2	229	295	436	97	68	39	7	65	0.22	58	6	36	33	60	126	70	17%	17%	110	16%	92%	10	20%	80%	-4.4	41	$13
1st Half	306	52	9	37	10	256		298	316	458	103	0	0	8	68	0.27	100	0	0	35	0	127	-36	0%		131	18%	90%	2	0%	100%	3.6	111	$19
2nd Half	158	23	7	18	3	209	2	201	253	396	85	75	41	6	60	0.15	55	6	39	29	59	124	76	17%	17%	81	10%	100%	8	25%	75%	-6.3	-85	$3
20 Proj	**245**	**35**	**11**	**28**	**6**	**236**		**213**	**291**	**444**	**99**	**87**	**105**	**7**	**65**	**0.21**	**39**	**13**	**48**	**32**	**80**	**129**	**116**	**15%**		**109**	**17%**	**75%**				**1.0**	**45**	**$8**

Bauers,Jake

Age: 24 Bats: L Pos: LF DH 1B | Ht: 6' 1" Wt: 195 | Health: A | PT/Exp: B | Consist: B | LIMA Plan: D+ | Rand Var: 0 | MM: 2223

12-43-.226 in 417 PA at CLE. Another touted youngster whose power metrics backed up in The Year of the HR. Still owns plus patience; sweet left-handed swing has been lauded by scouts since forever. But ct% has stagnated at higher levels, and numbers have yet to match the hype. Meh defense adds to murky outlook; age keeps us watching.

Yr Tm	PA	R	HR	RBI	SB	BA	xHR	xBA	OBP	SLG	OPS+	vL+	vR+	bb%	ct%	Eye	G	L	F	h%	HctX	PX	xPX	HR/F	xHR/F	Spd	SBO	SB%	#Wk	DOM	DIS	RAR	BPX	R$
15 aa	275	30	4	30	5	249			297	359	91			6	82	0.39				29		79				83	13%	61%					86	$4
16 aa	558	69	12	68	9	249			336	374	97			12	80	0.65				29		79				86	10%	57%					94	$12
17 aaa	560	74	12	59	19	245			345	379	97			13	74	0.59				31		87				91	14%	85%					67	$15
18 TAM *	605	75	15	69	15	219	11	236	316	380	96	83	102	12	69	0.46	43	21	36	28	104	114	132	14%	14%	76	20%	54%	18	44%	50%	-14.7	60	$13
19 CLE *	524	57	15	55	10	226	10	228	310	373	91	89	91	11	69	0.39	39	24	38	30	74	90	65	12%	10%	99	12%	64%	25	24%	40%	-19.4	0	$9
1st Half	287	32	10	29	2	226	8	228	300	389	92	89	93	9	70	0.34	43	19	38	28	76	92	64	15%	12%	107	6%	50%	15	27%	27%	-11.3	30	$7
2nd Half	237	25	5	26	8	225	2	234	326	354	90	92	87	13	67	0.45	29	34	38	32	72	88	67	7%	7%	104	18%	70%	10	20%	60%	-8.8	-15	$11
20 Proj	**350**	**41**	**10**	**39**	**7**	**229**		**240**	**321**	**390**	**96**	**91**	**97**	**12**	**71**	**0.45**	**38**	**25**	**37**	**29**	**86**	**98**	**92**	**13%**		**93**	**13%**	**60%**				**-4.8**	**33**	**$9**

Beaty,Matt

Age: 27 Bats: L Pos: 1B LF | Ht: 6' 0" Wt: 215 | Health: A | PT/Exp: D | Consist: C | LIMA Plan: D+ | Rand Var: +3 | MM: 2251

9-46-.265 in 266 PA at LA. Rode contact skills, .840 OPS vR and versatility to fantasy value in opportunistic MLB debut. But struggles vL, absence of plus power, speed will keep him from full-time role. Could disappear entirely, or BA could again make him modestly useful for stretches of a long season. Should be available on waivers in-season.

Yr Tm	PA	R	HR	RBI	SB	BA	xHR	xBA	OBP	SLG	OPS+	vL+	vR+	bb%	ct%	Eye	G	L	F	h%	HctX	PX	xPX	HR/F	xHR/F	Spd	SBO	SB%	#Wk	DOM	DIS	RAR	BPX	R$
15																																		
16																																		
17 aa	465	50	13	57	2	288			328	444	103			6	86	0.42				31		87				82	5%	42%					152	$12
18 aaa	110	10	1	9	0	231			291	338	87			8	80	0.42				28		81				91	0%	0%					97	-$2
19 LA *	396	48	11	59	5	258	6	284	303	424	96	43	112	6	87	0.49	48	19	33	27	121	83	93	13%	8%	88	8%	80%	21	48%	33%	-10.6	204	$9
1st Half	211	22	4	26	1	259	2	282	289	389	91	41	104	4	86	0.30	49	23	28	28	124	69	106	9%	9%	89	2%	100%	9	33%	33%	-7.5	130	$5
2nd Half	185	26	7	32	4	257	5	294	318	465	103	45	116	8	89	0.79	47	17	36	25	121	99	86	14%	10%	92	14%	77%	12	58%	33%	-0.5	296	$14
20 Proj	**245**	**27**	**8**	**31**	**2**	**251**		**281**	**307**	**432**	**99**	**43**	**107**	**7**	**85**	**0.48**	**48**	**19**	**33**	**27**	**122**	**95**	**94**	**12%**		**85**	**5%**	**76%**				**-0.8**	**181**	**$7**

Beckham,Tim

Age: 30 Bats: R Pos: SS | Ht: 6' 1" Wt: 205 | Health: C | PT/Exp: C | Consist: C | LIMA Plan: D | Rand Var: 0 | MM: 3213

Offers a modicum of thump with enough PA, but that's about the only good news. Streaky offense, abysmal glove had already cost him everyday AB before 80-game PED suspension shelved him in August. Plate skills stuck on abysmal, entrenched GB% caps HR upside, now out till the end of April. If he's your Opening Day SS, you're in trouble.

Yr Tm	PA	R	HR	RBI	SB	BA	xHR	xBA	OBP	SLG	OPS+	vL+	vR+	bb%	ct%	Eye	G	L	F	h%	HctX	PX	xPX	HR/F	xHR/F	Spd	SBO	SB%	#Wk	DOM	DIS	RAR	BPX	R$
15 TAM *	266	28	9	40	5	228	6	246	279	422	98	100	93	6	66	0.21	50	19	31	30	81	142	87	21%	14%	101	14%	68%	21	48%	38%	-4.2	68	$5
16 TAM	215	25	5	16	2	247	6	235	300	434	100	107	92	7	66	0.21	46	18	36	35	97	131	97	11%	13%	157	7%	67%	21	38%	43%	0.1	91	$2
17 2 AL	575	67	22	62	6	278	21	244	328	454	105	101	104	6	69	0.22	49	22	29	37	109	106	111	21%	20%	145	8%	55%	25	28%	48%	6.4	55	$16
18 BAL *	427	46	12	35	2	223	12	233	276	360	88	99	88	7	73	0.27	46	20	33	27	82	89	84	13%	13%	86	4%	46%	20	35%	50%	-10.7	13	$4
19 SEA	328	39	15	47	1	237	16	243	293	461	100	102	99	6	66	0.21	47	17	36	30	79	140	109	21%	22%	94	7%	25%	21	38%	48%	-8.3	78	$5
1st Half	252	29	12	37	1	226	11	243	278	451	97	101	96	6	66	0.18	50	17	34	29	75	143	102	23%	21%	75	11%	25%	16	44%	44%	-8.5	52	$7
2nd Half	76	10	3	10	0	275	5	234	342	493	110	108	111	9	68	0.32	36	19	45	36	90	127	134	14%	24%	139	0%	0%	5	20%	60%	1.9	133	-$2
20 Proj	**280**	**33**	**11**	**33**	**1**	**241**		**238**	**299**	**437**	**99**	**101**	**97**	**7**	**69**	**0.25**	**45**	**19**	**36**	**31**	**88**	**116**	**107**	**17%**		**123**	**5%**	**48%**				**1.0**	**27**	**$7**

JOCK THOMPSON

Bell,Josh

Age: 27	Bats: B	Pos: 1B	Health	C	LIMA Plan	A
Ht: 6' 4"	Wt: 240		PT/Exp	A	Rand Var	0
			Consist	B	MM	4045

Unlocked is one way to put it. Swing change in offseason made the most of his frame and resulted in massive jumps vR; HctX; xPX and HR/F—all while stellar plate skills did not budge. 2nd half fade due to h% and September groin injury, but age and batted-ball metrics point to relative repeatability, or... UP: 40/120/.300

Yr	Tm	PA	R	HR	RBI	SB	BA	xHR	xBA	OBP	SLG	OPS+	vL+	vR+	bb%	ct%	Eye	G	L	F	h%	HctX	PX	xPX	HR/F	xHR/F	Spd	SBO	SB%	#Wk	DOM	DIS	RAR	BPX	R$
15	a/a	543	57	5	66	8	285			356	390	104			10	86	0.77				32		65				116	8%	63%					141	$15
16	PIT *	626	71	15	75	3	275	4	274	362	427	107	70	110	12	82	0.76	50	21	29	31	110	89	96	9%	13%	81	7%	24%	9	56%	22%	-3.1	143	$15
17	PIT	620	75	26	90	2	255	20	275	334	466	107	101	107	11	79	0.56	51	18	31	28	104	113	95	19%	15%	98	4%	33%	27	56%	19%	-11.2	176	$14
18	PIT	583	74	12	62	2	261	18	256	357	411	106	102	107	13	79	0.74	49	19	33	31	99	93	88	9%	14%	100	4%	29%	27	52%	19%	-2.3	167	$13
19	PIT	613	94	37	116	0	277	38	291	367	569	124	99	133	12	78	0.63	44	19	37	29	122	150	135	24%	25%	71	1%	0%	25	64%	12%	28.3	289	$23
1st Half		356	61	22	70	0	301	24	309	376	625	134	123	137	11	77	0.53	44	20	36	33	128	172	150	25%	28%	75	1%	0%	15	80%	7%	28.6	341	$32
2nd Half		257	33	15	46	0	242	13	257	354	488	111	75	128	14	79	0.78	44	16	40	24	114	118	115	22%	19%	69	0%	0%	10	40%	20%	3.8	222	$11
20	**Proj**	**630**	**85**	**31**	**103**	**1**	**270**		**275**	**360**	**508**	**117**	**97**	**123**	**12**	**79**	**0.67**	**46**	**19**	**36**	**29**	**111**	**120**	**110**	**20%**		**84**	**3%**	**33%**				**27.4**	**208**	**$21**

Bellinger,Cody

Age: 24	Bats: L	Pos: RF 1B CF	Health	A	LIMA Plan	C
Ht: 6' 4"	Wt: 203		PT/Exp	A	Rand Var	0
			Consist	F	MM	4455

In first two years, established that he handles LHP/RHP equally, will take a walk, and can loft AND sting ball simultaneously. But staggering growth in ct% led gains in this MVP-level season. And don't dismiss his speed skills, which should drive draft value even higher in these environs. Suddenly, 2018 is the early-career outlier.

Yr	Tm	PA	R	HR	RBI	SB	BA	xHR	xBA	OBP	SLG	OPS+	vL+	vR+	bb%	ct%	Eye	G	L	F	h%	HctX	PX	xPX	HR/F	xHR/F	Spd	SBO	SB%	#Wk	DOM	DIS	RAR	BPX	R$
15																																			
16	a/a	457	56	23	60	7	248			325	458	107			10	75	0.45				28		124				86	8%	76%					134	$12
17	LA *	622	99	43	109	16	272	34	267	356	579	125	120	125	11	69	0.42	35	18	47	32	120	184	178	25%	22%	125	13%	84%	23	70%	17%	32.5	258	$29
18	LA	632	84	25	76	14	260	27	250	343	470	113	95	121	11	73	0.46	40	20	40	31	108	128	129	15%	16%	142	10%	93%	28	57%	25%	20.5	200	$22
19	LA	660	121	47	115	15	305	45	307	406	629	137	128	141	14	81	0.88	31	26	42	31	137	155	165	25%	24%	120	11%	75%	28	75%	7%	60.0	419	$37
1st Half		351	67	27	67	8	346	26	331	442	695	152	154	151	15	83	1.02	30	32	38	35	152	161	187	29%	28%	133	12%	62%	15	80%	7%	49.5	485	$47
2nd Half		309	54	20	48	7	259	20	281	366	555	121	104	131	14	78	0.75	33	19	47	26	121	148	139	21%	21%	105	9%	100%	13	69%	8%	14.5	344	$27
20	**Proj**	**630**	**106**	**41**	**104**	**14**	**287**		**279**	**378**	**581**	**129**	**117**	**134**	**13**	**76**	**0.61**	**35**	**22**	**43**	**31**	**123**	**150**	**151**	**23%**		**126**	**11%**	**83%**				**51.9**	**311**	**$35**

Belt,Brandon

Age: 32	Bats: L	Pos: 1B	Health	C	LIMA Plan	B+
Ht: 6' 4"	Wt: 235		PT/Exp	B	Rand Var	+2
			Consist	B	MM	3225

In 4 of 5 previous years, this note has ended with identical "UP: 30 HR." It was either delusional or stubborn, but at 32, he's probably ready to extinguish that torch. Once again his power metrics tout the upside, but current skills are showing some slippage. Plate approach and G/L/F both still very good, so of course in 2020 he'll slam 35.

Yr	Tm	PA	R	HR	RBI	SB	BA	xHR	xBA	OBP	SLG	OPS+	vL+	vR+	bb%	ct%	Eye	G	L	F	h%	HctX	PX	xPX	HR/F	xHR/F	Spd	SBO	SB%	#Wk	DOM	DIS	RAR	BPX	R$
15	SF	556	73	18	68	9	280	25	257	356	478	116	111	116	10	70	0.38	33	29	38	37	123	145	156	14%	19%	89	9%	75%	24	46%	33%	8.5	122	$20
16	SF	655	77	17	82	0	275	31	259	394	474	118	119	115	16	73	0.70	26	28	46	35	108	134	163	9%	17%	97	2%	0%	27	59%	30%	15.9	174	$15
17	SF	451	63	18	51	3	241	24	258	355	469	110	95	116	15	73	0.63	30	23	47	28	113	140	154	14%	19%	86	5%	60%	18	61%	28%	-4.7	182	$8
18	SF	456	50	14	46	4	253	24	235	342	414	105	87	113	11	73	0.46	24	29	47	31	112	100	146	10%	18%	103	3%	100%	22	36%	45%	-3.6	90	$10
19	SF	616	76	17	57	4	234	27	238	339	403	99	87	102	13	76	0.65	28	23	49	28	107	95	139	9%	14%	89	5%	57%	28	46%	39%	-14.6	130	$9
1st Half		307	42	10	31	2	227	15	243	358	422	104	98	107	17	78	0.85	31	21	40	26	100	106	130	11%	16%	91	4%	67%	15	53%	33%	-1.8	196	$9
2nd Half		309	34	7	26	2	240	11	234	320	385	93	73	99	11	75	0.49	26	25	49	30	105	85	147	7%	11%	90	5%	50%	13	38%	46%	-9.0	70	$9
20	**Proj**	**560**	**69**	**19**	**57**	**4**	**245**		**243**	**345**	**434**	**105**	**91**	**110**	**13**	**74**	**0.57**	**27**	**25**	**47**	**29**	**110**	**106**	**146**	**11%**		**94**	**4%**	**65%**				**6.2**	**122**	**$14**

Benintendi,Andrew

Age: 25	Bats: L	Pos: LF	Health	A	LIMA Plan	B+
Ht: 5' 10"	Wt: 170		PT/Exp	A	Rand Var	-2
			Consist	D	MM	3435

Again undershot his power projection; will the HR return? PRO: xHR says this is a mid-20s bat; evened his vL/vR splits; best MLB xPX since 2016. CON: The contact dip lasted all season; 2nd half fade. Still talented, still just 25, still seeking a consolidation year. A good bet to rebound.

Yr	Tm	PA	R	HR	RBI	SB	BA	xHR	xBA	OBP	SLG	OPS+	vL+	vR+	bb%	ct%	Eye	G	L	F	h%	HctX	PX	xPX	HR/F	xHR/F	Spd	SBO	SB%	#Wk	DOM	DIS	RAR	BPX	R$
15																																			
16	BOS *	375	48	8	50	7	289	3	288	345	481	112	58	131	8	84	0.53	36	25	39	33	112	117	116	6%	10%	117	18%	50%	8	50%	25%	12.8	231	$13
17	BOS	658	84	20	90	20	271	20	256	352	424	104	82	107	11	80	0.63	40	21	38	31	112	85	100	11%	11%	111	14%	80%	26	46%	23%	-3.4	139	$24
18	BOS	661	103	16	87	21	290	22	274	366	465	115	97	120	11	82	0.67	41	24	35	33	84	104	81	9%	13%	115	14%	88%	27	59%	4%	27.4	227	$30
19	BOS	615	72	13	68	10	266	23	243	343	431	103	104	102	10	74	0.42	38	21	41	34	98	99	107	8%	14%	120	9%	77%	27	33%	33%	-0.7	122	$15
1st Half		339	40	7	36	8	275	15	228	356	434	106	97	108	11	74	0.45	35	19	46	35	94	95	122	7%	15%	130	12%	80%	15	40%	20%	2.1	122	$18
2nd Half		276	32	6	32	2	256	7	259	327	427	99	108	93	9	75	0.39	42	23	35	32	102	103	89	9%	11%	110	5%	67%	12	25%	50%	-3.4	126	$12
20	**Proj**	**630**	**83**	**19**	**79**	**14**	**274**		**260**	**349**	**462**	**109**	**100**	**112**	**10**	**78**	**0.50**	**39**	**21**	**39**	**32**	**98**	**104**	**98**	**11%**		**119**	**12%**	**77%**				**18.1**	**185**	**$25**

Berti,Jon

Age: 30	Bats: R	Pos: SS CF 3B	Health	C	LIMA Plan	C
Ht: 5' 10"	Wt: 195		PT/Exp	D	Rand Var	-2
			Consist	B	MM	1543

6-24-.273 with 17 SB in 287 PA at MIA. Opened some eyes with unique (for this context) LD-and-SB game. His speed skill history says the bags are no fluke, as he checks all of the fast/chances/efficiency boxes. But there's just not enough punch in the stick to overcome his pedestrian ct%. His age points to this as his high-water mark.

Yr	Tm	PA	R	HR	RBI	SB	BA	xHR	xBA	OBP	SLG	OPS+	vL+	vR+	bb%	ct%	Eye	G	L	F	h%	HctX	PX	xPX	HR/F	xHR/F	Spd	SBO	SB%	#Wk	DOM	DIS	RAR	BPX	R$
15	a/a	439	48	3	29	19	223			283	292	80			8	82	0.46				27		48				112	26%	71%					46	$7
16	a/a	324	34	3	22	26	221			297	326	85			10	76	0.46				28		63				140	47%	71%					57	$9
17	aaa	233	23	3	18	20	186			248	296	73			8	71	0.28				25		67				138	57%	81%					-9	$4
18	TOR *	389	53	6	38	23	250	0	285	306	375	94	87	118	8	78	0.37	45	36	18	30	183	73	177	0%	0%	157	38%	66%	2	50%	50%	-6.5	117	$14
19	MIA *	361	63	9	30	21	264	6	264	339	400	98	115	96	10	73	0.41	53	26	21	34	91	79	59	16%	16%	130	25%	87%	15	20%	60%	3.7	56	$15
1st Half		121	22	5	9	4	236	2	283	348	406	101	200	73	15	77	0.73	56	26	19	26	84	84	33	25%	25%	112	12%	100%	5	20%	60%	1.0	144	-$2
2nd Half		240	41	4	22	17	277	4	255	335	398	97	96	104	8	71	0.29	52	26	21	38	93	77	67	13%	13%	128	32%	85%	10	20%	60%	1.6	4	$23
20	**Proj**	**350**	**52**	**7**	**30**	**20**	**252**		**266**	**333**	**381**	**96**	**124**	**89**	**9**	**75**	**0.40**	**54**	**26**	**20**	**32**	**89**	**72**	**53**	**15%**		**149**	**29%**	**77%**				**0.8**	**71**	**$15**

Betts,Mookie

Age: 27	Bats: R	Pos: RF	Health	A	LIMA Plan	C
Ht: 5' 9"	Wt: 180		PT/Exp	A	Rand Var	0
			Consist	F	MM	4555

Relative to his lofty draft price, a disappointing season. But fear not—that 2nd half was near vintage, comparable to his 2018 in almost every sense. When players with elite skills go on a short-term hot streak (say, hitting nearly one-third of your batted balls for line drives?), the results can be magical. Which means we can dream on UP: 40 HR

Yr	Tm	PA	R	HR	RBI	SB	BA	xHR	xBA	OBP	SLG	OPS+	vL+	vR+	bb%	ct%	Eye	G	L	F	h%	HctX	PX	xPX	HR/F	xHR/F	Spd	SBO	SB%	#Wk	DOM	DIS	RAR	BPX	R$
15	BOS	654	92	18	77	21	291	20	277	341	479	114	116	111	7	86	0.56	38	19	42	31	119	114	114	8%	9%	137	18%	78%	26	65%	12%	18.8	254	$30
16	BOS	730	122	31	113	26	318	24	295	363	534	122	110	122	7	88	0.61	41	19	39	33	119	114	107	13%	10%	128	16%	87%	27	56%	7%	48.8	280	$44
17	BOS	712	101	24	102	26	264	17	279	344	459	108	123	102	11	87	0.97	40	17	43	27	126	103	110	10%	7%	94	17%	90%	26	77%	4%	13.0	255	$28
18	BOS	614	129	32	80	30	346	44	302	438	640	149	168	142	13	83	0.89	34	21	45	37	135	166	151	16%	23%	140	20%	83%	26	77%	8%	87.0	443	$46
19	BOS	706	135	29	80	16	295	37	280	391	524	121	109	126	14	83	0.96	31	25	44	31	124	113	134	13%	17%	132	10%	84%	28	75%	14%	41.6	341	$31
1st Half		388	66	13	37	9	261	20	254	381	453	112	83	121	16	82	1.07	37	18	45	28	114	95	125	11%	17%	144	9%	90%	15	73%	13%	8.2	300	$26
2nd Half		318	69	16	43	7	335	17	308	403	607	133	135	132	11	84	0.81	26	32	42	35	134	133	143	16%	17%	113	10%	78%	13	77%	15%	31.1	378	$38
20	**Proj**	**665**	**128**	**32**	**86**	**22**	**309**		**288**	**392**	**565**	**129**	**130**	**127**	**12**	**84**	**0.87**	**32**	**23**	**44**	**32**	**128**	**126**	**133**	**15%**		**129**	**15%**	**84%**				**59.9**	**375**	**$40**

Bichette,Bo

Age: 22	Bats: R	Pos: SS	Health	A	LIMA Plan	D+
Ht: 6' 0"	Wt: 185		PT/Exp	D	Rand Var	0
			Consist	A	MM	4555

11-21-.311 with 4 SB in 212 PA at TOR. Was socked by two pitches all season—one broke his hand in AAA in April; the other resulted in a late-Sept concussion. But when his bat met the ball, good things happened. His MLB hard-hit and speed metrics give hints to a five-category future. With his age/pedigree, but there's star potential here.

Yr	Tm	PA	R	HR	RBI	SB	BA	xHR	xBA	OBP	SLG	OPS+	vL+	vR+	bb%	ct%	Eye	G	L	F	h%	HctX	PX	xPX	HR/F	xHR/F	Spd	SBO	SB%	#Wk	DOM	DIS	RAR	BPX	R$
15																																			
16																																			
17																																			
18	aa	582	84	10	66	28	281			333	442	107			7	81	0.41				33		104				108	30%	71%					183	$26
19	TOR *	451	62	18	49	17	287	10	279	335	508	112	141	116	7	76	0.30	44	23	34	34	86	125	97	22%	20%	121	28%	65%	8	75%	25%	7.8	204	$19
1st Half		127	18	3	16	9	283		256	347	447	106			9	76	0.41				35		98		0%		116	35%	81%				2.2	141	$3
2nd Half		323	44	15	33	8	288	10	286	331	531	114	139	116	6	76	0.26	44	23	34	34	86	136	97	22%	20%	120	24%	54%	8	75%	25%	7.7	230	$25
20	**Proj**	**595**	**84**	**25**	**67**	**24**	**275**		**286**	**329**	**507**	**113**	**130**	**104**	**7**	**78**	**0.35**	**44**	**23**	**34**	**31**	**77**	**127**	**87**	**17%**		**131**	**29%**	**68%**				**23.8**	**246**	**$29**

BRENT HERSHEY

Biggio,Cavan

Age: 25 Bats: L Pos: 2B | Health A | LIMA Plan B
Ht: 6' 2" Wt: 200 | PT/Exp D | Rand Var -1
Consist A | MM 4305

16-48-.234 with 14 SB in 430 PA at TOR. Surprised everyone as Jays' most valuable rookie. Power, patience, and speed carried over well from MiLB; SB% sets solid steals floor. But BA only overcame problematic ct% with help from unsustainable LD%; when distribution stabilizes, xBA looms. Buy for the power/speed, but be ready to take a BA hit.

Yr	Tm	PA	R	HR	RBI	SB	BA	xHR	xBA	OBP	SLG	OPS+	vL+	vR+	bb%	ct%	Eye	G	L	F	h%	HctX	PX	xPX	HR/F	xHR/F	Spd	SBO	SB%	#Wk	DOM	DIS	RAR	BPX	R$
15																																			
16																																			
17																																			
18	aa	533	68	22	84	17	233			355	450	111			16	64	0.53				31		150				104	18%	66%					140	$19
19	TOR *	595	85	21	71	18	249	15	228	375	439	108	97	109	17	69	0.64	25	28	47	32	94	112	151	15%	14%	105	11%	94%	20	30%	35%	15.0	115	$19
1st Half		288	40	11	41	8	262	6	231	389	459	113	83	122	17	72	0.74	24	24	52	32	140	109	251	18%	18%	97	11%	88%	7	29%	29%	11.5	152	$19
2nd Half		307	45	10	30	10	236	9	222	365	421	104	102	104	16	65	0.57	26	29	45	32	74	114	111	13%	12%	119	12%	100%	13	31%	38%	5.3	85	$20
20	Proj	595	82	23	79	19	241		226	365	445	109	99	113	16	67	0.58	30	24	46	31	100	123	167	15%		106	14%	80%				21.2	123	$20

Bird,Gregory

Age: 27 Bats: L Pos: 1B | Health F | LIMA Plan D+
Ht: 6' 4" Wt: 220 | PT/Exp F | Rand Var -3
Consist C | MM 4021

Torn plantar fascia ended season in April. Even before 2019, xPX, xBA, HctX had been fading since 2015 debut as bat continues to suffer from bad case of spherephobia. Has missed 525 days over past four seasons due to shoulder, ankle, and foot problems, stymieing development and casting real doubt on his ability to suit up.

Yr	Tm	PA	R	HR	RBI	SB	BA	xHR	xBA	OBP	SLG	OPS+	vL+	vR+	bb%	ct%	Eye	G	L	F	h%	HctX	PX	xPX	HR/F	xHR/F	Spd	SBO	SB%	#Wk	DOM	DIS	RAR	BPX	R$
15	NYY *	527	65	23	77	1	259	11	256	329	470	111	104	125	10	75	0.43	27	22	51	30	146	142	203	20%	20%	99	2%	45%	9	78%	22%	4.8	178	$15
16																																			
17	NYY *	226	30	12	34	0	209	8	248	310	449	102	131	85	13	73	0.54	30	18	52	22	108	140	162	16%	15%	86	0%	0%	12	50%	42%	-5.2	173	$2
18	NYY *	348	29	14	43	0	196	15	225	280	392	93	106	89	10	71	0.40	34	16	49	23	104	126	143	11%	16%	67	0%	0%	20	45%	25%	-8.9	87	$1
19	NYY	41	6	1	1	0	171	1	164	293	257	73	125	57	15	54	0.38	47	21	32	28	49	54	43	17%	17%	112	0%	0%	3	33%	67%	-2.9	-274	-$3
1st Half		41	6	1	1	0	171	1	164	293	257	73	128	57	15	54	0.38	47	21	32	28	49	54	43	17%	17%	112	0%	0%	3	33%	67%	-3.2	-278	-$3
2nd Half																																			
20	Proj	210	24	10	30	0	225		245	310	445	102	132	92	11	73	0.44	36	19	45	25	95	122	129	16%		76	1%	50%				-0.5	93	$5

Blackmon,Charlie

Age: 34 Bats: L Pos: RF | Health A | LIMA Plan D+
Ht: 6' 3" Wt: 220 | PT/Exp A | Rand Var 0
Consist C | MM 3255

Excelled as four-category stud, but what happened to SB—besides, you know, turning 33? Calf injury sustained end of May was likely culprit; with health, could post modest bounceback. While speed skills have begun descending a steep slope, batting skills, aided by remarkably consistent PA, appear headed down a gentle bunny hill trail. Still rock-solid.

Yr	Tm	PA	R	HR	RBI	SB	BA	xHR	xBA	OBP	SLG	OPS+	vL+	vR+	bb%	ct%	Eye	G	L	F	h%	HctX	PX	xPX	HR/F	xHR/F	Spd	SBO	SB%	#Wk	DOM	DIS	RAR	BPX	R$
15	COL	682	93	17	58	43	287	14	266	347	450	111	98	114	7	82	0.41	38	25	37	33	117	100	119	9%	8%	133	34%	77%	27	59%	22%	8.9	168	$36
16	COL	641	111	29	82	17	324	23	295	381	552	127	114	130	7	82	0.42	34	28	38	35	115	127	129	16%	13%	104	16%	65%	26	62%	23%	43.4	223	$36
17	COL	725	137	37	104	14	331	33	294	399	601	134	127	135	9	79	0.48	41	22	37	37	125	141	141	20%	17%	161	13%	58%	27	56%	7%	59.4	294	$42
18	COL	696	119	29	70	12	291	25	277	358	502	119	114	122	8	79	0.44	43	23	33	33	104	119	97	18%	15%	121	9%	75%	28	50%	18%	33.6	217	$30
19	COL	634	112	32	86	2	314	30	299	364	576	125	123	125	6	82	0.38	39	23	38	34	114	129	132	18%	17%	120	5%	29%	27	63%	19%	32.1	304	$27
1st Half		321	65	20	56	2	337	18	307	383	653	138	125	149	6	81	0.33	41	20	39	36	108	150	135	21%	19%	133	6%	50%	14	64%	14%	31.2	367	$37
2nd Half		313	47	12	30	0	290	12	294	345	495	111	122	106	7	83	0.45	37	26	37	32	120	107	129	14%	14%	102	4%	0%	13	62%	23%	4.7	233	$17
20	Proj	630	111	29	78	6	307		287	365	544	122	119	123	7	81	0.42	40	24	36	34	114	118	124	17%		125	7%	56%				39.9	245	$31

Bogaerts,Xander

Age: 27 Bats: R Pos: SS | Health A | LIMA Plan D+
Ht: 6' 1" Wt: 210 | PT/Exp A | Rand Var -3
Consist B | MM 3255

Four reasons why some regression is likely: PA will be tough to repeat; HR, PX, hr/f, BA all outperformed expected stats; Spd continued fade; h% could tick down a point or two. All that said, this is still an enviable skill set marked by outstanding BPX and high floors in average and power—just don't assume the next step.

Yr	Tm	PA	R	HR	RBI	SB	BA	xHR	xBA	OBP	SLG	OPS+	vL+	vR+	bb%	ct%	Eye	G	L	F	h%	HctX	PX	xPX	HR/F	xHR/F	Spd	SBO	SB%	#Wk	DOM	DIS	RAR	BPX	R$
15	BOS	654	84	7	81	10	320	8	269	355	421	108	123	101	5	84	0.32	53	21	26	37	100	71	60	5%	6%	116	7%	83%	27	33%	22%	20.0	103	$28
16	BOS	719	115	21	89	13	294	20	262	356	446	109	118	105	8	81	0.47	45	20	35	34	101	91	73	11%	11%	104	9%	76%	27	52%	19%	24.9	134	$29
17	BOS	635	94	10	62	15	273	7	262	343	403	100	103	98	9	80	0.48	49	21	30	33	101	77	54	7%	5%	134	10%	94%	26	42%	27%	4.6	121	$19
18	BOS	580	72	23	103	8	288	27	292	360	522	122	113	124	9	80	0.54	43	21	36	32	112	141	101	16%	18%	102	8%	80%	27	52%	7%	37.3	283	$25
19	BOS	698	110	33	117	4	309	28	284	384	555	125	119	126	11	80	0.62	41	19	40	34	107	130	116	17%	14%	88	3%	67%	28	71%	0%	45.4	278	$30
1st Half		365	63	16	57	3	299	16	284	392	540	124	133	122	14	80	0.78	40	20	40	33	108	130	119	16%	16%	94	4%	75%	15	73%	0%	23.9	300	$31
2nd Half		333	47	17	60	1	320	12	281	375	571	125	109	132	8	81	0.46	42	18	40	35	106	131	113	17%	12%	84	2%	50%	13	69%	0%	24.5	259	$30
20	Proj	665	98	27	106	6	295		279	363	513	118	114	118	10	80	0.54	44	20	36	33	107	117	98	15%		101	5%	73%				42.7	218	$30

Bohm,Alec

Age: 23 Bats: R Pos: 3B | Health A | LIMA Plan D
Ht: 6' 5" Wt: 225 | PT/Exp F | Rand Var
Consist F | MM 2231

Third overall pick in 2018 draft put that year's disappointing introduction to pro ball behind him as he bulldozed through three MiLB levels in 2019, finishing at AA. Exhibited strong plate skills with above-average power; unfavorable h% likely suppressed BA. Could start 2020 in AAA and move up quickly on his way to PHI. Invest.

Yr	Tm	PA	R	HR	RBI	SB	BA	xHR	xBA	OBP	SLG	OPS+	vL+	vR+	bb%	ct%	Eye	G	L	F	h%	HctX	PX	xPX	HR/F	xHR/F	Spd	SBO	SB%	#Wk	DOM	DIS	RAR	BPX	R$
15																																			
16																																			
17																																			
18																																			
19	aa	263	34	14	38	2	252			323	478	106			10	82	0.57				25		107				100	7%	45%					233	$6
1st Half		40	6	3	8	0	236			320	536	114			11	71	0.43				24		161				103	0%	0%				0.5	256	-$12
2nd Half		223	28	11	30	2	254			324	468	104			9	83	0.61				26		98				110	8%	45%				-1.4	241	$9
20	Proj	210	24	9	26	2	279		260	337	470	109	108	108	8	85	0.58	41	18	41	29	0	87		14%		112	6%	50%				4.9	162	$8

Bote,David

Age: 27 Bats: R Pos: 3B 2B | Health A | LIMA Plan D
Ht: 6' 1" Wt: 210 | PT/Exp C | Rand Var -2
Consist B | MM 2313

Productive utility player primed for more production? PRO: Improved Eye, leading to OBP surge; lowered sky-high GB%; positional flexibility. CON: Platoon splits flipped with poor showing vL; xPX sank well below league average; HctX cratered in 2nd half; GB% still blunting power development. Skills fluctuated wildly...there are better bets.

Yr	Tm	PA	R	HR	RBI	SB	BA	xHR	xBA	OBP	SLG	OPS+	vL+	vR+	bb%	ct%	Eye	G	L	F	h%	HctX	PX	xPX	HR/F	xHR/F	Spd	SBO	SB%	#Wk	DOM	DIS	RAR	BPX	R$
15																																			
16	a/a	50	4	1	3	0	240			289	290	79			6	73	0.26				31		27				105	0%	0%					-109	-$2
17	aa	515	58	12	53	4	247			313	396	95			9	75	0.39				30		92				100	6%	67%					76	$7
18	CHC *	465	48	15	63	5	230	11	242	295	399	96	121	92	8	68	0.29	57	18	24	30	97	111	101	19%	35%	120	11%	50%	19	32%	42%	-6.7	53	$9
19	CHC	356	47	11	41	5	257	8	249	362	422	104	89	109	12	69	0.47	50	23	27	34	87	101	78	19%	14%	97	6%	83%	27	44%	44%	5.4	52	$8
1st Half		234	30	9	34	4	257	6	264	338	451	105	78	114	10	73	0.43	50	22	28	31	98	112	75	21%	14%	87	9%	80%	15	47%	33%	3.3	111	$11
2nd Half		122	17	2	7	1	258	2	216	410	361	102	111	98	17	62	0.54	50	27	23	40	64	73	84	14%	14%	121	3%	100%	12	42%	58%	0.5	-81	$0
20	Proj	315	39	8	35	3	246		238	346	389	99	104	96	11	68	0.40	53	22	25	33	86	89	89	17%		116	6%	68%				-1.9	-29	$8

Bradley,Jackie

Age: 30 Bats: L Pos: CF | Health A | LIMA Plan B+
Ht: 5' 10" Wt: 200 | PT/Exp B | Rand Var +1
Consist A | MM 3325

2016 looking more and more like the outlier. Platoon splits will continue to cap PA, but elite defense will keep the floor from failing under the weight of all the collapsing skills metrics. Falling ct% and BA/xBA running in lockstep. Steals regressed thanks to career-low SB% efficiency. It's a flat profile, but 2019's line is highly repeatable.

Yr	Tm	PA	R	HR	RBI	SB	BA	xHR	xBA	OBP	SLG	OPS+	vL+	vR+	bb%	ct%	Eye	G	L	F	h%	HctX	PX	xPX	HR/F	xHR/F	Spd	SBO	SB%	#Wk	DOM	DIS	RAR	BPX	R$
15	BOS *	562	75	17	68	6	267	9	264	337	460	111	127	108	9	76	0.44	48	16	36	32	106	132	133	18%	16%	98	8%	59%	15	53%	47%	11.2	165	$17
16	BOS	636	94	26	87	9	267	26	269	349	486	114	91	120	10	74	0.44	47	18	34	32	109	133	109	18%	18%	101	7%	82%	27	56%	22%	22.9	160	$21
17	BOS	541	58	17	63	8	245	19	246	323	402	97	102	94	9	74	0.39	49	18	33	30	100	91	89	15%	16%	97	9%	73%	26	31%	38%	-7.2	58	$10
18	BOS	535	76	13	59	17	234	24	243	314	403	99	78	105	9	71	0.34	43	21	36	30	108	117	130	11%	20%	93	17%	94%	28	43%	36%	2.5	83	$15
19	BOS	567	69	21	62	8	225	23	242	317	421	98	84	105	10	69	0.36	50	17	33	28	85	117	99	18%	20%	102	12%	57%	28	36%	50%	-6.2	74	$10
1st Half		297	33	9	28	6	236	10	237	337	409	100	91	103	11	71	0.43	52	14	34	30	79	103	80	15%	16%	99	12%	75%	15	40%	60%	0.1	74	$10
2nd Half		270	36	12	34	2	213	12	247	296	433	96	77	107	9	66	0.30	46	21	33	27	92	132	121	23%	23%	103	13%	33%	13	31%	38%	-4.9	81	$11
20	Proj	560	74	20	66	10	233		245	317	424	100	87	104	9	70	0.35	47	19	34	29	96	112	110	16%		101	12%	70%				5.2	91	$16

ALAIN DE LEONARDIS

Brantley,Michael

Age: 33	Bats: L	Pos: LF DH	Health	C	LIMA Plan	B+
Ht: 6' 2"	Wt: 200		PT/Exp	B	Rand Var	-2
			Consist	A	MM	2255

Career-best HR count wasn't only about the ball, as trends have been following gradual power skills gains for years. Team context had more to do with SB drop than Spd dip. Core skills package remains one of the steadiest in the game even in his early 30s. The foundational contact skills ensure graceful aging, especially if health holds.

Yr	Tm	PA	R	HR	RBI	SB	BA	xHR	xBA	OBP	SLG	OPS+	vL+	vR+	bb%	ct%	Eye	G	L	F	h%	HctX	PX	xPX	HR/F	xHR/F	Spd	SBO	SB%	#Wk	DOM	DIS	RAR	BPX	R$
15	CLE	596	68	15	84	15	310	11	308	379	480	120	108	125	10	90	1.18	46	23	32	32	121	107	88	10%	7%	78	10%	94%	26	77%	0%	36.1	249	$28
16	CLE *	73	7	0	8	1	197	0	258	255	253	69	111	67	7	88	0.64	44	24	32	22	115	43	108	0%	0%	103	7%	100%	3	33%	67%	-4.5	91	-$2
17	CLE	375	47	9	52	11	299	9	288	357	444	107	92	113	8	85	0.62	49	22	28	33	117	81	74	11%	11%	98	12%	92%	20	50%	10%	4.5	161	$15
18	CLE	630	89	17	76	12	309	16	299	364	468	115	95	122	8	89	0.80	45	25	30	32	122	87	79	11%	10%	87	9%	80%	27	74%	11%	26.4	237	$27
19	HOU	637	88	22	90	3	311	21	306	372	503	116	97	124	8	89	0.77	45	24	31	32	128	92	89	14%	13%	79	3%	60%	28	68%	11%	25.9	256	$24
1st Half		347	40	11	43	3	313	11	299	372	491	115	117	114	8	89	0.79	47	22	31	32	124	85	82	13%	13%	89	5%	60%	15	73%	7%	12.4	259	$24
2nd Half		290	48	11	47	0	309	10	314	372	517	117	76	136	8	88	0.75	43	26	31	32	132	101	97	15%	14%	71	0%	0%	13	62%	15%	13.1	267	$24
20	Proj	595	84	18	84	6	308		301	367	484	115	94	123	8	88	0.76	46	24	30	32	125	87	85	13%		83	5%	78%				29.8	237	$24

Braun,Ryan

Age: 36	Bats: R	Pos: LF	Health	B	LIMA Plan	B
Ht: 6' 2"	Wt: 205		PT/Exp	B	Rand Var	-1
			Consist	B	MM	4353

Slowly eroding plate skills and widening platoon are marks of age, but health cooperated for the first time since 2016 to mitigate decline. As in the past, h% surge provided a BA/xBA near match. With years piling up, the draft price tends to sink, but power, speed, and contact fortify this profile and keep 20 HR/10 SB in play.

Yr	Tm	PA	R	HR	RBI	SB	BA	xHR	xBA	OBP	SLG	OPS+	vL+	vR+	bb%	ct%	Eye	G	L	F	h%	HctX	PX	xPX	HR/F	xHR/F	Spd	SBO	SB%	#Wk	DOM	DIS	RAR	BPX	R$
15	MIL	567	87	25	84	24	285	28	282	356	498	119	132	113	10	77	0.47	50	19	31	33	121	136	139	20%	23%	110	20%	86%	25	52%	28%	24.1	195	$31
16	MIL	564	80	30	91	16	305	24	303	365	538	123	136	116	8	81	0.47	56	19	25	33	113	127	97	29%	23%	109	14%	76%	26	58%	23%	35.0	217	$30
17	MIL	425	58	17	52	12	268	16	291	336	487	110	116	107	9	80	0.50	49	19	32	30	126	124	122	17%	16%	95	17%	75%	21	62%	24%	4.2	206	$15
18	MIL	444	59	20	64	11	254	22	290	313	469	108	120	102	8	79	0.40	48	23	28	28	125	125	120	22%	24%	83	18%	69%	27	48%	22%	3.5	193	$16
19	MIL	504	70	22	75	11	285	22	281	343	505	113	122	107	7	77	0.32	50	19	30	33	122	118	113	20%	20%	93	11%	92%	27	52%	22%	12.2	170	$20
1st Half		289	35	12	40	5	274	13	263	322	459	104	99	107	6	76	0.27	54	18	28	32	122	99	109	21%	22%	80	9%	83%	15	40%	33%	-0.1	81	$19
2nd Half		215	35	10	35	6	302	9	301	372	571	125	152	108	8	78	0.41	46	21	33	34	122	144	118	20%	18%	106	13%	100%	12	67%	8%	13.3	293	$22
20	Proj	441	64	20	66	12	279		286	340	506	114	128	107	8	78	0.39	49	20	30	31	123	120	117	21%		97	15%	82%				17.4	219	$21

Bregman,Alex

Age: 26	Bats: R	Pos: 3B SS	Health	A	LIMA Plan	C
Ht: 6' 0"	Wt: 180		PT/Exp	A	Rand Var	0
			Consist	C	MM	3355

Made good on a strong "UP: MVP" call from last year's book with a brilliant season. Career best HR total supported by xPX and HctX gains, but xHR strongly disagrees; power regression bet seems safe. More BB than K, xBA strong as ever, providing solid foundation. Heck, he's a stud even at a high-20s HR count.

Yr	Tm	PA	R	HR	RBI	SB	BA	xHR	xBA	OBP	SLG	OPS+	vL+	vR+	bb%	ct%	Eye	G	L	F	h%	HctX	PX	xPX	HR/F	xHR/F	Spd	SBO	SB%	#Wk	DOM	DIS	RAR	BPX	R$
15																																			
16	HOU *	570	91	25	86	8	273	6	287	343	504	115	99	109	10	81	0.57	29	28	43	29	106	131	118	13%	9%	124	9%	65%	9	56%	44%	17.2	254	$21
17	HOU	626	88	19	71	17	284	17	276	352	475	111	129	102	9	83	0.57	38	22	40	32	110	106	102	10%	9%	124	15%	77%	27	56%	26%	16.2	218	$24
18	HOU	705	105	31	103	10	286	26	298	394	532	128	135	125	14	86	1.13	35	22	43	29	112	137	127	14%	12%	102	8%	71%	28	68%	4%	49.3	373	$30
19	HOU	690	122	41	112	5	296	23	302	423	592	135	155	126	17	85	1.43	32	23	40	29	131	137	135	19%	10%	101	3%	83%	28	86%	0%	61.5	430	$31
1st Half		371	55	22	52	3	266	12	289	391	532	123	122	124	17	84	1.27	32	23	45	25	117	119	113	19%	10%	104	4%	75%	15	80%	0%	17.0	363	$26
2nd Half		319	67	19	60	2	332	10	321	461	664	148	187	129	19	86	1.66	31	22	48	33	148	159	161	18%	10%	106	2%	100%	13	92%	0%	42.5	530	$36
20	Proj	665	114	29	105	8	298		286	406	535	127	143	119	15	85	1.13	33	23	44	31	123	118	130	14%		109	6%	77%				50.7	335	$33

Brinson,Lewis

Age: 26	Bats: R	Pos: CF	Health	B	LIMA Plan	D
Ht: 6' 3"	Wt: 195		PT/Exp	C	Rand Var	+2
			Consist	C	MM	1403

0-15-.173 and 1 SB in 248 PA at MIA. He's wasting premium speed thanks to horrid contact and a poor eye, and minor league pop has yet to show up in the majors, too. Now in his mid-20s, it's hard to envision a scenario where he delivers on prospect pedigree. Could be on a Keon Broxton path if he doesn't cut his K rate soon.

Yr	Tm	PA	R	HR	RBI	SB	BA	xHR	xBA	OBP	SLG	OPS+	vL+	vR+	bb%	ct%	Eye	G	L	F	h%	HctX	PX	xPX	HR/F	xHR/F	Spd	SBO	SB%	#Wk	DOM	DIS	RAR	BPX	R$
15	a/a	151	19	6	22	4	291			343	482	115			7	74	0.30				36		131				96	14%	79%					124	$6
16	a/a	409	50	15	50	13	251			280	441	98			4	76	0.17				30		115				108	26%	66%					111	$12
17	MIL *	377	49	13	37	9	260	2	267	319	446	102	124	41	8	74	0.33	57	17	27	32	100	110	99	25%	25%	121	17%	61%	5	40%	40%	-3.6	118	$10
18	MIA *	457	32	12	45	3	194	19	218	228	327	77	89	76	4	69	0.15	52	17	31	25	99	82	109	13%	23%	159	5%	74%	21	24%	71%	-25.7	3	$0
19	MIA *	572	63	12	63	15	205	4	206	263	333	79	70	57	7	63	0.21	49	17	34	30	88	84	72	0%	8%	120	20%	68%	15	0%	80%	-25.0	-96	$8
1st Half		296	37	9	44	9	235	2	219	293	407	93	75	66	8	62	0.21	44	21	35	34	100	116	57	0%	12%	114	24%	60%	6	0%	100%	-5.2	-33	$15
2nd Half		276	26	3	20	6	173	2	192	230	256	64	66	53	7	65	0.21	52	15	33	25	83	51	79	0%	6%	141	15%	84%	9	0%	67%	-20.7	-152	$1
20	Proj	280	29	4	30	6	206		209	271	311	78	89	74	7	68	0.22	50	17	33	29	94	66	86	6%		136	15%	69%				-11.2	-95	$4

Brosseau,Michael

Age: 26	Bats: R	Pos: 2B	Health	A	LIMA Plan	D
Ht: 5' 10"	Wt: 215		PT/Exp	F	Rand Var	-1
			Consist	C	MM	3111

6-16-.273 in 142 PA at TAM. College product hit through minors and played ably in multiple call-ups. Couldn't replicate bb%/ct% combo (8/84 in MiLB; 5/70 in MLB), but power carried him. Small sample splits (OPS vR/vL: .829/.728) follows MiLB track record and platoon could be in his future. Strong xPX, but too soon to call it "real."

Yr	Tm	PA	R	HR	RBI	SB	BA	xHR	xBA	OBP	SLG	OPS+	vL+	vR+	bb%	ct%	Eye	G	L	F	h%	HctX	PX	xPX	HR/F	xHR/F	Spd	SBO	SB%	#Wk	DOM	DIS	RAR	BPX	R$
15																																			
16																																			
17																																			
18	aa	394	44	10	51	9	226			273	379	90			6	76	0.27				27		96				98	18%	67%					83	$8
19	TAM *	440	60	18	64	3	261	3	240	320	462	104	108	97	8	73	0.32	40	17	43	32	104	115	149	15%	8%	74	6%	43%	15	20%	60%	-1.0	81	$11
1st Half		275	42	11	49	2	266	0	264	338	478	109	166	100	10	74	0.43	17	33	50	32	86	121	130	0%	0%	78	8%	31%	2	100%	0%	0.8	144	$17
2nd Half		165	17	8	15	1	252	3	219	288	436	96	104	97	5	70	0.17	41	16	43	31	101	103	150	16%	8%	79	3%	100%	13	8%	69%	-4.1	-15	$3
20	Proj	245	29	10	32	3	246		237	306	443	101	109	90	7	73	0.27	41	16	43	29	91	110	135	15%		80	11%	60%				1.6	71	$8

Brown,Seth

Age: 27	Bats: L	Pos: LF	Health	A	LIMA Plan	D
Ht: 6' 3"	Wt: 220		PT/Exp	D	Rand Var	0
			Consist	A	MM	3311

0-13-.293 in 83 PA at OAK. Huge power explosion at AAA (.634 SLG, 37 HR) didn't travel in Sept. call-up, but a 42% h% padded his BA. Las Vegas venue and bouncy ball make HR surge tough to trust, and without it his Eye becomes especially problematic. At his age will need to prove himself at every stop.

Yr	Tm	PA	R	HR	RBI	SB	BA	xHR	xBA	OBP	SLG	OPS+	vL+	vR+	bb%	ct%	Eye	G	L	F	h%	HctX	PX	xPX	HR/F	xHR/F	Spd	SBO	SB%	#Wk	DOM	DIS	RAR	BPX	R$
15																																			
16																																			
17																																			
18	aa	536	49	10	67	4	233			282	366	90			6	67	0.21				33		102				90	3%	100%					-27	$8
19	OAK *	561	84	25	88	7	245	1	247	291	473	101	56	120	6	66	0.19	33	29	38	32	92	139	93	0%	5%	105	8%	85%	6	33%	33%	-5.5	78	$16
1st Half		285	41	12	40	3	218		240	250	430	91			4	66	0.12				29		130		0%		114	7%	100%				-13.9	41	$11
2nd Half		276	43	13	48	4	274	1	254	334	520	113	55	120	8	66	0.27	33	29	38	36	93	148	93	0%	5%	105	9%	76%	6	33%	33%	6.3	126	$23
20	Proj	245	31	7	36	3	244		230	306	426	98	82	101	7	66	0.23	35	25	40	33	84	116	84	12%		99	6%	89%				-1.3	24	$7

Broxton,Keon

Age: 30	Bats: R	Pos: CF LF	Health	A	LIMA Plan	F
Ht: 6' 3"	Wt: 195		PT/Exp	D	Rand Var	+2
			Consist	C	MM	3501

If it weren't for his premium glove, he likely wouldn't have 1026 MLB PA. Raw power and speed has its limits when you can't consistently make contact or get on base. Now 30, even the skills are dropping closer toward average. When three teams - including the 108-loss Orioles - could not find room for you... UP: AAA All-Star

Yr	Tm	PA	R	HR	RBI	SB	BA	xHR	xBA	OBP	SLG	OPS+	vL+	vR+	bb%	ct%	Eye	G	L	F	h%	HctX	PX	xPX	HR/F	xHR/F	Spd	SBO	SB%	#Wk	DOM	DIS	RAR	BPX	R$
15	PIT *	545	72	7	55	32	233		256	306	360	93	0	0	10	65	0.30	100	0	0	35	0	101	-16	0%		141	40%	64%	2	0%	50%	-20.0	8	$18
16	MIL *	435	48	15	37	35	238	8	227	324	434	103	124	93	11	58	0.31	45	25	30	37	102	152	139	26%	23%	137	48%	72%	17	29%	59%	-1.0	57	$18
17	MIL *	494	69	21	54	24	225	18	218	296	422	96	102	93	9	58	0.24	45	20	35	33	83	141	131	24%	22%	145	30%	77%	26	27%	62%	-15.7	24	$15
18	MIL *	406	43	11	33	21	187	3	193	245	326	79	71	107	7	52	0.16	55	20	24	32	73	120	90	33%	25%	137	38%	78%	13	38%	46%	-25.5	-127	$7
19	3 TM	228	24	6	16	10	167	6	157	242	275	69	77	61	9	49	0.19	49	17	34	30	51	85	81	18%	18%	105	36%	63%	26	15%	81%	-22.1	-311	$0
1st Half		145	16	3	8	8	185	4	165	236	274	68	85	55	6	53	0.14	49	18	34	32	58	67	81	13%	17%	109	36%	80%	15	13%	80%	-13.4	-319	$1
2nd Half		83	8	3	8	2	130	2	143	253	275	70	65	73	14	41	0.27	50	14	36	24	37	130	80	30%	20%	106	38%	33%	11	18%	82%	-8.9	-267	$0
20	Proj	175	20	6	15	8	199		179	278	345	84	82	84	10	51	0.21	50	18	32	35	64	112	96	22%		124	34%	62%				-5.5	-199	$5

PAUL SPORER

Bruce,Jay

Age: 33	Bats: L	Pos: LF RF	Health	C	LIMA Plan	D+
Ht: 6' 3"	Wt: 225		PT/Exp	C	Rand Var	+5
			Consist	C	MM	4023

Blasted 10 HR in 121 PA following June 2 trade from SEA to PHI, then injuries (oblique, flexor strain) shelved him for bulk of 2nd half. Overall, combo of elite xPX and extreme FB% helped him maximize HR output. Should remain a cheap power source, and h%/xBA even hints at some BA recovery. Durability will be a constant question, though.

Yr Tm	PA	R	HR	RBI	SB	BA	xHR	xBA	OBP	SLG	OPS+	vL+	vR+	bb%	ct%	Eye	G	L	F	h%	HctX	PX	xPX	HR/F	xHR/F	Spd	SBO	SB%	#Wk	DOM	DIS	RAR	BPX	R$
15 CIN	649	72	26	87	9	226	29	256	294	434	102	92	103	9	75	0.40	37	19	44	26	115	140	144	13%	15%	77	11%	64%	27	48%	26%	-9.8	149	$14
16 2 NL	589	74	33	99	4	250	29	279	309	506	111	92	116	7	77	0.35	37	22	41	27	119	147	153	19%	17%	95	5%	67%	27	56%	19%	9.8	200	$17
17 2 TM	617	82	36	101	1	254	31	267	324	508	112	95	117	9	75	0.41	33	21	47	28	122	143	161	18%	16%	78	2%	50%	27	44%	22%	5.3	176	$17
18 NYM	361	31	9	37	2	223	15	236	310	370	94	92	94	11	76	0.55	28	24	48	26	94	94	126	8%	13%	74	6%	40%	20	30%	35%	-9.2	93	$3
19 2 TM	333	43	26	59	1	216	25	263	261	523	104	104	104	6	74	0.23	29	17	54	20	110	160	161	21%	20%	61	2%	100%	23	57%	30%	-6.9	200	$7
1st Half	265	38	21	48	1	231	21	270	287	558	113	127	109	7	73	0.29	26	18	56	23	103	175	156	21%	21%	65	3%	100%	16	63%	19%	1.3	248	$12
2nd Half	68	5	5	11	0	162	5	215	162	397	74	26	90	0	76	0.00	37	15	48	13	137	110	180	20%	20%	78	0%	0%	7	43%	57%	-7.2	70	-$10
20 Proj	**385**	**41**	**22**	**58**	**1**	**229**		**248**	**279**	**461**	**100**	**85**	**104**	**6**	**75**	**0.28**	**32**	**19**	**49**	**24**	**115**	**120**	**156**	**17%**		**69**	**4%**	**54%**				**-3.3**	**96**	**$7**

Bryant,Kris

Age: 28	Bats: R	Pos: 3B RF LF	Health	B	LIMA Plan	B
Ht: 6' 5"	Wt: 230		PT/Exp	A	Rand Var	-1
			Consist	C	MM	4335

Put 2018's shoulder issues behind him as HR/F bounced back to historical norm. Now, a new concern: 2nd half ct% and xBA point to some BA downside, though lingering right knee soreness may have been a factor. 2016-17-19 set a pretty clear baseline for what to expect in a fully healthy season.

Yr Tm	PA	R	HR	RBI	SB	BA	xHR	xBA	OBP	SLG	OPS+	vL+	vR+	bb%	ct%	Eye	G	L	F	h%	HctX	PX	xPX	HR/F	xHR/F	Spd	SBO	SB%	#Wk	DOM	DIS	RAR	BPX	R$
15 CHC *	680	92	28	107	15	276	35	233	361	492	119	110	120	12	64	0.38	34	21	45	38	104	165	148	16%	21%	129	11%	78%	26	50%	35%	26.8	143	$29
16 CHC	699	121	39	102	8	292	44	273	385	554	128	143	120	11	74	0.49	31	24	46	33	122	158	159	19%	21%	113	7%	62%	27	59%	15%	38.4	234	$31
17 CHC	665	111	29	73	7	295	31	274	409	537	127	127	125	14	77	0.74	38	20	42	34	102	139	111	16%	17%	124	6%	58%	27	67%	19%	35.3	261	$25
18 CHC	457	59	13	52	2	272	20	252	374	460	115	158	103	11	72	0.45	34	25	41	35	83	125	119	11%	17%	121	5%	33%	22	45%	36%	9.2	163	$12
19 CHC	634	108	31	77	4	282	27	260	382	521	120	138	115	12	73	0.51	36	21	43	33	91	133	105	18%	16%	115	3%	100%	27	56%	30%	21.9	222	$22
1st Half	352	63	16	41	1	287	17	281	398	537	125	159	116	13	77	0.66	37	22	41	32	95	135	102	17%	18%	114	1%	100%	15	67%	20%	17.3	296	$24
2nd Half	282	45	15	36	3	275	10	234	362	502	114	112	115	11	68	0.38	34	19	47	34	85	129	108	19%	13%	112	4%	100%	12	42%	42%	7.7	126	$20
20 Proj	**630**	**102**	**30**	**79**	**5**	**281**		**255**	**380**	**514**	**120**	**138**	**115**	**12**	**73**	**0.49**	**35**	**22**	**43**	**34**	**92**	**131**	**115**	**17%**		**121**	**5%**	**67%**				**32.1**	**169**	**$26**

Buxton,Byron

Age: 26	Bats: R	Pos: CF	Health	F	LIMA Plan	B
Ht: 6' 2"	Wt: 190		PT/Exp	D	Rand Var	0
			Consist	D	MM	4525

Promising 1st half driven by concurrent gains in both ct% and quality of contact was stunted by multiple IL stints thereafter (wrist, concussion, shoulder). Season ended with Sept surgery to repair labrum in left shoulder; status for Opening Day uncertain. Still showing glimpses of being a force ... but staying on the field is required.

Yr Tm	PA	R	HR	RBI	SB	BA	xHR	xBA	OBP	SLG	OPS+	vL+	vR+	bb%	ct%	Eye	G	L	F	h%	HctX	PX	xPX	HR/F	xHR/F	Spd	SBO	SB%	#Wk	DOM	DIS	RAR	BPX	R$
15 MIN *	454	61	8	43	20	261	2	220	310	411	101	44	96	7	74	0.27	43	14	43	34	88	96	104	6%	6%	189	24%	79%	10	20%	70%	-0.9	122	$16
16 MIN *	533	81	20	60	16	250	7	232	301	469	105	99	94	7	64	0.20	35	22	43	35	70	158	85	14%	9%	174	19%	89%	20	30%	50%	7.7	137	$17
17 MIN	511	69	16	51	29	253	15	223	314	413	98	105	93	7	68	0.25	39	23	38	34	75	97	85	14%	13%	181	25%	97%	25	24%	52%	-0.6	58	$20
18 MIN *	238	27	4	16	9	212	0	222	248	330	80	31	58	5	67	0.14	43	23	33	30	75	92	48	0%	0%	123	24%	88%	7	14%	86%	-9.0	-30	$2
19 MIN	295	48	10	46	14	262	10	263	314	513	110	120	106	6	75	0.28	29	22	49	32	92	148	92	10%	10%	119	37%	82%	18	56%	17%	8.3	256	$12
1st Half	234	40	9	38	10	262	9	263	319	519	112	122	108	7	75	0.30	29	21	50	31	88	148	89	11%	11%	116	34%	77%	14	57%	14%	7.3	259	$16
2nd Half	61	8	1	8	4	263	2	269	295	491	104	123	100	5	74	0.20	30	26	44	34	107	150	103	5%	11%	126	50%	100%	4	50%	25%	1.8	237	-$3
20 Proj	**455**	**63**	**11**	**53**	**20**	**248**		**243**	**293**	**442**	**99**	**100**	**98**	**6**	**71**	**0.21**	**35**	**23**	**42**	**32**	**88**	**122**	**83**	**9%**		**141**	**30%**	**86%**				**7.2**	**160**	**$18**

Cabrera,Asdrubal

Age: 34	Bats: B	Pos: 3B 2B	Health	B	LIMA Plan	D+
Ht: 6' 0"	Wt: 205		PT/Exp	B	Rand Var	0
			Consist	A	MM	2235

Another solid season, sans fireworks. Problem is the bar keeps getting higher which now drops his solid productivity below replacement level. HR/xHR and BA/xBA are stable, but short-term bursts (2nd half ct%/xBA) can't be counted on to continue at his age. Positional flexiblity a plus, but more for in-season replacement than a March roster spot.

Yr Tm	PA	R	HR	RBI	SB	BA	xHR	xBA	OBP	SLG	OPS+	vL+	vR+	bb%	ct%	Eye	G	L	F	h%	HctX	PX	xPX	HR/F	xHR/F	Spd	SBO	SB%	#Wk	DOM	DIS	RAR	BPX	R$
15 TAM	551	66	15	58	6	265	18	248	315	430	104	100	103	7	79	0.34	36	21	44	31	92	107	107	9%	10%	100	7%	67%	25	48%	28%	-0.5	124	$14
16 NYM	568	65	23	62	5	280	18	273	336	474	110	113	107	7	80	0.37	37	23	40	31	119	114	142	14%	11%	80	5%	83%	26	38%	23%	8.3	146	$17
17 NYM	540	66	14	59	3	280	14	267	351	434	105	125	96	9	83	0.60	43	20	36	31	123	90	115	10%	10%	81	4%	60%	25	44%	28%	0.0	145	$13
18 2 NL	592	68	23	75	0	262	24	260	316	458	107	90	113	7	78	0.34	42	19	39	30	111	119	123	14%	15%	72	0%	0%	27	37%	22%	4.5	153	$15
19 2 TM	514	69	18	91	4	260	16	260	342	441	104	100	105	11	77	0.55	38	24	38	30	114	98	134	14%	12%	73	3%	100%	27	37%	33%	-2.0	119	$14
1st Half	287	37	11	43	3	228	8	243	310	406	96	78	102	10	73	0.43	35	24	41	27	102	98	115	14%	10%	74	5%	100%	15	27%	40%	-8.0	59	$12
2nd Half	227	32	7	48	1	301	7	282	383	487	115	135	109	13	82	0.80	43	24	34	34	129	97	156	13%	13%	78	2%	100%	12	50%	25%	9.1	207	$17
20 Proj	**455**	**56**	**13**	**66**	**1**	**263**		**257**	**335**	**427**	**102**	**103**	**102**	**10**	**79**	**0.51**	**40**	**22**	**38**	**30**	**116**	**90**	**130**	**11%**		**77**	**2%**	**77%**				**4.4**	**97**	**$13**

Cabrera,Melky

Age: 35	Bats: B	Pos: RF LF	Health	A	LIMA Plan	D+
Ht: 5' 10"	Wt: 210		PT/Exp	C	Rand Var	+1
			Consist	A	MM	1153

Signed to a minor league deal in February and worked his way into significant role. Customary robust ct% and good BA/xBA was again on display, but as his MO, the good news pretty much ends there. xPX and HctX highlight further degradation of power that's just not playable in today's game. Pass.

Yr Tm	PA	R	HR	RBI	SB	BA	xHR	xBA	OBP	SLG	OPS+	vL+	vR+	bb%	ct%	Eye	G	L	F	h%	HctX	PX	xPX	HR/F	xHR/F	Spd	SBO	SB%	#Wk	DOM	DIS	RAR	BPX	R$
15 CHW	683	70	12	77	3	273	8	278	314	394	99	83	103	6	86	0.45	46	24	30	30	101	79	66	7%	5%	71	2%	100%	26	35%	23%	-7.9	114	$16
16 CHW	646	70	14	86	2	296	8	289	345	455	109	114	105	7	88	0.68	43	22	35	32	103	92	79	8%	4%	83	1%	100%	27	67%	19%	17.6	194	$20
17 2 AL	661	76	16	81	1	283	13	284	322	416	99	99	97	5	88	0.49	49	22	29	30	102	70	74	10%	8%	76	2%	33%	27	48%	11%	-8.1	133	$17
18 CLE *	357	33	6	45	2	275	3	291	319	401	100	117	99	6	85	0.42	45	29	26	31	122	79	70	11%	5%	55	4%	70%	16	38%	25%	0.7	107	$7
19 PIT	397	43	7	47	2	280	5	286	313	399	95	87	98	4	89	0.41	47	23	29	30	96	61	48	7%	5%	80	2%	100%	28	36%	25%	-10.0	148	$8
1st Half	228	27	4	27	2	306	3	293	339	431	103	99	104	4	89	0.42	47	24	28	33	96	64	37	7%	6%	83	3%	100%	15	47%	27%	1.0	159	$11
2nd Half	169	16	3	20	0	247	2	271	278	358	84	76	89	4	90	0.41	47	22	31	26	96	57	64	7%	4%	76	0%	0%	13	23%	23%	-8.8	137	$4
20 Proj	**280**	**29**	**4**	**34**	**1**	**275**		**281**	**311**	**388**	**94**	**91**	**95**	**5**	**88**	**0.42**	**47**	**24**	**29**	**30**	**104**	**61**	**62**	**6%**		**75**	**2%**	**76%**				**-2.1**	**101**	**$7**

Cabrera,Miguel

Age: 37	Bats: R	Pos: DH 1B	Health	F	LIMA Plan	C+
Ht: 6' 4"	Wt: 249		PT/Exp	C	Rand Var	-2
			Consist	F	MM	2035

A chronic right knee issue will continue to be the backdrop for this former slugger. He can still tattoo lefties and hit line drives in bunches, but his power has dropped to below average and only some 1st half h% fortune kept his BA respectable. At his age and health level, the performance might only get worse from here.

Yr Tm	PA	R	HR	RBI	SB	BA	xHR	xBA	OBP	SLG	OPS+	vL+	vR+	bb%	ct%	Eye	G	L	F	h%	HctX	PX	xPX	HR/F	xHR/F	Spd	SBO	SB%	#Wk	DOM	DIS	RAR	BPX	R$
15 DET	511	64	18	76	1	338	29	290	440	534	136	140	132	15	81	0.94	42	25	33	39	142	126	124	16%	25%	80	1%	50%	21	52%	19%	39.3	216	$25
16 DET	679	92	38	108	0	316	54	293	393	563	130	125	129	11	81	0.65	42	23	36	34	134	137	144	22%	31%	73	0%	0%	27	52%	22%	43.7	223	$31
17 DET	529	50	16	60	0	249	24	265	329	399	98	123	89	10	77	0.49	40	27	33	29	132	88	125	13%	20%	64	1%	0%	24	29%	42%	-6.5	55	$7
18 DET	157	17	3	22	0	299	3	279	395	448	117	105	120	14	80	0.81	55	25	20	36	136	100	58	14%	14%	52	0%	0%	9	44%	44%	7.2	150	$2
19 DET	549	41	12	59	0	282	15	245	346	398	99	127	91	9	78	0.44	44	24	32	34	119	64	93	10%	12%	60	0%	0%	28	21%	57%	-5.2	4	$10
1st Half	299	19	4	34	0	298	6	238	365	385	100	131	94	10	77	0.47	45	25	29	37	117	51	86	7%	10%	69	0%	0%	15	20%	60%	-1.1	-30	$10
2nd Half	250	22	8	25	0	263	9	253	324	412	97	124	88	8	79	0.42	42	23	35	30	122	78	102	13%	14%	58	0%	0%	13	23%	54%	-4.3	52	$10
20 Proj	**490**	**47**	**13**	**60**	**0**	**272**		**255**	**346**	**417**	**103**	**117**	**98**	**10**	**78**	**0.51**	**46**	**24**	**31**	**32**	**128**	**81**	**94**	**12%**		**58**	**0%**	**21%**				**4.4**	**18**	**$13**

Cain,Lorenzo

Age: 34	Bats: R	Pos: CF	Health	B	LIMA Plan	B
Ht: 6' 2"	Wt: 205		PT/Exp	A	Rand Var	+3
			Consist	C	MM	1445

Disappointing season wasn't as bad as it seemed. Plate skills were in line with career marks, but low h% held BA down. While declining Spd comes with age, lingering knee soreness likely amplified it and contributed to SB% downturn. GB% and subpar xPX caps HR, but a modest BA/SB rebound is possible.

Yr Tm	PA	R	HR	RBI	SB	BA	xHR	xBA	OBP	SLG	OPS+	vL+	vR+	bb%	ct%	Eye	G	L	F	h%	HctX	PX	xPX	HR/F	xHR/F	Spd	SBO	SB%	#Wk	DOM	DIS	RAR	BPX	R$
15 KC	604	101	16	72	28	307	20	283	361	477	117	132	107	6	82	0.38	46	23	31	35	114	108	109	11%	14%	138	23%	82%	26	50%	31%	29.1	192	$35
16 KC	434	56	9	56	14	287	10	257	339	408	102	137	89	7	79	0.37	47	23	30	35	96	76	79	9%	11%	96	16%	74%	20	35%	30%	3.0	60	$17
17 KC	645	86	15	49	26	300	11	269	363	440	108	109	105	8	83	0.54	44	23	33	34	104	76	84	9%	7%	150	15%	93%	27	37%	22%	15.0	170	$28
18 MIL	620	90	10	38	30	308	9	273	395	417	112	136	103	11	83	0.76	55	22	23	36	116	66	72	10%	9%	143	19%	81%	26	31%	27%	27.9	170	$29
19 MIL	622	75	11	48	18	260	13	276	325	372	92	97	90	8	81	0.47	50	26	24	30	103	63	65	10%	12%	94	17%	69%	27	30%	44%	-3.8	78	$16
1st Half	348	47	4	28	10	248	6	279	313	350	89	93	87	8	80	0.44	54	25	21	30	89	63	52	8%	11%	91	17%	71%	15	20%	47%	-7.1	63	$16
2nd Half	274	28	7	20	8	274	6	273	339	399	97	103	95	8	82	0.52	46	26	28	31	119	64	81	12%	10%	100	16%	67%	12	42%	42%	1.6	107	$17
20 Proj	**595**	**78**	**12**	**47**	**22**	**282**		**271**	**350**	**401**	**101**	**112**	**96**	**9**	**82**	**0.53**	**49**	**24**	**26**	**33**	**109**	**64**	**75**	**10%**		**121**	**17%**	**77%**				**16.0**	**105**	**$25**

GREG PYRON

Calhoun,Kole

Calhoun,Kole	Health	A	LIMA Plan	B+
Age: 32 Bats: L Pos: RF	PT/Exp	A	Rand Var	0
Ht: 5' 10" Wt: 215	Consist	B	MM	3125

Managed to carry over new-found power, which dates back to a swing retooling during summer 2018 Triple-A stint. xHR fully validates the ensuing HR binge, even when FB% dipped in 2nd half. Best to treat this as a high-water mark, as high PA total, 2nd half ct% slip and age all feed headwinds to a full repeat.

Yr	Tm	PA	R	HR	RBI	SB	BA	xHR	xBA	OBP	SLG	OPS+	vL+	vR+	bb%	ct%	Eye	G	L	F	h%	HctX	PX	xPX	HR/F	xHR/F	Spd	SBO	SB%	#Wk	DOM	DIS	RAR	BPX	R$
15	LAA	686	78	26	83	4	256	25	248	308	422	102	91	105	7	74	0.27	42	23	35	31	90	109	116	16%	15%	75	3%	80%	27	26%	37%	-6.4	57	$17
16	LAA	672	91	18	75	2	271	23	261	348	438	107	112	103	10	80	0.57	38	22	40	31	115	100	113	9%	12%	77	3%	40%	27	41%	22%	8.3	131	$16
17	LAA	654	77	19	71	5	244	18	248	333	392	97	91	98	11	76	0.53	44	21	35	29	98	85	91	12%	12%	77	4%	83%	27	26%	37%	-9.5	64	$11
18	LAA	551	71	19	57	6	208	25	240	283	369	90	84	92	10	73	0.40	43	21	35	24	120	98	132	15%	20%	71	7%	75%	26	35%	46%	-17.3	40	$8
19	LAA	631	92	33	74	4	232	31	259	325	467	105	96	109	11	71	0.43	41	22	37	27	104	131	121	23%	22%	62	4%	80%	28	46%	29%	-1.3	111	$15
1st Half		330	48	17	41	3	225	17	259	315	457	103	95	107	11	74	0.48	38	21	41	24	111	122	140	20%	20%	80	6%	75%	15	53%	20%	-4.8	156	$15
2nd Half		301	44	16	33	1	240	14	258	336	479	108	99	111	11	67	0.39	44	24	32	29	95	143	98	28%	25%	52	2%	100%	13	38%	38%	0.5	85	$14
20	Proj	**595**	**82**	**26**	**68**	**4**	**232**		**251**	**316**	**432**	**101**	**93**	**103**	**10**	**72**	**0.42**	**42**	**22**	**36**	**27**	**106**	**111**	**116**	**19%**		**67**	**4%**	**78%**				**-0.9**	**89**	**$12**

Calhoun,Willie

Calhoun,Willie	Health	A	LIMA Plan	B+
Age: 25 Bats: L Pos: LF	PT/Exp	C	Rand Var	-1
Ht: 5' 8" Wt: 187	Consist	C	MM	3245

21-48-.269 in 337 AB at TEX. Called up in May, landed on IL (quad) within a week, then likely got off the Triple-A shuttle for good following late-July callup: 16-35-.265 over rest of season. Power skills don't rate as remarkable, but plus contact and lots of fly balls are a winning combo, both for power and a nice BA floor. A growth asset. UP: 30 HR

Yr	Tm	PA	R	HR	RBI	SB	BA	xHR	xBA	OBP	SLG	OPS+	vL+	vR+	bb%	ct%	Eye	G	L	F	h%	HctX	PX	xPX	HR/F	xHR/F	Spd	SBO	SB%	#Wk	DOM	DIS	RAR	BPX	R$
15																																			
16	aa	539	64	24	75	0	233			284	425	96			7	86	0.50				23		103				82	0%	0%					186	$8
17	TEX *	556	64	25	75	3	267	0	316	313	479	106	80	94	6	86	0.48	56	22	22	27	90	103	57	17%	0%	132	4%	58%	3	33%	67%	-4.4	242	$15
18	TEX *	565	57	9	46	3	252	2	248	293	366	91	62	92	6	86	0.41	39	19	42	28	78	72	77	6%	6%	88	2%	100%	10	30%	40%	-13.8	133	$8
19	TEX *	499	67	27	68	1	265	11	271	335	499	111	102	117	9	82	0.59	36	19	44	27	116	111	104	18%	10%	85	2%	38%	18	61%	17%	8.2	237	$14
1st Half		216	28	10	29	1	280	2	296	355	491	113	85	137	10	81	0.61	38	29	33	30	129	105	98	24%	12%	94	3%	38%	5	60%	20%	4.9	215	$9
2nd Half		283	40	17	39	0	254	9	269	319	505	109	104	111	9	83	0.57	36	17	47	24	113	115	105	18%	9%	89	0%	0%	13	62%	15%	2.7	263	$18
20	Proj	**525**	**65**	**26**	**65**	**2**	**265**		**267**	**324**	**485**	**109**	**90**	**116**	**8**	**84**	**0.52**	**38**	**18**	**44**	**27**	**103**	**104**	**92**	**15%**		**89**	**2%**	**67%**				**12.5**	**198**	**$17**

Camargo,Johan

Camargo,Johan	Health	B	LIMA Plan	D+
Age: 26 Bats: B Pos: SS	PT/Exp	D	Rand Var	0
Ht: 6' 0" Wt: 195	Consist	C	MM	2233

7-32-.233 in 248 PA at ATL. 2018's power spike (predictably) left as quickly as it appeared, and playing time dried up accordingly. Positional flexibility will keep him employed, and decent ct% is at least a foundation of a useful skill set. But to date, there's no first or second floor on top of that foundation.

Yr	Tm	PA	R	HR	RBI	SB	BA	xHR	xBA	OBP	SLG	OPS+	vL+	vR+	bb%	ct%	Eye	G	L	F	h%	HctX	PX	xPX	HR/F	xHR/F	Spd	SBO	SB%	#Wk	DOM	DIS	RAR	BPX	R$
15																																			
16	aa	471	46	4	43	1	236			277	320	81			5	79	0.26				29		52				119	3%	31%					11	$2
17	ATL *	392	45	7	44	1	278	5	265	314	422	99	150	84	5	79	0.25	48	21	31	34	91	89	64	7%	8%	106	1%	100%	18	33%	33%	-6.3	94	$8
18	ATL *	559	68	21	81	1	271	15	258	342	462	111	113	110	10	76	0.45	45	20	35	32	102	117	81	15%	12%	89	1%	50%	25	64%	16%	11.6	153	$17
19	ATL *	310	39	9	44	1	271	4	258	316	426	98	91	86	6	80	0.33	44	20	36	31	91	84	65	10%	6%	89	1%	100%	23	48%	30%	-5.7	107	$6
1st Half		152	20	3	22	1	241	2	260	276	379	88	84	89	5	83	0.28	44	20	36	27	88	74	59	7%	5%	104	3%	100%	15	47%	27%	-7.2	122	$2
2nd Half		158	19	6	22	0	300	2	252	354	473	109	105	83	8	78	0.38	43	20	36	35	96	94	76	16%	8%	82	0%	0%	8	50%	38%	3.5	107	$10
20	Proj	**280**	**34**	**9**	**38**	**1**	**273**		**257**	**326**	**442**	**103**	**115**	**98**	**7**	**79**	**0.36**	**45**	**20**	**35**	**32**	**96**	**91**	**73**	**12%**		**96**	**1%**	**73%**				**6.5**	**75**	**$9**

Candelario,Jeimer

Candelario,Jeimer	Health	C	LIMA Plan	D+
Age: 26 Bats: B Pos: 3B 1B	PT/Exp	B	Rand Var	0
Ht: 6' 1" Wt: 221	Consist	B	MM	2223

8-32-.203 in 386 PA at DET. Disappointing follow-up to first full-time MLB season, with two IL stints (shoulder in June, thumb in August), three round trips on the Triple-A shuttle. As bad as 1st half was, across-the-board skills rebound in 2nd half is just enough to hold our attention. End-game dart throw with upside.

Yr	Tm	PA	R	HR	RBI	SB	BA	xHR	xBA	OBP	SLG	OPS+	vL+	vR+	bb%	ct%	Eye	G	L	F	h%	HctX	PX	xPX	HR/F	xHR/F	Spd	SBO	SB%	#Wk	DOM	DIS	RAR	BPX	R$
15	aa	176	17	4	20	0	264			339	412	105			10	85	0.77				29		93				94	0%	0%					178	$2
16	CHC *	545	58	10	61	0	242	0	215	325	389	97	68	47	11	76	0.50	67	0	33	30	153	101	100	0%	0%	84	2%	0%	1	0%	100%	-11.6	91	$6
17	2 TM *	591	65	17	80	1	253	3	256	323	442	103	122	100	9	73	0.39	45	19	36	32	86	121	77	9%	9%	108	1%	100%	10	50%	40%	0.5	130	$10
18	DET	619	78	19	54	3	224	19	228	317	393	98	117	91	11	70	0.41	42	18	41	28	91	112	88	12%	12%	95	4%	60%	27	33%	37%	-6.0	77	$9
19	DET *	556	57	15	59	3	227	9	236	313	392	94	75	89	11	72	0.44	37	23	40	29	93	95	86	9%	10%	81	3%	75%	22	18%	45%	-14.5	41	$6
1st Half		289	32	6	29	3	238	3	222	312	380	93	69	81	10	69	0.35	35	24	41	32	79	85	73	4%	6%	102	6%	75%	12	8%	58%	-9.8	-11	$7
2nd Half		268	26	9	30	0	215	6	252	313	405	95	77	99	12	74	0.55	39	22	39	25	108	106	100	13%	13%	72	0%	0%	10	30%	30%	-7.8	111	$6
20	Proj	**420**	**50**	**12**	**49**	**2**	**240**		**240**	**338**	**410**	**101**	**102**	**100**	**12**	**74**	**0.51**	**40**	**20**	**39**	**29**	**93**	**97**	**87**	**11%**		**88**	**3%**	**78%**				**-0.6**	**79**	**$9**

Canha,Mark

Canha,Mark	Health	C	LIMA Plan	B
Age: 31 Bats: R Pos: CF RF	PT/Exp	C	Rand Var	-5
Ht: 6' 2" Wt: 212	Consist	C	MM	4235

Seemingly came into season looking to lift every pitch in the air. Landed on IL with a wrist injury at end of April, then it all clicked when he returned. FB% fell month over month, but power stuck around anyway and remained skill-supported. BA gains were fueled by fluky h% spike, particularly vs. RHP (36%), so expect some slippage there.

Yr	Tm	PA	R	HR	RBI	SB	BA	xHR	xBA	OBP	SLG	OPS+	vL+	vR+	bb%	ct%	Eye	G	L	F	h%	HctX	PX	xPX	HR/F	xHR/F	Spd	SBO	SB%	#Wk	DOM	DIS	RAR	BPX	R$
15	OAK	485	61	16	70	7	254	17	252	315	426	103	81	112	7	78	0.34	42	18	40	29	107	111	114	11%	12%	106	9%	78%	27	56%	37%	-0.6	132	$14
16	OAK	44	4	3	6	0	122	2	190	140	341	65	85	47	0	51	0.00	36	18	45	11	81	167	157	30%	20%	84	50%	0%	6	17%	67%	-4.9	-94	-$2
17	OAK *	483	53	13	50	5	218	5	234	269	395	89	77	91	6	71	0.24	33	20	47	28	80	119	75	9%	9%	96	6%	100%	16	38%	56%	-16.8	67	$3
18	OAK	411	60	17	52	1	249	19	259	328	449	108	131	91	8	76	0.39	38	22	40	28	104	123	114	15%	17%	98	3%	33%	26	50%	27%	7.0	167	$10
19	OAK	497	80	26	58	3	273	23	257	396	517	121	104	129	13	74	0.63	41	18	41	31	101	124	100	21%	19%	138	4%	60%	27	59%	26%	26.5	241	$15
1st Half		181	32	11	21	0	234	9	249	376	510	118	106	125	16	76	0.80	37	12	52	23	84	139	100	19%	16%	115	5%	0%	15	67%	13%	6.2	307	$3
2nd Half		316	48	15	37	3	294	13	261	408	521	123	103	131	13	73	0.54	44	22	34	35	111	116	101	23%	20%	143	3%	100%	12	50%	42%	21.6	204	$22
20	Proj	**490**	**75**	**24**	**61**	**3**	**256**		**254**	**355**	**484**	**113**	**107**	**115**	**11**	**74**	**0.47**	**39**	**19**	**42**	**29**	**99**	**121**	**101**	**18%**		**119**	**5%**	**62%**				**20.7**	**155**	**$17**

Cano,Robinson

Cano,Robinson	Health	F	LIMA Plan	B
Age: 37 Bats: L Pos: 2B	PT/Exp	B	Rand Var	+2
Ht: 6' 0" Wt: 210	Consist	D	MM	2045

Durability and a lot of contact were core to his value proposition at his peak. After three trips to IL with left leg injuries (twice for quad in 1st half, hamstring in August), durability now a weakness. Contact rate remains strong, but the after-contact profile is showing some wear. These trends rarely swing back to the positive at his age.

Yr	Tm	PA	R	HR	RBI	SB	BA	xHR	xBA	OBP	SLG	OPS+	vL+	vR+	bb%	ct%	Eye	G	L	F	h%	HctX	PX	xPX	HR/F	xHR/F	Spd	SBO	SB%	#Wk	DOM	DIS	RAR	BPX	R$
15	SEA	674	82	21	79	2	287	22	285	334	446	109	99	112	6	83	0.40	50	24	25	32	118	100	107	16%	17%	74	5%	25%	27	52%	11%	16.6	130	$22
16	SEA	715	107	39	103	0	298	30	290	350	533	120	104	127	7	85	0.47	46	18	36	30	122	124	96	19%	15%	75	1%	0%	27	59%	7%	31.8	217	$29
17	SEA	648	79	23	97	1	280	22	281	338	453	106	74	118	8	86	0.58	50	19	31	30	128	91	111	15%	14%	66	1%	100%	26	54%	27%	6.2	158	$19
18	SEA	348	44	10	50	0	303	14	284	374	471	117	124	112	9	85	0.68	48	23	29	33	130	99	110	13%	18%	75	0%	0%	15	47%	0%	17.6	203	$11
19	NYM	423	46	13	39	0	256	12	270	307	428	98	75	106	6	82	0.36	49	20	31	28	108	92	97	13%	12%	74	0%	0%	23	43%	17%	-1.2	144	$6
1st Half		238	18	4	18	0	238	6	249	286	368	87	63	97	6	80	0.29	51	20	29	28	110	79	100	8%	12%	76	0%	0%	13	23%	31%	-8.1	67	$0
2nd Half		185	28	9	21	0	281	6	296	335	509	111	90	120	7	86	0.50	47	21	33	28	106	109	94	19%	13%	76	0%	0%	10	70%	0%	6.1	252	$13
20	Proj	**476**	**60**	**15**	**59**	**0**	**272**		**276**	**331**	**443**	**104**	**91**	**109**	**7**	**84**	**0.50**	**48**	**21**	**31**	**29**	**118**	**89**	**103**	**13%**		**73**	**0%**	**43%**				**12.0**	**129**	**$14**

Caratini,Victor

Caratini,Victor	Health	B	LIMA Plan	D
Age: 26 Bats: B Pos: CA 1B	PT/Exp	D	Rand Var	-1
Ht: 6' 1" Wt: 215	Consist	D	MM	2233

Got first stretch of regular big-league playing time in 2nd half, and skills responded well. Contact rate spiked while power was emerging, a promising combo. Too many GB cap short-term power gains, but this is now a rosterable 2nd-C for AL/NL-only leagues, with raw materials in place to be a mixed league option if opportunity finds him.

Yr	Tm	PA	R	HR	RBI	SB	BA	xHR	xBA	OBP	SLG	OPS+	vL+	vR+	bb%	ct%	Eye	G	L	F	h%	HctX	PX	xPX	HR/F	xHR/F	Spd	SBO	SB%	#Wk	DOM	DIS	RAR	BPX	R$
15																																			
16	aa	458	47	5	39	2	259			333	357	94			10	78	0.51				32		68				96	2%	60%					49	$6
17	CHC *	379	44	9	49	1	286	2	281	335	449	105	157	73	7	80	0.36	65	15	20	34	99	98	61	11%	22%	84	1%	100%	14	21%	43%	12.9	118	$10
18	CHC *	329	31	5	37	0	243	4	236	303	336	89	62	89	8	76	0.36	53	23	24	30	79	63	62	6%	12%	90	0%	0%	23	9%	65%	-0.6	-3	$3
19	CHC	279	31	11	34	1	266	10	267	348	447	105	101	106	10	76	0.49	49	24	27	31	88	96	83	22%	20%	79	1%	100%	23	35%	30%	7.2	96	$5
1st Half		86	11	2	11	0	289	2	271	372	461	111	178	104	11	71	0.41	48	28	24	38	109	114	130	15%	15%	85	0%	0%	10	40%	20%	4.3	89	-$4
2nd Half		193	20	9	23	1	256	8	264	337	440	102	85	107	11	78	0.54	50	22	28	28	79	88	64	24%	22%	87	2%	100%	13	31%	38%	5.5	119	$9
20	Proj	**315**	**39**	**10**	**41**	**1**	**265**		**263**	**345**	**422**	**103**	**102**	**103**	**9**	**76**	**0.44**	**53**	**23**	**25**	**32**	**88**	**88**	**76**	**18%**		**85**	**1%**	**92%**				**12.4**	**38**	**$9**

RAY MURPHY

Carlson,Dylan

Age: 21 Bats: B Pos: LF
Ht: 6' 2" Wt: 205
Health A | PT/Exp F | Consist F
LIMA Plan D | Rand Var 0 | MM 3431

STL's #8 prospect entering the season, took a big step up in 2019 despite being one of the younger players in the high minors; now comfortably in the Top 25 overall. No single standout tool, but across-the-board skills that should translate well to MLB and gives him eventual 20/20 potential. Still not on 40-man, so expect more MiLB seasoning.

Yr	Tm	PA	R	HR	RBI	SB	BA	xHR	xBA	OBP	SLG	OPS+	vL+	vR+	bb%	ct%	Eye	G	L	F	h%	HctX	PX	xPX	HR/F	xHR/F	Spd	SBO	SB%	#Wk	DOM	DIS	RAR	BPX	R$
15																																			
16																																			
17																																			
18																																			
19	a/a	536	80	21	57	17	265			330	470	106			9	75	0.38				32		109				128	20%	66%					163	$20
1st Half		308	47	9	38	9	259			325	438	102			9	77	0.43				31		92				137	20%	64%				-4.2	163	$20
2nd Half		229	34	12	20	8	278			342	522	114			9	71	0.34				34		135				125	20%	70%				5.7	189	$19
20	Proj	210	31	9	21	7	271		253	336	483	110	109	110	9	74	0.38	40	21	39	32	0	116		16%		126	20%	69%				5.8	159	$6

Carpenter,Matt

Age: 34 Bats: L Pos: 3B
Ht: 6' 3" Wt: 205
Health B | PT/Exp A | Consist F
LIMA Plan B | Rand Var +1 | MM 4225

15-46-.226 in 492 PA at STL. Big steps back in power and hard-contact skills make us wonder if the bad back that put him on the IL mid-season (among other maladies) was a year-long problem. His expected power metrics aren't quite as bleak, so a rebound seems likely. But bid on that returning to 2016-17 levels, not 2018's.

Yr	Tm	PA	R	HR	RBI	SB	BA	xHR	xBA	OBP	SLG	OPS+	vL+	vR+	bb%	ct%	Eye	G	L	F	h%	HctX	PX	xPX	HR/F	xHR/F	Spd	SBO	SB%	#Wk	DOM	DIS	RAR	BPX	R$
15	STL	665	101	28	84	4	272	33	278	365	505	121	104	127	12	74	0.54	30	29	42	32	119	164	166	16%	19%	98	4%	57%	27	59%	26%	27.1	222	$23
16	STL	566	81	21	68	0	271	29	282	380	505	120	109	123	14	77	0.75	31	26	43	31	131	144	174	13%	18%	88	3%	0%	24	63%	21%	20.3	231	$15
17	STL	622	91	23	69	2	241	25	250	384	451	112	88	117	18	75	0.87	27	22	51	28	128	124	169	12%	13%	98	2%	67%	26	58%	12%	6.0	197	$11
18	STL	676	111	36	81	4	257	42	273	374	523	124	114	128	15	72	0.65	26	27	47	29	130	170	189	19%	22%	77	3%	80%	28	54%	25%	32.8	263	$23
19	STL *	523	60	15	48	6	216	20	224	320	374	92	89	98	13	69	0.49	32	25	43	28	99	94	138	12%	16%	104	6%	86%	25	36%	48%	-20.3	33	$6
1st Half		326	42	10	28	6	216	13	222	325	381	94	98	94	14	71	0.55	30	23	47	27	102	93	142	11%	14%	126	9%	86%	14	36%	43%	-10.0	96	$9
2nd Half		197	18	5	20	0	216	7	234	315	361	89	76	109	13	64	0.40	35	30	35	30	93	97	129	16%	22%	77	0%	0%	11	36%	55%	-7.7	-59	$0
20	Proj	490	66	22	54	3	240		251	356	461	110	96	114	14	70	0.57	30	27	43	29	113	129	157	17%		89	3%	77%				10.4	129	$13

Castellanos,Nick

Age: 28 Bats: R Pos: RF
Ht: 6' 4" Wt: 203
Health A | PT/Exp A | Consist C
LIMA Plan B | Rand Var 0 | MM 4145

Turned season around with torrid two months following escape from DET to CHC (16 HR in Aug/Sept); basically the exact power outburst that xHR has been begging for. Can that stick? Stable skills point to a blend of his 3-year scan as about what we should expect again, and his thump still comes mostly vL. Still, watch where he lands.

Yr	Tm	PA	R	HR	RBI	SB	BA	xHR	xBA	OBP	SLG	OPS+	vL+	vR+	bb%	ct%	Eye	G	L	F	h%	HctX	PX	xPX	HR/F	xHR/F	Spd	SBO	SB%	#Wk	DOM	DIS	RAR	BPX	R$
15	DET	595	42	15	73	0	255	22	243	303	419	101	134	90	7	72	0.26	36	23	40	33	103	118	118	9%	13%	102	2%	0%	27	33%	37%	-9.6	78	$9
16	DET	447	54	18	58	1	285	30	260	331	496	113	89	119	6	73	0.25	31	26	43	35	106	135	166	14%	23%	132	2%	50%	20	50%	30%	13.0	154	$13
17	DET	661	73	26	101	4	272	33	275	321	492	109	124	103	6	77	0.29	37	24	38	32	135	123	142	14%	18%	128	7%	44%	27	52%	30%	2.4	179	$19
18	DET	678	88	23	89	2	298	35	276	354	500	118	140	111	7	76	0.32	35	29	36	36	134	128	139	14%	21%	116	2%	67%	28	46%	32%	33.1	187	$25
19	2 TM	664	100	27	73	2	289	40	280	337	525	115	148	107	6	77	0.29	38	23	40	34	113	134	131	14%	21%	123	3%	50%	27	67%	7%	14.4	244	$21
1st Half		336	46	8	27	2	276	17	259	339	461	107	123	104	8	76	0.38	36	23	41	34	108	108	112	8%	18%	140	4%	67%	15	53%	13%	1.7	193	$13
2nd Half		328	54	19	46	0	302	23	299	335	588	122	169	111	4	77	0.20	39	22	39	34	119	159	150	20%	25%	105	2%	0%	12	83%	0%	15.7	289	$29
20	Proj	665	91	27	90	2	288		274	335	513	114	139	107	6	76	0.28	37	25	39	34	122	126	138	15%		118	3%	47%				26.3	153	$26

Castro,Harold

Age: 26 Bats: L Pos: 2B CF
Ht: 6' 0" Wt: 180
Health A | PT/Exp C | Consist C
LIMA Plan D | Rand Var -5 | MM 0333

5-38-.291 in 369 PA at DET. Speed and versatility are his calling cards—or should be. But SB% and inconsistent PT hold him back; elevated hit rate is certain to normalize, so you can dismiss gaudy BA. Factor in that his ability to walk rivals that of a newborn giraffe, and the position flexibility doesn't buy you much.

Yr	Tm	PA	R	HR	RBI	SB	BA	xHR	xBA	OBP	SLG	OPS+	vL+	vR+	bb%	ct%	Eye	G	L	F	h%	HctX	PX	xPX	HR/F	xHR/F	Spd	SBO	SB%	#Wk	DOM	DIS	RAR	BPX	R$
15	aa	348	33	1	21	14	234			260	286	76			3	81	0.18				29		38				114	31%	59%					-8	$5
16	aa	401	32	3	18	5	214			231	278	69			2	83	0.13				25		41				104	17%	37%					3	-$2
17	aa	429	42	1	25	17	258			284	318	81			4	86	0.26				30		35				134	26%	62%					64	$9
18	DET *	368	30	2	24	5	234	0	210	249	280	73	0	82	2	79	0.10	63	13	25	29	145	34	66	0%	0%	99	12%	53%	2	0%	50%	-20.3	-70	$2
19	DET *	498	46	8	58	5	290	7	254	313	394	94	58	99	3	76	0.14	52	25	22	37	104	55	67	8%	12%	136	8%	47%	20	15%	55%	-6.8	-7	$12
1st Half		216	23	4	25	3	279	1	280	313	394	94	0	90	5	75	0.20	52	33	15	35	98	61	26	11%	11%	118	13%	38%	8	13%	50%	-3.7	-19	$8
2nd Half		282	23	4	33	2	298	6	246	310	393	93	61	102	2	76	0.09	53	23	25	38	106	51	78	8%	12%	142	4%	67%	12	17%	58%	-1.6	-19	$15
20	Proj	350	32	5	31	4	265		264	283	355	86	52	92	3	79	0.14	52	27	21	32	103	49	57	9%		128	9%	54%				-6.7	-58	$8

Castro,Jason

Age: 33 Bats: L Pos: CA
Ht: 6' 3" Wt: 215
Health F | PT/Exp D | Consist F
LIMA Plan D | Rand Var -3 | MM 3203

Spot-starting served him well, as he (like several MIN teammates) posted career-best power skills in his limited PT. Hit them out to all fields, too, making his next home park less of an issue. BA will never be there, but power/patience combo makes him a decent late-round sim-league backup.

Yr	Tm	PA	R	HR	RBI	SB	BA	xHR	xBA	OBP	SLG	OPS+	vL+	vR+	bb%	ct%	Eye	G	L	F	h%	HctX	PX	xPX	HR/F	xHR/F	Spd	SBO	SB%	#Wk	DOM	DIS	RAR	BPX	R$
15	HOU	375	38	11	31	0	211	10	229	283	365	90	71	97	9	66	0.29	37	24	38	28	90	124	121	13%	12%	77	0%	0%	25	32%	44%	-4.3	14	$0
16	HOU	376	41	11	32	2	210	14	222	307	377	93	65	101	12	63	0.37	46	20	34	30	90	124	102	16%	20%	104	4%	67%	26	31%	46%	-1.7	20	$1
17	MIN	407	49	10	47	0	242	11	242	333	388	97	98	94	11	70	0.42	42	25	33	32	102	101	112	12%	13%	80	0%	0%	26	38%	50%	1.2	21	$4
18	MIN	74	4	1	3	0	143	1	194	257	238	68	52	69	12	59	0.35	42	26	32	22	80	84	111	8%	8%	83	0%	0%	6	33%	67%	-3.3	-153	-$4
19	MIN	275	39	13	30	0	232	17	228	332	435	102	45	113	12	63	0.38	36	25	39	31	112	125	177	22%	29%	108	0%	0%	28	32%	57%	7.8	37	$3
1st Half		145	25	8	19	0	233	11	252	317	465	104	61	113	10	71	0.38	34	23	43	26	121	127	173	20%	28%	113	0%	0%	15	47%	33%	3.0	156	$4
2nd Half		130	14	5	11	0	231	6	198	349	398	99	27	113	15	53	0.37	40	28	33	38	102	120	183	26%	32%	98	0%	0%	13	15%	85%	1.9	-119	$2
20	Proj	315	39	11	32	0	229		223	326	392	97	64	103	12	63	0.37	40	25	35	32	99	106	145	17%		92	0%	67%				6.5	-85	$6

Castro,Starlin

Age: 30 Bats: R Pos: 2B 3B
Ht: 6' 2" Wt: 230
Health B | PT/Exp A | Consist B
LIMA Plan B+ | Rand Var 0 | MM 2235

Huge 2nd half propelled him to... well, about where he usually ends up (note identical xPX from 2018). Tempting to wish on that finish, but did a simple mid-season bat change really make him a new man? Maybe, but regression is a powerful force. We're going out on a verrry shaky limb here and project... well, about where he usually ends up.

Yr	Tm	PA	R	HR	RBI	SB	BA	xHR	xBA	OBP	SLG	OPS+	vL+	vR+	bb%	ct%	Eye	G	L	F	h%	HctX	PX	xPX	HR/F	xHR/F	Spd	SBO	SB%	#Wk	DOM	DIS	RAR	BPX	R$
15	CHC	578	52	11	69	5	265	14	251	296	375	94	89	93	4	83	0.23	54	17	29	30	86	70	75	8%	11%	98	8%	50%	27	22%	41%	-7.6	76	$13
16	NYY	610	63	21	70	4	270	20	268	300	433	100	100	98	4	80	0.20	49	21	30	31	101	97	91	15%	14%	89	3%	100%	25	40%	36%	-4.8	91	$15
17	NYY *	505	69	17	65	2	299	12	263	333	450	105	111	103	5	79	0.24	52	20	28	35	93	84	69	16%	12%	100	2%	100%	22	36%	32%	5.9	73	$17
18	MIA	647	76	12	54	6	278	20	253	329	400	101	108	98	7	79	0.39	51	20	29	33	109	77	87	9%	15%	108	6%	60%	28	32%	39%	6.0	90	$17
19	MIA	676	68	22	86	2	270	22	265	300	436	98	115	91	4	83	0.25	48	19	33	30	120	82	87	13%	13%	91	3%	50%	28	36%	32%	0.0	122	$16
1st Half		345	22	5	33	1	230	8	228	258	313	76	101	68	4	82	0.24	52	17	31	27	114	43	72	6%	10%	89	3%	50%	15	7%	47%	-19.5	-4	$2
2nd Half		331	46	17	53	1	313	14	300	344	565	120	129	117	4	83	0.27	44	21	35	33	126	122	103	18%	15%	90	3%	50%	13	69%	15%	20.5	252	$31
20	Proj	602	68	18	71	3	276		263	312	431	100	110	96	5	81	0.28	49	20	31	31	111	80	86	13%		100	4%	60%				9.6	78	$19

Castro,Willi

Age: 23 Bats: B Pos: SS
Ht: 6' 1" Wt: 205
Health A | PT/Exp D | Consist A
LIMA Plan D+ | Rand Var -3 | MM 1413

1-8-.230 in 110 PA at DET. Youngster showed the warts you'd expect in debut from a hitter who had posted exactly one good half-year of hitting skills. Poor contact and just-okay power suppress BA, and low OBP tamps down excellent speed. Owns skills to eventually go for 10/20, but don't expect it in 2020. (See what I did there?)

Yr	Tm	PA	R	HR	RBI	SB	BA	xHR	xBA	OBP	SLG	OPS+	vL+	vR+	bb%	ct%	Eye	G	L	F	h%	HctX	PX	xPX	HR/F	xHR/F	Spd	SBO	SB%	#Wk	DOM	DIS	RAR	BPX	R$
15																																			
16																																			
17																																			
18	a/a	527	59	8	48	16	250			292	372	92			6	77	0.25				31		80				109	19%	75%					53	$13
19	DET *	607	76	11	63	15	279	2	239	324	431	100	100	78	6	74	0.26	36	24	39	36	64	87	43	4%	8%	137	14%	74%	7	29%	43%	-3.6	78	$19
1st Half		305	45	4	31	11	289		243	357	439	106			10	75	0.43				37		82		0%		152	18%	78%				5.4	126	$21
2nd Half		302	31	7	32	4	269	2	240	291	424	94	99	78	3	72	0.11	36	24	39	35	63	93	43	4%	8%	111	10%	63%	7	29%	43%	-6.1	19	$16
20	Proj	350	41	3	35	9	255		229	307	369	91	110	86	6	75	0.24	36	24	39	33	57	70	39	3%		128	16%	75%				-3.7	22	$10

ROD TRUESDELL

Cave,Jake

Age: 27 **Bats:** L **Pos:** RF CF | **Ht:** 6' 0" **Wt:** 200

Health A | **PT/Exp** C | **Consist** B | **LIMA Plan** D+ | **Rand Var** -3 | **MM** 4333

8-25-.258 in 228 PA at MIN. Rediscovered 2019 pop late after converting GB into liners and FB, which gives hope for more. But that in-season inconsistency is cemented in profile thanks to shaky ct%, so we have to view it more as a blip than a building block. Value him for what he is: a 5th OF or short-term injury replacement.

Yr	Tm	PA	R	HR	RBI	SB	BA	xHR	xBA	OBP	SLG	OPS+	vL+	vR+	bb%	ct%	Eye	G	L	F	h%	HctX	PX	xPX	HR/F	xHR/F	Spd	SBO	SB%	#Wk	DOM	DIS	RAR	BPX	R$
15	a/a	570	64	2	35	15	256			310	326	89			7	78	0.35				33		54				119	12%	82%					14	$11
16	a/a	458	53	8	50	5	244			298	388	93			7	72	0.27				32		97				114	13%	41%					43	$7
17	a/a	431	58	21	49	2	278			319	503	110			6	67	0.18				36		144				110	6%	34%					91	$13
18	MIN *	547	76	18	69	5	255	18	241	310	424	102	83	116	7	67	0.24	44	26	31	34	93	116	130	23%	32%	97	7%	62%	19	37%	42%	5.7	23	$15
19	MIN *	436	57	14	55	4	280	10	264	335	478	108	113	105	7	67	0.25	53	25	22	39	121	123	110	29%	36%	112	4%	100%	22	23%	55%	13.8	63	$12
1st Half		236	28	5	23	3	242	2	247	301	390	92	115	60	8	66	0.25	65	17	17	34	95	98	40	13%	25%	99	6%	100%	10	10%	70%	-2.3	-30	$6
2nd Half		200	29	9	32	1	325	9	283	375	581	126	111	132	7	68	0.25	46	29	24	44	137	153	149	35%	45%	126	2%	100%	12	33%	42%	18.6	178	$18
20	Proj	280	38	11	36	3	265		262	334	475	109	103	110	7	68	0.24	50	25	25	35	109	125	114	25%		114	6%	72%				5.2	75	$7

Cespedes,Yoenis

Age: 34 **Bats:** R **Pos:** DH | **Ht:** 5' 10" **Wt:** 220

Health F | **PT/Exp** F | **Consist** C | **LIMA Plan** C | **Rand Var** | **MM** 4233

Heel rehab ended poorly for his ankle, which he fractured in multiple places. All the injuries (and resulting PA slide) make him a dart throw on their own. Now, after another surgery, how lucky do you feel? Pre-injury power still legit, but given chronic foot and leg issues, we can't expect him to roam OF regularly. Likely needs a home at 1B/DH.

Yr	Tm	PA	R	HR	RBI	SB	BA	xHR	xBA	OBP	SLG	OPS+	vL+	vR+	bb%	ct%	Eye	G	L	F	h%	HctX	PX	xPX	HR/F	xHR/F	Spd	SBO	SB%	#Wk	DOM	DIS	RAR	BPX	R$
15	2 TM	676	101	35	105	7	291	40	289	328	542	121	101	125	5	78	0.23	42	20	38	33	124	160	131	19%	21%	97	9%	58%	27	56%	22%	26.4	216	$32
16	NYM	543	72	31	86	3	280	29	280	354	530	120	146	112	9	77	0.47	37	21	41	30	123	145	137	20%	19%	73	3%	75%	24	58%	17%	25.9	197	$20
17	NYM	321	46	17	42	0	292	17	264	352	540	120	120	117	8	79	0.43	34	16	50	32	135	134	159	15%	15%	93	1%	0%	16	63%	19%	11.8	212	$10
18	NYM	157	20	9	29	3	262	9	223	325	496	114	87	120	8	65	0.26	30	17	53	34	79	157	128	18%	18%	75	9%	100%	9	67%	22%	4.5	83	$5
19																																			
1st Half																																			
2nd Half																																			
20	Proj	315	44	18	52	3	279		253	340	524	116	113	116	8	74	0.34	35	19	46	32	112	131	138	18%		87	5%	80%				12.8	147	$14

Chapman,Matt

Age: 27 **Bats:** R **Pos:** 3B | **Ht:** 6' 0" **Wt:** 220

Health A | **PT/Exp** A | **Consist** C | **LIMA Plan** B | **Rand Var** +1 | **MM** 4135

Three signs of a breakout... (1) Plate skills continue to grow; (2) xHR validates jump in homers; (3) xBA points to batting average rebound. Plus, Statcast loves him too; exit velo top 4% of league last two years, barrel % up nearly 50% from 2019. Acing grades of health, consistency support another jump. UP: 40 HR

Yr	Tm	PA	R	HR	RBI	SB	BA	xHR	xBA	OBP	SLG	OPS+	vL+	vR+	bb%	ct%	Eye	G	L	F	h%	HctX	PX	xPX	HR/F	xHR/F	Spd	SBO	SB%	#Wk	DOM	DIS	RAR	BPX	R$
15																																			
16	a/a	570	77	27	80	6	210			287	434	98			10	64	0.30				27		156				103	10%	57%					97	$9
17	OAK *	520	63	25	64	4	228	15	233	305	469	104	104	104	10	65	0.32	34	16	51	29	95	159	134	14%	15%	108	11%	34%	16	56%	25%	-5.8	130	$8
18	OAK	616	100	24	68	1	278	23	266	356	508	120	113	122	9	73	0.40	40	20	39	34	117	148	114	15%	15%	114	2%	33%	26	50%	23%	28.2	223	$20
19	OAK	670	102	36	91	1	249	37	261	342	506	113	111	113	11	75	0.50	41	15	43	27	117	137	107	19%	20%	98	1%	50%	28	64%	25%	11.2	230	$18
1st Half		366	58	21	52	0	272	21	282	358	553	122	122	122	11	78	0.57	44	16	40	29	124	142	101	21%	21%	105	1%	0%	16	75%	19%	14.0	304	$24
2nd Half		304	44	15	39	1	221	16	236	322	449	102	101	102	11	71	0.43	37	15	48	25	109	130	115	17%	18%	88	2%	100%	12	50%	33%	-5.6	137	$11
20	Proj	665	100	37	101	1	262		254	347	526	117	114	118	10	71	0.40	39	16	45	31	113	148	115	20%		101	2%	42%				26.2	173	$25

Chavis,Michael

Age: 24 **Bats:** R **Pos:** 1B 2B | **Ht:** 5' 10" **Wt:** 216

Health B | **PT/Exp** D | **Consist** B | **LIMA Plan** C+ | **Rand Var** -2 | **MM** 4115

18-58-.254 in 382 PA at BOS. Pop from high minors converted well to majors—or did it? xHR tells us not so fast. And with growing holes in swing, we can't ignore that xBA. Late shoulder sprain to blame for 2nd half fade, but warts were spreading before that. A keeper hold, but likely overvalued in redraft leagues. DN: more AAA time

Yr	Tm	PA	R	HR	RBI	SB	BA	xHR	xBA	OBP	SLG	OPS+	vL+	vR+	bb%	ct%	Eye	G	L	F	h%	HctX	PX	xPX	HR/F	xHR/F	Spd	SBO	SB%	#Wk	DOM	DIS	RAR	BPX	R$
15																																			
16																																			
17	aa	264	32	11	32	1	239			287	450	99			6	77	0.28				27		128				83	2%	100%					145	$3
18	a/a	166	26	6	20	2	279			327	468	110			7	68	0.23				37		134				94	9%	69%					73	$4
19	BOS *	458	55	24	67	2	251	17	228	312	459	102	97	103	8	64	0.25	45	20	35	33	75	123	90	23%	22%	88	3%	67%	18	22%	61%	1.1	0	$11
1st Half		318	42	17	49	2	257	13	232	327	473	107	90	112	9	65	0.29	44	20	36	33	76	124	90	25%	24%	99	4%	67%	12	33%	50%	5.1	30	$17
2nd Half		141	13	6	18	0	238	4	213	280	429	94	108	75	6	63	0.16	47	18	35	33	73	121	88	17%	17%	79	0%	0%	6	0%	83%	-2.5	-56	-$2
20	Proj	490	61	22	62	3	241		236	301	442	100	109	94	7	67	0.22	46	19	35	31	74	123	89	21%		78	4%	69%				-2.8	-1	$13

Chirinos,Robinson

Age: 36 **Bats:** R **Pos:** CA | **Ht:** 6' 1" **Wt:** 210

Health B | **PT/Exp** C | **Consist** B | **LIMA Plan** C | **Rand Var** 0 | **MM** 4213

Even during these HR-happy times, there's value in predictability—especially when it comes to backstops. Here, high-teens homers is cemented in profile. While that BA might keep some away, the average CA hit .236 BA in 2019 (but in OBP leagues, he was the #10 ranked catcher). Sore shoulder likely behind 2nd half drop, so don't overreact to it.

Yr	Tm	PA	R	HR	RBI	SB	BA	xHR	xBA	OBP	SLG	OPS+	vL+	vR+	bb%	ct%	Eye	G	L	F	h%	HctX	PX	xPX	HR/F	xHR/F	Spd	SBO	SB%	#Wk	DOM	DIS	RAR	BPX	R$
15	TEX	273	33	10	34	0	232	11	253	325	438	106	117	98	10	73	0.45	35	19	45	27	89	145	133	13%	14%	86	0%	0%	19	53%	26%	5.8	157	$3
16	TEX *	191	21	9	20	0	206	7	240	271	432	96	111	106	8	69	0.29	40	14	45	24	111	155	156	19%	15%	69	3%	0%	19	42%	47%	-1.1	106	$0
17	TEX	309	46	17	38	1	255	16	246	360	506	116	148	102	11	70	0.43	40	14	46	30	100	150	124	20%	19%	103	1%	100%	26	50%	38%	13.6	167	$7
18	TEX	426	48	18	65	2	222	19	210	338	419	105	106	104	11	61	0.32	30	21	49	31	99	142	151	17%	18%	92	2%	100%	27	37%	48%	9.9	30	$8
19	HOU	437	57	17	58	1	238	16	241	347	443	105	119	99	12	66	0.41	35	26	40	31	90	128	109	18%	17%	92	3%	33%	27	37%	48%	13.2	70	$8
1st Half		250	36	12	39	0	236	10	239	371	477	113	120	111	16	65	0.54	33	21	46	30	88	148	134	20%	16%	86	3%	0%	15	33%	40%	9.0	144	$11
2nd Half		187	21	5	19	1	240	5	245	316	401	95	120	86	8	66	0.25	38	31	32	33	92	104	78	14%	14%	99	3%	100%	12	42%	58%	0.3	-15	$4
20	Proj	420	55	18	57	1	235		231	338	438	104	119	99	11	66	0.35	35	22	42	31	95	126	121	17%		94	2%	62%				13.8	23	$11

Choi,Ji-Man

Age: 29 **Bats:** L **Pos:** 1B | **Ht:** 6' 1" **Wt:** 250

Health A | **PT/Exp** C | **Consist** A | **LIMA Plan** C+ | **Rand Var** +2 | **MM** 4133

On surface, a steady mid-range contributor. Three reasons why there's more upside here... (1) HR/PA spike in 2nd half supported by huge xPX jump; (2) another year of ct% improvement; (3) xBA headed in right direction. Yeah, you still can't play him against lefties, but with 400 PA vR... UP: .270 BA, 25 HR

Yr	Tm	PA	R	HR	RBI	SB	BA	xHR	xBA	OBP	SLG	OPS+	vL+	vR+	bb%	ct%	Eye	G	L	F	h%	HctX	PX	xPX	HR/F	xHR/F	Spd	SBO	SB%	#Wk	DOM	DIS	RAR	BPX	R$
15	aaa	64	5	1	11	0	239			318	330	90			10	70	0.39				33		79				87	7%	0%					-19	-$1
16	LAA *	339	32	9	35	5	240	4	247	326	392	98	34	83	11	77	0.55	49	16	34	29	91	99	117	17%	14%	62	15%	39%	18	33%	50%	-8.3	86	$5
17	NYY *	339	37	17	63	3	254	2	230	330	496	111	0	161	10	65	0.32	64	0	36	34	119	167	178	50%	50%	50	5%	68%	3	67%	33%	1.6	88	$9
18	2 TM *	458	46	15	61	3	250	12	245	349	434	108	71	125	13	70	0.51	43	21	35	32	113	125	116	21%	25%	58	2%	100%	17	65%	24%	9.0	87	$10
19	TAM	487	54	19	63	2	261	22	259	363	459	109	82	116	13	74	0.59	42	24	35	31	109	107	120	18%	21%	77	4%	40%	27	37%	48%	8.0	119	$11
1st Half		271	27	9	31	1	261	10	253	347	423	103	75	109	11	76	0.52	46	22	31	31	103	85	86	16%	18%	83	6%	25%	14	29%	50%	-2.7	78	$9
2nd Half		216	27	10	32	1	261	12	265	384	506	117	91	125	17	70	0.67	35	26	39	32	117	139	168	20%	24%	72	2%	100%	13	46%	46%	8.0	185	$13
20	Proj	420	46	20	65	3	260		259	361	492	115	84	119	13	71	0.53	41	22	37	31	109	131	126	21%		66	5%	57%				15.5	131	$14

Choo,Shin-Soo

Age: 37 **Bats:** L **Pos:** DH RF LF | **Ht:** 5' 11" **Wt:** 210

Health C | **PT/Exp** A | **Consist** B | **LIMA Plan** B | **Rand Var** -1 | **MM** 3335

He's becoming the gold standard of consistency in his twilight years. With three 600+ PA seasons in last four, expect more of same, even as he gets closer to 40. The bonus in 2019 were those steals, but we can't expect him to hold Spd jump in late-30s, though SB acumen says he'll still give you a handful. A $20 lock.

Yr	Tm	PA	R	HR	RBI	SB	BA	xHR	xBA	OBP	SLG	OPS+	vL+	vR+	bb%	ct%	Eye	G	L	F	h%	HctX	PX	xPX	HR/F	xHR/F	Spd	SBO	SB%	#Wk	DOM	DIS	RAR	BPX	R$
15	TEX	653	94	22	82	4	276	24	267	375	463	117	98	126	12	74	0.52	51	21	28	34	104	130	122	19%	21%	85	3%	67%	27	48%	33%	6.9	132	$21
16	TEX *	244	28	8	21	7	251	9	250	340	403	101	137	89	11	74	0.51	47	22	31	31	129	96	127	18%	23%	74	19%	55%	13	23%	62%	-7.0	54	$6
17	TEX	636	96	22	78	12	261	25	268	357	423	105	100	104	12	75	0.57	49	25	26	31	110	92	107	20%	23%	81	9%	80%	26	35%	38%	4.9	76	$19
18	TEX	665	83	21	62	6	264	32	254	377	434	112	89	122	14	72	0.59	50	22	28	33	112	110	124	19%	28%	84	4%	86%	28	39%	39%	17.3	103	$18
19	TEX	660	93	24	61	15	265	28	257	371	455	110	89	118	12	71	0.47	49	22	29	33	110	110	106	21%	24%	104	9%	94%	28	36%	39%	7.6	104	$21
1st Half		344	53	12	34	6	278	14	269	378	481	115	78	127	11	72	0.46	47	24	29	35	118	118	110	20%	23%	115	8%	86%	15	47%	33%	7.8	156	$22
2nd Half		316	40	12	27	9	250	14	241	364	425	104	97	108	13	69	0.48	51	20	29	32	101	101	101	22%	26%	84	11%	100%	13	23%	46%	-0.1	37	$19
20	Proj	595	83	21	60	12	262		254	368	440	109	94	114	13	72	0.51	50	22	28	33	110	102	112	20%		91	8%	86%				11.9	84	$21

STEPHEN NICKRAND

Collins,Zack

Age: 25 Bats: L Pos: DH | Ht: 6' 3" Wt: 220

Health A | PT/Exp D | Consist C | LIMA Plan D | Rand Var -1 | MM 3103

3-12-.186 in 102 PA at CHW. Plus power held firm in jump to AAA, where he had a 1.022 OPS vR. The pop carried over in small MLB sample, which along with patience, gives him a hint of appeal in leagues where he's catcher eligible. But given history of poor defense and ct%, future may be as a 1B/DH who is a major BA drag.

Yr Tm	PA	R	HR	RBI	SB	BA	xHR	xBA	OBP	SLG	OPS+	vL+	vR+	bb%	ct%	Eye	G	L	F	h%	HctX	PX	xPX	HR/F	xHR/F	Spd	SBO	SB%	#Wk	DOM	DIS	RAR	BPX	R$
15																																		
16																																		
17 aa	45	7	2	5	0	229			421	465	119			25	64	0.93				29		159				103	0%	0%					203	-$1
18 aa	515	54	15	63	5	218			366	382	103			19	58	0.55				34		134				88	3%	100%					10	$8
19 CHW *	443	54	19	70	0	230	5	216	339	438	103	49	100	14	59	0.40	32	23	45	33	83	139	171	14%	24%	98	0%	0%	9	11%	78%	14.9	33	$7
1st Half	210	27	8	34	0	201	1	197	315	392	94	0	68	14	53	0.35	63	13	25	32	46	142	57	50%	50%	92	0%	0%	3	0%	67%	-0.3	-67	$3
2nd Half	233	27	10	37	0	257	4	237	360	479	111	56	108	14	66	0.47	26	26	49	34	99	136	194	11%	21%	106	0%	0%	6	17%	83%	11.3	122	$12
20 Proj	**280**	**32**	**7**	**41**	**1**	**214**		**196**	**346**	**366**	**96**	**58**	**109**	**16**	**59**	**0.46**	**36**	**22**	**43**	**33**	**89**	**109**	**175**	**12%**		**106**	**3%**	**53%**				**-5.1**	**-92**	**$2**

Conforto,Michael

Age: 27 Bats: L Pos: RF CF | Ht: 6' 1" Wt: 215

Health B | PT/Exp A | Consist C | LIMA Plan B | Rand Var +1 | MM 4235

Power metrics were nearly a carbon copy of 2018, and took positive steps elsewhere: ct% inched upward, GB% snapped back to normal, resulting in BA and HR improvements that had full support from xBA and xHR. Most signs point to a similar encore, minus a few SB, while last year's UP: 40 HR remains firmly in play.

Yr Tm	PA	R	HR	RBI	SB	BA	xHR	xBA	OBP	SLG	OPS+	vL+	vR+	bb%	ct%	Eye	G	L	F	h%	HctX	PX	xPX	HR/F	xHR/F	Spd	SBO	SB%	#Wk	DOM	DIS	RAR	BPX	R$
15 NYM *	387	48	13	48	1	277	11	274	346	479	115	66	120	10	77	0.47	39	23	39	32	137	137	157	17%	21%	95	2%	46%	12	83%	17%	14.7	186	$11
16 NYM *	486	59	19	61	3	257	14	250	329	459	107	40	107	9	74	0.41	36	19	45	31	120	129	153	12%	14%	71	6%	50%	22	36%	41%	5.2	120	$11
17 NYM	440	72	27	68	2	279	24	276	384	555	126	97	134	13	70	0.50	38	24	38	33	117	166	141	27%	24%	86	2%	100%	20	50%	20%	24.5	197	$16
18 NYM	638	78	28	82	3	243	26	245	350	448	110	112	109	13	71	0.53	44	20	37	29	93	128	130	20%	18%	85	4%	43%	27	41%	33%	13.7	130	$16
19 NYM	648	90	33	92	7	257	34	263	363	494	114	91	123	13	73	0.56	36	24	40	29	92	128	120	20%	21%	86	6%	78%	27	48%	30%	28.0	178	$20
1st Half	327	47	16	41	5	247	17	262	364	480	113	88	123	15	73	0.63	34	25	42	28	85	127	122	19%	20%	87	6%	100%	14	43%	21%	12.2	189	$18
2nd Half	321	43	17	51	2	266	17	264	361	507	115	95	124	12	73	0.50	38	23	38	31	99	129	117	22%	22%	91	5%	50%	13	54%	38%	14.0	174	$22
20 Proj	**630**	**88**	**32**	**90**	**5**	**260**		**258**	**362**	**493**	**115**	**97**	**121**	**13**	**72**	**0.53**	**39**	**22**	**39**	**30**	**100**	**129**	**129**	**21%**		**87**	**4%**	**65%**				**23.5**	**139**	**$23**

Contreras,Willson

Age: 28 Bats: R Pos: CA | Ht: 6' 1" Wt: 210

Health B | PT/Exp B | Consist D | LIMA Plan B | Rand Var -1 | MM 4245

Quickly put 2018 dud in the rearview with blistering start, but 2nd half injuries (foot, hamstring) and h% dip slowed him down. Consistently produces both vL and vR, while return of lofty HR/F, impressive PX/xPX, and rising FB% all suggest 30 HR is within reach. Should be safe to pay for repeat, which still leaves room for profit.

Yr Tm	PA	R	HR	RBI	SB	BA	xHR	xBA	OBP	SLG	OPS+	vL+	vR+	bb%	ct%	Eye	G	L	F	h%	HctX	PX	xPX	HR/F	xHR/F	Spd	SBO	SB%	#Wk	DOM	DIS	RAR	BPX	R$
15 aa	500	56	7	59	3	297			361	422	109			9	84	0.65				34		85				94	5%	41%					146	$15
16 CHC *	509	63	19	67	5	290	11	276	357	488	115	115	112	9	77	0.45	54	18	28	34	101	121	105	24%	22%	110	9%	43%	17	41%	29%	20.2	166	$18
17 CHC	428	50	21	74	5	276	19	268	356	499	115	122	109	11	74	0.46	53	17	29	32	106	131	101	26%	23%	78	8%	56%	22	45%	27%	21.4	142	$14
18 CHC	544	50	10	54	4	249	15	242	339	390	101	114	96	10	74	0.44	52	17	31	31	79	92	71	9%	14%	117	4%	80%	28	32%	46%	11.1	93	$9
19 CHC	409	57	24	64	1	272	21	263	355	533	118	134	113	9	72	0.37	50	16	34	32	92	140	128	27%	24%	106	3%	33%	23	48%	17%	19.8	189	$13
1st Half	279	38	17	48	1	285	15	260	380	556	125	133	123	11	69	0.41	49	16	35	34	86	150	125	29%	26%	107	4%	33%	15	60%	13%	20.7	200	$19
2nd Half	130	19	7	16	0	248	6	268	300	488	104	141	96	6	76	0.28	52	15	33	27	103	122	135	23%	20%	105	0%	0%	8	25%	25%	3.2	178	$1
20 Proj	**525**	**65**	**27**	**72**	**3**	**268**		**265**	**351**	**506**	**115**	**131**	**110**	**10**	**74**	**0.43**	**51**	**17**	**33**	**31**	**94**	**127**	**109**	**23%**		**105**	**4%**	**54%**				**34.7**	**151**	**$19**

Cooper,Garrett

Age: 29 Bats: R Pos: 1B RF | Ht: 6' 6" Wt: 230

Health F | PT/Exp D | Consist F | LIMA Plan C+ | Rand Var -5 | MM 3045

Recovered from two early IL stints to put together solid year, but a few reasons to be wary: h% fueled the high BA; ct%, xBA took turns for the worse in 2nd half; GB% stroke makes it tough to sustain power output even though xHR/F thinks there is a bit of headroom in HR/F. Bid on expectations around 2nd half times two and hope for profit.

Yr Tm	PA	R	HR	RBI	SB	BA	xHR	xBA	OBP	SLG	OPS+	vL+	vR+	bb%	ct%	Eye	G	L	F	h%	HctX	PX	xPX	HR/F	xHR/F	Spd	SBO	SB%	#Wk	DOM	DIS	RAR	BPX	R$
15 aa	35	3	0	4	0	504			591	623	169			17	92	2.65				55		71				112	0%	0%					257	$1
16 a/a	451	34	8	54	2	248			287	362	88			5	79	0.26				30		75				79	6%	40%					34	$5
17 NYY *	381	61	18	77	0	315	0	325	372	560	125	130	92	8	77	0.40	34	38	28	36	118	145	60	0%	0%	91	0%	0%	5	60%	40%	24.0	218	$17
18 MIA *	70	4	1	6	0	223	0	209	293	284	80	119	66	9	71	0.34	67	24	10	30	37	44	-27	0%	0%	88	0%	0%	5	20%	80%	-3.1	-113	-$2
19 MIA	421	52	15	50	0	281	18	255	344	446	105	84	113	8	71	0.30	52	25	23	36	100	93	93	24%	29%	101	0%	0%	21	24%	48%	-0.3	26	$10
1st Half	183	31	7	27	0	317	7	282	383	488	116	94	126	8	74	0.36	55	28	16	39	109	87	63	35%	35%	114	0%	0%	11	18%	45%	7.1	74	$12
2nd Half	238	21	8	23	0	253	11	230	315	415	96	76	104	8	69	0.26	50	21	29	33	94	98	118	19%	26%	94	0%	0%	10	30%	50%	-5.1	-4	$8
20 Proj	**455**	**59**	**18**	**68**	**0**	**275**		**273**	**337**	**468**	**108**	**87**	**116**	**8**	**74**	**0.32**	**52**	**24**	**24**	**33**	**100**	**108**	**96**	**24%**		**93**	**1%**	**33%**				**10.3**	**55**	**$16**

Cordell,Ryan

Age: 28 Bats: R Pos: RF | Ht: 6' 4" Wt: 195

Health A | PT/Exp F | Consist B | LIMA Plan D | Rand Var -2 | MM 2401

7-24-.221 with 3 SB in 247 PA at CHW. Couldn't take advantage of extended MLB opportunity, as lack of power and contact skills predictably led to poor results. Plus speed is his only asset, but history of low OBP and SB% suggest he's unlikely to capitalize on it. Look elsewhere for your end game flyer.

Yr Tm	PA	R	HR	RBI	SB	BA	xHR	xBA	OBP	SLG	OPS+	vL+	vR+	bb%	ct%	Eye	G	L	F	h%	HctX	PX	xPX	HR/F	xHR/F	Spd	SBO	SB%	#Wk	DOM	DIS	RAR	BPX	R$
15 aa	230	20	4	14	8	188			222	280	70			4	64	0.12				27		67				133	21%	87%					-105	-$1
16 aa	432	58	16	58	10	241			289	433	98			6	74	0.26				29		118				111	17%	69%					109	$11
17 aaa	278	33	8	30	6	232			279	402	91			6	70	0.22				30		108				115	21%	56%					45	$4
18 CHW *	238	17	5	25	6	192	1	169	227	304	74	88	27	4	68	0.14	29	13	58	26	94	78	150	7%	7%	114	21%	71%	5	20%	60%	-13.5	-63	$0
19 CHW *	301	28	8	28	4	221	7	199	280	358	85	74	94	7	66	0.24	38	17	45	30	70	86	81	11%	11%	129	10%	63%	28	39%	46%	-10.4	-37	$2
1st Half	181	16	4	16	2	231	4	201	278	353	84	71	90	6	63	0.18	40	22	39	34	65	82	90	9%	13%	133	5%	100%	15	40%	53%	-5.3	-100	$1
2nd Half	120	11	4	12	2	205	4	197	283	366	85	79	103	10	71	0.38	35	11	53	25	77	92	68	12%	12%	116	17%	44%	13	38%	38%	-4.3	52	$3
20 Proj	**210**	**20**	**6**	**22**	**4**	**212**		**213**	**263**	**363**	**84**	**75**	**92**	**6**	**68**	**0.19**	**40**	**18**	**41**	**28**	**72**	**91**	**77**	**11%**		**136**	**17%**	**65%**				**-9.9**	**-48**	**$4**

Cordero,Franchy

Age: 25 Bats: L Pos: CF | Ht: 6' 3" Wt: 175

Health F | PT/Exp F | Consist B | LIMA Plan D | Rand Var +3 | MM 4521

0-2-.333 in 20 PA at SD. More elbow issues put him on the shelf in April, and before he could make it back, June quad injury ended his season. Power/speed combo still intriguing, so buying low could pay dividends if news is positive this spring. But with more career IL days than PA in majors, you better have a backup plan.

Yr Tm	PA	R	HR	RBI	SB	BA	xHR	xBA	OBP	SLG	OPS+	vL+	vR+	bb%	ct%	Eye	G	L	F	h%	HctX	PX	xPX	HR/F	xHR/F	Spd	SBO	SB%	#Wk	DOM	DIS	RAR	BPX	R$
15																																		
16 a/a	273	25	5	15	9	264			305	387	94			6	70	0.20				36		76				147	24%	59%					0	$6
17 SD *	504	62	14	53	11	264	5	229	295	453	100	81	95	4	63	0.12	48	19	33	39	99	123	125	19%	31%	188	17%	67%	7	29%	57%	-10.4	58	$13
18 SD *	183	21	8	20	7	234	9	227	305	421	100	81	112	9	60	0.25	46	25	29	34	107	134	144	29%	38%	123	22%	78%	8	25%	63%	-1.6	17	$4
19 SD *	69	7	2	6	1	209	0	196	287	362	86	0	113	10	52	0.23	25	38	38	36	101	118	276	0%	0%	142	7%	100%	2	0%	100%	-3.2	-115	-$2
1st Half	69	7	2	6	1	209	0	196	287	362	87	0	114	10	52	0.23	25	38	38	36	101	118	276	0%	0%	141	7%	100%	2	0%	100%	-3.3	-119	-$2
2nd Half																																		
20 Proj	**210**	**23**	**11**	**23**	**4**	**243**		**245**	**297**	**485**	**105**	**86**	**111**	**7**	**63**	**0.21**	**47**	**23**	**31**	**33**	**104**	**145**	**136**	**28%**		**155**	**13%**	**79%**				**5.5**	**67**	**$7**

Correa,Carlos

Age: 25 Bats: R Pos: SS | Ht: 6' 4" Wt: 215

Health F | PT/Exp C | Consist F | LIMA Plan C+ | Rand Var -1 | MM 4345

21-59-.279 in 321 PA at HOU. Produced at high level when on the field, but with more injuries came further PA erosion. FB% spike in 2nd half boosted power numbers, but may have played role in h% collapse. He's young and very good, but since SB are gone and back woes aren't, both the massive ceiling and safe floor are lacking.

Yr Tm	PA	R	HR	RBI	SB	BA	xHR	xBA	OBP	SLG	OPS+	vL+	vR+	bb%	ct%	Eye	G	L	F	h%	HctX	PX	xPX	HR/F	xHR/F	Spd	SBO	SB%	#Wk	DOM	DIS	RAR	BPX	R$
15 HOU *	668	85	30	101	28	287	18	302	352	517	121	124	115	9	80	0.50	49	22	29	32	115	146	103	24%	20%	91	21%	84%	18	67%	6%	37.4	224	$36
16 HOU	660	76	20	96	13	274	24	275	361	451	110	99	112	11	76	0.54	50	22	27	33	115	113	100	17%	20%	109	9%	81%	26	46%	31%	22.9	149	$22
17 HOU *	506	84	24	88	2	312	22	283	386	535	123	143	120	11	78	0.55	48	20	32	35	125	125	108	23%	21%	94	2%	67%	20	60%	20%	36.1	194	$23
18 HOU	468	60	15	65	3	239	15	241	323	405	101	111	97	11	72	0.48	44	20	36	29	77	107	83	14%	14%	95	3%	100%	22	41%	36%	4.7	93	$10
19 HOU *	344	43	21	60	1	277	19	274	357	554	121	125	122	11	73	0.46	39	21	40	31	114	149	132	26%	23%	96	1%	100%	15	73%	7%	15.9	237	$11
1st Half	214	26	11	35	1	295	12	280	360	547	121	140	114	10	73	0.39	42	24	34	35	119	140	126	23%	26%	108	2%	100%	9	67%	0%	11.8	215	$13
2nd Half	130	17	10	25	0	248	7	259	348	566	121	84	136	13	73	0.57	33	15	52	25	102	165	146	29%	20%	85	0%	0%	6	83%	17%	5.7	289	$7
20 Proj	**525**	**71**	**28**	**89**	**3**	**269**		**265**	**351**	**511**	**116**	**115**	**115**	**11**	**74**	**0.49**	**43**	**20**	**37**	**31**	**110**	**130**	**116**	**22%**		**93**	**3%**	**87%**				**29.0**	**162**	**$21**

BRIAN RUDD

Crawford,Brandon

Age: 33 Bats: L Pos: SS	Health	A	LIMA Plan	C
Ht: 6' 2" Wt: 227	PT/Exp	A	Rand Var	+3
	Consist	B	MM	1135

Usually steady double-digit R$ tumbled. A few reasons why it might not return: 1) FB% decline, even with a decent xPX, limits HR; 2) BPX continues to freefall; 3) DIS% says he has a lot of unproductive weeks. While xBA, career-low h% vouch for a BA rebound, hope for much more at this age is dwindling.

Yr	Tm	PA	R	HR	RBI	SB	BA	xHR	xBA	OBP	SLG	OPS+	vL+	vR+	bb%	ct%	Eye	G	L	F	h%	HctX	PX	xPX	HR/F	xHR/F	Spd	SBO	SB%	#Wk	DOM	DIS	RAR	BPX	R$
15	SF	561	65	21	84	6	256	27	274	321	462	109	99	111	7	77	0.33	48	19	34	30	111	137	136	16%	21%	80	9%	60%	27	48%	19%	15.4	151	$16
16	SF	623	67	12	84	7	275	17	257	342	430	105	96	107	9	79	0.50	43	21	36	33	113	92	114	8%	11%	117	4%	100%	27	37%	30%	10.2	131	$16
17	SF	570	58	14	77	3	253	18	255	305	403	95	88	96	7	78	0.37	46	19	34	30	103	93	102	10%	13%	66	6%	38%	26	27%	35%	-6.2	73	$10
18	SF	594	63	14	54	4	254	13	258	325	394	99	106	95	8	77	0.41	44	25	31	31	103	88	91	11%	10%	78	6%	44%	28	29%	54%	5.3	70	$11
19	SF	560	58	11	59	3	228	16	253	304	350	87	78	90	9	77	0.45	48	23	28	28	104	69	106	10%	15%	79	4%	60%	28	25%	46%	-19.6	22	$5
1st Half		294	26	5	27	2	223	7	250	289	343	85	82	86	9	74	0.37	48	24	28	28	107	73	114	9%	13%	79	5%	67%	15	20%	47%	-13.8	-4	$2
2nd Half		266	32	6	32	1	234	8	255	320	357	89	74	95	11	79	0.57	48	23	29	27	101	64	98	11%	15%	83	3%	50%	13	31%	46%	-8.8	59	$9
20	**Proj**	**560**	**61**	**13**	**64**	**3**	**243**		**254**	**315**	**379**	**93**	**89**	**94**	**9**	**77**	**0.44**	**46**	**23**	**31**	**29**	**104**	**76**	**103**	**11%**		**80**	**5%**	**52%**				**-3.3**	**40**	**$9**

Crawford,J.P.

Age: 25 Bats: L Pos: SS	Health	C	LIMA Plan	B
Ht: 6' 2" Wt: 180	PT/Exp	D	Rand Var	0
	Consist	A	MM	1415

7-46-.226 in 396 PA at SEA. The ct% rebound was an encouraging sign, albeit with pedestrian results. Weak contact, GB% stroke point to a bleak HR outlook, which xHR confirms, while SBO tempers stolen base expectations. Defense, plate patience should keep him in the lineup vR, but his bat needs work.

Yr	Tm	PA	R	HR	RBI	SB	BA	xHR	xBA	OBP	SLG	OPS+	vL+	vR+	bb%	ct%	Eye	G	L	F	h%	HctX	PX	xPX	HR/F	xHR/F	Spd	SBO	SB%	#Wk	DOM	DIS	RAR	BPX	R$
15	aa	391	43	5	27	6	240			318	363	95			10	86	0.80				27		77				123	8%	73%					173	$4
16	a/a	533	54	6	37	10	226			315	306	84			12	81	0.68				27		51				97	12%	58%					54	$5
17	PHI *	631	75	14	62	5	223	0	240	329	364	93	50	104	14	76	0.66	31	27	43	27	44	81	20	0%	0%	142	6%	56%	5	20%	60%	-10.8	124	$5
18	PHI *	199	22	4	18	3	220	3	220	289	374	92	69	103	9	68	0.30	38	23	39	30	64	102	74	10%	10%	137	7%	100%	12	33%	50%	-1.0	40	$1
19	SEA *	527	58	9	57	7	236	5	242	321	371	92	58	105	11	75	0.51	45	20	35	29	74	79	69	8%	5%	119	8%	71%	20	35%	30%	-16.3	89	$8
1st Half		273	32	5	33	3	288	3	261	366	439	108	91	124	11	74	0.47	35	31	34	37	92	92	91	9%	9%	128	7%	62%	8	25%	13%	4.9	115	$12
2nd Half		254	26	4	24	4	178	2	230	275	297	75	47	92	11	77	0.56	50	15	35	21	64	66	56	7%	3%	121	10%	80%	12	42%	42%	-17.2	81	$3
20	**Proj**	**539**	**61**	**10**	**55**	**7**	**233**		**235**	**324**	**368**	**93**	**59**	**104**	**11**	**74**	**0.47**	**40**	**23**	**38**	**29**	**67**	**77**	**64**	**7%**		**129**	**8%**	**75%**				**-3.8**	**58**	**$11**

Cron,C.J.

Age: 30 Bats: R Pos: 1B	Health	B	LIMA Plan	B
Ht: 6' 4" Wt: 235	PT/Exp	B	Rand Var	+1
	Consist	B	MM	4035

Sustained power by crushing lefties, as two IL stints (thumb) were all that prevented 2018 repeat. Hard-hit skills support current HR pace, while xHR/F opens the door for even more. He's not selling out for it either, as contact gains, steady xBA suggest he can mash without tanking your batting average.

Yr	Tm	PA	R	HR	RBI	SB	BA	xHR	xBA	OBP	SLG	OPS+	vL+	vR+	bb%	ct%	Eye	G	L	F	h%	HctX	PX	xPX	HR/F	xHR/F	Spd	SBO	SB%	#Wk	DOM	DIS	RAR	BPX	R$
15	LAA *	499	47	20	66	3	260	18	263	290	448	103	93	106	4	79	0.20	45	18	37	29	96	120	107	14%	16%	79	4%	75%	25	44%	32%	-6.4	122	$13
16	LAA	443	51	16	69	2	278	17	270	325	467	108	91	110	5	82	0.32	41	20	39	31	107	111	106	12%	13%	85	5%	40%	22	41%	32%	2.8	151	$13
17	LAA *	457	46	19	71	4	239	17	240	284	419	94	105	96	6	73	0.23	33	23	45	29	105	107	129	15%	15%	77	6%	65%	23	26%	39%	-18.1	39	$8
18	TAM	560	68	30	74	1	253	34	260	323	493	113	129	105	7	71	0.26	40	21	39	30	104	151	115	21%	24%	84	3%	33%	28	50%	29%	9.3	150	$16
19	MIN	499	51	25	78	0	253	32	263	311	469	104	133	91	6	77	0.27	42	22	36	28	109	113	114	20%	25%	59	0%	0%	26	50%	38%	-1.9	104	$11
1st Half		316	34	17	52	0	271	19	282	329	503	111	140	101	7	78	0.34	39	25	36	29	108	118	117	21%	23%	65	0%	0%	15	60%	33%	3.9	159	$17
2nd Half		183	17	8	26	0	224	13	231	279	412	91	126	75	4	74	0.18	47	16	37	26	110	103	109	17%	28%	63	0%	0%	11	36%	45%	-8.6	22	$1
20	**Proj**	**525**	**61**	**30**	**79**	**1**	**253**		**261**	**310**	**490**	**108**	**129**	**98**	**6**	**74**	**0.23**	**41**	**20**	**38**	**28**	**107**	**126**	**115**	**21%**		**71**	**2%**	**53%**				**5.0**	**87**	**$17**

Cron,Kevin

Age: 27 Bats: R Pos: 1B	Health	A	LIMA Plan	D+
Ht: 6' 5" Wt: 250	PT/Exp	C	Rand Var	+3
	Consist	C	MM	4043

6-16-.211 in 78 PA at ARI. Showed off power with Pacific Coast League-leading 38 HR, and PX argues it wasn't just the new ball. Cut down on strikeouts in AAA with major bb% gains, but a 61% ct% in majors says he still carries BA risk. For now, he's just another cheap power source in reserve rounds.

Yr	Tm	PA	R	HR	RBI	SB	BA	xHR	xBA	OBP	SLG	OPS+	vL+	vR+	bb%	ct%	Eye	G	L	F	h%	HctX	PX	xPX	HR/F	xHR/F	Spd	SBO	SB%	#Wk	DOM	DIS	RAR	BPX	R$
15																																			
16	aa	494	53	24	77	3	212			258	413	91			6	69	0.20				25		131				83	5%	71%					54	$6
17	aa	561	62	21	75	1	259			320	448	103			8	71	0.30				33		122				77	1%	100%					70	$12
18	aaa	414	35	12	59	1	235			276	389	92			5	69	0.18				31		108				81	1%	100%					0	$6
19	ARI *	421	61	28	79	1	243	6	273	319	524	112	91	110	10	67	0.34	34	30	36	28	106	160	151	38%	38%	72	5%	15%	13	23%	31%	0.3	152	$13
1st Half		274	41	19	56	1	245	4	302	325	548	117	73	120	11	70	0.40	27	37	37	27	122	170	155	36%	36%	63	3%	38%	6	33%	33%	5.6	219	$18
2nd Half		147	20	9	23	0	241	2	225	309	482	104	113	87	9	62	0.26	50	14	36	31	76	141	142	40%	40%	110	8%	0%	7	14%	29%	-2.3	48	$3
20	**Proj**	**350**	**40**	**18**	**52**	**1**	**241**		**267**	**297**	**464**	**102**	**76**	**109**	**8**	**68**	**0.27**	**27**	**37**	**37**	**30**	**110**	**130**	**140**	**23%**		**74**	**4%**	**30%**				**0.5**	**24**	**$10**

Cruz,Nelson

Age: 40 Bats: R Pos: DH	Health	A	LIMA Plan	B
Ht: 6' 2" Wt: 230	PT/Exp	A	Rand Var	-5
	Consist	D	MM	4045

Scoffed at aging questions with 40+ HR despite two-wrist related IL trips. Even with ct% drop and inflated h%, plethora of hard-hit balls and favorable xBA provide safe BA floor. Career-high HR/F may regress, but elite xPX says not by much. Last call will be coming, but for now, order up another round of time-cultured power and enjoy.

Yr	Tm	PA	R	HR	RBI	SB	BA	xHR	xBA	OBP	SLG	OPS+	vL+	vR+	bb%	ct%	Eye	G	L	F	h%	HctX	PX	xPX	HR/F	xHR/F	Spd	SBO	SB%	#Wk	DOM	DIS	RAR	BPX	R$
15	SEA	655	90	44	93	3	302	40	277	369	566	130	153	119	9	72	0.36	46	20	34	35	113	169	137	30%	28%	87	3%	60%	26	50%	31%	33.1	189	$33
16	SEA	667	96	43	105	2	287	51	274	360	555	125	138	115	9	73	0.39	44	18	38	33	108	160	134	26%	31%	88	1%	100%	26	62%	23%	25.8	191	$27
17	SEA	645	91	39	119	1	288	43	268	375	549	124	111	125	11	75	0.50	40	18	42	32	123	146	150	22%	24%	60	1%	50%	27	52%	26%	36.0	176	$25
18	SEA	591	70	37	97	1	256	40	266	342	509	118	130	112	9	76	0.45	44	18	39	27	119	139	123	24%	26%	55	1%	100%	27	52%	37%	18.4	180	$20
19	MIN	520	81	41	108	0	311	44	281	392	639	137	157	130	11	71	0.43	40	20	40	35	129	177	156	31%	34%	72	1%	0%	24	58%	21%	46.7	263	$26
1st Half		247	35	16	46	0	284	21	269	372	572	126	135	123	11	67	0.38	37	24	39	35	128	170	162	29%	38%	82	0%	0%	13	54%	31%	13.0	196	$17
2nd Half		273	46	25	62	0	335	23	292	410	699	146	176	136	11	75	0.48	41	17	41	36	130	182	151	33%	31%	67	1%	0%	11	64%	9%	34.3	330	$34
20	**Proj**	**560**	**82**	**38**	**109**	**1**	**288**		**265**	**370**	**563**	**126**	**139**	**120**	**10**	**73**	**0.44**	**41**	**19**	**40**	**32**	**124**	**145**	**145**	**26%**		**68**	**1%**	**41%**				**36.2**	**155**	**$27**

Culberson,Charlie

Age: 31 Bats: R Pos: LF	Health	B	LIMA Plan	D
Ht: 6' 0" Wt: 200	PT/Exp	D	Rand Var	-5
	Consist	F	MM	2211

Fractured cheekbone (HBP) ended season in Sept. The results were forgettable, as xPX never bought into 2018's power spike, and inconsistent playing time cut into counting stats. Struggles vR (career 67% ct%, 87 PX) likely prevent everyday PA, while loss of multi-position eligibility cements waiver wire status.

Yr	Tm	PA	R	HR	RBI	SB	BA	xHR	xBA	OBP	SLG	OPS+	vL+	vR+	bb%	ct%	Eye	G	L	F	h%	HctX	PX	xPX	HR/F	xHR/F	Spd	SBO	SB%	#Wk	DOM	DIS	RAR	BPX	R$
15																																			
16	LA *	345	30	4	32	5	228	1	226	257	323	79	106	63	4	73	0.15	45	21	34	30	83	70	70	6%	6%	111	17%	47%	14	14%	43%	-23.5	-20	$2
17	LA *	416	27	3	24	5	194	0	203	231	256	65	57	72	5	77	0.21	56	11	33	24	70	39	-26	0%	0%	105	11%	58%	5	20%	20%	-40.4	-48	-$5
18	ATL	322	47	12	45	4	270	8	262	326	466	110	103	112	7	71	0.25	52	20	28	34	83	128	72	21%	14%	115	9%	67%	28	36%	39%	7.3	123	$10
19	ATL	144	14	5	20	0	259	4	229	294	437	97	112	86	4	67	0.14	42	22	36	35	93	101	90	15%	12%	148	3%	0%	25	40%	44%	-1.1	19	$0
1st Half		66	7	3	14	0	333	1	278	379	600	131	131	130	8	73	0.31	33	29	38	41	101	136	102	18%	6%	154	6%	0%	15	53%	27%	5.8	244	$1
2nd Half		78	7	2	6	0	200	3	181	221	307	70	98	51	1	63	0.04	50	15	35	29	86	68	78	13%	19%	106	0%	0%	10	20%	70%	-6.1	-219	$0
20	**Proj**	**210**	**22**	**7**	**26**	**1**	**246**		**237**	**286**	**414**	**94**	**101**	**88**	**5**	**70**	**0.16**	**46**	**21**	**33**	**32**	**88**	**96**	**80**	**15%**		**132**	**7%**	**45%**				**-4.1**	**-25**	**$5**

Cuthbert,Cheslor

Age: 27 Bats: R Pos: 1B 3B	Health	F	LIMA Plan	D
Ht: 6' 1" Wt: 210	PT/Exp	F	Rand Var	-2
	Consist	B	MM	1001

9-40-.246 in 330 PA at KC. Bloated h%, HR/F fueled 1st half that included May call-up, but fortunes reversed in 2nd half. Contact is the only average part of this skill set, but xBA says he won't find many hits (as seen in 0-for-40 Aug stretch!). With power skills on life support, MM score should keep him far from your roster.

Yr	Tm	PA	R	HR	RBI	SB	BA	xHR	xBA	OBP	SLG	OPS+	vL+	vR+	bb%	ct%	Eye	G	L	F	h%	HctX	PX	xPX	HR/F	xHR/F	Spd	SBO	SB%	#Wk	DOM	DIS	RAR	BPX	R$
15	KC *	477	51	9	50	4	247	0	263	300	371	94	88	91	7	83	0.46	46	22	32	28	49	81	38	8%	0%	99	6%	65%	8	25%	25%	-10.8	119	$7
16	KC *	611	60	17	67	2	276	6	252	324	428	102	111	94	7	80	0.36	48	17	35	32	101	92	74	9%	4%	107	2%	63%	23	39%	30%	1.0	120	$14
17	KC *	217	18	5	25	0	232	3	240	283	361	86	80	78	7	75	0.28	42	23	35	29	86	80	102	5%	8%	91	0%	0%	22	18%	64%	-8.9	15	$0
18	KC	117	11	3	7	0	194	3	194	282	301	81	99	69	9	78	0.48	48	11	41	22	88	60	41	9%	9%	82	4%	0%	8	25%	63%	-6.0	13	-$2
19	KC *	539	42	14	65	1	249	7	232	293	394	91	122	77	6	76	0.26	43	18	39	30	98	83	71	9%	7%	83	1%	100%	19	32%	42%	-16.4	33	$7
1st Half		317	28	9	40	1	270	2	238	310	434	99	139	97	5	73	0.22	48	17	35	34	72	98	32	15%	7%	95	1%	100%	6	17%	33%	-4.4	48	$12
2nd Half		222	14	5	25	0	218	5	223	275	335	80	115	66	6	80	0.34	40	19	41	25	114	63	89	7%	7%	77	0%	0%	13	38%	46%	-14.5	30	$0
20	**Proj**	**245**	**21**	**6**	**25**	**0**	**229**		**222**	**286**	**350**	**85**	**104**	**77**	**7**	**78**	**0.33**	**45**	**17**	**38**	**27**	**94**	**67**	**66**	**8%**		**85**	**2%**	**32%**				**-9.2**	**-34**	**$3**

BRANT CHESSER

D Arnaud,Travis

Age: 31 Bats: R Pos: CA 1B | Ht: 6' 2" Wt: 210

Health F | PT/Exp D | Consist B | LIMA Plan D+ | Rand Var -2 | MM 2023

Rehab from Tommy John surgery leaked into April; was released, signed, and traded in May; then surged with TAM (.263 BA, 16 HR in 365 PA). Power skills jibe with HR output and he's excellent vL, though xBA and h% baseline limit BA ceiling. Even if 2nd half skill growth doesn't stick, this profile plays well in two-catcher leagues.

Yr	Tm	PA	R	HR	RBI	SB	BA	xHR	xBA	OBP	SLG	OPS+	vL+	vR+	bb%	ct%	Eye	G	L	F	h%	HctX	PX	xPX	HR/F	xHR/F	Spd	SBO	SB%	#Wk	DOM	DIS	RAR	BPX	R$
15	NYM *	296	33	12	42	0	260	10	269	319	461	109	153	104	8	80	0.43	37	21	42	29	101	127	107	15%	13%	80	0%	0%	16	56%	19%	9.7	168	$7
16	NYM	276	27	4	15	0	247	5	217	307	323	86	61	91	7	80	0.38	52	17	31	29	105	47	85	6%	8%	90	0%	0%	19	11%	42%	-4.3	3	$1
17	NYM	376	39	16	57	0	244	12	263	293	443	99	119	90	6	83	0.39	42	17	41	25	109	105	114	13%	10%	74	0%	0%	24	50%	29%	2.1	161	$6
18	NYM	16	1	1	3	0	200	2	316	250	400	90	70	97	6	67	0.20	10	40	50	22	123	115	222	20%	40%	97	0%	0%	3	33%	67%	0.0	7	-$3
19	3 TM	391	52	16	69	0	251	15	248	312	433	99	116	88	8	76	0.38	41	21	39	29	109	97	100	15%	14%	70	1%	0%	25	28%	36%	9.9	74	$9
1st Half		138	18	5	19	0	206	7	230	261	365	84	90	79	7	74	0.27	41	19	40	24	89	86	100	13%	18%	74	4%	0%	12	33%	50%	-4.2	7	-$5
2nd Half		253	34	11	50	0	276	8	257	340	471	107	133	92	9	77	0.44	41	21	38	31	120	102	100	16%	12%	79	0%	0%	13	23%	23%	10.9	126	$16
20	**Proj**	**350**	**42**	**15**	**53**	**0**	**248**		**251**	**306**	**436**	**100**	**115**	**92**	**7**	**79**	**0.38**	**42**	**19**	**38**	**27**	**107**	**96**	**102**	**15%**		**75**	**1%**	**0%**				**10.3**	**70**	**$7**

Dahl,David

Age: 26 Bats: L Pos: CF LF RF | Ht: 6' 2" Wt: 200

Health F | PT/Exp F | Consist C | LIMA Plan C+ | Rand Var -5 | MM 4335

A familiar refrain, as injuries (Aug ankle sprain) derailed potential breakout. PRO: raw power/speed skills remain primo, LD stroke should soften BA regression. CON: Can't trust gains vL (45% h%), subpar SB% keeps his light red, nearly 300 IL days since 2017. Has to stay on the field, but don't give up on... UP: 30+ HR, 10 SB.

Yr	Tm	PA	R	HR	RBI	SB	BA	xHR	xBA	OBP	SLG	OPS+	vL+	vR+	bb%	ct%	Eye	G	L	F	h%	HctX	PX	xPX	HR/F	xHR/F	Spd	SBO	SB%	#Wk	DOM	DIS	RAR	BPX	R$
15	aa	297	38	5	20	18	274			296	408	98			3	76	0.13				34		93				123	40%	71%					65	$12
16	COL *	623	99	23	73	19	313	6	274	370	531	123	98	119	8	73	0.34	45	21	33	39	97	140	100	13%	11%	136	16%	72%	11	27%	27%	39.7	186	$32
17	aaa	72	9	2	10	1	229			252	376	84			3	76	0.13				28		77				140	14%	39%					42	-$1
18	COL *	349	35	17	54	6	267	12	264	308	498	112	97	125	6	73	0.22	39	23	38	32	101	140	124	23%	17%	100	13%	65%	15	67%	27%	5.8	157	$12
19	COL	413	67	15	61	4	302	18	268	353	524	116	117	115	7	71	0.25	41	26	32	39	89	131	129	17%	21%	122	9%	50%	19	47%	37%	13.6	144	$15
1st Half		310	53	12	51	2	317	14	274	362	552	122	128	119	7	72	0.25	41	26	33	41	91	136	125	17%	20%	120	8%	33%	15	47%	40%	14.8	178	$22
2nd Half		103	14	3	10	2	258	3	250	324	441	101	91	105	8	67	0.26	44	27	29	36	84	115	145	17%	17%	125	9%	100%	4	50%	25%	-0.6	52	-$5
20	**Proj**	**525**	**73**	**22**	**67**	**7**	**282**		**263**	**333**	**502**	**112**	**101**	**116**	**7**	**71**	**0.25**	**42**	**25**	**34**	**36**	**93**	**126**	**127**	**19%**		**122**	**10%**	**59%**				**25.6**	**122**	**$21**

Dalbec,Bobby

Age: 25 Bats: R Pos: 3B | Ht: 6' 4" Wt: 225

Health A | PT/Exp F | Consist A | LIMA Plan D | Rand Var | MM 3201

Didn't quite get The Call to Fenway, but a modest step forward regardless. Plus power and flyball stroke (46% FB%) should translate to HR in the majors, and has the plate patience and glove to stick. Contact remains an issue, though 2nd half ct%—most of which was at AAA—offers hope. Likely to get a shot at CI spot; just beware short-term BA risk.

Yr	Tm	PA	R	HR	RBI	SB	BA	xHR	xBA	OBP	SLG	OPS+	vL+	vR+	bb%	ct%	Eye	G	L	F	h%	HctX	PX	xPX	HR/F	xHR/F	Spd	SBO	SB%	#Wk	DOM	DIS	RAR	BPX	R$
15																																			
16																																			
17																																			
18	aa	116	11	4	19	0	240			269	447	99			4	56	0.09				39		176				95	0%	0%					7	$0
19	a/a	533	59	22	63	5	224			313	416	97			11	68	0.41				28		110				99	10%	44%					59	$9
1st Half		293	33	13	36	3	220			332	427	101			14	64	0.47				29		128				102	10%	38%				-6.6	70	$9
2nd Half		241	28	10	28	3	233			296	414	94			8	74	0.35				27		96				107	9%	54%				-8.6	85	$9
20	**Proj**	**245**	**26**	**9**	**34**	**2**	**233**		**217**	**293**	**420**	**96**	**95**	**96**	**8**	**64**	**0.24**	**39**	**19**	**42**	**32**	**85**	**120**		**15%**		**104**	**7%**	**52%**				**-4.7**	**-33**	**$6**

Davis,Chris

Age: 34 Bats: L Pos: 1B | Ht: 6' 3" Wt: 230

Health B | PT/Exp B | Consist A | LIMA Plan D | Rand Var 0 | MM 3103

Took him 33 at-bats to get first hit; didn't get much better from there. Once-mammoth raw power has dipped to mere mortal levels, which was no longer enough to cover for MLB-worst ct% (min. 300 PA), and he was even more futile vL. An easy name to cross off your list (easier than paying him $69 million through 2022).

Yr	Tm	PA	R	HR	RBI	SB	BA	xHR	xBA	OBP	SLG	OPS+	vL+	vR+	bb%	ct%	Eye	G	L	F	h%	HctX	PX	xPX	HR/F	xHR/F	Spd	SBO	SB%	#Wk	DOM	DIS	RAR	BPX	R$
15	BAL	670	100	47	117	2	262	55	271	361	562	129	110	135	13	64	0.40	32	25	43	32	115	224	195	29%	34%	62	3%	40%	27	56%	22%	31.1	216	$28
16	BAL	665	99	38	84	1	221	42	231	332	459	108	96	111	13	61	0.40	36	20	44	28	100	169	179	25%	28%	79	1%	100%	27	41%	41%	0.8	94	$12
17	BAL	524	65	26	61	1	215	26	216	309	423	98	82	104	12	57	0.31	37	23	40	31	96	149	152	25%	25%	73	2%	50%	24	17%	67%	-16.5	-12	$5
18	BAL	522	40	16	49	2	168	20	187	243	296	75	69	76	8	59	0.21	40	21	39	24	79	95	121	15%	18%	64	2%	100%	26	12%	73%	-34.8	-167	-$2
19	BAL	352	26	12	36	0	179	12	186	276	326	80	60	85	11	55	0.28	38	23	39	28	72	104	140	18%	18%	67	0%	0%	26	19%	65%	-21.4	-196	-$2
1st Half		198	13	5	18	0	169	6	178	253	281	71	32	82	9	56	0.22	38	23	39	26	72	80	143	13%	15%	80	0%	0%	14	14%	71%	-17.9	-252	-$6
2nd Half		154	13	7	18	0	194	6	197	305	388	91	109	88	15	53	0.36	38	24	38	30	72	140	136	26%	22%	65	0%	0%	12	25%	58%	-5.5	-96	$3
20	**Proj**	**315**	**29**	**13**	**35**	**0**	**190**		**196**	**285**	**358**	**87**	**77**	**89**	**11**	**57**	**0.29**	**38**	**23**	**39**	**28**	**81**	**115**	**141**	**20%**		**67**	**1%**	**74%**				**-12.2**	**-180**	**$3**

Davis,J.D.

Age: 27 Bats: R Pos: LF 3B | Ht: 6' 3" Wt: 225

Health A | PT/Exp C | Consist C | LIMA Plan B | Rand Var -4 | MM 3345

Last year, we said relevance "may require change of scenery". Sure enough, cracked NYM's Opening Day roster and didn't look back. A bit over his BA skis per h%, but everything else—from ct%/LD% combination to 2nd half loft/xPX gains—provides some staying power. Use xBA as your guide; the rest looks mostly repeatable.

Yr	Tm	PA	R	HR	RBI	SB	BA	xHR	xBA	OBP	SLG	OPS+	vL+	vR+	bb%	ct%	Eye	G	L	F	h%	HctX	PX	xPX	HR/F	xHR/F	Spd	SBO	SB%	#Wk	DOM	DIS	RAR	BPX	R$
15																																			
16	aa	523	52	20	69	1	241			296	432	99			7	66	0.23				32		140				80	4%	20%					43	$8
17	HOU *	509	51	23	64	5	233	4	248	283	430	96	127	85	6	68	0.22	60	16	23	29	109	125	125	40%	40%	73	8%	59%	10	40%	50%	-18.5	30	$8
18	HOU *	470	48	13	61	2	250	4	248	304	396	97	79	57	7	74	0.30	50	22	28	31	88	94	71	5%	19%	86	2%	100%	15	0%	60%	-6.1	47	$9
19	NYM	453	65	22	57	3	307	23	279	369	527	119	119	118	8	76	0.39	47	23	30	36	110	115	111	23%	24%	103	3%	100%	28	39%	36%	21.9	174	$17
1st Half		213	27	8	23	0	278	8	278	343	454	106	98	111	8	78	0.42	53	25	23	32	105	89	83	24%	24%	114	0%	0%	15	40%	33%	1.6	133	$7
2nd Half		240	38	14	34	3	333	14	278	392	593	130	142	124	8	75	0.37	41	21	37	39	114	139	137	23%	23%	97	5%	100%	13	38%	38%	21.4	219	$25
20	**Proj**	**455**	**57**	**20**	**59**	**3**	**277**		**265**	**334**	**479**	**109**	**119**	**103**	**8**	**74**	**0.32**	**50**	**21**	**29**	**33**	**102**	**111**	**101**	**22%**		**94**	**3%**	**82%**				**13.3**	**80**	**$17**

Davis,Khris

Age: 32 Bats: R Pos: DH | Ht: 5' 11" Wt: 203

Health B | PT/Exp A | Consist C | LIMA Plan B+ | Rand Var +1 | MM 4225

2018's home run leader + 2019 ball = ... just 23 HR? Hit 10 of them through April, then suffered hip injury in May, HBP (hand) in June. Power skills, xBA, FB% plunge all say he deserved this, but pristine PX/xPX history makes a compelling case for an injury-related pass. Offseason of R&R could yield a return to 40-HR plateau.

Yr	Tm	PA	R	HR	RBI	SB	BA	xHR	xBA	OBP	SLG	OPS+	vL+	vR+	bb%	ct%	Eye	G	L	F	h%	HctX	PX	xPX	HR/F	xHR/F	Spd	SBO	SB%	#Wk	DOM	DIS	RAR	BPX	R$
15	MIL	440	54	27	66	6	247	27	259	323	505	115	101	118	10	69	0.36	42	17	40	29	105	174	169	25%	25%	86	8%	75%	22	64%	18%	0.7	170	$15
16	OAK	610	85	42	102	1	247	47	266	307	524	113	119	109	7	70	0.25	43	17	40	27	111	171	145	27%	30%	84	3%	33%	26	54%	38%	-4.0	166	$18
17	OAK	652	91	43	110	4	247	45	257	336	528	116	104	117	11	66	0.37	38	19	42	30	112	177	174	27%	28%	73	3%	100%	27	56%	26%	19.0	152	$19
18	OAK	654	98	48	123	0	247	54	261	326	549	121	113	123	9	70	0.34	35	16	49	27	116	185	171	24%	27%	71	0%	0%	28	50%	14%	23.3	227	$25
19	OAK	533	61	23	73	0	220	24	222	293	387	90	120	78	9	70	0.32	42	20	37	27	111	89	126	18%	19%	81	0%	0%	29	28%	48%	-23.4	-19	$7
1st Half		277	35	16	43	0	248	15	243	310	461	103	127	95	7	70	0.27	40	22	38	29	113	111	139	24%	22%	89	0%	0%	16	31%	38%	-4.0	52	$13
2nd Half		256	26	7	30	0	189	9	200	273	304	76	113	60	11	69	0.38	45	18	37	24	108	65	111	12%	16%	79	0%	0%	13	23%	62%	-18.9	-96	$1
20	**Proj**	**595**	**77**	**38**	**94**	**1**	**241**		**246**	**317**	**490**	**109**	**122**	**103**	**9**	**70**	**0.35**	**38**	**20**	**42**	**27**	**112**	**135**	**146**	**24%**		**78**	**1%**	**81%**				**7.5**	**75**	**$19**

Dean,Austin

Age: 26 Bats: R Pos: LF | Ht: 6' 1" Wt: 190

Health A | PT/Exp D | Consist B | LIMA Plan B | Rand Var +1 | MM 2135

6-21-.225 in 189 PA at MIA. Dominant AAA performance didn't translate to majors until fourth call-up in Sept (.260 BA, 3 HR). Seeds of upside have been planted, as xBA hints at BA growth and HctX, xHR/F say there was enough hard contact. If 2nd half power skills hold, he's a launch angle tweak away from end game profit.

Yr	Tm	PA	R	HR	RBI	SB	BA	xHR	xBA	OBP	SLG	OPS+	vL+	vR+	bb%	ct%	Eye	G	L	F	h%	HctX	PX	xPX	HR/F	xHR/F	Spd	SBO	SB%	#Wk	DOM	DIS	RAR	BPX	R$
15																																			
16	aa	523	53	9	60	1	212			277	330	83			8	74	0.34				27		78				101	3%	29%					20	$1
17	aa	247	28	4	29	3	257			298	388	92			5	77	0.25				32		80				115	7%	72%					64	$3
18	MIA *	552	74	13	70	3	277	3	249	329	410	102	62	95	7	82	0.44	42	21	37	31	97	74	91	12%	9%	123	3%	53%	7	43%	14%	1.1	143	$16
19	MIA *	465	58	20	70	3	258	7	275	311	469	104	89	87	7	74	0.30	45	24	31	30	112	119	94	15%	17%	78	10%	38%	14	29%	50%	-5.0	119	$12
1st Half		246	29	8	38	3	254	1	274	304	429	98	68	79	7	79	0.34	49	22	29	29	92	95	44	11%	5%	95	11%	59%	7	29%	57%	-5.5	130	$11
2nd Half		219	29	12	31	0	263	6	277	319	515	110	127	93	8	69	0.27	40	27	33	32	127	151	143	18%	27%	74	8%	0%	7	29%	43%	0.9	141	$13
20	**Proj**	**455**	**57**	**15**	**61**	**3**	**263**		**261**	**320**	**440**	**102**	**98**	**103**	**7**	**76**	**0.33**	**43**	**23**	**34**	**31**	**106**	**98**	**97**	**14%**		**96**	**6%**	**43%**				**2.3**	**75**	**$14**

RYAN BLOOMFIELD

DeJong,Paul

Age: 26	Bats: R	Pos: SS	Health B	LIMA Plan B+	
Ht: 6' 0"	Wt: 200		PT/Exp B	Rand Var +3	
			Consist B	MM 3225	

Five reasons he's better than 2019's ugly BA says: (1) growth in both hard and overall contact, low h% point to BA upside; (2) power skills say 30 HR very repeatable; (3) walk-rate growth; (4) just tapping into speed skills; (5) pre-peak, so room for more growth. No, he'll never win a batting title, but at SS, you can do worse.

Yr	Tm	PA	R	HR	RBI	SB	BA	xHR	xBA	OBP	SLG	OPS+	vL+	vR+	bb%	ct%	Eye	G	L	F	h%	HctX	PX	xPX	HR/F	xHR/F	Spd	SBO	SB%	#Wk	DOM	DIS	RAR	BPX	R$
15																																			
16	aa	529	52	18	61	3	235			283	403	93			6	69	0.22				30		116				86	5%	53%					29	$7
17	STL *	627	77	35	92	1	279	20	261	311	517	111	126	110	4	71	0.16	34	23	43	34	104	145	133	20%	16%	83	3%	31%	19	53%	26%	18.2	106	$20
18	STL	489	68	19	68	1	241	24	245	313	433	103	90	107	7	72	0.29	32	24	44	29	102	125	134	14%	17%	102	2%	50%	22	50%	45%	6.5	113	$11
19	STL	664	97	30	78	9	233	30	246	318	444	101	88	104	9	74	0.42	38	18	44	26	107	114	123	15%	15%	101	10%	64%	28	54%	32%	-5.3	148	$17
1st Half		351	53	13	36	6	260	14	258	345	458	107	120	105	10	78	0.52	36	21	43	29	118	106	119	13%	13%	113	9%	86%	15	60%	33%	3.5	200	$19
2nd Half		313	44	17	42	3	204	16	230	288	429	95	62	104	9	70	0.33	40	14	46	22	95	123	128	19%	18%	88	13%	43%	13	46%	31%	-12.0	96	$14
20	**Proj**	**630**	**88**	**29**	**83**	**5**	**251**		**242**	**321**	**460**	**105**	**92**	**108**	**8**	**72**	**0.31**	**35**	**20**	**44**	**30**	**103**	**117**	**129**	**16%**		**98**	**7%**	**57%**				**10.8**	**79**	**$17**

Demeritte,Travis

Age: 25	Bats: R	Pos: RF	Health A	LIMA Plan D+	
Ht: 6' 0"	Wt: 180		PT/Exp B	Rand Var -3	
			Consist A	MM 3403	

3-10-.225 in 186 PA at DET. Toolsy former first-round pick played his way back onto prospect radars with strong work at AAA. But all those Ks after his trade/call-up couldn't have impressed his new employers. He'll get more chances to show early 2019 wasn't a fluke, but there's little in skills to say it'll stick.

Yr	Tm	PA	R	HR	RBI	SB	BA	xHR	xBA	OBP	SLG	OPS+	vL+	vR+	bb%	ct%	Eye	G	L	F	h%	HctX	PX	xPX	HR/F	xHR/F	Spd	SBO	SB%	#Wk	DOM	DIS	RAR	BPX	R$
15																																			
16																																			
17	aa	508	60	13	44	5	203			281	341	83			10	66	0.32				28		86				141	11%	39%					-6	$1
18	aa	476	61	15	55	5	204			284	376	91			10	64	0.31				28		123				109	8%	70%					30	$6
19	DET *	566	80	19	71	6	242	5	226	316	429	99	82	84	10	64	0.30	39	21	39	34	78	123	55	7%	12%	131	8%	65%	10	10%	70%	-13.4	59	$13
1st Half		283	41	12	47	3	264		255	345	498	112			11	67	0.37				35		147		0%		108	11%	49%				3.7	159	$18
2nd Half		284	39	7	24	3	220	5	200	288	361	86	81	84	9	61	0.24	39	21	39	33	74	96	55	7%	12%	150	5%	100%	10	10%	70%	-13.7	-56	$8
20	**Proj**	**385**	**51**	**11**	**43**	**4**	**220**		**214**	**299**	**382**	**92**	**87**	**93**	**10**	**64**	**0.31**	**39**	**21**	**39**	**31**	**67**	**105**	**50**	**12%**		**142**	**8%**	**64%**				**-9.1**	**-25**	**$8**

DeShields Jr.,Delino

Age: 27	Bats: R	Pos: CF	Health B	LIMA Plan C	
Ht: 5' 9"	Wt: 200		PT/Exp C	Rand Var -1	
			Consist C	MM 1503	

4-32-.249 with 24 SB in 408 PA at TEX. Still a one-trick pony, but another year in, the lack of skills growth looms larger. Track record of consistent 50%+ DISaster weeks is damning. And remember, TEX actually resorted to Joey Gallo in CF for a while. With another 400-ish PA, he'll get 20+ SB again. But... DN: <200 PA, 10 SB.

Yr	Tm	PA	R	HR	RBI	SB	BA	xHR	xBA	OBP	SLG	OPS+	vL+	vR+	bb%	ct%	Eye	G	L	F	h%	HctX	PX	xPX	HR/F	xHR/F	Spd	SBO	SB%	#Wk	DOM	DIS	RAR	BPX	R$
15	TEX *	519	85	2	39	25	262	4	237	340	374	100	106	95	10	76	0.50	47	19	34	34	72	80	56	2%	4%	167	24%	76%	25	32%	48%	-1.0	111	$18
16	TEX *	437	64	6	26	24	218	2	218	295	307	82	73	82	10	69	0.35	55	17	28	30	57	66	51	12%	6%	105	33%	69%	18	22%	50%	-18.1	-49	$10
17	TEX	440	75	6	22	29	269	5	218	347	367	96	100	92	10	71	0.40	45	20	35	36	69	65	68	7%	6%	168	30%	78%	27	22%	52%	-2.4	27	$19
18	TEX *	429	54	2	22	22	214	2	215	308	275	81	92	76	11	75	0.55	49	19	32	28	77	44	58	3%	3%	114	26%	78%	23	22%	57%	-13.4	-10	$8
19	TEX *	480	49	6	40	29	244	5	229	314	348	88	103	81	9	72	0.37	43	25	32	33	77	62	65	5%	6%	141	30%	83%	26	15%	54%	-8.0	0	$15
1st Half		267	27	3	24	17	238	2	229	329	331	88	89	90	12	74	0.51	44	23	33	31	76	56	79	3%	5%	116	30%	81%	13	15%	46%	-3.9	0	$15
2nd Half		213	22	3	16	12	250	3	228	300	367	88	113	72	6	69	0.22	41	27	32	35	78	70	53	7%	7%	150	29%	86%	13	16%	62%	-3.1	-26	$15
20	**Proj**	**350**	**45**	**4**	**24**	**21**	**240**		**223**	**317**	**334**	**88**	**99**	**81**	**10**	**72**	**0.38**	**45**	**22**	**32**	**32**	**75**	**57**	**62**	**5%**		**141**	**29%**	**80%**				**-2.6**	**-12**	**$13**

Desmond,Ian

Age: 34	Bats: R	Pos: CF LF	Health B	LIMA Plan B	
Ht: 6' 3"	Wt: 220		PT/Exp B	Rand Var +2	
			Consist A	MM 3335	

PRO: Reached 20 HR again via recovered flyball rate; most other skills stable. CON: Wow, the SBO just went *poof* and the SB with it. Some reported leg soreness may have factored in, but at 34, we can't assume running game simply returns. So adjust value accordingly; his other, stable skills mean a $10 bid is likely to earn a profit.

Yr	Tm	PA	R	HR	RBI	SB	BA	xHR	xBA	OBP	SLG	OPS+	vL+	vR+	bb%	ct%	Eye	G	L	F	h%	HctX	PX	xPX	HR/F	xHR/F	Spd	SBO	SB%	#Wk	DOM	DIS	RAR	BPX	R$
15	WAS	641	69	19	62	13	233	21	229	290	384	94	104	89	7	68	0.24	53	16	31	31	83	113	91	15%	17%	111	14%	72%	27	26%	48%	-11.5	30	$13
16	TEX	677	107	22	86	21	285	24	264	335	446	106	119	101	6	74	0.28	53	21	26	35	92	101	81	18%	20%	116	16%	78%	26	46%	38%	11.2	80	$30
17	COL	373	47	7	40	15	274	4	244	326	375	94	88	94	6	74	0.28	63	16	21	35	82	61	60	13%	8%	110	19%	79%	18	11%	61%	-7.4	-15	$13
18	COL	619	82	22	88	20	236	21	269	307	422	101	117	93	9	74	0.36	62	16	22	28	93	109	87	25%	24%	138	20%	77%	28	39%	32%	0.2	143	$21
19	COL	482	64	20	65	3	255	22	274	310	479	105	127	87	7	73	0.29	47	22	30	31	98	126	93	20%	22%	104	7%	50%	28	43%	46%	8.6	152	$12
1st Half		270	40	11	42	1	276	14	278	333	512	113	144	91	8	72	0.29	45	24	31	35	103	140	116	20%	26%	105	6%	33%	15	53%	40%	10.0	174	$16
2nd Half		212	24	9	23	2	228	8	269	280	437	94	109	83	7	75	0.29	49	20	30	26	92	110	87	20%	18%	103	8%	67%	13	31%	54%	-2.4	130	$6
20	**Proj**	**455**	**59**	**16**	**58**	**8**	**250**		**263**	**309**	**436**	**100**	**117**	**90**	**7**	**74**	**0.31**	**54**	**19**	**27**	**30**	**93**	**103**	**83**	**20%**		**118**	**12%**	**70%**				**7.2**	**98**	**$15**

Devers,Rafael

Age: 23	Bats: L	Pos: 3B	Health B	LIMA Plan B+	
Ht: 6' 0"	Wt: 237		PT/Exp B	Rand Var -2	
			Consist D	MM 4145	

Breakout fueled by terrific contact growth. Held back early by lingering GB tilt, then exploded May-Aug. A strikeout spike dampened Sept; that's possibly fatigue, as the 21-year-old saw most PA in career. Next steps? Maintaining consistency over full year, further gains vL—both attainable with experience. UP: .315/40/125, MVP candidate

Yr	Tm	PA	R	HR	RBI	SB	BA	xHR	xBA	OBP	SLG	OPS+	vL+	vR+	bb%	ct%	Eye	G	L	F	h%	HctX	PX	xPX	HR/F	xHR/F	Spd	SBO	SB%	#Wk	DOM	DIS	RAR	BPX	R$
15																																			
16																																			
17	BOS *	592	81	27	83	3	298	8	273	355	523	118	142	98	8	78	0.40	49	15	36	34	109	129	98	17%	14%	83	5%	42%	11	27%	18%	25.7	173	$22
18	BOS *	512	62	22	68	5	244	19	242	302	439	102	86	106	8	73	0.31	46	15	39	29	93	123	95	17%	15%	62	7%	71%	25	48%	40%	1.4	87	$14
19	BOS	702	129	32	115	8	311	32	298	361	555	122	97	133	7	82	0.40	44	21	34	34	107	126	93	18%	18%	85	10%	50%	28	57%	11%	36.5	252	$34
1st Half		348	62	12	50	8	322	15	295	372	525	120	102	126	7	83	0.43	46	23	31	36	101	106	77	15%	19%	97	15%	62%	15	53%	7%	15.6	222	$34
2nd Half		354	67	20	65	0	300	18	302	350	584	123	94	140	7	81	0.38	42	20	38	32	112	146	109	20%	18%	73	4%	0%	13	62%	15%	17.2	285	$34
20	**Proj**	**665**	**104**	**33**	**101**	**6**	**294**		**276**	**347**	**534**	**119**	**104**	**124**	**7**	**78**	**0.36**	**44**	**19**	**37**	**33**	**103**	**128**	**96**	**18%**		**76**	**7%**	**53%**				**33.5**	**198**	**$31**

Diaz,Aledmys

Age: 29	Bats: R	Pos: 1B 2B	Health D	LIMA Plan D+	
Ht: 6' 1"	Wt: 195		PT/Exp D	Rand Var +1	
			Consist B	MM 2233	

9-40-.271 in 247 PA at HOU. Injuries sidelined him for much of the mid-season; otherwise, took to part-time role with aplomb and alacrity. Superb plate skills provide a BA floor even without elite hard contact, and he'd again be a 20-HR threat with full-time PA. So watch 2020 role closely; for now, solid bench filler.

Yr	Tm	PA	R	HR	RBI	SB	BA	xHR	xBA	OBP	SLG	OPS+	vL+	vR+	bb%	ct%	Eye	G	L	F	h%	HctX	PX	xPX	HR/F	xHR/F	Spd	SBO	SB%	#Wk	DOM	DIS	RAR	BPX	R$
15	a/a	451	43	9	37	4	225			269	349	86			6	80	0.31				26		85				91	13%	38%					84	$3
16	STL	460	71	17	65	4	300	13	284	369	510	120	98	126	9	85	0.68	46	16	39	32	109	118	108	13%	10%	139	7%	50%	22	55%	14%	25.4	277	$18
17	STL *	478	45	10	40	6	240	4	246	273	362	85	80	92	4	83	0.27	46	17	38	27	79	71	69	8%	4%	113	11%	58%	16	44%	38%	-17.8	103	$5
18	TOR	452	55	18	55	3	263	18	269	303	453	105	98	106	5	85	0.37	41	18	41	27	100	105	105	12%	12%	94	8%	43%	26	46%	23%	5.6	220	$12
19	HOU *	270	37	9	40	2	253	7	266	334	431	101	99	114	10	84	0.76	46	17	37	27	94	87	70	13%	10%	109	3%	100%	20	50%	25%	-1.1	226	$5
1st Half		109	17	5	22	0	286	4	283	321	510	111	117	108	7	87	0.54	52	13	35	29	101	101	62	16%	13%	127	0%	0%	10	50%	20%	3.1	300	$4
2nd Half		161	20	4	18	2	229	3	252	334	372	93	83	118	14	82	0.88	40	20	39	25	89	75	77	10%	8%	94	5%	100%	10	50%	30%	-3.0	170	$6
20	**Proj**	**350**	**45**	**12**	**46**	**3**	**253**		**262**	**320**	**428**	**101**	**90**	**104**	**8**	**84**	**0.56**	**44**	**17**	**39**	**27**	**95**	**88**	**83**	**12%**		**109**	**6%**	**63%**				**-0.1**	**167**	**$10**

Diaz,Elias

Age: 29	Bats: R	Pos: CA	Health C	LIMA Plan D	
Ht: 6' 1"	Wt: 220		PT/Exp D	Rand Var -1	
			Consist F	MM 1013	

2-28-.241 in 332 PA at PIT. Well, so much for the shiny, happy power skills. Had a real chance to duplicate 2018 heroics, but 2019 looked a lot like the rest of his career. He may still own those skills. But now it looks like they're either buried somewhere in the garage or the neighbor borrowed them. Either way, they're probably long gone.

Yr	Tm	PA	R	HR	RBI	SB	BA	xHR	xBA	OBP	SLG	OPS+	vL+	vR+	bb%	ct%	Eye	G	L	F	h%	HctX	PX	xPX	HR/F	xHR/F	Spd	SBO	SB%	#Wk	DOM	DIS	RAR	BPX	R$
15	PIT *	351	28	3	40	1	235	0	102	287	324	85	0	0	7	84	0.45	0	0	100	27	363	59	732	0%	0%	98	7%	15%	2	0%	50%	-8.8	76	$1
16	PIT *	108	3	0	10	1	224		249	248	249	68	0	0	3	80	0.16	33	33	33	28	0	21	-24	0%		78	3%	100%	1	0%	100%	-7.4	-89	-$2
17	PIT *	426	34	3	41	3	225	2	238	260	300	75	86	74	5	80	0.24	52	18	30	27	84	52	70	2%	4%	64	4%	100%	15	27%	53%	-17.8	-15	$0
18	PIT	277	33	10	34	0	286	8	263	339	452	110	129	100	8	84	0.53	45	20	35	31	112	92	104	13%	11%	81	1%	0%	25	48%	36%	13.4	173	$7
19	PIT *	362	35	2	31	0	249	4	236	299	317	82	85	78	7	81	0.38	47	21	31	30	88	43	46	3%	5%	74	0%	0%	22	14%	55%	-10.9	-7	$1
1st Half		206	23	1	22	0	286	2	257	334	368	94	101	89	7	83	0.43	47	23	29	34	97	53	35	3%	5%	85	0%	0%	11	27%	36%	2.2	59	$4
2nd Half		156	12	1	9	0	199	2	208	258	248	67	68	66	7	79	0.33	47	19	34	25	79	30	60	3%	5%	76	0%	0%	11	0%	73%	-8.8	-85	-$3
20	**Proj**	**315**	**30**	**5**	**30**	**1**	**245**		**239**	**296**	**343**	**86**	**97**	**81**	**7**	**82**	**0.38**	**47**	**20**	**33**	**29**	**95**	**55**	**72**	**6%**		**75**	**1%**	**50%**				**0.0**	**-17**	**$5**

ROD TRUESDELL

Diaz,Isan

Age: 24 Bats: L Pos: 2B	Health A	LIMA Plan D+	
Ht: 5' 10" Wt: 185	PT/Exp D	Rand Var -1	
	Consist B	MM 2205	

5-23-.173 in 201 PA at MIA. After rough intro to Triple-A in 2018, rebounded to post HR total more befitting of his talent. And while intro to majors was equally rough, 135 xPX in Sept offers hope he'll again fare better second time around. Low-LD%, low ct% approach makes BA problematic; might be wise to hedge on PA.

Yr Tm	PA	R	HR	RBI	SB	BA	xHR	xBA	OBP	SLG	OPS+	vL+	vR+	bb%	ct%	Eye	G	L	F	h%	HctX	PX	xPX	HR/F	xHR/F	Spd	SBO	SB%	#Wk	DOM	DIS	RAR	BPX	R$
15																																		
16																																		
17																																		
18 a/a	490	54	10	48	12	205			301	343	89			12	64	0.38				29		101				112	13%	79%					-10	$7
19 MIA *	623	97	26	86	5	239	5	221	317	435	100	53	81	10	70	0.38	41	13	45	30	94	110	106	9%	9%	105	8%	38%	9	22%	56%	-5.6	78	$16
1st Half	315	60	15	47	2	262		258	341	483	110			11	72	0.43				31		122		0%		113	7%	35%				4.2	163	$21
2nd Half	308	38	11	39	3	216	5	205	293	387	90	52	81	10	67	0.33	41	13	45	28	91	97	106	9%	9%	109	10%	40%	9	22%	56%	-12.4	7	$10
20 Proj	**490**	**66**	**11**	**59**	**7**	**223**		**206**	**314**	**360**	**91**	**61**	**99**	**11**	**67**	**0.38**	**40**	**18**	**41**	**30**	**88**	**85**	**95**	**9%**		**106**	**10%**	**61%**				**-7.0**	**-32**	**$8**

Diaz,Yandy

Age: 28 Bats: R Pos: 3B 1B	Health D	LIMA Plan B	
Ht: 6' 2" Wt: 215	PT/Exp C	Rand Var 0	
	Consist B	MM 2135	

Rays' gamble that small-sample HctX could lead to more power with FB% increase paid off... when healthy, which was only about half the season. Platoon splits were exaggerated by hit rate (35% vL, 27% vR), though power was clearly better vL (138 PX). With health, next step forward should be double-digit value, and maybe... UP: 20 HR

Yr Tm	PA	R	HR	RBI	SB	BA	xHR	xBA	OBP	SLG	OPS+	vL+	vR+	bb%	ct%	Eye	G	L	F	h%	HctX	PX	xPX	HR/F	xHR/F	Spd	SBO	SB%	#Wk	DOM	DIS	RAR	BPX	R$
15 a/a	562	54	6	49	8	286			371	368	103			12	85	0.89				33		51				112	9%	50%					105	$14
16 a/a	503	53	8	47	9	287			370	398	105			12	80	0.67				34		70				99	8%	72%					89	$14
17 CLE *	536	69	4	39	3	293	2	264	385	379	102	96	86	13	80	0.74	59	22	19	36	106	56	60	0%	9%	107	3%	54%	11	27%	55%	4.6	73	$12
18 CLE *	520	54	3	44	1	264	2	246	353	353	98	101	116	12	76	0.58	53	23	23	34	125	65	84	5%	10%	107	3%	29%	10	40%	40%	-1.6	50	$7
19 TAM	347	53	14	38	2	267	13	276	340	476	108	128	98	10	80	0.57	51	17	32	29	118	108	115	18%	16%	102	5%	50%	18	61%	22%	4.7	222	$8
1st Half	268	40	11	32	1	284	11	284	354	500	114	131	106	10	82	0.63	52	17	31	31	119	110	108	18%	18%	101	3%	50%	14	64%	14%	7.1	252	$12
2nd Half	79	13	3	6	1	211	2	249	291	394	90	127	67	10	75	0.44	47	17	36	24	112	102	143	16%	11%	105	13%	50%	4	50%	50%	-3.7	126	-$5
20 Proj	**455**	**61**	**15**	**50**	**3**	**269**		**264**	**350**	**444**	**107**	**119**	**98**	**11**	**78**	**0.57**	**50**	**20**	**30**	**31**	**117**	**95**	**103**	**16%**		**101**	**6%**	**48%**				**8.5**	**118**	**$14**

Diaz,Yusniel

Age: 23 Bats: R Pos: DH	Health A	LIMA Plan D	
Ht: 6' 1" Wt: 195	PT/Exp D	Rand Var	
	Consist B	MM 2121	

Season shortened by series of injuries likely kept promising BAL prospect from getting call-up. Patience is already a positive, and scouts see raw plus power, .290ish BA in future. Running game is a bigger question mark, as minor league success rate has been terrible (28-for-66, 42%). Any bid for 2020 is speculative at this point.

Yr Tm	PA	R	HR	RBI	SB	BA	xHR	xBA	OBP	SLG	OPS+	vL+	vR+	bb%	ct%	Eye	G	L	F	h%	HctX	PX	xPX	HR/F	xHR/F	Spd	SBO	SB%	#Wk	DOM	DIS	RAR	BPX	R$
15																																		
16																																		
17 aa	116	13	3	11	2	309			357	456	109			7	70	0.25				42		104				92	23%	24%					24	$3
18 aa	399	45	9	34	9	253			338	386	100			11	80	0.63				29		75				121	21%	39%					133	$9
19 aa	316	41	11	49	0	243			314	436	100			9	75	0.42				29		105				110	5%	0%					141	$5
1st Half	171	23	7	26	0	213			298	400	93			11	74	0.46				24		97				133	6%	0%				-7.6	133	$3
2nd Half	144	18	4	22	0	278			334	477	107			8	77	0.36				34		114				116	4%	0%				0.9	185	$7
20 Proj	**175**	**21**	**5**	**21**	**2**	**261**		**244**	**332**	**431**	**103**	**102**	**102**	**10**	**76**	**0.45**	**40**	**20**	**40**	**32**	**92**	**93**		**10%**		**124**	**14%**	**31%**				**-0.8**	**98**	**$5**

Dickerson,Alex

Age: 30 Bats: L Pos: LF	Health F	LIMA Plan D+	
Ht: 6' 3" Wt: 235	PT/Exp F	Rand Var -2	
	Consist F	MM 3333	

6-28-.276 in 190 PA at SD/SF. Missed all of 2017-18 with herniated disc, Tommy John surgery. Returned with modest power intact, only to have oblique issue tank his numbers in Aug/Sept (.164 BA, 0 HR). xHR, xHR/F hint at untapped potential, but given injury history, struggles vL, middling xBA, and age, overall upside is limited.

Yr Tm	PA	R	HR	RBI	SB	BA	xHR	xBA	OBP	SLG	OPS+	vL+	vR+	bb%	ct%	Eye	G	L	F	h%	HctX	PX	xPX	HR/F	xHR/F	Spd	SBO	SB%	#Wk	DOM	DIS	RAR	BPX	R$
15 SD *	497	53	8	46	3	243	0	254	288	380	93	0	91	6	74	0.24	20	40	40	31	128	101	84	0%	0%	98	3%	100%	4	0%	75%	-13.9	51	$6
16 SD *	511	72	16	70	5	279	9	274	329	460	107	97	108	7	84	0.45	37	22	40	30	116	104	105	12%	11%	93	5%	83%	17	53%	35%	9.8	174	$16
17																																		
18																																		
19 2 NL *	316	43	9	43	1	270	9	252	329	450	103	73	114	8	77	0.38	35	23	41	32	108	97	108	11%	16%	114	3%	50%	18	39%	44%	-0.5	137	$6
1st Half	178	22	5	29	1	276	3	245	340	442	104	30	135	9	76	0.41	45	18	37	33	139	88	167	14%	21%	118	4%	50%	7	43%	43%	0.2	115	$7
2nd Half	139	21	4	14	0	262	5	260	315	460	102	104	106	7	77	0.33	32	25	43	31	95	108	85	10%	12%	108	0%	0%	11	36%	45%	-0.6	159	$5
20 Proj	**280**	**38**	**10**	**35**	**2**	**268**		**262**	**326**	**466**	**107**	**79**	**112**	**7**	**79**	**0.36**	**37**	**22**	**41**	**31**	**114**	**104**	**114**	**12%**		**107**	**3%**	**75%**				**5.1**	**154**	**$9**

Dickerson,Corey

Age: 31 Bats: L Pos: LF	Health D	LIMA Plan B	
Ht: 6' 1" Wt: 210	PT/Exp B	Rand Var 0	
	Consist A	MM 4255	

12-59-.304 in 279 PA at PIT/PHI. Not bad for injury-plagued season. Posted best xBA and highest OPS since leaving Coors, though xPX continues to warn against fully buying into his power. xBA concurs that .285 is probably his ceiling. Good chance he'll rebound, just not to 2017-18 levels.

Yr Tm	PA	R	HR	RBI	SB	BA	xHR	xBA	OBP	SLG	OPS+	vL+	vR+	bb%	ct%	Eye	G	L	F	h%	HctX	PX	xPX	HR/F	xHR/F	Spd	SBO	SB%	#Wk	DOM	DIS	RAR	BPX	R$
15 COL *	263	32	11	33	0	296	13	293	325	514	117	91	129	4	76	0.18	38	30	32	35	123	149	135	19%	24%	113	2%	0%	16	44%	25%	8.5	181	$9
16 TAM	547	57	24	70	0	245	26	256	293	469	104	80	108	6	74	0.25	38	17	45	29	95	144	119	14%	15%	85	2%	0%	27	52%	33%	-1.5	143	$10
17 TAM	628	84	27	62	4	282	25	265	325	490	109	109	107	6	74	0.23	42	22	36	34	101	122	106	17%	16%	112	5%	57%	27	37%	37%	4.6	124	$19
18 PIT	533	65	13	55	8	300	18	284	330	474	111	102	113	4	84	0.26	38	27	35	34	106	100	101	9%	12%	123	9%	73%	27	44%	30%	14.0	210	$19
19 2 NL *	314	36	12	62	1	286	11	287	327	520	113	104	125	6	78	0.28	36	25	39	33	105	133	112	15%	14%	90	2%	100%	17	59%	12%	7.5	211	$9
1st Half	107	11	2	18	0	252	1	262	309	423	98	103	125	8	76	0.34	44	21	35	31	91	113	88	11%	6%	79	0%	0%	7	43%	29%	-2.0	126	-$5
2nd Half	207	25	10	44	1	303	10	296	333	569	119	102	126	5	78	0.24	34	26	40	34	110	143	120	16%	16%	99	3%	100%	10	70%	0%	10.1	259	$16
20 Proj	**490**	**59**	**18**	**63**	**3**	**286**		**280**	**324**	**503**	**111**	**98**	**114**	**5**	**78**	**0.26**	**38**	**25**	**37**	**33**	**104**	**120**	**107**	**13%**		**104**	**4%**	**71%**				**16.9**	**172**	**$18**

Dietrich,Derek

Age: 30 Bats: L Pos: 2B 1B	Health A	LIMA Plan D	
Ht: 6' 0" Wt: 205	PT/Exp C	Rand Var +5	
	Consist B	MM 3113	

Had one insane month (.304 BA, 12 HR in May) amid season marred by on/off shoulder problem and career marked by swings in FB%/xPX, h%, results vL. But those 1st half skills! To quote noted baseball analyst Winston Churchill, he's "a riddle wrapped in a mystery inside an enigma." Let crummy R$ history be your guide amidst uncertainty.

Yr Tm	PA	R	HR	RBI	SB	BA	xHR	xBA	OBP	SLG	OPS+	vL+	vR+	bb%	ct%	Eye	G	L	F	h%	HctX	PX	xPX	HR/F	xHR/F	Spd	SBO	SB%	#Wk	DOM	DIS	RAR	BPX	R$
15 MIA *	493	58	15	46	0	241	12	243	297	422	100	72	118	7	74	0.30	37	20	43	30	112	125	159	12%	15%	110	5%	0%	18	39%	39%	-1.8	119	$7
16 MIA	412	39	7	42	1	279	11	245	374	425	109	75	114	8	76	0.38	40	22	38	35	86	93	99	7%	11%	109	1%	100%	26	46%	31%	2.4	83	$8
17 MIA	464	56	13	53	0	249	13	252	334	424	102	108	98	8	76	0.37	37	23	41	30	98	102	106	10%	10%	115	1%	0%	26	42%	42%	-7.2	112	$6
18 MIA	551	72	16	45	2	265	17	240	330	421	104	98	104	5	72	0.21	41	23	36	34	97	103	88	12%	13%	99	2%	100%	28	29%	46%	2.9	40	$12
19 CIN	305	41	19	43	1	187	15	246	328	462	105	55	110	9	71	0.38	35	17	48	18	95	143	127	22%	18%	97	4%	50%	26	35%	50%	-5.5	170	$3
1st Half	218	36	18	40	1	222	13	274	353	567	123	66	130	10	74	0.45	35	17	48	19	107	165	149	28%	20%	114	5%	50%	15	53%	40%	4.9	315	$10
2nd Half	87	5	1	3	0	99	1	173	264	197	61	0	65	9	62	0.26	35	16	49	14	63	76	57	5%	5%	81	0%	0%	11	9%	64%	-9.2	-174	-$13
20 Proj	**315**	**39**	**13**	**36**	**1**	**245**		**231**	**350**	**440**	**106**	**89**	**108**	**8**	**70**	**0.29**	**37**	**20**	**43**	**30**	**89**	**111**	**98**	**15%**		**91**	**2%**	**54%**				**3.5**	**26**	**$8**

Dixon,Brandon

Age: 28 Bats: R Pos: 1B LF	Health A	LIMA Plan D+	
Ht: 6' 2" Wt: 215	PT/Exp C	Rand Var -1	
	Consist B	MM 3313	

15-52-.248 with 5 SB in 420 PA at DET. Hit 11 HR in May/June, then pitchers shut him down in 2nd half; that'll happen with plate discipline this bad. And that's the crux—plus power and speed should make him worth targeting, but poor ct% has led to career .225 xBA that undercuts his value. Playing time could be next... DN: 300 PA, 10 HR

Yr Tm	PA	R	HR	RBI	SB	BA	xHR	xBA	OBP	SLG	OPS+	vL+	vR+	bb%	ct%	Eye	G	L	F	h%	HctX	PX	xPX	HR/F	xHR/F	Spd	SBO	SB%	#Wk	DOM	DIS	RAR	BPX	R$
15 aa	346	29	7	34	14	221			243	340	81			3	68	0.09				30		93				92	34%	68%					-51	$6
16 aa	447	55	16	59	14	242			290	411	95			6	62	0.18				35		128				85	21%	71%					-20	$12
17 aaa	470	46	14	51	14	228			278	394	90			6	66	0.20				31		116				92	27%	61%					0	$8
18 CIN *	313	36	10	28	7	249	5	232	286	433	99	77	80	5	63	0.14	43	22	35	36	90	142	131	19%	19%	111	19%	66%	18	28%	50%	-9.0	40	$7
19 DET *	466	46	16	54	5	237	19	220	272	410	91	99	95	5	65	0.14	36	24	40	33	92	107	126	14%	18%	130	7%	83%	24	29%	33%	-15.3	-15	$8
1st Half	225	22	12	34	3	226	11	215	250	422	90	98	102	3	66	0.09	36	18	46	28	100	114	147	21%	21%	101	8%	100%	11	36%	27%	-10.7	-30	$8
2nd Half	241	24	4	20	2	249	8	222	303	398	92	100	89	6	64	0.18	36	28	36	37	86	99	109	8%	16%	141	6%	67%	13	23%	38%	-8.0	-33	$7
20 Proj	**385**	**40**	**14**	**41**	**5**	**239**		**227**	**281**	**425**	**95**	**93**	**95**	**5**	**64**	**0.15**	**39**	**23**	**38**	**33**	**91**	**119**	**127**	**16%**		**119**	**13%**	**60%**				**-7.6**	**-27**	**$10**

BRANDON KRUSE

Donaldson,Josh

Age: 34	Bats: R	Pos: 3B	Health	D	LIMA Plan	A
Ht: 6' 1"	Wt: 210		PT/Exp	B	Rand Var	0
			Consist	C	MM	4245

First clean bill of health in 3 years fueled successful rebound. Concessions to age are visible in ct%, BA history, but xBA, HctX and that torrid 2nd half say decline isn't precipitous. More importantly, power, bb%, and performance vR looked near-vintage. Best seasons are in the rear-view, but he's still a fine component of any fantasy risk portfolio.

Yr	Tm	PA	R	HR	RBI	SB	BA	xHR	xBA	OBP	SLG	OPS+	vL+	vR+	bb%	ct%	Eye	G	L	F	h%	HctX	PX	xPX	HR/F	xHR/F	Spd	SBO	SB%	#Wk	DOM	DIS	RAR	BPX	R$
15	TOR	711	122	41	123	6	297	44	297	371	568	131	141	126	10	79	0.55	45	17	38	32	129	170	140	22%	23%	92	3%	100%	27	74%	19%	51.7	270	$37
16	TOR	700	122	37	99	7	284	41	289	404	549	130	126	128	16	79	0.92	38	21	41	30	130	148	135	20%	22%	110	4%	88%	27	74%	11%	46.4	291	$29
17	TOR	496	65	33	78	2	270	30	272	385	559	127	139	121	15	73	0.68	41	17	42	29	108	164	132	26%	23%	65	3%	50%	21	62%	24%	24.8	230	$16
18	2 AL	219	30	8	23	2	246	9	252	352	449	111	125	104	14	71	0.57	48	17	35	30	108	138	113	17%	19%	92	4%	100%	12	58%	33%	4.2	177	$4
19	ATL	659	96	37	94	4	259	37	271	379	521	120	110	122	15	72	0.65	42	21	36	29	118	145	124	26%	26%	77	3%	67%	27	48%	26%	19.5	215	$21
1st Half		338	44	15	39	2	253	18	260	358	478	112	98	115	13	70	0.49	43	23	34	31	112	134	110	21%	26%	80	4%	67%	15	40%	33%	3.7	144	$15
2nd Half		321	52	22	55	2	265	19	282	402	569	128	121	131	18	74	0.84	41	20	38	28	124	157	138	30%	26%	78	3%	67%	12	58%	17%	19.4	304	$27
20	Proj	**560**	**83**	**30**	**80**	**4**	**261**		**265**	**376**	**515**	**120**	**121**	**119**	**15**	**73**	**0.66**	**43**	**19**	**37**	**30**	**116**	**140**	**125**	**23%**		**83**	**3%**	**75%**				**28.3**	**192**	**$18**

Dozier,Brian

Age: 33	Bats: R	Pos: 2B	Health	A	LIMA Plan	C+
Ht: 5' 11"	Wt: 200		PT/Exp	A	Rand Var	0
			Consist	C	MM	3223

Lost playing time as season progressed, and it had nothing to do with injuries. Patience remains stellar, but .221 BA vR turned him into a bench player by September. One-time plus power didn't return in record MLB HR year, and running game just vanished. Now an aging free agent with an uncertain outlook.

Yr	Tm	PA	R	HR	RBI	SB	BA	xHR	xBA	OBP	SLG	OPS+	vL+	vR+	bb%	ct%	Eye	G	L	F	h%	HctX	PX	xPX	HR/F	xHR/F	Spd	SBO	SB%	#Wk	DOM	DIS	RAR	BPX	R$
15	MIN	704	101	28	77	12	236	22	261	307	444	105	105	102	9	76	0.41	33	23	44	27	100	138	129	13%	10%	102	12%	75%	26	58%	19%	5.8	178	$18
16	MIN	691	104	42	99	18	268	34	276	340	546	121	130	115	9	78	0.44	36	16	48	28	109	159	137	18%	15%	123	14%	90%	26	65%	19%	28.3	269	$30
17	MIN	705	106	34	93	16	269	32	264	357	496	114	140	104	11	77	0.55	38	19	43	30	106	124	138	17%	16%	116	13%	70%	27	63%	22%	17.2	203	$26
18	2 TM	632	81	21	72	12	215	20	240	305	391	96	89	98	11	77	0.54	39	17	44	24	105	107	112	11%	11%	93	11%	80%	28	43%	29%	-6.6	147	$13
19	WAS	482	54	20	50	3	238	18	243	340	430	102	117	96	13	75	0.58	35	21	44	27	100	103	117	15%	13%	78	6%	43%	28	43%	29%	1.9	119	$8
1st Half		288	30	12	29	1	230	12	235	309	424	98	143	82	10	73	0.39	37	18	45	27	106	109	140	14%	14%	81	3%	50%	15	40%	27%	-3.5	85	$8
2nd Half		194	24	8	21	2	252	6	257	387	440	109	87	120	18	78	0.97	33	24	43	28	91	94	82	15%	11%	80	8%	40%	13	46%	31%	3.9	178	$9
20	Proj	**420**	**54**	**18**	**48**	**6**	**241**		**247**	**341**	**438**	**105**	**107**	**103**	**13**	**76**	**0.62**	**36**	**20**	**44**	**27**	**101**	**104**	**115**	**14%**		**93**	**9%**	**62%**				**8.5**	**138**	**$12**

Dozier,Hunter

Age: 28	Bats: R	Pos: 3B RF	Health	B	LIMA Plan	B
Ht: 6' 4"	Wt: 220		PT/Exp	C	Rand Var	-3
			Consist	C	MM	4215

Breakout from 2013 1st-rounder who was nearing journeyman status. What next? PRO: Power held up reasonably well all season; bb%, ct%, FB% upticks were all positives. CON: 2nd half across-the-board fade vR following June IL stint; HR/F, xBA history says this isn't big-time upside. Bid the under, hope for a surprise. DN: 400 PA.

Yr	Tm	PA	R	HR	RBI	SB	BA	xHR	xBA	OBP	SLG	OPS+	vL+	vR+	bb%	ct%	Eye	G	L	F	h%	HctX	PX	xPX	HR/F	xHR/F	Spd	SBO	SB%	#Wk	DOM	DIS	RAR	BPX	R$
15	aa	509	50	9	41	5	183			238	294	74			7	65	0.21				26		95				90	8%	67%					-51	-$3
16	KC *	549	67	17	61	6	259	0	255	319	448	104	74	73	8	71	0.31	45	18	36	33	53	136	44	0%	0%	91	6%	83%	3	0%	100%	2.1	111	$13
17	a/a	110	12	3	9	1	200			272	369	86			9	49	0.20				37		160				108	10%	40%					-67	-$2
18	KC *	524	49	12	42	3	225	16	221	287	367	91	84	97	8	67	0.26	41	22	37	31	111	102	132	12%	17%	107	7%	45%	20	30%	35%	-14.2	0	$5
19	KC	586	75	26	84	2	279	27	253	348	522	116	119	114	9	72	0.37	34	22	44	34	112	132	144	16%	16%	155	3%	50%	26	58%	31%	19.6	222	$18
1st Half		256	30	13	44	1	294	13	272	379	566	126	94	136	12	75	0.55	34	21	44	34	126	143	167	17%	17%	114	3%	50%	13	62%	23%	14.8	278	$16
2nd Half		330	45	13	40	1	268	14	238	324	490	107	138	98	8	69	0.27	35	22	44	35	102	122	125	14%	15%	182	3%	50%	13	54%	38%	2.2	170	$19
20	Proj	**560**	**65**	**21**	**64**	**3**	**248**		**234**	**315**	**456**	**104**	**101**	**104**	**9**	**67**	**0.29**	**37**	**22**	**41**	**33**	**112**	**127**	**138**	**15%**		**133**	**5%**	**51%**				**3.1**	**54**	**$14**

Drury,Brandon

Age: 27	Bats: R	Pos: 3B	Health	C	LIMA Plan	D+
Ht: 6' 2"	Wt: 215		PT/Exp	C	Rand Var	+4
			Consist	B	MM	2023

Found and fumbled opportunity on rebuilding team awaiting prospect infusion. Even with poor h% luck, BA and contact skills have deteriorated. The HRs weren't special in 2019, and he's not hitting enough FB to grow them. Apart from age and positional versatility, there's nothing optimistic here. You can do better.

Yr	Tm	PA	R	HR	RBI	SB	BA	xHR	xBA	OBP	SLG	OPS+	vL+	vR+	bb%	ct%	Eye	G	L	F	h%	HctX	PX	xPX	HR/F	xHR/F	Spd	SBO	SB%	#Wk	DOM	DIS	RAR	BPX	R$
15	ARI *	606	51	6	53	3	260	2	267	291	362	91	126	60	4	84	0.27	56	21	23	30	106	75	109	18%	18%	69	9%	25%	5	20%	40%	-21.9	73	$8
16	ARI	499	59	16	53	1	282	14	271	329	458	107	109	104	6	78	0.31	50	20	30	33	105	111	97	15%	13%	97	2%	50%	27	44%	37%	6.3	131	$13
17	ARI	480	41	13	63	1	267	13	275	317	447	102	98	102	6	77	0.27	49	22	29	32	99	114	87	13%	13%	87	2%	50%	27	41%	30%	-0.6	115	$9
18	2 AL *	334	32	7	36	2	226	2	212	312	347	91	66	74	11	65	0.36	42	23	35	32	64	91	91	5%	10%	79	4%	67%	8	13%	38%	-6.9	-53	$3
19	TOR	447	43	15	41	0	218	18	248	262	380	85	81	87	6	73	0.22	42	24	34	26	97	92	99	14%	17%	79	1%	0%	27	30%	44%	-23.3	7	$2
1st Half		244	23	6	19	0	207	9	239	254	348	80	59	90	6	69	0.20	44	26	30	27	99	88	95	13%	19%	93	0%	0%	15	27%	40%	-16.9	-48	-$1
2nd Half		203	20	9	22	0	230	9	258	271	419	91	103	83	5	78	0.26	40	22	38	25	94	97	103	16%	16%	73	3%	0%	12	33%	50%	-9.0	89	$6
20	Proj	**315**	**30**	**9**	**33**	**1**	**235**		**243**	**293**	**385**	**91**	**91**	**90**	**7**	**73**	**0.27**	**44**	**23**	**33**	**29**	**89**	**89**	**96**	**12%**		**84**	**3%**	**40%**				**-8.3**	**-26**	**$5**

Dubon,Mauricio

Age: 25	Bats: R	Pos: 2B	Health	A	LIMA Plan	B
Ht: 6' 0"	Wt: 160		PT/Exp	C	Rand Var	+4
			Consist	B	MM	2355

4-9-.274 and 3 SB in 111 PA at SF. Torn ACL in 2018 stalled rookie's advance and running game, but still some pluses here. Career .300 minors hitter doesn't walk enough, but owns fine contact skills. Added weight, improved conditioning contributed to HR spike though metrics look skeptical. Low ceiling, but signs hint at worthy end-gamer.

Yr	Tm	PA	R	HR	RBI	SB	BA	xHR	xBA	OBP	SLG	OPS+	vL+	vR+	bb%	ct%	Eye	G	L	F	h%	HctX	PX	xPX	HR/F	xHR/F	Spd	SBO	SB%	#Wk	DOM	DIS	RAR	BPX	R$
15																																			
16	aa	260	39	5	32	5	328			352	512	118			3	85	0.24				37		110				112	13%	60%					203	$12
17	a/a	524	61	8	47	31	247			293	346	86			6	83	0.37				29		61				87	40%	65%					58	$17
18	aaa	109	12	3	12	4	283			292	460	104			1	79	0.06				34		109				107	37%	53%					130	$2
19	2 NL *	636	76	17	53	11	260	2	288	291	393	91	107	94	4	84	0.28	48	27	26	29	91	68	74	18%	9%	123	15%	51%	7	14%	43%	-14.6	141	$15
1st Half		328	35	8	31	5	260		250	285	383	89			3	83	0.21				29		62		0%		123	16%	48%				-10.6	104	$13
2nd Half		308	41	9	21	5	259	2	295	297	404	93	106	94	5	85	0.36	48	27	26	28	92	73	74	18%	9%	127	15%	54%	7	14%	43%	-6.1	181	$16
20	Proj	**455**	**55**	**13**	**42**	**11**	**267**		**292**	**294**	**428**	**97**	**107**	**92**	**4**	**83**	**0.22**	**48**	**27**	**26**	**30**	**83**	**84**	**67**	**14%**		**131**	**22%**	**53%**				**-0.2**	**130**	**$16**

Duffy,Matt

Age: 29	Bats: R	Pos: 3B	Health	F	LIMA Plan	C+
Ht: 6' 2"	Wt: 190		PT/Exp	F	Rand Var	+1
			Consist	D	MM	1333

1-12-.252 in 166 PA at TAM. Hamstring woes shelved him until late July and put a serious dent in any residual 2nd half value. Plus contact; improving bb%; legs may again outrun xBA and find double-digit SB if healthy. But durability has never been a sure thing. Only constant is ceding a ton of HR at a corner spot. High risk, low reward.

Yr	Tm	PA	R	HR	RBI	SB	BA	xHR	xBA	OBP	SLG	OPS+	vL+	vR+	bb%	ct%	Eye	G	L	F	h%	HctX	PX	xPX	HR/F	xHR/F	Spd	SBO	SB%	#Wk	DOM	DIS	RAR	BPX	R$
15	SF	612	77	12	77	12	295	15	276	334	428	106	89	110	5	83	0.31	53	21	27	34	103	83	90	9%	12%	128	8%	100%	27	44%	26%	10.6	135	$24
16	2 TM	366	41	5	28	8	258	8	263	310	357	91	95	87	6	84	0.43	50	21	29	29	90	59	67	6%	10%	127	15%	62%	17	35%	24%	-11.3	103	$7
17																																			
18	TAM	560	59	4	44	12	294	5	264	361	366	101	100	100	8	82	0.51	54	25	20	35	93	48	44	5%	6%	111	11%	67%	27	26%	37%	4.1	57	$16
19	TAM *	203	15	2	19	0	245	2	246	319	322	85	68	101	10	80	0.56	54	23	24	30	100	48	52	4%	7%	87	2%	0%	11	27%	36%	-8.7	26	-$1
1st Half		6	0	0	0	0	0	0	0	0	0	0			0	79	0.00				0		0		0%	#N/A	115	0%	0%				-1.2	-174	-$15
2nd Half		197	15	2	19	0	254	2	247	330	334	87	68	101	10	80	0.58	54	23	24	31	100	49	52	4%	7%	87	2%	0%	11	27%	36%	-8.0	33	-$1
20	Proj	**350**	**36**	**4**	**32**	**7**	**269**		**262**	**330**	**359**	**93**	**83**	**96**	**8**	**82**	**0.47**	**52**	**23**	**25**	**32**	**96**	**51**	**61**	**6%**		**113**	**11%**	**71%**				**-4.9**	**43**	**$10**

Duggar,Steven

Age: 26	Bats: L	Pos: CF RF	Health	D	LIMA Plan	C+
Ht: 6' 2"	Wt: 189		PT/Exp	F	Rand Var	0
			Consist	A	MM	2313

4-28-.234 in 277 PA at SF. Couldn't shake injury bug as surgically-repaired shoulder ended his season again in August. But Health isn't the only problem here. He's never had any power to speak of, and his running game has never developed. Toss in poor contact and nothing-special patience and you have a recipe for mediocrity. Just say no.

Yr	Tm	PA	R	HR	RBI	SB	BA	xHR	xBA	OBP	SLG	OPS+	vL+	vR+	bb%	ct%	Eye	G	L	F	h%	HctX	PX	xPX	HR/F	xHR/F	Spd	SBO	SB%	#Wk	DOM	DIS	RAR	BPX	R$
15																																			
16	aa	268	31	1	21	8	303			369	412	106			9	77	0.45				39		75				122	20%	51%					71	$9
17	aaa	53	6	1	5	2	224			321	331	87			13	70	0.48				29		63				104	32%	52%					-30	-$1
18	SF *	495	56	4	32	13	232	3	214	290	352	89	118	86	8	64	0.23	43	23	34	35	70	102	72	6%	9%	137	18%	69%	8	25%	50%	-14.7	-13	$7
19	SF *	378	44	6	38	3	246	6	232	306	365	89	63	92	8	70	0.29	50	21	29	33	80	74	73	8%	12%	130	11%	25%	15	20%	60%	-20.1	-7	$4
1st Half		274	26	4	28	1	235	5	226	277	351	84	62	94	6	68	0.19	52	21	28	33	79	73	68	9%	11%	137	9%	20%	13	15%	62%	-17.1	-48	$4
2nd Half		104	18	2	10	2	278	0	252	382	404	104	258	64	14	75	0.68	25	33	42	35	65	77	151	0%	0%	110	16%	30%	2	50%	50%	-1.1	96	$5
20	Proj	**280**	**36**	**4**	**24**	**6**	**238**		**234**	**309**	**364**	**91**	**83**	**94**	**9**	**70**	**0.35**	**48**	**22**	**30**	**32**	**75**	**82**	**70**	**8%**		**135**	**19%**	**46%**				**-3.2**	**-9**	**$6**

JOCK THOMPSON

Duvall,Adam

Age: 31	Bats: R	Pos: LF	Health	A	LIMA Plan	D+
Ht: 6' 1"	Wt: 215		PT/Exp	B	Rand Var	0
			Consist	C	MM	4223

10-19-.267 in 127 PA at ATL. Pre-All-Star break performance (26 HR, 77% ct% in 297 AB) at AAA fueled MLB opportunity in late July. Power stayed intact, resurgent h% kept BA afloat in sporadic playing time. 2018 disaster was overdone, but he's still the same streaky low-BA, high-power guy as always. Plenty of those around these days.

Yr Tm	PA	R	HR	RBI	SB	BA	xHR	xBA	OBP	SLG	OPS+	vL+	vR+	bb%	ct%	Eye	G	L	F	h%	HctX	PX	xPX	HR/F	xHR/F	Spd	SBO	SB%	#Wk	DOM	DIS	RAR	BPX	R$
15 CIN *	594	62	31	77	4	224	3	248	265	444	99	69	123	5	70	0.18	29	24	47	26	111	153	128	28%	17%	76	5%	77%	6	50%	50%	-14.6	97	$11
16 CIN	607	85	33	103	6	241	35	256	297	498	108	107	106	7	70	0.25	34	19	47	28	111	163	155	18%	19%	111	11%	55%	27	44%	33%	2.3	171	$17
17 CIN	647	78	31	99	5	249	26	247	301	480	105	122	97	6	71	0.23	33	18	49	30	91	143	116	15%	13%	87	7%	63%	27	37%	37%	-8.7	118	$16
18 2 NL	427	48	15	61	2	195	21	224	274	365	88	89	88	9	70	0.32	30	22	48	24	94	114	116	12%	16%	71	5%	50%	28	29%	43%	-19.2	33	$4
19 ATL *	534	72	33	89	1	223	12	221	284	479	101	147	101	8	70	0.29	27	12	60	25	109	138	182	20%	24%	103	1%	100%	11	64%	27%	-10.6	144	$12
1st Half	288	39	17	49	1	207		265	270	451	96			8	74	0.33				21		127		0%		97	2%	100%				-10.1	159	$12
2nd Half	246	33	16	40	0	241	12	218	302	511	107	146	101	8	66	0.25	27	12	60	29	103	153	182	20%	24%	112	0%	0%	11	64%	27%	0.2	141	$13
20 Proj	**280**	**36**	**16**	**44**	**1**	**235**		**240**	**301**	**478**	**105**	**116**	**100**	**8**	**70**	**0.27**	**33**	**19**	**48**	**27**	**100**	**136**	**143**	**19%**		**93**	**3%**	**62%**				**1.0**	**88**	**$5**

Dyson,Jarrod

Age: 35	Bats: L	Pos: CF RF	Health	D	LIMA Plan	B
Ht: 5' 10"	Wt: 165		PT/Exp	C	Rand Var	0
			Consist	B	MM	0523

Return to health fueled running game rebound in the most plate appearances of his 10-year career. But 2nd half FB% spike and poor h% crushed his BA, costing him Sept PA. Needs to keep the ball on the ground, now less predictable as he ages. Relevant because of SB scarcity, but he's still a risky one-trick pony.

Yr Tm	PA	R	HR	RBI	SB	BA	xHR	xBA	OBP	SLG	OPS+	vL+	vR+	bb%	ct%	Eye	G	L	F	h%	HctX	PX	xPX	HR/F	xHR/F	Spd	SBO	SB%	#Wk	DOM	DIS	RAR	BPX	R$
15 KC	225	31	2	18	26	250	1	278	311	380	96	80	98	6	82	0.38	54	23	23	30	68	77	28	6%	3%	168	60%	90%	26	42%	38%	0.0	141	$12
16 KC *	362	51	1	26	33	275	1	280	335	378	97	136	93	8	86	0.65	56	20	24	32	60	57	32	2%	2%	161	42%	82%	25	52%	24%	0.1	163	$18
17 SEA	390	56	5	30	28	251	3	251	324	350	90	50	96	7	84	0.51	47	19	34	29	54	54	41	5%	3%	145	37%	80%	21	38%	24%	-13.3	121	$15
18 ARI	237	29	2	12	16	189	2	240	282	257	75	97	68	11	83	0.79	46	23	31	22	70	36	45	4%	4%	131	33%	84%	15	33%	40%	-11.5	90	$3
19 ARI	452	65	7	27	30	230	4	234	313	320	84	94	83	10	79	0.55	49	19	32	28	80	47	54	7%	4%	147	29%	88%	28	25%	50%	-8.6	67	$15
1st Half	238	38	5	18	19	260	2	256	349	375	97	88	98	12	78	0.62	51	23	26	31	84	56	58	12%	5%	145	30%	90%	15	33%	40%	3.2	100	$20
2nd Half	214	27	2	9	11	198	2	208	272	260	70	102	67	9	79	0.46	48	14	38	24	75	37	50	4%	4%	131	27%	85%	13	15%	62%	-12.2	11	$9
20 Proj	**315**	**44**	**4**	**19**	**22**	**223**		**240**	**302**	**312**	**83**	**88**	**81**	**10**	**81**	**0.57**	**49**	**20**	**32**	**26**	**71**	**46**	**47**	**6%**		**148**	**33%**	**85%**				**-5.5**	**101**	**$12**

Eaton,Adam

Age: 31	Bats: L	Pos: RF	Health	F	LIMA Plan	B
Ht: 5' 9"	Wt: 176		PT/Exp	C	Rand Var	-1
			Consist	B	MM	1535

Amazing what IL avoidance can do. Turned improved health into PA, counting stats spikes. Strong 2nd half fueled rebound near 2016 value. Rock-solid plate skills and speed offer foundation for more BA excellence and double-digit SB. Subpar power a fixed reality, but that's not the target here. Bid the under, hope for more durability and a SBO bump.

Yr Tm	PA	R	HR	RBI	SB	BA	xHR	xBA	OBP	SLG	OPS+	vL+	vR+	bb%	ct%	Eye	G	L	F	h%	HctX	PX	xPX	HR/F	xHR/F	Spd	SBO	SB%	#Wk	DOM	DIS	RAR	BPX	R$
15 CHW	689	98	14	56	18	287	12	267	361	431	110	89	116	8	79	0.44	51	22	27	35	91	93	69	11%	9%	150	14%	69%	26	38%	35%	9.9	141	$26
16 CHW	706	91	14	59	14	284	14	276	362	428	108	98	108	9	81	0.55	54	21	26	33	104	83	90	11%	11%	136	10%	74%	27	52%	11%	12.2	151	$22
17 WAS	107	24	2	13	3	297	3	273	393	462	115	79	118	13	80	0.78	53	15	32	35	101	99	87	9%	13%	143	13%	75%	4	50%	0%	3.2	215	$3
18 WAS	370	55	5	33	9	301	6	267	394	411	111	77	116	10	80	0.59	47	26	26	36	96	72	66	8%	9%	130	9%	90%	21	24%	48%	10.2	130	$13
19 WAS	656	103	15	49	15	279	14	247	365	428	105	103	106	10	81	0.61	40	20	40	32	96	74	95	8%	8%	157	10%	83%	28	46%	25%	3.6	196	$20
1st Half	352	47	6	21	6	279	6	226	364	384	100	99	100	11	81	0.63	43	18	40	33	90	51	86	6%	6%	158	9%	67%	15	33%	20%	-3.2	126	$16
2nd Half	304	56	9	28	9	280	8	268	366	479	111	109	112	10	82	0.60	36	23	41	31	103	100	104	10%	9%	144	13%	100%	13	62%	31%	7.4	270	$26
20 Proj	**490**	**85**	**11**	**45**	**13**	**288**		**260**	**376**	**436**	**109**	**96**	**112**	**11**	**81**	**0.62**	**44**	**21**	**34**	**34**	**98**	**79**	**86**	**9%**		**151**	**11%**	**84%**				**15.3**	**179**	**$21**

Edman,Tommy

Age: 25	Bats: R	Pos: 3B 2B	Health	A	LIMA Plan	B
Ht: 5' 10"	Wt: 180		PT/Exp	C	Rand Var	-2
			Consist	B	MM	2543

11-36-.304 and 15 SB in 342 PA at STL. Fine debut from unheralded prospect. Minor league ct%, base-running skills held up at MLB level; power surged into average territory. Patience and h% sustainability remain question marks; BA is likely to regress. But SB, positional versatility provide foundation for something more than just bench utility value.

Yr Tm	PA	R	HR	RBI	SB	BA	xHR	xBA	OBP	SLG	OPS+	vL+	vR+	bb%	ct%	Eye	G	L	F	h%	HctX	PX	xPX	HR/F	xHR/F	Spd	SBO	SB%	#Wk	DOM	DIS	RAR	BPX	R$
15																																		
16																																		
17 aa	233	18	2	23	4	232			278	323	80			6	84	0.40				27		55				103	13%	67%					76	$1
18 a/a	550	65	5	32	23	263			306	342	90			6	81	0.34				31		50				121	20%	80%					53	$16
19 STL *	557	89	16	59	22	288	10	273	323	470	105	126	107	5	81	0.28	41	25	35	33	116	90	108	12%	11%	153	18%	96%	18	61%	22%	13.1	204	$24
1st Half	242	36	7	26	9	263	2	255	297	438	98	61	138	5	81	0.26	52	11	37	30	146	86	130	20%	20%	154	18%	100%	5	60%	20%	-1.5	189	$13
2nd Half	315	53	9	33	13	307	8	277	356	495	112	134	104	5	81	0.29	39	26	34	35	112	93	105	11%	10%	150	19%	93%	13	62%	23%	12.1	211	$33
20 Proj	**420**	**56**	**17**	**37**	**16**	**271**		**273**	**327**	**472**	**107**	**98**	**111**	**5**	**82**	**0.32**	**44**	**20**	**35**	**30**	**126**	**97**	**115**	**15%**		**142**	**20%**	**86%**				**7.4**	**215**	**$19**

Encarnacion,Edwin

Age: 37	Bats: R	Pos: 1B DH	Health	B	LIMA Plan	C+
Ht: 6' 1"	Wt: 230		PT/Exp	A	Rand Var	+2
			Consist	B	MM	4135

Unfortunate 1st half h% slowed him down before correcting (and then some) after June. Only 2nd half injuries (fractured wrist, strained oblique) cut into his PA. By all measures, a surprisingly stable skill set at a career point when players begin to struggle. Another year adds to risk, but this "decline" looks gentle. Age could keep him cheap.

Yr Tm	PA	R	HR	RBI	SB	BA	xHR	xBA	OBP	SLG	OPS+	vL+	vR+	bb%	ct%	Eye	G	L	F	h%	HctX	PX	xPX	HR/F	xHR/F	Spd	SBO	SB%	#Wk	DOM	DIS	RAR	BPX	R$
15 TOR	624	94	39	111	3	277	37	297	372	557	129	115	130	12	81	0.79	36	19	45	27	129	166	142	20%	19%	54	3%	60%	27	81%	4%	25.9	273	$28
16 TOR	701	99	42	127	2	263	43	284	357	529	121	122	118	12	77	0.63	38	20	41	28	118	155	137	22%	22%	55	1%	100%	27	78%	7%	18.1	217	$24
17 CLE	668	96	38	107	2	258	37	269	377	504	118	114	118	16	76	0.78	37	21	42	27	116	131	136	21%	21%	62	1%	100%	27	52%	19%	26.7	185	$20
18 CLE	578	74	32	107	3	246	34	250	336	474	112	103	114	11	74	0.48	36	20	44	27	115	130	142	20%	21%	64	2%	100%	27	48%	33%	12.2	137	$20
19 2 AL	486	81	34	86	0	244	30	264	344	531	116	126	112	12	75	0.56	31	19	51	24	104	144	132	21%	19%	77	1%	0%	22	50%	18%	8.8	244	$15
1st Half	339	58	24	55	0	225	21	261	342	511	114	120	112	14	75	0.67	30	19	51	21	101	139	128	22%	19%	85	1%	0%	16	50%	25%	2.6	252	$20
2nd Half	147	23	10	31	0	284	9	267	347	575	122	144	113	8	75	0.33	33	17	50	31	111	153	142	20%	18%	67	0%	0%	6	50%	0%	6.2	226	$6
20 Proj	**504**	**77**	**32**	**84**	**1**	**257**		**260**	**349**	**520**	**117**	**122**	**114**	**11**	**75**	**0.53**	**34**	**19**	**47**	**27**	**112**	**135**	**138**	**20%**		**68**	**1%**	**74%**				**20.4**	**181**	**$20**

Engel,Adam

Age: 28	Bats: R	Pos: CF	Health	A	LIMA Plan	C+
Ht: 6' 2"	Wt: 210		PT/Exp	C	Rand Var	-2
			Consist	A	MM	2501

6-26-.242 and 3 SB in 241 PA at CHW. As expected, PA in majors dropped off precipitously. SBO did likewise, and the combo sent his SB and value plummeting. HR/F uptick notwithstanding, this is a mediocre across-the-board skill set in which little has changed. Consistency here isn't a good thing. Even second tier clubs and rebuilders should do better.

Yr Tm	PA	R	HR	RBI	SB	BA	xHR	xBA	OBP	SLG	OPS+	vL+	vR+	bb%	ct%	Eye	G	L	F	h%	HctX	PX	xPX	HR/F	xHR/F	Spd	SBO	SB%	#Wk	DOM	DIS	RAR	BPX	R$
15																																		
16 a/a	496	58	6	32	30	215			279	337	84			8	68	0.28				30		85				138	45%	65%					3	$11
17 CHW *	516	49	12	35	11	172	6	191	228	316	73	86	62	7	62	0.19	41	14	45	25	64	104	98	8%	8%	137	20%	71%	19	11%	79%	-39.0	-39	-$3
18 CHW	463	49	6	29	16	235	7	200	279	336	85	82	86	4	70	0.14	41	18	41	32	66	69	64	5%	6%	150	26%	67%	27	15%	63%	-15.1	-30	$9
19 CHW *	512	57	13	47	12	227	5	225	272	370	85	110	80	6	67	0.19	44	23	33	31	65	87	73	13%	11%	146	19%	65%	18	17%	44%	-18.5	-19	$9
1st Half	261	29	8	23	6	201	1	207	238	356	79	68	94	5	66	0.14	38	21	41	27	76	89	101	8%	8%	158	23%	65%	6	17%	50%	-14.0	-30	$5
2nd Half	251	28	5	23	6	255	4	231	309	385	92	122	76	7	68	0.25	46	23	31	35	63	84	65	14%	11%	120	16%	64%	12	17%	42%	-2.8	-26	$13
20 Proj	**245**	**27**	**5**	**19**	**7**	**232**		**210**	**292**	**365**	**88**	**97**	**84**	**6**	**67**	**0.19**	**42**	**19**	**39**	**32**	**67**	**83**	**77**	**9%**		**142**	**22%**	**67%**				**-4.6**	**-55**	**$6**

Ervin,Phillip

Age: 27	Bats: R	Pos: LF CF	Health	A	LIMA Plan	C+
Ht: 5' 10"	Wt: 207		PT/Exp	D	Rand Var	-2
			Consist	A	MM	2323

7-23-.271 and 4 SB in 260 PA at CIN. Decent 2nd half bench production from ex-1st-rounder, but limitations seem apparent. HctX, ct% are nothing special; neither is career .232 BA vR. Power metrics are stuck on average. Spd perked up, but SB% is trending poorly. Absence of carrying skill, lack of opportunity keep him unrosterable for now.

Yr Tm	PA	R	HR	RBI	SB	BA	xHR	xBA	OBP	SLG	OPS+	vL+	vR+	bb%	ct%	Eye	G	L	F	h%	HctX	PX	xPX	HR/F	xHR/F	Spd	SBO	SB%	#Wk	DOM	DIS	RAR	BPX	R$
15 aa	62	6	2	7	3	216			358	381	103			18	66	0.65				29		130				94	38%	51%					92	$0
16 aa	480	65	13	41	33	221			320	374	95			13	76	0.60				26		95				108	37%	75%					111	$16
17 CIN *	457	45	9	42	22	226	2	205	284	343	84	125	91	8	73	0.30	33	19	49	29	67	75	107	14%	10%	103	30%	74%	10	30%	30%	-26.9	0	$10
18 CIN *	436	46	11	60	14	249	6	245	312	406	99	104	98	8	73	0.33	36	28	36	32	92	101	86	12%	11%	96	24%	60%	18	28%	50%	-6.3	60	$13
19 CIN *	421	51	12	44	9	261	6	245	321	446	102	135	88	8	72	0.32	39	23	37	33	94	100	101	11%	9%	145	20%	46%	21	33%	43%	-7.5	111	$11
1st Half	207	27	6	26	5	250	1	231	325	418	99	171	32	10	68	0.34	38	25	38	34	78	100	89	11%	11%	110	26%	37%	9	22%	67%	-6.9	22	$9
2nd Half	214	24	6	18	4	272	6	259	327	472	105	123	96	6	76	0.28	40	23	37	33	102	100	103	11%	11%	162	13%	67%	12	42%	25%	-0.1	181	$12
20 Proj	**280**	**33**	**9**	**31**	**7**	**250**		**244**	**320**	**428**	**101**	**127**	**84**	**8**	**73**	**0.33**	**37**	**24**	**38**	**31**	**88**	**98**	**95**	**12%**		**125**	**19%**	**60%**				**-1.4**	**87**	**$9**

JOCK THOMPSON

Escobar,Eduardo

Age: 31	Bats: B	Pos: 3B 2B	Health	A	LIMA Plan	B+
Ht: 5' 10"	Wt: 185		PT/Exp	A	Rand Var	0
			Consist	B	MM	3235

Huge step forward on the surface, but other than xPX jump, skills looked very similar to 2018. The xHR increase was minimal, as much of his value was tied to maxing out PA and RBI. Plus power, "AAA" reliability, and multi-position eligibility are all appealing, but good chance he falls short of 30 HR and 100 RBI in 2020.

Yr	Tm	PA	R	HR	RBI	SB	BA	xHR	xBA	OBP	SLG	OPS+	vL+	vR+	bb%	ct%	Eye	G	L	F	h%	HctX	PX	xPX	HR/F	xHR/F	Spd	SBO	SB%	#Wk	DOM	DIS	RAR	BPX	R$
15	MIN	446	48	12	58	2	262	15	267	309	445	105	109	101	6	79	0.33	42	19	39	31	101	125	118	10%	12%	105	6%	40%	27	44%	30%	-0.6	168	$10
16	MIN	377	32	6	37	1	236	8	240	280	338	84	75	87	6	80	0.29	39	23	37	28	84	63	73	6%	8%	84	5%	25%	25	36%	44%	-20.6	20	$2
17	MIN	499	62	21	73	5	254	22	250	309	449	102	97	102	7	79	0.34	34	21	45	28	100	102	114	13%	13%	115	6%	83%	27	33%	44%	-8.4	136	$12
18	2 TM	631	75	23	84	2	272	26	275	334	489	114	108	116	8	78	0.41	32	25	43	31	109	136	133	12%	13%	74	5%	33%	27	52%	30%	14.7	200	$19
19	ARI	699	94	35	118	5	269	30	268	320	511	110	115	108	7	80	0.38	33	23	45	29	114	116	152	15%	13%	116	4%	83%	28	50%	25%	5.9	230	$24
1st Half		367	55	18	64	3	292	14	269	351	541	119	148	104	8	78	0.41	31	25	45	33	104	124	151	15%	12%	119	5%	75%	15	40%	33%	14.6	241	$30
2nd Half		332	39	17	54	2	244	16	267	286	479	101	68	112	6	81	0.35	35	21	44	25	124	107	154	15%	14%	114	3%	100%	13	62%	15%	-4.6	222	$18
20	**Proj**	**665**	**84**	**28**	**92**	**4**	**263**		**262**	**315**	**477**	**107**	**103**	**107**	**7**	**79**	**0.36**	**34**	**23**	**44**	**29**	**110**	**108**	**136**	**13%**		**103**	**4%**	**66%**				**10.5**	**170**	**$19**

Farmer,Kyle

Age: 29	Bats: R	Pos: 2B	Health	A	LIMA Plan	D
Ht: 6' 0"	Wt: 214		PT/Exp	D	Rand Var	-3
			Consist	B	MM	2121

A surprising HR/SB source in limited 1st half action, but predictably, it didn't last. A couple IL stints (concussion, oblique) can't explain all of his struggles, as there's not a plus skill to be found now that ct% has gone M.I.A. Still catcher-eligible in some leagues (15 games), which would be the only reason to keep him on your radar.

Yr	Tm	PA	R	HR	RBI	SB	BA	xHR	xBA	OBP	SLG	OPS+	vL+	vR+	bb%	ct%	Eye	G	L	F	h%	HctX	PX	xPX	HR/F	xHR/F	Spd	SBO	SB%	#Wk	DOM	DIS	RAR	BPX	R$
15	aa	294	21	2	33	0	238			266	345	85			4	77	0.17				30		90				79	2%	0%					41	$0
16	aa	284	24	4	24	2	214			264	328	81			6	80	0.34				25		76				92	3%	100%					69	-$1
17	LA *	387	41	8	44	1	261	0	367	300	385	92	66	99	5	83	0.32	35	53	12	30	118	73	106	0%	0%	70	6%	13%	7	14%	29%	-3.1	67	$6
18	LA *	376	27	5	34	1	227	0	265	261	343	84	87	88	4	78	0.21	43	28	28	28	112	80	81	0%	0%	91	3%	36%	15	27%	47%	-6.5	47	$1
19	CIN	197	22	9	27	4	230	7	235	279	410	91	107	82	5	68	0.17	40	24	35	29	94	102	80	20%	16%	68	14%	80%	24	17%	54%	-3.7	-52	$3
1st Half		107	13	6	20	4	242	4	243	290	455	99	121	78	5	66	0.15	43	25	32	31	103	121	106	29%	19%	69	25%	80%	14	14%	50%	0.8	-30	$5
2nd Half		90	9	3	7	0	214	3	227	267	357	82	72	85	6	70	0.20	37	24	39	27	82	82	53	13%	13%	88	0%	0%	10	20%	60%	-2.5	-52	$0
20	**Proj**	**210**	**20**	**6**	**23**	**2**	**231**		**242**	**287**	**369**	**88**	**91**	**85**	**5**	**72**	**0.20**	**41**	**26**	**33**	**29**	**99**	**81**	**77**	**12%**		**78**	**7%**	**66%**				**-4.9**	**-54**	**$4**

Fisher,Derek

Age: 26	Bats: L	Pos: LF	Health	A	LIMA Plan	D
Ht: 6' 3"	Wt: 205		PT/Exp	D	Rand Var	+3
			Consist	B	MM	2303

7-17-.185 with 5 SB in 167 PA at HOU/TOR. Power/speed combo was on display, as were the flaws that keep him from living up to prospect hype. Abysmal ct% led to poor OBP that negates speed; career .167 BA vR says he's not even a fit for a strong-side platoon. You better have a rock-solid BA foundation if chasing these HR and SB.

Yr	Tm	PA	R	HR	RBI	SB	BA	xHR	xBA	OBP	SLG	OPS+	vL+	vR+	bb%	ct%	Eye	G	L	F	h%	HctX	PX	xPX	HR/F	xHR/F	Spd	SBO	SB%	#Wk	DOM	DIS	RAR	BPX	R$
15																																			
16	a/a	545	59	18	63	23	228			323	394	98			12	63	0.38				32		120				105	23%	75%					11	$15
17	HOU *	532	62	19	60	14	241	3	266	298	416	96	85	88	7	70	0.27	54	24	21	31	108	110	101	26%	16%	114	25%	48%	13	15%	54%	-25.5	61	$13
18	HOU *	351	43	11	34	9	188	3	201	260	344	84	130	72	9	55	0.21	50	21	29	30	83	125	144	36%	27%	116	16%	89%	10	30%	60%	-17.1	-83	$4
19	2 AL *	418	52	17	41	10	207	5	215	298	379	90	106	77	11	62	0.34	49	18	33	28	82	105	80	24%	17%	113	10%	69%	15	13%	53%	-17.9	-30	$7
1st Half		231	28	6	21	8	222	1	219	290	363	87	119	77	9	66	0.28	51	18	31	31	82	85	79	8%	8%	130	20%	78%	5	0%	40%	-10.9	-41	$7
2nd Half		186	24	10	20	2	187	4	210	307	400	93	99	77	15	57	0.40	47	18	35	24	79	136	81	35%	24%	98	11%	49%	10	20%	60%	-7.6	-4	$6
20	**Proj**	**315**	**38**	**10**	**33**	**8**	**222**		**210**	**305**	**371**	**91**	**113**	**82**	**11**	**61**	**0.31**	**50**	**20**	**30**	**33**	**85**	**97**	**106**	**19%**		**114**	**15%**	**68%**				**-7.4**	**-95**	**$8**

Fletcher,David

Age: 26	Bats: R	Pos: 3B 2B SS	Health	A	LIMA Plan	B+
Ht: 5' 9"	Wt: 185		PT/Exp	B	Rand Var	-1
			Consist	B	MM	0345

A fine year overall, but did fall off in 2nd half: ct% went from elite to very good; already-modest power slipped further; no SB attempts in final two months. Can't count on double-digit HR or SB, but LD stroke should yield another high BA, which along with multi-position eligibility, still gives him some fringe value.

Yr	Tm	PA	R	HR	RBI	SB	BA	xHR	xBA	OBP	SLG	OPS+	vL+	vR+	bb%	ct%	Eye	G	L	F	h%	HctX	PX	xPX	HR/F	xHR/F	Spd	SBO	SB%	#Wk	DOM	DIS	RAR	BPX	R$
15																																			
16	aa	83	10	0	6	1	284			309	355	90			3	82	0.20				35		58				95	5%	100%					31	$0
17	a/a	469	48	2	32	16	230			265	290	74			5	86	0.34				26		37				103	22%	71%					45	$6
18	LAA *	571	70	5	49	7	274	1	280	306	388	96	93	94	4	89	0.42	39	27	34	30	95	69	49	1%	1%	110	8%	76%	15	40%	20%	1.3	180	$13
19	LAA	653	83	6	49	8	290	4	284	350	384	97	96	98	8	89	0.86	44	26	30	32	99	49	56	4%	3%	122	6%	73%	28	43%	7%	1.0	193	$16
1st Half		306	39	5	30	5	288	3	294	350	399	100	87	107	9	92	1.23	45	26	30	30	108	52	68	7%	4%	118	9%	63%	15	60%	0%	2.1	241	$16
2nd Half		347	44	1	19	3	292	1	276	350	371	95	107	91	8	87	0.67	43	27	30	33	91	46	44	1%	1%	124	3%	100%	13	23%	15%	0.8	144	$16
20	**Proj**	**595**	**73**	**4**	**46**	**8**	**281**		**277**	**328**	**371**	**94**	**93**	**94**	**6**	**88**	**0.59**	**42**	**27**	**31**	**31**	**97**	**50**	**52**	**3%**		**117**	**7%**	**71%**				**-4.5**	**133**	**$17**

Flores,Wilmer

Age: 28	Bats: R	Pos: 2B	Health	C	LIMA Plan	C+
Ht: 6' 3"	Wt: 205		PT/Exp	C	Rand Var	-4
			Consist	B	MM	2143

Slow out of the gate, then May foot fracture cost him two months. Finished strong upon return, and while h% spike helped, power and contact skills returned to near-peak levels. There's still untapped upside if he ever got full-time PA, but time's running out on shaking platoon label. UP: 20+ HR, .300 BA (which is what this proj. scales to in 600 PA).

Yr	Tm	PA	R	HR	RBI	SB	BA	xHR	xBA	OBP	SLG	OPS+	vL+	vR+	bb%	ct%	Eye	G	L	F	h%	HctX	PX	xPX	HR/F	xHR/F	Spd	SBO	SB%	#Wk	DOM	DIS	RAR	BPX	R$
15	NYM	510	55	16	59	0	263	8	267	295	408	98	132	87	4	87	0.30	42	21	37	27	109	86	95	10%	5%	92	1%	0%	26	46%	23%	-1.4	146	$11
16	NYM	335	38	16	49	1	267	9	274	319	469	107	148	86	7	84	0.48	33	22	45	27	93	108	107	14%	8%	96	3%	50%	21	48%	29%	2.4	197	$9
17	NYM	362	42	18	52	1	271	13	271	307	488	107	114	101	5	84	0.31	36	18	46	28	120	111	127	14%	10%	97	3%	50%	21	52%	10%	1.4	197	$9
18	NYM	429	43	11	51	0	267	8	261	319	417	102	85	110	7	89	0.69	36	19	45	28	108	85	109	7%	5%	82	0%	0%	25	60%	20%	3.8	217	$9
19	ARI	285	31	9	37	0	317	7	290	361	487	113	128	101	5	88	0.48	37	25	38	33	114	84	93	10%	8%	82	0%	0%	21	48%	10%	13.4	211	$7
1st Half		138	13	2	14	0	281	2	280	326	398	97	115	85	4	89	0.43	41	24	35	30	113	64	74	5%	5%	81	0%	0%	9	33%	11%	-0.8	159	$0
2nd Half		147	18	7	23	0	350	5	301	395	569	127	140	117	6	88	0.53	33	25	42	36	116	103	111	14%	10%	96	0%	0%	12	58%	8%	14.2	281	$14
20	**Proj**	**350**	**39**	**12**	**47**	**0**	**283**		**275**	**327**	**457**	**106**	**115**	**100**	**6**	**88**	**0.47**	**36**	**22**	**42**	**29**	**113**	**86**	**105**	**10%**		**87**	**1%**	**46%**				**10.6**	**150**	**$12**

Flowers,Tyler

Age: 34	Bats: R	Pos: CA	Health	B	LIMA Plan	D
Ht: 6' 4"	Wt: 260		PT/Exp	D	Rand Var	-1
			Consist	B	MM	2003

Kept head above water early on thanks to inflated h% and HR/F, but the big jump in strikeouts caught up to him, and he hit just .198 after April 28. Still has patience, power, and defense going for him, but unless ct% bounces back, the potential BA damage could more than offset any positive contributions.

Yr	Tm	PA	R	HR	RBI	SB	BA	xHR	xBA	OBP	SLG	OPS+	vL+	vR+	bb%	ct%	Eye	G	L	F	h%	HctX	PX	xPX	HR/F	xHR/F	Spd	SBO	SB%	#Wk	DOM	DIS	RAR	BPX	R$
15	CHW	361	21	9	39	0	239	10	194	295	356	91	104	86	6	69	0.20	47	17	36	32	93	88	85	11%	12%	66	1%	0%	26	27%	54%	-4.6	-57	$2
16	ATL	325	27	8	41	0	270	14	217	357	420	106	104	104	9	68	0.32	42	19	39	37	120	113	153	11%	18%	80	0%	0%	22	36%	45%	4.5	14	$5
17	ATL	370	41	12	49	0	281	10	255	378	445	110	110	108	8	74	0.38	42	24	33	35	111	99	99	15%	13%	64	1%	0%	27	30%	33%	11.8	42	$9
18	ATL	296	34	8	30	0	227	10	215	341	359	97	155	74	12	70	0.46	41	21	38	29	126	86	132	12%	15%	71	0%	0%	24	29%	54%	2.2	-13	$2
19	ATL	310	36	11	34	0	229	13	217	319	413	97	71	109	10	61	0.30	45	20	35	33	88	117	106	19%	22%	120	0%	0%	27	26%	52%	-1.1	-11	$2
1st Half		169	19	7	15	0	250	9	215	337	446	105	76	117	11	61	0.31	47	19	34	36	74	118	95	23%	29%	135	0%	0%	15	33%	60%	4.5	7	$2
2nd Half		141	17	4	19	0	203	4	219	298	374	89	67	99	10	62	0.28	43	22	35	29	105	115	119	15%	15%	87	0%	0%	12	17%	42%	-2.4	-48	$3
20	**Proj**	**301**	**35**	**10**	**36**	**0**	**235**		**221**	**331**	**397**	**98**	**97**	**98**	**10**	**66**	**0.33**	**43**	**21**	**35**	**32**	**105**	**100**	**114**	**15%**		**94**	**0%**	**0%**				**6.0**	**-64**	**$6**

Ford,Mike

Age: 27	Bats: L	Pos: 1B	Health	A	LIMA Plan	D+
Ht: 6' 0"	Wt: 225		PT/Exp	C	Rand Var	+1
			Consist	F	MM	3041

12-25-.259 in 163 PA at NYY. Unlucky h% (14% in first 90 MLB PA) suppressed numbers for awhile, but got it going with .379 BA, 8 HR in last 73 PA. Though xHR/F warns against fully buying in, 2nd half surges in ct%, FB%, and HctX at least make him worth keeping an eye on. With opportunity, could again be cheap source of power.

Yr	Tm	PA	R	HR	RBI	SB	BA	xHR	xBA	OBP	SLG	OPS+	vL+	vR+	bb%	ct%	Eye	G	L	F	h%	HctX	PX	xPX	HR/F	xHR/F	Spd	SBO	SB%	#Wk	DOM	DIS	RAR	BPX	R$
15																																			
16	aa	174	19	5	23	0	259			390	432	112			18	80	1.08				29		106				83	0%	0%					194	$2
17	a/a	511	70	21	75	1	246			368	442	109			16	81	0.99				26		105				86	1%	100%					200	$10
18	aaa	396	38	14	41	1	215			273	373	89			7	77	0.35				24		95				85	1%	100%					90	$3
19	NYY *	492	74	32	69	0	255	6	270	334	523	114	181	102	11	78	0.55	37	18	44	26	111	133	135	24%	12%	57	1%	0%	13	62%	31%	12.6	222	$14
1st Half		280	39	17	39	0	257	1	317	357	524	118	133	91	14	75	0.62	28	39	33	28	100	139	102	17%	17%	80	2%	0%	4	50%	50%	8.1	233	$15
2nd Half		212	34	14	30	0	252	6	271	302	522	109	177	106	7	83	0.42	39	14	46	24	118	126	141	24%	13%	62	0%	0%	9	67%	22%	1.3	244	$12
20	**Proj**	**245**	**32**	**12**	**32**	**0**	**262**		**273**	**356**	**483**	**113**	**146**	**105**	**11**	**79**	**0.59**	**35**	**24**	**41**	**28**	**111**	**112**	**125**	**17%**		**63**	**1%**	**55%**				**7.3**	**146**	**$8**

BRIAN RUDD

Forsythe,Logan

Age: 33 Bats: R Pos: 1B 3B
Ht: 6' 1" Wt: 205

Health	C	LIMA Plan	D
PT/Exp	C	Rand Var	0
Consist	A	MM	1303

Hit .302 through May, but gradually lost playing time before rib injury ended season in Sept. Hot start was a h%-fueled mirage, as contact sunk to new lows, xBA remained on life support, and he couldn't recover dominance vL. There's hope for some minor power gains, but BPX trend at this age says his run is in cool-down mode.

Yr	Tm	PA	R	HR	RBI	SB	BA	xHR	xBA	OBP	SLG	OPS+	vL+	vR+	bb%	ct%	Eye	G	L	F	h%	HctX	PX	xPX	HR/F	xHR/F	Spd	SBO	SB%	#Wk	DOM	DIS	RAR	BPX	R$
15	TAM	615	69	17	68	9	281	16	255	359	444	112	134	100	9	79	0.50	40	20	41	33	108	109	105	10%	9%	106	8%	69%	26	46%	27%	13.3	154	$20
16	TAM	567	76	20	52	6	264	24	259	333	444	106	105	104	8	75	0.36	42	23	35	32	110	110	115	15%	18%	121	9%	50%	24	50%	25%	0.5	123	$14
17	LA	439	56	6	36	3	224	9	225	351	327	91	115	76	16	70	0.63	44	23	33	30	103	74	111	7%	11%	92	4%	60%	23	30%	52%	-12.5	0	$2
18	2 TM	416	37	2	27	3	232	4	217	313	291	84	76	88	10	78	0.49	49	19	32	29	97	45	69	2%	4%	97	3%	100%	24	21%	50%	-14.6	-7	$2
19	TEX	366	38	7	39	2	227	11	223	325	353	90	76	97	12	68	0.44	42	23	35	31	112	81	133	9%	14%	89	2%	100%	24	21%	71%	-11.9	-30	$2
1st Half		222	25	3	31	1	259	6	241	360	402	102	92	107	13	68	0.48	39	27	34	37	117	102	150	7%	14%	92	2%	100%	14	29%	64%	-1.3	33	$5
2nd Half		144	13	4	8	1	180	5	194	271	281	73	54	83	10	70	0.38	46	17	37	22	105	53	109	12%	15%	90	3%	100%	10	10%	80%	-11.8	-107	-$2
20	**Proj**	**315**	**33**	**5**	**27**	**2**	**225**		**220**	**317**	**330**	**87**	**81**	**90**	**11**	**72**	**0.45**	**45**	**21**	**35**	**29**	**106**	**65**	**108**	**8%**		**95**	**3%**	**82%**				**-9.7**	**-64**	**$1**

Fowler,Dexter

Age: 34 Bats: B Pos: RF CF
Ht: 6' 5" Wt: 195

Health	C	LIMA Plan	C+
PT/Exp	B	Rand Var	0
Consist	F	MM	2325

Modest rebound from injury-riddled 2018, but with hints of decline. xBA, another uptick in Ks suggest BA will remain a liability; quickly becoming ineffective on basepaths; not enough FBs to complement his last remaining plus skill (xPX). At an age where SB dry up fast and don't return, there's little left to buoy his value.

Yr	Tm	PA	R	HR	RBI	SB	BA	xHR	xBA	OBP	SLG	OPS+	vL+	vR+	bb%	ct%	Eye	G	L	F	h%	HctX	PX	xPX	HR/F	xHR/F	Spd	SBO	SB%	#Wk	DOM	DIS	RAR	BPX	R$
15	CHC	690	102	17	46	20	250	13	245	346	411	106	119	99	12	74	0.55	43	20	36	31	90	109	98	11%	8%	164	15%	74%	26	50%	27%	-1.3	159	$19
16	CHC	551	84	13	48	13	276	15	250	393	447	114	118	110	14	73	0.64	41	24	36	35	90	110	100	11%	13%	143	11%	76%	23	48%	35%	18.0	151	$18
17	STL	491	68	18	64	7	264	16	269	363	488	114	100	117	13	76	0.62	39	22	38	31	117	124	150	15%	13%	148	8%	70%	24	54%	38%	10.4	227	$14
18	STL	334	40	8	31	5	180	5	217	278	298	80	77	80	11	74	0.51	42	18	39	21	93	74	89	9%	6%	92	10%	71%	19	26%	47%	-17.3	27	$1
19	STL	574	69	19	67	8	238	18	245	346	409	100	89	103	13	71	0.52	39	25	36	30	92	99	129	15%	14%	91	9%	62%	28	43%	43%	-12.3	67	$12
1st Half		256	27	8	27	4	243	7	251	349	394	99	102	99	12	72	0.49	40	28	32	30	96	86	102	16%	14%	84	9%	67%	15	47%	47%	-5.3	30	$6
2nd Half		318	42	11	40	4	234	11	241	343	420	101	81	107	14	70	0.54	38	23	39	29	89	110	150	15%	15%	102	9%	57%	13	38%	38%	-4.4	104	$16
20	**Proj**	**490**	**63**	**15**	**55**	**8**	**242**		**240**	**343**	**407**	**101**	**93**	**102**	**13**	**73**	**0.53**	**40**	**23**	**37**	**30**	**96**	**93**	**120**	**13%**		**110**	**9%**	**67%**				**0.6**	**74**	**$14**

Fowler,Dustin

Age: 25 Bats: L Pos: OF
Ht: 6' 0" Wt: 190

Health	B	LIMA Plan	D
PT/Exp	C	Rand Var	
Consist	C	MM	2411

A step back for this once-trendy prospect, as he spent most of the season at AAA. Warning signs are plentiful—from the jump in strikeouts to another year of subpar on-base skills, stagnant PX, and he mostly stopped running. We've seen better skills before, so can't rule out a post-hype rebound, but it's best to track that from afar.

Yr	Tm	PA	R	HR	RBI	SB	BA	xHR	xBA	OBP	SLG	OPS+	vL+	vR+	bb%	ct%	Eye	G	L	F	h%	HctX	PX	xPX	HR/F	xHR/F	Spd	SBO	SB%	#Wk	DOM	DIS	RAR	BPX	R$
15																																			
16	aa	562	63	13	83	24	268			295	434	99			4	83	0.22				30		93				119	31%	67%					143	$22
17	NYY *	310	44	14	38	12	273		276	304	505	109	0	0	4	76	0.19	44	20	36	32	0	129	-26	0%		136	29%	68%	1	0%	100%	3.6	182	$12
18	OAK *	439	48	9	44	16	266	7	237	292	410	97	41	87	3	78	0.16	41	20	39	32	113	83	88	10%	12%	132	25%	72%	17	18%	59%	0.4	90	$14
19	aaa	587	73	17	67	8	230			271	379	86			5	70	0.18				30		84				127	11%	64%					-11	$10
1st Half		338	42	10	44	4	233			275	394	89			5	71	0.20				30		88				138	12%	56%				-8.7	41	$12
2nd Half		250	31	8	22	4	227			266	360	83			5	67	0.16				31		78				118	10%	76%				-8.9	-81	$8
20	**Proj**	**210**	**26**	**5**	**23**	**5**	**249**		**229**	**282**	**399**	**92**	**44**	**95**	**4**	**74**	**0.17**	**41**	**20**	**39**	**31**	**102**	**82**	**79**	**9%**		**132**	**16%**	**65%**				**-5.8**	**27**	**$6**

Fraley,Jake

Age: 25 Bats: L Pos: CF
Ht: 6' 0" Wt: 195

Health	A	LIMA Plan	D+
PT/Exp	F	Rand Var	-3
Consist	F	MM	4321

0-1-.150 in 41 PA at SEA. Thumb injury during Sept audition soured otherwise productive season. Took advantage of green light and made gains elsewhere, as PX, FB stroke (44% FB% in minors) say the power can stick. Iffy contact, plate patience say it might not always be smooth, but SB upside alone gives him end game intrigue.

Yr	Tm	PA	R	HR	RBI	SB	BA	xHR	xBA	OBP	SLG	OPS+	vL+	vR+	bb%	ct%	Eye	G	L	F	h%	HctX	PX	xPX	HR/F	xHR/F	Spd	SBO	SB%	#Wk	DOM	DIS	RAR	BPX	R$
15																																			
16																																			
17																																			
18																																			
19	SEA *	452	60	16	68	18	251	0	207	299	444	99	29	55	6	72	0.24	31	12	58	31	38	111	2	0%	0%	107	29%	70%	3	0%	100%	-8.3	81	$17
1st Half		293	43	10	49	16	276		251	330	474	107			8	72	0.29				35		111		0%		119	34%	70%				0.6	111	$26
2nd Half		159	17	6	19	3	207	0	204	241	390	83	29	55	4	70	0.15	31	12	58	25	37	111	2	0%	0%	92	16%	69%	3	0%	100%	-10.6	30	$0
20	**Proj**	**245**	**30**	**11**	**34**	**8**	**251**		**245**	**308**	**466**	**104**	**107**	**103**	**6**	**71**	**0.20**	**33**	**24**	**44**	**31**	**90**	**125**	**2**	**15%**		**101**	**26%**	**71%**				**4.4**	**111**	**$10**

France,Ty

Age: 25 Bats: R Pos: 3B 2B
Ht: 6' 0" Wt: 205

Health	A	LIMA Plan	D
PT/Exp	C	Rand Var	-3
Consist	C	MM	3031

7-24-.234 in 201 PA at SD. Breakout season—even by Pacific Coast League standards—led to a couple of chances in majors. Finished with 5 HR in 60 PA in September, and while PX growth supports the power spike, MLB plate skills (0.18 Eye, .240 xBA) hint at short-term BA risk. Still, BPX says he's worth a dart throw on the possiblity of an everyday gig.

Yr	Tm	PA	R	HR	RBI	SB	BA	xHR	xBA	OBP	SLG	OPS+	vL+	vR+	bb%	ct%	Eye	G	L	F	h%	HctX	PX	xPX	HR/F	xHR/F	Spd	SBO	SB%	#Wk	DOM	DIS	RAR	BPX	R$
15																																			
16																																			
17	aa	382	38	4	36	1	259			297	353	87			5	80	0.27				31		60				91	1%	100%					21	$4
18	a/a	543	63	16	72	2	223			272	372	89			6	80	0.33				25		88				89	6%	33%					100	$8
19	SD *	518	77	24	85	1	288	7	270	330	510	111	101	88	6	77	0.27	43	21	37	33	112	118	96	14%	14%	106	2%	25%	14	36%	57%	6.6	174	$18
1st Half		273	41	14	48	1	282	3	274	317	519	112	61	96	5	77	0.23	50	16	34	32	105	122	82	8%	12%	128	3%	41%	7	29%	71%	3.9	211	$20
2nd Half		245	36	10	37	0	294	3	271	343	499	111	142	79	7	76	0.32	34	26	40	35	119	114	113	20%	12%	76	2%	0%	7	43%	43%	5.3	130	$16
20	**Proj**	**210**	**27**	**9**	**30**	**1**	**262**		**264**	**329**	**460**	**106**	**127**	**96**	**6**	**78**	**0.30**	**40**	**22**	**38**	**29**	**113**	**105**	**101**	**15%**		**98**	**4%**	**32%**				**1.1**	**100**	**$7**

Franco,Maikel

Age: 27 Bats: R Pos: 3B
Ht: 6' 1" Wt: 215

Health	A	LIMA Plan	D+
PT/Exp	B	Rand Var	+3
Consist	D	MM	2333

17-56-.234 in 428 PA at PHI. Early power surge (6 HR in 16 games) evaporated, as struggles led to AAA demotion in August. Continued to put bat on ball with ease, but without enough oomph (HctX, xPX) to make the FB% spike count. Minor BA recovery is likely, but recapturing 2016-18's HR baseline seems unrealistic.

Yr	Tm	PA	R	HR	RBI	SB	BA	xHR	xBA	OBP	SLG	OPS+	vL+	vR+	bb%	ct%	Eye	G	L	F	h%	HctX	PX	xPX	HR/F	xHR/F	Spd	SBO	SB%	#Wk	DOM	DIS	RAR	BPX	R$
15	PHI *	483	57	18	70	3	291	10	283	340	492	116	114	116	7	82	0.40	47	18	35	32	105	130	120	16%	11%	91	2%	100%	16	69%	25%	17.1	200	$18
16	PHI	630	67	25	88	1	255	22	263	306	427	100	116	93	6	82	0.38	44	20	35	27	102	95	91	15%	13%	76	1%	50%	27	48%	26%	-9.8	117	$14
17	PHI	623	66	24	76	0	230	18	264	281	409	92	87	93	7	83	0.43	45	18	37	24	105	95	86	13%	10%	64	0%	0%	27	52%	22%	-26.1	133	$7
18	PHI	465	48	22	68	1	270	17	272	314	467	108	90	113	6	86	0.47	49	17	34	27	87	100	88	17%	13%	89	1%	100%	27	52%	30%	6.1	213	$14
19	PHI *	472	52	19	60	0	225	16	250	291	402	92	104	90	8	84	0.57	43	17	40	23	96	84	78	13%	12%	83	0%	0%	26	42%	27%	-20.5	170	$6
1st Half		277	34	12	40	0	227	12	256	296	414	95	84	98	9	87	0.76	45	15	40	22	102	86	73	14%	14%	81	0%	0%	15	47%	20%	-8.9	226	$9
2nd Half		195	18	7	20	0	223	4	244	282	385	88	127	72	8	79	0.40	40	20	40	25	88	82	88	11%	9%	91	0%	0%	11	36%	36%	-9.1	100	$2
20	**Proj**	**350**	**37**	**13**	**45**	**0**	**248**		**258**	**303**	**422**	**98**	**105**	**94**	**7**	**84**	**0.51**	**45**	**18**	**38**	**26**	**95**	**84**	**86**	**13%**		**87**	**0%**	**92%**				**-2.0**	**120**	**$9**

Frazier,Adam

Age: 28 Bats: L Pos: 2B
Ht: 5' 10" Wt: 180

Health	A	LIMA Plan	B
PT/Exp	B	Rand Var	0
Consist	A	MM	1255

Hit rate pendulum swung wildly, as hits started to drop in 2nd half. Excellent contact skills, LD% stroke lock in BA value, but there's not much else to like. Raw speed hasn't translated to SB success, which has limited his opps, while PX/xPX set him back in today's HR environment. Reliability scores confirm: plan for more of the same.

Yr	Tm	PA	R	HR	RBI	SB	BA	xHR	xBA	OBP	SLG	OPS+	vL+	vR+	bb%	ct%	Eye	G	L	F	h%	HctX	PX	xPX	HR/F	xHR/F	Spd	SBO	SB%	#Wk	DOM	DIS	RAR	BPX	R$
15	aa	404	47	1	24	9	281			328	356	95			7	88	0.57				32		51				115	15%	52%					111	$10
16	PIT *	448	52	2	31	19	306	2	298	366	400	104	113	101	9	86	0.70	44	33	23	35	110	59	93	7%	7%	140	28%	52%	16	25%	56%	1.9	154	$18
17	PIT	454	55	6	53	9	276	6	288	344	399	100	90	100	8	86	0.63	48	25	27	31	96	66	59	6%	6%	124	12%	64%	25	44%	24%	-7.6	158	$12
18	PIT *	481	59	10	48	2	251	7	266	309	397	98	81	117	8	83	0.49	49	20	31	28	106	87	79	12%	8%	108	8%	21%	22	59%	14%	-8.9	167	$8
19	PIT	608	80	10	50	5	278	10	283	336	417	100	88	104	7	86	0.53	41	26	33	31	89	70	69	6%	6%	129	7%	50%	28	46%	18%	-8.0	207	$13
1st Half		307	38	3	19	2	254	5	273	311	361	90	81	93	6	86	0.50	41	26	32	28	95	54	67	4%	6%	138	6%	50%	15	40%	20%	-12.6	167	$6
2nd Half		301	42	7	31	3	303	6	294	361	474	110	97	115	7	86	0.57	41	26	34	33	83	87	70	9%	8%	119	8%	50%	13	54%	15%	5.9	252	$21
20	**Proj**	**525**	**68**	**10**	**49**	**6**	**275**		**283**	**335**	**420**	**102**	**87**	**105**	**7**	**86**	**0.53**	**44**	**25**	**31**	**30**	**96**	**74**	**72**	**8%**		**123**	**10%**	**48%**				**7.5**	**171**	**$16**

RYAN BLOOMFIELD

Frazier,Clint

Age: 25 Bats: R Pos: RF		Health	D	LIMA Plan	D+
Ht: 6' 1" Wt: 190		PT/Exp	D	Rand Var	0
		Consist	D	MM	4313

12-38-.267 in 246 PA at NYY. Weak glove, stacked NYY lineup made it tough to stick in majors, though fading skills didn't help his cause. Declining HctX and xPX, and at risk of becoming BA liability as well. SBO, SB% trends don't bode well for return to SB relevance. Despite all that, there is a history of better, so still too talented to give up on.

Yr Tm	PA	R	HR	RBI	SB	BA	xHR	xBA	OBP	SLG	OPS+	vL+	vR+	bb%	ct%	Eye	G	L	F	h%	HctX	PX	xPX	HR/F	xHR/F	Spd	SBO	SB%	#Wk	DOM	DIS	RAR	BPX	R$
15																																		
16 a/a	508	70	18	51	12	253			319	436	103			9	71	0.34				32		120				108	14%	74%					94	$14
17 NYY *	448	57	17	54	9	237	5	242	305	449	101	102	92	9	71	0.33	38	17	45	29	115	132	158	10%	12%	121	13%	80%	11	36%	36%	-4.1	133	$9
18 NYY *	250	40	10	18	3	274	1	276	345	487	115	159	73	10	67	0.33	52	29	19	37	106	147	139	0%	25%	129	9%	59%	7	14%	71%	8.1	157	$6
19 NYY *	511	60	20	59	3	240	11	240	287	430	95	95	111	6	72	0.23	39	20	42	29	86	112	101	18%	17%	100	7%	38%	16	38%	50%	-14.7	74	$9
1st Half	255	28	12	36	3	267	10	248	313	485	107	106	114	6	70	0.22	39	21	40	33	84	129	110	20%	19%	97	9%	57%	11	45%	45%	-0.4	96	$14
2nd Half	257	32	8	23	0	213	1	212	261	377	84	71	84	6	73	0.24	35	13	52	26	88	97	51	8%	8%	104	5%	0%	5	20%	60%	-16.3	59	$5
20 Proj	**350**	**47**	**15**	**38**	**4**	**246**		**234**	**303**	**457**	**102**	**95**	**105**	**8**	**71**	**0.28**	**37**	**17**	**46**	**30**	**98**	**124**	**109**	**14%**		**118**	**9%**	**60%**				**0.7**	**93**	**$7**

Frazier,Todd

Age: 34 Bats: R Pos: 3B		Health	C	LIMA Plan	D
Ht: 6' 3" Wt: 220		PT/Exp	B	Rand Var	-1
		Consist	B	MM	2113

Spring training oblique injury delayed start of season, likely led to 1st half drops in PX, xPX; hit 18 of 21 HR after June 1. Even career-low HctX followed same line of demarcation: 71 before 6/1, 94 after. Still, can't dismiss eroding Eye, xHR/F decline, disappearance of running game. Aging Axiom #3: Negatives tend to snowball as you age.

Yr Tm	PA	R	HR	RBI	SB	BA	xHR	xBA	OBP	SLG	OPS+	vL+	vR+	bb%	ct%	Eye	G	L	F	h%	HctX	PX	xPX	HR/F	xHR/F	Spd	SBO	SB%	#Wk	DOM	DIS	RAR	BPX	R$
15 CIN	678	82	35	89	13	255	31	273	309	498	112	125	106	6	78	0.32	33	19	48	28	125	157	155	15%	13%	79	17%	62%	27	63%	30%	6.1	205	$24
16 CHW	666	89	40	98	15	225	32	245	302	464	104	108	101	10	72	0.39	36	16	49	24	92	142	111	19%	15%	71	15%	75%	27	44%	30%	-7.3	131	$19
17 2 AL	571	73	27	76	4	214	25	243	342	430	103	117	97	14	74	0.64	34	18	47	23	96	122	123	16%	15%	76	5%	57%	27	44%	33%	-11.6	133	$8
18 NYM	472	54	18	59	9	213	16	228	303	390	96	74	103	10	73	0.43	36	19	46	25	109	110	132	13%	12%	81	13%	69%	23	39%	39%	-12.3	83	$10
19 NYM	499	63	21	67	1	251	16	248	329	443	102	119	95	8	76	0.38	35	22	43	28	88	99	107	14%	11%	100	3%	33%	24	33%	42%	-10.5	119	$11
1st Half	228	27	11	34	1	261	7	261	342	463	108	133	99	9	79	0.48	38	23	40	28	87	95	92	17%	11%	92	4%	50%	11	45%	45%	-0.4	152	$10
2nd Half	271	36	10	33	0	242	9	237	317	426	98	110	93	8	74	0.31	33	21	46	29	89	102	120	12%	11%	107	2%	0%	13	23%	38%	-7.4	96	$11
20 Proj	**280**	**36**	**11**	**38**	**2**	**234**		**236**	**320**	**420**	**100**	**105**	**97**	**10**	**75**	**0.42**	**35**	**20**	**45**	**27**	**97**	**99**	**119**	**13%**		**92**	**5%**	**48%**				**-2.7**	**63**	**$7**

Freeman,Freddie

Age: 30 Bats: L Pos: 1B		Health	B	LIMA Plan	D+
Ht: 6' 5" Wt: 220		PT/Exp	A	Rand Var	0
		Consist	B	MM	4255

Bone spurs in right elbow flared up in Sept (.754 OPS, 93 PX, .248 xBA) and took bite out of 2nd half skills. Eye vL dropped to 0.25, lowest rate since 2011. The rest of this skill set is outstanding; he can do this again, and perhaps take a shot at more. xHR suggests it should've happened twice already, so let's make it official... UP: 40 HR

Yr Tm	PA	R	HR	RBI	SB	BA	xHR	xBA	OBP	SLG	OPS+	vL+	vR+	bb%	ct%	Eye	G	L	F	h%	HctX	PX	xPX	HR/F	xHR/F	Spd	SBO	SB%	#Wk	DOM	DIS	RAR	BPX	R$
15 ATL	481	62	18	66	3	276	27	279	370	471	117	91	125	12	76	0.57	37	28	36	32	129	133	152	16%	24%	82	3%	75%	22	45%	23%	7.6	168	$16
16 ATL	693	102	34	91	6	302	43	279	400	569	132	122	134	13	71	0.52	30	29	41	38	125	173	177	20%	25%	110	4%	86%	27	59%	15%	46.4	237	$29
17 ATL	514	84	28	71	8	307	32	300	403	586	133	117	136	13	78	0.68	35	24	41	34	119	157	156	20%	23%	102	10%	62%	21	76%	10%	29.5	294	$24
18 ATL	707	94	23	98	10	309	36	290	388	505	124	128	120	11	79	0.58	36	32	31	36	121	119	123	15%	23%	82	7%	77%	28	61%	25%	34.6	193	$31
19 ATL	692	113	38	121	6	295	41	296	389	549	125	98	134	13	79	0.09	38	28	34	32	128	127	133	24%	25%	90	5%	67%	28	71%	18%	36.0	263	$31
1st Half	381	63	22	65	3	312	24	310	399	592	132	122	136	12	79	0.64	36	30	34	34	140	141	145	24%	27%	95	5%	60%	15	80%	7%	30.1	311	$36
2nd Half	311	50	16	56	3	273	17	279	376	496	115	74	132	14	78	0.74	41	25	34	29	112	111	117	23%	24%	86	5%	75%	13	62%	31%	10.2	211	$23
20 Proj	**665**	**103**	**37**	**106**	**7**	**300**		**295**	**391**	**559**	**128**	**110**	**135**	**12**	**78**	**0.65**	**37**	**28**	**35**	**33**	**122**	**134**	**135**	**23%**		**91**	**6%**	**70%**				**52.7**	**255**	**$34**

Gallo,Joey

Age: 26 Bats: L Pos: CF LF		Health	D	LIMA Plan	B
Ht: 6' 5" Wt: 235		PT/Exp	B	Rand Var	-5
		Consist	C	MM	5115

Oblique injury cost him most of June, broken hamate ended season in late July. Too bad, because stellar 1st half featured more walks and LD%, lower FB% yet higher HR/F—a continuation of changes that began in 2nd half of 2018. It resulted in .263 xBA over 410 AB, and eye-popping 1st half xHR pace. If wrist is healthy... UP: .260 BA, 50 HR

Yr Tm	PA	R	HR	RBI	SB	BA	xHR	xBA	OBP	SLG	OPS+	vL+	vR+	bb%	ct%	Eye	G	L	F	h%	HctX	PX	xPX	HR/F	xHR/F	Spd	SBO	SB%	#Wk	DOM	DIS	RAR	BPX	R$
15 TEX *	486	49	24	64	5	210	7	217	303	433	103	66	115	12	52	0.28	35	27	37	33	115	206	185	32%	37%	81	5%	100%	10	40%	50%	-2.8	62	$7
16 TEX *	443	57	21	52	3	204	1	184	310	434	101	34	50	13	53	0.33	17	17	67	31	36	185	100	25%	25%	120	3%	100%	7	0%	86%	-0.3	74	$4
17 TEX	532	85	41	80	7	209	42	237	333	537	117	111	116	14	56	0.38	28	18	54	25	106	231	206	30%	31%	110	8%	78%	27	59%	30%	11.5	221	$13
18 TEX	577	82	40	92	3	206	48	238	312	498	112	114	110	13	59	0.36	30	21	50	25	105	213	180	28%	33%	81	6%	43%	28	64%	25%	12.1	190	$16
19 TEX	297	54	22	49	4	253	29	241	389	598	131	153	120	18	53	0.46	27	26	47	37	95	251	199	37%	49%	96	8%	67%	15	60%	27%	23.3	285	$11
1st Half	238	45	20	46	3	286	26	269	426	683	148	156	144	20	56	0.55	27	29	43	40	106	270	199	43%	57%	98	6%	75%	12	67%	17%	31.7	411	$17
2nd Half	59	9	2	3	1	135	3	124	237	288	69	153	37	10	40	0.19	26	5	68	26	53	153	200	15%	23%	107	22%	50%	3	33%	67%	-4.7	-226	-$13
20 Proj	**560**	**90**	**41**	**90**	**3**	**242**		**235**	**370**	**559**	**125**	**152**	**113**	**16**	**56**	**0.44**	**29**	**22**	**49**	**33**	**102**	**215**	**194**	**32%**		**86**	**5%**	**50%**				**39.8**	**188**	**$22**

Galvis,Freddy

Age: 30 Bats: B Pos: SS 2B		Health	A	LIMA Plan	D+
Ht: 5' 10" Wt: 185		PT/Exp	A	Rand Var	-2
		Consist	A	MM	2323

Transition to more homers and fewer steals has basically been a wash, value-wise, and xHR suggests we shouldn't trust the two 20+ HR seasons. (The corresponding HR/F outliers would seem to second that notion.) When you add in career-low ct% that got worse in 2nd half, good chance BA goes backward, too.

Yr Tm	PA	R	HR	RBI	SB	BA	xHR	xBA	OBP	SLG	OPS+	vL+	vR+	bb%	ct%	Eye	G	L	F	h%	HctX	PX	xPX	HR/F	xHR/F	Spd	SBO	SB%	#Wk	DOM	DIS	RAR	BPX	R$
15 PHI	603	63	7	50	10	263	8	229	302	343	90	83	91	5	82	0.29	41	22	37	31	88	49	89	4%	5%	139	7%	91%	27	19%	41%	-8.4	51	$13
16 PHI	624	61	20	67	17	241	12	253	274	399	92	73	95	4	77	0.18	40	23	36	28	83	95	80	13%	8%	99	20%	74%	27	37%	30%	-22.0	63	$14
17 PHI	663	71	12	61	14	255	12	252	309	382	93	85	94	7	82	0.41	37	24	39	29	84	71	85	6%	6%	126	12%	74%	27	44%	30%	-18.5	112	$14
18 SD	656	62	13	67	8	248	15	239	299	380	94	108	87	7	76	0.31	41	22	37	31	112	85	118	8%	9%	105	10%	57%	28	43%	43%	-9.0	60	$13
19 2 TM	589	67	23	70	4	260	17	245	296	438	97	94	99	5	74	0.19	40	21	39	31	97	98	100	14%	11%	93	5%	67%	25	28%	44%	-1.6	52	$14
1st Half	320	37	12	38	3	257	8	241	297	426	97	93	99	5	75	0.23	43	19	38	31	89	92	87	14%	9%	85	6%	75%	15	27%	40%	-2.9	48	$15
2nd Half	269	30	11	32	1	264	8	248	295	453	99	97	100	4	72	0.16	37	24	39	32	107	106	115	15%	11%	108	4%	50%	10	30%	50%	-0.7	63	$13
20 Proj	**350**	**38**	**11**	**38**	**4**	**250**		**244**	**291**	**406**	**94**	**93**	**93**	**5**	**76**	**0.24**	**40**	**22**	**38**	**30**	**99**	**86**	**103**	**11%**		**108**	**8%**	**67%**				**-1.7**	**30**	**$9**

Gamel,Ben

Age: 28 Bats: L Pos: LF RF CF		Health	A	LIMA Plan	D
Ht: 5' 11" Wt: 185		PT/Exp	C	Rand Var	-2
		Consist	B	MM	1323

If 2019 season was an attempt to trade ct% for power, it fell apart in 2nd half, and did further damage to BA that was already overdue for regression. Sudden surge in vL+ was driven by 52% hit rate, while slide in vR+ was more legit. He's providing less value with each passing year; xBA, BPX don't offer much hope for reversing course.

Yr Tm	PA	R	HR	RBI	SB	BA	xHR	xBA	OBP	SLG	OPS+	vL+	vR+	bb%	ct%	Eye	G	L	F	h%	HctX	PX	xPX	HR/F	xHR/F	Spd	SBO	SB%	#Wk	DOM	DIS	RAR	BPX	R$
15 aaa	541	68	10	56	11	276			331	427	106			8	76	0.34				35		100				130	13%	67%					105	$17
16 2 AL *	579	81	7	51	17	273	1	237	330	375	96	157	54	8	77	0.36	44	22	34	34	80	68	69	9%	9%	114	17%	66%	9	22%	56%	-6.0	37	$18
17 SEA *	619	73	12	65	5	273	10	247	326	404	98	93	98	7	76	0.34	45	22	33	34	91	79	80	8%	8%	123	4%	69%	24	29%	38%	-10.7	67	$14
18 SEA *	384	51	2	31	10	276	4	256	349	387	102	92	102	10	78	0.51	47	25	28	35	75	74	50	2%	7%	130	13%	77%	23	22%	39%	1.7	103	$10
19 MIL	356	47	7	33	2	248	6	232	337	373	94	118	87	11	67	0.38	44	26	29	35	87	85	89	11%	10%	108	4%	50%	28	32%	57%	-9.6	-30	$4
1st Half	207	29	5	18	1	260	5	239	348	398	100	114	96	11	67	0.37	42	28	30	36	102	90	128	14%	14%	110	6%	33%	15	33%	67%	-3.5	-7	$5
2nd Half	149	18	2	15	1	231	1	223	322	338	87	124	76	12	65	0.40	48	24	28	34	66	79	33	8%	4%	107	3%	100%	13	31%	46%	-5.8	-63	$3
20 Proj	**280**	**36**	**4**	**26**	**4**	**247**		**240**	**327**	**363**	**93**	**104**	**89**	**10**	**72**	**0.40**	**46**	**25**	**29**	**33**	**80**	**74**	**65**	**7%**		**120**	**8%**	**70%**				**-4.1**	**-9**	**$6**

Garcia,Avisail

Age: 29 Bats: R Pos: RF DH		Health	C	LIMA Plan	C+
Ht: 6' 4" Wt: 250		PT/Exp	B	Rand Var	-2
		Consist	C	MM	2225

xHR suggests that 20 HR is just scratching the surface of what he's capable of, but that's the lone positive. xBA indicates he got lucky on hit rate, xPX has been subpar every year but one, and double-digit SB stands as pretty big outlier. Has hit IL at least once in six of last seven seasons, making step back seem more likely than a repeat.

Yr Tm	PA	R	HR	RBI	SB	BA	xHR	xBA	OBP	SLG	OPS+	vL+	vR+	bb%	ct%	Eye	G	L	F	h%	HctX	PX	xPX	HR/F	xHR/F	Spd	SBO	SB%	#Wk	DOM	DIS	RAR	BPX	R$
15 CHW	601	66	13	59	7	257	15	243	309	365	94	105	89	6	75	0.26	49	25	27	32	96	73	90	12%	14%	93	10%	50%	27	33%	48%	-18.3	-3	$13
16 CHW	453	59	12	51	4	245	15	252	307	385	94	91	93	8	72	0.30	55	22	23	31	101	92	77	17%	21%	88	8%	50%	25	36%	40%	-11.0	17	$8
17 CHW	556	75	18	77	5	327	25	275	378	503	118	135	110	6	79	0.30	52	20	27	39	113	98	90	16%	23%	131	5%	63%	25	48%	44%	27.3	139	$25
18 CHW *	412	51	22	56	3	240	21	247	282	455	102	113	95	5	70	0.20	48	17	34	28	99	130	101	21%	24%	108	5%	75%	21	33%	48%	-2.3	100	$11
19 TAM	530	61	20	72	10	282	26	260	332	464	106	102	107	6	74	0.25	46	22	32	34	103	100	90	17%	22%	97	11%	71%	28	36%	46%	3.7	78	$18
1st Half	311	37	12	37	8	274	15	258	331	453	105	100	107	6	75	0.27	47	21	32	33	109	96	82	17%	22%	98	14%	80%	15	27%	47%	-1.0	78	$20
2nd Half	219	24	8	35	2	294	10	262	333	480	107	105	108	6	74	0.22	45	24	31	37	95	105	100	17%	21%	94	8%	50%	13	46%	46%	2.3	70	$15
20 Proj	**525**	**64**	**19**	**73**	**6**	**271**		**252**	**320**	**444**	**103**	**107**	**100**	**6**	**74**	**0.24**	**48**	**21**	**31**	**33**	**102**	**95**	**94**	**17%**		**106**	**8%**	**65%**				**4.1**	**35**	**$19**

BRANDON KRUSE

Garcia,Greg

Age: 30	Bats: L	Pos: 2B	Health	C	LIMA Plan	D
Ht: 6' 0"	Wt: 190		PT/Exp	D	Rand Var	-1
			Consist	B	MM	1221

In today's low-contact, launch angle environment, you don't see many OBPs higher than SLGs. He's actually there for his CAREER, which speaks to both his plate discipline, and the fact that nothing good happens when he does swing. Positional flexibility and respectable performance vR could yield a little deep NL-only value, if you squint.

Yr Tm	PA	R	HR	RBI	SB	BA	xHR	xBA	OBP	SLG	OPS+	vL+	vR+	bb%	ct%	Eye	G	L	F	h%	HctX	PX	xPX	HR/F	xHR/F	Spd	SBO	SB%	#Wk	DOM	DIS	RAR	BPX	R$
15 STL *	452	41	2	30	11	236	2	243	312	307	86	162	94	10	80	0.55	57	18	25	29	103	56	71	13%	13%	94	13%	76%	12	58%	17%	-11.3	38	$5
16 STL *	369	42	3	23	2	256	3	249	350	334	93	78	108	12	77	0.62	50	25	24	32	74	55	67	8%	8%	108	5%	41%	23	22%	39%	-9.1	31	$4
17 STL	290	27	2	20	2	253	2	253	365	332	93	45	100	13	73	0.58	48	30	22	34	50	52	41	5%	5%	121	4%	67%	27	30%	48%	-7.2	0	$2
18 STL	208	15	3	15	3	221	4	232	309	304	85	86	84	10	80	0.54	46	22	32	26	82	51	68	7%	9%	101	8%	75%	28	18%	46%	-7.1	33	$0
19 SD	372	52	4	31	0	248	4	243	364	354	95	67	99	14	73	0.64	55	22	23	33	81	62	46	8%	8%	133	2%	0%	28	29%	46%	-3.2	48	$3
1st Half	182	30	3	20	0	259	3	267	352	411	102	20	109	13	73	0.55	56	23	21	34	82	87	44	13%	13%	130	2%	0%	15	40%	40%	1.1	111	$4
2nd Half	190	22	1	11	0	235	1	217	376	294	88	90	88	16	73	0.73	54	20	26	32	80	35	48	3%	3%	126	2%	0%	13	15%	54%	-5.6	-26	$2
20 Proj	**245**	**28**	**3**	**19**	**2**	**240**		**241**	**348**	**334**	**92**	**75**	**94**	**13**	**75**	**0.60**	**52**	**23**	**26**	**31**	**77**	**54**	**53**	**7%**		**121**	**4%**	**53%**				**-2.3**	**-23**	**$1**

Garcia,Leury

Age: 29	Bats: B	Pos: CF RF LF	Health	D	LIMA Plan	C+
Ht: 5' 8"	Wt: 180		PT/Exp	C	Rand Var	-2
			Consist	A	MM	1533

Earned a nice profit for those who took a flyer, scratching max value out of a lackluster skill set. GB/LD swing complemented his speed and lack of power. However, OBP was still below average due to puny bb%. The bags aren't worth the price even in a speed-starved era, and it's doubtful the PT is repeatable.

Yr Tm	PA	R	HR	RBI	SB	BA	xHR	xBA	OBP	SLG	OPS+	vL+	vR+	bb%	ct%	Eye	G	L	F	h%	HctX	PX	xPX	HR/F	xHR/F	Spd	SBO	SB%	#Wk	DOM	DIS	RAR	BPX	R$
15 CHW *	382	47	3	27	26	257		266	293	336	88	74	61	5	77	0.22	100	0	0	33	95	60	-16	0%		119	43%	65%	9	0%	67%	-13.8	3	$14
16 CHW *	380	42	6	33	16	264	1	238	305	363	91	48	101	6	75	0.24	54	20	26	34	78	59	68	11%	11%	115	28%	61%	5	0%	80%	-7.3	-14	$11
17 CHW	321	40	9	33	8	274	7	272	318	429	100	95	100	4	77	0.19	55	20	24	33	84	91	67	16%	13%	101	19%	62%	16	44%	44%	-9.1	64	$9
18 CHW	275	23	4	32	12	271	4	248	303	376	94	110	86	3	73	0.13	49	29	23	36	81	63	63	10%	10%	137	20%	92%	22	14%	59%	-3.6	-20	$8
19 CHW	618	93	8	40	15	279	10	253	310	378	91	103	85	3	76	0.15	55	22	24	36	75	59	45	8%	10%	147	14%	75%	27	15%	48%	-17.5	15	$18
1st Half	311	56	5	23	8	290	6	261	327	393	96	112	90	4	76	0.17	55	24	22	37	71	63	53	10%	13%	129	16%	67%	15	20%	47%	-6.4	15	$21
2nd Half	307	37	3	17	7	268	4	243	292	362	86	96	81	3	76	0.13	55	19	25	35	78	55	37	5%	7%	151	12%	88%	12	8%	50%	-11.7	0	$14
20 Proj	**420**	**48**	**7**	**36**	**12**	**268**		**253**	**302**	**377**	**91**	**101**	**86**	**4**	**75**	**0.15**	**53**	**24**	**24**	**34**	**79**	**62**	**54**	**10%**		**134**	**17%**	**73%**				**-0.6**	**-20**	**$14**

Gardner,Brett

Age: 36	Bats: L	Pos: CF LF	Health	A	LIMA Plan	C+
Ht: 5' 11"	Wt: 195		PT/Exp	A	Rand Var	+1
			Consist	B	MM	2523

Nice rebound from down 2018, as career-best HR buoyed by increased FB%, fortuitous hr/f, and torrid Sept (10 HR in 94 PA). But xHR and wide PX/xPX gap tell us to expect a major pullback. Speed skills still look strong, but he's at an age where one muscle pull erases double-digit SB. Wherever he lands in 2020, don't pay for a repeat of this.

Yr Tm	PA	R	HR	RBI	SB	BA	xHR	xBA	OBP	SLG	OPS+	vL+	vR+	bb%	ct%	Eye	G	L	F	h%	HctX	PX	xPX	HR/F	xHR/F	Spd	SBO	SB%	#Wk	DOM	DIS	RAR	BPX	R$
15 NYY	656	94	16	66	20	259	15	247	343	399	103	105	101	10	76	0.50	45	21	34	31	88	94	87	11%	10%	115	15%	80%	27	37%	48%	5.1	103	$22
16 NYY	634	80	7	41	16	261	8	256	351	362	97	87	99	11	81	0.66	52	21	27	31	84	61	42	6%	7%	129	11%	80%	27	30%	37%	1.6	97	$15
17 NYY	682	96	21	63	23	264	13	266	350	428	104	78	111	11	79	0.59	44	22	33	30	92	89	79	13%	8%	124	16%	82%	26	38%	46%	-4.7	148	$23
18 NYY	609	95	12	45	16	236	10	247	322	368	96	87	98	11	80	0.61	49	18	33	27	81	75	58	8%	7%	154	12%	89%	28	36%	61%	-8.7	163	$15
19 NYY	550	86	28	74	10	251	12	276	325	503	110	85	119	9	78	0.48	44	18	38	27	92	125	80	19%	8%	130	11%	83%	27	52%	33%	6.2	267	$18
1st Half	298	49	12	36	6	236	5	267	319	441	102	67	112	10	83	0.68	47	15	38	24	94	93	67	14%	6%	140	12%	75%	15	53%	40%	-4.4	267	$16
2nd Half	252	37	16	38	4	268	7	284	333	575	120	101	129	9	72	0.34	40	22	38	30	90	167	98	26%	11%	112	8%	100%	12	50%	25%	10.5	278	$20
20 Proj	**420**	**64**	**10**	**47**	**10**	**257**		**248**	**335**	**410**	**100**	**85**	**105**	**10**	**78**	**0.51**	**45**	**19**	**35**	**31**	**88**	**81**	**76**	**10%**		**131**	**11%**	**85%**				**9.4**	**143**	**$15**

Garver,Mitch

Age: 29	Bats: R	Pos: CA	Health	A	LIMA Plan	C+
Ht: 6' 1"	Wt: 220		PT/Exp	D	Rand Var	-2
			Consist	D	MM	4133

Suddenly started hitting the ball harder, and more often, in 2nd half 2018. Then added more FBs and the result was a breakout 2019. Impressive xPX/FB% combo backs most of this HR surge. HctX and plate skills imply the (elite for a C) BA should stick too. Crushed both vR and vL, so only suspect-but-improving defense stands in way of more PA.

Yr Tm	PA	R	HR	RBI	SB	BA	xHR	xBA	OBP	SLG	OPS+	vL+	vR+	bb%	ct%	Eye	G	L	F	h%	HctX	PX	xPX	HR/F	xHR/F	Spd	SBO	SB%	#Wk	DOM	DIS	RAR	BPX	R$
15																																		
16 a/a	475	42	10	62	1	241			306	373	92			9	73	0.35				31		94				74	4%	20%					29	$5
17 MIN *	416	55	15	44	2	255	1	254	344	471	109	101	70	12	70	0.46	45	16	39	32	92	140	95	0%	8%	106	2%	100%	8	13%	50%	15.3	158	$8
18 MIN	335	38	7	45	0	268	9	246	335	414	104	87	111	9	76	0.40	40	23	38	33	114	95	122	8%	10%	107	0%	0%	26	46%	46%	12.3	107	$7
19 MIN	359	70	31	67	0	273	26	279	365	630	132	153	120	11	72	0.47	39	14	47	28	118	186	159	29%	24%	90	0%	0%	25	60%	16%	38.2	330	$15
1st Half	160	30	12	32	0	284	9	267	369	603	130	155	116	10	71	0.39	38	16	46	32	113	169	146	26%	20%	109	0%	0%	13	54%	23%	14.6	274	$11
2nd Half	199	40	19	35	0	265	17	287	362	653	134	151	124	13	73	0.54	40	12	48	25	122	199	170	31%	28%	77	0%	0%	12	67%	8%	20.3	378	$19
20 Proj	**385**	**61**	**23**	**61**	**0**	**265**		**259**	**349**	**530**	**118**	**126**	**113**	**11**	**73**	**0.44**	**39**	**17**	**44**	**30**	**117**	**144**	**145**	**21%**		**96**	**1%**	**60%**				**29.0**	**181**	**$15**

Gennett,Scooter

Age: 30	Bats: L	Pos: 2B	Health	D	LIMA Plan	C
Ht: 5' 10"	Wt: 185		PT/Exp	C	Rand Var	+2
			Consist	F	MM	2225

Right groin strain suffered in March wiped out 1st half, and never found his footing after that; ultimately released by SF in August. However, 2017-18 performance plus still-prime age say he deserves a mulligan. With health and opportunity, should bounce back some, though 2017-18 xHR and xBA point to something short of a full recovery.

Yr Tm	PA	R	HR	RBI	SB	BA	xHR	xBA	OBP	SLG	OPS+	vL+	vR+	bb%	ct%	Eye	G	L	F	h%	HctX	PX	xPX	HR/F	xHR/F	Spd	SBO	SB%	#Wk	DOM	DIS	RAR	BPX	R$
15 MIL *	469	50	7	37	1	262	4	262	285	384	93	43	98	3	82	0.19	49	22	30	30	78	80	77	7%	4%	123	5%	19%	24	38%	25%	-6.9	103	$7
16 MIL	541	58	14	56	8	263	10	255	317	412	99	96	98	7	77	0.33	45	21	35	32	91	97	90	11%	8%	90	7%	89%	26	42%	38%	-4.5	83	$13
17 CIN	497	80	27	97	3	295	17	272	342	531	117	92	123	6	75	0.26	41	21	38	34	105	131	125	21%	13%	107	4%	60%	27	44%	41%	18.0	158	$22
18 CIN	638	86	23	92	4	310	19	264	357	490	117	108	121	7	79	0.34	40	24	36	36	112	105	113	14%	11%	97	4%	67%	27	41%	30%	33.9	143	$27
19 2 NL	139	15	2	11	0	226	2	222	245	323	75	58	80	1	69	0.05	43	24	33	31	85	67	53	7%	7%	90	0%	0%	9	11%	78%	-8.0	-137	-$2
1st Half	8	0	0	0	0	125		131	125	125	33	44	0	0	88	0.00	57	14	29	14	130	0	-1	0%		104	0%	0%	2	0%	100%	-1.2	-63	-$13
2nd Half	131	15	2	11	0	232	2	222	252	336	78	61	82	2	68	0.05	42	25	33	33	82	72	58	7%	7%	92	0%	0%	7	14%	71%	-7.3	-141	-$1
20 Proj	**455**	**60**	**14**	**59**	**2**	**271**		**248**	**310**	**428**	**99**	**86**	**103**	**5**	**75**	**0.20**	**43**	**23**	**35**	**33**	**95**	**89**	**92**	**12%**		**99**	**4%**	**66%**				**5.7**	**13**	**$15**

Goldschmidt,Paul

Age: 32	Bats: R	Pos: 1B	Health	A	LIMA Plan	B
Ht: 6' 3"	Wt: 225		PT/Exp	A	Rand Var	+2
			Consist	C	MM	4235

Strong 2nd half brought full-season numbers somewhat in line with history. Both xPX and xHR think the power could have been even better. 2nd half xBA/LD% indicate he can still keep the average up too and should drive a mild rebound. Even with SB likely gone for good, he's aging gracefully and is still a potential four-category stud.

Yr Tm	PA	R	HR	RBI	SB	BA	xHR	xBA	OBP	SLG	OPS+	vL+	vR+	bb%	ct%	Eye	G	L	F	h%	HctX	PX	xPX	HR/F	xHR/F	Spd	SBO	SB%	#Wk	DOM	DIS	RAR	BPX	R$
15 ARI	694	103	33	110	21	321	39	284	435	570	140	149	135	17	73	0.78	42	23	35	39	132	169	152	22%	26%	96	11%	81%	27	70%	7%	61.9	251	$42
16 ARI	704	106	24	95	32	297	25	274	411	489	122	144	114	16	74	0.73	46	25	29	37	113	122	106	19%	20%	97	17%	86%	27	52%	22%	34.6	160	$37
17 ARI	664	117	36	120	18	297	38	284	404	563	130	134	126	14	74	0.64	46	19	35	35	132	154	160	25%	26%	105	12%	78%	27	59%	15%	34.7	242	$35
18 ARI	689	95	33	83	7	290	43	267	389	533	128	134	124	13	71	0.52	39	25	36	36	121	153	139	22%	28%	118	6%	64%	28	54%	29%	35.7	230	$28
19 STL	680	97	34	97	3	260	39	251	346	476	109	125	105	11	72	0.47	38	22	39	30	119	116	140	20%	23%	98	2%	75%	28	46%	32%	4.2	133	$20
1st Half	351	46	14	31	0	246	17	222	336	405	99	109	97	11	71	0.44	43	20	37	30	122	84	145	17%	21%	100	1%	0%	15	40%	40%	-6.2	22	$11
2nd Half	329	51	20	66	3	274	22	277	356	552	120	141	115	12	74	0.50	33	25	42	31	115	149	134	22%	24%	99	4%	100%	13	54%	23%	15.3	256	$30
20 Proj	**630**	**95**	**32**	**96**	**4**	**280**		**262**	**374**	**515**	**120**	**132**	**115**	**13**	**72**	**0.53**	**40**	**23**	**37**	**33**	**121**	**129**	**141**	**21%**		**106**	**4%**	**59%**				**33.8**	**154**	**$26**

Gomes,Yan

Age: 32	Bats: R	Pos: CA	Health	B	LIMA Plan	D+
Ht: 6' 2"	Wt: 215		PT/Exp	C	Rand Var	0
			Consist	B	MM	3313

Probably safe to blame 1st half woes on AL-to-NL move, as 2nd half was much more in line with past levels. Don't read too much into bb% spike; 28 of 38 walks came in 209 PA batting eighth. Track record of durability is a plus, but long-term vL/vR split tamps any optimism of what he could do in an expanded role.

Yr Tm	PA	R	HR	RBI	SB	BA	xHR	xBA	OBP	SLG	OPS+	vL+	vR+	bb%	ct%	Eye	G	L	F	h%	HctX	PX	xPX	HR/F	xHR/F	Spd	SBO	SB%	#Wk	DOM	DIS	RAR	BPX	R$
15 CLE	389	38	12	45	0	231	15	248	267	391	92	75	96	3	71	0.13	34	26	40	29	86	120	102	11%	14%	63	0%	0%	20	40%	40%	-5.1	24	$4
16 CLE	264	22	9	34	0	167	10	221	201	327	72	100	59	3	73	0.13	39	16	45	19	80	102	99	11%	12%	80	0%	0%	18	33%	33%	-20.0	14	-$4
17 CLE	383	43	14	56	0	232	11	223	309	399	95	112	85	8	71	0.31	41	17	42	29	84	103	109	14%	11%	74	0%	0%	27	33%	41%	-1.4	21	$4
18 CLE	435	52	16	48	0	266	20	251	313	449	105	117	100	5	70	0.18	32	27	41	34	112	125	142	14%	17%	96	0%	0%	27	44%	44%	13.8	73	$10
19 WAS	358	36	12	43	2	223	13	231	316	389	93	115	87	11	73	0.45	39	19	42	27	83	94	91	12%	13%	82	3%	100%	27	26%	44%	-3.8	59	$3
1st Half	184	13	3	20	0	220	4	216	304	317	83	129	69	9	74	0.40	39	21	39	28	63	59	66	6%	8%	91	0%	0%	15	13%	53%	-4.8	-26	-$3
2nd Half	174	23	9	23	2	227	9	247	328	467	105	100	106	12	72	0.50	39	16	45	25	105	134	119	18%	18%	78	5%	100%	12	42%	33%	4.8	167	$10
20 Proj	**350**	**39**	**13**	**44**	**1**	**233**		**234**	**305**	**409**	**96**	**110**	**91**	**8**	**72**	**0.32**	**37**	**20**	**42**	**28**	**93**	**103**	**111**	**13%**		**81**	**2%**	**100%**				**6.3**	**6**	**$8**

GREG PYRON

Gonzalez,Erik

Age: 28	Bats: R	Pos: SS	Health D	LIMA Plan D	
Ht: 6' 3"	Wt: 205		PT/Exp F	Rand Var +1	
			Consist C	MM 1511	

1-6-.254 in 156 PA with PIT. Began 2019 as primary shortstop, but suffered a broken clavicle in mid-April and was relegated to bench upon August return. Speed is his one plus asset, but it's completely shackled by insufficient contact (see Lilliputian Eye ratios). File under "noodle bat."

Yr	Tm	PA	R	HR	RBI	SB	BA	xHR	xBA	OBP	SLG	OPS+	vL+	vR+	bb%	ct%	Eye	G	L	F	h%	HctX	PX	xPX	HR/F	xHR/F	Spd	SBO	SB%	#Wk	DOM	DIS	RAR	BPX	R$
15	a/a	571	61	8	60	16	237			267	343	85			4	80	0.20				28		70				108	20%	67%					46	$11
16	CLE *	462	53	9	43	10	272		274	299	407	96	72	97	4	78	0.17	75	13	13	33	119	92	7	0%		106	23%	44%	7	0%	100%	-13.2	77	$12
17	CLE *	281	34	9	21	5	236	4	239	260	385	86	79	97	3	66	0.09	58	21	22	33	85	97	93	25%	25%	140	16%	61%	18	28%	50%	-14.6	-24	$3
18	CLE	143	17	1	16	3	265	2	257	301	375	94	79	104	3	75	0.15	55	22	23	35	108	82	77	4%	9%	109	10%	100%	26	23%	50%	-1.3	23	$1
19	PIT *	236	19	2	13	5	219	1	212	257	287	72	96	74	5	68	0.16	56	20	24	32	64	44	31	4%	4%	149	14%	68%	13	0%	54%	-14.6	-137	-$1
1st Half		65	2	0	2	3	193	0	209	270	263	71	101	71	10	73	0.39	61	11	28	26	51	42	33	0%	0%	134	21%	100%	4	0%	25%	-3.9	-48	-$9
2nd Half		171	17	2	11	2	228	1	215	252	296	72	94	77	3	66	0.09	53	25	22	34	72	45	30	7%	7%	145	11%	44%	9	0%	67%	-11.6	-185	$2
20	**Proj**	**210**	**20**	**2**	**16**	**5**	**234**		**234**	**274**	**334**	**82**	**80**	**82**	**5**	**71**	**0.17**	**56**	**21**	**23**	**32**	**82**	**63**	**57**	**7%**		**133**	**15%**	**77%**				**-6.9**	**-87**	**$1**

Gonzalez,Marwin

Age: 31	Bats: B	Pos: RF 3B 1B	Health A	LIMA Plan C	
Ht: 6' 1"	Wt: 205		PT/Exp B	Rand Var 0	
			Consist D	MM 2133	

Missed most of Sept due to abdomen and oblique injuries. Flashed a flicker of that 2017 power in 1st half, but unsurprisingly it didn't last. xHR never bought the 2017 power spike; 2016-19 xHR show a narrow range for power output. Decent plate skills and multi-position eligibility make him a mid-tier—but useful—Swiss Army Knife.

Yr	Tm	PA	R	HR	RBI	SB	BA	xHR	xBA	OBP	SLG	OPS+	vL+	vR+	bb%	ct%	Eye	G	L	F	h%	HctX	PX	xPX	HR/F	xHR/F	Spd	SBO	SB%	#Wk	DOM	DIS	RAR	BPX	R$
15	HOU	370	44	12	34	4	279	6	265	317	442	106	116	96	4	78	0.22	44	23	33	33	109	107	100	14%	7%	94	11%	44%	27	48%	44%	2.2	103	$11
16	HOU	518	55	13	51	12	254	15	253	293	401	94	98	90	4	76	0.19	47	21	32	31	102	94	99	12%	13%	98	17%	67%	27	30%	37%	-6.4	51	$12
17	HOU	515	67	23	90	8	303	14	283	377	530	122	105	125	10	78	0.49	44	20	36	35	104	132	94	18%	11%	83	8%	73%	27	56%	30%	21.2	194	$23
18	HOU	552	61	16	68	2	247	18	246	324	409	101	105	99	10	74	0.42	42	23	36	30	105	101	123	13%	14%	90	4%	40%	28	25%	29%	-3.2	87	$11
19	MIN	463	52	15	55	1	264	15	257	322	414	98	103	95	7	77	0.32	45	24	31	31	110	81	99	15%	15%	82	1%	100%	25	36%	40%	-7.4	48	$9
1st Half		263	28	9	26	1	250	10	258	316	408	97	111	92	8	75	0.34	46	24	29	30	112	86	98	17%	19%	78	2%	100%	15	33%	40%	-6.1	41	$8
2nd Half		200	24	6	29	0	281	5	254	330	422	99	95	101	6	79	0.28	43	23	34	33	106	74	100	12%	10%	97	0%	0%	10	40%	40%	-1.8	63	$11
20	**Proj**	**420**	**49**	**14**	**56**	**2**	**268**		**256**	**331**	**433**	**103**	**103**	**102**	**8**	**77**	**0.36**	**44**	**23**	**34**	**32**	**107**	**90**	**104**	**14%**		**89**	**4%**	**62%**				**3.7**	**50**	**$13**

Goodrum,Niko

Age: 28	Bats: B	Pos: SS 2B LF	Health B	LIMA Plan B	
Ht: 6' 3"	Wt: 218		PT/Exp C	Rand Var -2	
			Consist B	MM 3425	

Groin strain cost him the final month of 2019, but this was a solid followup to pleasantly surprising 2018 campaign. Above-average Spd/SB% could prompt more green lights. Meanwhile, xHR/F says the HR output was sustainable. That nets out to an appealing power/speed/versatility combo. With a few more FBs ... UP: 20 HR/20 SB.

Yr	Tm	PA	R	HR	RBI	SB	BA	xHR	xBA	OBP	SLG	OPS+	vL+	vR+	bb%	ct%	Eye	G	L	F	h%	HctX	PX	xPX	HR/F	xHR/F	Spd	SBO	SB%	#Wk	DOM	DIS	RAR	BPX	R$
15	aa	229	25	4	14	13	214			283	327	85			9	74	0.37				27		72				146	34%	75%					46	$4
16	aa	200	21	5	22	7	248			315	398	97			9	69	0.31				33		104				102	19%	75%					29	$4
17	MIN *	506	66	12	61	10	240	0	226	281	383	89	22	22	5	71	0.20	71	0	29	31	124	90	81	0%	0%	117	18%	56%	6	0%	83%	-17.2	15	$10
18	DET	492	55	16	53	12	245	19	253	315	432	103	109	100	9	70	0.32	44	23	33	31	96	127	102	16%	18%	105	10%	75%	27	37%	33%	5.5	110	$13
19	DET	472	61	12	45	12	248	12	245	322	421	99	121	92	10	67	0.33	41	28	31	34	93	109	87	13%	13%	123	14%	80%	22	18%	41%	-6.4	56	$11
1st Half		302	39	6	25	7	234	9	241	311	387	93	109	90	10	68	0.35	35	31	34	32	89	97	91	10%	15%	121	13%	78%	15	20%	47%	-7.6	30	$11
2nd Half		170	22	6	20	5	273	3	253	341	481	108	135	97	9	66	0.31	51	21	28	38	101	129	80	21%	11%	120	15%	83%	7	14%	29%	3.8	93	$12
20	**Proj**	**504**	**62**	**16**	**53**	**14**	**249**		**249**	**315**	**435**	**101**	**118**	**94**	**9**	**69**	**0.30**	**44**	**24**	**31**	**33**	**96**	**112**	**92**	**16%**		**121**	**17%**	**75%**				**6.5**	**79**	**$17**

Goodwin,Brian

Age: 29	Bats: L	Pos: LF CF	Health F	LIMA Plan C	
Ht: 6' 0"	Wt: 200		PT/Exp D	Rand Var -3	
			Consist B	MM 4313	

Logged career-high number of MLB PA and recaptured once-intriguing power/speed blend. Sold out for power while hitting bushels of flyballs in 2nd half. Plate skills suffered under the strain, but change was still a net positive. Lack of platoon splits helps his cause for more PT and makes a repeat season possible.

Yr	Tm	PA	R	HR	RBI	SB	BA	xHR	xBA	OBP	SLG	OPS+	vL+	vR+	bb%	ct%	Eye	G	L	F	h%	HctX	PX	xPX	HR/F	xHR/F	Spd	SBO	SB%	#Wk	DOM	DIS	RAR	BPX	R$
15	aa	460	46	6	37	12	196			250	282	74			7	76	0.29				25		62				103	22%	60%					-3	$1
16	WAS *	521	46	12	64	13	250	1	241	312	388	95	101	100	8	71	0.32	59	15	26	33	114	96	105	0%	14%	98	14%	79%	7	14%	43%	-7.1	29	$12
17	WAS *	376	48	14	38	8	240	11	244	303	445	100	133	102	8	70	0.30	38	19	43	30	96	135	133	16%	14%	101	12%	86%	14	50%	21%	-4.8	106	$8
18	2 TM *	240	27	8	34	5	223	6	224	293	379	93	89	98	9	66	0.29	43	23	34	30	81	110	83	17%	17%	93	13%	70%	20	30%	50%	-2.7	-3	$4
19	LAA	458	65	17	47	7	262	16	242	326	470	106	106	105	8	69	0.29	33	24	43	34	90	127	126	14%	13%	109	10%	70%	27	44%	33%	8.5	104	$12
1st Half		243	39	7	25	3	279	7	251	335	438	103	94	106	8	73	0.32	37	28	36	35	83	92	95	12%	12%	117	8%	60%	15	40%	47%	4.5	70	$12
2nd Half		215	26	10	22	4	242	8	236	316	505	108	117	105	9	64	0.27	27	20	53	32	98	172	167	15%	12%	95	14%	80%	12	50%	17%	5.1	152	$12
20	**Proj**	**350**	**44**	**14**	**40**	**7**	**243**		**238**	**312**	**447**	**102**	**107**	**100**	**8**	**68**	**0.29**	**36**	**22**	**41**	**31**	**89**	**126**	**118**	**15%**		**102**	**13%**	**74%**				**0.9**	**72**	**$11**

Gordon,Alex

Age: 36	Bats: L	Pos: LF	Health B	LIMA Plan C+	
Ht: 6' 1"	Wt: 225		PT/Exp A	Rand Var 0	
			Consist B	MM 1135	

Tepid late-career revival continued, led by his best ct% yet and BA/xBA uptick. xHR says there's latent power here, but he's been underperforming that metric for a while. Though HctX and xPX still slightly above average, FB trend is dubious and thump doesn't grow at his age. There's not much meat on this bone.

Yr	Tm	PA	R	HR	RBI	SB	BA	xHR	xBA	OBP	SLG	OPS+	vL+	vR+	bb%	ct%	Eye	G	L	F	h%	HctX	PX	xPX	HR/F	xHR/F	Spd	SBO	SB%	#Wk	DOM	DIS	RAR	BPX	R$
15	KC *	456	44	14	52	2	276	12	250	367	435	112	113	110	12	74	0.55	38	25	38	34	108	111	125	13%	12%	74	6%	29%	20	45%	35%	10.9	89	$12
16	KC *	532	64	18	44	8	223	20	226	306	382	94	90	94	10	67	0.36	38	24	38	30	100	107	147	15%	18%	89	7%	89%	24	17%	46%	-5.4	6	$7
17	KC	541	52	9	45	7	208	12	236	293	315	82	80	80	8	74	0.36	43	24	33	26	87	68	82	8%	10%	85	10%	64%	27	22%	52%	-40.0	-18	$1
18	KC	568	56	13	54	12	245	20	252	324	370	96	77	103	9	75	0.40	44	26	30	30	105	81	112	11%	17%	59	10%	86%	26	19%	42%	-9.1	13	$13
19	KC	633	77	13	76	5	266	20	267	345	396	98	90	101	8	82	0.51	46	23	31	30	110	70	107	9%	14%	71	5%	63%	28	32%	29%	-10.5	85	$14
1st Half		337	45	10	52	4	266	14	270	345	447	106	96	110	8	80	0.44	46	20	35	30	106	99	104	12%		64	6%	100%	15	40%	33%	0.0	133	$20
2nd Half		296	32	3	24	1	266	6	267	345	338	90	84	92	9	84	0.61	47	27	27	31	115	40	110	5%		82	5%	25%	13	23%	23%	-11.0	52	$8
20	**Proj**	**455**	**51**	**9**	**48**	**3**	**251**		**253**	**332**	**370**	**95**	**86**	**97**	**9**	**78**	**0.45**	**44**	**25**	**31**	**30**	**105**	**68**	**108**	**9%**		**73**	**5%**	**56%**				**-7.0**	**14**	**$10**

Gordon,Dee

Age: 32	Bats: L	Pos: 2B	Health B	LIMA Plan C+	
Ht: 5' 11"	Wt: 170		PT/Exp A	Rand Var 0	
			Consist B	MM 0545	

Injuries (right wrist contusion, left quad strain) prompted two IL stints. Speed is what you come here for, but leg ailments have now dampened Spd/SBO in back-to-back seasons. Given his age, we can't assume a full rebound and pop is non-existent. In theory, lack of MLB bags props up his value, but there's also now DN: under 20 SB.

Yr	Tm	PA	R	HR	RBI	SB	BA	xHR	xBA	OBP	SLG	OPS+	vL+	vR+	bb%	ct%	Eye	G	L	F	h%	HctX	PX	xPX	HR/F	xHR/F	Spd	SBO	SB%	#Wk	DOM	DIS	RAR	BPX	R$
15	MIA	653	88	4	46	58	333	4	280	359	418	108	114	104	4	85	0.27	60	22	19	39	68	54	40	4%	4%	170	40%	74%	25	44%	24%	22.6	122	$47
16	MIA *	381	52	1	16	32	262	1	256	298	329	85	78	88	5	83	0.31	59	19	23	31	57	36	29	2%	2%	203	40%	82%	15	13%	40%	-13.9	94	$16
17	MIA	694	114	2	33	60	308	2	281	341	375	96	86	98	4	86	0.27	58	23	20	36	56	37	20	2%	2%	198	39%	79%	27	22%	22%	1.1	124	$43
18	SEA	588	62	4	36	30	268	2	270	288	349	88	82	90	2	86	0.11	55	22	22	31	64	44	28	4%	2%	159	33%	71%	27	22%	37%	-12.5	100	$20
19	SEA	421	36	3	34	22	275	1	264	304	359	88	96	85	4	84	0.30	53	21	25	32	64	41	21	4%	1%	152	26%	81%	26	35%	42%	-9.1	100	$13
1st Half		237	23	3	24	14	268	1	251	298	359	88	108	81	4	84	0.28	49	20	31	31	70	45	27	5%	2%	124	28%	88%	14	21%	57%	-4.5	67	$15
2nd Half		184	13	0	10	8	283	0	282	311	358	88	82	91	4	86	0.32	60	23	18	33	57	36	13	0%	0%	166	23%	73%	12	50%	25%	-3.4	119	$10
20	**Proj**	**455**	**49**	**2**	**30**	**27**	**270**		**270**	**303**	**347**	**87**	**85**	**88**	**4**	**85**	**0.30**	**56**	**22**	**22**	**31**	**62**	**38**	**23**	**3%**		**169**	**31%**	**77%**				**-5.3**	**92**	**$19**

Grandal,Yasmani

Age: 31	Bats: B	Pos: CA 1B	Health A	LIMA Plan B	
Ht: 6' 1"	Wt: 235		PT/Exp B	Rand Var +1	
			Consist A	MM 3125	

Career year more a result of increased workload than increased skills. Scuffled in Jul-Aug (.220 BA, 3 HR, 44% GB% in 205 PA), but found a second wind down the stretch. Added LD% now raises his BA floor a bit. Stable plate skills, power metrics, ability to hit both vR/vL, and track record of durability make him a terrific option in all formats.

Yr	Tm	PA	R	HR	RBI	SB	BA	xHR	xBA	OBP	SLG	OPS+	vL+	vR+	bb%	ct%	Eye	G	L	F	h%	HctX	PX	xPX	HR/F	xHR/F	Spd	SBO	SB%	#Wk	DOM	DIS	RAR	BPX	R$
15	LA	426	43	16	47	0	234	17	229	353	403	105	110	103	15	74	0.71	46	17	37	27	97	110	117	16%	17%	62	1%	0%	27	37%	52%	9.2	95	$6
16	LA	457	49	27	72	1	228	25	251	339	477	111	105	110	14	70	0.55	45	16	39	25	111	152	155	25%	23%	61	4%	25%	26	46%	31%	9.1	146	$9
17	LA	482	50	22	58	0	247	16	239	308	459	103	89	104	8	70	0.31	44	16	40	30	104	134	125	18%	13%	63	1%	0%	27	48%	33%	9.1	79	$8
18	LA	518	65	24	68	2	241	27	248	349	466	113	101	116	14	72	0.58	41	17	42	28	108	139	140	18%	20%	58	2%	67%	28	54%	32%	25.0	153	$13
19	MIL	632	79	28	77	5	246	28	259	380	468	113	121	108	17	73	0.78	39	23	38	28	114	120	133	20%	20%	72	3%	83%	28	50%	32%	25.1	170	$15
1st Half		314	41	18	46	3	265	16	272	376	531	121	122	120	15	75	0.69	37	23	40	29	128	133	144	23%	20%	84	4%	100%	15	53%	27%	22.4	233	$20
2nd Half		318	38	10	31	2	225	12	245	384	403	104	120	97	20	71	0.86	41	23	36	28	100	106	121	16%	19%	68	3%	67%	13	46%	38%	8.3	111	$10
20	**Proj**	**560**	**68**	**25**	**70**	**3**	**241**		**248**	**358**	**454**	**109**	**112**	**108**	**15**	**72**	**0.64**	**41**	**20**	**39**	**28**	**109**	**119**	**132**	**18%**		**66**	**3%**	**69%**				**28.8**	**121**	**$15**

GREG PYRON

Granderson,Curtis	Health	A	LIMA Plan	F
Age: 39 Bats: L Pos: LF	PT/Exp	C	Rand Var	+5
Ht: 6' 1" Wt: 200	Consist	C	MM	3111

Those looking for signs of late-career rebound will only find chutes downward. Fly balls returned, but most of them landed in gloves instead of seats. While unlucky h% didn't help, lack of contact got worse as season progressed, and xBA still makes him a BA liability. It's been a fun run, but time to unbuckle and hop off for good.

Yr Tm	PA	R	HR	RBI	SB	BA	xHR	xBA	OBP	SLG	OPS+	vL+	vR+	bb%	ct%	Eye	G	L	F	h%	HctX	PX	xPX	HR/F	xHR/F	Spd	SBO	SB%	#Wk	DOM	DIS	RAR	BPX	R$
15 NYM	682	98	26	70	11	259	27	259	364	457	114	77	122	13	74	0.60	31	27	42	31	118	135	154	14%	15%	102	9%	65%	27	44%	19%	11.8	170	$21
16 NYM	633	88	30	59	4	237	24	265	335	464	109	98	110	12	76	0.57	36	22	42	26	114	131	127	17%	14%	98	4%	67%	27	48%	22%	6.2	183	$12
17 2 NL	527	74	26	64	6	212	23	250	323	452	104	89	106	13	73	0.58	33	19	49	23	104	140	154	16%	14%	112	7%	75%	26	50%	31%	-7.3	197	$8
18 2 TM	403	60	13	38	2	242	13	253	351	431	108	77	109	13	69	0.51	32	31	37	31	95	130	133	15%	15%	86	3%	67%	28	43%	29%	6.0	117	$8
19 MIA	363	44	12	34	0	183	12	226	281	356	85	107	80	11	69	0.42	33	22	45	22	106	104	154	12%	12%	85	4%	0%	28	36%	46%	-25.0	37	-$1
1st Half	230	29	7	22	0	191	9	229	274	368	86	112	81	10	71	0.37	32	21	47	23	109	106	154	10%	13%	93	8%	0%	15	33%	53%	-15.1	67	$0
2nd Half	133	15	5	12	0	168	3	221	293	336	83	100	80	14	65	0.49	34	24	42	20	101	101	153	16%	10%	80	0%	0%	13	38%	38%	-8.3	-11	-$2
20 Proj	**175**	**23**	**6**	**17**	**1**	**206**		**234**	**312**	**388**	**94**	**95**	**94**	**13**	**70**	**0.48**	**33**	**24**	**43**	**25**	**103**	**108**	**147**	**14%**		**92**	**4%**	**49%**				**-3.5**	**48**	**$0**

Gregorius,Didi	Health	D	LIMA Plan	B+
Age: 30 Bats: L Pos: SS	PT/Exp	B	Rand Var	+4
Ht: 6' 3" Wt: 205	Consist	B	MM	2235

16-61-.238 in 344 PA at NYY. Returned in June from TJ surgery; power followed in 2nd half. Steady contact, xBA say he deserved a better fate, so BA should rebound with h% bump. Don't expect him to keep outhitting xHR/F though, and SBO return limits value in SS-rich environment. Without bags, this profile blends in instead of sticking out.

Yr Tm	PA	R	HR	RBI	SB	BA	xHR	xBA	OBP	SLG	OPS+	vL+	vR+	bb%	ct%	Eye	G	L	F	h%	HctX	PX	xPX	HR/F	xHR/F	Spd	SBO	SB%	#Wk	DOM	DIS	RAR	BPX	R$
15 NYY	578	57	9	56	5	265	6	252	318	370	96	86	98	6	84	0.39	45	21	34	30	82	68	64	6%	4%	103	6%	63%	27	33%	30%	-7.4	92	$11
16 NYY	597	68	20	70	7	276	9	271	304	447	102	113	96	3	85	0.23	40	20	40	29	85	96	78	10%	5%	103	7%	88%	27	56%	19%	6.9	166	$18
17 NYY	569	73	25	87	3	287	10	274	318	478	107	87	112	4	87	0.36	36	20	44	29	81	96	67	12%	5%	97	3%	75%	23	57%	17%	11.9	194	$20
18 NYY	569	89	27	86	10	268	15	282	335	494	115	106	117	8	86	0.70	39	20	42	26	114	114	100	15%	8%	110	13%	63%	26	54%	15%	21.3	293	$23
19 NYY *	369	48	16	62	2	227	12	258	263	416	90	95	95	5	84	0.31	38	18	44	23	100	88	99	13%	10%	97	5%	67%	18	50%	33%	-16.3	174	$7
1st Half	97	13	3	9	0	237	2	248	261	354	82	23	129	3	84	0.19	43	21	36	26	88	54	66	15%	10%	112	0%	0%	5	40%	40%	-5.2	70	-$10
2nd Half	272	35	13	53	2	224	10	263	265	439	93	112	85	5	84	0.35	36	18	46	22	104	100	107	13%	10%	94	7%	67%	13	54%	31%	-9.2	215	$13
20 Proj	**560**	**77**	**21**	**85**	**5**	**251**		**259**	**293**	**423**	**96**	**84**	**100**	**5**	**85**	**0.37**	**39**	**19**	**42**	**26**	**98**	**81**	**87**	**11%**		**105**	**6%**	**66%**				**0.2**	**164**	**$18**

Greiner,Grayson	Health	C	LIMA Plan	F
Age: 27 Bats: R Pos: CA	PT/Exp	D	Rand Var	0
Ht: 6' 6" Wt: 239	Consist	B	MM	1001

5-19-.202 in 224 PA at DET. From paltry production to a two-month back injury; this was a grind. Extreme GB% tilt and below-average xPX capped HR total, while poor contact skills point to a BA that will hurt your roster. Owners looking for second-catcher viability should look elsewhere, unless negative BPX is a category.

Yr Tm	PA	R	HR	RBI	SB	BA	xHR	xBA	OBP	SLG	OPS+	vL+	vR+	bb%	ct%	Eye	G	L	F	h%	HctX	PX	xPX	HR/F	xHR/F	Spd	SBO	SB%	#Wk	DOM	DIS	RAR	BPX	R$
15																																		
16 a/a	220	16	6	24	1	251			278	397	92			4	71	0.13				33		93				115	2%	100%					0	$2
17 a/a	376	29	12	37	0	207			279	370	87			9	76	0.41				24		97				88	0%	0%					82	-$1
18 DET *	291	19	3	31	0	228	4	219	319	327	89	135	72	12	69	0.43	45	24	31	32	91	75	85	0%	19%	88	1%	0%	14	29%	50%	0.1	-37	$0
19 DET *	275	24	7	22	0	204	6	191	251	312	75	64	76	6	65	0.18	53	15	32	28	89	64	84	11%	13%	105	0%	0%	17	6%	65%	-8.7	-152	-$2
1st Half	170	13	5	14	0	161	3	176	229	277	68	74	66	8	63	0.23	53	14	33	22	80	70	72	15%	9%	74	0%	0%	12	8%	75%	-10.6	-189	-$5
2nd Half	105	11	2	8	0	269	3	208	290	365	86	32	106	3	69	0.10	53	18	30	37	111	56	113	0%	25%	140	0%	0%	5	0%	40%	-0.8	-107	$3
20 Proj	**210**	**17**	**4**	**19**	**0**	**215**		**213**	**269**	**328**	**80**	**91**	**78**	**7**	**69**	**0.25**	**49**	**19**	**31**	**29**	**95**	**68**	**92**	**10%**		**107**	**1%**	**32%**				**-3.0**	**-138**	**$2**

Grichuk,Randal	Health	B	LIMA Plan	B+
Age: 28 Bats: R Pos: RF CF	PT/Exp	B	Rand Var	+2
Ht: 6' 2" Wt: 213	Consist	B	MM	4325

Just another 30+ HR, sub-.250 BA OF out of central casting? HctX and xPX are foundational to that power skill, and they were trending badly... until the second half. Suddenly, ct% jumps, xBA and xPX join the party; he even hits RHPs for a couple of months. Need to see it again, but there's a chance he's a lead instead of an extra.

Yr Tm	PA	R	HR	RBI	SB	BA	xHR	xBA	OBP	SLG	OPS+	vL+	vR+	bb%	ct%	Eye	G	L	F	h%	HctX	PX	xPX	HR/F	xHR/F	Spd	SBO	SB%	#Wk	DOM	DIS	RAR	BPX	R$
15 STL	350	49	17	47	4	276	20	265	329	548	122	113	124	6	66	0.20	38	21	42	37	107	202	139	19%	22%	137	9%	67%	22	55%	14%	12.5	219	$13
16 STL *	560	75	28	81	5	238	26	252	278	474	102	109	101	5	70	0.19	41	16	44	28	114	154	142	18%	19%	110	10%	56%	25	48%	32%	-5.9	143	$13
17 STL *	511	63	27	69	6	236	25	249	279	478	101	88	104	6	67	0.18	36	21	43	29	109	154	152	18%	21%	108	8%	86%	24	29%	29%	-10.3	112	$11
18 TOR	462	60	25	61	3	245	29	260	301	502	111	113	110	6	71	0.22	35	18	47	29	96	167	136	18%	20%	91	7%	60%	25	56%	24%	4.4	200	$13
19 TOR	628	75	31	80	2	232	27	248	280	457	98	102	95	6	72	0.21	39	19	42	27	93	122	93	17%	15%	119	3%	67%	28	36%	46%	-15.2	130	$12
1st Half	341	41	15	34	1	227	14	224	287	419	94	108	88	7	69	0.26	38	18	44	28	78	109	85	16%	15%	117	1%	100%	15	20%	60%	-12.1	52	$10
2nd Half	287	34	16	46	1	238	13	274	272	502	102	97	105	4	76	0.15	40	20	41	26	110	135	101	19%	15%	115	5%	50%	13	54%	31%	-6.7	207	$15
20 Proj	**595**	**75**	**31**	**81**	**4**	**248**		**250**	**295**	**489**	**106**	**105**	**105**	**5**	**71**	**0.20**	**38**	**19**	**43**	**29**	**100**	**136**	**118**	**18%**		**113**	**5%**	**66%**				**3.9**	**120**	**$19**

Grisham,Trent	Health	A	LIMA Plan	B
Age: 23 Bats: L Pos: CF	PT/Exp	D	Rand Var	0
Ht: 6' 0" Wt: 205	Consist	F	MM	2315

6-24-.231 in 183 PA at MIL. Posted 26 HR/12 SB in AA/AAA; power/speed skills provided modest cover. Plate patience carried over after August call-up and should keep OBP from sinking, but 69% ct% and .222 xBA in majors could drive down BA. At this age, multi-category potential makes him a worthy flyer.

Yr Tm	PA	R	HR	RBI	SB	BA	xHR	xBA	OBP	SLG	OPS+	vL+	vR+	bb%	ct%	Eye	G	L	F	h%	HctX	PX	xPX	HR/F	xHR/F	Spd	SBO	SB%	#Wk	DOM	DIS	RAR	BPX	R$
15																																		
16																																		
17																																		
18 aa	394	42	7	29	10	225			341	330	93			15	72	0.62				29		67				116	12%	76%					27	$6
19 MIL *	613	87	31	87	12	267	4	262	364	520	117	93	98	13	75	0.62	38	19	43	30	94	129	90	13%	8%	97	11%	68%	10	40%	40%	19.8	230	$23
1st Half	318	37	16	44	6	244		276	351	495	113			14	76	0.68				27		130		0%		106	14%	59%				4.1	256	$19
2nd Half	295	50	15	43	5	292	4	260	379	547	122	92	98	12	75	0.56	38	19	43	34	94	128	90	13%	8%	111	8%	83%	10	40%	40%	16.6	233	$27
20 Proj	**525**	**69**	**16**	**61**	**11**	**253**		**228**	**363**	**426**	**106**	**101**	**107**	**14**	**73**	**0.59**	**38**	**19**	**43**	**31**	**85**	**94**	**81**	**11%**		**98**	**10%**	**74%**				**16.9**	**114**	**$17**

Grossman,Robert	Health	A	LIMA Plan	D+
Age: 30 Bats: B Pos: LF RF	PT/Exp	B	Rand Var	+2
Ht: 6' 0" Wt: 215	Consist	B	MM	1223

SB spike was the sole source of R$, as playing time vL dried up. LD stroke with strong Eye suggest we'll see a BA rebound, though speed skills support only a handful of bags. His "A" consistency hints at more of the same for a possible platoon player with no power; you want someone with more upside in the end game.

Yr Tm	PA	R	HR	RBI	SB	BA	xHR	xBA	OBP	SLG	OPS+	vL+	vR+	bb%	ct%	Eye	G	L	F	h%	HctX	PX	xPX	HR/F	xHR/F	Spd	SBO	SB%	#Wk	DOM	DIS	RAR	BPX	R$
15 HOU *	437	42	5	29	9	191	0	176	267	266	74	48	78	9	69	0.34	55	6	39	26	47	61	56	8%	0%	84	19%	49%	6	33%	50%	-29.7	-76	-$1
16 MIN *	527	62	16	49	5	265	9	249	365	426	108	134	97	14	72	0.58	38	25	37	33	92	107	96	13%	10%	83	6%	56%	21	38%	38%	13.5	83	$12
17 MIN	456	62	9	45	3	246	8	262	361	380	99	92	101	15	79	0.85	41	25	34	29	99	81	83	9%	8%	91	3%	75%	25	36%	36%	-9.4	124	$6
18 MIN	465	50	5	48	0	273	7	247	367	384	104	123	94	13	79	0.72	39	24	37	33	92	77	58	4%	6%	103	1%	0%	27	48%	37%	3.7	120	$8
19 OAK	482	57	6	38	9	240	8	250	334	348	90	71	93	12	80	0.69	41	25	34	29	95	60	81	5%	7%	104	10%	69%	29	21%	31%	-15.6	89	$7
1st Half	252	32	5	22	5	243	4	263	329	383	95	60	99	12	81	0.67	36	26	37	28	91	78	75	7%	6%	86	14%	56%	16	31%	25%	-7.2	133	$8
2nd Half	230	25	1	16	4	237	3	238	339	308	85	78	87	13	78	0.70	46	24	31	30	99	41	87	2%	6%	123	6%	100%	13	8%	38%	-9.2	41	$6
20 Proj	**315**	**37**	**4**	**28**	**4**	**255**		**248**	**352**	**366**	**97**	**103**	**94**	**13**	**79**	**0.71**	**40**	**25**	**35**	**31**	**95**	**64**	**78**	**6%**		**102**	**6%**	**68%**				**-1.0**	**68**	**$7**

Guerrero Jr.,Vladimir	Health	A	LIMA Plan	D+
Age: 21 Bats: R Pos: 3B DH	PT/Exp	D	Rand Var	-1
Ht: 6' 2" Wt: 250	Consist	F	MM	2045

15-69-.272 in 514 PA at TOR. Hype didn't carry over to field, as knee issues may have driven late power outage. Hardest-hit ball in MLB (118.9 mph) points to immense power upside, but he needs to add loft to make it count. Plus ct% backs a BA repeat, and while breakout seems inevitable given pedigree, it may not be in 2020.

Yr Tm	PA	R	HR	RBI	SB	BA	xHR	xBA	OBP	SLG	OPS+	vL+	vR+	bb%	ct%	Eye	G	L	F	h%	HctX	PX	xPX	HR/F	xHR/F	Spd	SBO	SB%	#Wk	DOM	DIS	RAR	BPX	R$
15																																		
16																																		
17																																		
18 a/a	378	59	19	71	3	383			438	634	148			9	89	0.89				39		133				86	5%	48%					360	$25
19 TOR *	548	58	18	76	1	277	17	259	343	448	105	84	109	9	81	0.53	50	17	33	31	98	88	89	12%	14%	78	1%	48%	23	35%	26%	4.9	144	$13
1st Half	260	28	11	30	1	265	9	256	335	451	105	94	101	10	81	0.56	49	17	34	29	106	92	105	15%	16%	69	3%	48%	11	36%	27%	-0.3	148	$10
2nd Half	288	30	7	46	0	287	9	258	351	444	105	76	116	9	81	0.51	50	18	32	33	92	83	77	10%	13%	89	0%	0%	12	33%	25%	2.4	137	$16
20 Proj	**630**	**69**	**22**	**81**	**2**	**296**		**270**	**362**	**484**	**114**	**93**	**121**	**9**	**83**	**0.59**	**50**	**17**	**33**	**33**	**98**	**97**	**88**	**14%**		**77**	**2%**	**50%**				**27.0**	**160**	**$23**

BRANT CHESSER

Gurriel,Lourdes

Age: 26 Bats: R Pos: LF	Health	C	LIMA Plan	B+
Ht: 6' 3" Wt: 215	PT/Exp	D	Rand Var	-1
	Consist	B	MM	3235

20-50-6-.277 in 343 PA at TOR. Soared in May/June after his call-up, hitting 14 of his 20 HRs and batting .349 in 132 AB, mostly supported by the metrics. A left quadriceps strain landed him on the IL in August and he never recovered (.184 xBA with 63% ct% in Aug/Sept). Power growth is the key takeaway looking forward.

Yr Tm	PA	R	HR	RBI	SB	BA	xHR	xBA	OBP	SLG	OPS+	vL+	vR+	bb%	ct%	Eye	G	L	F	h%	HctX	PX	xPX	HR/F	xHR/F	Spd	SBO	SB%	#Wk	DOM	DIS	RAR	BPX	R$
15																																		
16																																		
17 aa	178	17	4	23	2	220			257	340	80			5	80	0.25				26		74				83	5%	100%					48	$0
18 TOR *	475	52	17	71	4	276	11	253	299	432	101	115	100	3	77	0.14	43	24	33	33	86	92	92	17%	17%	104	9%	44%	15	33%	47%	-3.0	63	$15
19 TOR *	468	66	23	71	6	268	20	260	303	508	108	130	107	5	74	0.20	39	18	43	31	112	133	145	20%	20%	113	15%	49%	18	50%	33%	-0.2	181	$16
1st Half	311	44	17	54	2	281	13	272	312	545	115	150	121	4	75	0.18	38	19	43	32	114	147	159	26%	24%	107	12%	32%	11	55%	27%	4.6	219	$22
2nd Half	157	22	6	17	4	239	7	236	295	430	96	104	92	6	73	0.24	42	16	42	29	109	104	128	13%	16%	126	21%	67%	7	43%	43%	-5.1	104	$3
20 Proj	**525**	**66**	**27**	**74**	**7**	**258**		**261**	**297**	**480**	**104**	**118**	**98**	**4**	**76**	**0.19**	**41**	**20**	**39**	**29**	**101**	**118**	**121**	**18%**		**112**	**13%**	**58%**				**1.7**	**118**	**$17**

Gurriel,Yulieski

Age: 36 Bats: R Pos: 1B 3B	Health	A	LIMA Plan	B+
Ht: 6' 0" Wt: 190	PT/Exp	B	Rand Var	0
	Consist	B	MM	2255

We looked at that HR to xHR variance and thought, "Holy cow, that has to be wrong" - but it's not. Most of his HRs had marginal exit velocities and/or low launch angles, so the odds of anything close to a repeat are remote... especially at age 36. But the rest of his skills are solid, so he will probably flirt with .300 again. Use 2017 as your guide.

Yr Tm	PA	R	HR	RBI	SB	BA	xHR	xBA	OBP	SLG	OPS+	vL+	vR+	bb%	ct%	Eye	G	L	F	h%	HctX	PX	xPX	HR/F	xHR/F	Spd	SBO	SB%	#Wk	DOM	DIS	RAR	BPX	R$
15																																		
16 HOU *	173	15	4	19	1	234	2	250	262	348	83	72	99	4	85	0.25	42	20	38	26	98	68	74	7%	4%	84	6%	50%	6	67%	0%	-9.3	80	$0
17 HOU	564	69	18	75	3	299	12	293	332	486	110	92	114	4	88	0.35	46	19	35	31	125	102	99	11%	7%	89	4%	60%	27	67%	15%	4.9	215	$19
18 HOU *	594	72	13	87	5	292	7	271	320	431	104	124	95	4	88	0.34	44	20	36	31	99	80	87	8%	4%	118	4%	83%	26	46%	23%	8.8	200	$21
19 HOU	612	85	31	104	5	298	13	306	343	541	117	105	122	6	88	0.57	38	22	39	29	118	113	79	16%	7%	90	6%	63%	28	61%	11%	26.5	319	$25
1st Half	330	40	8	37	3	267	4	284	303	423	97	93	98	5	89	0.50	35	25	40	28	114	77	62	7%	4%	110	9%	50%	15	47%	7%	-7.2	233	$15
2nd Half	282	45	23	67	2	335	9	332	390	681	141	117	152	7	88	0.65	42	19	39	31	123	156	100	26%	10%	73	3%	100%	13	77%	15%	32.8	426	$38
20 Proj	**595**	**76**	**19**	**88**	**5**	**292**		**282**	**331**	**468**	**108**	**100**	**110**	**5**	**88**	**0.44**	**42**	**21**	**38**	**30**	**113**	**88**	**86**	**10%**		**97**	**5%**	**69%**				**14.8**	**202**	**$24**

Guzman,Ronald

Age: 25 Bats: L Pos: 1B	Health	B	LIMA Plan	D+
Ht: 6' 5" Wt: 225	PT/Exp	C	Rand Var	+1
	Consist	A	MM	3133

10-36-.219 in 295 PA at TEX. Hit .305 in 59 AB after Sept recall from AAA, but you can thank a 46% hit rate. Otherwise, marginal improvement here and there, flashes a fine mitt, and owns some impressive physical tools. But overall? In today's MLB, a 1B with this little production is a waste of a roster spot.

Yr Tm	PA	R	HR	RBI	SB	BA	xHR	xBA	OBP	SLG	OPS+	vL+	vR+	bb%	ct%	Eye	G	L	F	h%	HctX	PX	xPX	HR/F	xHR/F	Spd	SBO	SB%	#Wk	DOM	DIS	RAR	BPX	R$
15																																		
16 a/a	496	50	14	56	2	256			306	411	98			7	76	0.30				31		92				114	3%	44%					80	$9
17 aaa	507	60	9	48	3	264			318	376	93			7	80	0.40				31		64				110	3%	73%					67	$9
18 TEX	428	46	16	58	1	235	12	235	306	416	100	80	106	8	69	0.27	41	22	37	30	83	119	81	16%	12%	91	1%	100%	26	27%	46%	-3.6	50	$8
19 TEX *	444	53	15	50	1	200	13	256	316	424	98	70	105	10	68	0.37	37	29	34	31	92	120	92	17%	22%	72	3%	33%	19	37%	32%	-6.2	44	$6
1st Half	213	24	8	29	1	211	10	269	287	426	95	74	108	10	69	0.35	36	29	35	26	99	137	106	17%	24%	74	9%	33%	11	36%	18%	-8.2	115	$3
2nd Half	231	29	7	22	0	259	3	247	343	422	101	62	101	11	67	0.38	39	30	31	35	81	104	61	18%	18%	88	0%	0%	8	38%	50%	-1.1	4	$8
20 Proj	**280**	**33**	**11**	**33**	**1**	**245**		**252**	**321**	**432**	**101**	**75**	**110**	**9**	**71**	**0.34**	**39**	**26**	**35**	**31**	**86**	**110**	**80**	**17%**		**90**	**2%**	**52%**				**-0.2**	**26**	**$7**

Gyorko,Jedd

Age: 31 Bats: R Pos: 3B	Health	D	LIMA Plan	D
Ht: 5' 10" Wt: 215	PT/Exp	D	Rand Var	+5
	Consist	D	MM	1213

2-9-.174 in 101 PA at STL/LA. Main accomplishment in 2019 was managing to injure most regions of his body (calf, back, wrist). Otherwise—and consequently—a lost season. While 2016 now looks ominously like an age-27 career peak, his base power skills haven't deteriorated that much. Could provide pop in part-time role.

Yr Tm	PA	R	HR	RBI	SB	BA	xHR	xBA	OBP	SLG	OPS+	vL+	vR+	bb%	ct%	Eye	G	L	F	h%	HctX	PX	xPX	HR/F	xHR/F	Spd	SBO	SB%	#Wk	DOM	DIS	RAR	BPX	R$
15 SD *	523	39	19	63	0	242	17	231	289	391	95	111	90	6	75	0.26	42	21	37	29	113	96	129	14%	15%	59	2%	0%	25	20%	56%	-13.8	22	$8
16 STL	438	58	30	59	0	243	25	265	306	495	109	99	112	8	76	0.39	41	19	40	24	107	137	135	24%	20%	85	0%	0%	27	56%	19%	1.5	166	$10
17 STL	481	52	20	67	6	272	20	257	341	472	109	129	101	10	75	0.45	41	20	39	32	94	114	114	16%	16%	79	7%	75%	24	38%	33%	4.6	115	$14
18 STL	402	49	11	47	2	262	15	245	346	416	105	128	96	11	78	0.57	40	21	40	31	107	94	105	10%	14%	84	2%	100%	25	36%	36%	3.2	120	$9
19 2 NL *	131	11	3	14	2	193	2	209	265	295	74	50	77	9	74	0.38	41	19	40	23	110	52	110	7%	7%	70	7%	100%	17	24%	59%	-10.8	-70	-$2
1st Half	62	5	2	7	2	196	2	201	274	304	77	49	88	10	75	0.43	48	14	38	23	117	49	130	13%	13%	75	13%	100%	10	20%	60%	-4.3	-63	-$4
2nd Half	69	6	1	7	0	190	0	226	257	287	72	50	46	8	74	0.34	31	27	42	23	98	54	79	0%	0%	83	0%	0%	7	29%	57%	-5.8	-70	-$1
20 Proj	**350**	**35**	**12**	**41**	**3**	**243**		**234**	**314**	**391**	**95**	**87**	**99**	**9**	**76**	**0.43**	**39**	**21**	**40**	**28**	**105**	**77**	**106**	**12%**		**74**	**4%**	**92%**				**-3.8**	**16**	**$9**

Hamilton,Billy

Age: 29 Bats: B Pos: CF	Health	A	LIMA Plan	D
Ht: 6' 0" Wt: 160	PT/Exp	B	Rand Var	0
	Consist	B	MM	0501

Well, this just isn't good at all. Already weak contact has slid to unacceptably low levels, dragging all-important OBP even further south. Needs playing time to amass SB totals and that's in serious jeopardy. Worse still, raw speed skills took a dip. Those 50-steal seasons seem like a distant memory now. DN: single-digit SB

Yr Tm	PA	R	HR	RBI	SB	BA	xHR	xBA	OBP	SLG	OPS+	vL+	vR+	bb%	ct%	Eye	G	L	F	h%	HctX	PX	xPX	HR/F	xHR/F	Spd	SBO	SB%	#Wk	DOM	DIS	RAR	BPX	R$
15 CIN	454	56	4	28	57	226	2	216	274	289	78	88	73	6	82	0.37	43	20	38	27	69	38	58	3%	2%	164	61%	88%	22	18%	55%	-16.6	57	$23
16 CIN	460	69	3	17	58	260	1	239	321	343	90	78	93	8	77	0.39	48	22	30	33	60	57	32	3%	1%	183	56%	88%	23	35%	57%	-4.6	80	$28
17 CIN	633	85	4	38	59	247	2	238	299	335	85	71	89	7	77	0.33	46	24	31	31	50	49	24	3%	2%	199	46%	82%	26	27%	46%	-25.8	70	$29
18 CIN	556	74	4	29	34	236	1	221	299	327	87	84	87	8	74	0.35	38	27	35	31	52	57	21	3%	1%	192	32%	77%	28	25%	64%	-13.8	57	$17
19 2 TM	353	41	0	15	22	218	0	211	289	275	75	71	76	9	72	0.37	39	25	36	30	59	41	41	0%	0%	155	33%	79%	28	14%	50%	-15.3	-37	$7
1st Half	254	28	0	9	16	220	0	222	291	273	75	70	78	9	74	0.40	42	26	32	30	58	35	34	0%	0%	156	32%	80%	15	7%	40%	-11.6	-26	$8
2nd Half	99	13	0	6	6	213	0	186	283	281	74	75	74	9	67	0.31	31	21	48	32	61	58	62	0%	0%	141	36%	75%	13	23%	62%	-4.9	-78	$4
20 Proj	**245**	**32**	**1**	**13**	**18**	**229**		**212**	**291**	**304**	**80**	**76**	**81**	**8**	**73**	**0.34**	**38**	**24**	**38**	**31**	**57**	**49**	**39**	**2%**		**165**	**38%**	**80%**				**-5.8**	**-18**	**$9**

Hampson,Garrett

Age: 25 Bats: R Pos: 2B CF	Health	A	LIMA Plan	C
Ht: 5' 11" Wt: 188	PT/Exp	F	Rand Var	-1
	Consist	D	MM	2513

8-27-15-.247 in 327 PA at COL. Say, do you remember Hampson in September? Unlike his slow start, there was never a cloudy day (5 HR, 9 SB, 80% ct%, 126 xPX, 160 Spd, .903 OPS). Regular playing time helped prospect look like a budding multi-category threat. Sure, it was only 95 PA. But given pre-2019 intrigue, it's something to hope on.

Yr Tm	PA	R	HR	RBI	SB	BA	xHR	xBA	OBP	SLG	OPS+	vL+	vR+	bb%	ct%	Eye	G	L	F	h%	HctX	PX	xPX	HR/F	xHR/F	Spd	SBO	SB%	#Wk	DOM	DIS	RAR	BPX	R$
15																																		
16																																		
17																																		
18 COL *	528	60	8	32	27	281	1	249	341	411	104	143	101	8	81	0.48	44	20	36	33	85	77	113	0%	11%	151	24%	83%	9	33%	56%	11.3	167	$20
19 COL *	439	50	9	33	19	243	6	224	290	378	89	94	89	6	72	0.24	43	19	37	32	75	77	73	11%	8%	154	26%	79%	24	17%	54%	-10.0	33	$11
1st Half	246	27	2	14	7	217	0	235	247	324	76	67	74	4	73	0.15	45	23	32	29	60	66	18	4%	0%	140	28%	63%	11	0%	73%	-16.0	-11	$4
2nd Half	193	23	7	19	12	277	6	220	344	451	105	116	98	9	70	0.35	42	17	42	36	85	93	116	15%	13%	157	25%	92%	13	31%	38%	5.8	81	$21
20 Proj	**350**	**40**	**9**	**26**	**18**	**264**		**238**	**317**	**421**	**99**	**103**	**96**	**7**	**75**	**0.32**	**43**	**19**	**38**	**32**	**75**	**84**	**77**	**10%**		**158**	**25%**	**83%**				**6.1**	**94**	**$15**

Haniger,Mitch

Age: 29 Bats: R Pos: RF CF	Health	F	LIMA Plan	B
Ht: 6' 2" Wt: 215	PT/Exp	C	Rand Var	+3
	Consist	A	MM	4235

Unfortunate season-ending injury aside, skills took a tumble. While flyball jump helped prop up power metrics, that big K spike and related hard-contact dip can't be ignored. Three solid skills years prior weigh in his favor, but this stumble—along with injury history—makes bidding on a full rebound a risky proposition.

Yr Tm	PA	R	HR	RBI	SB	BA	xHR	xBA	OBP	SLG	OPS+	vL+	vR+	bb%	ct%	Eye	G	L	F	h%	HctX	PX	xPX	HR/F	xHR/F	Spd	SBO	SB%	#Wk	DOM	DIS	RAR	BPX	R$
15 aa	166	18	1	15	3	250			307	340	90			8	76	0.35				32		73				100	20%	41%					27	$1
16 ARI *	632	68	24	87	9	268	5	253	341	476	111	79	101	10	75	0.44	39	18	43	32	113	128	135	14%	14%	113	9%	66%	7	57%	14%	14.7	163	$19
17 SEA *	454	63	18	52	5	275	14	267	334	484	110	97	116	8	76	0.36	44	19	37	32	106	124	120	16%	14%	101	9%	56%	19	53%	32%	7.1	152	$13
18 SEA	683	90	26	93	8	285	35	265	366	493	119	124	116	10	75	0.47	42	21	36	34	103	128	109	16%	21%	105	6%	80%	27	56%	26%	30.9	190	$26
19 SEA	283	46	15	32	4	220	15	240	314	463	103	120	98	11	67	0.37	35	20	45	26	82	143	116	20%	20%	99	7%	100%	12	50%	33%	-2.4	133	$5
1st Half	283	46	15	32	4	220	15	240	314	463	104	122	98	11	67	0.37	35	20	45	26	82	143	116	20%	20%	99	7%	100%	12	50%	33%	-3.9	133	$5
2nd Half																																		
20 Proj	**455**	**64**	**20**	**55**	**6**	**257**		**252**	**338**	**475**	**109**	**107**	**109**	**10**	**73**	**0.39**	**40**	**20**	**40**	**31**	**99**	**122**	**119**	**17%**		**105**	**9%**	**66%**				**9.0**	**141**	**$16**

ROD TRUESDELL

Happ,Ian

Age: 25 Bats: B Pos: LF | Ht: 6' 0" Wt: 205
Health A | PT/Exp C | Consist B
LIMA Plan D+ | Rand Var 0 | MM 4313

11-30-.264 with 2 SB in 156 PA at CHC. Best performance yet at MLB level (see 2nd half line), however: 1) HctX still well below average; 2) PX not supported by xPX; 3) PX regression would drag down xBA; 4) vL+ gains were only 30 AB sample. No denying he's talented, but breakout might not as imminent as it appears.

Yr	Tm	PA	R	HR	RBI	SB	BA	xHR	xBA	OBP	SLG	OPS+	vL+	vR+	bb%	ct%	Eye	G	L	F	h%	HctX	PX	xPX	HR/F	xHR/F	Spd	SBO	SB%	#Wk	DOM	DIS	RAR	BPX	R$
15																																			
16	aa	265	30	7	27	5	236			286	369	89			7	73	0.26				30		90				87	13%	70%					14	$4
17	CHC *	526	78	31	88	10	254	21	253	323	513	112	105	114	9	66	0.30	40	20	40	32	87	163	122	25%	22%	100	13%	65%	22	41%	45%	7.0	133	$19
18	CHC	462	56	15	44	8	233	20	206	353	408	105	85	112	15	57	0.42	40	23	38	37	80	141	126	18%	24%	104	10%	67%	28	25%	57%	5.0	13	$10
19	CHC *	569	77	23	72	9	225	10	222	319	420	98	100	124	12	66	0.41	43	16	42	29	79	117	102	26%	24%	102	9%	80%	11	45%	55%	-1.8	56	$13
1st Half		325	40	9	33	6	190		203	289	324	82			12	62	0.37				27		90		0%		92	11%	71%				-15.7	-93	$6
2nd Half		244	38	15	40	4	271	10	261	358	547	120	99	124	12	72	0.48	43	16	42	31	85	147	102	26%	24%	113	6%	100%	11	45%	55%	14.2	233	$21
20	**Proj**	**280**	**38**	**14**	**36**	**5**	**239**		**235**	**330**	**468**	**107**	**93**	**112**	**12**	**65**	**0.39**	**41**	**19**	**40**	**31**	**85**	**138**	**116**	**22%**		**105**	**10%**	**76%**				**4.8**	**90**	**$7**

Harper,Bryce

Age: 27 Bats: L Pos: RF | Ht: 6' 3" Wt: 220
Health A | PT/Exp A | Consist D
LIMA Plan D+ | Rand Var 0 | MM 4345

Moved to new city, had first child, and dealt with $330M of daily pressure, so perhaps that lends significance to 2nd half gains. Lower ct% approach—and BA trade-off—appears to be here to stay, but as xHR, xHR/F show, it could lead to even more power. 2018-19 gives us solid baseline; if these other factors move you, go the extra buck.

Yr	Tm	PA	R	HR	RBI	SB	BA	xHR	xBA	OBP	SLG	OPS+	vL+	vR+	bb%	ct%	Eye	G	L	F	h%	HctX	PX	xPX	HR/F	xHR/F	Spd	SBO	SB%	#Wk	DOM	DIS	RAR	BPX	R$
15	WAS	654	118	42	99	6	330	33	309	460	649	155	136	159	19	75	0.95	39	22	39	37	134	208	161	27%	21%	99	5%	60%	27	81%	7%	87.2	365	$40
16	WAS	627	84	24	86	21	243	24	252	373	441	111	103	111	17	77	0.92	40	17	42	27	106	117	111	14%	14%	89	17%	68%	26	54%	31%	12.3	183	$21
17	WAS	492	95	29	87	4	319	25	293	413	595	135	106	144	14	76	0.69	40	22	38	36	106	155	105	24%	21%	115	4%	67%	21	62%	24%	44.7	285	$26
18	WAS	695	103	34	100	13	249	37	262	393	496	123	119	124	19	69	0.77	40	22	38	30	108	161	148	23%	25%	82	8%	81%	28	61%	25%	37.0	233	$26
19	PHI	682	98	35	114	15	260	40	261	372	510	117	124	113	15	69	0.56	38	24	38	32	115	145	152	23%	27%	82	10%	83%	28	50%	29%	19.2	174	$27
1st Half		367	50	15	59	4	250	19	251	368	471	112	122	107	15	67	0.55	40	23	38	32	108	139	155	19%	25%	72	7%	57%	15	40%	27%	4.8	126	$22
2nd Half		315	48	20	55	11	272	21	273	378	555	123	127	121	14	71	0.56	37	25	38	31	122	152	149	28%	29%	104	14%	100%	13	62%	31%	17.7	244	$33
20	**Proj**	**665**	**105**	**36**	**109**	**14**	**270**		**266**	**387**	**527**	**123**	**120**	**123**	**16**	**71**	**0.65**	**39**	**23**	**38**	**32**	**113**	**145**	**142**	**24%**		**92**	**9%**	**82%**				**42.4**	**224**	**$32**

Haseley,Adam

Age: 24 Bats: L Pos: CF LF | Ht: 6' 1" Wt: 195
Health A | PT/Exp F | Consist C
LIMA Plan D+ | Rand Var +1 | MM 1233

5-26-.266 with 4 SB in 242 PA at PHI. Too many grounders, not enough hard contact puts even meager power output in question, and struggles vL likely make him a platoon bat at best. Sudden SB jump bears watching; 1st half skills suggest there could be something to it. Young enough to grow, but nothing looks to be sprouting yet.

Yr	Tm	PA	R	HR	RBI	SB	BA	xHR	xBA	OBP	SLG	OPS+	vL+	vR+	bb%	ct%	Eye	G	L	F	h%	HctX	PX	xPX	HR/F	xHR/F	Spd	SBO	SB%	#Wk	DOM	DIS	RAR	BPX	R$
15																																			
16																																			
17																																			
18	aa	149	18	5	14	0	282			344	425	106			9	84	0.58				30		74				102	3%	0%					147	$2
19	PHI *	499	62	14	51	8	257	4	271	315	417	97	69	104	8	74	0.33	57	22	20	32	93	92	53	15%	12%	104	10%	71%	14	36%	50%	2.6	70	$11
1st Half		227	29	8	24	4	246		231	317	428	100	0	83	9	74	0.39	67	0	33	30	43	101	-36	0%		122	15%	56%	1	100%	0%	0.1	126	$8
2nd Half		272	33	7	28	4	266	4	268	313	408	95	70	104	6	74	0.27	57	23	20	33	95	85	57	16%	13%	94	6%	100%	13	31%	54%	1.1	33	$14
20	**Proj**	**350**	**43**	**6**	**31**	**3**	**266**		**262**	**336**	**374**	**96**	**73**	**102**	**8**	**78**	**0.38**	**57**	**23**	**20**	**32**	**86**	**61**	**51**	**13%**		**105**	**6%**	**61%**				**2.4**	**-4**	**$9**

Hays,Austin

Age: 24 Bats: R Pos: CF | Ht: 6' 1" Wt: 195
Health A | PT/Exp D | Consist D
LIMA Plan C | Rand Var 0 | MM 2333

4-13-.309 with 2 SB in 75 PA at BAL. Highly-touted prospect brings emerging pop to the table, but high BA in majors was driven by 81% ct%, 138 PX -- skill levels he has yet to own outside of small MLB sample. Running game also a concern due to poor SB% history. Anyone projecting .300, 30 HR, 15 SB out of his Sept call-up is likely to get burnt.

Yr	Tm	PA	R	HR	RBI	SB	BA	xHR	xBA	OBP	SLG	OPS+	vL+	vR+	bb%	ct%	Eye	G	L	F	h%	HctX	PX	xPX	HR/F	xHR/F	Spd	SBO	SB%	#Wk	DOM	DIS	RAR	BPX	R$
15																																			
16																																			
17	BAL *	336	37	15	54	1	273	1	262	303	460	102	95	67	4	79	0.20	56	16	29	31	99	100	79	8%	8%	98	3%	43%	5	20%	60%	0.8	103	$9
18	aa	282	25	10	32	4	209			234	363	83			3	77	0.14				24		89				99	17%	57%					53	$2
19	BAL *	384	55	15	45	10	242	2	260	282	438	96	45	172	5	75	0.22	41	22	37	28	80	111	107	20%	10%	118	22%	63%	5	80%	20%	-5.5	133	$10
1st Half		99	11	4	11	3	217		254	264	394	88			6	75	0.26				25		101		0%		101	22%	69%				-3.1	96	-$9
2nd Half		286	45	12	34	7	250	2	262	288	453	98	45	172	5	75	0.21	41	22	37	29	80	114	107	20%	10%	123	22%	61%	5	80%	20%	-1.2	144	$17
20	**Proj**	**403**	**47**	**16**	**49**	**8**	**251**		**254**	**282**	**431**	**96**	**104**	**91**	**4**	**76**	**0.19**	**44**	**20**	**36**	**29**	**88**	**98**	**96**	**15%**		**112**	**16%**	**62%**				**1.5**	**70**	**$13**

Healy,Ryon

Age: 28 Bats: R Pos: 3B | Ht: 6' 5" Wt: 225
Health F | PT/Exp C | Consist B
LIMA Plan D+ | Rand Var +4 | MM 3033

Season cut short by back, hip injuries makes him a question mark as he hits peak age. FB% increase was offset by continued slide in HctX, and career power skills (104 PX, 101 xPX, 15% HR/F) paint him as decidedly average at this point. Might be time to demote him from mid-level to bench option in most leagues.

Yr	Tm	PA	R	HR	RBI	SB	BA	xHR	xBA	OBP	SLG	OPS+	vL+	vR+	bb%	ct%	Eye	G	L	F	h%	HctX	PX	xPX	HR/F	xHR/F	Spd	SBO	SB%	#Wk	DOM	DIS	RAR	BPX	R$
15	aa	529	47	7	46	0	258			290	357	90			4	82	0.25				30		70				85	1%	0%					57	$6
16	OAK *	645	85	23	90	1	296	14	268	336	499	114	120	114	6	77	0.26	42	20	39	35	93	130	102	16%	17%	103	1%	42%	13	54%	15%	19.7	157	$22
17	OAK	605	66	25	78	0	271	24	246	302	451	101	116	95	4	75	0.16	43	19	38	32	104	106	115	15%	14%	91	1%	0%	27	44%	37%	-11.5	70	$15
18	SEA	524	51	24	73	0	235	23	240	277	412	95	88	98	5	77	0.24	44	19	37	26	97	99	100	17%	17%	74	0%	0%	26	19%	35%	-9.5	73	$10
19	SEA	187	24	7	26	0	237	8	259	289	456	99	76	107	7	76	0.33	38	17	44	27	89	128	116	12%	14%	88	0%	0%	10	60%	30%	-2.4	185	$1
1st Half		187	24	7	26	0	237	8	259	289	456	99	78	107	7	76	0.33	38	17	44	27	89	128	116	12%	14%	88	0%	0%	10	60%	30%	-3.7	185	$1
2nd Half																																			
20	**Proj**	**350**	**40**	**15**	**47**	**0**	**256**		**253**	**297**	**457**	**101**	**98**	**102**	**5**	**77**	**0.24**	**42**	**19**	**40**	**29**	**96**	**110**	**110**	**15%**		**92**	**1%**	**22%**				**0.5**	**70**	**$10**

Hedges,Austin

Age: 27 Bats: R Pos: CA | Ht: 6' 1" Wt: 206
Health A | PT/Exp D | Consist D
LIMA Plan D | Rand Var +3 | MM 2203

We keep waiting for power breakout that never materializes, and xHR suggests maybe we should stop. Has never been able to maintain even league average HctX, and all 2nd half leap to 50%+ fly ball rate did was kill his BA, with help of career-worst ct%. Thin CA pool lets him hang on to relevance, but only as a deep league flyer.

Yr	Tm	PA	R	HR	RBI	SB	BA	xHR	xBA	OBP	SLG	OPS+	vL+	vR+	bb%	ct%	Eye	G	L	F	h%	HctX	PX	xPX	HR/F	xHR/F	Spd	SBO	SB%	#Wk	DOM	DIS	RAR	BPX	R$
15	SD *	228	21	4	21	1	202	1	226	250	308	78	58	66	6	77	0.28	45	19	36	24	67	74	55	8%	3%	76	2%	100%	23	17%	74%	-8.7	11	-$2
16	SD *	348	39	13	56	1	256	1	219	275	433	96	135	20	2	80	0.13	44	6	50	28	109	104	59	0%	11%	78	5%	24%	3	33%	67%	-4.3	100	$7
17	SD	417	36	18	55	4	214	13	223	262	398	88	80	90	6	68	0.19	37	18	46	26	92	116	114	15%	11%	69	7%	80%	24	38%	54%	-8.5	0	$3
18	SD *	355	34	16	44	3	239	11	235	288	445	102	94	100	6	69	0.23	38	18	44	30	94	133	116	15%	12%	93	4%	100%	21	38%	43%	8.2	87	$7
19	SD	347	28	11	36	1	176	10	200	252	311	75	63	78	8	65	0.25	32	22	46	23	71	81	89	12%	11%	62	2%	100%	27	19%	56%	-20.1	-141	-$2
1st Half		205	14	6	22	1	185	6	214	249	312	75	64	78	6	65	0.17	30	28	42	25	77	78	92	12%	12%	69	3%	100%	15	13%	67%	-10.3	-159	-$3
2nd Half		142	14	5	14	0	163	4	179	257	309	75	60	79	12	65	0.37	35	14	52	20	62	86	84	12%	10%	79	0%	0%	12	25%	42%	-6.2	-81	-$1
20	**Proj**	**315**	**29**	**11**	**36**	**2**	**208**		**209**	**272**	**366**	**86**	**77**	**89**	**8**	**68**	**0.26**	**36**	**19**	**45**	**26**	**78**	**93**	**95**	**13%**		**76**	**3%**	**89%**				**-2.0**	**-78**	**$4**

Hernandez,Cesar

Age: 30 Bats: B Pos: 2B | Ht: 5' 10" Wt: 160
Health A | PT/Exp A | Consist B
LIMA Plan B+ | Rand Var 0 | MM 1535

Gave up on 2018's free-swinging quest for power and instead posted career highs in ct%, HctX, xBA. But he offset those gains by following up career-best bb% with career-worst, as well as lowest SB total, SBO since he became a starter. Volatility makes projections difficult, but one thing you can count on is lots and lots of PAs - which has great value.

Yr	Tm	PA	R	HR	RBI	SB	BA	xHR	xBA	OBP	SLG	OPS+	vL+	vR+	bb%	ct%	Eye	G	L	F	h%	HctX	PX	xPX	HR/F	xHR/F	Spd	SBO	SB%	#Wk	DOM	DIS	RAR	BPX	R$
15	PHI	452	57	1	35	19	272	3	257	339	348	96	106	89	9	79	0.47	54	24	22	34	80	58	67	2%	5%	150	19%	79%	24	38%	42%	0.3	70	$14
16	PHI	622	67	6	39	17	294	5	263	371	393	104	107	101	11	79	0.57	55	24	21	36	83	55	58	7%	6%	186	15%	57%	27	26%	33%	2.1	109	$20
17	PHI	577	85	9	34	15	294	10	273	373	421	106	107	104	11	80	0.59	53	23	25	35	71	74	61	9%	10%	185	12%	75%	22	41%	18%	8.3	173	$19
18	PHI	708	91	15	60	19	253	13	225	356	362	99	97	99	13	74	0.61	46	21	34	32	66	65	63	10%	9%	146	12%	76%	28	29%	36%	2.6	73	$20
19	PHI	667	77	14	71	9	279	11	274	333	408	98	84	104	7	84	0.45	49	23	29	32	95	67	55	10%	7%	123	7%	82%	28	43%	21%	4.2	152	$18
1st Half		342	41	7	37	5	284	6	284	339	429	103	75	112	7	86	0.50	47	23	30	31	95	73	67	9%	7%	117	7%	83%	15	40%	13%	3.9	193	$18
2nd Half		325	36	7	34	4	275	5	261	326	387	94	92	95	7	81	0.41	50	22	27	32	95	60	41	11%	8%	127	6%	80%	13	46%	31%	-1.7	104	$17
20	**Proj**	**595**	**74**	**11**	**54**	**12**	**275**		**258**	**346**	**393**	**99**	**94**	**101**	**9**	**80**	**0.52**	**49**	**22**	**28**	**33**	**83**	**63**	**57**	**9%**		**145**	**9%**	**74%**				**10.0**	**77**	**$19**

BRANDON KRUSE

Hernandez,Enrique

Age: 28	Bats: R	Pos: 2B CF	Health	B	LIMA Plan	D+
Ht: 5' 11"	Wt: 192		PT/Exp	C	Rand Var	0
			Consist	C	MM	2323

Unable to build on 2018 gains after winning Opening Day 2B gig, eventually ceding PA by mid-season. Late July hand injury may have factored into Aug/Sept power drop-off, but bb%, ct% each took a step back, and success vL now less automatic than in platoon bat days. Worth monitoring, though time is running out for him to put it all together.

Yr	Tm	PA	R	HR	RBI	SB	BA	xHR	xBA	OBP	SLG	OPS+	vL+	vR+	bb%	ct%	Eye	G	L	F	h%	HctX	PX	xPX	HR/F	xHR/F	Spd	SBO	SB%	#Wk	DOM	DIS	RAR	BPX	R$
15	LA *	280	28	8	29	1	269	7	261	306	427	102	168	81	5	76	0.22	46	23	30	33	110	106	98	15%	15%	122	5%	27%	20	45%	40%	1.9	103	$5
16	LA	244	25	7	18	2	190	7	211	283	324	83	90	70	11	70	0.44	41	17	42	23	79	89	91	11%	11%	92	4%	100%	23	26%	48%	-13.2	14	-$2
17	LA	342	46	11	37	3	215	10	259	308	421	98	125	66	12	73	0.51	42	19	40	26	116	132	122	13%	11%	98	4%	100%	27	48%	37%	-6.4	161	$3
18	LA	462	67	21	52	3	256	18	260	336	470	112	108	114	11	81	0.64	38	19	44	27	105	115	105	15%	13%	110	3%	100%	28	61%	14%	14.5	237	$13
19	LA	460	57	17	64	4	237	15	242	304	411	95	99	92	8	77	0.37	36	21	43	27	107	92	107	12%	11%	87	4%	100%	25	36%	32%	-4.9	89	$9
1st Half		296	34	13	41	2	215	12	236	287	404	92	106	84	8	75	0.34	38	18	44	24	120	97	123	15%	14%	86	4%	100%	15	40%	33%	-7.9	74	$10
2nd Half		164	23	4	23	2	275	3	254	335	423	100	89	106	8	80	0.43	33	24	43	32	85	83	80	8%	6%	100	5%	100%	10	30%	30%	1.7	126	$7
20	Proj	420	56	15	53	4	245		247	317	425	100	106	94	9	77	0.45	38	20	42	28	103	97	103	12%		99	4%	96%				5.4	119	$9

Hernandez,Teoscar

Age: 27	Bats: R	Pos: CF LF	Health	A	LIMA Plan	B
Ht: 6' 2"	Wt: 205		PT/Exp	C	Rand Var	0
			Consist	B	MM	4325

26-65-.230 with 6 SB in 464 PA at TOR. Returned from mid-May demotion to put on big-time HR display, backed by elite power metrics and improved patience. The problem? Contact woes point to continued streakiness, and subpar defense could ultimately cut into playing time. Pay for power, but don't go overboard staring at that 2nd half line.

Yr	Tm	PA	R	HR	RBI	SB	BA	xHR	xBA	OBP	SLG	OPS+	vL+	vR+	bb%	ct%	Eye	G	L	F	h%	HctX	PX	xPX	HR/F	xHR/F	Spd	SBO	SB%	#Wk	DOM	DIS	RAR	BPX	R$
15	aa	495	70	14	36	25	191			231	310	75			5	69	0.17				24		81				124	37%	76%					-19	$9
16	HOU *	571	75	12	54	28	262	3	234	323	404	99	119	84	8	76	0.38	48	12	40	32	102	94	75	14%	10%	123	34%	59%	9	56%	22%	-3.8	103	$21
17	2 AL *	538	78	25	81	15	253	7	246	322	495	109	86	134	9	69	0.33	28	23	49	32	79	152	139	31%	27%	115	22%	60%	7	57%	43%	5.9	161	$19
18	TOR	523	67	22	57	5	239	36	238	302	468	107	103	107	8	66	0.25	36	20	44	32	91	157	149	16%	26%	147	10%	50%	26	65%	27%	7.4	170	$12
19	TOR *	544	67	30	74	8	228	25	226	299	461	101	109	100	9	64	0.28	39	18	43	29	97	138	144	23%	22%	118	10%	74%	26	38%	35%	0.4	78	$14
1st Half		297	32	11	33	6	203	8	204	266	363	84	95	76	8	67	0.26	40	17	44	26	84	90	120	12%	14%	132	12%	86%	13	15%	46%	-10.6	-15	$8
2nd Half		247	35	19	41	2	259	17	252	340	562	122	121	121	11	60	0.30	38	19	43	33	107	203	168	33%	30%	104	8%	50%	13	62%	23%	14.1	219	$21
20	Proj	525	69	31	79	5	239		241	307	500	109	108	108	9	66	0.28	38	19	44	30	94	155	140	22%		124	9%	60%				16.2	123	$18

Herrera,Odubel

Age: 28	Bats: L	Pos: CF	Health	A	LIMA Plan	C
Ht: 5' 11"	Wt: 205		PT/Exp	C	Rand Var	+4
			Consist	C	MM	2323

Suffered April hamstring injury, fell into strong-side platoon, then came 85-game suspension in June. Not a good year. Skills-wise, story wasn't much better, as previously overperforming PX and HR/F couldn't repeat while xBA/Spd reinforced disappearance of multi-category ways. A long way from being an appealing fantasy option.

Yr	Tm	PA	R	HR	RBI	SB	BA	xHR	xBA	OBP	SLG	OPS+	vL+	vR+	bb%	ct%	Eye	G	L	F	h%	HctX	PX	xPX	HR/F	xHR/F	Spd	SBO	SB%	#Wk	DOM	DIS	RAR	BPX	R$
15	PHI	537	64	8	41	16	297	9	248	344	418	106	99	106	5	74	0.22	47	23	29	39	85	93	83	8%	9%	129	18%	67%	27	44%	30%	8.7	57	$20
16	PHI	656	87	15	49	25	286	14	249	361	420	106	81	112	10	77	0.47	46	22	32	35	85	79	88	11%	10%	150	17%	78%	27	26%	26%	12.2	106	$26
17	PHI	563	67	14	56	8	281	13	265	325	452	104	105	102	6	76	0.25	44	21	35	35	90	110	79	10%	9%	95	11%	62%	25	40%	36%	-0.2	103	$16
18	PHI	597	64	22	71	5	255	15	245	310	420	101	103	100	6	78	0.31	45	18	37	29	71	93	64	14%	9%	110	5%	71%	28	25%	46%	1.5	110	$15
19	PHI	139	12	1	10	2	222	2	243	288	341	84	77	86	8	74	0.33	40	24	35	29	79	80	62	3%	6%	90	15%	50%	9	22%	44%	-4.8	15	-$1
1st Half		139	12	1	16	2	222	2	243	288	341	84	78	85	8	74	0.33	40	24	35	29	79	80	62	3%	6%	90	15%	50%	9	22%	44%	-5.3	15	-$1
2nd Half																																			
20	Proj	350	39	7	36	6	251		247	309	395	95	90	96	7	76	0.31	44	22	34	31	82	84	73	9%		107	11%	67%				1.2	50	$9

Heyward,Jason

Age: 30	Bats: L	Pos: RF CF	Health	B	LIMA Plan	B+
Ht: 6' 5"	Wt: 240		PT/Exp	B	Rand Var	0
			Consist	A	MM	1335

At first blush, HR outburst driven by contact-for-power trade-off. But beware HR/xHR gap before penciling in another 20 HR, and "improved" xPX still sitting well below league average. SB uptick added to R$ gains, though mediocre SB% and inconsistent SBO speak to SB volatility. A decent back-end piece but not at the price that those 20 HRs will likely draw.

Yr	Tm	PA	R	HR	RBI	SB	BA	xHR	xBA	OBP	SLG	OPS+	vL+	vR+	bb%	ct%	Eye	G	L	F	h%	HctX	PX	xPX	HR/F	xHR/F	Spd	SBO	SB%	#Wk	DOM	DIS	RAR	BPX	R$
15	STL	608	79	13	60	23	293	11	288	359	439	111	98	114	9	84	0.62	57	19	23	33	105	94	73	12%	10%	113	16%	88%	27	48%	19%	23.3	173	$27
16	CHC	592	61	7	49	11	230	8	249	306	325	86	79	86	9	82	0.58	46	21	33	27	88	62	72	5%	5%	89	11%	73%	27	26%	37%	-22.6	74	$6
17	CHC	480	59	11	59	4	259	10	262	326	389	96	88	97	9	84	0.61	47	20	33	29	87	66	70	9%	8%	113	7%	50%	24	33%	17%	-10.6	133	$10
18	CHC	488	67	8	57	1	270	10	260	335	395	101	100	101	9	86	0.70	48	18	34	30	95	71	69	6%	8%	107	2%	50%	26	54%	8%	4.4	180	$11
19	CHC	589	78	21	62	8	251	13	259	343	429	102	72	111	12	79	0.62	46	20	34	28	96	88	82	15%	9%	110	7%	73%	27	33%	33%	10.0	159	$14
1st Half		315	41	14	37	5	271	7	266	362	473	111	75	122	13	80	0.72	46	19	35	29	93	92	76	18%	9%	127	7%	83%	15	33%	33%	12.9	222	$19
2nd Half		274	37	7	25	3	229	7	250	321	379	92	70	99	11	77	0.52	47	20	33	27	99	83	91	11%	11%	93	8%	60%	12	33%	33%	-3.9	89	$9
20	Proj	525	70	14	57	6	256		258	335	404	100	83	104	10	82	0.62	47	19	33	29	95	75	78	11%		108	6%	68%				0.5	134	$15

Hicks,Aaron

Age: 30	Bats: B	Pos: CF	Health	F	LIMA Plan	C+
Ht: 6' 1"	Wt: 202		PT/Exp	C	Rand Var	-2
			Consist	B	MM	3221

Hit IL for seventh straight year, as fairly significant back/elbow injuries bookended forgettable season. On the field, plate skills cratered and speed game dried up, while even modest power enjoyed touch of good fortune. That said, can't write off the skills growth from 2017-18. But TJS will now shelve him into the summer. Late season FAAB flyer.

Yr	Tm	PA	R	HR	RBI	SB	BA	xHR	xBA	OBP	SLG	OPS+	vL+	vR+	bb%	ct%	Eye	G	L	F	h%	HctX	PX	xPX	HR/F	xHR/F	Spd	SBO	SB%	#Wk	DOM	DIS	RAR	BPX	R$
15	MIN *	553	69	13	49	15	268	10	259	331	418	104	120	91	9	80	0.48	42	23	35	31	90	94	93	11%	10%	125	13%	78%	18	39%	22%	4.8	141	$17
16	NYY	361	32	8	31	3	217	7	232	281	336	84	65	92	8	79	0.44	46	17	37	25	93	72	104	8%	7%	93	9%	43%	25	28%	36%	-14.1	60	$1
17	NYY *	387	60	16	54	11	267	11	266	370	481	114	120	108	14	78	0.76	44	16	40	30	98	122	119	16%	12%	92	15%	68%	19	47%	26%	12.7	206	$14
18	NYY	581	90	27	79	11	248	25	264	366	467	115	111	116	15	77	0.81	40	22	38	27	112	122	131	19%	18%	112	8%	85%	27	41%	30%	26.1	240	$21
19	NYY	255	41	12	36	1	235	10	228	325	443	102	88	109	12	67	0.43	43	16	41	29	89	122	98	19%	16%	94	5%	33%	12	33%	42%	1.6	81	$4
1st Half		151	24	6	24	1	217	6	228	311	395	94	80	101	13	71	0.50	41	18	40	26	88	100	91	16%	16%	87	6%	50%	8	38%	38%	-1.5	59	$4
2nd Half		104	17	6	12	0	261	4	227	346	511	113	99	122	12	63	0.35	47	12	41	35	90	156	110	25%	17%	112	4%	0%	4	25%	50%	4.0	133	$5
20	Proj	224	35	10	30	3	248		243	344	461	108	101	111	13	72	0.53	43	17	40	29	96	118	112	19%		105	8%	61%				8.2	122	$8

Hicks,John

Age: 30	Bats: R	Pos: CA 1B	Health	B	LIMA Plan	D
Ht: 6' 2"	Wt: 230		PT/Exp	D	Rand Var	+1
			Consist	C	MM	2103

Team context afforded enough PA to sniff fantasy relevance, but plate skills took a tumble as bottom fell out of BA—with h% not there to bail him out this time around. While 2nd half xPX boost offers slight encouragement, overall profile provides little in the way of either ceiling or floor. Not a good combo, even for a catcher.

Yr	Tm	PA	R	HR	RBI	SB	BA	xHR	xBA	OBP	SLG	OPS+	vL+	vR+	bb%	ct%	Eye	G	L	F	h%	HctX	PX	xPX	HR/F	xHR/F	Spd	SBO	SB%	#Wk	DOM	DIS	RAR	BPX	R$
15	SEA *	343	26	4	24	7	174	0	197	202	249	63	28	24	3	67	0.11	14	36	50	24	117	63	198	0%	0%	77	20%	67%	6	17%	67%	-23.9	-127	-$4
16	DET *	342	36	8	36	3	255		330	292	392	93	0	401	5	74	0.20	50	50	0	33	0	95	-24	0%		81	6%	72%	1	100%	0%	0.4	17	$5
17	DET *	397	42	12	50	6	244	6	241	276	398	90	97	105	4	70	0.14	50	19	30	32	101	101	89	17%	17%	68	14%	57%	19	37%	37%	-6.4	-24	$7
18	DET	312	35	9	32	0	260	10	221	312	403	99	114	92	7	71	0.26	43	19	38	34	96	93	98	12%	13%	106	1%	0%	19	32%	47%	7.6	20	$5
19	DET	333	29	13	35	1	210	10	215	240	379	82	90	79	4	66	0.12	41	19	40	27	86	105	103	15%	12%	56	4%	50%	28	25%	57%	-6.8	-93	$1
1st Half		158	10	3	9	1	187	3	198	222	313	71	71	72	4	65	0.13	40	16	43	26	80	91	87	7%	7%	57	5%	100%	15	27%	53%	-8.4	-141	-$7
2nd Half		175	19	10	26	0	231	7	229	257	438	92	97	88	3	66	0.11	41	21	38	28	92	117	117	24%	17%	72	3%	0%	13	23%	62%	-1.8	-41	$8
20	Proj	280	28	10	31	1	230		222	265	395	89	96	85	4	68	0.15	43	19	38	30	92	100	100	15%		78	5%	50%				0.0	-77	$5

Hiura,Keston

Age: 23	Bats: R	Pos: 2B	Health	A	LIMA Plan	D+
Ht: 5' 11"	Wt: 190		PT/Exp	F	Rand Var	-2
			Consist	F	MM	4335

19-49-.303 with 9 SB in 348 PA at MIL. Praised by scouts for quick hands and contact ability, rookie sensation flipped power switch at both AAA/MLB. Underlying xPX/xHR says 30+ HR in play, while average Spd tempers SB expectations. Pedigree suggests BA goodness lies ahead even if xBA raises question as to when. Time to buy is now.

Yr	Tm	PA	R	HR	RBI	SB	BA	xHR	xBA	OBP	SLG	OPS+	vL+	vR+	bb%	ct%	Eye	G	L	F	h%	HctX	PX	xPX	HR/F	xHR/F	Spd	SBO	SB%	#Wk	DOM	DIS	RAR	BPX	R$
15																																			
16																																			
17																																			
18	aa	300	34	6	19	10	264			315	408	100			7	78	0.34				32		92				112	23%	66%					120	$8
19	MIL *	579	85	35	85	14	298	21	262	351	577	123	88	136	7	66	0.24	38	24	38	39	100	170	140	24%	27%	110	16%	73%	18	44%	44%	39.9	178	$28
1st Half		311	42	21	45	6	286	6	261	335	561	120	102	110	7	65	0.21	40	25	35	37	94	164	120	29%	35%	102	15%	66%	6	17%	67%	15.4	141	$27
2nd Half		268	43	14	40	8	313	15	268	381	596	129	83	144	8	66	0.27	38	24	39	42	103	178	146	23%	24%	115	17%	80%	12	58%	33%	23.0	226	$29
20	Proj	630	86	28	73	11	275		264	344	503	114	88	121	7	70	0.26	43	23	33	35	100	136	136	20%		119	13%	67%				26.8	132	$26

BRIAN SLACK

Holt,Brock

Age: 32 Bats: L Pos: 2B — Ht: 5' 10" Wt: 180
Health: F | PT/Exp: D | Consist: D
LIMA Plan: D | Rand Var: -5 | MM: 1223

3-31-.297 in 295 PA at BOS. Cornea scratched by toddler son, shoulder injury led to slow start; from June 1 on, batted .316 (thanks, h%). Still, Brockstar? More like one-hit wonder. Only 1 SB try, so he's no (Dexy's Midnight) runner. Has never had pop, so he's too unsexy for your roster. An OK roster filler, but keep big bids on (Vanilla) ice.

Yr Tm	PA	R	HR	RBI	SB	BA	xHR	xBA	OBP	SLG	OPS+	vL+	vR+	bb%	ct%	Eye	G	L	F	h%	HctX	PX	xPX	HR/F	xHR/F	Spd	SBO	SB%	#Wk	DOM	DIS	RAR	BPX	R$
15 BOS	509	56	2	45	8	280	3	263	349	379	101	111	96	9	79	0.47	53	24	24	35	89	74	62	2%	4%	127	7%	89%	26	31%	35%	5.6	86	$12
16 BOS *	353	47	7	36	4	258	4	276	325	382	96	46	102	9	80	0.49	54	24	22	30	75	81	50	14%	8%	98	8%	57%	22	41%	32%	-5.1	94	$7
17 BOS *	252	28	2	14	2	193	0	226	275	253	71	90	68	10	77	0.48	60	17	23	24	66	40	18	0%	0%	103	5%	67%	15	33%	53%	-17.1	-24	-$3
18 BOS	367	41	7	46	7	277	8	266	362	411	107	100	108	10	77	0.51	51	24	25	34	83	86	56	11%	13%	102	14%	50%	27	41%	37%	6.9	103	$10
19 BOS *	332	43	4	33	2	287	4	250	363	394	101	73	111	10	75	0.48	48	25	28	37	92	65	59	5%	7%	130	2%	100%	21	33%	52%	3.1	56	$6
1st Half	140	20	2	18	2	288	1	255	365	396	102	70	110	11	70	0.40	58	27	15	40	92	68	48	9%	9%	121	4%	100%	8	25%	63%	2.1	-22	$4
2nd Half	192	23	2	15	0	286	3	250	365	393	100	73	111	11	79	0.57	42	24	34	35	93	64	65	4%	7%	129	0%	0%	13	38%	46%	2.0	111	$7
20 Proj	**315**	**39**	**4**	**32**	**2**	**269**		**251**	**351**	**372**	**97**	**82**	**101**	**10**	**77**	**0.49**	**51**	**23**	**25**	**34**	**85**	**62**	**51**	**7%**		**118**	**5%**	**55%**				**2.5**	**1**	**$5**

Hoskins,Rhys

Age: 27 Bats: R Pos: 1B — Ht: 6' 4" Wt: 225
Health: A | PT/Exp: A | Consist: C
LIMA Plan: B+ | Rand Var: +2 | MM: 4225

Hit on hand by pitch on 8/15; stats suffered thereafter (.182 BA, 5 HR in 40 games). Before that, 2019 looked like it would be bit better than 2018, if not quite as exciting as end of 2017. Still plenty of power, patience, and loft, paired with adequate contact. If injury indeed depressed totals, this may be buying opportunity... UP: 45 HR, still

Yr Tm	PA	R	HR	RBI	SB	BA	xHR	xBA	OBP	SLG	OPS+	vL+	vR+	bb%	ct%	Eye	G	L	F	h%	HctX	PX	xPX	HR/F	xHR/F	Spd	SBO	SB%	#Wk	DOM	DIS	RAR	BPX	R$
15																																		
16 aa	551	71	31	87	6	240			313	470	107			10	71	0.36				28		144				82	8%	64%					123	$15
17 PHI *	668	104	45	126	5	256	13	287	359	551	122	133	134	14	77	0.69	31	24	45	26	143	158	178	32%	23%	85	5%	71%	9	56%	33%	14.0	267	$24
18 PHI	659	89	34	96	5	246	34	256	354	496	118	93	124	13	73	0.58	29	19	52	28	93	157	145	16%	16%	74	5%	63%	28	54%	32%	10.9	230	$21
19 PHI	703	86	29	85	2	226	30	237	364	454	109	128	102	17	70	0.67	29	21	50	27	111	131	143	14%	15%	114	2%	50%	28	54%	25%	-1.8	193	$12
1st Half	364	43	19	55	1	261	15	251	393	522	122	138	117	17	71	0.70	28	22	50	31	114	144	154	18%	14%	104	3%	33%	15	67%	20%	14.5	241	$20
2nd Half	339	43	10	30	1	189	15	221	333	382	94	119	85	17	69	0.64	30	19	51	23	108	116	131	10%	15%	124	1%	100%	13	38%	31%	-10.9	148	$4
20 Proj	**665**	**89**	**34**	**93**	**4**	**247**		**247**	**365**	**499**	**116**	**118**	**115**	**15**	**72**	**0.61**	**29**	**20**	**50**	**28**	**109**	**140**	**148**	**17%**		**98**	**3%**	**63%**				**24.5**	**189**	**$21**

Hosmer,Eric

Age: 30 Bats: L Pos: 1B — Ht: 6' 4" Wt: 225
Health: A | PT/Exp: A | Consist: D
LIMA Plan: B | Rand Var: -1 | MM: 2135

Totals say, "Ho-hum. Another steady-if-boring season." But some creeping concerns, like, "What's up with 2nd half contact rate?" For two years, has been punchless vL and heavy GB tilt leaves HR at mercy of HR/F (though xHR/F says not to worry). Ultra-reliable, but 2019 seems about as good as it's going to get.

Yr Tm	PA	R	HR	RBI	SB	BA	xHR	xBA	OBP	SLG	OPS+	vL+	vR+	bb%	ct%	Eye	G	L	F	h%	HctX	PX	xPX	HR/F	xHR/F	Spd	SBO	SB%	#Wk	DOM	DIS	RAR	BPX	R$
15 KC	667	98	18	93	7	297	24	290	363	459	115	101	121	9	82	0.56	52	24	24	34	116	102	94	15%	20%	108	5%	70%	27	48%	19%	10.4	168	$27
16 KC	667	80	25	104	5	266	26	263	328	433	104	89	109	9	78	0.43	59	16	25	30	109	97	89	21%	22%	77	5%	63%	26	46%	27%	-7.5	94	$19
17 KC	671	98	25	94	6	318	21	298	385	498	118	101	124	10	83	0.63	56	22	22	35	99	96	65	23%	19%	92	3%	86%	27	70%	7%	21.0	173	$30
18 SD	677	72	18	69	7	253	21	266	322	398	100	73	114	9	77	0.44	60	20	20	30	98	90	68	19%	23%	86	7%	64%	28	43%	43%	-14.2	87	$15
19 SD	667	72	22	99	0	265	22	253	310	425	98	78	104	6	74	0.25	56	21	23	33	102	89	77	21%	21%	86	2%	0%	28	21%	46%	-16.9	22	$15
1st Half	350	48	13	60	0	302	14	280	354	474	111	87	117	7	80	0.38	57	22	21	35	107	86	77	25%	26%	94	1%	0%	15	27%	20%	7.6	122	$25
2nd Half	317	24	9	39	0	225	9	226	262	372	84	72	89	5	67	0.15	55	19	26	30	97	93	78	17%	17%	80	4%	0%	13	15%	77%	-18.8	-81	$5
20 Proj	**665**	**73**	**20**	**87**	**2**	**261**		**259**	**317**	**414**	**98**	**80**	**106**	**8**	**76**	**0.34**	**57**	**21**	**23**	**31**	**101**	**85**	**75**	**19%**		**88**	**3%**	**43%**				**-1.9**	**14**	**$18**

Iglesias,Jose

Age: 30 Bats: R Pos: SS — Ht: 5' 11" Wt: 194
Health: B | PT/Exp: B | Consist: A
LIMA Plan: B | Rand Var: -2 | MM: 1255

Need more juiced ball evidence? Guy with flat, even declining, power skills doubles prior HR output thanks to HR/F. He credits taking fewer first pitches, but c'mon. High GB%, ct%, decent wheels have some value—though SB%, declining SBO are concerning. Glove will keep him in lineup, but prime candidate to feel effects if "old" ball magically reappears.

Yr Tm	PA	R	HR	RBI	SB	BA	xHR	xBA	OBP	SLG	OPS+	vL+	vR+	bb%	ct%	Eye	G	L	F	h%	HctX	PX	xPX	HR/F	xHR/F	Spd	SBO	SB%	#Wk	DOM	DIS	RAR	BPX	R$
15 DET	454	44	2	23	11	300	1	273	347	370	100	123	91	6	89	0.57	56	21	23	33	65	46	30	2%	1%	135	15%	58%	22	36%	18%	7.3	130	$13
16 DET	513	57	4	32	7	255	3	271	306	336	87	95	83	5	89	0.56	51	20	28	28	66	53	28	3%	3%	109	9%	64%	26	46%	27%	-17.2	129	$7
17 DET	484	56	6	54	7	258	3	288	291	373	89	86	88	4	86	0.33	50	23	27	29	100	71	47	6%	3%	78	11%	64%	26	42%	31%	-11.6	109	$9
18 DET	464	43	5	48	15	269	5	279	310	389	97	120	90	4	89	0.40	44	23	34	29	88	73	45	4%	4%	105	22%	71%	23	57%	26%	2.2	190	$13
19 CIN	530	62	11	59	6	288	8	285	318	407	96	90	98	4	86	0.29	52	24	24	32	91	58	53	10%	8%	114	9%	50%	27	41%	30%	-4.8	130	$14
1st Half	272	31	5	32	2	288	4	285	324	405	97	84	102	5	84	0.32	51	26	23	33	88	59	62	10%	8%	126	7%	40%	15	40%	33%	-3.4	122	$12
2nd Half	258	31	6	27	4	287	4	285	311	409	95	97	94	3	88	0.24	54	21	25	31	94	58	44	11%	7%	97	11%	57%	12	42%	25%	-4.3	133	$16
20 Proj	**490**	**53**	**7**	**49**	**6**	**277**		**281**	**312**	**386**	**94**	**98**	**92**	**4**	**87**	**0.34**	**51**	**23**	**26**	**31**	**89**	**57**	**47**	**6%**		**106**	**10%**	**52%**				**-1.4**	**108**	**$14**

Inciarte,Ender

Age: 29 Bats: L Pos: CF — Ht: 5' 11" Wt: 190
Health: F | PT/Exp: B | Consist: B
LIMA Plan: C+ | Rand Var: +3 | MM: 1445

5-24-.246 with 7 SB in 230 PA at ATL. Shhh... Keep this between us, OK? In and around injuries, guy who posted three $20+ seasons still lives. Indeed, 2nd half bb%, Eye were best yet, while ct% just a tick off lofty career norm. If you can stomach risk (it's not as great as some think), there's lots of profit here, especially in SB-poor environment.

Yr Tm	PA	R	HR	RBI	SB	BA	xHR	xBA	OBP	SLG	OPS+	vL+	vR+	bb%	ct%	Eye	G	L	F	h%	HctX	PX	xPX	HR/F	xHR/F	Spd	SBO	SB%	#Wk	DOM	DIS	RAR	BPX	R$
15 ARI	561	73	6	45	21	303	4	284	338	408	104	73	113	5	89	0.45	52	22	26	33	102	66	72	5%	3%	129	21%	68%	23	43%	13%	2.4	159	$24
16 ATL	578	85	3	29	16	291	3	275	351	381	100	101	97	8	87	0.66	49	24	27	33	80	53	50	2%	2%	157	14%	70%	24	46%	33%	1.2	157	$18
17 ATL	718	93	11	57	22	304	6	274	350	409	102	94	102	7	86	0.52	47	24	29	34	77	57	54	7%	4%	135	15%	71%	27	41%	30%	-0.9	136	$29
18 ATL	660	83	10	61	28	265	7	269	325	380	98	93	99	7	86	0.57	45	24	31	30	100	65	68	6%	4%	121	26%	67%	28	43%	29%	-9.3	160	$24
19 ATL *	264	35	5	25	8	242	2	271	328	377	94	91	100	11	81	0.66	48	24	28	28	91	71	67	12%	5%	116	15%	78%	13	38%	38%	-6.8	141	$5
1st Half	140	13	2	9	3	218	1	273	300	323	83	97	80	9	78	0.44	56	26	18	26	86	57	41	12%	6%	107	13%	75%	8	25%	38%	-8.2	37	-$1
2nd Half	124	22	3	16	5	271	1	260	373	440	107	86	135	14	83	0.98	36	21	43	30	99	87	107	12%	4%	127	17%	80%	5	60%	40%	2.0	263	$12
20 Proj	**525**	**73**	**11**	**50**	**19**	**267**		**271**	**342**	**405**	**101**	**88**	**104**	**10**	**84**	**0.64**	**45**	**23**	**31**	**30**	**93**	**70**	**72**	**9%**		**127**	**18%**	**74%**				**11.3**	**178**	**$21**

Jansen,Danny

Age: 25 Bats: R Pos: CA — Ht: 6' 2" Wt: 230
Health: A | PT/Exp: D | Consist: D
LIMA Plan: D+ | Rand Var: +5 | MM: 2133

Last year, we warned "road ahead could be bumpy." Sure enough, he veered straight into ditch, as woes from prior Sept persisted. But he turned corner in 2nd half, even while losing some PA. You'd take CA with 2nd half xBA, HctX, league-average power, regained FB%. He's still young, and if xPX continues upward trajectory... UP: 25 HR

Yr Tm	PA	R	HR	RBI	SB	BA	xHR	xBA	OBP	SLG	OPS+	vL+	vR+	bb%	ct%	Eye	G	L	F	h%	HctX	PX	xPX	HR/F	xHR/F	Spd	SBO	SB%	#Wk	DOM	DIS	RAR	BPX	R$
15																																		
16																																		
17 a/a	276	29	5	28	1	295			373	451	110			11	89	1.09				32		88				99	1%	100%					239	$6
18 TOR *	432	52	14	59	4	257	4	256	340	441	108	98	110	11	82	0.68	32	20	48	28	60	111	69	10%	13%	100	4%	100%	7	43%	43%	20.4	230	$11
19 TOR	384	41	13	43	0	207	13	237	279	360	85	95	79	8	77	0.39	39	20	41	23	114	78	97	12%	12%	83	1%	0%	27	30%	56%	-5.2	52	$1
1st Half	209	16	4	20	0	188	5	216	269	290	75	105	60	10	75	0.43	43	20	37	23	106	58	89	8%	10%	76	0%	0%	15	20%	67%	-9.2	-30	-$4
2nd Half	175	25	9	23	0	230	7	254	291	441	97	85	102	6	80	0.33	34	21	45	24	122	99	106	16%	12%	99	3%	0%	12	42%	42%	-0.1	156	$8
20 Proj	**420**	**49**	**15**	**52**	**1**	**241**		**253**	**326**	**423**	**101**	**100**	**100**	**9**	**81**	**0.53**	**35**	**20**	**44**	**26**	**93**	**93**	**87**	**11%**		**87**	**1%**	**47%**				**11.4**	**125**	**$10**

Jimenez,Eloy

Age: 23 Bats: R Pos: LF — Ht: 6' 4" Wt: 205
Health: B | PT/Exp: D | Consist: D
LIMA Plan: B | Rand Var: +2 | MM: 4045

31-79-.267 in 504 PA at CHW. In 1st half, xPX cast doubt on legitimacy of power, but that worm turned in 2nd half. Contact rate, HctX also paint picture of player for whom light is coming on. You'd maybe like to see a few more fly balls, but there's still plenty here to take first of many runs at 40 HR, with decent BA. Prime growth stock.

Yr Tm	PA	R	HR	RBI	SB	BA	xHR	xBA	OBP	SLG	OPS+	vL+	vR+	bb%	ct%	Eye	G	L	F	h%	HctX	PX	xPX	HR/F	xHR/F	Spd	SBO	SB%	#Wk	DOM	DIS	RAR	BPX	R$
15																																		
16																																		
17 aa	73	11	3	7	1	346			392	556	127			7	74	0.30				43		131				99	10%	48%					142	$2
18 a/a	446	58	21	68	0	315			361	544	125			7	81	0.39				35		128				95	1%	0%					240	$19
19 CHW *	526	71	32	80	0	268	30	256	310	509	109	102	113	6	71	0.21	48	18	34	31	94	128	102	27%	26%	121	0%	0%	24	50%	29%	6.6	141	$16
1st Half	251	32	15	34	0	250	13	230	298	475	103	92	108	6	69	0.22	49	15	36	30	82	123	82	27%	25%	100	0%	0%	12	33%	42%	-2.8	67	$10
2nd Half	275	39	17	46	0	284	18	273	327	541	114	108	117	5	74	0.21	47	20	32	32	104	131	117	27%	29%	137	0%	0%	12	67%	17%	7.0	200	$21
20 Proj	**595**	**80**	**36**	**92**	**0**	**288**		**271**	**334**	**541**	**118**	**111**	**120**	**6**	**76**	**0.26**	**48**	**18**	**34**	**32**	**95**	**130**	**103**	**25%**		**123**	**0%**	**0%**				**29.1**	**133**	**$26**

KRISTOPHER OLSON

Jones,Adam

Age: 34 Bats: R Pos: RF	Health	C	LIMA Plan	D
Ht: 6' 2" Wt: 215	PT/Exp	A	Rand Var	0
	Consist	B	MM	1223

Tailed off sharply after May, with growing cracks in once-consistent contact. Ugly 2nd-half BPX tells the story. Taking the season as a whole, though, it's a relatively slower decline. Power metrics have actually held steady, even increased a tad, but the overall package is uninspiring. Double-digit roto value is now at risk.

Yr Tm	PA	R	HR	RBI	SB	BA	xHR	xBA	OBP	SLG	OPS+	vL+	vR+	bb%	ct%	Eye	G	L	F	h%	HctX	PX	xPX	HR/F	xHR/F	Spd	SBO	SB%	#Wk	DOM	DIS	RAR	BPX	R$
15 BAL	581	74	27	82	3	269	29	274	308	474	109	104	109	4	81	0.24	46	18	36	29	109	122	120	17%	18%	97	3%	75%	25	44%	36%	1.5	168	$20
16 BAL	672	86	29	83	2	265	30	248	310	436	102	78	106	6	81	0.34	43	17	41	28	108	92	110	14%	15%	86	1%	100%	27	44%	26%	0.1	111	$18
17 BAL	635	82	26	73	2	285	22	271	322	466	106	98	106	4	81	0.24	45	21	34	31	102	97	84	16%	13%	101	2%	67%	26	38%	15%	0.6	130	$19
18 BAL	613	54	15	63	7	281	17	260	313	419	101	99	101	4	84	0.26	43	21	37	31	97	83	81	8%	10%	73	6%	88%	28	43%	21%	3.9	113	$17
19 ARI	527	66	16	67	2	260	19	249	313	414	97	95	97	6	79	0.31	43	19	38	30	103	82	95	11%	13%	81	3%	67%	27	30%	41%	-14.9	78	$11
1st Half	324	40	13	43	2	264	16	257	315	448	102	105	100	6	82	0.33	44	17	39	29	115	93	119	14%	17%	71	4%	67%	15	47%	33%	-4.2	130	$16
2nd Half	203	26	3	24	0	253	3	236	310	360	89	80	92	7	75	0.28	41	24	35	32	85	64	53	6%	6%	101	0%	0%	12	8%	50%	-8.2	-7	$3
20 Proj	**427**	**51**	**12**	**51**	**2**	**268**		**251**	**315**	**416**	**98**	**94**	**100**	**5**	**80**	**0.29**	**43**	**20**	**36**	**31**	**99**	**79**	**84**	**11%**		**90**	**3%**	**79%**				**-0.6**	**57**	**$10**

Jones,JaCoby

Age: 28 Bats: R Pos: CF	Health	D	LIMA Plan	C+
Ht: 6' 2" Wt: 201	PT/Exp	C	Rand Var	-1
	Consist	A	MM	3413

11-26-.235 in 333 PA at DET. Season ended in early Aug with wrist fracture. PRO: Small gains in power skills, HctX, and plate skills. CON: Ct% still subpar, speed skills starting to tail off. VERDICT: Those gains in plate approach are just enough to hold our interest. With another step there, these tools can get playable fast.

Yr Tm	PA	R	HR	RBI	SB	BA	xHR	xBA	OBP	SLG	OPS+	vL+	vR+	bb%	ct%	Eye	G	L	F	h%	HctX	PX	xPX	HR/F	xHR/F	Spd	SBO	SB%	#Wk	DOM	DIS	RAR	BPX	R$
15 aa	161	22	5	18	9	241			311	408	100			9	63	0.27				35		130				120	33%	73%					30	$5
16 DET *	425	38	6	37	10	228	2	221	279	358	87	40	121	7	64	0.20	44	25	31	34	97	98	147	0%	40%	146	19%	65%	5	20%	40%	-14.0	-17	$4
17 DET *	535	65	11	52	17	206	4	211	264	326	79	74	65	7	63	0.21	51	19	31	30	78	85	90	13%	17%	120	22%	72%	14	14%	79%	-31.3	-76	$6
18 DET	467	54	11	34	13	207	13	230	266	364	87	86	87	5	67	0.17	43	24	33	28	89	108	88	12%	14%	154	24%	72%	27	22%	41%	-15.6	40	$7
19 DET *	355	42	11	29	7	244	13	241	305	435	98	73	104	8	68	0.28	40	23	37	32	103	115	107	15%	17%	117	13%	78%	17	35%	41%	-0.1	67	$6
1st Half	252	28	9	24	6	251	11	240	306	457	102	89	105	7	67	0.24	38	23	39	33	101	125	111	16%	19%	112	14%	86%	13	31%	54%	2.9	74	$9
2nd Half	103	14	2	5	1	228	2	246	302	379	90	44	102	10	71	0.36	45	24	31	30	107	93	95	12%	12%	125	9%	50%	4	50%	0%	-2.0	63	-$2
20 Proj	**420**	**52**	**11**	**33**	**10**	**238**		**233**	**308**	**402**	**96**	**77**	**101**	**8**	**67**	**0.25**	**44**	**23**	**33**	**32**	**95**	**102**	**95**	**13%**		**135**	**16%**	**70%**				**0.1**	**17**	**$11**

Judge,Aaron

Age: 28 Bats: R Pos: RF	Health	D	LIMA Plan	C+
Ht: 6' 7" Wt: 282	PT/Exp	B	Rand Var	-2
	Consist	C	MM	5125

Strained oblique took away May and much of June, but put up something close to typical levels in 2nd half. In fact, injuries aside, he's posted remarkably consistent skills over the last few seasons. With health, that 2nd-half xPX shows he still has it in him to do this... UP: 2017 redux

Yr Tm	PA	R	HR	RBI	SB	BA	xHR	xBA	OBP	SLG	OPS+	vL+	vR+	bb%	ct%	Eye	G	L	F	h%	HctX	PX	xPX	HR/F	xHR/F	Spd	SBO	SB%	#Wk	DOM	DIS	RAR	BPX	R$
15 a/a	525	55	20	63	6	238			306	422	102			9	66	0.29				31		138				91	7%	74%					62	$11
16 NYY *	489	65	24	68	4	237	4	215	317	446	104	39	91	10	65	0.33	35	14	51	31	129	142	196	18%	18%	74	5%	82%	6	33%	50%	0.3	51	$11
17 NYY	678	128	52	114	9	284	58	267	422	627	141	124	142	19	62	0.61	35	22	43	36	113	223	175	36%	40%	94	6%	69%	26	58%	23%	67.0	282	$33
18 NYY	498	77	27	67	6	278	29	251	392	528	127	135	124	15	63	0.50	42	23	35	38	112	175	126	29%	31%	77	6%	67%	22	46%	36%	31.0	100	$20
19 NYY	446	75	27	55	3	272	30	256	381	540	122	147	113	14	63	0.45	40	27	32	36	117	163	150	35%	39%	88	4%	60%	20	50%	35%	22.1	141	$15
1st Half	119	19	7	17	2	299	7	259	420	536	128	147	122	17	66	0.61	38	31	31	39	109	130	94	35%	35%	90	8%	67%	7	43%	29%	7.7	115	-$1
2nd Half	327	56	20	38	1	263	23	257	367	541	120	145	109	14	62	0.41	41	26	33	35	119	176	171	35%	40%	89	2%	50%	13	54%	38%	12.4	159	$20
20 Proj	**560**	**92**	**35**	**82**	**4**	**275**		**251**	**387**	**546**	**126**	**135**	**121**	**15**	**63**	**0.49**	**39**	**24**	**36**	**36**	**115**	**164**	**147**	**32%**		**83**	**4%**	**56%**				**37.5**	**136**	**$25**

Kelenic,Jarred

Age: 20 Bats: L Pos: LF	Health	A	LIMA Plan	D
Ht: 6' 1" Wt: 196	PT/Exp	F	Rand Var	0
	Consist	F	MM	2521

SEA's top prospect slashed .291/.364/.540 with 23 HR, 20 SB in 117 games across three minor league levels, finishing in AA at age 19. It may be a stretch for him to see the majors in 2020, from a service-time perspective if nothing else. But keeper-league owners? Get this skilled youngster on your radar.

Yr Tm	PA	R	HR	RBI	SB	BA	xHR	xBA	OBP	SLG	OPS+	vL+	vR+	bb%	ct%	Eye	G	L	F	h%	HctX	PX	xPX	HR/F	xHR/F	Spd	SBO	SB%	#Wk	DOM	DIS	RAR	BPX	R$
15																																		
16																																		
17																																		
18																																		
19 aa	91	12	6	18	3	255			324	556	117			9	78	0.46				25		145				111	17%	100%					300	$1
1st Half																																		
2nd Half	91	12	6	18	3	255			324	556	116			9	78	0.46				25		145				117	17%	100%				4.9	307	$1
20 Proj	**175**	**21**	**7**	**31**	**5**	**228**		**250**	**290**	**417**	**95**	**94**	**95**	**8**	**80**	**0.45**	**39**	**18**	**43**	**24**	**95**	**93**		**12%**		**119**	**15%**	**100%**				**-1.6**	**183**	**$6**

Kelly,Carson

Age: 25 Bats: R Pos: CA	Health	A	LIMA Plan	C
Ht: 6' 2" Wt: 220	PT/Exp	D	Rand Var	-1
	Consist	C	MM	3035

May be ready to fulfill long-held promise. Exciting power growth, and xPX shows there's plenty of room for more. Despite ct% dip, growing walk rate shows he knows what he's doing up there. That xBA points to BA upside, too. Only a Sept crash (.494 OPS) casts doubt. May be ready to take the next step. UP: 30 HR

Yr Tm	PA	R	HR	RBI	SB	BA	xHR	xBA	OBP	SLG	OPS+	vL+	vR+	bb%	ct%	Eye	G	L	F	h%	HctX	PX	xPX	HR/F	xHR/F	Spd	SBO	SB%	#Wk	DOM	DIS	RAR	BPX	R$
15																																		
16 STL *	363	36	5	27	0	259		210	300	349	88	225	12	6	80	0.30	64	9	27	31	59	61	-1	0%		93	1%	0%	5	20%	40%	-8.5	29	$3
17 STL *	346	35	8	40	0	236	1	244	307	360	89	37	64	9	83	0.59	56	16	28	26	110	70	123	0%	6%	68	3%	0%	12	42%	33%	-4.5	85	$2
18 STL *	372	30	5	34	0	217	1	186	300	304	84	25	51	10	82	0.64	54	7	39	25	87	53	98	0%	9%	83	0%	0%	5	0%	80%	-5.5	53	$0
19 ARI	365	46	18	47	0	245	15	263	348	478	110	147	94	13	75	0.61	37	22	41	27	126	126	168	19%	15%	74	0%	0%	27	48%	26%	11.4	189	$7
1st Half	189	20	9	26	0	275	7	284	354	527	118	165	99	11	78	0.54	40	22	38	31	125	138	150	18%	14%	77	0%	0%	15	60%	13%	12.2	252	$7
2nd Half	176	26	9	21	0	211	8	237	341	422	101	129	90	16	71	0.67	34	21	45	23	127	110	189	19%	17%	87	0%	0%	12	33%	42%	2.8	126	$6
20 Proj	**490**	**55**	**22**	**67**	**0**	**250**		**253**	**342**	**448**	**106**	**140**	**96**	**12**	**78**	**0.59**	**40**	**20**	**39**	**27**	**120**	**102**	**153**	**16%**		**71**	**0%**	**0%**				**21.7**	**96**	**$13**

Kemp,Anthony

Age: 28 Bats: L Pos: 2B LF	Health	A	LIMA Plan	D
Ht: 5' 6" Wt: 165	PT/Exp	C	Rand Var	+3
	Consist	C	MM	1321

Season sabotaged by hit-rate misfortune, even as he pumped up the power a bit. That said, he owns a pretty marginal skill set to begin with and his one distinguishing asset, speed, is suddenly on life support due to volatile SB%. Without double-digit bags, not much to see here.

Yr Tm	PA	R	HR	RBI	SB	BA	xHR	xBA	OBP	SLG	OPS+	vL+	vR+	bb%	ct%	Eye	G	L	F	h%	HctX	PX	xPX	HR/F	xHR/F	Spd	SBO	SB%	#Wk	DOM	DIS	RAR	BPX	R$
15 a/a	504	56	2	35	25	259			319	324	90			8	83	0.52				31		44				118	30%	61%					59	$15
16 HOU *	417	43	3	26	10	247	1	250	319	334	89	59	88	10	82	0.58	45	24	31	30	108	50	77	4%	4%	132	18%	49%	15	40%	47%	-17.3	80	$6
17 HOU *	565	66	6	43	16	252	0	217	282	346	84	69	65	4	89	0.37	44	9	47	27	90	48	75	0%	0%	153	20%	65%	7	14%	43%	-29.0	148	$11
18 HOU *	467	59	6	43	18	259	2	261	331	363	96	93	106	9	85	0.70	45	23	32	29	95	61	80	9%	3%	108	19%	76%	21	48%	29%	-1.2	137	$14
19 2 TM	279	31	8	29	4	212	3	241	291	380	89	97	88	8	81	0.49	41	16	43	23	99	80	110	10%	4%	121	15%	50%	28	32%	43%	-9.8	156	$2
1st Half	162	21	5	14	4	232	2	251	311	408	96	100	95	10	82	0.60	44	15	41	25	95	84	87	11%	4%	123	20%	57%	15	40%	47%	-3.2	204	$3
2nd Half	117	10	3	15	0	184	1	229	265	340	80	95	77	7	79	0.36	35	19	46	21	105	74	144	8%	3%	115	5%	0%	13	23%	38%	-7.3	93	$0
20 Proj	**210**	**24**	**5**	**21**	**5**	**230**		**252**	**300**	**373**	**91**	**89**	**90**	**8**	**83**	**0.50**	**42**	**20**	**38**	**25**	**100**	**69**	**100**	**8%**		**118**	**17%**	**60%**				**-3.8**	**140**	**$5**

Kendrick,Howie

Age: 36 Bats: R Pos: 1B 2B	Health	F	LIMA Plan	C+
Ht: 5' 11" Wt: 220	PT/Exp	D	Rand Var	-5
	Consist	C	MM	2253

Not only recovered from torn Achilles, did so with arguably his best season ever at 35. Even in this juiced ball season, power spike was remarkable—and fully supported by metrics (see xHR). No, he won't hit .344 again, but xBA shows BA shouldn't fall far. And if his newfound pop sticks, he could have some deep-league value.

Yr Tm	PA	R	HR	RBI	SB	BA	xHR	xBA	OBP	SLG	OPS+	vL+	vR+	bb%	ct%	Eye	G	L	F	h%	HctX	PX	xPX	HR/F	xHR/F	Spd	SBO	SB%	#Wk	DOM	DIS	RAR	BPX	R$
15 LA	495	64	9	54	6	295	11	286	336	409	104	99	103	5	82	0.33	59	24	17	34	108	75	71	14%	17%	93	6%	75%	22	27%	36%	10.0	81	$17
16 LA	543	65	8	40	10	255	15	272	326	366	94	84	96	9	80	0.52	61	19	20	30	110	72	63	10%	19%	95	9%	83%	26	31%	38%	-10.8	80	$10
17 2 NL	334	40	9	41	12	315	12	285	368	475	113	119	108	7	78	0.32	58	22	20	38	99	93	84	19%	25%	110	19%	71%	19	37%	37%	10.3	100	$16
18 WAS	160	17	4	12	1	303	5	287	331	474	111	93	118	3	81	0.17	48	24	28	35	118	112	82	11%	14%	72	6%	50%	8	50%	25%	5.2	143	$3
19 WAS	370	61	17	62	2	344	23	296	395	572	128	135	124	7	85	0.55	48	19	33	37	134	110	120	18%	24%	83	3%	67%	25	48%	16%	35.9	263	$17
1st Half	222	39	12	45	2	325	15	298	378	569	126	138	121	8	85	0.57	46	20	34	34	128	115	126	20%	25%	65	5%	67%	14	50%	7%	17.8	256	$22
2nd Half	148	22	5	17	0	372	8	292	419	577	131	134	129	7	86	0.53	52	17	31	41	144	103	111	14%	22%	103	0%	0%	11	45%	27%	17.1	274	$11
20 Proj	**350**	**49**	**12**	**44**	**4**	**306**		**288**	**353**	**491**	**114**	**115**	**112**	**6**	**83**	**0.38**	**51**	**21**	**28**	**34**	**124**	**98**	**98**	**15%**		**90**	**6%**	**67%**				**15.1**	**173**	**$15**

ROD TRUESDELL

Kepler,Max

Age: 27 Bats: L Pos: RF CF	Health C	LIMA Plan A	
Ht: 6' 4" Wt: 220	PT/Exp A	Rand Var +1	
	Consist B	MM 3135	

Huge power breakout? Not so fast. Expected-power metrics show no real change from 2018. It's not all bad news: Sept injury may have cut into those skills, and BA would actually improve with a hit-rate regression. But those who expect him to repeat that HR total will likely overbid; best to use a blend of 2018 and 2019 as your baseline.

Yr	Tm	PA	R	HR	RBI	SB	BA	xHR	xBA	OBP	SLG	OPS+	vL+	vR+	bb%	ct%	Eye	G	L	F	h%	HctX	PX	xPX	HR/F	xHR/F	Spd	SBO	SB%	#Wk	DOM	DIS	RAR	BPX	R$
15	MIN *	464	58	7	54	14	288		280	365	457	115	0	46	11	83	0.72	75	0	25	33	90	107	-16	0%		124	15%	76%	2	0%	100%	14.0	214	$17
16	MIN *	571	66	18	80	7	243	7	259	319	426	101	80	106	10	79	0.52	47	16	36	28	106	105	103	15%	6%	106	8%	69%	22	55%	36%	-2.5	149	$12
17	MIN	568	67	19	69	6	243	11	256	312	425	99	60	109	8	78	0.41	43	18	40	28	104	107	93	12%	7%	87	6%	86%	26	46%	35%	-7.8	124	$10
18	MIN	611	80	20	58	4	224	20	249	319	408	101	104	99	12	82	0.74	38	16	46	24	112	104	120	10%	10%	99	7%	44%	28	68%	14%	-6.6	220	$10
19	MIN	596	98	36	90	1	252	22	275	336	519	113	115	112	10	81	0.61	36	17	47	25	119	131	113	18%	11%	70	5%	17%	26	62%	15%	9.0	267	$18
1st Half		334	53	21	53	1	269	14	287	344	548	119	107	124	10	82	0.62	36	19	45	26	124	135	103	19%	13%	66	7%	20%	15	67%	7%	8.6	289	$24
2nd Half		262	45	15	37	0	230	8	261	324	483	106	127	99	11	80	0.59	37	15	48	22	113	125	125	17%	9%	88	2%	0%	11	55%	27%	-2.2	259	$12
20	**Proj**	**595**	**92**	**27**	**83**	**4**	**255**		**257**	**339**	**474**	**109**	**107**	**110**	**10**	**81**	**0.60**	**38**	**17**	**46**	**27**	**113**	**111**	**112**	**14%**		**88**	**5%**	**47%**				**11.8**	**211**	**$17**

Kieboom,Carter

Age: 22 Bats: R Pos: SS	Health A	LIMA Plan C+	
Ht: 6' 2" Wt: 190	PT/Exp F	Rand Var -3	
	Consist B	MM 3313	

2-2-.128 in 43 PA at WAS. Top SS prospect got his feet wet early, then put up another solid MiLB season, although power went missing in 2nd half (only 3 HR in Jul/Aug). Continued to show strong plate skills though, and overall, another solid growth season. Keeper-league gem at a prime position who could arrive quickly.

Yr	Tm	PA	R	HR	RBI	SB	BA	xHR	xBA	OBP	SLG	OPS+	vL+	vR+	bb%	ct%	Eye	G	L	F	h%	HctX	PX	xPX	HR/F	xHR/F	Spd	SBO	SB%	#Wk	DOM	DIS	RAR	BPX	R$
15																																			
16																																			
17																																			
18	aa	267	31	4	20	3	247			300	366	92			7	75	0.30				31		83				101	6%	70%					40	$3
19	WAS *	507	65	15	63	4	262	2	221	344	418	101	51	68	11	72	0.45	48	13	39	33	109	90	137	22%	22%	105	4%	64%	3	0%	67%	2.1	59	$12
1st Half		305	45	12	47	2	267	2	241	361	482	113	52	69	13	71	0.50	48	13	39	33	107	122	137	22%	22%	110	6%	52%	3	0%	67%	7.5	152	$18
2nd Half		203	20	2	16	2	253		210	318	327	85			9	74	0.37				33		45		0%		108	3%	100%				-7.3	-59	$2
20	**Proj**	**350**	**41**	**15**	**34**	**3**	**254**		**236**	**323**	**450**	**104**	**109**	**102**	**9**	**73**	**0.38**	**48**	**13**	**39**	**30**	**96**	**108**	**123**	**16%**		**105**	**5%**	**75%**				**7.6**	**77**	**$10**

Kiermaier,Kevin

Age: 30 Bats: L Pos: CF	Health F	LIMA Plan B	
Ht: 6' 1" Wt: 210	PT/Exp C	Rand Var +3	
	Consist B	MM 2533	

Still managed decent counting stats despite losing time to injury for the fourth season in a row. It's clearly too much to expect him to stay healthy. Skills consistent, if mediocre—other than fine speed, of course. But now on the wrong side of 30, how long will that last? May never reach that 25-steal potential, but might have a tick of BA upside.

Yr	Tm	PA	R	HR	RBI	SB	BA	xHR	xBA	OBP	SLG	OPS+	vL+	vR+	bb%	ct%	Eye	G	L	F	h%	HctX	PX	xPX	HR/F	xHR/F	Spd	SBO	SB%	#Wk	DOM	DIS	RAR	BPX	R$
15	TAM	535	62	10	40	18	263	9	275	298	420	100	86	103	4	81	0.25	48	23	29	31	88	96	58	8%	8%	151	21%	78%	26	46%	31%	-2.8	157	$16
16	TAM	414	55	12	37	21	246	9	260	331	410	101	110	96	10	80	0.54	42	21	38	28	102	98	78	11%	8%	99	25%	88%	19	42%	26%	2.7	137	$14
17	TAM	421	56	15	39	16	276	11	252	338	450	106	90	112	7	74	0.31	50	18	32	34	95	99	70	17%	12%	134	22%	70%	17	18%	29%	3.9	97	$16
18	TAM	367	44	7	29	10	217	7	240	282	370	90	76	95	7	73	0.27	50	19	31	28	84	91	70	10%	10%	152	22%	67%	19	16%	47%	-8.7	80	$5
19	TAM	480	60	14	55	19	228	14	262	278	398	90	102	85	5	77	0.25	54	17	29	27	88	88	59	14%	14%	136	28%	79%	27	37%	44%	-12.5	115	$13
1st Half		283	38	9	36	14	244	9	267	294	431	97	98	97	6	77	0.30	54	18	28	29	89	92	64	16%	16%	145	30%	82%	15	40%	40%	-0.5	144	$19
2nd Half		197	22	5	19	5	205	6	251	254	351	80	107	65	4	77	0.19	53	16	30	24	86	81	52	12%	14%	114	23%	71%	12	33%	50%	-10.2	59	$5
20	**Proj**	**420**	**53**	**11**	**41**	**15**	**237**		**252**	**291**	**399**	**93**	**85**	**96**	**6**	**76**	**0.26**	**51**	**18**	**31**	**29**	**88**	**86**	**63**	**13%**		**140**	**24%**	**74%**				**-2.3**	**102**	**$13**

Kiner-Falefa,Isiah

Age: 25 Bats: R Pos: CA 3B	Health B	LIMA Plan D	
Ht: 5' 10" Wt: 176	PT/Exp C	Rand Var 0	
	Consist B	MM 1321	

1-21-.238 in 222 PA at TEX. Struggled as primary CA early. Then TEX abandoned that project and returned him to the minors to re-learn the infield. Split time at 3B upon his return, but didn't fare much better at the dish. Qualifying at CA with multi-position eligibility keeps him on the margins of our radar, but that's the epitome of faint praise.

Yr	Tm	PA	R	HR	RBI	SB	BA	xHR	xBA	OBP	SLG	OPS+	vL+	vR+	bb%	ct%	Eye	G	L	F	h%	HctX	PX	xPX	HR/F	xHR/F	Spd	SBO	SB%	#Wk	DOM	DIS	RAR	BPX	R$
15																																			
16	aa	439	48	0	24	5	245			308	274	79			8	87	0.70				28		18				125	9%	45%					54	$3
17	aa	550	52	5	43	15	275			324	370	93			7	85	0.50				31		58				103	15%	70%					106	$14
18	TEX	396	43	4	34	7	261	2	271	325	357	94	111	85	7	83	0.45	51	25	24	31	89	60	34	6%	3%	118	12%	58%	25	32%	44%	-6.0	100	$8
19	TEX *	324	31	3	31	5	230	2	236	283	327	81	70	88	7	78	0.33	50	17	33	29	98	62	85	2%	4%	108	7%	100%	20	15%	45%	-16.7	37	$2
1st Half		121	15	1	13	1	231	1	237	308	343	87	89	86	8	69	0.30	53	21	25	32	73	76	77	5%	5%	115	4%	100%	11	18%	55%	-5.9	-30	-$3
2nd Half		203	16	2	18	4	230	1	222	274	319	78	57	91	6	83	0.36	47	13	41	27	120	55	93	0%	3%	109	9%	100%	9	11%	33%	-12.7	81	$5
20	**Proj**	**245**	**25**	**2**	**22**	**4**	**246**		**247**	**310**	**337**	**87**	**84**	**88**	**7**	**81**	**0.40**	**50**	**20**	**30**	**30**	**96**	**55**	**65**	**4%**		**114**	**10%**	**74%**				**0.1**	**30**	**$5**

Kingery,Scott

Age: 26 Bats: R Pos: CF 3B	Health B	LIMA Plan B	
Ht: 5' 10" Wt: 180	PT/Exp B	Rand Var -2	
	Consist D	MM 3515	

Rebounded to a level much closer to those 2017 MLEs, which gives us more confidence that it'll stick. Ebbing contact will keep BA in check, but fills the boxes across the rest of the Roto categories. Position flexibility adds to value and keeps him in the lineup. High LD + FB numbers and growing xPX/HctX could lead to ... UP: 25 HR/25 SB

Yr	Tm	PA	R	HR	RBI	SB	BA	xHR	xBA	OBP	SLG	OPS+	vL+	vR+	bb%	ct%	Eye	G	L	F	h%	HctX	PX	xPX	HR/F	xHR/F	Spd	SBO	SB%	#Wk	DOM	DIS	RAR	BPX	R$
15																																			
16	aa	160	12	2	14	3	213			232	282	70			2	73	0.09				28		51				88	18%	58%					-89	-$1
17	a/a	578	89	24	56	25	275			319	478	107			6	77	0.28				32		112				132	24%	82%					155	$25
18	PHI	484	55	8	35	10	226	12	220	267	338	84	82	84	5	72	0.19	35	24	41	30	71	79	101	6%	9%	122	14%	77%	28	18%	57%	-18.1	0	$7
19	PHI	500	64	19	55	15	258	18	248	315	474	105	115	101	7	68	0.23	34	26	40	34	108	134	123	15%	14%	124	20%	79%	23	30%	39%	6.5	115	$16
1st Half		190	28	10	26	5	313	9	282	363	585	127	125	127	5	72	0.20	37	26	37	39	124	160	120	21%	19%	119	16%	83%	11	27%	36%	14.1	233	$14
2nd Half		310	36	9	29	10	223	10	226	285	404	91	108	85	8	66	0.25	32	26	42	31	98	116	125	12%	13%	124	23%	77%	12	33%	42%	-7.7	37	$17
20	**Proj**	**595**	**74**	**19**	**58**	**17**	**248**		**239**	**296**	**424**	**97**	**102**	**94**	**6**	**71**	**0.21**	**34**	**25**	**40**	**32**	**94**	**105**	**114**	**12%**		**126**	**19%**	**77%**				**4.8**	**61**	**$20**

Kipnis,Jason

Age: 33 Bats: L Pos: 2B	Health C	LIMA Plan B	
Ht: 5' 11" Wt: 200	PT/Exp C	Rand Var +1	
	Consist A	MM 2225	

17-65-.245 in 511 PA at CLE. The slow decline continues. It's not showing up in the stats, particularly. But you can see it in the BPX trend. Sure, he stepped up power a bit in 2nd half, but that late surge averted a complete disaster; overall, those skills still fell off. Decent hard contact will keep him from the edge of the cliff for now.

Yr	Tm	PA	R	HR	RBI	SB	BA	xHR	xBA	OBP	SLG	OPS+	vL+	vR+	bb%	ct%	Eye	G	L	F	h%	HctX	PX	xPX	HR/F	xHR/F	Spd	SBO	SB%	#Wk	DOM	DIS	RAR	BPX	R$
15	CLE	641	86	9	52	12	303	12	284	372	451	115	94	124	9	81	0.53	45	27	28	36	109	103	97	7%	9%	116	12%	60%	24	50%	21%	25.1	165	$23
16	CLE	688	91	23	82	15	275	22	267	343	469	110	107	110	9	76	0.41	39	24	37	33	110	123	122	13%	13%	89	11%	83%	27	52%	26%	16.3	140	$24
17	CLE *	410	44	13	37	6	223	11	253	278	400	91	84	98	7	78	0.35	36	20	44	25	95	108	122	10%	9%	91	11%	75%	18	44%	28%	-11.1	124	$4
18	CLE	601	65	18	75	7	230	19	243	315	389	97	90	99	10	79	0.54	34	22	45	26	101	95	120	10%	10%	67	6%	88%	28	43%	32%	-0.9	113	$12
19	CLE *	534	53	17	66	7	238	14	248	299	400	93	83	101	8	80	0.43	40	19	41	27	102	84	108	11%	9%	81	8%	78%	23	39%	30%	-10.8	107	$10
1st Half		289	23	6	31	5	234	8	242	292	363	87	64	106	8	81	0.42	43	18	39	27	95	70	105	8%	11%	74	10%	83%	12	17%	42%	-8.5	67	$6
2nd Half		245	30	11	35	2	243	7	255	309	445	99	108	96	8	79	0.44	37	19	44	26	110	102	112	14%	9%	95	6%	67%	11	64%	18%	-0.6	170	$14
20	**Proj**	**455**	**51**	**15**	**56**	**6**	**239**		**250**	**306**	**410**	**96**	**88**	**99**	**8**	**79**	**0.44**	**38**	**20**	**42**	**27**	**102**	**91**	**114**	**11%**		**86**	**8%**	**77%**				**0.9**	**115**	**$12**

La Stella,Tommy

Age: 31 Bats: L Pos: 2B 3B	Health F	LIMA Plan B	
Ht: 5' 11" Wt: 180	PT/Exp F	Rand Var -1	
	Consist C	MM 1055	

July 2 tibia fracture essentially ended surprising mid-career breakout. He couldn't have scripted it better: a springtime swing-path adjustment led to a stunning and simultaneous spike in ct%, HctX and xPX. While the breakout was fully skills supported, regression is likely given his long history of marginal power.

Yr	Tm	PA	R	HR	RBI	SB	BA	xHR	xBA	OBP	SLG	OPS+	vL+	vR+	bb%	ct%	Eye	G	L	F	h%	HctX	PX	xPX	HR/F	xHR/F	Spd	SBO	SB%	#Wk	DOM	DIS	RAR	BPX	R$
15	CHC *	148	13	2	18	2	254	1	302	306	379	95	0	106	7	91	0.86	38	30	33	27	91	81	74	5%	5%	86	6%	100%	8	63%	13%	-2.4	192	$1
16	CHC *	219	22	3	13	0	261	4	267	333	382	97	116	100	10	80	0.55	36	28	36	31	105	82	100	5%	9%	92	2%	0%	20	40%	30%	-3.8	103	$1
17	CHC *	266	28	6	26	0	231	3	249	311	345	88	133	112	10	81	0.59	43	23	34	27	105	65	95	14%	8%	78	2%	0%	20	55%	20%	-13.0	61	$0
18	CHC	188	23	1	19	0	266	2	258	340	331	93	53	97	9	84	0.63	53	24	23	31	96	45	56	3%	6%	86	2%	0%	27	44%	41%	-2.8	60	$1
19	LAA	315	49	16	44	0	295	11	291	346	486	110	93	117	6	90	0.71	45	21	33	28	135	80	104	18%	13%	91	0%	0%	17	53%	6%	7.6	252	$10
1st Half		303	49	16	44	0	304	11	295	356	500	114	98	121	7	91	0.77	46	22	33	29	135	81	96	20%	13%	94	0%	0%	15	53%	7%	9.0	263	$11
2nd Half		12	0	0	0	0	83	0	154	83	167	33	0	44	0	83	0.00	40	10	50	10	144	58	288	0%	0%	101	0%	0%	2	50%	0%	-2.1	44	-$21
20	**Proj**	**490**	**61**	**18**	**54**	**1**	**273**		**281**	**342**	**440**	**105**	**95**	**107**	**9**	**86**	**0.68**	**44**	**23**	**33**	**28**	**111**	**79**	**86**	**14%**		**85**	**2%**	**33%**				**13.2**	**145**	**$15**

ROD TRUESDELL

Lagares,Juan

Age: 31 Bats: R Pos: CF
Ht: 6' 1" Wt: 215

Health	F	LIMA Plan	D
PT/Exp	F	Rand Var	+1
Consist	F	MM	1411

As glove-first reserve OF, 42% of 133 games played in 2019 resulted in 0 or 1 PA; in those games, he hit .174 with 1 RBI, 1 SB. So he spent nearly half the season providing no fantasy value whatsoever. Rest of year wasn't much better, resulting in career lows in ct%, HctX, xBA, Spd, SBO. Only a matter of time before the bat defeats the glove.

Yr Tm	PA	R	HR	RBI	SB	BA	xHR	xBA	OBP	SLG	OPS+	vL+	vR+	bb%	ct%	Eye	G	L	F	h%	HctX	PX	xPX	HR/F	xHR/F	Spd	SBO	SB%	#Wk	DOM	DIS	RAR	BPX	R$
15 NYM	465	47	6	41	7	259	6	236	289	358	90	106	82	3	80	0.18	55	14	31	31	107	64	72	6%	6%	127	10%	70%	27	26%	41%	-10.7	51	$9
16 NYM	160	15	3	9	4	239	3	259	301	380	93	88	95	7	81	0.41	42	22	35	28	71	83	68	7%	7%	125	18%	67%	19	32%	42%	-4.2	123	$1
17 NYM *	301	40	3	15	7	245	4	251	281	348	84	80	91	5	77	0.22	51	20	29	31	93	68	77	5%	7%	138	16%	70%	18	28%	50%	-15.1	48	$4
18 NYM	64	9	0	6	3	339	0	255	375	390	106	92	119	5	85	0.33	56	22	22	40	73	26	-7	0%	0%	142	19%	75%	8	13%	63%	2.1	47	$1
19 NYM	285	38	5	27	4	213	3	219	279	326	80	84	78	8	71	0.29	47	18	35	28	59	69	57	8%	5%	107	8%	80%	28	29%	61%	-10.7	-41	$1
1st Half	155	18	2	15	3	179	2	196	247	257	67	70	66	7	66	0.23	58	13	29	25	46	53	54	8%	8%	92	14%	75%	15	20%	73%	-11.2	-178	-$2
2nd Half	130	20	3	12	1	254	1	243	318	407	96	95	96	9	76	0.39	35	24	42	31	75	86	59	8%	3%	116	3%	100%	13	38%	46%	0.3	104	$5
20 Proj	**245**	**32**	**3**	**19**	**4**	**235**		**236**	**291**	**339**	**85**	**83**	**85**	**7**	**76**	**0.29**	**49**	**20**	**31**	**30**	**73**	**63**	**45**	**5%**		**126**	**11%**	**73%**				**-4.7**	**-2**	**$2**

Lamb,Jacob

Age: 29 Bats: L Pos: 3B 1B
Ht: 6' 3" Wt: 215

Health	F	LIMA Plan	C
PT/Exp	C	Rand Var	+5
Consist	D	MM	3223

6-30-.193 in 226 PA at ARI. Quad injury in 5th game of season kept him out of action 'til June, then sat vs. LHP after that. The latter may have done some good, as he posted career highs in HctX, xPX—though vR+ was held down by low h%. Given his history of plus power, could provide decent value as platoon bat if given the chance.

Yr Tm	PA	R	HR	RBI	SB	BA	xHR	xBA	OBP	SLG	OPS+	vL+	vR+	bb%	ct%	Eye	G	L	F	h%	HctX	PX	xPX	HR/F	xHR/F	Spd	SBO	SB%	#Wk	DOM	DIS	RAR	BPX	R$
15 ARI	390	38	6	34	3	263	10	234	331	386	100	75	102	9	72	0.37	45	23	32	35	115	87	114	7%	12%	124	5%	60%	21	29%	57%	-3.0	43	$6
16 ARI	594	81	29	91	6	249	28	271	332	509	114	84	120	11	71	0.42	46	17	37	30	113	164	149	21%	20%	112	6%	86%	27	67%	22%	11.6	200	$17
17 ARI	635	89	30	105	6	248	26	264	357	487	113	74	124	14	72	0.57	41	21	38	29	104	142	125	20%	17%	96	6%	60%	27	48%	26%	6.9	176	$17
18 ARI	238	34	6	31	1	222	8	216	307	348	91	69	96	11	69	0.40	51	18	31	29	107	86	127	13%	18%	109	5%	33%	13	31%	38%	-8.0	0	$2
19 ARI *	269	29	7	34	1	180	8	223	293	326	82	152	81	13	69	0.51	39	23	38	23	126	85	170	12%	16%	103	2%	100%	17	35%	41%	-17.6	11	-$1
1st Half	72	5	1	7	0	168	1	182	260	245	67	0	104	11	61	0.31	43	21	36	27	70	64	177	0%	20%	95	0%	0%	4	25%	50%	-6.8	-200	-$11
2nd Half	197	24	6	27	1	185	7	237	320	358	89	180	77	15	72	0.62	39	23	39	22	139	92	169	13%	15%	111	2%	100%	13	38%	38%	-9.2	100	$3
20 Proj	**385**	**50**	**14**	**55**	**2**	**238**		**241**	**337**	**422**	**102**	**77**	**107**	**12**	**71**	**0.50**	**44**	**21**	**36**	**29**	**109**	**103**	**150**	**17%**		**108**	**3%**	**59%**				**0.9**	**59**	**$10**

Laureano,Ramon

Age: 25 Bats: R Pos: CF
Ht: 5' 11" Wt: 200

Health	B	LIMA Plan	C+
PT/Exp	C	Rand Var	-2
Consist	C	MM	4435

Stress reaction in shin stole six weeks of 2nd half, drove down SBO, and leaves us pining for larger data sample of possible breakout. Still, signs of growth abound: 2nd half ct%, FB%, xPX increase. 2nd half BA/xBA likely inflated by h%, outsized PX, respectively; don't expect him to hit .300. But 20/20 is on the table.

Yr Tm	PA	R	HR	RBI	SB	BA	xHR	xBA	OBP	SLG	OPS+	vL+	vR+	bb%	ct%	Eye	G	L	F	h%	HctX	PX	xPX	HR/F	xHR/F	Spd	SBO	SB%	#Wk	DOM	DIS	RAR	BPX	R$
15																																		
16 aa	141	17	4	11	9	300			385	508	122			12	70	0.45				40		141				116	30%	73%					149	$6
17 aa	496	55	9	47	20	206			259	334	80			7	73	0.26				26		78				129	28%	79%					21	$6
18 OAK *	446	62	15	47	16	269	9	247	335	449	109	110	116	9	68	0.31	44	25	31	36	100	124	86	15%	26%	113	18%	83%	10	30%	50%	9.4	83	$17
19 OAK	481	79	24	67	13	288	21	263	340	521	114	100	110	8	72	0.22	36	25	39	35	99	133	108	19%	17%	101	15%	87%	24	42%	42%	14.5	137	$21
1st Half	331	45	13	40	9	258	12	241	305	441	100	93	102	5	70	0.16	35	25	40	33	97	109	102	15%	14%	99	17%	82%	16	38%	50%	-6.7	30	$22
2nd Half	150	34	11	27	4	359	9	315	416	711	149	136	156	9	76	0.39	36	25	38	41	104	188	123	28%	23%	103	11%	100%	8	50%	25%	21.9	385	$20
20 Proj	**525**	**86**	**26**	**69**	**17**	**281**		**264**	**346**	**517**	**116**	**110**	**118**	**8**	**72**	**0.32**	**37**	**25**	**38**	**34**	**101**	**134**	**103**	**20%**		**118**	**17%**	**83%**				**32.5**	**185**	**$27**

LeMahieu,DJ

Age: 31 Bats: R Pos: 2B 3B 1B
Ht: 6' 4" Wt: 215

Health	B	LIMA Plan	B
PT/Exp	A	Rand Var	-3
Consist	C	MM	1255

Another Coors-aided hitter leaves COL and falls ap-- wait, what?! Plate skills held steady, Yankee Stadium brought out his power (19 of 26 HR), and xHR says it was the real deal! But, but... it's probably not. His historically below league average xPX is completely flat from past years, and only his juiced up HR/F has changed. His fate rests with the ball.

Yr Tm	PA	R	HR	RBI	SB	BA	xHR	xBA	OBP	SLG	OPS+	vL+	vR+	bb%	ct%	Eye	G	L	F	h%	HctX	PX	xPX	HR/F	xHR/F	Spd	SBO	SB%	#Wk	DOM	DIS	RAR	BPX	R$
15 COL	620	85	6	61	23	301	9	271	358	388	104	104	102	8	81	0.47	54	26	19	36	95	58	75	7%	10%	136	14%	88%	26	38%	35%	5.0	78	$27
16 COL	635	104	11	66	11	348	14	303	416	495	124	126	121	10	86	0.83	51	27	23	39	122	84	95	10%	13%	150	9%	61%	26	62%	19%	43.4	220	$32
17 COL	682	95	8	64	6	310	6	289	374	409	105	127	96	9	85	0.66	56	25	20	35	105	56	60	8%	6%	112	5%	55%	27	37%	30%	2.1	118	$23
18 COL	581	90	15	62	6	276	15	280	321	428	104	125	93	6	85	0.45	50	21	29	30	109	88	97	11%	11%	104	8%	55%	25	56%	24%	4.8	183	$18
19 NYY	655	109	26	102	5	327	25	302	375	518	119	139	110	7	85	0.51	50	24	26	35	119	92	90	19%	19%	110	4%	71%	28	57%	21%	38.5	233	$31
1st Half	343	62	12	61	4	345	12	304	392	534	124	125	123	7	85	0.50	49	25	26	38	110	93	82	17%	17%	132	4%	100%	15	60%	13%	24.8	256	$37
2nd Half	312	47	14	41	1	308	13	296	356	502	113	149	95	7	85	0.52	51	23	26	32	129	91	99	22%	20%	82	4%	33%	13	54%	31%	10.1	204	$24
20 Proj	**630**	**100**	**19**	**80**	**6**	**309**		**290**	**360**	**467**	**111**	**132**	**102**	**7**	**85**	**0.52**	**51**	**23**	**26**	**34**	**115**	**79**	**88**	**15%**		**110**	**6%**	**62%**				**32.3**	**162**	**$28**

Lewis,Kyle

Age: 24 Bats: R Pos: RF
Ht: 6' 4" Wt: 210

Health	A	LIMA Plan	D+
PT/Exp	F	Rand Var	-3
Consist	C	MM	4313

6-13-.268 in 75 PA at SEA. Went all-in on swapping ct% for power, and it paid off in 2nd half. But count the red flags: poor HctX; 2nd half erosion of bb%, Eye; only 11 HR in 517 Triple-A PA; dangerously low xBA. Prior to 2019, never posted more than 363 PA due to injuries. He served us a tasty cup of coffee, but isn't ready to make a meal.

Yr Tm	PA	R	HR	RBI	SB	BA	xHR	xBA	OBP	SLG	OPS+	vL+	vR+	bb%	ct%	Eye	G	L	F	h%	HctX	PX	xPX	HR/F	xHR/F	Spd	SBO	SB%	#Wk	DOM	DIS	RAR	BPX	R$
15																																		
16																																		
17																																		
18 aa	146	15	3	16	1	190			268	318	81			10	72	0.38				24		88				91	3%	100%					20	-$2
19 SEA *	587	70	17	74	3	248	6	203	323	404	97	67	136	10	61	0.28	51	14	35	37	69	108	144	40%	40%	111	4%	57%	4	75%	25%	-11.4	-48	$11
1st Half	301	37	4	39	2	237		193	340	346	92			13	61	0.40				37		80		0%		118	2%	100%				-9.2	-107	$8
2nd Half	287	33	13	35	1	259	6	214	305	461	101	67	136	6	61	0.17	51	14	35	37	69	134	144	40%	40%	101	5%	31%	4	75%	25%	-3.7	-7	$15
20 Proj	**350**	**34**	**17**	**34**	**2**	**225**		**230**	**293**	**447**	**100**	**63**	**112**	**9**	**66**	**0.29**	**51**	**14**	**35**	**28**	**62**	**136**	**130**	**24%**		**110**	**4%**	**71%**				**-1.7**	**20**	**$7**

Lindor,Francisco

Age: 26 Bats: B Pos: SS
Ht: 5' 11" Wt: 190

Health	A	LIMA Plan	D+
PT/Exp	A	Rand Var	0
Consist	A	MM	3355

Third straight 30+ HR season, but first without underlying skill support, as 2nd half xHR, xPX, xHR/F all say his total was inflated. However, if preseason calf/ankle injuries hadn't cost him PA, xHR probably would've reached 30 anyway. So we'll pencil him in for a fourth season, along with more of the goodies that landed him on our cover.

Yr Tm	PA	R	HR	RBI	SB	BA	xHR	xBA	OBP	SLG	OPS+	vL+	vR+	bb%	ct%	Eye	G	L	F	h%	HctX	PX	xPX	HR/F	xHR/F	Spd	SBO	SB%	#Wk	DOM	DIS	RAR	BPX	R$
15 CLE *	689	73	14	71	20	298	8	274	349	443	111	123	110	7	82	0.45	51	21	29	34	92	92	75	13%	9%	136	17%	68%	17	71%	18%	19.1	165	$28
16 CLE	684	99	15	78	19	301	16	282	358	435	108	101	109	8	85	0.65	49	22	28	33	95	77	74	10%	11%	118	13%	79%	27	44%	19%	24.6	163	$29
17 CLE	723	99	33	89	15	273	31	289	337	505	113	118	108	8	86	0.65	39	18	42	28	122	120	122	14%	13%	100	11%	83%	27	74%	7%	25.0	267	$26
18 CLE	745	129	38	92	25	277	36	292	352	519	121	140	113	9	84	0.65	39	22	40	28	129	131	135	17%	16%	93	20%	71%	28	68%	25%	40.1	297	$38
19 CLE	654	101	32	74	22	284	25	292	335	518	113	101	119	7	84	0.47	44	20	37	29	122	115	104	17%	14%	105	19%	81%	25	60%	12%	18.3	274	$30
1st Half	289	41	12	27	12	291	11	288	349	498	113	99	120	8	82	0.49	44	23	33	32	127	104	109	17%	15%	107	19%	92%	12	50%	8%	11.0	230	$22
2nd Half	365	60	20	47	10	279	13	295	324	534	113	103	118	6	85	0.45	43	17	39	28	118	123	99	18%	12%	105	19%	71%	13	69%	15%	10.3	311	$36
20 Proj	**700**	**110**	**31**	**84**	**22**	**282**		**284**	**339**	**500**	**113**	**111**	**113**	**8**	**84**	**0.53**	**42**	**20**	**37**	**30**	**121**	**107**	**111**	**15%**		**105**	**18%**	**77%**				**33.9**	**269**	**$35**

Locastro,Tim

Age: 27 Bats: R Pos: LF RF CF
Ht: 6' 1" Wt: 200

Health	A	LIMA Plan	D+
PT/Exp	D	Rand Var	0
Consist	A	MM	1513

1-17-.250 with 17 SB in 250 PA at ARI. Incredibly efficient base-stealer, yet to be thrown out in majors (21-0 SB/CS). Unfortunately, that's his only plus skill. Ct% has fallen as he's moved up the ladder, and even with HctX boost, power is an afterthought. Defensive versatility (can also play INF) should provide enough PA to drive modest value.

Yr Tm	PA	R	HR	RBI	SB	BA	xHR	xBA	OBP	SLG	OPS+	vL+	vR+	bb%	ct%	Eye	G	L	F	h%	HctX	PX	xPX	HR/F	xHR/F	Spd	SBO	SB%	#Wk	DOM	DIS	RAR	BPX	R$
15																																		
16 aa	197	22	1	11	7	242			265	300	77			3	90	0.33				26		37				106	22%	77%					89	$2
17 LA *	492	69	8	32	28	261		106	292	382	90	0	0	4	83	0.25	0	0	100	30	0	72	-26	0%		121	34%	77%	2	0%	50%	-16.8	109	$18
18 LA *	335	51	3	18	17	225	0	207	275	326	83	88	69	6	78	0.32	33	17	50	28	48	72	98	0%	0%	130	29%	88%	8	13%	75%	-10.6	80	$7
19 ARI *	379	58	6	29	22	241	1	245	284	373	87	93	91	5	78	0.27	44	20	36	29	84	75	60	2%	2%	163	33%	95%	23	26%	48%	-4.4	122	$12
1st Half	223	35	5	21	12	247	1	250	299	407	94	92	96	7	81	0.40	44	16	40	28	87	80	78	0%	3%	170	29%	90%	11	27%	45%	-0.3	207	$14
2nd Half	156	23	1	8	11	232	1	235	262	326	78	95	87	4	73	0.15	44	24	33	31	80	68	43	4%	4%	131	39%	100%	12	25%	50%	-5.0	-15	$10
20 Proj	**280**	**42**	**2**	**18**	**16**	**239**		**236**	**340**	**330**	**90**	**92**	**88**	**5**	**79**	**0.26**	**44**	**21**	**36**	**30**	**83**	**57**	**57**	**2%**		**149**	**31%**	**91%**				**-9.7**	**73**	**$10**

BRANDON KRUSE

Long,Shed

Age: 24 Bats: L Pos: 2B | Ht: 5' 8" Wt: 184
Health C | PT/Exp D | Consist A
LIMA Plan D | Rand Var -1 | MM 2311

5-15-.263 with 3 SB in 168 PA at SEA. Returned from broken finger to hit .289 with 4 HR in Sept, but that doesn't erase struggles to that point: ct% is a problem, especially factoring in modest power; bb% is in free fall; low SB% put green light on hold. Could eventually become decent SB source, but has a few obstacles to clear first.

Yr Tm	PA	R	HR	RBI	SB	BA	xHR	xBA	OBP	SLG	OPS+	vL+	vR+	bb%	ct%	Eye	G	L	F	h%	HctX	PX	xPX	HR/F	xHR/F	Spd	SBO	SB%	#Wk	DOM	DIS	RAR	BPX	R$
15																																		
16																																		
17 aa	162	14	4	15	4	230			329	372	94			13	76	0.61				28		82				119	13%	80%					100	$1
18 aa	502	64	11	48	16	239			314	375	95			10	69	0.36				32		92				114	19%	71%					23	$13
19 SEA *	409	49	12	41	4	241	4	236	298	400	93	130	96	8	69	0.26	47	21	31	32	78	94	64	14%	11%	112	11%	37%	11	45%	45%	-11.4	0	$6
1st Half	292	35	7	30	4	237	1	238	302	382	91	173	73	8	69	0.30	41	27	33	32	83	87	76	6%	6%	108	12%	45%	6	50%	50%	-8.2	-7	$8
2nd Half	117	13	5	11	0	253	3	236	291	444	97	102	117	5	67	0.16	52	17	30	34	74	112	55	21%	16%	116	9%	0%	5	40%	40%	-2.0	19	$1
20 Proj	**245**	**28**	**6**	**24**	**4**	**241**		**232**	**305**	**385**	**93**	**82**	**96**	**8**	**69**	**0.30**	**48**	**21**	**31**	**32**	**78**	**86**	**63**	**12%**		**118**	**14%**	**57%**				**-2.0**	**-18**	**$3**

Longoria,Evan

Age: 34 Bats: R Pos: 3B | Ht: 6' 1" Wt: 215
Health C | PT/Exp A | Consist B
LIMA Plan B+ | Rand Var -1 | MM 2335

Skills were nearly identical in 1st/2nd half, but h% and HR/F swings led to contrasting results, which balanced out to look a lot like 2018. Doesn't offer much upside or BA at this point, but other than some ct% erosion and injury creep, he's aging pretty gracefully. No reason to think his numbers will look that different in 2020.

Yr Tm	PA	R	HR	RBI	SB	BA	xHR	xBA	OBP	SLG	OPS+	vL+	vR+	bb%	ct%	Eye	G	L	F	h%	HctX	PX	xPX	HR/F	xHR/F	Spd	SBO	SB%	#Wk	DOM	DIS	RAR	BPX	R$
15 TAM	670	74	21	73	3	270	29	253	328	435	106	132	95	8	78	0.39	39	21	40	31	105	111	121	11%	15%	87	3%	75%	27	44%	33%	4.9	122	$18
16 TAM	685	81	36	98	0	273	42	276	318	521	114	102	115	6	77	0.29	32	21	47	30	114	148	146	16%	18%	96	2%	0%	27	59%	26%	13.2	203	$21
17 TAM	677	71	20	86	6	261	19	266	313	424	99	90	100	7	82	0.42	43	20	37	29	114	91	91	11%	10%	83	5%	86%	27	37%	22%	-12.5	127	$15
18 SF	512	51	16	54	3	244	20	250	281	413	96	103	92	4	79	0.22	42	18	39	28	120	99	114	11%	13%	103	4%	75%	23	43%	39%	-11.7	120	$9
19 SF	508	59	20	69	3	254	24	251	325	437	101	111	96	8	75	0.38	41	22	37	30	115	96	123	16%	19%	116	3%	75%	26	31%	38%	-8.9	119	$11
1st Half	277	29	7	27	2	222	12	243	300	371	90	88	90	9	76	0.44	39	22	38	26	112	81	119	10%	16%	115	3%	100%	15	40%	40%	-12.1	93	$5
2nd Half	231	30	13	42	1	293	12	258	355	517	115	143	103	8	74	0.32	43	21	36	34	118	114	128	23%	21%	103	4%	50%	11	18%	36%	6.5	133	$20
20 Proj	**525**	**60**	**21**	**71**	**3**	**259**		**253**	**316**	**444**	**102**	**111**	**98**	**7**	**77**	**0.33**	**41**	**20**	**38**	**30**	**116**	**97**	**118**	**14%**		**107**	**4%**	**71%**				**2.4**	**87**	**$16**

Lopez,Nicky

Age: 25 Bats: L Pos: 2B SS | Ht: 5' 11" Wt: 175
Health A | PT/Exp C | Consist D
LIMA Plan B+ | Rand Var +2 | MM 0335

2-30-.240 with 1 SB in 402 PA at KC. Generated a lot of buzz upon May call-up, but fell flat. Quietly hit .301 in last 96 PA, but while ct% is elite, low HctX and LD% warn against banking on BA boost. With no power, he needs to run to have value, so non-existent 2nd half SBO and SB% history don't bode well for 2020 outlook.

Yr Tm	PA	R	HR	RBI	SB	BA	xHR	xBA	OBP	SLG	OPS+	vL+	vR+	bb%	ct%	Eye	G	L	F	h%	HctX	PX	xPX	HR/F	xHR/F	Spd	SBO	SB%	#Wk	DOM	DIS	RAR	BPX	R$
15																																		
16																																		
17 aa	246	23	0	10	6	248			291	284	77			6	87	0.47				29		23				122	16%	60%					52	$2
18 a/a	553	61	7	43	12	281			345	376	100			9	89	0.87				31		48				140	12%	65%					187	$15
19 KC *	533	65	4	40	8	257	3	278	304	349	87	85	77	6	89	0.59	62	16	22	28	78	50	5	3%	4%	124	10%	64%	20	35%	30%	-17.2	170	$8
1st Half	307	46	3	18	8	272	1	287	330	371	94	110	72	8	88	0.73	61	18	21	30	82	52	-10	4%	4%	137	15%	64%	8	13%	38%	-3.9	196	$14
2nd Half	226	19	1	22	0	237	2	256	268	321	78	68	82	4	89	0.39	63	14	23	26	75	48	15	2%	5%	111	0%	0%	12	50%	25%	-11.5	144	$2
20 Proj	**525**	**57**	**5**	**39**	**9**	**262**		**264**	**313**	**348**	**89**	**95**	**86**	**7**	**89**	**0.63**	**55**	**18**	**27**	**29**	**78**	**45**	**5**	**4%**		**134**	**10%**	**63%**				**-6.0**	**122**	**$12**

Lowe,Brandon

Age: 25 Bats: L Pos: 2B | Ht: 5' 10" Wt: 185
Health C | PT/Exp D | Consist C
LIMA Plan C+ | Rand Var -5 | MM 4423

Provided plenty of power before leg injuries wiped out 2nd half. PRO: xHR, xHR/F indicate he deserved more HR; speed hints at some value on bases. CON: Bloated h% hid some major contact issues; jury still out on whether he can hit LHP (45% ct% in 68 PA). Has a lower BA floor than many may realize, but with enough AB, UP: 30 HR

Yr Tm	PA	R	HR	RBI	SB	BA	xHR	xBA	OBP	SLG	OPS+	vL+	vR+	bb%	ct%	Eye	G	L	F	h%	HctX	PX	xPX	HR/F	xHR/F	Spd	SBO	SB%	#Wk	DOM	DIS	RAR	BPX	R$
15																																		
16																																		
17 aa	97	7	2	10	1	225			239	339	77			2	68	0.06				31		78				106	12%	44%					-76	-$1
18 TAM *	576	78	24	89	9	251	8	254	335	467	111	98	109	11	69	0.40	43	22	35	32	88	146	100	19%	25%	96	10%	66%	9	33%	33%	17.8	147	$19
19 TAM	327	42	17	51	5	270	21	236	336	514	113	88	120	8	62	0.22	30	27	43	38	92	156	130	22%	27%	117	7%	100%	16	25%	38%	10.2	93	$10
1st Half	300	39	15	47	4	271	18	236	333	513	113	94	119	7	62	0.20	31	25	43	38	91	156	123	21%	25%	115	7%	100%	15	27%	33%	9.6	93	$12
2nd Half	27	3	2	4	1	261	3	250	370	522	118	0	135	15	57	0.40	15	46	38	36	105	157	213	40%	60%	118	13%	100%	1	0%	100%	1.5	70	-$13
20 Proj	**385**	**50**	**18**	**59**	**6**	**243**		**240**	**318**	**473**	**106**	**91**	**110**	**9**	**65**	**0.27**	**36**	**24**	**40**	**32**	**90**	**144**	**114**	**20%**		**111**	**9%**	**83%**				**8.9**	**88**	**$13**

Lowe,Nate

Age: 24 Bats: L Pos: 1B | Ht: 6' 4" Wt: 245
Health A | PT/Exp F | Consist D
LIMA Plan C | Rand Var 0 | MM 3133

7-19-.263 in 169 PA at TAM. Bounced back and forth between AAA and majors; plate discipline didn't carry over well (0.26 Eye in MLB, 0.88 in AAA). But lofty HR/F was supported by xHR/F, suggesting league-average power could surge with uptick in FB%. For now, gradual improvement more likely than full-fledged breakout.

Yr Tm	PA	R	HR	RBI	SB	BA	xHR	xBA	OBP	SLG	OPS+	vL+	vR+	bb%	ct%	Eye	G	L	F	h%	HctX	PX	xPX	HR/F	xHR/F	Spd	SBO	SB%	#Wk	DOM	DIS	RAR	BPX	R$
15																																		
16																																		
17																																		
18 a/a	325	47	14	50	1	278			360	483	117			11	77	0.55				32		121				93	2%	43%					187	$10
19 TAM *	558	76	20	71	1	252	7	244	350	432	104	128	98	13	69	0.49	40	24	36	32	99	110	93	19%	19%	66	1%	100%	13	15%	54%	3.5	44	$12
1st Half	316	43	7	35	1	244	2	244	350	389	99	53	88	14	68	0.51	29	32	39	33	101	95	106	0%	18%	76	1%	100%	4	25%	75%	-4.5	7	$10
2nd Half	242	32	12	36	0	261	5	251	351	488	111	144	101	12	70	0.46	45	21	34	32	99	128	89	27%	19%	72	0%	0%	9	11%	44%	4.6	111	$14
20 Proj	**350**	**49**	**14**	**50**	**1**	**264**		**255**	**355**	**455**	**109**	**80**	**114**	**12**	**72**	**0.50**	**38**	**26**	**36**	**32**	**100**	**109**	**96**	**17%**		**73**	**1%**	**62%**				**9.0**	**61**	**$11**

Lowrie,Jed

Age: 36 Bats: B Pos: 2B | Ht: 6' 0" Wt: 180
Health F | PT/Exp B | Consist F
LIMA Plan D+ | Rand Var +5 | MM 1223

0-0-.000 in 8 PA at NYM. Feb knee injury put him on the shelf to start season, subsequent hamstring and calf maladies kept him out until Sept. Skills supported late-career resurgence in 2017-18, so he can't be dismissed. But coming off lost season at his age, it's hard to put much faith in health or performance fully returning.

Yr Tm	PA	R	HR	RBI	SB	BA	xHR	xBA	OBP	SLG	OPS+	vL+	vR+	bb%	ct%	Eye	G	L	F	h%	HctX	PX	xPX	HR/F	xHR/F	Spd	SBO	SB%	#Wk	DOM	DIS	RAR	BPX	R$
15 HOU	263	35	9	30	1	222	5	263	312	400	99	125	88	11	81	0.65	35	21	44	24	128	115	153	11%	6%	88	2%	100%	15	60%	27%	-4.4	181	$2
16 OAK	369	30	2	27	0	263	4	239	314	322	87	90	84	7	81	0.40	43	25	32	32	91	40	81	2%	5%	112	0%	0%	17	24%	53%	-14.1	14	$3
17 OAK	645	86	14	69	0	277	19	280	360	448	108	99	109	11	82	0.73	29	27	43	32	115	103	115	7%	9%	101	1%	0%	27	63%	15%	5.3	203	$14
18 OAK	680	78	23	99	0	267	21	260	353	448	111	99	115	11	79	0.61	33	23	43	31	117	110	125	11%	10%	96	0%	0%	28	46%	29%	13.8	187	$19
19 NYM *	55	5	1	2	0	160		209	221	258	63	0	19	7	60	0.19	33	33	33	23	0	61	-36	0%		106	0%	0%	5	20%	60%	-6.1	-226	-$4
1st Half	25	1	1	1	0	123		143	173	210	51			6	50	0.12				20		59		0%		107	0%	0%				-3.4	-400	-$7
2nd Half	29	4	1	1	0	196		240	264	303	75	0	19	8	70	0.31	33	33	33	25	0	62	-36	0%		105	0%	0%	5	20%	60%	-2.3	-74	-$1
20 Proj	**350**	**39**	**8**	**38**	**0**	**261**		**249**	**334**	**396**	**98**	**98**	**98**	**10**	**80**	**0.55**	**35**	**24**	**41**	**30**	**109**	**75**	**112**	**7%**		**104**	**0%**	**65%**				**-1.3**	**58**	**$8**

Lucroy,Jonathan

Age: 34 Bats: R Pos: CA | Ht: 6' 0" Wt: 200
Health B | PT/Exp C | Consist B
LIMA Plan D | Rand Var +2 | MM 1331

Decent start with .273/.340/.460 slash line through late May, but talk about a rough summer. Memorial Day: extended slump began; July: suffered concussion, broken nose; August: was DFA'd, then didn't see field much with CHC. Offers neither power nor average at this point, so look for downward PA trend to continue.

Yr Tm	PA	R	HR	RBI	SB	BA	xHR	xBA	OBP	SLG	OPS+	vL+	vR+	bb%	ct%	Eye	G	L	F	h%	HctX	PX	xPX	HR/F	xHR/F	Spd	SBO	SB%	#Wk	DOM	DIS	RAR	BPX	R$
15 MIL	415	51	7	43	1	264	9	275	326	391	100	88	102	9	83	0.56	44	26	29	30	124	83	104	8%	10%	95	1%	100%	21	38%	29%	7.0	122	$8
16 2 TM	544	67	24	81	5	292	21	276	355	500	116	108	117	9	80	0.47	37	24	39	33	114	118	131	16%	14%	105	4%	100%	27	48%	22%	27.6	183	$21
17 2 TM	481	45	6	40	1	265	6	270	345	371	96	85	98	10	88	0.90	53	19	28	29	80	59	46	6%	6%	103	1%	100%	27	48%	26%	3.6	155	$6
18 OAK	454	41	4	51	0	241	7	254	291	325	85	92	82	6	84	0.45	42	25	33	28	108	55	78	3%	6%	82	0%	0%	28	29%	46%	-4.1	70	$4
19 2 TM	328	30	8	36	0	232	8	249	305	355	88	80	91	8	83	0.53	45	21	34	26	101	60	73	10%	10%	93	0%	0%	25	32%	44%	-7.4	93	$1
1st Half	247	27	7	26	0	232	6	251	308	350	88	79	92	9	85	0.62	49	20	30	25	95	54	51	12%	11%	89	0%	0%	15	27%	40%	-3.4	104	$3
2nd Half	81	3	1	10	0	233	2	237	296	370	88	85	89	8	77	0.35	32	23	46	29	121	81	143	4%	8%	86	0%	0%	10	40%	50%	-0.9	56	-$4
20 Proj	**175**	**15**	**4**	**20**	**0**	**244**		**255**	**310**	**373**	**92**	**88**	**93**	**8**	**82**	**0.50**	**42**	**22**	**36**	**28**	**102**	**68**	**91**	**7%**		**93**	**0%**	**100%**				**2.2**	**61**	**$3**

BRIAN RUDD

Lugo,Dawel

Lugo,Dawel	Health	A	LIMA Plan	D+
Age: 25 Bats: R Pos: 3B	PT/Exp	B	Rand Var	-2
Ht: 6' 0" Wt: 220	Consist	B	MM	1341

6-26-.245 in 288 PA at DET. Didn't do much with May or August call-ups. Three reasons why future is similarly bleak: 1) Plenty of grounders with ho-hum xPX cap HR; 2) Even with plus Spd, didn't attempt a single bag in majors; 3) Weak Eye and poor patience limit OBP. Even if contact bounces back, there isn't enough here to roster.

Yr	Tm	PA	R	HR	RBI	SB	BA	xHR	xBA	OBP	SLG	OPS+	vL+	vR+	bb%	ct%	Eye	G	L	F	h%	HctX	PX	xPX	HR/F	xHR/F	Spd	SBO	SB%	#Wk	DOM	DIS	RAR	BPX	R$
15																																			
16	aa	177	22	4	18	1	302			316	449	104			2	91	0.22				32		77				115	5%	46%					186	$4
17	aa	545	50	11	56	3	256			295	390	92			5	85	0.38				28		71				115	3%	70%					136	$8
18	DET *	618	60	4	60	11	245	0	280	263	325	81	112	72	2	85	0.17	66	19	15	28	93	50	24	9%	0%	106	12%	71%	6	33%	17%	-26.4	63	$11
19	DET *	582	67	10	61	5	276	6	268	301	416	95	73	91	4	79	0.18	48	24	28	33	91	75	58	10%	10%	121	7%	60%	15	13%	53%	-10.8	81	$13
1st Half		246	27	4	26	3	295	2	285	332	441	103	79	77	5	81	0.28	50	27	23	35	91	75	61	7%	13%	127	9%	60%	7	14%	71%	-0.3	122	$10
2nd Half		337	40	6	35	2	262	4	260	279	398	89	70	97	2	78	0.11	48	22	30	32	90	75	57	11%	9%	113	4%	60%	8	13%	38%	-13.5	52	$15
20	**Proj**	**245**	**27**	**5**	**25**	**2**	**267**		**277**	**293**	**403**	**94**	**97**	**92**	**3**	**83**	**0.19**	**50**	**24**	**26**	**31**	**91**	**70**	**45**	**9%**		**115**	**7%**	**67%**				**-3.7**	**86**	**$4**

Luplow,Jordan

Luplow,Jordan	Health	A	LIMA Plan	C+
Age: 26 Bats: R Pos: RF LF	PT/Exp	D	Rand Var	-4
Ht: 6' 1" Wt: 195	Consist	D	MM	4233

15-38-.276 in 261 PA at CLE. Walloped lefties (14 HR, .439 OBP in 155 PA) before hamstring strain cut short a 2nd half that teased with FB%, xPX gains. Struggles vR limit him to short-side platoon, which caps PA, while h% questions BA repeat. BPX growth makes him appealing, but only in daily leagues when used wisely.

Yr	Tm	PA	R	HR	RBI	SB	BA	xHR	xBA	OBP	SLG	OPS+	vL+	vR+	bb%	ct%	Eye	G	L	F	h%	HctX	PX	xPX	HR/F	xHR/F	Spd	SBO	SB%	#Wk	DOM	DIS	RAR	BPX	R$
15																																			
16																																			
17	PIT *	541	71	22	60	4	263	2	242	326	453	104	88	87	8	78	0.42	38	16	46	30	88	105	103	12%	8%	98	8%	44%	8	38%	38%	-4.6	133	$13
18	PIT *	447	48	9	45	7	231	3	232	300	379	94	98	79	9	78	0.44	42	15	42	28	66	91	75	10%	10%	122	12%	63%	12	33%	33%	-11.2	133	$7
19	CLE *	314	51	17	43	5	275	12	266	370	533	120	154	76	13	71	0.53	40	21	39	33	100	145	110	23%	19%	102	10%	59%	22	59%	32%	12.8	222	$11
1st Half		198	32	11	29	4	267	7	257	348	512	115	151	64	11	68	0.39	44	21	35	33	81	145	72	26%	21%	99	12%	62%	13	54%	38%	4.5	152	$13
2nd Half		116	20	6	15	1	289	5	281	408	570	129	162	99	17	78	0.90	34	21	45	32	132	145	165	20%	17%	111	6%	50%	9	67%	22%	8.1	352	$6
20	**Proj**	**315**	**45**	**16**	**38**	**4**	**262**		**263**	**355**	**507**	**116**	**143**	**89**	**12**	**76**	**0.55**	**40**	**18**	**42**	**29**	**92**	**130**	**106**	**17%**		**112**	**9%**	**59%**				**11.7**	**220**	**$12**

Lux,Gavin

Lux,Gavin	Health	A	LIMA Plan	B
Age: 22 Bats: L Pos: 2B	PT/Exp	F	Rand Var	-2
Ht: 6' 2" Wt: 190	Consist	C	MM	2325

2-2-.240 in 82 PA at LA. Swatted 26 HR with 10 SB at AA/AAA with notable PX growth. xPX says it carried over in Sept call-up. Line drive stroke (23% LD% in minors) hints at favorable BA, but while he owns plus Spd, low SB% could limit steals. May not reach elite ceiling in 2020, but he's worth the price tag in keeper leagues.

Yr	Tm	PA	R	HR	RBI	SB	BA	xHR	xBA	OBP	SLG	OPS+	vL+	vR+	bb%	ct%	Eye	G	L	F	h%	HctX	PX	xPX	HR/F	xHR/F	Spd	SBO	SB%	#Wk	DOM	DIS	RAR	BPX	R$
15																																			
16																																			
17																																			
18	aa	115	17	3	7	2	287			352	424	107			9	79	0.47				34		79				120	11%	42%					113	$1
19	LA *	588	94	24	72	10	304	2	260	369	513	117	54	101	9	74	0.40	39	27	33	37	135	112	164	12%	12%	132	10%	65%	5	20%	60%	33.3	170	$25
1st Half		296	42	12	32	6	295			351	482	111			8	74	0.34				36		97		0%	#VALUE!	135	11%	64%				10.1	122	$21
2nd Half		293	52	12	40	5	313	2	276	387	546	123	54	101	11	73	0.46	39	27	33	39	135	128	164	12%	12%	129	8%	67%	5	20%	60%	21.8	219	$29
20	**Proj**	**455**	**71**	**13**	**45**	**8**	**273**		**250**	**342**	**438**	**105**	**66**	**111**	**9**	**76**	**0.43**	**44**	**21**	**34**	**33**	**122**	**89**	**148**	**13%**		**135**	**11%**	**60%**				**12.2**	**102**	**$17**

Machado,Manny

Machado,Manny	Health	A	LIMA Plan	B
Age: 27 Bats: R Pos: 3B SS	PT/Exp	A	Rand Var	0
Ht: 6' 3" Wt: 215	Consist	F	MM	3235

Fifth straight 30+ HR season, but rising power tide with dips in BA/SB cut R$ nearly in half. Did SD marine layer dampen output? Plus power skills are entrenched, but erosion in ct% and xBA fog his BA outlook, while he nearly stopped running on basepaths. Again. Forecast: slightly clearer skies, but nowhere near as nice as 2018.

Yr	Tm	PA	R	HR	RBI	SB	BA	xHR	xBA	OBP	SLG	OPS+	vL+	vR+	bb%	ct%	Eye	G	L	F	h%	HctX	PX	xPX	HR/F	xHR/F	Spd	SBO	SB%	#Wk	DOM	DIS	RAR	BPX	R$
15	BAL	713	102	35	86	20	286	27	279	359	502	120	105	123	10	82	0.63	44	18	38	30	119	127	122	18%	14%	100	15%	71%	27	63%	4%	29.3	224	$35
16	BAL	696	105	37	96	0	294	36	283	343	533	119	124	115	7	81	0.40	37	20	43	31	117	136	118	17%	16%	98	2%	0%	27	63%	4%	26.6	226	$27
17	BAL	690	81	33	95	9	259	33	266	310	471	105	110	101	7	82	0.43	42	16	42	27	131	112	131	15%	15%	95	9%	69%	27	59%	22%	-5.2	188	$20
18	2 TM	709	84	37	107	14	297	37	281	367	538	125	128	123	10	84	0.67	40	18	42	31	119	128	115	16%	16%	96	9%	88%	28	64%	14%	45.1	290	$34
19	SD	661	81	32	85	5	256	26	251	334	462	106	142	95	10	78	0.51	42	17	41	28	118	101	121	17%	14%	100	5%	63%	28	46%	39%	-4.6	167	$18
1st Half		349	51	20	56	2	277	16	257	352	516	116	176	104	10	77	0.47	39	18	43	30	114	120	135	19%	15%	92	3%	67%	15	47%	47%	9.6	193	$26
2nd Half		312	30	12	29	3	231	9	243	314	401	94	121	84	10	80	0.55	45	17	39	25	122	79	106	14%	10%	117	7%	60%	13	46%	31%	-10.1	148	$9
20	**Proj**	**630**	**77**	**31**	**84**	**7**	**267**		**259**	**338**	**479**	**110**	**127**	**103**	**9**	**81**	**0.53**	**42**	**17**	**41**	**28**	**121**	**103**	**119**	**16%**		**101**	**6%**	**69%**				**16.2**	**174**	**$23**

Madrigal,Nick

Madrigal,Nick	Health	A	LIMA Plan	B
Age: 23 Bats: R Pos: 2B	PT/Exp	F	Rand Var	0
Ht: 5' 7" Wt: 165	Consist	F	MM	1553

Potential rabbit climbed three levels in CHW organization and swiped 35 bags. He has more than one trick too, as absurd bat-to-ball skills (just 16 Ks in 532 PA!) support excellent BA, while plus raw speed and SBO stand out with SB at a premium. Power is non-existent, but there's late-round value if he gets a playing time carrot in 2020.

Yr	Tm	PA	R	HR	RBI	SB	BA	xHR	xBA	OBP	SLG	OPS+	vL+	vR+	bb%	ct%	Eye	G	L	F	h%	HctX	PX	xPX	HR/F	xHR/F	Spd	SBO	SB%	#Wk	DOM	DIS	RAR	BPX	R$
15																																			
16																																			
17																																			
18																																			
19	a/a	306	51	2	25	16	314			369	408	103			8	96	2.17				32		46				125	28%	63%					281	$13
1st Half		85	16	0	10	9	364			416	449	116			8	97	3.19				37		37				160	44%	68%				4.8	315	$5
2nd Half		222	36	2	16	8	301			358	400	100			8	96	2.01				31		51				123	21%	60%				1.7	289	$17
20	**Proj**	**350**	**62**	**3**	**32**	**20**	**286**		**288**	**343**	**395**	**99**	**98**	**99**	**8**	**91**	**0.94**	**53**	**20**	**27**	**31**	**95**	**55**		**4%**		**150**	**33%**	**64%**				**-1.3**	**252**	**$18**

Maldonado,Martin

Maldonado,Martin	Health	A	LIMA Plan	D
Age: 33 Bats: R Pos: CA	PT/Exp	C	Rand Var	+2
Ht: 6' 0" Wt: 230	Consist	A	MM	2011

Traded twice in July, then hit 6 HR in final two months to thrust R$ above zero. Some modest gains if we squint—HctX, xHR/F reflect power growth—but BA will be a drag, as he's not beating out many of those ground balls. Defense, bb% spike might yield part-time role, but BPX baseline seals his fate as a fringe second catcher.

Yr	Tm	PA	R	HR	RBI	SB	BA	xHR	xBA	OBP	SLG	OPS+	vL+	vR+	bb%	ct%	Eye	G	L	F	h%	HctX	PX	xPX	HR/F	xHR/F	Spd	SBO	SB%	#Wk	DOM	DIS	RAR	BPX	R$
15	MIL	256	19	4	22	0	210	3	205	282	293	80	112	69	9	72	0.35	47	20	33	28	91	62	99	8%	6%	51	2%	0%	25	12%	68%	-8.0	-76	-$2
16	MIL	253	21	8	21	1	202	9	225	332	351	93	91	92	14	73	0.63	44	18	38	24	84	92	90	14%	16%	50	2%	100%	25	44%	40%	-1.8	29	-$1
17	LAA	471	43	14	38	0	221	15	221	276	368	86	84	86	3	72	0.13	49	15	37	27	78	91	78	13%	14%	72	3%	0%	26	19%	50%	-16.0	-21	$1
18	2 AL	404	39	9	44	0	225	9	227	276	351	87	90	85	4	74	0.16	41	21	38	28	86	83	86	9%	9%	67	1%	0%	27	15%	63%	-4.9	-27	$3
19	3 TM	374	46	12	27	0	213	13	237	293	378	89	90	88	9	74	0.37	48	17	35	25	103	95	95	14%	15%	67	0%	0%	28	29%	54%	-1.4	44	$1
1st Half		234	22	5	16	0	229	8	232	300	362	88	67	97	7	77	0.35	50	17	33	27	108	78	90	9%	15%	67	0%	0%	15	20%	67%	-3.5	30	$0
2nd Half		140	24	7	11	0	187	5	242	281	407	91	123	72	11	69	0.39	44	18	38	21	95	125	103	22%	16%	70	0%	0%	13	38%	38%	-1.8	78	$3
20	**Proj**	**245**	**29**	**8**	**22**	**0**	**212**		**230**	**284**	**371**	**88**	**97**	**83**	**7**	**73**	**0.29**	**45**	**18**	**37**	**25**	**92**	**92**	**92**	**14%**		**66**	**1%**	**13%**				**-1.3**	**-21**	**$3**

Mancini,Trey

Mancini,Trey	Health	A	LIMA Plan	B
Age: 28 Bats: R Pos: RF 1B	PT/Exp	A	Rand Var	+1
Ht: 6' 4" Wt: 215	Consist	D	MM	3245

"Boomer" lived up to his nickname with first $20+ season. Three reasons to buy another one: 1) Added FB% to drive xPX growth, while xHR and xHR/F held firm; 2) Minor upticks in ct% and LD% support favorable BA; 3) Not vulnerable to platoon splits. While minor regression seems likely, BPX says it will be soft.

Yr	Tm	PA	R	HR	RBI	SB	BA	xHR	xBA	OBP	SLG	OPS+	vL+	vR+	bb%	ct%	Eye	G	L	F	h%	HctX	PX	xPX	HR/F	xHR/F	Spd	SBO	SB%	#Wk	DOM	DIS	RAR	BPX	R$
15	aa	345	52	12	49	2	332			368	540	127			5	81	0.30				38		137				94	3%	61%					197	$17
16	BAL *	614	69	20	63	2	243	3	220	309	392	95	243	87	9	70	0.31	40	20	40	31	169	94	250	75%	75%	123	3%	43%	2	50%	50%	-13.8	29	$9
17	BAL	586	65	24	78	1	293	27	263	338	488	111	98	114	6	74	0.24	51	19	30	36	103	112	113	20%	22%	128	1%	100%	27	37%	37%	7.5	118	$19
18	BAL	636	69	24	58	0	242	29	249	299	416	99	91	102	7	74	0.29	55	19	26	29	91	104	95	21%	25%	109	1%	0%	28	25%	39%	-5.5	87	$11
19	BAL	679	106	35	97	1	291	31	284	364	535	119	119	119	9	76	0.44	46	22	32	33	98	129	118	24%	21%	109	1%	100%	28	61%	18%	33.1	230	$25
1st Half		336	53	17	40	1	302	17	287	357	544	120	127	117	8	77	0.36	43	24	33	34	99	126	133	21%	21%	124	1%	100%	15	67%	13%	15.9	241	$24
2nd Half		343	53	18	57	0	279	14	276	370	525	118	111	121	11	75	0.51	49	20	30	32	97	132	101	26%	21%	96	0%	0%	13	54%	23%	13.0	219	$26
20	**Proj**	**630**	**87**	**29**	**83**	**1**	**277**		**268**	**342**	**489**	**112**	**107**	**113**	**8**	**75**	**0.36**	**50**	**20**	**29**	**32**	**96**	**114**	**107**	**22%**		**110**	**1%**	**65%**				**21.0**	**103**	**$23**

BRANT CHESSER

Margot,Manuel

Age: 25 Bats: R Pos: CF	Health A	LIMA Plan C+	
Ht: 5' 11" Wt: 180	PT/Exp B	Rand Var 0	
	Consist A	MM 1523	

Teased us with hot summer stretch (8 HR/9 SB in July-Aug), but surrounding struggles look here to stay. xHR and xPX show that HR spike was not real, and sub-par xBA has been flat now for three years. Issues vR will cost him playing time. Primo wheels and SB success look sustainable, but there are too many other holes to count on further growth.

Yr	Tm	PA	R	HR	RBI	SB	BA	xHR	xBA	OBP	SLG	OPS+	vL+	vR+	bb%	ct%	Eye	G	L	F	h%	HctX	PX	xPX	HR/F	xHR/F	Spd	SBO	SB%	#Wk	DOM	DIS	RAR	BPX	R$
15	aa	275	31	2	27	16	263			309	403	99			6	85	0.45				30		98				104	42%	65%					176	$9
16	SD *	578	72	4	41	23	258	0	301	289	350	87	104	78	4	86	0.32	63	23	13	29	140	53	51	0%	0%	173	27%	65%	3	33%	67%	-21.8	140	$16
17	SD	529	53	13	39	17	263	8	251	313	409	97	110	90	7	78	0.33	41	23	36	31	80	79	75	9%	6%	167	19%	71%	22	27%	32%	-10.3	124	$14
18	SD	519	50	8	51	11	245	10	251	292	384	93	91	94	6	82	0.36	43	20	37	29	118	81	106	6%	7%	149	20%	52%	28	36%	29%	-9.8	167	$10
19	SD	441	59	12	37	20	234	6	238	304	387	92	116	82	9	78	0.43	43	16	40	27	90	81	82	10%	5%	152	25%	83%	27	37%	48%	-3.7	152	$12
1st Half		195	25	3	15	10	238	2	219	289	337	84	125	74	6	77	0.29	41	18	41	29	87	60	73	5%	4%	129	23%	100%	15	27%	53%	-4.8	30	$6
2nd Half		246	34	9	22	10	230	4	254	316	429	98	111	91	11	79	0.57	45	15	39	25	93	98	90	13%	6%	158	26%	71%	12	50%	42%	-0.2	241	$17
20	Proj	420	50	9	37	17	243		243	302	385	92	104	87	8	80	0.40	43	19	39	29	99	75	90	7%		155	23%	77%				0.1	127	$11

Marisnick,Jake

Age: 29 Bats: R Pos: CF	Health A	LIMA Plan D	
Ht: 6' 4" Wt: 220	PT/Exp D	Rand Var 0	
	Consist B	MM 3501	

Had a sneaky-good start, but it all fell apart as PT dried up in 2nd half. Another ct% uptick was nice, though still too many Ks and not enough hard contact (HctX, xPX) to move the BA needle, while meager bb% hampers on-base ability. His light is green, but SB volume isn't enough to ease the pain in every other category.

Yr	Tm	PA	R	HR	RBI	SB	BA	xHR	xBA	OBP	SLG	OPS+	vL+	vR+	bb%	ct%	Eye	G	L	F	h%	HctX	PX	xPX	HR/F	xHR/F	Spd	SBO	SB%	#Wk	DOM	DIS	RAR	BPX	R$
15	HOU	372	46	9	36	24	236	10	223	281	383	93	92	91	5	69	0.17	42	20	38	32	72	107	93	10%	11%	136	47%	73%	25	32%	48%	-11.6	38	$13
16	HOU *	339	42	5	22	11	204	6	224	245	321	77	95	69	5	70	0.18	45	19	36	28	74	90	68	7%	9%	114	31%	64%	26	19%	50%	-19.7	-6	$2
17	HOU	259	50	16	35	9	243	14	227	319	496	109	108	107	8	61	0.22	37	15	48	32	71	171	119	25%	22%	107	26%	69%	24	50%	42%	1.1	91	$9
18	HOU *	317	48	13	38	9	225	9	219	273	423	96	96	90	6	64	0.18	32	23	45	31	68	140	123	18%	16%	135	22%	73%	24	33%	63%	-2.5	70	$8
19	HOU	318	46	10	34	10	233	8	231	289	411	93	93	92	5	67	0.18	45	18	36	31	74	108	66	14%	11%	124	23%	77%	28	21%	50%	-6.6	22	$7
1st Half		189	29	8	24	6	256	6	262	312	477	105	139	89	5	70	0.17	48	21	32	32	78	131	68	22%	16%	108	25%	75%	15	33%	33%	1.7	104	$11
2nd Half		129	17	2	10	4	200	2	183	256	317	75	38	99	6	64	0.19	41	15	44	29	66	72	64	6%	6%	142	21%	80%	13	8%	69%	-6.9	-107	$2
20	Proj	245	38	9	27	8	235		218	292	423	96	92	98	6	65	0.18	40	19	42	32	70	116	89	15%		128	24%	74%				0.0	33	$9

Markakis,Nick

Age: 36 Bats: L Pos: RF	Health C	LIMA Plan B+	
Ht: 6' 1" Wt: 210	PT/Exp A	Rand Var 0	
	Consist C	MM 1255	

Like an old washing machine, you never really want to use him, but he's dependable and you know the end result. July HBP (wrist) sent him in for repairs for six weeks; otherwise churned out loads of hits. Elite contact/LD% combo locks in that plus BA, but all other features are lacking. Should last another year; so rinse, repeat for 2020.

Yr	Tm	PA	R	HR	RBI	SB	BA	xHR	xBA	OBP	SLG	OPS+	vL+	vR+	bb%	ct%	Eye	G	L	F	h%	HctX	PX	xPX	HR/F	xHR/F	Spd	SBO	SB%	#Wk	DOM	DIS	RAR	BPX	R$
15	ATL	686	73	3	53	2	296	4	261	370	376	104	88	109	10	86	0.84	52	21	27	34	97	60	55	2%	3%	95	1%	67%	27	44%	19%	2.4	122	$16
16	ATL	684	67	13	89	0	269	15	259	346	397	101	83	107	10	83	0.70	43	22	35	31	111	82	105	7%	8%	63	1%	0%	27	44%	19%	0.9	114	$13
17	ATL	670	76	8	76	0	275	9	260	354	384	99	96	98	10	81	0.62	49	22	29	33	109	71	71	6%	6%	77	1%	0%	27	33%	26%	-8.8	85	$13
18	ATL	705	78	14	93	1	297	13	293	366	440	112	106	114	10	87	0.90	43	27	30	32	130	84	89	8%	8%	87	1%	50%	28	50%	14%	25.4	213	$22
19	ATL	469	61	9	62	2	285	8	289	356	420	103	85	109	10	86	0.80	48	25	27	32	122	70	83	9%	8%	88	2%	100%	22	59%	18%	0.1	178	$11
1st Half		342	54	8	48	0	275	7	291	354	426	104	75	113	11	86	0.88	48	24	27	30	115	76	72	11%	10%	92	0%	0%	15	73%	13%	1.2	204	$16
2nd Half		127	7	1	14	2	310	2	284	362	405	101	111	98	7	86	0.56	47	27	27	35	139	57	110	4%	7%	83	6%	100%	7	29%	29%	1.0	119	-$1
20	Proj	560	59	10	69	3	292		283	358	419	105	98	106	9	85	0.71	47	25	28	33	124	70	88	8%		84	2%	83%				12.7	131	$18

Marte,Ketel

Age: 26 Bats: B Pos: CF 2B	Health A	LIMA Plan A	
Ht: 6' 1" Wt: 165	PT/Exp B	Rand Var -5	
	Consist C	MM 3555	

Holy breakout. Easy to say he'll "regress," but to what? 2nd half h% was fluky, but xBA says he can flirt with .300, while SB% hints at more bags if he starts running. HR looks least likely to repeat given outlier HR/F, tepid xPX, and Sept back injury adds some uncertainty. He won't crash; it's just tough to turn profit after a career year.

Yr	Tm	PA	R	HR	RBI	SB	BA	xHR	xBA	OBP	SLG	OPS+	vL+	vR+	bb%	ct%	Eye	G	L	F	h%	HctX	PX	xPX	HR/F	xHR/F	Spd	SBO	SB%	#Wk	DOM	DIS	RAR	BPX	R$
15	SEA *	531	58	4	39	24	279	2	266	333	375	99	99	107	7	84	0.50	52	22	26	33	82	66	45	4%	4%	151	23%	71%	11	55%	18%	0.6	132	$19
16	SEA *	496	59	1	35	13	254	2	253	284	318	82	71	87	4	82	0.23	52	22	26	31	71	47	41	1%	2%	127	16%	72%	22	14%	41%	-21.7	34	$9
17	ARI *	582	70	9	45	8	276	5	273	332	416	100	96	99	8	86	0.59	45	21	34	31	98	76	77	8%	8%	158	8%	69%	15	53%	7%	-3.3	206	$13
18	ARI	580	68	14	59	6	260	14	285	332	437	106	135	89	9	85	0.68	51	20	29	28	113	93	84	11%	11%	149	5%	86%	28	61%	7%	11.3	263	$14
19	ARI	628	97	32	92	10	329	28	308	389	592	130	130	130	8	85	0.62	43	22	35	34	123	122	107	19%	17%	138	7%	83%	26	73%	15%	66.6	359	$32
1st Half		361	55	20	52	4	309	17	300	357	571	124	129	121	7	84	0.44	42	22	36	32	127	121	124	20%	17%	130	5%	100%	15	53%	27%	28.8	319	$34
2nd Half		267	42	12	40	6	356	10	319	431	623	139	136	140	11	86	0.91	45	23	33	38	117	123	83	18%	15%	146	10%	75%	11	100%	0%	36.5	415	$30
20	Proj	595	82	22	71	10	292		295	356	506	116	120	113	9	85	0.64	47	21	32	31	111	101	87	15%		147	9%	78%				38.6	282	$26

Marte,Starling

Age: 31 Bats: R Pos: CF	Health A	LIMA Plan D+	
Ht: 6' 1" Wt: 190	PT/Exp B	Rand Var 0	
	Consist A	MM 2555	

Yet another $30 season, even as he missed most of Sept (wrist). BPX hints this was his best year yet: ct% growth with h% baseline say BA gains were legit; ditto for HR, as xHR/F continued to climb; SB skills showed little sign of age-related decline. Assuming health checks out this spring, he's a five-category building block.

Yr	Tm	PA	R	HR	RBI	SB	BA	xHR	xBA	OBP	SLG	OPS+	vL+	vR+	bb%	ct%	Eye	G	L	F	h%	HctX	PX	xPX	HR/F	xHR/F	Spd	SBO	SB%	#Wk	DOM	DIS	RAR	BPX	R$
15	PIT	633	84	19	81	30	287	23	283	337	444	109	99	109	4	79	0.22	54	24	23	34	101	103	94	19%	23%	117	28%	75%	27	48%	22%	11.1	116	$32
16	PIT	529	71	9	46	47	311	14	274	362	456	111	99	112	4	79	0.22	48	23	28	38	111	95	98	8%	13%	147	46%	80%	25	36%	40%	15.6	131	$35
17	PIT *	377	51	8	33	23	275	9	245	318	376	93	54	107	6	79	0.30	49	21	30	33	84	54	77	10%	13%	142	28%	85%	15	20%	40%	-6.6	45	$16
18	PIT	606	81	20	72	33	277	27	272	327	460	109	101	111	6	81	0.32	51	17	32	31	99	105	106	14%	19%	139	35%	70%	28	57%	18%	12.0	203	$31
19	PIT	586	97	23	82	25	295	26	296	342	503	112	101	116	4	83	0.27	50	21	28	32	108	101	88	19%	21%	136	25%	81%	23	52%	4%	25.1	230	$30
1st Half		325	50	12	39	12	276	13	287	319	465	105	88	109	4	81	0.23	50	22	28	30	104	93	89	18%	19%	128	21%	86%	13	46%	0%	6.1	181	$27
2nd Half		261	47	11	43	13	319	13	309	372	550	122	113	125	5	84	0.32	51	21	28	34	112	112	88	19%	23%	140	29%	76%	10	60%	10%	17.9	293	$35
20	Proj	595	93	21	78	29	291		281	342	476	110	96	114	5	81	0.28	50	20	29	33	102	93	92	16%		141	26%	80%				27.3	199	$35

Martin,Richie

Age: 25 Bats: R Pos: SS	Health A	LIMA Plan D	
Ht: 5' 11" Wt: 190	PT/Exp C	Rand Var +1	
	Consist D	MM 1321	

First overall pick from 2018 Rule 5 Draft somehow stuck around all year. The old "can't steal first" adage applies here, as wheels made him useful on basepaths, but he was the only MLB hitter (min. 295 PA) with THIS bad of an Eye/HctX combination. Safe to say those SB opps will be sparse, as are his odds of fantasy relevance.

Yr	Tm	PA	R	HR	RBI	SB	BA	xHR	xBA	OBP	SLG	OPS+	vL+	vR+	bb%	ct%	Eye	G	L	F	h%	HctX	PX	xPX	HR/F	xHR/F	Spd	SBO	SB%	#Wk	DOM	DIS	RAR	BPX	R$
15																																			
16																																			
17	aa	305	34	2	22	10	198			247	274	70			6	79	0.31				24		46				126	21%	74%					12	$0
18	aa	486	53	4	33	19	261			312	379	96			7	79	0.35				32		75				128	27%	63%					97	$13
19	BAL	309	29	6	23	10	208	4	224	260	322	77	84	68	5	71	0.17	49	20	31	27	61	63	56	10%	7%	138	20%	91%	28	21%	68%	-21.9	-48	$2
1st Half		188	17	4	8	5	174	2	212	232	297	71	73	68	5	65	0.17	49	20	31	24	61	73	70	12%	6%	139	17%	100%	15	13%	73%	-15.8	-96	-$2
2nd Half		121	12	2	15	5	261	2	241	303	360	87	98	69	3	79	0.17	50	20	30	31	61	50	37	8%	8%	127	22%	83%	13	31%	62%	-4.2	15	$9
20	Proj	245	24	4	17	9	234		240	289	350	86	96	73	5	76	0.23	50	20	31	29	61	63	50	8%		136	24%	75%				-6.6	19	$6

Martinez,J.D.

Age: 32 Bats: R Pos: DH RF	Health B	LIMA Plan D+	
Ht: 6' 3" Wt: 220	PT/Exp A	Rand Var 0	
	Consist C	MM 4355	

Dealt with nagging back issues for most of the year, which likely drove some skills decay. The raw power (xPX, xHR/F) dipped from elite to very good, as xBA now questions another .300 season. Could reclaim 2017-18 greatness with healthy off-season, but at an age where injuries tend to linger, it's best to "settle" for a repeat.

Yr	Tm	PA	R	HR	RBI	SB	BA	xHR	xBA	OBP	SLG	OPS+	vL+	vR+	bb%	ct%	Eye	G	L	F	h%	HctX	PX	xPX	HR/F	xHR/F	Spd	SBO	SB%	#Wk	DOM	DIS	RAR	BPX	R$
15	DET	657	93	38	102	3	282	49	265	344	535	123	126	119	8	70	0.30	34	22	43	34	131	175	182	21%	27%	97	3%	60%	27	52%	30%	16.3	184	$28
16	DET *	554	71	22	72	2	300	33	265	364	517	120	116	123	9	71	0.35	42	21	36	38	119	147	144	18%	27%	92	3%	47%	21	48%	14%	17.5	146	$20
17	2 TM	485	85	45	104	4	306	46	306	379	696	144	180	132	11	70	0.42	38	19	43	34	140	226	192	34%	35%	96	4%	100%	22	73%	5%	58.1	348	$28
18	BOS	649	111	43	130	6	330	49	298	402	629	143	134	144	11	74	0.47	43	23	34	38	123	178	148	29%	34%	110	4%	86%	28	71%	7%	77.4	320	$41
19	BOS	656	98	36	105	2	304	38	281	383	557	125	180	106	11	76	0.52	43	22	35	35	121	131	127	23%	25%	94	1%	100%	28	46%	29%	40.1	226	$27
1st Half		334	49	18	47	1	298	23	281	374	549	123	165	111	11	78	0.55	38	22	39	33	124	128	140	20%	25%	95	1%	100%	15	53%	27%	17.9	248	$25
2nd Half		322	49	18	58	1	311	15	280	391	564	126	193	100	12	74	0.50	48	22	30	37	117	135	112	29%	24%	94	1%	100%	13	38%	31%	22.2	207	$30
20	Proj	609	92	38	100	2	301		282	378	578	129	162	117	11	74	0.47	43	22	35	35	124	148	144	27%		101	2%	84%				49.0	215	$30

RYAN BLOOMFIELD

Martinez,Jose

Age: 31 Bats: R Pos: RF	Health B	LIMA Plan D+	Even before August shoulder injury, power was off, and now has three straight half-seasons with sub-90 xPX. BA might bounce back some, but likely not to .300 again given ct% tumble. Odds against HR catching up to xHR given sub-30% FB rate, and awful defense puts PT at risk. Even with full health... DN: 250 PA
Ht: 6' 6" Wt: 215	PT/Exp C	Rand Var -1	
	Consist D	MM 2443	

Yr	Tm	PA	R	HR	RBI	SB	BA	xHR	xBA	OBP	SLG	OPS+	vL+	vR+	bb%	ct%	Eye	G	L	F	h%	HctX	PX	xPX	HR/F	xHR/F	Spd	SBO	SB%	#Wk	DOM	DIS	RAR	BPX	R$
15	aaa	377	43	7	45	6	324			388	467	119			9	81	0.55				38		97				95	7%	71%					138	$16
16	STL *	487	40	7	42	8	226	0	266	271	328	82	146	100	6	80	0.32	60	20	20	27	152	67	9	0%	0%	88	9%	86%	5	20%	0%	-23.1	46	$3
17	STL	307	47	14	46	4	309	17	286	379	518	120	178	102	10	78	0.53	42	27	31	35	117	115	123	21%	25%	113	5%	100%	24	42%	33%	15.9	182	$13
18	STL	590	64	17	83	0	305	26	273	364	457	114	108	114	8	81	0.47	46	26	28	35	120	91	101	14%	22%	85	2%	0%	28	46%	29%	19.9	130	$20
19	STL	373	45	10	42	3	269	13	258	340	410	100	130	91	9	75	0.43	50	24	26	33	97	75	85	15%	20%	116	3%	100%	25	32%	52%	-2.6	63	$7
1st Half		240	26	5	28	1	281	9	260	346	392	99	136	89	9	79	0.46	47	26	27	34	103	61	89	11%	20%	92	1%	100%	15	27%	47%	-2.1	41	$8
2nd Half		133	19	5	14	2	248	4	256	331	444	102	124	96	11	69	0.39	55	21	24	32	85	106	76	25%	20%	145	6%	100%	10	40%	60%	-0.4	104	$6
20	Proj	**315**	**40**	**12**	**39**	**3**	**281**		**276**	**345**	**461**	**109**	**130**	**102**	**9**	**79**	**0.47**	**46**	**24**	**29**	**32**	**106**	**92**	**94**	**18%**		**115**	**4%**	**85%**				**9.2**	**125**	**$9**

Maybin,Cameron

Age: 33 Bats: R Pos: LF RF	Health C	LIMA Plan D+	11-32-.285 with 9 SB in 269 PA at NYY. Injuries (calf, wrist) cropped up again as SB% continued downward trend. Meanwhile, sold out for power at expense of ct%, but lucky h% saved BA. Still a good bet for double-digit SB, which is clearest path to value, as it's doubtful he can maintain both power gains and decent BA.
Ht: 6' 3" Wt: 215	PT/Exp C	Rand Var -5	
	Consist B	MM 2323	

Yr	Tm	PA	R	HR	RBI	SB	BA	xHR	xBA	OBP	SLG	OPS+	vL+	vR+	bb%	ct%	Eye	G	L	F	h%	HctX	PX	xPX	HR/F	xHR/F	Spd	SBO	SB%	#Wk	DOM	DIS	RAR	BPX	R$
15	ATL	555	65	10	59	23	267	8	266	327	370	97	98	95	8	80	0.44	58	22	20	32	75	67	46	12%	10%	100	19%	79%	26	31%	38%	-3.2	57	$20
16	DET *	487	76	6	51	18	282	5	269	352	392	101	108	107	10	79	0.52	57	22	22	35	80	69	48	7%	8%	142	18%	71%	19	21%	26%	6.1	103	$18
17	2 AL	450	63	10	35	33	228	7	254	318	365	92	85	93	11	76	0.54	58	14	28	27	84	83	65	12%	8%	116	38%	80%	24	29%	58%	-9.8	94	$16
18	2 TM	384	32	4	28	10	249	7	244	326	336	92	89	93	10	78	0.51	49	24	28	31	96	57	62	5%	9%	110	15%	67%	28	25%	43%	-4.0	43	$6
19	NYY *	343	54	12	37	10	267	12	231	353	453	107	97	122	12	67	0.40	41	19	39	36	87	119	104	17%	18%	124	21%	53%	19	42%	37%	6.1	93	$11
1st Half		193	30	5	17	7	268	5	212	360	411	103	86	130	13	65	0.41	41	20	39	39	80	96	93	16%	16%	133	22%	55%	9	33%	44%	2.1	7	$10
2nd Half		150	24	7	19	3	267	6	257	344	506	112	103	112	11	70	0.39	41	18	40	33	96	147	116	18%	18%	100	18%	50%	10	50%	30%	5.1	181	$12
20	Proj	**315**	**43**	**9**	**30**	**11**	**258**		**243**	**340**	**414**	**101**	**92**	**106**	**11**	**73**	**0.45**	**47**	**20**	**33**	**33**	**89**	**94**	**83**	**13%**		**113**	**21%**	**64%**				**1.2**	**68**	**$12**

Mazara,Nomar

Age: 25 Bats: L Pos: RF	Health B	LIMA Plan B	August oblique injury sent him to IL, but lingered and led to frequent days off in Sept. Overall, he made modest power gains, but this was more or less the same in just about every phase of his game. There's value in his consistency, but those waiting on him reaching next level could be disappointed once again.
Ht: 6' 4" Wt: 215	PT/Exp B	Rand Var -1	
	Consist A	MM 3235	

Yr	Tm	PA	R	HR	RBI	SB	BA	xHR	xBA	OBP	SLG	OPS+	vL+	vR+	bb%	ct%	Eye	G	L	F	h%	HctX	PX	xPX	HR/F	xHR/F	Spd	SBO	SB%	#Wk	DOM	DIS	RAR	BPX	R$
15	a/a	535	56	11	57	2	272			333	398	102			8	78	0.42				33		85				91	1%	100%					73	$12
16	TEX	568	59	20	64	0	266	20	254	320	419	101	74	106	7	78	0.35	49	21	30	30	91	84	77	16%	16%	119	1%	0%	26	38%	35%	-2.6	91	$12
17	TEX	616	64	20	101	2	253	21	256	323	422	100	80	104	9	77	0.43	47	19	34	29	102	99	87	14%	14%	83	3%	50%	27	33%	19%	-5.8	97	$13
18	TEX	536	61	20	77	1	258	24	260	317	436	104	97	107	7	76	0.34	55	18	27	30	105	108	80	20%	24%	92	1%	100%	23	48%	39%	2.8	120	$14
19	TEX	469	69	19	66	4	268	22	265	318	469	104	84	112	6	75	0.26	47	20	33	32	117	111	109	18%	21%	99	5%	80%	26	35%	42%	1.0	119	$14
1st Half		318	47	12	46	3	264	16	267	318	449	102	87	109	6	76	0.28	49	21	30	31	127	100	111	18%	24%	104	6%	75%	15	27%	40%	-3.6	115	$18
2nd Half		151	22	7	20	1	277	6	262	318	511	109	80	120	6	72	0.23	42	20	38	34	97	139	103	18%	15%	97	3%	100%	11	45%	45%	2.5	152	$5
20	Proj	**525**	**69**	**21**	**75**	**3**	**265**		**259**	**319**	**457**	**104**	**86**	**111**	**7**	**75**	**0.30**	**48**	**20**	**32**	**31**	**105**	**107**	**94**	**18%**		**95**	**3%**	**79%**				**7.0**	**81**	**$18**

McBroom,Ryan

Age: 28 Bats: R Pos: RF	Health A	LIMA Plan D	0-6-.293 in 83 PA at KC. Showed improved power in Triple-A; path to majors opened up after August trade. Didn't show much in small MLB sample, and was lucky to hit for such a high BA. There's not much to see here, as the low ct% more than offsets the decent power, and he's not at an age when we can expect much more growth.
Ht: 6' 3" Wt: 235	PT/Exp B	Rand Var -3	
	Consist B	MM 2023	

Yr	Tm	PA	R	HR	RBI	SB	BA	xHR	xBA	OBP	SLG	OPS+	vL+	vR+	bb%	ct%	Eye	G	L	F	h%	HctX	PX	xPX	HR/F	xHR/F	Spd	SBO	SB%	#Wk	DOM	DIS	RAR	BPX	R$
15																																			
16	aa	31	2	1	2	0	123			191	211	55			8	77	0.36				13		45				104	0%	0%					-20	-$3
17	aa	525	51	17	63	1	226			284	375	88			7	73	0.30				27		90				78	4%	21%					18	$4
18	a/a	487	50	14	48	1	258			297	396	96			5	65	0.16				36		98				95	8%	9%					-60	$9
19	KC *	540	72	22	55	1	266	3	264	336	460	106	99	94	9	70	0.35	50	26	24	34	82	114	44	0%	25%	81	3%	38%	5	20%	80%	5.1	59	$12
1st Half		275	40	14	27	1	261		261	319	485	107			8	74	0.32				30		124		0%	#VALUE!	90	3%	38%				0.5	141	$12
2nd Half		265	32	9	28	1	272	3	242	354	433	104	98	94	11	66	0.37	50	26	24	38	77	102	44	0%	25%	80	3%	38%	5	20%	80%	0.8	-22	$12
20	Proj	**315**	**37**	**9**	**33**	**1**	**258**		**242**	**324**	**397**	**97**	**105**	**92**	**8**	**68**	**0.27**	**50**	**26**	**24**	**35**	**69**	**87**	**40**	**18%**		**81**	**5%**	**26%**				**-2.9**	**-97**	**$8**

McCann,Brian

Age: 36 Bats: L Pos: CA	Health D	LIMA Plan F	Returned to solid No. 2 catcher status in 1st half, but limped to finish line, as plummeting xBA and HR/F were accompanied by August knee injury. Would still offer decent power if he kept playing, but announced his retirement. Fine career: 10 seasons with 20+ HR, seven All-Star appearances, and a World Series ring.
Ht: 6' 3" Wt: 225	PT/Exp D	Rand Var -2	
	Consist D	MM 0000	

Yr	Tm	PA	R	HR	RBI	SB	BA	xHR	xBA	OBP	SLG	OPS+	vL+	vR+	bb%	ct%	Eye	G	L	F	h%	HctX	PX	xPX	HR/F	xHR/F	Spd	SBO	SB%	#Wk	DOM	DIS	RAR	BPX	R$
15	NYY	535	68	26	94	0	232	18	248	320	437	105	104	104	10	79	0.54	36	17	47	24	110	120	131	15%	10%	65	0%	0%	27	48%	30%	9.3	143	$12
16	NYY	492	56	20	58	1	242	18	242	335	413	102	89	103	11	77	0.55	34	21	44	27	111	97	120	14%	12%	71	1%	100%	27	44%	41%	1.9	86	$8
17	HOU	399	47	18	62	1	241	13	261	323	436	102	98	101	10	83	0.66	41	17	41	24	99	97	98	15%	11%	77	1%	100%	26	50%	12%	5.9	167	$7
18	HOU *	240	23	8	25	0	204	4	218	276	327	83	83	89	9	78	0.45	28	22	50	22	74	66	74	9%	5%	78	2%	0%	19	32%	47%	-4.5	27	$0
19	ATL	316	28	12	45	0	249	10	240	323	412	97	65	102	10	81	0.58	44	19	37	27	112	78	98	14%	12%	64	0%	0%	26	46%	38%	1.5	100	$4
1st Half		171	17	8	30	0	267	7	264	339	466	108	56	115	11	83	0.72	43	21	37	27	115	92	102	17%	15%	68	0%	0%	14	50%	36%	6.9	185	$6
2nd Half		145	11	4	15	0	229	3	212	303	351	86	73	89	9	79	0.46	46	17	38	26	108	62	92	10%	8%	73	0%	0%	12	42%	42%	-2.0	22	$2
20	Proj																																		

McCann,James

Age: 30 Bats: R Pos: CA	Health A	LIMA Plan C	A career year, but sustainable? PRO: Made strides vR with as many HR (14) as past three years combined; jump in xHR/F supported HR/F bump. CON: 1st half h% was a fluke; ct% crashed in 2nd half; GB% spike prevented even more HR. BA doesn't look repeatable, but if FB% returns, there's 20+ HR potential at a scarce position.
Ht: 6' 3" Wt: 225	PT/Exp C	Rand Var -5	
	Consist D	MM 2123	

Yr	Tm	PA	R	HR	RBI	SB	BA	xHR	xBA	OBP	SLG	OPS+	vL+	vR+	bb%	ct%	Eye	G	L	F	h%	HctX	PX	xPX	HR/F	xHR/F	Spd	SBO	SB%	#Wk	DOM	DIS	RAR	BPX	R$
15	DET	425	32	7	41	0	264	9	254	297	387	95	126	83	4	78	0.18	50	23	27	33	90	82	63	8%	11%	103	1%	0%	27	30%	48%	1.6	43	$6
16	DET *	399	33	12	50	0	212	17	204	267	341	83	115	68	7	68	0.23	41	18	41	28	94	83	112	13%	18%	93	1%	0%	25	20%	56%	-10.9	-43	$1
17	DET	391	39	13	49	1	253	15	260	318	415	98	123	86	7	75	0.29	38	28	34	30	116	93	101	14%	16%	98	1%	100%	25	24%	28%	1.9	55	$6
18	DET	457	31	8	39	0	220	12	211	267	314	80	71	83	6	73	0.22	38	22	39	28	98	63	90	7%	10%	66	3%	0%	28	11%	57%	-9.8	-80	$1
19	CHW	476	62	18	60	4	273	19	249	328	460	105	113	101	6	69	0.22	44	24	32	36	95	113	89	19%	20%	82	5%	80%	27	22%	41%	19.6	19	$13
1st Half		229	36	9	28	4	319	11	264	376	514	119	130	115	7	73	0.30	44	24	32	40	86	114	89	18%	22%	88	7%	100%	15	33%	33%	18.5	96	$18
2nd Half		247	26	9	32	0	231	8	234	285	410	92	99	89	5	65	0.16	44	23	32	31	104	113	89	19%	17%	79	2%	0%	12	8%	50%	-2.4	-48	$9
20	Proj	**420**	**44**	**16**	**49**	**2**	**250**		**242**	**302**	**422**	**97**	**108**	**93**	**6**	**71**	**0.21**	**42**	**24**	**34**	**32**	**100**	**100**	**91**	**16%**		**84**	**3%**	**56%**				**9.1**	**-26**	**$10**

McCutchen,Andrew

Age: 33 Bats: R Pos: LF	Health F	LIMA Plan B	In the midst of another solid year, but torn ACL brought it to a halt. Given injury, age, and poor SB%/SBO, can't count on more than a handful of bags. But excellent plate discipline remains intact, and power skills are still above league average. If knee checks out in spring, he'll be an attractive high-floor option in middle rounds.
Ht: 5' 11" Wt: 195	PT/Exp B	Rand Var 0	
	Consist B	MM 3235	

Yr	Tm	PA	R	HR	RBI	SB	BA	xHR	xBA	OBP	SLG	OPS+	vL+	vR+	bb%	ct%	Eye	G	L	F	h%	HctX	PX	xPX	HR/F	xHR/F	Spd	SBO	SB%	#Wk	DOM	DIS	RAR	BPX	R$
15	PIT	685	91	23	96	11	292	33	268	401	488	124	127	121	14	77	0.74	38	24	38	35	131	132	158	14%	20%	107	8%	69%	27	59%	30%	32.2	200	$28
16	PIT	675	81	24	79	6	256	27	249	336	430	104	100	103	10	76	0.48	36	22	42	30	111	104	134	13%	14%	107	8%	46%	27	37%	30%	0.9	120	$16
17	PIT	650	94	28	88	11	279	24	276	363	486	114	150	102	11	80	0.63	41	22	37	31	114	113	109	16%	14%	91	9%	69%	27	52%	15%	15.3	185	$24
18	2 TM	682	83	20	65	14	255	25	250	368	424	110	114	107	14	75	0.66	41	23	36	31	119	105	125	13%	16%	101	12%	61%	27	44%	26%	11.8	140	$19
19	PHI	262	45	10	29	2	256	9	255	378	457	111	110	111	16	75	0.78	45	18	37	30	95	109	101	17%	15%	98	4%	67%	11	55%	27%	3.2	189	$5
1st Half		262	45	10	29	2	256	9	255	378	457	111	112	111	16	75	0.78	45	18	37	30	95	109	101	17%	15%	98	4%	67%	11	55%	27%	4.3	189	$5
2nd Half																																			
20	Proj	**553**	**80**	**20**	**66**	**4**	**265**		**256**	**370**	**456**	**111**	**120**	**108**	**14**	**76**	**0.68**	**41**	**21**	**38**	**31**	**111**	**102**	**118**	**15%**		**101**	**3%**	**71%**				**17.7**	**147**	**$18**

BRIAN RUDD

McGuire,Reese

Age: 25 Bats: L Pos: CA	Health	A	LIMA Plan	D+
	PT/Exp	F	Rand Var	+2
Ht: 6' 0" Wt: 215	Consist	C	MM	2333

5-11-.299 in 105 PA at TOR. Sprung up as useful part-time catcher after July call-up. Fluky LD% in majors won't last (22% in AAA) which should deflate xBA, while recent PX baseline and HctX hint plus ct% will be hollow at best. It's a low bar in two-catcher leagues, but with low BA and little pop, he still might struggle to reach it.

Yr	Tm	PA	R	HR	RBI	SB	BA	xHR	xBA	OBP	SLG	OPS+	vL+	vR+	bb%	ct%	Eye	G	L	F	h%	HctX	PX	xPX	HR/F	xHR/F	Spd	SBO	SB%	#Wk	DOM	DIS	RAR	BPX	R$
15																																			
16	aa	350	29	1	36	5	242			309	320	86			9	89	0.85				27		52				92	13%	45%					123	$3
17	aa	129	17	6	17	2	266			345	470	109			11	82	0.68				28		105				109	9%	62%					209	$3
18	TOR *	384	32	8	37	4	224	1	233	287	338	87	87	138	8	74	0.34	36	27	36	28	99	71	166	25%	13%	92	7%	63%	5	60%	40%	-2.3	-3	$3
19	TOR *	368	39	9	35	3	246	2	273	303	387	92	89	123	8	80	0.41	40	28	32	28	88	76	85	20%	8%	94	4%	100%	10	50%	30%	4.2	100	$4
1st Half		201	17	3	18	3	214		235	285	318	81			9	78	0.46				26		61		0%		95	6%	100%				-5.4	37	$0
2nd Half		167	22	7	18	1	283	2	294	324	468	104	88	123	6	83	0.35	40	28	32	31	91	93	85	20%	8%	94	2%	100%	10	50%	30%	6.4	174	$10
20	**Proj**	**315**	**33**	**11**	**33**	**4**	**247**		**261**	**308**	**417**	**98**	**80**	**102**	**8**	**80**	**0.44**	**42**	**22**	**36**	**27**	**82**	**87**	**77**	**13%**		**101**	**7%**	**73%**				**8.2**	**113**	**$5**

McKinney,Billy

Age: 25 Bats: L Pos: RF LF	Health	B	LIMA Plan	D+
	PT/Exp	C	Rand Var	+2
Ht: 6' 1" Wt: 205	Consist	B	MM	3221

12-28-.215 in 276 PA at TOR. Provided OF depth as he shuttled between AAA and MLB. Skills paint a pretty "meh" picture, as xHR/F questions true power ceiling, plate skills remain iffy, and he barely plays vL. Maybe 2nd half h% sticks and he doesn't kill your BA, but if that's the best we can come up with, it's best to move on.

Yr	Tm	PA	R	HR	RBI	SB	BA	xHR	xBA	OBP	SLG	OPS+	vL+	vR+	bb%	ct%	Eye	G	L	F	h%	HctX	PX	xPX	HR/F	xHR/F	Spd	SBO	SB%	#Wk	DOM	DIS	RAR	BPX	R$
15	aa	296	23	3	32	0	260			315	381	97			8	81	0.43				31		95				82	0%	0%					114	$3
16	aa	482	49	4	41	4	235			323	321	88			12	75	0.52				30		59				105	8%	37%					14	$3
17	a/a	477	61	17	59	2	260			316	460	104			8	76	0.34				31		115				112	3%	63%					145	$10
18	2 AL *	453	47	19	47	2	217	6	253	283	433	99	77	114	8	72	0.33	37	24	39	25	88	130	79	18%	18%	114	4%	62%	9	33%	44%	-6.9	147	$6
19	TOR *	423	51	15	44	1	225	8	248	294	426	95	81	95	9	73	0.36	39	21	41	27	95	111	99	16%	11%	126	5%	21%	22	36%	41%	-12.2	144	$4
1st Half		254	27	6	23	0	207	4	245	269	370	85	60	92	8	75	0.34	40	21	39	25	86	95	84	10%	10%	122	7%	0%	11	27%	45%	-16.0	107	$1
2nd Half		169	24	9	21	1	254	4	252	330	510	111	115	100	10	71	0.40	37	20	44	30	108	136	122	26%	13%	126	2%	100%	11	45%	36%	2.5	200	$10
20	**Proj**	**245**	**29**	**9**	**27**	**1**	**226**		**248**	**296**	**428**	**97**	**78**	**101**	**9**	**74**	**0.36**	**37**	**22**	**41**	**27**	**95**	**110**	**95**	**13%**		**122**	**4%**	**50%**				**-3.0**	**109**	**$5**

McMahon,Ryan

Age: 25 Bats: L Pos: 2B 3B	Health	A	LIMA Plan	C+
	PT/Exp	C	Rand Var	-2
Ht: 6' 2" Wt: 208	Consist	F	MM	4225

Finally got regular playing time after early IL trip (elbow). Flashed plus raw power (see xHR/F), but don't expect 2nd half HR pace to continue, particularly if he keeps pounding GBs. Shaky contact caps BA too, so while bb% gains and competence vL say he can hold everyday gig, a repeat seems more likely than a breakout.

Yr	Tm	PA	R	HR	RBI	SB	BA	xHR	xBA	OBP	SLG	OPS+	vL+	vR+	bb%	ct%	Eye	G	L	F	h%	HctX	PX	xPX	HR/F	xHR/F	Spd	SBO	SB%	#Wk	DOM	DIS	RAR	BPX	R$
15																																			
16	aa	513	42	11	64	9	247			316	403	98			9	67	0.30				35		114				99	13%	60%					23	$9
17	COL *	526	59	17	69	8	333	0	291	380	534	122	27	84	7	80	0.38	86	0	14	39	70	117	81	0%	0%	90	8%	72%	7	14%	71%	34.4	173	$25
18	COL *	436	42	13	49	3	243	4	242	292	410	97	135	85	6	68	0.21	46	24	30	33	85	114	99	14%	11%	88	6%	56%	21	29%	67%	-3.6	17	$8
19	COL	539	70	24	83	5	250	20	247	329	450	103	102	103	10	67	0.35	51	21	28	32	102	119	112	27%	22%	83	5%	83%	27	33%	48%	7.1	37	$15
1st Half		248	35	7	35	1	248	8	229	327	392	96	105	91	10	68	0.37	49	21	30	33	98	90	108	16%	18%	101	2%	100%	14	36%	50%	-1.9	-11	$7
2nd Half		291	35	17	48	4	252	12	259	331	500	110	101	113	10	66	0.34	52	22	26	32	105	144	114	39%	27%	75	8%	80%	13	31%	46%	7.4	85	$21
20	**Proj**	**560**	**64**	**23**	**78**	**4**	**261**		**251**	**327**	**462**	**106**	**120**	**101**	**9**	**68**	**0.29**	**49**	**22**	**29**	**34**	**95**	**120**	**107**	**23%**		**88**	**4%**	**75%**				**15.8**	**38**	**$18**

McNeil,Jeff

Age: 28 Bats: L Pos: LF RF 2B	Health	A	LIMA Plan	B+
	PT/Exp	C	Rand Var	-4
Ht: 6' 1" Wt: 195	Consist	D	MM	2355

A pair of hammy-related IL stints didn't faze him, as he put the juiced ball in play often (ct%) and with more pop (HctX). Sure, 1st half h% and 2nd half HR/F were over his head, but year-long xBA says he can flirt with .300, while xHR/HR gap was minimal. Had wrist surgery in Oct, so check spring reports, but this has staying power.

Yr	Tm	PA	R	HR	RBI	SB	BA	xHR	xBA	OBP	SLG	OPS+	vL+	vR+	bb%	ct%	Eye	G	L	F	h%	HctX	PX	xPX	HR/F	xHR/F	Spd	SBO	SB%	#Wk	DOM	DIS	RAR	BPX	R$
15																																			
16																																			
17	aaa	73	8	1	4	1	196			221	281	67			3	82	0.18				23		55				101	12%	100%					33	-$2
18	NYM *	613	85	16	68	11	292	6	270	339	464	111	113	119	7	86	0.52	39	22	40	32	96	92	103	4%	8%	141	8%	92%	11	73%	9%	17.1	253	$23
19	NYM	567	83	23	75	5	318	19	296	384	531	122	108	126	6	85	0.47	43	22	35	34	111	106	94	15%	13%	106	8%	45%	26	58%	0%	20.6	267	$23
1st Half		296	37	6	34	3	348	8	290	412	509	123	123	123	6	87	0.50	44	23	33	39	119	87	81	8%	11%	118	9%	43%	14	43%	0%	15.2	244	$21
2nd Half		271	46	17	41	2	284	10	305	354	556	120	96	131	7	84	0.44	43	21	36	28	102	128	109	23%	14%	94	7%	50%	12	75%	0%	7.9	304	$25
20	**Proj**	**595**	**90**	**21**	**77**	**8**	**303**		**287**	**368**	**497**	**116**	**105**	**120**	**7**	**86**	**0.49**	**43**	**22**	**35**	**32**	**104**	**96**	**100**	**13%**		**120**	**8%**	**65%**				**26.8**	**230**	**$27**

Meadows,Austin

Age: 25 Bats: L Pos: RF DH LF	Health	A	LIMA Plan	D+
	PT/Exp	C	Rand Var	-2
Ht: 6' 3" Wt: 220	Consist	C	MM	4445

Full-fledged breakout despite three-week IL stint (thumb) in April. It came loaded with encouraging signs: xHR and HR were in lockstep; mashed nearly equally vL/R; 2nd half contact/power skills sent BPX flying. Lack of SB success is our one nitpick, but he's young enough to turn that around. If so... UP: first-round pick in 2021.

Yr	Tm	PA	R	HR	RBI	SB	BA	xHR	xBA	OBP	SLG	OPS+	vL+	vR+	bb%	ct%	Eye	G	L	F	h%	HctX	PX	xPX	HR/F	xHR/F	Spd	SBO	SB%	#Wk	DOM	DIS	RAR	BPX	R$
15	aa	27	4	0	1	1	340			381	597	136			6	79	0.33				43		151				145	14%	100%					262	-$1
16	a/a	321	44	10	43	15	261			326	514	114			9	77	0.42				31		150				130	33%	74%					249	$12
17	aaa	306	43	3	33	10	236			291	336	84			7	82	0.43				28		66				89	20%	76%					70	$5
18	2 TM *	467	59	16	54	15	276	6	272	314	463	108	128	97	5	81	0.30	41	21	37	31	111	111	139	12%	12%	118	19%	83%	13	31%	38%	8.2	203	$18
19	TAM	591	83	33	89	12	291	34	271	364	558	122	109	128	9	75	0.41	34	23	43	33	118	137	139	19%	20%	109	14%	63%	25	44%	20%	28.6	237	$26
1st Half		284	34	12	41	8	291	14	256	366	516	118	102	123	9	74	0.39	33	25	42	35	114	119	121	15%	18%	119	17%	67%	13	31%	38%	8.8	170	$21
2nd Half		307	49	21	48	4	290	20	286	362	598	127	115	133	9	77	0.44	35	21	44	31	122	154	156	23%	22%	103	10%	57%	12	58%	0%	17.1	304	$31
20	**Proj**	**595**	**83**	**31**	**86**	**16**	**275**		**274**	**337**	**529**	**116**	**117**	**115**	**8**	**78**	**0.38**	**36**	**22**	**42**	**30**	**116**	**130**	**140**	**17%**		**113**	**18%**	**72%**				**24.5**	**253**	**$29**

Mejia,Francisco

Age: 24 Bats: B Pos: CA	Health	B	LIMA Plan	C+
	PT/Exp	D	Rand Var	-2
Ht: 5' 10" Wt: 180	Consist	C	MM	3133

8-22-.265 in 244 PA at SD. Premier catcher prospect got first extended look; results were underwhelming. Hit a ton of FBs, but just a few cleared the fence (deservedly so, per xHR/F). That typically leads to a lower h%, and xBA confirms the 2nd half BA gains were fluky. That all considered, the thin CA pool still makes him a potential high-end pick.

Yr	Tm	PA	R	HR	RBI	SB	BA	xHR	xBA	OBP	SLG	OPS+	vL+	vR+	bb%	ct%	Eye	G	L	F	h%	HctX	PX	xPX	HR/F	xHR/F	Spd	SBO	SB%	#Wk	DOM	DIS	RAR	BPX	R$
15																																			
16																																			
17	CLE *	382	44	12	44	6	278		320	319	447	103	44	52	6	85	0.40	50	30	20	30	138	91	49	0%		93	9%	73%	4	0%	50%	9.7	164	$11
18	2 TM *	507	44	12	56	0	234	2	234	269	373	89	71	104	4	76	0.19	54	16	30	28	98	90	74	27%	18%	88	0%	0%	6	33%	50%	-2.5	43	$5
19	SD *	311	37	11	30	1	273	7	248	312	467	103	91	103	5	77	0.24	36	20	44	32	94	105	94	11%	9%	136	3%	50%	21	43%	43%	5.9	163	$6
1st Half		152	18	5	14	0	249	3	263	288	457	100	116	75	5	76	0.22	39	21	39	30	84	116	84	9%	14%	136	0%	0%	10	40%	50%	2.0	181	$1
2nd Half		159	19	6	16	1	295	4	237	340	477	108	81	119	6	77	0.26	35	19	47	35	100	94	98	11%	8%	126	5%	50%	11	45%	36%	7.0	130	$10
20	**Proj**	**385**	**42**	**14**	**41**	**1**	**262**		**253**	**312**	**449**	**102**	**89**	**109**	**5**	**78**	**0.25**	**44**	**18**	**38**	**30**	**95**	**101**	**85**	**13%**		**118**	**2%**	**38%**				**13.0**	**78**	**$10**

Mercado,Oscar

Age: 25 Bats: R Pos: CF LF	Health	A	LIMA Plan	B
	PT/Exp	B	Rand Var	0
Ht: 6' 2" Wt: 197	Consist	A	MM	1525

15-54-.269 with 15 SB in 482 PA at CLE. Never looked back after May call-up. SB prowess carried over to majors (15-for-19), though PX history, xHR/F say power might be maxed out. Wild h% swing drove 1st/2nd half BA variance; xBA says to split the difference. Five-category production should stick, but more value in bags than bombs.

Yr	Tm	PA	R	HR	RBI	SB	BA	xHR	xBA	OBP	SLG	OPS+	vL+	vR+	bb%	ct%	Eye	G	L	F	h%	HctX	PX	xPX	HR/F	xHR/F	Spd	SBO	SB%	#Wk	DOM	DIS	RAR	BPX	R$
15																																			
16																																			
17	aa	504	66	11	40	33	265			305	386	93			5	75	0.23				33		72				122	45%	61%					24	$21
18	aaa	524	66	6	36	29	251			307	348	91			7	80	0.40				30		64				105	33%	68%					63	$18
19	CLE *	614	89	18	66	26	268	11	257	318	441	101	101	100	7	78	0.34	40	22	39	31	108	94	105	11%	8%	120	25%	78%	21	33%	14%	6.4	148	$24
1st Half		299	47	7	29	17	291	4	255	340	458	107	95	123	7	76	0.30	42	21	36	36	114	99	118	9%	9%	133	32%	76%	8	38%	13%	9.0	137	$26
2nd Half		315	42	11	37	9	246	7	261	296	425	95	105	89	7	81	0.39	39	22	40	27	106	89	98	12%	8%	113	17%	82%	13	31%	15%	-0.7	167	$22
20	**Proj**	**595**	**82**	**15**	**55**	**29**	**259**		**246**	**316**	**403**	**97**	**96**	**96**	**7**	**79**	**0.35**	**40**	**22**	**38**	**31**	**109**	**79**	**106**	**9%**		**119**	**29%**	**72%**				**5.3**	**110**	**$25**

RYAN BLOOMFIELD

Mercer,Jordy

Age: 33	Bats: R	Pos: SS	Health	C	LIMA Plan	D+
Ht: 6' 3"	Wt: 210		PT/Exp	C	Rand Var	-1
			Consist	A	MM	2133

9-22-.270 in 271 PA at DET. Missed nearly two months (quad), which is the only thing stopping us from just copy/pasting last year's box. Okay fine, subtle power uptick is worth noting, but lack of FB% caps any semblance of HR hope, and Eye tumbled even further. He'll be there in the end game; opt for someone with a higher ceiling.

Yr	Tm	PA	R	HR	RBI	SB	BA	xHR	xBA	OBP	SLG	OPS+	vL+	vR+	bb%	ct%	Eye	G	L	F	h%	HctX	PX	xPX	HR/F	xHR/F	Spd	SBO	SB%	#Wk	DOM	DIS	RAR	BPX	R$
15	PIT *	456	36	4	36	3	240	7	238	288	317	84	102	80	6	81	0.35	49	21	31	29	89	58	87	3%	7%	86	5%	60%	23	26%	52%	-9.2	30	$3
16	PIT	584	66	11	59	1	256	8	257	328	374	95	112	89	9	84	0.61	49	20	32	29	86	68	60	8%	6%	115	1%	50%	26	31%	15%	-2.8	129	$9
17	PIT	558	52	14	58	0	255	9	268	326	406	98	96	97	9	82	0.58	48	21	31	28	104	82	87	11%	7%	114	3%	0%	25	48%	20%	-4.0	152	$7
18	PIT	436	43	6	39	2	251	9	260	315	381	96	105	92	7	78	0.37	38	27	34	31	86	89	78	6%	8%	98	2%	100%	26	23%	42%	-0.9	97	$6
19	DET *	318	32	9	25	0	257	10	258	297	409	94	117	93	5	79	0.26	42	23	35	30	101	85	102	13%	14%	95	0%	0%	20	35%	35%	-8.4	85	$3
1st Half		117	11	1	6	0	196	4	218	256	284	72	95	75	7	80	0.41	44	16	40	24	116	56	118	5%	20%	87	0%	0%	7	43%	57%	-8.9	30	-$9
2nd Half		201	21	8	19	0	292	6	274	323	479	106	119	101	4	78	0.19	42	26	33	34	96	102	96	16%	12%	98	0%	0%	13	31%	23%	3.0	115	$9
20	**Proj**	**420**	**42**	**10**	**36**	**1**	**253**		**258**	**307**	**396**	**95**	**108**	**90**	**7**	**79**	**0.34**	**43**	**23**	**34**	**30**	**98**	**80**	**92**	**10%**		**100**	**1%**	**53%**				**-0.8**	**44**	**$5**

Merrifield,Whit

Age: 31	Bats: R	Pos: 2B RF	Health	A	LIMA Plan	D+
Ht: 6' 0"	Wt: 195		PT/Exp	A	Rand Var	-3
			Consist	B	MM	2545

Another strong R$ despite curious SB plunge. Maybe 1st half SB% turned his light yellow, as Spd shows no sign of injury/skill decline. BA profile remains rock-solid with LD% stroke, and there's enough pop to keep HR hole from getting too deep. Not a given he'll run wild again, but high-floor BA/SB sources like him are hard to find.

Yr	Tm	PA	R	HR	RBI	SB	BA	xHR	xBA	OBP	SLG	OPS+	vL+	vR+	bb%	ct%	Eye	G	L	F	h%	HctX	PX	xPX	HR/F	xHR/F	Spd	SBO	SB%	#Wk	DOM	DIS	RAR	BPX	R$
15	aaa	573	63	4	29	24	226			266	310	80			5	86	0.39				26		57				122	30%	70%					105	$9
16	KC *	621	76	7	49	22	252	7	257	293	364	89	120	88	5	77	0.25	45	26	30	32	111	81	87	3%	10%	124	21%	80%	17	24%	47%	-17.7	63	$15
17	KC *	665	84	21	85	35	291	20	274	323	469	106	106	103	4	85	0.32	38	22	40	31	105	94	111	9%	10%	131	30%	79%	25	44%	12%	8.8	200	$34
18	KC	707	88	12	60	45	304	20	269	367	438	112	131	103	9	82	0.54	35	30	35	36	111	85	100	7%	11%	107	28%	82%	28	43%	21%	26.1	157	$38
19	KC	735	105	16	74	20	302	17	277	348	463	108	106	108	6	81	0.36	38	29	33	35	108	83	95	9%	9%	159	16%	67%	28	54%	25%	12.5	200	$29
1st Half		382	59	11	42	11	301	10	291	351	497	113	107	116	7	81	0.37	37	32	32	35	115	99	107	12%	11%	162	20%	61%	15	67%	20%	7.9	248	$33
2nd Half		353	46	5	32	9	304	7	260	346	426	102	106	100	6	82	0.34	40	25	35	36	101	67	82	5%	7%	142	13%	75%	13	38%	31%	1.2	141	$26
20	**Proj**	**665**	**89**	**17**	**65**	**23**	**298**		**274**	**346**	**460**	**108**	**117**	**105**	**7**	**82**	**0.39**	**38**	**27**	**35**	**34**	**108**	**85**	**96**	**9%**		**140**	**18%**	**74%**				**27.7**	**175**	**$31**

Miller,Brad

Age: 30	Bats: L	Pos: 3B	Health	B	LIMA Plan	D
Ht: 6' 2"	Wt: 215		PT/Exp	D	Rand Var	-2
			Consist	B	MM	4213

13-25-.260 in 170 PA at CLE/PHI. DFA'd in April, traded in June, then morphed into fantasy hero in Sept (.327 BA, 8 HR). Power gains have some legs—xHR/F was in lockstep with HR/F—but not enough to cover for BA deficiencies, and issues vL curb PA ceiling. There's a chance he parlays this into 2016 repeat, but don't bet on it.

Yr	Tm	PA	R	HR	RBI	SB	BA	xHR	xBA	OBP	SLG	OPS+	vL+	vR+	bb%	ct%	Eye	G	L	F	h%	HctX	PX	xPX	HR/F	xHR/F	Spd	SBO	SB%	#Wk	DOM	DIS	RAR	BPX	R$
15	SEA	497	44	11	46	13	258	11	254	329	402	102	71	110	9	77	0.47	48	20	31	31	106	97	97	10%	10%	108	14%	76%	27	22%	41%	5.1	105	$12
16	TAM	601	73	30	81	6	243	25	268	304	482	107	92	108	8	73	0.32	45	19	37	28	104	147	116	20%	17%	100	9%	60%	26	62%	19%	-0.9	160	$15
17	TAM	407	43	9	40	5	201	13	214	327	337	89	90	87	15	67	0.57	47	17	36	27	105	88	94	11%	16%	120	8%	63%	22	32%	45%	-16.4	27	$1
18	2 TM *	283	23	8	30	1	236	11	210	300	391	96	91	101	8	64	0.25	40	20	40	34	98	114	150	12%	18%	107	1%	100%	17	18%	65%	-2.5	-10	$2
19	2 TM *	323	48	21	45	3	246	12	238	322	518	112	77	125	10	67	0.33	40	13	47	29	97	154	110	26%	24%	106	10%	41%	19	47%	32%	7.4	163	$9
1st Half		213	30	11	28	2	247	4	239	336	491	110	111	127	12	65	0.38	39	19	42	32	83	146	75	20%	27%	103	11%	31%	7	43%	29%	3.1	126	$9
2nd Half		110	18	10	17	1	245	8	251	300	569	115	58	124	6	70	0.23	40	10	50	25	109	169	128	29%	23%	103	5%	100%	12	50%	33%	3.1	219	$7
20	**Proj**	**280**	**35**	**13**	**35**	**3**	**237**		**228**	**311**	**452**	**103**	**80**	**107**	**9**	**67**	**0.32**	**41**	**16**	**42**	**30**	**100**	**124**	**116**	**19%**		**111**	**7%**	**62%**				**0.2**	**48**	**$8**

Molina,Yadier

Age: 37	Bats: R	Pos: CA	Health	C	LIMA Plan	B
Ht: 5' 11"	Wt: 205		PT/Exp	B	Rand Var	+1
			Consist	A	MM	1245

Has to slow down one of these years, right? Two thumb injuries cost him six weeks, but no signs of decay in BA, as ct%/LD% combo supports repeat. Power was another story, though xHR trend paints a less volatile HR picture, and xPX says there's some juice left in his bat. If age presents discount, you're probably good to buy in once more.

Yr	Tm	PA	R	HR	RBI	SB	BA	xHR	xBA	OBP	SLG	OPS+	vL+	vR+	bb%	ct%	Eye	G	L	F	h%	HctX	PX	xPX	HR/F	xHR/F	Spd	SBO	SB%	#Wk	DOM	DIS	RAR	BPX	R$
15	STL	530	34	4	61	3	270	7	253	310	350	92	79	94	6	88	0.54	48	20	32	30	99	54	79	3%	5%	77	3%	75%	25	36%	28%	0.6	86	$9
16	STL	581	56	8	58	3	307	13	282	360	427	107	105	106	7	88	0.62	48	22	30	34	111	75	88	6%	9%	77	3%	60%	27	48%	26%	16.2	146	$17
17	STL	543	60	18	82	9	273	19	274	312	439	101	113	96	5	85	0.38	42	20	37	29	126	88	118	11%	12%	75	11%	69%	26	42%	23%	9.9	139	$17
18	STL	503	55	20	74	4	261	18	279	314	436	104	111	101	6	86	0.44	39	24	37	27	140	92	130	14%	12%	64	6%	57%	23	57%	26%	13.3	163	$15
19	STL	452	45	10	57	6	270	13	282	312	399	94	112	90	5	86	0.40	39	27	34	29	125	67	108	8%	11%	65	6%	100%	22	41%	41%	0.2	111	$10
1st Half		267	24	4	35	4	265	7	284	292	375	89	92	89	3	87	0.28	41	27	32	29	128	61	105	6%	10%	52	7%	100%	14	43%	43%	-0.8	85	$10
2nd Half		185	21	6	22	2	277	6	280	341	434	102	138	93	8	84	0.54	37	27	36	30	119	77	113	12%	12%	93	4%	100%	8	38%	38%	5.6	163	$10
20	**Proj**	**490**	**52**	**14**	**66**	**6**	**271**		**275**	**319**	**416**	**99**	**113**	**94**	**6**	**86**	**0.44**	**40**	**25**	**35**	**29**	**126**	**73**	**113**	**10%**		**74**	**6%**	**80%**				**15.8**	**123**	**$16**

Moncada,Yoan

Age: 25	Bats: B	Pos: 3B	Health	B	LIMA Plan	B
Ht: 6' 2"	Wt: 205		PT/Exp	B	Rand Var	-5
			Consist	C	MM	4425

25-79-.315 with 10 SB at CHW. BA explosion driven by MLB's highest h%... since 1977. Made legit ct% strides, and xBA bump should help prevent a total crash. Missed three weeks (hamstring), which gives room for counting stat growth given xHR/F, SB% gains. Sure, "regression" is coming, but it might be softer than most think.

Yr	Tm	PA	R	HR	RBI	SB	BA	xHR	xBA	OBP	SLG	OPS+	vL+	vR+	bb%	ct%	Eye	G	L	F	h%	HctX	PX	xPX	HR/F	xHR/F	Spd	SBO	SB%	#Wk	DOM	DIS	RAR	BPX	R$
15																																			
16	BOS *	219	33	9	24	7	259	0	273	339	457	108	68	69	11	60	0.30	71	29	0	39	70	144	12	0%		129	21%	64%	3	0%	67%	1.8	51	$7
17	CHW *	583	78	18	52	17	246	7	213	339	405	100	85	106	12	63	0.38	46	19	35	36	91	105	112	18%	16%	142	18%	61%	11	36%	36%	-6.0	12	$15
18	CHW	650	73	17	61	12	235	24	213	315	400	99	81	104	10	62	0.31	37	23	40	35	85	123	113	12%	17%	129	12%	67%	27	26%	44%	-3.5	30	$14
19	CHW *	581	88	27	84	10	317	28	264	365	551	122	110	126	7	70	0.25	42	23	35	41	96	135	103	20%	23%	134	9%	77%	26	46%	35%	35.2	170	$27
1st Half		312	44	14	44	5	304	17	259	357	528	118	104	123	7	70	0.24	43	24	34	39	96	128	106	21%	25%	131	11%	63%	15	47%	27%	11.2	133	$26
2nd Half		269	44	13	40	5	332	11	270	379	578	126	117	130	7	71	0.27	42	22	36	42	96	143	99	19%	19%	132	7%	100%	11	45%	45%	21.4	207	$29
20	**Proj**	**630**	**89**	**24**	**76**	**13**	**270**		**242**	**338**	**473**	**109**	**97**	**114**	**9**	**68**	**0.31**	**41**	**22**	**37**	**36**	**91**	**122**	**107**	**17%**		**138**	**13%**	**70%**				**15.0**	**93**	**$25**

Mondesi,Adalberto

Age: 24	Bats: B	Pos: SS	Health	C	LIMA Plan	D
Ht: 6' 1"	Wt: 190		PT/Exp	D	Rand Var	-3
			Consist	B	MM	3515

9-62-.263 with 43 SB in 443 PA at KC. Separated shoulder derailed 2nd half, though breakneck SB pace continued despite orders not to dive. Already-shaky plate skills deteriorated even further, while raw power (xPX, xHR/F) also crashed. Opening Day outlook is in question, so while UP: 60 SB is in play, so is... DN: .240 BA, 10 HR.

Yr	Tm	PA	R	HR	RBI	SB	BA	xHR	xBA	OBP	SLG	OPS+	vL+	vR+	bb%	ct%	Eye	G	L	F	h%	HctX	PX	xPX	HR/F	xHR/F	Spd	SBO	SB%	#Wk	DOM	DIS	RAR	BPX	R$
15	aa	318	30	5	27	16	230			264	344	85			4	71	0.15				31		80				128	35%	71%					-11	$7
16	KC *	334	41	7	35	28	232	3	208	275	375	89	59	73	6	68	0.19	49	12	39	32	86	89	137	7%	10%	168	45%	93%	10	20%	80%	-5.0	17	$13
17	KC *	395	47	11	46	22	270	1	259	302	453	101	61	61	4	70	0.16	34	34	31	36	73	114	120	11%	11%	142	35%	81%	10	10%	70%	1.8	76	$17
18	KC *	417	62	18	54	40	262	17	254	293	479	107	116	108	4	72	0.16	41	21	38	32	115	132	130	20%	24%	134	61%	85%	16	44%	31%	10.3	153	$27
19	KC *	488	62	10	64	45	258	14	227	293	418	94	83	100	5	67	0.15	47	19	34	37	88	95	82	9%	14%	157	55%	85%	20	20%	50%	-10.2	11	$27
1st Half		321	40	6	44	28	267	12	239	304	438	99	92	103	5	70	0.18	48	18	34	36	94	99	88	8%	17%	149	48%	90%	14	29%	43%	0.0	63	$32
2nd Half		167	22	4	20	18	242	3	205	271	382	86	62	95	4	61	0.10	45	22	33	37	76	87	63	12%	12%	160	69%	78%	6	0%	67%	-7.4	-100	$18
20	**Proj**	**525**	**69**	**15**	**65**	**42**	**255**		**232**	**288**	**429**	**96**	**88**	**99**	**4**	**68**	**0.14**	**43**	**22**	**35**	**35**	**90**	**102**	**101**	**12%**		**157**	**49%**	**83%**				**2.8**	**60**	**$30**

Moore,Dylan

Age: 27	Bats: R	Pos: SS LF	Health	A	LIMA Plan	D
Ht: 6' 0"	Wt: 200		PT/Exp	C	Rand Var	0
			Consist	D	MM	3411

9-28-.206 with 11 SB in 282 PA at SEA. Broke camp with utility role; plugged holes all over the field after May wrist injury. Likely to leave holes in your roster, however. xBA hints that Mendoza-level BA is here to stay; xHR/F points to scant power despite all those fly balls; SB% should lead to a red light. A pretty easy pass.

Yr	Tm	PA	R	HR	RBI	SB	BA	xHR	xBA	OBP	SLG	OPS+	vL+	vR+	bb%	ct%	Eye	G	L	F	h%	HctX	PX	xPX	HR/F	xHR/F	Spd	SBO	SB%	#Wk	DOM	DIS	RAR	BPX	R$
15																																			
16																																			
17	aa	465	45	6	39	9	175			253	238	66			9	72	0.38				23		39				91	18%	50%					-91	-$3
18	a/a	433	51	11	42	17	250			294	429	100			6	80	0.31				29		106				118	30%	67%					177	$13
19	SEA *	313	33	9	33	12	199	8	202	270	362	84	98	88	9	65	0.28	37	16	47	27	75	104	100	13%	11%	117	40%	55%	27	33%	52%	-21.4	-7	$5
1st Half		166	17	3	15	7	183	3	188	255	286	72	86	82	9	69	0.31	44	12	44	24	78	66	97	9%	9%	97	39%	58%	15	27%	60%	-14.0	-89	$1
2nd Half		147	16	6	18	5	215	4	215	306	446	99	110	94	9	61	0.25	30	19	51	30	72	152	103	15%	10%	128	40%	50%	12	42%	42%	-5.5	85	$9
20	**Proj**	**210**	**23**	**8**	**22**	**8**	**215**		**228**	**301**	**411**	**96**	**104**	**92**	**8**	**71**	**0.30**	**39**	**16**	**45**	**26**	**74**	**112**	**101**	**13%**		**123**	**34%**	**58%**				**-4.4**	**91**	**$6**

RYAN BLOOMFIELD

Moran,Colin

Age: 27	Bats: L	Pos: 3B	Health	B	LIMA Plan	B
Ht: 6' 4"	Wt: 205		PT/Exp	C	Rand Var	-3
			Consist	B	MM	2035

On the surface, a near carbon copy of 2018, as fortunate h% masked down-tick in plate skills and fluky RBI total boosted value. Owns below-average HctX and FB%, and while xHR/F suggests a few more dingers, nothing points to a breakout. Only draftable skill is BA that won't hurt you; without power or speed, anything more depends on luck.

Yr	Tm	PA	R	HR	RBI	SB	BA	xHR	xBA	OBP	SLG	OPS+	vL+	vR+	bb%	ct%	Eye	G	L	F	h%	HctX	PX	xPX	HR/F	xHR/F	Spd	SBO	SB%	#Wk	DOM	DIS	RAR	BPX	R$
15	aa	399	36	8	52	1	268			328	399	101			8	75	0.36				34		97				88	1%	100%					62	$8
16	HOU *	521	41	8	57	2	218	1	263	275	306	79	0	50	7	68	0.24	47	40	13	31	73	65	76	0%	50%	92	4%	51%	4	25%	75%	-33.7	-94	$1
17	HOU *	333	37	13	43	0	244	0	259	291	415	95	186	145	6	77	0.29	50	20	30	28	94	93	74	33%	0%	113	5%	0%	3	67%	33%	-13.5	100	$4
18	PIT	465	49	11	58	0	277	13	265	340	407	103	70	108	8	80	0.48	45	26	29	32	97	78	91	11%	13%	103	2%	0%	28	43%	25%	1.3	110	$11
19	PIT	503	46	13	80	0	277	18	255	322	429	100	89	102	6	75	0.26	44	24	32	35	89	90	80	12%	16%	80	1%	0%	27	26%	37%	-8.2	37	$11
1st Half		246	26	10	44	0	271	9	264	317	459	104	82	106	7	75	0.28	43	25	32	32	95	104	82	18%	16%	81	0%	0%	15	27%	33%	-0.8	78	$12
2nd Half		257	20	3	36	0	283	9	245	327	401	96	93	97	6	75	0.24	45	23	32	37	83	76	78	5%	16%	88	2%	0%	12	25%	42%	-4.8	4	$10
20	Proj	**490**	**45**	**14**	**64**	**0**	**263**		**258**	**316**	**415**	**98**	**81**	**101**	**7**	**76**	**0.32**	**44**	**25**	**31**	**32**	**92**	**86**	**84**	**13%**		**93**	**2%**	**7%**				**-2.0**	**-1**	**$9**

Moreland,Mitch

Age: 34	Bats: L	Pos: 1B	Health	C	LIMA Plan	B
Ht: 6' 2"	Wt: 230		PT/Exp	B	Rand Var	0
			Consist	A	MM	4145

Season totals look mundane, including tepid xPX and HctX, but that obscures a 1st half power spike backed by surges in bb%, xHR/F, xBA. Then he missed two months with two different IL stints, and that likely hurt 2nd half output. Steady plate skills support solid BA and OBP. Pay for 2019; profit if Apr/May wasn't a fluke.

Yr	Tm	PA	R	HR	RBI	SB	BA	xHR	xBA	OBP	SLG	OPS+	vL+	vR+	bb%	ct%	Eye	G	L	F	h%	HctX	PX	xPX	HR/F	xHR/F	Spd	SBO	SB%	#Wk	DOM	DIS	RAR	BPX	R$
15	TEX	515	51	23	85	1	278	27	265	330	482	113	94	120	6	76	0.29	46	20	35	32	120	135	131	18%	21%	61	1%	100%	26	38%	38%	7.9	124	$17
16	TEX	503	49	22	60	1	233	25	252	298	422	98	108	93	7	74	0.30	42	21	37	27	110	116	111	17%	20%	61	1%	100%	26	35%	31%	-11.4	69	$7
17	BOS	576	73	22	79	0	246	31	264	326	443	103	91	103	10	76	0.48	43	20	36	28	120	118	119	15%	22%	60	1%	0%	26	35%	42%	-8.8	121	$10
18	BOS	459	57	15	68	2	245	26	252	325	433	105	95	107	11	75	0.49	43	20	37	29	96	116	121	13%	23%	71	2%	100%	28	39%	25%	4.9	123	$11
19	BOS	335	48	19	58	1	252	18	276	328	507	111	78	118	10	75	0.46	45	20	35	27	92	134	101	24%	23%	60	1%	100%	21	57%	19%	6.7	178	$9
1st Half		174	25	13	34	1	225	13	285	316	543	115	68	122	12	75	0.57	44	16	40	21	101	163	136	28%	28%	54	3%	100%	10	60%	10%	2.7	278	$9
2nd Half		161	23	6	24	0	279	5	267	342	469	107	84	114	8	75	0.35	46	24	30	34	82	104	64	18%	15%	79	0%	0%	11	55%	27%	1.8	89	$8
20	Proj	**455**	**61**	**22**	**72**	**1**	**252**		**267**	**326**	**482**	**109**	**88**	**113**	**10**	**75**	**0.43**	**44**	**20**	**35**	**28**	**98**	**123**	**107**	**20%**		**65**	**1%**	**90%**				**9.7**	**148**	**$15**

Moustakas,Mike

Age: 31	Bats: L	Pos: 3B 2B	Health	C	LIMA Plan	B+
Ht: 6' 0"	Wt: 225		PT/Exp	A	Rand Var	+1
			Consist	B	MM	3145

Superb 1st half was supported by HctX, xPX, with plate skills suggesting an even higher BA. Unfortunately, in playing through multiple hand injuries in Aug/Sep, all his peripherals sagged—along with playing time. His skills have been remarkably consistent, so health is all that stands between him and a 2019 repeat.

Yr	Tm	PA	R	HR	RBI	SB	BA	xHR	xBA	OBP	SLG	OPS+	vL+	vR+	bb%	ct%	Eye	G	L	F	h%	HctX	PX	xPX	HR/F	xHR/F	Spd	SBO	SB%	#Wk	DOM	DIS	RAR	BPX	R$
15	KC	614	73	22	82	1	284	20	274	348	470	114	114	112	7	86	0.57	40	19	41	30	117	112	114	11%	10%	65	2%	33%	27	63%	19%	13.5	189	$20
16	KC	113	12	7	13	0	240	5	301	301	500	109	114	106	8	88	0.69	42	19	40	21	133	134	135	19%	14%	70	5%	0%	7	71%	29%	-0.3	274	$1
17	KC	598	75	38	85	0	272	29	279	314	521	112	101	114	6	83	0.36	35	20	46	27	107	124	119	18%	14%	68	0%	0%	27	59%	15%	6.6	197	$18
18	2 TM	635	66	28	95	4	251	29	264	315	459	107	100	109	8	82	0.48	34	20	46	26	124	116	130	13%	13%	70	4%	80%	28	54%	14%	3.1	197	$18
19	MIL	584	80	35	87	3	254	31	278	329	516	112	114	111	9	81	0.54	36	19	45	25	117	127	129	18%	16%	76	3%	100%	28	61%	14%	4.7	256	$18
1st Half		328	51	23	49	3	275	19	293	348	569	122	125	121	9	80	0.47	33	23	44	27	123	144	146	22%	18%	74	4%	100%	15	73%	13%	13.4	285	$26
2nd Half		256	29	12	38	0	228	11	253	305	447	99	101	98	10	83	0.64	39	14	47	23	108	105	108	13%	12%	82	0%	0%	13	46%	15%	-5.1	230	$7
20	Proj	**595**	**73**	**32**	**88**	**2**	**262**		**270**	**328**	**500**	**111**	**110**	**111**	**8**	**83**	**0.52**	**36**	**19**	**45**	**26**	**117**	**115**	**124**	**16%**		**73**	**2%**	**78%**				**16.1**	**208**	**$21**

Mullins II,Cedric

Age: 25	Bats: B	Pos: CF	Health	A	LIMA Plan	D
Ht: 5' 8"	Wt: 175		PT/Exp	C	Rand Var	+3
			Consist	C	MM	0411

0-4-.094 in 74 PA with 1 SB at BAL. Marginal prospect floundered in majors, then AAA, before modest success at AA (.743 OPS, 20 SB in 51 games). Defense should earn him another chance, and his Spd/SB history is interesting, but GB tendencies will likely limit power and overall value. He's far from a sure thing.

Yr	Tm	PA	R	HR	RBI	SB	BA	xHR	xBA	OBP	SLG	OPS+	vL+	vR+	bb%	ct%	Eye	G	L	F	h%	HctX	PX	xPX	HR/F	xHR/F	Spd	SBO	SB%	#Wk	DOM	DIS	RAR	BPX	R$
15																																			
16																																			
17	aa	333	44	11	31	7	220			277	365	86			7	78	0.35				25		80				105	22%	49%					70	$4
18	BAL *	663	83	14	48	18	247	3	246	300	389	95	63	103	7	82	0.41	51	12	37	28	81	84	65	9%	7%	135	16%	82%	9	44%	44%	-0.6	170	$17
19	BAL *	580	68	9	38	28	188	1	211	249	279	70	32	49	7	80	0.41	53	8	39	22	52	47	18	0%	5%	121	31%	78%	5	20%	60%	-38.8	41	$9
1st Half		336	35	4	21	9	161	1	200	216	239	61	32	49	7	79	0.34	53	8	39	19	52	38	18	0%	5%	140	24%	67%	5	20%	60%	-29.3	15	$1
2nd Half		243	31	4	16	18	220		243	284	323	80			8	81	0.48				25		56		0%		108	39%	84%				-8.4	78	$20
20	Proj	**175**	**22**	**2**	**13**	**7**	**243**		**231**	**316**	**326**	**86**	**61**	**94**	**7**	**81**	**0.41**	**46**	**18**	**35**	**29**	**64**	**47**	**37**	**3%**		**117**	**22%**	**76%**				**-2.9**	**39**	**$5**

Muncy,Max

Age: 29	Bats: L	Pos: 2B 1B 3B	Health	A	LIMA Plan	B
Ht: 6' 0"	Wt: 218		PT/Exp	C	Rand Var	0
			Consist	F	MM	4135

Excellent follow-up to surprising 2018 breakout was cut short by broken wrist in Aug. While xPX, HctX, and FB% regressed and year-to-year totals look flat, much of that was due to post-injury sag. His power remains elite, and excellent bb% balances low ct%, keeps xBA from tanking. All signs point to continued mashing.

Yr	Tm	PA	R	HR	RBI	SB	BA	xHR	xBA	OBP	SLG	OPS+	vL+	vR+	bb%	ct%	Eye	G	L	F	h%	HctX	PX	xPX	HR/F	xHR/F	Spd	SBO	SB%	#Wk	DOM	DIS	RAR	BPX	R$
15	OAK *	345	33	6	37	0	226	4	196	293	361	91	69	90	9	69	0.31	32	13	55	31	108	109	209	8%	10%	74	2%	0%	17	29%	47%	-7.0	19	$1
16	OAK *	383	39	8	28	4	202	3	227	299	304	82	54	76	12	75	0.55	51	19	30	25	89	61	74	8%	12%	105	4%	100%	15	13%	53%	-20.0	14	$0
17	aaa	357	46	9	33	2	251			328	394	97			10	67	0.35				34		99				94	11%	23%					0	$5
18	LA *	517	80	36	82	3	262	32	267	382	571	132	124	137	16	68	0.60	34	21	45	30	118	192	176	29%	27%	77	2%	100%	25	60%	12%	41.0	273	$21
19	LA	589	101	35	98	4	251	31	262	374	515	118	117	118	15	69	0.60	38	23	39	29	110	146	150	27%	23%	80	3%	80%	27	48%	30%	27.4	189	$20
1st Half		334	52	20	57	3	276	18	275	377	541	123	125	121	15	73	0.63	39	24	37	31	111	138	137	26%	23%	85	4%	75%	15	47%	20%	20.8	219	$25
2nd Half		255	49	15	41	1	216	14	245	369	480	112	107	114	17	64	0.58	36	22	42	25	108	157	170	27%	25%	80	2%	100%	12	50%	42%	5.2	159	$13
20	Proj	**560**	**90**	**33**	**88**	**3**	**253**		**253**	**369**	**514**	**119**	**122**	**117**	**15**	**69**	**0.55**	**37**	**22**	**41**	**30**	**108**	**147**	**154**	**25%**		**81**	**4%**	**62%**				**31.0**	**162**	**$22**

Munoz,Yairo

Age: 25	Bats: R	Pos: 3B	Health	A	LIMA Plan	D
Ht: 6' 1"	Wt: 201		PT/Exp	D	Rand Var	-2
			Consist	A	MM	1431

Could not build on extremely modest 2018 breakout, and wound up in limited bench role. Walk rate and power metrics cratered, but SB% improvement and extreme ground ball rate are good to see—future fantasy value will come from his legs. A decent end game flyer in very deep leagues.

Yr	Tm	PA	R	HR	RBI	SB	BA	xHR	xBA	OBP	SLG	OPS+	vL+	vR+	bb%	ct%	Eye	G	L	F	h%	HctX	PX	xPX	HR/F	xHR/F	Spd	SBO	SB%	#Wk	DOM	DIS	RAR	BPX	R$
15																																			
16	aa	406	38	7	34	5	222			259	330	80			5	80	0.25				26		66				106	16%	41%					46	$2
17	a/a	463	54	10	56	18	272			298	407	95			4	81	0.20				32		78				104	23%	77%					82	$16
18	STL *	432	48	10	52	6	269	7	260	327	400	101	117	100	8	77	0.37	54	22	23	33	105	83	85	15%	13%	91	11%	49%	24	21%	46%	6.1	63	$11
19	STL	181	20	2	13	8	267	2	250	298	355	87	86	87	4	78	0.19	58	19	24	33	86	50	45	6%	6%	141	26%	73%	26	19%	58%	-5.7	22	$3
1st Half		74	9	0	5	3	319	1	233	338	375	95	104	92	3	78	0.13	64	15	22	41	82	42	32	0%	8%	132	24%	60%	14	21%	57%	-1.0	-30	-$1
2nd Half		107	11	2	8	5	230	2	257	271	340	81	68	84	5	79	0.24	54	21	25	27	89	55	54	10%	10%	136	27%	83%	12	17%	58%	-5.7	44	$6
20	Proj	**245**	**27**	**4**	**23**	**8**	**263**		**257**	**304**	**372**	**91**	**94**	**89**	**5**	**79**	**0.25**	**56**	**20**	**24**	**32**	**94**	**61**	**61**	**10%**		**129**	**20%**	**68%**				**-5.5**	**18**	**$8**

Murphy,Daniel

Age: 35	Bats: L	Pos: 1B	Health	D	LIMA Plan	C+
Ht: 6' 1"	Wt: 221		PT/Exp	B	Rand Var	+1
			Consist	D	MM	2155

Missed most of April with broken finger. Owners expected more upon move to Coors Field, but HctX and xPX reveal struggle to hit the ball with authority. Posted solid results vL, but they were h%-driven. Usually solid ct% slipped, too, and while that and LD% are still enough to make him a BA asset, the days of 20+ HR appear to be gone.

Yr	Tm	PA	R	HR	RBI	SB	BA	xHR	xBA	OBP	SLG	OPS+	vL+	vR+	bb%	ct%	Eye	G	L	F	h%	HctX	PX	xPX	HR/F	xHR/F	Spd	SBO	SB%	#Wk	DOM	DIS	RAR	BPX	R$
15	NYM	538	56	14	73	2	281	16	299	322	449	107	87	112	6	92	0.82	43	21	36	28	124	101	108	8%	10%	62	3%	50%	24	63%	4%	-4.1	222	$15
16	WAS	582	88	25	104	5	347	31	314	390	595	134	125	135	6	89	0.61	36	22	42	35	138	135	138	12%	15%	105	6%	63%	26	77%	0%	48.3	317	$34
17	WAS	593	94	23	93	2	322	18	307	384	543	124	109	127	9	86	0.68	33	28	39	34	124	119	120	13%	10%	86	1%	100%	27	63%	19%	27.4	252	$27
18	2 NL *	392	46	13	47	3	288	10	278	332	444	107	78	118	6	88	0.54	35	26	39	30	84	82	82	11%	9%	78	3%	100%	17	53%	18%	2.3	180	$12
19	COL	476	56	13	78	1	279	8	282	328	452	104	115	99	7	83	0.43	40	24	36	31	88	94	92	10%	6%	71	2%	50%	25	48%	28%	-2.5	163	$12
1st Half		221	24	6	42	1	282	4	267	330	450	104	119	99	7	83	0.46	36	23	41	32	94	89	102	9%	6%	87	2%	100%	12	50%	25%	1.3	167	$11
2nd Half		255	32	7	36	0	275	5	294	325	453	103	113	98	6	83	0.41	43	25	32	31	82	99	83	11%	8%	64	2%	0%	13	46%	31%	-0.9	174	$14
20	Proj	**525**	**67**	**15**	**80**	**2**	**291**		**283**	**338**	**460**	**107**	**104**	**108**	**7**	**85**	**0.49**	**38**	**25**	**37**	**32**	**92**	**89**	**96**	**10%**		**76**	**2%**	**71%**				**14.1**	**169**	**$20**

ARIK FLORIMONTE

Murphy,Sean

Age: 25	Bats: R	Pos: CA	Health C	LIMA Plan D+
Ht: 6' 3"	Wt: 232		PT/Exp F	Rand Var 0
			Consist C	MM 3133

4-8-.245 in 60 PA at OAK. 104 days on Triple-A IL with multiple injuries, culminating in Oct knee surgery. In between, a 2nd half homer binge turned heads, with HR/F rate (28%, all levels) exceeding any previous mark. HR will be capped without more FB, and mediocre Eye will limit him to an average BA, but that's still pretty useful from a CA.

Yr	Tm	PA	R	HR	RBI	SB	BA	xHR	xBA	OBP	SLG	OPS+	vL+	vR+	bb%	ct%	Eye	G	L	F	h%	HctX	PX	xPX	HR/F	xHR/F	Spd	SBO	SB%	#Wk	DOM	DIS	RAR	BPX	R$
15																																			
16																																			
17	aa	207	20	3	18	0	183			248	261	68			8	81	0.46				21		47				93	0%	0%					24	-$4
18	a/a	285	42	6	34	2	248			301	416	99			7	79	0.36				29		110				99	4%	100%					170	$5
19	OAK *	191	33	11	31	0	253	3	282	320	512	111	96	131	9	70	0.33	46	27	27	30	85	147	99	40%	30%	86	3%	0%	6	33%	50%	9.4	156	$4
1st Half		82	11	1	7	0	270		215	330	379	95	0	0	8	69	0.29	44	20	36	38	0	73	-36	0%		116	6%	0%	1	0%	100%	0.2	-48	-$4
2nd Half		109	22	10	24	0	240	3	315	313	615	122	95	134	10	70	0.36	46	27	27	23	85	203	99	40%	30%	74	0%	0%	5	40%	40%	7.3	322	$10
20	**Proj**	**350**	**54**	**12**	**49**	**1**	**251**		**255**	**323**	**437**	**102**	**94**	**106**	**8**	**72**	**0.33**	**46**	**22**	**32**	**31**	**96**	**109**	**89**	**16%**		**78**	**2%**	**50%**				**11.5**	**68**	**$7**

Murphy,Tom

Age: 29	Bats: R	Pos: CA	Health B	LIMA Plan D
Ht: 6' 1"	Wt: 218		PT/Exp F	Rand Var -3
			Consist D	MM 4211

Finally delivered on power potential, built on breakout vL that was part real (189 PX) but also lucky (43% h%). HR/F is backed by xHR/F, as he makes the most of FB despite lacking HctX, though plate skills will limit BA. Recent history vR suggests value won't increase proportionally with more PA, making him viable for deep-leaguers only.

Yr	Tm	PA	R	HR	RBI	SB	BA	xHR	xBA	OBP	SLG	OPS+	vL+	vR+	bb%	ct%	Eye	G	L	F	h%	HctX	PX	xPX	HR/F	xHR/F	Spd	SBO	SB%	#Wk	DOM	DIS	RAR	BPX	R$
15	COL *	453	44	19	54	4	232	3	228	273	433	98	57	187	5	68	0.18	33	17	50	29	142	146	213	25%	25%	96	9%	51%	4	50%	25%	0.0	86	$8
16	COL *	364	46	20	56	2	297	3	274	327	584	124	88	154	4	71	0.16	28	24	48	37	139	184	225	42%	25%	124	4%	60%	6	83%	17%	23.5	226	$14
17	COL *	173	16	3	14	0	196	0	192	233	320	74	37	0	5	58	0.12	40	20	40	32	47	104	40	0%	0%	86	0%	0%	6	0%	83%	-8.7	-139	-$3
18	COL *	345	29	13	40	2	214	3	234	252	415	92	89	87	5	60	0.13	31	33	37	31	73	154	85	11%	17%	103	12%	41%	13	15%	62%	-2.7	23	$3
19	SEA	281	32	18	40	2	273	15	241	324	535	114	144	87	7	67	0.22	34	19	47	34	87	150	133	22%	19%	90	3%	100%	27	37%	48%	18.4	107	$8
1st Half		118	12	8	18	1	268	6	232	297	527	110	112	107	3	63	0.10	28	21	51	35	94	159	168	22%	17%	78	5%	100%	15	40%	53%	4.7	33	$3
2nd Half		163	20	10	22	1	277	8	250	344	541	117	173	74	9	70	0.33	39	17	44	33	82	145	109	22%	18%	103	3%	100%	12	33%	42%	11.0	170	$11
20	**Proj**	**245**	**25**	**12**	**31**	**1**	**246**		**228**	**290**	**463**	**101**	**125**	**84**	**6**	**64**	**0.17**	**34**	**22**	**44**	**33**	**90**	**136**	**114**	**18%**		**96**	**5%**	**69%**				**7.6**	**-1**	**$7**

Myers,Wil

Age: 29	Bats: R	Pos: LF CF	Health C	LIMA Plan C+
Ht: 6' 3"	Wt: 205		PT/Exp B	Rand Var -3
			Consist A	MM 3415

Value rebounded, carried by speed and improved health, but struggles vR cost him playing time as the year went on. And while xPX and xHR/F show he still has power, plummeting ct% plus consistently subpar FB rate equals disappointing HR totals. 2019 is a good baseline, with slight risk of... DN: the short end of a platoon.

Yr	Tm	PA	R	HR	RBI	SB	BA	xHR	xBA	OBP	SLG	OPS+	vL+	vR+	bb%	ct%	Eye	G	L	F	h%	HctX	PX	xPX	HR/F	xHR/F	Spd	SBO	SB%	#Wk	DOM	DIS	RAR	BPX	R$
15	SD	253	40	8	29	5	253	9	254	336	427	106	109	103	11	76	0.49	48	17	36	30	115	119	107	14%	15%	111	11%	71%	12	50%	33%	3.4	146	$7
16	SD	676	99	28	94	28	259	26	263	336	461	108	110	106	10	73	0.43	45	21	34	31	100	125	111	19%	17%	121	21%	82%	27	48%	33%	12.7	149	$28
17	SD	649	80	30	74	20	243	27	242	328	464	106	105	105	11	68	0.39	38	20	43	30	114	138	144	18%	16%	126	18%	77%	26	46%	31%	0.6	136	$19
18	SD	343	39	11	39	13	253	11	266	318	440	100	112	101	9	70	0.32	44	28	20	33	120	137	121	17%	17%	95	19%	93%	19	42%	42%	7.3	123	$11
19	SD	490	58	18	53	16	239	20	220	321	418	98	114	94	10	61	0.30	43	22	35	35	100	119	121	20%	22%	114	20%	70%	28	21%	50%	1.4	-4	$14
1st Half		277	40	11	24	9	219	11	215	315	401	96	119	91	12	59	0.32	44	22	34	32	98	124	117	23%	23%	115	19%	75%	15	27%	53%	-2.5	-19	$13
2nd Half		213	18	7	29	7	264	9	226	329	440	101	111	99	9	64	0.28	42	22	36	38	103	114	125	16%	20%	114	22%	64%	13	15%	46%	2.6	7	$14
20	**Proj**	**504**	**59**	**18**	**59**	**17**	**248**		**236**	**327**	**433**	**102**	**110**	**99**	**10**	**66**	**0.34**	**43**	**23**	**35**	**34**	**108**	**117**	**124**	**17%**		**112**	**19%**	**76%**				**3.6**	**42**	**$19**

Naquin,Tyler

Age: 29	Bats: L	Pos: RF	Health F	LIMA Plan C+
Ht: 6' 2"	Wt: 195		PT/Exp F	Rand Var -1
			Consist B	MM 2231

10-34-.288 in 294 PA at CLE. Torn ACL will likely keep him out until at least mid-April, possibly mid-season. Found a few more fly balls, and xPX validates his mini power bump from "atrocious" to "below average." To be fantasy viable, needs to capitalize on HctX (more fly balls) and/or speed (higher SBO), but biggest obstacle is Health.

Yr	Tm	PA	R	HR	RBI	SB	BA	xHR	xBA	OBP	SLG	OPS+	vL+	vR+	bb%	ct%	Eye	G	L	F	h%	HctX	PX	xPX	HR/F	xHR/F	Spd	SBO	SB%	#Wk	DOM	DIS	RAR	BPX	R$
15	a/a	361	44	6	24	11	279			347	416	106			9	76	0.44				35		106				99	16%	77%					105	$11
16	CLE *	442	57	15	50	7	289	13	253	359	486	115	105	120	10	67	0.34	46	23	30	40	105	133	127	22%	21%	132	11%	56%	26	50%	46%	19.8	106	$15
17	CLE *	359	37	8	41	4	257	0	261	311	392	94	66	69	7	75	0.31	59	21	21	32	94	82	69	0%	0%	113	10%	46%	9	22%	56%	-14.0	45	$6
18	CLE	183	22	3	23	1	264	4	242	295	356	90	78	91	3	76	0.14	54	23	23	33	107	61	63	10%	13%	90	5%	50%	14	29%	50%	-5.4	-37	$2
19	CLE *	317	37	12	39	4	286	12	263	318	486	107	109	104	4	76	0.19	44	21	36	34	106	112	84	13%	16%	99	9%	67%	20	55%	35%	2.7	122	$9
1st Half		182	17	8	24	3	254	7	260	283	470	101	87	99	4	73	0.15	46	19	35	30	104	121	96	15%	18%	94	13%	75%	12	50%	33%	-3.3	104	$7
2nd Half		135	20	4	15	1	331	5	269	373	508	116	133	111	5	79	0.27	41	22	37	39	109	101	71	11%	14%	110	6%	50%	8	63%	38%	5.8	159	$10
20	**Proj**	**245**	**30**	**8**	**29**	**3**	**266**		**259**	**309**	**431**	**99**	**106**	**98**	**5**	**76**	**0.22**	**47**	**22**	**31**	**32**	**105**	**94**	**82**	**14%**		**103**	**9%**	**60%**				**-0.5**	**48**	**$8**

Narvaez,Omar

Age: 28	Bats: B	Pos: CA	Health A	LIMA Plan C+
Ht: 5' 11"	Wt: 220		PT/Exp C	Rand Var -2
			Consist A	MM 1035

Breakout season was fueled by 1st half HctX, xPX improvements, that gave way to smoke and mirrors in 2nd half, when fortunate HR/F rate carried him. Plate skills are good, and pair with consistent LD% to lay down a solid BA/OBP floor. Given historically poor HctX, expect power regression; what remains will still be above average for a catcher.

Yr	Tm	PA	R	HR	RBI	SB	BA	xHR	xBA	OBP	SLG	OPS+	vL+	vR+	bb%	ct%	Eye	G	L	F	h%	HctX	PX	xPX	HR/F	xHR/F	Spd	SBO	SB%	#Wk	DOM	DIS	RAR	BPX	R$
15																																			
16	CHW *	316	27	3	23	0	227	1	263	289	293	79	128	82	8	85	0.58	40	28	31	26	50	43	40	4%	4%	79	0%	0%	11	36%	27%	-9.3	46	-$1
17	CHW	295	23	2	14	0	277	1	257	373	340	96	89	95	13	82	0.84	44	28	29	33	65	41	27	3%	2%	75	0%	0%	26	23%	38%	2.2	36	$2
18	CHW	322	30	9	30	0	275	5	270	366	429	110	79	115	12	77	0.58	42	29	29	33	81	94	84	15%	8%	77	2%	0%	26	38%	35%	15.5	103	$6
19	SEA	482	63	22	55	0	278	15	263	353	460	108	91	111	10	79	0.51	33	26	41	31	81	88	94	16%	11%	81	0%	0%	29	41%	28%	25.1	111	$12
1st Half		267	39	11	29	0	288	8	263	363	458	110	118	108	10	78	0.53	32	28	41	33	91	83	103	14%	11%	78	0%	0%	16	31%	38%	12.8	96	$14
2nd Half		215	24	11	26	0	266	7	263	340	464	106	73	116	9	79	0.49	35	25	40	29	68	94	84	18%	11%	92	0%	0%	13	54%	15%	7.8	141	$10
20	**Proj**	**490**	**53**	**14**	**48**	**0**	**270**		**259**	**349**	**406**	**102**	**87**	**104**	**10**	**79**	**0.56**	**38**	**27**	**35**	**31**	**80**	**70**	**75**	**12%**		**80**	**1%**	**0%**				**18.7**	**15**	**$12**

Naylor,Josh

Age: 23	Bats: L	Pos: LF RF	Health A	LIMA Plan B
Ht: 5' 11"	Wt: 250		PT/Exp C	Rand Var 0
			Consist C	MM 2035

8-32-.249 in 279 PA at SD. Passable debut was consistent with skills displayed in minors. Has power potential and solid plate skills, but with excessive GB and few LD (18% career, all levels), batted ball profile has not played to his strengths. There's a path to success, but it's a narrow one and may take time. Deep sleeper.

Yr	Tm	PA	R	HR	RBI	SB	BA	xHR	xBA	OBP	SLG	OPS+	vL+	vR+	bb%	ct%	Eye	G	L	F	h%	HctX	PX	xPX	HR/F	xHR/F	Spd	SBO	SB%	#Wk	DOM	DIS	RAR	BPX	R$
15																																			
16																																			
17	aa	171	17	2	18	2	247			312	341	88			9	77	0.41				31		65				88	7%	65%					12	$1
18	aa	557	63	14	65	4	274			347	404	104			10	85	0.73				30		72				90	6%	45%					153	$15
19	SD *	522	65	15	62	2	257	6	261	321	420	98	88	97	9	80	0.46	53	17	30	30	114	91	89	14%	11%	48	2%	63%	19	16%	63%	-8.0	93	$10
1st Half		292	38	9	37	2	239	2	244	303	393	93	57	84	8	81	0.48	55	12	33	27	94	81	68	10%	10%	53	4%	63%	7	0%	86%	-9.6	89	$11
2nd Half		230	27	6	25	0	279	4	267	345	455	106	100	104	9	78	0.45	52	19	28	33	122	103	98	16%	11%	55	0%	0%	12	25%	50%	2.3	107	$9
20	**Proj**	**455**	**53**	**12**	**52**	**1**	**265**		**253**	**331**	**415**	**100**	**95**	**101**	**9**	**81**	**0.52**	**52**	**17**	**30**	**30**	**111**	**82**	**86**	**12%**		**50**	**2%**	**33%**				**2.8**	**77**	**$12**

Neuse,Sheldon

Age: 25	Bats: R	Pos: 2B	Health A	LIMA Plan D
Ht: 6' 0"	Wt: 218		PT/Exp D	Rand Var +3
			Consist F	MM 2103

0-7-.250 in 61 PA at OAK. Succeeded at AAA in second go-round—albeit in extremely hitter-friendly Las Vegas/PCL—earning him Aug call-up. Scouts see plus raw power, but low FB% over all pro seasons has hampered HR output. Even with fly ball growth, he'll need more hard contact to overcome dismal ct% and avoid being a BA drag.

Yr	Tm	PA	R	HR	RBI	SB	BA	xHR	xBA	OBP	SLG	OPS+	vL+	vR+	bb%	ct%	Eye	G	L	F	h%	HctX	PX	xPX	HR/F	xHR/F	Spd	SBO	SB%	#Wk	DOM	DIS	RAR	BPX	R$
15																																			
16																																			
17	aa	72	7	0	5	0	335			379	390	103			7	66	0.21				51		53				99	0%	0%					-142	$0
18	aaa	524	38	4	43	3	228			264	307	79			5	62	0.13				36		69				98	4%	74%					-187	$2
19	OAK *	601	78	19	84	2	263	1	260	319	428	99	68	94	8	68	0.26	42	32	26	35	100	102	102	0%	10%	77	4%	39%	7	14%	71%	-6.4	-11	$15
1st Half		320	46	9	44	2	262		237	329	430	101	0	0	9	70	0.33	44	20	36	35	0	104	-36	0%		96	5%	39%	1	0%	100%	-4.0	41	$15
2nd Half		281	32	10	40	1	265	1	254	309	425	97	67	98	6	67	0.19	42	32	26	36	98	99	102	0%	10%	68	3%	39%	6	17%	67%	-5.7	-67	$14
20	**Proj**	**315**	**33**	**8**	**37**	**2**	**233**		**224**	**281**	**373**	**88**	**75**	**107**	**7**	**66**	**0.21**	**45**	**24**	**31**	**33**	**88**	**92**	**92**	**13%**		**84**	**4%**	**59%**				**-5.2**	**-104**	**$6**

ARIK FLORIMONTE

Newman,Kevin

Age: 26 Bats: R Pos: SS 2B | Ht: 6' 0" Wt: 195

Health C | PT/Exp B | Consist B | LIMA Plan B+ | Rand Var -3 | MM 1445

12-64-.308 with 16 SB in 531 PA at PIT. Put aside April finger injury to provide sneaky good R$—especially in 2nd half, atop PIT lineup. Impatience mitigated by high-contact ways, while paltry xHR/xPX says inflated HR total unlikely to repeat. SB% growth not a given, but with lofty SBO, could provide nice BA/SB at reasonable cost.

Yr	Tm	PA	R	HR	RBI	SB	BA	xHR	xBA	OBP	SLG	OPS+	vL+	vR+	bb%	ct%	Eye	G	L	F	h%	HctX	PX	xPX	HR/F	xHR/F	Spd	SBO	SB%	#Wk	DOM	DIS	RAR	BPX	R$
15																																			
16	aa	255	34	2	23	5	261			324	340	90			9	89	0.86				29		47				110	12%	60%					131	$5
17	a/a	535	57	3	36	10	245			281	331	82			5	87	0.39				28		52				113	11%	74%					106	$6
18	PIT *	558	64	3	33	22	250	1	263	288	326	85	120	55	5	85	0.35	55	20	25	29	59	51	45	0%	6%	105	28%	61%	8	13%	88%	-13.0	80	$14
19	PIT *	565	65	12	65	16	302	7	282	342	435	103	95	110	6	87	0.46	49	22	28	33	80	63	50	10%	6%	150	17%	64%	26	46%	27%	7.2	204	$21
1st Half		250	25	5	30	5	310	3	279	360	453	109	92	120	7	84	0.50	54	19	27	35	83	74	51	11%	7%	128	12%	61%	13	54%	31%	5.7	189	$13
2nd Half		315	40	7	35	11	296	4	282	341	422	101	96	102	5	88	0.41	46	24	30	32	79	55	49	9%	5%	167	21%	65%	13	38%	23%	-1.2	219	$27
20	Proj	**595**	**70**	**8**	**55**	**18**	**280**		**274**	**327**	**385**	**96**	**110**	**91**	**6**	**87**	**0.45**	**52**	**21**	**27**	**31**	**72**	**54**	**48**	**6%**		**139**	**19%**	**65%**				**1.7**	**128**	**$19**

Nido,Tomas

Age: 26 Bats: R Pos: CA | Ht: 6' 0" Wt: 210

Health A | PT/Exp F | Consist B | LIMA Plan F | Rand Var -3 | MM 1001

4-14-.191 in 144 PA at NYM. If he's good enough for Noah Syndergaard, he's good enough for your fantasy roster, right?... Um, no. Woeful offensive profile didn't improve with off-season Lasik surgery, and GB-hitting ways, uninspiring plate skills, and lackluster power give little reason to expect more. Looking elsewhere is advised.

Yr	Tm	PA	R	HR	RBI	SB	BA	xHR	xBA	OBP	SLG	OPS+	vL+	vR+	bb%	ct%	Eye	G	L	F	h%	HctX	PX	xPX	HR/F	xHR/F	Spd	SBO	SB%	#Wk	DOM	DIS	RAR	BPX	R$
15																																			
16																																			
17	NYM *	409	40	8	62	0	217	0	286	279	336	82	0	103	8	80	0.43	25	38	38	25	81	70	161	0%	0%	75	0%	0%	4	25%	25%	-11.7	52	$1
18	NYM *	329	28	4	31	0	204	1	252	230	312	75	87	54	3	77	0.15	51	24	25	25	91	75	74	7%	7%	92	0%	0%	13	8%	62%	-11.9	13	-$1
19	NYM *	183	11	4	17	0	202	3	189	236	304	72	84	68	4	70	0.15	55	15	30	27	79	62	66	14%	10%	68	0%	0%	23	35%	57%	-11.1	-148	-$3
1st Half		119	7	3	12	0	242	3	193	260	335	79	138	69	2	69	0.08	54	19	26	33	95	52	86	20%	20%	90	0%	0%	11	36%	45%	-3.6	-181	-$3
2nd Half		64	4	1	5	0	121	1	195	190	241	57	34	68	8	71	0.29	56	10	34	15	58	82	37	7%	7%	68	0%	0%	12	33%	67%	-5.3	-48	-$4
20	Proj	**175**	**13**	**4**	**18**	**0**	**219**		**223**	**257**	**339**	**80**	**91**	**76**	**5**	**74**	**0.21**	**54**	**18**	**29**	**28**	**80**	**73**	**64**	**10%**		**70**	**0%**	**0%**				**-2.7**	**-98**	**$1**

Nimmo,Brandon

Age: 27 Bats: L Pos: CF LF | Ht: 6' 3" Wt: 207

Health F | PT/Exp C | Consist F | LIMA Plan B | Rand Var +3 | MM 4425

8-29-.221 with 3 SB in 254 PA at NYM. Lingering neck injury finally sent him to IL in May, costing him 3 months. Improved on elite bb% while upping FB%, and 2nd half xPX bump an encouraging sign. That said, xHR and xHR/F say power over-performed, and success vL driven by 52% h%. Mildly intriguing, even with BA and injury risk.

Yr	Tm	PA	R	HR	RBI	SB	BA	xHR	xBA	OBP	SLG	OPS+	vL+	vR+	bb%	ct%	Eye	G	L	F	h%	HctX	PX	xPX	HR/F	xHR/F	Spd	SBO	SB%	#Wk	DOM	DIS	RAR	BPX	R$
15	a/a	395	35	4	19	4	237			304	324	88			9	76	0.41				30		61				122	11%	37%					30	$2
16	NYM *	506	61	9	47	5	279	1	261	337	398	100	89	89	8	76	0.36	42	30	28	35	87	76	79	7%	7%	123	10%	33%	10	20%	50%	-3.0	57	$12
17	NYM *	403	42	7	33	2	221	6	225	335	353	92	70	116	14	65	0.49	43	24	33	32	92	99	106	13%	15%	101	2%	100%	13	31%	69%	-12.0	0	$1
18	NYM	535	77	17	47	9	263	15	254	404	483	123	103	130	15	68	0.57	45	22	33	35	93	148	114	18%	15%	145	11%	60%	26	46%	35%	24.4	213	$16
19	NYM *	295	42	9	34	5	212	5	227	356	386	99	155	90	18	65	0.65	39	23	38	28	81	110	103	16%	10%	96	7%	100%	14	57%	36%	2.2	59	$4
1st Half		170	22	3	15	2	191	3	209	334	309	86	137	76	18	64	0.59	38	25	37	27	74	82	87	10%	10%	91	4%	100%	9	44%	56%	-4.6	-56	-$1
2nd Half		125	20	6	19	4	241	3	252	386	494	116	197	116	19	68	0.73	40	21	40	29	93	147	130	26%	16%	112	10%	100%	5	80%	0%	6.7	230	$10
20	Proj	**525**	**74**	**18**	**57**	**10**	**243**		**241**	**376**	**440**	**110**	**106**	**110**	**16**	**67**	**0.58**	**41**	**23**	**35**	**32**	**88**	**120**	**109**	**17%**		**116**	**8%**	**81%**				**20.4**	**119**	**$16**

Nola,Austin

Age: 30 Bats: R Pos: 1B | Ht: 6' 0" Wt: 195

Health A | PT/Exp D | Consist B | LIMA Plan D | Rand Var -4 | MM 2311

10-31-.269 in 267 PA at SEA. Journeyman rode passable plate skills to solid 2nd half production after June debut, though xBA and MiLB history warn against buying into BA. Ditto for power, which popped up out of nowhere and outpaced xHR. No longer CA-eligible; best to let someone else buy into small-sample success.

Yr	Tm	PA	R	HR	RBI	SB	BA	xHR	xBA	OBP	SLG	OPS+	vL+	vR+	bb%	ct%	Eye	G	L	F	h%	HctX	PX	xPX	HR/F	xHR/F	Spd	SBO	SB%	#Wk	DOM	DIS	RAR	BPX	R$
15	a/a	502	34	1	34	0	205			266	263	74			8	78	0.37				26		48				94	1%	0%					-11	-$5
16	aaa	391	27	4	35	3	213			252	306	76			5	81	0.28				25		63				81	6%	73%					34	-$1
17	a/a	286	23	2	25	2	189			271	252	70			10	79	0.54				23		41				83	7%	50%					-6	-$3
18	aaa	246	19	1	23	1	212			276	283	77			8	75	0.36				28		56				82	3%	100%					-33	-$2
19	SEA *	482	60	15	55	4	256	6	232	322	417	98	117	100	9	73	0.36	40	19	41	32	85	93	90	14%	8%	114	4%	73%	16	50%	50%	-4.0	70	$10
1st Half		230	26	6	26	3	249	0	270	315	388	94	200	110	9	71	0.33	38	38	25	32	61	84	89	50%	0%	102	7%	66%	3	33%	67%	-6.5	7	$6
2nd Half		252	34	9	29	1	262	6	240	335	444	103	110	99	9	74	0.38	40	18	42	32	88	101	90	13%	9%	117	2%	100%	13	54%	46%	-0.6	122	$13
20	Proj	**245**	**25**	**8**	**25**	**2**	**231**		**233**	**304**	**395**	**94**	**102**	**90**	**9**	**75**	**0.38**	**40**	**18**	**42**	**27**	**79**	**91**	**81**	**12%**		**108**	**4%**	**74%**				**-4.4**	**33**	**$5**

Nunez,Renato

Age: 26 Bats: R Pos: DH 1B | Ht: 6' 1" Wt: 220

Health A | PT/Exp B | Consist B | LIMA Plan B | Rand Var 0 | MM 3225

Set career-high HR/RBI marks thanks to extended run in middle of BAL lineup. Aug/Sept bumps and bruises (ankle, hamstring, hand) possible culprits for late-season xHR/xPX slippage. Middling HctX and fly ball tilt say h% may stick in current range, capping BA upside. Really though, FB-driven power potential is the only allure here.

Yr	Tm	PA	R	HR	RBI	SB	BA	xHR	xBA	OBP	SLG	OPS+	vL+	vR+	bb%	ct%	Eye	G	L	F	h%	HctX	PX	xPX	HR/F	xHR/F	Spd	SBO	SB%	#Wk	DOM	DIS	RAR	BPX	R$
15	aa	402	47	13	46	1	243			283	398	95			5	82	0.30				27		100				82	1%	100%					116	$7
16	OAK *	546	51	18	63	2	203		271	240	347	80	45	0	5	76	0.20	75	17	8	23	26	87	-3	0%		86	2%	100%	3	0%	100%	-45.8	26	$1
17	OAK *	526	60	24	65	2	216	1	281	272	422	93	84	86	7	67	0.24	29	43	29	27	78	132	116	50%	50%	92	3%	59%	4	0%	75%	-17.3	58	$5
18	2 AL *	511	51	13	46	1	262	8	220	321	403	100	93	107	8	74	0.33	39	17	43	33	74	94	78	11%	11%	108	1%	100%	16	38%	19%	-0.4	67	$9
19	BAL	599	72	31	90	1	244	29	246	311	460	102	109	98	7	74	0.31	33	21	46	28	93	115	104	17%	16%	77	2%	50%	28	36%	32%	-9.8	96	$14
1st Half		307	39	18	44	0	235	18	249	300	480	104	116	97	7	72	0.28	35	18	46	26	101	134	121	19%	19%	81	2%	0%	15	40%	33%	-5.8	137	$13
2nd Half		292	33	13	46	1	254	11	244	322	438	100	103	98	8	75	0.34	30	24	46	29	85	95	87	14%	12%	80	2%	100%	13	31%	31%	-4.3	67	$15
20	Proj	**560**	**64**	**28**	**78**	**1**	**243**		**242**	**308**	**456**	**103**	**104**	**101**	**7**	**74**	**0.30**	**34**	**20**	**46**	**28**	**85**	**115**	**92**	**16%**		**90**	**2%**	**72%**				**-1.5**	**60**	**$16**

O Hearn,Ryan

Age: 26 Bats: L Pos: 1B | Ht: 6' 3" Wt: 200

Health A | PT/Exp C | Consist A | LIMA Plan D | Rand Var +4 | MM 4123

14-38-.195 in 370 PA at KC. Couldn't carry over MLB success (12 HR, .262 BA in 149 PA) from 2018, as abysmal 1st half set stage for June demotion. Is there hope? Struggles vL are severe, while GB/FB rate moved more in line with minor-league track record. Looking like a strong-side platoon bat, and not necessarily one worth rostering.

Yr	Tm	PA	R	HR	RBI	SB	BA	xHR	xBA	OBP	SLG	OPS+	vL+	vR+	bb%	ct%	Eye	G	L	F	h%	HctX	PX	xPX	HR/F	xHR/F	Spd	SBO	SB%	#Wk	DOM	DIS	RAR	BPX	R$
15																																			
16	aa	457	45	12	55	3	247			318	410	99			9	67	0.31				34		121				89	8%	34%					31	$7
17	a/a	523	45	16	53	1	227			292	393	92			8	68	0.29				30		110				91	1%	100%					24	$3
18	KC *	557	59	20	70	2	219	9	230	295	408	97	65	152	10	70	0.36	35	19	46	27	108	127	160	25%	19%	87	1%	100%	10	70%	10%	-7.2	90	$8
19	KC *	512	47	20	58	0	209	15	234	289	397	91	66	90	10	71	0.38	46	18	36	25	103	107	97	17%	18%	90	1%	0%	23	35%	43%	-17.7	63	$4
1st Half		274	22	7	23	0	189	8	214	279	327	81	76	84	11	72	0.44	50	14	36	23	90	81	86	12%	16%	96	2%	0%	12	33%	33%	-18.1	19	-$3
2nd Half		237	25	13	35	0	232	7	257	301	475	102	53	98	9	69	0.32	42	23	35	27	122	137	112	24%	21%	98	0%	0%	11	36%	55%	-2.7	130	$11
20	Proj	**315**	**31**	**14**	**38**	**1**	**221**		**240**	**297**	**437**	**99**	**59**	**108**	**10**	**69**	**0.34**	**41**	**19**	**40**	**27**	**108**	**125**	**125**	**18%**		**95**	**2%**	**50%**				**-3.0**	**46**	**$6**

O Neill,Tyler

Age: 25 Bats: R Pos: LF | Ht: 5' 11" Wt: 210

Health B | PT/Exp C | Consist D | LIMA Plan C | Rand Var -2 | MM 3303

5-16-.262 in 151 PA at STL. Bum elbow in April, then wrist injury derailed him after steady PA in July. Glaring bat-to-ball issues a concern, putting BA at risk when MLB 39% h% slides back. Surprisingly low power after near-elite 2018 levels and in minors. Needs opportunity and ct% growth, but hardly a lost cause. Low-risk, high-reward.

Yr	Tm	PA	R	HR	RBI	SB	BA	xHR	xBA	OBP	SLG	OPS+	vL+	vR+	bb%	ct%	Eye	G	L	F	h%	HctX	PX	xPX	HR/F	xHR/F	Spd	SBO	SB%	#Wk	DOM	DIS	RAR	BPX	R$
15																																			
16	aa	547	61	22	92	11	272			345	468	111			10	66	0.33				37		135				90	9%	83%					60	$20
17	aaa	540	64	25	79	12	224			288	434	97			8	68	0.28				28		131				94	13%	84%					76	$12
18	STL *	402	77	28	73	4	265	10	240	319	539	119	111	110	7	64	0.22	29	23	48	33	107	179	169	25%	28%	117	7%	79%	15	33%	53%	16.6	170	$18
19	STL *	337	42	15	38	3	236	6	214	283	413	92	85	98	6	62	0.17	38	23	40	33	100	111	108	14%	17%	91	5%	100%	17	29%	59%	-13.5	-74	$6
1st Half		209	25	10	25	2	218	1	215	257	402	88	22	104	5	61	0.13	41	23	36	30	105	116	100	13%	13%	96	6%	100%	8	25%	63%	-10.8	-89	$6
2nd Half		127	17	5	13	1	266	5	217	326	430	100	133	96	8	65	0.25	36	23	41	37	102	102	111	15%	19%	92	3%	100%	9	33%	56%	-1.0	-52	$5
20	Proj	**350**	**49**	**15**	**49**	**4**	**249**		**218**	**310**	**435**	**100**	**91**	**102**	**7**	**63**	**0.22**	**37**	**23**	**41**	**34**	**105**	**115**	**131**	**18%**		**98**	**6%**	**89%**				**0.5**	**-44**	**$12**

BRIAN SLACK

Odor,Rougned

Age: 26 Bats: L Pos: 2B	Health B	LIMA Plan B	Knee sprain may have contributed to slow start, and by Sept, team was dropping gauntlet about future role. His response? Best month: 9 HR, 138 HctX, .286 xBA. Success rate jeopardizes SB (note 2nd half SBO), and BA may not crack .240 due to boatload of Ks. But sustaining 2nd half FB% and HctX could lead to ... UP: 40 HR
Ht: 5' 11" Wt: 195	PT/Exp A	Rand Var +2	
	Consist B	MM 4225	

Yr	Tm	PA	R	HR	RBI	SB	BA	xHR	xBA	OBP	SLG	OPS+	vL+	vR+	bb%	ct%	Eye	G	L	F	h%	HctX	PX	xPX	HR/F	xHR/F	Spd	SBO	SB%	#Wk	DOM	DIS	RAR	BPX	R$
15	TEX *	588	76	20	77	9	273	12	277	316	486	112	108	107	6	83	0.37	46	15	40	30	106	126	102	12%	9%	132	14%	51%	22	55%	18%	13.3	235	$21
16	TEX	632	89	33	88	14	271	29	269	296	502	109	103	108	3	78	0.14	40	18	42	30	112	135	131	17%	15%	90	19%	67%	26	54%	19%	4.8	154	$25
17	TEX	651	79	30	75	15	204	23	239	252	397	87	60	95	5	73	0.20	42	16	42	23	109	109	116	16%	12%	92	21%	71%	27	30%	41%	-30.2	61	$9
18	TEX	535	76	18	63	12	253	19	238	326	424	104	99	106	8	73	0.34	41	20	39	31	122	107	121	14%	15%	102	20%	50%	25	24%	40%	2.1	90	$17
19	TEX	581	77	30	93	11	205	33	230	283	439	96	106	90	9	66	0.29	35	17	48	25	104	142	157	19%	21%	85	20%	55%	27	41%	44%	-17.8	85	$14
1st Half		271	36	10	37	7	187	13	214	259	370	84	93	81	8	66	0.26	38	17	46	24	87	114	122	14%	18%	93	30%	54%	14	29%	50%	-15.7	4	$6
2nd Half		310	41	20	56	4	221	20	245	303	500	106	116	100	10	66	0.32	32	18	50	25	120	167	188	22%	22%	87	13%	57%	13	54%	38%	0.5	167	$21
20	**Proj**	**525**	**72**	**28**	**76**	**10**	**231**		**239**	**299**	**462**	**102**	**103**	**101**	**8**	**70**	**0.28**	**37**	**18**	**45**	**27**	**111**	**130**	**140**	**18%**		**94**	**17%**	**57%**				**2.4**	**115**	**$15**

Ohtani,Shohei

Age: 25 Bats: L Pos: DH	Health C	LIMA Plan C+	Started year on IL (recovery from TJ surgery), ended it there, too (knee surgery). In between, showed modest gains in ct%, HctX, but rise in GB% kept HR total down, even as courage on basepaths grew. If plan to return to two-way duty holds, won't amass enough PA for monster counting stats, but can still offer HR/SB help in part-time role.
Ht: 6' 4" Wt: 210	PT/Exp D	Rand Var 0	
	Consist D	MM 4543	

Yr	Tm	PA	R	HR	RBI	SB	BA	xHR	xBA	OBP	SLG	OPS+	vL+	vR+	bb%	ct%	Eye	G	L	F	h%	HctX	PX	xPX	HR/F	xHR/F	Spd	SBO	SB%	#Wk	DOM	DIS	RAR	BPX	R$
15																																			
16																																			
17																																			
18	LAA	366	59	22	61	10	285	24	279	361	564	128	91	143	10	69	0.36	44	24	33	35	109	181	129	30%	32%	113	16%	71%	25	60%	28%	23.9	253	$19
19	LAA	423	51	18	62	12	286	19	276	343	505	113	104	115	8	71	0.30	50	26	24	36	123	120	111	26%	28%	141	15%	80%	19	42%	37%	10.2	152	$17
1st Half		194	25	12	35	4	299	9	293	356	552	121	115	124	8	72	0.33	52	28	20	35	126	131	106	48%	36%	121	10%	80%	9	56%	33%	9.3	174	$16
2nd Half		229	26	6	27	8	276	9	262	332	467	105	92	110	7	71	0.28	47	24	29	36	119	112	115	14%	21%	149	20%	80%	10	30%	40%	1.2	130	$17
20	**Proj**	**350**	**49**	**18**	**54**	**10**	**285**		**275**	**347**	**534**	**119**	**98**	**126**	**8**	**70**	**0.31**	**47**	**25**	**28**	**35**	**117**	**140**	**118**	**29%**		**131**	**16%**	**76%**				**17.0**	**176**	**$18**

Olson,Matt

Age: 26 Bats: L Pos: 1B	Health B	LIMA Plan B	36-91-.267 in 547 PA at OAK. To his owners' relief, shrugged off idea that full recovery from hamate surgery requires time, as mashing resumed unabated after mid-May return. Makes enough contact for BA not to kill you, and FB%, xPX say you can take power to the bank. With health, first of several 40 HR seasons seems like a good bet.
Ht: 6' 5" Wt: 230	PT/Exp B	Rand Var 0	
	Consist B	MM 4235	

Yr	Tm	PA	R	HR	RBI	SB	BA	xHR	xBA	OBP	SLG	OPS+	vL+	vR+	bb%	ct%	Eye	G	L	F	h%	HctX	PX	xPX	HR/F	xHR/F	Spd	SBO	SB%	#Wk	DOM	DIS	RAR	BPX	R$
15	aa	545	62	12	57	4	217			331	366	97			15	68	0.54				29		123				81	4%	78%					76	$5
16	OAK *	551	61	13	51	1	207	0	203	302	359	90	0	70	12	71	0.46	47	6	47	26	51	110	-9	0%	0%	89	1%	100%	4	50%	25%	-20.6	69	$0
17	OAK *	545	78	41	93	2	245	16	257	325	536	116	101	143	11	69	0.38	38	16	46	27	113	168	178	41%	28%	79	2%	100%	16	44%	44%	7.8	176	$16
18	OAK	660	85	29	84	2	247	37	247	335	453	109	97	114	11	72	0.43	36	21	43	29	125	132	140	16%	21%	82	2%	67%	28	50%	25%	10.1	137	$17
19	OAK *	570	75	37	92	0	262	38	209	330	531	114	100	127	9	72	0.37	31	24	45	29	125	145	161	24%	25%	74	0%	0%	22	59%	23%	16.7	170	$18
1st Half		239	31	17	33	0	236	19	261	309	518	110	139	110	10	74	0.41	30	19	51	24	136	145	173	23%	28%	79	0%	0%	10	70%	10%	1.2	211	$8
2nd Half		331	44	20	59	0	281	20	274	363	541	119	80	140	9	71	0.34	32	27	40	33	118	145	154	24%	24%	81	0%	0%	12	50%	33%	12.1	159	$25
20	**Proj**	**595**	**79**	**40**	**100**	**1**	**260**		**264**	**348**	**538**	**119**	**100**	**127**	**10**	**71**	**0.40**	**34**	**22**	**44**	**29**	**123**	**152**	**157**	**24%**		**76**	**1%**	**79%**				**25.9**	**146**	**$23**

Osuna,Jose

Age: 27 Bats: R Pos: 1B RF	Health B	LIMA Plan C+	10-36-.264 in 285 PA at PIT. Rough Sept (.541 OPS) put damper on under-the-radar intrigue built over prior three months, as FB% jump fizzled, power went back into hibernation. Aside from new success vR, what's left looks too akin to 2018 to inspire faith. Could he recapture June-Aug groove? Sure, but don't spend too much to find out.
Ht: 6' 2" Wt: 240	PT/Exp D	Rand Var 0	
	Consist A	MM 3143	

Yr	Tm	PA	R	HR	RBI	SB	BA	xHR	xBA	OBP	SLG	OPS+	vL+	vR+	bb%	ct%	Eye	G	L	F	h%	HctX	PX	xPX	HR/F	xHR/F	Spd	SBO	SB%	#Wk	DOM	DIS	RAR	BPX	R$
15	aa	337	37	6	42	5	253			283	371	91			4	80	0.21				30		83				91	12%	59%					62	$7
16	a/a	505	53	11	60	3	254			300	408	96			6	82	0.37				29		97				93	7%	37%					134	$8
17	PIT *	267	36	7	31	1	231	7	283	270	416	92	98	87	5	80	0.27	53	18	29	26	96	106	65	14%	14%	95	5%	43%	25	56%	36%	-11.5	139	$2
18	PIT *	437	48	10	56	4	258	3	272	303	404	98	116	61	6	80	0.33	47	24	29	30	94	96	79	12%	12%	67	8%	51%	15	40%	40%	-3.5	103	$10
19	PIT *	362	51	11	46	2	256	10	273	308	442	100	80	113	7	78	0.34	47	21	32	30	92	106	95	14%	14%	81	2%	100%	19	53%	26%	-6.7	133	$7
1st Half		127	19	5	22	2	258	4	252	316	498	109	119	151	8	68	0.26	36	21	42	34	92	151	175	29%	29%	86	6%	100%	6	83%	17%	0.9	130	$3
2nd Half		235	32	6	24	0	255	6	276	298	412	94	70	106	6	83	0.42	49	21	30	28	96	86	80	11%	11%	81	0%	0%	13	38%	31%	-5.9	152	$9
20	**Proj**	**350**	**46**	**13**	**45**	**2**	**252**		**277**	**302**	**453**	**102**	**102**	**100**	**6**	**79**	**0.31**	**47**	**21**	**32**	**29**	**95**	**111**	**96**	**15%**		**82**	**6%**	**66%**				**0.2**	**152**	**$10**

Ozuna,Marcell

Age: 29 Bats: R Pos: LF	Health B	LIMA Plan B	1st half power surge was fueled by unsustainable monster April (36% HR/F); conversely, forgive late struggles due to 15% hit rate in Sept. Gave back 2018's ct% gains, but HctX has held steady, and xHR, xHR/F encouraging. Spd makes rise in SBO look dubious, but he's not getting caught... yet. Bid to $20 confidently, but not much further.
Ht: 6' 1" Wt: 225	PT/Exp A	Rand Var +4	
	Consist C	MM 3245	

Yr	Tm	PA	R	HR	RBI	SB	BA	xHR	xBA	OBP	SLG	OPS+	vL+	vR+	bb%	ct%	Eye	G	L	F	h%	HctX	PX	xPX	HR/F	xHR/F	Spd	SBO	SB%	#Wk	DOM	DIS	RAR	BPX	R$
15	MIA *	623	64	14	53	3	263	15	255	310	402	99	122	89	6	77	0.29	48	21	31	32	115	102	106	9%	14%	79	4%	48%	23	30%	43%	-8.1	70	$12
16	MIA	608	75	23	76	0	266	24	262	321	452	105	125	98	7	79	0.37	44	20	37	30	121	105	121	14%	15%	135	2%	0%	26	38%	35%	4.2	166	$14
17	MIA	679	93	37	124	1	312	34	275	376	548	124	107	126	9	77	0.44	47	19	34	36	121	130	106	23%	22%	90	2%	25%	27	52%	22%	37.6	176	$31
18	STL	627	69	23	88	3	280	33	248	325	433	105	125	98	6	81	0.35	47	18	35	31	135	81	112	14%	20%	95	2%	100%	26	38%	38%	6.5	107	$21
19	STL	549	80	29	89	12	243	31	275	330	474	107	98	108	11	76	0.54	41	23	35	26	127	118	119	22%	24%	77	11%	86%	24	42%	29%	1.9	178	$19
1st Half		326	52	20	62	8	259	22	279	331	515	113	83	118	10	77	0.46	40	22	38	27	129	130	133	23%		82	13%	89%	14	50%	21%	6.8	211	$28
2nd Half		223	28	9	27	4	219	9	270	327	411	97	116	93	14	76	0.67	44	25	31	24	124	99	97	20%		79	9%	80%	10	30%	40%	-4.3	137	$5
20	**Proj**	**595**	**77**	**29**	**93**	**8**	**261**		**267**	**334**	**471**	**108**	**114**	**106**	**10**	**78**	**0.49**	**44**	**21**	**35**	**29**	**127**	**106**	**111**	**20%**		**86**	**7%**	**81%**				**14.5**	**155**	**$23**

Pache,Cristian

Age: 21 Bats: R Pos: OF	Health A	LIMA Plan D	Fast-rising ATL prospect's glove may already be ready, but offensive refinement needed. Second tour of AA went better, but still featured less-than-ideal ct%, and SB technique needs work. Held his own at AAA (.748 OPS in 105 PA), where he'll likely start 2020. If he can smooth out rough edges, he'll be a potential SB boon.
Ht: 6' 2" Wt: 185	PT/Exp F	Rand Var 0	
	Consist C	MM 2223	

Yr	Tm	PA	R	HR	RBI	SB	BA	xHR	xBA	OBP	SLG	OPS+	vL+	vR+	bb%	ct%	Eye	G	L	F	h%	HctX	PX	xPX	HR/F	xHR/F	Spd	SBO	SB%	#Wk	DOM	DIS	RAR	BPX	R$
15																																			
16																																			
17																																			
18	aa	108	9	1	7	0	256			287	329	85			4	72	0.16				35		49				116	8%	0%					-83	-$1
19	a/a	528	62	11	60	8	273			330	448	103			8	74	0.33				35		103				117	16%	41%					119	$13
1st Half		313	46	11	53	8	307			367	545	122			9	75	0.38				37		131				143	24%	43%				17.6	252	$25
2nd Half		218	21	1	13	1	246			306	361	88			8	73	0.32				33		77				138	4%	48%				-4.3	56	-$4
20	**Proj**	**280**	**29**	**6**	**25**	**2**	**270**		**249**	**319**	**422**	**100**	**99**	**99**	**7**	**73**	**0.27**	**48**	**22**	**30**	**35**	**91**	**88**		**10%**		**146**	**11%**	**32%**				**-2.3**	**22**	**$7**

Panik,Joe

Age: 29 Bats: L Pos: 2B	Health C	LIMA Plan D+	When Giants DFA'd him, looked like it was time to push, well... you know... but he landed new gig, kept doing his thing. Unfortunately, that "thing" involves excellent contact and nothing else, though xPX says he could pick up HR pace a bit, especially in a friendlier park. Still, even with regular PA, he'd be no more than an average Joe.
Ht: 6' 1" Wt: 200	PT/Exp B	Rand Var +2	
	Consist C	MM 0341	

Yr	Tm	PA	R	HR	RBI	SB	BA	xHR	xBA	OBP	SLG	OPS+	vL+	vR+	bb%	ct%	Eye	G	L	F	h%	HctX	PX	xPX	HR/F	xHR/F	Spd	SBO	SB%	#Wk	DOM	DIS	RAR	BPX	R$
15	SF	432	59	8	37	3	312	7	288	378	455	116	106	117	9	89	0.90	43	23	34	33	115	91	89	7%	6%	106	4%	60%	18	72%	11%	21.5	216	$15
16	SF	526	67	10	62	5	239	14	270	315	379	95	80	98	10	90	1.06	45	18	37	25	94	73	87	6%	9%	122	4%	100%	24	67%	13%	-11.3	214	$8
17	SF	573	60	10	53	4	288	10	282	347	421	103	92	106	8	89	0.85	44	22	34	31	94	70	78	6%	6%	116	3%	80%	27	59%	15%	3.0	203	$14
18	SF	392	38	4	24	4	254	6	271	307	332	88	68	97	7	92	0.87	48	23	30	27	105	44	56	4%	6%	97	6%	67%	21	43%	10%	-8.7	153	$5
19	2 NL	491	50	5	39	4	244	8	267	315	336	86	98	83	9	89	0.91	43	23	34	26	114	47	93	4%	6%	96	5%	67%	28	50%	21%	-13.3	159	$5
1st Half		304	26	3	22	3	232	6	263	313	326	85	98	81	10	88	0.94	42	23	35	25	118	50	101	4%	7%	90	7%	60%	15	47%	27%	-10.9	152	$3
2nd Half		187	24	2	17	1	263	2	275	319	351	88	102	85	7	91	0.87	46	23	31	28	106	43	81	4%	4%	107	2%	100%	13	54%	15%	-3.9	178	$6
20	**Proj**	**245**	**27**	**3**	**20**	**2**	**260**		**272**	**321**	**358**	**91**	**88**	**92**	**8**	**90**	**0.88**	**45**	**23**	**33**	**28**	**106**	**49**	**79**	**5%**		**105**	**4%**	**72%**				**-1.2**	**149**	**$5**

KRISTOPHER OLSON

Parra,Gerardo

Age: 33 Bats: L Pos: RF LF | Ht: 5' 11" Wt: 210

Health B | PT/Exp C | Consist C | LIMA Plan D+ | Rand Var +4 | MM 1241

Managed to extend career after early-season DFA, but this skill set, while mostly stable, is as boring as they come. Rebound of unlucky hit rate might help OBP recover, though Spd and SB% suggest SBO unwarranted, so helpful handful of SB could dry up nonetheless. If he can't recapture HctX of old, next DFA may be it. UPDATE: Signed with JPN

Yr Tm	PA	R	HR	RBI	SB	BA	xHR	xBA	OBP	SLG	OPS+	vL+	vR+	bb%	ct%	Eye	G	L	F	h%	HctX	PX	xPX	HR/F	xHR/F	Spd	SBO	SB%	#Wk	DOM	DIS	RAR	BPX	R$
15 2 TM	589	83	14	51	14	291	13	287	328	452	109	91	111	5	83	0.30	47	24	29	33	109	104	97	11%	10%	113	14%	78%	27	44%	22%	8.5	165	$23
16 COL *	408	47	7	41	6	247	11	271	265	384	88	86	91	2	79	0.12	55	19	26	29	103	90	100	9%	14%	92	14%	60%	19	53%	37%	-15.1	69	$6
17 COL	425	56	10	71	2	309	8	277	341	452	106	107	104	5	83	0.30	47	23	30	35	117	83	113	10%	8%	76	7%	29%	24	42%	29%	1.9	97	$16
18 COL	443	52	6	53	11	284	8	254	342	372	99	71	106	7	81	0.43	47	25	28	34	102	55	96	7%	9%	68	12%	73%	28	25%	54%	-1.6	20	$14
19 2 NL	301	38	9	48	8	234	8	267	293	391	91	85	92	6	78	0.32	47	23	30	27	85	84	93	14%	13%	65	19%	73%	28	43%	36%	-12.8	56	$7
1st Half	177	18	5	21	5	217	4	258	282	354	85	97	81	6	77	0.30	45	25	30	25	90	74	104	14%	11%	65	21%	71%	15	47%	40%	-10.6	7	$4
2nd Half	124	20	4	27	3	257	4	280	309	442	99	67	108	7	81	0.36	50	20	30	29	78	96	77	15%	15%	74	16%	75%	13	38%	31%	-1.8	133	$11
20 Proj																																		

Pederson,Joc

Age: 28 Bats: L Pos: LF RF 1B | Ht: 6' 1" Wt: 220

Health A | PT/Exp C | Consist B | LIMA Plan B | Rand Var +1 | MM 4135

We now know who he is: a premium power source in perpetual need of a platoon partner. Batting average may never live up to promise of xBA, as hit rate seems to be settling in mid-20s. But he lofts plenty of fly balls that neither shifts nor stadium walls can contain. Set baseline at 25 HR (see xHR), hope for favorable gusts.

Yr Tm	PA	R	HR	RBI	SB	BA	xHR	xBA	OBP	SLG	OPS+	vL+	vR+	bb%	ct%	Eye	G	L	F	h%	HctX	PX	xPX	HR/F	xHR/F	Spd	SBO	SB%	#Wk	DOM	DIS	RAR	BPX	R$
15 LA	585	67	26	54	4	210	26	224	346	417	106	95	107	16	65	0.54	42	16	42	26	104	152	147	20%	20%	84	7%	36%	27	41%	37%	-5.6	105	$7
16 LA	476	64	25	68	6	246	22	261	352	495	115	63	123	13	68	0.48	40	21	40	30	107	169	134	23%	20%	77	7%	75%	25	56%	36%	14.2	169	$13
17 LA *	392	50	13	42	5	199	11	258	288	379	89	79	101	11	75	0.50	47	19	34	22	100	110	101	15%	15%	72	10%	61%	23	43%	35%	-19.7	100	$2
18 LA	443	65	25	56	1	248	21	281	321	522	117	70	122	9	78	0.47	39	17	44	26	122	156	134	18%	15%	89	7%	17%	28	68%	14%	8.6	283	$13
19 LA	514	83	36	74	1	249	26	272	339	538	116	66	122	10	75	0.45	42	17	41	25	118	141	124	26%	19%	108	2%	50%	28	50%	32%	9.1	252	$16
1st Half	278	48	20	40	0	243	14	276	335	539	117	46	125	10	77	0.47	44	16	40	23	119	137	112	27%	19%	136	0%	0%	15	60%	33%	4.2	300	$17
2nd Half	236	35	16	34	1	256	12	266	343	536	116	88	120	10	73	0.43	39	19	42	27	116	147	138	25%	19%	79	4%	50%	13	38%	31%	5.4	207	$15
20 Proj	**490**	**74**	**27**	**66**	**2**	**247**		**259**	**336**	**489**	**111**	**74**	**116**	**10**	**75**	**0.46**	**41**	**18**	**41**	**27**	**115**	**127**	**127**	**20%**		**91**	**5%**	**44%**				**9.8**	**168**	**$16**

Pence,Hunter

Age: 37 Bats: R Pos: DH | Ht: 6' 4" Wt: 230

Health F | PT/Exp C | Consist F | LIMA Plan D | Rand Var -4 | MM 2423

Improbable resuscitation was petering out before back injury ended year in late August, 5th straight year with significant IL time. Gargantuan 1st half somewhat legit, per exit velo, HctX, PX and, to lesser extent, xPX. But age-36 "breakouts" are rare, to say the least. Wide range of outcomes, but if this was last hurrah, no one would be surprised.

Yr Tm	PA	R	HR	RBI	SB	BA	xHR	xBA	OBP	SLG	OPS+	vL+	vR+	bb%	ct%	Eye	G	L	F	h%	HctX	PX	xPX	HR/F	xHR/F	Spd	SBO	SB%	#Wk	DOM	DIS	RAR	BPX	R$
15 SF	223	30	9	40	4	275	11	279	327	478	112	79	118	7	77	0.33	54	17	29	32	119	135	117	20%	24%	86	10%	80%	11	73%	9%	4.4	154	$8
16 SF *	466	62	15	62	1	290	16	258	356	460	111	111	107	9	76	0.43	55	17	28	35	93	108	79	15%	19%	100	2%	50%	20	40%	35%	13.6	120	$15
17 SF	539	55	13	67	2	260	18	239	315	385	94	103	89	7	79	0.39	57	13	29	30	94	66	76	11%	16%	143	4%	40%	24	33%	42%	-11.9	91	$9
18 SF *	355	26	5	32	5	224	5	225	257	312	79	79	83	4	73	0.16	50	21	29	29	82	61	64	8%	10%	106	8%	83%	22	27%	55%	-17.9	-50	$2
19 TEX	316	53	18	59	6	297	15	279	358	552	121	132	112	8	76	0.38	45	20	36	34	111	133	106	23%	19%	111	9%	86%	19	58%	26%	17.0	230	$14
1st Half	215	44	15	48	3	294	12	299	353	608	128	141	121	8	76	0.36	46	19	36	32	121	164	126	28%	23%	113	9%	75%	13	62%	23%	13.2	319	$21
2nd Half	101	9	3	11	3	304	4	236	366	435	106	121	91	9	76	0.41	43	21	36	37	90	69	64	12%	16%	94	10%	100%	6	50%	33%	2.2	30	$1
20 Proj	**280**	**33**	**10**	**38**	**5**	**262**		**250**	**316**	**429**	**100**	**107**	**95**	**7**	**76**	**0.33**	**49**	**19**	**32**	**31**	**96**	**90**	**82**	**16%**		**109**	**8%**	**86%**				**0.3**	**59**	**$10**

Peralta,David

Age: 32 Bats: L Pos: LF | Ht: 6' 1" Wt: 210

Health F | PT/Exp B | Consist D | LIMA Plan B+ | Rand Var 0 | MM 2345

Shoulder woes arose in mid-May; "Freight Train" then derailed entirely in late August, undergoing season-ending surgery. Even accounting for injury, return to 30-HR level seems like pipe dream given high ground ball rate. Still, HctX raises floor; xBA consistency says you can lock in .275 BA. Health permitting, a solid rebound candidate.

Yr Tm	PA	R	HR	RBI	SB	BA	xHR	xBA	OBP	SLG	OPS+	vL+	vR+	bb%	ct%	Eye	G	L	F	h%	HctX	PX	xPX	HR/F	xHR/F	Spd	SBO	SB%	#Wk	DOM	DIS	RAR	BPX	R$
15 ARI	517	61	17	78	9	312	16	286	371	522	124	95	128	9	77	0.41	52	21	27	38	118	133	115	18%	17%	123	10%	69%	26	46%	15%	29.8	189	$24
16 ARI *	221	28	4	17	2	244	4	269	281	414	95	97	98	5	76	0.22	51	21	28	30	107	107	99	11%	11%	116	8%	62%	10	30%	30%	-4.6	103	$2
17 ARI	577	82	14	57	8	293	13	278	352	444	107	94	109	7	82	0.46	55	18	26	34	106	86	80	12%	11%	116	8%	67%	26	46%	23%	3.3	148	$19
18 ARI	614	75	30	87	4	293	26	280	352	516	120	96	130	8	78	0.39	51	20	29	33	140	124	120	23%	20%	107	3%	100%	27	52%	26%	30.0	200	$25
19 ARI	423	48	12	57	0	275	10	275	343	461	107	92	113	8	77	0.40	51	21	28	33	116	105	89	15%	12%	104	0%	0%	19	47%	21%	2.7	159	$9
1st Half	317	38	9	44	0	286	7	275	350	477	111	80	124	8	76	0.37	50	22	28	35	114	112	86	15%	12%	108	0%	0%	14	43%	21%	5.8	159	$13
2nd Half	106	10	3	13	0	242	3	272	321	411	96	135	81	9	82	0.53	53	19	28	27	120	84	98	14%	14%	97	0%	0%	5	60%	20%	-2.6	163	-$4
20 Proj	**595**	**67**	**20**	**70**	**3**	**275**		**275**	**340**	**461**	**108**	**104**	**108**	**8**	**79**	**0.42**	**52**	**20**	**28**	**32**	**121**	**98**	**99**	**16%**		**110**	**3%**	**75%**				**13.8**	**139**	**$19**

Peraza,Jose

Age: 26 Bats: R Pos: 2B SS LF | Ht: 6' 0" Wt: 196

Health A | PT/Exp B | Consist D | LIMA Plan C+ | Rand Var +2 | MM 1433

Cold comfort for those who paid for 2018 repeat: from skills perspective, it sorta was. Main changes were dip in PA as he got lost in logjam and lackluster SB%, which led to 2nd half SBO degradation. Lack of bb% continues to suppress OBP, fly ball rate heading in wrong direction, too. Until he rectifies these issues, PT may become more elusive.

Yr Tm	PA	R	HR	RBI	SB	BA	xHR	xBA	OBP	SLG	OPS+	vL+	vR+	bb%	ct%	Eye	G	L	F	h%	HctX	PX	xPX	HR/F	xHR/F	Spd	SBO	SB%	#Wk	DOM	DIS	RAR	BPX	R$
15 LA *	519	54	3	35	30	255	0	231	276	324	84	107	17	3	90	0.28	37	21	42	28	37	40	37	0%	0%	132	31%	79%	5	40%	20%	-15.7	103	$16
16 CIN *	564	61	5	44	30	292	3	268	325	378	96	107	101	5	85	0.33	43	28	29	34	73	52	55	5%	5%	145	32%	63%	18	28%	39%	-11.2	100	$24
17 CIN	518	50	5	37	23	259	5	248	297	324	83	87	80	4	86	0.29	47	22	31	29	74	33	43	4%	4%	150	24%	74%	26	19%	38%	-26.1	73	$14
18 CIN	683	85	14	58	23	288	10	269	326	416	103	108	100	4	88	0.39	37	26	38	31	96	70	57	7%	5%	114	18%	79%	28	46%	18%	9.1	177	$27
19 CIN	403	37	6	33	7	239	4	242	285	346	84	96	78	4	85	0.29	36	21	43	27	93	56	71	4%	3%	111	16%	54%	28	36%	29%	-17.5	100	$4
1st Half	235	22	5	20	5	222	3	227	277	338	82	89	79	5	84	0.32	35	18	47	24	90	57	75	6%	4%	121	20%	56%	15	40%	27%	-13.0	115	$4
2nd Half	168	15	1	13	2	263	2	263	298	356	86	107	77	4	85	0.25	37	26	37	30	97	55	65	2%	4%	100	11%	50%	13	31%	31%	-5.8	85	$5
20 Proj	**350**	**36**	**5**	**28**	**12**	**261**		**254**	**302**	**363**	**90**	**99**	**85**	**4**	**86**	**0.31**	**39**	**24**	**38**	**29**	**90**	**53**	**61**	**5%**		**119**	**21%**	**71%**				**-4.9**	**101**	**$11**

Perez,Hernan

Age: 29 Bats: R Pos: 2B SS | Ht: 6' 1" Wt: 215

Health A | PT/Exp C | Consist A | LIMA Plan D | Rand Var +1 | MM 1313

8-18-.228 with 5 SB in 246 PA at MIL. Retains some utility vL, though best skill, Spd, waned in 2019, and it's not like he was getting on base enough to deploy it. And while HR pace looks OK, xHR and xHR/F scream, "Fool's gold!" Days of 400+ PA may be gone for good, so at best, he's a cheap source of SB, and maybe not even that.

Yr Tm	PA	R	HR	RBI	SB	BA	xHR	xBA	OBP	SLG	OPS+	vL+	vR+	bb%	ct%	Eye	G	L	F	h%	HctX	PX	xPX	HR/F	xHR/F	Spd	SBO	SB%	#Wk	DOM	DIS	RAR	BPX	R$
15 2 TM	272	14	1	21	5	243	4	233	257	327	81	88	76	2	78	0.08	43	22	34	31	102	66	98	1%	6%	91	12%	83%	26	23%	58%	-14.1	-8	$1
16 MIL *	494	57	14	64	35	273	9	249	303	424	99	106	93	4	77	0.19	43	20	36	33	100	91	97	12%	8%	118	39%	83%	24	33%	29%	-4.7	77	$25
17 MIL	458	47	14	51	13	259	9	263	289	414	94	105	89	4	82	0.25	48	18	34	29	100	83	81	12%	8%	99	18%	76%	27	37%	37%	-14.7	103	$12
18 MIL	334	36	9	29	11	253	9	237	290	386	94	109	84	5	78	0.24	42	21	37	30	99	77	104	10%	10%	137	19%	79%	28	29%	46%	-7.5	83	$9
19 MIL *	363	41	12	31	9	229	5	240	273	388	88	95	74	6	72	0.22	52	16	32	28	97	95	77	15%	9%	86	15%	90%	21	14%	67%	-18.8	11	$6
1st Half	160	20	5	11	4	235	3	232	277	383	88	96	80	6	72	0.21	52	16	32	29	96	86	75	14%	9%	93	16%	80%	13	8%	62%	-7.5	-11	$2
2nd Half	203	21	7	20	5	224	2	247	269	393	87	96	65	6	72	0.22	53	17	31	28	99	102	82	17%	11%	86	15%	100%	8	25%	75%	-9.4	33	$9
20 Proj	**280**	**30**	**7**	**26**	**7**	**241**		**236**	**280**	**371**	**88**	**98**	**79**	**5**	**75**	**0.22**	**48**	**18**	**33**	**30**	**99**	**75**	**88**	**10%**		**102**	**15%**	**82%**				**-4.4**	**6**	**$8**

Perez,Roberto

Age: 31 Bats: R Pos: CA | Ht: 5' 11" Wt: 220

Health B | PT/Exp D | Consist D | LIMA Plan D | Rand Var -5 | MM 3103

Our encyclopedia has long promoted idea of catcher late-career "spikes," but it would've been hard to see this coming. Yet with doubters, Statcast has got his back (see xHR/F). With so few fly balls, he'll have to keep stinging it to maintain HR, and xBA suggests he'll still be a BA bane. But least he's gone from punchline to punch source.

Yr Tm	PA	R	HR	RBI	SB	BA	xHR	xBA	OBP	SLG	OPS+	vL+	vR+	bb%	ct%	Eye	G	L	F	h%	HctX	PX	xPX	HR/F	xHR/F	Spd	SBO	SB%	#Wk	DOM	DIS	RAR	BPX	R$
15 CLE	226	30	7	21	0	228	7	237	348	402	105	116	98	15	65	0.52	53	20	27	31	89	134	121	21%	21%	93	0%	0%	26	38%	50%	4.7	73	$1
16 CLE	184	14	3	17	0	183	4	213	285	294	79	92	71	13	71	0.52	54	15	31	24	72	75	94	9%	12%	83	0%	0%	15	33%	53%	-5.8	-6	-$3
17 CLE	248	22	8	38	0	207	7	222	291	373	89	107	79	10	67	0.37	50	17	32	27	87	112	94	17%	15%	51	2%	0%	26	23%	54%	-4.7	-6	$0
18 CLE	210	16	2	19	1	168	5	182	256	263	72	90	67	10	61	0.30	50	15	36	26	91	81	106	5%	13%	70	3%	100%	26	23%	73%	-7.5	-160	-$3
19 CLE	449	46	24	63	0	239	23	229	321	452	103	113	97	10	67	0.35	51	17	32	29	94	116	120	28%	27%	79	0%	0%	27	22%	52%	14.1	30	$8
1st Half	219	24	14	31	0	238	13	231	327	481	108	131	97	11	66	0.38	50	18	32	28	96	133	131	35%	33%	65	0%	0%	15	27%	47%	7.0	56	$8
2nd Half	230	22	10	32	0	240	9	222	316	425	98	97	98	10	69	0.33	51	16	33	30	92	100	110	22%	20%	93	0%	0%	12	17%	58%	2.8	11	$9
20 Proj	**420**	**41**	**15**	**54**	**1**	**229**		**215**	**313**	**397**	**95**	**111**	**88**	**11**	**66**	**0.35**	**51**	**17**	**33**	**30**	**91**	**101**	**111**	**19%**		**73**	**1%**	**67%**				**7.8**	**-75**	**$8**

KRISTOPHER OLSON

Perez,Salvador

Age: 30 Bats: R Pos: CA | Ht: 6' 4" Wt: 240

Health F | PT/Exp D | Consist C | LIMA Plan C+ | Rand Var -1 | MM 3125

Missed 2019 due to Tommy John surgery. MLB ban on playing in Venezuela deprived him of DH time to knock rust off in winter, but otherwise, recovery has had no reported hiccups. When last seen in 2018 2nd half, power was as good as it's ever been. As long as he didn't leave that on operating table, return to catcher pool will be most welcome.

Yr	Tm	PA	R	HR	RBI	SB	BA	xHR	xBA	OBP	SLG	OPS+	vL+	vR+	bb%	ct%	Eye	G	L	F	h%	HctX	PX	xPX	HR/F	xHR/F	Spd	SBO	SB%	#Wk	DOM	DIS	RAR	BPX	R$
15	KC	553	52	21	70	1	260	16	268	280	426	98	77	106	2	85	0.16	42	21	37	27	88	99	87	12%	9%	66	1%	100%	27	48%	22%	5.2	119	$13
16	KC	546	57	22	64	0	247	17	246	288	438	99	103	95	4	77	0.18	35	18	47	28	105	116	107	12%	9%	67	0%	0%	27	44%	26%	3.8	86	$9
17	KC	498	57	27	80	1	268	29	266	297	495	106	104	105	3	80	0.18	33	20	47	28	123	121	142	15%	16%	56	1%	100%	24	63%	29%	12.4	127	$14
18	KC *	568	55	28	84	1	238	29	258	262	444	98	98	98	3	79	0.15	35	20	45	25	134	116	149	15%	16%	50	2%	50%	24	54%	25%	7.9	110	$13
19																																			
1st Half																																			
2nd Half																																			
20	Proj	490	51	23	68	1	250		251	284	448	99	96	99	3	79	0.17	35	20	45	27	115	101	124	13%		63	1%	69%				-6.9	72	$10

Pham,Thomas

Age: 32 Bats: R Pos: LF DH | Ht: 6' 1" Wt: 215

Health B | PT/Exp A | Consist B | LIMA Plan D+ | Rand Var +2 | MM 3445

Don't be too concerned about power, HctX dip in 2nd half; he gutted out last two months of playoff chase with hand, elbow injuries. He offset that with bump in SB chances, nearly impeccable SB%. Even with full health, heavy dose of ground balls may keep him below 30 HR plateau. But if ct% gains hold... UP: .290 BA, 30 SB well within reach.

Yr	Tm	PA	R	HR	RBI	SB	BA	xHR	xBA	OBP	SLG	OPS+	vL+	vR+	bb%	ct%	Eye	G	L	F	h%	HctX	PX	xPX	HR/F	xHR/F	Spd	SBO	SB%	#Wk	DOM	DIS	RAR	BPX	R$
15	STL *	360	48	9	45	8	262	5	258	334	427	106	108	114	10	73	0.40	51	21	27	33	120	111	119	16%	16%	110	9%	100%	12	42%	33%	3.5	95	$11
16	STL *	322	39	12	31	8	214	9	228	301	383	93	99	105	11	62	0.32	45	25	30	30	107	124	126	35%	35%	100	19%	58%	18	33%	56%	-9.4	0	$5
17	STL *	631	107	26	87	29	292	21	277	384	497	118	128	122	13	73	0.56	52	22	26	36	106	121	104	27%	24%	104	22%	73%	22	55%	23%	23.0	148	$33
18	2 TM	570	102	21	63	15	275	26	258	367	464	115	122	112	12	72	0.48	48	24	28	35	128	113	123	21%	26%	148	14%	68%	27	41%	37%	17.2	157	$24
19	TAM	654	77	21	68	25	273	23	281	369	450	109	123	102	12	78	0.66	53	22	25	32	118	94	95	19%	21%	109	16%	86%	28	50%	29%	12.7	178	$25
1st Half		349	39	13	35	7	284	15	279	384	468	114	118	112	13	77	0.68	54	23	23	33	127	93	102	25%	28%	125	10%	70%	15	40%	33%	9.5	185	$21
2nd Half		305	38	8	33	18	261	8	282	351	429	103	130	91	12	79	0.64	52	21	27	30	108	96	86	14%	14%	93	25%	95%	13	62%	23%	2.6	178	$28
20	Proj	630	91	23	71	27	272		271	365	461	111	122	106	12	75	0.55	51	22	26	33	117	103	105	21%		118	19%	82%				22.1	164	$30

Phegley,Joshua

Age: 32 Bats: R Pos: CA | Ht: 5' 10" Wt: 225

Health D | PT/Exp F | Consist A | LIMA Plan D | Rand Var +1 | MM 1011

Injuries opened door to bounty of 1st half playing time, and he took advantage, though xHR, xHR/F, xPX never bought power output. 2nd half was different story: less contact, drop in HctX, missed time with thumb injury. Makes competent enough contact to kick around as backup for a few more years, but 2019 may well be his high water mark.

Yr	Tm	PA	R	HR	RBI	SB	BA	xHR	xBA	OBP	SLG	OPS+	vL+	vR+	bb%	ct%	Eye	G	L	F	h%	HctX	PX	xPX	HR/F	xHR/F	Spd	SBO	SB%	#Wk	DOM	DIS	RAR	BPX	R$
15	OAK	243	27	9	34	0	249	6	265	300	449	104	109	97	6	77	0.27	37	21	43	28	101	136	121	12%	8%	70	0%	0%	23	39%	48%	4.8	143	$4
16	OAK	86	11	1	10	0	256	2	250	314	372	93	89	95	6	83	0.38	39	20	41	30	108	80	108	4%	7%	83	0%	0%	11	45%	45%	0.0	103	$0
17	OAK *	191	15	4	13	0	208	5	235	251	340	79	80	77	5	82	0.32	35	17	48	23	96	82	91	5%	8%	52	3%	0%	20	35%	35%	-8.1	67	-$2
18	OAK *	231	21	4	27	0	192	2	208	250	327	80	70	88	7	69	0.25	44	15	41	26	64	95	87	7%	7%	105	0%	0%	18	22%	50%	-5.3	0	-$2
19	OAK	342	44	12	62	0	230	7	267	282	411	92	110	83	4	80	0.24	35	25	40	26	95	91	79	12%	7%	55	2%	0%	28	29%	39%	0.9	74	$6
1st Half		215	31	9	42	0	263	5	287	304	470	103	125	95	4	82	0.23	33	27	41	28	102	107	82	13%	7%	69	0%	0%	16	38%	31%	4.3	167	$10
2nd Half		127	13	3	20	0	198	2	232	246	310	73	93	62	6	76	0.25	39	23	38	24	84	61	72	9%	6%	51	4%	0%	12	17%	50%	-6.2	-70	-$2
20	Proj	245	26	6	35	0	234		233	283	368	88	93	84	6	76	0.26	38	21	41	28	86	78	85	8%		66	2%	0%				-0.3	-15	$4

Phillips,Brett

Age: 26 Bats: L Pos: CF | Ht: 6' 0" Wt: 185

Health A | PT/Exp C | Consist D | LIMA Plan D | Rand Var +3 | MM 3503

2-6-.138 with 3 SB in 79 PA in KC. For a guy who shares his surname with a bulb company, it's sure taking a long time for light to come on. Ingredients of intriguing power/speed combo still here (18 HR, 22 SB in 414 PA at AAA), but whiffs remain a major issue. Might still flip the switch, but getting to the age where prospects begin to dim.

Yr	Tm	PA	R	HR	RBI	SB	BA	xHR	xBA	OBP	SLG	OPS+	vL+	vR+	bb%	ct%	Eye	G	L	F	h%	HctX	PX	xPX	HR/F	xHR/F	Spd	SBO	SB%	#Wk	DOM	DIS	RAR	BPX	R$
15	aa	234	33	1	22	8	285			347	421	107			9	72	0.34				39		103				133	19%	72%					84	$7
16	aa	507	59	18	61	12	230			330	410	101			13	63	0.40				32		124				122	15%	62%					40	$11
17	MIL *	513	65	20	67	11	265	3	226	324	466	106	41	113	8	61	0.22	38	25	38	39	73	139	101	20%	15%	147	11%	91%	11	18%	64%	3.6	55	$16
18	2 TM *	428	42	6	27	8	192	2	190	257	314	79	53	86	8	56	0.20	49	21	31	32	76	97	87	9%	9%	154	11%	89%	15	13%	80%	-20.2	-107	$1
19	KC *	466	62	14	46	19	196	1	200	307	382	91	83	65	14	61	0.41	42	16	42	28	83	108	132	11%	6%	183	19%	94%	8	13%	38%	-7.0	56	$10
1st Half		249	32	6	20	10	193		198	306	355	88			14	59	0.40				29		98		0%		189	18%	89%				-5.4	4	$6
2nd Half		217	31	8	26	10	200	1	216	307	413	95	82	65	13	64	0.43	42	16	42	26	86	119	132	11%	8%	164	20%	100%	8	13%	38%	-0.3	107	$14
20	Proj	280	35	8	28	9	212		207	299	388	92	62	98	11	61	0.32	42	21	37	31	78	109	108	14%		162	17%	92%				-0.1	-10	$7

Pillar,Kevin

Age: 31 Bats: R Pos: CF RF | Ht: 6' 0" Wt: 210

Health A | PT/Exp A | Consist A | LIMA Plan B+ | Rand Var +1 | MM 2345

May have overachieved by cracking 20 HR barrier for first time - note the consistently subpar power metrics - otherwise, he was the same guy as ever. Speed isn't elite, but it's holding steady, and you can see where SB total is bound to land. Contact rate is rock solid, too, so BA unlikely to bottom out. He's vanilla, but in that pleasing, sugar cookie sort of way.

Yr	Tm	PA	R	HR	RBI	SB	BA	xHR	xBA	OBP	SLG	OPS+	vL+	vR+	bb%	ct%	Eye	G	L	F	h%	HctX	PX	xPX	HR/F	xHR/F	Spd	SBO	SB%	#Wk	DOM	DIS	RAR	BPX	R$
15	TOR	628	76	12	56	25	278	8	261	314	399	99	94	99	4	85	0.33	41	22	37	31	92	78	72	7%	4%	106	20%	86%	27	33%	22%	3.3	127	$24
16	TOR	584	59	7	53	14	266	8	259	303	376	92	96	89	4	84	0.27	46	20	34	31	92	72	73	5%	5%	98	16%	70%	25	32%	28%	-13.0	91	$14
17	TOR	632	72	16	42	15	256	13	269	300	404	94	125	83	5	84	0.35	43	20	36	28	93	85	69	9%	7%	102	16%	71%	26	38%	12%	-17.8	139	$14
18	TOR	542	65	15	59	14	252	15	273	282	426	98	95	98	3	81	0.18	36	27	38	29	101	108	90	9%	9%	93	19%	82%	26	50%	23%	-2.7	157	$16
19	2 TM	645	83	21	88	14	259	17	277	287	432	95	107	91	3	85	0.20	44	20	36	27	110	86	71	11%	9%	100	17%	74%	28	43%	21%	-2.9	178	$20
1st Half		321	42	11	43	8	240	8	268	268	408	90	95	88	3	85	0.22	40	20	39	25	104	82	74	11%	8%	94	16%	89%	15	47%	27%	-6.4	159	$17
2nd Half		324	41	10	45	6	277	8	284	306	456	101	120	93	3	86	0.18	48	19	33	30	116	90	69	11%	9%	104	17%	60%	13	38%	15%	1.6	196	$23
20	Proj	560	70	16	66	14	260		272	292	424	96	107	92	4	84	0.23	42	22	36	28	104	86	76	10%		100	17%	75%				3.7	166	$20

Pinder,Chad

Age: 28 Bats: R Pos: LF RF 2B | Ht: 6' 2" Wt: 207

Health B | PT/Exp D | Consist B | LIMA Plan D | Rand Var +1 | MM 3023

Coming into 2019, some interesting power skills seemed to be percolating, but they never materialized. 1st half ct% jump faded, and throughout, contact was less hard, produced more ground balls. 2nd half was particularly ominous for playing-time prospects. Can move around diamond, but no sign he'll break out of utility role anytime soon.

Yr	Tm	PA	R	HR	RBI	SB	BA	xHR	xBA	OBP	SLG	OPS+	vL+	vR+	bb%	ct%	Eye	G	L	F	h%	HctX	PX	xPX	HR/F	xHR/F	Spd	SBO	SB%	#Wk	DOM	DIS	RAR	BPX	R$
15	aa	498	53	10	64	5	272			302	403	98			4	76	0.18				34		96				85	10%	48%					49	$13
16	OAK *	501	62	11	45	4	226	2	224	262	360	85	109	60	5	72	0.17	50	13	37	29	132	91	173	7%	14%	108	6%	78%	8	38%	38%	-16.9	17	$4
17	OAK *	377	38	16	44	4	235	18	231	282	430	96	98	99	6	66	0.19	41	19	40	31	89	127	119	19%	23%	106	8%	62%	18	50%	39%	-15.2	33	$5
18	OAK	333	43	13	27	0	258	20	233	332	436	106	116	98	8	70	0.31	44	19	37	32	120	112	136	17%	26%	117	3%	0%	26	38%	38%	0.7	83	$6
19	OAK	370	45	13	47	0	240	13	258	290	416	94	98	89	5	74	0.23	49	22	29	29	105	101	91	17%	17%	77	1%	0%	28	39%	36%	-12.4	48	$5
1st Half		198	28	8	26	0	255	6	275	298	451	100	106	95	4	77	0.19	51	22	28	29	104	107	78	20%	15%	86	3%	0%	16	50%	31%	-4.6	111	$7
2nd Half		172	17	5	21	0	223	7	238	281	376	87	90	82	7	71	0.26	46	22	31	28	106	93	109	14%	20%	78	0%	0%	12	25%	42%	-8.3	-11	$3
20	Proj	315	38	12	36	1	243		241	297	418	96	102	90	6	72	0.24	46	20	34	30	109	102	117	16%		92	3%	38%				-4.4	-6	$7

Piscotty,Stephen

Age: 29 Bats: R Pos: RF | Ht: 6' 4" Wt: 205

Health C | PT/Exp C | Consist D | LIMA Plan B | Rand Var 0 | MM 2135

13-44-.249 in 393 PA at OAK. After decent first couple of months, rest of season went in fits and starts due to health woes. Got things rolling again in Aug, only to have ankle sprain sink Sept. Struggles vR bear watching, but xPX remains somewhat bullish, so staying on right side of IL may be all he may needs to return to 20 HR level.

Yr	Tm	PA	R	HR	RBI	SB	BA	xHR	xBA	OBP	SLG	OPS+	vL+	vR+	bb%	ct%	Eye	G	L	F	h%	HctX	PX	xPX	HR/F	xHR/F	Spd	SBO	SB%	#Wk	DOM	DIS	RAR	BPX	R$
15	STL *	611	69	15	69	6	259	11	264	326	428	105	122	115	9	76	0.42	45	21	34	31	127	119	136	12%	18%	141	10%	42%	12	50%	33%	-4.7	170	$14
16	STL	648	86	22	85	7	273	27	264	343	457	109	129	100	8	77	0.38	44	20	36	32	100	114	105	13%	17%	121	8%	58%	27	48%	19%	8.3	154	$20
17	STL *	446	46	12	45	3	235	12	240	336	384	97	96	93	13	75	0.60	49	18	33	28	99	91	112	11%	14%	89	8%	33%	22	27%	45%	-12.7	79	$4
18	OAK	605	78	27	88	2	267	31	287	331	491	114	108	115	7	79	0.37	45	22	33	29	124	134	113	19%	22%	78	2%	100%	28	64%	21%	15.2	210	$20
19	OAK *	417	49	14	46	2	248	16	246	304	406	94	133	83	7	77	0.34	44	20	36	29	105	84	102	13%	16%	95	2%	100%	20	35%	35%	-9.0	70	$7
1st Half		328	37	9	34	2	242	13	243	306	391	93	127	83	8	76	0.39	44	20	37	29	100	82	102	11%	15%	101	3%	100%	15	40%	33%	-10.2	74	$9
2nd Half		89	12	5	12	0	270	3	263	299	462	100	165	87	4	77	0.18	45	23	32	30	130	93	102	27%	20%	91	0%	0%	5	20%	40%	-0.9	74	$0
20	Proj	557	70	20	71	2	257		255	320	424	100	123	91	7	77	0.34	45	21	34	30	116	90	108	15%		86	3%	57%				-0.6	56	$16

KRISTOPHER OLSON

Polanco,Gregory

Age: 28 Bats: L Pos: RF | Ht: 6' 5" Wt: 235

Health F | PT/Exp C | Consist C | LIMA Plan C+ | Rand Var -3 | MM 3323

6-17-.242 in 167 PA at PIT. Returned from off-season left shoulder surgery in late April, but ended up back on the IL for the same shoulder by mid-June. Pre-injury, 2018 skill set was compelling. Can't just run back last year's "UP: 30 HR, 20 SB" amid health questions, but still young enough to own those skills if you can buy them at a discount.

Yr	Tm	PA	R	HR	RBI	SB	BA	xHR	xBA	OBP	SLG	OPS+	vL+	vR+	bb%	ct%	Eye	G	L	F	h%	HctX	PX	xPX	HR/F	xHR/F	Spd	SBO	SB%	#Wk	DOM	DIS	RAR	BPX	R$
15	PIT	652	83	9	52	27	256	13	250	320	381	98	73	102	8	80	0.45	45	20	35	31	103	87	95	6%	8%	116	24%	73%	27	41%	22%	-12.6	114	$20
16	PIT	587	79	22	86	17	258	19	274	323	463	107	106	105	9	77	0.45	39	24	37	30	112	125	110	14%	12%	84	18%	74%	26	58%	23%	7.1	157	$21
17	PIT	410	39	11	35	8	251	9	262	305	391	93	78	96	7	84	0.45	42	20	38	27	88	78	77	9%	8%	80	10%	89%	23	39%	30%	-12.5	115	$7
18	PIT	532	75	23	81	12	254	25	257	340	499	116	107	119	11	75	0.52	33	19	48	29	94	150	123	14%	15%	106	12%	86%	24	67%	21%	20.1	250	$20
19	PIT *	218	27	7	25	4	236	6	215	302	405	94	90	98	9	66	0.28	37	19	44	33	87	109	120	13%	13%	97	12%	82%	9	33%	33%	-7.4	-4	$3
1st Half		188	24	6	21	4	242	6	213	297	409	94	92	99	7	66	0.23	37	19	44	33	88	104	120	13%	13%	103	14%	82%	9	33%	33%	-5.6	-19	$4
2nd Half		30	2	1	4	0	195		223	334	380	94			17	62	0.55				28		142		0%		93	0%	0%				-0.9	96	-$6
20	**Proj**	**420**	**53**	**14**	**49**	**10**	**251**		**244**	**314**	**431**	**100**	**90**	**103**	**8**	**75**	**0.36**	**39**	**20**	**41**	**30**	**94**	**100**	**106**	**12%**		**99**	**14%**	**80%**				**0.9**	**118**	**$11**

Polanco,Jorge

Age: 26 Bats: B Pos: SS | Ht: 5' 11" Wt: 200

Health A | PT/Exp B | Consist A | LIMA Plan B | Rand Var -3 | MM 2245

Sometimes we don't need the full suite of advanced metrics to diagnose a breakout. Simply put, he hit the ball hard a lot more often. Also hit balls in the air more often, in the Year of the Juiced Ball. Both xPX and xHR say the power can stick. More questionable is BA: more FBs should push h% lower, so set BA expectations against 2nd half xBA.

Yr	Tm	PA	R	HR	RBI	SB	BA	xHR	xBA	OBP	SLG	OPS+	vL+	vR+	bb%	ct%	Eye	G	L	F	h%	HctX	PX	xPX	HR/F	xHR/F	Spd	SBO	SB%	#Wk	DOM	DIS	RAR	BPX	R$
15	MIN *	525	52	5	45	17	266		268	313	350	92	184	65	6	84	0.43	56	22	22	31	41	56	-16	0%		101	20%	60%	2	50%	50%	-11.1	73	$14
16	MIN *	587	53	12	62	9	272	3	274	323	428	102	116	96	7	82	0.41	33	30	37	31	78	90	64	5%	4%	102	12%	54%	16	50%	25%	5.4	129	$14
17	MIN	544	60	13	74	13	256	10	258	313	410	97	89	99	8	84	0.53	38	19	43	28	94	86	89	7%	6%	97	15%	72%	26	54%	23%	-3.7	155	$14
18	MIN	333	38	6	42	7	288	6	255	345	427	107	87	116	8	79	0.40	36	26	38	35	94	86	76	7%	7%	110	16%	50%	14	21%	21%	6.9	123	$10
19	MIN	704	107	22	79	4	295	25	267	356	485	112	95	119	9	82	0.52	29	26	44	33	112	97	132	10%	11%	125	4%	57%	28	57%	4%	18.1	226	$23
1st Half		366	55	11	39	3	320	15	265	378	521	120	95	131	9	84	0.60	24	25	51	35	116	100	136	8%	11%	144	6%	50%	15	67%	0%	20.1	293	$26
2nd Half		338	52	11	40	1	267	10	270	332	446	103	96	106	9	79	0.45	35	28	38	31	107	94	126	12%	11%	103	1%	100%	13	46%	8%	1.8	152	$19
20	**Proj**	**595**	**79**	**19**	**72**	**8**	**272**		**267**	**333**	**457**	**106**	**95**	**111**	**8**	**81**	**0.47**	**33**	**26**	**41**	**31**	**101**	**95**	**104**	**11%**		**114**	**10%**	**58%**				**16.5**	**177**	**$21**

Pollock,A.J.

Age: 32 Bats: R Pos: CF | Ht: 6' 1" Wt: 212

Health F | PT/Exp C | Consist A | LIMA Plan C+ | Rand Var -2 | MM 3443

Elbow infection cost him six weeks in 1st half, then returned for a second half that was pretty much vintage. The PA column reminds us that stringing together consecutive vintage half-seasons is where things break down (pun intended). Age, checkered injury history suggest double-digit SB now at risk, but the bat still plays... in stretches.

Yr	Tm	PA	R	HR	RBI	SB	BA	xHR	xBA	OBP	SLG	OPS+	vL+	vR+	bb%	ct%	Eye	G	L	F	h%	HctX	PX	xPX	HR/F	xHR/F	Spd	SBO	SB%	#Wk	DOM	DIS	RAR	BPX	R$
15	ARI	673	111	20	76	39	315	18	299	367	498	121	121	118	8	85	0.60	50	21	29	34	128	111	99	13%	12%	120	26%	85%	27	70%	15%	45.0	227	$44
16	ARI	46	9	2	4	4	244	2	209	326	390	97	57	105	11	80	0.63	42	9	48	26	89	71	119	13%	13%	112	31%	100%	3	33%	33%	0.3	103	$1
17	ARI	466	73	14	49	20	266	13	299	330	471	107	113	102	8	83	0.49	45	23	32	29	118	113	111	12%	12%	116	27%	77%	21	52%	19%	2.0	227	$18
18	ARI	460	61	21	65	13	257	23	265	316	484	111	103	114	7	76	0.31	42	19	38	29	124	132	146	17%	19%	116	17%	87%	22	59%	18%	11.6	197	$18
19	LA	342	49	15	47	5	266	14	259	327	468	106	118	99	7	76	0.31	43	20	37	31	115	106	94	17%	16%	96	8%	83%	19	37%	37%	8.0	122	$10
1st Half		115	15	2	14	0	223	3	226	287	330	82	110	71	8	78	0.39	48	17	35	27	102	55	70	7%	10%	119	4%	0%	6	33%	50%	-4.5	33	-$8
2nd Half		227	34	13	33	5	288	11	274	348	537	117	121	114	6	75	0.27	41	21	37	33	122	132	107	22%	19%	84	10%	100%	13	38%	31%	12.5	170	$19
20	**Proj**	**420**	**62**	**17**	**56**	**10**	**267**		**265**	**325**	**467**	**107**	**113**	**103**	**7**	**78**	**0.34**	**44**	**20**	**36**	**30**	**119**	**104**	**109**	**16%**		**111**	**13%**	**87%**				**15.0**	**177**	**$18**

Posey,Buster

Age: 33 Bats: R Pos: CA | Ht: 6' 1" Wt: 210

Health C | PT/Exp B | Consist D | LIMA Plan B | Rand Var +1 | MM 1245

A relatively healthy year, with just two min-length IL stints (concussion, hamstring), but skills decline now in full effect. Accumulation of a decade's worth of wear-and-tear is the likely root cause, rather than acute injury. Straight-line decline of HctX and recent BPX string tell the tale. Still has value in CA pool—but not the Buster of old, for sure.

Yr	Tm	PA	R	HR	RBI	SB	BA	xHR	xBA	OBP	SLG	OPS+	vL+	vR+	bb%	ct%	Eye	G	L	F	h%	HctX	PX	xPX	HR/F	xHR/F	Spd	SBO	SB%	#Wk	DOM	DIS	RAR	BPX	R$
15	SF	623	74	19	95	2	318	23	287	379	470	118	118	116	9	91	1.08	44	22	34	33	137	87	113	11%	13%	60	1%	100%	27	63%	11%	43.1	189	$27
16	SF	614	82	14	80	6	288	23	289	362	434	108	121	100	10	87	0.94	49	22	30	31	128	84	111	10%	16%	93	4%	86%	27	59%	15%	19.2	194	$19
17	SF	568	62	12	67	6	320	15	285	400	462	115	135	106	11	87	0.92	44	23	33	35	116	81	113	8%	10%	81	4%	86%	27	52%	11%	37.2	179	$21
18	SF	448	47	5	41	3	284	11	264	359	382	103	115	96	10	87	0.85	47	22	31	32	116	61	93	5%	10%	79	4%	60%	22	50%	23%	14.5	137	$10
19	SF	445	43	7	38	0	257	14	260	320	368	91	75	98	8	82	0.48	49	23	28	30	102	63	87	7%	15%	78	0%	0%	27	30%	33%	-4.4	78	$4
1st Half		219	20	3	20	0	251	7	271	315	382	93	77	100	8	83	0.55	44	23	32	29	99	78	85	6%	13%	65	0%	0%	14	36%	21%	0.6	126	$1
2nd Half		226	23	4	18	0	262	7	250	324	354	90	73	96	7	82	0.42	54	22	24	30	105	49	89	10%	17%	94	0%	0%	13	23%	46%	-0.7	37	$7
20	**Proj**	**504**	**51**	**9**	**48**	**2**	**261**		**267**	**330**	**376**	**95**	**93**	**95**	**9**	**85**	**0.63**	**48**	**23**	**30**	**29**	**111**	**63**	**95**	**8%**		**81**	**2%**	**73%**				**11.1**	**81**	**$11**

Profar,Jurickson

Age: 27 Bats: B Pos: 2B | Ht: 6' 0" Wt: 190

Health B | PT/Exp B | Consist D | LIMA Plan B | Rand Var +5 | MM 2345

Park factor change in TEX-to-OAK would have suggested a power loss, instead it was BA that tumbled. Hidden behind that h% dip are nothing but positive signs: xBA held steady, plate skills actually improved in 2nd half, power played just fine in larger home park. Rand Var confirms him as a premium rebound candidate.

Yr	Tm	PA	R	HR	RBI	SB	BA	xHR	xBA	OBP	SLG	OPS+	vL+	vR+	bb%	ct%	Eye	G	L	F	h%	HctX	PX	xPX	HR/F	xHR/F	Spd	SBO	SB%	#Wk	DOM	DIS	RAR	BPX	R$
15																																			
16	TEX *	489	57	9	40	5	244	4	247	311	350	90	62	97	9	80	0.48	53	19	28	29	78	62	47	8%	7%	121	8%	54%	20	25%	65%	-15.0	71	$7
17	TEX *	430	46	5	39	5	236	1	274	311	338	87	97	63	10	87	0.83	41	25	34	26	92	62	82	0%	7%	92	6%	83%	7	43%	57%	-12.5	139	$4
18	TEX	594	82	20	77	10	254	16	288	335	458	110	111	109	9	83	0.61	44	22	34	27	114	115	98	13%	11%	111	8%	100%	28	61%	11%	16.9	260	$19
19	OAK	518	65	20	67	9	218	17	277	301	410	94	109	90	9	84	0.64	41	22	37	22	109	93	98	14%	12%	79	10%	90%	29	52%	10%	-11.3	196	$10
1st Half		310	33	10	40	6	215	11	266	277	377	87	112	80	7	83	0.41	42	22	37	23	107	81	95	11%	13%	82	11%	100%	16	38%	19%	-11.3	133	$10
2nd Half		208	32	10	27	3	223	7	297	337	463	105	106	105	14	85	1.08	41	22	37	21	113	112	104	18%	13%	87	9%	75%	13	69%	0%	1.9	319	$10
20	**Proj**	**560**	**76**	**19**	**72**	**9**	**253**		**277**	**338**	**434**	**104**	**113**	**100**	**10**	**84**	**0.71**	**43**	**22**	**35**	**27**	**105**	**90**	**92**	**13%**		**92**	**8%**	**85%**				**12.2**	**218**	**$18**

Puig,Yasiel

Age: 29 Bats: R Pos: RF | Ht: 6' 2" Wt: 240

Health B | PT/Exp B | Consist B | LIMA Plan B | Rand Var -1 | MM 3335

Gets a deserved "A" for consistency (see R$ stability), but in-season he continues to bounce around wildly. For second straight year, he spent half the season trying to loft balls over fences, and other half trying to swing hard and level. You aren't paying us for ¯_(ツ)_/¯, so best to focus on that R$ and not worry about how he gets there.

Yr	Tm	PA	R	HR	RBI	SB	BA	xHR	xBA	OBP	SLG	OPS+	vL+	vR+	bb%	ct%	Eye	G	L	F	h%	HctX	PX	xPX	HR/F	xHR/F	Spd	SBO	SB%	#Wk	DOM	DIS	RAR	BPX	R$
15	LA	311	30	11	38	3	255	11	249	322	436	106	127	96	8	77	0.39	44	17	39	30	107	114	89	13%	13%	104	8%	50%	18	39%	28%	-1.3	127	$7
16	LA *	441	54	14	54	5	268	11	252	316	428	101	106	95	6	79	0.34	48	16	35	31	100	92	90	12%	12%	101	8%	61%	22	27%	36%	-0.6	100	$12
17	LA	570	72	28	74	15	263	26	277	346	487	112	79	120	11	80	0.64	48	16	36	28	107	119	95	19%	18%	94	15%	71%	27	56%	22%	12.0	206	$20
18	LA	444	60	23	63	15	267	19	278	327	494	114	89	126	8	79	0.41	43	21	36	29	111	129	107	20%	17%	83	20%	75%	26	58%	31%	12.2	200	$20
19	2 TM	611	76	24	84	19	267	24	252	327	458	104	103	104	7	76	0.33	38	21	41	31	102	102	107	14%	14%	89	19%	73%	27	37%	37%	0.0	107	$23
1st Half		307	35	17	45	13	239	17	244	290	458	100	107	97	6	75	0.25	31	22	46	26	93	110	111	17%	17%	87	27%	81%	15	40%	33%	-7.1	100	$23
2nd Half		304	41	7	39	6	295	7	259	365	458	109	100	112	9	77	0.43	45	20	35	36	111	95	103	9%	9%	93	13%	60%	12	33%	42%	3.9	122	$23
20	**Proj**	**595**	**77**	**25**	**81**	**17**	**269**		**259**	**334**	**466**	**108**	**96**	**111**	**8**	**78**	**0.41**	**42**	**20**	**38**	**31**	**106**	**104**	**103**	**15%**		**92**	**17%**	**71%**				**12.0**	**150**	**$26**

Pujols,Albert

Age: 40 Bats: R Pos: 1B DH | Ht: 6' 3" Wt: 235

Health B | PT/Exp A | Consist A | LIMA Plan B | Rand Var +1 | MM 2135

After cratering his RAR and BPX in 2017, he's managed to claw back onto the gentle glide path to retirement. Chronically low h%, underpinned by appalling Spd, locks BA below xBA. Power mired consistently below average, but bulk PAs prop up counting stats and value. Watch the 2nd half xHR/F and xPX, could be another crater ahead.

Yr	Tm	PA	R	HR	RBI	SB	BA	xHR	xBA	OBP	SLG	OPS+	vL+	vR+	bb%	ct%	Eye	G	L	F	h%	HctX	PX	xPX	HR/F	xHR/F	Spd	SBO	SB%	#Wk	DOM	DIS	RAR	BPX	R$
15	LAA	661	85	40	95	5	244	32	286	307	480	110	104	109	8	88	0.69	42	16	42	22	127	125	130	18%	14%	59	6%	63%	27	70%	11%	-1.8	235	$21
16	LAA	650	71	31	119	4	268	34	269	323	457	106	110	103	8	87	0.65	44	17	40	26	129	95	132	15%	16%	60	3%	100%	26	50%	23%	5.8	171	$21
17	LAA	636	53	23	101	3	241	22	251	286	386	90	81	91	6	84	0.40	43	18	38	25	120	72	105	12%	11%	52	2%	100%	27	30%	22%	-28.9	73	$10
18	LAA	498	50	19	64	1	245	19	272	289	411	97	94	97	6	86	0.43	40	22	37	25	135	88	122	13%	13%	57	1%	100%	22	41%	14%	-5.6	150	$10
19	LAA	545	55	23	93	3	244	20	262	305	430	97	108	91	8	86	0.63	46	15	39	24	116	86	90	14%	12%	59	3%	100%	28	54%	25%	-6.6	181	$12
1st Half		280	29	13	43	0	235	14	248	304	433	98	103	95	9	87	0.81	44	14	43	22	131	89	102	14%	15%	66	0%	0%	15	53%	27%	-5.6	226	$9
2nd Half		265	26	10	50	3	254	6	266	306	426	97	116	88	7	85	0.49	48	17	34	26	101	83	77	14%	8%	60	5%	100%	13	54%	23%	-4.6	144	$16
20	**Proj**	**490**	**50**	**20**	**79**	**3**	**246**		**261**	**299**	**420**	**97**	**103**	**94**	**7**	**86**	**0.53**	**44**	**18**	**38**	**25**	**121**	**81**	**103**	**13%**		**58**	**3%**	**96%**				**-3.8**	**141**	**$14**

RAY MURPHY

Quinn,Roman

Age: 27	Bats: B	Pos: CF	Health	F	LIMA Plan	D
Ht: 5' 10"	Wt: 170		PT/Exp	F	Rand Var	-1
			Consist	C	MM	1501

4-11-.213 with 8 SB in 122 PA at PHI. Injuries (oblique in spring, groin x2 in-season) keep us wondering what he might do in extended look. Did have 4 HR and 6 SB in 63 AB over three weeks right after ASB. Scoff at that sample all you want, but as this box shows, such scraps are all he's given us to date. If he gets even 300 AB... UP: 30 SB.

Yr	Tm	PA	R	HR	RBI	SB	BA	xHR	xBA	OBP	SLG	OPS+	vL+	vR+	bb%	ct%	Eye	G	L	F	h%	HctX	PX	xPX	HR/F	xHR/F	Spd	SBO	SB%	#Wk	DOM	DIS	RAR	BPX	R$
15	aa	246	35	4	12	23	272			314	378	96			6	79	0.30				33		62				165	53%	67%					78	$12
16	PHI *	377	53	5	25	28	246	1	247	307	357	90	123	84	8	71	0.31	57	22	22	33	51	77	50	0%	13%	170	42%	74%	3	33%	33%	-10.2	43	$14
17	aaa	190	21	2	11	9	242			304	340	86			8	67	0.27				35		67				132	28%	66%					-58	$3
18	PHI *	251	25	4	21	20	256	1	236	307	394	97	123	90	7	74	0.29	49	18	33	33	59	81	79	7%	3%	183	43%	80%	11	45%	27%	-0.1	110	$10
19	PHI *	150	23	4	13	9	216	3	206	288	354	85	85	89	9	65	0.29	48	16	36	30	72	79	62	18%	14%	142	30%	88%	11	36%	55%	-3.1	-44	$2
1st Half		78	10	0	4	3	154	0	151	226	190	56	38	47	8	56	0.21	60	10	30	28	44	26	-24	0%	0%	147	25%	70%	5	20%	60%	-7.4	-344	-$5
2nd Half		72	13	4	9	6	286	3	267	366	540	120	106	128	10	76	0.47	41	20	39	32	97	122	104	25%	19%	124	33%	100%	6	50%	50%	5.6	230	$11
20	**Proj**	**245**	**34**	**5**	**21**	**20**	**243**		**224**	**313**	**375**	**93**	**98**	**88**	**8**	**70**	**0.30**	**50**	**18**	**32**	**32**	**66**	**73**	**62**	**10%**		**163**	**40%**	**84%**				**1.0**	**30**	**$9**

Ramirez,Harold

Age: 25	Bats: R	Pos: LF RF CF	Health	A	LIMA Plan	C
Ht: 5' 10"	Wt: 220		PT/Exp	B	Rand Var	-1
			Consist	C	MM	1243

11-50-.276 in 446 PA at MIA. Started hot after May callup as h% was off the charts (44% over first 57 AB), which was key as it earned him a lineup spot for rest of season. Second half line (all in MIA) much more representative of his true skill level, which is fringe-average across the board. Any value hinges on finding more PA than he deserves.

Yr	Tm	PA	R	HR	RBI	SB	BA	xHR	xBA	OBP	SLG	OPS+	vL+	vR+	bb%	ct%	Eye	G	L	F	h%	HctX	PX	xPX	HR/F	xHR/F	Spd	SBO	SB%	#Wk	DOM	DIS	RAR	BPX	R$
15																																			
16	aa	402	52	2	43	6	295			328	387	97			5	81	0.26				36		58				124	16%	36%					57	$12
17	aa	471	39	5	45	4	247			291	335	84			6	84	0.38				28		51				96	7%	57%					58	$4
18	aa	485	50	9	58	13	292			324	429	104			5	79	0.23				35		94				81	14%	86%					87	$18
19	MIA *	560	71	14	62	3	282	11	271	312	433	99	86	100	4	79	0.21	57	20	23	34	95	82	63	14%	14%	107	4%	57%	22	23%	36%	-6.8	81	$14
1st Half		287	41	5	31	3	306	2	277	338	439	104	80	106	5	79	0.23	62	19	19	37	87	79	37	8%	8%	94	6%	71%	9	11%	56%	2.0	74	$17
2nd Half		273	30	9	31	0	256	9	266	293	426	95	90	97	4	78	0.18	54	20	26	30	100	86	80	17%	17%	121	2%	0%	13	31%	23%	-8.2	96	$11
20	**Proj**	**385**	**44**	**9**	**43**	**4**	**278**		**272**	**319**	**423**	**100**	**90**	**103**	**5**	**80**	**0.24**	**57**	**20**	**23**	**33**	**95**	**79**	**63**	**14%**		**101**	**8%**	**64%**				**0.8**	**68**	**$12**

Ramirez,Jose

Age: 27	Bats: B	Pos: 3B	Health	B	LIMA Plan	C
Ht: 5' 9"	Wt: 190		PT/Exp	A	Rand Var	+3
			Consist	D	MM	4355

So much hand-wringing about that 1st half as it happened. Easy to see there'd be some bounceback as most skills were intact, except power. But xHR and xPX remind us that his power comes from lots of contact and FBs rather than raw skill. Speed is most stable element here, so in order of likelihood to return: 1) 30 SB, 2) 30 HR, 3) .300 BA.

Yr	Tm	PA	R	HR	RBI	SB	BA	xHR	xBA	OBP	SLG	OPS+	vL+	vR+	bb%	ct%	Eye	G	L	F	h%	HctX	PX	xPX	HR/F	xHR/F	Spd	SBO	SB%	#Wk	DOM	DIS	RAR	BPX	R$
15	CLE *	544	76	7	38	23	240	4	264	306	355	92	79	90	9	90	0.96	48	16	36	25	94	71	69	6%	4%	122	25%	74%	20	35%	20%	-13.9	197	$14
16	CLE	618	84	11	76	22	312	11	290	363	462	112	114	109	7	89	0.71	41	23	36	34	97	91	77	6%	6%	96	18%	76%	27	81%	7%	21.0	211	$30
17	CLE	645	107	29	83	17	318	19	320	374	583	128	126	127	8	88	0.75	39	21	40	32	121	138	102	14%	9%	104	15%	77%	27	85%	4%	51.2	342	$35
18	CLE	698	110	39	105	34	270	30	299	387	552	130	113	136	15	86	1.33	33	21	46	25	115	146	119	17%	13%	88	22%	85%	28	79%	4%	53.6	400	$40
19	CLE	542	68	23	83	24	255	20	274	327	479	107	103	108	10	85	0.70	33	21	46	26	118	109	114	12%	10%	93	24%	86%	23	65%	17%	6.6	278	$23
1st Half		340	32	5	30	18	214	11	225	309	325	85	98	78	12	85	0.93	32	19	50	23	105	57	89	4%	9%	120	26%	86%	15	53%	27%	-16.6	181	$16
2nd Half		202	36	18	53	6	321	10	345	356	722	142	112	156	6	83	0.39	35	24	42	30	138	193	155	27%	15%	68	21%	86%	8	88%	0%	23.1	456	$33
20	**Proj**	**609**	**93**	**28**	**100**	**27**	**282**		**290**	**353**	**529**	**119**	**108**	**123**	**10**	**86**	**0.78**	**35**	**21**	**43**	**28**	**119**	**120**	**117**	**14%**		**89**	**23%**	**85%**				**33.7**	**367**	**$35**

Ramos,Wilson

Age: 32	Bats: R	Pos: CA	Health	C	LIMA Plan	C+
Ht: 6' 1"	Wt: 245		PT/Exp	C	Rand Var	0
			Consist	D	MM	1135

Nudged his contact back to near-elite level, but still lost nearly 20 pts of BA. That may look like h% variance at work, but it's more a matter of a 60+% GB rate combined with being a 245-lb catcher. Extreme G/L/F split should revert closer to historical levels, which could mean a few more HR if he gets to 500 PA again. Overall picture is stable.

Yr	Tm	PA	R	HR	RBI	SB	BA	xHR	xBA	OBP	SLG	OPS+	vL+	vR+	bb%	ct%	Eye	G	L	F	h%	HctX	PX	xPX	HR/F	xHR/F	Spd	SBO	SB%	#Wk	DOM	DIS	RAR	BPX	R$
15	WAS	504	41	15	68	0	229	16	240	258	358	86	85	84	4	79	0.21	55	20	25	26	93	81	84	16%	17%	54	0%	0%	26	27%	42%	-10.2	16	$5
16	WAS	523	58	22	80	0	307	23	280	354	496	116	136	108	7	84	0.44	54	20	25	33	120	105	97	21%	22%	54	0%	0%	26	62%	23%	26.8	143	$20
17	TAM *	251	22	13	39	0	252	11	258	287	444	98	107	93	5	84	0.31	52	18	30	25	113	94	106	21%	21%	48	0%	0%	15	40%	47%	2.0	115	$4
18	2 TM	416	39	15	70	0	306	16	266	358	487	117	127	112	8	79	0.40	55	20	25	36	114	107	90	20%	21%	64	0%	0%	24	25%	38%	30.4	127	$15
19	NYM	524	52	14	73	1	288	13	269	351	416	102	123	95	8	85	0.64	62	18	19	31	94	63	50	18%	17%	52	1%	100%	28	36%	25%	11.3	96	$13
1st Half		265	35	9	41	0	270	8	264	343	414	101	137	89	10	82	0.62	63	19	18	30	96	68	54	26%	23%	58	0%	0%	15	33%	40%	6.5	85	$13
2nd Half		259	17	5	32	1	305	5	266	359	419	103	110	101	7	89	0.67	62	18	20	33	93	58	45	12%	12%	54	1%	100%	13	38%	8%	9.7	122	$12
20	**Proj**	**490**	**46**	**16**	**73**	**1**	**287**		**263**	**339**	**440**	**105**	**119**	**100**	**7**	**84**	**0.48**	**58**	**19**	**23**	**31**	**103**	**76**	**72**	**19%**		**54**	**0%**	**100%**				**24.8**	**70**	**$16**

Realmuto,J.T.

Age: 29	Bats: R	Pos: CA	Health	A	LIMA Plan	B
Ht: 6' 1"	Wt: 210		PT/Exp	A	Rand Var	0
			Consist	B	MM	3445

First half-season in PHI was a slight disappointment. He followed up with an absolutely stellar 2nd half that was littered with skill levels that matched or exceeded career bests. Even his sneaky SB game re-emerged. Prime age, durability, status as position's only five-category contributor make him the top catcher on your 2020 ranking list.

Yr	Tm	PA	R	HR	RBI	SB	BA	xHR	xBA	OBP	SLG	OPS+	vL+	vR+	bb%	ct%	Eye	G	L	F	h%	HctX	PX	xPX	HR/F	xHR/F	Spd	SBO	SB%	#Wk	DOM	DIS	RAR	BPX	R$
15	MIA	467	49	10	47	8	259	10	269	290	406	97	109	92	4	84	0.27	45	21	34	29	106	88	105	8%	8%	125	13%	67%	25	44%	16%	1.8	149	$11
16	MIA	545	60	11	48	12	303	12	261	343	428	105	83	108	5	80	0.28	49	20	30	36	97	82	86	9%	10%	102	11%	75%	26	27%	35%	12.4	86	$20
17	MIA	579	68	17	65	8	278	17	267	332	451	105	111	101	6	80	0.34	48	18	34	32	108	97	98	12%	12%	126	8%	80%	27	37%	37%	16.9	152	$17
18	MIA	529	74	21	74	3	277	24	272	340	484	114	91	120	7	78	0.37	40	23	37	32	111	123	110	15%	17%	108	4%	60%	24	58%	13%	28.0	200	$18
19	PHI	592	92	25	83	9	275	22	273	328	493	109	110	108	7	77	0.33	39	23	38	32	122	117	118	16%	14%	111	8%	90%	27	37%	19%	21.0	189	$21
1st Half		310	49	10	37	3	265	12	251	319	431	100	118	93	7	75	0.30	42	22	35	32	112	92	103	13%		107	6%	75%	15	20%	27%	6.0	78	$17
2nd Half		282	43	15	46	6	286	11	296	337	561	118	103	124	7	80	0.38	36	25	40	31	132	142	134	18%		112	11%	100%	12	58%	8%	21.1	304	$27
20	**Proj**	**560**	**86**	**22**	**82**	**8**	**278**		**270**	**330**	**481**	**109**	**104**	**110**	**7**	**79**	**0.34**	**41**	**22**	**37**	**32**	**116**	**108**	**113**	**14%**		**116**	**8%**	**83%**				**32.2**	**180**	**$24**

Reddick,Josh

Age: 33	Bats: L	Pos: RF LF	Health	B	LIMA Plan	B
Ht: 6' 2"	Wt: 195		PT/Exp	B	Rand Var	0
			Consist	C	MM	1335

Not necessarily related to his value, but still fascinating: long-time platoon bat has actually learned to hit vL in recent years, but slipping vR concurrently. Quintessential "better real life player than fantasy": makes lots of contact, runs pretty well, plays strong defense. Just not enough HctX to make it all go, for our purposes.

Yr	Tm	PA	R	HR	RBI	SB	BA	xHR	xBA	OBP	SLG	OPS+	vL+	vR+	bb%	ct%	Eye	G	L	F	h%	HctX	PX	xPX	HR/F	xHR/F	Spd	SBO	SB%	#Wk	DOM	DIS	RAR	BPX	R$
15	OAK	578	67	20	77	10	272	15	276	333	449	109	90	113	8	88	0.75	38	21	41	28	99	100	93	11%	8%	113	8%	83%	26	58%	12%	7.8	224	$20
16	2 TM *	464	54	11	38	8	270	9	259	333	392	99	49	116	9	85	0.63	41	22	37	30	105	70	90	8%	7%	121	9%	73%	22	50%	27%	-1.9	149	$11
17	HOU	533	77	13	82	7	314	12	275	363	484	114	101	115	8	85	0.60	34	24	42	35	107	95	97	7%	7%	118	7%	70%	26	58%	12%	22.0	209	$23
18	HOU	485	63	17	47	7	242	11	241	318	400	99	115	92	10	82	0.64	37	19	44	26	91	83	91	11%	7%	108	7%	78%	27	52%	22%	-2.5	167	$11
19	HOU	547	57	14	56	5	275	11	266	319	409	97	110	93	7	87	0.55	39	23	37	29	97	62	57	8%	7%	104	5%	71%	27	44%	26%	-5.4	159	$12
1st Half		311	36	10	29	4	297	8	274	334	444	104	115	101	6	89	0.59	38	24	39	31	105	66	71	10%	8%	108	7%	67%	15	53%	20%	1.7	204	$17
2nd Half		236	21	4	27	1	247	2	258	298	363	87	104	83	7	84	0.50	41	23	36	28	85	58	37	6%	3%	101	2%	100%	12	33%	33%	-9.4	111	$6
20	**Proj**	**455**	**54**	**12**	**51**	**5**	**268**		**257**	**322**	**410**	**99**	**104**	**96**	**8**	**85**	**0.57**	**38**	**22**	**40**	**29**	**96**	**69**	**72**	**9%**		**109**	**6%**	**75%**				**1.6**	**137**	**$14**

Rendon,Anthony

Age: 30	Bats: R	Pos: 3B	Health	B	LIMA Plan	C
Ht: 6' 1"	Wt: 200		PT/Exp	A	Rand Var	-3
			Consist	A	MM	4255

Bryce who? Stellar season in which he took already-impressive broad base of skills and sprinkled in more HctX, a few more FBs, and an astounding fourth straight year of improvement vR. Best to treat this as his ceiling, especially given lofty PA total. Expect a tick of pullback across the board, but that still leaves him in a ritzy neighborhood.

Yr	Tm	PA	R	HR	RBI	SB	BA	xHR	xBA	OBP	SLG	OPS+	vL+	vR+	bb%	ct%	Eye	G	L	F	h%	HctX	PX	xPX	HR/F	xHR/F	Spd	SBO	SB%	#Wk	DOM	DIS	RAR	BPX	R$
15	WAS *	381	44	5	25	1	261	8	238	337	361	97	103	96	10	78	0.52	45	21	33	32	111	76	104	6%	10%	106	3%	33%	16	19%	44%	-5.5	70	$5
16	WAS	647	91	20	85	12	270	21	258	348	450	109	110	106	10	79	0.56	36	21	44	31	117	111	116	10%	11%	107	11%	67%	26	54%	12%	5.7	174	$21
17	WAS	605	81	25	100	7	301	21	282	403	533	126	150	117	14	84	1.02	34	19	47	32	116	127	112	12%	10%	91	5%	78%	27	67%	15%	34.8	285	$25
18	WAS	597	88	24	92	2	308	31	292	374	535	126	129	124	9	84	0.67	33	24	44	33	118	130	122	12%	16%	94	2%	67%	26	69%	19%	38.3	303	$26
19	WAS	646	117	34	126	5	319	37	297	412	598	134	137	133	12	84	0.93	33	21	46	33	130	136	160	16%	17%	95	3%	83%	26	73%	12%	53.9	374	$33
1st Half		299	63	19	58	1	311	23	297	398	630	137	143	135	11	82	0.70	30	20	50	32	147	156	205	18%	21%	104	3%	50%	14	64%	21%	25.9	400	$31
2nd Half		347	54	15	68	4	326	14	297	424	569	131	132	131	14	86	1.20	36	22	42	34	115	118	123	14%	13%	89	4%	100%	12	83%	0%	30.5	356	$35
20	**Proj**	**595**	**97**	**30**	**105**	**5**	**303**		**291**	**389**	**563**	**128**	**135**	**125**	**12**	**84**	**0.83**	**34**	**21**	**44**	**31**	**122**	**129**	**136**	**15%**		**97**	**4%**	**77%**				**48.4**	**324**	**$30**

RAY MURPHY

Renfroe,Hunter

Age: 28 Bats: R Pos: RF LF | Ht: 6' 1" Wt: 220

Health B | PT/Exp C | Consist A | LIMA Plan B | Rand Var +3 | MM 4325

Bum ankle likely to blame for 2nd-half collapse. Before that, light-tower power was on full display, and was even driving potential BA growth (see 1st-half xBA) despite very shaky ct%. Improved pitch selectivity bodes well, FB% on the rise and xHR/F locked in the 20s. Price in a BA hit, but the power points to ... UP: 40 HR

Yr	Tm	PA	R	HR	RBI	SB	BA	xHR	xBA	OBP	SLG	OPS+	vL+	vR+	bb%	ct%	Eye	G	L	F	h%	HctX	PX	xPX	HR/F	xHR/F	Spd	SBO	SB%	#Wk	DOM	DIS	RAR	BPX	R$
15	a/a	538	48	15	57	4	231			271	380	91			5	70	0.18				30		108				97	5%	77%					16	$6
16	SD *	583	72	23	84	3	255	2	242	275	443	98	159	159	3	76	0.11	43	13	43	30	82	116	125	31%	15%	89	6%	59%	3	100%	0%	-9.2	89	$14
17	SD *	538	63	29	70	4	253	21	251	296	493	106	143	84	6	70	0.21	38	17	45	30	99	149	131	19%	15%	87	4%	100%	22	41%	36%	-2.3	121	$13
18	SD *	483	57	27	71	2	241	25	259	291	483	107	113	110	6	73	0.26	37	20	43	27	126	148	136	20%	20%	83	3%	67%	23	52%	26%	3.8	163	$13
19	SD	494	64	33	64	5	216	28	236	289	489	103	118	98	9	65	0.30	36	16	48	25	106	159	144	24%	20%	80	6%	100%	27	41%	48%	-9.6	119	$11
1st Half		261	36	24	45	4	248	18	280	310	609	123	165	112	8	71	0.31	36	17	47	24	121	191	154	30%	23%	81	9%	100%	15	60%	33%	9.3	289	$20
2nd Half		233	28	9	19	1	178	9	183	266	347	81	85	78	11	58	0.29	37	15	49	25	87	113	130	15%	15%	88	2%	100%	12	17%	67%	-15.2	-96	$0
20	Proj	490	60	30	63	4	243		243	303	497	108	119	102	8	70	0.28	36	17	47	28	115	142	137	20%		85	4%	90%				7.5	114	$13

Rengifo,Luis

Age: 23 Bats: R Pos: 2B | Ht: 5' 10" Wt: 195

Health A | PT/Exp D | Consist B | LIMA Plan D+ | Rand Var 0 | MM 1323

7-33-.238 in 406 PA at LAA. Owns fine speed, and he'll draw a walk. But so-so pop plus a big contact-rate dip in majors hurt OBP, and awful SB conversion rate earned a frequent red light. Contact better in minors, and they can coach up his baserunning. So while there's some long-term hope, don't expect much in 2020.

Yr	Tm	PA	R	HR	RBI	SB	BA	xHR	xBA	OBP	SLG	OPS+	vL+	vR+	bb%	ct%	Eye	G	L	F	h%	HctX	PX	xPX	HR/F	xHR/F	Spd	SBO	SB%	#Wk	DOM	DIS	RAR	BPX	R$
15																																			
16																																			
17																																			
18	a/a	376	55	4	36	14	246			317	364	94			9	82	0.59				29		68				135	25%	62%					153	$10
19	LAA *	523	54	11	42	4	234	9	242	304	362	88	79	96	9	74	0.39	48	22	30	29	83	73	50	9%	11%	131	10%	32%	22	23%	55%	-19.1	52	$5
1st Half		297	31	7	28	2	238	5	238	299	368	89	100	90	8	75	0.34	48	20	32	30	97	73	70	8%	13%	132	11%	27%	11	27%	55%	-10.3	56	$6
2nd Half		226	23	4	14	2	227	4	244	323	354	89	65	102	11	73	0.45	47	24	29	29	72	73	33	10%	10%	127	9%	40%	11	18%	55%	-7.3	48	$3
20	Proj	350	42	7	29	7	238		251	318	368	92	80	98	10	77	0.47	48	22	30	29	82	71	48	9%		139	16%	52%				-4.7	67	$8

Reyes,Franmil

Age: 24 Bats: R Pos: RF DH | Ht: 6' 5" Wt: 275

Health A | PT/Exp B | Consist C | LIMA Plan C+ | Rand Var +2 | MM 4035

Impressive power even by today's standards. BA won't kill you too much, and small platoon split points to full-time AB. Bigger question is G/F profile; FB% and HR spiked in 1st half, but both regressed to 2018 levels in 2nd half. What's his true FB level? If it's only 30%, then expect a HR pullback. If closer to 40%, than UP: 45 HR, .270 BA.

Yr	Tm	PA	R	HR	RBI	SB	BA	xHR	xBA	OBP	SLG	OPS+	vL+	vR+	bb%	ct%	Eye	G	L	F	h%	HctX	PX	xPX	HR/F	xHR/F	Spd	SBO	SB%	#Wk	DOM	DIS	RAR	BPX	R$
15																																			
16																																			
17	aa	550	73	22	95	4	246			306	433	99			8	72	0.31				30		114				82	7%	47%					70	$13
18	SD *	521	71	27	68	0	275	14	246	345	487	115	143	103	10	68	0.34	49	21	30	35	111	135	115	30%	26%	76	0%	0%	18	33%	44%	18.7	83	$17
19	2 TM	548	69	37	81	0	249	37	256	310	512	109	115	107	9	68	0.30	44	21	34	29	112	145	140	31%	31%	45	0%	0%	28	43%	39%	3.0	81	$15
1st Half		279	35	24	41	0	248	23	270	301	559	115	97	118	8	70	0.28	39	22	39	25	121	160	156	34%	32%	55	0%	0%	15	47%	33%	4.0	163	$17
2nd Half		269	34	13	40	0	250	14	241	320	463	103	123	92	10	66	0.32	49	21	30	32	102	128	122	27%	29%	52	0%	0%	13	38%	46%	-1.2	15	$13
20	Proj	595	78	35	87	1	257		253	323	498	110	127	103	9	69	0.32	47	21	32	31	110	135	128	30%		56	1%	50%				16.1	53	$21

Reyes,Pablo

Age: 26 Bats: R Pos: LF | Ht: 5' 8" Wt: 175

Health A | PT/Exp C | Consist A | LIMA Plan D | Rand Var +1 | MM 2323

2-19-.203 in 157 PA at PIT. Awful start to 2019 (.128/.190/.319 in Apr/May) earned a quick demotion. Fared better in 2nd half, though, and actually hit better vR than vL in minors, so vR+ issues fixable. Versatile glove helps. No outstanding skill, but history of decent contact and power metrics give him room to grow.

Yr	Tm	PA	R	HR	RBI	SB	BA	xHR	xBA	OBP	SLG	OPS+	vL+	vR+	bb%	ct%	Eye	G	L	F	h%	HctX	PX	xPX	HR/F	xHR/F	Spd	SBO	SB%	#Wk	DOM	DIS	RAR	BPX	R$
15																																			
16																																			
17	aa	465	54	8	44	18	250			323	369	93			10	82	0.60				29		67				109	28%	54%					109	$12
18	PIT *	489	52	9	39	13	251	2	233	298	372	93	169	82	6	79	0.31	48	15	37	30	74	75	114	18%	12%	144	20%	58%	5	60%	20%	-14.0	113	$11
19	PIT *	342	35	9	42	5	224	2	235	277	389	88	97	66	7	75	0.30	47	13	40	27	88	94	84	5%	5%	104	15%	52%	16	25%	50%	-17.6	85	$4
1st Half		156	14	4	16	2	194	0	206	234	334	76	47	35	5	71	0.18	42	13	46	25	39	91	-26	0%	0%	95	15%	66%	6	0%	100%	-12.9	-19	-$4
2nd Half		187	22	6	26	3	251	2	254	314	437	99	134	72	8	80	0.45	49	13	38	29	107	97	116	6%	6%	115	15%	43%	10	40%	20%	-4.0	181	$10
20	Proj	280	30	8	29	6	248		239	306	405	96	121	76	7	79	0.38	47	14	39	29	88	85	80	9%		117	19%	56%				-4.3	104	$8

Reyes,Victor

Age: 25 Bats: B Pos: CF LF | Ht: 6' 5" Wt: 215

Health A | PT/Exp C | Consist D | LIMA Plan C | Rand Var -2 | MM 1433

3-25-.304 with 9 SB in 292 PA at DET. PRO: Flashed solid line-drive stroke in second MLB go-round; owns above-par wheels. CON: Poor patience hurts SB opps; low FB% caps power. Something of a unicorn; despite size, profiles as line-drive, gap-power BA guy. But note xBA when setting value; it shows he's not a .300 hitter just yet.

Yr	Tm	PA	R	HR	RBI	SB	BA	xHR	xBA	OBP	SLG	OPS+	vL+	vR+	bb%	ct%	Eye	G	L	F	h%	HctX	PX	xPX	HR/F	xHR/F	Spd	SBO	SB%	#Wk	DOM	DIS	RAR	BPX	R$
15																																			
16																																			
17	aa	501	49	3	43	15	276			309	382	93			4	82	0.26				33		65				117	21%	61%					76	$13
18	DET	219	35	1	12	9	222	3	246	239	288	73	68	73	2	78	0.11	50	26	24	28	100	39	63	3%	8%	145	23%	90%	26	12%	62%	-14.3	-17	$3
19	DET *	592	71	12	73	17	287	3	279	318	428	99	92	105	4	79	0.21	45	29	26	35	110	78	70	5%	5%	111	20%	64%	19	16%	26%	-7.2	81	$21
1st Half		262	38	8	47	6	275	0	307	300	431	98	0	78	3	81	0.19	63	25	13	31	70	82	26	0%	0%	102	23%	46%	7	14%	43%	-7.7	107	$19
2nd Half		330	33	4	27	12	297	3	270	332	426	100	93	106	5	77	0.23	44	29	27	37	109	74	72	6%	6%	125	18%	79%	12	17%	17%	-0.2	67	$23
20	Proj	315	41	5	29	11	274		258	298	390	92	85	94	4	79	0.18	45	26	30	33	105	63	68	6%		123	21%	73%				1.3	59	$12

Reynolds,Bryan

Age: 25 Bats: B Pos: LF RF CF | Ht: 6' 3" Wt: 205

Health A | PT/Exp D | Consist C | LIMA Plan B | Rand Var -2 | MM 2345

16-68-.314 in 546 PA at PIT. Terrific debut, with line drives and solid hard contact driving the bus. Unheralded pre-2019, but has bested .300 in every pro season. And before we decide 2019 h% was over his head, note that career MiLB rate was nearly as good (38%), so this may be close to his level. Expect some pullback, but not much.

Yr	Tm	PA	R	HR	RBI	SB	BA	xHR	xBA	OBP	SLG	OPS+	vL+	vR+	bb%	ct%	Eye	G	L	F	h%	HctX	PX	xPX	HR/F	xHR/F	Spd	SBO	SB%	#Wk	DOM	DIS	RAR	BPX	R$
15																																			
16																																			
17																																			
18	a/a	383	48	6	40	3	280			348	398	103			10	77	0.48				35		75				75	7%	50%					37	$9
19	PIT *	603	92	20	78	6	316	20	281	379	516	119	99	124	9	75	0.39	46	24	30	39	111	119	108	14%	18%	135	6%	58%	24	46%	29%	37.0	215	$24
1st Half		280	43	10	38	3	351	5	294	413	568	131	132	128	9	76	0.42	46	27	27	43	132	128	111	14%	12%	145	7%	45%	12	50%	33%	32.1	263	$25
2nd Half		323	49	10	40	3	285	14	266	350	471	108	80	121	8	75	0.37	47	22	31	35	97	106	105	14%	20%	121	5%	75%	12	42%	25%	10.7	148	$23
20	Proj	595	87	18	73	5	294		268	362	472	112	95	119	9	76	0.41	46	24	30	36	111	99	107	14%		130	5%	59%				22.7	110	$23

Riley,Austin

Age: 23 Bats: R Pos: LF | Ht: 6' 3" Wt: 220

Health B | PT/Exp D | Consist C | LIMA Plan C+ | Rand Var +4 | MM 4105

18-49-.226 in 297 PA at ATL. Partially torn knee ligament took a chunk out of season, but was already in a tailspin (2 HR, .480 OPS in July) as pitchers adjusted after hot start (14 HR in May/Jun). Extreme FB lean says he'll hit his share of bombs, but that coupled with poor ct% mean potential BA issues. It's his turn to adjust now.

Yr	Tm	PA	R	HR	RBI	SB	BA	xHR	xBA	OBP	SLG	OPS+	vL+	vR+	bb%	ct%	Eye	G	L	F	h%	HctX	PX	xPX	HR/F	xHR/F	Spd	SBO	SB%	#Wk	DOM	DIS	RAR	BPX	R$
15																																			
16																																			
17	aa	200	29	8	28	2	296			372	467	112			11	69	0.39				39		103				109	3%	100%					39	$6
18	a/a	419	51	16	59	1	280			329	484	113			7	67	0.22				38		144				94	1%	100%					87	$13
19	ATL *	488	75	30	85	0	244	17	248	296	505	106	128	90	7	67	0.22	26	25	49	29	97	152	160	22%	21%	83	2%	0%	18	33%	44%	-3.2	107	$14
1st Half		338	60	26	72	0	274	13	279	326	592	123	161	110	7	71	0.26	25	28	47	30	112	172	167	28%	26%	95	3%	0%	8	38%	25%	12.7	241	$26
2nd Half		151	15	4	14	0	176	4	179	230	312	71	93	57	7	58	0.17	28	20	52	27	72	101	148	13%	13%	83	0%	0%	10	30%	60%	-13.2	-174	-$14
20	Proj	455	60	21	65	1	249		226	310	459	104	133	93	8	65	0.23	29	23	48	33	88	131	156	16%		81	2%	67%				3.1	2	$14

ROD TRUESDELL

Rizzo,Anthony

Age: 30 Bats: L Pos: 1B | Ht: 6' 3" Wt: 240

Health B | PT/Exp A | Consist A | LIMA Plan B+ | Rand Var 0 | MM 3155

Back tightness started in May; flared periodically rest of year. That may have contributed to 2nd half shift to LDs instead of FBs, which benefitted BA at the expense of HR. Superb plate skills and that LD stroke give him a high BA floor, but xPX, FB% and xHR all say return to 30 HR is not automatic. Even minor back issues can be worrisome.

Yr Tm	PA	R	HR	RBI	SB	BA	xHR	xBA	OBP	SLG	OPS+	vL+	vR+	bb%	ct%	Eye	G	L	F	h%	HctX	PX	xPX	HR/F	xHR/F	Spd	SBO	SB%	#Wk	DOM	DIS	RAR	BPX	R$
15 CHC	701	94	31	101	17	278	31	285	387	512	125	122	124	11	82	0.74	35	22	44	29	121	143	131	15%	15%	76	14%	74%	27	70%	15%	19.1	243	$31
16 CHC	676	94	32	109	3	292	31	293	385	544	126	112	130	11	81	0.69	38	20	41	31	113	145	120	16%	16%	73	5%	38%	27	74%	7%	28.4	251	$26
17 CHC	691	99	32	109	10	273	31	291	392	507	121	117	120	13	84	1.01	41	20	39	28	117	119	107	17%	16%	70	8%	71%	27	70%	7%	11.0	248	$25
18 CHC	665	74	25	101	6	283	22	286	376	470	117	95	124	11	86	0.88	38	25	37	29	108	100	93	14%	12%	76	6%	60%	27	59%	22%	13.6	230	$24
19 CHC	613	89	27	94	5	293	22	301	405	520	123	105	128	12	83	0.83	43	25	32	31	107	109	95	20%	16%	77	4%	71%	27	56%	26%	23.7	252	$23
1st Half	348	54	19	56	3	270	16	291	382	519	120	90	129	12	83	0.80	44	20	36	27	115	117	110	22%	18%	65	6%	60%	15	67%	33%	10.5	259	$26
2nd Half	265	35	8	38	2	324	6	315	434	521	126	122	127	12	84	0.86	42	32	26	36	97	98	74	16%	12%	95	3%	100%	12	42%	17%	16.7	256	$18
20 Proj	**630**	**89**	**27**	**101**	**5**	**291**		**293**	**396**	**506**	**121**	**108**	**125**	**12**	**84**	**0.83**	**40**	**25**	**35**	**31**	**108**	**104**	**96**	**17%**		**80**	**4%**	**61%**				**34.1**	**245**	**$24**

Robert,Luis

Age: 22 Bats: R Pos: LF | Ht: 6' 3" Wt: 185

Health A | PT/Exp F | Consist F | LIMA Plan C+ | Rand Var 0 | MM 3513

Highly regarded CHW prospect didn't disappoint, appearing at three different levels of the minors, capping the year batting .297 with 16 HR and 7 SB in just 47 games at AAA. Aggressive approach and pitch recognition issues foretell a bumpy MLB transition, but the power/speed combo is elite and the long-term upside is immense.

Yr Tm	PA	R	HR	RBI	SB	BA	xHR	xBA	OBP	SLG	OPS+	vL+	vR+	bb%	ct%	Eye	G	L	F	h%	HctX	PX	xPX	HR/F	xHR/F	Spd	SBO	SB%	#Wk	DOM	DIS	RAR	BPX	R$
15																																		
16																																		
17																																		
18																																		
19 a/a	449	79	23	61	25	288			322	535	114			5	72	0.18				35		134				132	37%	75%					167	$26
1st Half	218	37	7	27	16	313			351	519	116			5	72	0.21				40		118				144	41%	75%				12.5	148	$22
2nd Half	233	45	16	37	11	276			310	579	117			5	72	0.17				32		157				169	34%	77%				11.6	270	$29
20 Proj	**350**	**52**	**13**	**44**	**15**	**238**		**233**	**276**	**445**	**97**	**96**	**97**	**5**	**72**	**0.19**	**34**	**20**	**46**	**29**	**91**	**115**		**12%**		**158**	**32%**	**79%**				**-4.1**	**152**	**$15**

Robles,Victor

Age: 23 Bats: R Pos: CF | Ht: 6' 0" Wt: 190

Health A | PT/Exp D | Consist C | LIMA Plan B | Rand Var 0 | MM 2535

Showed off an awfully appealing HR/SB combo in strong rookie campaign. xHR largely backs power output, but big drop in FB% from 1st half/2nd half tempers HR upside. Elite Spd is his best asset; upgraded SB% means he should keep getting lots of green lights. 2nd half ct%/GB/SBO plays to his strengths and hints at... UP: 40 SB.

Yr Tm	PA	R	HR	RBI	SB	BA	xHR	xBA	OBP	SLG	OPS+	vL+	vR+	bb%	ct%	Eye	G	L	F	h%	HctX	PX	xPX	HR/F	xHR/F	Spd	SBO	SB%	#Wk	DOM	DIS	RAR	BPX	R$
15																																		
16																																		
17 WAS *	177	23	3	16	10	298	0	264	341	455	107	0	110	6	82	0.36	53	12	35	35	105	93	135	0%	0%	131	33%	70%	5	40%	40%	1.7	170	$7
18 WAS *	240	30	5	19	16	271	2	237	332	411	103	135	110	8	82	0.51	27	24	49	31	107	84	106	14%	9%	131	40%	65%	5	20%	20%	1.3	173	$9
19 WAS	617	86	17	65	28	255	15	249	326	419	99	97	99	6	74	0.25	41	20	37	31	64	95	57	12%	10%	131	31%	76%	28	25%	32%	-0.3	96	$23
1st Half	308	44	12	36	11	244	10	237	314	435	100	122	93	6	72	0.21	35	22	43	29	60	104	84	15%	13%	136	27%	73%	15	27%	33%	-2.2	100	$20
2nd Half	309	42	5	29	17	265	5	260	338	404	98	75	106	6	76	0.29	46	23	31	33	68	86	32	8%	8%	125	34%	77%	13	23%	31%	0.0	100	$26
20 Proj	**630**	**87**	**16**	**61**	**32**	**269**		**255**	**340**	**431**	**104**	**111**	**99**	**7**	**78**	**0.34**	**38**	**23**	**38**	**32**	**82**	**90**	**75**	**9%**		**141**	**32%**	**72%**				**13.0**	**152**	**$30**

Rodgers,Brendan

Age: 23 Bats: R Pos: 2B | Ht: 6' 0" Wt: 180

Health D | PT/Exp D | Consist A | LIMA Plan D+ | Rand Var -4 | MM 1323

0-7-.224 in 81 PA at COL. Top prospect struggled upon mid-May promotion before hitting the IL with a right shoulder impingement; ultimately required July surgery to repair torn labrum. Decent ct%/power/Spd blend makes him a possible five-category contributor at peak, but lingering questions about shoulder cast doubt on 2020 impact.

Yr Tm	PA	R	HR	RBI	SB	BA	xHR	xBA	OBP	SLG	OPS+	vL+	vR+	bb%	ct%	Eye	G	L	F	h%	HctX	PX	xPX	HR/F	xHR/F	Spd	SBO	SB%	#Wk	DOM	DIS	RAR	BPX	R$
15																																		
16																																		
17 aa	157	17	6	15	0	263			295	412	95			4	77	0.20				31		83				96	6%	0%					42	$1
18 a/a	449	39	14	49	9	250			289	416	98			5	78	0.25				29		102				92	14%	73%					113	$11
19 COL *	234	31	7	21	0	284	1	254	325	436	101	62	72	6	75	0.24	49	22	29	35	79	87	66	0%	7%	139	0%	0%	7	0%	71%	1.8	85	$3
1st Half	234	31	7	21	0	284	1	254	325	436	102	64	72	6	75	0.24	49	22	29	35	79	87	66	0%	7%	139	0%	0%	7	0%	71%	0.6	85	$3
2nd Half																																		
20 Proj	**350**	**39**	**8**	**34**	**4**	**266**		**248**	**311**	**392**	**95**	**90**	**96**	**5**	**77**	**0.23**	**45**	**23**	**32**	**33**	**71**	**71**	**59**	**10%**		**132**	**7%**	**61%**				**-0.3**	**-16**	**$10**

Rodriguez,Ronny

Age: 28 Bats: R Pos: 2B SS | Ht: 6' 0" Wt: 200

Health A | PT/Exp C | Consist A | LIMA Plan C+ | Rand Var 0 | MM 3323

14-43-.221 in 294 PA at DET. Jumped on the launch angle train with some success, as both xPX and xHR/F endorsed the resulting power surge. Does he have a second trick to add to that? Simply dreadful eye closes the door on any BA value. Raw Spd skill is interesting, but only if he shows that the SB% gains were more than a seven-event fluke.

Yr Tm	PA	R	HR	RBI	SB	BA	xHR	xBA	OBP	SLG	OPS+	vL+	vR+	bb%	ct%	Eye	G	L	F	h%	HctX	PX	xPX	HR/F	xHR/F	Spd	SBO	SB%	#Wk	DOM	DIS	RAR	BPX	R$
15 aa	278	31	10	26	4	272			295	460	105			3	76	0.14				32		123				111	17%	40%					124	$7
16 aaa	469	48	9	49	3	240			270	366	87			4	80	0.22				28		79				98	9%	43%					71	$5
17 aaa	466	48	14	51	12	261			291	401	93			4	79	0.20				30		78				93	17%	68%					48	$12
18 DET *	474	52	13	53	10	266	5	251	295	428	100	102	74	4	79	0.19	45	18	37	31	102	96	82	9%	9%	120	20%	53%	17	35%	65%	0.2	130	$14
19 DET *	471	55	23	68	7	241	14	240	270	461	97	95	90	4	71	0.14	38	19	43	29	100	119	131	17%	17%	120	10%	87%	20	45%	45%	-7.2	96	$12
1st Half	212	20	7	26	4	209	9	234	242	404	86	100	89	4	70	0.14	40	18	42	26	104	112	142	14%		109	19%	81%	12	50%	33%	-9.3	52	$1
2nd Half	259	35	16	42	3	267	5	245	293	508	106	91	92	4	72	0.13	36	20	45	31	94	124	115	21%		133	5%	100%	8	38%	63%	4.2	130	$20
20 Proj	**350**	**40**	**15**	**45**	**6**	**244**		**245**	**270**	**444**	**96**	**107**	**91**	**4**	**75**	**0.16**	**40**	**19**	**41**	**28**	**100**	**105**	**109**	**14%**		**116**	**15%**	**66%**				**-0.9**	**94**	**$11**

Rogers,Jake

Age: 25 Bats: R Pos: CA | Ht: 6' 1" Wt: 205

Health A | PT/Exp F | Consist A | LIMA Plan D+ | Rand Var 0 | MM 3203

4-8-.125 in 128 PA at DET. Regarded as the top defensive catcher in the 2016 draft. He has shown patience and decent power, but will need to improve horrid ct% (54% at DET) to be more than a low-end starter/backup in MLB. Age and defensive skills will buy him time to do that, but you can watch from a safe distance.

Yr Tm	PA	R	HR	RBI	SB	BA	xHR	xBA	OBP	SLG	OPS+	vL+	vR+	bb%	ct%	Eye	G	L	F	h%	HctX	PX	xPX	HR/F	xHR/F	Spd	SBO	SB%	#Wk	DOM	DIS	RAR	BPX	R$
15																																		
16																																		
17																																		
18 aa	385	47	14	46	6	197			266	362	87			9	66	0.28				25		111				97	9%	84%					10	$5
19 DET *	412	52	17	54	0	199	3	207	287	391	90	130	48	11	63	0.33	37	17	46	26	62	119	99	15%	11%	97	0%	0%	9	11%	56%	-0.3	0	$3
1st Half	221	33	11	38	0	240		233	335	450	105			13	66	0.43				30		118		0%		116	0%	0%				6.2	81	$9
2nd Half	191	19	6	16	0	153	3	195	231	323	73	128	48	9	59	0.25	37	17	46	21	58	120	99	15%	11%	96	0%	0%	9	11%	56%	-9.8	-70	-$4
20 Proj	**350**	**43**	**12**	**42**	**2**	**207**		**201**	**290**	**375**	**90**	**189**	**66**	**10**	**64**	**0.30**	**37**	**17**	**46**	**28**	**52**	**106**	**89**	**13%**		**85**	**3%**	**86%**				**0.6**	**-55**	**$6**

Rojas,Josh

Age: 26 Bats: L Pos: LF | Ht: 6' 1" Wt: 185

Health A | PT/Exp D | Consist C | LIMA Plan C | Rand Var 0 | MM 1433

2-16-.217 in 157 PA at ARI. Utility-type enjoyed a breakout minors season, boosting power while maintaining solid plate skills. Speed game is much more established. Questions abound: Did the ball juice his power? Will shaky SB% draw him red lights? Potential power/speed/versatility (also plays infield) package makes for a nice end-game flyer.

Yr Tm	PA	R	HR	RBI	SB	BA	xHR	xBA	OBP	SLG	OPS+	vL+	vR+	bb%	ct%	Eye	G	L	F	h%	HctX	PX	xPX	HR/F	xHR/F	Spd	SBO	SB%	#Wk	DOM	DIS	RAR	BPX	R$
15																																		
16																																		
17																																		
18 aa	436	56	6	40	23	222			304	339	89			11	78	0.53				27		75				111	38%	59%					93	$12
19 ARI *	616	82	18	76	28	265	5	270	338	450	105	101	77	10	78	0.50	44	23	33	31	111	99	139	6%	16%	116	28%	67%	8	25%	63%	-2.0	174	$25
1st Half	314	39	9	36	16	260		277	325	459	105			9	81	0.52				29		103		0%		129	34%	69%				-1.8	244	$23
2nd Half	302	43	9	40	12	271	5	254	351	441	105	100	77	11	74	0.48	44	23	33	34	106	94	139	6%	16%	111	23%	64%	8	25%	63%	0.2	107	$28
20 Proj	**280**	**37**	**6**	**31**	**13**	**249**		**253**	**331**	**390**	**97**	**120**	**90**	**10**	**78**	**0.51**	**44**	**23**	**33**	**30**	**95**	**79**	**125**	**9%**		**113**	**31%**	**63%**				**-3.3**	**118**	**$11**

GREG PYRON

Rojas,Miguel

Age: 31	Bats: R	Pos: SS	Health	C	LIMA Plan	B+
Ht: 5' 11"	Wt: 195		PT/Exp	B	Rand Var	-1
			Consist	B	MM	1245

HctX has been rising last couple seasons. 2nd half FB%, xPX growth suggests he might be figuring out what to do with it, though Aug hamstring injury set him back. Outlook is less optimistic for SB upside, as Spd, SBO, and SB% histories all look pretty mediocre. Likeliest outcome is simply another year of modest, BA/PA-driven value.

Yr	Tm	PA	R	HR	RBI	SB	BA	xHR	xBA	OBP	SLG	OPS+	vL+	vR+	bb%	ct%	Eye	G	L	F	h%	HctX	PX	xPX	HR/F	xHR/F	Spd	SBO	SB%	#Wk	DOM	DIS	RAR	BPX	R$
15	MIA *	417	39	3	35	2	268	1	289	307	369	94	45	105	5	88	0.47	55	24	21	30	88	64	42	4%	4%	111	9%	19%	16	38%	31%	-11.6	135	$6
16	MIA	214	27	1	14	2	247	1	267	288	325	83	94	77	5	86	0.41	54	20	26	28	70	55	37	2%	2%	98	7%	67%	27	37%	44%	-10.5	86	$1
17	MIA	306	37	1	26	2	290	1	285	361	375	99	94	98	9	88	0.84	48	25	27	33	72	52	32	2%	2%	116	3%	67%	18	22%	28%	-4.1	148	$6
18	MIA	527	44	11	53	6	252	6	260	297	346	89	88	89	5	86	0.35	47	24	29	27	85	51	45	9%	5%	72	7%	67%	27	33%	44%	-18.8	57	$10
19	MIA	526	52	5	46	9	284	6	276	331	379	94	98	92	6	87	0.52	47	24	30	32	107	54	65	4%	5%	98	10%	64%	24	38%	33%	-14.8	130	$12
1st Half		311	29	0	23	6	287	3	275	350	358	95	77	101	8	86	0.66	49	24	26	33	102	48	37	0%	5%	89	11%	67%	15	33%	33%	-6.8	107	$11
2nd Half		215	23	5	23	3	279	4	274	304	407	94	126	80	3	88	0.29	43	23	34	30	115	61	102	8%	6%	114	10%	60%	9	44%	33%	-5.7	163	$13
20	**Proj**	**525**	**54**	**9**	**50**	**7**	**274**		**276**	**318**	**383**	**94**	**101**	**91**	**5**	**87**	**0.45**	**47**	**24**	**29**	**30**	**95**	**57**	**58**	**7%**		**101**	**8%**	**62%**				**0.2**	**102**	**$12**

Romine,Austin

Age: 31	Bats: R	Pos: CA	Health	A	LIMA Plan	D
Ht: 6' 1"	Wt: 220		PT/Exp	D	Rand Var	-4
			Consist	B	MM	2121

Second-CA-caliber pop looks legit, but career-high BA was not supported by skills, even with ct% rebound. And higher 2nd half xBA looks like small-sample fluke boosted by inflated PX, with BA aided by h%. It was brief, it was profitable, it may never come again... it was the Rominaissance. (If history holds, 2020 should be his Age of Enlightenmine.)

Yr	Tm	PA	R	HR	RBI	SB	BA	xHR	xBA	OBP	SLG	OPS+	vL+	vR+	bb%	ct%	Eye	G	L	F	h%	HctX	PX	xPX	HR/F	xHR/F	Spd	SBO	SB%	#Wk	DOM	DIS	RAR	BPX	R$
15	NYY *	358	30	6	39	0	219		355	258	321	81	0	0	5	81	0.28	50	50	0	25	0	70	-16	0%		69	2%	0%	1	0%	0%	-11.2	35	$0
16	NYY	176	17	4	26	1	242	4	260	269	382	89	98	74	4	81	0.23	47	19	33	28	88	90	100	9%	9%	79	3%	100%	26	38%	42%	-1.5	86	$1
17	NYY	252	19	2	21	0	218	3	235	272	293	76	66	77	6	75	0.28	45	25	30	28	84	50	66	4%	6%	83	0%	0%	27	11%	56%	-10.9	-58	-$2
18	NYY	265	30	10	42	1	244	7	243	295	417	99	99	98	6	72	0.25	49	19	32	30	95	111	89	18%	12%	64	2%	100%	25	28%	48%	5.6	40	$5
19	NYY	240	29	8	35	1	281	8	251	310	439	99	107	96	4	78	0.20	48	19	33	33	99	85	79	14%	14%	76	4%	50%	26	31%	46%	7.5	48	$5
1st Half		105	9	2	16	0	216	3	197	231	304	71	50	79	2	76	0.08	51	13	36	26	90	49	73	7%	11%	73	0%	0%	14	14%	57%	-5.3	-100	-$4
2nd Half		135	20	6	19	1	333	5	288	370	548	121	140	111	6	79	0.31	46	24	31	38	106	114	85	19%	16%	88	6%	50%	12	50%	33%	12.2	181	$12
20	**Proj**	**245**	**27**	**8**	**34**	**1**	**247**		**247**	**286**	**396**	**92**	**97**	**89**	**5**	**77**	**0.23**	**48**	**20**	**32**	**29**	**95**	**83**	**82**	**13%**		**75**	**3%**	**60%**				**2.9**	**-4**	**$6**

Rosario,Amed

Age: 24	Bats: R	Pos: SS	Health	A	LIMA Plan	B
Ht: 6' 2"	Wt: 189		PT/Exp	A	Rand Var	-1
			Consist	A	MM	1535

xBA pumps the brakes on BA-fueled 2nd half breakout, but that doesn't take away from ct% growth or rising HctX. Will likely remain stuck on 20ish SB plateau until he gets more efficient; 1st half SB% suggests he can. Even as he passes $20 mark, his youth, talent could mean we still haven't yet seen his best.

Yr	Tm	PA	R	HR	RBI	SB	BA	xHR	xBA	OBP	SLG	OPS+	vL+	vR+	bb%	ct%	Eye	G	L	F	h%	HctX	PX	xPX	HR/F	xHR/F	Spd	SBO	SB%	#Wk	DOM	DIS	RAR	BPX	R$
15																																			
16	aa	232	33	2	27	5	307			362	422	107			8	72	0.31				42		83				114	11%	71%					20	$8
17	NYM *	582	65	10	53	21	267	2	246	294	381	91	110	81	4	77	0.17	51	20	29	33	75	65	73	12%	6%	170	23%	68%	10	20%	50%	-11.9	58	$18
18	NYM	592	76	9	51	24	256	11	253	295	381	94	103	90	5	79	0.24	50	21	30	31	80	75	71	7%	9%	163	27%	69%	28	25%	43%	-1.8	117	$19
19	NYM	655	75	15	72	19	287	14	267	323	432	100	116	95	5	80	0.25	48	22	29	34	92	75	65	10%	10%	148	19%	66%	28	29%	25%	0.8	130	$23
1st Half		337	36	9	42	10	255	8	254	293	414	94	112	89	5	75	0.23	45	22	33	31	91	86	93	12%	10%	144	17%	83%	15	20%	27%	-6.6	100	$19
2nd Half		318	39	6	30	9	321	5	280	355	450	106	119	102	4	84	0.28	51	23	26	37	94	65	38	9%	7%	147	20%	53%	13	38%	23%	4.3	163	$27
20	**Proj**	**630**	**77**	**15**	**64**	**22**	**282**		**260**	**320**	**428**	**101**	**116**	**95**	**5**	**79**	**0.24**	**48**	**22**	**30**	**34**	**86**	**77**	**66**	**10%**		**157**	**22%**	**68%**				**9.1**	**96**	**$27**

Rosario,Eddie

Age: 28	Bats: L	Pos: LF	Health	A	LIMA Plan	B+
Ht: 6' 1"	Wt: 180		PT/Exp	A	Rand Var	+1
			Consist	A	MM	3245

New HR peak came with xHR, xHR/F support, but best part of 2019 skill line is that the guy who swings at everything is putting bat on ball more than ever, easing downside concerns that have flared up in xBA history. Ct% was the same vL, too. Injuries likely played role in 2nd half downturn, so perhaps next we'll see... UP: 40 HR

Yr	Tm	PA	R	HR	RBI	SB	BA	xHR	xBA	OBP	SLG	OPS+	vL+	vR+	bb%	ct%	Eye	G	L	F	h%	HctX	PX	xPX	HR/F	xHR/F	Spd	SBO	SB%	#Wk	DOM	DIS	RAR	BPX	R$
15	MIN *	573	69	15	60	12	259	16	242	284	438	101	112	100	3	75	0.14	39	20	41	32	96	110	110	10%	12%	173	17%	62%	22	41%	27%	-4.3	132	$16
16	MIN *	520	75	16	54	9	275	11	257	301	441	101	80	100	3	76	0.15	46	19	34	33	93	106	102	12%	13%	128	14%	63%	18	28%	50%	3.8	106	$16
17	MIN	589	79	27	78	9	290	26	281	328	507	112	90	120	6	80	0.33	42	20	37	32	103	119	121	16%	16%	107	13%	53%	27	52%	22%	5.3	191	$23
18	MIN	592	87	24	77	8	288	25	259	323	479	111	101	115	5	81	0.29	36	20	44	32	109	108	126	12%	13%	105	7%	80%	26	62%	27%	15.5	187	$24
19	MIN	590	91	32	109	3	276	31	279	300	500	106	100	108	4	85	0.26	37	20	42	28	114	104	120	16%	15%	86	3%	75%	25	52%	12%	3.3	211	$22
1st Half		324	51	20	60	3	285	20	285	312	529	112	108	114	4	85	0.31	37	20	43	28	123	111	135	18%	18%	104	6%	75%	14	57%	7%	6.3	267	$28
2nd Half		266	40	12	49	0	268	11	271	286	465	99	92	102	3	84	0.20	38	21	41	28	103	96	102	13%	12%	76	0%	0%	11	45%	18%	-3.4	159	$16
20	**Proj**	**602**	**89**	**30**	**101**	**6**	**279**		**270**	**307**	**497**	**108**	**98**	**112**	**4**	**82**	**0.25**	**37**	**20**	**42**	**29**	**108**	**107**	**118**	**15%**		**98**	**7%**	**67%**				**14.3**	**185**	**$27**

Ruiz,Rio

Age: 26	Bats: L	Pos: 3B	Health	A	LIMA Plan	D+
Ht: 6' 1"	Wt: 215		PT/Exp	C	Rand Var	0
			Consist	A	MM	1013

12-46-.232 in 413 PA at BAL. HctX, xPX samples prior to 2019 were total of 195 PA, so first near-full season's skills should carry more weight. Can't hit LHP (2nd half vL+ was 23 AB), and xHR, xHR/F splash cold water on potential 2nd half power breakout, which leaves us without much to be excited about. Well, except for that sweet alliteration.

Yr	Tm	PA	R	HR	RBI	SB	BA	xHR	xBA	OBP	SLG	OPS+	vL+	vR+	bb%	ct%	Eye	G	L	F	h%	HctX	PX	xPX	HR/F	xHR/F	Spd	SBO	SB%	#Wk	DOM	DIS	RAR	BPX	R$
15	aa	477	43	4	41	2	214			308	295	84			12	75	0.54				28		63				89	3%	45%					5	-$1
16	ATL *	530	48	8	58	2	235	0	242	318	332	88	0	114	11	71	0.42	20	40	40	31	173	64	225	0%	0%	111	4%	30%	2	0%	0%	-22.5	-20	$4
17	ATL *	599	64	17	68	2	199	5	214	277	335	82	189	68	10	68	0.33	56	13	30	26	91	87	123	12%	15%	78	3%	45%	12	42%	33%	-40.6	-39	$0
18	ATL *	543	58	7	57	2	234	0	233	280	332	85	0	48	6	79	0.31	57	14	29	28	125	62	116	0%	0%	91	2%	59%	5	0%	60%	-24.4	27	$6
19	BAL *	436	36	13	52	0	231	8	240	303	372	90	82	92	9	76	0.44	45	21	34	27	92	73	91	13%	8%	95	1%	0%	26	35%	50%	-15.7	48	$3
1st Half		247	19	4	21	0	230	3	216	304	315	83	58	89	10	75	0.43	45	22	34	29	90	49	79	7%	5%	96	0%	0%	15	13%	73%	-13.7	-41	$0
2nd Half		189	17	9	31	0	232	5	268	301	447	99	128	98	9	79	0.46	45	21	34	24	94	103	108	20%	13%	96	3%	0%	11	64%	18%	-4.6	170	$8
20	**Proj**	**420**	**40**	**11**	**50**	**1**	**225**		**233**	**292**	**360**	**88**	**118**	**83**	**9**	**76**	**0.40**	**49**	**18**	**33**	**27**	**92**	**72**	**107**	**11%**		**92**	**2%**	**36%**				**-13.3**	**-9**	**$6**

Russell,Addison

Age: 26	Bats: R	Pos: 2B SS	Health	B	LIMA Plan	D
Ht: 6' 0"	Wt: 200		PT/Exp	C	Rand Var	-1
			Consist	C	MM	2313

9-23-.237 in 241 PA at CHC. 2016's HR surge is fading into memory as HctX hits new low. Forget about new HR/F high, as xHR/F says that's not real either. Given lousy xBA history, power was always his best—and perhaps only—shot at value. Now, instead of building to age-appropriate peak, seems to be disappearing before our eyes.

Yr	Tm	PA	R	HR	RBI	SB	BA	xHR	xBA	OBP	SLG	OPS+	vL+	vR+	bb%	ct%	Eye	G	L	F	h%	HctX	PX	xPX	HR/F	xHR/F	Spd	SBO	SB%	#Wk	DOM	DIS	RAR	BPX	R$
15	CHC *	568	66	14	61	5	246	12	226	303	393	97	73	102	8	70	0.27	41	18	41	33	83	115	105	10%	9%	96	6%	61%	25	36%	40%	-2.8	46	$11
16	CHC	598	67	21	95	5	238	22	251	321	417	100	108	96	9	74	0.41	41	21	38	28	88	111	96	14%	15%	110	5%	83%	27	44%	33%	-8.0	111	$12
17	CHC	385	52	12	43	2	239	10	256	304	418	97	109	91	8	74	0.32	40	23	37	29	97	109	83	13%	10%	111	4%	67%	22	32%	45%	-9.3	103	$5
18	CHC	465	52	5	38	4	250	5	236	317	340	91	104	86	9	76	0.40	42	25	33	32	82	63	79	5%	5%	116	3%	100%	26	31%	46%	-6.9	33	$7
19	CHC *	349	45	14	44	3	239	6	235	309	415	96	85	95	9	72	0.36	48	17	35	29	78	93	90	16%	11%	116	6%	55%	19	21%	47%	-2.9	67	$6
1st Half		182	23	7	22	1	235	4	235	315	409	97	100	97	10	71	0.41	48	19	33	28	88	90	105	18%	14%	121	7%	26%	9	33%	33%	-2.9	59	$4
2nd Half		167	22	7	21	2	244	2	233	304	423	96	71	93	8	73	0.32	48	15	37	29	66	96	73	15%	7%	110	5%	100%	10	10%	60%	-1.1	70	$8
20	**Proj**	**280**	**35**	**8**	**32**	**2**	**244**		**234**	**315**	**390**	**95**	**95**	**94**	**9**	**74**	**0.35**	**45**	**20**	**35**	**30**	**81**	**83**	**85**	**12%**		**114**	**5%**	**74%**				**-0.4**	**6**	**$7**

Sanchez,Gary

Age: 27	Bats: R	Pos: CA	Health	D	LIMA Plan	B
Ht: 6' 2"	Wt: 230		PT/Exp	C	Rand Var	+3
			Consist	D	MM	4035

xHR says there's 40 HR power—maybe even 50!—in his bat if he can ever log 500+ PA again. Health grade says you should continue targeting mid-30s. Contact concerns have been exacerbated by ailments, so while he might not hit .275 again, 2018-19's .211 is equally out of line. Moderation in all things, especially injury-prone catchers.

Yr	Tm	PA	R	HR	RBI	SB	BA	xHR	xBA	OBP	SLG	OPS+	vL+	vR+	bb%	ct%	Eye	G	L	F	h%	HctX	PX	xPX	HR/F	xHR/F	Spd	SBO	SB%	#Wk	DOM	DIS	RAR	BPX	R$
15	NYY *	393	44	18	55	6	255		164	304	459	106	0	0	7	76	0.29	0	0	100	29	0	135	-16	0%		70	10%	74%	2	0%	50%	10.8	130	$12
16	NYY *	532	69	31	87	7	275	17	288	334	530	118	117	146	8	78	0.40	49	16	34	30	132	150	159	40%	34%	72	7%	87%	11	45%	36%	33.2	203	$21
17	NYY	525	79	33	90	2	278	31	275	345	531	117	117	115	8	75	0.33	42	21	37	31	111	140	114	25%	24%	84	3%	67%	23	39%	22%	28.2	158	$20
18	NYY *	402	54	22	56	1	184	23	241	279	417	96	121	87	11	70	0.44	43	14	43	19	91	147	115	18%	23%	50	1%	100%	22	36%	32%	3.0	123	$5
19	NYY	446	62	34	77	0	232	36	252	316	525	112	99	115	9	68	0.32	32	20	48	24	100	156	140	26%	28%	75	1%	0%	25	44%	40%	19.3	152	$12
1st Half		264	38	23	54	0	261	27	267	330	588	123	125	122	8	71	0.31	29	21	51	27	115	168	170	27%	32%	87	0%	0%	14	50%	29%	17.8	230	$19
2nd Half		182	24	11	23	0	190	9	232	297	430	96	70	106	10	65	0.33	38	19	43	21	77	138	92	25%	20%	73	3%	0%	11	36%	55%	-2.0	59	$1
20	**Proj**	**455**	**64**	**33**	**75**	**1**	**245**		**256**	**327**	**531**	**115**	**109**	**117**	**9**	**70**	**0.34**	**39**	**18**	**43**	**27**	**104**	**154**	**123**	**27%**		**66**	**2%**	**53%**				**27.3**	**135**	**$17**

BRANDON KRUSE

Sanchez,Yolmer

Age: 28 Bats: B Pos: 2B	Health C	LIMA Plan D+	On the plus side, set career highs in bb% and vL+; on the minus side...pretty much everything else. Impressive speed, but poor SB% track record may have finally sunk SBO. Only two MLB regulars posted lower HctX; could power crash have been linked to shoulder issues from spring? Even if "power" returns, curb your "enthusiasm."
Ht: 5' 11" Wt: 185	PT/Exp A	Rand Var -2	
	Consist B	MM 1313	

Yr	Tm	PA	R	HR	RBI	SB	BA	xHR	xBA	OBP	SLG	OPS+	vL+	vR+	bb%	ct%	Eye	G	L	F	h%	HctX	PX	xPX	HR/F	xHR/F	Spd	SBO	SB%	#Wk	DOM	DIS	RAR	BPX	R$
15	CHW *	555	54	7	45	6	244	3	261	276	349	87	84	81	4	78	0.20	54	23	23	30	76	79	48	7%	4%	89	10%	59%	23	22%	61%	-17.0	32	$7
16	CHW *	413	40	11	44	8	217	3	232	255	362	84	55	88	5	73	0.18	39	21	40	27	67	95	75	9%	7%	102	19%	59%	17	35%	53%	-22.3	23	$4
17	CHW	531	62	12	59	8	266	10	251	317	413	98	86	100	6	77	0.31	45	21	34	32	75	82	72	9%	8%	160	14%	47%	27	33%	33%	-5.5	109	$13
18	CHW	662	62	8	55	14	242	11	254	306	372	94	72	99	7	77	0.36	49	22	29	30	80	83	67	6%	8%	114	14%	70%	28	29%	39%	-6.8	83	$12
19	CHW	555	59	2	43	5	252	6	220	318	321	85	96	81	8	76	0.38	43	21	36	33	72	42	49	1%	4%	155	6%	56%	28	7%	57%	-20.6	11	$6
1st Half		253	24	1	19	3	250	2	211	321	313	85	97	82	8	75	0.35	45	20	35	33	70	38	54	2%	3%	157	9%	50%	15	7%	60%	-9.8	-22	$2
2nd Half		302	35	1	24	2	254	4	228	314	327	85	96	80	8	78	0.40	42	22	36	32	73	46	45	1%	5%	142	4%	67%	13	8%	54%	-9.2	33	$9
20	**Proj**	**420**	**45**	**4**	**37**	**6**	**249**		**235**	**309**	**352**	**89**	**87**	**89**	**7**	**77**	**0.33**	**45**	**22**	**33**	**32**	**74**	**59**	**58**	**4%**		**140**	**10%**	**59%**				**-6.3**	**-1**	**$6**

Sandoval,Pablo

Age: 33 Bats: B Pos: 3B 1B	Health F	LIMA Plan D	The Panda is back...or is he? Ended famine vL; power rebounded as he took better advantage of solid HctX while lowering GB%; but the pièce de résistance was actually a h% that didn't sink like a ruined soufflé for a change. TJ surgery in Sept cut season short and will take a big bite out of 2020—perhaps it's best to skip this course.
Ht: 5' 11" Wt: 268	PT/Exp D	Rand Var -5	
	Consist B	MM 3031	

Yr	Tm	PA	R	HR	RBI	SB	BA	xHR	xBA	OBP	SLG	OPS+	vL+	vR+	bb%	ct%	Eye	G	L	F	h%	HctX	PX	xPX	HR/F	xHR/F	Spd	SBO	SB%	#Wk	DOM	DIS	RAR	BPX	R$
15	BOS	505	43	10	47	0	245	11	253	292	366	92	64	102	5	84	0.34	49	19	32	27	88	79	68	8%	9%	41	0%	0%	25	36%	36%	-16.4	68	$5
16	BOS	7	0	0	0	0	0	0	0	143	0	19	0	19	14	33	0.25	0	0	100	0	0	0	-24	0%	0%	57	0%	0%	2	0%	100%	-1.1	-623	-$2
17	2 TM *	392	35	10	37	0	204	9	226	250	326	77	52	93	6	79	0.29	47	16	36	23	104	70	87	12%	12%	34	1%	0%	18	22%	33%	-31.1	-12	-$2
18	SF	252	22	9	40	0	248	8	255	310	417	101	61	112	8	77	0.37	50	20	30	28	116	99	94	17%	15%	46	0%	0%	19	37%	32%	-2.3	67	$4
19	SF	296	42	14	41	1	268	12	281	313	507	109	122	106	6	75	0.27	47	21	32	31	108	135	108	21%	18%	32	2%	100%	21	43%	14%	1.1	122	$7
1st Half		182	26	10	29	1	284	10	290	320	556	117	97	122	5	73	0.20	44	22	33	33	114	158	122	24%	24%	37	3%	100%	15	47%	13%	5.5	159	$10
2nd Half		114	16	4	12	0	243	2	265	301	427	96	174	82	8	79	0.41	51	18	30	27	98	101	85	16%	8%	41	0%	0%	6	33%	17%	-2.6	96	$2
20	**Proj**	**140**	**16**	**5**	**18**	**0**	**247**		**261**	**298**	**433**	**98**	**91**	**100**	**7**	**78**	**0.32**	**49**	**19**	**32**	**28**	**106**	**101**	**93**	**16%**		**42**	**1%**	**74%**				**-0.9**	**73**	**$3**

Sano,Miguel

Age: 27 Bats: R Pos: 3B	Health D	LIMA Plan B	34-79-.247 in 439 PA at MIN. Heel laceration kept him out until mid-May, then he showed off that Bunyanesque power that always keeps us coming back for more. Skills are consistent but we never really know how much of him we're going to get, as he's missed at least three weeks in each of last four seasons. Still, with health... UP: 45 HR
Ht: 6' 4" Wt: 272	PT/Exp C	Rand Var -2	
	Consist F	MM 5015	

Yr	Tm	PA	R	HR	RBI	SB	BA	xHR	xBA	OBP	SLG	OPS+	vL+	vR+	bb%	ct%	Eye	G	L	F	h%	HctX	PX	xPX	HR/F	xHR/F	Spd	SBO	SB%	#Wk	DOM	DIS	RAR	BPX	R$
15	MIN *	604	88	29	89	5	257	22	249	357	496	119	122	127	13	63	0.43	33	25	42	35	122	188	175	26%	32%	86	5%	70%	15	53%	20%	22.4	157	$20
16	MIN *	524	60	27	68	1	231	28	224	317	459	106	110	103	11	59	0.31	34	20	46	32	96	173	157	21%	23%	76	1%	100%	24	38%	42%	0.6	66	$9
17	MIN	483	75	28	77	0	264	28	229	352	507	115	132	108	11	59	0.31	39	21	40	38	107	166	148	27%	27%	99	0%	0%	22	36%	41%	15.2	73	$14
18	MIN *	334	34	15	45	0	204	15	201	290	404	96	89	95	11	58	0.29	44	15	41	29	91	156	121	21%	24%	70	0%	0%	17	24%	65%	-5.2	7	$3
19	MIN *	474	78	35	84	0	246	34	247	336	562	110	131	110	12	50	0.32	37	21	42	33	105	210	175	37%	37%	89	1%	0%	21	57%	19%	15.7	189	$15
1st Half		178	25	13	27	0	214	12	229	293	523	109	126	108	10	54	0.24	39	14	47	29	99	225	202	36%	36%	59	0%	0%	8	50%	13%	-1.3	133	$1
2nd Half		296	53	22	57	0	264	22	255	368	587	126	135	123	13	60	0.38	36	24	39	35	109	202	162	37%	37%	110	1%	0%	13	62%	23%	14.8	233	$24
20	**Proj**	**525**	**76**	**34**	**85**	**0**	**247**		**232**	**336**	**526**	**116**	**123**	**113**	**12**	**58**	**0.31**	**39**	**19**	**42**	**34**	**102**	**185**	**158**	**30%**		**86**	**1%**	**30%**				**18.5**	**82**	**$19**

Santana,Carlos

Age: 34 Bats: B Pos: 1B DH	Health A	LIMA Plan B+	Arguably the finest season of 10-year MLB career: Eye, splits, HctX contributed to yet another magnificent BPX. Bested sub-par 2018 by altering spray distribution from both sides, which helped beat shift, buoyed h%, and allowed BA to finally catch up to xBA. Even if HR regress a bit, still one of the most reliable bats in the business.
Ht: 5' 11" Wt: 210	PT/Exp A	Rand Var -2	
	Consist C	MM 3245	

Yr	Tm	PA	R	HR	RBI	SB	BA	xHR	xBA	OBP	SLG	OPS+	vL+	vR+	bb%	ct%	Eye	G	L	F	h%	HctX	PX	xPX	HR/F	xHR/F	Spd	SBO	SB%	#Wk	DOM	DIS	RAR	BPX	R$
15	CLE	666	72	19	85	11	231	21	252	357	395	105	104	103	16	78	0.89	45	18	37	26	101	108	95	12%	13%	73	8%	79%	27	56%	22%	-3.8	146	$14
16	CLE	688	89	34	87	5	259	34	281	366	498	118	100	122	14	83	1.00	43	16	41	26	122	129	122	17%	17%	80	4%	71%	27	74%	7%	24.1	257	$20
17	CLE	667	90	23	79	5	259	24	278	363	455	110	103	111	13	84	0.94	41	20	39	28	112	106	102	12%	13%	86	3%	83%	27	63%	11%	4.2	221	$16
18	PHI	679	82	24	86	2	229	24	253	352	414	106	114	102	16	83	1.18	40	16	44	23	101	101	112	12%	12%	81	2%	67%	28	64%	14%	7.3	243	$13
19	CLE	686	110	34	93	4	281	29	276	397	515	121	128	117	16	81	1.00	45	17	38	29	121	114	112	19%	16%	76	2%	100%	28	71%	21%	37.9	267	$24
1st Half		353	55	18	50	3	293	17	283	411	534	126	118	130	16	82	1.07	49	17	35	31	129	116	114	22%	20%	73	3%	100%	15	80%	20%	22.8	281	$27
2nd Half		333	55	16	43	1	269	11	267	381	495	116	140	104	15	81	0.93	41	18	41	28	112	112	109	17%	12%	83	1%	100%	13	62%	23%	11.3	256	$21
20	**Proj**	**665**	**96**	**29**	**87**	**4**	**260**		**266**	**373**	**473**	**114**	**120**	**110**	**15**	**82**	**1.00**	**43**	**17**	**40**	**27**	**113**	**105**	**110**	**16%**		**81**	**2%**	**85%**				**25.3**	**238**	**$22**

Santana,Daniel

Age: 29 Bats: B Pos: 1B CF	Health C	LIMA Plan B	28-81-.283 with 21 SB in 511 PA at TEX. Finally followed up promising 2014 rookie season with five-category breakout. Solving righties was key, but other puzzles remain: Low ct% was offset by h%, but xBA looms; OBP—hence SB—at risk with h% regression due to weak bb%; outperformed xPX by large margin. Don't overpay.
Ht: 5' 11" Wt: 185	PT/Exp D	Rand Var -5	
	Consist C	MM 3525	

Yr	Tm	PA	R	HR	RBI	SB	BA	xHR	xBA	OBP	SLG	OPS+	vL+	vR+	bb%	ct%	Eye	G	L	F	h%	HctX	PX	xPX	HR/F	xHR/F	Spd	SBO	SB%	#Wk	DOM	DIS	RAR	BPX	R$
15	MIN *	435	50	2	34	13	243	1	249	263	347	85	86	68	3	77	0.12	54	20	26	31	88	72	56	0%	2%	140	25%	64%	22	9%	50%	-19.5	38	$7
16	MIN	248	29	2	14	12	240	5	246	279	326	82	55	88	5	76	0.22	53	22	25	31	93	58	76	5%	12%	127	39%	57%	19	26%	63%	-11.9	6	$5
17	2 TM	178	19	4	23	7	202	5	255	243	357	80	55	87	4	76	0.20	54	15	31	24	103	94	121	11%	14%	108	27%	100%	19	32%	63%	-9.6	64	$1
18	ATL *	364	46	12	31	10	211	2	244	240	382	86	104	67	4	69	0.12	35	29	35	27	90	118	149	0%	33%	101	32%	58%	4	50%	50%	-16.4	33	$6
19	TEX *	548	84	28	85	22	282	26	257	319	526	112	112	114	5	68	0.17	40	25	35	36	105	139	111	24%	23%	131	26%	75%	25	48%	36%	19.9	126	$28
1st Half		248	41	9	29	10	295	9	255	329	507	112	83	125	5	70	0.17	37	28	35	39	106	123	107	18%	18%	133	28%	65%	12	50%	42%	8.6	111	$20
2nd Half		300	43	19	56	12	272	17	258	317	541	113	126	106	5	66	0.17	43	22	35	34	104	152	113	29%	26%	125	24%	86%	13	46%	31%	12.8	137	$35
20	**Proj**	**490**	**67**	**17**	**63**	**17**	**252**		**247**	**291**	**441**	**98**	**93**	**100**	**4**	**70**	**0.16**	**43**	**23**	**34**	**32**	**101**	**109**	**103**	**16%**		**122**	**26%**	**72%**				**-4.9**	**77**	**$20**

Santana,Domingo

Age: 27 Bats: R Pos: LF RF	Health C	LIMA Plan C+	It was the best of times, it was the worst of times, as great 1st half had expectations of 2017 repeat written all over it until a strained right elbow ruined 2nd half. Before injury, parlayed HctX and career-low GB% into MLB career-best xPX; xHR says results could've been even better. If elbow doesn't hurt like the dickens... UP: 35 HR
Ht: 6' 5" Wt: 220	PT/Exp B	Rand Var 0	
	Consist C	MM 4305	

Yr	Tm	PA	R	HR	RBI	SB	BA	xHR	xBA	OBP	SLG	OPS+	vL+	vR+	bb%	ct%	Eye	G	L	F	h%	HctX	PX	xPX	HR/F	xHR/F	Spd	SBO	SB%	#Wk	DOM	DIS	RAR	BPX	R$
15	2 TM *	580	74	21	81	5	271	10	237	347	457	112	131	93	10	64	0.32	52	19	29	39	92	146	135	28%	34%	115	8%	45%	11	55%	36%	9.1	78	$19
16	MIL	281	34	11	32	2	256	11	252	345	447	108	127	97	11	63	0.35	44	30	26	36	98	143	107	28%	28%	87	7%	40%	17	29%	47%	5.5	49	$6
17	MIL	607	88	30	85	15	278	23	266	371	505	117	118	115	12	66	0.41	45	27	28	37	106	148	120	31%	24%	96	12%	79%	26	46%	35%	16.4	115	$25
18	MIL *	445	40	11	42	2	245	9	209	318	391	98	75	112	10	57	0.25	49	23	28	40	85	123	95	13%	24%	118	3%	69%	18	28%	50%	-4.9	-50	$6
19	SEA	505	63	21	69	8	253	27	238	329	441	102	107	100	10	64	0.30	43	27	31	35	92	118	128	24%	30%	87	9%	73%	25	28%	60%	-2.8	-7	$14
1st Half		374	48	18	62	5	278	25	257	348	499	113	124	110	9	67	0.32	39	28	33	36	102	131	145	24%	33%	89	9%	63%	16	38%	44%	7.8	78	$22
2nd Half		131	15	3	7	3	181	3	180	275	276	73	78	68	11	53	0.28	56	21	23	31	63	68	64	21%	21%	103	10%	100%	9	11%	89%	-10.0	-281	-$10
20	**Proj**	**525**	**70**	**22**	**72**	**8**	**246**		**222**	**326**	**432**	**102**	**100**	**102**	**10**	**60**	**0.29**	**43**	**24**	**32**	**36**	**96**	**124**	**102**	**24%**		**95**	**8%**	**78%**				**3.4**	**-49**	**$17**

Santander,Anthony

Age: 25 Bats: B Pos: RF LF CF	Health C	LIMA Plan B+	20-59-.261 in 405 PA at BAL. Unheralded prospect made 2019 splash after falling under the radar when right elbow injury cost him most of 2017, possibly hampering 2018 performance. Most skills improved after promotion, with HctX, PX, xPX, FB% surging in 2nd half and supporting the kind of power production that could lead to... UP: 30 HR
Ht: 6' 2" Wt: 190	PT/Exp D	Rand Var -1	
	Consist F	MM 2225	

Yr	Tm	PA	R	HR	RBI	SB	BA	xHR	xBA	OBP	SLG	OPS+	vL+	vR+	bb%	ct%	Eye	G	L	F	h%	HctX	PX	xPX	HR/F	xHR/F	Spd	SBO	SB%	#Wk	DOM	DIS	RAR	BPX	R$
15																																			
16																																			
17	BAL *	87	12	4	14	0	300	0	304	352	535	119	50	94	7	76	0.34	22	35	43	35	121	139	115	0%	0%	96	0%	0%	7	29%	43%	4.3	188	$2
18	BAL *	370	31	7	29	4	209	3	236	242	327	79	79	74	4	81	0.23	39	20	41	24	94	69	77	3%	9%	114	8%	78%	7	14%	14%	-21.5	83	$1
19	BAL *	608	69	24	80	3	246	17	245	282	431	95	106	100	5	78	0.23	39	18	43	28	102	99	110	16%	13%	105	7%	43%	18	50%	28%	-17.7	119	$13
1st Half		298	36	8	34	2	236	3	239	280	383	89	78	130	6	79	0.29	45	15	39	27	92	83	101	14%	11%	110	8%	50%	6	50%	33%	-14.7	107	$8
2nd Half		310	33	16	46	1	255	14	252	285	476	100	115	92	4	76	0.17	37	18	44	28	103	115	113	16%	14%	105	5%	33%	12	50%	25%	-6.1	141	$18
20	**Proj**	**560**	**57**	**22**	**63**	**4**	**243**		**248**	**282**	**425**	**95**	**95**	**95**	**5**	**79**	**0.23**	**40**	**18**	**42**	**27**	**97**	**94**	**96**	**12%**		**111**	**7%**	**59%**				**-9.7**	**84**	**$14**

ALAIN DE LEONARDIS

Schoop,Jonathan

Age: 28 Bats: R Pos: 2B
Ht: 6' 1" Wt: 225

Health	B	LIMA Plan	D+
PT/Exp	B	Rand Var	0
Consist	C	MM	3023

Skills-wise, 2019 was more or less in line with his overall career averages. Whatever growth he displayed in 2nd half was mostly due to mashing vL and facing a lower percentage of righties, something to keep in mind. Scan the column on the far right and notice how much 2017 sticks out—don't chase that high.

Yr	Tm	PA	R	HR	RBI	SB	BA	xHR	xBA	OBP	SLG	OPS+	vL+	vR+	bb%	ct%	Eye	G	L	F	h%	HctX	PX	xPX	HR/F	xHR/F	Spd	SBO	SB%	#Wk	DOM	DIS	RAR	BPX	R$
15	BAL *	347	36	18	44	2	274	14	264	295	493	110	79	122	3	74	0.11	43	19	38	32	115	147	123	17%	16%	65	3%	100%	15	47%	27%	8.1	111	$11
16	BAL	647	82	25	82	1	267	21	266	298	454	102	93	103	3	78	0.15	45	20	35	31	84	116	74	15%	13%	81	2%	33%	27	41%	26%	-3.5	106	$17
17	BAL	675	92	32	105	1	293	22	270	338	503	113	127	106	5	77	0.25	42	21	37	33	113	120	113	18%	12%	67	1%	100%	27	41%	19%	23.7	112	$25
18	2 TM	501	61	21	61	1	233	14	249	266	416	94	90	96	4	76	0.17	45	18	37	26	78	110	79	16%	11%	73	2%	50%	25	36%	32%	-6.7	73	$10
19	MIN	464	61	23	59	1	256	18	256	304	473	103	120	97	4	73	0.17	43	20	37	30	98	118	103	20%	15%	78	2%	50%	28	39%	32%	-1.3	78	$11
1st Half		286	39	13	34	1	251	10	261	301	457	101	97	102	4	74	0.16	45	21	34	29	101	114	94	19%	15%	76	2%	100%	15	40%	27%	-2.1	74	$13
2nd Half		178	22	10	25	0	265	8	247	309	500	107	142	87	5	72	0.19	40	18	42	31	93	125	118	20%	16%	91	3%	0%	13	38%	38%	2.2	96	$8
20	**Proj**	**350**	**45**	**17**	**47**	**1**	**259**		**252**	**300**	**467**	**103**	**114**	**98**	**4**	**74**	**0.18**	**43**	**19**	**38**	**30**	**95**	**112**	**101**	**18%**		**78**	**2%**	**43%**				**5.2**	**51**	**$8**

Schwarber,Kyle

Age: 27 Bats: L Pos: LF
Ht: 6' 0" Wt: 235

Health	C	LIMA Plan	C+
PT/Exp	B	Rand Var	-4
Consist	A	MM	4135

Improvement vL unlocked more PA and helped him finish just shy of 40 HR—can he get there in 2020? Consistently hard contact, rising FB% and xPX, track record of elevated xHR/F confirm elite power; improving ct% and BPX attest to increasing abundance of quality AB. Building off exciting 2nd half could lead to... UP: 45 HR, .260 BA

Yr	Tm	PA	R	HR	RBI	SB	BA	xHR	xBA	OBP	SLG	OPS+	vL+	vR+	bb%	ct%	Eye	G	L	F	h%	HctX	PX	xPX	HR/F	xHR/F	Spd	SBO	SB%	#Wk	DOM	DIS	RAR	BPX	R$
15	CHC *	570	88	29	82	4	271	15	247	368	505	122	66	131	13	68	0.48	40	17	42	34	116	164	157	24%	23%	94	4%	56%	14	57%	21%	23.8	159	$21
16	CHC	5	0	0	0	0	0		0	200	0	27	0	27	20	50	0.50	100	0	0	0	203	0	-24	0%		87	0%	0%	1	0%	100%	-0.6	-374	-$2
17	CHC *	527	74	33	66	1	217	29	234	315	476	106	86	108	12	64	0.40	38	15	46	25	94	163	125	24%	23%	71	2%	50%	26	42%	23%	-5.7	106	$8
18	CHC	510	64	26	61	4	238	26	243	356	467	114	91	118	15	67	0.56	44	19	37	29	100	143	119	25%	25%	94	5%	57%	28	43%	36%	11.3	147	$13
19	CHC	610	82	38	92	2	250	40	264	339	531	116	99	120	11	71	0.45	38	20	42	28	102	154	140	24%	25%	71	4%	40%	28	50%	25%	12.3	189	$18
1st Half		325	43	18	40	1	234	18	244	320	475	106	97	109	12	68	0.41	38	20	41	28	99	135	141	23%	23%	71	4%	33%	15	40%	27%	-1.5	100	$14
2nd Half		285	39	20	52	1	267	22	286	361	595	126	102	133	12	73	0.50	38	19	43	29	106	174	139	26%	28%	78	3%	50%	13	62%	23%	14.8	300	$22
20	**Proj**	**560**	**77**	**35**	**81**	**2**	**254**		**255**	**355**	**531**	**119**	**96**	**125**	**13**	**69**	**0.48**	**40**	**19**	**42**	**30**	**102**	**154**	**134**	**25%**		**80**	**2%**	**51%**				**26.0**	**166**	**$20**

Seager,Corey

Age: 26 Bats: L Pos: SS
Ht: 6' 4" Wt: 215

Health	F	LIMA Plan	B
PT/Exp	C	Rand Var	+2
Consist	B	MM	3255

Returned from Tommy John and hip surgeries to post decent season, but couldn't quite stay off the trainer's table, as a bad left hamstring strain kept him out a month. Batting skills are there: impressive BPX, xPX, HctX persisted even while bb% and ct% took a small hit. Recent health woes dampen otherwise positive outlook.

Yr	Tm	PA	R	HR	RBI	SB	BA	xHR	xBA	OBP	SLG	OPS+	vL+	vR+	bb%	ct%	Eye	G	L	F	h%	HctX	PX	xPX	HR/F	xHR/F	Spd	SBO	SB%	#Wk	DOM	DIS	RAR	BPX	R$
15	LA *	643	86	20	82	5	280	5	296	328	462	110	128	141	7	83	0.42	53	20	27	31	168	118	139	19%	24%	94	5%	83%	6	83%	17%	27.4	189	$22
16	LA	687	105	26	72	3	308	31	290	365	512	119	97	127	8	79	0.41	46	24	29	36	127	122	130	18%	21%	114	3%	50%	27	59%	19%	36.4	186	$27
17	LA	613	85	22	77	4	295	25	271	375	479	114	121	109	11	76	0.51	42	25	33	35	135	111	136	16%	18%	80	4%	67%	27	52%	33%	28.5	118	$21
18	LA	115	13	2	13	0	267	4	280	348	396	103	92	108	10	83	0.65	45	28	27	30	108	74	79	9%	17%	109	0%	0%	6	33%	17%	2.5	153	$0
19	LA	541	82	19	87	1	272	21	279	335	483	108	92	117	8	80	0.45	39	22	39	31	117	117	130	12%	14%	86	1%	100%	25	48%	16%	12.1	215	$16
1st Half		270	40	8	38	1	278	9	263	359	468	111	84	125	11	78	0.55	37	21	43	33	111	110	142	10%	11%	98	2%	100%	12	50%	17%	6.4	204	$13
2nd Half		271	42	11	49	0	266	12	294	310	496	106	100	109	6	81	0.34	41	23	36	29	122	123	119	15%	16%	81	0%	0%	13	46%	15%	2.8	230	$18
20	**Proj**	**560**	**81**	**21**	**86**	**1**	**278**		**283**	**345**	**481**	**111**	**101**	**116**	**9**	**80**	**0.49**	**42**	**24**	**34**	**31**	**121**	**109**	**118**	**15%**		**91**	**1%**	**75%**				**24.1**	**175**	**$21**

Seager,Kyle

Age: 32 Bats: L Pos: 3B
Ht: 6' 0" Wt: 210

Health	C	LIMA Plan	B+
PT/Exp	B	Rand Var	+2
Consist	B	MM	3035

23-63-.239 in 443 PA at SEA. Spring training injury to tendon in left hand required surgery, shelving him until late May. Took awhile to get going but really turned on the jets in 2nd half, with boosts to BPX, PX, ct%. That 137 OPS+ vL was in just 93 AB, though, and shouldn't be taken too strongly. Could still offer late-round profit potential.

Yr	Tm	PA	R	HR	RBI	SB	BA	xHR	xBA	OBP	SLG	OPS+	vL+	vR+	bb%	ct%	Eye	G	L	F	h%	HctX	PX	xPX	HR/F	xHR/F	Spd	SBO	SB%	#Wk	DOM	DIS	RAR	BPX	R$
15	SEA	686	85	26	74	6	266	25	280	328	451	109	115	102	8	84	0.55	35	24	41	28	122	113	112	12%	12%	81	8%	50%	27	70%	15%	6.9	186	$20
16	SEA	676	89	30	99	3	278	31	281	359	499	117	98	124	10	82	0.64	36	22	42	30	129	125	135	15%	15%	72	2%	75%	27	67%	11%	24.0	206	$22
17	SEA	650	72	27	88	2	249	28	251	323	450	104	102	102	9	81	0.53	31	17	52	27	117	110	142	11%	12%	78	2%	67%	27	48%	7%	-0.3	167	$13
18	SEA	630	62	22	78	2	221	22	247	273	400	93	98	90	6	76	0.28	34	21	45	25	104	112	127	11%	11%	64	4%	50%	28	36%	32%	-15.3	93	$9
19	SEA *	484	58	23	68	2	234	21	262	308	446	100	123	95	9	78	0.48	33	23	44	25	102	107	140	17%	16%	69	4%	50%	20	55%	20%	-6.7	144	$9
1st Half		184	19	5	20	1	210	7	214	292	342	85	92	93	10	74	0.46	29	20	51	25	103	73	146	11%	15%	73	2%	100%	7	29%	29%	-10.0	4	-$5
2nd Half		300	39	18	48	1	249	14	288	323	509	110	137	96	9	80	0.50	34	25	41	25	102	126	138	20%	16%	74	5%	33%	13	69%	15%	0.9	233	$18
20	**Proj**	**595**	**69**	**27**	**81**	**2**	**244**		**258**	**315**	**449**	**103**	**112**	**98**	**9**	**79**	**0.46**	**34**	**22**	**44**	**26**	**107**	**105**	**136**	**14%**		**70**	**4%**	**53%**				**1.1**	**131**	**$16**

Segura,Jean

Age: 30 Bats: R Pos: SS
Ht: 5' 10" Wt: 205

Health	B	LIMA Plan	B
PT/Exp	A	Rand Var	+2
Consist	B	MM	1455

Suffered string of lower half injuries (hamstring, heel, shin) that may have gnawed at his SBO and Spd; could 2018's SB% have been yet another culprit? Otherwise, enjoyed typically fine season making plenty of hard contact on the ground. Hit rate regression should buy him back some BA. Good to go for another round.

Yr	Tm	PA	R	HR	RBI	SB	BA	xHR	xBA	OBP	SLG	OPS+	vL+	vR+	bb%	ct%	Eye	G	L	F	h%	HctX	PX	xPX	HR/F	xHR/F	Spd	SBO	SB%	#Wk	DOM	DIS	RAR	BPX	R$
15	MIL	584	57	6	50	25	257	6	252	281	336	86	94	81	2	83	0.14	59	17	24	30	71	49	48	5%	5%	128	24%	81%	26	15%	38%	-9.1	49	$17
16	ARI	694	102	20	64	33	319	26	296	368	499	118	103	120	6	84	0.39	53	19	28	35	101	103	93	14%	18%	143	25%	77%	27	41%	15%	34.9	214	$39
17	SEA	565	80	11	45	22	300	11	279	349	427	104	109	101	6	84	0.41	54	19	26	34	96	73	66	9%	9%	120	20%	73%	23	35%	22%	11.0	136	$24
18	SEA	632	91	10	63	20	304	13	272	341	415	105	112	101	5	88	0.46	51	19	29	33	84	63	59	7%	9%	123	18%	65%	27	52%	22%	19.0	173	$27
19	PHI	618	79	12	60	10	280	13	292	323	420	99	118	92	5	87	0.41	52	21	27	30	100	72	61	9%	9%	112	9%	83%	27	52%	22%	-0.5	193	$17
1st Half		327	49	10	38	5	272	8	291	316	452	103	141	92	5	87	0.43	52	18	31	29	86	87	63	12%		122	9%	83%	15	53%	27%	0.0	244	$20
2nd Half		291	30	2	22	5	288	5	292	330	384	94	97	93	5	88	0.39	52	25	23	32	116	55	58	4%		95	9%	83%	12	50%	17%	-3.8	130	$13
20	**Proj**	**595**	**79**	**10**	**56**	**16**	**290**		**281**	**332**	**413**	**100**	**110**	**96**	**5**	**87**	**0.40**	**53**	**20**	**27**	**32**	**96**	**64**	**62**	**8%**		**119**	**15%**	**74%**				**10.9**	**159**	**$24**

Semien,Marcus

Age: 29 Bats: R Pos: SS
Ht: 6' 0" Wt: 195

Health	B	LIMA Plan	B+
PT/Exp	A	Rand Var	0
Consist	B	MM	3345

That escalated quickly! Skills and expected stats suggest production was deserved, and 2nd half—especially huge shift in G/L/F—was bonkers. Is there a catch? Regression will almost certainly claw back some PA along with counting stats. But this was such a wholesale evolution, even a partial skills fade would leave him sitting pretty.

Yr	Tm	PA	R	HR	RBI	SB	BA	xHR	xBA	OBP	SLG	OPS+	vL+	vR+	bb%	ct%	Eye	G	L	F	h%	HctX	PX	xPX	HR/F	xHR/F	Spd	SBO	SB%	#Wk	DOM	DIS	RAR	BPX	R$
15	OAK	601	65	15	45	11	257	14	242	310	405	100	121	90	7	76	0.32	38	23	39	31	98	96	119	9%	8%	138	11%	69%	27	37%	30%	-2.5	105	$14
16	OAK	621	72	27	75	10	238	24	249	300	435	100	110	94	8	76	0.37	39	18	43	27	88	119	114	15%	13%	110	9%	83%	27	41%	22%	1.5	140	$14
17	OAK	386	53	10	40	12	249	9	237	325	398	97	89	98	10	75	0.45	37	20	42	30	92	92	110	9%	8%	107	14%	92%	16	31%	38%	-1.0	85	$10
18	OAK	703	89	15	70	14	255	19	248	318	388	98	105	94	9	79	0.47	39	23	38	30	95	83	90	8%	10%	107	12%	70%	28	36%	25%	2.0	117	$19
19	OAK	747	123	33	92	10	285	32	290	369	522	118	121	117	12	84	0.85	41	20	39	30	122	113	105	15%	15%	134	9%	56%	29	69%	7%	28.2	348	$29
1st Half		395	57	11	42	5	271	12	266	352	434	105	114	102	11	84	0.80	47	18	36	30	110	82	72	10%	11%	122	8%	56%	16	63%	13%	2.7	237	$22
2nd Half		352	66	22	50	5	300	20	314	389	622	133	129	135	12	85	0.91	35	23	42	29	136	149	143	20%	18%	139	11%	56%	13	77%	0%	30.0	467	$36
20	**Proj**	**665**	**100**	**24**	**84**	**11**	**275**		**269**	**349**	**474**	**111**	**114**	**109**	**10**	**82**	**0.62**	**39**	**21**	**40**	**30**	**115**	**101**	**108**	**13%**		**124**	**10%**	**66%**				**27.4**	**223**	**$27**

Senzel,Nick

Age: 25 Bats: R Pos: CF
Ht: 6' 1" Wt: 205

Health	D	LIMA Plan	B
PT/Exp	D	Rand Var	+1
Consist	F	MM	2425

12-42-.256 with 14 SB in 414 PA at CIN. Vertigo, finger and elbow surgeries have taken some shine off former #2 overall pick. MLB debut marred by more injuries (ankle, hamstring, "allergies," elbow, thumb). Still, showed off surprising speed, moderate power, passable plate skills before season-ending labrum surgery. Talented and RISKY.

Yr	Tm	PA	R	HR	RBI	SB	BA	xHR	xBA	OBP	SLG	OPS+	vL+	vR+	bb%	ct%	Eye	G	L	F	h%	HctX	PX	xPX	HR/F	xHR/F	Spd	SBO	SB%	#Wk	DOM	DIS	RAR	BPX	R$
15																																			
16																																			
17	aa	237	42	12	36	5	345			423	588	135			12	78	0.61				40		137				98	13%	56%					227	$13
18	aaa	187	19	5	21	7	280			342	457	111			9	74	0.36				35		114				102	19%	75%					123	$5
19	CIN *	447	61	13	44	14	254	14	243	309	419	97	118	92	7	72	0.28	48	19	33	32	100	95	77	13%	16%	145	19%	74%	19	37%	47%	1.2	85	$13
1st Half		254	37	9	29	8	263	10	245	323	456	104	130	97	8	70	0.30	43	20	37	34	108	113	108	15%	19%	138	19%	73%	10	50%	30%	4.4	119	$16
2nd Half		193	24	4	15	6	242	4	240	301	371	89	97	87	6	73	0.25	53	18	28	31	91	72	42	11%	11%	145	19%	75%	9	22%	67%	-4.2	30	$8
20	**Proj**	**455**	**59**	**13**	**50**	**15**	**263**		**247**	**329**	**426**	**102**	**120**	**95**	**8**	**73**	**0.34**	**47**	**20**	**33**	**33**	**98**	**94**	**68**	**13%**		**130**	**19%**	**73%**				**9.9**	**82**	**$18**

ALAIN DE LEONARDIS

Severino,Pedro

Age: 26 Bats: R Pos: CA | Ht: 6' 1" Wt: 219

Health A | PT/Exp D | Consist B | LIMA Plan D+ | Rand Var -1 | MM 2123

Waived by WAS in March, took trip around the Beltway and "surged" (by catcher standards) for a half with BAL. Gains in xPX and xHR/F lend some credence to HR repeat, and while xBA jumped with them, things came back to Earth in 2nd half. Finding a usable second catcher is like sitting in traffic; he's just another stopped car in front of you.

Yr	Tm	PA	R	HR	RBI	SB	BA	xHR	xBA	OBP	SLG	OPS+	vL+	vR+	bb%	ct%	Eye	G	L	F	h%	HctX	PX	xPX	HR/F	xHR/F	Spd	SBO	SB%	#Wk	DOM	DIS	RAR	BPX	R$
15	WAS *	349	29	4	29	1	229	1	271	265	305	80	0	103	5	84	0.30	33	33	33	26	120	53	233	0%	100%	76	4%	28%	2	50%	50%	-12.2	30	$0
16	WAS *	343	30	4	24	3	263	0	212	313	345	90	166	135	7	84	0.45	60	8	32	30	82	53	76	25%	0%	99	8%	39%	9	56%	33%	-7.8	69	$4
17	WAS *	254	14	4	27	1	207	0	192	252	275	71	76	52	6	76	0.24	47	16	37	26	64	40	66	0%	0%	80	3%	42%	8	13%	75%	-13.9	-82	-$2
18	WAS *	347	26	7	26	1	197	3	230	248	309	77	78	66	6	77	0.30	40	21	38	23	63	71	49	4%	6%	75	2%	100%	18	17%	61%	-10.7	10	-$2
19	BAL	341	37	13	44	3	249	12	252	321	420	98	106	90	9	76	0.40	40	23	37	29	87	90	91	15%	14%	66	5%	75%	26	27%	38%	7.8	56	$6
1st Half		180	19	9	23	1	277	7	280	346	491	112	132	95	9	77	0.43	36	28	35	31	89	109	95	20%	16%	70	2%	100%	14	43%	29%	9.0	130	$7
2nd Half		161	18	4	21	2	219	5	223	292	342	84	82	84	8	75	0.36	44	17	39	26	85	69	87	10%	12%	78	9%	67%	12	8%	50%	-3.8	-7	$5
20	**Proj**	**350**	**32**	**12**	**38**	**2**	**232**		**243**	**297**	**385**	**92**	**104**	**83**	**7**	**77**	**0.34**	**41**	**22**	**38**	**27**	**77**	**81**	**74**	**13%**		**69**	**5%**	**67%**				**2.6**	**11**	**$4**

Shaw,Travis

Age: 30 Bats: L Pos: 3B | Ht: 6' 4" Wt: 230

Health A | PT/Exp B | Consist D | LIMA Plan D | Rand Var +4 | MM 3203

7-16-.157 in 270 PA at MIL. A total disaster. Sent to IL (wrist) with .163 BA in May; demoted to AAA in June, again in Aug. Once-stable power skills crashed, while ct% sunk more than any hitter from 2018. BPX confirms there's no way to sugarcoat this, so while maybe it was injury-fueled and he bounces back, don't pay much to find out.

Yr	Tm	PA	R	HR	RBI	SB	BA	xHR	xBA	OBP	SLG	OPS+	vL+	vR+	bb%	ct%	Eye	G	L	F	h%	HctX	PX	xPX	HR/F	xHR/F	Spd	SBO	SB%	#Wk	DOM	DIS	RAR	BPX	R$
15	BOS *	559	56	17	61	0	248	11	237	302	397	97	134	99	7	77	0.34	37	20	43	29	98	98	128	18%	15%	87	2%	0%	16	31%	31%	-21.1	78	$9
16	BOS	530	63	16	71	5	242	21	240	306	421	99	81	102	8	72	0.32	36	19	45	30	98	123	122	10%	13%	80	6%	83%	26	35%	38%	-14.5	86	$10
17	MIL	606	84	31	101	10	273	22	274	349	513	116	103	118	10	74	0.43	43	20	38	31	112	141	128	21%	15%	76	7%	100%	26	69%	19%	6.8	167	$23
18	MIL	587	73	32	86	5	241	29	263	345	480	114	83	123	13	78	0.72	37	18	45	25	115	133	132	18%	17%	61	5%	71%	28	71%	4%	6.1	220	$18
19	MIL *	428	40	16	38	2	180	8	194	297	332	84	34	83	14	62	0.44	29	22	49	24	76	92	101	10%	12%	67	3%	61%	21	19%	71%	-27.5	-100	$0
1st Half		251	23	7	14	1	166	7	186	273	282	74	31	88	13	63	0.39	33	21	46	23	88	72	116	12%	13%	74	3%	35%	12	25%	58%	-20.4	-152	-$4
2nd Half		177	18	9	24	1	201	1	205	333	406	97	51	67	16	61	0.51	11	26	63	25	31	123	38	6%	6%	92	3%	100%	9	11%	89%	-3.7	19	$6
20	**Proj**	**315**	**36**	**13**	**40**	**2**	**226**		**223**	**336**	**406**	**100**	**81**	**104**	**13**	**69**	**0.48**	**33**	**21**	**45**	**28**	**82**	**103**	**99**	**15%**		**76**	**4%**	**80%**				**-1.6**	**7**	**$7**

Sierra,Magneuris

Age: 24 Bats: L Pos: CF | Ht: 5' 11" Wt: 160

Health A | PT/Exp C | Consist C | LIMA Plan D+ | Rand Var 0 | MM 0533

0-1-.350 with 3 SB in 42 PA at MIA. Swiped 33 bags at AA/AAA before Sept cup of coffee. Spd score confirms the raw wheels are elite and he puts them to use with GB% stroke, though xBA leaves little room for BA growth with zero pop. OBP deficiencies might keep him off the field, so while steals are scarce, don't get too desperate.

Yr	Tm	PA	R	HR	RBI	SB	BA	xHR	xBA	OBP	SLG	OPS+	vL+	vR+	bb%	ct%	Eye	G	L	F	h%	HctX	PX	xPX	HR/F	xHR/F	Spd	SBO	SB%	#Wk	DOM	DIS	RAR	BPX	R$
15																																			
16																																			
17	STL *	408	38	1	36	17	266	0	275	305	331	85	122	81	5	81	0.29	53	28	19	33	21	44	-3	0%	0%	160	24%	70%	8	0%	88%	-18.2	58	$11
18	MIA *	513	51	2	21	15	219	0	240	245	272	72	104	52	3	76	0.14	57	23	19	29	55	36	18	0%	0%	176	21%	67%	11	9%	73%	-32.4	-20	$5
19	MIA *	587	80	6	28	35	202	0	255	299	361	88	261	99	5	81	0.28	62	14	24	31	76	50	33	0%	0%	188	35%	70%	4	25%	75%	-11.0	119	$21
1st Half		317	38	2	13	16	263		230	299	338	85			5	81	0.28				32		40		0%	#VALUE!	171	25%	78%				-7.4	74	$16
2nd Half		270	42	4	16	20	261	0	263	299	388	91	258	99	5	80	0.28	62	14	24	31	76	61	33	0%	0%	187	48%	65%	4	25%	75%	-5.7	144	$27
20	**Proj**	**350**	**42**	**3**	**19**	**12**	**248**		**258**	**281**	**329**	**82**	**127**	**75**	**4**	**79**	**0.22**	**57**	**22**	**21**	**31**	**49**	**44**	**15**	**5%**		**184**	**22%**	**68%**				**-8.5**	**6**	**$9**

Simmons,Andrelton

Age: 30 Bats: R Pos: SS | Ht: 6' 2" Wt: 195

Health C | PT/Exp A | Consist B | LIMA Plan B | Rand Var 0 | MM 1345

Ankle sprains in May and August cost him nearly two months. Elite bat-to-ball skills held firm, and while 2nd half h% tanked BA, complete absence of already-shaky power hint some of it was deserved. A green light would work wonders here, as SB% continues to be excellent. We'll have to settle for just a partial rebound instead.

Yr	Tm	PA	R	HR	RBI	SB	BA	xHR	xBA	OBP	SLG	OPS+	vL+	vR+	bb%	ct%	Eye	G	L	F	h%	HctX	PX	xPX	HR/F	xHR/F	Spd	SBO	SB%	#Wk	DOM	DIS	RAR	BPX	R$
15	ATL	583	60	4	44	5	265	4	279	321	338	92	78	94	7	91	0.81	56	22	22	29	92	47	61	4%	4%	108	5%	63%	27	56%	22%	-11.2	132	$10
16	LAA	483	48	4	44	10	281	4	282	324	366	94	102	90	6	92	0.74	55	20	26	30	87	51	54	4%	4%	109	9%	91%	23	48%	9%	0.0	151	$12
17	LAA	647	77	14	69	19	278	11	286	331	421	101	92	102	7	89	0.70	50	19	31	30	105	78	82	8%	7%	104	16%	76%	27	56%	15%	5.0	197	$22
18	LAA	600	68	11	75	10	292	11	281	337	417	104	104	104	6	92	0.80	50	19	31	30	122	65	82	7%	7%	139	8%	83%	27	56%	7%	14.9	253	$21
19	LAA	424	47	7	40	10	264	5	262	309	364	89	108	83	6	91	0.65	54	14	32	28	108	51	33	6%	4%	91	12%	83%	22	50%	23%	-14.1	163	$9
1st Half		206	23	3	21	5	291	4	269	316	402	96	100	94	3	91	0.33	54	14	31	31	123	59	50	5%	7%	94	13%	83%	11	55%	27%	-2.1	174	$9
2nd Half		218	24	4	19	5	236	1	251	303	327	83	121	73	8	90	0.95	53	14	32	24	92	42	16	7%	2%	95	11%	83%	11	45%	18%	-9.7	156	$10
20	**Proj**	**595**	**67**	**10**	**65**	**13**	**279**		**270**	**326**	**388**	**96**	**106**	**92**	**6**	**91**	**0.71**	**52**	**17**	**31**	**29**	**107**	**54**	**53**	**7%**		**108**	**10%**	**81%**				**5.4**	**175**	**$21**

Sisco,Chance

Age: 25 Bats: L Pos: CA | Ht: 6' 2" Wt: 195

Health A | PT/Exp D | Consist C | LIMA Plan D | Rand Var +2 | MM 3103

8-20-.210 in 198 PA at BAL. Scorching May in AAA (.348 BA, 9 HR) led to June call-up, but production didn't carry over. MLB plate skills (63% ct%, .215 xBA) suggest he was overmatched and he barely played vL. Power stroke held strong, but while prospect pedigree and bb% give him staying power, don't count on this all coming together.

Yr	Tm	PA	R	HR	RBI	SB	BA	xHR	xBA	OBP	SLG	OPS+	vL+	vR+	bb%	ct%	Eye	G	L	F	h%	HctX	PX	xPX	HR/F	xHR/F	Spd	SBO	SB%	#Wk	DOM	DIS	RAR	BPX	R$
15	aa	82	8	2	7	0	248			321	379	98			10	81	0.56				28		87				94	5%	0%					114	-$1
16	a/a	486	52	5	46	2	282			370	363	100			12	76	0.59				36		55				91	3%	45%					9	$10
17	BAL *	397	46	8	47	2	237	1	204	303	349	87	22	216	9	67	0.28	45	18	36	33	172	79	223	50%	25%	88	4%	45%	5	20%	40%	-7.2	-73	$4
18	BAL *	326	32	5	26	1	199	5	176	267	292	77	91	75	8	64	0.25	47	13	40	29	78	74	126	5%	14%	88	1%	100%	18	17%	72%	-7.9	-133	-$1
19	BAL *	382	53	16	49	0	231	8	226	309	422	97	52	103	10	67	0.34	38	20	42	29	97	113	151	18%	18%	95	1%	0%	17	24%	59%	6.7	37	$5
1st Half		238	34	12	43	0	255	4	259	324	490	109	67	141	9	69	0.33	36	25	39	31	111	138	151	36%		92	2%	0%	5	60%	20%	8.5	130	$11
2nd Half		144	19	4	6	0	189	4	183	313	303	81	47	87	12	64	0.36	39	18	43	26	88	67	152	12%		129	0%	0%	12	8%	75%	-5.0	-100	-$4
20	**Proj**	**280**	**35**	**11**	**27**	**1**	**221**		**213**	**335**	**393**	**98**	**71**	**100**	**10**	**67**	**0.33**	**41**	**18**	**41**	**28**	**90**	**103**	**141**	**16%**		**100**	**2%**	**49%**				**3.2**	**-64**	**$5**

Slater,Austin

Age: 27 Bats: R Pos: RF | Ht: 6' 2" Wt: 197

Health B | PT/Exp D | Consist A | LIMA Plan D | Rand Var -1 | MM 2323

5-21-.238 in 192 PA at SF. Earned July call-up after slashing .308/.436/.529 with 6 SB at AAA, but success quickly vanished. Uptick in Ks hurt xBA/BA, and he stopped running in majors. Meager FB% also caps HR despite flashy power skills, so while he's a launch-angle adjustment away from relevance, he'll still cost you in BA.

Yr	Tm	PA	R	HR	RBI	SB	BA	xHR	xBA	OBP	SLG	OPS+	vL+	vR+	bb%	ct%	Eye	G	L	F	h%	HctX	PX	xPX	HR/F	xHR/F	Spd	SBO	SB%	#Wk	DOM	DIS	RAR	BPX	R$
15	aa	212	20	0	12	1	279			324	344	93			6	73	0.25				38		58				106	4%	46%					-38	$2
16	a/a	439	47	12	56	7	265			347	413	103			11	74	0.48				33		95				87	12%	46%					60	$11
17	SF *	323	37	6	38	3	277	3	235	322	391	96	108	94	6	75	0.27	61	14	25	35	73	71	48	14%	14%	121	8%	48%	9	22%	56%	-7.7	24	$7
18	SF *	435	43	4	45	13	263	3	251	323	371	96	91	86	8	70	0.30	63	21	16	37	97	83	31	5%	14%	108	14%	84%	17	12%	76%	-1.8	-3	$11
19	SF *	467	55	13	55	5	245	8	246	337	410	99	109	89	12	65	0.40	52	25	23	34	102	107	113	20%	32%	116	7%	69%	14	29%	50%	-9.0	30	$9
1st Half		275	35	8	34	4	250		222	345	405	100			13	66	0.42				35		103		0%		96	10%	65%	1	100%	0%	-3.8	4	$11
2nd Half		192	20	5	21	1	238	8	247	333	417	99	108	89	12	65	0.37	52	25	23	34	101	111	113	20%	32%	141	2%	100%	13	23%	54%	-3.1	59	$4
20	**Proj**	**280**	**31**	**7**	**31**	**3**	**256**		**247**	**340**	**408**	**101**	**108**	**95**	**10**	**69**	**0.36**	**55**	**22**	**23**	**35**	**89**	**95**	**67**	**17%**		**125**	**7%**	**66%**				**0.3**	**-10**	**$7**

Smith,Dominic

Age: 25 Bats: L Pos: 1B LF | Ht: 6' 0" Wt: 239

Health C | PT/Exp C | Consist F | LIMA Plan C | Rand Var -2 | MM 3033

Squeezed for playing time in April (thanks, Pete); July foot injury shelved him for over two months. Take this sample with a grain of salt, but bb%/ct% took steps forward; xBA supports BA gains; BPX surged above league average. Don't extrapolate HR pace—xHR/F says he's not there yet—but this once-top prospect has life again.

Yr	Tm	PA	R	HR	RBI	SB	BA	xHR	xBA	OBP	SLG	OPS+	vL+	vR+	bb%	ct%	Eye	G	L	F	h%	HctX	PX	xPX	HR/F	xHR/F	Spd	SBO	SB%	#Wk	DOM	DIS	RAR	BPX	R$
15																																			
16	aa	532	56	13	79	2	272			337	410	102			9	82	0.56				31		83				82	2%	61%					114	$13
17	NYM *	672	74	22	82	1	256	8	242	307	418	97	58	94	7	75	0.30	50	16	34	31	113	98	112	23%	20%	50	1%	40%	9	33%	44%	-27.9	33	$12
18	NYM *	509	48	9	38	2	208	6	228	251	328	80	81	94	5	71	0.20	34	26	40	27	80	86	105	13%	16%	72	2%	100%	14	43%	50%	-36.2	-33	$1
19	NYM	197	35	11	25	1	282	8	274	355	525	117	114	117	10	75	0.43	40	23	37	32	96	129	89	22%	16%	78	6%	33%	19	53%	37%	4.6	178	$5
1st Half		141	29	8	14	1	328	6	279	418	590	135	131	136	13	74	0.56	42	22	36	39	96	143	96	25%	19%	91	5%	50%	15	53%	33%	12.7	237	$8
2nd Half		56	6	3	11	0	182	2	262	196	382	76	82	75	2	78	0.08	37	23	40	18	94	99	74	18%	12%	76	17%	0%	4	50%	50%	-5.6	74	-$2
20	**Proj**	**385**	**51**	**19**	**53**	**1**	**263**		**258**	**315**	**472**	**106**	**98**	**107**	**6**	**74**	**0.27**	**39**	**23**	**38**	**31**	**92**	**114**	**95**	**18%**		**67**	**5%**	**31%**				**4.0**	**63**	**$13**

RYAN BLOOMFIELD

Smith,Dwight

Age: 27 Bats: L Pos: LF
Ht: 6' 0" Wt: 210

Health	B	LIMA Plan	D+
PT/Exp	D	Rand Var	0
Consist	A	MM	2223

13-53-.241 with 5 SB in 392 PA at BAL. Did most of his "damage" during Apr/May (10 HR in 195 AB) with an out-of-character 19% HR/F. Then injuries (concussion, calf strain) limited his opportunity, and when your history of hit and power metrics are this low, the leash is short even on a rebuilding club. Next.

Yr	Tm	PA	R	HR	RBI	SB	BA	xHR	xBA	OBP	SLG	OPS+	vL+	vR+	bb%	ct%	Eye	G	L	F	h%	HctX	PX	xPX	HR/F	xHR/F	Spd	SBO	SB%	#Wk	DOM	DIS	RAR	BPX	R$
15	aa	499	62	6	37	3	244			304	350	91			8	84	0.55				28		73				101	6%	50%					119	$5
16	aa	508	46	13	61	10	242			297	392	94			7	78	0.36				28		91				99	16%	56%					91	$9
17	TOR *	467	54	8	43	8	264	0	257	334	378	95	103	118	9	79	0.49	59	18	24	32	37	72	18	0%	0%	120	14%	48%	5	20%	80%	-16.5	88	$10
18	TOR *	421	41	7	43	7	242	1	239	320	384	98	53	127	10	80	0.59	48	12	40	28	73	96	98	10%	5%	93	11%	68%	13	46%	31%	-5.4	160	$7
19	BAL *	439	53	15	62	5	242	10	254	292	415	94	83	98	6	77	0.31	47	19	34	28	78	89	80	14%	11%	111	7%	83%	22	27%	32%	-12.1	104	$9
1st Half		286	37	12	45	4	250	9	267	296	453	100	100	102	6	77	0.29	44	21	35	28	77	105	93	16%	13%	109	9%	80%	14	29%	21%	-4.6	152	$14
2nd Half		153	16	4	17	1	228	1	223	285	344	83	32	90	7	77	0.35	55	13	32	27	81	59	44	8%	4%	113	3%	100%	8	25%	50%	-7.9	22	-$1
20	**Proj**	**315**	**35**	**9**	**36**	**4**	**244**		**242**	**313**	**397**	**96**	**60**	**106**	**8**	**79**	**0.41**	**50**	**14**	**36**	**28**	**77**	**83**	**78**	**11%**		**102**	**9%**	**66%**				**-4.1**	**85**	**$5**

Smith,Mallex

Age: 27 Bats: L Pos: CF RF
Ht: 5' 10" Wt: 180

Health	B	LIMA Plan	C
PT/Exp	B	Rand Var	+2
Consist	D	MM	1525

6-37-.227 with 46 SB in 566 PA at SEA. The two-trick-pony hopes of 2018 crumbled in a mountainous heap of give-backs in just about every offensive metric, from xBA to OPS to Eye to HctX. Obviously SB game is still elite, and there's some time to recapture his LD stroke, but there are shades of a Billy Hamiltonesque career path here.

Yr	Tm	PA	R	HR	RBI	SB	BA	xHR	xBA	OBP	SLG	OPS+	vL+	vR+	bb%	ct%	Eye	G	L	F	h%	HctX	PX	xPX	HR/F	xHR/F	Spd	SBO	SB%	#Wk	DOM	DIS	RAR	BPX	R$
15	a/a	531	75	2	31	51	283			346	353	97			9	80	0.48				35		47				148	41%	78%					57	$30
16	ATL *	250	37	3	26	20	258	3	253	331	388	98	40	109	10	74	0.42	61	16	23	34	60	79	59	11%	11%	147	45%	68%	15	27%	40%	-3.1	69	$11
17	TAM *	484	56	5	21	35	256	1	238	315	352	89	80	92	8	74	0.34	50	22	28	34	64	57	29	4%	2%	186	39%	71%	19	21%	47%	-13.8	48	$18
18	TAM	544	65	2	40	40	296	5	265	367	406	107	114	104	9	80	0.48	50	25	25	37	80	70	57	2%	5%	157	35%	77%	27	41%	37%	17.5	137	$27
19	SEA *	613	76	7	41	51	231	7	233	287	338	83	89	82	7	74	0.30	51	19	30	30	67	60	54	6%	6%	171	44%	85%	27	22%	48%	-18.0	37	$24
1st Half		341	47	6	27	26	235	4	241	291	363	87	96	86	7	75	0.31	47	20	32	30	79	72	73	8%	6%	148	38%	93%	14	29%	43%	-5.0	67	$26
2nd Half		272	29	1	14	25	224	2	222	299	306	80	84	77	8	72	0.29	55	18	27	31	55	45	34	2%	4%	183	52%	78%	13	15%	54%	-11.1	-11	$22
20	**Proj**	**525**	**65**	**4**	**35**	**43**	**254**		**241**	**323**	**358**	**92**	**89**	**92**	**8**	**75**	**0.36**	**52**	**21**	**28**	**33**	**68**	**58**	**49**	**4%**		**173**	**42%**	**79%**				**0.5**	**57**	**$26**

Smith,Will

Age: 25 Bats: R Pos: CA
Ht: 5' 10" Wt: 195

Health	A	LIMA Plan	C
PT/Exp	F	Rand Var	+1
Consist	D	MM	4313

15-42-.253 in 196 PA at LA. Impactful debut, but sustainable? PRO: Impressive HctX/xPX; big jump in ct% at AAA; lots of FB in the minors. CON: xHR skeptical of power; ct% reverted to 69% in MLB; HR spike coincides with questions on AAA/MLB baseball. Young and useful, but prime overbid candidate due to batted ball profile.

Yr	Tm	PA	R	HR	RBI	SB	BA	xHR	xBA	OBP	SLG	OPS+	vL+	vR+	bb%	ct%	Eye	G	L	F	h%	HctX	PX	xPX	HR/F	xHR/F	Spd	SBO	SB%	#Wk	DOM	DIS	RAR	BPX	R$
15																																			
16																																			
17																																			
18	a/a	383	44	15	45	4	200			265	376	89			8	64	0.25				26		126				86	5%	100%					0	$4
19	LA *	447	65	30	81	3	236	10	248	315	515	110	89	136	10	72	0.41	29	17	54	25	111	147	168	23%	15%	93	3%	100%	14	50%	36%	12.9	211	$13
1st Half		231	31	13	34	2	244	1	280	326	500	110	63	177	11	73	0.44	35	29	35	27	118	136	154	50%	17%	97	3%	100%	3	67%	0%	9.6	193	$11
2nd Half		216	33	16	47	1	227	8	250	302	531	110	94	129	10	72	0.38	28	15	57	22	110	159	170	20%	14%	90	3%	100%	11	45%	45%	7.6	230	$16
20	**Proj**	**385**	**52**	**20**	**63**	**3**	**240**		**232**	**322**	**460**	**105**	**73**	**122**	**10**	**69**	**0.34**	**31**	**21**	**48**	**29**	**113**	**125**	**164**	**17%**		**91**	**4%**	**100%**				**15.4**	**62**	**$13**

Smoak,Justin

Age: 33 Bats: B Pos: 1B DH
Ht: 6' 4" Wt: 220

Health	A	LIMA Plan	D+
PT/Exp	A	Rand Var	+5
Consist	C	MM	3023

Has power; will be traveling. Rock-solid history of FB%, xPX and high-teens HR/F points to bunches of long balls. But notice the relationship of HR and contact: 2017 and 1st half of 2019 writes one story; 2018 and 2nd half of 2019, another. At his age, we're projecting the latter outcome only accelerates. A tough profile these days.

Yr	Tm	PA	R	HR	RBI	SB	BA	xHR	xBA	OBP	SLG	OPS+	vL+	vR+	bb%	ct%	Eye	G	L	F	h%	HctX	PX	xPX	HR/F	xHR/F	Spd	SBO	SB%	#Wk	DOM	DIS	RAR	BPX	R$
15	TOR	328	44	18	59	0	226	17	274	299	470	107	116	104	9	71	0.34	43	24	34	26	112	166	141	25%	24%	72	0%	0%	27	52%	33%	-3.2	157	$7
16	TOR	341	33	14	34	1	217	15	223	314	391	96	84	99	12	63	0.36	30	27	42	29	99	123	144	18%	19%	80	1%	100%	26	27%	58%	-8.1	-3	$2
17	TOR	637	85	38	90	0	270	38	277	355	529	118	130	113	11	77	0.57	34	21	44	29	123	141	158	20%	20%	68	1%	0%	27	56%	19%	17.8	203	$19
18	TOR	594	67	25	77	0	242	29	239	350	457	112	96	119	14	69	0.53	39	18	43	30	86	147	140	17%	19%	70	1%	0%	27	44%	30%	13.5	150	$13
19	TOR	500	54	22	61	0	208	25	242	342	406	99	88	104	16	74	0.75	37	21	43	22	110	103	144	17%	19%	58	0%	0%	27	41%	37%	-7.0	115	$5
1st Half		274	31	14	37	0	227	17	256	361	440	107	75	123	16	78	0.90	33	22	45	23	119	101	161	18%	21%	71	0%	0%	14	43%	29%	-0.3	185	$8
2nd Half		226	23	8	24	0	185	8	227	319	365	90	106	83	16	70	0.61	42	19	39	22	99	106	121	15%	15%	61	0%	0%	13	38%	46%	-9.6	59	$1
20	**Proj**	**350**	**40**	**16**	**45**	**0**	**224**		**242**	**339**	**433**	**104**	**98**	**106**	**14**	**72**	**0.60**	**38**	**20**	**42**	**26**	**104**	**117**	**141**	**17%**		**67**	**0%**	**18%**				**1.8**	**71**	**$7**

Sogard,Eric

Age: 34 Bats: L Pos: 2B
Ht: 5' 10" Wt: 185

Health	D	LIMA Plan	D+
PT/Exp	D	Rand Var	-5
Consist	F	MM	1333

13-40-.290 with 8 SB in 442 PA at TOR/TAM. Not even the Bespectacled One could see this season coming into focus: ct% return; FB spike, fortunate HR/F, SB perfection plus an MLB opportunity. Base skills intact, but with his age and defensive limits, the future is fuzzy (and not repeatable). 2019 owners: just be grateful for 2020 hindsight.

Yr	Tm	PA	R	HR	RBI	SB	BA	xHR	xBA	OBP	SLG	OPS+	vL+	vR+	bb%	ct%	Eye	G	L	F	h%	HctX	PX	xPX	HR/F	xHR/F	Spd	SBO	SB%	#Wk	DOM	DIS	RAR	BPX	R$
15	OAK	401	40	1	37	6	247	1	240	294	304	83	75	83	6	87	0.46	44	22	34	28	63	37	40	1%	1%	115	7%	86%	26	19%	46%	-13.5	65	$5
16																																			
17	MIL *	399	56	5	29	6	265	3	279	366	378	100	99	102	14	84	1.02	39	29	33	30	90	68	62	4%	4%	94	8%	67%	21	43%	29%	-2.3	148	$8
18	MIL *	208	13	0	8	3	146	1	214	220	178	55	70	54	9	76	0.40	36	27	36	19	96	28	101	0%	4%	76	11%	70%	14	21%	64%	-19.3	-100	-$6
19	2 AL *	477	64	14	44	8	285	5	267	351	449	106	111	106	9	84	0.63	32	26	42	31	102	83	84	9%	4%	110	6%	100%	23	39%	35%	11.8	204	$14
1st Half		273	40	10	29	6	300	3	268	374	489	115	131	113	11	84	0.76	32	24	44	32	103	90	90	12%		123	8%	100%	12	42%	25%	14.4	259	$19
2nd Half		204	24	4	15	2	266	2	270	324	399	95	84	99	7	84	0.48	32	28	41	30	101	74	78	6%		92	4%	100%	11	36%	45%	-0.8	141	$7
20	**Proj**	**350**	**40**	**5**	**26**	**4**	**240**		**252**	**314**	**345**	**89**	**96**	**86**	**9**	**82**	**0.56**	**35**	**26**	**38**	**28**	**95**	**59**	**80**	**5%**		**96**	**6%**	**82%**				**-4.7**	**71**	**$6**

Solak,Nick

Age: 25 Bats: R Pos: 3B
Ht: 5' 11" Wt: 190

Health	A	LIMA Plan	C+
PT/Exp	C	Rand Var	0
Consist	A	MM	2425

5-17-.293 with 2 SB in 135 PA at TEX. Solid debut, but 4 cautions before you dive in: 1) 35% MLB hit rate reinforces xBA; 2) consistent 50%+ GB% in MiLB; 3) history of low-70s ct%; 4) 2019 his first HR/F over 16%. Has good foundation from which to improve, but likely to come slower than Aug/Sep would lead you to believe.

Yr	Tm	PA	R	HR	RBI	SB	BA	xHR	xBA	OBP	SLG	OPS+	vL+	vR+	bb%	ct%	Eye	G	L	F	h%	HctX	PX	xPX	HR/F	xHR/F	Spd	SBO	SB%	#Wk	DOM	DIS	RAR	BPX	R$
15																																			
16																																			
17	aa	129	15	2	9	1	275			330	416	100			8	78	0.37				34		89				108	7%	48%					100	$1
18	aa	536	77	16	65	18	250			331	389	100			11	73	0.44				31		85				110	17%	73%					50	$19
19	TEX *	588	77	26	71	6	264	5	261	326	461	105	141	100	8	73	0.34	53	20	28	31	73	105	64	21%	21%	123	6%	71%	7	29%	0%	6.5	122	$17
1st Half		296	39	12	33	2	248		244	320	436	101			9	73	0.38				30		101		0%		111	6%	49%				-0.4	93	$12
2nd Half		292	38	14	38	3	280	5	267	333	487	108	139	100	7	74	0.30	53	20	28	33	74	110	64	21%	21%	121	5%	100%	7	29%	0%	8.8	137	$21
20	**Proj**	**490**	**66**	**16**	**56**	**9**	**264**		**249**	**347**	**425**	**104**	**124**	**89**	**9**	**74**	**0.37**	**51**	**20**	**30**	**32**	**67**	**89**	**58**	**17%**		**131**	**10%**	**71%**				**3.0**	**51**	**$17**

Soler,Jorge

Age: 28 Bats: R Pos: DH RF
Ht: 6' 4" Wt: 230

Health	D	LIMA Plan	B
PT/Exp	C	Rand Var	-2
Consist	C	MM	4225

Via plate approach and batted ball distribution, this has been one stable skill set in recent years. But then health, prime age, and the Rabbit Ball converge for six months and ... holy moly. If the gains in HctX, xPX and HR/F can at least partially stick, this is an impact bat—though not without injury risk.

Yr	Tm	PA	R	HR	RBI	SB	BA	xHR	xBA	OBP	SLG	OPS+	vL+	vR+	bb%	ct%	Eye	G	L	F	h%	HctX	PX	xPX	HR/F	xHR/F	Spd	SBO	SB%	#Wk	DOM	DIS	RAR	BPX	R$
15	CHC	404	39	10	47	3	262	11	236	324	399	101	101	99	8	67	0.26	42	28	30	37	110	107	123	14%	15%	98	4%	75%	20	30%	50%	-10.7	0	$8
16	CHC *	310	40	12	33	0	224	12	215	325	394	98	110	100	13	68	0.47	40	17	43	28	86	112	91	17%	17%	85	0%	0%	19	47%	37%	-10.3	43	$3
17	KC *	421	45	19	52	1	205	3	217	300	394	93	77	61	12	65	0.39	38	18	44	26	82	122	88	7%	11%	64	1%	100%	13	0%	69%	-12.2	12	$2
18	KC	257	27	9	28	3	265	13	251	354	466	114	148	102	11	69	0.41	47	19	34	34	109	144	110	17%	25%	94	7%	75%	12	42%	42%	7.0	143	$5
19	KC	676	95	48	117	3	265	51	271	354	569	122	113	125	11	70	0.41	39	20	41	30	113	168	140	28%	30%	72	3%	75%	28	68%	18%	26.4	219	$25
1st Half		346	41	22	55	0	233	25	245	301	498	107	92	112	7	67	0.24	43	18	40	27	99	155	130	26%	30%	69	2%	0%	15	53%	27%	-4.9	107	$17
2nd Half		330	54	26	62	3	301	26	293	409	649	140	143	139	15	73	0.65	36	22	43	32	129	181	151	30%	30%	83	3%	100%	13	85%	8%	33.2	348	$35
20	**Proj**	**630**	**82**	**32**	**94**	**4**	**258**		**248**	**350**	**492**	**113**	**117**	**111**	**11**	**69**	**0.42**	**41**	**20**	**40**	**32**	**108**	**137**	**123**	**21%**		**81**	**3%**	**80%**				**18.2**	**104**	**$22**

BRENT HERSHEY

Soto,Juan

Age: 21 Bats: L Pos: LF | Ht: 6' 1" Wt: 185
Health C | PT/Exp C | Consist B | LIMA Plan A | Rand Var 0 | MM 4455

2nd half h% a hiccup in near carbon-copy followup to fine rookie season, with all signs pointing upward. Running game blossomed; SB%, youth tease more with SBO cooperation. Sharp cut in GB% bolstered power, now with full xPX support. Sturdy ct%, elite bb% never wavered; 2nd half HctX soared. Stud in the making. UP: .300 BA, 40 HR.

Yr	Tm	PA	R	HR	RBI	SB	BA	xHR	xBA	OBP	SLG	OPS+	vL+	vR+	bb%	ct%	Eye	G	L	F	h%	HctX	PX	xPX	HR/F	xHR/F	Spd	SBO	SB%	#Wk	DOM	DIS	RAR	BPX	R$
15																																			
16																																			
17																																			
18	WAS *	528	80	24	79	6	293	24	277	404	519	128	118	130	16	76	0.78	54	17	29	34	98	135	105	25%	27%	110	5%	75%	21	71%	19%	36.4	263	$23
19	WAS	659	110	34	110	12	282	39	280	401	548	126	111	133	16	76	0.82	42	21	37	32	108	138	139	22%	25%	117	7%	92%	28	61%	18%	42.1	307	$29
1st Half		316	49	14	52	5	297	17	272	402	534	125	128	123	15	74	0.66	45	22	33	36	91	127	117	22%	26%	125	5%	100%	15	53%	20%	20.2	241	$25
2nd Half		343	61	20	58	7	268	22	287	399	562	127	94	143	18	78	1.00	39	20	41	28	124	147	158	23%	25%	111	8%	88%	13	69%	15%	22.4	370	$33
20	Proj	630	103	33	102	10	286		279	401	545	127	112	133	16	76	0.81	45	20	35	32	105	136	127	23%		116	6%	86%				50.1	285	$28

Souza,Steven

Age: 31 Bats: R Pos: OF | Ht: 6' 4" Wt: 225
Health F | PT/Exp D | Consist D | LIMA Plan D | Rand Var | MM 3313

Torn ACL in March torpedoed 2019. Projects to be ready for Opening Day, but on heels of injury-plagued 2018, lost year now clouds his future. At least some of the power should return and bb% should work again. But ct%, BA skills (.229 BA vR) have never been pluses; running game now a question mark. He'll be inexpensive for good reason.

Yr	Tm	PA	R	HR	RBI	SB	BA	xHR	xBA	OBP	SLG	OPS+	vL+	vR+	bb%	ct%	Eye	G	L	F	h%	HctX	PX	xPX	HR/F	xHR/F	Spd	SBO	SB%	#Wk	DOM	DIS	RAR	BPX	R$
15	TAM	426	59	16	40	12	225	15	220	318	399	100	101	98	11	61	0.32	45	20	35	32	92	138	100	21%	19%	105	18%	67%	21	24%	48%	-10.1	30	$10
16	TAM	468	58	17	49	7	247	20	224	303	409	97	90	98	7	63	0.19	41	25	34	35	83	118	110	18%	22%	119	13%	54%	24	25%	58%	-9.4	-6	$10
17	TAM	617	78	30	78	16	239	28	246	351	459	109	104	108	14	66	0.47	45	21	34	30	91	139	100	26%	24%	96	13%	80%	27	48%	26%	2.2	97	$17
18	ARI	272	21	5	29	6	220	8	229	309	369	94	108	86	10	69	0.37	37	24	39	30	112	106	122	8%	13%	107	12%	86%	18	33%	56%	-5.1	50	$2
19																																			
1st Half																																			
2nd Half																																			
20	Proj	280	32	10	31	6	234		227	316	410	98	99	97	10	65	0.31	41	23	36	32	95	110	110	17%		114	14%	71%				-4.0	-10	$8

Springer,George

Age: 30 Bats: R Pos: CF RF | Ht: 6' 3" Wt: 215
Health C | PT/Exp A | Consist D | LIMA Plan B+ | Rand Var -1 | MM 4345

Strained hamstring cost him a 1st half month, mild concussion limited him in Sept. Unlike nagging 2018 injuries, neither slowed him down. Power, HctX rebounded in a big way; new ball likely helped HR. Plate skills stable as ever; torched RHPs all season. Once a BA/xBA combo in question; now a premium bat unlikely to be discounted.

Yr	Tm	PA	R	HR	RBI	SB	BA	xHR	xBA	OBP	SLG	OPS+	vL+	vR+	bb%	ct%	Eye	G	L	F	h%	HctX	PX	xPX	HR/F	xHR/F	Spd	SBO	SB%	#Wk	DOM	DIS	RAR	BPX	R$
15	HOU	451	59	16	41	16	276	17	261	367	459	115	129	105	11	72	0.46	45	24	30	35	106	127	112	19%	20%	120	17%	80%	19	58%	32%	14.8	132	$18
16	HOU	744	116	29	82	9	261	32	259	359	457	111	128	103	12	72	0.49	48	20	31	32	99	122	111	20%	22%	125	10%	47%	27	41%	26%	17.2	143	$22
17	HOU	627	112	34	85	5	283	30	285	367	522	119	129	114	10	80	0.58	48	18	34	30	119	128	112	23%	20%	98	8%	42%	25	64%	12%	25.5	221	$24
18	HOU	616	102	22	71	6	265	30	249	346	434	108	116	104	10	78	0.52	49	16	35	31	96	101	100	15%	20%	112	6%	60%	28	46%	25%	16.3	157	$20
19	HOU	556	96	39	96	6	292	38	290	383	591	120	118	133	12	76	0.60	45	20	36	31	110	140	127	30%	29%	115	6%	75%	24	58%	21%	47.5	307	$26
1st Half		243	43	18	45	4	306	19	289	387	617	134	128	136	12	75	0.54	43	20	37	33	123	154	128	31%	32%	105	8%	80%	11	64%	27%	25.3	300	$24
2nd Half		313	53	21	51	2	281	18	289	380	570	125	110	131	13	77	0.64	45	20	35	29	117	139	126	29%	25%	120	4%	67%	13	54%	15%	23.7	311	$28
20	Proj	595	102	35	88	7	281		275	370	532	121	120	121	12	77	0.56	47	19	35	31	112	126	116	25%		115	7%	65%				43.1	216	$28

Stallings,Jacob

Age: 30 Bats: R Pos: CA | Ht: 6' 4" Wt: 220
Health A | PT/Exp F | Consist C | LIMA Plan D+ | Rand Var -2 | MM 2023

6-13-.262 in 207 PA at PIT. Journeyman gained 2nd half playing time fueled partly by plus defense and noteworthy 40% CS%. Bat cooperated, as decent ct% run continued; even HR, power metrics and patience peaked. But nothing in history, peripherals or age hints at big upside from here. These may well be the best of times.

Yr	Tm	PA	R	HR	RBI	SB	BA	xHR	xBA	OBP	SLG	OPS+	vL+	vR+	bb%	ct%	Eye	G	L	F	h%	HctX	PX	xPX	HR/F	xHR/F	Spd	SBO	SB%	#Wk	DOM	DIS	RAR	BPX	R$
15	aa	276	19	2	24	3	227			258	299	78			4	72	0.15				31		60				88	7%	72%					-73	$0
16	PIT *	282	20	5	26	1	198	0	246	225	311	73	0	116	3	71	0.12	45	27	27	26	105	85	67	0%	0%	84	5%	46%	3	0%	67%	-19.0	-37	-$3
17	PIT *	246	31	3	33	1	258	0	301	305	365	90	106	133	6	84	0.42	42	33	25	30	57	68	57	0%	0%	90	6%	25%	4	50%	50%	-2.6	94	$3
18	PIT *	308	28	2	33	1	222	0	245	256	307	78	39	77	4	75	0.19	52	24	24	29	96	65	33	0%	0%	91	6%	22%	8	0%	75%	-9.3	-23	$0
19	PIT *	264	34	7	18	0	252	7	244	306	395	93	126	83	7	79	0.37	48	19	34	29	95	77	74	12%	14%	102	0%	0%	21	33%	48%	-1.5	89	$2
1st Half		102	15	2	9	0	277	1	285	333	442	104	33	132	8	80	0.41	37	29	34	33	87	98	35	8%	8%	84	0%	0%	8	38%	38%	3.2	148	-$1
2nd Half		162	19	5	9	0	236	6	224	298	365	87	143	67	7	78	0.34	51	16	34	27	97	64	86	13%	15%	112	0%	0%	13	31%	54%	-2.0	52	$4
20	Proj	350	40	10	32	1	241		249	293	386	91	108	86	6	78	0.30	45	21	34	28	93	81	66	11%		94	3%	35%				2.8	20	$6

Stanton,Giancarlo

Age: 30 Bats: R Pos: LF | Ht: 6' 6" Wt: 245
Health F | PT/Exp B | Consist C | LIMA Plan C+ | Rand Var -5 | MM 4125

Biceps injury kicked off year-long IL run early. Shoulder woes, strained calf then stalled his rehab. June return lasted 6 games, as strained knee shelved him until mid-Sept. Strained quad then curtailed his post-season. Plus power, patience haven't vanished, but physical woes leave him more high-risk/high-reward than ever. DN: 300 PA.

Yr	Tm	PA	R	HR	RBI	SB	BA	xHR	xBA	OBP	SLG	OPS+	vL+	vR+	bb%	ct%	Eye	G	L	F	h%	HctX	PX	xPX	HR/F	xHR/F	Spd	SBO	SB%	#Wk	DOM	DIS	RAR	BPX	R$
15	MIA	318	47	27	67	4	265	27	282	346	606	133	162	122	11	66	0.36	35	20	45	30	142	236	209	32%	32%	90	9%	67%	12	67%	25%	22.3	278	$16
16	MIA	469	56	27	74	0	240	26	243	326	489	111	128	104	11	66	0.36	40	17	43	29	115	167	156	23%	22%	84	0%	0%	24	46%	46%	12.3	134	$10
17	MIA	692	123	59	132	2	281	52	296	376	631	135	161	125	12	73	0.52	45	16	39	29	114	197	131	34%	30%	59	2%	50%	27	74%	15%	47.0	282	$32
18	NYY	705	102	38	100	5	266	40	250	343	509	118	144	109	10	66	0.33	45	19	37	34	103	164	113	25%	26%	105	3%	100%	27	48%	37%	26.4	160	$26
19	NYY	72	8	3	13	0	288	4	219	403	492	119	138	112	17	59	0.50	44	22	33	44	86	138	116	25%	33%	76	0%	0%	7	29%	57%	3.4	22	-$1
1st Half		38	4	1	7	0	290	1	209	421	419	112	74	125	18	58	0.54	50	28	22	47	89	89	47	25%	25%	89	0%	0%	4	25%	75%	1.0	-115	-$3
2nd Half		34	4	2	6	0	286	3	236	382	571	126	235	99	15	61	0.45	39	17	44	40	82	189	185	25%	38%	78	0%	0%	3	33%	33%	2.3	185	$2
20	Proj	525	77	31	90	2	260		251	338	515	115	146	105	11	67	0.37	43	19	37	32	98	149	131	27%		74	3%	75%				20.5	110	$21

Starling,Bubba

Age: 27 Bats: R Pos: CF RF | Ht: 6' 4" Wt: 215
Health B | PT/Exp F | Consist A | LIMA Plan D | Rand Var -2 | MM 1201

4-12-.215 and 2 SB in 195 PA at KC. Disappointing 2011 1st-rounder now beyond post-hype finally made MLB debut in 2nd half—and it went about as well as expected. Small sample 70% ct%, 70 HctX, power metrics in KC just more evidence of inability to make good hard contact anywhere. Raw power/speed promise is long gone. Pass.

Yr	Tm	PA	R	HR	RBI	SB	BA	xHR	xBA	OBP	SLG	OPS+	vL+	vR+	bb%	ct%	Eye	G	L	F	h%	HctX	PX	xPX	HR/F	xHR/F	Spd	SBO	SB%	#Wk	DOM	DIS	RAR	BPX	R$
15	aa	354	40	7	25	3	228			279	371	91			7	71	0.24				30		107				118	12%	36%					49	$2
16	a/a	416	34	5	32	9	164			199	264	63			4	61	0.11				25		89				88	18%	89%					-137	-$5
17	aaa	292	27	5	16	4	215			253	321	77			5	74	0.20				27		69				105	15%	46%					-15	-$1
18	aaa	39	4	0	2	1	219			295	272	78			10	80	0.55				27		43				103	8%	100%					30	-$2
19	KC *	473	50	9	39	8	238	3	225	277	340	82	68	79	5	72	0.19	43	24	34	31	72	61	66	9%	7%	106	12%	70%	12	17%	67%	-18.3	-70	$6
1st Half		248	21	3	22	6	252	#N/A	217	294	346	85			6	73	0.22				33		55		0%	#N/A	122	17%	64%				-7.1	-48	$6
2nd Half		225	29	5	17	2	222	3	224	258	334	78	67	79	5	70	0.17	43	24	34	29	71	67	66	9%	7%	96	4%	100%	12	17%	67%	-9.8	-93	$6
20	Proj	210	21	4	15	3	218		225	262	331	80	73	82	5	71	0.19	43	24	34	29	64	70	59	8%		106	13%	61%				-7.3	-88	$3

Stewart,Christin

Age: 26 Bats: L Pos: LF | Ht: 6' 0" Wt: 205
Health B | PT/Exp C | Consist B | LIMA Plan D+ | Rand Var -1 | MM 2213

10-40-.233 in 403 PA at DET. Plus power promise fueled prospect's ascent, stagnated in first extended MLB look. BA, ct% look chronically sub-par; neither speed nor defense are special. Patience, handedness can work, but only if he regains that HR stroke. 2nd-half xPX offers just a glimmer of hope at an age where he needs to step up.

Yr	Tm	PA	R	HR	RBI	SB	BA	xHR	xBA	OBP	SLG	OPS+	vL+	vR+	bb%	ct%	Eye	G	L	F	h%	HctX	PX	xPX	HR/F	xHR/F	Spd	SBO	SB%	#Wk	DOM	DIS	RAR	BPX	R$
15																																			
16	aa	96	13	5	15	0	188			267	368	86			10	68	0.34				22		111				96	0%	0%					29	-$1
17	aa	532	55	23	71	2	225			293	433	97			9	69	0.31				28		130				97	2%	100%					85	$6
18	DET *	572	66	22	75	0	240	2	235	328	425	104	87	113	12	74	0.51	38	19	44	28	97	110	108	10%	10%	104	0%	0%	3	67%	33%	1.4	137	$12
19	DET *	513	43	13	51	1	236	17	238	310	388	93	86	93	9	71	0.37	33	25	41	30	88	93	97	9%	15%	78	2%	45%	22	36%	36%	-15.2	11	$5
1st Half		248	20	6	27	0	224	11	244	310	383	93	79	95	11	74	0.47	32	24	44	27	83	94	82	8%	15%	84	2%	0%	13	38%	23%	-8.8	78	$1
2nd Half		265	23	7	24	1	247	5	234	311	393	93	90	91	9	68	0.29	36	27	37	33	96	92	119	10%	13%	83	1%	100%	9	33%	56%	-7.0	-37	$8
20	Proj	420	42	10	49	1	237		227	323	381	95	86	96	10	72	0.40	36	23	41	30	93	86	105	9%		90	1%	67%				-5.6	-25	$7

JOCK THOMPSON

Stewart,D.J.

Age: 26 Bats: L Pos: RF
Ht: 6' 0" Wt: 230

Health	C	LIMA Plan	D+
PT/Exp	C	Rand Var	0
Consist	B	MM	2103

4-15-.238 and 2 SB in 140 PA at BAL. 2015 1st-rounder with .948 OPS at AAA got late-season MLB look. Firm plate skills; BA and HctX took baby steps. Power continues to languish with big GB% spike; once-productive running game has crumbled along with SB%. Handedness offers a career shot; don't bet on more until you see more.

Yr	Tm	PA	R	HR	RBI	SB	BA	xHR	xBA	OBP	SLG	OPS+	vL+	vR+	bb%	ct%	Eye	G	L	F	h%	HctX	PX	xPX	HR/F	xHR/F	Spd	SBO	SB%	#Wk	DOM	DIS	RAR	BPX	R$
15																																			
16																																			
17	aa	514	65	17	64	16	229			314	379	93			11	77	0.55				26		82				99	16%	78%					85	$12
18	BAL *	512	56	14	55	11	209	1	204	284	354	88	46	126	9	73	0.38	34	14	52	26	74	95	119	20%	7%	81	16%	66%	4	50%	0%	-20.3	40	$8
19	BAL *	418	53	15	58	5	244	4	248	330	434	101	97	90	11	76	0.55	48	14	37	28	92	103	87	11%	11%	71	12%	43%	10	40%	50%	-6.1	126	$9
1st Half		202	22	6	27	4	250	0	275	339	435	103	89	10	12	77	0.59	56	19	25	29	100	100	73	0%	0%	86	11%	77%	2	0%	100%	-0.7	148	$7
2nd Half		215	29	8	29	1	233	4	236	312	419	96	100	103	10	76	0.47	47	13	40	27	89	102	90	12%	12%	68	13%	13%	8	50%	38%	-7.7	100	$11
20	Proj	**350**	**42**	**10**	**44**	**6**	**228**		**226**	**311**	**382**	**93**	**94**	**93**	**10**	**75**	**0.46**	**47**	**13**	**40**	**27**	**80**	**87**	**81**	**11%**		**69**	**14%**	**54%**				**-7.8**	**56**	**$6**

Story,Trevor

Age: 27 Bats: R Pos: SS
Ht: 6' 2" Wt: 214

Health	B	LIMA Plan	D+
PT/Exp	A	Rand Var	-3
Consist	C	MM	4525

Thumb injury IL'd him for two weeks in late June, fueling poor July—but otherwise a model of H2H consistency. Consolidated most of 2018 ct% gains; Spd uptick bolstered BA, running game. Power still plus, though xHR, xHR/F say another 30 HR season isn't a slam dunk. More faint warning signs: .260 BA, 11 HR on the road. Just sayin'...

Yr	Tm	PA	R	HR	RBI	SB	BA	xHR	xBA	OBP	SLG	OPS+	vL+	vR+	bb%	ct%	Eye	G	L	F	h%	HctX	PX	xPX	HR/F	xHR/F	Spd	SBO	SB%	#Wk	DOM	DIS	RAR	BPX	R$
15	a/a	549	60	16	58	16	259			309	463	108			7	73	0.26				33		144				117	18%	83%					151	$17
16	COL	415	67	27	72	8	272	25	259	341	567	124	132	118	8	65	0.27	29	24	47	34	119	200	191	24%	22%	112	15%	62%	17	53%	12%	19.3	209	$18
17	COL	555	68	24	82	7	239	21	224	308	457	103	137	88	9	62	0.26	34	18	48	33	101	156	166	16%	14%	118	8%	78%	26	38%	38%	2.5	85	$12
18	COL	656	88	37	108	27	291	38	271	348	567	127	149	117	7	72	0.28	34	23	43	35	118	172	155	20%	20%	118	24%	82%	28	57%	25%	53.5	257	$38
19	COL	656	111	35	85	23	294	26	260	363	554	122	122	121	9	70	0.33	33	24	42	36	107	147	132	20%	15%	137	20%	74%	26	54%	27%	37.9	222	$34
1st Half		328	65	17	48	12	294	14	258	360	547	121	119	122	8	71	0.31	35	22	43	36	113	144	141	19%	16%	114	21%	75%	14	50%	21%	16.1	193	$36
2nd Half		328	46	18	37	11	295	12	262	366	562	122	126	121	10	70	0.35	32	26	42	37	102	150	124	21%	14%	152	19%	73%	12	58%	33%	18.7	244	$32
20	Proj	**630**	**94**	**30**	**90**	**20**	**282**		**250**	**348**	**525**	**117**	**129**	**112**	**8**	**69**	**0.30**	**34**	**23**	**43**	**36**	**110**	**142**	**148**	**18%**		**132**	**19%**	**76%**				**36.5**	**175**	**$33**

Straw,Myles

Age: 25 Bats: R Pos: SS
Ht: 5' 10" Wt: 180

Health	A	LIMA Plan	D
PT/Exp	D	Rand Var	-3
Consist	B	MM	0511

0-7-.269 and 7 SB in 127 PA at HOU. Blazing speed is front-and-center here. Decent ct% and career .305 minor league BA hint he'll out-run xBA, soft HctX. Plus bb%, OF defense and now infield versatility work in his favor. Power vacuum (5 HR in 1950 professional AB) caps upside at bench utility. But with opportunity... UP: 30+ SB.

Yr	Tm	PA	R	HR	RBI	SB	BA	xHR	xBA	OBP	SLG	OPS+	vL+	vR+	bb%	ct%	Eye	G	L	F	h%	HctX	PX	xPX	HR/F	xHR/F	Spd	SBO	SB%	#Wk	DOM	DIS	RAR	BPX	R$
15																																			
16																																			
17	aa	52	8	0	3	2	214			303	214	69			11	77	0.56				28		0				117	11%	100%					-91	-$1
18	HOU *	581	78	2	25	57	246	0	181	318	298	85	0	146	10	77	0.47	44	11	44	31	95	34	139	25%	0%	168	41%	84%	4	25%	25%	-7.9	27	$27
19	HOU *	427	59	1	30	21	259	1	234	330	317	86	102	92	10	78	0.48	48	23	29	33	86	34	60	0%	4%	166	22%	78%	18	28%	39%	-8.9	37	$12
1st Half		261	32	1	15	15	242	0	240	313	294	81	129	92	9	73	0.39	40	34	26	33	87	31	71	0%	0%	176	25%	82%	6	17%	17%	-8.1	-30	$12
2nd Half		166	27	0	15	6	286	0	242	358	354	94	79	92	10	85	0.76	54	15	31	34	88	39	52	0%	0%	135	17%	71%	12	33%	50%	0.5	130	$12
20	Proj	**175**	**25**	**0**	**11**	**14**	**258**		**235**	**329**	**311**	**86**	**94**	**82**	**10**	**79**	**0.51**	**48**	**23**	**29**	**33**	**88**	**32**	**60**	**0%**		**149**	**32%**	**85%**				**-1.6**	**23**	**$8**

Suarez,Eugenio

Age: 28 Bats: R Pos: 3B
Ht: 5' 11" Wt: 213

Health	A	LIMA Plan	B
PT/Exp	A	Rand Var	-2
Consist	B	MM	4225

Opened up swing after June, traded ct% for loft and thump, turned OK year into a great one. Firm LD%, elevated h%, 2nd-half Spd bump helped late BA spike. But double-down focus on power was key as he maintained elite bb% and crushed RHP. Per xHR and xHR/F, HR will likely regress, but he's healthy and in his prime. Pay the price.

Yr	Tm	PA	R	HR	RBI	SB	BA	xHR	xBA	OBP	SLG	OPS+	vL+	vR+	bb%	ct%	Eye	G	L	F	h%	HctX	PX	xPX	HR/F	xHR/F	Spd	SBO	SB%	#Wk	DOM	DIS	RAR	BPX	R$
15	CIN *	623	67	21	69	7	263	11	248	310	429	103	113	102	6	75	0.28	41	21	38	32	95	111	105	12%	10%	107	9%	54%	18	39%	39%	-3.4	100	$17
16	CIN	627	78	21	70	11	248	21	241	317	411	99	119	91	8	73	0.33	41	22	38	31	103	104	105	13%	13%	94	11%	69%	27	30%	37%	-12.0	57	$15
17	CIN	632	87	26	82	4	260	19	258	367	461	111	119	106	13	72	0.57	39	24	37	31	99	118	116	18%	13%	82	5%	44%	27	37%	37%	4.3	115	$16
18	CIN	606	79	34	104	1	283	34	269	366	526	123	142	115	11	73	0.45	38	25	37	33	131	143	150	23%	23%	94	1%	50%	27	56%	26%	30.1	193	$25
19	CIN	662	87	49	103	3	271	39	260	358	572	123	130	121	11	67	0.37	36	22	42	32	108	166	145	30%	23%	96	3%	60%	28	61%	18%	25.2	196	$25
1st Half		340	38	17	48	1	248	15	252	329	470	107	126	100	10	71	0.40	41	22	38	29	122	123	130	21%	19%	66	4%	33%	15	47%	20%	-1.5	93	$16
2nd Half		322	49	32	55	2	296	24	267	388	682	141	137	143	12	63	0.35	30	22	48	35	94	218	164	38%	28%	136	3%	100%	13	77%	15%	31.7	337	$35
20	Proj	**630**	**86**	**37**	**101**	**3**	**274**		**251**	**361**	**520**	**118**	**127**	**115**	**11**	**70**	**0.40**	**37**	**23**	**41**	**33**	**110**	**135**	**141**	**23%**		**99**	**4%**	**59%**				**29.1**	**108**	**$26**

Suzuki,Kurt

Age: 36 Bats: R Pos: CA
Ht: 5' 11" Wt: 210

Health	A	LIMA Plan	C
PT/Exp	D	Rand Var	+2
Consist	B	MM	2043

More solid-not-special offense from veteran in career twilight age-wise. Average power helped by a few more FBs and, yes, a friendly ball. History and peripherals say he'll give back some HR, but it's that durable near-elite ct% and firm LD% that keep him relevant. Risk is rising, but hard to beat for a cheap, do-no-harm catching option.

Yr	Tm	PA	R	HR	RBI	SB	BA	xHR	xBA	OBP	SLG	OPS+	vL+	vR+	bb%	ct%	Eye	G	L	F	h%	HctX	PX	xPX	HR/F	xHR/F	Spd	SBO	SB%	#Wk	DOM	DIS	RAR	BPX	R$
15	MIN	479	36	5	50	0	240	5	229	296	314	85	91	81	6	86	0.49	43	19	38	27	100	50	84	4%	4%	75	0%	0%	26	38%	35%	-10.0	59	$3
16	MIN	373	34	8	49	0	258	6	270	301	403	96	101	91	5	86	0.38	40	21	39	28	103	88	79	7%	5%	57	0%	0%	26	54%	27%	-3.2	126	$5
17	ATL	309	38	19	50	0	283	11	284	351	536	119	158	106	6	86	0.44	35	18	47	27	116	123	124	17%	10%	61	0%	0%	27	56%	33%	16.5	221	$10
18	ATL	388	45	12	50	0	271	10	281	332	444	107	113	105	6	88	0.51	35	23	41	28	125	97	105	9%	8%	49	0%	0%	27	56%	19%	13.5	187	$9
19	WAS	309	37	17	63	0	264	10	289	324	486	107	125	102	6	87	0.56	34	23	43	25	104	98	101	16%	9%	53	2%	0%	27	59%	11%	6.8	215	$8
1st Half		166	18	9	35	0	273	5	276	313	494	108	129	102	4	84	0.29	36	21	43	27	106	102	122	16%	9%	62	3%	0%	15	53%	20%	5.0	181	$8
2nd Half		143	19	8	28	0	254	4	304	336	476	107	122	102	9	90	1.08	31	26	43	23	101	92	77	16%	8%	59	0%	0%	12	67%	0%	4.8	274	$9
20	Proj	**315**	**39**	**13**	**56**	**0**	**266**		**274**	**327**	**443**	**104**	**118**	**98**	**6**	**87**	**0.53**	**35**	**23**	**43**	**27**	**110**	**83**	**101**	**11%**		**56**	**1%**	**0%**				**11.7**	**149**	**$11**

Swanson,Dansby

Age: 26 Bats: R Pos: SS
Ht: 6' 1" Wt: 190

Health	B	LIMA Plan	C+
PT/Exp	B	Rand Var	0
Consist	A	MM	2325

Big 1st half eclipsed disappointing 2018 as LD%, HctX surges, broad power metrics spike revived early promise. But unraveled after July foot injury IL'd him for 5 weeks, as ct% collapsed and he was homerless in final 147 AB. Could deserve an injury mulligan, though, as that April-June points to ... UP: .270 BA, 25 HR.

Yr	Tm	PA	R	HR	RBI	SB	BA	xHR	xBA	OBP	SLG	OPS+	vL+	vR+	bb%	ct%	Eye	G	L	F	h%	HctX	PX	xPX	HR/F	xHR/F	Spd	SBO	SB%	#Wk	DOM	DIS	RAR	BPX	R$
15																																			
16	ATL *	515	74	10	62	10	258	4	243	331	382	97	137	103	10	75	0.44	46	23	31	32	106	75	97	10%	13%	162	9%	82%	8	25%	63%	-3.0	89	$13
17	ATL *	594	63	7	55	4	229	7	239	314	321	85	98	81	11	75	0.49	47	23	29	29	89	60	73	6%	6%	107	4%	56%	26	19%	42%	-19.6	15	$4
18	ATL	533	51	14	59	10	238	13	240	304	395	97	89	98	8	74	0.36	42	20	38	29	98	99	89	10%	10%	121	12%	71%	26	31%	23%	2.2	107	$11
19	ATL	545	77	17	65	10	251	22	253	325	422	99	105	98	9	74	0.41	37	26	37	30	109	96	106	13%	16%	119	12%	67%	24	42%	29%	-2.9	111	$14
1st Half		362	55	15	52	7	269	19	274	332	483	109	111	108	8	77	0.40	36	27	37	31	112	110	112	16%	20%	119	14%	64%	15	60%	7%	4.3	193	$23
2nd Half		183	22	2	13	3	213	4	208	311	300	81	94	78	12	68	0.43	39	23	38	30	104	62	92	5%	10%	116	9%	75%	9	11%	67%	-9.6	-63	-$4
20	Proj	**560**	**70**	**17**	**67**	**9**	**253**		**244**	**328**	**416**	**100**	**108**	**98**	**10**	**73**	**0.41**	**41**	**23**	**36**	**31**	**102**	**92**	**93**	**13%**		**120**	**10%**	**71%**				**7.2**	**63**	**$17**

Tapia,Raimel

Age: 26 Bats: L Pos: LF
Ht: 6' 3" Wt: 185

Health	A	LIMA Plan	C+
PT/Exp	C	Rand Var	-1
Consist	C	MM	1543

Touted prospect's opportunity yielded mixed results. BA/ct% drove value with assist from plus Spd, but running game capped by SBO. Power drifted from meh to poor in 2nd half, and season-long love of GBs didn't help. Chronically sub-par HctX; .221 hitter away from Coors. Has yet to prove he can translate .319 MiLB BA to the bigs.

Yr	Tm	PA	R	HR	RBI	SB	BA	xHR	xBA	OBP	SLG	OPS+	vL+	vR+	bb%	ct%	Eye	G	L	F	h%	HctX	PX	xPX	HR/F	xHR/F	Spd	SBO	SB%	#Wk	DOM	DIS	RAR	BPX	R$
15																																			
16	COL *	591	79	7	42	22	322	0	292	349	441	108	68	76	4	88	0.34	37	33	30	36	76	65	59	0%	0%	166	24%	55%	6	0%	67%	10.6	177	$28
17	COL *	443	59	4	37	14	325	2	283	352	468	110	85	105	4	81	0.22	42	28	29	39	71	85	69	6%	6%	154	16%	76%	19	42%	42%	10.5	152	$20
18	COL *	482	57	9	45	13	261	1	229	296	424	100	55	120	5	79	0.23	24	24	53	32	64	100	120	11%	11%	131	18%	80%	9	44%	44%	-3.6	150	$13
19	COL	447	54	9	44	9	275	9	264	309	415	96	91	98	5	77	0.21	52	22	26	34	80	78	64	11%	11%	136	12%	75%	27	33%	52%	-8.4	78	$11
1st Half		256	34	6	27	3	267	6	263	305	449	101	107	98	5	74	0.20	49	21	29	34	85	103	72	12%	12%	146	12%	50%	15	33%	47%	-4.2	122	$11
2nd Half		191	20	3	17	6	284	2	264	314	372	90	65	97	4	80	0.22	54	24	22	34	72	49	55	9%	6%	111	12%	100%	12	33%	58%	-4.1	15	$12
20	Proj	**385**	**47**	**7**	**35**	**10**	**285**		**272**	**319**	**424**	**100**	**87**	**104**	**4**	**79**	**0.22**	**48**	**25**	**27**	**34**	**75**	**76**	**65**	**8%**		**142**	**15%**	**76%**				**2.7**	**98**	**$15**

JOCK THOMPSON

Tatis Jr.,Fernando

Age: 21 | Bats: R | Pos: SS | Ht: 6' 3" | Wt: 185
Health: C | PT/Exp: D | Consist: D | LIMA Plan: C+ | Rand Var: -5 | MM: 4535

Precocious rookie with off-the-charts athleticism leap-frogged AAA into NL ROY conversation before back injury stopped him in August. Plate skills could use polish; baseball instincts, youth say this may yet happen. But HR/F, Spd suggest huge upside regardless. Hair-on-fire play, resulting durability issues are only obstacles to greatness.

Yr	Tm	PA	R	HR	RBI	SB	BA	xHR	xBA	OBP	SLG	OPS+	vL+	vR+	bb%	ct%	Eye	G	L	F	h%	HctX	PX	xPX	HR/F	xHR/F	Spd	SBO	SB%	#Wk	DOM	DIS	RAR	BPX	R$
15																																			
16																																			
17	aa	57	6	1	6	3	268			294	341	85			3	71	0.12				36		45				104	21%	100%					-124	$0
18	aa	383	70	14	39	14	274			331	472	111			8	67	0.26				37		136				122	22%	74%					107	$17
19	SD	372	61	22	53	16	317	20	265	379	590	129	165	119	8	67	0.27	47	22	31	42	97	150	126	32%	29%	189	23%	73%	17	47%	24%	29.8	233	$22
1st Half		205	40	11	28	12	337	12	262	405	613	136	153	133	10	67	0.32	49	17	34	45	88	156	131	27%	29%	196	27%	80%	11	55%	18%	21.4	267	$26
2nd Half		167	21	11	25	4	294	8	271	347	562	120	171	99	7	67	0.22	44	28	27	37	107	143	120	39%	29%	155	18%	57%	6	33%	33%	7.0	170	$16
20	**Proj**	**525**	**88**	**28**	**68**	**20**	**287**		**260**	**350**	**531**	**119**	**159**	**106**	**8**	**67**	**0.27**	**46**	**24**	**30**	**37**	**99**	**139**	**124**	**28%**		**174**	**23%**	**71%**				**30.8**	**150**	**$27**

Tauchman,Mike

Age: 29 | Bats: L | Pos: LF | Ht: 6' 2" | Wt: 220
Health: A | PT/Exp: D | Consist: B | LIMA Plan: D+ | Rand Var: -2 | MM: 4251

13-47-.277 and 6 SB in 294 PA at NYY. Older rookie rode 2nd half h%, power bump to .988 OPS after June; perfect base-running a plus. But peripherals look mixed. Improving patience, mid-season ct% rebound are encouraging. SB%, FB% still need confirmation; xHR/F, xPX are skeptical about big power. With opportunity, he's flyer-worthy.

Yr	Tm	PA	R	HR	RBI	SB	BA	xHR	xBA	OBP	SLG	OPS+	vL+	vR+	bb%	ct%	Eye	G	L	F	h%	HctX	PX	xPX	HR/F	xHR/F	Spd	SBO	SB%	#Wk	DOM	DIS	RAR	BPX	R$
15	aa	543	47	3	33	19	270			318	351	93			7	86	0.50				31		52				124	24%	57%					103	$14
16	aaa	503	51	1	36	16	256			298	334	86			6	83	0.34				31		50				121	23%	58%					60	$10
17	COL *	478	56	12	55	12	281	0	279	328	452	105	129	73	7	80	0.35	65	12	24	33	76	96	18	0%	0%	132	20%	53%	10	30%	70%	-4.5	155	$16
18	COL *	476	54	13	47	8	246	1	262	310	411	100	33	50	8	78	0.41	65	12	24	29	64	97	61	0%	25%	115	19%	39%	6	17%	67%	-9.5	140	$11
19	NYY *	403	62	15	58	9	259	9	271	344	470	108	127	110	11	74	0.50	42	25	33	31	86	119	93	21%	14%	89	9%	100%	21	33%	57%	6.3	159	$13
1st Half		227	32	6	25	4	209	4	241	299	383	91	112	87	11	71	0.44	53	13	34	27	69	107	59	17%	17%	108	8%	100%	12	17%	75%	-8.5	96	$6
2nd Half		176	30	9	33	5	325	5	304	403	584	130	132	129	11	79	0.61	36	31	33	37	100	134	112	23%	13%	76	10%	100%	9	56%	33%	16.3	256	$22
20	**Proj**	**210**	**29**	**10**	**27**	**5**	**269**		**285**	**338**	**512**	**114**	**123**	**110**	**9**	**78**	**0.45**	**42**	**24**	**33**	**30**	**88**	**125**	**91**	**20%**		**97**	**16%**	**67%**				**7.5**	**229**	**$9**

Taylor,Chris

Age: 29 | Bats: R | Pos: LF SS 2B | Ht: 6' 1" | Wt: 196
Health: B | PT/Exp: B | Consist: B | LIMA Plan: C+ | Rand Var: -1 | MM: 3523

Swiss army knife with value despite 2nd half wrist injury that shelved him for 5 weeks. Ct% has faded, but Spd and line-drive bat keep BA afloat. Power still a tick above average; running game still effective even with SBO decline. Regular AB no longer a given; might be too volatile for H2Hers. Versatility, secondary skills keep him relevant.

Yr	Tm	PA	R	HR	RBI	SB	BA	xHR	xBA	OBP	SLG	OPS+	vL+	vR+	bb%	ct%	Eye	G	L	F	h%	HctX	PX	xPX	HR/F	xHR/F	Spd	SBO	SB%	#Wk	DOM	DIS	RAR	BPX	R$
15	SEA *	477	47	3	22	14	221	2	210	285	302	82	88	49	8	75	0.36	32	24	44	29	126	60	161	0%	7%	133	23%	54%	10	10%	70%	-21.2	22	$4
16	2 TM *	394	45	3	35	13	258	1	243	312	380	94	87	81	7	74	0.30	44	22	33	34	79	87	98	7%	7%	132	21%	69%	12	17%	50%	-9.4	63	$9
17	LA *	614	91	22	76	18	280	19	263	343	483	111	111	113	9	73	0.36	42	23	36	35	96	123	103	16%	14%	142	17%	73%	25	40%	24%	12.4	164	$25
18	LA	604	85	17	63	9	254	23	238	331	444	107	105	108	9	67	0.31	34	28	39	35	95	134	117	12%	16%	152	11%	60%	28	43%	32%	8.0	133	$16
19	LA	414	52	12	52	8	262	11	254	333	462	105	112	100	9	60	0.32	38	27	35	35	90	126	106	14%	13%	117	9%	100%	24	33%	38%	9.2	111	$11
1st Half		262	29	8	39	6	266	6	259	331	472	107	128	93	9	70	0.32	40	25	35	35	88	130	90	14%	11%	109	11%	100%	15	33%	40%	6.4	130	$14
2nd Half		152	23	4	13	2	256	5	247	336	444	103	84	113	10	67	0.32	35	31	34	35	94	118	134	13%	16%	132	6%	100%	9	33%	33%	1.6	85	$5
20	**Proj**	**420**	**58**	**12**	**46**	**10**	**259**		**246**	**332**	**447**	**105**	**104**	**104**	**9**	**69**	**0.33**	**37**	**27**	**36**	**35**	**94**	**116**	**116**	**12%**		**135**	**14%**	**81%**				**6.2**	**108**	**$15**

Tellez,Rowdy

Age: 25 | Bats: L | Pos: 1B DH | Ht: 6' 4" | Wt: 255
Health: A | PT/Exp: C | Consist: B | LIMA Plan: B | Rand Var: 0 | MM: 4045

21-54-.227 in 399 PA at TOR. Slugger with promising power scuffled through streaky rookie season that included July demotion. Monthly BAs from April: .219, .247, .205, .240, .167, .257. He'll never win a batting title, but ct%, LD% history hints at more than this. Patience, h% improved after MLB return, HR/F looks legit. Still growing.

Yr	Tm	PA	R	HR	RBI	SB	BA	xHR	xBA	OBP	SLG	OPS+	vL+	vR+	bb%	ct%	Eye	G	L	F	h%	HctX	PX	xPX	HR/F	xHR/F	Spd	SBO	SB%	#Wk	DOM	DIS	RAR	BPX	R$
15																																			
16	aa	493	61	21	70	3	285			364	504	118			11	77	0.55				33		134				87	5%	52%					191	$16
17	aaa	491	44	6	55	6	223			296	339	85			9	78	0.46				27		78				84	6%	85%					58	$3
18	TOR *	501	48	15	58	6	263	4	268	318	431	104	45	165	7	78	0.37	38	26	36	31	115	106	138	22%	22%	69	9%	59%	5	40%	60%	1.5	117	$13
19	TOR *	514	66	27	72	1	249	20	257	310	484	105	108	93	8	69	0.28	39	24	38	30	99	138	114	22%	21%	54	2%	50%	25	36%	44%	-2.7	74	$12
1st Half		260	30	14	37	1	226	14	251	281	448	97	103	95	6	69	0.21	37	25	38	27	97	126	120	22%	22%	64	4%	50%	15	27%	60%	-9.3	33	$9
2nd Half		254	36	13	35	0	273	7	262	346	522	114	119	92	10	69	0.36	41	22	37	34	103	149	104	21%	21%	57	0%	0%	10	50%	20%	6.9	130	$16
20	**Proj**	**546**	**64**	**29**	**75**	**3**	**255**		**272**	**324**	**498**	**111**	**89**	**120**	**9**	**73**	**0.35**	**39**	**24**	**37**	**29**	**106**	**136**	**122**	**22%**		**56**	**5%**	**63%**				**12.2**	**135**	**$18**

Thaiss,Matt

Age: 25 | Bats: L | Pos: 3B | Ht: 6' 0" | Wt: 215
Health: A | PT/Exp: C | Consist: B | LIMA Plan: D | Rand Var: +5 | MM: 4131

8-23-.211 in 164 PA at LAA. A tale of divergent skills. Rookie maintained plus patience, continued to show power growth following July MLB promotion, though xHR/F suggests it needs confirmation. Ct% went backwards, dragging average down with it, though BA history suggests a moderate rebound. Work-in-progress needs more AAA time.

Yr	Tm	PA	R	HR	RBI	SB	BA	xHR	xBA	OBP	SLG	OPS+	vL+	vR+	bb%	ct%	Eye	G	L	F	h%	HctX	PX	xPX	HR/F	xHR/F	Spd	SBO	SB%	#Wk	DOM	DIS	RAR	BPX	R$
15																																			
16																																			
17	aa	213	28	1	24	4	277			396	367	102			17	69	0.63				40		77				88	10%	55%					-6	$4
18	a/a	556	57	12	56	6	233			276	372	90			6	77	0.26				28		87				108	10%	56%					80	$8
19	LAA *	512	56	18	54	1	212	5	234	296	375	89	91	95	11	72	0.42	37	22	40	25	107	92	126	21%	13%	64	1%	100%	14	36%	64%	-20.1	11	$4
1st Half		343	39	10	31	1	213		237	299	357	88			11	75	0.50				25		79		0%		97	1%	100%	1	0%	100%	-16.5	63	$5
2nd Half		169	17	8	23	0	209	5	229	288	413	92	90	95	10	65	0.32	37	22	40	26	97	124	126	21%		58	0%	0%	13	38%	62%	-6.6	-4	$2
20	**Proj**	**175**	**19**	**9**	**19**	**1**	**228**		**253**	**303**	**453**	**102**	**102**	**101**	**10**	**72**	**0.38**	**37**	**22**	**40**	**26**	**87**	**125**	**113**	**19%**		**70**	**6%**	**58%**				**-0.5**	**99**	**$4**

Thames,Eric

Age: 33 | Bats: L | Pos: 1B | Ht: 6' 0" | Wt: 210
Health: B | PT/Exp: C | Consist: B | LIMA Plan: B | Rand Var: 0 | MM: 5325

Firm power-and-patience combo, inflated h% helped him win strong-side platoon AB in May; held on despite 2nd half h%, BA plunges. Career .843 OPS vR suggests a repeat is doable, .198 BA vL caps his upside. Abysmal ct%, in-season streakiness keep his playing time hanging by a thread. Don't bid full value and have a backup plan.

Yr	Tm	PA	R	HR	RBI	SB	BA	xHR	xBA	OBP	SLG	OPS+	vL+	vR+	bb%	ct%	Eye	G	L	F	h%	HctX	PX	xPX	HR/F	xHR/F	Spd	SBO	SB%	#Wk	DOM	DIS	RAR	BPX	R$
15	for	595	127	28	137	36	355			452	656	154			15	82	0.96				39		184				104	26%	80%				87.6	370	$54
16	for	529	115	24	118	12	299			383	555	128			12	78	0.61				34		151				101	12%	72%				38.8	251	$30
17	MIL	551	83	31	63	4	247	25	256	359	518	118	88	124	14	65	0.46	38	20	41	31	110	174	162	25%	20%	98	5%	67%	27	48%	44%	2.9	179	$14
18	MIL	278	41	16	37	7	219	17	228	306	478	108	85	110	10	61	0.30	33	20	47	28	103	180	186	23%	24%	109	13%	100%	21	48%	38%	-1.9	140	$8
19	MIL	459	67	25	61	3	247	22	240	346	505	113	89	117	11	65	0.36	33	21	46	32	109	157	158	21%	18%	99	5%	60%	28	39%	32%	2.7	141	$12
1st Half		216	32	12	35	2	272	10	235	384	539	123	114	125	15	60	0.43	36	21	43	39	100	173	147	26%	21%	108	5%	67%	15	40%	33%	10.0	156	$13
2nd Half		243	35	13	26	1	227	12	243	313	477	104	70	110	8	69	0.29	31	20	49	27	117	145	166	18%	17%	89	5%	50%	13	38%	31%	-4.2	133	$11
20	**Proj**	**455**	**72**	**27**	**65**	**7**	**247**		**243**	**343**	**518**	**116**	**90**	**119**	**11**	**66**	**0.37**	**34**	**20**	**46**	**31**	**108**	**162**	**169**	**22%**		**101**	**9%**	**79%**				**15.4**	**183**	**$18**

Toro,Abraham

Age: 23 | Bats: S | Pos: 3B | Ht: 6' 1" | Wt: 190
Health: A | PT/Exp: F | Consist: C | LIMA Plan: D | Rand Var: 0 | MM: 2231

2-9-.218 in 87 PA at HOU. Prospect elevated status with .324/.411/.527 line over 442 AB at AA/AAA, made MLB jump in late August. Intriguing plate skills held up well as 26% h% suppressed BA in HOU. GB%, power metrics are less impressive. Despite decent Spd, running game looks undeveloped. Watch from a distance.

Yr	Tm	PA	R	HR	RBI	SB	BA	xHR	xBA	OBP	SLG	OPS+	vL+	vR+	bb%	ct%	Eye	G	L	F	h%	HctX	PX	xPX	HR/F	xHR/F	Spd	SBO	SB%	#Wk	DOM	DIS	RAR	BPX	R$
15																																			
16																																			
17																																			
18	aa	193	15	2	20	3	211			273	337	84			8	72	0.30				28		96				97	17%	46%					37	$0
19	HOU *	577	78	16	73	4	271	2	260	341	437	103	36	114	10	78	0.49	50	18	32	32	90	89	64	11%	11%	119	5%	56%	7	29%	14%	1.5	148	$15
1st Half		305	39	12	49	4	257		249	344	437	104			12	75	0.54				30		93		0%	#VALUE!	115	4%	100%				0.1	133	$16
2nd Half		277	44	5	29	1	300	2	276	360	471	110	36	114	9	82	0.51	50	18	32	35	94	94	64	11%	11%	126	6%	23%	7	29%	14%	4.7	219	$14
20	**Proj**	**175**	**21**	**4**	**21**	**2**	**254**		**254**	**327**	**412**	**100**	**40**	**124**	**9**	**76**	**0.43**	**50**	**18**	**32**	**31**	**85**	**92**	**58**	**9%**		**117**	**9%**	**52%**				**-0.7**	**97**	**$5**

JOCK THOMPSON

Torres,Gleyber

Age: 23	Bats: R	Pos: SS 2B	Health	A	LIMA Plan	B
Ht: 6' 1"	Wt: 200		PT/Exp	C	Rand Var	0
			Consist	A	MM	3235

Second-year player used ct% bump, PA hike, sturdy FB%, HR/F—and new ball—to fashion big HR year that drove value. Some volatility is visible in DOM%/DIS% (22 HR came in May and August), and PX/xPX say this isn't 40 HR power. But these are minor quibbles for roto players. Believe in the youth, pedigree and the sum of the parts.

Yr Tm	PA	R	HR	RBI	SB	BA	xHR	xBA	OBP	SLG	OPS+	vL+	vR+	bb%	ct%	Eye	G	L	F	h%	HctX	PX	xPX	HR/F	xHR/F	Spd	SBO	SB%	#Wk	DOM	DIS	RAR	BPX	R$
15																																		
16																																		
17 a/a	230	29	8	32	7	280			372	476	114			13	75	0.59				34		117				100	20%	51%					158	$8
18 NYY *	537	59	25	87	7	276	24	247	340	479	113	127	108	9	72	0.35	33	25	43	33	102	122	115	18%	18%	106	7%	69%	22	32%	14%	22.0	127	$21
19 NYY	604	96	38	90	5	278	31	270	337	535	116	118	115	8	76	0.37	37	21	42	30	105	130	116	21%	18%	89	5%	71%	28	43%	39%	24.2	200	$24
1st Half	319	54	19	47	3	295	16	265	365	548	122	105	127	10	75	0.46	39	20	42	33	109	131	122	21%	18%	100	5%	75%	15	53%	33%	20.4	215	$27
2nd Half	285	42	19	43	2	260	15	276	305	521	109	128	100	6	78	0.27	36	22	42	27	100	128	111	22%	17%	85	6%	67%	13	31%	46%	5.6	193	$20
20 Proj	**595**	**82**	**31**	**92**	**8**	**276**		**256**	**341**	**499**	**113**	**122**	**109**	**9**	**75**	**0.38**	**35**	**22**	**42**	**32**	**103**	**118**	**115**	**18%**		**96**	**9%**	**63%**				**26.8**	**128**	**$23**

Travis,Sam

Age: 26	Bats: R	Pos: 1B	Health	A	LIMA Plan	F
Ht: 6' 0"	Wt: 205		PT/Exp	D	Rand Var	-1
			Consist	B	MM	1201

6-16-.215 in 155 PA at BOS. Prospect once praised for his hit tool is regressing at higher levels. Effort to overhaul swing for more power has yet to produce any gains as ct% dwindles and woeful GB% remains chronic. Handedness works against him, and he's at wrong position to be dealing with these issues. There's just nothing to like here.

Yr Tm	PA	R	HR	RBI	SB	BA	xHR	xBA	OBP	SLG	OPS+	vL+	vR+	bb%	ct%	Eye	G	L	F	h%	HctX	PX	xPX	HR/F	xHR/F	Spd	SBO	SB%	#Wk	DOM	DIS	RAR	BPX	R$
15 aa	270	29	3	31	7	286			358	412	107			10	85	0.74				33		87				93	19%	53%					162	$8
16 aaa	187	24	5	27	1	273			328	433	104			8	76	0.35				33		106				84	2%	100%					91	$4
17 BOS *	420	48	5	22	6	261	1	236	330	358	92	127	38	8	78	0.47	51	17	32	32	95	65	87	0%	6%	103	8%	74%	13	31%	46%	-14.4	48	$6
18 BOS *	423	34	7	43	1	237	0	208	283	334	85	43	124	6	73	0.24	58	15	27	31	72	66	59	14%	0%	70	3%	27%	7	43%	57%	-15.9	-63	$3
19 BOS *	417	46	11	42	6	235	5	227	299	381	90	89	81	8	72	0.33	55	12	33	30	92	84	85	17%	14%	97	8%	84%	17	29%	47%	-12.4	15	$6
1st Half	249	26	4	24	4	236	0	251	304	350	87	67	24	9	71	0.34	70	17	13	32	75	74	7	0%	0%	99	9%	77%	6	0%	50%	-10.9	-30	$5
2nd Half	168	19	8	18	2	233	5	233	291	426	95	94	97	8	74	0.32	51	10	38	26	99	99	106	18%	15%	106	6%	100%	11	45%	45%	-4.5	96	$7
20 Proj	**175**	**18**	**2**	**17**	**2**	**244**		**221**	**309**	**339**	**87**	**105**	**57**	**8**	**75**	**0.34**	**56**	**15**	**30**	**32**	**91**	**59**	**74**	**6%**		**96**	**6%**	**75%**				**-5.0**	**-59**	**$3**

Trevino,Jose

Age: 27	Bats: R	Pos: CA	Health	A	LIMA Plan	D+
Ht: 5' 11"	Wt: 211		PT/Exp	D	Rand Var	0
			Consist	A	MM	1221

2-13-.258 in 123 PA at TEX. Given first extended MLB opportunity beginning in August. Plus ct% held up nicely, small sample BA exceeded expectations thanks to 32% h% and decent LD%. But particularly minus power and speed, nothing in his history suggests that even this meager production can continue. File under "avoid" for now.

Yr Tm	PA	R	HR	RBI	SB	BA	xHR	xBA	OBP	SLG	OPS+	vL+	vR+	bb%	ct%	Eye	G	L	F	h%	HctX	PX	xPX	HR/F	xHR/F	Spd	SBO	SB%	#Wk	DOM	DIS	RAR	BPX	R$
15																																		
16																																		
17 aa	418	33	6	35	1	215			245	285	71			4	88	0.33				23		37				85	4%	27%					52	-$2
18 TEX *	202	14	2	15	0	203	0	167	243	280	72	70	69	5	84	0.32	57	0	43	23	44	45	-27	0%	0%	94	3%	0%	2	0%	50%	-7.5	33	-$3
19 TEX *	278	28	3	28	1	219	2	251	243	323	75	115	73	3	78	0.15	46	23	31	27	104	66	77	7%	7%	89	3%	100%	10	20%	30%	-8.2	0	-$1
1st Half	106	9	1	9	1	194		234	226	273	67			4	81	0.22				23		51		0%		86	4%	100%				-6.4	0	-$8
2nd Half	171	19	3	19	1	234	2	251	254	354	80	113	73	3	76	0.11	46	23	31	29	101	77	77	7%	7%	92	2%	100%	10	20%	30%	-4.7	0	$3
20 Proj	**245**	**21**	**4**	**22**	**1**	**212**		**252**	**240**	**310**	**74**	**97**	**62**	**4**	**81**	**0.22**	**46**	**23**	**31**	**25**	**91**	**56**	**69**	**6%**		**99**	**4%**	**62%**				**-7.0**	**-20**	**$2**

Trout,Mike

Age: 28	Bats: R	Pos: CF	Health	B	LIMA Plan	C
Ht: 6' 2"	Wt: 235		PT/Exp	A	Rand Var	+1
			Consist	C	MM	5455

Otherworldly again, leading AL in HR before Sept season-ending toe surgery. Third straight season with an IL stint, PAs have slid from once-lofty levels. Running game slowed by nagging groin/calf/foot injuries, but should rebound some. Try to devalue him with leaguemates; it won't work, but it's all you've got. He still checks all the boxes.

Yr Tm	PA	R	HR	RBI	SB	BA	xHR	xBA	OBP	SLG	OPS+	vL+	vR+	bb%	ct%	Eye	G	L	F	h%	HctX	PX	xPX	HR/F	xHR/F	Spd	SBO	SB%	#Wk	DOM	DIS	RAR	BPX	R$
15 LAA	682	104	41	90	11	299	41	289	402	590	138	142	134	13	73	0.58	37	24	38	35	129	190	152	25%	25%	122	10%	61%	27	70%	7%	60.4	292	$35
16 LAA	681	123	29	100	30	315	37	276	441	550	135	131	133	17	75	0.85	41	22	37	38	127	142	142	19%	24%	118	17%	81%	27	63%	19%	69.4	243	$42
17 LAA	507	92	33	72	22	306	32	296	442	629	144	120	147	19	78	1.04	37	18	45	32	120	173	133	23%	23%	116	17%	85%	22	73%	9%	61.1	373	$31
18 LAA	607	101	39	79	24	312	40	281	460	628	151	138	153	20	74	0.98	31	23	45	35	121	182	156	25%	25%	120	13%	92%	26	69%	15%	87.6	397	$38
19 LAA	600	110	45	104	11	291	49	291	438	645	144	129	150	18	74	0.92	24	27	49	30	113	180	172	26%	28%	89	8%	85%	24	79%	8%	71.6	396	$31
1st Half	361	63	22	57	8	297	27	290	452	606	141	131	146	20	77	1.08	27	27	46	32	119	157	166	22%	27%	78	9%	80%	15	80%	13%	41.0	363	$35
2nd Half	239	47	23	47	3	283	22	294	418	702	148	128	155	17	71	0.73	20	25	54	27	104	216	182	31%	29%	108	5%	100%	9	78%	0%	31.6	470	$25
20 Proj	**609**	**113**	**43**	**100**	**18**	**299**		**282**	**437**	**629**	**143**	**130**	**147**	**18**	**74**	**0.87**	**30**	**24**	**46**	**32**	**116**	**170**	**161**	**25%**		**111**	**12%**	**84%**				**82.4**	**387**	**$39**

Tsutsugo,Yoshitomo

Age: 28	Bats: L	Pos: LF	Health	A	LIMA Plan	C+
Ht: 6' 5"	Wt: 225		PT/Exp	A	Rand Var	0
			Consist	C	MM	3043

Japanese slugger with intriguing history chases American dream as club announced his MLB posting in October. Mostly a blank slate, but per the equivalencies, bb% looks solid, power looks volatile, recent ct% plunge puts BA in question. Handedness works for him, OF glove is suspect. A reasonable flyer in OBP leagues.

Yr Tm	PA	R	HR	RBI	SB	BA	xHR	xBA	OBP	SLG	OPS+	vL+	vR+	bb%	ct%	Eye	G	L	F	h%	HctX	PX	xPX	HR/F	xHR/F	Spd	SBO	SB%	#Wk	DOM	DIS	RAR	BPX	R$
15 for	551	77	14	91	0	295			365	444	113			10	81	0.59				34		97				86	0%	0%				9.8	135	$20
16 for	539	87	27	107	0	300			391	555	129			13	79	0.71				33		145				104	1%	0%				35.5	260	$24
17 for	578	83	17	92	1	265			360	426	105			13	78	0.69				31		96				79	1%	100%				-4.3	127	$14
18 for	559	75	23	87	0	275			358	486	117			12	80	0.64				31		124				88	0%	0%				19.1	230	$18
19 for	535	72	18	77	0	253			352	417	102			13	71	0.53				32		96				85	0%	0%				-2.0	59	$11
1st Half																																		
2nd Half																																		
20 Proj	**420**	**62**	**16**	**73**	**0**	**271**		**267**	**359**	**472**	**112**	**111**	**111**	**12**	**79**	**0.67**	**44**	**20**	**36**	**30**	**100**	**105**		**15%**		**100**	**0%**	**35%**				**14.9**	**169**	**$15**

Tucker,Cole

Age: 23	Bats: B	Pos: SS	Health	A	LIMA Plan	F
Ht: 6' 3"	Wt: 205		PT/Exp	C	Rand Var	+2
			Consist	B	MM	1533

2-13-.211 with 0 SB in 157 PA at PIT. Wiry prospect with defensive chops, legit wheels and great hair teased scouts with March power before turning into a pumpkin after promotion. BA dropped, ct% plunged, GB% rate, HR/F remain issues, absence of SBO killed running game. Athleticism, age buy him time, and he needs it. Hard pass for now.

Yr Tm	PA	R	HR	RBI	SB	BA	xHR	xBA	OBP	SLG	OPS+	vL+	vR+	bb%	ct%	Eye	G	L	F	h%	HctX	PX	xPX	HR/F	xHR/F	Spd	SBO	SB%	#Wk	DOM	DIS	RAR	BPX	R$
15																																		
16																																		
17 aa	186	23	2	17	10	251			330	364	93			10	81	0.62				30		55				170	26%	76%					130	$5
18 aa	564	66	4	38	30	240			304	326	87			8	79	0.43				30		53				132	30%	70%					53	$16
19 PIT *	501	58	8	36	9	228	3	254	293	363	87	75	87	8	74	0.35	49	24	27	29	83	77	58	7%	10%	119	12%	73%	14	43%	57%	-17.4	48	$6
1st Half	262	28	7	21	7	242	2	257	289	401	92	76	75	6	74	0.25	48	22	30	30	94	94	71	9%	9%	104	21%	69%	8	38%	63%	-8.4	59	$8
2nd Half	238	30	2	16	2	213	0	260	297	319	81	74	129	11	75	0.47	52	28	21	28	53	59	24	0%	0%	141	3%	100%	6	50%	50%	-12.0	41	$3
20 Proj	**280**	**33**	**3**	**23**	**10**	**241**		**260**	**320**	**355**	**91**	**78**	**97**	**9**	**77**	**0.43**	**50**	**25**	**24**	**30**	**69**	**62**	**43**	**6%**		**130**	**19%**	**73%**				**-3.4**	**68**	**$8**

Tucker,Kyle

Age: 23	Bats: L	Pos: LF	Health	A	LIMA Plan	C+
Ht: 6' 4"	Wt: 190		PT/Exp	C	Rand Var	+2
			Consist	B	MM	2313

4-11-.269 and 5 SB in 71 PA at HOU. Poor AAA start turned torrid as prospect posted 30/30 season that segued into September call-up. Swing-and-miss, streakiness (.165 BA in Apr, .194 in July) keep growth stock's BA, playing time in question. But power and running game look ready for an extended audition. With some h% luck... UP: 20/20.

Yr Tm	PA	R	HR	RBI	SB	BA	xHR	xBA	OBP	SLG	OPS+	vL+	vR+	bb%	ct%	Eye	G	L	F	h%	HctX	PX	xPX	HR/F	xHR/F	Spd	SBO	SB%	#Wk	DOM	DIS	RAR	BPX	R$
15																																		
16																																		
17 aa	306	35	15	42	7	251			299	481	105			6	75	0.28				29		136				88	20%	63%					158	$8
18 HOU *	514	73	19	73	16	264	2	256	323	447	107	137	42	8	77	0.38	49	16	35	31	95	109	76	0%	11%	114	18%	74%	9	33%	33%	6.2	157	$21
19 HOU *	578	81	29	81	27	229	4	239	292	452	99	110	116	8	71	0.31	34	19	47	26	116	124	176	18%	18%	98	29%	83%	5	60%	20%	-9.9	119	$23
1st Half	314	44	18	43	14	230		259	285	479	102			7	69	0.25				27		140		0%		122	27%	92%				-4.6	156	$24
2nd Half	264	37	11	38	13	227	4	235	300	419	95	108	116	9	74	0.40	34	19	47	26	120	105	176	18%	18%	91	31%	74%	5	60%	20%	-8.3	104	$21
20 Proj	**385**	**53**	**13**	**56**	**13**	**250**		**232**	**322**	**420**	**100**	**128**	**87**	**8**	**74**	**0.33**	**36**	**20**	**44**	**30**	**110**	**96**	**136**	**11%**		**101**	**19%**	**80%**				**-0.6**	**95**	**$16**

JOCK THOMPSON

Turner,Justin

Age: 35 Bats: R Pos: 3B	Health C	LIMA Plan B+	PRO: Expected rates of homers, power, and BA all support more seasons in the $20 range. CON: Yo-yo counting stats result of spotty health that won't likely get better now that he's in mid-30s; plate skills no longer elite. Still, you can use his perceived volatility to your advantage, since the foundation it rests upon remains very solid.
Ht: 5' 11" Wt: 202	PT/Exp B	Rand Var 0	
	Consist B	MM 3255	

Yr	Tm	PA	R	HR	RBI	SB	BA	xHR	xBA	OBP	SLG	OPS+	vL+	vR+	bb%	ct%	Eye	G	L	F	h%	HctX	PX	xPX	HR/F	xHR/F	Spd	SBO	SB%	#Wk	DOM	DIS	RAR	BPX	R$
15	LA	439	55	16	60	5	294	14	291	370	491	120	104	124	8	82	0.51	36	28	36	33	113	126	117	14%	12%	77	7%	71%	25	40%	28%	16.7	184	$17
16	LA	622	79	27	90	4	275	26	283	339	493	113	86	123	8	81	0.45	36	24	40	30	123	125	123	15%	14%	93	4%	80%	27	56%	26%	12.6	194	$20
17	LA	543	72	21	71	7	322	25	282	415	530	127	157	111	11	88	1.05	31	21	48	33	138	108	154	11%	13%	71	5%	88%	25	64%	12%	32.9	248	$24
18	LA	426	62	14	52	2	312	17	290	406	518	128	143	120	11	85	0.87	29	26	44	34	141	120	154	10%	12%	80	3%	67%	21	62%	14%	27.7	283	$16
19	LA	549	80	27	67	2	290	25	283	372	509	117	122	113	9	82	0.58	34	26	40	31	142	106	151	17%	16%	90	1%	100%	26	54%	19%	15.5	219	$18
1st Half		316	44	9	33	1	301	14	275	386	452	112	109	114	10	82	0.60	34	28	38	34	149	78	152	10%	16%	96	1%	100%	15	40%	33%	6.6	156	$17
2nd Half		233	36	18	34	1	275	11	298	352	585	123	144	114	10	81	0.55	33	23	44	26	134	145	149	25%	15%	83	2%	100%	11	73%	0%	11.2	315	$19
20	**Proj**	**525**	**78**	**25**	**70**	**3**	**298**		**284**	**382**	**524**	**122**	**134**	**115**	**10**	**83**	**0.68**	**32**	**25**	**43**	**31**	**138**	**112**	**149**	**15%**		**84**	**3%**	**83%**				**32.1**	**233**	**$20**

Turner,Trea

Age: 27 Bats: R Pos: SS	Health C	LIMA Plan D+	On surface, 2019 was a season similar to the year prior. But he did it in 170 fewer plate appearances. Homers backed by xHR, so he can repeat that level. He's outproduced xBA routinely, so don't assume a big BA backslide. Spd + acumen on basepaths remain elite. In short, a top-level, multi-category bat worthy of 1st round/$30+ consideration.
Ht: 6' 2" Wt: 185	PT/Exp A	Rand Var -2	
	Consist B	MM 2545	

Yr	Tm	PA	R	HR	RBI	SB	BA	xHR	xBA	OBP	SLG	OPS+	vL+	vR+	bb%	ct%	Eye	G	L	F	h%	HctX	PX	xPX	HR/F	xHR/F	Spd	SBO	SB%	#Wk	DOM	DIS	RAR	BPX	R$
15	WAS *	532	64	7	48	27	295	1	248	345	405	105	113	78	7	77	0.33	50	21	29	37	36	79	11	13%	13%	121	24%	76%	8	13%	50%	18.1	62	$25
16	WAS *	690	111	18	71	57	313	12	276	362	498	117	101	132	7	78	0.36	43	25	32	38	111	109	122	17%	15%	204	36%	87%	14	64%	21%	41.3	223	$49
17	WAS	447	75	11	45	46	284	11	268	338	451	106	84	110	7	81	0.38	52	15	34	33	87	94	85	10%	10%	183	51%	85%	18	61%	28%	12.7	206	$30
18	WAS	740	103	19	73	43	271	18	253	344	416	105	111	103	9	80	0.52	49	18	33	31	93	82	79	11%	10%	159	26%	83%	28	50%	18%	24.2	180	$36
19	WAS	569	96	19	57	35	298	19	276	353	497	113	106	115	8	78	0.38	47	20	33	35	102	108	87	14%	14%	157	29%	88%	23	52%	13%	26.0	237	$32
1st Half		202	32	6	19	17	274	7	257	332	473	108	100	111	8	73	0.32	49	16	35	35	84	114	71	13%	15%	160	42%	89%	10	30%	10%	4.7	181	$14
2nd Half		367	64	13	38	18	310	13	288	365	510	116	111	117	7	81	0.43	46	22	32	35	113	105	95	15%	15%	146	23%	86%	13	69%	15%	18.5	259	$42
20	**Proj**	**630**	**101**	**20**	**63**	**43**	**289**		**267**	**347**	**471**	**110**	**102**	**112**	**8**	**79**	**0.40**	**48**	**19**	**33**	**34**	**98**	**97**	**87**	**13%**		**168**	**32%**	**85%**				**30.8**	**209**	**$39**

Upton,Justin

Age: 32 Bats: R Pos: LF	Health D	LIMA Plan C+	Turf toe sidelined him until mid-season, then barking knee required platelet injection in Sept. Long string of pre-2019 durability says not to panic. But strikeouts have been on a steady incline, which means his reliable power now will come with a suspect BA. And lack of SB opps are here to stay given knee concerns. A power-only pony.
Ht: 6' 1" Wt: 215	PT/Exp B	Rand Var +2	
	Consist D	MM 4115	

Yr	Tm	PA	R	HR	RBI	SB	BA	xHR	xBA	OBP	SLG	OPS+	vL+	vR+	bb%	ct%	Eye	G	L	F	h%	HctX	PX	xPX	HR/F	xHR/F	Spd	SBO	SB%	#Wk	DOM	DIS	RAR	BPX	R$
15	SD	619	85	26	81	19	251	28	240	336	454	110	77	116	11	71	0.43	39	17	44	31	108	140	131	15%	16%	120	16%	79%	26	50%	38%	12.7	149	$23
16	DET	626	81	31	87	9	246	34	243	310	465	105	102	105	8	69	0.28	39	18	43	30	106	144	126	18%	20%	90	10%	69%	27	44%	48%	8.1	100	$17
17	2 AL	631	99	35	109	13	273	35	265	361	542	121	153	110	12	68	0.41	37	20	43	34	112	178	151	21%	21%	66	12%	72%	27	52%	26%	20.8	176	$27
18	LAA	613	80	30	85	8	257	31	239	344	463	112	82	120	10	67	0.36	42	22	36	33	108	132	137	23%	24%	98	7%	80%	28	31%	46%	12.2	83	$21
19	LAA	250	34	12	40	1	215	11	211	309	416	96	71	107	13	64	0.41	38	16	46	27	92	120	114	18%	16%	73	3%	50%	13	38%	54%	-6.2	7	$3
1st Half		49	5	3	4	0	273	3	257	347	500	113	0	149	10	73	0.42	28	25	47	31	102	114	104	20%	20%	92	0%	0%	3	33%	67%	1.2	119	-$10
2nd Half		207	29	9	36	1	200	8	203	300	394	92	82	96	13	62	0.41	40	14	46	26	89	122	117	17%	15%	72	4%	50%	10	40%	50%	-7.5	-11	$6
20	**Proj**	**560**	**80**	**28**	**90**	**4**	**242**		**233**	**327**	**465**	**107**	**78**	**116**	**11**	**66**	**0.38**	**38**	**19**	**43**	**30**	**102**	**134**	**126**	**20%**		**81**	**5%**	**64%**				**8.2**	**65**	**$19**

Urias,Luis

Age: 23 Bats: R Pos: SS 2B	Health A	LIMA Plan D+	4-24-.223 in 249 PA at SD. Consistent .300 hitter in minors couldn't carry that over to MLB. Blame ct% that dipped in each of final three months (masked by a fluky 39% h% in Sept). Underlying HR and power metrics point to thump as a work-in-progress too. At age 23, he's got time. Value limited to keeper leagues for now.
Ht: 5' 9" Wt: 185	PT/Exp C	Rand Var +1	
	Consist B	MM 1325	

Yr	Tm	PA	R	HR	RBI	SB	BA	xHR	xBA	OBP	SLG	OPS+	vL+	vR+	bb%	ct%	Eye	G	L	F	h%	HctX	PX	xPX	HR/F	xHR/F	Spd	SBO	SB%	#Wk	DOM	DIS	RAR	BPX	R$
15																																			
16																																			
17	aa	505	74	3	36	7	294			382	373	101			13	85	0.96				34		48				123	7%	56%					130	$14
18	SD *	551	65	8	37	2	248	1	243	318	366	95	171	55	9	73	0.38	63	16	21	33	83	81	78	25%	13%	120	3%	69%	3	67%	33%	1.9	47	$7
19	SD *	570	71	17	60	5	248	5	254	317	408	96	116	76	9	75	0.41	49	20	31	30	95	87	89	8%	10%	130	6%	60%	14	7%	43%	-6.5	111	$11
1st Half		311	42	11	32	5	256	1	258	323	451	104	0	63	9	74	0.38	54	15	31	31	118	108	117	0%	25%	115	10%	69%	2	0%	100%	-0.1	137	$15
2nd Half		259	29	5	28	0	238	4	242	309	355	88	128	78	9	77	0.45	49	21	31	29	95	63	87	9%	9%	125	2%	0%	12	8%	33%	-9.2	67	$6
20	**Proj**	**455**	**57**	**8**	**40**	**3**	**253**		**244**	**348**	**376**	**97**	**139**	**82**	**10**	**76**	**0.45**	**49**	**21**	**31**	**31**	**86**	**70**	**78**	**8%**		**142**	**4%**	**59%**				**0.0**	**29**	**$10**

Urshela,Giovanny

Age: 28 Bats: R Pos: 3B	Health B	LIMA Plan D	Journeyman turned a good 1st half into a great 2nd. In aggregate, surprising HR and sexy BA both came close to expected returns. That will prevent regression from reaching prior baseline. Still, we simply can't overlook long history of mediocrity, and eroding ct% puts plate skills on shakier ground. Expect moderate pullback.
Ht: 6' 0" Wt: 220	PT/Exp D	Rand Var -5	
	Consist B	MM 2043	

Yr	Tm	PA	R	HR	RBI	SB	BA	xHR	xBA	OBP	SLG	OPS+	vL+	vR+	bb%	ct%	Eye	G	L	F	h%	HctX	PX	xPX	HR/F	xHR/F	Spd	SBO	SB%	#Wk	DOM	DIS	RAR	BPX	R$
15	CLE *	372	35	9	29	0	231	7	250	274	352	87	93	80	6	80	0.29	42	24	34	27	77	77	74	8%	10%	94	1%	0%	17	18%	41%	-14.8	57	$1
16	aaa	481	44	7	47	0	249			269	346	84			3	87	0.21				27		59				84	0%	0%					83	$4
17	CLE *	478	40	6	41	0	231	2	254	269	313	78	71	74	5	85	0.35	46	23	31	26	84	48	60	2%	5%	83	0%	0%	14	21%	29%	-28.2	42	$0
18	TOR *	280	28	3	22	0	234	1	195	267	320	81	143	70	4	82	0.25	45	9	45	28	64	55	41	7%	7%	120	0%	0%	8	13%	63%	-11.9	60	$0
19	NYY	476	73	21	74	1	314	20	293	355	534	118	114	119	5	80	0.29	41	25	33	35	122	116	122	18%	17%	75	2%	50%	26	46%	35%	22.6	181	$19
1st Half		230	32	6	38	1	303	7	282	352	457	108	86	116	6	82	0.38	41	27	33	35	127	84	121	11%	12%	75	2%	100%	14	50%	21%	3.4	122	$13
2nd Half		246	41	15	36	0	325	13	304	358	603	127	132	123	4	79	0.22	42	24	34	36	118	147	122	24%	21%	81	2%	0%	12	42%	50%	16.9	252	$24
20	**Proj**	**420**	**53**	**14**	**50**	**0**	**274**		**276**	**311**	**446**	**102**	**101**	**102**	**5**	**82**	**0.27**	**43**	**24**	**33**	**31**	**102**	**90**	**93**	**13%**		**84**	**1%**	**40%**				**2.7**	**86**	**$13**

VanMeter,Josh

Age: 25 Bats: L Pos: LF	Health A	LIMA Plan C+	8-23-.237 with 9 SB in 260 PA at CIN. Blistering start at AAA earned him super-utility role in majors. While stats didn't convert, underlying power blossomed in 2nd half while plate skills held sturdy. With routine work, a sleeper multi-category bat that will qualify all over diamond. UP: 20 HR, 20 SB
Ht: 5' 11" Wt: 165	PT/Exp B	Rand Var -2	
	Consist B	MM 2323	

Yr	Tm	PA	R	HR	RBI	SB	BA	xHR	xBA	OBP	SLG	OPS+	vL+	vR+	bb%	ct%	Eye	G	L	F	h%	HctX	PX	xPX	HR/F	xHR/F	Spd	SBO	SB%	#Wk	DOM	DIS	RAR	BPX	R$
15																																			
16	aa	112	9	2	5	2	189			234	257	67			6	82	0.33				21		38				103	17%	47%					11	-$2
17	aa	533	48	6	58	16	257			337	359	93			11	77	0.53				32		70				83	13%	83%					39	$12
18	a/a	472	45	11	50	8	235			306	408	99			9	76	0.42				29		114				101	14%	60%					147	$8
19	CIN *	462	69	21	59	16	273	7	264	352	499	113	60	102	11	76	0.50	36	23	41	31	124	122	132	11%	10%	103	20%	71%	21	38%	29%	10.1	200	$19
1st Half		221	34	13	35	7	299	0	282	375	562	125	84	82	11	76	0.50	36	25	39	34	112	139	71	0%	0%	104	18%	68%	8	13%	63%	12.5	252	$20
2nd Half		242	35	8	24	9	248	7	252	331	442	102	52	107	11	75	0.50	36	22	42	29	126	107	144	13%	12%	116	21%	74%	13	54%	8%	-1.5	170	$17
20	**Proj**	**420**	**51**	**13**	**46**	**12**	**258**		**250**	**343**	**433**	**104**	**72**	**108**	**10**	**76**	**0.47**	**36**	**23**	**41**	**31**	**120**	**98**	**115**	**11%**		**103**	**17%**	**70%**				**4.0**	**127**	**$15**

Vargas,Ildemaro

Age: 28 Bats: B Pos: 2B	Health A	LIMA Plan D+	6-24-.269 in 211 PA at ARI. First extended MLB look shined light on his path to value as a high-contact bat with speed. The latter was hidden due to lack of green light; double-digit steals in play if that flickers. Elite bat-to-ball skills put .300 BA within sight, as shown by xBA. BA/SB profile makes him a profit target in very deep leagues.
Ht: 6' 0" Wt: 170	PT/Exp C	Rand Var 0	
	Consist C	MM 1451	

Yr	Tm	PA	R	HR	RBI	SB	BA	xHR	xBA	OBP	SLG	OPS+	vL+	vR+	bb%	ct%	Eye	G	L	F	h%	HctX	PX	xPX	HR/F	xHR/F	Spd	SBO	SB%	#Wk	DOM	DIS	RAR	BPX	R$
15																																			
16	a/a	554	58	5	28	16	269			312	353	91			6	92	0.78				29		50				109	12%	93%					154	$13
17	ARI *	518	58	6	44	5	252	0	282	279	365	86	166	59	4	90	0.36	50	20	30	27	36	63	49	0%	0%	121	8%	58%	6	17%	50%	-24.0	167	$7
18	ARI *	575	48	5	36	7	229	1	293	254	320	79	55	103	3	89	0.30	40	33	27	25	87	51	56	25%	25%	146	11%	57%	5	20%	40%	-27.9	160	$4
19	ARI *	342	37	7	38	2	283	4	300	316	419	98	134	80	5	91	0.51	53	23	25	29	107	63	60	14%	9%	129	4%	55%	23	30%	26%	1.0	233	$7
1st Half		198	22	5	21	1	266	2	300	313	398	95	143	68	6	88	0.59	55	23	21	28	110	64	64	14%	7%	117	2%	100%	14	21%	29%	-1.6	204	$6
2nd Half		144	14	3	16	1	305	1	283	319	446	101	100	113	2	93	0.33	44	20	36	31	93	62	47	13%	6%	139	6%	31%	9	44%	22%	1.5	263	$8
20	**Proj**	**210**	**21**	**6**	**19**	**4**	**281**		**294**	**308**	**437**	**100**	**115**	**95**	**4**	**91**	**0.42**	**49**	**21**	**30**	**29**	**100**	**71**	**54**	**10%**		**131**	**11%**	**78%**				**3.9**	**214**	**$7**

STEPHEN NICKRAND

Vazquez,Christian

Age: 29	Bats: R	Pos: CA	Health C	LIMA Plan B	
Ht: 5' 9"	Wt: 195		PT/Exp C	Rand Var -2	
			Consist F	MM 1235	

Power output exploded and there was at least some skills support. But really? He more than doubled his *career* HR total in one season. It's not a leap to recommend that you side with the rabbit ball here. Yes, his floor is higher now, so he won't come crashing back down to 2018. But best case is likely a blend of the two.

Yr Tm	PA	R	HR	RBI	SB	BA	xHR	xBA	OBP	SLG	OPS+	vL+	vR+	bb%	ct%	Eye	G	L	F	h%	HctX	PX	xPX	HR/F	xHR/F	Spd	SBO	SB%	#Wk	DOM	DIS	RAR	BPX	R$
15																																		
16 BOS *	349	38	3	26	2	240	2	271	291	329	84	109	70	7	77	0.32	60	25	15	30	87	65	53	5%	10%	91	2%	100%	16	13%	56%	-5.9	11	$2
17 BOS	345	43	5	32	7	290	5	268	330	404	99	99	97	5	80	0.27	47	25	28	35	86	70	58	7%	7%	91	10%	78%	27	41%	44%	5.4	48	$10
18 BOS	269	24	3	16	4	207	4	237	257	283	75	84	71	5	84	0.32	42	21	36	24	85	48	51	4%	5%	79	10%	80%	20	20%	50%	-8.6	27	-$1
19 BOS	521	66	23	72	4	276	19	270	320	477	106	117	100	6	79	0.33	39	23	38	31	92	103	100	16%	13%	86	5%	67%	28	39%	36%	24.3	144	$16
1st Half	244	31	11	34	1	289	9	265	325	482	108	121	102	5	79	0.28	41	22	37	32	85	94	92	16%	13%	117	5%	33%	15	40%	33%	9.7	152	$14
2nd Half	277	35	12	38	3	264	10	274	316	472	104	114	98	7	79	0.37	38	24	39	29	98	111	107	16%	13%	62	5%	100%	13	38%	38%	9.4	144	$18
20 Proj	**490**	**57**	**14**	**54**	**6**	**261**		**257**	**306**	**410**	**96**	**110**	**91**	**6**	**80**	**0.31**	**40**	**23**	**37**	**30**	**89**	**79**	**77**	**10%**		**82**	**7%**	**77%**				**11.9**	**76**	**$11**

Verdugo,Alex

Age: 24	Bats: L	Pos: CF RF LF	Health B	LIMA Plan C+	
Ht: 6' 0"	Wt: 212		PT/Exp C	Rand Var +1	
			Consist B	MM 2155	

Ingredients of a breakout... (1) Now showing thump vL; (2) Slowly buying into launch angle revolution; (3) Exit velo up another couple ticks; (4) Still a high-contact bat even with those gains. Late oblique strain will cause his growth to stay under radar. If playing time and health align, there's a $20 bat here... UP: .320 BA, 20 HR

Yr Tm	PA	R	HR	RBI	SB	BA	xHR	xBA	OBP	SLG	OPS+	vL+	vR+	bb%	ct%	Eye	G	L	F	h%	HctX	PX	xPX	HR/F	xHR/F	Spd	SBO	SB%	#Wk	DOM	DIS	RAR	BPX	R$
15																																		
16 aa	513	51	12	56	2	256			308	381	94			7	85	0.50				28		73				84	7%	22%					111	$8
17 LA *	498	57	6	53	8	279	0	328	340	387	98	53	77	8	87	0.70	58	32	11	31	74	62	40	50%	0%	88	9%	64%	6	17%	33%	-6.1	127	$12
18 LA *	455	47	9	40	6	287	2	265	341	409	104	77	103	7	84	0.52	62	16	22	32	121	73	68	7%	14%	93	7%	74%	10	30%	40%	8.7	133	$12
19 LA	377	43	12	44	4	294	10	296	342	475	109	110	107	7	86	0.53	49	23	29	32	129	89	91	14%	12%	85	5%	80%	20	65%	25%	15.6	204	$10
1st Half	278	32	9	37	4	311	8	308	360	506	116	118	114	7	89	0.74	48	22	31	32	132	93	99	13%	11%	92	6%	100%	15	80%	20%	17.0	281	$16
2nd Half	99	11	3	7	0	250	2	265	293	391	90	92	89	6	76	0.27	52	25	23	30	122	77	66	19%	13%	82	5%	0%	5	20%	40%	-1.8	19	-$4
20 Proj	**455**	**50**	**16**	**45**	**4**	**291**		**278**	**339**	**462**	**108**	**103**	**109**	**7**	**83**	**0.45**	**48**	**22**	**30**	**32**	**124**	**87**	**75**	**15%**		**77**	**6%**	**58%**				**19.7**	**131**	**$16**

Villar,Jonathan

Age: 29	Bats: B	Pos: 2B SS	Health A	LIMA Plan D	
Ht: 6' 1"	Wt: 215		PT/Exp A	Rand Var 0	
			Consist B	MM 2525	

One of nine hitters in 2019 to top 700 PA; that durability returned him to elite value. R$ confirms upper-tier returns are tied to PA, which remain volatile. And xBA, xPX keep redux of 2015 and 2017 in play. Legs are his consistent tool, and with strong Spd + SB%, that's what to target here. Sum of these parts is a good bat, not a great one.

Yr Tm	PA	R	HR	RBI	SB	BA	xHR	xBA	OBP	SLG	OPS+	vL+	vR+	bb%	ct%	Eye	G	L	F	h%	HctX	PX	xPX	HR/F	xHR/F	Spd	SBO	SB%	#Wk	DOM	DIS	RAR	BPX	R$
15 HOU *	426	58	6	33	31	242	2	239	293	356	91	105	102	7	70	0.24	57	20	23	33	75	85	44	10%	10%	139	45%	71%	15	33%	40%	-12.1	14	$16
16 MIL	679	92	19	63	62	285	16	264	369	457	112	126	105	12	70	0.45	56	20	24	38	101	120	101	20%	16%	110	43%	78%	27	44%	48%	29.7	103	$43
17 MIL	436	49	11	40	23	241	9	240	293	372	89	80	91	7	67	0.23	57	21	22	33	90	89	83	19%	16%	105	32%	74%	25	20%	64%	-12.2	-36	$13
18 2 TM	515	54	14	46	35	260	15	235	325	384	98	101	96	8	70	0.30	56	20	24	34	80	79	71	18%	19%	112	30%	88%	26	23%	50%	5.1	-10	$23
19 BAL	713	111	24	73	40	274	23	253	339	453	105	97	109	9	73	0.35	49	20	31	34	73	100	70	17%	16%	122	28%	82%	28	29%	43%	5.8	96	$35
1st Half	353	51	10	35	16	254	10	253	325	416	99	87	106	9	74	0.39	50	19	31	31	64	94	56	14%	14%	101	26%	76%	15	27%	33%	-3.5	81	$24
2nd Half	360	60	14	38	24	294	14	253	353	489	111	108	112	8	71	0.31	48	20	32	37	82	107	84	19%	19%	139	30%	86%	13	31%	54%	13.3	115	$45
20 Proj	**665**	**88**	**18**	**60**	**37**	**261**		**243**	**324**	**408**	**98**	**95**	**99**	**8**	**71**	**0.30**	**53**	**20**	**27**	**34**	**80**	**86**	**74**	**15%**		**124**	**28%**	**80%**				**8.8**	**34**	**$31**

Vogelbach,Daniel

Age: 27	Bats: L	Pos: DH 1B	Health A	LIMA Plan C+	
Ht: 6' 0"	Wt: 250		PT/Exp C	Rand Var +2	
			Consist B	MM 3015	

Broke through with a bang, but look under hood reveals a mixed bag. PRO: Power mostly validated by xPX; xBA doesn't profile him at Mendoza level; astute Eye gives him extra value in OBP leagues. CON: Strikeouts piled up as season went along; rough 2nd half as pitchers adjusted. Expect at least moderate regression.

Yr Tm	PA	R	HR	RBI	SB	BA	xHR	xBA	OBP	SLG	OPS+	vL+	vR+	bb%	ct%	Eye	G	L	F	h%	HctX	PX	xPX	HR/F	xHR/F	Spd	SBO	SB%	#Wk	DOM	DIS	RAR	BPX	R$
15 aa	300	32	6	31	1	241			356	371	101			15	73	0.66				31		98				91	2%	41%					78	$3
16 SEA *	549	63	19	77	0	246		255	353	417	105	0	34	14	73	0.62	67	17	17	30	0	108	-24	0%		57	0%	0%	4	0%	75%	-7.0	77	$10
17 SEA *	550	51	14	69	2	242	0	273	328	372	94	66	72	11	74	0.49	32	37	32	30	141	81	145	0%	0%	56	2%	67%	7	29%	71%	-11.0	3	$7
18 SEA *	457	49	19	58	0	229	5	246	349	416	106	38	112	15	74	0.71	44	21	34	26	143	112	161	19%	24%	57	1%	0%	13	23%	38%	2.6	117	$8
19 SEA	558	73	30	76	0	208	25	240	341	439	104	79	112	16	68	0.62	33	22	45	23	90	130	123	21%	18%	42	0%	0%	29	41%	48%	-6.5	85	$9
1st Half	317	47	20	48	0	244	17	265	379	519	120	63	137	18	72	0.79	28	23	49	26	107	144	146	22%	18%	54	0%	0%	16	50%	38%	10.6	219	$17
2nd Half	241	26	10	28	0	162	9	208	290	338	83	94	78	15	62	0.46	41	21	38	20	68	109	88	21%	19%	49	0%	0%	13	31%	62%	-15.4	-70	-$2
20 Proj	**525**	**60**	**25**	**64**	**0**	**231**		**239**	**353**	**438**	**107**	**75**	**117**	**15**	**70**	**0.59**	**39**	**22**	**39**	**27**	**108**	**116**	**132**	**20%**		**45**	**1%**	**41%**				**4.7**	**42**	**$12**

Vogt,Stephen

Age: 35	Bats: L	Pos: CA	Health F	LIMA Plan D	
Ht: 6' 0"	Wt: 225		PT/Exp F	Rand Var 0	
			Consist A	MM 3133	

10-40-.263 in 280 PA at SF. Nice rebound after shoulder surgery wiped out 2018. Statcast loved new approach: exit velocity, launch angle, barrels, and hard-hit % all better than ever. If he were ten years younger, that would make him an intriguing target. But in his mid-30s and with whiffs growing, he's second-catcher material only.

Yr Tm	PA	R	HR	RBI	SB	BA	xHR	xBA	OBP	SLG	OPS+	vL+	vR+	bb%	ct%	Eye	G	L	F	h%	HctX	PX	xPX	HR/F	xHR/F	Spd	SBO	SB%	#Wk	DOM	DIS	RAR	BPX	R$
15 OAK	511	58	18	71	0	261	14	258	341	443	109	87	114	11	78	0.58	38	22	40	30	96	115	110	13%	10%	86	2%	0%	25	48%	32%	17.3	149	$12
16 OAK	532	54	14	56	0	251	15	260	305	406	97	74	100	7	83	0.42	30	23	46	28	90	93	106	7%	8%	69	0%	0%	27	52%	26%	-3.5	120	$7
17 2 TM	303	25	12	40	0	233	10	255	285	423	95	67	97	7	80	0.38	38	19	44	25	106	105	122	12%	10%	82	2%	0%	23	57%	26%	-0.7	133	$2
18																																		
19 SF *	348	36	12	45	3	247	14	255	313	463	103	86	111	9	74	0.38	27	24	49	29	107	125	136	11%	15%	77	6%	75%	22	45%	32%	5.1	148	$6
1st Half	175	19	4	17	0	238	5	237	326	438	102	74	121	12	71	0.45	23	24	53	31	97	123	141	6%	14%	101	3%	0%	10	50%	50%	3.1	144	$0
2nd Half	173	17	8	28	3	256	9	272	295	488	103	93	106	6	78	0.28	29	24	46	28	114	127	133	14%	15%	57	10%	100%	12	42%	17%	5.3	156	$11
20 Proj	**280**	**28**	**10**	**37**	**1**	**246**		**254**	**305**	**439**	**100**	**79**	**104**	**8**	**78**	**0.39**	**31**	**23**	**46**	**28**	**103**	**107**	**126**	**11%**		**79**	**4%**	**68%**				**8.7**	**119**	**$7**

Voit,Luke

Age: 29	Bats: R	Pos: 1B DH	Health B	LIMA Plan B	
Ht: 6' 3"	Wt: 225		PT/Exp C	Rand Var -2	
			Consist C	MM 4035	

On his way to a career year before mid-season sports hernia got in way. Consistently above-par power skills backed by xPX, and xHR says 20-25 HR is his new baseline now. Further, those BB make him a boon in OBP leagues. But heed dwindling ct%. As the Ks keep piling up, his damage to your BA will grow, and PT will be at risk.

Yr Tm	PA	R	HR	RBI	SB	BA	xHR	xBA	OBP	SLG	OPS+	vL+	vR+	bb%	ct%	Eye	G	L	F	h%	HctX	PX	xPX	HR/F	xHR/F	Spd	SBO	SB%	#Wk	DOM	DIS	RAR	BPX	R$
15																																		
16 aa	524	57	15	60	1	259			318	404	98			8	81	0.45				29		82				105	2%	26%					111	$10
17 STL *	415	45	14	57	1	268	5	261	320	455	104	106	94	7	76	0.32	48	18	34	32	126	116	142	14%	18%	73	2%	39%	14	36%	50%	-9.9	106	$9
18 2 TM *	458	60	25	68	0	276	16	274	347	512	119	163	139	10	73	0.40	35	28	37	32	126	141	158	41%	43%	112	1%	0%	14	50%	29%	20.7	197	$16
19 NYY	510	72	21	62	0	263	25	246	378	464	112	103	114	14	67	0.50	40	26	35	35	90	120	118	21%	25%	94	0%	0%	23	39%	48%	12.3	81	$12
1st Half	349	53	17	50	0	280	19	262	393	509	120	103	125	14	69	0.54	39	27	34	35	93	129	118	24%	27%	98	0%	0%	14	57%	36%	14.3	148	$20
2nd Half	161	19	4	12	0	228	7	208	348	368	94	105	88	14	62	0.42	42	23	36	34	84	97	118	13%	23%	93	0%	0%	9	11%	67%	-4.5	-67	-$5
20 Proj	**455**	**58**	**25**	**55**	**0**	**260**		**263**	**353**	**505**	**115**	**123**	**111**	**11**	**70**	**0.43**	**40**	**25**	**36**	**31**	**107**	**138**	**136**	**25%**		**94**	**1%**	**30%**				**16.4**	**103**	**$15**

Votto,Joey

Age: 36	Bats: L	Pos: 1B	Health B	LIMA Plan B	
Ht: 6' 2"	Wt: 220		PT/Exp A	Rand Var +1	
			Consist F	MM 2245	

So much for a rebound. Steep two-year declines in plate and underlying power skills paint a pessimistic picture. Statcast tells the story: he's barreling the ball at one-third of his pre-2018 rate. xHR puts rebound to 20 HR in cards, but that no longer carries much value by itself, and xBA confirms days of pairing it with a .300 BA are over.

Yr Tm	PA	R	HR	RBI	SB	BA	xHR	xBA	OBP	SLG	OPS+	vL+	vR+	bb%	ct%	Eye	G	L	F	h%	HctX	PX	xPX	HR/F	xHR/F	Spd	SBO	SB%	#Wk	DOM	DIS	RAR	BPX	R$
15 CIN	695	95	29	80	11	314	34	285	459	541	139	139	137	21	75	1.06	42	25	33	37	126	151	150	22%	25%	81	6%	79%	27	59%	22%	56.7	241	$33
16 CIN	677	101	29	97	8	326	30	298	434	550	134	116	138	16	78	0.90	43	27	30	37	123	133	134	22%	23%	84	4%	89%	27	52%	22%	55.9	226	$33
17 CIN	707	106	36	100	5	320	33	309	454	578	138	131	138	19	85	1.61	39	23	38	33	125	130	141	20%	18%	85	2%	83%	27	85%	11%	58.4	333	$32
18 CIN	623	67	12	67	2	284	21	276	417	419	116	105	121	17	80	1.07	38	31	31	34	121	83	129	10%	17%	81	1%	100%	27	44%	26%	15.0	157	$16
19 CIN	608	79	15	47	5	261	21	253	357	411	102	86	108	13	77	0.62	37	25	38	32	110	86	116	10%	14%	87	3%	100%	27	37%	22%	-4.7	104	$12
1st Half	319	41	8	21	2	267	11	238	361	415	104	96	107	12	74	0.54	35	24	42	33	102	85	134	9%	13%	109	2%	100%	15	40%	27%	0.2	89	$11
2nd Half	289	38	7	26	3	254	10	271	353	407	100	75	111	13	79	0.73	39	27	34	30	119	87	97	10%	15%	65	4%	100%	12	33%	17%	-1.2	126	$13
20 Proj	**630**	**84**	**17**	**67**	**5**	**281**		**267**	**383**	**442**	**111**	**98**	**116**	**14**	**79**	**0.76**	**38**	**27**	**35**	**33**	**118**	**88**	**124**	**12%**		**82**	**3%**	**94%**				**22.1**	**140**	**$21**

STEPHEN NICKRAND

Walker,Christian

Age: 29	Bats: R	Pos: 1B	Health C	LIMA Plan D+
Ht: 6' 0"	Wt: 220		PT/Exp C	Rand Var +1
			Consist D	MM 4325

PRO: Power skills have been good for a while; xHR supported even more homers; Statcast exit velocity and hard hit % were upper-crust; plate skills matured late. CON: Flyball rate keeps declining, which leaves him hr/f dependent; Ks are in his DNA, so he'll never help you in BA. Overall, buy the power...if he has path to 600 PA again.

Yr	Tm	PA	R	HR	RBI	SB	BA	xHR	xBA	OBP	SLG	OPS+	vL+	vR+	bb%	ct%	Eye	G	L	F	h%	HctX	PX	xPX	HR/F	xHR/F	Spd	SBO	SB%	#Wk	DOM	DIS	RAR	BPX	R$
15	BAL *	592	64	19	70	1	241		274	304	404	99	59	69	8	72	0.32	80	20	0	30	125	118	34	0%		77	3%	22%	4	50%	50%	-21.7	68	$10
16	aaa	543	58	16	58	1	223			278	359	87			7	67	0.23				30		92				94	4%	21%					-37	$4
17	ARI *	566	66	23	73	3	250	2	229	301	464	103	200	53	7	75	0.29	29	14	57	29	174	122	330	50%	50%	111	5%	56%	4	50%	50%	-18.8	142	$12
18	ARI *	392	46	13	47	2	211	4	198	248	383	87	96	63	5	65	0.14	37	11	52	29	53	123	111	21%	29%	99	3%	100%	13	38%	54%	-23.2	0	$4
19	ARI	603	86	29	73	8	259	34	248	348	476	109	103	111	11	71	0.43	42	20	38	31	113	121	127	20%	24%	85	6%	89%	28	43%	32%	4.0	107	$18
1st Half		320	42	14	36	5	256	20	245	328	474	107	95	112	9	69	0.32	40	20	40	33	117	131	148	18%	25%	88	9%	83%	15	40%	27%	1.1	96	$17
2nd Half		283	44	15	37	3	263	14	251	371	479	112	114	111	14	73	0.59	44	20	37	30	108	110	105	23%	22%	82	4%	100%	13	46%	38%	6.5	130	$20
20	Proj	**560**	**74**	**28**	**69**	**5**	**244**		**249**	**319**	**470**	**106**	**101**	**107**	**9**	**70**	**0.33**	**42**	**20**	**38**	**29**	**112**	**127**	**122**	**21%**		**96**	**5%**	**84%**				**6.1**	**107**	**$14**

Walker,Neil

Age: 34	Bats: B	Pos: 1B 3B	Health C	LIMA Plan D+
Ht: 6' 3"	Wt: 210		PT/Exp C	Rand Var 0
			Consist C	MM 1233

As power continues to erode, so does his value; nowadays, it's hard to cover for a bat that struggles to reach double-digit HR in 400 PA. Three-year dive in flyball rate confirms it's not coming back. And mediocre batting average has been validated by xBA for years. As a CI-only bat now, there's nothing here worthy of your time.

Yr	Tm	PA	R	HR	RBI	SB	BA	xHR	xBA	OBP	SLG	OPS+	vL+	vR+	bb%	ct%	Eye	G	L	F	h%	HctX	PX	xPX	HR/F	xHR/F	Spd	SBO	SB%	#Wk	DOM	DIS	RAR	BPX	R$
15	PIT	603	69	16	71	4	269	18	261	328	427	105	79	109	7	80	0.40	42	21	37	31	112	105	113	10%	11%	96	4%	80%	27	44%	22%	-8.3	130	$16
16	NYM	458	57	23	55	3	282	22	255	347	476	112	135	102	9	80	0.50	35	21	43	30	116	102	136	16%	15%	100	3%	75%	21	52%	24%	6.2	143	$15
17	2 NL	448	59	14	49	0	265	12	260	362	439	107	81	113	12	80	0.71	36	22	42	30	106	97	114	11%	9%	95	2%	0%	21	71%	24%	-6.4	161	$9
18	NYY	398	48	11	46	0	219	15	235	309	354	92	66	98	11	75	0.48	37	24	39	26	105	82	124	11%	15%	85	0%	0%	28	32%	57%	-16.9	47	$4
19	MIA	381	37	8	38	3	261	12	262	344	395	98	89	100	11	77	0.55	42	27	31	32	100	76	100	10%	15%	89	3%	100%	24	38%	42%	-6.5	74	$5
1st Half		185	15	5	17	2	279	8	252	357	430	105	80	110	10	75	0.46	38	25	37	34	103	88	135	11%	17%	88	4%	100%	12	42%	50%	1.4	74	$4
2nd Half		196	22	3	21	1	244	4	274	332	360	91	99	90	12	79	0.64	45	29	26	29	98	66	68	9%	11%	95	2%	100%	12	33%	33%	-5.5	85	$7
20	Proj	**350**	**40**	**9**	**38**	**2**	**251**		**253**	**335**	**392**	**98**	**84**	**100**	**11**	**77**	**0.54**	**40**	**25**	**35**	**30**	**104**	**77**	**108**	**10%**		**91**	**2%**	**83%**				**-0.9**	**49**	**$8**

Walsh,Jared

Age: 26	Bats: L	Pos: 1B	Health A	LIMA Plan F
Ht: 6' 0"	Wt: 210		PT/Exp D	Rand Var 0
			Consist B	MM 4301

1-5-.203 in 87 PA at LAA. Dual batter/mop-up pitcher role got him noticed, but that's where intrigue ends. While LH power is backed by xPX and HR/F should've been better, the holes in his swing are huge and chronic. At best, he's a power dart-throw at your corner spot in deep AL-only leagues.

Yr	Tm	PA	R	HR	RBI	SB	BA	xHR	xBA	OBP	SLG	OPS+	vL+	vR+	bb%	ct%	Eye	G	L	F	h%	HctX	PX	xPX	HR/F	xHR/F	Spd	SBO	SB%	#Wk	DOM	DIS	RAR	BPX	R$
15																																			
16																																			
17	aa	72	7	3	8	1	210			240	367	81			4	51	0.08				36		133				95	8%	100%					-152	-$1
18	a/a	352	41	11	44	1	221			277	388	92			7	62	0.20				32		131				83	1%	100%					-23	$4
19	LAA *	505	60	25	57	0	239	3	242	303	466	102	98	78	8	61	0.23	39	27	34	33	115	150	134	7%	20%	76	0%	0%	11	0%	73%	-2.5	19	$9
1st Half		258	28	9	22	0	236	1	262	304	409	95	200	73	9	63	0.26	42	37	21	34	126	118	69	0%	25%	84	0%	0%	5	0%	80%	-7.2	-37	$3
2nd Half		247	32	16	35	0	243	3	236	303	525	109	64	82	8	59	0.21	36	20	44	33	106	186	183	9%	27%	84	0%	0%	6	0%	67%	1.3	100	$14
20	Proj	**175**	**21**	**7**	**21**	**0**	**232**		**220**	**309**	**430**	**99**	**108**	**98**	**8**	**61**	**0.22**	**38**	**22**	**40**	**33**	**114**	**136**	**137**	**18%**		**84**	**1%**	**100%**				**-1.8**	**-61**	**$4**

Wendle,Joe

Age: 30	Bats: L	Pos: 2B 3B	Health D	LIMA Plan D
Ht: 6' 1"	Wt: 200		PT/Exp C	Rand Var +4
			Consist F	MM 1433

It was clear his $20 season in 2018 was a fluke, foretold by xBA and xPX. Disastrous 1st half validated it, but path to value via SB reappeared in 2nd half. Upper-scale Statcast sprint speed confirms he still has talent there, but at 30, the window is only open a crack. There's profit potential here now, but only at $5 or under. UP: 20 SB

Yr	Tm	PA	R	HR	RBI	SB	BA	xHR	xBA	OBP	SLG	OPS+	vL+	vR+	bb%	ct%	Eye	G	L	F	h%	HctX	PX	xPX	HR/F	xHR/F	Spd	SBO	SB%	#Wk	DOM	DIS	RAR	BPX	R$
15	aaa	595	64	7	45	10	252			274	380	91			3	78	0.14				31		93				112	11%	81%					73	$10
16	OAK *	615	74	9	58	13	240	1	256	272	361	86	101	76	4	76	0.18	54	21	25	30	94	78	65	5%	5%	139	14%	73%	6	0%	50%	-25.6	49	$10
17	OAK *	506	52	6	45	10	234	0	257	256	350	81	0	128	3	80	0.15	50	20	30	28	129	69	124	33%	0%	118	16%	66%	4	50%	25%	-25.3	55	$6
18	TAM	545	62	7	61	16	300	10	261	354	435	109	113	108	7	80	0.39	46	22	32	36	109	86	76	5%	8%	101	15%	80%	28	36%	29%	20.3	120	$21
19	TAM	263	32	3	19	8	231	2	254	293	340	84	46	95	5	80	0.30	44	23	32	28	89	62	56	5%	3%	120	22%	73%	17	24%	53%	-12.3	70	$3
1st Half		83	4	0	4	1	176	0	217	253	216	63	46	67	4	77	0.18	48	21	31	23	74	31	45	0%	0%	93	8%	100%	7	0%	71%	-7.7	-107	-$12
2nd Half		180	28	3	15	7	256	2	268	311	396	93	46	108	6	82	0.37	43	24	33	30	96	75	61	7%	4%	131	26%	70%	10	40%	40%	-3.1	152	$10
20	Proj	**280**	**32**	**3**	**24**	**8**	**247**		**253**	**297**	**358**	**88**	**70**	**92**	**5**	**80**	**0.26**	**47**	**22**	**31**	**30**	**96**	**64**	**64**	**5%**		**115**	**17%**	**75%**				**-5.2**	**62**	**$7**

Wieters,Matt

Age: 34	Bats: B	Pos: CA	Health C	LIMA Plan D
Ht: 6' 5"	Wt: 235		PT/Exp D	Rand Var +1
			Consist B	MM 2021

On surface, his worst season yet, but as a second-catcher, you could do much worse, because... (1) Mendoza-ish BA debunked by xBA; (2) HctX, xPX trends put power resurrection in play; (3) Above-average 2nd-half BPX. While prior upside is long gone and so-so durability relegates him to PT work, there's also profit here under $5.

Yr	Tm	PA	R	HR	RBI	SB	BA	xHR	xBA	OBP	SLG	OPS+	vL+	vR+	bb%	ct%	Eye	G	L	F	h%	HctX	PX	xPX	HR/F	xHR/F	Spd	SBO	SB%	#Wk	DOM	DIS	RAR	BPX	R$
15	BAL	282	24	8	25	0	267	9	255	319	422	103	100	102	7	74	0.31	43	25	32	33	101	109	113	13%	15%	77	0%	0%	19	53%	37%	6.8	62	$4
16	BAL	464	48	17	66	1	243	17	261	302	409	97	87	98	7	80	0.38	36	24	40	27	107	94	113	13%	13%	81	1%	100%	27	41%	44%	-3.7	100	$8
17	WAS	465	43	10	52	1	225	10	239	288	344	85	91	82	8	78	0.40	42	21	36	27	86	72	100	8%	8%	66	1%	100%	27	30%	41%	-9.9	21	$2
18	WAS	271	24	8	30	0	238	9	234	330	374	97	98	96	11	81	0.67	34	21	45	26	102	76	137	9%	10%	83	1%	0%	18	39%	28%	3.4	110	$2
19	STL	183	15	11	27	1	214	7	244	268	435	93	102	90	7	72	0.26	38	21	41	23	120	112	163	22%	14%	64	6%	50%	23	39%	43%	-3.4	44	$1
1st Half		73	6	4	12	1	221	3	226	260	426	92	45	112	4	68	0.14	38	19	43	26	124	114	134	20%	15%	71	17%	50%	14	36%	43%	-1.4	-22	-$3
2nd Half		110	9	7	15	0	210	4	248	273	440	94	155	78	8	75	0.36	38	22	39	21	116	111	180	23%	13%	76	0%	0%	9	44%	44%	-0.2	111	$3
20	Proj	**245**	**24**	**12**	**36**	**1**	**239**		**244**	**301**	**427**	**98**	**104**	**96**	**8**	**76**	**0.35**	**38**	**21**	**41**	**27**	**108**	**96**	**141**	**17%**		**68**	**3%**	**46%**				**5.7**	**19**	**$6**

Wilkerson,Steve

Age: 28	Bats: B	Pos: CF LF	Health B	LIMA Plan D
Ht: 6' 1"	Wt: 195		PT/Exp F	Rand Var -1
			Consist B	MM 2103

10-35-.225 in 361 PA at BAL. If you can't offset whiffs with homers or steals in today's times, you're in trouble. Even as xPX inched to average, xHR and bottom-scale exit velocity + hard hit % give little hope he can sustain this tiny power spike. And career-best h% in 2nd half couldn't move needle on BA as strikeouts piled up. Pass.

Yr	Tm	PA	R	HR	RBI	SB	BA	xHR	xBA	OBP	SLG	OPS+	vL+	vR+	bb%	ct%	Eye	G	L	F	h%	HctX	PX	xPX	HR/F	xHR/F	Spd	SBO	SB%	#Wk	DOM	DIS	RAR	BPX	R$
15																																			
16																																			
17	aa	262	27	5	24	4	239			289	327	83			7	73	0.26				31		54				92	10%	63%					-61	$2
18	BAL *	147	14	3	13	1	195	0	218	240	322	78	35	79	6	71	0.21	47	17	37	25	35	90	56	0%	0%	85	14%	30%	6	33%	67%	-7.8	-13	-$2
19	BAL *	425	51	12	42	5	231	6	225	276	379	87	61	104	6	70	0.20	45	19	36	30	80	88	100	13%	8%	104	10%	63%	24	21%	54%	-12.7	-19	$6
1st Half		242	31	8	26	4	229	3	233	265	373	85	30	105	5	71	0.17	47	21	32	29	79	78	85	17%	8%	110	13%	68%	11	27%	64%	-8.2	-30	$7
2nd Half		183	20	4	16	1	235	3	218	308	389	92	77	104	7	67	0.25	44	16	40	32	79	102	116	9%	7%	104	6%	50%	13	15%	46%	-3.3	-4	$3
20	Proj	**280**	**30**	**6**	**26**	**3**	**220**		**218**	**281**	**349**	**85**	**63**	**97**	**6**	**70**	**0.22**	**45**	**18**	**37**	**29**	**79**	**80**	**104**	**9%**		**95**	**10%**	**51%**				**-7.7**	**-65**	**$4**

Winker,Jesse

Age: 26	Bats: L	Pos: LF CF	Health D	LIMA Plan B
Ht: 6' 3"	Wt: 215		PT/Exp C	Rand Var +3
			Consist C	MM 2055

Four reasons he's still a post-hype play worth taking: (1) Steady BPX growth crested in 2nd half; (2) Back strain behind late power dip; (3) .300 BA potential supported by xBA; (4) 80% higher launch angle from 2018 gives him blueprint to unlock power. Even with chronic woes vL, there's still a step forward in sight. UP: .300 BA, 25 HR

Yr	Tm	PA	R	HR	RBI	SB	BA	xHR	xBA	OBP	SLG	OPS+	vL+	vR+	bb%	ct%	Eye	G	L	F	h%	HctX	PX	xPX	HR/F	xHR/F	Spd	SBO	SB%	#Wk	DOM	DIS	RAR	BPX	R$
15	aa	509	60	13	48	7	264			359	407	107			13	78	0.69				31		96				95	8%	62%					127	$13
16	aaa	434	35	3	40	0	280			369	357	99			12	82	0.80				33		55				80	0%	0%					69	$6
17	CIN *	468	48	9	49	3	283	4	247	355	409	103	47	138	10	81	0.60	53	16	31	33	118	77	100	23%	13%	80	6%	32%	13	54%	15%	-3.6	100	$11
18	CIN	334	38	7	43	0	299	10	265	405	431	116	96	120	15	84	1.07	42	24	34	34	135	79	107	9%	13%	68	0%	0%	18	56%	22%	13.2	167	$9
19	CIN	384	51	16	38	0	269	11	302	357	473	110	58	119	10	82	0.63	49	26	25	29	117	99	88	23%	16%	102	2%	0%	22	45%	23%	3.4	226	$8
1st Half		262	36	12	25	0	248	9	298	328	457	105	57	114	9	81	0.51	51	26	24	26	114	102	99	27%	20%	98	2%	0%	15	53%	27%	-2.5	200	$9
2nd Half		122	15	4	13	0	317	2	310	418	510	122	63	130	13	86	1.00	45	28	27	34	123	92	65	17%	8%	116	3%	0%	7	29%	14%	6.4	289	$4
20	Proj	**525**	**63**	**19**	**58**	**1**	**289**		**287**	**383**	**476**	**116**	**72**	**123**	**12**	**83**	**0.81**	**46**	**24**	**29**	**31**	**125**	**93**	**92**	**17%**		**89**	**3%**	**23%**				**23.0**	**166**	**$18**

STEPHEN NICKRAND

Wolters,Tony

Age: 28 Bats: L Pos: CA	Health	C	LIMA Plan	D+
	PT/Exp	D	Rand Var	-1
Ht: 5' 10" Wt: 197	Consist	B	MM	0223

Hitters with zero pop—even catchers—need to give you something else to offset the ground you'll lose in HR. Early on, he did that with BA, but pullback was inevitable due to inflated h% and suspect xBA. History of intriguing Spd points to potential for a few steals, but likelihood he ever gets a green light is nearly nil. FA fodder.

Yr	Tm	PA	R	HR	RBI	SB	BA	xHR	xBA	OBP	SLG	OPS+	vL+	vR+	bb%	ct%	Eye	G	L	F	h%	HctX	PX	xPX	HR/F	xHR/F	Spd	SBO	SB%	#Wk	DOM	DIS	RAR	BPX	R$
15	aa	258	21	2	15	3	198			256	263	72			7	72	0.28				27		49				111	9%	55%					-57	-$3
16	COL	230	27	3	30	4	259	3	258	327	395	98	78	101	9	74	0.40	48	23	29	34	64	98	72	7%	7%	104	9%	80%	25	36%	48%	0.4	74	$4
17	COL *	322	34	2	22	0	239	1	236	323	312	85	66	87	11	75	0.50	55	22	24	31	64	51	42	0%	2%	98	2%	0%	24	21%	54%	-6.6	-15	$0
18	COL	216	19	3	27	2	170	3	246	292	286	80	84	78	12	82	0.79	57	15	28	19	64	58	38	7%	7%	120	4%	100%	28	39%	29%	-6.2	120	-$2
19	COL	411	42	1	42	0	262	2	255	337	329	88	97	84	9	81	0.53	44	27	29	32	84	42	66	1%	2%	117	1%	0%	28	36%	36%	-6.7	44	$3
1st Half		215	27	1	23	0	296	1	278	364	392	101	100	102	9	84	0.63	44	28	28	35	84	55	64	2%	2%	119	2%	0%	15	47%	27%	5.4	133	$6
2nd Half		196	15	0	19	0	225	1	227	308	260	75	95	66	9	78	0.45	44	25	30	29	85	26	69	0%	2%	107	0%	0%	13	23%	46%	-7.7	-56	$1
20	Proj	**420**	**42**	**3**	**44**	**2**	**241**		**243**	**327**	**319**	**87**	**91**	**85**	**10**	**79**	**0.53**	**49**	**23**	**28**	**30**	**74**	**45**	**57**	**3%**		**116**	**2%**	**61%**				**-0.1**	**-13**	**$3**

Wong,Kolten

Age: 29 Bats: L Pos: 2B	Health	B	LIMA Plan	B
	PT/Exp	B	Rand Var	-3
Ht: 5' 9" Wt: 185	Consist	C	MM	1435

Finally resurrected the multi-category value he showed four years prior. But skills suggest not much has changed from before: HR growth product of few more FB, spike in steals driven by green light and return of SB acumen more than tools. With exit velocity in bottom 2% of league, xBA pessimism remains warranted. DN: .250 BA, 10 SB

Yr	Tm	PA	R	HR	RBI	SB	BA	xHR	xBA	OBP	SLG	OPS+	vL+	vR+	bb%	ct%	Eye	G	L	F	h%	HctX	PX	xPX	HR/F	xHR/F	Spd	SBO	SB%	#Wk	DOM	DIS	RAR	BPX	R$
15	STL	613	71	11	61	15	262	10	262	321	386	99	76	106	6	83	0.38	45	22	33	30	98	80	86	7%	7%	107	17%	65%	27	30%	26%	-2.9	111	$17
16	STL *	392	46	8	31	8	249	5	253	323	384	96	88	92	9	83	0.63	46	20	34	28	87	67	79	6%	6%	155	8%	100%	26	35%	38%	-5.1	149	$7
17	STL	411	55	4	42	8	285	4	270	376	412	106	93	107	10	83	0.68	48	20	32	33	95	79	72	4%	4%	112	9%	80%	22	55%	18%	3.1	155	$11
18	STL	407	41	9	38	6	249	7	263	332	388	100	85	103	8	83	0.52	49	20	31	28	86	80	59	10%	8%	97	12%	55%	25	44%	36%	-3.5	140	$7
19	STL	549	61	11	59	24	285	9	259	361	423	104	96	106	9	83	0.57	44	20	36	33	97	71	83	8%	7%	106	20%	86%	26	42%	31%	11.8	141	$21
1st Half		303	32	7	33	14	239	6	240	325	371	93	106	89	10	83	0.67	41	17	42	26	107	67	105	8%	7%	93	19%	100%	15	40%	20%	-3.3	133	$18
2nd Half		246	29	4	26	10	341	3	281	407	486	118	84	127	7	82	0.45	48	24	28	40	86	76	57	8%	6%	117	20%	71%	11	45%	45%	14.3	156	$25
20	Proj	**525**	**63**	**11**	**56**	**17**	**270**		**262**	**347**	**410**	**102**	**88**	**105**	**8**	**83**	**0.52**	**46**	**20**	**34**	**31**	**92**	**73**	**72**	**8%**		**111**	**17%**	**76%**				**9.0**	**157**	**$20**

Yastrzemski,Mike

Age: 29 Bats: L Pos: LF RF	Health	A	LIMA Plan	B
	PT/Exp	C	Rand Var	-3
Ht: 5' 11" Wt: 180	Consist	C	MM	4225

21-55-.272 in 411 PA at SF. Did granddaddy proud in MLB debut, as launch angle and barrel rate teamed to uncork power. While xPX and xHR both support 20+ HR, we can't ignore history of so-so pop and bad MLEs, nor that he needed 2,300 PA in high minors before getting a sniff in majors—even with surname on his side. Expect regression.

Yr	Tm	PA	R	HR	RBI	SB	BA	xHR	xBA	OBP	SLG	OPS+	vL+	vR+	bb%	ct%	Eye	G	L	F	h%	HctX	PX	xPX	HR/F	xHR/F	Spd	SBO	SB%	#Wk	DOM	DIS	RAR	BPX	R$
15	aa	511	52	5	48	7	215			268	320	82			7	76	0.31				27		78				103	14%	45%					41	$2
16	a/a	520	55	11	48	11	185			269	295	77			10	69	0.37				24		74				108	13%	76%					-29	$0
17	a/a	388	48	12	47	2	213			282	361	86			9	67	0.29				28		92				115	6%	49%					-9	$2
18	a/a	467	44	8	43	6	198			265	321	81			8	71	0.31				26		85				105	13%	48%					3	$2
19	SF *	563	91	28	73	3	264	22	253	328	508	111	123	110	9	70	0.32	34	23	43	32	103	139	142	18%	19%	113	8%	34%	20	50%	30%	4.8	163	$17
1st Half		273	45	12	33	1	243	5	249	310	464	103	126	90	9	67	0.30	35	27	39	31	94	131	123	17%	17%	116	11%	24%	7	43%	43%	-4.9	107	$11
2nd Half		290	46	16	40	2	285	18	262	349	550	119	121	118	8	72	0.33	34	21	45	34	109	146	150	19%	21%	111	6%	50%	13	54%	23%	10.7	215	$23
20	Proj	**490**	**66**	**22**	**59**	**4**	**245**		**246**	**313**	**460**	**104**	**102**	**104**	**8**	**70**	**0.31**	**36**	**23**	**41**	**30**	**103**	**123**	**139**	**17%**		**115**	**9%**	**44%**				**1.3**	**86**	**$15**

Yelich,Christian

Age: 28 Bats: L Pos: RF	Health	A	LIMA Plan	C
	PT/Exp	A	Rand Var	-3
Ht: 6' 3" Wt: 195	Consist	F	MM	4455

40/40 in sights before broken kneecap got in way. Former GB tilt now long in the past, pushing xPX to elite heights. Statcast exit velocity, barrel%, and hard hit% all in top 4% of league, further cementing new .300-BA, 40-HR baseline. Don't hesitate to bid $40 unless knee recovery is slow; even then, any pullback will be SB-only.

Yr	Tm	PA	R	HR	RBI	SB	BA	xHR	xBA	OBP	SLG	OPS+	vL+	vR+	bb%	ct%	Eye	G	L	F	h%	HctX	PX	xPX	HR/F	xHR/F	Spd	SBO	SB%	#Wk	DOM	DIS	RAR	BPX	R$
15	MIA	525	63	7	44	16	300	11	282	366	416	109	97	111	9	79	0.47	62	23	15	37	114	85	82	13%	20%	121	14%	76%	25	48%	32%	8.7	105	$20
16	MIA	659	78	21	98	9	298	26	289	376	483	117	97	121	11	76	0.52	57	23	20	36	117	118	97	24%	29%	93	7%	69%	27	52%	22%	29.6	146	$25
17	MIA	694	100	18	81	16	282	21	272	369	439	108	96	111	12	77	0.58	55	19	25	34	110	94	77	15%	18%	109	9%	89%	27	48%	30%	10.9	127	$25
18	MIL	651	118	36	110	22	326	38	310	402	598	138	137	138	10	76	0.50	52	25	24	37	134	156	128	35%	37%	135	15%	85%	27	56%	22%	71.3	313	$44
19	MIL	580	100	44	97	30	329	41	306	429	671	146	122	159	14	76	0.68	43	21	36	36	133	172	146	33%	31%	113	19%	94%	25	60%	20%	74.9	389	$42
1st Half		341	64	29	63	18	328	29	317	425	704	151	130	161	14	78	0.75	43	18	39	33	145	182	173	33%	33%	119	20%	95%	15	73%	13%	49.2	459	$52
2nd Half		239	36	15	34	12	332	12	292	435	624	140	114	156	14	73	0.60	43	25	32	39	116	156	104	33%	26%	107	18%	92%	10	40%	30%	28.1	289	$29
20	Proj	**630**	**104**	**43**	**102**	**23**	**319**		**298**	**408**	**624**	**139**	**123**	**146**	**12**	**76**	**0.58**	**44**	**23**	**34**	**35**	**125**	**157**	**118**	**30%**		**117**	**15%**	**85%**				**74.1**	**330**	**$43**

Zimmer,Bradley

Age: 27 Bats: L Pos: RF	Health	F	LIMA Plan	D
	PT/Exp	F	Rand Var	+3
Ht: 6' 5" Wt: 220	Consist	C	MM	3501

0-0-.000 in 14 PA at CLE. That MLB line is a microcosm of the development of this former top prospect. Huge holes in swing are showing no signs of abating. Without that, the power/speed tools he does flash have little shot at manifesting. Steep GB tilt dampens hope for sustained power anyway. Nothing more than a dart throw now.

Yr	Tm	PA	R	HR	RBI	SB	BA	xHR	xBA	OBP	SLG	OPS+	vL+	vR+	bb%	ct%	Eye	G	L	F	h%	HctX	PX	xPX	HR/F	xHR/F	Spd	SBO	SB%	#Wk	DOM	DIS	RAR	BPX	R$
15	aa	203	22	6	22	11	208			270	354	87			8	70	0.28				27		108				95	33%	83%					30	$4
16	a/a	533	62	13	51	31	230			324	382	96			12	63	0.38				33		115				105	36%	67%					11	$17
17	CLE *	469	58	12	50	25	248	12	236	309	410	96	83	94	8	66	0.26	48	20	32	35	90	112	83	13%	20%	121	29%	85%	18	17%	61%	-3.9	27	$16
18	CLE *	146	16	3	10	6	208	4	195	259	306	78	107	75	6	58	0.16	48	24	28	33	94	82	123	13%	25%	103	24%	86%	9	11%	78%	-5.8	-183	$0
19	CLE *	51	7	2	4	2	218	0	232	270	407	90	0	17	7	61	0.18	80	0	20	32	35	127	113	0%	0%	124	18%	100%	4	0%	75%	-1.0	-7	-$2
1st Half																																			
2nd Half		51	7	2	4	2	218	0	232	270	407	89	0	17	7	61	0.18	80	0	20	32	35	127	113	0%	0%	126	18%	100%	4	0%	75%	-0.9	-11	-$2
20	Proj	**210**	**26**	**5**	**19**	**8**	**221**		**217**	**289**	**370**	**89**	**97**	**85**	**8**	**63**	**0.23**	**50**	**19**	**31**	**32**	**92**	**101**	**107**	**13%**		**123**	**24%**	**81%**				**-6.3**	**-36**	**$6**

Zimmerman,Ryan

Age: 35 Bats: R Pos: 1B	Health	F	LIMA Plan	C+
	PT/Exp	C	Rand Var	0
Ht: 6' 3" Wt: 215	Consist	D	MM	3133

Post-season heroics put a positive spin on another abbreviated campaign. Plantar fasciitis was the culprit this time, but it won't be the last. "F" health advises this is who he is, and that 2017 is looking like a clear aberration now. Best-case scenario is 400 AB and 20 HR. Problem is, that production doesn't mean what it used to.

Yr	Tm	PA	R	HR	RBI	SB	BA	xHR	xBA	OBP	SLG	OPS+	vL+	vR+	bb%	ct%	Eye	G	L	F	h%	HctX	PX	xPX	HR/F	xHR/F	Spd	SBO	SB%	#Wk	DOM	DIS	RAR	BPX	R$
15	WAS	390	43	16	73	1	249	19	275	308	465	108	146	92	8	77	0.42	48	17	35	28	124	146	141	16%	20%	78	1%	100%	17	47%	35%	-3.9	184	$10
16	WAS	467	60	15	46	4	218	16	243	272	370	87	92	84	6	76	0.28	49	17	35	25	106	94	99	13%	14%	92	6%	80%	24	50%	46%	-27.5	57	$4
17	WAS	576	90	36	108	1	303	33	289	358	573	125	138	118	8	76	0.35	46	20	34	34	124	152	138	26%	24%	88	1%	100%	27	59%	30%	22.8	209	$26
18	WAS	323	33	13	51	1	264	19	282	337	486	114	159	98	9	81	0.55	49	17	34	29	118	129	128	16%	24%	96	3%	50%	18	61%	22%	3.7	253	$8
19	WAS	190	20	6	27	0	257	7	246	321	415	98	126	86	9	77	0.44	47	20	33	30	110	86	118	14%	16%	87	0%	0%	15	27%	27%	-3.8	85	$1
1st Half		94	7	3	11	0	207	2	199	298	354	87	90	86	12	77	0.58	47	13	41	23	83	77	108	12%	8%	99	0%	0%	7	43%	14%	-4.4	89	-$4
2nd Half		96	13	3	16	0	303	5	281	344	472	108	160	86	6	78	0.30	47	27	26	36	134	95	128	17%	28%	79	0%	0%	8	13%	38%	2.0	93	$6
20	Proj	**385**	**45**	**15**	**61**	**1**	**267**		**263**	**328**	**462**	**106**	**138**	**94**	**8**	**78**	**0.41**	**48**	**20**	**33**	**30**	**116**	**105**	**125**	**17%**		**88**	**1%**	**64%**				**7.3**	**101**	**$13**

Zunino,Mike

Age: 29 Bats: R Pos: CA	Health	B	LIMA Plan	D
	PT/Exp	C	Rand Var	+5
Ht: 6' 2" Wt: 235	Consist	D	MM	4003

Actually improved strikeout rate but lost nearly 50 points in BA. Easy to blame a career-worst hit rate, but the problems run deeper. Mendoza-ish xBA 3 of past 5 years; xPX on steady decline; Statcast metrics worst since 2015 debacle. Even those still placing hope on his draft pick pedigree need to use 2018 as an optimistic baseline.

Yr	Tm	PA	R	HR	RBI	SB	BA	xHR	xBA	OBP	SLG	OPS+	vL+	vR+	bb%	ct%	Eye	G	L	F	h%	HctX	PX	xPX	HR/F	xHR/F	Spd	SBO	SB%	#Wk	DOM	DIS	RAR	BPX	R$
15	SEA *	427	33	13	33	0	183	14	186	224	315	75	72	73	5	64	0.15	33	17	50	25	81	102	121	10%	13%	72	1%	0%	21	14%	62%	-19.6	-78	-$4
16	SEA *	499	53	26	76	0	228	11	227	304	446	102	113	103	10	66	0.32	29	18	53	28	94	146	155	23%	21%	83	1%	0%	14	29%	43%	7.4	83	$8
17	SEA *	479	57	29	72	1	250	24	245	317	515	112	117	109	9	61	0.25	32	22	46	34	96	186	141	24%	23%	75	1%	100%	24	50%	50%	18.0	109	$11
18	SEA	405	37	20	44	0	201	23	212	259	410	93	80	98	6	60	0.16	37	19	44	27	87	156	131	20%	23%	67	0%	0%	22	27%	45%	-1.2	-3	$3
19	TAM	289	30	9	32	0	165	13	187	232	312	72	61	78	7	63	0.20	40	14	46	22	85	93	96	12%	17%	67	0%	0%	26	23%	69%	-12.8	-133	-$3
1st Half		164	16	3	18	0	182	8	207	232	318	73	72	74	4	68	0.14	40	16	43	25	103	91	110	7%	18%	71	0%	0%	13	23%	69%	-9.0	-93	-$4
2nd Half		125	14	6	14	0	143	5	158	232	304	71	52	84	10	57	0.27	41	9	50	17	59	96	73	19%	16%	77	0%	0%	13	23%	69%	-7.1	-181	-$1
20	Proj	**315**	**33**	**14**	**37**	**0**	**205**		**198**	**271**	**394**	**89**	**76**	**95**	**7**	**61**	**0.20**	**38**	**16**	**47**	**28**	**83**	**121**	**112**	**17%**		**67**	**0%**	**59%**				**-0.7**	**-110**	**$4**

STEPHEN NICKRAND

THE NEXT TIER (*=includes MLEs)

Batters

The preceding section provided player boxes and analysis for 427 batters. As we know, far more than 427 batters will play in the major leagues in 2020. Many of those additional hitters are covered in the minor league section, but that still leaves a gap: established major leaguers who don't play enough, or well enough, to merit a player box.

This section looks to fill that gap. Here, you will find "The Next Tier" of batters who are mostly past their growth years, but who are likely to see some playing time in 2020. We are including their 2018-19 statline here for reference for you to do your own analysis. This way, if Wilmer Difo looks like an intriguing deep-league FAAB possibility, you can find solace in the fact that he's contributed near-double digit SB the past two seasons. Or if you're dredging through the catcher pool in May and Kevan Smith has come upon some MLB playing time, this is a good reminder that he did hit .289 in not quite 200 AB in 2019.

Batter	Yr	B	Age	Pos	PA	R	HR	RBI	SB	BA	xBA	OPS+	vL+	vR+	bb%	ct%	Eye	G/L/F	HctX	PX	xPX	Spd	SBO	SB%	BPX
Austin, Tyler	18*	R	26	37	412	51	25	65	1	227	246	105	118	99	6	62	0.18	38/24/38	83	177	124	73	4	33	93
	19*	R	27		239	40	12	31	4	208	204	97	106	72	12	57	0.33	41/15/44	86	144	167	102	10	77	7
Avila, Alex	18	L	31	2	234	13	7	20	0	165	170	83	93	81	16	54	0.41	49/22/29	101	115	154	53	0	0	-143
	19	L	32		201	22	9	24	1	207	230	103	89	106	18	59	0.53	52/23/25	108	145	153	78	2	100	41
Beckham, Gordon	18*	R	31	4	448	47	7	36	5	221	196	86	95	48	10	80	0.53	42/9/48	67	65	101	116	7	66	90
	19	R	32		240	29	6	15	3	215	231	85	57	95	5	70	0.19	40/22/38	101	96	121	126	10	75	22
Bonifacio, Jorge	18*	R	25	o	326	40	4	30	0	247	226	98	108	86	11	71	0.41	34/23/43	93	100	111	97	1	0	50
	19*	R	26		500	51	13	48	4	190	214	76	148	74	6	69	0.20	46/15/38	74	83	21	132	11	48	-11
Bour, Justin	18	L	30	3	501	49	20	59	2	227	231	103	79	112	15	71	0.59	45/19/36	97	108	109	58	1	100	60
	19*	L	31		380	43	18	50	1	199	218	91	68	85	11	66	0.35	46/14/40	94	120	133	50	3	45	-4
Casali, Curtis	18*	R	29	2	256	25	7	31	0	259	259	99	137	97	7	75	0.30	37/28/35	91	96	93	65	3	0	47
	19	R	30		236	24	8	32	0	251	248	98	96	99	11	71	0.42	29/28/42	95	91	109	83	0	0	26
Castillo, Welington	18*	R	31	02	220	18	6	17	1	238	217	89	104	95	5	71	0.19	41/21/38	97	82	102	67	2	100	-60
	19	R	32		272	20	13	45	0	207	213	88	89	91	6	67	0.20	45/16/39	81	122	106	56	0	0	-4
Cervelli, Francisco	18	R	32	2	404	39	12	57	2	259	237	112	112	111	13	75	0.61	39/19/42	93	103	110	118	5	40	147
	19	R	33		160	15	3	12	1	213	217	86	67	92	8	71	0.32	43/17/40	92	83	108	91	3	100	-11
Cozart, Zack	18	R	32	5	253	29	5	18	0	219	249	91	77	95	8	81	0.45	38/21/41	110	86	113	108	0	0	143
	19	R	33		107	4	0	7	0	124	202	43	42	43	5	84	0.31	31/21/48	89	14	80	74	0	0	-74
Descalso, Daniel	18	L	31	4	422	54	13	57	0	238	235	109	124	105	15	68	0.58	30/24/46	109	134	168	97	1	0	143
	19*	L	32		224	24	3	18	2	164	196	69	60	70	12	66	0.40	45/20/35	72	55	102	111	6	67	-122
Difo, Wilmer	18	R	26	6	456	55	7	42	10	230	246	90	63	97	9	80	0.48	42/24/34	62	67	54	150	12	77	123
	19*	R	27		394	49	5	29	9	247	240	85	101	78	7	75	0.32	48/24/28	53	51	33	112	16	56	-30
Duda, Lucas	18	L	32	3	367	35	14	50	1	241	231	101	71	111	8	69	0.27	29/26/45	98	115	135	72	1	100	20
	19*	L	33		225	14	5	22	0	166	181	68	41	85	8	64	0.25	32/19/49	91	75	107	49	0	0	-189
Freeman, Michael	18*	L	30	4	321	34	4	25	4	205	204	74	0	0	5	72	0.20	44/20/36	265	59	-27	106	19	34	-67
	19*	L	31		244	31	6	26	2	264	228	100	105	97	12	65	0.41	49/25/26	77	84	58	109	6	46	-48
Freese, David	18	R	35	3	312	38	11	51	0	296	259	115	122	108	8	74	0.33	52/22/26	99	105	104	121	0	0	117
	19	R	36		186	35	11	29	0	315	295	133	117	156	12	73	0.52	44/25/31	120	160	105	84	0	0	263
Gallagher, Cameron	18*	R	25	2	356	26	4	39	1	221	205	79	47	89	6	82	0.39	29/18/53	61	52	54	61	1	100	53
	19	R	26		142	14	3	12	0	238	240	90	89	90	8	78	0.39	39/22/40	86	73	81	81	3	0	41
Goins, Ryan	18*	L	30	5	256	24	2	12	3	196	226	71	63	81	5	70	0.19	45/27/29	72	63	63	102	9	69	-80
	19*	L	31		463	46	9	44	2	247	214	93	147	74	10	65	0.30	51/18/31	55	91	52	105	6	30	-56
Gonzalez, Carlos	18	L	32	7	504	71	16	64	5	276	257	110	100	114	7	76	0.33	48/16/36	98	120	99	100	6	71	150
	19	L	33		202	22	4	13	0	209	203	80	44	86	11	66	0.38	56/19/24	72	58	62	83	6	0	-144
Harrison, Josh	18	R	30	4	374	41	8	37	3	250	245	91	94	89	5	80	0.26	38/25/37	97	67	114	100	4	100	53
	19*	R	31		174	11	1	10	4	170	213	62	65	64	6	80	0.33	36/18/45	77	48	54	102	22	67	11
Hechavarria, Adeiny	18	R	29	46	321	34	6	31	2	247	241	86	105	79	5	80	0.28	38/25/37	106	59	112	100	3	100	37
	19*	R	30		317	45	9	46	4	247	244	93	114	94	6	77	0.27	47/15/38	104	91	113	95	11	66	85
Heredia, Guillermo	18*	R	27	89	369	32	5	20	3	235	250	89	93	89	9	83	0.63	43/23/33	82	61	64	96	10	40	97
	19*	R	28		260	33	6	23	2	218	229	83	104	68	7	69	0.26	40/24/35	69	87	59	89	10	38	-44
Hernandez, Marco	19*	L	26	4	297	36	3	20	3	251	248	83	95	75	3	72	0.10	52/24/23	66	70	19	115	14	43	-44
Herrera, Rosell	18*	B	25	8	436	39	4	32	7	235	270	88	70	89	6	80	0.33	57/22/22	109	76	77	116	17	51	97
	19*	B	26		296	27	6	31	6	233	238	86	52	92	8	75	0.34	46/20/34	69	74	20	109	12	72	41
Holaday, Bryan	18	R	30	2	166	7	1	16	0	205	219	72	58	77	6	81	0.34	39/23/38	64	36	45	75	0	0	-33
	19*	R	31		235	18	5	21	1	238	264	91	83	111	10	82	0.67	49/22/28	119	71	87	84	5	25	130
Iannetta, Chris	18	R	35	2	360	36	11	36	0	224	232	101	97	103	14	71	0.57	38/23/39	102	103	133	75	0	0	60
	19	R	36		164	20	6	21	0	222	241	97	90	100	11	63	0.33	40/27/33	102	133	131	60	0	0	-4
Jay, Jon	18	L	33	9	586	74	3	40	4	268	273	94	84	97	6	82	0.35	59/24/17	107	48	52	130	5	57	60
	19*	L	34		247	18	0	14	1	266	253	80	80	84	4	81	0.22	51/26/22	60	30	31	92	1	100	-48

THE NEXT TIER (*=includes MLEs)

Batter	Yr	B	Age	Pos	PA	R	HR	RBI	SB	BA	xBA	OPS+	vL+	vR+	bb%	ct%	Eye	G/L/F	HctX	PX	xPX	Spd	SBO	SB%	BPX
Joyce, Matt	18*	L	33	9	280	37	7	17	0	209	242	91	94	93	13	75	0.63	35/26/39	99	87	134	79	3	0	73
	19	L	34		238	32	7	23	0	295	270	114	98	116	16	78	0.84	34/29/36	109	84	95	95	0	0	148
Kang, Jung-ho	18*	R	31	5	42	3	0	3	0	203	283	64	0	91	5	82	0.29	40/40/20	121	16	23	83	14	0	-70
	19*	R	32		215	18	11	28	0	194	234	88	66	93	6	65	0.20	41/21/38	91	132	121	78	0	0	11
Kemp, Matt	18	R	33	7	506	62	21	85	0	290	265	113	115	111	7	75	0.31	35/27/38	120	117	143	61	0	0	93
	19*	R	34		97	6	2	7	0	191	188	63	118	49	3	70	0.09	43/19/38	98	44	83	80	0	0	-200
Kinsler, Ian	18	R	36	4	534	66	14	48	16	240	259	94	68	104	7	87	0.63	37/21/42	94	79	81	85	20	70	177
	19	R	37		281	28	9	22	2	217	234	86	86	85	7	79	0.35	41/17/42	91	79	72	80	11	33	70
Knapp, Andrew	18	B	26	2	215	19	4	15	1	198	196	84	89	82	11	60	0.32	38/26/36	72	88	113	130	2	100	-87
	19	B	27		160	12	2	8	0	213	213	85	84	85	11	63	0.35	37/27/37	81	86	95	88	0	0	-107
Leon, Sandy	18	B	29	2	288	30	5	22	1	177	203	71	65	72	5	72	0.20	41/17/41	70	72	74	64	2	100	-77
	19*	B	30		217	15	5	19	0	180	196	67	67	76	6	72	0.25	35/20/45	64	48	70	86	3	0	-111
Maile, Luke	18	R	27	2	231	22	3	27	2	248	216	97	114	90	11	67	0.37	46/20/34	85	94	100	122	3	100	10
	19	R	28		129	9	2	9	1	151	218	58	36	68	6	72	0.24	42/24/34	71	44	62	103	5	100	-107
Martin, Leonys	18	L	30	8	353	48	11	33	7	255	231	103	80	110	8	76	0.39	36/18/46	106	102	120	130	13	64	143
	19	L	31		264	32	9	19	4	199	198	82	60	91	8	67	0.27	41/15/44	70	84	74	107	17	44	-52
Martin, Russell	18	R	35	2	352	37	10	25	0	194	201	92	95	90	16	72	0.68	51/14/35	79	81	83	82	3	0	33
	19	R	36		249	29	6	20	1	220	224	89	98	85	12	71	0.50	50/21/28	82	61	56	77	2	100	-59
Mathis, Jeff	18	R	35	2	218	15	1	20	0	200	195	75	86	69	9	66	0.30	37/24/39	98	60	126	82	0	0	-137
	19	R	36		244	17	2	12	1	158	179	57	56	58	6	62	0.17	40/22/39	69	52	52	83	3	100	-263
Morales, Kendrys	18	B	35	3	471	47	21	57	2	249	246	107	81	118	11	77	0.53	46/18/36	115	107	135	51	4	40	107
	19	B	36		201	16	2	12	0	194	228	75	74	75	13	85	1.00	54/17/28	121	26	74	76	0	0	37
Nunez, Eduardo	18	R	31	4	502	56	10	44	7	265	262	94	89	95	3	86	0.23	49/19/32	86	70	47	122	8	78	147
	19	R	32		174	13	2	20	5	228	250	73	72	72	2	84	0.15	54/18/27	75	44	24	92	18	83	19
Owings, Christopher	18*	R	26	4	401	43	5	28	12	207	219	77	98	64	6	74	0.26	39/22/38	106	65	123	109	23	64	-13
	19*	R	27		370	33	11	40	10	204	209	81	66	54	7	60	0.18	57/15/28	82	104	65	100	25	58	-111
Pearce, Steve	18	R	35	3	251	35	11	42	0	284	283	123	133	114	12	81	0.71	44/20/36	110	129	122	95	0	0	270
	19*	R	36		124	11	1	10	0	171	189	63	70	63	7	62	0.21	41/24/36	58	56	91	95	0	0	-226
Peterson, Jace	18	L	28	o	246	21	3	28	13	200	232	88	54	93	13	72	0.53	48/19/34	74	88	65	80	29	81	37
	19*	L	29		467	55	9	44	13	236	257	89	93	75	8	78	0.41	43/25/32	95	74	97	95	17	73	67
Pina, Manny	18	R	31	2	337	39	9	28	2	252	260	97	80	101	6	80	0.34	40/26/34	99	83	103	87	3	100	87
	19	R	32		179	10	7	25	0	228	221	96	126	70	9	68	0.32	36/21/43	91	110	108	58	0	0	0
Plawecki, Kevin	18	R	27	2	277	33	7	30	0	210	229	95	97	93	10	73	0.43	48/14/38	95	104	95	105	2	0	93
	19	R	28		174	13	3	17	0	222	233	84	74	88	7	80	0.39	42/18/40	83	70	48	72	3	0	56
Prado, Martin	18	R	34	35	209	16	1	18	1	244	247	82	73	83	5	82	0.31	47/25/28	92	44	58	83	4	50	7
	19	R	35		260	26	2	15	0	233	243	74	82	68	5	83	0.29	50/22/29	103	36	58	89	0	0	0
Rickard, Joey	18*	R	27	79	403	47	10	44	6	238	235	95	110	92	9	76	0.40	35/22/43	82	93	101	105	9	76	100
	19*	R	28		446	54	9	34	5	247	242	94	97	79	9	75	0.38	41/21/38	79	88	80	150	9	51	126
Riddle, J.T.	18*	L	26	8	426	41	11	51	2	241	255	93	65	97	6	78	0.30	48/23/29	92	80	87	116	5	34	83
	19*	L	27		265	33	9	27	2	189	245	76	129	68	4	74	0.15	50/17/33	110	95	122	88	7	100	22
Robertson, Daniel	18	R	24	45	340	46	9	34	2	262	241	110	116	107	13	73	0.56	51/19/30	93	102	77	94	4	50	93
	19	R	25		354	32	4	26	3	214	213	78	87	75	10	71	0.41	53/19/28	80	45	44	98	5	58	-96
Rodriguez, Sean	18*	R	33	5	212	24	6	24	2	171	186	81	110	69	12	61	0.35	33/19/48	60	103	105	113	7	57	-43
	19*	R	34		186	29	7	20	1	219	210	95	95	93	11	58	0.32	42/23/35	81	126	94	104	5	50	-44
Smith, Kevan	18*	R	30	2	305	30	6	33	1	258	251	90	154	79	5	85	0.38	63/16/21	75	54	52	80	1	100	70
	19	R	31		211	21	5	20	2	251	289	94	119	79	8	81	0.43	50/28/23	112	79	70	69	4	100	85
Solano, Donovan	18*	R	30	4	324	26	3	29	3	241	237	81	0	0	3	83	0.20	44/20/36	0	55	-27	85	6	68	33
	19*	R	31		321	35	5	34	0	307	280	101	110	104	5	79	0.26	37/34/29	104	64	77	111	1	0	48
Taylor, Michael	18	R	27	8	385	46	6	28	24	227	227	89	86	90	8	67	0.25	51/18/31	80	99	83	127	38	80	10
	19*	R	28		336	41	9	33	15	226	225	91	101	79	8	62	0.24	46/21/33	103	119	141	104	33	67	-22
Tilson, Charlie	18*	L	25	9	403	28	0	31	11	219	225	72	48	92	6	78	0.28	65/16/19	42	27	11	113	17	66	-63
	19*	L	26		407	43	3	37	7	230	237	77	43	83	6	76	0.26	56/20/25	84	46	44	115	12	66	-41
Trumbo, Mark	18*	R	32	0	383	42	17	46	0	254	247	102	109	104	7	74	0.27	42/23/35	109	107	111	80	0	0	67
	19*	R	33		90	5	3	10	0	171	229	77	67	63	7	68	0.24	50/21/29	98	117	57	68	0	0	4
White, Tyler	18*	R	27	3	521	62	21	76	1	261	256	111	140	115	10	79	0.53	39/19/43	95	118	101	88	2	22	190
	19	R	28		279	18	3	23	0	208	214	81	62	92	13	68	0.46	41/24/35	82	69	82	49	0	0	-115
Williams, Nick	18	L	24	7	448	53	17	50	3	256	248	104	87	107	7	73	0.29	44/24/32	81	99	87	115	5	60	70
	19*	L	25		312	34	10	24	1	223	234	86	38	62	5	63	0.13	40/29/32	69	112	94	109	1	100	-48
Zobrist, Ben	18	B	37	4	520	67	9	58	3	305	277	113	109	114	11	87	0.92	48/22/30	114	78	95	112	5	43	220
	19	B	38	0	176	24	1	17	0	260	236	89	76	91	13	84	0.96	55/19/26	73	31	33	93	0	0	63

The following section contains player boxes for every pitcher who had significant playing time in 2019 and/or is expected to get fantasy roster-worthy innings in 2020. You will find some prospects here, specifically the most impactful names who we project to play in 2020. For more complete prospect coverage, see our Prospects section.

Snapshot Section

The top band of each player box contains the following information:

Age as of Opening Day 2020.

Throws right (R) or left (L).

Role: Starters (SP) are those projected to face 20+ batters per game; the rest are relievers (RP).

Ht/Wt: Each batter's height and weight.

Type evaluates the extent to which a pitcher allows the ball to be put into play and his ground ball or fly ball tendency. CON (contact) represents pitchers who allow the ball to be put into play a great deal. PWR (power) represents those with high strikeout and/or walk totals who keep the ball out of play. GB are those who have a ground ball rate more than 50%; xGB are those who have a GB rate more than 55%. FB are those who have a fly ball rate more than 40%; xFB are those who have a FB rate more than 45%.

Reliability Grades analyze each pitcher's forecast risk, on an A-F scale. High grades go to those who have accumulated few disabled list days (Health), have a history of substantial and regular major league playing time (PT/Exp) and have displayed consistent performance over the past three years, using xERA (Consist).

LIMA Plan Grade evaluates how well that pitcher would be a good fit for a team using the LIMA Plan draft strategy. Best grades go to pitchers who have excellent base skills and had a 2019 dollar value less than $20. Lowest grades will go to poor skills and values more than $20.

Random Variance Score (Rand Var) measures the impact random variance had on the pitcher's 2019 stats and the probability that his 2020 performance will exceed or fall short of 2019. The variables tracked are those prone to regression—H%, S%, HR/F and xERA to ERA variance. Players are rated on a scale of −5 to +5 with positive scores indicating rebounds and negative scores indicating corrections. Note that this score is computer-generated and the projections will override it on occasion.

Mayberry Method (MM) acknowledges the imprecision of the forecasting process by projecting player performance in broad strokes. The four digits of MM each represent a fantasy-relevant skill—ERA, strikeout rate, saves potential and playing time (IP)—and are all on a scale of 0 to 5.

Commentaries for each pitcher provide a brief analysis of his skills and the potential impact on performance in 2020. MLB statistics are listed first for those who played only a portion of 2019 at the major league level. Note that these commentaries generally look at performance related issues only. Role and playing time expectations may impact these analyses, so you will have to adjust accordingly. Upside (UP) and downside (DN) statistical potential appears for some players; these are less grounded in hard data and more speculative of skills potential.

Player Stat Section

The past five years' statistics represent the total accumulated in the majors as well as in Triple-A, Double-A ball and various foreign leagues during each year. All non-major league stats have been converted to a major league equivalent (MLE) performance level. Minor league levels below Double-A are not included.

Nearly all baseball publications separate a player's statistical experiences in the major leagues from the minor leagues and outside leagues. While this may be appropriate for official record-keeping purposes, it is not an easy-to-analyze snapshot of a player's complete performance for a given year.

Bill James has proven that minor league statistics (converted to MLEs), at Double-A level or above, provide as accurate a record of a player's performance as major league statistics. Other researchers have also devised conversion factors for foreign leagues. Since these are adequate barometers, we include them in the pool of historical data for each year.

Team designations: An asterisk (*) appearing with a team name means that Triple-A and/or Double-A numbers are included in that year's stat line. Any stints of less than 10 IP are not included (to screen out most rehab appearances). A designation of "a/a" means the stats were accumulated at both AA and AAA levels that year. "for" represents a foreign or independent league. The designation "2TM" appears whenever a player was on more than one major league team, crossing leagues, in a season. "2AL" and "2NL" represent more than one team in the same league. Players who were cut during the season and finished 2019 as a free agent are designated as FAA (Free agent, AL) and FAN (Free agent, NL).

Stats: Descriptions of all the categories appear in the Encyclopedia.

- The leading decimal point has been suppressed on some categories to conserve space.
- Data for platoons (vL+, vR+), Ball% and SwK, balls-in-play (G/L/F), HR/F and xHR/F, consistency (Wk#, DOM, DIS), xWHIP and velocity (Vel) are for major league performance only.
- Formulas that use BIP data, like xERA and BPV, are used for years in which G/L/F data is available. Where feasible, older versions of these formulas are used otherwise.

Earned run average is presented alongside skills-based xERA. WHIP appears next, next to skill-based expected WHIP (xWHIP), followed by opponents' OPS splits vs. left-handed and right-handed batters (indexed to league average). Batters faced per game (BF/G) provide a quick view of a pitcher's role—starters will generally have levels over 20.

Basic pitching skills are measured with Control, or walk rate (Ctl), Dominance, or strikeout rate (Dom), and Command, or strikeout-to-walk rate (Cmd). Ball% and Swinging strike rate (SwK) are also presented with these basic skills. Our research shows that Ball% serves as a useful tool for validating Ctl, and SwK serves as a similar check on Dom. Vel is the pitcher's average fastball velocity.

Once the ball leaves the bat, it will either be a (G)round ball, (L)ine drive or (F)ly ball.

Random variance indicators include hit rate (H%)—often referred to as batting average on balls-in-play (BABIP)—which tends to regress to 30%. Normal strand rates (S%) fall within the tolerances of 65% to 80%. The ratio of home runs to fly balls (HR/F) is another sanity check; levels far from the league average of 14% are prone to regression, as is HR/F vs. xHR/F disparity.

In looking at consistency for starting pitchers, we track games started (GS), average pitch counts (APC) for all outings (for starters and relievers), the percentage of DOMinating starts (PQS 4 or 5) and DISaster starts (PQS 0 or 1). The larger the variance between DOM and DIS, the greater the consistency of good or bad performance.

For relievers, we look at their saves success rate (Sv%) and Leverage Index (LI). A Doug Dennis study showed little correlation between saves success and future opportunity. However, you can increase your odds by prospecting for pitchers who have *both* a high saves percentage (80% or better) *and* high skills. Relievers with LI levels over 1.0 are being used more often by managers to win ballgames.

The final section includes several overall performance measures: runs above replacement (RAR), Base performance index (BPX, which is BPV indexed to each year's league average) and the Rotisserie value (R$).

2020 Projections

Forecasts are computed from a player's trends over the past five years. Adjustments were made for leading indicators and variances between skill and statistical output. After reviewing the leading indicators, you might opt to make further adjustments.

Although each year's numbers include all playing time at the Double-A level or above, the 2020 forecast only represents potential playing time at the major league level, and again is highly preliminary.

Note that the projected Rotisserie values in this book will not necessarily align with each player's historical actuals. Since we currently have no idea who is going to close games for the Giants, or whether Forrest Whitley is going to break camp with the Astros, it is impossible to create a finite pool of playing time, something which is required for valuation. So the projections are roughly based on a 12-team AL/NL league, and include an inflated number of innings, league-wide. This serves to flatten the spread of values and depress individual player dollar projections. In truth, a $25 player in this book might actually be worth $21, or $28. This level of precision is irrelevant in a process that is driven by market forces anyway. So, don't obsess over it.

Be aware of other sources that publish perfectly calibrated Rotisserie values over the winter. They are likely making arbitrary decisions as to where free agents are going to sign and who is going to land jobs in the spring. We do not make those leaps of faith here.

Bottom line… It is far too early to be making definitive projections for 2020, especially on playing time. Focus on the skill levels and trends, then consult BaseballHQ.com for playing time revisions as players change teams and roles become more defined. A free projections update will be available online in March.

Do-it-yourself analysis

Here are some data points you can look at in doing your own player analysis:

- Variance between vL+ and vR+ (opposition OPS)
- Variance in 2019 HR/F rate from 14%
- Variance in HR/F and xHR/F each year
- Variance in 2019 hit rate (H%) from 30%
- Variance in 2019 strand rate (S%) to tolerances (65% - 80%)
- Variance between ERA and xERA each year
- Growth or decline in base performance index (BPX)
- Spikes in innings pitched
- Trends in average pitch counts (APC)
- Trends in DOM/DIS splits
- Trends in saves success rate (Sv%)
- Variance between Dom changes and corresponding SwK levels
- Variance between Ctl changes and corresponding Ball% levels
- Improvement or decline in velocity

Adams,Austin L

Age: 29	Th: R	Role: RP	Health: A	LIMA Plan: C+	
Ht: 6' 3"	Wt: 225	Type: Pwr xGB	PT/Exp: D	Rand Var: +5	
			Consist: F	MM: 5500	

2-2, 3.94 ERA in 32 IP at WAS/SEA. Missed two months (shoulder strain), then returned in Sept, only to suffer torn ACL that will cost him a portion of 2020. Slider-heavy mix generated plenty of whiffs, and shaky Ctl headed in right direction with Ball% support. Keep on your radar; he has the goods to sneak into high-leverage role upon return.

Yr Tm	W	Sv	IP	K	ERA	xERA	WHIP	xWHIP	vL+	vR+	BF/G	Ctl	Dom	Cmd	Ball%	SwK	Vel	G	L	F	H%	S%	HR/F	xHR/F	GS	APC	DOM%	DIS%	Sv%	LI	RAR	BPX	R$
15 a/a	1	1	40	43	3.94	2.84	1.59				6.1	8.6	9.5	1.1							26%	73%									0.1	117	-$4
16 aa	0	4	41	52	4.33	3.88	1.53				5.6	5.7	11.2	2.0							35%	71%									-0.7	118	-$2
17 WAS *	6	5	64	82	2.90	4.16	1.68		99	91	5.8	6.9	11.6	1.7		13.0%	94.9	40	30	30	37%	83%	0%	1%	0	22			83	0.06	11.5	121	$3
18 WAS *	1	9	48	60	4.77	5.56	1.83		171	47	5.2	4.8	11.2	2.3		4.2%	94.8	50	25	25	45%	72%	0%		0	12			90	2.59	-3.7	117	-$5
19 2 TM *	3	1	49	79	3.33	2.15	1.06	1.14	66	93	4.3	4.0	14.4	3.6	38%	17.0%	95.2	50	18	32	31%	71%	21%	19%	2	18	0%	50%	33	1.05	7.1	173	$4
1st Half	0	1	35	57	2.68	1.70	1.01	1.12	51	88	4.5	3.9	14.5	3.8	40%	14.9%	95.0	53	18	29	30%	75%	18%	8%	2	20	0%	50%	50	1.09	8.0	187	$5
2nd Half	3	0	14	21	4.61	2.97	1.12		106	103	3.8	4.1	14.1	3.4		22.5%	95.6	45	18	36	29%	62%	25%	35%	0	15			0	0.97	-0.2	146	$2
20 Proj	1	0	36	49	3.60	3.00	1.29	1.23	64	110	5.0	4.3	12.1	2.8	44%	14.9%	95.0	53	18	29	32%	76%	16%		0						2.4	152	-$2

Agrazal,Dario

Age: 25	Th: R	Role: SP	Health: A	LIMA Plan: A	
Ht: 6' 2"	Wt: 240	Type: Con GB	PT/Exp: D	Rand Var: +3	
			Consist: A	MM: 1001	

4-5, 4.91 ERA in 73 IP at PIT. Recorded a 2.25 ERA in first 5 starts thanks to H% and S%, then the wheels fell off with a 6.55 mark the rest of the way. Awful vR, as he threw four-seam or sinker 72% of the time against them, with a combined 4% SwK. Stellar Ctl isn't nearly enough to overcome the lack of swing-and-miss stuff. Stay away.

Yr Tm	W	Sv	IP	K	ERA	xERA	WHIP	xWHIP	vL+	vR+	BF/G	Ctl	Dom	Cmd	Ball%	SwK	Vel	G	L	F	H%	S%	HR/F	xHR/F	GS	APC	DOM%	DIS%	Sv%	LI	RAR	BPX	R$
15																																	
16																																	
17																																	
18 aa	5	0	87	42	4.93	5.11	1.40				24.5	1.4	4.3	3.1							33%	66%									-8.4	62	-$6
19 PIT *	9	0	162	99	5.64	5.56	1.41	1.43	95	129	22.2	1.7	5.5	3.2	35%	6.7%	91.2	40	21	40	32%	63%	15%	13%	14	77	0%	43%	0	0.73	-22.7	51	-$6
1st Half	6	0	89	55	5.13	5.03	1.36		17	147	24.8	1.6	5.5	3.6		7.6%	91.6	39	30	30	32%	65%	10%	13%	2	79	0%	50%			-6.8	74	-$2
2nd Half	3	0	73	44	6.26	6.22	1.46	1.36	104	124	19.6	2.0	5.5	2.8	35%	6.6%	91.1	40	19	41	32%	62%	16%	14%	12	76	0%	42%	0	0.71	-15.9	26	-$11
20 Proj	5	0	87	48	5.46	4.52	1.43	1.49	99	122	22.7	1.6	5.0	3.0	39%	6.6%	91.1	46	20	34	32%	66%	15%		16						-14.1	81	-$6

Alcantara,Sandy

Age: 24	Th: R	Role: SP	Health: B	LIMA Plan: C	
Ht: 6' 4"	Wt: 170	Type: Con	PT/Exp: B	Rand Var: -1	
			Consist: C	MM: 1105	

At first glance, looks like prime regression candidate due to ERA/xERA gap and longstanding issue with walks. But seemed to turn a corner in final 10 starts with increased sinker usage, higher velocity, and a 2.3 Ctl with support from Ball%. League-average SwK says 2nd half Dom bump may stick, but ERA still more likely to go up than down.

Yr Tm	W	Sv	IP	K	ERA	xERA	WHIP	xWHIP	vL+	vR+	BF/G	Ctl	Dom	Cmd	Ball%	SwK	Vel	G	L	F	H%	S%	HR/F	xHR/F	GS	APC	DOM%	DIS%	Sv%	LI	RAR	BPX	R$
15																																	
16																																	
17 STL *	7	0	134	98	5.36	5.38	1.61		108	126	17.9	4.1	6.6	1.6		17.4%	98.3	26	43	30	33%	68%	29%	16%	0	19			0	0.08	-16.5	45	-$9
18 MIA *	8	0	151	106	4.13	3.93	1.36	1.67	86	112	25.3	3.6	6.3	1.7	39%	10.6%	95.5	48	16	36	29%	70%	9%	9%	6	95	33%	33%			0.4	65	$1
19 MIA	6	0	197	151	3.88	5.14	1.32	1.49	100	90	26.2	3.7	6.9	1.9	35%	11.4%	95.6	45	19	36	28%	74%	11%	14%	32	97	25%	28%			15.3	51	$7
1st Half	4	0	96	65	3.86	5.32	1.40	1.52	93	106	25.6	4.0	6.1	1.5	37%	11.4%	95.3	46	21	33	29%	74%	9%	13%	16	93	19%	38%			7.7	27	$4
2nd Half	2	0	102	86	3.90	4.93	1.24	1.36	106	76	26.8	3.4	7.6	2.3	34%	11.4%	95.8	43	18	39	27%	73%	12%	15%	16	100	31%	19%			7.7	73	$10
20 Proj	7	0	181	140	4.19	4.31	1.34	1.52	103	106	23.7	3.5	7.0	2.0	37%	11.4%	95.6	46	18	36	29%	73%	12%		32						-0.8	64	$4

Alcantara,Victor

Age: 27	Th: R	Role: RP	Health: B	LIMA Plan: B	
Ht: 6' 2"	Wt: 190	Type: Con	PT/Exp: D	Rand Var: +4	
			Consist: B	MM: 0000	

3-2, 4.85 ERA in 43 IP at DET. Sinkerballer got a little help from H% to stay afloat in 1st half, but then train went off the rails. In addition to a couple brief IL stints (tooth surgery, finger), Ctl and Ball% went up, and he was hurt by unlucky S% and HR/F. Even with GB tilt, three 5.00+ xERAs in one box are a good sign he's safe to avoid.

Yr Tm	W	Sv	IP	K	ERA	xERA	WHIP	xWHIP	vL+	vR+	BF/G	Ctl	Dom	Cmd	Ball%	SwK	Vel	G	L	F	H%	S%	HR/F	xHR/F	GS	APC	DOM%	DIS%	Sv%	LI	RAR	BPX	R$
15																																	
16 aa	3	0	111	70	5.86	5.43	1.71				17.3	4.9	5.6	1.2							33%	66%									-22.8	34	-$15
17 DET *	1	1	82	64	5.18	5.12	1.82		154	96	8.5	5.9	7.0	1.2		11.9%	92.1	54	21	25	36%	69%	14%	10%	0	22			50	0.11	-8.3	67	-$11
18 DET *	6	3	82	58	3.37	4.41	1.28	1.24	94	94	6.0	1.5	6.3	4.2	34%	10.5%	93.9	50	18	32	32%	77%	17%	13%	0	16			75	0.70	7.9	109	$4
19 DET *	3	0	62	36	5.81	5.42	1.43	1.52	90	121	4.5	3.1	5.3	1.7	35%	10.5%	93.4	54	14	32	28%	63%	18%	22%	0	15			0	0.95	-9.9	16	-$7
1st Half	3	0	36	20	4.29	5.06	1.29	1.42	86	113	3.8	2.8	5.0	1.8	34%	10.6%	93.4	53	15	32	26%	73%	16%	23%	0	14			0	1.02	0.9	51	-$2
2nd Half	0	0	26	16	7.88	6.58	1.62		102	176	5.8	3.6	5.6	1.5		9.8%	93.5	56	12	32	31%	53%	25%	19%	0	18			0	0.59	-10.9	-1	-$12
20 Proj	2	0	58	38	5.44	4.66	1.52	1.35	104	122	6.0	3.5	5.9	1.7	34%	10.6%	93.6	50	16	34	31%	67%	14%		0						-9.2	46	-$7

Allard,Kolby

Age: 22	Th: L	Role: SP	Health: A	LIMA Plan: B	
Ht: 6' 1"	Wt: 190	Type: Con	PT/Exp: D	Rand Var: 0	
			Consist: B	MM: 1101	

4-2, 4.96 ERA in 45 IP at TEX. Acquired in deadline deal and was decent for five Aug starts, but faded badly in Sept (6 K, 10 BB). The prospect shine has worn off a bit over past two seasons, as he hasn't been missing many bats, but late velocity bump at least offers hope that Dom gains are coming. Only 22, he's worth tracking, but from a distance.

Yr Tm	W	Sv	IP	K	ERA	xERA	WHIP	xWHIP	vL+	vR+	BF/G	Ctl	Dom	Cmd	Ball%	SwK	Vel	G	L	F	H%	S%	HR/F	xHR/F	GS	APC	DOM%	DIS%	Sv%	LI	RAR	BPX	R$
15																																	
16																																	
17 aa	8	0	150	120	4.34	4.77	1.49				24.0	3.0	7.2	2.4							35%	72%									0.4	82	$0
18 ATL *	7	0	121	80	3.77	4.39	1.39		203	158	23.2	2.6	5.9	2.2		4.3%	89.4	32	29	39	32%	74%	20%	27%	1	54	0%	100%	0	0.56	5.7	70	$0
19 TEX *	11	0	160	121	4.71	5.36	1.54	1.50	100	98	23.3	3.2	6.8	2.1	36%	8.2%	92.5	45	26	29	34%	72%	7%	8%	9	93	11%	44%			-4.0	52	-$3
1st Half	6	0	89	61	4.20	5.23	1.49		0	0	24.0	3.3	6.2	1.9							32%	76%	0%		0	0					3.3	41	$0
2nd Half	5	0	71	60	5.34	5.51	1.60	1.45	100	97	22.5	3.2	7.5	2.4	36%	8.2%	92.5	45	26	29	36%	67%	7%	8%	9	93	11%	44%			-7.3	66	-$6
20 Proj	7	0	109	81	4.41	4.33	1.49	1.60	93	94	23.2	3.0	6.7	2.2	40%	8.2%	92.5	45	26	29	34%	72%	9%		20						-3.5	72	-$2

Allen,Logan

Age: 23	Th: L	Role: SP	Health: A	LIMA Plan: F	
Ht: 6' 3"	Wt: 200	Type:	PT/Exp: D	Rand Var: +5	
			Consist: F	MM: 0100	

2-3, 6.18 ERA in 28 IP at SD/CLE. First taste of majors didn't go well, as inability to put hitters away, along with Ctl woes and H%/S% misfortune, led to ugly results. Two most often-used pitches (four-seamer, slider) allowed ISOs of .256 and .344, respectively. Still young with likely future as back-end starter, but more AAA seasoning is needed.

Yr Tm	W	Sv	IP	K	ERA	xERA	WHIP	xWHIP	vL+	vR+	BF/G	Ctl	Dom	Cmd	Ball%	SwK	Vel	G	L	F	H%	S%	HR/F	xHR/F	GS	APC	DOM%	DIS%	Sv%	LI	RAR	BPX	R$
15																																	
16																																	
17																																	
18 a/a	14	0	150	134	2.62	2.58	1.09				23.5	2.8	8.0	2.9							27%	78%									28.3	118	$21
19 2 TM *	7	0	108	87	7.08	6.97	1.78	1.60	147	121	18.4	4.0	7.3	1.8	37%	10.2%	92.7	49	29	22	36%	63%	20%	27%	4	50	25%	50%	0	0.60	-34.2	22	-$17
1st Half	6	0	72	64	5.45	5.22	1.51		113	79	20.9	3.4	8.0	2.4		11.7%	92.3	56	26	18	34%	66%	0%	12%	2	90	50%	0%			-8.4	66	-$9
2nd Half	1	0	38	23	9.77	9.72	2.19		166	150	15.8	5.1	5.4	1.0		9.2%	92.9	46	31	24	37%	58%	29%	33%	2	39	0%	100%	0	0.55	-24.5	-47	-$31
20 Proj	3	0	44	34	5.43	4.66	1.58				21.3	3.8	7.1	1.9				43	20	37	32%	70%	15%		9						-6.9	54	-$6

Alvarado,Jose

Age: 25	Th: L	Role: RP	Health: D	LIMA Plan: C	
Ht: 6' 2"	Wt: 245	Type: Pwr	PT/Exp: D	Rand Var: +1	
			Consist: C	MM: 3510	

Dominant again for first month and a half, but unsightly Ctl and missed time (personal, oblique, elbow) littered the rest of his season. He was finished after the August elbow injury, which may have contributed to late velocity dip. Check health status in spring, as he could still deliver both strong ratios and saves if back to full strength.

Yr Tm	W	Sv	IP	K	ERA	xERA	WHIP	xWHIP	vL+	vR+	BF/G	Ctl	Dom	Cmd	Ball%	SwK	Vel	G	L	F	H%	S%	HR/F	xHR/F	GS	APC	DOM%	DIS%	Sv%	LI	RAR	BPX	R$
15																																	
16																																	
17 TAM *	2	1	59	65	3.92	2.41	1.17		97	61	3.9	4.2	9.8	2.3		11.4%	98.2	54	16	30	27%	66%	4%	12%	0	13			33	1.15	3.2	131	$2
18 TAM	1	8	64	80	2.39	3.16	1.11	1.25	79	69	3.8	4.1	11.3	2.8	38%	13.2%	97.4	55	17	28	29%	77%	2%	9%	0	15			67	1.48	13.9	144	$8
19 TAM	1	7	30	39	4.80	5.41	1.87	1.70	71	113	4.2	8.1	11.7	1.4	42%	12.8%	98.2	48	22	30	37%	74%	9%	10%	1	17	0%	100%	78	1.17	-1.1	19	-$3
1st Half	0	6	24	32	3.33	4.29	1.44	1.43	73	90	3.9	5.9	11.8	2.0	40%	14.5%	98.5	43	23	34	33%	76%	5%	7%	0	16			75	1.25	3.5	81	-$2
2nd Half	1	1	6	7	11.12	12.47	3.71		63	172	5.0	17.5	11.1	0.6		8.4%	97.4	62	19	19	50%	70%	25%	22%	1	21	0%	100%	100	0.90	-4.6	-253	-$10
20 Proj	1	5	58	70	3.50	3.43	1.28	1.36	80	90	3.8	4.8	10.9	2.3	39%	12.5%	98.1	48	21	31	29%	75%	12%		0						4.7	106	$2

BRIAN RUDD

Alzolay,Adbert

			Health	A	LIMA Plan	C
Age: 25	Th: R	Role: SP	PT/Exp	F	Rand Var	+5
Ht: 6' 0"	Wt: 179	Type: Pwr FB	Consist	C	MM	0201

1-1, 7.30 ERA in 12 IP at CHC. Flashed improved skills in AAA before short summer stint in majors, but everything collapsed in 2nd half. Plus fastball and curveball drove Dom growth, though Ctl spike hints that wildness will inflate WHIP. Sprinkle in some HR risk (51% FB% in AAA), and he's likely another year away.

Yr	Tm	W	Sv	IP	K	ERA	xERA	WHIP	xWHIP	vL+	vR+	BF/G	Ctl	Dom	Cmd	Ball%	SwK	Vel	G	L	F	H%	S%	HR/F	xHR/F	GS	APC	DOM%	DIS%	Sv%	LI	RAR	BPX	R$
15																																		
16																																		
17	aa	0	0	33	26	3.92	3.23	1.37				19.5	3.5	7.3	2.1							33%	68%									1.8	109	-$4
18	aaa	2	0	41	23	5.06	4.91	1.47				22.1	2.8	5.0	1.8							32%	66%									-4.6	43	-$6
19	CHC *	3	0	78	88	5.84	5.34	1.52	1.67	133	109	17.9	4.9	10.1	2.1	39%	11.1%	94.4	32	24	43	32%	66%	25%	19%	2	56	0%	100%	0	0.54	-12.9	60	-$7
1st Half		3	0	41	47	3.55	3.26	1.06		16	123	19.7	2.8	10.4	3.8		11.3%	94.7	37	11	53	26%	74%	20%	14%	1	71	0%	100%	0	0.69	4.8	121	$3
2nd Half		0	0	38	41	8.30	7.58	2.01		251	86	16.6	7.2	9.8	1.4		10.8%	93.9	28	39	33	36%	61%	33%	27%	1	42	0%	100%	0	0.38	-17.7	21	-$18
20	**Proj**	**2**	**0**	**73**	**63**	**5.05**	**4.82**	**1.54**				**20.5**	**4.3**	**7.8**	**1.8**	**39%**	**11.0%**		**33**	**23**	**44**	**31%**	**73%**	**15%**		**15**						**-8.0**	**43**	**-$6**

Anderson,Brett

			Health	F	LIMA Plan	C
Age: 32	Th: L	Role: SP	PT/Exp	C	Rand Var	0
Ht: 6' 4"	Wt: 230	Type: Con GB	Consist	C	MM	1001

Overcame peppered injury history, only missing time with finger issue to post positive R$. Skills metrics say it's not happening again. GB% can limit ERA damage, but he was the only SP with a sub-5.0 Dom (min. 175 IP), while both xERA, xWHIP point to rising ratios. Let someone else spin the roulette wheel.

Yr	Tm	W	Sv	IP	K	ERA	xERA	WHIP	xWHIP	vL+	vR+	BF/G	Ctl	Dom	Cmd	Ball%	SwK	Vel	G	L	F	H%	S%	HR/F	xHR/F	GS	APC	DOM%	DIS%	Sv%	LI	RAR	BPX	R$
15	LA	10	0	180	116	3.69	3.53	1.33	1.32	96	104	24.2	2.3	5.8	2.5	36%	8.1%	90.7	66	15	19	31%	75%	17%	17%	31	88	13%	39%			6.0	103	$5
16	LA	1	0	11	5	11.91	6.27	2.56		172	161	15.5	3.2	4.0	1.3		6.2%	91.3	50	29	21	44%	56%	36%	22%	3	52	0%	100%	0	0.71	-10.8	16	-$9
17	2 TM *	7	0	92	52	6.14	6.04	1.75	1.43	143	112	20.1	3.4	5.0	1.5	37%	8.9%	90.5	49	29	22	36%	64%	12%	16%	13	69	0%	46%			-20.3	33	-$12
18	OAK *	6	0	113	73	4.25	4.51	1.34	1.26	99	109	19.6	1.6	5.8	3.7	36%	7.8%	90.3	56	20	25	33%	69%	15%	17%	17	71	12%	47%			-1.3	98	-$1
19	OAK	13	0	176	90	3.89	5.01	1.31	1.46	77	103	24.0	2.5	4.6	1.8	36%	8.0%	90.8	54	20	25	28%	73%	13%	20%	31	86	0%	42%			13.4	51	$9
1st Half		8	0	96	48	3.92	5.27	1.33	1.49	100	92	24.2	3.1	4.5	1.5	37%	8.1%	90.5	52	21	27	28%	72%	10%	18%	17	88	0%	29%			6.9	30	$10
2nd Half		5	0	80	42	3.84	4.52	1.28	1.33	54	117	23.6	1.8	4.7	2.6	35%	7.9%	91.2	57	20	23	29%	75%	18%	23%	14	83	0%	57%			6.5	78	$7
20	**Proj**	**6**	**0**	**87**	**48**	**4.30**	**4.17**	**1.38**	**1.36**	**89**	**108**	**21.9**	**2.3**	**5.0**	**2.2**	**36%**	**8.1%**	**90.7**	**54**	**22**	**25**	**31%**	**71%**	**13%**		**17**						**-1.6**	**68**	**-$1**

Anderson,Chase

			Health	D	LIMA Plan	A
Age: 32	Th: R	Role: SP	PT/Exp	A	Rand Var	0
Ht: 6' 1"	Wt: 200	Type: FB	Consist	A	MM	1203

Moved back to rotation after May blister and provided serviceable results, even as ERA expectedly rose from 2018. Look for the subpar Dom to continue, while steady Ball% points to a Ctl stuck in neutral. His FB% tilt, rising xERA magnify ERA risk, so in the end game, he's a back-end arm with little upside.

Yr	Tm	W	Sv	IP	K	ERA	xERA	WHIP	xWHIP	vL+	vR+	BF/G	Ctl	Dom	Cmd	Ball%	SwK	Vel	G	L	F	H%	S%	HR/F	xHR/F	GS	APC	DOM%	DIS%	Sv%	LI	RAR	BPX	R$
15	ARI	6	0	153	111	4.30	4.16	1.30	1.30	102	107	23.7	2.4	6.5	2.8	36%	8.4%	91.5	42	24	34	30%	69%	11%	10%	27	91	11%	26%			-6.4	88	$0
16	MIL	9	0	152	120	4.39	4.75	1.37	1.36	90	128	20.9	3.1	7.1	2.3	39%	8.8%	91.1	36	23	41	29%	74%	15%	14%	30	85	13%	47%	0	0.78	-3.8	68	$1
17	MIL	12	0	141	133	2.74	4.11	1.09	1.23	80	92	22.8	2.6	8.5	3.2	36%	10.6%	93.1	39	18	43	27%	79%	0%	8%	25	90	36%	20%			28.2	119	$20
18	MIL	9	0	158	128	3.93	4.60	1.19	1.37	93	110	21.6	3.2	7.3	2.2	00%	9.7%	92.4	34	21	44	24%	75%	15%	14%	30	87	10%	40%			4.3	64	$8
19	MIL	8	0	139	124	4.21	5.04	1.27	1.39	80	118	18.5	3.2	8.0	2.5	35%	11.2%	93.4	35	20	45	28%	73%	13%	11%	27	75	4%	33%	0	0.73	5.1	76	$6
1st Half		4	0	57	61	4.42	4.63	1.33	1.27	73	127	16.7	3.5	9.6	2.8	35%	12.3%	93.5	37	23	39	31%	72%	14%	14%	10	69	10%	20%	0	0.69	0.6	104	$2
2nd Half		4	0	82	63	4.06	5.40	1.22	1.37	86	112	20.1	3.1	6.9	2.3	35%	10.4%	93.3	33	18	48	26%	73%	12%	10%	17	80	0%	41%			4.5	58	$9
20	**Proj**	**9**	**0**	**160**	**138**	**4.16**	**4.31**	**1.31**	**1.32**	**91**	**120**	**20.5**	**3.2**	**7.8**	**2.4**	**36%**	**10.5%**	**92.9**	**36**	**21**	**44**	**29%**	**75%**	**14%**		**32**						**-0.1**	**77**	**$5**

Anderson,Justin

			Health	C	LIMA Plan	D
Age: 27	Th: R	Role: RP	PT/Exp	D	Rand Var	+3
Ht: 6' 3"	Wt: 230	Type: Pwr	Consist	D	MM	1400

Adding fly balls and home runs to already-shaky Ctl created a ratio explosion; August lat injury didn't help. Ball% says the walks will continue in droves, which will keep WHIP elevated, and xERA claims ERA isn't safe either. While SwK supports a fair amount of whiffs, the rest of this profile is a minefield.

Yr	Tm	W	Sv	IP	K	ERA	xERA	WHIP	xWHIP	vL+	vR+	BF/G	Ctl	Dom	Cmd	Ball%	SwK	Vel	G	L	F	H%	S%	HR/F	xHR/F	GS	APC	DOM%	DIS%	Sv%	LI	RAR	BPX	R$
15																																		
16																																		
17	aa	3	1	59	30	7.20	6.18	1.76				6.4	4.9	4.7	1.0							32%	60%									-20.5	3	-$12
18	LAA	3	4	55	67	4.07	4.11	1.48	1.55	91	85	4.2	6.5	10.9	1.7	44%	14.0%	97.3	51	19	30	30%	72%	8%	7%	0	18			67	1.06	0.6	57	-$1
19	LAA	3	1	47	60	5.55	5.05	1.57	1.52	111	96	4.0	6.1	11.5	1.9	41%	12.4%	94.7	35	25	39	33%	66%	13%	12%	0	17			50	0.81	-6.1	59	-$5
1st Half		2	1	29	38	3.77	4.59	1.40	1.36	114	77	4.0	5.3	11.9	2.2	41%	11.6%	94.8	31	29	40	33%	74%	7%	8%	0	17			50	0.80	2.6	86	-$2
2nd Half		1	0	18	22	8.35	5.73	1.85	1.63	106	124	4.0	7.4	10.8	1.5	42%	13.6%	94.4	42	20	38	34%	57%	21%	18%	0	16			0	0.81	-8.7	17	-$10
20	**Proj**	**2**	**0**	**44**	**51**	**4.93**	**4.35**	**1.62**	**1.53**	**110**	**104**	**4.2**	**6.3**	**10.5**	**1.7**	**42%**	**13.2%**	**95.7**	**43**	**22**	**36**	**32%**	**73%**	**16%**		**0**						**-4.2**	**47**	**-$5**

Anderson,Nick

			Health	A	LIMA Plan	F
Age: 29	Th: R	Role: RP	PT/Exp	D	Rand Var	+5
Ht: 6' 5"	Wt: 195	Type: Pwr FB	Consist	F	MM	5510

Posted elite ratios once 2nd half S% swung in his favor; BPX growth says it wasn't just luck. Elite SwK backs double-digit Dom and Ball% makes a Ctl repeat possible, so while fly balls carry ERA risk, his xERA backs a repeat. Late LI pairs well with closer-worthy skills, so if that continues... UP: 25 Saves

Yr	Tm	W	Sv	IP	K	ERA	xERA	WHIP	xWHIP	vL+	vR+	BF/G	Ctl	Dom	Cmd	Ball%	SwK	Vel	G	L	F	H%	S%	HR/F	xHR/F	GS	APC	DOM%	DIS%	Sv%	LI	RAR	BPX	R$
15																																		
16																																		
17	aa	2	9	34	27	1.66	1.77	1.01				4.4	2.2	7.3	3.4							28%	82%									11.2	152	$6
18	aaa	8	4	60	65	5.26	5.86	1.52				6.7	3.4	9.7	2.8							35%	71%									-8.3	71	-$2
19	2 TM	5	1	65	110	3.32	2.73	1.08	0.94	102	72	3.9	2.5	15.2	6.1	31%	20.3%	96.1	29	30	42	38%	74%	15%	17%	0	16			20	1.19	9.5	233	$7
1st Half		2	1	34	56	4.46	3.12	1.28	1.03	84	103	4.1	3.4	14.7	4.3	32%	18.4%	95.8	29	35	36	40%	68%	15%	17%	0	17			50	0.97	0.2	196	$2
2nd Half		3	0	31	54	2.05	2.49	0.85	0.75	123	36	3.7	1.5	15.8	10.8	29%	22.4%	96.3	28	23	49	34%	86%	14%	16%	0	16			0	1.43	9.3	275	$12
20	**Proj**	**6**	**9**	**58**	**84**	**3.28**	**2.86**	**1.11**	**0.86**	**114**	**69**	**4.5**	**2.7**	**13.0**	**4.9**	**30%**	**20.8%**	**96.1**	**29**	**28**	**44**	**33%**	**76%**	**14%**		**0**						**6.3**	**193**	**$9**

Anderson,Shaun

			Health	B	LIMA Plan	B
Age: 25	Th: R	Role: RP	PT/Exp	D	Rand Var	+2
Ht: 6' 4"	Wt: 225	Type: Con	Consist	B	MM	1110

3-5, 5.44 ERA with 2 Sv in 96 IP at SF. May call-up started 16 games, worked through blister before ending year in bullpen. More sliders in relief drove 2nd half SwK bump, but Ctl hints he sold out for Ks. Both xERA and xWHIP should keep him from relevance, so no matter his role, invest in someone with stronger skills.

Yr	Tm	W	Sv	IP	K	ERA	xERA	WHIP	xWHIP	vL+	vR+	BF/G	Ctl	Dom	Cmd	Ball%	SwK	Vel	G	L	F	H%	S%	HR/F	xHR/F	GS	APC	DOM%	DIS%	Sv%	LI	RAR	BPX	R$
15																																		
16																																		
17																																		
18	a/a	8	0	142	105	4.17	4.38	1.35				23.7	2.1	6.7	3.2							33%	70%									-0.4	96	$1
19	SF *	5	2	135	103	5.21	5.16	1.53	1.49	111	107	16.3	3.5	6.8	2.0	38%	9.8%	92.6	41	28	31	33%	67%	14%	14%	16	57	0%	44%	100	0.99	-11.8	52	-$6
1st Half		5	0	86	58	4.40	4.49	1.41	1.42	105	86	22.8	2.9	6.1	2.1	36%	7.0%	92.2	46	29	25	32%	70%	12%	12%	9	90	0%	33%			1.1	61	-$1
2nd Half		0	2	49	44	6.64	6.35	1.73	1.44	116	127	11.1	4.5	8.2	1.8	39%	12.7%	93.0	36	27	37	36%	63%	15%	16%	7	41	0%	57%	100	1.10	-12.9	40	-$16
20	**Proj**	**2**	**2**	**58**	**45**	**4.47**	**4.21**	**1.36**	**1.44**	**99**	**100**	**16.1**	**3.1**	**7.0**	**2.3**	**38%**	**10.5%**	**92.7**	**40**	**28**	**32**	**30%**	**70%**	**13%**		**9**						**-2.3**	**69**	**-$2**

Andriese,Matt

			Health	D	LIMA Plan	A
Age: 30	Th: R	Role: RP	PT/Exp	C	Rand Var	+4
Ht: 6' 2"	Wt: 225	Type: Pwr	Consist	A	MM	2300

Bad fortune mostly drove poor start; HR luck reversed in 2nd half. Stable xERA says he belongs between the extremes, as plus GB% should keep ERA in check. However, don't expect Dom repeat given SwK drop. Steady BPX, "A" Consistency say to plan for more of the same, which makes him a reserve pick.

Yr	Tm	W	Sv	IP	K	ERA	xERA	WHIP	xWHIP	vL+	vR+	BF/G	Ctl	Dom	Cmd	Ball%	SwK	Vel	G	L	F	H%	S%	HR/F	xHR/F	GS	APC	DOM%	DIS%	Sv%	LI	RAR	BPX	R$
15	TAM *	6	2	131	105	3.59	4.31	1.36	1.31	108	95	14.4	2.0	7.3	3.7	36%	8.9%	91.3	48	17	35	35%	75%	11%	14%	8	44	13%	50%	100	0.77	6.0	115	$3
16	TAM *	9	1	162	145	4.49	4.24	1.27	1.18	96	100	19.0	1.8	8.0	4.3	33%	11.0%	91.8	43	19	38	33%	67%	11%	14%	19	68	11%	26%	100	0.81	-6.1	127	$4
17	TAM	5	1	86	76	4.50	4.43	1.37	1.30	82	126	20.8	2.9	8.0	2.7	35%	11.5%	92.1	45	20	35	31%	74%	17%	16%	17	80	12%	41%	100	0.73	-1.5	105	$0
18	2 TM	3	0	79	78	5.26	3.85	1.39	1.24	99	124	8.3	2.9	8.9	3.1	34%	12.8%	92.2	49	20	31	32%	67%	21%	22%	5	33	0%	60%	0	0.86	-10.8	127	-$6
19	ARI	5	1	71	79	4.71	4.00	1.40	1.29	100	101	5.7	3.4	10.1	2.9	35%	11.0%	92.5	50	20	29	35%	68%	14%	16%	0	22			25	1.02	-1.8	127	-$1
1st Half		4	1	42	44	5.83	4.30	1.51	1.34	109	106	5.6	4.1	9.5	2.3	37%	9.9%	92.3	51	22	28	34%	63%	18%	16%	0	22			50	0.99	-6.8	97	-$2
2nd Half		1	0	29	35	3.10	3.56	1.24	1.11	85	95	5.9	2.5	10.9	4.4	33%	12.9%	92.9	49	18	32	36%	76%	8%	16%	0	22			0	1.07	5.0	170	$1
20	**Proj**	**3**	**0**	**58**	**58**	**4.49**	**3.64**	**1.36**	**1.23**	**95**	**109**	**7.4**	**3.2**	**9.0**	**2.8**	**34%**	**11.7%**	**92.3**	**47**	**21**	**32**	**32%**	**71%**	**17%**		**0**						**-2.4**	**116**	**-$2**

BRANT CHESSER

Archer,Chris

Age: 31	Th: R	Role: SP	Health: F	LIMA Plan: A
Ht: 6' 2"	Wt: 195	Type: Pwr	PT/Exp: A	Rand Var: +4
			Consist: A	MM: 3503

Another year, another ERA/xERA gap; this time with some skills decline. Still got plenty of whiffs, but early wildness, FB% spike coupled with fluky HR/F torpedoed his ratios. IL stints piled up too (thumb in May; shoulder in August), so while he should improve, we can no longer count on 200 IP/200+ K as part of the package.

Yr	Tm	W	Sv	IP	K	ERA	xERA	WHIP	xWHIP	vL+	vR+	BF/G	Ctl	Dom	Cmd	Ball%	SwK	Vel	G	L	F	H%	S%	HR/F	xHR/F	GS	APC	DOM%	DIS%	Sv%	LI	RAR	BPX	R$
15	TAM	12	0	212	252	3.23	3.12	1.14	1.14	83	88	25.5	2.8	10.7	3.8	35%	13.3%	95.2	46	20	34	31%	74%	10%	10%	34	101	44%	15%			19.2	168	$22
16	TAM	9	0	201	233	4.02	3.50	1.24	1.18	95	97	25.8	3.0	10.4	3.5	37%	12.5%	94.3	48	18	35	31%	73%	16%	18%	33	103	36%	27%			4.1	158	$12
17	TAM	10	0	201	249	4.07	3.50	1.26	1.12	101	90	25.1	2.7	11.1	4.2	36%	13.8%	95.5	42	22	36	34%	72%	14%	12%	34	100	35%	12%			7.0	178	$14
18	2 TM	6	0	148	162	4.31	3.71	1.38	1.21	110	103	23.6	3.0	9.8	3.3	35%	13.4%	94.7	45	23	32	35%	72%	14%	16%	27	93	26%	33%			-2.9	138	$0
19	PIT	3	0	120	143	5.19	4.46	1.41	1.34	105	106	22.9	4.1	10.8	2.6	37%	13.3%	94.1	36	24	39	31%	69%	20%	19%	23	91	17%	39%			-10.1	104	-$4
1st Half		3	0	74	80	5.50	4.89	1.47	1.39	109	114	23.1	4.6	9.8	2.1	38%	12.6%	93.8	38	22	40	29%	70%	23%	22%	14	92	21%	43%			-9.0	72	-$4
2nd Half		0	0	46	63	4.70	3.84	1.33	1.13	97	95	22.4	3.3	12.3	3.7	35%	14.4%	94.5	34	27	38	36%	69%	16%	13%	9	90	11%	33%			-1.1	157	-$3
20	**Proj**	**6**	**0**	**160**	**192**	**4.56**	**3.53**	**1.36**	**1.20**	**103**	**100**	**23.5**	**3.5**	**10.8**	**3.1**	**36%**	**13.5%**	**94.6**	**38**	**24**	**38**	**33%**	**71%**	**16%**		**28**						**-8.0**	**135**	**$2**

Armstrong,Shawn

Age: 29	Th: R	Role: RP	Health: B	LIMA Plan: F
Ht: 6' 2"	Wt: 225	Type: Pwr FB	PT/Exp: D	Rand Var: +3
			Consist: F	MM: 1310

DFA'd in April and quickly fell into high-leverage role with BAL, which says more about the club than the pitcher. Control issues intensified with no sign of relief from Ball%, while xHR/F hints this could've been worse with so many FBs. 2018 looks like the outlier here, as xERA/xWHIP point to more middle-inning futility.

Yr	Tm	W	Sv	IP	K	ERA	xERA	WHIP	xWHIP	vL+	vR+	BF/G	Ctl	Dom	Cmd	Ball%	SwK	Vel	G	L	F	H%	S%	HR/F	xHR/F	GS	APC	DOM%	DIS%	Sv%	LI	RAR	BPX	R$
15	CLE *	1	16	58	74	3.16	3.27	1.43		57	108	4.5	4.7	11.5	2.4		13.7%	93.5	35	24	41	37%	76%	14%	11%	0	16			94	0.08	5.7	146	$5
16	CLE *	3	9	60	58	2.68	2.82	1.41		76	108	4.4	5.9	8.8	1.5		10.4%	92.5	52	16	32	28%	80%	10%	10%	0	20			90	0.59	11.1	110	$5
17	CLE *	2	10	54	45	4.43	5.35	1.52		95	100	4.8	3.9	7.5	2.0		10.9%	93.2	39	17	44	32%	76%	15%	13%	0	20			77	0.14	-0.5	48	$0
18	SEA *	2	16	71	80	1.99	2.95	1.23		68	83	4.5	4.0	10.2	2.6		11.8%	93.8	40	17	43	30%	86%	7%	8%	0	15			89	0.81	18.8	126	$12
19	2 AL	1	4	58	63	5.74	5.42	1.64	1.44	81	125	4.9	4.5	9.8	2.2	38%	12.5%	93.4	29	25	45	37%	67%	10%	13%	0	21			44	1.07	-8.8	67	-$6
1st Half		0	1	28	33	5.46	5.07	1.46	1.34	60	138	5.2	4.5	10.6	2.4	37%	14.6%	93.0	31	22	47	32%	67%	14%	18%	0	21			50	0.89	-3.3	86	-$7
2nd Half		1	3	30	30	6.00	5.82	1.80	1.42	102	114	4.7	4.5	9.0	2.0	38%	10.6%	93.8	28	28	44	40%	67%	7%	9%	0	20			43	1.23	-5.5	51	-$6
20	**Proj**	**2**	**2**	**58**	**61**	**4.37**	**4.42**	**1.51**	**1.39**	**81**	**120**	**4.6**	**4.3**	**9.5**	**2.2**	**38%**	**12.1%**	**93.5**	**29**	**26**	**45**	**33%**	**77%**	**14%**		**0**						**-1.6**	**70**	**-$3**

Arrieta,Jake

Age: 34	Th: R	Role: SP	Health: D	LIMA Plan: A
Ht: 6' 4"	Wt: 225	Type: Con GB	PT/Exp: A	Rand Var: +3
			Consist: A	MM: 2103

Pitched with a bone spur in elbow, which inevitably led to season-ending surgery in August. Year-over-year declines are visible in almost every phase: he keeps missing fewer bats (SwK); xERA continued its steady ascent; spiraling R$, BPX show just how far he's fallen. Durability concerns at this age add even more risk.

Yr	Tm	W	Sv	IP	K	ERA	xERA	WHIP	xWHIP	vL+	vR+	BF/G	Ctl	Dom	Cmd	Ball%	SwK	Vel	G	L	F	H%	S%	HR/F	xHR/F	GS	APC	DOM%	DIS%	Sv%	LI	RAR	BPX	R$
15	CHC	22	0	229	236	1.77	2.62	0.86	1.09	62	79	26.4	1.9	9.3	4.9	35%	11.5%	94.6	56	21	23	25%	81%	8%	8%	33	104	67%	3%			62.0	179	$51
16	CHC	18	0	197	190	3.10	3.60	1.08	1.31	83	76	25.6	3.5	8.7	2.5	37%	10.8%	93.7	53	20	28	25%	74%	11%	12%	31	101	42%	19%			26.5	111	$26
17	CHC	14	0	168	163	3.53	4.03	1.22	1.25	112	83	23.6	2.9	8.7	3.0	37%	9.0%	92.1	45	21	34	29%	76%	14%	12%	30	91	20%	27%			17.2	121	$16
18	PHI	10	0	173	138	3.96	4.07	1.29	1.33	111	92	23.4	3.0	7.2	2.4	36%	8.4%	93.0	52	20	29	29%	73%	14%	15%	31	89	23%	39%			4.0	91	$6
19	PHI	8	0	136	110	4.64	4.65	1.47	1.42	123	91	24.8	3.4	7.3	2.2	37%	7.6%	92.5	51	23	26	32%	73%	19%	20%	24	91	8%	33%			-2.3	75	-$2
1st Half		8	0	104	81	4.43	4.63	1.42	1.40	121	92	26.2	3.5	7.0	2.0	36%	7.9%	92.7	52	22	26	30%	74%	21%	22%	17	97	12%	29%			1.0	69	$3
2nd Half		0	0	32	29	5.34	4.41	1.66	1.30	126	91	21.1	3.1	8.2	2.6	38%	6.8%	92.1	49	27	24	39%	68%	13%	13%	7	78	0%	43%			-3.3	99	-$16
20	**Proj**	**7**	**0**	**131**	**105**	**4.25**	**3.91**	**1.38**	**1.31**	**116**	**89**	**22.7**	**3.1**	**7.2**	**2.4**	**37%**	**8.2%**	**92.7**	**50**	**23**	**27**	**31%**	**72%**	**14%**		**24**						**-1.6**	**87**	**$1**

Baez,Pedro

Age: 32	Th: R	Role: RP	Health: D	LIMA Plan: A
Ht: 6' 0"	Wt: 232	Type: Pwr xFB	PT/Exp: C	Rand Var: -5
			Consist: A	MM: 2300

One of the steadiest ERA columns you'll find in this book. Early Dom plunge recovered in 2nd half; elite SwK suggests to trust the latter. Other signs are not so hot: extreme FB% tilt says he's reliant on fortunate HR/F to stick, Ball% trending in wrong direction, H% won't repeat. Next entry in ERA column likely won't be as pretty.

Yr	Tm	W	Sv	IP	K	ERA	xERA	WHIP	xWHIP	vL+	vR+	BF/G	Ctl	Dom	Cmd	Ball%	SwK	Vel	G	L	F	H%	S%	HR/F	xHR/F	GS	APC	DOM%	DIS%	Sv%	LI	RAR	BPX	R$
15	LA	4	0	51	60	3.35	3.27	1.14	1.06	101	95	4.0	1.9	10.6	5.5	33%	15.5%	97.1	38	19	44	34%	72%	7%	11%	0	16			0	1.20	3.8	184	$2
16	LA	3	0	74	83	3.04	3.39	1.00	1.15	75	89	4.0	2.7	10.1	3.8	33%	15.0%	96.7	43	20	38	25%	78%	16%	15%	0	16			0	1.02	10.5	155	$7
17	LA	3	0	64	64	2.95	4.82	1.33	1.37	90	103	4.2	4.1	9.0	2.2	35%	16.4%	97.0	35	22	43	29%	84%	11%	8%	0	18			0	1.00	11.1	78	$2
18	LA	4	0	56	62	2.88	4.14	1.22	1.28	83	94	4.3	3.7	9.9	2.7	36%	15.5%	96.0	35	22	44	30%	78%	6%	8%	0	18			0	0.78	8.9	106	$2
19	LA	7	1	70	69	3.10	4.41	0.95	1.30	70	74	3.9	3.0	8.9	3.0	37%	15.7%	95.9	34	18	48	22%	70%	7%	7%	0	16			14	1.39	12.1	100	$9
1st Half		3	0	37	32	2.65	4.66	0.88	1.30	43	81	3.9	2.9	7.7	2.7	37%	16.1%	95.8	36	18	46	21%	69%	2%	4%	0	15			0	1.43	8.5	82	$8
2nd Half		4	1	32	37	3.62	4.28	1.02	1.19	104	67	3.9	3.1	10.3	3.4	36%	15.3%	95.9	33	18	50	24%	71%	13%	10%	0	16			20	1.34	3.5	124	$10
20	**Proj**	**5**	**0**	**65**	**69**	**3.79**	**3.83**	**1.20**	**1.25**	**91**	**97**	**4.0**	**3.3**	**9.5**	**2.9**	**36%**	**15.7%**	**96.2**	**35**	**19**	**46**	**29%**	**73%**	**11%**		**0**						**2.9**	**110**	**$3**

Bailey,Homer

Age: 34	Th: R	Role: SP	Health: F	LIMA Plan: D
Ht: 6' 4"	Wt: 223	Type: Con	PT/Exp: B	Rand Var: +1
			Consist: D	MM: 1103

Traded to OAK in July; surged with a 3.22 ERA in Aug/Sep. Ramped up use of dominant splitter (20% SwK, 60% GB%) to drive Dom gains, but with just one sub-5.00 xERA on this page, be careful extrapolating late-season surge. A mid-30s pitcher with extensive arm issues suddenly thriving? The exception, not the rule.

Yr	Tm	W	Sv	IP	K	ERA	xERA	WHIP	xWHIP	vL+	vR+	BF/G	Ctl	Dom	Cmd	Ball%	SwK	Vel	G	L	F	H%	S%	HR/F	xHR/F	GS	APC	DOM%	DIS%	Sv%	LI	RAR	BPX	R$
15	CIN	0	0	11	3	5.56	5.64	1.76		196	100	25.5	3.2	2.4	0.8		7.0%	91.1	52	17	31	31%	76%	23%	24%	2	86	0%	100%			-2.2	-15	-$6
16	CIN *	3	0	51	44	7.51	9.32	2.13		131	96	18.0	3.7	7.7	2.1		10.0%	92.7	45	30	25	43%	69%	11%	16%	6	76	17%	33%			-20.9	-1	-$15
17	CIN	6	0	91	67	6.43	5.19	1.69	1.49	108	126	23.3	4.2	6.6	1.6	38%	10.0%	93.5	45	27	28	35%	62%	13%	12%	18	88	6%	61%			-23.2	36	-$12
18	CIN *	3	0	146	96	6.24	6.82	1.66	1.36	130	120	24.2	2.8	5.9	2.1	33%	9.4%	93.1	43	24	33	35%	66%	19%	18%	20	89	15%	65%			-37.6	20	-$22
19	2 AL	13	0	163	149	4.57	4.51	1.32	1.33	86	106	22.5	2.9	8.2	2.8	35%	11.2%	93.0	44	22	34	31%	68%	13%	12%	31	91	23%	32%			-1.4	99	$6
1st Half		7	0	85	78	4.87	4.67	1.40	1.38	90	105	21.6	3.8	8.3	2.2	36%	10.9%	92.8	46	22	32	31%	68%	14%	13%	17	91	24%	35%			-3.8	76	$4
2nd Half		6	0	78	71	4.25	4.33	1.23	1.18	81	107	23.4	2.0	8.2	4.2	35%	11.5%	93.2	43	22	36	32%	69%	12%	12%	14	93	21%	29%			2.5	125	$9
20	**Proj**	**8**	**0**	**131**	**107**	**4.98**	**4.18**	**1.45**	**1.33**	**102**	**112**	**21.7**	**3.0**	**7.4**	**2.4**	**35%**	**10.4%**	**93.1**	**44**	**23**	**33**	**32%**	**69%**	**15%**		**26**						**-13.4**	**83**	**-$4**

Barlow,Scott

Age: 27	Th: R	Role: RP	Health: A	LIMA Plan: F
Ht: 6' 3"	Wt: 215	Type: Pwr	PT/Exp: D	Rand Var: +2
			Consist: F	MM: 2300

Classic case of luck factors toying with results, as 2nd half ERA was elite despite dip in skills. Through the big H%, S%, and HR/F swings was a consistently-wild Ctl and mediocre xERA, though SwK gives Dom growth some legs. Splitting 1st/2nd half ERA seems safe, which nets us just another "meh" middle reliever.

Yr	Tm	W	Sv	IP	K	ERA	xERA	WHIP	xWHIP	vL+	vR+	BF/G	Ctl	Dom	Cmd	Ball%	SwK	Vel	G	L	F	H%	S%	HR/F	xHR/F	GS	APC	DOM%	DIS%	Sv%	LI	RAR	BPX	R$
15																																		
16	aa	4	0	124	86	4.77	4.90	1.56				22.7	3.5	6.2	1.8							34%	70%									-8.9	58	-$7
17	a/a	7	0	140	132	3.92	3.42	1.22				21.7	3.6	8.5	2.3							27%	71%									7.6	94	$8
18	KC *	2	1	66	57	6.59	6.65	1.70		84	101	15.0	3.5	7.8	2.2		11.4%	90.6	38	26	36	37%	64%	12%	19%	0	40			50	1.33	-19.9	42	-$13
19	KC	3	1	70	92	4.22	4.19	1.44	1.35	112	88	5.1	4.7	11.8	2.5	37%	14.8%	94.1	40	23	37	35%	72%	9%	11%	0	21			33	1.13	2.5	111	-$1
1st Half		2	1	36	52	6.19	4.06	1.54	1.20	127	102	5.5	4.2	12.9	3.1	36%	13.1%	93.7	33	28	39	40%	62%	17%	15%	0	23			50	1.29	-7.6	141	-$4
2nd Half		1	0	34	40	2.12	4.31	1.32	1.42	93	73	4.6	5.3	10.6	2.0	38%	16.7%	94.6	48	18	34	31%	82%	0%	5%	0	19			0	0.96	10.0	80	$3
20	**Proj**	**2**	**0**	**65**	**70**	**4.57**	**3.99**	**1.47**	**1.33**	**124**	**96**	**7.6**	**4.2**	**9.6**	**2.3**	**37%**	**15.2%**	**94.2**	**42**	**22**	**36**	**34%**	**70%**	**11%**		**0**						**-3.4**	**90**	**-$4**

Barnes,Matt

Age: 30	Th: R	Role: RP	Health: A	LIMA Plan: A
Ht: 6' 4"	Wt: 210	Type: Pwr	PT/Exp: C	Rand Var: +5
			Consist: A	MM: 5510

Flirted with closer gig early, but gopheritis and H% didn't subside until 2nd half. Threw his curveball (19% SwK, 61% GB%) more than half the time, which pushed elite Dom up further, but also came at the expense of control, which is a deal-breaker for 9th inning work. xERA/BPX hold some merit, but role may elude unless he limits the free pass.

Yr	Tm	W	Sv	IP	K	ERA	xERA	WHIP	xWHIP	vL+	vR+	BF/G	Ctl	Dom	Cmd	Ball%	SwK	Vel	G	L	F	H%	S%	HR/F	xHR/F	GS	APC	DOM%	DIS%	Sv%	LI	RAR	BPX	R$
15	BOS *	4	0	81	72	5.68	6.34	1.77	1.31	110	135	7.6	4.5	8.1	1.8	35%	10.1%	94.8	39	22	40	37%	71%	16%	15%	2	25	0%	100%	0	0.88	-17.1	44	-$12
16	BOS	4	1	67	71	4.05	4.03	1.40	1.35	100	95	4.6	4.2	9.6	2.3	40%	11.3%	96.8	46	21	33	32%	72%	10%	13%	0	19			50	1.08	1.1	99	$0
17	BOS	7	1	70	83	3.88	3.41	1.22	1.23	105	78	4.1	3.6	10.7	3.0	39%	12.9%	95.2	49	23	28	31%	71%	14%	11%	0	17			33	0.95	4.1	147	$5
18	BOS	6	0	62	96	3.65	2.88	1.26	1.17	88	85	4.3	4.5	14.0	3.1	40%	14.9%	96.6	53	14	33	35%	73%	11%	16%	0	18			0	1.08	3.8	185	$3
19	BOS	5	4	64	110	3.78	3.11	1.38	1.22	84	91	4.1	5.3	15.4	2.9	39%	15.4%	96.7	47	22	31	38%	77%	20%	14%	0	19			33	1.42	5.8	173	$4
1st Half		3	4	35	62	4.93	2.51	1.36	1.09	83	95	4.1	4.7	16.1	3.4	39%	15.2%	96.5	52	25	23	41%	65%	25%	18%	0	19			40	1.42	-1.8	211	$4
2nd Half		2	0	30	48	2.43	3.81	1.42	1.31	85	87	4.0	6.1	14.6	2.4	39%	15.7%	96.9	41	19	40	34%	89%	16%	12%	0	18			0	1.42	7.6	128	$4
20	**Proj**	**5**	**5**	**58**	**88**	**3.54**	**2.82**	**1.25**	**1.22**	**82**	**80**	**4.0**	**4.9**	**13.6**	**2.8**	**39%**	**14.5%**	**96.4**	**48**	**20**	**33**	**32%**	**74%**	**14%**		**0**						**4.4**	**160**	**$5**

RYAN BLOOMFIELD

Barria,Jaime		Health	A	LIMA Plan	C
Age: 23	Th: R Role SP	PT/Exp	D	Rand Var	+5
Ht: 6' 1"	Wt: 210 Type Con FB	Consist	C	MM	0101

4-10, 6.42 ERA in 83 IP at LAA. Spent most of 1st half in AAA before getting extended look in majors. Delivered shaky results, as Ball% and SwK crashed, while sky-high FB% led to 16 HR in just 127 PA vR. Can't write him off yet given age and likely S%, HR/F regression, but has a lot of work to do in order to become interesting again.

Yr	Tm	W	Sv	IP	K	ERA	xERA	WHIP	xWHIP	vL+	vR+	BF/G	Ctl	Dom	Cmd	Ball%	SwK	Vel	G	L	F	H%	S%	HR/F	xHR/F	GS	APC	DOM%	DIS%	Sv%	LI	RAR	BPX	R$
15																																		
16																																		
17	a/a	3	0	76	54	3.38	3.99	1.26				20.7	2.0	6.4	3.2							31%	76%									9.2	97	$2
18	LAA *	10	0	147	115	3.37	4.02	1.27	1.39	84	115	19.5	3.1	7.0	2.2	38%	10.8%	91.2	37	20	43	28%	78%	10%	12%	26	84	15%	42%			14.2	70	$9
19	LAA *	7	0	132	113	7.17	6.90	1.52	1.35	96	142	19.7	2.4	7.7	3.2	39%	9.6%	91.7	34	19	46	33%	59%	20%	16%	13	79	0%	62%	0	0.81	-43.3	30	-$14
1st Half		5	0	66	53	6.19	5.66	1.41	1.18	93	124	19.8	1.9	7.3	3.8	34%	11.6%	91.4	35	23	42	33%	59%	9%	9%	2	71	0%	50%	0	0.64	-13.6	73	-$9
2nd Half		2	0	69	60	7.87	7.76	1.57	1.34	97	150	20.1	2.9	7.9	2.7	41%	8.9%	91.8	34	18	48	31%	58%	24%	19%	11	83	0%	64%	0	0.88	-28.4	-2	-$20
20	**Proj**	**7**	**0**	**123**	**99**	**4.92**	**4.57**	**1.43**	**1.32**	**94**	**134**	**20.9**	**3.0**	**7.2**	**2.4**	**38%**	**10.3%**	**91.5**	**35**	**20**	**45**	**31%**	**72%**	**15%**		**21**						**-11.7**	**72**	**-$3**

Bass,Anthony		Health	C	LIMA Plan	F
Age: 32	Th: R Role RP	PT/Exp	D	Rand Var	0
Ht: 6' 2"	Wt: 200 Type GB	Consist	F	MM	2210

2-4, 3.56 ERA with 5 Sv in 48 IP at SEA. Had H% in his corner this time around, but even with added velocity, was just another back end bullpen arm in 1st half. Missed a lot more bats in 2nd half, including 22%+ SwK on slider and splitter. Small sample, shaky track record warn against fully buying in, but a decent saves flyer in an -only league.

Yr	Tm	W	Sv	IP	K	ERA	xERA	WHIP	xWHIP	vL+	vR+	BF/G	Ctl	Dom	Cmd	Ball%	SwK	Vel	G	L	F	H%	S%	HR/F	xHR/F	GS	APC	DOM%	DIS%	Sv%	LI	RAR	BPX	R$
15	TEX	0	0	64	45	4.50	4.16	1.34	1.36	109	102	8.2	2.8	6.3	2.3	38%	8.9%	92.6	49	23	28	31%	67%	9%	12%	0	32			0	0.55	-4.2	77	-$5
16																																		
17	TEX *	3	0	81	63	6.38	6.89	1.87		168	135	19.0	3.7	7.0	1.9		8.1%	92.3	43	27	30	40%	67%	11%	1%	0	56			0	0.39	-20.2	42	-$14
18	CHC *	0	3	47	32	3.86	5.36	1.50		112	93	4.8	1.9	6.2	3.3		8.2%	94.1	53	27	20	36%	76%	11%	5%	0	15			60	0.69	1.7	83	-$4
19	SEA *	3	14	69	58	3.44	2.48	1.05	1.35	69	79	4.2	3.2	7.5	2.4	38%	11.4%	95.4	52	21	28	23%	70%	14%	16%	0	17			64	1.28	9.1	93	$10
1st Half		2	10	39	25	3.34	3.28	1.17	1.52	73	106	4.7	3.4	5.8	1.7	41%	7.6%	95.2	54	15	31	24%	76%	19%	22%	0	19			63	1.31	5.6	55	$11
2nd Half		1	4	30	33	3.56	3.37	0.89	1.19	67	63	4.0	3.0	9.8	3.3	37%	13.5%	95.4	50	24	26	22%	60%	11%	11%	0	16			67	1.26	3.5	135	$10
20	**Proj**	**1**	**2**	**44**	**39**	**3.86**	**3.64**	**1.31**	**1.34**	**96**	**102**	**5.3**	**3.1**	**8.1**	**2.7**	**38%**	**10.2%**	**94.3**	**50**	**22**	**28**	**32%**	**72%**	**11%**		**0**						**1.6**	**106**	**-$1**

Bassitt,Chris		Health	F	LIMA Plan	B
Age: 31	Th: R Role RP	PT/Exp	C	Rand Var	0
Ht: 6' 5"	Wt: 220 Type	Consist	B	MM	1201

Joined rotation in late April; surprisingly held on most of the year. Jumps in velocity and Dom helped him post solid ERA, but there are reasons to be skeptical: SwK continues to be well below average; Ball% didn't come close to supporting 2nd half Ctl gains; xERA improved, but still very mediocre. Count on him taking a step back.

Yr	Tm	W	Sv	IP	K	ERA	xERA	WHIP	xWHIP	vL+	vR+	BF/G	Ctl	Dom	Cmd	Ball%	SwK	Vel	G	L	F	H%	S%	HR/F	xHR/F	GS	APC	DOM%	DIS%	Sv%	LI	RAR	BPX	R$
15	OAK *	3	0	155	118	4.07	3.35	1.30	1.38	89	103	20.6	2.9	6.8	2.3	38%	8.8%	93.1	44	21	34	31%	67%	6%	11%	13	79	31%	8%	0	0.65	-2.1	99	$0
16	OAK	0	0	28	23	6.11	5.33	1.75		90	146	26.6	4.5	7.4	1.6		8.7%	92.5	46	18	36	35%	68%	15%	23%	5	101	0%	60%			-6.6	42	-$7
17	aaa	4	0	38	23	7.95	6.15	1.82				10.3	4.1	5.4	1.3							37%	54%									-16.7	33	-$10
18	OAK *	7	0	131	101	4.68	4.89	1.51	1.38	79	93	19.8	3.2	7.0	2.2	37%	7.2%	92.0	45	22	34	34%	60%	9%	13%	7	73	14%	43%	0	0.69	-8.6	71	-$6
19	OAK	10	0	144	141	3.81	4.41	1.19	1.30	92	93	21.9	2.9	8.8	3.0	35%	9.3%	93.5	41	21	38	28%	74%	14%	13%	25	87	24%	36%	0	0.71	12.3	107	$11
1st Half		5	0	73	72	3.80	4.69	1.21	1.36	98	84	24.0	3.9	8.8	2.3	36%	9.1%	93.3	42	20	39	26%	73%	12%	14%	13	98	23%	23%			6.3	79	$10
2nd Half		5	0	71	69	3.82	4.16	1.17	1.14	86	102	20.0	1.9	8.8	4.6	35%	9.4%	93.7	41	22	37	30%	75%	16%	12%	12	77	25%	50%	0	0.67	6.0	137	$12
20	**Proj**	**8**	**0**	**116**	**104**	**4.51**	**4.11**	**1.42**	**1.30**	**101**	**112**	**17.5**	**3.1**	**8.0**	**2.6**	**36%**	**8.5%**	**92.9**	**42**	**21**	**37**	**33%**	**72%**	**13%**		**21**						**-5.1**	**92**	**$0**

Bauer,Trevor		Health	C	LIMA Plan	B
Age: 29	Th: R Role SP	PT/Exp	A	Rand Var	+2
Ht: 6' 1"	Wt: 205 Type Pwr	Consist	B	MM	3405

A frustratingly inconsistent season from an expected ace. Results were more bad than good in 2nd half, but SwK was back in full force, and other than the FB% spike, it sure looked a lot like 2018 if you strip away luck factors. A little too risky to build a staff around, but at reduced cost, he offers plenty of profit potential heading into 2020.

Yr	Tm	W	Sv	IP	K	ERA	xERA	WHIP	xWHIP	vL+	vR+	BF/G	Ctl	Dom	Cmd	Ball%	SwK	Vel	G	L	F	H%	S%	HR/F	xHR/F	GS	APC	DOM%	DIS%	Sv%	LI	RAR	BPX	R$
15	CLE	11	0	176	170	4.55	4.21	1.31	1.38	97	102	24.0	4.0	8.7	2.2	39%	9.9%	92.8	39	20	41	28%	68%	12%	10%	30	93	40%	27%	0	0.76	-12.8	77	$2
16	CLE	12	0	190	168	4.26	4.11	1.31	1.33	94	100	23.2	3.3	8.0	2.4	38%	9.4%	93.2	49	20	31	30%	69%	12%	13%	28	88	25%	39%	0	0.74	-1.7	96	$7
17	CLE	17	0	176	196	4.19	3.72	1.37	1.21	111	97	23.4	3.1	10.0	3.3	39%	9.5%	94.0	46	22	32	34%	74%	16%	14%	31	98	19%	23%	0	0.77	3.8	146	$11
18	CLE	12	1	175	221	2.21	3.15	1.09	1.12	78	83	25.6	2.9	11.3	3.9	37%	13.7%	94.5	45	21	34	31%	81%	6%	10%	27	102	59%	11%	100	0.80	42.0	171	$28
19	2 TM	11	0	213	253	4.48	4.14	1.25	1.26	108	91	26.8	3.5	10.7	3.1	37%	12.6%	94.6	38	22	40	30%	69%	15%	16%	34	108	47%	15%			0.7	125	$12
1st Half		6	0	119	134	3.55	4.11	1.14	1.25	106	80	27.8	3.6	10.1	2.9	37%	11.9%	94.7	41	21	38	27%	74%	13%	17%	18	112	50%	6%			14.0	115	$20
2nd Half		5	0	94	119	5.65	4.26	1.38	1.18	109	107	25.7	3.4	11.4	3.4	37%	13.5%	94.4	33	23	44	34%	64%	18%	14%	16	104	44%	25%			-13.3	137	$1
20	**Proj**	**12**	**0**	**189**	**222**	**3.98**	**3.36**	**1.23**	**1.20**	**98**	**92**	**24.3**	**3.3**	**10.6**	**3.2**	**37%**	**13.0%**	**94.3**	**41**	**22**	**38**	**31%**	**72%**	**14%**		**31**						**4.0**	**139**	**$14**

Bedrosian,Cam		Health	D	LIMA Plan	A
Age: 28	Th: R Role RP	PT/Exp	C	Rand Var	0
Ht: 6' 1"	Wt: 225 Type Pwr	Consist	A	MM	2300

Provided value early on, as SwK and Dom bounced back and luck was on his side. But 1st half success proved unsustainable, as luck factors started to correct, then forearm strain ended season in late August. Expected to be good to go by spring, but even so, this looks like a 4.00 ERA pitcher who is probably far from save opps.

Yr	Tm	W	Sv	IP	K	ERA	xERA	WHIP	xWHIP	vL+	vR+	BF/G	Ctl	Dom	Cmd	Ball%	SwK	Vel	G	L	F	H%	S%	HR/F	xHR/F	GS	APC	DOM%	DIS%	Sv%	LI	RAR	BPX	R$
15	LAA *	2	3	69	70	3.99	4.18	1.52	1.47	144	101	5.2	4.1	9.1	2.2	40%	7.1%	94.4	43	23	34	36%	73%	9%	11%	0	19			60	0.73	-0.3	107	-$3
16	LAA	2	1	40	51	1.12	2.94	1.09	1.13	79	66	3.6	3.1	11.4	3.6	37%	11.3%	95.3	49	21	29	32%	91%	4%	10%	0	15			50	0.78	15.3	175	$5
17	LAA	6	6	45	53	4.43	3.91	1.30	1.22	103	86	4.0	3.4	10.7	3.1	36%	13.1%	93.9	43	17	40	33%	68%	10%	10%	0	16			55	1.12	-0.4	145	$3
18	LAA	5	1	64	57	3.80	4.21	1.39	1.37	102	102	3.8	3.7	8.0	2.2	38%	8.8%	93.1	47	21	32	31%	76%	12%	14%	0	15			13	0.96	2.8	81	-$1
19	LAA	3	1	61	64	3.23	4.11	1.14	1.30	73	91	4.4	3.2	9.4	2.9	38%	12.6%	93.0	48	19	33	27%	76%	13%	15%	7	17	0%	43%	33	0.94	9.7	118	$4
1st Half		3	1	39	44	2.54	3.96	1.10	1.29	56	87	4.3	3.9	10.2	2.6	37%	12.9%	92.8	51	16	33	26%	80%	9%	11%	7	18	0%	43%	50	0.91	9.5	116	$7
2nd Half		0	0	22	20	4.43	4.33	1.21	1.19	100	100	4.5	2.0	8.1	4.0	39%	12.2%	93.2	42	24	34	30%	70%	17%	20%	0	17			0	0.98	0.2	121	-$3
20	**Proj**	**3**	**0**	**58**	**57**	**4.02**	**3.78**	**1.33**	**1.27**	**97**	**99**	**4.1**	**3.3**	**8.8**	**2.6**	**38%**	**11.3%**	**93.4**	**45**	**21**	**34**	**31%**	**74%**	**14%**		**0**						**0.9**	**104**	**-$1**

Beede,Tyler		Health	A	LIMA Plan	B
Age: 27	Th: R Role SP	PT/Exp	D	Rand Var	+2
Ht: 6' 3"	Wt: 211 Type Pwr	Consist	B	MM	2303

5-10, 5.08 ERA in 117 IP at SF. PRO: Velocity took big step forward; missed more bats in 2nd half with major Ctl improvement. CON: Though Ball% was better, it was not enough to support Ctl improvement; sub-2.0 Cmd vL and on road. May be an out pitch vs lefties (curveball?) away from a sub-4.00 ERA.

Yr	Tm	W	Sv	IP	K	ERA	xERA	WHIP	xWHIP	vL+	vR+	BF/G	Ctl	Dom	Cmd	Ball%	SwK	Vel	G	L	F	H%	S%	HR/F	xHR/F	GS	APC	DOM%	DIS%	Sv%	LI	RAR	BPX	R$
15	aa	3	0	72	43	6.81	4.21	1.53				24.2	4.6	5.4	1.2							30%	52%									-25.4	52	-$13
16	aa	8	0	147	115	3.70	4.33	1.48				26.4	3.4	7.0	2.0							34%	75%									8.9	81	$2
17	aaa	6	0	109	70	5.74	5.82	1.66				25.7	3.3	5.7	1.7							35%	66%									-18.6	38	-$11
18	SF *	4	0	82	70	7.53	6.37	1.97		111	131	11.2	6.8	7.7	1.1		11.4%	92.3	45	27	27	36%	61%	0%	1%	2	83	0%	0%			-34.0	44	-$21
19	SF *	7	0	153	151	4.56	4.93	1.42	1.37	109	105	21.0	3.6	8.9	2.5	38%	11.7%	94.3	44	22	34	32%	73%	18%	20%	22	85	14%	41%	0	0.74	-1.0	69	$0
1st Half		3	0	74	77	4.70	4.88	1.55	1.63	133	100	20.2	5.3	9.4	1.8	40%	11.2%	94.5	46	21	33	32%	73%	19%	20%	7	83	0%	57%	0	0.65	-1.8	67	-$4
2nd Half		4	0	79	74	4.42	4.33	1.30	1.18	98	105	22.7	2.0	8.4	4.1	37%	12.0%	94.2	43	23	34	32%	73%	18%	20%	15	85	20%	33%			0.8	128	$5
20	**Proj**	**8**	**0**	**160**	**153**	**4.42**	**3.99**	**1.45**	**1.36**	**106**	**97**	**21.3**	**3.6**	**8.7**	**2.4**	**38%**	**11.6%**	**94.3**	**44**	**22**	**34**	**33%**	**73%**	**14%**		**29**						**-5.3**	**93**	**$0**

Beeks,Jalen		Health	A	LIMA Plan	A
Age: 26	Th: L Role RP	PT/Exp	C	Rand Var	+1
Ht: 5' 11"	Wt: 200 Type	Consist	A	MM	1201

Provided value in primary pitcher role during 1st half, but netted very different results in 2nd half, as H%, S%, and HR/F all took a turn for the worse. Other than SwK downturn, skills were about the same throughout; blame random H%/S% shift and HR/F spike. Heed xERA; odds appear stacked against him recapturing early-season magic.

Yr	Tm	W	Sv	IP	K	ERA	xERA	WHIP	xWHIP	vL+	vR+	BF/G	Ctl	Dom	Cmd	Ball%	SwK	Vel	G	L	F	H%	S%	HR/F	xHR/F	GS	APC	DOM%	DIS%	Sv%	LI	RAR	BPX	R$
15																																		
16	aa	5	0	65	46	6.09	6.03	1.77				23.1	4.1	6.3	1.6							36%	66%									-15.3	40	-$10
17	a/a	11	0	145	125	4.69	4.68	1.48				24.0	3.8	7.7	2.0							33%	70%									-5.9	71	$0
18	2 AL *	10	0	139	134	4.73	4.75	1.41	1.47	80	120	19.6	3.4	8.7	2.6	39%	11.9%	91.8	47	21	32	33%	69%	13%	12%	1	63	0%	100%	0	0.88	-9.9	81	-$2
19	TAM	6	1	104	89	4.31	4.83	1.49	1.41	114	102	14.1	3.5	7.7	2.2	37%	10.2%	92.2	46	24	31	33%	73%	12%	14%	3	55	0%	67%	100	0.77	2.5	75	-$1
1st Half		5	1	61	51	2.79	4.68	1.29	1.35	95	90	13.8	3.2	7.5	2.3	37%	10.9%	92.1	44	24	32	31%	79%	5%	11%	0	54			100	0.82	13.0	75	$8
2nd Half		1	0	43	38	6.49	4.94	1.77	1.38	136	118	14.4	3.8	8.0	2.1	38%	9.2%	92.3	48	23	28	37%	67%	23%	20%	3	57	0%	67%	0	0.69	-10.5	74	-$13
20	**Proj**	**5**	**0**	**87**	**75**	**4.59**	**4.18**	**1.48**	**1.41**	**106**	**111**	**16.5**	**3.6**	**7.7**	**2.1**	**38%**	**10.7%**	**92.1**	**46**	**23**	**32**	**32%**	**73%**	**15%**		**15**						**-4.7**	**76**	**-$3**

BRIAN RUDD

Berrios,Jose

Berrios,Jose				Health	A	LIMA Plan	A
Age: 26	Th: R	Role	SP	PT/Exp	A	Rand Var	0
Ht: 6' 0"	Wt: 205	Type		Consist	A	MM	2305

Different results in 1st/2nd half thanks to swings in H%/S%, jump in Ctl. But most skills held firm throughout—Ball% says Ctl will be fine—and he continued to gradually increase workload. May not offer the upside many were expecting, but there's plenty of value in his steady BPX and "AAA" reliability once the big guns are off the board.

Yr Tm	W	Sv	IP	K	ERA	xERA	WHIP	xWHIP	vL+	vR+	BF/G	Ctl	Dom	Cmd	Ball%	SwK	Vel	G	L	F	H%	S%	HR/F	xHR/F	GS	APC	DOM%	DIS%	Sv%	LI	RAR	BPX	R$
15 a/a	14	0	166	147	3.41	3.11	1.14				24.4	2.0	7.9	4.0							30%	72%									11.4	140	$15
16 MIN *	13	0	170	152	5.05	4.36	1.40	1.58	113	141	23.1	3.8	8.0	2.1	42%	8.6%	93.3	38	22	40	30%	66%	16%	16%	14	82	7%	50%			-18.0	72	-$1
17 MIN *	17	0	185	170	3.43	3.28	1.18	1.27	104	83	23.2	2.8	8.3	3.0	37%	10.0%	93.5	39	21	40	29%	74%	9%	10%	25	92	32%	32%	0	0.78	21.3	114	$21
18 MIN	12	0	192	202	3.84	3.76	1.14	1.21	93	91	24.9	2.9	9.5	3.3	36%	11.7%	93.2	42	20	38	28%	71%	13%	12%	32	96	38%	25%			7.4	130	$16
19 MIN	14	0	200	195	3.68	4.26	1.22	1.23	93	95	26.3	2.3	8.8	3.8	33%	11.2%	92.8	42	21	37	31%	74%	12%	14%	32	98	25%	25%			20.3	126	$17
1st Half	8	0	112	102	2.89	4.19	1.08	1.13	82	94	26.9	1.6	8.2	5.1	31%	11.1%	92.7	41	21	38	29%	79%	11%	14%	17	99	24%	12%			22.3	134	$26
2nd Half	6	0	88	93	4.69	4.42	1.40	1.25	105	96	25.7	3.2	9.5	3.0	34%	11.4%	92.8	44	19	37	34%	70%	13%	14%	15	97	27%	40%			-2.0	117	$6
20 Proj	**14**	**0**	**189**	**186**	**3.79**	**3.66**	**1.23**	**1.25**	**95**	**94**	**25.2**	**2.7**	**8.9**	**3.3**	**35%**	**11.2%**	**93.0**	**41**	**20**	**38**	**30%**	**73%**	**12%**		**30**						**8.4**	**123**	**$15**

Betances,Dellin

Betances,Dellin				Health	F	LIMA Plan	D
Age: 32	Th: R	Role	RP	PT/Exp	D	Rand Var	+5
Ht: 6' 8"	Wt: 265	Type	Pwr	Consist	D	MM	5510

March shoulder issue was originally thought to be minor, but instead was the beginning of long, injury-filled season. Finally came back in September after multiple setbacks, only to tear his Achilles in lone appearance. He won't need surgery, but he clearly carries risk. If health and velocity check out in spring, could be a high-impact arm again.

Yr Tm	W	Sv	IP	K	ERA	xERA	WHIP	xWHIP	vL+	vR+	BF/G	Ctl	Dom	Cmd	Ball%	SwK	Vel	G	L	F	H%	S%	HR/F	xHR/F	GS	APC	DOM%	DIS%	Sv%	LI	RAR	BPX	R$
15 NYY	6	9	84	131	1.50	2.43	1.01	1.13	62	79	4.5	4.3	14.0	3.3	38%	15.5%	97.0	48	21	32	27%	90%	12%	12%	0	19			69	1.42	25.5	194	$19
16 NYY	3	12	73	126	3.08	2.09	1.12	0.98	86	73	4.1	3.5	15.5	4.5	37%	16.0%	97.7	54	19	27	38%	74%	13%	13%	0	17			71	1.19	10.0	260	$12
17 NYY	3	10	60	100	2.87	3.21	1.22	1.34	58	84	4.0	6.6	15.1	2.3	41%	12.9%	98.5	49	13	38	28%	77%	8%	9%	0	17			77	1.09	11.0	143	$9
18 NYY	4	4	67	115	2.70	2.18	1.05	0.98	84	77	4.1	3.5	15.5	4.4	35%	15.2%	97.8	44	28	28	34%	79%	21%	14%	0	17			57	1.09	11.9	238	$9
19 NYY	0	0	1	2	0.00	0.00	0.00		0	0	2.0	0.0	27.0	0.0	13%	0.0%	94.4	0	0	0	0%	0%	0%		0	8			0	0.89	0.4	505	-$5
1st Half																																	
2nd Half	0	0	1	2	0.00	0.00	0.00		0	0	2.0	0.0	27.0	0.0		0.0%	94.4	0	0	0	0%	0%	0%		0	8			0	0.89	0.4	506	-$5
20 Proj	**3**	**2**	**58**	**90**	**3.00**	**2.65**	**1.17**	**1.07**	**78**	**79**	**4.0**	**4.5**	**14.0**	**3.1**	**38%**	**13.8%**	**97.8**	**46**	**21**	**33**	**32%**	**77%**	**12%**		**0**						**8.3**	**176**	**$5**

Bettis,Chad

Bettis,Chad				Health	F	LIMA Plan	B
Age: 31	Th: R	Role	RP	PT/Exp	C	Rand Var	+5
Ht: 6' 0"	Wt: 201	Type	Con GB	Consist	B	MM	1001

Move to 'pen added velocity, but didn't move the needle on SwK or xERA, and more GB couldn't even help his HR issues. Sure, he was a little unlucky, but he's simply not the answer vL or vR, as he hasn't struck out 20% of either since way back in 2015. Until he shows the ability to get more whiffs, he's safe to avoid.

Yr Tm	W	Sv	IP	K	ERA	xERA	WHIP	xWHIP	vL+	vR+	BF/G	Ctl	Dom	Cmd	Ball%	SwK	Vel	G	L	F	H%	S%	HR/F	xHR/F	GS	APC	DOM%	DIS%	Sv%	LI	RAR	BPX	R$
15 COL *	11	0	157	125	4.29	4.79	1.46	1.35	101	114	24.1	3.2	7.1	2.3	39%	10.3%	92.0	49	22	28	33%	73%	11%	14%	20	94	20%	40%			-6.4	69	-$2
16 COL	14	0	186	138	4.79	4.31	1.41	1.35	94	116	25.4	2.9	6.7	2.3	38%	9.2%	91.7	51	22	27	32%	68%	14%	15%	32	95	19%	44%			-13.8	86	$0
17 COL *	2	0	70	42	5.62	5.95	1.53	1.31	105	116	20.2	2.5	5.4	2.1	36%	9.6%	90.2	48	19	33	32%	67%	16%	9%	9	82	11%	44%			-10.8	26	-$8
18 COL	5	0	120	80	5.01	4.78	1.40	1.46	99	117	19.2	3.5	6.0	1.7	38%	8.7%	90.5	49	19	32	28%	67%	15%	16%	20	71	5%	40%	0	0.75	-12.8	46	-$6
19 COL	1	1	64	42	6.08	4.70	1.55	1.43	121	110	7.4	3.0	5.9	2.0	36%	9.5%	93.0	61	19	20	33%	63%	23%	18%	3	26	0%	100%	33	0.79	-12.4	72	-$9
1st Half	1	1	45	33	5.76	4.07	1.50	1.36	116	101	8.1	3.0	6.6	2.2	36%	9.7%	92.4	67	17	16	34%	62%	21%	25%	3	29	0%	100%	33	1.01	-7.0	90	-$8
2nd Half	0	0	18	9	6.87	5.82	1.69	1.47	133	131	6.1	2.9	4.4	1.5	37%	9.2%	94.1	47	24	29	32%	65%	25%	11%	0	22			0	0.39	-5.4	27	-$11
20 Proj	**2**	**0**	**73**	**48**	**5.38**	**4.38**	**1.57**	**1.41**	**118**	**123**	**8.5**	**3.0**	**6.0**	**2.0**	**37%**	**9.3%**	**92.1**	**52**	**20**	**28**	**33%**	**70%**	**19%**		**0**						**-11.0**	**64**	**-$8**

Biagini,Joe

Biagini,Joe				Health	A	LIMA Plan	D
Age: 30	Th: R	Role	RP	PT/Exp	D	Rand Var	+5
Ht: 6' 5"	Wt: 235	Type		Consist	D	MM	1100

First, the good news: brought SwK up to career-best mark, struck out a batter per inning in 1st half. The bad news list is much longer: Ball% and Ctl headed in wrong direction; LHB continued to crush him; HR issues worsened; 2nd half was absolute train wreck. Middle relievers with poor ratios don't make for very intriguing targets.

Yr Tm	W	Sv	IP	K	ERA	xERA	WHIP	xWHIP	vL+	vR+	BF/G	Ctl	Dom	Cmd	Ball%	SwK	Vel	G	L	F	H%	S%	HR/F	xHR/F	GS	APC	DOM%	DIS%	Sv%	LI	RAR	BPX	R$
15 aa	10	0	130	70	3.35	3.89	1.38				23.8	2.6	4.8	1.8							31%	75%									9.8	66	$4
16 TOR	4	1	68	62	3.06	3.75	1.30	1.24	98	88	4.9	2.5	8.2	3.3	35%	11.9%	94.3	52	21	26	34%	76%	6%	8%	0	19			33	0.91	9.4	131	$3
17 TOR *	4	1	137	108	5.31	4.64	1.41	1.35	104	98	12.1	3.2	7.1	2.2	36%	8.7%	93.8	56	18	27	31%	64%	15%	11%	18	44	17%	39%	33	1.22	-16.1	64	-$5
18 TOR *	4	0	95	63	6.08	6.22	1.63	1.37	131	122	7.8	3.2	5.9	1.9	36%	9.0%	94.3	48	20	32	34%	65%	18%	18%	4	25	0%	100%	0	0.69	-22.6	28	-$14
19 2AL	3	1	65	60	4.59	4.53	1.50	1.39	140	98	4.5	3.6	8.4	2.3	39%	12.3%	94.0	46	27	26	32%	77%	27%	26%	0	18			33	0.88	-0.7	83	-$3
1st Half	2	1	37	37	3.41	3.88	1.22	1.21	107	95	4.1	2.7	9.0	3.4	38%	14.0%	94.2	48	25	28	29%	79%	21%	24%	0	17			33	1.12	5.0	126	$1
2nd Half	1	0	28	23	6.18	5.31	1.88	1.53	173	102	5.1	4.9	7.5	1.5	39%	10.2%	93.8	44	31	25	36%	75%	36%	28%	0	20			0	0.53	-5.7	28	-$9
20 Proj	**3**	**0**	**58**	**47**	**4.86**	**4.33**	**1.56**	**1.37**	**127**	**100**	**6.0**	**3.5**	**7.3**	**2.1**	**37%**	**10.6%**	**94.1**	**46**	**23**	**31**	**34%**	**72%**	**15%**		**0**						**-5.1**	**69**	**-$6**

Bieber,Shane

Bieber,Shane				Health	A	LIMA Plan	A
Age: 25	Th: R	Role	SP	PT/Exp	B	Rand Var	+1
Ht: 6' 3"	Wt: 200	Type	Pwr	Consist	A	MM	5405

Lived up to spring hype and then some, combining heavy workload, pinpoint Ctl, and much-improved SwK on way to breakout. Solved LHB by throwing more curves, a pitch that generated more whiffs against both sides. Still gave up a lot of hard contact, but that's the only blemish in these skills. Looks like a good bet to do it again.

Yr Tm	W	Sv	IP	K	ERA	xERA	WHIP	xWHIP	vL+	vR+	BF/G	Ctl	Dom	Cmd	Ball%	SwK	Vel	G	L	F	H%	S%	HR/F	xHR/F	GS	APC	DOM%	DIS%	Sv%	LI	RAR	BPX	R$
15																																	
16																																	
17 aa	2	0	54	38	2.99	4.13	1.31				25.0	0.9	6.3	7.2							36%	77%									9.2	205	$0
18 CLE *	17	0	196	183	3.45	3.64	1.16	1.11	124	91	23.6	1.4	8.4	6.0	33%	11.8%	93.1	47	22	31	33%	73%	12%	17%	19	90	42%	21%	0	0.79	16.9	178	$19
19 CLE	15	0	214	259	3.28	3.30	1.05	1.05	90	86	25.3	1.7	10.9	6.5	34%	14.3%	93.1	44	21	35	31%	76%	16%	17%	33	98	48%	9%	0	0.76	32.5	188	$30
1st Half	7	0	104	133	3.54	3.24	1.04	1.01	93	86	23.3	2.0	11.5	5.8	35%	15.0%	93.2	45	20	35	30%	73%	18%	22%	17	92	41%	12%	0	0.74	12.5	192	$26
2nd Half	8	0	110	126	3.03	3.43	1.06	1.01	88	86	27.4	1.4	10.3	7.4	32%	13.6%	93.0	43	22	35	32%	78%	15%	13%	16	105	56%	6%			20.1	184	$33
20 Proj	**14**	**0**	**203**	**229**	**3.31**	**3.00**	**1.12**	**1.05**	**100**	**84**	**24.3**	**1.7**	**10.2**	**6.1**	**33%**	**13.2%**	**93.1**	**44**	**20**	**36**	**32%**	**75%**	**13%**		**33**						**21.0**	**184**	**$25**

Blach,Ty

Blach,Ty				Health	A	LIMA Plan	F
Age: 29	Th: L	Role	SP	PT/Exp	B	Rand Var	+5
Ht: 6' 1"	Wt: 213	Type	Con	Consist	F	MM	0000

1-3, 12.00 ERA in 27 IP at SF/BAL. Made just seven appearances in majors; allowed 5+ ER in five of them. His already weak skills got even worse, as he struggled to throw strikes, missed fewer bats, and posted ugly 2.7 hr/9. Health Grade is the only positive in his entire box, but in life's grand scheme, if you've got your health, you've got everything.

Yr Tm	W	Sv	IP	K	ERA	xERA	WHIP	xWHIP	vL+	vR+	BF/G	Ctl	Dom	Cmd	Ball%	SwK	Vel	G	L	F	H%	S%	HR/F	xHR/F	GS	APC	DOM%	DIS%	Sv%	LI	RAR	BPX	R$
15 aaa	11	0	165	77	4.82	4.94	1.46				26.2	1.7	4.2	2.5							34%	67%									-17.5	58	-$7
16 SF *	15	0	180	101	3.89	3.56	1.28		51	68	24.5	2.3	5.0	2.2		5.8%	91.1	58	9	33	30%	69%	7%	3%	2	60	50%	50%	0	0.40	6.7	77	$9
17 SF	8	0	164	73	4.78	5.20	1.36	1.43	78	112	20.4	2.4	4.0	1.7	36%	6.6%	90.1	47	21	32	29%	66%	10%	10%	24	74	8%	38%	0	0.72	-8.6	40	-$1
18 SF	6	0	119	75	4.25	4.47	1.47	1.42	99	106	10.9	3.1	5.7	1.8	36%	7.3%	90.0	54	23	23	32%	71%	9%	14%	13	40	0%	62%	0	0.89	-1.4	58	-$4
19 2TM *	4	0	124	70	9.45	9.65	2.20	1.70	195	132	24.0	3.5	5.1	1.5	40%	6.5%	90.3	35	25	39	41%	58%	20%	15%	5	74	0%	80%	0	0.60	-75.6	-23	-$40
1st Half	3	0	85	44	8.48	8.73	2.03		92	226	25.7	2.8	4.6	1.7		3.0%	89.8	31	13	56	40%	59%	22%	12%	0	66			0	0.38	-41.5	-11	-$41
2nd Half	1	0	42	27	10.86	10.82	2.42	1.57	214	116	21.9	4.7	5.8	1.2	40%	7.0%	90.4	36	28	36	43%	56%	19%	16%	5	76	0%	80%	0	0.64	-32.8	-40	-$40
20 Proj	**2**	**0**	**58**	**33**	**5.97**	**5.07**	**1.75**	**1.48**	**141**	**119**	**22.4**	**3.3**	**5.2**	**1.6**	**38%**	**7.0%**	**90.2**	**45**	**24**	**31**	**35%**	**68%**	**14%**		**10**						**-13.0**	**31**	**-$11**

Boyd,Matt

Boyd,Matt				Health	A	LIMA Plan	B
Age: 29	Th: L	Role	SP	PT/Exp	A	Rand Var	+3
Ht: 6' 3"	Wt: 234	Type	Pwr xFB	Consist	B	MM	3403

Went primarily with four-seamer/slider, and got a lot more whiffs on both pitches, posting career-best Dom and SwK. But 1st half Ctl proved unsustainable, and high FB% caught up to him with 2.6 hr/9 in last 19 starts. The strikeout gains look legit and xERA gives hope for a step forward, but FB% and xHR/F will keep his ERA combustible.

Yr Tm	W	Sv	IP	K	ERA	xERA	WHIP	xWHIP	vL+	vR+	BF/G	Ctl	Dom	Cmd	Ball%	SwK	Vel	G	L	F	H%	S%	HR/F	xHR/F	GS	APC	DOM%	DIS%	Sv%	LI	RAR	BPX	R$
15 2AL *	10	0	172	128	3.84	3.77	1.17	1.38	156	129	21.5	2.5	6.7	2.6	38%	8.6%	91.1	32	16	52	26%	73%	18%	16%	12	77	0%	50%	0	0.74	2.6	74	$9
16 DET *	8	0	161	127	3.95	4.39	1.31	1.29	81	109	21.5	2.7	7.1	2.6	34%	9.9%	91.2	38	17	45	30%	75%	13%	12%	18	84	22%	44%	0	0.87	4.8	72	$5
17 DET *	9	0	181	148	4.95	4.94	1.43	1.39	94	114	23.4	3.3	7.3	2.2	36%	10.5%	92.1	37	22	41	31%	69%	11%	12%	24	90	13%	46%	0	0.74	-13.1	60	-$2
18 DET	9	0	170	159	4.39	4.46	1.16	1.25	89	100	22.9	2.7	8.4	3.1	37%	10.7%	90.4	29	21	50	27%	67%	11%	10%	31	92	16%	26%			-5.0	98	$8
19 DET	9	0	185	238	4.56	3.81	1.23	1.12	94	104	24.6	2.4	11.6	4.8	34%	14.8%	92.0	36	20	45	33%	71%	18%	16%	32	97	34%	13%			-1.4	170	$10
1st Half	5	0	102	129	3.72	3.58	1.09	1.00	95	94	24.6	1.8	11.4	6.5	33%	14.5%	91.6	36	21	43	32%	73%	15%	16%	17	97	41%	6%			9.9	187	$17
2nd Half	4	0	84	109	5.59	4.29	1.40	1.15	92	116	24.6	3.2	11.7	3.6	35%	15.2%	92.5	35	18	47	34%	68%	21%	17%	15	98	27%	20%			-11.2	150	$1
20 Proj	**9**	**0**	**174**	**202**	**4.29**	**3.60**	**1.27**	**1.20**	**94**	**105**	**24.4**	**2.7**	**10.5**	**3.8**	**35%**	**13.6%**	**91.6**	**34**	**20**	**46**	**32%**	**73%**	**16%**		**29**						**-3.0**	**145**	**$8**

BRIAN RUDD

Bradley,Archie

Age: 27	Th: R	Role: RP	Health	B	LIMA Plan	A
Ht: 6' 4"	Wt: 225	Type: Pwr	PT/Exp	C	Rand Var	0
			Consist	A	MM	3331

Walk explosion, skyrocketing H% sent 1st half ERA into atmosphere, but luck paid him back after July. Although Ball% increase says he deserved some of the added walks, expect Ctl to settle near 2nd half mark. While late-season ERA is unsustainable, GB% tilt and Dom make him a mid-tier saves option with ERA in the 2018-19 range.

Yr	Tm	W	Sv	IP	K	ERA	xERA	WHIP	xWHIP	vL+	vR+	BF/G	Ctl	Dom	Cmd	Ball%	SwK	Vel	G	L	F	H%	S%	HR/F	xHR/F	GS	APC	DOM%	DIS%	Sv%	LI	RAR	BPX	R$
15	ARI *	3	0	57	40	4.70	4.90	1.57	1.70	81	139	20.8	4.2	6.3	1.5	42%	6.4%	92.2	58	14	28	32%	71%	10%	13%	8	81	0%	63%			-5.2	49	-$6
16	ARI *	13	0	182	182	4.42	4.29	1.47	1.38	127	91	23.7	4.2	9.0	2.1	38%	8.7%	92.4	45	25	30	34%	71%	13%	13%	26	99	15%	38%			-5.2	92	$1
17	ARI	3	1	73	79	1.73	3.32	1.04	1.16	77	75	4.6	2.6	9.7	3.8	34%	10.5%	96.4	48	23	29	29%	86%	7%	12%	0	18			14	1.29	23.7	158	$10
18	ARI	4	3	72	75	3.64	3.50	1.14	1.17	67	111	3.9	2.5	9.4	3.8	32%	9.3%	95.6	49	17	33	29%	73%	14%	16%	0	16			27	1.37	4.5	148	$4
19	ARI	4	18	72	87	3.52	4.14	1.44	1.36	104	88	4.8	4.5	10.9	2.4	36%	10.6%	95.5	45	25	30	35%	77%	9%	12%	1	19	0%	100%	86	1.11	8.7	106	$9
1st Half		2	0	38	50	5.21	4.29	1.76	1.35	104	115	5.3	5.2	11.8	2.3	36%	11.4%	95.6	46	26	27	42%	70%	10%	15%	1	21	0%	100%	0	1.05	-3.3	105	-$5
2nd Half		2	18	34	37	1.60	3.86	1.07	1.28	105	54	4.3	3.7	9.9	2.6	36%	9.6%	95.4	44	23	34	26%	88%	7%	10%	0	18			95	1.18	12.0	108	$24
20	**Proj**	**4**	**30**	**73**	**77**	**3.15**	**3.49**	**1.27**	**1.27**	**93**	**94**	**4.7**	**3.6**	**9.5**	**2.7**	**35%**	**9.8%**	**95.3**	**47**	**22**	**31**	**30%**	**79%**	**13%**		**0**						**8.9**	**115**	**$16**

Brault,Steven

Age: 28	Th: L	Role: SP	Health	C	LIMA Plan	B
Ht: 6' 0"	Wt: 195	Type: Pwr	PT/Exp	C	Rand Var	+1
			Consist	B	MM	1201

Scanning across xERA and xWHIP, he deserved the poor ratios and yet another season of negative R$. Continued to hand out plenty of free passes, while subpar Dom says you're losing strikeout pace with him on roster. While GB% may sneak his ERA below 5.00, BPX is forgettable. Let someone else take the R$ loss.

Yr	Tm	W	Sv	IP	K	ERA	xERA	WHIP	xWHIP	vL+	vR+	BF/G	Ctl	Dom	Cmd	Ball%	SwK	Vel	G	L	F	H%	S%	HR/F	xHR/F	GS	APC	DOM%	DIS%	Sv%	LI	RAR	BPX	R$
15	aa	9	0	90	65	2.32	2.46	1.11				23.6	1.8	6.5	3.5							30%	78%									18.3	139	$11
16	PIT *	2	0	105	93	5.42	5.93	1.78	1.47	112	123	20.0	4.9	8.0	1.7	41%	10.3%	91.0	45	26	29	37%	71%	15%	13%	7	83	0%	71%	0	0.71	-15.9	53	-$13
17	PIT *	11	1	155	108	3.13	3.66	1.36	1.47	87	112	20.3	3.7	6.3	1.7	39%	8.1%	91.9	42	20	38	30%	78%	7%	9%	4	58	25%	50%	100	0.49	23.4	75	$11
18	PIT	6	0	92	82	4.61	4.93	1.54	1.59	87	112	9.2	5.6	8.1	1.4	41%	10.6%	92.5	48	19	33	30%	72%	12%	16%	5	37	0%	60%	0	0.83	-5.3	23	-$5
19	PIT	4	0	113	100	5.16	5.10	1.50	1.49	91	110	20.2	4.2	7.9	1.9	38%	10.1%	92.0	45	21	34	32%	68%	13%	14%	19	80	11%	37%	0	0.76	-9.2	57	-$6
1st Half		3	0	57	49	4.29	5.43	1.59	1.51	86	114	18.3	4.8	7.8	1.6	39%	10.0%	91.9	45	18	38	33%	75%	10%	14%	8	75	0%	38%	0	0.73	1.5	37	-$4
2nd Half		1	0	57	51	6.04	4.70	1.41	1.37	96	105	22.6	3.7	8.1	2.2	38%	10.2%	92.0	45	25	31	31%	59%	18%	15%	11	87	18%	36%			-10.7	76	-$7
20	**Proj**	**6**	**0**	**116**	**99**	**4.68**	**4.41**	**1.47**	**1.48**	**86**	**106**	**20.2**	**4.3**	**7.7**	**1.8**	**39%**	**9.9%**	**92.0**	**45**	**21**	**34**	**31%**	**70%**	**11%**		**25**						**-7.5**	**51**	**-$3**

Brebbia,John

Age: 30	Th: R	Role: RP	Health	A	LIMA Plan	B
Ht: 6' 1"	Wt: 185	Type: Pwr xFB	PT/Exp	D	Rand Var	-2
			Consist	B	MM	2401

Fared well in slightly higher leverage role. Even with velocity down a tick, consistent SwK should keep double-digit Dom as a feature, and Ball% says he could even shave off a few walks. FB% tilt adds some ERA risk if HR/F corrects, but when searching for cheap LIMA targets, he's a potential gem.

Yr	Tm	W	Sv	IP	K	ERA	xERA	WHIP	xWHIP	vL+	vR+	BF/G	Ctl	Dom	Cmd	Ball%	SwK	Vel	G	L	F	H%	S%	HR/F	xHR/F	GS	APC	DOM%	DIS%	Sv%	LI	RAR	BPX	R$
15																																		
16	a/a	5	2	68	52	6.31	6.72	1.76				7.2	2.6	6.9	2.6							39%	65%									-17.8	51	-$10
17	STL *	1	3	78	73	2.37	2.59	0.94	1.13	98	78	4.5	1.9	8.3	4.4	31%	13.2%	94.2	25	19	56	24%	84%	10%	8%	0	16			75	0.68	19.3	146	$10
18	STL *	5	4	60	70	3.03	3.00	1.26	1.16	107	73	4.8	2.8	10.6	3.9	34%	12.8%	94.6	33	20	48	34%	75%	8%	12%	0	19			100	0.48	4.2	133	$3
19	STL	3	0	73	87	3.59	4.41	1.18	1.26	98	76	4.6	3.3	10.8	3.2	33%	13.8%	93.5	27	23	51	31%	71%	6%	8%	0	18			0	0.77	8.2	118	$3
1st Half		1	0	40	46	3.40	4.56	1.18	1.22	114	76	4.6	3.4	10.4	3.1	34%	14.1%	93.6	28	24	48	29%	76%	10%	11%	0	19			0	0.80	5.4	111	$2
2nd Half		2	0	33	41	3.82	4.44	1.18	1.17	81	77	4.6	3.3	11.2	3.4	32%	13.5%	93.3	26	21	54	33%	66%	2%	4%	0	18			0	0.74	2.8	127	$4
20	**Proj**	**4**	**0**	**73**	**81**	**3.62**	**3.82**	**1.22**	**1.17**	**111**	**84**	**4.7**	**2.9**	**10.1**	**3.5**	**33%**	**13.3%**	**94.0**	**28**	**21**	**51**	**31%**	**75%**	**10%**		**0**						**4.7**	**126**	**$3**

Brennan,Brandon

Age: 28	Th: R	Role: RP	Health	D	LIMA Plan	C
Ht: 6' 4"	Wt: 220	Type: Pwr xGB	PT/Exp	D	Rand Var	+1
			Consist	C	MM	1210

Ugly 1st half came with boatload of BBs and some bad luck before shoulder started barking in mid-June. SwK looks promising, but Dom history suggests pullback is coming. Ball% (and initials!) hint that walks will continue to haunt, so while GB% could limit ERA damage, uninspiring BPX says he isn't worth chasing for saves.

Yr	Tm	W	Sv	IP	K	ERA	xERA	WHIP	xWHIP	vL+	vR+	BF/G	Ctl	Dom	Cmd	Ball%	SwK	Vel	G	L	F	H%	S%	HR/F	xHR/F	GS	APC	DOM%	DIS%	Sv%	LI	RAR	BPX	R$
15																																		
16	aa	2	0	66	46	9.78	7.53	2.10				13.5	4.4	6.2	1.4							42%	50%									-45.3	31	-$24
17	a/a	2	15	60	45	6.36	5.75	1.91				6.7	5.2	6.9	1.3							39%	64%									-14.7	65	-$6
18	a/a	5	1	76	63	4.48	3.85	1.34				7.2	3.3	7.5	2.2							31%	67%									-3.1	87	-$2
19	SEA	3	0	47	47	4.56	4.23	1.23	1.46	104	74	4.5	4.6	8.9	2.0	39%	15.7%	94.8	55	18	26	24%	65%	18%	17%	0	16			0	0.99	-0.3	77	-$1
1st Half		2	0	34	35	5.56	4.35	1.38	1.49	118	76	4.9	5.3	9.3	1.8	39%	14.3%	94.9	55	21	24	27%	60%	18%	20%	0	18			0	0.96	-4.4	62	-$2
2nd Half		1	0	13	12	2.03	3.68	0.83		61	68	3.5	2.7	8.1	3.0		20.4%	94.4	55	12	33	16%	89%	18%	9%	0	12			0	1.06	4.1	115	$1
20	**Proj**	**2**	**2**	**51**	**47**	**4.82**	**4.06**	**1.55**	**1.64**	**127**	**80**	**6.4**	**4.7**	**8.3**	**1.8**	**42%**	**14.3%**	**94.9**	**55**	**21**	**24**	**33%**	**70%**	**14%**		**0**						**-4.2**	**64**	**-$4**

Brewer,Colten

Age: 27	Th: R	Role: RP	Health	B	LIMA Plan	D
Ht: 6' 4"	Wt: 230	Type: Pwr	PT/Exp	D	Rand Var	0
			Consist	D	MM	2300

Pitched backwards with curveball-first approach, but expected ratios say he didn't fool anybody. Inability to throw strikes should continue to inflate WHIP, and even with GB% tilt, struggles vR cap ERA upside. His Dom no longer stands out, while poor Cmd should tell you to rummage through a different bargain bin.

Yr	Tm	W	Sv	IP	K	ERA	xERA	WHIP	xWHIP	vL+	vR+	BF/G	Ctl	Dom	Cmd	Ball%	SwK	Vel	G	L	F	H%	S%	HR/F	xHR/F	GS	APC	DOM%	DIS%	Sv%	LI	RAR	BPX	R$
15																																		
16																																		
17	a/a	3	12	51	45	4.82	5.57	1.68				6.6	3.0	7.8	2.6							40%	71%									-2.9	92	$0
18	SD *	4	3	58	61	4.16	3.88	1.40		120	122	5.1	3.3	9.5	2.8		10.8%		50	25	25	36%	69%	0%	1%	0	18			75	0.34	-0.1	122	-$1
19	BOS	1	0	55	52	4.12	5.22	1.70	1.59	91	117	4.4	5.6	8.6	1.5	39%	11.4%	94.9	50	23	26	34%	78%	14%	13%	0	18			0	0.79	2.6	34	-$6
1st Half		1	0	35	35	4.08	5.17	1.75	1.58	85	103	5.1	6.1	8.9	1.5	40%	11.7%	94.9	53	21	26	36%	75%	4%	5%	0	20			0	0.88	1.9	29	-$6
2nd Half		0	0	19	17	4.19	4.99	1.60	1.49	102	145	3.4	4.7	7.9	1.7	39%	10.9%		45	28	28	30%	85%	31%	25%	0	14			0	0.69	0.8	43	-$5
20	**Proj**	**2**	**0**	**51**	**49**	**4.61**	**4.01**	**1.57**	**1.53**	**92**	**122**	**4.5**	**4.2**	**8.7**	**2.1**	**39%**	**11.2%**	**94.5**	**48**	**25**	**27**	**35%**	**72%**	**14%**		**0**						**-2.9**	**79**	**-$5**

Brice,Austin

Age: 28	Th: R	Role: RP	Health	F	LIMA Plan	A
Ht: 6' 4"	Wt: 235	Type:	PT/Exp	D	Rand Var	0
			Consist	A	MM	1100

Rode wave of early fortune before forearm issues cost him most of 2nd half. Trading sinkers for curveballs and four-seamers boosted SwK but cost him GB%, while Dom baseline questions small-sample spike. Steady xERA/xWHIP forecast league-average ratios, and as a middle reliever, that's a pass in reserve rounds.

Yr	Tm	W	Sv	IP	K	ERA	xERA	WHIP	xWHIP	vL+	vR+	BF/G	Ctl	Dom	Cmd	Ball%	SwK	Vel	G	L	F	H%	S%	HR/F	xHR/F	GS	APC	DOM%	DIS%	Sv%	LI	RAR	BPX	R$
15	aa	6	0	125	105	5.67	4.73	1.61				22.2	5.1	7.6	1.5							33%	64%									-26.4	66	-$13
16	MIA *	4	4	116	90	3.82	3.27	1.22		84	77	10.0	2.8	7.0	2.5		12.6%	94.1	53	16	32	29%	69%	17%	14%	0	14			100	0.47	5.3	96	$6
17	CIN *	2	1	57	46	4.93	4.75	1.45	1.22	95	106	6.1	3.0	7.3	2.5	34%	11.3%	93.8	51	17	32	34%	67%	19%	15%	0	23			50	0.56	-4.0	78	-$4
18	CIN *	5	1	61	52	4.69	4.95	1.34	1.33	143	106	5.1	3.1	7.6	2.5	36%	9.6%	94.0	51	19	30	29%	71%	26%	23%	0	18			100	0.65	-4.1	56	-$2
19	MIA	1	0	45	46	3.43	4.51	1.23	1.35	103	80	5.5	3.6	9.3	2.6	36%	12.1%	93.2	42	23	34	27%	79%	16%	10%	0	22			0	0.71	6.0	97	-$1
1st Half		1	0	32	29	2.23	4.59	1.18	1.39	87	74	5.7	3.9	8.1	2.1	36%	12.1%	93.0	48	22	30	25%	86%	11%	8%	0	22			0	0.75	9.1	72	$1
2nd Half		0	0	12	17	6.57	4.28	1.38		135	100	5.2	2.9	12.4	4.3		12.0%	93.6	26	26	47	34%	62%	25%	13%	0	22			0	0.63	-3.1	162	-$6
20	**Proj**	**2**	**0**	**44**	**37**	**4.38**	**4.05**	**1.42**	**1.31**	**113**	**102**	**6.5**	**3.5**	**7.6**	**2.2**	**35%**	**11.1%**	**93.6**	**50**	**19**	**31**	**31%**	**74%**	**17%**		**0**						**-1.2**	**81**	**-$4**

Britton,Zach

Age: 32	Th: L	Role: RP	Health	F	LIMA Plan	A
Ht: 6' 3"	Wt: 195	Type: Pwr xGB	PT/Exp	C	Rand Var	-5
			Consist	A	MM	4210

Provided deep-league value; mostly thanks to H%/S% combo. Wowzers, that MLB-leading GB% (min. 60 IP) sure keeps ERA in check, but look for the free passes to continue in droves given ugly Ball%. With meager Dom baseline, velocity dip, and a tough path to repeat 2019 ratios, that value may dry up.

Yr	Tm	W	Sv	IP	K	ERA	xERA	WHIP	xWHIP	vL+	vR+	BF/G	Ctl	Dom	Cmd	Ball%	SwK	Vel	G	L	F	H%	S%	HR/F	xHR/F	GS	APC	DOM%	DIS%	Sv%	LI	RAR	BPX	R$
15	BAL	4	36	66	79	1.92	1.75	0.99	1.02	45	90	4.0	1.9	10.8	5.6	31%	16.7%	95.9	79	11	9	31%	82%	20%	19%	0	14			90	1.17	16.5	238	$23
16	BAL	2	47	67	74	0.54	2.03	0.84	1.11	67	56	3.7	2.4	9.9	4.1	37%	17.6%	96.3	80	11	9	24%	95%	7%	17%	0	15			100	1.31	30.2	204	$32
17	BAL	2	15	37	29	2.89	3.73	1.53	1.49	95	92	4.2	4.3	7.0	1.6	40%	12.4%	96.1	73	19	8	33%	80%	11%	14%	0	15			88	1.05	6.7	72	$4
18	2 AL	2	7	41	34	3.10	3.45	1.23	1.51	94	80	4.1	4.6	7.5	1.6	42%	12.8%	94.9	73	16	11	24%	77%	25%	30%	0	16			70	0.86	5.3	70	$2
19	NYY	3	3	61	53	1.91	3.48	1.14	1.52	61	77	3.7	4.7	7.8	1.7	41%	10.9%	94.8	77	13	9	23%	85%	20%	26%	0	14			43	1.02	19.7	74	$7
1st Half		3	3	35	26	2.55	3.74	1.27	1.62	53	88	3.9	5.1	6.6	1.3	42%	9.2%	94.8	78	12	9	24%	81%	22%	26%	0	15			50	1.07	8.5	41	$7
2nd Half		0	0	26	27	1.04	2.80	0.96	1.35	66	57	3.5	4.2	9.3	2.3	39%	13.7%	94.6	75	15	10	21%	92%	17%	27%	0	13			0	0.94	11.1	119	$6
20	**Proj**	**2**	**2**	**58**	**50**	**3.39**	**3.14**	**1.31**	**1.43**	**82**	**86**	**3.9**	**4.6**	**7.8**	**1.7**	**40%**	**12.6%**	**95.1**	**75**	**15**	**10**	**28%**	**74%**	**18%**		**0**						**5.4**	**80**	**$1**

BRANT CHESSER

Brooks,Aaron

Age: 30	Th: R	Role RP	Health D	LIMA Plan D
Ht: 6' 4"	Wt: 230	Type Con	PT/Exp C	Rand Var +4
			Consist D	MM 0001

Ugly results with OAK/BAL; the skills hint at more of the same. He barely misses bats, so strikeouts are limited. xERA and xWHIP say he'll damage your ratios. And even decent Ctl can be questioned thanks to barely average Ball%. DIS % points out that he's not just bad, he's consistently bad. Another negative R$ warns to stay away from the wreckage.

Yr Tm	W	Sv	IP	K	ERA	xERA	WHIP	xWHIP	vL+	vR+	BF/G	Ctl	Dom	Cmd	Ball%	SwK	Vel	G	L	F	H%	S%	HR/F	xHR/F	GS	APC	DOM%	DIS%	Sv%	LI	RAR	BPX	R$
15 2AL *	10	0	174	119	5.19	5.38	1.51	1.31	114	133	22.8	1.9	6.2	3.3	36%	8.0%	91.5	43	22	34	36%	67%	14%	17%	9	68	22%	33%	0	0.89	-26.4	81	-$11
16 aaa	1	0	16	10	8.71	8.87	1.87				15.3	2.3	5.4	2.3							37%	58%									-9.1	-25	-$8
17 aaa	8	0	146	85	6.93	7.72	1.74				25.5	1.8	5.2	2.9							37%	65%									-46.1	15	-$21
18 OAK *	9	0	103	58	3.60	4.73	1.44		0	279	15.1	2.7	5.1	1.9		0.0%	91.5	71	0	29	32%	77%	0%		0	14			0	0.02	7.0	51	$0
19 2AL	6	0	110	82	5.65	5.15	1.38	1.40	114	106	16.6	2.8	6.7	2.4	37%	8.4%	92.0	44	18	38	30%	63%	16%	16%	18	65	11%	67%	0	0.56	-15.5	74	-$5
1st Half	2	0	50	43	5.01	4.81	1.25	1.26	113	100	14.3	2.5	7.7	3.1	36%	8.9%	92.2	41	18	41	27%	69%	19%	20%	6	57	17%	67%	0	0.38	-3.1	98	-$4
2nd Half	4	0	60	39	6.18	5.47	1.49	1.41	114	112	19.1	3.0	5.9	2.0	38%	8.0%	91.7	46	18	36	32%	60%	13%	13%	12	75	8%	67%	0	0.76	-12.4	53	-$6
20 Proj	**6**	**0**	**116**	**74**	**5.31**	**4.65**	**1.49**	**1.33**	**113**	**116**	**17.5**	**2.7**	**5.7**	**2.1**	**37%**	**8.2%**	**91.8**	**44**	**20**	**37**	**32%**	**68%**	**13%**		**21**						**-16.6**	**60**	**-$7**

Buehler,Walker

Age: 25	Th: R	Role SP	Health B	LIMA Plan B
Ht: 6' 2"	Wt: 185	Type Pwr	PT/Exp B	Rand Var 0
			Consist B	MM 5405

An impressive follow-up to 2018's breakout. Missed bats with four pitches that each had a 10%+ SwK, so double-digit Dom seems entrenched, and steady Ball% backs pinpoint Ctl. More cutters instead of sinkers cut into GB%, but expected ratios didn't skip a beat. Elite (and upward trending) BPX hints at... UP: Cy Young.

Yr Tm	W	Sv	IP	K	ERA	xERA	WHIP	xWHIP	vL+	vR+	BF/G	Ctl	Dom	Cmd	Ball%	SwK	Vel	G	L	F	H%	S%	HR/F	xHR/F	GS	APC	DOM%	DIS%	Sv%	LI	RAR	BPX	R$
15																																	
16																																	
17 LA *	4	1	82	97	4.79	3.90	1.33		67	172	10.9	3.5	10.6	3.1		10.4%	98.1	67	17	17	34%	65%	50%	29%	0	24			100	0.33	-4.4	126	$0
18 LA	8	0	137	151	2.62	3.14	0.96	1.13	78	76	22.5	2.4	9.9	4.1	33%	11.8%	96.2	50	18	32	26%	77%	11%	11%	23	91	39%	9%	0	0.79	25.9	162	$21
19 LA	14	0	182	215	3.26	3.42	1.04	1.08	81	88	24.6	1.8	10.6	5.8	32%	12.8%	96.6	43	23	35	31%	73%	12%	11%	30	95	43%	13%			28.1	177	$26
1st Half	8	0	97	104	3.43	3.54	0.97	1.02	77	86	23.9	1.3	9.6	7.4	32%	12.4%	96.7	41	24	35	29%	68%	11%	13%	16	94	50%	19%			12.8	172	$27
2nd Half	6	0	85	111	3.06	3.35	1.13	1.05	86	89	25.4	2.4	11.7	4.8	32%	13.1%	96.5	44	21	34	33%	78%	14%	9%	14	95	36%	7%			15.2	183	$24
20 Proj	**15**	**0**	**189**	**220**	**3.14**	**2.93**	**1.07**	**1.08**	**83**	**85**	**23.8**	**2.3**	**10.5**	**4.5**	**32%**	**12.7%**	**96.4**	**46**	**21**	**34**	**30%**	**74%**	**12%**		**31**						**23.6**	**172**	**$27**

Bumgarner,Madison

Age: 30	Th: L	Role SP	Health D	LIMA Plan A
Ht: 6' 4"	Wt: 242	Type Con	PT/Exp A	Rand Var 0
			Consist A	MM 3205

Greeted owners with a rebound that offered rare 200+ IP in this era of "opener." Curveball and cutter drove SwK recovery, while 2018 Ctl is the only blip in otherwise elite Cmd history. Velocity rebound should keep decline at bay and full 34 GS instills confidence in health, so if mileage keeps price down, pay for a repeat.

Yr Tm	W	Sv	IP	K	ERA	xERA	WHIP	xWHIP	vL+	vR+	BF/G	Ctl	Dom	Cmd	Ball%	SwK	Vel	G	L	F	H%	S%	HR/F	xHR/F	GS	APC	DOM%	DIS%	Sv%	LI	RAR	BPX	R$
15 SF	18	0	218	234	2.93	3.10	1.01	1.06	74	88	27.2	1.6	9.6	6.0	33%	13.0%	92.1	42	23	36	30%	75%	10%	10%	32	104	59%	6%			27.9	179	$32
16 SF	15	0	227	251	2.74	3.48	1.03	1.10	70	88	26.8	2.1	10.0	4.6	34%	11.9%	90.9	40	19	41	28%	79%	11%	13%	34	105	56%	9%			40.5	166	$34
17 SF	4	0	111	101	3.32	3.99	1.09	1.14	70	100	26.5	1.6	8.2	5.1	33%	10.6%	91.0	41	18	41	28%	77%	13%	13%	17	98	53%	12%			14.2	147	$10
18 SF	6	0	130	109	3.26	4.35	1.24	1.32	87	99	26.2	3.0	7.6	2.5	36%	9.4%	90.9	43	22	35	29%	78%	10%	16%	21	98	29%	14%			14.2	88	$7
19 SF	9	0	208	203	3.90	4.16	1.13	1.18	73	102	24.8	1.9	8.8	4.7	33%	12.0%	91.4	36	23	42	30%	71%	13%	16%	34	95	35%	18%			15.5	133	$17
1st Half	5	0	110	113	4.02	4.08	1.19	1.12	69	108	25.2	2.0	9.3	4.7	33%	12.1%	91.7	36	26	38	31%	72%	15%	18%	18	98	28%	17%			6.6	139	$16
2nd Half	4	0	98	90	3.77	4.37	1.06	1.14	77	96	24.4	1.7	8.3	4.7	33%	11.8%	91.0	36	19	45	28%	69%	10%	14%	16	93	44%	19%			8.9	126	$19
20 Proj	**11**	**0**	**189**	**177**	**3.82**	**3.58**	**1.13**	**1.18**	**76**	**99**	**24.7**	**2.1**	**8.4**	**4.0**	**34%**	**11.1%**	**91.2**	**40**	**21**	**39**	**29%**	**71%**	**12%**		**30**						**7.7**	**130**	**$16**

Bummer,Aaron

Age: 26	Th: L	Role RP	Health A	LIMA Plan A
Ht: 6' 3"	Wt: 200	Type xGB	PT/Exp D	Rand Var -4
			Consist A	MM 4201

Shift in fortune definitely wasn't a bummer. But it wasn't all luck. Elite GB% says he can hold strong ERA, even if H% shifts. Velocity jump, SwK should keep Dom from falling further. And it's not all roses: xERA/xWHIP say that a ratio repeat just isn't realistic. Rising LI is intriguing, but he's bullpen depth for now.

Yr Tm	W	Sv	IP	K	ERA	xERA	WHIP	xWHIP	vL+	vR+	BF/G	Ctl	Dom	Cmd	Ball%	SwK	Vel	G	L	F	H%	S%	HR/F	xHR/F	GS	APC	DOM%	DIS%	Sv%	LI	RAR	BPX	R$
15																																	
16																																	
17 CHW *	2	3	60	51	4.00	4.22	1.47		82	105	5.2	5.1	7.6	1.5		11.5%	93.2	54	14	32	29%	75%	22%	15%	0	12			75	1.55	2.7	65	-$1
18 CHW *	2	0	64	60	3.72	4.16	1.48	1.19	82	114	4.0	3.1	8.5	2.7	40%	10.5%	93.1	61	22	16	37%	73%	6%	16%	0	16			0	0.92	3.4	117	-$3
19 CHW	0	1	68	60	2.13	3.24	0.99	1.34	60	75	4.5	3.2	8.0	2.5	37%	11.0%	95.6	72	11	17	23%	81%	14%	9%	0	18			33	1.23	19.8	117	$7
1st Half	0	1	29	30	1.84	3.04	0.95	1.20	77	66	4.7	2.8	9.2	3.3	36%	9.9%	95.4	64	16	19	25%	81%	7%	5%	0	19			50	1.08	9.6	146	$5
2nd Half	0	0	38	30	2.35	3.23	1.02	1.40	46	82	4.4	3.5	7.0	2.0	37%	11.9%	95.7	78	7	15	21%	81%	20%	14%	0	17			0	1.34	10.2	95	$8
20 Proj	**1**	**0**	**73**	**65**	**3.09**	**3.10**	**1.24**	**1.27**	**69**	**92**	**4.4**	**3.5**	**8.1**	**2.3**	**38%**	**10.8%**	**94.6**	**68**	**16**	**17**	**29%**	**76%**	**14%**		**0**						**9.5**	**112**	**$2**

Bundy,Dylan

Age: 27	Th: R	Role SP	Health B	LIMA Plan A
Ht: 6' 1"	Wt: 200	Type Pwr FB	PT/Exp A	Rand Var +2
			Consist A	MM 2303

Breakout didn't happen (yet again) despite a modest ERA rebound. Stagnant xERA, BPX continuing to hover near league-average and "A" consistency suggest more of the same. Small positive signs: SwK backs a strikeout per inning, 2nd half FB% helps, though HR risk still lurks. For now, he's back-end rotation filler with a few extra Ks.

Yr Tm	W	Sv	IP	K	ERA	xERA	WHIP	xWHIP	vL+	vR+	BF/G	Ctl	Dom	Cmd	Ball%	SwK	Vel	G	L	F	H%	S%	HR/F	xHR/F	GS	APC	DOM%	DIS%	Sv%	LI	RAR	BPX	R$
15 aa	0	0	22	21	4.91	3.74	1.39				11.6	2.1	8.5	4.0							38%	61%									-2.6	156	-$5
16 BAL	10	0	110	104	4.02	4.51	1.38	1.32	103	106	13.2	3.4	8.5	2.5	35%	11.2%	93.8	36	22	42	31%	77%	13%	11%	14	54	14%	43%	0	0.82	2.3	89	$3
17 BAL	13	0	170	152	4.24	4.55	1.20	1.26	102	91	24.9	2.7	8.1	3.0	35%	11.8%	92.2	33	20	47	28%	69%	11%	12%	28	101	25%	29%			2.4	100	$12
18 BAL	8	0	172	184	5.45	4.29	1.41	1.21	128	108	24.2	2.8	9.6	3.4	33%	13.2%	91.6	34	20	46	33%	69%	18%	15%	31	92	35%	32%			-27.6	126	-$7
19 BAL	7	0	162	162	4.79	4.58	1.35	1.33	103	105	23.3	3.2	9.0	2.8	35%	13.3%	91.2	41	21	38	31%	70%	16%	13%	30	93	17%	37%			-5.6	103	$1
1st Half	3	0	84	90	4.91	4.67	1.34	1.25	102	114	23.0	3.2	9.6	3.0	36%	13.5%	91.1	36	21	43	30%	71%	18%	16%	16	93	6%	31%			-4.2	110	$0
2nd Half	4	0	77	72	4.66	4.52	1.37	1.31	104	96	23.7	3.3	8.4	2.6	34%	13.0%	91.3	47	21	32	32%	69%	14%	9%	14	92	29%	43%			-1.4	96	$2
20 Proj	**9**	**0**	**160**	**158**	**4.67**	**4.01**	**1.36**	**1.27**	**110**	**104**	**21.4**	**3.1**	**8.9**	**2.9**	**34%**	**12.8%**	**91.7**	**37**	**21**	**42**	**31%**	**72%**	**15%**		**31**						**-10.2**	**107**	**$2**

Burke,Brock

Age: 23	Th: L	Role SP	Health A	LIMA Plan F
Ht: 6' 4"	Wt: 180	Type GB	PT/Exp F	Rand Var +5
			Consist F	MM 2201

0-2, 7.43 ERA in 27 IP at TEX. Shoulder injury, blister limited IP before making six rocky starts in Aug/Sept. While small-sample MLB skills (14/11 K/BB, 13 BPV) warn of more bumps in the road, his 10.1 Dom in AA/AAA hints at possible strikeout upside. GB% tilt should help smooth out ERA, but at this age, he needs more seasoning.

Yr Tm	W	Sv	IP	K	ERA	xERA	WHIP	xWHIP	vL+	vR+	BF/G	Ctl	Dom	Cmd	Ball%	SwK	Vel	G	L	F	H%	S%	HR/F	xHR/F	GS	APC	DOM%	DIS%	Sv%	LI	RAR	BPX	R$
15																																	
16																																	
17																																	
18 aa	6	0	56	64	2.28	2.20	1.03				24.0	2.2	10.3	4.6							31%	78%									13.0	185	$7
19 TEX *	3	0	81	63	5.83	4.70	1.42	1.60	129	113	20.2	3.3	7.0	2.1	38%	5.3%	91.6	50	18	32	31%	60%	21%	19%	6	79	0%	67%			-13.2	59	-$7
1st Half	0	0	19	15	6.29	4.54	1.44		0	0	20.5	2.7	7.2	2.6							34%	54%	0%		0	0					-4.2	83	-$13
2nd Half	3	0	64	47	5.70	4.62	1.39	1.54	130	112	20.7	3.4	6.7	2.0	38%	5.3%	91.6	50	18	32	30%	60%	21%	19%	6	79	0%	67%			-9.4	51	-$5
20 Proj	**6**	**0**	**94**	**84**	**4.39**	**3.92**	**1.29**	**1.70**	**100**	**88**	**21.9**	**3.0**	**8.0**	**2.7**	**42%**	**8.0%**	**91.6**	**47**	**18**	**35**	**29%**	**70%**	**14%**		**18**						**-2.8**	**102**	**$1**

Burnes,Corbin

Age: 25	Th: R	Role RP	Health B	LIMA Plan F
Ht: 6' 3"	Wt: 205	Type Pwr	PT/Exp D	Rand Var +5
			Consist F	MM 2301

1-5, 8.82 ERA in 49 IP at MIL. Struck out 12 in season debut, but went into tailspin with AAA/bullpen demotions, July shoulder injury. Slider (35% SwK!) should keep strikeouts coming, and while fastball isn't fooling hitters, his 3.88 xERA in majors deserved a better fate. Skills are worth a flyer, as luck factor correction should help ratios.

Yr Tm	W	Sv	IP	K	ERA	xERA	WHIP	xWHIP	vL+	vR+	BF/G	Ctl	Dom	Cmd	Ball%	SwK	Vel	G	L	F	H%	S%	HR/F	xHR/F	GS	APC	DOM%	DIS%	Sv%	LI	RAR	BPX	R$
15																																	
16																																	
17 aa	3	0	86	73	3.22	3.35	1.26				21.9	2.4	7.6	3.2							33%	74%									12.1	126	$3
18 MIL *	10	1	118	103	4.33	3.99	1.32	1.23	70	89	10.0	3.0	7.9	2.6	33%	15.9%	95.3	49	21	30	31%	68%	13%	13%	0	19			33	0.96	-2.6	92	$2
19 MIL *	1	1	72	91	9.06	8.03	1.84	1.20	167	111	8.4	3.6	11.3	3.1	36%	17.7%	95.2	45	24	31	43%	53%	39%	29%	4	28	0%	75%	100	1.05	-40.5	53	-$19
1st Half	1	1	53	69	6.81	6.86	1.62	1.23	170	109	8.7	4.1	11.7	2.9	37%	17.2%	95.0	45	23	32	37%	65%	39%	31%	4	32	0%	75%	100	1.08	-15.0	55	-$16
2nd Half	0	0	22	22	13.61	9.73	2.19		144	126	8.3	2.1	9.1	4.3		20.8%	96.9	43	30	26	49%	34%	33%	21%	0	16			0	0.97	-24.2	70	-$27
20 Proj	**3**	**0**	**73**	**72**	**4.77**	**3.83**	**1.45**	**1.23**	**131**	**94**	**9.4**	**3.1**	**9.0**	**2.9**	**36%**	**16.8%**	**95.1**	**44**	**22**	**34**	**33%**	**73%**	**19%**		**0**						**-5.5**	**114**	**-$4**

BRANT CHESSER

Buttrey,Ty

Age: 27	Th: R	Role RP	Health A
Ht: 6' 6"	Wt: 240	Type Pwr	PT/Exp D
LIMA Plan D	Rand Var +2	MM 4410	Consist D

Dominated with a 1.27 ERA through May, but had just one other month (August) with a sub-5.00 mark. Major swings in S%, HR/F were the main culprits, as he mostly held 2018's Ctl/Dom gains with backing from SwK and Ball%. So while xERA suggests he's an RP that won't hurt you, there are plenty of those to go around.

Yr Tm	W	Sv	IP	K	ERA	xERA	WHIP	xWHIP	vL+	vR+	BF/G	Ctl	Dom	Cmd	Ball%	SwK	Vel	G	L	F	H%	S%	HR/F	xHR/F	GS	APC	DOM%	DIS%	Sv%	LI	RAR	BPX	R$
15																																	
16 aa	1	0	79	43	5.78	5.75	1.83				11.1	5.5	4.9	0.9							33%	68%									-15.5	23	-$14
17 a/a	2	4	64	60	6.85	5.33	1.77				7.3	5.2	8.4	1.6							38%	59%									-19.6	77	-$10
18 LAA *	1	5	64	79	2.41	2.75	1.13		109	56	4.9	2.5	11.0	4.3		14.3%	96.0	57	23	20	33%	80%	0%	15%	0	19			50	1.41	13.8	174	$6
19 LAA	6	2	72	84	3.98	3.84	1.27	1.21	88	95	4.3	2.9	10.5	3.7	35%	12.3%	97.1	46	20	34	34%	71%	12%	14%	0	17			33	1.31	4.7	147	$4
1st Half	4	2	39	47	2.33	3.69	1.19	1.11	83	90	4.3	2.6	10.9	4.3	35%	13.7%	97.0	43	21	37	34%	84%	8%	14%	0	17			40	1.38	10.4	162	$9
2nd Half	2	0	34	37	5.86	4.05	1.37	1.23	94	99	4.3	3.2	9.9	3.1	35%	10.8%	97.2	49	20	31	33%	59%	17%	14%	0	17			0	1.22	-5.7	129	-$2
20 Proj	**3**	**2**	**65**	**73**	**3.73**	**3.25**	**1.27**	**1.18**	**89**	**95**	**4.9**	**3.0**	**10.1**	**3.3**	**35%**	**11.9%**	**97.1**	**48**	**20**	**31**	**32%**	**74%**	**15%**		**0**						**3.4**	**145**	**$2**

Cabrera,Genesis

Age: 23	Th: L	Role RP	Health A
Ht: 6' 2"	Wt: 190	Type FB	PT/Exp D
LIMA Plan F	Rand Var +3	MM 0200	Consist F

0-2, 4.87 ERA in 20 IP at STL. First chapter of MLB career started in May with two spot starts; returned as reliever in September. Needs more AAA seasoning, as nearly every skill in this box was below average, while lack of a reliable third pitch might eventually move him to 'pen. No matter the role, he's safe to avoid for 2020.

Yr Tm	W	Sv	IP	K	ERA	xERA	WHIP	xWHIP	vL+	vR+	BF/G	Ctl	Dom	Cmd	Ball%	SwK	Vel	G	L	F	H%	S%	HR/F	xHR/F	GS	APC	DOM%	DIS%	Sv%	LI	RAR	BPX	R$
15																																	
16																																	
17 aa	5	0	65	46	4.36	5.94	1.74				24.6	3.8	6.4	1.7							37%	76%									-0.1	47	-$5
18 a/a	8	0	141	125	4.41	3.68	1.33				21.7	4.2	8.0	1.9							29%	68%									-4.5	83	$1
19 STL *	5	1	119	107	6.49	6.11	1.61	1.54	157	83	16.0	3.6	8.1	2.2	36%	7.8%	96.3	36	26	38	35%	62%	8%	13%	2	29	0%	100%	50	0.57	-29.2	44	-$13
1st Half	3	0	63	52	6.10	6.34	1.63		189	103	17.5	4.0	7.5	1.9		5.2%	95.9	33	28	40	33%	67%	13%	17%	2	42	0%	100%	0	0.39	-12.4	26	-$14
2nd Half	2	1	59	55	6.65	5.52	1.52		131	49	15.0	3.1	8.4	2.7		11.1%	97.1	42	23	35	35%	57%	0%	5%	0	20			100	0.68	-15.5	67	-$11
20 Proj	**3**	**0**	**51**	**44**	**5.39**	**4.55**	**1.51**				**18.6**	**3.7**	**7.8**	**2.1**	**36%**	**9.0%**		**39**	**20**	**41**	**31%**	**69%**	**15%**		**10**						**-7.8**	**64**	**-$6**

Cahill,Trevor

Age: 32	Th: R	Role SP	Health F
Ht: 6' 4"	Wt: 230	Type	PT/Exp C
LIMA Plan D	Rand Var +5	MM 1201	Consist D

Sore elbow cost him most of June, then moved to bullpen with only marginally better results. Once-elite GB% has eroded into just an average asset, while SwK/Dom took another tumble, and strike-throwing inability persists. So sure, Rand Var says he was unlucky, but a "rebound" to xERA doesn't mean he's rosterable.

Yr Tm	W	Sv	IP	K	ERA	xERA	WHIP	xWHIP	vL+	vR+	BF/G	Ctl	Dom	Cmd	Ball%	SwK	Vel	G	L	F	H%	S%	HR/F	xHR/F	GS	APC	DOM%	DIS%	Sv%	LI	RAR	BPX	R$
15 2 NL *	2	0	80	55	5.72	4.86	1.55	1.35	94	106	9.4	3.9	6.2	1.6	39%	10.2%	91.5	63	19	18	32%	63%	17%	22%	3	26	0%	100%	0	0.63	-17.3	52	-$11
16 CHC *	4	0	85	85	3.35	4.38	1.49	1.44	90	81	6.6	5.1	9.0	1.8	42%	11.5%	92.0	57	22	22	31%	82%	18%	17%	1	23	0%	0%	0	0.70	8.8	77	$1
17 2 TM	4	0	84	87	4.93	4.28	1.62	1.43	102	124	18.1	4.8	9.3	1.9	40%	11.6%	90.9	56	18	26	33%	75%	25%	18%	14	73	21%	29%	0	0.66	-5.9	86	-$6
18 OAK *	7	0	125	112	3.60	2.88	1.19	1.32	92	88	20.9	3.6	8.1	2.2	39%	11.9%	91.8	53	19	27	27%	69%	10%	15%	20	85	25%	20%	0	0.77	7.0	103	$7
19 LAA	4	0	102	81	5.98	5.15	1.47	1.44	125	110	12.3	3.4	7.1	2.1	38%	10.2%	91.7	46	20	34	29%	66%	23%	17%	11	48	9%	64%	0	0.65	-18.6	65	-$8
1st Half	2	0	62	48	6.93	5.16	1.41	1.36	133	106	19.6	3.0	6.9	2.3	38%	9.8%	91.4	42	22	35	28%	56%	24%	22%	11	76	9%	64%	0	0.81	-18.6	69	-$11
2nd Half	2	0	40	33	4.50	5.05	1.55	1.44	110	116	7.8	4.1	7.4	1.8	39%	10.8%	92.4	52	17	32	31%	78%	20%	9%	0	32			0	0.55	0.0	59	-$5
20 Proj	**5**	**0**	**102**	**88**	**4.76**	**4.17**	**1.44**	**1.39**	**106**	**106**	**20.2**	**3.9**	**7.8**	**2.0**	**39%**	**11.0%**	**91.8**	**48**	**20**	**32**	**30%**	**71%**	**16%**		**16**						**-7.6**	**70**	**-$3**

Canning,Griffin

Age: 24	Th: R	Role SP	Health D
Ht: 6' 2"	Wt: 180	Type Pwr FB	PT/Exp D
LIMA Plan A	Rand Var +1	MM 2301	Consist A

5-6, 4.58 ERA in 90 IP at LAA. Called up in April and thrived in 1st half, though August elbow inflammation cut season short. Racked up whiffs with knockout slider (22% SwK), so Ks should be plentiful, but Ball% says walks might be too. Didn't have this FB% tilt in minors, so if health checks out, he's a growth stock worth tracking.

Yr Tm	W	Sv	IP	K	ERA	xERA	WHIP	xWHIP	vL+	vR+	BF/G	Ctl	Dom	Cmd	Ball%	SwK	Vel	G	L	F	H%	S%	HR/F	xHR/F	GS	APC	DOM%	DIS%	Sv%	LI	RAR	BPX	R$
15																																	
16																																	
17																																	
18 a/a	4	0	106	100	4.02	3.61	1.29				19.0	3.1	8.4	2.7							32%	69%									1.7	107	$1
19 LAA *	6	0	106	111	3.97	3.61	1.17	1.27	92	104	20.2	2.7	9.4	3.5	38%	14.0%	93.9	38	18	44	29%	70%	13%	12%	17	86	35%	29%	0	0.86	7.0	111	$6
1st Half	4	0	78	78	3.12	3.02	0.97	1.13	79	106	21.0	1.8	9.0	4.9	37%	15.3%	93.8	36	15	49	25%	77%	15%	14%	11	92	27%	18%			13.3	139	$12
2nd Half	2	0	29	33	6.28	4.87	1.71	1.40	114	100	19.3	5.0	10.4	2.1	40%	11.6%	94.1	40	25	35	39%	62%	7%	10%	6	77	50%	50%	0	0.95	-6.3	75	-$11
20 Proj	**6**	**0**	**123**	**127**	**4.28**	**3.88**	**1.29**	**1.29**	**101**	**100**	**21.3**	**3.5**	**9.3**	**2.7**	**39%**	**12.9%**	**94.0**	**39**	**21**	**41**	**30%**	**72%**	**14%**		**22**						**-2.0**	**103**	**$3**

Carrasco,Carlos

Age: 33	Th: R	Role RP	Health F
Ht: 6' 4"	Wt: 224	Type Pwr	PT/Exp A
LIMA Plan A	Rand Var +5	MM 4403	Consist A

Leukemia diagnosis put everything in perspective, as he missed three months before inspirational return in September. Pre-diagnosis skills were on track with 2017-18 peak, but trifecta of bad luck (H%, S%, HR/F) destroyed surface stats. Hoping for good vibes on the recovery trail, as he's good enough to be an ace once more.

Yr Tm	W	Sv	IP	K	ERA	xERA	WHIP	xWHIP	vL+	vR+	BF/G	Ctl	Dom	Cmd	Ball%	SwK	Vel	G	L	F	H%	S%	HR/F	xHR/F	GS	APC	DOM%	DIS%	Sv%	LI	RAR	BPX	R$
15 CLE	14	0	184	216	3.63	2.75	1.07	1.06	88	92	24.3	2.1	10.6	5.0	32%	14.3%	94.5	51	19	30	31%	69%	13%	11%	30	93	57%	20%			7.6	194	$19
16 CLE	11	0	146	150	3.32	3.41	1.15	1.14	100	94	24.0	2.1	9.2	4.4	34%	12.7%	93.8	49	20	31	30%	78%	16%	14%	25	90	32%	20%			15.7	162	$15
17 CLE	18	0	200	226	3.29	3.23	1.10	1.08	96	85	24.9	2.1	10.2	4.9	34%	13.9%	94.3	45	22	33	31%	74%	12%	14%	32	96	50%	13%			26.5	180	$28
18 CLE	17	0	192	231	3.38	3.05	1.13	1.05	96	89	24.5	2.0	10.8	5.4	33%	15.7%	93.5	47	21	32	33%	74%	13%	15%	30	93	47%	17%	0	0.80	18.3	191	$23
19 CLE	6	1	80	96	5.29	3.68	1.35	1.09	111	118	14.8	1.8	10.8	6.0	33%	15.3%	93.5	41	23	36	36%	68%	22%	21%	12	55	42%	25%	50	0.70	-7.7	180	-$1
1st Half	4	0	65	79	4.98	3.73	1.31	1.01	119	109	22.9	1.5	10.9	7.2	33%	14.2%	93.4	39	22	39	37%	69%	20%	21%	12	85	42%	25%			-3.8	189	$1
2nd Half	2	1	15	17	6.60	3.78	1.53	1.19	83	169	6.0	3.0	10.2	3.4	33%	19.8%	94.0	48	26	26	36%	63%	36%	23%	0	23			50	0.64	-3.9	140	-$8
20 Proj	**14**	**0**	**174**	**202**	**3.73**	**3.09**	**1.17**	**1.10**	**84**	**103**	**11.8**	**2.3**	**10.5**	**4.5**	**33%**	**16.2%**	**93.8**	**43**	**23**	**35**	**32%**	**73%**	**14%**		**10**						**9.0**	**168**	**$17**

Cashner,Andrew

Age: 33	Th: R	Role RP	Health D
Ht: 6' 6"	Wt: 235	Type Con	PT/Exp A
LIMA Plan A	Rand Var 0	MM 0003	Consist A

Ever had a job title that was a bit over your head? He kicked off the year as "Opening Day starter" in BAL, finished it as middle reliever in BOS. Through it all, another modicum of skill here, capped off by a third straight 5.00+ xERA. A lot of zeros in his MM score, which coincides with the number of reasons to roster him.

Yr Tm	W	Sv	IP	K	ERA	xERA	WHIP	xWHIP	vL+	vR+	BF/G	Ctl	Dom	Cmd	Ball%	SwK	Vel	G	L	F	H%	S%	HR/F	xHR/F	GS	APC	DOM%	DIS%	Sv%	LI	RAR	BPX	R$
15 SD	6	0	185	165	4.34	3.95	1.44	1.32	123	94	25.9	3.2	8.0	2.5	35%	8.6%	94.8	47	23	30	34%	72%	12%	11%	31	100	23%	26%			-8.6	99	-$4
16 2 NL	5	0	132	112	5.25	4.65	1.53	1.44	122	108	21.0	4.1	7.6	1.9	39%	7.6%	93.5	46	20	33	32%	68%	15%	17%	27	85	11%	37%	0	1.05	-17.3	61	-$8
17 TEX	11	0	167	86	3.40	5.24	1.32	1.53	93	92	25.1	3.5	4.6	1.3	38%	6.4%	93.4	49	19	32	27%	77%	9%	7%	28	94	7%	43%			19.7	21	$10
18 BAL	4	0	153	99	5.29	5.39	1.58	1.50	116	120	24.3	3.8	5.8	1.5	39%	7.2%	92.4	40	23	36	31%	70%	14%	14%	28	95	7%	57%			-21.6	23	-$15
19 2 AL	11	1	150	108	4.68	5.11	1.35	1.48	84	111	15.1	3.5	6.5	1.9	39%	9.7%	93.9	48	17	34	28%	68%	12%	17%	23	60	17%	39%	100	0.86	-3.2	53	$3
1st Half	8	0	89	62	4.03	5.02	1.25	1.38	67	117	23.5	2.9	6.2	2.1	39%	8.9%	93.5	49	16	35	27%	71%	11%	16%	16	94	13%	31%			5.2	66	$9
2nd Half	3	1	61	46	5.64	5.16	1.48	1.51	112	104	10.0	4.3	6.8	1.6	39%	10.8%	94.4	47	20	33	30%	63%	14%	18%	7	39	29%	57%	100	0.91	-8.5	35	-$7
20 Proj	**7**	**0**	**131**	**90**	**4.81**	**4.59**	**1.44**	**1.47**	**102**	**108**	**16.7**	**3.7**	**6.2**	**1.7**	**39%**	**8.6%**	**93.6**	**46**	**20**	**34**	**30%**	**69%**	**12%**		**22**						**-10.6**	**41**	**-$3**

Castillo,Diego

Age: 26	Th: R	Role RP	Health B
Ht: 6' 3"	Wt: 250	Type Pwr GB	PT/Exp D
LIMA Plan C	Rand Var +1	MM 5410	Consist C

Booted from closer role after 10-ER stretch from 5/31 to 6/22; returned from IL (shoulder) in July as an opener. Post-injury skills were elite, as he racked up more whiffs, reined in control with support from Ball%, and induced a ton of ground balls. String of closer-worthy BPX says last year's "UP: 25 Sv" still applies.

Yr Tm	W	Sv	IP	K	ERA	xERA	WHIP	xWHIP	vL+	vR+	BF/G	Ctl	Dom	Cmd	Ball%	SwK	Vel	G	L	F	H%	S%	HR/F	xHR/F	GS	APC	DOM%	DIS%	Sv%	LI	RAR	BPX	R$
15																																	
16																																	
17 a/a	4	15	72	79	3.55	3.29	1.26				5.7	2.7	9.9	3.7							35%	71%									7.1	155	$10
18 TAM *	4	4	84	93	2.55	1.99	0.94	1.15	70	81	5.1	2.7	10.0	3.7	37%	13.7%	97.7	45	18	37	25%	77%	12%	14%	11	21	0%	36%	57	1.20	16.5	152	$12
19 TAM	5	8	69	81	3.41	3.55	1.24	1.24	101	85	4.5	3.4	10.6	3.1	36%	14.0%	98.3	57	13	30	31%	77%	15%	15%	6	17	0%	83%	80	1.16	9.3	146	$7
1st Half	1	7	34	38	3.93	4.04	1.31	1.33	95	99	4.5	4.2	10.0	2.4	37%	12.3%	98.2	53	15	32	29%	75%	18%	17%	0	17			88	1.34	2.4	106	$4
2nd Half	4	1	34	43	2.88	3.06	1.17	1.09	106	73	4.5	2.6	11.3	4.3	34%	15.9%	98.3	61	11	28	33%	78%	13%	13%	6	17	0%	83%	50	0.98	6.9	187	$10
20 Proj	**4**	**5**	**65**	**75**	**3.08**	**3.02**	**1.13**	**1.18**	**88**	**83**	**4.7**	**3.0**	**10.4**	**3.5**	**36%**	**14.1%**	**98.1**	**53**	**15**	**32**	**30%**	**76%**	**11%**		**0**						**8.6**	**158**	**$7**

RYAN BLOOMFIELD

Castillo,Luis

Age: 27	Th: R	Role: SP	Health	A	LIMA Plan	A
Ht: 6' 2"	Wt: 190	Type: Pwr GB	PT/Exp	A	Rand Var	+2
			Consist	A	MM	5405

Last year, we said "let the hype build anew"... and he delivered. SwK entered the stratosphere with nasty change-up that also produced GBs in bunches. Even reined in early wildness with 2nd half Ball% and Ctl gains, so while others may see late fade and run, we see S%, HR/F misfortune with room for... UP: sub-3.00 ERA, 250 K.

Yr Tm	W	Sv	IP	K	ERA	xERA	WHIP	xWHIP	vL+	vR+	BF/G	Ctl	Dom	Cmd	Ball%	SwK	Vel	G	L	F	H%	S%	HR/F	xHR/F	GS	APC	DOM%	DIS%	Sv%	LI	RAR	BPX	R$
15																																	
16																																	
17 CIN *	7	0	170	166	3.70	3.71	1.22	1.22	83	87	23.6	2.6	8.8	3.4	37%	13.2%	97.5	59	12	29	31%	73%	17%	11%	15	99	40%	20%			13.8	120	$12
18 CIN	10	0	170	165	4.30	3.77	1.22	1.22	120	82	22.8	2.6	8.8	3.4	35%	13.9%	95.8	46	22	32	29%	70%	18%	19%	31	90	26%	32%			-3.1	128	$7
19 CIN	15	0	191	226	3.40	3.47	1.14	1.27	89	78	24.4	3.7	10.7	2.9	39%	16.4%	96.5	55	18	27	27%	74%	18%	15%	32	99	28%	16%			26.0	135	$23
1st Half	7	0	98	115	2.47	3.64	1.15	1.36	89	67	23.7	4.8	10.5	2.2	41%	15.5%	96.3	56	17	27	24%	83%	15%	13%	17	97	24%	24%			24.7	104	$26
2nd Half	8	0	92	111	4.39	3.22	1.14	1.11	90	89	25.2	2.6	10.8	4.1	36%	17.5%	96.6	54	19	27	30%	65%	21%	17%	15	100	33%	7%			1.4	170	$20
20 Proj	**14**	**0**	**189**	**219**	**3.58**	**2.99**	**1.18**	**1.22**	**100**	**83**	**23.1**	**3.0**	**10.5**	**3.4**	**37%**	**15.2%**	**96.4**	**52**	**19**	**29**	**30%**	**74%**	**17%**		**33**						**13.2**	**157**	**$19**

Castro,Miguel

Age: 25	Th: R	Role: RP	Health	A	LIMA Plan	C
Ht: 6' 7"	Wt: 205	Type: Pwr	PT/Exp	C	Rand Var	0
			Consist	C	MM	1111

Stumbled upon 2nd half success in relief, but it was all luck-fueled. Upticks in fastball velocity and SwK do support Dom growth, but inability to find the plate resulted in a fifth straight sub-2.0 Cmd. Multi-inning volume would boost value if his ratios were any good, but they're not, and xERA/xWHIP say they shouldn't be.

Yr Tm	W	Sv	IP	K	ERA	xERA	WHIP	xWHIP	vL+	vR+	BF/G	Ctl	Dom	Cmd	Ball%	SwK	Vel	G	L	F	H%	S%	HR/F	xHR/F	GS	APC	DOM%	DIS%	Sv%	LI	RAR	BPX	R$
15 2 TM *	3	4	51	43	4.57	5.75	1.67		126	134	5.4	5.0	7.5	1.5		11.3%	96.4	33	24	43	32%	77%	17%	23%	0	16			36	1.04	-3.9	35	-$5
16 COL *	2	0	30	24	10.27	8.39	1.84		151	105	4.0	3.7	7.1	1.9		10.4%	96.1	54	19	27	35%	46%	23%	20%	0	13			0	1.27	-22.7	-21	-$12
17 BAL *	6	0	91	48	4.05	3.59	1.26	1.54	112	77	8.2	3.4	4.7	1.4	38%	10.2%	95.6	49	17	34	25%	70%	12%	13%	1	26	0%	100%	0	0.90	3.4	45	$2
18 BAL	2	0	86	57	3.96	5.33	1.45	1.67	106	94	6.0	5.2	5.9	1.1	39%	10.1%	95.5	49	19	32	26%	75%	11%	16%	1	23	0%	100%	0	0.99	2.0	-8	-$4
19 BAL	1	2	73	71	4.66	4.98	1.42	1.54	102	91	4.9	5.0	8.7	1.7	40%	12.1%	97.4	49	17	34	28%	70%	14%	13%	0	19			40	0.87	-1.4	52	-$3
1st Half	0	2	42	38	5.36	5.00	1.50	1.46	108	101	5.5	4.5	8.1	1.8	38%	12.4%	97.2	50	18	32	30%	68%	17%	15%	0	21			50	0.84	-4.4	57	-$6
2nd Half	1	0	31	33	3.73	4.85	1.31	1.54	87	78	4.3	5.7	9.5	1.7	42%	11.7%	97.7	48	16	36	25%	74%	10%	10%	0	17			0	0.91	3.0	45	$0
20 Proj	**2**	**2**	**73**	**60**	**4.79**	**4.50**	**1.42**	**1.57**	**108**	**92**	**5.2**	**4.9**	**7.4**	**1.5**	**40%**	**11.1%**	**96.5**	**49**	**18**	**34**	**27%**	**69%**	**13%**		**0**						**-5.7**	**33**	**-$3**

Cease,Dylan

Age: 24	Th: R	Role: SP	Health	A	LIMA Plan	F
Ht: 6' 2"	Wt: 190	Type: Pwr GB	PT/Exp	D	Rand Var	+5
			Consist	F	MM	1303

4-7, 5.79 ERA in 73 IP at CHW. Called up in July with plenty of hype, but debut was a dud. Ball% says the control issues aren't going away any time soon, and while upper-90s fastball helped drive elite Dom in majors, league-average SwK tempers expectations. Long-term outlook is dreamy, but this might take a while.

Yr Tm	W	Sv	IP	K	ERA	xERA	WHIP	xWHIP	vL+	vR+	BF/G	Ctl	Dom	Cmd	Ball%	SwK	Vel	G	L	F	H%	S%	HR/F	xHR/F	GS	APC	DOM%	DIS%	Sv%	LI	RAR	BPX	R$
15																																	
16																																	
17																																	
18 aa	3	0	53	68	2.33	2.60	1.16				21.1	4.2	11.5	2.8							29%	83%									11.9	141	$4
19 CHW *	9	0	142	143	5.56	5.65	1.63	1.39	120	102	21.8	4.3	9.1	2.1	40%	11.1%	96.5	46	21	34	36%	68%	21%	16%	14	97	14%	36%			-18.4	64	-$8
1st Half	5	0	69	62	5.30	5.54	1.72		0	0	20.9	4.2	8.1	1.9							38%	68%	0%		0	0					-6.8	71	-$10
2nd Half	4	0	73	81	5.79	4.54	1.55	1.34	121	101	23.3	4.3	10.0	2.3	40%	11.1%	96.5	46	21	34	34%	67%	21%	16%	14	97	14%	36%			-11.6	95	-$7
20 Proj	**10**	**0**	**160**	**164**	**4.31**	**4.04**	**1.44**	**1.48**	**98**	**84**	**23.1**	**4.4**	**9.3**	**2.1**	**44%**	**11.1%**	**96.5**	**46**	**21**	**34**	**31%**	**74%**	**14%**		**29**						**-3.2**	**84**	**$2**

Cessa,Luis

Age: 28	Th: R	Role: RP	Health	D	LIMA Plan	C
Ht: 6' 0"	Wt: 210	Type:	PT/Exp	D	Rand Var	+2
			Consist	C	MM	2201

Ate more innings in middle relief; they tasted marginally better than before. Missed more bats than ever, as slider became his primary pitch (50% usage; 20% SwK), but he couldn't hold on to 2018's Ctl gains thanks to iffy Ball%. If Dom growth sticks, GB% tilt makes him deep-league worthy should he slide into rotation gig.

Yr Tm	W	Sv	IP	K	ERA	xERA	WHIP	xWHIP	vL+	vR+	BF/G	Ctl	Dom	Cmd	Ball%	SwK	Vel	G	L	F	H%	S%	HR/F	xHR/F	GS	APC	DOM%	DIS%	Sv%	LI	RAR	BPX	R$
15 a/a	8	0	139	96	5.35	5.21	1.60				24.6	2.4	6.2	2.6							38%	65%									-23.8	81	-$13
16 NYY *	10	0	148	104	4.30	4.61	1.26	1.27	104	99	18.8	2.4	6.4	2.7	37%	11.0%	94.6	43	20	37	28%	73%	20%	13%	9	62	11%	33%	0	0.53	-2.0	54	$4
17 NYY *	4	0	114	85	4.80	5.46	1.55	1.46	73	139	20.8	3.6	6.7	1.9	38%	10.6%	95.6	45	18	36	32%	73%	18%	18%	5	62	0%	60%	0	0.60	-6.3	42	-$6
18 NYY *	4	2	82	69	4.54	3.76	1.24	1.27	99	110	13.8	2.1	7.6	3.7	35%	12.4%	94.8	47	23	30	32%	63%	12%	13%	5	44	0%	60%	67	0.39	-4.0	120	$0
19 NYY	2	1	81	75	4.11	4.48	1.31	1.38	102	99	8.0	3.4	8.3	2.4	37%	13.2%	94.5	49	18	33	28%	75%	18%	12%	0	31			100	0.67	3.9	92	$0
1st Half	0	0	41	41	4.61	4.37	1.37	1.28	117	103	7.7	3.3	9.0	2.7	38%	13.6%	94.3	45	22	33	31%	73%	21%	15%	0	30			0	0.68	-0.5	105	-$4
2nd Half	2	1	40	34	3.60	4.55	1.25	1.38	89	94	8.3	3.6	7.7	2.1	37%	12.9%	94.7	52	15	33	26%	77%	16%	10%	0	33			100	0.65	4.5	77	$4
20 Proj	**4**	**0**	**87**	**80**	**4.33**	**3.80**	**1.34**	**1.33**	**94**	**105**	**15.3**	**3.0**	**8.2**	**2.7**	**37%**	**12.4%**	**94.8**	**48**	**19**	**33**	**31%**	**71%**	**14%**		**17**						**-2.0**	**106**	**$0**

Chacin,Jhoulys

Age: 32	Th: R	Role: SP	Health	F	LIMA Plan	A
Ht: 6' 3"	Wt: 215	Type:	PT/Exp	A	Rand Var	+5
			Consist	A	MM	1201

Talk about a rough year: IL stints in June (back) and July (lat); released in August; and through it all, zero PQS-DOMinant starts in 24 tries. Sure, Rand Var says he was "unlucky," but stagnant SwK questions Dom spike, control deteriorated, and xERA hit career high. Nothing but more rough skies ahead.

Yr Tm	W	Sv	IP	K	ERA	xERA	WHIP	xWHIP	vL+	vR+	BF/G	Ctl	Dom	Cmd	Ball%	SwK	Vel	G	L	F	H%	S%	HR/F	xHR/F	GS	APC	DOM%	DIS%	Sv%	LI	RAR	BPX	R$
15 ARI *	9	0	155	89	3.39	3.82	1.35		135	70	25.9	3.1	5.2	1.7		9.6%	88.6	47	19	33	30%	76%	15%	24%	4	85	50%	50%	0	0.84	11.0	61	$4
16 2 TM	6	0	144	119	4.81	4.36	1.44	1.37	103	99	18.6	3.4	7.4	2.2	37%	8.4%	90.8	48	23	29	33%	68%	11%	13%	22	70	18%	59%	0	0.68	-11.1	80	-$4
17 SD	13	0	180	153	3.89	4.38	1.27	1.38	104	81	23.9	3.6	7.6	2.1	37%	8.3%	91.4	49	19	32	28%	72%	11%	12%	32	92	22%	28%			10.3	81	$12
18 MIL	15	0	193	156	3.50	4.36	1.16	1.37	107	74	22.7	3.3	7.3	2.2	37%	8.8%	90.1	42	22	36	26%	72%	9%	12%	35	86	23%	34%			15.4	71	$17
19 2 TM	3	0	103	101	6.01	5.16	1.56	1.43	121	113	18.8	4.0	8.8	2.2	39%	8.2%	90.0	38	24	38	32%	68%	21%	17%	24	78	0%	42%	0	0.74	-19.2	72	-$10
1st Half	3	0	72	60	5.60	5.66	1.52	1.48	106	115	21.7	4.4	7.5	1.7	39%	7.7%	89.8	35	25	40	29%	68%	17%	13%	15	89	0%	53%			-9.8	33	-$8
2nd Half	0	0	31	41	6.97	4.04	1.65	1.15	148	109	14.5	3.2	11.9	3.7	37%	9.4%	90.5	43	23	34	39%	66%	32%	27%	9	61	0%	22%	0	0.70	-9.4	163	-$13
20 Proj	**4**	**0**	**87**	**74**	**4.98**	**4.24**	**1.42**	**1.33**	**120**	**98**	**20.5**	**3.5**	**7.6**	**2.2**	**37%**	**8.6%**	**90.4**	**43**	**22**	**35**	**30%**	**70%**	**18%**		**14**						**-8.8**	**72**	**-$4**

Chafin,Andrew

Age: 30	Th: L	Role: RP	Health	B	LIMA Plan	A
Ht: 6' 2"	Wt: 225	Type: Pwr	PT/Exp	D	Rand Var	+4
			Consist	A	MM	4400

Couldn't top 2018's ERA despite some underlying growth. Leaned on killer slider (27% SwK) to fuel career-high Dom, while Ball% gains drove improved Ctl. But new three-batter minimum rule for RP could magnify struggles vR (career 2.3 Cmd, .333 oOBP), while ever-elusive save opps make him just another decent middle reliever.

Yr Tm	W	Sv	IP	K	ERA	xERA	WHIP	xWHIP	vL+	vR+	BF/G	Ctl	Dom	Cmd	Ball%	SwK	Vel	G	L	F	H%	S%	HR/F	xHR/F	GS	APC	DOM%	DIS%	Sv%	LI	RAR	BPX	R$
15 ARI	5	2	75	58	2.76	3.70	1.15	1.42	72	89	4.6	3.6	7.0	1.9	39%	8.7%	92.5	58	19	23	26%	76%	6%	9%	0	18			100	1.29	11.1	76	$6
16 ARI	0	0	23	28	6.75	3.40	1.46		77	112	3.1	4.4	11.1	2.5		15.1%	92.8	51	24	25	37%	50%	7%	7%	0	11			0	0.94	-7.2	132	-$6
17 ARI	1	0	51	61	3.51	3.31	1.34	1.24	75	107	3.1	3.7	10.7	2.9	39%	11.7%	93.7	56	21	22	34%	77%	17%	17%	0	12			0	1.02	5.4	153	-$1
18 ARI	1	0	49	53	3.10	3.79	1.34	1.38	91	80	2.7	4.6	9.7	2.1	39%	14.6%	93.5	50	26	24	32%	74%	0%	10%	0	11			0	1.20	6.4	91	-$1
19 ARI	2	0	53	68	3.76	3.50	1.33	1.17	89	95	2.9	3.1	11.6	3.8	35%	15.8%	93.8	43	28	29	36%	75%	15%	17%	0	12			0	1.23	4.8	160	-$1
1st Half	0	0	28	33	3.25	3.56	1.37	1.22	81	106	2.8	3.6	10.7	3.0	37%	15.2%	93.8	45	30	25	36%	78%	12%	16%	0	11			0	1.07	4.3	130	-$2
2nd Half	2	0	25	35	4.32	3.42	1.28	1.04	97	84	3.0	2.5	12.6	5.0	34%	16.3%	93.9	41	25	34	37%	71%	18%	17%	0	12			0	1.41	0.6	194	$2
20 Proj	**2**	**0**	**58**	**69**	**3.52**	**3.11**	**1.26**	**1.23**	**86**	**91**	**2.9**	**3.5**	**10.6**	**3.0**	**37%**	**14.3%**	**93.6**	**48**	**25**	**27**	**32%**	**75%**	**15%**		**0**						**4.5**	**141**	**$1**

Chapman,Aroldis

Age: 32	Th: L	Role: RP	Health	D	LIMA Plan	B
Ht: 6' 4"	Wt: 212	Type: Pwr	PT/Exp	B	Rand Var	-3
			Consist	B	MM	5530

Another drop in fastball velocity didn't faze him, as he countered with more sliders (20% SwK) to dominate once again. Mostly moved past 2018's wildness, and with ironclad Dom baseline, both xERA/xWHIP point to another year of ratio goodness. If paying up for a closer, he should live near the top of your list.

Yr Tm	W	Sv	IP	K	ERA	xERA	WHIP	xWHIP	vL+	vR+	BF/G	Ctl	Dom	Cmd	Ball%	SwK	Vel	G	L	F	H%	S%	HR/F	xHR/F	GS	APC	DOM%	DIS%	Sv%	LI	RAR	BPX	R$
15 CIN	4	33	66	116	1.63	2.55	1.15	1.08	62	78	4.3	4.5	15.7	3.5	37%	19.7%	99.5	37	22	41	36%	88%	6%	7%	0	18			92	1.24	19.1	211	$23
16 2 TM	4	36	58	90	1.55	2.24	0.86	0.96	63	61	3.8	2.8	14.0	5.0	32%	19.1%	100.4	46	25	29	29%	83%	6%	6%	0	17			92	1.39	18.9	238	$25
17 NYY	4	22	50	69	3.22	3.15	1.13	1.14	76	80	4.0	3.6	12.3	3.5	32%	14.2%	100.1	49	16	35	32%	72%	7%	9%	0	17			85	1.14	7.1	183	$13
18 NYY	3	32	51	93	2.45	2.47	1.05	1.13	64	70	3.9	5.3	16.3	3.1	37%	16.2%	98.9	44	19	37	30%	77%	6%	8%	0	17			94	1.10	10.7	200	$19
19 NYY	3	37	57	85	2.21	3.10	1.11	1.16	61	75	3.9	3.9	13.4	3.4	35%	14.7%	98.4	42	28	30	32%	82%	8%	8%	0	16			88	1.05	16.1	169	$22
1st Half	1	23	33	47	1.36	2.60	0.97	0.99	36	79	3.8	2.5	12.8	5.2	33%	13.7%	98.3	47	29	24	32%	87%	6%	11%	0	16			92	1.02	12.8	207	$25
2nd Half	2	14	24	38	3.38	3.81	1.29	1.32	92	70	4.1	6.0	14.3	2.4	38%	15.8%	98.5	35	27	39	30%	76%	11%	5%	0	18			82	1.08	3.3	117	$19
20 Proj	**4**	**35**	**58**	**92**	**2.54**	**2.59**	**1.11**	**1.15**	**69**	**73**	**3.8**	**4.5**	**14.3**	**3.2**	**36%**	**15.6%**	**98.5**	**42**	**23**	**34**	**31%**	**78%**	**8%**		**0**						**11.5**	**178**	**$21**

RYAN BLOOMFIELD

Chatwood,Tyler

Age: 30	Th: R	Role RP	Health B	LIMA Plan D
Ht: 6' 0"	Wt: 185	Type Pwr GB	PT/Exp B	Rand Var +2
			Consist D	MM 3301

Velocity ramped up after move to 'pen, though 1st half skills were still unsightly, and so was HR/F. But then: nudged Ball% down further, leading to decent Ctl; SwK surge led to never-before-seen Dom; put the clamp down on RHB. Sample too small to erase all of the recent struggles, but he's at least back on deep-league radars.

Yr Tm	W	Sv	IP	K	ERA	xERA	WHIP	xWHIP	vL+	vR+	BF/G	Ctl	Dom	Cmd	Ball%	SwK	Vel	G	L	F	H%	S%	HR/F	xHR/F	GS	APC	DOM%	DIS%	Sv%	LI	RAR	BPX	R$
15																																	
16 COL	12	0	158	117	3.87	4.31	1.37	1.48	102	95	24.8	4.0	6.7	1.7	40%	8.4%	92.2	57	17	26	29%	74%	12%	12%	27	94	22%	37%			6.2	56	$5
17 COL	8	1	148	120	4.69	4.39	1.44	1.52	111	100	19.1	4.7	7.3	1.6	42%	10.3%	94.7	58	20	22	28%	70%	22%	17%	25	75	16%	52%	100	0.72	-6.1	49	-$1
18 CHC	4	0	104	85	5.30	5.98	1.80	1.94	126	81	20.3	8.2	7.4	0.9	44%	8.1%	93.1	54	18	28	29%	71%	11%	15%	20	81	0%	45%	0	0.63	-14.7	-67	-$14
19 CHC	5	2	77	74	3.76	4.15	1.33	1.44	108	78	8.5	4.3	8.7	2.0	40%	10.1%	95.9	51	29	19	29%	74%	20%	12%	5	34	0%	40%	50	1.03	7.1	74	$3
1st Half	4	1	44	35	4.50	4.92	1.55	1.61	117	96	10.1	5.3	7.2	1.3	41%	9.1%	95.7	52	26	21	28%	75%	26%	13%	3	39	0%	67%	100	1.06	0.0	17	$0
2nd Half	1	1	33	39	2.76	2.97	1.04	1.15	97	51	7.0	3.0	10.7	3.5	39%	11.6%	96.2	50	34	16	29%	73%	8%	10%	2	28	0%	0%	33	1.00	7.1	152	$6
20 Proj	**4**	**0**	**73**	**77**	**4.14**	**3.44**	**1.34**	**1.53**	**110**	**78**	**11.3**	**4.4**	**9.5**	**2.2**	**41%**	**10.2%**	**94.7**	**53**	**25**	**22**	**30%**	**71%**	**16%**		**3**						**0.1**	**96**	**$0**

Chavez,Jesse

Age: 36	Th: R	Role RP	Health D	LIMA Plan B
Ht: 6' 2"	Wt: 175	Type	PT/Exp B	Rand Var -2
			Consist B	MM 1201

Underwent surgery after an August elbow injury put end to disastrous 2nd half. But even when early results were OK, he had mostly given back 2018 Ctl gains, while velocity and SwK hit rock bottom. Not worth considering until he proves he can miss some bats, even with promising news on health front this spring.

Yr Tm	W	Sv	IP	K	ERA	xERA	WHIP	xWHIP	vL+	vR+	BF/G	Ctl	Dom	Cmd	Ball%	SwK	Vel	G	L	F	H%	S%	HR/F	xHR/F	GS	APC	DOM%	DIS%	Sv%	LI	RAR	BPX	R$
15 OAK	7	1	157	136	4.18	4.04	1.35	1.28	113	87	22.4	2.8	7.8	2.8	38%	9.3%	91.2	43	23	34	32%	72%	11%	10%	26	86	23%	38%	100	0.74	-4.3	104	$1
16 2 TM	2	0	67	63	4.43	4.05	1.33	1.21	113	101	4.5	2.4	8.5	3.5	34%	9.9%	93.2	43	18	39	32%	73%	15%	16%	0	18			0	0.90	-2.0	128	-$2
17 LAA	7	0	138	119	5.35	4.51	1.40	1.30	103	117	15.4	2.9	7.8	2.6	38%	8.3%	92.0	41	22	37	31%	67%	18%	16%	21	61	10%	43%	0	0.74	-16.8	95	-$3
18 2 TM	5	5	95	92	2.55	3.50	1.06	1.10	89	90	6.1	1.6	8.7	5.4	33%	11.1%	93.0	44	20	36	29%	84%	14%	15%	0	24			83	0.83	18.8	155	$12
19 TEX	3	1	78	72	4.85	4.49	1.33	1.29	92	114	7.0	2.5	8.3	3.3	37%	7.0%	91.2	42	24	34	32%	67%	15%	18%	9	27	11%	33%	50	1.02	-3.3	110	-$2
1st Half	3	0	58	56	2.97	4.06	1.18	1.19	67	114	6.6	2.3	8.7	3.7	36%	7.1%	91.3	44	22	34	30%	82%	15%	17%	6	26	17%	0%	0	1.02	11.0	127	$3
2nd Half	0	1	20	16	10.18	5.76	1.77	1.36	140	116	8.3	3.1	7.1	2.3	39%	6.8%	90.9	35	30	35	38%	41%	15%	21%	3	32	0%	100%	50	1.05	-14.2	62	-$17
20 Proj	**3**	**0**	**73**	**65**	**4.90**	**4.14**	**1.42**	**1.24**	**114**	**111**	**7.5**	**2.7**	**8.0**	**2.9**	**36%**	**8.4%**	**91.8**	**39**	**22**	**39**	**32%**	**71%**	**16%**		**0**						**-6.7**	**100**	**-$4**

Chen,Wei-Yin

Age: 34	Th: L	Role RP	Health F	LIMA Plan A
Ht: 6' 0"	Wt: 200	Type Con FB	PT/Exp C	Rand Var +2
			Consist A	MM 1100

With shift to bullpen, he was able to stay healthy and bump up SwK/Dom a bit, but that's where the good news ends. The trifecta of bad luck (H%, S%, HR/F) was a contributing factor, but part of that was his own doing with all of the line drives/hard contact he allowed. No matter what role he's in, xERA shows that he'll be safe to avoid.

Yr Tm	W	Sv	IP	K	ERA	xERA	WHIP	xWHIP	vL+	vR+	BF/G	Ctl	Dom	Cmd	Ball%	SwK	Vel	G	L	F	H%	S%	HR/F	xHR/F	GS	APC	DOM%	DIS%	Sv%	LI	RAR	BPX	R$
15 BAL	11	0	191	153	3.34	4.01	1.22	1.22	79	115	25.5	1.9	7.2	3.7	32%	9.2%	91.4	40	20	39	30%	79%	12%	11%	31	97	26%	19%			14.7	114	$13
16 MIA	5	0	123	100	4.96	4.23	1.28	1.20	105	108	23.6	1.8	7.3	4.2	34%	9.6%	90.7	40	21	38	31%	66%	15%	15%	22	87	27%	27%			-11.8	121	-$1
17 MIA	2	0	33	25	3.82	4.56	1.03	1.30	69	87	14.7	2.5	6.8	2.8	34%	9.5%	90.9	37	19	44	24%	65%	7%	8%	5	55	0%	40%	0	0.52	2.2	86	-$1
18 MIA	6	0	133	111	4.79	4.77	1.34	1.35	76	111	22.0	3.2	7.5	2.4	36%	8.8%	91.1	37	20	43	30%	67%	11%	10%	26	86	27%	46%			-10.0	74	-$3
19 MIA	0	0	68	63	6.59	4.84	1.54	1.28	120	123	6.8	2.4	8.3	3.5	33%	10.0%	91.3	37	25	38	36%	61%	18%	16%	0	26			0	0.51	-17.5	109	-$11
1st Half	0	0	32	31	8.16	5.01	1.66	1.25	93	145	6.2	2.8	8.7	3.1	32%	10.4%	91.1	38	23	38	38%	52%	18%	14%	0	24			0	0.75	-14.4	106	-$15
2nd Half	0	0	36	32	5.20	4.76	1.43	1.20	144	103	7.5	2.0	7.9	4.0	34%	9.6%	91.6	35	27	38	34%	70%	18%	19%	0	28			0	0.23	-3.1	111	-$7
20 Proj	**1**	**0**	**58**	**48**	**4.91**	**4.51**	**1.56**	**1.26**	**122**	**126**	**10.2**	**2.8**	**7.4**	**2.6**	**34%**	**9.5%**	**91.2**	**37**	**23**	**40**	**34%**	**75%**	**16%**		**0**						**-5.4**	**84**	**-$6**

Chirinos,Yonny

Age: 26	Th: R	Role SP	Health D	LIMA Plan A
Ht: 6' 2"	Wt: 240	Type Con	PT/Exp C	Rand Var 0
			Consist A	MM 2103

Split time between starter and primary pitcher, and results were excellent early on. But luck swung the other way in 2nd half before finger injury knocked him out for six weeks. Strong Ctl provides decent floor, but sinker-heavy approach limits strikeout upside, and H% likely isn't done correcting. Use xERA, xWHIP as your guides.

Yr Tm	W	Sv	IP	K	ERA	xERA	WHIP	xWHIP	vL+	vR+	BF/G	Ctl	Dom	Cmd	Ball%	SwK	Vel	G	L	F	H%	S%	HR/F	xHR/F	GS	APC	DOM%	DIS%	Sv%	LI	RAR	BPX	R$
15																																	
16 aa	5	0	67	38	5.39	4.96	1.47				20.4	1.7	5.1	3.1							35%	63%									-9.8	78	-$5
17 a/a	13	0	168	122	3.58	3.65	1.16				24.8	1.5	6.5	4.3							30%	72%									16.2	126	$16
18 TAM *	5	0	122	101	4.29	4.36	1.30	1.27	93	97	19.3	2.4	7.5	3.1	35%	11.5%	93.7	44	24	32	32%	70%	8%	13%	7	73	29%	43%	0	0.90	-2.1	91	$0
19 TAM	9	0	133	114	3.85	4.09	1.05	1.23	78	101	20.4	1.9	7.7	4.1	35%	10.7%	93.9	43	23	33	25%	71%	18%	18%	18	76	33%	22%	0	0.73	10.8	118	$12
1st Half	7	0	93	76	3.10	4.10	1.00	1.21	80	94	21.3	2.0	7.4	3.6	35%	10.7%	93.7	43	24	33	24%	77%	16%	19%	11	80	36%	18%	0	0.75	16.2	107	$19
2nd Half	2	0	40	38	5.58	4.09	1.17	1.12	76	118	18.7	1.6	8.5	5.4	35%	10.7%	94.1	44	22	34	29%	58%	22%	15%	7	70	29%	29%	0	0.70	-5.3	145	-$4
20 Proj	**9**	**0**	**145**	**119**	**4.07**	**3.66**	**1.19**	**1.20**	**87**	**110**	**20.6**	**1.9**	**7.4**	**4.0**	**35%**	**11.0%**	**93.8**	**44**	**23**	**33**	**30%**	**71%**	**15%**		**28**						**1.5**	**120**	**$8**

Cimber,Adam

Age: 29	Th: R	Role RP	Health A	LIMA Plan B
Ht: 6' 4"	Wt: 195	Type Con GB	PT/Exp D	Rand Var +1
			Consist B	MM 2000

With mid-80s sinker as his primary offering, his success relies on the defense behind him. 1st half/2nd half swings in H% and S%, and in turn, his ERA, show just how thin the line is. Has just a 5.9 Dom in career vR, but also only 9 HR in 560 PA, which should afford him more chances. But path to fantasy relevance is murky to say the least.

Yr Tm	W	Sv	IP	K	ERA	xERA	WHIP	xWHIP	vL+	vR+	BF/G	Ctl	Dom	Cmd	Ball%	SwK	Vel	G	L	F	H%	S%	HR/F	xHR/F	GS	APC	DOM%	DIS%	Sv%	LI	RAR	BPX	R$
15 a/a	4	1	59	39	3.31	4.54	1.41				5.4	2.3	5.9	2.6							33%	79%									4.7	76	-$1
16 a/a	3	3	57	24	4.62	4.57	1.44				5.3	2.4	3.8	1.6							31%	68%									-3.1	38	-$3
17 a/a	5	5	81	50	3.67	3.78	1.09				6.4	1.2	5.5	4.7							27%	73%									6.8	116	$7
18 2 TM	3	0	68	58	3.42	3.44	1.24	1.23	145	85	4.1	2.2	7.6	3.4	29%	10.4%	86.5	57	21	21	32%	74%	12%	7%	0	14			0	0.88	6.1	129	$1
19 CLE	6	1	57	41	4.45	4.54	1.32	1.41	124	86	3.6	3.0	6.5	2.2	32%	10.2%	85.2	56	20	24	30%	68%	14%	13%	0	12			33	1.32	0.4	76	$0
1st Half	3	0	29	20	3.38	4.48	1.16	1.40	119	75	3.5	3.1	6.1	2.0	34%	10.0%	84.7	59	15	25	24%	77%	17%	11%	0	12			0	1.00	4.1	71	$1
2nd Half	3	1	27	21	5.60	4.42	1.50	1.35	130	96	3.7	3.0	6.9	2.3	30%	10.3%	85.7	52	26	22	35%	62%	11%	17%	0	11			33	1.65	-3.7	82	-$1
20 Proj	**5**	**0**	**58**	**42**	**4.31**	**3.74**	**1.30**	**1.31**	**135**	**88**	**4.0**	**2.5**	**6.5**	**2.7**	**31%**	**10.3%**	**85.8**	**54**	**21**	**25**	**31%**	**68%**	**13%**		**0**						**-1.2**	**96**	**-$1**

Cishek,Steve

Age: 34	Th: R	Role RP	Health B	LIMA Plan B
Ht: 6' 6"	Wt: 215	Type Pwr	PT/Exp C	Rand Var -5
			Consist B	MM 2210

A fourth straight sub-3.00 ERA, but skills fell off a cliff in 2nd half, as August hip injury may have bothered him for longer than short IL stint. The struggles do add a little more uncertainty to a profile that is reliant on limiting hard contact, keeping H% low, and keeping S% high. It's a dangerous balancing act. One of these years he won't be so lucky.

Yr Tm	W	Sv	IP	K	ERA	xERA	WHIP	xWHIP	vL+	vR+	BF/G	Ctl	Dom	Cmd	Ball%	SwK	Vel	G	L	F	H%	S%	HR/F	xHR/F	GS	APC	DOM%	DIS%	Sv%	LI	RAR	BPX	R$
15 2 NL	2	4	55	48	3.58	4.42	1.48	1.46	104	98	4.1	4.4	7.8	1.8	39%	9.7%	90.8	46	22	32	32%	77%	8%	12%	0	16			44	0.91	2.6	55	-$1
16 SEA	4	25	64	76	2.81	3.35	1.02	1.15	99	68	4.2	3.0	10.7	3.6	38%	11.5%	91.4	44	17	39	26%	79%	13%	10%	0	17			78	1.52	10.9	160	$17
17 2 AL	3	1	45	41	2.01	3.42	0.90	1.25	88	56	3.6	2.8	8.3	2.9	37%	10.7%	90.3	56	18	26	21%	81%	10%	10%	0	15			25	1.16	12.9	128	$6
18 CHC	4	4	70	78	2.18	3.51	1.04	1.26	99	74	3.6	3.6	10.0	2.8	38%	11.9%	90.3	47	18	35	25%	82%	8%	10%	0	14			57	1.46	17.1	124	$10
19 CHC	4	7	64	57	2.95	4.58	1.20	1.47	96	78	3.8	4.1	8.0	2.0	38%	9.8%	90.5	50	16	34	25%	80%	12%	13%	0	16			64	1.14	12.3	68	$7
1st Half	2	7	36	39	2.97	3.55	1.05	1.23	90	66	3.9	3.2	9.7	3.0	37%	10.9%	90.5	53	16	31	26%	74%	11%	15%	0	17			78	1.09	6.9	129	$10
2nd Half	2	0	28	18	2.93	6.01	1.41	1.67	107	90	3.7	5.2	5.9	1.1	39%	8.5%	90.6	46	15	38	24%	86%	13%	11%	0	15			0	1.20	5.4	-12	$2
20 Proj	**4**	**2**	**58**	**54**	**3.41**	**3.86**	**1.25**	**1.38**	**111**	**86**	**3.7**	**3.9**	**8.3**	**2.1**	**38%**	**10.3%**	**90.5**	**49**	**17**	**34**	**27%**	**78%**	**14%**		**0**						**5.3**	**83**	**$2**

Civale,Aaron

Age: 25	Th: R	Role SP	Health A	LIMA Plan F
Ht: 6' 2"	Wt: 215	Type Con FB	PT/Exp D	Rand Var -3
			Consist F	MM 1101

3-4, 2.34 ERA in 58 IP at CLE. Made quite a splash during final two months, thanks in large part to fortunate S% and HR/F. Stellar Ctl carried over from minors, but he isn't missing enough bats to bank on Dom gains. A decent back-of-rotation option, but regression is looming, and even a sub-4.00 ERA might be wishful thinking.

Yr Tm	W	Sv	IP	K	ERA	xERA	WHIP	xWHIP	vL+	vR+	BF/G	Ctl	Dom	Cmd	Ball%	SwK	Vel	G	L	F	H%	S%	HR/F	xHR/F	GS	APC	DOM%	DIS%	Sv%	LI	RAR	BPX	R$
15																																	
16																																	
17																																	
18 aa	5	0	107	66	5.27	5.91	1.53				22.2	1.9	5.5	2.9							35%	68%									-14.8	54	-$10
19 CLE *	10	0	132	104	2.83	3.59	1.19	1.33	91	81	23.0	2.2	7.1	3.2	38%	9.0%	92.6	40	22	37	29%	80%	7%	6%	10	86	40%	40%			27.2	95	$14
1st Half	7	0	56	44	2.89	3.68	1.22		0	56	25.3	2.3	7.1	3.1		4.6%	91.4	50	14	36	30%	80%	0%	1%	1	87	0%	0%			11.2	94	$12
2nd Half	3	0	78	60	2.70	3.32	1.13	1.26	97	83	22.0	2.1	6.9	3.2	38%	9.5%	92.8	40	23	38	28%	81%	7%	7%	9	86	44%	44%			17.4	97	$16
20 Proj	**6**	**0**	**102**	**75**	**4.03**	**4.33**	**1.34**	**1.39**	**115**	**106**	**22.9**	**2.3**	**6.7**	**2.9**	**41%**	**9.5%**	**92.8**	**40**	**23**	**38**	**31%**	**75%**	**12%**		**18**						**1.5**	**87**	**$1**

BRIAN RUDD

Clarke,Taylor

Age: 27 Th: R Role RP	Health B	LIMA Plan C	
Ht: 6' 4" Wt: 200 Type Con FB	PT/Exp D	Rand Var +3	
	Consist C	MM 0001	

5-5, 5.32 ERA in 85 IP at ARI. Recorded save in lone April appearance, but things went downhill from there with an xERA over 5.00 in every month. Pumped up velocity, SwK, and Dom after returning from July back injury, though it was mostly in long relief. Regardless of role, short-term outlook is pretty shaky.

Yr Tm	W	Sv	IP	K	ERA	xERA	WHIP	xWHIP	vL+	vR+	BF/G	Ctl	Dom	Cmd	Ball%	SwK	Vel	G	L	F	H%	S%	HR/F	xHR/F	GS	APC	DOM%	DIS%	Sv%	LI	RAR	BPX	R$
15																																	
16 aa	8	0	98	61	5.21	5.48	1.52				24.9	2.1	5.6	2.7							34%	67%									-12.3	57	-$6
17 a/a	12	0	145	114	4.03	4.21	1.35				22.4	3.3	7.1	2.2							30%	73%									5.8	72	$7
18 aaa	13	0	152	101	3.72	3.68	1.27				23.0	2.4	6.0	2.5							31%	71%									8.1	87	$8
19 ARI *	8	1	123	90	5.59	5.66	1.43	1.42	114	120	16.9	3.4	6.6	1.9	38%	10.4%	93.7	40	17	44	28%	67%	20%	19%	15	66	7%	53%	100	0.76	-16.5	21	-$4
1st Half	5	1	74	50	6.41	5.96	1.54	1.37	131	119	20.0	3.2	6.1	1.9	38%	9.6%	93.0	41	17	41	32%	61%	18%	21%	8	80	0%	63%	100	0.73	-17.3	22	-$8
2nd Half	3	0	49	40	4.38	5.22	1.28	1.35	97	120	13.5	3.6	7.3	2.0	38%	11.1%	94.3	38	17	45	23%	80%	22%	17%	7	57	14%	43%	0	0.78	0.8	19	$0
20 Proj	**5**	**0**	**73**	**53**	**4.65**	**4.57**	**1.39**	**1.36**	**110**	**117**	**18.8**	**3.0**	**6.5**	**2.1**	**38%**	**10.5%**	**93.8**	**39**	**20**	**41**	**29%**	**74%**	**16%**		**14**						**-4.5**	**61**	**-$2**

Clase,Emmanuel

Age: 22 Th: R Role RP	Health A	LIMA Plan F	
Ht: 6' 2" Wt: 206 Type Con xGB	PT/Exp F	Rand Var +2	
	Consist F	MM 4210	

2-3, 2.31 ERA with 1 Sv in 21 IP at TEX. Whiffs haven't caught up to the stuff just yet, but plenty of reasons to be intrigued by this young arm: top-notch velocity, extreme GB tilt, stellar Ctl, and 12 Sv in minors before call-up. Could be just a minor tweak away from unleashing more Ks and emerging as late-inning force. UP: 20 Sv

Yr Tm	W	Sv	IP	K	ERA	xERA	WHIP	xWHIP	vL+	vR+	BF/G	Ctl	Dom	Cmd	Ball%	SwK	Vel	G	L	F	H%	S%	HR/F	xHR/F	GS	APC	DOM%	DIS%	Sv%	LI	RAR	BPX	R$
15																																	
16																																	
17																																	
18																																	
19 TEX *	3	12	63	54	3.78	3.46	1.24	1.24	90	90	4.7	2.2	7.7	3.6	34%	11.3%	99.3	61	20	20	32%	69%	15%	17%	1	16	0%	100%	86	1.00	5.6	119	$6
1st Half	1	4	24	18	7.03	5.21	1.67		0	0	4.9	2.5	6.6	2.6							40%	53%	0%		0	0					-7.5	90	-$9
2nd Half	2	8	38	36	1.74	2.36	0.96	1.21	91	88	4.5	1.9	8.4	4.4	34%	11.3%	99.3	61	20	20	26%	88%	15%	17%	1	16	0%	100%	100	1.00	13.1	143	$15
20 Proj	**3**	**5**	**65**	**56**	**3.41**	**3.15**	**1.23**	**1.33**	**89**	**88**	**4.7**	**2.2**	**7.7**	**3.6**	**38%**	**11.3%**	**99.3**	**61**	**20**	**20**	**32%**	**72%**	**7%**		**0**						**6.0**	**137**	**$4**

Claudio,Alex

Age: 28 Th: L Role RP	Health D	LIMA Plan B	
Ht: 6' 3" Wt: 180 Type Con xGB	PT/Exp C	Rand Var +2	
	Consist B	MM 1000	

Led majors in appearances, but BF/G continued downward trend as exposure to RHB was limited. Given low velocity and Dom, his margin for error is very thin, which makes Ctl/Ball% spikes all the more concerning. Odds are against both a sub-4.00 ERA and positive R$.

Yr Tm	W	Sv	IP	K	ERA	xERA	WHIP	xWHIP	vL+	vR+	BF/G	Ctl	Dom	Cmd	Ball%	SwK	Vel	G	L	F	H%	S%	HR/F	xHR/F	GS	APC	DOM%	DIS%	Sv%	LI	RAR	BPX	R$
15 TEX *	4	0	56	42	3.38	4.48	1.35		98	115	4.9	2.2	6.8	3.1		11.2%	84.1	51	16	33	33%	79%	27%	12%	0	14			0	1.16	4.0	89	-$1
16 TEX *	4	1	68	40	2.28	2.78	1.14	1.26	61	103	6.0	1.9	5.4	2.8	33%	10.6%	85.5	63	17	20	29%	80%	6%	9%	0	20			100	0.72	16.0	106	$6
17 TEX	4	11	83	56	2.50	3.31	1.04	1.23	49	94	4.6	1.6	6.1	3.7	32%	10.1%	86.7	67	17	17	27%	78%	12%	9%	1	16	0%	100%	73	1.18	18.9	133	$13
18 TEX	4	1	68	41	4.48	3.91	1.52	1.28	82	130	4.5	1.7	5.4	3.2	33%	11.6%	86.0	61	23	16	36%	70%	11%	18%	1	16	0%	100%	33	1.14	-2.8	104	-$5
19 MIL	2	0	62	44	4.06	4.58	1.31	1.47	89	111	3.2	3.5	6.4	1.8	36%	10.8%	85.7	57	20	22	27%	73%	19%	14%	0	12			0	1.15	3.4	61	-$2
1st Half	1	0	34	23	4.46	4.62	1.28	1.41	78	121	3.4	3.1	6.0	1.9	36%	10.7%	85.2	58	17	25	26%	71%	22%	13%	0	13			0	1.06	0.2	65	-$3
2nd Half	1	0	28	21	3.58	4.30	1.34	1.46	106	99	3.0	3.9	6.8	1.8	36%	11.0%	86.3	57	25	19	29%	74%	13%	17%	0	11			0	1.25	3.2	57	$0
20 Proj	**3**	**0**	**58**	**39**	**4.21**	**4.04**	**1.39**	**1.35**	**86**	**113**	**3.7**	**3.3**	**6.1**	**1.9**	**34%**	**10.9%**	**86.0**	**56**	**21**	**23**	**30%**	**71%**	**12%**		**0**						**-0.4**	**64**	**-$3**

Clevinger,Mike

Age: 29 Th: R Role SP	Health D	LIMA Plan A	
Ht: 6' 4" Wt: 215 Type Pwr	PT/Exp B	Rand Var -1	
	Consist A	MM 4505	

April back injury was a major scare, but returned sooner than expected and quickly shook off the rust. Though the velocity did slip a bit in August/September, SwK and Dom remained way above previous levels. Ball% doesn't fully support Ctl gains, but even with a few more BB, he's a rotation anchor and potential top 5 SP.

Yr Tm	W	Sv	IP	K	ERA	xERA	WHIP	xWHIP	vL+	vR+	BF/G	Ctl	Dom	Cmd	Ball%	SwK	Vel	G	L	F	H%	S%	HR/F	xHR/F	GS	APC	DOM%	DIS%	Sv%	LI	RAR	BPX	R$
15 aa	9	0	158	114	3.95	3.82	1.31				24.2	2.5	6.5	2.6							32%	70%									0.3	91	$3
16 CLE *	14	0	146	119	4.73	4.91	1.53	1.49	69	133	18.7	4.3	7.4	1.7	40%	9.8%	93.4	38	22	40	31%	72%	13%	13%	10	57	0%	60%	0	0.84	-9.8	54	-$2
17 CLE *	15	0	156	164	3.27	3.64	1.32	1.35	108	77	19.0	4.4	9.5	2.1	40%	12.8%	92.5	39	24	36	29%	79%	12%	13%	21	78	33%	24%	0	0.71	20.8	98	$15
18 CLE	13	0	200	207	3.02	3.82	1.16	1.23	99	82	25.3	3.0	9.3	3.1	36%	12.4%	93.6	40	20	39	29%	78%	10%	11%	32	102	31%	13%			28.0	120	$22
19 CLE	13	0	126	169	2.71	3.19	1.06	1.09	85	74	23.8	2.6	12.1	4.6	37%	15.7%	95.5	41	24	36	32%	77%	10%	13%	21	100	57%	10%			27.8	180	$21
1st Half	1	0	18	31	5.89	3.14	1.09	1.15	102	41	18.8	4.9	15.2	3.1	38%	16.4%	95.9	31	28	41	28%	44%	15%	18%	4	81	50%	25%			-3.1	164	-$22
2nd Half	12	0	108	138	2.17	3.23	1.05	1.03	82	77	24.9	2.3	11.5	5.1	36%	15.6%	95.4	42	23	35	32%	83%	9%	12%	17	104	59%	6%			31.0	182	$28
20 Proj	**15**	**0**	**189**	**237**	**3.27**	**3.10**	**1.10**	**1.20**	**91**	**78**	**24.9**	**3.2**	**11.3**	**3.5**	**37%**	**15.0%**	**94.4**	**39**	**23**	**38**	**29%**	**74%**	**12%**		**30**						**20.4**	**153**	**$25**

Clippard,Tyler

Age: 35 Th: R Role RP	Health A	LIMA Plan A	
Ht: 6' 3" Wt: 200 Type Pwr xFB	PT/Exp C	Rand Var -5	
	Consist A	MM 2400	

Topped 60 IP for 11th straight year, and rode fortunate H% (14% vL) and HR/F to lowest ERA since 2014. Ball% backed up Ctl gains and SwK still strong, but the latter will be tough to sustain with velocity on the decline. Still a fine RP, but sky-high FB% is a problem if ball stays the same. xERA warns us not to pay for a repeat.

Yr Tm	W	Sv	IP	K	ERA	xERA	WHIP	xWHIP	vL+	vR+	BF/G	Ctl	Dom	Cmd	Ball%	SwK	Vel	G	L	F	H%	S%	HR/F	xHR/F	GS	APC	DOM%	DIS%	Sv%	LI	RAR	BPX	R$
15 2 TM	5	19	71	64	2.92	4.96	1.13	1.41	64	105	4.4	3.9	8.1	2.1	36%	12.3%	91.5	21	18	61	23%	79%	7%	8%	0	18			76	1.25	9.2	46	$13
16 2 TM	4	3	63	72	3.57	4.15	1.27	1.26	102	93	3.8	3.7	10.3	2.8	37%	13.0%	91.1	31	19	50	29%	79%	13%	8%	0	15			50	1.05	4.8	112	$3
17 3 AL	2	5	60	72	4.77	4.60	1.29	1.35	90	99	3.9	4.6	10.7	2.3	37%	14.4%	91.1	32	17	51	27%	68%	13%	9%	0	17			45	1.11	-3.1	94	$1
18 TOR	4	7	69	85	3.67	4.12	1.17	1.15	82	115	3.9	3.0	11.1	3.7	35%	15.1%	90.9	19	20	60	29%	78%	13%	11%	1	16	0%	100%	54	1.02	4.1	134	$6
19 CLE	1	0	62	64	2.90	4.18	0.85	1.19	61	100	4.5	2.2	9.3	4.3	34%	14.1%	90.0	32	13	56	21%	73%	9%	10%	3	18	0%	67%	0	0.82	12.3	129	$6
1st Half	0	0	24	24	3.38	4.63	0.92	1.24	52	91	4.2	3.0	9.0	3.0	37%	13.5%	90.3	31	14	56	23%	62%	3%	9%	1	16	0%	100%	0	0.68	3.3	98	-$1
2nd Half	1	0	38	40	2.61	4.11	0.82	1.06	65	107	4.8	1.7	9.5	5.7	32%	14.4%	89.8	32	12	56	20%	83%	13%	11%	2	19	0%	50%	0	0.92	8.9	148	$10
20 Proj	**2**	**0**	**65**	**72**	**3.97**	**3.89**	**1.16**	**1.19**	**82**	**118**	**4.1**	**2.9**	**10.0**	**3.4**	**35%**	**14.2%**	**90.5**	**28**	**16**	**56**	**28%**	**73%**	**13%**		**0**						**1.5**	**122**	**$1**

Cobb,Alex

Age: 32 Th: R Role SP	Health F	LIMA Plan B	
Ht: 6' 3" Wt: 205 Type Con	PT/Exp B	Rand Var +5	
	Consist B	MM 1001	

Ineffective in three April starts that were sandwiched between groin, back, and hip injuries, the last of which required season-ending surgery. Small sample 2019 aside, it's been five years since he's even topped 8% SwK, and the F Health Grade is well-deserved. Time to give up on a potential return to form.

Yr Tm	W	Sv	IP	K	ERA	xERA	WHIP	xWHIP	vL+	vR+	BF/G	Ctl	Dom	Cmd	Ball%	SwK	Vel	G	L	F	H%	S%	HR/F	xHR/F	GS	APC	DOM%	DIS%	Sv%	LI	RAR	BPX	R$
15																																	
16 TAM *	1	0	37	24	9.18	9.27	2.12		164	101	20.3	3.2	5.8	1.8		8.0%	90.4	53	19	29	41%	59%	22%	22%	5	77	20%	60%			-22.8	-18	-$15
17 TAM	12	0	179	128	3.66	4.29	1.22	1.29	90	99	25.6	2.2	6.4	2.9	36%	7.1%	91.7	48	22	30	29%	74%	13%	13%	29	98	38%	17%			15.4	98	$14
18 BAL	5	0	152	102	4.90	4.59	1.41	1.35	105	120	23.6	2.5	6.0	2.4	36%	7.6%	92.0	50	19	31	31%	69%	15%	16%	28	87	21%	36%			-14.2	78	-$7
19 BAL	0	0	12	8	10.95	5.51	1.86	1.31	130	203	20.0	1.5	5.8	4.0	35%	10.5%	92.3	46	24	30	31%	57%	60%	55%	3	76	0%	67%			-9.8	98	-$9
1st Half	0	0	12	8	10.95	5.49	1.86		129	206	20.0	1.5	5.8	4.0		10.5%	92.3	46	24	30	31%	57%	60%	55%	3	76	0%	67%			-9.8	98	-$9
2nd Half																																	
20 Proj	**3**	**0**	**73**	**46**	**5.21**	**4.48**	**1.44**	**1.32**	**105**	**116**	**21.1**	**2.7**	**5.7**	**2.1**	**36%**	**7.4%**	**91.8**	**46**	**21**	**33**	**31%**	**67%**	**14%**		**15**						**-9.5**	**61**	**-$6**

Cole,A.J.

Age: 28 Th: R Role RP	Health D	LIMA Plan C	
Ht: 6' 5" Wt: 238 Type Pwr xFB	PT/Exp D	Rand Var 0	
	Consist C	MM 1300	

3-1, 3.86 ERA in 26 IP at CLE. He's added velocity and whiffs since move to 'pen, and before August shoulder injury ended season, made strides with Ball%/Ctl. But with high FB%, even a friendly HR/F couldn't prevent some issues with the long ball. Should continue to rack up fair share of Ks, but won't help your ratios.

Yr Tm	W	Sv	IP	K	ERA	xERA	WHIP	xWHIP	vL+	vR+	BF/G	Ctl	Dom	Cmd	Ball%	SwK	Vel	G	L	F	H%	S%	HR/F	xHR/F	GS	APC	DOM%	DIS%	Sv%	LI	RAR	BPX	R$
15 WAS *	5	1	115	72	4.25	4.35	1.40		128	81	20.2	2.9	5.6	1.9		10.2%	90.5	36	27	36	31%	71%	8%	9%	1	52	0%	100%	100	0.48	-4.1	58	-$3
16 WAS *	9	0	163	129	6.02	5.97	1.59	1.28	106	105	24.0	3.0	7.1	2.4	36%	10.7%	91.0	32	13	55	35%	65%	11%	10%	8	84	13%	38%			-36.8	48	-$14
17 WAS *	7	0	145	109	6.28	6.65	1.87	1.51	130	81	23.5	4.1	6.7	1.7	38%	10.4%	93.1	44	17	39	39%	67%	14%	12%	8	85	0%	50%	0	0.67	-34.5	40	-$21
18 2 TM	4	0	48	59	6.14	4.49	1.59	1.28	160	105	6.9	4.1	11.0	2.7	36%	14.8%	93.4	32	20	47	34%	71%	23%	17%	2	27	0%	50%	0	0.47	-11.9	112	-$7
19 CLE *	3	3	43	46	4.07	4.65	1.34	1.24	117	104	4.7	2.9	9.7	3.4	33%	14.6%	94.4	31	19	50	33%	75%	10%	8%	0	19			100	0.73	2.3	97	$0
1st Half	2	2	33	35	4.43	4.95	1.34	1.23	125	118	4.6	3.2	9.5	3.0	32%	14.5%	94.6	32	22	46	31%	74%	17%	13%	0	19			100	0.69	0.3	76	$0
2nd Half	1	1	10	11	2.79	4.76	1.34		101	81	5.1	1.9	10.2	5.5		14.6%	93.9	29	14	57	40%	77%	0%	1%	0	21			100	0.80	2.0	153	-$2
20 Proj	**3**	**0**	**58**	**62**	**4.64**	**4.04**	**1.36**	**1.35**	**119**	**93**	**8.4**	**3.2**	**9.6**	**3.0**	**36%**	**12.6%**	**93.3**	**33**	**20**	**47**	**32%**	**72%**	**14%**		**0**						**-3.5**	**111**	**-$2**

BRIAN RUDD

Cole,Gerrit

Age: 29	Th: R	Role: SP	Health	B	LIMA Plan	B
			PT/Exp	A	Rand Var	0
Ht: 6' 4"	Wt: 225	Type: Pwr	Consist	B	MM	5505

Epic 300-K performance featured electric 2nd half skills and results, even with August hamstring injury. Created absurd SwK with four-seamer and slider to support primo Dom, and pinpoint Ctl seems locked in, so xERA backs stellar repeat. World-class skills make him a worthy candidate for the first SP off the board.

Yr Tm	W	Sv	IP	K	ERA	xERA	WHIP	xWHIP	vL+	vR+	BF/G	Ctl	Dom	Cmd	Ball%	SwK	Vel	G	L	F	H%	S%	HR/F	xHR/F	GS	APC	DOM%	DIS%	Sv%	LI	RAR	BPX	R$
15 PIT	19	0	208	202	2.60	3.16	1.09	1.13	82	91	26.0	1.9	8.7	4.6	35%	10.7%	95.6	48	22	30	31%	77%	7%	12%	32	101	59%	13%			35.0	157	$30
16 PIT	7	0	116	98	3.88	4.17	1.44	1.30	118	89	24.1	2.8	7.6	2.7	35%	8.8%	95.2	46	25	29	35%	73%	7%	8%	21	92	24%	29%			4.4	102	$1
17 PIT	12	0	203	196	4.26	3.91	1.25	1.20	105	93	25.7	2.4	8.7	3.6	35%	9.9%	96.0	46	21	34	31%	71%	16%	15%	33	100	24%	18%			2.6	138	$12
18 HOU	15	0	200	276	2.88	3.08	1.03	1.06	71	94	25.0	2.9	12.4	4.3	33%	14.7%	96.6	36	21	43	30%	76%	10%	12%	32	102	50%	0%			31.5	184	$31
19 HOU	20	0	212	326	2.50	2.65	0.89	0.93	77	76	24.8	2.0	13.8	6.8	33%	17.6%	97.2	40	20	39	29%	81%	17%	13%	33	102	42%	12%			52.5	231	$46
1st Half	8	0	110	161	3.28	2.94	1.04	0.96	88	83	24.3	2.3	13.2	5.8	33%	16.6%	96.8	41	22	36	32%	76%	19%	14%	18	102	33%	22%			16.5	213	$35
2nd Half	12	0	103	165	1.67	2.47	0.74	0.82	65	68	25.3	1.8	14.5	8.3	33%	18.8%	97.6	39	18	43	26%	89%	14%	12%	15	102	53%	0%			36.0	251	$58
20 Proj	**17**	**0**	**203**	**275**	**2.84**	**2.67**	**1.00**	**1.01**	**81**	**84**	**24.2**	**2.3**	**12.2**	**5.3**	**33%**	**16.5%**	**96.7**	**40**	**21**	**39**	**30%**	**78%**	**14%**		**32**						**32.9**	**202**	**$35**

Cole,Taylor

Age: 30	Th: R	Role: RP	Health	B	LIMA Plan	F
			PT/Exp	D	Rand Var	+2
Ht: 6' 1"	Wt: 200	Type:	Consist	F	MM	1200

3-4, 5.92 ERA in 52 IP at LAA. Started season with shoulder injury, rode the AAA shuttle, and opened a few games while posting ugly results. Even with favorable GB%, inability to find the zone and likely HR/F bump say that elevated ratios should continue. Tack on just league-average Dom, and you should mine for R$ elsewhere.

Yr Tm	W	Sv	IP	K	ERA	xERA	WHIP	xWHIP	vL+	vR+	BF/G	Ctl	Dom	Cmd	Ball%	SwK	Vel	G	L	F	H%	S%	HR/F	xHR/F	GS	APC	DOM%	DIS%	Sv%	LI	RAR	BPX	R$
15 aa	7	0	164	105	5.46	6.25	1.70				26.5	3.3	5.7	1.7							35%	70%									-30.2	27	-$19
16 aa	3	0	62	42	5.33	6.70	1.79				23.7	2.8	6.2	2.2							39%	72%									-8.7	41	-$9
17 TOR	0	0	1	1	36.00	0.00	7.00		188	248	10.0	9.0	9.0	1.0		9.8%	92.8	57	43	0	77%	43%	0%		0	41			0	0.98	-3.9	-55	-$7
18 LAA *	7	6	92	88	4.38	3.72	1.31	1.19	75	74	7.3	3.7	8.6	2.3	39%	15.1%	92.8	51	19	30	30%	68%	13%	6%	2	32	0%	50%	67	0.62	-2.6	94	$3
19 LAA *	6	3	74	68	5.63	5.50	1.64	1.43	93	108	6.1	3.7	8.3	2.3	38%	12.2%	93.2	48	30	22	37%	66%	6%	8%	6	24	0%	50%	75	0.92	-10.3	71	-$5
1st Half	3	3	36	36	4.82	6.02	1.65	1.39	83	103	6.4	3.5	9.1	2.6	39%	11.0%	93.2	50	23	27	38%	74%	0%	5%	1	27	0%	100%	100	0.68	-1.4	69	-$3
2nd Half	3	0	38	32	6.40	5.01	1.62	1.39	98	110	5.8	3.8	7.5	2.0	38%	12.8%	93.2	48	33	20	37%	58%	10%	10%	5	23	0%	40%	0	1.01	-8.9	74	-$7
20 Proj	**4**	**0**	**58**	**50**	**5.30**	**4.10**	**1.60**	**1.31**	**110**	**123**	**8.0**	**3.7**	**7.7**	**2.1**	**39%**	**13.2%**	**93.0**	**49**	**25**	**26**	**36%**	**67%**	**13%**		**0**						**-8.2**	**78**	**-$6**

Colome,Alex

Age: 31	Th: R	Role: RP	Health	B	LIMA Plan	B
			PT/Exp	B	Rand Var	-5
Ht: 6' 1"	Wt: 220	Type: Pwr	Consist	B	MM	2330

Kept closer job with 1st half H% fortune and rode Sv train to profit. Increase in walks dampens Cmd outlook, but even with cutter missing fewer bats, SwK hints at slight Dom bump. Luck correction should add to 2020 ratios, and if they reach xERA/xWHIP, he could lose ninth-inning chances. Tread carefully, as he needs Sv for value.

Yr Tm	W	Sv	IP	K	ERA	xERA	WHIP	xWHIP	vL+	vR+	BF/G	Ctl	Dom	Cmd	Ball%	SwK	Vel	G	L	F	H%	S%	HR/F	xHR/F	GS	APC	DOM%	DIS%	Sv%	LI	RAR	BPX	R$
15 TAM	8	0	110	88	3.94	4.06	1.30	1.29	101	93	10.6	2.5	7.2	2.8	37%	10.9%	94.1	40	25	35	32%	71%	8%	11%	13	40	8%	38%	0	1.06	0.3	94	$2
16 TAM	2	37	57	71	1.91	2.85	1.02	1.06	65	87	4.0	2.4	11.3	4.7	34%	15.7%	94.7	47	23	30	29%	88%	15%	10%	0	15			93	1.23	16.0	194	$22
17 TAM	2	47	67	58	3.24	4.26	1.20	1.32	90	81	4.3	3.1	7.8	2.5	35%	12.0%	95.1	49	18	34	29%	74%	6%	9%	0	15			89	1.41	9.2	101	$23
18 2 AL	7	12	68	72	3.04	3.51	1.18	1.19	67	106	4.0	2.8	9.5	3.4	34%	14.2%	95.1	46	24	30	30%	78%	13%	16%	0	16			71	1.37	9.3	139	$10
19 CHW	4	30	61	55	2.80	4.53	1.07	1.38	77	86	4.0	3.4	8.1	2.4	37%	13.5%	94.4	45	18	37	23%	79%	11%	18%	0	16			91	1.18	12.8	84	$18
1st Half	3	18	33	26	2.16	4.47	0.66	1.31	53	67	3.7	2.7	7.0	2.6	37%	13.1%	94.4	41	13	46	11%	78%	10%	16%	0	14			95	1.16	9.6	79	$23
2nd Half	1	12	28	29	3.58	4.55	1.55	1.36	104	102	4.4	4.2	9.4	2.2	38%	14.0%	94.4	49	23	28	36%	80%	13%	21%	0	17			86	1.20	3.2	91	$12
20 Proj	**4**	**28**	**58**	**56**	**3.51**	**3.66**	**1.26**	**1.28**	**87**	**100**	**4.1**	**3.2**	**8.7**	**2.7**	**36%**	**13.5%**	**94.7**	**46**	**21**	**33**	**30%**	**76%**	**13%**		**0**						**4.6**	**108**	**$13**

Conley,Adam

Age: 30	Th: L	Role: RP	Health	B	LIMA Plan	C
			PT/Exp	D	Rand Var	+5
Ht: 6' 3"	Wt: 200	Type:	Consist	C	MM	0110

Secured two early saves, but ratios imploded and eventually relegated him to low-leverage bullpen role. SwK drop with slider questions the Dom spike, and battles with control expect more WHIP ugliness. While GB% and fortune could bounce back some, xERA will damage any team, and has not been roster-worthy for years.

Yr Tm	W	Sv	IP	K	ERA	xERA	WHIP	xWHIP	vL+	vR+	BF/G	Ctl	Dom	Cmd	Ball%	SwK	Vel	G	L	F	H%	S%	HR/F	xHR/F	GS	APC	DOM%	DIS%	Sv%	LI	RAR	BPX	R$
15 MIA *	13	0	174	123	3.51	3.72	1.35	1.28	105	101	21.3	3.3	6.4	1.9	34%	10.7%	91.3	41	19	41	30%	75%	9%	12%	11	73	18%	36%	0	0.72	9.6	77	$7
16 MIA	8	0	133	124	3.85	4.67	1.40	1.41	103	100	23.4	4.2	8.4	2.0	38%	10.4%	91.0	38	21	41	31%	75%	8%	12%	25	91	24%	32%			5.6	64	$3
17 MIA *	11	0	165	105	6.46	5.90	1.63	1.46	109	116	21.6	3.8	5.7	1.5	37%	10.0%	89.5	40	19	42	32%	62%	14%	12%	20	78	15%	55%	0	0.83	-42.8	21	-$16
18 MIA *	5	3	91	69	5.15	4.59	1.39	1.27	80	96	6.4	3.3	6.9	2.1	37%	15.4%	95.3	44	20	36	30%	65%	11%	12%	0	15			60	1.26	-11.2	61	-$4
19 MIA	2	2	61	53	6.53	5.63	1.73	1.51	118	123	4.7	4.3	7.9	1.8	36%	11.5%	95.4	38	24	38	36%	64%	14%	14%	0	18			50	1.19	-15.1	45	-$10
1st Half	1	2	32	31	7.31	4.73	1.59	1.31	112	127	4.5	3.4	8.7	2.6	36%	11.8%	95.7	41	28	32	36%	56%	19%	20%	0	17			67	1.52	-11.1	92	-$10
2nd Half	1	0	29	22	5.65	6.64	1.88	1.61	124	118	5.0	5.3	6.9	1.3	36%	11.2%	95.0	35	21	45	36%	72%	10%	10%	0	19			0	0.78	-4.1	-8	-$10
20 Proj	**3**	**2**	**58**	**46**	**5.16**	**4.80**	**1.56**	**1.42**	**110**	**116**	**6.2**	**4.1**	**7.1**	**1.8**	**36%**	**12.0%**	**94.0**	**40**	**21**	**39**	**32%**	**70%**	**12%**		**0**						**-7.2**	**42**	**-$5**

Corbin,Patrick

Age: 30	Th: L	Role: SP	Health	B	LIMA Plan	C
			PT/Exp	A	Rand Var	0
Ht: 6' 3"	Wt: 210	Type: Pwr	Consist	C	MM	4405

Successful follow-up, as slider-first approach kept the strikeouts coming in waves. Velocity uptick, strong SwK support another double-digit Dom, and steady ground balls will keep ERA far from wipeout. While control may not drop to 2018 level, xWHIP is a reasonable expectation. Hang loose with him as your SP #2.

Yr Tm	W	Sv	IP	K	ERA	xERA	WHIP	xWHIP	vL+	vR+	BF/G	Ctl	Dom	Cmd	Ball%	SwK	Vel	G	L	F	H%	S%	HR/F	xHR/F	GS	APC	DOM%	DIS%	Sv%	LI	RAR	BPX	R$
15 ARI *	7	0	101	87	3.63	4.07	1.28	1.16	79	111	21.9	2.0	7.7	3.9	33%	11.5%	92.4	47	23	30	33%	74%	12%	16%	16	78	25%	19%			4.2	119	$3
16 ARI	5	1	156	131	5.15	4.39	1.56	1.41	101	116	19.5	3.8	7.6	2.0	39%	9.9%	91.7	54	19	27	33%	70%	18%	21%	24	71	21%	42%	100	0.89	-18.4	78	-$9
17 ARI	14	0	190	178	4.03	4.08	1.42	1.27	86	112	25.0	2.9	8.4	2.9	36%	11.5%	92.4	50	20	30	34%	76%	15%	15%	32	93	31%	28%	0	0.76	7.6	122	$8
18 ARI	11	0	200	246	3.15	2.82	1.05	1.05	95	81	24.2	2.2	11.1	5.1	36%	16.2%	90.8	48	24	27	32%	72%	11%	16%	33	95	39%	0%			24.7	192	$25
19 WAS	14	0	202	238	3.25	3.65	1.18	1.22	67	94	25.3	3.1	10.6	3.4	38%	14.7%	91.9	50	18	33	30%	77%	14%	19%	33	100	30%	27%			31.2	147	$24
1st Half	7	0	99	111	3.71	3.91	1.16	1.19	70	93	25.5	3.0	10.1	3.4	38%	13.3%	91.4	46	18	37	29%	73%	14%	19%	16	99	38%	38%			9.7	136	$20
2nd Half	7	0	103	127	2.81	3.39	1.21	1.17	63	95	25.1	3.2	11.1	3.4	38%	16.0%	92.3	53	18	29	32%	81%	15%	20%	17	101	24%	18%			21.5	157	$27
20 Proj	**12**	**0**	**189**	**213**	**3.46**	**3.10**	**1.21**	**1.17**	**80**	**96**	**23.7**	**2.8**	**10.2**	**3.6**	**37%**	**14.3%**	**91.8**	**50**	**20**	**30**	**32%**	**75%**	**14%**		**32**						**16.0**	**154**	**$18**

Cortes,Nestor

Age: 25	Th: L	Role: RP	Health	A	LIMA Plan	C
			PT/Exp	D	Rand Var	+3
Ht: 5' 11"	Wt: 210	Type: xFB	Consist	C	MM	0200

5-1, 5.67 ERA in 67 IP at NYY. Buoyed between AAA and majors for much of 1st half, then 2nd half FB% spike opened the floodgates. He's mediocre everywhere you look—bland SwK/Dom is forgettable, xERA should keep ERA inflated, subpar Ball% won't help WHIP—and mediocre just doesn't cut it in middle relief.

Yr Tm	W	Sv	IP	K	ERA	xERA	WHIP	xWHIP	vL+	vR+	BF/G	Ctl	Dom	Cmd	Ball%	SwK	Vel	G	L	F	H%	S%	HR/F	xHR/F	GS	APC	DOM%	DIS%	Sv%	LI	RAR	BPX	R$
15																																	
16																																	
17 a/a	7	0	100	88	2.86	3.18	1.26				14.1	3.0	7.9	2.6							31%	77%									18.5	115	$8
18 BAL *	6	0	122	87	4.91	5.18	1.43		196	183	18.5	3.3	6.4	1.9		10.2%	88.0	47	16	37	30%	70%	29%	19%	0	27			0	0.97	-11.5	39	-$6
19 NYY *	7	0	108	103	5.27	5.02	1.39	1.38	131	103	11.3	3.3	8.6	2.6	37%	10.9%	89.6	34	22	44	31%	67%	18%	15%	1	39	0%	100%	0	0.72	-10.2	64	-$2
1st Half	5	0	71	65	4.87	3.89	1.18	1.10	109	97	17.7	2.3	8.3	3.7	37%	9.7%	89.5	41	23	36	29%	62%	19%	16%	0	59			0	0.53	-3.2	103	$3
2nd Half	2	0	37	38	6.03	6.09	1.77	1.50	144	107	7.3	5.3	9.2	1.7	37%	11.7%	89.6	29	21	50	34%	73%	18%	15%	1	32	0%	100%	0	0.78	-7.0	32	-$11
20 Proj	**3**	**0**	**58**	**51**	**4.94**	**4.74**	**1.48**	**1.34**	**126**	**98**	**11.9**	**3.8**	**7.8**	**2.0**	**37%**	**11.0%**	**89.6**	**33**	**20**	**47**	**30%**	**74%**	**16%**		**4**						**-5.6**	**56**	**-$4**

Covey,Dylan

Age: 28	Th: R	Role: RP	Health	F	LIMA Plan	D
			PT/Exp	D	Rand Var	+3
Ht: 6' 1"	Wt: 220	Type: Con	Consist	D	MM	1003

1-8, 7.98 ERA in 59 IP at CHW. Ugly results mirrored MM score; June shoulder injury ended season in September. Three reasons to steer clear: 1) Sinker lost sink, combined with HR/F for ERA explosion; 2) Anemic SwK doesn't offer strikeouts; 3) DIS% reflects frequent blowup potential. An extreme ratio risk, even if the shoulder checks out.

Yr Tm	W	Sv	IP	K	ERA	xERA	WHIP	xWHIP	vL+	vR+	BF/G	Ctl	Dom	Cmd	Ball%	SwK	Vel	G	L	F	H%	S%	HR/F	xHR/F	GS	APC	DOM%	DIS%	Sv%	LI	RAR	BPX	R$
15																																	
16 aa	2	0	29	20	2.33	3.76	1.46				20.9	5.4	6.2	1.2							27%	86%									6.7	60	-$2
17 CHW	0	0	70	41	7.71	5.67	1.67	1.59	118	143	17.2	4.4	5.3	1.2	41%	6.6%	92.6	48	16	35	29%	59%	25%	19%	12	64	0%	58%	0	0.66	-29.0	3	-$16
18 CHW *	8	0	162	119	4.63	4.68	1.47	1.45	108	93	20.4	3.8	6.6	1.7	37%	7.4%	94.1	55	20	25	31%	70%	13%	17%	21	76	24%	52%	0	0.79	-9.6	56	-$5
19 CHW *	3	0	110	77	5.98	6.78	1.71	1.58	143	97	16.0	3.1	6.3	2.0	37%	7.8%	94.4	42	26	32	36%	68%	18%	20%	12	57	0%	67%	0	1.03	-20.0	24	-$14
1st Half	1	0	54	35	4.00	5.23	1.47	1.65	125	67	15.6	4.0	5.7	1.4	39%	6.7%	93.8	38	26	37	28%	79%	14%	20%	7	69	0%	57%	0	1.12	3.4	19	-$8
2nd Half	2	0	58	42	7.61	7.85	1.87	1.34	181	126	16.9	2.1	6.6	3.2	34%	9.5%	95.3	48	27	25	41%	60%	29%	20%	5	45	0%	80%	0	0.95	-22.1	46	-$20
20 Proj	**5**	**0**	**145**	**105**	**5.24**	**4.49**	**1.51**	**1.48**	**118**	**98**	**17.3**	**3.4**	**6.5**	**1.9**	**37%**	**7.8%**	**94.2**	**45**	**24**	**32**	**31%**	**70%**	**18%**		**27**						**-19.5**	**56**	**-$9**

BRANT CHESSER

Crick,Kyle

Age: 27 Th: R Role RP	Health C	LIMA Plan B	
Ht: 6' 4" Wt: 220 Type Pwr FB	PT/Exp D	Rand Var +3	
	Consist B	MM 1400	

Still brings good velocity; power fastball/slider combo has produced a healthy Dom trend. But fortunate 1st-half H%, S% couldn't survive season-long FB spike, and his collapse wasn't just about poor HR/F luck. Control isn't his thing, and he won't be trustworthy until it is. SwK, stuff keep us watching, but from a distance.

Yr	Tm	W	Sv	IP	K	ERA	xERA	WHIP	xWHIP	vL+	vR+	BF/G	Ctl	Dom	Cmd	Ball%	SwK	Vel	G	L	F	H%	S%	HR/F	xHR/F	GS	APC	DOM%	DIS%	Sv%	LI	RAR	BPX	R$
15	aa	3	0	63	63	4.37	4.96	2.03				8.5	10.2	9.0	0.9							32%	77%									-3.2	84	-$10
16	aa	4	0	109	72	6.63	5.84	1.89				22.3	6.0	5.9	1.0							35%	64%									-32.8	37	-$20
17	SF *	1	6	62	60	3.21	3.07	1.32	1.52	69	88	4.7	4.5	8.8	2.0	38%	11.7%	95.5	38	16	46	29%	76%	5%	6%	0	20			55	0.56	8.7	109	$3
18	PIT	3	2	60	65	2.39	3.80	1.13	1.26	92	66	4.0	3.4	9.7	2.8	36%	11.7%	95.9	40	25	35	29%	80%	5%	8%	0	16			67	0.92	13.1	115	$5
19	PIT	3	0	49	61	4.96	4.99	1.55	1.56	96	114	4.3	6.4	11.2	1.7	38%	13.1%	95.3	44	14	42	29%	74%	20%	14%	0	18			0	1.03	-2.7	55	-$4
1st Half		3	0	29	35	2.79	4.94	1.45	1.67	90	86	4.3	7.4	10.9	1.5	40%	12.8%	95.2	48	13	39	24%	85%	13%	9%	0	17			0	1.33	6.1	23	$0
2nd Half		0	0	20	26	8.10	4.99	1.70	1.33	103	148	4.4	5.0	11.7	2.4	35%	13.4%	95.4	39	16	46	34%	59%	27%	19%	0	19			0	0.64	-8.9	102	-$10
20	Proj	2	0	58	66	4.62	4.20	1.47	1.40	96	106	4.4	5.3	10.2	1.9	37%	12.5%	95.6	41	19	41	30%	73%	14%		0						-3.3	67	-$4

Cueto,Johnny

Age: 34 Th: R Role SP	Health F	LIMA Plan B	
Ht: 5' 11" Wt: 229 Type	PT/Exp C	Rand Var +1	
	Consist B	MM 2103	

Can't take much away from late-season return from Tommy John surgery, but 34/10 K/BB over 37 MLB/rehab IP combined offers some hope. For the past three seasons, once-dominant starter with fine control hasn't been healthy, as reflected in both IP and results. Now in his mid-30s, an intriguing low-cost flyer if he can stay in one piece.

Yr	Tm	W	Sv	IP	K	ERA	xERA	WHIP	xWHIP	vL+	vR+	BF/G	Ctl	Dom	Cmd	Ball%	SwK	Vel	G	L	F	H%	S%	HR/F	xHR/F	GS	APC	DOM%	DIS%	Sv%	LI	RAR	BPX	R$
15	2 TM	11	0	212	176	3.44	3.76	1.13	1.21	82	105	27.1	2.0	7.5	3.8	34%	10.4%	92.5	43	22	36	29%	73%	9%	12%	32	102	34%	28%			13.7	122	$17
16	SF	18	0	220	198	2.79	3.43	1.09	1.16	91	82	27.5	1.8	8.1	4.4	34%	10.0%	91.5	50	21	29	30%	76%	8%	11%	32	103	53%	16%			38.0	148	$30
17	SF	8	0	147	136	4.52	4.53	1.45	1.31	110	107	25.9	3.2	8.3	2.6	36%	11.1%	91.3	39	25	36	33%	73%	14%	15%	25	101	20%	40%			-2.9	95	$0
18	SF	3	0	53	38	3.23	4.20	1.11	1.28	96	98	23.8	2.2	6.5	2.9	38%	9.6%	89.4	44	19	37	25%	78%	14%	18%	9	88	33%	56%			6.0	90	$1
19	SF	1	0	16	13	5.06	5.02	1.25	1.62	149	60	16.8	5.1	7.3	1.4	40%	7.9%	91.3	53	16	30	20%	65%	23%	26%	4	66	0%	25%			-1.1	28	-$4
1st Half																																		
2nd Half		1	0	16	13	5.06	4.92	1.25	1.57	150	59	16.8	5.1	7.3	1.4	40%	7.9%	91.3	53	16	30	20%	65%	23%	26%	4	66	0%	25%			-1.1	29	-$4
20	Proj	9	0	145	121	4.06	3.93	1.24	1.35	112	86	21.5	3.2	7.5	2.3	37%	9.6%	91.1	46	20	33	27%	72%	15%		27						1.7	83	$7

Darvish,Yu

Age: 33 Th: R Role SP	Health F	LIMA Plan B	
Ht: 6' 5" Wt: 220 Type Pwr	PT/Exp B	Rand Var +5	
	Consist B	MM 4505	

Big rebound from multiple arm issues and lost 2018, fueled by 2nd-half Ctl turnaround. Health key to across-the-board jump in peripherals and results after June; avoided IL for the first time since 2012. Velocity, Dom, SwK were better than ever. Ditto GB% even with HR/F that seems likely to regress. With more durability... UP: 3.30 ERA, 15 wins.

Yr	Tm	W	Sv	IP	K	ERA	xERA	WHIP	xWHIP	vL+	vR+	BF/G	Ctl	Dom	Cmd	Ball%	SwK	Vel	G	L	F	H%	S%	HR/F	xHR/F	GS	APC	DOM%	DIS%	Sv%	LI	RAR	BPX	R$
15																																		
16	TEX *	8	0	127	154	3.42	3.21	1.16	1.09	82	90	21.1	3.1	10.9	3.6	35%	13.1%	93.3	40	20	40	30%	75%	12%	11%	17	93	47%	12%			12.0	141	$12
17	2 TM	10	0	187	209	3.86	3.68	1.16	1.17	103	81	24.7	2.8	10.1	3.6	35%	12.6%	94.2	41	22	37	29%	72%	15%	11%	31	99	35%	26%			11.5	150	$17
18	CHC	1	0	40	49	4.95	4.15	1.43	1.34	115	97	22.5	4.7	11.0	2.3	39%	11.2%	93.9	38	23	40	31%	70%	18%	20%	8	93	13%	50%			-3.9	100	-$5
19	CHC	6	0	179	229	3.98	3.35	1.10	1.14	101	83	23.6	2.8	11.5	4.1	34%	14.0%	94.2	45	21	34	28%	72%	23%	19%	31	92	32%	16%			11.6	168	$15
1st Half		2	0	90	105	4.98	4.26	1.36	1.38	111	88	23.0	4.9	10.5	2.1	38%	13.0%	93.8	47	21	32	27%	70%	24%	22%	17	92	12%	29%			-5.3	89	$2
2nd Half		4	0	88	124	2.95	2.60	0.83	0.81	90	75	24.3	0.7	12.6	17.7	30%	15.4%	94.8	44	21	35	29%	76%	21%	16%	14	92	57%	0%			16.9	251	$29
20	Proj	11	0	181	226	3.74	3.08	1.18	1.14	104	88	22.4	2.9	11.2	3.8	33%	13.5%	94.1	42	22	36	31%	75%	18%		32						9.2	164	$17

Davies,Zachary

Age: 27 Th: R Role SP	Health F	LIMA Plan A	
Ht: 6' 0" Wt: 155 Type Con	PT/Exp B	Rand Var -2	
	Consist A	MM 1003	

IP, Ctl, ERA returned as 2018 shoulder woes vanished, bringing more double-digit wins and modest profitability. Kept HR from becoming a problem despite GB% plunge. Ability to pitch in and out of traffic wrings the most from unsexy skill set. You'll need to compensate for poor Dom and hope the floor holds. Per xERA, at some point again it won't.

Yr	Tm	W	Sv	IP	K	ERA	xERA	WHIP	xWHIP	vL+	vR+	BF/G	Ctl	Dom	Cmd	Ball%	SwK	Vel	G	L	F	H%	S%	HR/F	xHR/F	GS	APC	DOM%	DIS%	Sv%	LI	RAR	BPX	R$
15	MIL *	9	0	162	112	3.53	3.71	1.36	1.49	60	104	22.6	3.2	6.2	1.9	38%	10.6%	88.8	58	21	21	31%	74%	10%	8%	6	90	33%	50%			8.7	80	$4
16	MIL	11	0	163	135	3.97	3.98	1.25	1.23	104	94	24.4	2.1	7.4	3.6	36%	8.8%	89.3	45	22	33	31%	72%	12%	10%	28	92	25%	29%			4.5	119	$8
17	MIL	17	0	191	124	3.90	4.54	1.35	1.36	104	98	24.8	2.6	5.8	2.3	38%	7.8%	89.7	50	23	27	31%	74%	12%	11%	33	94	12%	48%			10.7	76	$10
18	MIL *	3	0	94	70	5.35	4.46	1.43	1.35	107	105	20.0	3.6	6.7	1.9	38%	8.5%	89.9	48	22	30	31%	63%	13%	13%	13	86	8%	38%			-13.9	62	-$8
19	MIL	10	0	160	102	3.55	5.32	1.29	1.46	99	95	21.7	2.9	5.7	2.0	39%	7.4%	88.5	40	24	36	28%	77%	11%	13%	31	86	6%	32%			18.8	48	$9
1st Half		7	0	92	59	3.24	5.26	1.40	1.40	112	97	23.0	2.8	5.8	2.0	38%	7.6%	88.3	41	24	35	31%	81%	11%	11%	17	90	12%	41%			14.3	51	$11
2nd Half		3	0	68	43	3.97	5.35	1.15	1.41	80	92	20.1	2.9	5.7	2.0	40%	7.1%	88.8	39	23	38	24%	70%	11%	15%	14	83	0%	21%			4.5	44	$7
20	Proj	9	0	160	108	4.20	4.33	1.32	1.38	98	99	21.1	3.0	6.1	2.0	38%	7.9%	89.1	44	23	33	29%	71%	11%		31						-0.9	59	$4

Davis,Wade

Age: 34 Th: R Role RP	Health D	LIMA Plan C	
Ht: 6' 5" Wt: 227 Type Pwr	PT/Exp B	Rand Var +5	
	Consist C	MM 1400	

Lost closer role in July as poor 2018 morphed into nightmarish cliff-fall. Ugly Ball% trend a harbinger of Ctl collapse. Dom, SwK no longer elite as velocity continued to drift; RHBs began pummeling him at will. 2nd-half FB% problems now a legit concern as he enters his mid-30s. Laws of regression hint at an uptick, but not enough to matter.

Yr	Tm	W	Sv	IP	K	ERA	xERA	WHIP	xWHIP	vL+	vR+	BF/G	Ctl	Dom	Cmd	Ball%	SwK	Vel	G	L	F	H%	S%	HR/F	xHR/F	GS	APC	DOM%	DIS%	Sv%	LI	RAR	BPX	R$
15	KC	8	17	67	78	0.94	3.04	0.79	1.12	62	63	3.6	2.7	10.4	3.9	36%	12.0%	95.9	38	21	41	21%	92%	5%	8%	0	15			94	1.22	25.1	157	$23
16	KC	2	27	43	47	1.87	3.47	1.13	1.24	66	80	3.9	3.3	9.8	2.9	37%	13.1%	94.9	49	18	33	30%	82%	0%	4%	0	16			90	1.00	12.4	134	$14
17	CHC	4	32	59	79	2.30	3.49	1.14	1.23	65	93	4.1	4.3	12.1	2.8	38%	15.5%	94.3	40	21	38	28%	85%	12%	12%	0	18			97	1.15	14.9	144	$20
18	COL	3	43	65	78	4.13	3.52	1.06	1.22	66	103	3.8	3.6	10.7	3.0	41%	12.3%	93.8	42	18	40	25%	64%	13%	7%	0	16			88	1.21	0.1	134	$20
19	COL	1	15	43	42	8.65	6.11	1.88	1.65	103	126	4.1	6.1	8.9	1.4	41%	11.0%	93.2	38	23	38	36%	53%	14%	14%	0	17			83	1.13	-21.8	11	-$7
1st Half		1	12	25	26	5.76	5.20	1.76	1.53	83	130	4.2	5.8	9.4	1.6	41%	11.0%	93.7	47	22	31	36%	68%	13%	16%	0	17			86	1.44	-3.9	42	-$2
2nd Half		0	3	18	16	12.74	7.25	2.04	1.68	130	122	4.0	6.6	8.2	1.2	41%	10.9%	92.6	27	25	47	36%	34%	14%	12%	0	16			75	0.74	-17.9	-29	-$14
20	Proj	2	0	44	48	5.04	4.25	1.49	1.42	89	112	3.9	5.0	9.8	2.0	40%	12.1%	93.7	38	22	40	32%	69%	13%		0						-4.8	68	-$5

deGrom,Jacob

Age: 32 Th: R Role SP	Health A	LIMA Plan B	
Ht: 6' 4" Wt: 180 Type Pwr	PT/Exp A	Rand Var -2	
	Consist B	MM 5505	

Squinting reveals slight HR uptick, but that was laid to rest in ridiculous 2nd half (see that DOM%/DIS%). Emerged from MLB HR debacle year with premier skill set intact, more valuable than ever. Velocity, Dom, Ctl and underlying metrics all rock-solid. Three straight 200 IP seasons. Still nowhere to go but down, still ace-worthy.

Yr	Tm	W	Sv	IP	K	ERA	xERA	WHIP	xWHIP	vL+	vR+	BF/G	Ctl	Dom	Cmd	Ball%	SwK	Vel	G	L	F	H%	S%	HR/F	xHR/F	GS	APC	DOM%	DIS%	Sv%	LI	RAR	BPX	R$
15	NYM	14	0	191	205	2.54	3.04	0.98	1.07	91	67	25.0	1.8	9.7	5.4	32%	13.3%	95.0	44	21	35	29%	78%	9%	8%	30	99	63%	13%			33.4	176	$30
16	NYM	7	0	148	143	3.04	3.57	1.20	1.17	85	102	25.2	2.2	8.7	4.0	34%	11.4%	93.4	46	23	32	32%	79%	12%	14%	24	98	38%	13%			21.0	144	$13
17	NYM	15	0	201	239	3.53	3.39	1.19	1.12	92	90	26.7	2.6	10.7	4.1	33%	14.0%	95.2	45	21	34	32%	76%	16%	12%	31	102	48%	23%			20.5	173	$22
18	NYM	10	0	217	269	1.70	2.73	0.91	1.01	79	64	26.1	1.9	11.2	5.8	31%	15.9%	96.0	46	22	32	29%	84%	6%	9%	32	100	75%	0%			65.6	200	$44
19	NYM	11	0	204	255	2.43	3.15	0.97	1.05	82	74	25.1	1.9	11.3	5.8	33%	16.1%	96.9	44	21	35	30%	80%	11%	10%	32	103	66%	13%			52.3	187	$36
1st Half		4	0	103	128	3.32	3.41	1.11	1.03	92	87	24.8	1.9	11.2	5.8	32%	15.3%	96.8	42	22	36	33%	75%	14%	11%	17	104	47%	24%			15.1	185	$24
2nd Half		7	0	101	127	1.51	2.95	0.83	1.00	70	59	25.5	2.0	11.3	5.8	33%	17.0%	97.1	47	20	33	26%	86%	8%	9%	15	102	87%	0%			37.3	191	$47
20	Proj	14	0	203	247	2.80	2.74	1.01	1.04	84	75	25.0	2.0	10.9	5.4	32%	15.4%	96.2	45	21	33	30%	76%	11%		31						33.9	190	$32

DeSclafani,Anthony

Age: 30 Th: R Role SP	Health F	LIMA Plan C	
Ht: 6' 1" Wt: 195 Type	PT/Exp C	Rand Var +1	
	Consist C	MM 2203	

Fine year, errr... 2nd half, as inconsistent SP improved with health, began dominating LHB, surging in June. Stable Cmd still a plus; late GB% spike kept HR problem from getting much worse and he benefitted from a 19% H% over final five starts. Still intriguing, but Consistency grade should be heeded. In-season surge isn't likely a new benchmark.

Yr	Tm	W	Sv	IP	K	ERA	xERA	WHIP	xWHIP	vL+	vR+	BF/G	Ctl	Dom	Cmd	Ball%	SwK	Vel	G	L	F	H%	S%	HR/F	xHR/F	GS	APC	DOM%	DIS%	Sv%	LI	RAR	BPX	R$
15	CIN	9	0	185	151	4.05	4.04	1.35	1.30	108	98	25.3	2.7	7.4	2.7	35%	9.9%	92.5	45	21	34	32%	72%	9%	10%	31	94	29%	23%			-1.9	99	$2
16	CIN *	9	0	140	118	3.93	4.43	1.23	1.22	114	80	23.7	2.0	7.6	3.8	37%	9.7%	92.9	42	23	35	30%	75%	13%	11%	20	98	25%	30%			4.6	95	$7
17																																		
18	CIN *	7	0	135	125	5.15	5.42	1.32	1.21	125	94	22.4	2.2	8.3	3.7	35%	10.2%	93.6	41	22	36	31%	69%	20%	15%	21	85	14%	24%			-16.6	76	-$3
19	CIN	9	0	167	167	3.89	4.27	1.20	1.26	105	85	22.5	2.6	9.0	3.4	36%	10.4%	94.7	43	19	38	29%	75%	16%	14%	31	86	23%	26%			12.7	122	$12
1st Half		5	0	81	84	4.35	4.50	1.34	1.20	127	83	21.6	2.7	9.4	3.5	36%	11.3%	94.5	38	21	41	32%	74%	16%	16%	16	82	13%	31%			1.5	122	$6
2nd Half		4	0	86	83	3.45	4.10	1.07	1.22	80	87	23.3	2.6	8.7	3.3	36%	9.6%	94.9	48	17	35	25%	76%	17%	11%	15	91	33%	20%			11.2	122	$17
20	Proj	9	0	174	163	4.18	3.67	1.24	1.22	111	90	22.5	2.5	8.4	3.4	36%	10.1%	93.9	43	20	37	29%	73%	17%		31						-0.6	123	$9

JOCK THOMPSON

Devenski,Christopher

Age: 29	Th: R	Role RP	Health B	LIMA Plan B	
Ht: 6' 3"	Wt: 210	Type Pwr xFB	PT/Exp C	Rand Var +1	
			Consist B	MM 2300	

2018's xERA had us holding out hope for a rebound, but that collapsed under the weight of rising FB, HR and falling strand rate. That HR/F looks entrenched now, and struggles vL only add to his issues. Still, owns premium SwK, good velocity and Ctl. Watchable, but unrosterable until we see more consistency.

Yr	Tm	W	Sv	IP	K	ERA	xERA	WHIP	xWHIP	vL+	vR+	BF/G	Ctl	Dom	Cmd	Ball%	SwK	Vel	G	L	F	H%	S%	HR/F	xHR/F	GS	APC	DOM%	DIS%	Sv%	LI	RAR	BPX	R$
15	aa	7	2	120	87	3.54	4.76	1.42				21.1	2.5	6.5	2.6							33%	79%									6.2	71	$2
16	HOU	4	1	108	104	2.16	3.48	0.91	1.10	87	63	8.5	1.7	8.6	5.2	32%	13.8%	92.4	33	26	41	27%	77%	4%	7%	5	33	40%	40%	100	0.91	27.1	145	$17
17	HOU	8	4	81	100	2.68	3.39	0.94	1.12	55	103	5.1	2.9	11.2	3.8	34%	17.4%	94.1	40	15	45	23%	80%	14%	12%	0	20			40	1.51	16.7	169	$15
18	HOU	2	2	47	51	4.18	3.87	1.16	1.16	97	101	3.9	2.5	9.7	3.9	34%	14.8%	94.2	34	20	46	29%	72%	16%	11%	1	16	0%	100%	40	1.35	-0.2	138	$0
19	HOU	2	0	69	72	4.83	4.70	1.30	1.27	109	98	4.9	2.7	9.4	3.4	36%	13.4%	94.8	33	21	47	31%	69%	14%	12%	1	19	0%	100%	0	0.54	-2.7	116	-$2
1st Half		2	0	35	39	4.58	4.58	1.27	1.16	106	108	5.0	2.5	9.9	3.9	36%	14.1%	94.6	29	23	48	32%	71%	15%	13%	0	19			0	0.46	-0.3	128	-$1
2nd Half		0	0	34	33	5.08	5.00	1.34	1.26	113	87	4.7	2.9	8.8	3.0	35%	12.7%	94.9	36	19	45	31%	67%	13%	11%	1	18	0%	100%	0	0.61	-2.4	102	-$4
20	**Proj**	**3**	**0**	**65**	**69**	**4.17**	**3.72**	**1.20**	**1.18**	**99**	**97**	**4.7**	**2.7**	**9.5**	**3.6**	**35%**	**14.3%**	**94.3**	**34**	**20**	**45**	**30%**	**72%**	**14%**		**0**						**-0.2**	**128**	**$0**

Diaz,Edwin

Age: 26	Th: R	Role RP	Health A	LIMA Plan C	
Ht: 6' 3"	Wt: 165	Type Pwr FB	PT/Exp A	Rand Var +5	
			Consist C	MM 5530	

Poster-boy to explain 1) why closers will be devalued in 2020, and 2) the MLB HR onslaught. Elite Dom, SwK and velocity all steadfast as ever. Ctl waivered a tad, but it was tangential to the primary issues. RHBs teed off, FB% jumped, HR and H% went through the roof. Some bad luck here will regress - heed xERA - and Ks, Sv upside keep him attractive.

Yr	Tm	W	Sv	IP	K	ERA	xERA	WHIP	xWHIP	vL+	vR+	BF/G	Ctl	Dom	Cmd	Ball%	SwK	Vel	G	L	F	H%	S%	HR/F	xHR/F	GS	APC	DOM%	DIS%	Sv%	LI	RAR	BPX	R$
15	aa	5	0	104	93	4.88	3.76	1.36				21.8	2.9	8.1	2.8							34%	62%									-11.8	114	-$4
16	SEA *	3	19	92	137	2.73	3.03	1.12	0.92	82	88	5.6	2.1	13.3	6.2	33%	19.4%	97.3	47	23	31	37%	79%	15%	13%	0	17			86	1.34	16.7	230	$18
17	SEA	4	34	66	89	3.27	3.78	1.15	1.24	87	80	4.2	4.4	12.1	2.8	36%	16.8%	97.3	39	15	46	26%	79%	14%	8%	0	17			87	1.64	8.8	141	$20
18	SEA	0	57	73	124	1.96	1.96	0.79	0.83	61	68	3.8	2.1	15.2	7.3	33%	19.7%	97.3	44	20	35	30%	79%	11%	9%	0	16			93	1.40	19.8	276	$36
19	NYM	2	26	58	99	5.59	3.12	1.38	1.04	91	124	3.8	3.4	15.4	4.5	34%	18.5%	97.5	37	20	44	40%	68%	27%	13%	0	16			79	1.18	-7.7	217	$8
1st Half		1	17	32	52	4.78	3.21	1.38	0.98	93	119	4.1	2.8	14.6	5.2	34%	18.6%	97.0	36	23	41	41%	73%	23%	10%	0	17			81	1.48	-1.1	220	$10
2nd Half		1	9	26	47	6.58	3.17	1.38	1.04	88	131	3.6	4.2	16.3	3.9	35%	18.3%	98.0	38	15	47	38%	61%	32%	17%	0	15			75	0.87	-6.6	214	$6
20	**Proj**	**2**	**35**	**65**	**105**	**3.47**	**2.56**	**1.19**	**0.99**	**77**	**96**	**3.9**	**3.2**	**14.5**	**4.5**	**34%**	**18.6%**	**97.4**	**40**	**19**	**41**	**37%**	**75%**	**14%**		**0**						**5.5**	**220**	**$18**

Diaz,Jairo

Age: 29	Th: R	Role RP	Health F	LIMA Plan F	
Ht: 6' 0"	Wt: 200	Type Pwr	PT/Exp F	Rand Var +1	
			Consist F	MM 2220	

6-4, 4.53 ERA with 5 Sv in 58 IP at COL. Live arm re-flashed promise after long road back from TJ surgery and subsequent forearm issues. Premium velocity is intact; power fastball/slider combo generated plenty of SwK, GB%; kept a lid on HR. Health remains his primary issue. But 5-for-6 in September save opps is intriguing.

Yr	Tm	W	Sv	IP	K	ERA	xERA	WHIP	xWHIP	vL+	vR+	BF/G	Ctl	Dom	Cmd	Ball%	SwK	Vel	G	L	F	H%	S%	HR/F	xHR/F	GS	APC	DOM%	DIS%	Sv%	LI	RAR	BPX	R$
15	COL *	3	8	74	56	4.76	5.02	1.61		84	87	4.8	5.3	6.8	1.3		10.8%	97.2	57	17	26	30%	73%	14%	9%	0	13			53	0.95	-7.3	42	-$4
16																																		
17	COL *	0	3	23	14	7.43	6.48	1.97		165	172	4.6	5.0	5.6	1.1		5.0%	97.3	59	27	14	38%	60%	0%	2%	0	30			75	0.02	-8.7	35	-$8
18																																		
19	COL *	7	11	78	79	3.50	3.52	1.24	1.24	84	112	4.4	2.9	9.1	3.1	35%	14.6%	97.0	49	19	31	31%	74%	14%	10%	0	16			79	0.96	9.6	111	$10
1st Half		2	6	41	38	2.92	3.31	1.16	1.27	101	124	4.4	3.2	8.4	2.6	35%	12.5%	97.3	49	14	37	26%	80%	24%	14%	0	16			86	0.93	7.9	90	$9
2nd Half		5	5	37	41	4.14	3.70	1.32	1.17	75	104	4.5	2.7	10.0	3.7	35%	15.9%	96.9	50	22	28	36%	68%	7%	7%	0	16			71	0.97	1.7	147	$11
20	**Proj**	**3**	**14**	**44**	**40**	**4.06**	**4.00**	**1.45**	**1.21**	**93**	**121**	**4.6**	**3.9**	**8.3**	**2.2**	**35%**	**14.5%**	**97.0**	**49**	**19**	**32**	**32%**	**76%**	**16%**		**0**						**0.5**	**84**	**$3**

Dobnak,Randy

Age: 25	Th: R	Role SP	Health A	LIMA Plan F	
Ht: 6' 1"	Wt: 230	Type Con xGB	PT/Exp F	Rand Var -1	
			Consist F	MM 2001	

2-1, 1.59 ERA in 28 IP at MIN. Unheralded xGBer rocketed to MLB debut just 2 years after being signed from indy league. Plus Ctl, HR-stinginess never missed a beat along the way. SwK came alive at higher levels, though Dom and velocity warn about expecting too much. Back-end SP upside; check his progress and opportunity in March.

Yr	Tm	W	Sv	IP	K	ERA	xERA	WHIP	xWHIP	vL+	vR+	BF/G	Ctl	Dom	Cmd	Ball%	SwK	Vel	G	L	F	H%	S%	HR/F	xHR/F	GS	APC	DOM%	DIS%	Sv%	LI	RAR	BPX	R$
15																																		
16																																		
17																																		
18																																		
19	MIN *	11	1	143	100	2.93	3.17	1.16	1.21	54	105	19.6	2.0	6.3	3.2	32%	13.8%	92.7	53	25	22	29%	76%	5%	11%	5	47	20%	40%	100	0.50	27.7	103	$16
1st Half		4	0	58	43	3.84	5.03	1.42		0	0	22.4	2.4	6.7	2.8							33%	77%	0%		0	0					4.8	66	$0
2nd Half		7	1	87	57	2.24	1.77	0.95	1.17	55	104	18.2	1.7	5.9	3.6	32%	13.8%	92.7	53	25	22	26%	75%	5%	11%	5	47	20%	40%	100	0.50	24.2	131	$27
20	**Proj**	**7**	**0**	**87**	**60**	**3.74**	**3.72**	**1.22**	**1.29**	**53**	**115**	**20.2**	**1.9**	**6.2**	**3.2**	**35%**	**13.8%**	**92.7**	**51**	**24**	**25**	**30%**	**72%**	**11%**		**17**						**4.4**	**102**	**$4**

Dominguez,Seranthony

Age: 25	Th: R	Role RP	Health F	LIMA Plan F	
Ht: 6' 1"	Wt: 185	Type Pwr xGB	PT/Exp F	Rand Var +3	
			Consist F	MM 4410	

Skills are still visible, but late-inning reliever struggled from the get-go before being shelved with elbow issues in early June, and he never returned. Velocity, SwK, GB% still look sturdy, but Ctl waivered and HR, H% took a hit. Possibility of Tommy John surgery hangs over rebound and closer upside. Avoid for now.

Yr	Tm	W	Sv	IP	K	ERA	xERA	WHIP	xWHIP	vL+	vR+	BF/G	Ctl	Dom	Cmd	Ball%	SwK	Vel	G	L	F	H%	S%	HR/F	xHR/F	GS	APC	DOM%	DIS%	Sv%	LI	RAR	BPX	R$
15																																		
16																																		
17																																		
18	PHI *	4	16	76	92	2.67	1.24	0.87	1.16	86	52	4.4	3.0	10.9	3.7	35%	16.0%	98.1	56	15	29	23%	70%	11%	12%	0	18			76	1.48	13.9	174	$17
19	PHI	3	0	25	29	4.01	4.06	1.46	1.36	133	67	4.1	4.4	10.6	2.4	36%	14.0%	97.4	55	17	29	34%	76%	16%	11%	0	17			0	1.11	1.5	115	-$3
1st Half		3	0	25	29	4.01	4.02	1.46	1.32	132	68	4.1	4.4	10.6	2.4	36%	14.0%	97.4	55	17	29	34%	76%	16%	11%	0	17			0	1.11	1.5	114	-$3
2nd Half																																		
20	**Proj**	**3**	**2**	**36**	**42**	**3.49**	**3.25**	**1.30**	**1.25**	**118**	**64**	**4.2**	**4.1**	**10.4**	**2.6**	**36%**	**14.7%**	**97.6**	**55**	**16**	**29**	**31%**	**76%**	**13%**		**0**						**2.9**	**128**	**$0**

Doolittle,Sean

Age: 33	Th: L	Role RP	Health F	LIMA Plan C	
Ht: 6' 2"	Wt: 204	Type Pwr xFB	PT/Exp B	Rand Var 0	
			Consist C	MM 3430	

Elite SwK ebbed all season. Historically lofty FB% was just that; HR became a problem beginning in late July. Terrible August ended with 2-week IL stint (knee tendinitis); Dom was slow to rebound. Lost Sept save opps due to 2nd-half struggles vR. Age, health both look like factors, though still a decent bet for 25 Sv if you aren't risk-averse.

Yr	Tm	W	Sv	IP	K	ERA	xERA	WHIP	xWHIP	vL+	vR+	BF/G	Ctl	Dom	Cmd	Ball%	SwK	Vel	G	L	F	H%	S%	HR/F	xHR/F	GS	APC	DOM%	DIS%	Sv%	LI	RAR	BPX	R$
15	OAK	1	4	14	15	3.95	3.99	1.24		146	75	4.8	3.3	9.9	3.0		10.2%	92.4	32	19	49	32%	69%	6%	6%	0	21			80	0.75	0.0	118	-$2
16	OAK	2	4	39	45	3.23	3.65	1.05	1.05	79	109	3.5	1.8	10.4	5.6	30%	16.1%	94.8	29	16	55	29%	77%	12%	14%	0	14			67	1.18	4.6	171	$3
17	2 TM	2	24	51	62	2.81	3.42	0.86	1.01	49	76	3.7	1.8	10.9	6.2	26%	16.3%	94.7	31	19	50	26%	72%	8%	7%	0	15			92	1.26	9.8	189	$16
18	WAS	3	25	45	60	1.60	2.64	0.60	0.87	28	61	3.8	1.2	12.0	10.0	30%	17.7%	93.9	32	19	48	21%	79%	7%	8%	0	14			96	1.40	14.2	223	$19
19	WAS	6	29	60	66	4.05	4.80	1.30	1.20	86	110	4.1	2.3	9.9	4.4	30%	12.8%	93.5	25	19	56	34%	76%	11%	13%	0	17			83	1.22	3.4	131	$14
1st Half		4	18	34	40	3.18	4.93	1.32	1.15	73	105	4.1	2.6	10.6	4.0	30%	13.4%	93.6	23	19	58	36%	79%	5%	7%	0	17			86	1.43	5.6	131	$17
2nd Half		2	11	26	26	5.19	4.98	1.27	1.13	102	117	4.1	1.7	9.0	5.2	31%	12.2%	93.4	28	19	53	30%	72%	19%	20%	0	18			79	0.92	-2.2	132	$10
20	**Proj**	**4**	**25**	**51**	**56**	**3.69**	**3.62**	**1.11**	**1.04**	**78**	**98**	**3.8**	**2.2**	**10.0**	**4.6**	**30%**	**13.6%**	**93.9**	**29**	**19**	**53**	**29%**	**73%**	**12%**		**0**						**2.9**	**147**	**$13**

Drake,Oliver

Age: 33	Th: R	Role RP	Health A	LIMA Plan A	
Ht: 6' 4"	Wt: 215	Type Pwr	PT/Exp D	Rand Var +5	
			Consist A	MM 4400	

5-2, 3.21 ERA with 2 Sv in 56 IP at TAM. Two bad July outings the only blips in stellar MLB performance following late May call-up. PRO: Ctl suddenly looking healthier; SwK, GB% shot into elite territory. CON: HR spiked; xHR/F trend looks dismal; age isn't his friend. More interesting than previously, but long-ball woes allow little room for error.

Yr	Tm	W	Sv	IP	K	ERA	xERA	WHIP	xWHIP	vL+	vR+	BF/G	Ctl	Dom	Cmd	Ball%	SwK	Vel	G	L	F	H%	S%	HR/F	xHR/F	GS	APC	DOM%	DIS%	Sv%	LI	RAR	BPX	R$
15	BAL *	1	23	60	66	1.78	3.03	1.31		84	109	4.5	4.4	10.0	2.3		14.1%	90.6	48	15	37	31%	88%	6%	9%	0	23			100	0.48	16.0	125	$12
16	BAL *	2	10	74	82	4.30	4.73	1.54		81	80	5.3	4.9	9.9	2.0		14.9%	90.3	49	14	37	33%	75%	13%	8%	0	21			77	0.72	-1.0	84	$1
17	2 TM	3	1	56	62	4.66	4.01	1.57	1.31	92	139	3.9	4.0	10.0	2.5	37%	12.3%	91.9	49	25	26	37%	72%	14%	14%	0	16			25	0.75	-2.1	118	-$4
18	5 TM	1	0	48	51	5.29	3.81	1.45	1.24	118	94	4.8	3.2	9.6	3.0	36%	13.5%	92.5	45	26	29	37%	63%	10%	15%	0	19			0	0.41	-6.7	126	-$6
19	TAM *	6	8	81	101	4.19	3.20	1.10	1.16	47	116	4.6	3.0	11.2	3.7	34%	17.3%	93.6	52	16	31	28%	66%	23%	19%	0	19			89	1.09	3.1	130	$9
1st Half		1	6	43	53	4.96	4.00	1.29	1.20	43	129	5.2	3.2	11.0	3.5	37%	14.8%	93.5	49	16	36	34%	63%	19%	21%	0	23			100	0.70	-2.4	120	$3
2nd Half		5	2	38	48	3.32	2.91	0.89	1.09	49	107	4.1	2.8	11.4	4.0	33%	18.7%	93.6	54	17	29	21%	71%	25%	18%	0	17			67	1.26	5.6	175	$15
20	**Proj**	**3**	**0**	**44**	**51**	**4.32**	**3.16**	**1.26**	**1.20**	**80**	**109**	**4.4**	**3.3**	**10.5**	**3.1**	**35%**	**15.0%**	**92.9**	**49**	**21**	**30**	**32%**	**68%**	**15%**		**0**						**-0.9**	**145**	**-$2**

JOCK THOMPSON

Duffey,Tyler

Age: 29	Th: R	Role RP	
Ht: 6' 3"	Wt: 220	Type Pwr	
Health	A	LIMA Plan	D
PT/Exp	D	Rand Var	-1
Consist	D	MM	4401

5-1, 2.50 ERA in 58 IP at MIN. Fastballs-up-in-the-zone convert. Season-long SwK, Dom spikes fueled career year. Elevated S%, stable Ctl also helped one-time GBer minimize HR damage, despite more suspect G/L/F. xERA, 2nd-half BPX grab our attention; so do historical HR/F, consistency grade. Entering consolidation year with much to prove.

Yr Tm	W	Sv	IP	K	ERA	xERA	WHIP	xWHIP	vL+	vR+	BF/G	Ctl	Dom	Cmd	Ball%	SwK	Vel	G	L	F	H%	S%	HR/F	xHR/F	GS	APC	DOM%	DIS%	Sv%	LI	RAR	BPX	R$
15 MIN *	12	0	196	148	3.20	3.33	1.28	1.30	91	104	25.1	2.3	6.8	2.9	36%	10.1%	90.2	50	19	31	33%	74%	8%	13%	10	91	50%	20%			18.3	115	$12
16 MIN *	10	0	164	133	6.06	5.74	1.49	1.23	97	142	22.8	2.5	7.3	2.9	35%	8.9%	90.4	48	23	29	34%	63%	20%	22%	26	88	23%	42%			-37.7	59	-$11
17 MIN	2	1	71	67	4.94	4.02	1.37	1.20	99	96	5.5	2.3	8.5	3.7	33%	11.4%	92.1	50	19	31	34%	66%	13%	18%	0	20			33	1.00	-5.1	143	-$3
18 MIN *	6	3	84	65	5.39	5.25	1.44		126	101	7.2	3.0	7.0	2.3		10.5%	93.0	34	28	38	32%	66%	19%	25%	1	22	0%	100%	38	0.99	-12.9	54	-$5
19 MIN *	5	1	73	98	2.34	2.69	1.03	1.02	77	80	4.3	2.5	12.1	4.9	34%	16.0%	94.0	38	25	37	30%	84%	16%	16%	0	17			33	0.97	19.5	173	$10
1st Half	1	1	41	50	2.17	3.13	1.14	1.04	90	84	5.6	2.6	10.9	4.2	34%	13.7%	93.7	43	23	33	32%	86%	17%	16%	0	21			100	0.53	11.9	148	$8
2nd Half	4	0	32	48	2.56	2.87	0.88	0.93	65	77	3.4	2.3	13.6	6.0	34%	18.2%	94.3	32	28	40	28%	79%	15%	16%	0	14			0	1.24	7.6	212	$13
20 Proj	**5**	**0**	**73**	**81**	**3.75**	**3.24**	**1.20**	**1.10**	**85**	**94**	**5.2**	**2.5**	**10.0**	**3.9**	**34%**	**13.4%**	**92.6**	**43**	**23**	**34**	**32%**	**73%**	**14%**		**0**						**3.6**	**152**	**$3**

Duffy,Danny

Age: 31	Th: L	Role SP	
Ht: 6' 3"	Wt: 205	Type FB	
Health	F	LIMA Plan	A
PT/Exp	A	Rand Var	0
Consist	A	MM	1203

No stranger to IL, missed the first month of the season with shoulder tightness; 4 more weeks in August with a balky hamstring. Through it all, skills remained surprisingly stable as FB pitcher managed to avoid 2019 HR onslaught. Durability uptick might yield a little more, but it's not worth chasing.

Yr Tm	W	Sv	IP	K	ERA	xERA	WHIP	xWHIP	vL+	vR+	BF/G	Ctl	Dom	Cmd	Ball%	SwK	Vel	G	L	F	H%	S%	HR/F	xHR/F	GS	APC	DOM%	DIS%	Sv%	LI	RAR	BPX	R$
15 KC	7	1	137	102	4.08	4.56	1.39	1.42	81	111	19.6	3.5	6.7	1.9	36%	9.0%	93.8	39	25	36	30%	73%	10%	10%	24	79	8%	29%	100	0.75	-2.0	52	$0
16 KC	12	0	180	188	3.51	3.72	1.14	1.13	61	104	17.4	2.1	9.4	4.5	33%	13.3%	94.8	36	21	43	30%	76%	13%	15%	26	64	38%	15%	0	0.72	15.1	151	$17
17 KC	9	0	146	130	3.81	4.34	1.26	1.25	60	104	25.4	2.5	8.0	3.2	33%	12.1%	92.8	39	20	41	32%	71%	8%	10%	24	95	38%	25%			9.8	111	$9
18 KC	8	0	155	141	4.88	4.99	1.49	1.41	90	110	24.7	4.1	8.2	2.0	38%	10.1%	93.1	35	22	43	32%	71%	11%	14%	28	99	11%	39%			-13.9	58	-$6
19 KC	7	0	131	115	4.34	4.96	1.31	1.38	104	101	24.1	3.2	7.9	2.5	36%	10.7%	92.4	36	22	42	29%	72%	13%	15%	23	94	13%	30%			2.7	77	$3
1st Half	3	0	69	58	4.43	5.08	1.33	1.34	116	98	24.4	3.1	7.6	2.4	36%	10.3%	92.2	37	22	41	29%	72%	13%	16%	12	95	8%	25%			0.6	72	$1
2nd Half	4	0	62	57	4.23	4.90	1.28	1.31	83	103	23.8	3.2	8.3	2.6	37%	11.3%	92.5	35	22	43	29%	72%	13%	14%	11	93	18%	36%			2.1	83	$6
20 Proj	**8**	**0**	**145**	**128**	**4.45**	**4.31**	**1.37**	**1.33**	**92**	**107**	**23.2**	**3.3**	**7.9**	**2.4**	**36%**	**10.8%**	**92.8**	**36**	**22**	**42**	**30%**	**72%**	**12%**		**26**						**-5.4**	**78**	**$2**

Dugger,Robert

Age: 24	Th: R	Role SP	
Ht: 6' 2"	Wt: 180	Type Con FB	
Health	A	LIMA Plan	D
PT/Exp	D	Rand Var	+5
Consist	D	MM	0100

0-4, 5.77 ERA in 34 IP at MIA. Fringe SP prospect with average stuff, subpar velocity has struggled mightily above AA, as FB% lean and HR have become issues. Small sample, inexperience also in play here. But he whiffed less than a batter per IP in the minors, and all the luck in the world isn't likely to help with this at higher levels. Pass.

Yr Tm	W	Sv	IP	K	ERA	xERA	WHIP	xWHIP	vL+	vR+	BF/G	Ctl	Dom	Cmd	Ball%	SwK	Vel	G	L	F	H%	S%	HR/F	xHR/F	GS	APC	DOM%	DIS%	Sv%	LI	RAR	BPX	R$
15																																	
16																																	
17																																	
18 aa	7	0	110	92	4.39	4.43	1.36				25.6	3.0	7.6	2.5							32%	70%									-3.2	79	-$1
19 MIA *	8	0	161	127	6.98	6.12	1.62	1.60	127	92	23.8	3.3	7.1	2.1	39%	9.9%	89.9	39	21	40	35%	58%	14%	14%	7	81	14%	71%			-49.0	39	-$19
1st Half	7	0	83	68	5.46	4.62	1.43		0	0	23.6	2.9	7.3	2.5							33%	62%	0%		0	0					-9.8	75	-$6
2nd Half	1	0	77	59	8.61	7.73	1.82	1.54	128	91	23.9	3.8	6.9	1.8	39%	9.9%	89.9	39	21	40	36%	55%	14%	14%	7	81	14%	71%			-39.2	2	-$33
20 Proj	**2**	**0**	**44**	**35**	**5.12**	**4.56**	**1.47**	**1.69**	**126**	**91**	**24.0**	**3.0**	**7.2**	**2.4**	**43%**	**9.9%**	**89.9**	**39**	**21**	**40**	**33%**	**69%**	**11%**		**8**						**-5.2**	**75**	**-$5**

Dunn,Justin

Age: 24	Th: R	Role SP	
Ht: 6' 2"	Wt: 185	Type Pwr FB	
Health	A	LIMA Plan	B
PT/Exp	D	Rand Var	0
Consist	B	MM	1301

0-0, 2.70 ERA in 7 IP at SEA. Ctl-challenged (9 BB) during brief September debut. But legit prospect led AA-Texas League in Ks; mid-rotation upside can be seen in 10.8 Dom that let him bypass AAA for the time being. Has opportunity, but broad repertoire with work-in-progress secondaries are likely a year away from being helpful.

Yr Tm	W	Sv	IP	K	ERA	xERA	WHIP	xWHIP	vL+	vR+	BF/G	Ctl	Dom	Cmd	Ball%	SwK	Vel	G	L	F	H%	S%	HR/F	xHR/F	GS	APC	DOM%	DIS%	Sv%	LI	RAR	BPX	R$
15																																	
16																																	
17																																	
18 aa	6	0	91	92	4.67	4.33	1.45				26.0	3.7	9.0	2.4							35%	68%									-5.8	99	-$3
19 SEA *	9	0	140	143	5.22	5.12	1.50	2.69	88	40	20.9	3.5	9.2	2.6	46%	6.6%	92.5	44	6	50	35%	67%	0%	3%	4	34	0%	0%			-12.3	80	-$3
1st Half	5	0	71	78	5.20	4.96	1.54		0	0	22.1	3.1	9.9	3.2							39%	66%	0%		0	0					-6.1	111	-$3
2nd Half	4	0	69	64	5.24	5.28	1.47		88	40	19.7	3.9	8.4	2.2		6.6%	92.5	44	6	50	31%	69%	0%	3%	4	34	0%	0%			-6.2	52	-$3
20 Proj	**5**	**0**	**73**	**73**	**4.98**	**4.25**	**1.48**				**22.5**	**3.9**	**9.0**	**2.3**	**37%**	**9.5%**		**37**	**22**	**41**	**33%**	**69%**	**12%**		**14**						**-7.5**	**84**	**-$4**

Duplantier,Jon

Age: 25	Th: R	Role RP	
Ht: 6' 4"	Wt: 225	Type Pwr	
Health	C	LIMA Plan	A
PT/Exp	F	Rand Var	0
Consist	A	MM	0201

1-1, 4.42 ERA in 37 IP at ARI. Injuries continue to dog athletic SP prospect with lively stuff and GB tilt. Ctl deteriorated along with shoulder inflammation; now owns just 154 professional IP over the past two seasons. Worked out of the pen in 2nd half in attempt to clean up funky arm action. Still has a mid-rotation future, but now health is everything.

Yr Tm	W	Sv	IP	K	ERA	xERA	WHIP	xWHIP	vL+	vR+	BF/G	Ctl	Dom	Cmd	Ball%	SwK	Vel	G	L	F	H%	S%	HR/F	xHR/F	GS	APC	DOM%	DIS%	Sv%	LI	RAR	BPX	R$
15																																	
16																																	
17																																	
18 aa	5	0	67	56	3.27	3.57	1.34				19.9	3.9	7.6	1.9							30%	76%									7.2	88	$1
19 ARI *	2	1	75	69	4.70	4.02	1.55	1.49	91	112	11.7	5.4	8.4	1.6	39%	8.7%	92.2	44	19	37	33%	68%	5%	14%	3	45	0%	67%	100	0.71	-1.8	84	-$5
1st Half	1	1	42	39	4.42	3.46	1.35	1.29	82	109	12.5	4.6	8.4	1.8	38%	10.0%	92.2	41	23	36	29%	67%	8%	16%	3	51	0%	67%	100	0.92	0.5	87	-$3
2nd Half	1	0	33	30	5.08	4.75	1.81		109	119	10.8	6.4	8.3	1.3		6.8%	92.1	51	11	37	37%	69%	0%	9%	0	38			0	0.47	-2.3	83	-$7
20 Proj	**4**	**0**	**87**	**79**	**4.36**	**4.60**	**1.51**	**1.42**	**83**	**114**	**13.7**	**4.7**	**8.2**	**1.7**	**42%**	**10.0%**	**92.2**	**41**	**23**	**36**	**31%**	**75%**	**12%**		**10**						**-2.2**	**45**	**-$3**

Dyson,Sam

Age: 32	Th: R	Role RP	
Ht: 6' 1"	Wt: 212	Type Con xGB	
Health	B	LIMA Plan	C
PT/Exp	C	Rand Var	0
Consist	C	MM	3110

Shelved with biceps tendinitis in early August, recurrence finished him in early September. Subsequent surgery to repair shoulder capsule and 12-month return timeline now jeopardize his 2020. Physical issues clearly fueled 2nd half downturn; GB% still the bedrock of his success, though trend isn't comforting. Unrosterable until he's pitching again.

Yr Tm	W	Sv	IP	K	ERA	xERA	WHIP	xWHIP	vL+	vR+	BF/G	Ctl	Dom	Cmd	Ball%	SwK	Vel	G	L	F	H%	S%	HR/F	xHR/F	GS	APC	DOM%	DIS%	Sv%	LI	RAR	BPX	R$
15 2TM	5	2	75	71	2.63	2.74	1.14	1.21	77	89	4.1	2.5	8.5	3.4	35%	12.9%	95.8	69	17	14	30%	78%	13%	15%	0	15			50	1.02	12.4	157	$7
16 TEX	3	38	70	55	2.43	3.38	1.22	1.33	100	81	3.9	2.9	7.0	2.4	35%	9.0%	95.3	65	19	16	29%	83%	16%	11%	0	14			88	1.32	15.3	107	$20
17 2TM	4	14	55	34	6.09	5.28	1.77	1.62	122	110	4.7	4.9	5.6	1.1	37%	8.1%	95.1	63	17	20	33%	67%	21%	18%	0	17			67	1.32	-11.7	10	-$3
18 SF	4	3	70	56	2.69	3.39	1.08	1.28	100	85	3.7	2.6	7.2	2.8	36%	11.5%	93.6	61	15	24	26%	77%	11%	17%	0	13			38	1.08	12.7	114	$7
19 2TM	5	2	62	55	3.32	3.70	1.06	1.21	84	85	4.1	1.9	7.9	4.2	33%	8.8%	93.9	54	18	28	28%	72%	13%	14%	0	14			50	1.10	9.1	135	$5
1st Half	2	1	39	33	2.54	3.31	0.92	1.12	90	72	4.1	1.4	7.6	5.5	33%	8.8%	93.9	57	18	25	26%	76%	12%	14%	0	13			100	0.97	9.5	147	$7
2nd Half	3	1	23	22	4.63	4.29	1.29	1.24	77	106	4.1	2.7	8.5	3.1	33%	8.9%	93.9	49	18	34	31%	67%	13%	13%	0	15			33	1.30	-0.4	116	$2
20 Proj	**2**	**2**	**29**	**24**	**3.73**	**3.48**	**1.22**	**1.29**	**94**	**93**	**4.0**	**2.7**	**7.5**	**2.7**	**35%**	**9.6%**	**94.2**	**58**	**17**	**26**	**29%**	**72%**	**13%**		**0**						**1.5**	**110**	**-$1**

Eflin,Zach

Age: 26	Th: R	Role SP	
Ht: 6' 6"	Wt: 215	Type Con	
Health	D	LIMA Plan	C
PT/Exp	C	Rand Var	0
Consist	C	MM	1103

Strong start gutted by horrendous six-game stretch (7 HR, 31 runs over 27 IP) beginning in late June; banished to the pen in late July. Reclaimed rotation spot later in August; posted 3.20 ERA over final 8 starts (45 IP) with more GB-oriented, pitch-to-contact approach. Still the seeds of something good here, but consistency has been elusive.

Yr Tm	W	Sv	IP	K	ERA	xERA	WHIP	xWHIP	vL+	vR+	BF/G	Ctl	Dom	Cmd	Ball%	SwK	Vel	G	L	F	H%	S%	HR/F	xHR/F	GS	APC	DOM%	DIS%	Sv%	LI	RAR	BPX	R$
15 aa	8	0	132	62	4.09	4.31	1.29				23.5	1.5	4.2	2.8							30%	70%									-2.0	64	$1
16 PHI *	8	0	132	80	4.67	3.62	1.17	1.42	127	99	23.9	2.0	5.5	2.8	36%	6.3%	92.3	36	24	40	28%	62%	13%	13%	11	90	18%	64%			-7.9	79	$3
17 PHI *	2	0	108	68	6.02	5.96	1.52	1.31	123	116	24.6	2.3	5.7	2.5	34%	7.5%	92.7	44	18	38	33%	64%	19%	17%	11	93	0%	36%			-22.0	36	-$11
18 PHI *	13	0	148	136	4.46	4.29	1.32	1.23	115	93	21.9	2.6	8.3	3.2	34%	11.1%	94.3	41	21	38	33%	68%	11%	12%	24	85	29%	29%			-5.7	103	$4
19 PHI	10	0	163	129	4.13	4.84	1.35	1.36	113	95	22.0	2.6	7.1	2.7	34%	9.4%	93.6	45	21	35	30%	76%	16%	13%	28	80	21%	43%	0	0.74	7.5	87	$6
1st Half	7	0	97	80	3.34	4.74	1.25	1.24	107	91	25.6	2.2	7.4	3.3	34%	10.0%	93.5	41	20	39	30%	80%	13%	13%	16	92	31%	44%			13.9	101	$14
2nd Half	3	0	66	49	5.29	4.96	1.49	1.39	121	101	18.4	3.3	6.6	2.0	35%	8.7%	93.6	49	23	28	31%	70%	22%	14%	12	69	8%	42%	0	0.70	-6.4	64	-$6
20 Proj	**9**	**0**	**145**	**111**	**4.40**	**4.19**	**1.38**	**1.31**	**116**	**98**	**21.4**	**2.6**	**6.9**	**2.7**	**34%**	**9.1%**	**93.5**	**44**	**21**	**36**	**31%**	**73%**	**14%**		**28**						**-4.4**	**87**	**$1**

JOCK THOMPSON

Eickhoff,Jerad

Age: 29	Th: R	Role SP	Health F	PT/Exp D	Consist B
Ht: 6' 4"	Wt: 245	Type Con FB	LIMA Plan B	Rand Var +5	MM 0100

3-4, 5.71 ERA in 58 IP at PHI. 1.50 ERA, no HR, 31 Ks over 30 IP in first 5 starts before things abruptly turned ugly. 18 HR over next 22 IP got him bounced from the rotation in mid-June. More injuries (biceps, blisters) kept him from resurfacing, have now helped derail his career for the past 3 seasons. Still flashes, still not a skill set to depend on.

Yr Tm	W	Sv	IP	K	ERA	xERA	WHIP	xWHIP	vL+	vR+	BF/G	Ctl	Dom	Cmd	Ball%	SwK	Vel	G	L	F	H%	S%	HR/F	xHR/F	GS	APC	DOM%	DIS%	Sv%	LI	RAR	BPX	R$
15 PHI *	15	0	184	155	4.14	4.08	1.27	1.18	114	65	24.3	2.6	7.6	2.9	34%	10.8%	91.0	38	22	40	30%	71%	9%	14%	8	92	50%	13%			-4.1	89	$7
16 PHI	11	0	197	167	3.65	4.06	1.16	1.20	111	88	24.6	1.9	7.6	4.0	37%	9.7%	91.0	41	20	39	29%	75%	13%	10%	33	92	24%	24%			13.2	124	$15
17 PHI	4	0	128	118	4.71	4.94	1.52	1.37	119	91	24.0	3.7	8.3	2.2	38%	9.0%	90.4	38	22	40	34%	72%	10%	12%	24	89	17%	38%			-5.6	78	-$4
18 PHI *	0	0	30	21	4.00	5.86	1.62		169	93	16.5	3.1	6.5	2.1		19.4%	91.3	20	40	40	35%	78%	17%	32%	1	33	0%	0%	0	0.28	0.5	49	-$6
19 PHI *	6	1	85	68	6.48	6.00	1.38	1.34	152	99	19.7	3.3	7.3	2.2	38%	11.1%	89.5	36	18	46	26%	61%	23%	20%	10	81	10%	30%	100	0.65	-20.6	13	-$6
1st Half	5	1	68	59	5.74	5.86	1.33	1.28	151	100	20.2	3.0	7.8	2.6	38%	11.1%	89.5	36	18	46	26%	67%	23%	20%	10	81	10%	30%	100	0.65	-10.4	25	-$4
2nd Half	1	0	16	9	9.34	6.34	1.56		0	0	17.8	4.5	5.2	1.2							26%	41%	0%		0	0					-9.7	-17	-$15
20 Proj	3	0	58	45	4.89	4.58	1.41	1.26	131	96	20.8	3.4	7.0	2.1	37%	10.2%	90.4	38	20	42	29%	72%	16%		12						-5.3	59	-$4

Elias,Roenis

Age: 31	Th: L	Role RP	Health F	PT/Exp D	Consist F
Ht: 6' 1"	Wt: 205	Type	LIMA Plan F	Rand Var 0	MM 1200

Per Consistency, Health, Dom, not exactly a high-leverage profile, but deviant saves total fueled modest value. Lefty with reverse splits was in the right place at the right time, enjoyed SwK surge, 1st-half HR luck. July trade, more injuries (hamstring) torpedoed his 2nd-half, but he now has "closer experience" and a WS ring. What a country!

Yr Tm	W	Sv	IP	K	ERA	xERA	WHIP	xWHIP	vL+	vR+	BF/G	Ctl	Dom	Cmd	Ball%	SwK	Vel	G	L	F	H%	S%	HR/F	xHR/F	GS	APC	DOM%	DIS%	Sv%	LI	RAR	BPX	R$
15 SEA *	9	0	177	135	5.20	4.78	1.43	1.37	84	108	22.1	3.1	6.9	2.2	37%	10.2%	91.7	44	19	36	32%	66%	12%	12%	20	84	25%	45%	0	0.73	-27.0	62	-$9
16 BOS *	10	0	133	86	6.70	6.96	1.98		172	160	26.5	5.4	5.9	1.1		3.9%	92.6	36	30	33	37%	67%	18%	25%	1	42	0%	100%	0	0.37	-41.1	14	-$24
17 BOS *	1	0	37	20	10.06	10.26	2.08		132	0	20.2	3.3	4.8	1.5		18.2%	92.3	0	0	0	37%	56%	0%		0	11			0	0.03	-26.0	-75	-$16
18 SEA *	6	1	92	65	3.73	3.58	1.35	1.39	93	87	10.4	3.4	6.3	1.8	38%	9.7%	94.2	34	24	42	31%	71%	2%	7%	4	36	0%	25%	100	0.40	4.8	81	$1
19 2 TM	4	14	50	47	3.96	4.89	1.28	1.36	145	76	4.5	3.2	8.5	2.6	36%	12.2%	94.0	34	26	39	28%	78%	17%	16%	0	18			82	1.39	3.4	84	$6
1st Half	2	10	38	38	3.55	4.72	1.24	1.34	117	70	5.0	3.8	9.0	2.4	36%	12.2%	93.9	37	27	36	28%	74%	10%	12%	0	20			91	1.23	4.5	82	$8
2nd Half	2	4	12	9	5.25	5.47	1.42		242	94	3.5	1.5	6.8	4.5		12.0%	94.4	28	25	48	27%	91%	32%	23%	0	13			67	1.73	-1.1	94	$0
20 Proj	3	0	58	50	4.28	4.28	1.41	1.36	118	107	9.4	3.3	7.7	2.4	37%	10.8%	93.1	39	23	38	31%	75%	15%		0						-0.9	77	-$3

Eovaldi,Nathan

Age: 30	Th: R	Role RP	Health F	PT/Exp D	Consist C
Ht: 6' 2"	Wt: 225	Type Pwr	LIMA Plan C	Rand Var +5	MM 2303

Missed more than three months following another round of arthroscopic elbow surgery. Subsequent bullpen experiment ended in mid-August; finished up with plenty of SwK and velocity, but Ctl, HR were persistent issues. That 2018 2nd half still tugs at us, but arm hasn't stayed fully intact since 2016 Tommy John surgery. End-game only.

Yr Tm	W	Sv	IP	K	ERA	xERA	WHIP	xWHIP	vL+	vR+	BF/G	Ctl	Dom	Cmd	Ball%	SwK	Vel	G	L	F	H%	S%	HR/F	xHR/F	GS	APC	DOM%	DIS%	Sv%	LI	RAR	BPX	R$
15 NYY	14	0	154	121	4.20	3.98	1.45	1.33	107	93	24.9	2.9	7.1	2.5	35%	9.1%	96.7	52	22	26	34%	71%	8%	10%	27	98	19%	30%			-4.5	95	$1
16 NYY	9	0	125	97	4.76	4.27	1.31	1.34	118	96	21.9	2.9	7.0	2.4	35%	9.9%	97.1	50	18	32	28%	69%	19%	19%	21	86	19%	38%	0	0.70	-8.8	90	$1
17																																	
18 2 AL	6	0	111	101	3.81	3.72	1.13	1.14	101	88	20.7	1.6	8.2	5.1	31%	11.3%	97.2	46	19	35	30%	70%	12%	12%	21	82	24%	19%	0	0.75	4.6	147	$6
19 BOS	2	0	68	70	5.99	4.91	1.58	1.46	126	107	13.1	4.7	9.3	2.0	38%	10.9%	97.5	45	19	36	32%	68%	23%	18%	12	55	8%	58%	0	0.88	-12.3	71	-$8
1st Half	0	0	21	16	6.00	5.60	1.52	1.55	136	109	23.3	4.7	6.9	1.5	39%	8.5%	97.1	48	15	37	26%	69%	25%	23%	4	95	25%	75%			-3.9	24	-$12
2nd Half	2	0	47	54	5.98	4.59	1.61	1.36	123	105	11.0	4.6	10.4	2.3	38%	12.0%	97.6	43	21	36	35%	68%	22%	16%	8	47	0%	50%	0	0.89	-8.5	91	-$7
20 Proj	6	0	131	128	4.87	3.85	1.41	1.33	117	99	16.5	3.5	8.9	2.6	36%	10.5%	97.3	46	19	34	31%	71%	19%		22						-11.6	104	-$2

Erlin,Robert

Age: 29	Th: L	Role RP	Health F	PT/Exp D	Consist F
Ht: 6' 0"	Wt: 190	Type Con	LIMA Plan F	Rand Var +5	MM 2100

0-1, 5.37 ERA in 55 IP at SD. Soft-tossing swing-man with fine Ctl coming off career-best 2018 that was more valuable in the real game. Shifted to bullpen full-time in multi-inning role, where he was hit hard all season; spent 2nd half as a shuttle piece. H% will regress and luck should improve a tad. Just not enough to matter.

Yr Tm	W	Sv	IP	K	ERA	xERA	WHIP	xWHIP	vL+	vR+	BF/G	Ctl	Dom	Cmd	Ball%	SwK	Vel	G	L	F	H%	S%	HR/F	xHR/F	GS	APC	DOM%	DIS%	Sv%	LI	RAR	BPX	R$
15 SD *	8	0	142	99	5.41	5.53	1.50		137	83	22.8	2.3	6.2	2.7		8.6%	90.1	47	25	27	34%	67%	7%	6%	3	73	33%	33%			-25.5	56	-$11
16 SD	1	0	16	13	4.02	3.49	0.96		58	120	19.3	1.7	7.5	4.3		10.3%	88.0	43	24	33	22%	67%	21%	14%	2	68	50%	50%	0	0.74	0.3	129	-$2
17																																	
18 SD	4	0	109	88	4.21	3.62	1.14	1.11	97	96	11.3	1.0	7.3	7.3	33%	9.7%	90.3	47	23	30	31%	65%	12%	15%	12	41	0%	50%	0	0.67	-0.8	149	$3
19 SD *	0	1	71	62	6.29	6.30	1.68	1.27	105	105	6.8	2.2	7.8	3.6	36%	10.7%	90.6	45	25	30	41%	63%	11%	14%	1	26	0%	100%	20	0.66	-15.7	88	-$12
1st Half	0	1	40	38	5.57	5.23	1.50	1.18	113	96	5.9	2.3	8.7	3.8	36%	12.6%	90.7	42	25	33	38%	63%	13%	16%	1	23	0%	100%	33	0.82	-5.2	108	-$9
2nd Half	0	0	32	24	7.18	7.66	1.90	1.28	93	116	8.3	2.0	6.8	3.4	37%	8.3%	90.6	48	26	26	43%	62%	9%	12%	0	31			0	0.38	-10.5	64	-$14
20 Proj	1	0	51	41	4.84	4.00	1.45	1.19	104	107	9.1	2.3	7.2	3.2	35%	9.9%	90.5	44	25	32	34%	70%	14%		0						-4.3	104	-$5

Estevez,Carlos

Age: 27	Th: R	Role RP	Health D	PT/Exp D	Consist F
Ht: 6' 6"	Wt: 275	Type Pwr	LIMA Plan F	Rand Var 0	MM 2310

Imposing high-octane reliever rebounded from 2018 oblique, elbow woes into high-leverage MLB IP. Early SwK, Dom spikes began to fade in August, but markedly improved Ctl, HR avoidance fueled 2nd half gains. Volatility, suspect G/L/F and injury history leave us unconvinced, but he has skills to build on. With another year of health... UP: 20 Sv.

Yr Tm	W	Sv	IP	K	ERA	xERA	WHIP	xWHIP	vL+	vR+	BF/G	Ctl	Dom	Cmd	Ball%	SwK	Vel	G	L	F	H%	S%	HR/F	xHR/F	GS	APC	DOM%	DIS%	Sv%	LI	RAR	BPX	R$
15 aa	0	13	36	33	6.56	5.64	1.65				4.7	2.5	8.3	3.4							40%	59%									-11.5	105	-$4
16 COL	3	11	55	59	5.24	4.42	1.42	1.39	73	117	3.9	4.6	9.7	2.1	38%	11.8%	97.3	44	16	40	31%	64%	10%	10%	0	16			61	1.21	-7.1	86	$1
17 COL *	6	4	66	56	3.66	4.21	1.41	1.36	105	104	4.1	3.4	7.7	2.3	38%	11.3%	97.1	45	28	26	32%	76%	11%	8%	0	16			57	0.62	5.7	86	$3
18 aaa	0	1	29	26	7.52	8.38	1.92				4.9	3.6	8.1	2.2							40%	65%									-12.1	15	-$11
19 COL	2	0	72	81	3.75	4.32	1.29	1.24	112	91	4.3	2.9	10.1	3.5	34%	14.4%	97.9	38	20	42	32%	78%	14%	14%	0	17			0	0.93	6.7	131	$1
1st Half	1	0	38	47	4.46	4.38	1.49	1.22	141	88	4.3	3.5	11.0	3.1	35%	16.0%	97.6	39	23	38	36%	78%	19%	20%	0	17			0	0.86	0.2	132	-$3
2nd Half	1	0	34	34	2.94	4.36	1.07	1.15	72	94	4.4	2.1	9.1	4.3	33%	12.4%	98.3	37	16	47	28%	78%	9%	8%	0	18			0	1.01	6.5	132	$5
20 Proj	3	5	65	66	4.13	3.79	1.35	1.27	98	98	4.1	3.1	9.1	2.9	36%	12.6%	97.6	41	22	37	33%	73%	12%		0						0.2	113	$1

Familia,Jeurys

Age: 30	Th: R	Role RP	Health F	PT/Exp C	Consist C
Ht: 6' 3"	Wt: 240	Type Pwr GB	LIMA Plan C	Rand Var +4	MM 2410

Return of shoulder woes took an early toll. Missed 4+ weeks over two IL stints, as BB-HR-S% combo crushed his 1st half. More effective afterward, but Ctl remained a year-long problem. Still owns good Dom, partial GB% rebound was a plus, 9th-inning history still points to flyer upside. But he's now another inconsistent RP with durability issues.

Yr Tm	W	Sv	IP	K	ERA	xERA	WHIP	xWHIP	vL+	vR+	BF/G	Ctl	Dom	Cmd	Ball%	SwK	Vel	G	L	F	H%	S%	HR/F	xHR/F	GS	APC	DOM%	DIS%	Sv%	LI	RAR	BPX	R$
15 NYM	2	43	78	86	1.85	2.62	1.00	1.10	85	75	4.1	2.2	9.9	4.5	33%	16.3%	97.1	58	20	22	28%	86%	14%	13%	0	15			90	1.29	20.4	185	$27
16 NYM	3	51	78	84	2.55	3.08	1.21	1.27	85	72	4.1	3.6	9.7	2.7	35%	15.5%	96.2	63	18	19	31%	77%	3%	6%	0	16			91	1.22	15.7	142	$27
17 NYM	2	6	25	25	4.38	4.17	1.46		101	73	4.3	5.5	9.1	1.7		10.5%	95.9	60	21	19	31%	69%	8%	6%	0	16			86	1.08	-0.1	65	-$1
18 2 TM	8	18	72	83	3.13	3.58	1.22	1.23	99	69	4.3	3.5	10.4	3.0	35%	14.7%	96.2	46	21	33	32%	74%	5%	9%	0	17			75	1.28	9.1	134	$13
19 NYM	4	0	60	63	5.70	5.15	1.73	1.63	117	106	4.2	6.3	9.5	1.5	39%	11.3%	96.0	51	19	30	34%	68%	14%	13%	0	16			0	0.81	-8.8	32	-$8
1st Half	2	0	28	28	7.81	5.52	1.84	1.66	157	104	4.5	6.8	9.1	1.3	39%	12.0%	95.8	51	17	32	33%	59%	20%	12%	0	16			0	0.99	-11.3	9	-$12
2nd Half	2	0	32	35	3.90	4.67	1.64	1.52	89	107	3.9	5.8	9.7	1.7	40%	10.8%	96.2	51	21	28	35%	76%	8%	15%	0	15			0	0.67	2.4	51	-$4
20 Proj	5	2	65	71	4.08	3.70	1.45	1.40	102	90	4.1	4.8	9.8	2.1	37%	13.2%	96.2	52	19	28	33%	72%	10%		0						0.6	90	$0

Farmer,Buck

Age: 29	Th: R	Role RP	Health A	PT/Exp C	Consist B
Ht: 6' 4"	Wt: 232	Type Pwr	LIMA Plan B	Rand Var 0	MM 1201

Near-across-the-board gains always get our attention. Velocity continued to tick upward as Dom, SwK jumped. Ctl improved all season, even GB% looks healthier. But Ball% history hints that the walks will return. FB% spiked, swing-and-miss fell off in 2nd half partly fueled by HR/F and H% luck. Still too many moving parts; call us mildly intrigued.

Yr Tm	W	Sv	IP	K	ERA	xERA	WHIP	xWHIP	vL+	vR+	BF/G	Ctl	Dom	Cmd	Ball%	SwK	Vel	G	L	F	H%	S%	HR/F	xHR/F	GS	APC	DOM%	DIS%	Sv%	LI	RAR	BPX	R$
15 DET *	7	0	127	84	5.70	5.29	1.53	1.52	147	130	18.4	3.0	5.9	2.0	38%	8.0%	92.5	45	15	40	33%	64%	18%	16%	5	50	0%	80%	0	0.58	-27.2	45	-$12
16 DET *	5	0	129	100	5.11	5.57	1.60		122	82	16.8	3.5	7.0	2.0		10.7%	92.9	52	11	37	34%	71%	13%	13%	1	36	0%	100%	0	0.28	-14.7	49	-$9
17 DET *	11	0	172	137	6.07	6.02	1.67	1.33	116	109	24.1	2.9	7.2	2.4	38%	11.3%	91.7	32	21	47	38%	64%	13%	9%	11	82	18%	64%			-36.3	62	-$15
18 DET	3	0	69	57	4.15	5.33	1.56	1.59	84	121	4.7	5.3	7.4	1.4	39%	11.2%	94.5	40	23	37	31%	75%	8%	8%	1	19	0%	0%	0	0.73	0.0	9	-$5
19 DET	6	0	68	73	3.72	4.02	1.27	1.28	99	99	3.9	3.2	9.7	3.0	38%	13.2%	95.1	47	20	33	31%	74%	13%	18%	1	16	0%	0%	0	1.22	6.5	124	$3
1st Half	4	0	31	35	4.31	3.81	1.47	1.25	125	108	3.8	3.4	10.1	2.9	38%	14.3%	94.9	52	23	25	36%	74%	18%	27%	1	15	0%	0%	0	1.24	0.8	129	$0
2nd Half	2	0	36	38	3.22	4.18	1.10	1.22	80	89	4.1	3.0	9.4	3.2	38%	12.3%	95.2	43	17	40	27%	75%	11%	13%	0	16			0	1.20	5.8	120	$5
20 Proj	5	0	73	68	4.32	4.14	1.42	1.37	101	106	5.1	3.7	8.4	2.3	38%	11.8%	94.2	43	20	37	32%	72%	10%		0						-1.5	83	-$1

JOCK THOMPSON

Fedde,Erick

Age: 27	Th: R	Role: RP	Health: D	LIMA Plan: A
Ht: 6' 4"	Wt: 195	Type: Con	PT/Exp: D	Rand Var: +1
			Consist: A	MM: 1001

4-2, 4.50 ERA in 78 IP at WAS. Stayed off the IL for a change, but that was the biggest plus in a no-growth season for ex-1st-rounder. Ctl is still nothing special while Dom plunged to unrosterable levels with full SwK support. GB% still plays, but he's never been stingy with the HR ball. LHBs still own him, but you shouldn't.

Yr Tm	W	Sv	IP	K	ERA	xERA	WHIP	xWHIP	vL+	vR+	BF/G	Ctl	Dom	Cmd	Ball%	SwK	Vel	G	L	F	H%	S%	HR/F	xHR/F	GS	APC	DOM%	DIS%	Sv%	LI	RAR	BPX	R$
15																																	
16 aa	2	0	29	24	5.30	5.47	1.72				26.7	3.3	7.3	2.2							40%	67%									-4.0	83	-$6
17 WAS *	4	0	106	80	5.38	5.04	1.47		111	196	14.2	2.8	6.9	2.5		5.7%	93.0	62	17	21	34%	65%	50%	32%	3	99	0%	100%			-13.3	69	-$6
18 WAS *	5	0	122	105	5.58	5.61	1.63	1.39	120	115	21.8	3.2	7.8	2.4	41%	9.1%	93.7	53	22	24	38%	66%	22%	28%	11	86	9%	64%			-21.6	75	-$13
19 WAS *	7	0	114	70	5.36	5.55	1.50	1.61	121	91	17.6	3.4	5.5	1.6	40%	7.3%	92.3	51	22	27	30%	68%	16%	18%	12	61	0%	67%	0	0.60	-12.1	20	-$6
1st Half	3	0	71	46	4.64	4.89	1.43	1.61	120	83	17.6	3.4	5.8	1.7	40%	7.9%	92.2	53	17	30	29%	71%	14%	16%	6	59	0%	50%	0	0.62	-1.2	36	-$4
2nd Half	4	0	44	25	6.53	6.62	1.61	1.51	122	103	17.6	3.3	5.1	1.5	41%	6.7%	92.4	49	26	25	31%	64%	19%	21%	6	64	0%	83%	0	0.58	-10.9	-6	-$9
20 Proj	**4**	**0**	**73**	**51**	**5.66**	**4.50**	**1.58**	**1.49**	**129**	**108**	**18.3**	**3.4**	**6.3**	**1.8**	**41%**	**8.0%**	**92.9**	**49**	**22**	**29**	**33%**	**67%**	**16%**		**14**						**-13.5**	**55**	**-$8**

Feliz,Michael

Age: 27	Th: R	Role: RP	Health: C	LIMA Plan: A
Ht: 6' 4"	Wt: 240	Type: Pwr FB	PT/Exp: D	Rand Var: 0
			Consist: A	MM: 3510

4-4, 3.99 ERA in 56 IP at PIT. Healthy after 2 years of a balky shoulder, with notable 2nd-half results. Velocity, SwK turned around as he finished with a 13+ Dom in Aug/Sept. GB% began spiking in July. Suddenly began to find the plate, and Ctl gains kept lid on poor HR luck. Even 2nd-half H%, S% cooperated. With more health, luck... UP: 20 Sv

Yr Tm	W	Sv	IP	K	ERA	xERA	WHIP	xWHIP	vL+	vR+	BF/G	Ctl	Dom	Cmd	Ball%	SwK	Vel	G	L	F	H%	S%	HR/F	xHR/F	GS	APC	DOM%	DIS%	Sv%	LI	RAR	BPX	R$
15 HOU *	6	1	87	69	2.91	2.50	1.03		119	127	16.7	2.4	7.2	3.0		12.6%	93.5	38	31	31	25%	75%	25%	17%	0	35			100	0.05	11.2	114	$9
16 HOU	8	0	65	95	4.43	2.94	1.18	1.06	96	84	5.7	3.0	13.2	4.3	37%	14.3%	94.9	42	21	37	34%	67%	18%	17%	0	24			0	0.99	-1.9	207	$4
17 HOU	4	0	48	70	5.63	3.89	1.56	1.19	116	114	4.7	4.1	13.1	3.2	35%	14.9%	96.2	31	27	42	41%	67%	15%	12%	0	20			0	0.67	-7.5	161	-$4
18 PIT	1	0	48	55	5.66	4.43	1.51	1.33	100	114	4.6	4.3	10.4	2.4	38%	10.4%	94.7	32	29	39	35%	64%	11%	15%	0	20			0	0.76	-8.9	92	-$7
19 PIT *	4	2	71	90	3.49	4.26	1.33	1.31	91	100	4.4	4.4	11.3	2.6	36%	13.1%	95.2	34	21	45	30%	81%	18%	15%	1	18	0%	100%	50	0.84	8.9	93	$3
1st Half	2	0	21	27	6.00	4.87	1.38	1.41	100	81	4.6	5.6	11.6	2.1	39%	11.2%	94.6	20	33	47	30%	56%	9%	12%	1	22	0%	100%	0	0.51	-3.9	61	-$4
2nd Half	2	0	35	46	2.80	3.89	1.19	1.18	86	111	3.9	3.6	11.7	3.3	33%	14.5%	95.6	42	14	44	26%	94%	24%	17%	0	15			0	1.01	7.4	147	$6
20 Proj	**4**	**5**	**65**	**83**	**3.98**	**3.49**	**1.26**	**1.25**	**92**	**98**	**4.3**	**3.9**	**11.4**	**2.9**	**36%**	**12.7%**	**95.2**	**34**	**24**	**42**	**30%**	**75%**	**16%**		**0**						**1.4**	**129**	**$3**

Ferguson,Caleb

Age: 23	Th: L	Role: RP	Health: B	LIMA Plan: B
Ht: 6' 3"	Wt: 226	Type: Pwr	PT/Exp: D	Rand Var: +2
			Consist: B	MM: 2400

1-2, 4.84 ERA in 45 IP at LA. Struggled early in follow-up to promising 2018 debut. HR issues that helped put him on the minor league shuttle subsided in the 2nd half, but Ctl a season-long problem. SwK drop, volatile G/L/F also disconcerting. Historical sub-3 ERA, 10+ Dom as minor league SP points to upside; age buys time. Work-in-progress.

Yr Tm	W	Sv	IP	K	ERA	xERA	WHIP	xWHIP	vL+	vR+	BF/G	Ctl	Dom	Cmd	Ball%	SwK	Vel	G	L	F	H%	S%	HR/F	xHR/F	GS	APC	DOM%	DIS%	Sv%	LI	RAR	BPX	R$
15																																	
16																																	
17																																	
18 LA *	10	2	96	105	2.57	3.26	1.14	1.07	100	92	9.7	2.5	9.8	3.9	32%	12.0%	93.9	45	25	30	30%	82%	21%	15%	3	29	0%	67%	67	0.79	18.7	139	$13
19 LA *	1	1	61	77	4.02	3.77	1.32	1.47	95	109	4.3	4.7	11.4	2.5	36%	9.8%	94.5	39	25	37	30%	73%	17%	13%	2	18	0%	50%	100	0.51	3.6	104	$0
1st Half	0	0	30	37	4.20	5.21	1.46	1.38	100	138	4.6	4.4	11.2	2.5	36%	9.8%	94.3	41	27	32	33%	79%	29%	17%	1	20	0%	100%	0	0.61	1.1	77	-$4
2nd Half	1	1	31	40	3.85	2.37	1.18	1.48	88	75	4.0	4.9	11.6	2.4	36%	9.9%	94.8	35	21	44	27%	67%	5%	10%	1	16	0%	0%	100	0.41	2.5	132	$3
20 Proj	**2**	**0**	**44**	**50**	**4.01**	**3.87**	**1.40**	**1.29**	**96**	**101**	**5.6**	**4.5**	**10.4**	**2.3**	**34%**	**10.7%**	**94.3**	**39**	**23**	**38**	**32%**	**74%**	**12%**		**0**						**0.7**	**95**	**-$2**

Fernandez,Junior

Age: 23	Th: R	Role: RP	Health: A	LIMA Plan: F
Ht: 6' 1"	Wt: 180	Type: Pwr	PT/Exp: F	Rand Var: +5
			Consist: F	MM: 3410

0-1, 5.40 ERA in 12 IP at STL. Light flicked on a year after prospect's move to the pen. SwK, Dom jumped as he roared through three levels with a sub-2 ERA before his MLB debut. Rookie wasn't overmatched; unscored upon in 10 of 13 MLB appearances, as one bad outing did the damage. Ctl is a project, GB% is a plus. Looks closer-ish down the road.

Yr Tm	W	Sv	IP	K	ERA	xERA	WHIP	xWHIP	vL+	vR+	BF/G	Ctl	Dom	Cmd	Ball%	SwK	Vel	G	L	F	H%	S%	HR/F	xHR/F	GS	APC	DOM%	DIS%	Sv%	LI	RAR	BPX	R$
15																																	
16																																	
17																																	
18 aa	0	0	21	15	5.33	4.32	1.64				5.9	6.2	6.2	1.0							30%	66%									-3.1	59	-$7
19 STL *	3	7	66	74	2.39	2.27	1.14	1.28	75	95	5.3	3.7	10.2	2.8	44%	19.3%	96.8	50	36	14	29%	79%	50%	29%	0	17			64	1.22	17.1	136	$9
1st Half	1	5	34	41	1.84	1.51	1.00		0	0	6.5	2.8	10.7	3.9							30%	79%	0%		0	0					11.2	176	$10
2nd Half	2	2	32	34	2.98	3.09	1.30		75	94	4.5	4.7	9.6	2.1		19.3%	96.8	50	36	14	29%	78%	50%	29%	0	17			40	1.22	5.9	104	$8
20 Proj	**3**	**2**	**58**	**65**	**3.38**	**3.44**	**1.23**				**5.2**	**3.8**	**10.1**	**2.7**				**45**	**21**	**34**	**30%**	**75%**	**11%**		**0**						**5.6**	**118**	**$2**

Fiers,Mike

Age: 35	Th: R	Role: SP	Health: B	LIMA Plan: A
Ht: 6' 2"	Wt: 202	Type: Con	PT/Exp: A	Rand Var: -2
			Consist: A	MM: 1103

More good health, plus Ctl and ability to contain HR damage again the keys to outpitching a subpar skill set. 2.91/5.15 home/road ERA splits also notable. But SwK/Dom decay continues, and he isn't getting any younger. Sometimes the magic works (sub-3 ERA May through Aug); sometimes not (7.83 ERA in Apr, Sept). Eventually it just disappears.

Yr Tm	W	Sv	IP	K	ERA	xERA	WHIP	xWHIP	vL+	vR+	BF/G	Ctl	Dom	Cmd	Ball%	SwK	Vel	G	L	F	H%	S%	HR/F	xHR/F	GS	APC	DOM%	DIS%	Sv%	LI	RAR	BPX	R$
15 2 TM	7	0	180	180	3.69	4.00	1.25	1.27	91	107	24.5	3.2	9.0	2.8	36%	10.3%	89.4	38	20	42	30%	75%	11%	11%	30	98	20%	20%	0	0.78	6.0	109	$8
16 HOU	11	0	169	134	4.48	4.25	1.36	1.26	102	115	23.4	2.2	7.2	3.2	36%	9.3%	89.6	42	26	32	32%	71%	15%	14%	30	89	30%	40%	0	0.76	-6.1	105	$2
17 HOU	8	0	153	146	5.22	4.48	1.43	1.34	107	114	23.1	3.6	8.6	2.4	37%	9.5%	89.7	43	20	37	30%	70%	20%	14%	28	91	18%	36%	0	0.75	-16.4	92	-$3
18 2 AL	12	0	172	139	3.56	4.35	1.18	1.22	97	110	23.0	1.9	7.3	3.8	35%	8.9%	89.4	39	17	43	28%	79%	14%	18%	30	87	20%	40%	0	0.76	12.5	110	$13
19 OAK	15	0	185	126	3.90	5.01	1.19	1.41	90	99	22.8	2.6	6.1	2.4	35%	8.2%	90.4	40	21	39	26%	74%	14%	15%	33	88	15%	36%			13.8	64	$15
1st Half	9	0	101	66	4.01	5.25	1.12	1.37	87	92	23.0	2.7	5.9	2.2	35%	8.1%	90.4	39	18	43	24%	69%	12%	14%	18	88	17%	39%			6.2	55	$18
2nd Half	6	0	84	60	3.76	4.74	1.27	1.32	95	106	22.7	2.5	6.5	2.6	35%	8.3%	90.4	41	25	34	28%	78%	17%	18%	15	88	13%	33%			7.6	75	$11
20 Proj	**12**	**0**	**174**	**132**	**4.27**	**4.20**	**1.27**	**1.30**	**97**	**108**	**22.6**	**2.6**	**6.8**	**2.6**	**35%**	**8.8%**	**89.9**	**40**	**21**	**39**	**28%**	**73%**	**15%**		**31**						**-2.6**	**82**	**$8**

Flaherty,Jack

Age: 24	Th: R	Role: SP	Health: A	LIMA Plan: B
Ht: 6' 4"	Wt: 205	Type: Pwr	PT/Exp: B	Rand Var: -2
			Consist: B	MM: 4405

Everything clicked except offensive support in near-flawless 2nd half: Improved Ctl in concert with SwK, Dom, GB% bumps as velocity ticked up, and he dominated hitters on both sides of the plate. H%, S%, HR/F luck couldn't have been better. Likely overpriced on draft day. But he's really good, and we wouldn't bet against a worthy follow-up.

Yr Tm	W	Sv	IP	K	ERA	xERA	WHIP	xWHIP	vL+	vR+	BF/G	Ctl	Dom	Cmd	Ball%	SwK	Vel	G	L	F	H%	S%	HR/F	xHR/F	GS	APC	DOM%	DIS%	Sv%	LI	RAR	BPX	R$
15																																	
16																																	
17 STL *	14	0	170	142	3.12	3.59	1.21		145	79	22.1	2.4	7.5	3.2		14.2%	93.2	48	22	30	30%	78%	21%	16%	5	60	0%	80%	0	0.65	25.9	108	$18
18 STL *	12	0	184	216	3.17	2.83	1.07	1.21	83	92	21.7	3.2	10.6	3.3	37%	14.1%	92.7	42	21	37	27%	76%	15%	11%	28	92	21%	18%			22.3	132	$23
19 STL	11	0	196	231	2.75	3.56	0.97	1.15	81	76	23.4	2.5	10.6	4.2	36%	14.2%	93.9	40	22	38	25%	79%	14%	13%	33	96	42%	12%			42.5	153	$32
1st Half	4	0	85	94	4.75	4.17	1.23	1.19	111	92	22.3	2.8	9.9	3.5	37%	13.1%	93.6	36	25	38	29%	69%	21%	16%	16	94	19%	19%			-2.5	127	$7
2nd Half	7	0	111	137	1.22	3.17	0.77	1.04	60	59	24.4	2.3	11.1	4.9	34%	15.2%	94.1	42	19	38	22%	90%	7%	10%	17	98	65%	6%			45.0	174	$51
20 Proj	**13**	**0**	**189**	**212**	**3.09**	**3.18**	**1.03**	**1.14**	**82**	**83**	**22.2**	**2.7**	**10.1**	**3.7**	**36%**	**14.2%**	**93.4**	**41**	**22**	**38**	**27%**	**75%**	**13%**		**33**						**24.8**	**146**	**$27**

Floro,Dylan

Age: 29	Th: R	Role: RP	Health: B	LIMA Plan: D
Ht: 6' 2"	Wt: 203	Type: Con GB	PT/Exp: D	Rand Var: 0
			Consist: D	MM: 2200

Unscored upon in first 16 appearances, but fast start was forgotten by late May as LHBs began to hammer him. Nagging injuries (neck, intercoastal strain) and Ctl then became problems until September. Still owns some appreciable skills, notably that GB%, Ball% trend and rising SwK. But Consistency isn't one of them.

Yr Tm	W	Sv	IP	K	ERA	xERA	WHIP	xWHIP	vL+	vR+	BF/G	Ctl	Dom	Cmd	Ball%	SwK	Vel	G	L	F	H%	S%	HR/F	xHR/F	GS	APC	DOM%	DIS%	Sv%	LI	RAR	BPX	R$
15 aaa	9	0	133	68	6.38	5.89	1.62				23.6	1.5	4.6	3.1							37%	59%									-39.6	66	-$18
16 TAM *	1	7	65	47	4.12	6.03	1.64		105	114	6.6	2.1	6.5	3.1		9.3%	92.5	55	21	25	38%	78%	0%	6%	0	21			78	0.77	0.6	72	-$3
17 CHC *	3	2	70	36	5.31	6.79	1.65		135	129	8.6	1.6	4.7	2.8		9.0%	91.3	50	19	31	36%	72%	18%	12%	0	44			67	0.15	-8.2	32	-$7
18 2 NL	6	0	64	58	2.25	3.84	1.25	1.31	103	78	5.0	3.2	8.2	2.5	35%	11.6%	93.3	55	18	26	31%	83%	6%	8%	0	18			0	1.06	15.0	106	$5
19 LA	5	0	47	42	4.24	4.25	1.29	1.30	123	75	4.0	2.7	8.1	3.0	33%	13.1%	93.9	51	20	28	32%	68%	10%	11%	0	15			0	1.14	1.5	111	$0
1st Half	3	0	29	23	4.60	4.26	1.23	1.22	135	72	4.1	1.8	7.1	3.8	34%	12.5%	93.8	49	22	28	31%	64%	12%	11%	0	15			0	1.25	-0.3	114	$0
2nd Half	2	0	17	19	3.63	4.11	1.38	1.33	105	81	3.9	4.2	9.9	2.4	31%	14.1%	93.9	54	17	29	33%	74%	7%	12%	0	15			0	0.96	1.9	106	-$1
20 Proj	**5**	**0**	**51**	**43**	**3.89**	**3.73**	**1.38**	**1.30**	**123**	**86**	**4.8**	**2.9**	**7.7**	**2.7**	**33%**	**12.7%**	**93.6**	**53**	**19**	**28**	**33%**	**73%**	**10%**		**0**						**1.6**	**106**	**-$1**

JOCK THOMPSON

Foltynewicz,Mike

Age: 28	Th: R	Role SP	Health D	LIMA Plan B
Ht: 6' 4"	Wt: 200	Type	PT/Exp B	Rand Var +2
			Consist B	MM 2203

8-6, 4.54 ERA in 117 IP at ATL. Missed the first month with a bum elbow. Upon return, Ks were down, hits and HR up, and ratios wrecked. Rebounded in 2nd half closer to 2018. However, mediocre Ball% and SwK, along with questionable LD% and FB% serve as a reality check on the eye-popping velocity. He's had his career year.

Yr Tm	W	Sv	IP	K	ERA	xERA	WHIP	xWHIP	vL+	vR+	BF/G	Ctl	Dom	Cmd	Ball%	SwK	Vel	G	L	F	H%	S%	HR/F	xHR/F	GS	APC	DOM%	DIS%	Sv%	LI	RAR	BPX	R$
15 ATL *	5	0	143	132	5.26	5.96	1.62	1.31	130	119	22.7	3.6	8.3	2.3	35%	9.6%	95.0	33	23	44	36%	72%	14%	11%	15	82	13%	40%	0	0.99	-22.9	55	-$13
16 ATL *	10	0	150	132	3.93	3.89	1.28	1.25	105	102	22.8	3.0	7.9	2.6	34%	10.2%	95.2	41	21	37	30%	73%	13%	14%	22	96	23%	32%			4.8	89	$7
17 ATL	10	0	154	143	4.79	4.68	1.48	1.33	116	97	23.9	3.4	8.4	2.4	38%	9.9%	95.3	39	24	36	34%	70%	12%	13%	28	96	11%	36%	0	0.76	-8.2	89	-$1
18 ATL	13	0	183	202	2.85	3.68	1.08	1.24	84	81	24.0	3.3	9.9	3.0	37%	10.8%	96.4	43	19	38	26%	77%	10%	11%	31	98	39%	23%			29.3	126	$25
19 ATL *	13	0	169	139	4.84	4.66	1.36	1.34	97	105	22.8	3.0	7.4	2.5	35%	10.8%	94.9	37	23	40	31%	68%	17%	15%	21	90	24%	29%			-7.0	64	$3
1st Half	4	0	85	66	6.57	5.59	1.46	1.33	118	119	22.9	3.3	7.0	2.1	34%	11.0%	95.2	35	23	43	30%	58%	21%	17%	11	86	9%	36%			-21.7	34	-$10
2nd Half	9	0	84	72	3.08	3.72	1.27	1.23	73	91	22.8	2.7	7.8	2.9	36%	10.7%	94.6	39	24	37	31%	78%	12%	13%	10	94	40%	20%			14.7	96	$16
20 Proj	**12**	**0**	**160**	**146**	**4.08**	**4.02**	**1.31**	**1.27**	**97**	**99**	**22.9**	**3.1**	**8.3**	**2.6**	**36%**	**10.5%**	**95.3**	**39**	**22**	**39**	**31%**	**72%**	**11%**		**29**						**1.4**	**93**	**$8**

Font,Wilmer

Age: 30	Th: R	Role RP	Health D	LIMA Plan B
Ht: 6' 4"	Wt: 250	Type Pwr FB	PT/Exp C	Rand Var +2
			Consist B	MM 2300

Throughout his recent travels around the continent (6 MLB teams in three years), his skills have improved but his results largely have not. Ball% and SwK support Ctl/Dom gains, but a persistent FB lean has unleashed a HR epidemic. Even his foray into the world of Openers has not cured the disease (7 HR in 17 games started). Risky.

Yr Tm	W	Sv	IP	K	ERA	xERA	WHIP	xWHIP	vL+	vR+	BF/G	Ctl	Dom	Cmd	Ball%	SwK	Vel	G	L	F	H%	S%	HR/F	xHR/F	GS	APC	DOM%	DIS%	Sv%	LI	RAR	BPX	R$
15																																	
16 a/a	4	0	66	44	5.38	5.40	1.42				23.3	1.9	6.0	3.2							33%	66%									-9.7	63	-$5
17 LA *	10	0	138	144	4.51	4.20	1.33		125	225	20.4	2.5	9.4	3.8		11.0%	93.8	27	27	47	35%	68%	29%	20%	0	30			0	0.33	-2.6	130	$5
18 3 TM	2	0	44	36	5.93	4.84	1.41	1.36	114	118	10.1	3.3	7.4	2.3	36%	10.0%	94.4	43	14	42	28%	66%	20%	16%	5	44	20%	0%	0	0.54	-9.7	75	-$7
19 3 TM	4	0	84	95	4.48	4.36	1.27	1.26	113	101	7.4	3.1	10.1	3.3	35%	12.7%	94.3	37	18	45	30%	72%	17%	14%	17	32	6%	47%	0	0.81	0.2	124	$1
1st Half	2	0	41	39	4.87	4.96	1.33	1.35	108	104	7.5	3.8	8.6	2.3	36%	12.8%	93.8	41	14	45	28%	68%	14%	14%	3	33	0%	100%	0	0.76	-1.8	80	-$3
2nd Half	2	0	44	56	4.12	3.98	1.21	1.07	117	99	7.4	2.5	11.5	4.7	34%	12.6%	94.7	32	22	46	32%	77%	19%	14%	14	31	7%	36%	0	0.85	2.1	165	$4
20 Proj	**3**	**0**	**58**	**58**	**4.59**	**3.93**	**1.32**	**1.26**	**111**	**106**	**9.4**	**2.9**	**9.0**	**3.1**	**36%**	**12.0%**	**94.4**	**39**	**17**	**44**	**31%**	**73%**	**16%**		**0**						**-3.1**	**117**	**-$2**

Freeland,Kyle

Age: 27	Th: L	Role SP	Health D	LIMA Plan D
Ht: 6' 4"	Wt: 201	Type Con	PT/Exp B	Rand Var +5
			Consist D	MM 1103

3-11, 6.73 ERA in 104 IP at COL. Ho-hum ... just your normal, everyday -$43 earnings swing. Amazingly, sub-indicators (Ball%, SwK) and batted ball metrics were nearly identical from 2018 to 2019—which points to the inconvenient truth that he's just not that good. Truly one who lived and died by strand rate. A resurrection? Highly unlikely.

Yr Tm	W	Sv	IP	K	ERA	xERA	WHIP	xWHIP	vL+	vR+	BF/G	Ctl	Dom	Cmd	Ball%	SwK	Vel	G	L	F	H%	S%	HR/F	xHR/F	GS	APC	DOM%	DIS%	Sv%	LI	RAR	BPX	R$
15																																	
16 a/a	11	0	162	84	5.76	5.94	1.60				27.6	2.7	4.7	1.7							33%	66%									-31.4	19	-$14
17 COL	11	0	156	107	4.10	4.80	1.49	1.40	100	109	20.0	3.0	6.2	1.7	30%	8.0%	92.0	54	19	28	31%	75%	13%	11%	28	78	14%	68%	0	0.69	5.0	54	$2
18 COL	17	0	202	173	2.85	4.20	1.25	1.33	71	98	25.6	3.1	7.7	2.5	36%	9.6%	91.6	46	19	35	29%	80%	8%	11%	33	98	33%	21%			32.5	90	$21
19 COL *	3	0	136	100	7.40	6.80	1.68	1.45	103	126	21.8	3.7	6.6	1.8	36%	9.9%	91.9	47	21	33	34%	59%	22%	18%	22	81	9%	59%			-48.4	13	-$22
1st Half	2	0	84	63	8.54	7.31	1.79	1.41	123	120	22.6	4.2	6.8	1.6	36%	10.8%	91.3	43	19	38	34%	54%	22%	21%	12	84	17%	58%			-41.6	4	-$29
2nd Half	1	0	52	37	5.57	5.98	1.51	1.37	82	134	20.5	2.8	6.4	2.3	36%	8.9%	92.6	52	22	26	32%	68%	22%	14%	10	77	0%	60%			-6.8	31	-$12
20 Proj	**5**	**0**	**131**	**96**	**5.27**	**4.39**	**1.51**	**1.38**	**91**	**119**	**22.5**	**3.3**	**6.6**	**2.0**	**37%**	**9.4%**	**91.9**	**48**	**20**	**32**	**32%**	**68%**	**15%**		**25**						**-18.0**	**65**	**-$8**

Fried,Max

Age: 26	Th: L	Role SP	Health B	LIMA Plan B
Ht: 6' 4"	Wt: 190	Type Pwr GB	PT/Exp C	Rand Var +5
			Consist B	MM 3305

Quiet consolidation year; is a 2020 breakout looming? PRO: Cmd on the rise with Ball% and SwK support; plus velocity; extreme GBer; big step up in 2nd half. CON: Consistently outrageous HR/F and line drive after line drive seems like a recipe for continued ERA/xERA, WHIP/xWHIP disparity. Still, signs here of UP: 3.25 ERA, 200 K

Yr Tm	W	Sv	IP	K	ERA	xERA	WHIP	xWHIP	vL+	vR+	BF/G	Ctl	Dom	Cmd	Ball%	SwK	Vel	G	L	F	H%	S%	HR/F	xHR/F	GS	APC	DOM%	DIS%	Sv%	LI	RAR	BPX	R$
15																																	
16																																	
17 ATL *	3	0	119	103	6.63	5.41	1.69		91	118	17.8	4.7	7.8	1.7		9.0%	92.4	65	18	17	35%	60%	21%	24%	4	47	0%	75%	0	0.38	-33.2	61	-$16
18 ATL *	4	0	113	115	4.40	4.12	1.46	1.36	114	88	16.7	4.3	9.2	2.1	39%	14.4%	93.0	51	28	20	34%	70%	20%	14%	5	41	20%	20%	0	0.64	-3.4	98	-$4
19 ATL	17	0	166	173	4.02	3.59	1.33	1.21	86	103	21.3	2.6	9.4	3.7	35%	11.9%	93.8	54	24	22	34%	74%	20%	16%	30	81	17%	23%	0	0.80	9.9	144	$12
1st Half	9	0	94	90	4.04	3.69	1.36	1.23	82	106	20.9	2.7	8.6	3.2	36%	11.4%	94.0	55	24	21	34%	73%	20%	15%	17	80	12%	18%	0	0.85	5.4	127	$12
2nd Half	8	0	72	83	4.00	3.35	1.31	1.12	93	99	21.7	2.4	10.4	4.4	35%	12.5%	93.6	52	24	24	35%	74%	21%	16%	13	83	23%	31%	0	0.73	4.5	166	$12
20 Proj	**14**	**0**	**181**	**186**	**3.94**	**3.32**	**1.34**	**1.24**	**98**	**98**	**20.9**	**3.5**	**9.2**	**2.7**	**37%**	**13.0%**	**93.5**	**52**	**26**	**22**	**32%**	**73%**	**18%**		**30**						**4.8**	**118**	**$11**

Fry,Paul

Age: 27	Th: L	Role RP	Health A	LIMA Plan D
Ht: 6' 0"	Wt: 190	Type Pwr xGB	PT/Exp D	Rand Var +5
			Consist D	MM 2310

Three reasons to dismiss his 2nd half Dom increase: 1) In-season SwK did not change; 2) Ball% says there is very little hope for improvement in Ctl (and thus Cmd) or WHIP; 3) "Meh" velocity and reverse platoon split just muddies potential role. Grounders? Yes. Grounded in skill? Um ... No.

Yr Tm	W	Sv	IP	K	ERA	xERA	WHIP	xWHIP	vL+	vR+	BF/G	Ctl	Dom	Cmd	Ball%	SwK	Vel	G	L	F	H%	S%	HR/F	xHR/F	GS	APC	DOM%	DIS%	Sv%	LI	RAR	BPX	R$
15 aa	0	7	25	38	1.98	3.06	1.34				4.7	3.4	13.6	4.1							43%	84%									6.1	203	$2
16 aaa	3	0	55	56	3.22	3.87	1.55				5.0	5.0	9.2	1.8							35%	78%									6.6	108	-$1
17 a/a	3	1	60	61	5.77	6.16	1.85				8.5	5.6	9.1	1.6							38%	70%									-10.5	60	-$9
18 BAL *	4	4	81	80	3.73	3.51	1.28	1.33	96	78	5.3	3.5	8.9	2.6	38%	10.2%	91.3	58	21	21	31%	72%	5%	5%	0	18			57	1.28	4.2	108	$3
19 BAL	1	3	57	55	5.34	4.36	1.45	1.47	110	91	3.9	4.6	8.6	1.9	40%	10.3%	90.7	58	19	23	31%	64%	19%	15%	0	16			38	1.31	-5.9	75	-$4
1st Half	1	1	32	26	4.45	4.10	1.30	1.50	70	104	4.1	4.5	7.2	1.6	40%	10.3%	90.4	65	17	17	27%	65%	13%	18%	0	18			50	1.22	0.2	58	-$3
2nd Half	0	2	25	29	6.48	4.45	1.64	1.36	146	72	3.6	4.7	10.4	2.2	39%	10.3%	91.1	49	21	30	36%	64%	24%	13%	0	15			33	1.41	-6.1	96	-$6
20 Proj	**2**	**5**	**58**	**57**	**4.64**	**3.76**	**1.50**	**1.38**	**121**	**87**	**4.5**	**4.5**	**8.8**	**2.0**	**39%**	**10.3%**	**91.0**	**56**	**20**	**23**	**33%**	**71%**	**17%**		**0**						**-3.5**	**82**	**-$3**

Fulmer,Michael

Age: 27	Th: R	Role SP	Health F	LIMA Plan A
Ht: 6' 3"	Wt: 246	Type Con	PT/Exp C	Rand Var 0
			Consist A	MM 2101

Burst onto scene with Rookie of the Year 2016, but since then results (and most indicators) have slid in wrong direction, culminating with TJ surgery in March 2019. Best case, could find his way back for a half a season, but shaky Cmd and a lack of swing and miss despite high velocity only dampens expectations. Needs to prove health first.

Yr Tm	W	Sv	IP	K	ERA	xERA	WHIP	xWHIP	vL+	vR+	BF/G	Ctl	Dom	Cmd	Ball%	SwK	Vel	G	L	F	H%	S%	HR/F	xHR/F	GS	APC	DOM%	DIS%	Sv%	LI	RAR	BPX	R$
15 aa	10	0	118	95	2.53	3.32	1.22				22.6	2.3	7.3	3.1							31%	81%									20.8	115	$11
16 DET *	12	0	174	148	3.26	3.40	1.16	1.25	84	93	23.9	2.4	7.7	3.1	36%	10.8%	94.8	49	19	32	28%	76%	11%	13%	26	95	35%	31%			20.0	105	$17
17 DET	10	0	165	114	3.83	4.22	1.15	1.29	90	83	27.0	2.2	6.2	2.9	36%	9.8%	95.8	49	22	29	28%	68%	9%	11%	25	99	36%	32%			10.8	96	$12
18 DET	3	0	132	110	4.69	4.31	1.31	1.34	108	100	23.3	3.1	7.5	2.4	35%	11.1%	95.8	44	22	34	29%	68%	15%	15%	24	90	25%	33%			-8.9	83	-$3
19																																	
1st Half																																	
2nd Half																																	
20 Proj	**4**	**0**	**73**	**58**	**4.06**	**3.92**	**1.28**	**1.29**	**102**	**100**	**24.2**	**2.6**	**7.3**	**2.8**	**35%**	**10.7%**	**95.4**	**45**	**21**	**34**	**30%**	**72%**	**13%**		**12**						**0.8**	**97**	**$0**

Gallegos,Giovanny

Age: 28	Th: R	Role RP	Health A	LIMA Plan B
Ht: 6' 2"	Wt: 210	Type Pwr xFB	PT/Exp D	Rand Var -5
			Consist B	MM 4411

Rose quickly with first extended MLB chance, and though 2nd half was H%/S% heaven, his more neutral 1st half was plenty fine, too. Stellar Cmd history, season-long Ball%/SwK support and ability to steer clear of the HR (ONE long ball surrendered from May 25 to Sept 1) point to potentially a bigger role. With opportunity, UP: 35 Sv

Yr Tm	W	Sv	IP	K	ERA	xERA	WHIP	xWHIP	vL+	vR+	BF/G	Ctl	Dom	Cmd	Ball%	SwK	Vel	G	L	F	H%	S%	HR/F	xHR/F	GS	APC	DOM%	DIS%	Sv%	LI	RAR	BPX	R$
15																																	
16 a/a	7	4	78	88	2.00	2.70	1.04				7.2	2.2	10.1	4.6							29%	87%									21.1	168	$14
17 NYY *	4	5	64	78	3.58	3.72	1.17		108	94	5.8	2.5	11.0	4.5		14.3%	94.1	36	22	42	32%	75%	12%	14%	0	23			63	0.43	6.1	153	$6
18 2 TM *	2	4	56	55	3.29	2.69	1.09		138	81	6.1	2.1	8.8	4.2		9.3%	94.4	34	24	41	30%	70%	17%	15%	0	30			80	0.16	6.0	155	$3
19 STL	3	1	74	93	2.31	3.35	0.81	1.04	68	76	4.2	1.9	11.3	5.8	32%	16.7%	93.7	34	19	47	23%	80%	11%	13%	0	17			25	0.94	20.0	178	$12
1st Half	1	0	38	54	2.63	2.95	0.85	0.89	73	76	4.3	1.7	12.9	7.7	30%	17.2%	93.8	33	24	44	29%	75%	11%	12%	0	18			0	0.63	8.7	216	$9
2nd Half	2	1	36	39	1.98	3.98	0.77	1.11	64	76	4.1	2.2	9.7	4.3	33%	16.0%	93.6	34	15	51	18%	87%	11%	13%	0	17			25	1.26	11.3	138	$15
20 Proj	**4**	**5**	**73**	**83**	**2.68**	**3.21**	**0.95**	**1.02**	**75**	**87**	**4.9**	**2.1**	**10.3**	**4.9**	**32%**	**16.5%**	**93.7**	**34**	**18**	**48**	**27%**	**77%**	**9%**		**0**						**13.1**	**162**	**$10**

BRENT HERSHEY

Gallen,Zac

Age: 24	Th: R	Role SP	Health A	LIMA Plan D
Ht: 6' 2"	Wt: 191	Type FB	PT/Exp D	Rand Var -3
			Consist D	MM 2203

3-6, 2.81 ERA in 80 IP at MIA/ARI. Breakout season at Triple-A and majors due to uptick in velocity and change-up development. Improved his Ball% and strikeout rate throughout season and stayed mostly away from HR barrage, but MLB xERA of 4.09 and S% provide a check on expectations. Solid foundation with room to grow.

Yr Tm	W	Sv	IP	K	ERA	xERA	WHIP	xWHIP	vL+	vR+	BF/G	Ctl	Dom	Cmd	Ball%	SwK	Vel	G	L	F	H%	S%	HR/F	xHR/F	GS	APC	DOM%	DIS%	Sv%	LI	RAR	BPX	R$
15																																	
16																																	
17 a/a	5	0	92	54	4.54	4.96	1.44				23.1	2.4	5.3	2.2							32%	71%									-2.1	51	-$3
18 aaa	8	0	134	117	4.08	5.41	1.59				23.6	3.2	7.9	2.5							37%	76%									1.1	77	-$4
19 2 NL *	12	0	172	190	2.54	2.51	1.01	1.32	88	87	22.7	2.8	9.9	3.5	35%	13.2%	92.9	39	24	37	26%	81%	11%	12%	15	92	27%	7%			41.8	130	$28
1st Half	9	0	102	108	2.42	2.01	0.87		48	89	23.6	2.0	9.5	4.9		13.2%	92.7	24	40	36	24%	79%	0%	7%	2	95	50%	0%			26.2	162	$37
2nd Half	3	0	70	82	2.70	4.13	1.21	1.29	93	85	22.4	4.1	10.5	2.6	35%	13.2%	93.0	41	21	38	28%	83%	12%	12%	13	92	23%	8%			15.6	107	$15
20 Proj	**10**	**0**	**174**	**166**	**3.39**	**3.97**	**1.31**	**1.42**	**97**	**91**	**23.0**	**3.1**	**8.6**	**2.8**	**39%**	**13.2%**	**93.0**	**41**	**21**	**38**	**32%**	**78%**	**9%**		**31**						**16.3**	**103**	**$12**

Gant,John

Age: 27	Th: R	Role RP	Health C	LIMA Plan C
Ht: 6' 3"	Wt: 200	Type Pwr	PT/Exp C	Rand Var -1
			Consist C	MM 1211

Big velocity boost with move to reliever, but four reasons why saves are a longshot: 1) Extra oomph had minuscule effect on SwK; 2) Dom still below par; 3) 1st half Ctl improvement only temporary; 4) 2nd half handed out line drives like candy. Deftly avoided HR; but walk + ringing double serves the same purpose. Trust xERA in this case.

Yr Tm	W	Sv	IP	K	ERA	xERA	WHIP	xWHIP	vL+	vR+	BF/G	Ctl	Dom	Cmd	Ball%	SwK	Vel	G	L	F	H%	S%	HR/F	xHR/F	GS	APC	DOM%	DIS%	Sv%	LI	RAR	BPX	R$
15 aa	8	0	100	76	4.28	4.28	1.53				24.2	3.8	6.9	1.8							34%	71%									-3.9	82	-$4
16 ATL *	4	0	106	99	5.17	5.30	1.60	1.34	104	124	14.6	3.9	8.4	2.2	36%	9.9%	91.8	42	24	34	36%	69%	14%	14%	7	47	14%	29%	0	0.46	-12.8	72	-$8
17 STL *	6	0	121	88	4.81	5.38	1.53		131	109	21.0	2.7	6.6	2.4		10.0%	93.0	54	13	33	35%	71%	22%	8%	2	41	0%	100%	0	0.38	-6.7	62	-$4
18 STL *	12	0	163	128	3.01	3.70	1.33	1.49	90	88	19.9	4.0	7.1	1.7	36%	12.0%	93.3	45	21	34	28%	80%	8%	9%	19	72	16%	26%	0	0.79	22.8	73	$11
19 STL	11	3	66	60	3.66	4.56	1.28	1.52	102	76	4.2	4.6	8.1	1.8	37%	12.6%	95.9	46	27	27	27%	72%	9%	7%	0	17			50	1.17	6.9	50	$6
1st Half	7	3	43	38	2.32	3.78	0.89	1.28	71	64	4.3	3.0	8.0	2.7	35%	12.9%	95.9	48	23	29	20%	77%	10%	6%	0	18			60	1.32	11.5	98	$14
2nd Half	4	0	24	22	6.08	5.90	1.99	1.79	152	95	4.1	7.6	8.4	1.1	39%	12.0%	95.8	44	32	24	37%	67%	6%	8%	0	16			0	0.97	-4.6	-36	-$7
20 Proj	**8**	**7**	**73**	**61**	**4.24**	**4.43**	**1.49**	**1.52**	**109**	**95**	**6.9**	**4.7**	**7.6**	**1.6**	**37%**	**11.8%**	**94.3**	**45**	**25**	**30**	**31%**	**72%**	**8%**		**0**						**-0.8**	**39**	**$2**

Garcia,Jarlin

Age: 27	Th: L	Role RP	Health B	LIMA Plan B
Ht: 6' 3"	Wt: 215	Type Con	PT/Exp D	Rand Var -4
			Consist B	MM 1010

Was getting late-innings work by the end of the season, but this is not an impactful skill set despite impressive surface ratios. Experienced growth in GB%, Ball% and velocity, but just doesn't come up with enough swings and misses to make it work. Made the best of fortunate H%/S% and HR/F in 2019. Unlikely to repeat.

Yr Tm	W	Sv	IP	K	ERA	xERA	WHIP	xWHIP	vL+	vR+	BF/G	Ctl	Dom	Cmd	Ball%	SwK	Vel	G	L	F	H%	S%	HR/F	xHR/F	GS	APC	DOM%	DIS%	Sv%	LI	RAR	BPX	R$
15 aa	1	0	37	30	5.84	5.28	1.64				23.4	4.2	7.3	1.7							35%	64%									-8.5	59	-$8
16 aa	1	0	40	24	5.54	4.53	1.39				18.6	2.6	5.3	2.1							31%	60%									-6.6	55	-$5
17 MIA	1	0	53	42	4.73	4.71	1.20	1.33	80	106	3.3	2.9	7.1	2.5	37%	12.0%	94.2	39	20	41	27%	62%	9%	9%	0	13			0	0.96	-2.4	81	-$2
18 MIA *	5	0	116	67	5.15	5.36	1.44	1.53	109	110	12.7	3.3	5.2	1.6	38%	8.3%	92.1	43	20	37	29%	69%	21%	23%	7	36	0%	29%	0	0.86	-14.4	18	-$8
19 MIA	4	0	51	39	3.02	4.61	1.11	1.38	79	81	3.9	2.8	6.9	2.4	35%	9.1%	93.3	47	18	35	26%	75%	8%	13%	0	14			0	0.90	9.3	79	$3
1st Half	2	0	22	16	3.63	4.79	1.12	1.36	65	89	5.1	2.8	6.4	2.3	36%	8.9%	93.3	49	15	36	27%	67%	4%	8%	0	19			0	0.48	2.4	73	$0
2nd Half	2	0	28	23	2.54	4.45	1.09	1.32	89	73	3.3	2.9	7.3	2.6	34%	9.3%	93.4	45	21	35	25%	82%	11%	18%	0	12			0	1.12	6.9	84	$5
20 Proj	**3**	**2**	**58**	**42**	**4.53**	**4.37**	**1.35**	**1.40**	**99**	**104**	**5.0**	**3.0**	**6.5**	**2.1**	**37%**	**9.3%**	**93.0**	**44**	**19**	**37**	**30%**	**69%**	**11%**		**0**						**-2.7**	**66**	**-$2**

Garcia,Yimi

Age: 29	Th: R	Role RP	Health F	LIMA Plan D
Ht: 6' 0"	Wt: 225	Type xFB	PT/Exp D	Rand Var -3
			Consist D	MM 2300

Made some 2nd half strides as Dom took off—but on second look, sub-indicators didn't budge. Gets a lot of Ctl mileage out of purely "meh" Ball%, but according to LI, pitched in bigger spots as the season wore on. But with that FB%, do you trust him with the game on the line, knowing that H%/S% will come calling at some point? Me neither.

Yr Tm	W	Sv	IP	K	ERA	xERA	WHIP	xWHIP	vL+	vR+	BF/G	Ctl	Dom	Cmd	Ball%	SwK	Vel	G	L	F	H%	S%	HR/F	xHR/F	GS	APC	DOM%	DIS%	Sv%	LI	RAR	BPX	R$
15 LA	3	1	57	68	3.34	3.35	0.95	1.00	80	84	3.8	1.6	10.8	6.8	31%	15.3%	93.4	28	17	54	28%	72%	10%	11%	1	14	0%	100%	17	1.05	4.4	188	$4
16 LA	0	0	8	4	3.24	4.93	1.20		110	70	3.9	1.1	4.3	4.0		9.4%	92.8	35	19	46	32%	70%	0%	6%	0	14			0	0.87	1.0	73	-$4
17																																	
18 LA *	2	1	39	30	5.26	6.16	1.36		113	146	4.1	0.9	7.0	7.5		12.4%	94.5	36	21	43	33%	69%	21%	23%	0	16			33	0.56	-5.3	146	-$5
19 LA	1	0	62	66	3.61	4.24	0.87	1.16	91	88	3.9	2.0	9.5	4.7	34%	12.4%	94.2	30	14	56	19%	74%	17%	11%	0	16			0	0.63	6.9	136	$4
1st Half	0	0	32	29	4.22	4.78	0.81	1.23	87	84	3.8	2.5	8.2	3.2	34%	12.2%	94.4	33	9	59	13%	61%	17%	13%	0	16			0	0.51	1.1	98	$1
2nd Half	1	0	30	37	2.97	3.97	0.92	0.99	97	91	3.9	1.5	11.0	7.4	34%	12.7%	94.1	26	21	53	25%	86%	17%	9%	0	15			0	0.75	5.8	176	$7
20 Proj	**2**	**0**	**65**	**65**	**4.11**	**4.02**	**1.22**	**1.05**	**110**	**110**	**3.9**	**2.1**	**9.0**	**4.3**	**33%**	**13.6%**	**93.9**	**29**	**16**	**55**	**30%**	**76%**	**14%**		**0**						**0.3**	**130**	**$0**

Garrett,Amir

Age: 28	Th: L	Role RP	Health C	LIMA Plan D
Ht: 6' 5"	Wt: 228	Type Pwr	PT/Exp D	Rand Var 0
			Consist D	MM 2400

On the rise: velocity, strikeout and walk rates, off-the-mound sprint speed, left hooks and overall drama. Wacky 1st half strand rate kept seasonal ERA respectable; but it's the mid-90s fastball, big GB spike and low xHR/F that continue to whisper "What if?" But will need to overcome being better known for boxing and basketball than his pitching.

Yr Tm	W	Sv	IP	K	ERA	xERA	WHIP	xWHIP	vL+	vR+	BF/G	Ctl	Dom	Cmd	Ball%	SwK	Vel	G	L	F	H%	S%	HR/F	xHR/F	GS	APC	DOM%	DIS%	Sv%	LI	RAR	BPX	R$
15																																	
16 a/a	7	0	145	114	3.60	3.30	1.33				24.0	4.2	7.1	1.7							28%	73%									10.4	84	$6
17 CIN *	5	0	138	115	7.42	6.79	1.71	1.53	126	126	20.9	4.3	7.4	1.7	38%	9.1%	91.7	43	18	38	33%	60%	28%	18%	14	77	14%	50%	0	0.77	-52.3	15	-$22
18 CIN	1	0	63	71	4.29	3.82	1.29	1.25	99	103	4.0	3.6	10.1	2.8	39%	14.3%	95.1	38	25	37	31%	70%	13%	11%	0	15			0	0.97	-1.1	118	-$2
19 CIN	5	0	56	78	3.21	3.72	1.41	1.39	84	99	3.6	5.6	12.5	2.2	39%	16.6%	95.3	54	18	28	32%	82%	19%	12%	0	14			0	1.47	8.9	115	$2
1st Half	3	0	36	51	1.75	3.29	1.25	1.28	71	94	3.7	5.0	12.8	2.6	39%	16.6%	95.3	52	21	27	30%	90%	14%	7%	0	15			0	1.39	12.2	136	$6
2nd Half	2	0	20	27	5.85	4.39	1.70	1.49	120	104	3.4	6.8	12.2	1.8	40%	16.4%	95.4	57	14	29	34%	70%	27%	19%	0	13			0	1.58	-3.3	78	-$5
20 Proj	**4**	**0**	**58**	**68**	**4.65**	**3.77**	**1.47**	**1.37**	**99**	**107**	**4.5**	**5.0**	**10.6**	**2.1**	**39%**	**14.6%**	**94.7**	**47**	**20**	**33**	**32%**	**72%**	**18%**		**0**						**-3.6**	**93**	**-$3**

Gausman,Kevin

Age: 29	Th: R	Role RP	Health D	LIMA Plan A
Ht: 6' 3"	Wt: 190	Type Pwr	PT/Exp A	Rand Var +5
			Consist A	MM 3410

Reasons to continue the 2nd half bullpen experiment: 1) In fastball/splitter, has two outstanding pitches; 2) threw a ton more strikes and Cmd more than doubled; 3) whiffs were up and Ks followed; 4) fluky LD%, H% and S% ruined his decimals and hid the growth. Should be no doubt on his most impactful role. With opportunity, UP: 25 Sv

Yr Tm	W	Sv	IP	K	ERA	xERA	WHIP	xWHIP	vL+	vR+	BF/G	Ctl	Dom	Cmd	Ball%	SwK	Vel	G	L	F	H%	S%	HR/F	xHR/F	GS	APC	DOM%	DIS%	Sv%	LI	RAR	BPX	R$
15 BAL *	4	0	130	118	4.28	4.42	1.25	1.21	88	119	18.2	2.5	8.2	3.3	36%	11.6%	95.3	44	17	38	30%	72%	13%	14%	17	75	35%	24%	0	0.72	-5.2	88	$0
16 BAL	9	0	180	174	3.61	3.84	1.28	1.19	89	111	25.2	2.4	8.7	3.7	36%	11.3%	94.7	44	21	35	32%	78%	15%	16%	30	104	30%	20%			12.9	137	$11
17 BAL	11	0	187	179	4.68	4.44	1.49	1.32	107	109	24.0	3.4	8.6	2.5	37%	11.3%	95.0	43	22	35	34%	73%	15%	15%	34	99	29%	35%			-7.3	101	$0
18 2 TM	10	0	184	148	3.92	4.21	1.30	1.28	98	110	25.0	2.5	7.3	3.0	35%	11.6%	93.6	46	21	33	31%	75%	14%	16%	31	97	26%	42%			5.2	102	$6
19 2 NL	3	0	102	114	5.72	4.23	1.42	1.24	105	106	14.5	2.8	10.0	3.6	33%	15.5%	94.0	38	27	35	36%	62%	15%	17%	17	54	29%	41%	0	0.79	-15.3	131	-$6
1st Half	2	0	62	64	6.21	4.71	1.51	1.29	105	111	21.8	3.5	9.2	2.7	34%	14.1%	93.9	41	23	36	36%	59%	12%	14%	13	78	31%	38%			-13.1	100	-$8
2nd Half	1	0	40	50	4.95	3.56	1.28	1.02	103	98	9.3	1.8	11.3	6.3	30%	17.7%	94.1	31	35	35	36%	66%	19%	22%	4	36	25%	50%	0	0.81	-2.2	177	-$2
20 Proj	**3**	**2**	**65**	**71**	**4.11**	**3.52**	**1.31**	**1.20**	**99**	**104**	**7.2**	**2.6**	**9.7**	**3.7**	**34%**	**14.5%**	**94.2**	**40**	**23**	**37**	**33%**	**74%**	**15%**		**0**						**0.3**	**141**	**$0**

Gaviglio,Sam

Age: 30	Th: R	Role RP	Health A	LIMA Plan B
Ht: 6' 2"	Wt: 205	Type Con	PT/Exp C	Rand Var +2
			Consist B	MM 2101

Sinker/slider reliever added a tick of velocity and several ticks of swing and miss, and now sports a very good Cmd. But he'll likely continue to run into HR problems despite a GB tendency. That ERA/xERA and Dom history makes it tough to take the leap unless he proves the SwK can be sustained. Best left for someone else to find out.

Yr Tm	W	Sv	IP	K	ERA	xERA	WHIP	xWHIP	vL+	vR+	BF/G	Ctl	Dom	Cmd	Ball%	SwK	Vel	G	L	F	H%	S%	HR/F	xHR/F	GS	APC	DOM%	DIS%	Sv%	LI	RAR	BPX	R$
15 aaa	8	0	102	67	4.82	4.47	1.35				20.2	2.8	5.9	2.1							30%	67%									-10.8	54	-$3
16 a/a	8	0	165	102	4.99	4.80	1.43				25.0	2.1	5.5	2.7							33%	66%									-16.2	69	-$5
17 2 AL *	7	0	146	95	4.59	4.95	1.38	1.42	111	116	21.2	2.4	5.8	2.5	37%	7.6%	88.6	49	18	32	31%	71%	21%	17%	13	73	0%	54%	0	0.64	-4.1	53	-$1
18 TOR *	3	0	153	127	4.83	5.19	1.38	1.29	109	113	20.7	2.5	7.5	3.0	37%	8.9%	88.0	49	19	32	32%	70%	17%	15%	24	79	8%	54%	0	0.81	-12.8	68	-$6
19 TOR	4	0	96	88	4.61	4.15	1.12	1.23	105	89	7.5	2.1	8.3	4.0	34%	12.1%	89.3	47	16	37	27%	65%	18%	17%	0	27			0	0.42	-1.2	129	$3
1st Half	4	0	55	48	4.58	4.24	1.15	1.14	117	97	8.1	1.5	7.9	5.3	34%	11.9%	89.2	47	15	38	28%	70%	21%	21%	0	29			0	0.35	-0.5	138	$4
2nd Half	0	0	41	40	4.65	4.10	1.08	1.24	86	77	6.9	2.9	8.9	3.1	34%	12.3%	89.4	47	17	35	26%	59%	13%	11%	0	26			0	0.51	-0.7	117	$0
20 Proj	**3**	**0**	**87**	**73**	**4.59**	**3.81**	**1.29**	**1.26**	**106**	**100**	**10.9**	**2.4**	**7.5**	**3.2**	**35%**	**10.2%**	**88.7**	**48**	**18**	**34**	**30%**	**69%**	**16%**		**3**						**-4.8**	**112**	**-$2**

BRENT HERSHEY

German,Domingo			Health	B	LIMA Plan	A
Age: 27	Th: R	Role SP	PT/Exp	C	Rand Var	+2
Ht: 6' 2"	Wt: 175	Type Pwr FB	Consist	A	MM	3403

Missed time with June hip strain and Sept alleged domestic violence incident, but otherwise met the workload challenge. Ball% didn't support Ctl improvement, but fewer walks kept runners off base—a good thing considering his HR/F and FB%. A solid K-per-inning starter, though unlikely to win 18 again and Opening Day status an open question.

Yr	Tm	W	Sv	IP	K	ERA	xERA	WHIP	xWHIP	vL+	vR+	BF/G	Ctl	Dom	Cmd	Ball%	SwK	Vel	G	L	F	H%	S%	HR/F	xHR/F	GS	APC	DOM%	DIS%	Sv%	LI	RAR	BPX	R$
15																																		
16																																		
17	NYY *	8	0	124	117	4.05	4.50	1.40		82	94	19.3	3.3	8.5	2.6		11.5%	96.4	55	21	24	33%	74%	13%	8%	0	36			0	0.35	4.7	89	$3
18	NYY	2	0	86	102	5.57	3.94	1.33	1.22	114	100	17.9	3.5	10.7	3.1	35%	15.2%	94.7	37	22	40	32%	62%	16%	12%	14	70	14%	36%	0	0.68	-15.0	132	-$6
19	NYY	18	0	143	153	4.03	4.15	1.15	1.21	103	87	22.0	2.5	9.6	3.9	34%	13.4%	93.6	38	21	41	28%	75%	19%	15%	24	83	25%	13%	0	0.90	8.4	134	$16
1st Half		9	0	70	77	3.86	4.06	1.11	1.15	85	92	22.4	2.4	9.9	4.1	34%	14.3%	93.7	39	23	38	28%	73%	16%	15%	12	85	25%	8%	0	0.80	5.6	141	$16
2nd Half		9	0	73	76	4.19	4.33	1.18	1.17	122	83	21.6	2.5	9.4	3.8	34%	12.6%	93.5	37	19	43	27%	76%	21%	16%	12	82	25%	17%	0	0.99	2.8	128	$16
20	**Proj**	**12**	**0**	**145**	**156**	**4.09**	**3.58**	**1.24**	**1.18**	**109**	**93**	**21.1**	**2.7**	**9.7**	**3.6**	**34%**	**14.1%**	**94.0**	**38**	**21**	**41**	**30%**	**75%**	**17%**		**24**						**1.0**	**135**	**$10**

Gibson,Kyle			Health	C	LIMA Plan	B
Age: 32	Th: R	Role SP	PT/Exp	A	Rand Var	+5
Ht: 6' 6"	Wt: 215	Type Pwr GB	Consist	B	MM	2305

Another incremental step in SwK pushed Dom and Cmd to a career high; is he a candidate for early-30s breakout? PRO: Established GBer; velocity ticked up also; xERA stable. CON: Ball% firmly worse than league average, which is bad when you give up this many line drives and HR. Even if he lands with a superb infield defense, this is his ceiling.

Yr	Tm	W	Sv	IP	K	ERA	xERA	WHIP	xWHIP	vL+	vR+	BF/G	Ctl	Dom	Cmd	Ball%	SwK	Vel	G	L	F	H%	S%	HR/F	xHR/F	GS	APC	DOM%	DIS%	Sv%	LI	RAR	BPX	R$
15	MIN	11	0	195	145	3.84	3.94	1.29	1.36	96	98	25.7	3.0	6.7	2.2	38%	10.1%	91.8	53	20	27	29%	72%	11%	12%	32	101	31%	31%			3.0	84	$7
16	MIN	6	0	147	104	5.07	4.70	1.56	1.42	120	104	26.1	3.4	6.4	1.9	39%	10.0%	91.0	49	23	29	33%	70%	14%	15%	25	99	16%	56%			-16.0	60	-$9
17	MIN *	13	0	175	137	4.93	5.34	1.53	1.40	110	111	23.8	3.4	7.0	2.1	38%	10.4%	92.0	51	23	26	33%	71%	18%	18%	29	90	17%	45%			-12.3	52	-$3
18	MIN	10	0	197	179	3.62	4.00	1.30	1.35	100	94	25.8	3.6	8.2	2.3	40%	11.7%	93.0	50	22	28	29%	76%	15%	15%	32	101	22%	28%			13.0	90	$10
19	MIN	13	0	160	160	4.84	4.08	1.44	1.30	107	100	20.8	3.2	9.0	2.9	38%	13.4%	93.3	51	25	24	34%	70%	20%	21%	29	81	21%	31%	0	0.88	-6.6	115	$2
1st Half		8	0	88	88	4.21	3.80	1.23	1.18	96	95	23.0	2.4	9.0	3.8	38%	14.1%	93.3	47	25	27	31%	70%	18%	21%	15	88	27%	27%	0	0.87	3.2	135	$10
2nd Half		5	0	72	72	5.60	4.29	1.70	1.37	121	105	18.8	4.1	9.0	2.2	39%	12.7%	93.4	56	24	20	37%	70%	24%	20%	14	75	14%	36%	0	0.89	-9.8	92	-$8
20	**Proj**	**13**	**0**	**189**	**183**	**4.47**	**3.68**	**1.42**	**1.33**	**106**	**99**	**21.6**	**3.4**	**8.7**	**2.5**	**39%**	**12.7%**	**92.9**	**50**	**21**	**28**	**33%**	**72%**	**17%**		**37**						**-7.3**	**107**	**$3**

Giles,Ken			Health	A	LIMA Plan	A
Age: 29	Th: R	Role RP	PT/Exp	B	Rand Var	-5
Ht: 6' 3"	Wt: 210	Type Pwr	Consist	A	MM	5530

Seems curiously undervalued each year, when in fact his skills are remarkably consistent: 1) High-90s heat; 2) elite SwK; 3) yearly 4.0+ Cmd; 4) minimal platoon split; 5) ability to dodge the longball (in HR-friendly home parks, no less). That's what you want from a closer, right? Reliabilty ratings; a BPX scan confirm ... UP: 45 Sv

Yr	Tm	W	Sv	IP	K	ERA	xERA	WHIP	xWHIP	vL+	vR+	BF/G	Ctl	Dom	Cmd	Ball%	SwK	Vel	G	L	F	H%	S%	HR/F	xHR/F	GS	APC	DOM%	DIS%	Sv%	LI	RAR	BPX	R$
15	PHI	6	15	70	87	1.80	3.24	1.20	1.17	79	80	4.3	3.2	11.2	3.5	35%	15.2%	96.5	45	22	33	34%	85%	3%	9%	0	17			75	1.15	18.7	164	$14
16	HOU	2	15	66	102	4.11	2.96	1.29	1.07	80	112	4.1	3.4	14.0	4.1	33%	20.2%	97.2	40	25	36	38%	71%	15%	12%	0	16			75	1.25	0.6	210	$7
17	HOU	1	34	63	83	2.30	3.11	1.04	1.09	77	74	3.9	3.0	11.9	4.0	33%	16.6%	98.1	44	18	38	30%	80%	7%	7%	0	15			89	1.11	15.9	186	$21
18	2 AL	0	20	50	53	4.65	3.40	1.21	1.06	89	110	3.9	1.3	9.5	7.6	30%	16.4%	97.3	44	20	36	35%	64%	11%	14%	0	14			100	0.99	-3.1	183	$7
19	TOR	2	23	53	83	1.87	2.87	1.00	1.01	75	77	3.9	2.9	14.1	4.9	33%	19.3%	97.0	39	19	42	32%	88%	11%	12%	0	15			96	1.10	17.2	210	$17
1st Half		1	12	28	49	1.29	2.52	1.04	0.88	53	100	4.0	2.6	15.8	6.1	33%	21.4%	97.4	41	19	41	40%	89%	5%	10%	0	16			92	1.16	11.1	254	$16
2nd Half		1	11	25	34	2.52	3.43	0.96	1.10	102	53	3.9	3.2	12.2	3.8	34%	16.6%	96.5	38	19	43	23%	85%	17%	15%	0	14			100	1.03	6.1	162	$17
20	**Proj**	**2**	**30**	**58**	**79**	**2.82**	**2.78**	**1.08**	**1.04**	**83**	**84**	**3.8**	**2.6**	**12.2**	**4.7**	**32%**	**17.7%**	**97.1**	**41**	**19**	**39**	**32%**	**78%**	**12%**		**0**						**9.6**	**195**	**$17**

Ginkel,Kevin			Health	A	LIMA Plan	A
Age: 26	Th: R	Role RP	PT/Exp	F	Rand Var	-5
Ht: 6' 4"	Wt: 210	Type Pwr xFB	Consist	A	MM	4500

3-0, 1.48 ERA with 2 Sv in 24 IP at ARI. Rode a four-seamer and swing-and-miss slider to the majors and was quickly thrust into significant late-inning role (LI). Deft command is his ticket—totaled 91 K vs. 23 BB across 80 IP in 2019—with velocity to boot. Will need to keep tabs on fly balls, but skills worth keeping an eye on.

Yr	Tm	W	Sv	IP	K	ERA	xERA	WHIP	xWHIP	vL+	vR+	BF/G	Ctl	Dom	Cmd	Ball%	SwK	Vel	G	L	F	H%	S%	HR/F	xHR/F	GS	APC	DOM%	DIS%	Sv%	LI	RAR	BPX	R$
15																																		
16																																		
17																																		
18	aa	5	5	44	50	1.98	1.86	0.90				4.8	1.9	10.1	5.3							27%	82%									11.8	196	$8
19	ARI *	5	13	61	78	1.81	2.11	0.98	1.26	81	62	4.3	3.3	11.5	3.4	39%	14.4%	93.5	34	24	41	25%	89%	8%	9%	0	16			93	1.11	20.2	146	$15
1st Half		2	6	26	35	2.01	2.06	0.90		0	0	4.9	2.5	12.1	4.8							25%	87%	0%		0	0					8.1	176	$10
2nd Half		3	7	35	42	1.65	2.14	1.04	1.21	81	61	3.9	4.0	11.1	2.8	39%	14.4%	93.5	34	24	41	24%	90%	8%	9%	0	16			100	1.11	12.2	132	$19
20	**Proj**	**3**	**0**	**29**	**35**	**3.12**	**3.30**	**1.11**	**1.33**	**105**	**66**	**4.7**	**2.7**	**10.9**	**4.0**	**43%**	**14.4%**	**93.5**	**34**	**24**	**41**	**29%**	**80%**	**14%**		**0**						**3.7**	**156**	**$0**

Giolito,Lucas			Health	C	LIMA Plan	C
Age: 25	Th: R	Role SP	PT/Exp	B	Rand Var	0
Ht: 6' 6"	Wt: 245	Type Pwr FB	Consist	C	MM	4505

Showed up in Feb with a shorter arm stroke and entered a new world of more strikes, more missed bats, more mph, and eventually more BF/G. Most exciting? Nearly every metric improved in the 2nd half—advance scouting reports, pressure of success, and a long season be damned—which points to repeatability. Took a while, but he's arrived.

Yr	Tm	W	Sv	IP	K	ERA	xERA	WHIP	xWHIP	vL+	vR+	BF/G	Ctl	Dom	Cmd	Ball%	SwK	Vel	G	L	F	H%	S%	HR/F	xHR/F	GS	APC	DOM%	DIS%	Sv%	LI	RAR	BPX	R$
15	aa	4	0	47	38	4.63	4.44	1.52				25.7	3.3	7.3	2.2							36%	68%									-3.9	90	-$4
16	WAS *	6	0	130	108	4.31	4.93	1.57		119	152	21.1	4.1	7.5	1.8		6.3%	93.4	41	27	32	34%	74%	29%	21%	4	66	0%	75%	0	0.68	-1.9	65	-$4
17	CHW *	9	0	174	152	4.49	4.63	1.40	1.29	84	88	23.7	3.9	7.9	2.0	36%	10.7%	92.1	45	20	35	30%	72%	18%	11%	7	101	29%	14%			-2.8	62	$2
18	CHW	10	0	173	125	6.13	5.33	1.48	1.57	114	105	24.2	4.7	6.5	1.4	40%	8.6%	92.4	44	18	37	28%	60%	13%	14%	32	94	16%	41%			-42.3	15	-$14
19	CHW	14	0	177	228	3.41	3.60	1.06	1.15	74	96	24.3	2.9	11.6	4.0	34%	15.5%	94.3	36	21	43	28%	74%	14%	12%	29	97	38%	10%			23.8	158	$24
1st Half		11	0	96	115	2.72	3.78	1.02	1.16	66	86	23.7	3.1	10.8	3.5	34%	14.5%	94.2	37	22	41	26%	78%	10%	8%	16	94	50%	19%			21.2	137	$33
2nd Half		3	0	81	113	4.24	3.51	1.12	1.04	84	108	25.1	2.7	12.6	4.7	33%	16.7%	94.4	34	20	45	31%	69%	18%	16%	13	101	23%	0%			2.6	182	$14
20	**Proj**	**12**	**0**	**189**	**230**	**3.61**	**3.18**	**1.13**	**1.28**	**88**	**96**	**22.8**	**3.0**	**11.0**	**3.7**	**36%**	**13.5%**	**93.3**	**40**	**20**	**40**	**29%**	**74%**	**15%**		**33**						**12.7**	**156**	**$20**

Givens,Mychal			Health	A	LIMA Plan	A
Age: 30	Th: R	Role RP	PT/Exp	C	Rand Var	+5
Ht: 6' 0"	Wt: 210	Type Pwr	Consist	A	MM	3520

Increased effectiveness (23% SwK) and frequency of change-up led to elite SwK/Dom. Pull up a chair for the But List, though: stubborn Ball%/Ctl, widening platoon splits, gobs of line drives, notorious inconsistency (ERAs by month: 4.82/6.39/3.68/2.79/2.70/6.35). Expect premium velocity/Ks; some saves—and bring a seat cushion.

Yr	Tm	W	Sv	IP	K	ERA	xERA	WHIP	xWHIP	vL+	vR+	BF/G	Ctl	Dom	Cmd	Ball%	SwK	Vel	G	L	F	H%	S%	HR/F	xHR/F	GS	APC	DOM%	DIS%	Sv%	LI	RAR	BPX	R$
15	BAL *	6	15	87	101	2.19	2.07	1.05	0.99	76	74	5.9	2.4	10.4	4.3	33%	12.7%	94.3	39	30	31	31%	79%	5%	5%	0	21			88	0.79	19.0	187	$18
16	BAL	8	0	75	96	3.13	3.64	1.27	1.27	139	69	4.7	4.3	11.6	2.7	35%	15.3%	94.3	35	25	39	32%	78%	9%	8%	0	20			0	1.10	9.7	124	$6
17	BAL	8	0	79	88	2.75	3.61	1.04	1.17	82	83	4.6	2.9	10.1	3.5	36%	12.5%	95.6	43	17	40	26%	81%	13%	12%	0	19			0	1.13	15.6	150	$11
18	BAL	0	9	77	79	3.99	4.07	1.19	1.29	94	81	4.6	3.5	9.3	2.6	34%	12.1%	95.1	36	24	39	29%	66%	5%	8%	0	18			69	1.34	1.5	99	$3
19	BAL	2	11	63	86	4.57	3.62	1.19	1.20	122	79	4.5	3.7	12.3	3.3	35%	16.7%	95.3	38	23	39	28%	69%	23%	18%	0	19			58	1.45	-0.5	149	$5
1st Half		0	6	32	46	5.06	3.79	1.31	1.19	101	110	4.9	4.2	12.9	3.1	36%	16.0%	95.1	38	20	42	30%	71%	26%	19%	0	20			55	1.65	-2.2	147	$1
2nd Half		2	5	31	40	4.06	3.50	1.06	1.13	141	41	4.1	3.2	11.6	3.6	35%	17.4%	95.6	38	25	37	26%	68%	19%	18%	0	17			63	1.27	1.7	151	$9
20	**Proj**	**3**	**24**	**58**	**69**	**3.91**	**3.47**	**1.24**	**1.19**	**120**	**82**	**4.5**	**3.6**	**10.7**	**3.0**	**35%**	**14.8%**	**95.2**	**38**	**23**	**39**	**30%**	**74%**	**16%**		**0**						**1.7**	**128**	**$11**

Glasnow,Tyler			Health	F	LIMA Plan	B
Age: 26	Th: R	Role SP	PT/Exp	C	Rand Var	-4
Ht: 6' 8"	Wt: 230	Type Pwr	Consist	B	MM	5401

Early on, newfound Cmd due to tightened delivery had many (justifiably) abuzz. But a seemingly minor early-May forearm strain stretched all the way into September. Dominates almost exclusively with top-scale FB and elite-spin CB (combined 97% usage) which often points to a bullpen role. Sky-high ceiling, but with more risk than you may realize.

Yr	Tm	W	Sv	IP	K	ERA	xERA	WHIP	xWHIP	vL+	vR+	BF/G	Ctl	Dom	Cmd	Ball%	SwK	Vel	G	L	F	H%	S%	HR/F	xHR/F	GS	APC	DOM%	DIS%	Sv%	LI	RAR	BPX	R$
15	a/a	7	0	104	108	2.78	2.52	1.19				20.8	3.4	9.3	2.7							30%	76%									15.2	138	$9
16	PIT *	8	0	140	141	2.82	3.03	1.36		110	102	20.2	5.5	9.1	1.7		12.1%	93.5	48	21	32	28%	80%	10%	12%	4	63	0%	50%	0	0.55	23.6	104	$10
17	PIT *	11	0	155	167	4.64	4.59	1.48	1.65	139	128	22.3	4.6	9.7	2.1	41%	8.4%	94.6	43	21	36	33%	71%	18%	16%	13	81	8%	54%	0	0.81	-5.4	86	$1
18	2 TM	2	0	112	136	4.27	3.46	1.27	1.29	93	97	10.4	4.3	11.0	2.6	39%	12.2%	96.6	50	20	30	29%	70%	18%	21%	11	41	27%	9%	0	0.56	-1.7	127	$1
19	TAM	6	0	61	76	1.78	2.95	0.89	1.05	55	78	19.2	2.1	11.3	5.4	35%	12.1%	97.0	50	16	34	27%	84%	9%	11%	12	75	58%	8%			20.4	190	$11
1st Half		6	0	48	55	1.86	3.03	0.91	1.02	62	75	22.9	1.7	10.2	6.1	34%	12.1%	96.7	52	18	31	28%	83%	8%	10%	8	87	63%	13%			15.8	184	$14
2nd Half		0	0	12	21	1.46	2.81	0.81		33	98	11.8	3.6	15.3	4.2		11.9%	97.6	43	5	52	22%	89%	9%	13%	4	53	50%	0%			4.6	216	-$3
20	**Proj**	**9**	**0**	**116**	**129**	**3.27**	**3.03**	**1.08**	**1.34**	**86**	**82**	**20.1**	**2.4**	**10.0**	**4.1**	**38%**	**10.5%**	**95.8**	**48**	**20**	**33**	**29%**	**73%**	**12%**		**23**						**12.6**	**161**	**$13**

BRENT HERSHEY

Gonsolin,Tony	Health	A	LIMA Plan	C
Age: 26 Th: R Role RP	PT/Exp	F	Rand Var	0
Ht: 6' 3" Wt: 205 Type Pwr xFB	Consist	C	MM	1201

4-2, 2.93 ERA in 40 IP at LA. Mid-rotation SP prospect with high-spin fastball and three plus breaking pitches. Solid debut, but before we go gaga: intriguing SwK was boosted by appearances as RP; MLB 22% H% reveals just how lucky he got on batted balls; Ball% and Ctl just okay; LD% unsustainable; BPX meh. Interesting, but don't overpay.

Yr Tm	W	Sv	IP	K	ERA	xERA	WHIP	xWHIP	vL+	vR+	BF/G	Ctl	Dom	Cmd	Ball%	SwK	Vel	G	L	F	H%	S%	HR/F	xHR/F	GS	APC	DOM%	DIS%	Sv%	LI	RAR	BPX	R$
15																																	
16																																	
17																																	
18 aa	6	0	45	41	2.58	2.64	1.10				19.7	2.9	8.3	2.8							27%	79%									8.8	119	$4
19 LA *	6	1	82	78	3.83	3.67	1.30	1.38	75	79	14.1	3.8	8.6	2.3	39%	12.3%	93.7	42	15	44	29%	73%	9%	9%	6	63	17%	50%	100	0.65	6.8	87	$3
1st Half	1	0	30	29	3.84	3.74	1.35		143	81	13.9	3.6	8.6	2.4		13.0%	94.5	67	7	27	32%	72%	25%	7%	1	77	0%	100%			2.5	96	-$5
2nd Half	5	1	52	50	3.83	3.64	1.27	1.36	64	78	14.2	3.9	8.6	2.2	39%	12.2%	93.6	38	16	46	28%	73%	7%	9%	5	62	20%	40%	100	0.64	4.3	83	$8
20 Proj	**11**	**0**	**116**	**109**	**3.89**	**4.39**	**1.36**	**1.49**	**88**	**109**	**19.7**	**3.7**	**8.5**	**2.3**	**43%**	**12.2%**	**93.6**	**36**	**21**	**44**	**30%**	**76%**	**11%**		**24**						**3.8**	**75**	**$5**

Gonzales,Marco	Health	A	LIMA Plan	C
Age: 28 Th: L Role SP	PT/Exp	B	Rand Var	-1
Ht: 6' 1" Wt: 195 Type Con	Consist	C	MM	1103

When your average fastball velocity is a number usually reserved for public radio stations, you don't have much margin for error. Gave back most skills gains from 2018 and even lost a tick. One of only 15 SP to crack 200 IP, but then you see the xERA and xWHIP and rightly wonder if that's a good thing. Consider this your PSA... DN: 5.00 ERA

Yr Tm	W	Sv	IP	K	ERA	xERA	WHIP	xWHIP	vL+	vR+	BF/G	Ctl	Dom	Cmd	Ball%	SwK	Vel	G	L	F	H%	S%	HR/F	xHR/F	GS	APC	DOM%	DIS%	Sv%	LI	RAR	BPX	R$
15 STL *	1	0	79	52	5.67	6.53	1.75		69	181	21.1	2.8	5.9	2.1		3.0%	89.4	36	36	29	38%	69%	25%	34%	1	66	0%	100%			-16.5	38	-$14
16																																	
17 2 TM *	9	0	120	88	4.52	4.60	1.37	1.29	110	129	21.0	2.5	6.6	2.6	36%	9.7%	91.5	45	23	32	32%	70%	18%	14%	8	64	0%	75%	0	0.59	-2.3	73	$1
18 SEA	13	0	167	145	4.00	3.71	1.22	1.17	95	101	23.7	1.7	7.8	4.5	32%	9.7%	90.1	45	25	30	32%	70%	11%	13%	29	88	28%	14%			3.2	135	$9
19 SEA	16	0	203	147	3.99	5.11	1.31	1.38	108	95	25.5	2.5	6.5	2.6	34%	8.3%	88.9	41	21	38	31%	72%	9%	10%	34	95	26%	32%			12.9	75	$12
1st Half	9	0	107	76	4.39	5.35	1.40	1.34	101	105	24.4	2.6	6.4	2.5	33%	7.5%	88.7	40	21	39	32%	70%	8%	12%	19	90	16%	37%			1.6	68	$9
2nd Half	7	0	96	71	3.55	4.87	1.21	1.29	116	84	26.8	2.3	6.6	2.8	34%	9.1%	89.2	42	22	36	29%	75%	11%	8%	15	101	40%	27%			11.4	83	$15
20 Proj	**12**	**0**	**174**	**132**	**4.55**	**4.17**	**1.35**	**1.26**	**106**	**101**	**23.5**	**2.5**	**6.8**	**2.7**	**34%**	**9.1%**	**89.8**	**42**	**23**	**35**	**31%**	**69%**	**11%**		**31**						**-8.5**	**86**	**$3**

Gonzalez,Gio	Health	D	LIMA Plan	A
Age: 34 Th: L Role SP	PT/Exp	B	Rand Var	0
Ht: 6' 0" Wt: 205 Type	Consist	A	MM	2203

3-2, 3.50 ERA in 87 IP at MIL. Signed late and pitched effectively before missing seven weeks due to arm fatigue. Second half xWHIP veered into troubling territory as scary Ball% pointed to a Ctl that could easily have topped 5.0. Sure, he keeps the ball on the ground with change-up heavy pitch mix, but there are better bets for a buck.

Yr Tm	W	Sv	IP	K	ERA	xERA	WHIP	xWHIP	vL+	vR+	BF/G	Ctl	Dom	Cmd	Ball%	SwK	Vel	G	L	F	H%	S%	HR/F	xHR/F	GS	APC	DOM%	DIS%	Sv%	LI	RAR	BPX	R$
15 WAS	11	0	176	169	3.79	3.66	1.42	1.32	88	103	24.5	3.5	8.7	2.4	37%	10.2%	92.0	54	20	27	35%	73%	6%	12%	31	95	23%	29%			3.7	110	$4
16 WAS	11	0	177	171	4.57	3.87	1.34	1.26	86	103	23.9	3.0	8.7	2.9	39%	10.0%	90.8	48	23	30	33%	68%	13%	15%	32	97	28%	31%			-8.3	120	$3
17 WAS	15	0	201	188	2.96	4.17	1.18	1.34	67	92	25.8	3.5	8.4	2.4	40%	9.1%	89.9	46	19	35	27%	79%	11%	11%	32	105	38%	16%			34.8	96	$25
18 2 NL	10	0	171	148	4.21	4.61	1.44	1.44	82	107	23.3	4.2	7.8	1.9	40%	10.0%	89.8	45	23	32	31%	73%	10%	14%	32	94	13%	38%			-1.3	57	$0
19 MIL *	5	0	109	95	4.00	4.26	1.39	1.43	63	103	19.9	3.6	7.9	2.2	42%	11.1%	89.3	44	24	31	31%	74%	12%	16%	17	79	12%	41%	0	0.78	6.8	74	$1
1st Half	4	0	46	40	4.69	4.62	1.48	1.27	57	107	22.0	3.1	7.9	2.6	36%	11.2%	89.4	45	24	31	35%	68%	7%	14%	6	88	17%	33%			-1.0	87	-$2
2nd Half	1	0	63	55	3.50	3.99	1.32	1.45	67	100	18.5	4.0	7.9	2.0	44%	11.0%	89.2	44	24	32	28%	78%	14%	17%	11	75	9%	45%	0	0.78	7.8	67	$4
20 Proj	**8**	**0**	**145**	**129**	**4.14**	**4.02**	**1.37**	**1.38**	**73**	**106**	**23.1**	**3.7**	**8.0**	**2.1**	**40%**	**10.4%**	**89.7**	**46**	**23**	**32**	**31%**	**72%**	**11%**		**26**						**0.2**	**77**	**$3**

Goody,Nick	Health	F	LIMA Plan	C
Age: 28 Th: R Role RP	PT/Exp	D	Rand Var	+1
Ht: 5' 11" Wt: 200 Type Pwr xFB	Consist	C	MM	0400

3-2, 3.54 ERA in 40 IP at CLE. Returned after arthroscopic elbow surgery ended his 2018, posting mixed results. PRO: Nasty slider; added velocity; SwK% supports higher Dom; Ball% suggests he underperformed Ctl rate. CON: FB rate could lead to whiplash; unremarkable fastball; marginal LI; low BPX. Seeds are there but needs nurturing.

Yr Tm	W	Sv	IP	K	ERA	xERA	WHIP	xWHIP	vL+	vR+	BF/G	Ctl	Dom	Cmd	Ball%	SwK	Vel	G	L	F	H%	S%	HR/F	xHR/F	GS	APC	DOM%	DIS%	Sv%	LI	RAR	BPX	R$
15 NYY *	2	8	68	74	2.39	2.98	1.26		114	103	5.5	3.4	9.8	2.8		10.7%	90.9	47	21	32	32%	82%	0%	0%	0	17			73	0.66	13.2	137	$7
16 NYY *	0	5	52	63	3.82	4.55	1.18		149	103	4.7	2.8	10.8	3.8		15.2%	90.9	23	21	56	28%	81%	16%	16%	0	20			100	0.45	2.4	101	$2
17 CLE	1	0	55	72	2.80	3.60	1.08	1.13	78	88	3.9	3.3	11.9	3.6	35%	16.9%	91.7	28	23	48	28%	81%	12%	11%	0	16			0	0.55	10.5	157	$4
18 CLE	0	0	12	12	6.94	5.48	1.71		113	157	4.8	3.9	9.3	2.4		14.1%	91.3	28	21	51	34%	69%	20%	22%	0	17			0	1.57	-4.0	79	-$7
19 CLE *	3	0	66	76	6.32	6.28	1.59	1.41	97	88	4.8	5.1	10.4	2.0	36%	15.9%	92.7	26	21	53	31%	67%	13%	7%	0	18			0	0.93	-14.7	37	-$8
1st Half	0	0	36	43	8.51	8.50	1.90		104	94	5.7	5.6	10.7	1.9		21.4%	92.2	33	29	38	36%	62%	22%	7%	0	22			0	0.42	-17.9	2	-$16
2nd Half	3	0	30	33	3.64	5.35	1.21	1.38	95	84	4.2	4.6	10.0	2.2	35%	13.8%	92.9	23	18	58	24%	77%	11%	7%	0	17			0	1.08	3.2	64	$2
20 Proj	**2**	**0**	**58**	**65**	**5.07**	**4.53**	**1.47**	**1.28**	**114**	**111**	**4.6**	**4.7**	**10.1**	**2.2**	**35%**	**15.0%**	**92.4**	**25**	**20**	**54**	**31%**	**71%**	**14%**		**0**						**-6.6**	**68**	**-$5**

Gore,MacKenzie	Health	A	LIMA Plan	F
Age: 21 Th: L Role SP	PT/Exp	F	Rand Var	0
Ht: 6' 3" Wt: 195 Type Pwr FB	Consist	F	MM	1301

Third overall pick of 2017 draft bounced back from an injury-plagued 2018. Dominated Single-A, then faced somewhat stiffer competition in AA over five-start sample before he was shut down in early August to manage his workload. Showed advanced command of four-pitch arsenal; has #1/2 SP ceiling for SD and could move quickly. Dynasty darling.

Yr Tm	W	Sv	IP	K	ERA	xERA	WHIP	xWHIP	vL+	vR+	BF/G	Ctl	Dom	Cmd	Ball%	SwK	Vel	G	L	F	H%	S%	HR/F	xHR/F	GS	APC	DOM%	DIS%	Sv%	LI	RAR	BPX	R$
15																																	
16																																	
17																																	
18																																	
19 aa	2	0	23	22	4.64	4.22	1.31				19.2	3.1	8.5	2.8							31%	67%									-0.4	84	-$3
1st Half																																	
2nd Half	2	0	23	22	4.64	4.22	1.31		0	0	19.2	3.1	8.5	2.8							31%	67%			0	0					-0.4	85	-$3
20 Proj	**7**	**0**	**73**	**72**	**4.74**	**4.14**	**1.42**				**20.3**	**3.4**	**8.9**	**2.6**	**35%**	**11.5%**		**38**	**20**	**42**	**33%**	**70%**	**12%**		**15**						**-5.3**	**96**	**-$1**

Gott,Trevor	Health	D	LIMA Plan	C
Age: 27 Th: R Role RP	PT/Exp	D	Rand Var	+3
Ht: 6' 0" Wt: 185 Type Pwr	Consist	C	MM	2300

Skills surged in 2019, highlighted by big progress in SwK%, Ball%, vL+. Outperformed xWHIP, underperformed xERA, but BPX describes a LIMA-worthy RP. Unfortunately, injury bug bit hard, as a right forearm strain in May presaged season-ending UCL sprain in his pitching elbow in August. Left groin surgery caps it all off. DN: Lots of IL days

Yr Tm	W	Sv	IP	K	ERA	xERA	WHIP	xWHIP	vL+	vR+	BF/G	Ctl	Dom	Cmd	Ball%	SwK	Vel	G	L	F	H%	S%	HR/F	xHR/F	GS	APC	DOM%	DIS%	Sv%	LI	RAR	BPX	R$
15 LAA *	5	8	76	53	2.80	3.19	1.30	1.45	98	77	4.3	3.3	6.3	1.9	38%	6.5%	96.2	57	16	26	30%	78%	5%	8%	0	15			62	1.13	10.8	91	$6
16 WAS *	3	1	45	32	5.76	5.81	1.77		105	87	5.0	3.5	6.3	1.8		6.9%	94.3	39	17	44	38%	66%	0%	0%	0	11			33	0.70	-8.8	58	-$8
17 WAS *	3	4	40	31	6.88	6.51	1.88		203	160	5.6	3.8	7.0	1.8		8.9%	95.0	35	29	35	40%	62%	17%	14%	0	25			100	0.47	-12.6	55	-$8
18 WAS *	1	3	49	45	5.25	4.25	1.37		139	112	4.3	3.5	8.2	2.4		6.6%	94.9	57	14	29	32%	62%	25%	25%	0	15			75	0.55	-6.7	85	-$5
19 SF	7	1	53	57	4.44	3.95	1.10	1.24	66	88	4.3	2.9	9.7	3.4	34%	11.3%	94.7	43	20	37	29%	59%	8%	15%	0	18			50	0.98	0.4	128	$3
1st Half	4	0	34	37	3.93	3.99	0.99	1.19	56	87	4.4	2.9	9.7	3.4	34%	11.4%	94.7	41	18	40	25%	61%	9%	19%	0	18			0	0.80	2.4	127	$5
2nd Half	3	1	18	20	5.40	3.94	1.31	1.20	84	89	4.1	2.9	9.8	3.3	36%	11.1%	94.6	46	22	32	35%	57%	6%	7%	0	19			50	1.26	-2.0	132	$0
20 Proj	**4**	**0**	**44**	**42**	**4.17**	**3.89**	**1.37**	**1.30**	**97**	**108**	**4.4**	**3.2**	**8.6**	**2.7**	**36%**	**9.5%**	**95.3**	**44**	**20**	**36**	**32%**	**74%**	**14%**		**0**						**-0.1**	**103**	**-$2**

Graterol,Brusdar	Health	A	LIMA Plan	F
Age: 21 Th: R Role RP	PT/Exp	F	Rand Var	0
Ht: 6' 1" Wt: 265 Type Pwr	Consist	F	MM	2300

1-1, 4.66 ERA in 9 IP at MIN. Advanced #2/3 SP prospect ran roughshod over AA hitters before retooling as RP in AAA and reaching MLB in Sept. Three-pitch mix features two-seamer with plus-plus velocity and slider with tight, two-plane break. Durability issues may eventually lead to bullpen assignment, but could be an asset in any role for 2020.

Yr Tm	W	Sv	IP	K	ERA	xERA	WHIP	xWHIP	vL+	vR+	BF/G	Ctl	Dom	Cmd	Ball%	SwK	Vel	G	L	F	H%	S%	HR/F	xHR/F	GS	APC	DOM%	DIS%	Sv%	LI	RAR	BPX	R$
15																																	
16																																	
17																																	
18																																	
19 MIN *	8	1	70	59	2.84	2.60	1.12	1.14	100	91	10.6	3.3	7.6	2.3	30%	9.0%	99.0	48	30	22	26%	76%	17%	13%	0	14			100	1.49	14.4	96	$8
1st Half	5	0	49	39	2.51	2.63	1.17		0	0	21.8	3.7	7.2	2.0							26%	80%	0%		0	0					12.1	90	$10
2nd Half	3	1	21	19	3.87	2.82	1.06		101	90	4.7	2.7	8.4	3.2		9.0%	99.0	48	30	22	26%	66%	17%	13%	0	14			100	1.49	1.6	109	$3
20 Proj	**6**	**0**	**44**	**42**	**3.98**	**3.84**	**1.34**				**7.4**	**3.4**	**8.6**	**2.5**	**35%**	**11.0%**		**45**	**22**	**33**	**31%**	**74%**	**13%**		**0**						**0.9**	**98**	**$0**

ALAIN DE LEONARDIS

Gray,Jonathan

Age: 28	Th: R	Role SP	Health F	LIMA Plan A
Ht: 6' 4"	Wt: 227	Type	PT/Exp A	Rand Var +1
			Consist A	MM 3303

Regained velocity, posting solid 1st half before broken left foot ended his season in Aug. Control slumped but Ball% suggests ability to throw strikes didn't change much. BPX, xERA, and xWHIP from 2016-18 justified fantasy GMs' stubbornness (and frustration!) as they kept hoping for a breakout, but all three backed up in 2019. Wait and see.

Yr Tm	W	Sv	IP	K	ERA	xERA	WHIP	xWHIP	vL+	vR+	BF/G	Ctl	Dom	Cmd	Ball%	SwK	Vel	G	L	F	H%	S%	HR/F	xHR/F	GS	APC	DOM%	DIS%	Sv%	LI	RAR	BPX	R$
15 COL *	6	0	155	123	5.35	5.68	1.67	1.27	104	134	23.2	3.2	7.1	2.2	37%	10.4%	94.4	42	25	33	37%	68%	10%	9%	9	76	22%	33%			-26.5	65	-$16
16 COL	10	0	168	185	4.61	3.60	1.26	1.22	94	97	24.6	3.2	9.9	3.1	35%	12.4%	95.1	44	24	32	32%	65%	13%	13%	29	96	41%	34%			-8.7	137	$6
17 COL	10	0	110	112	3.67	3.63	1.30	1.18	92	101	23.1	2.4	9.1	3.7	35%	9.4%	96.0	49	23	29	34%	74%	11%	10%	20	92	35%	20%			9.4	151	$8
18 COL	12	0	172	183	5.12	3.64	1.35	1.19	113	100	24.0	2.7	9.6	3.5	36%	12.9%	94.8	47	22	30	34%	65%	18%	15%	31	90	29%	29%			-20.6	142	-$1
19 COL	11	0	150	150	3.84	4.08	1.35	1.33	108	96	24.5	3.4	9.0	2.7	36%	12.3%	96.1	50	23	26	32%	76%	17%	17%	25	91	28%	32%	0	1.01	12.3	108	$8
1st Half	9	0	103	111	3.84	3.91	1.35	1.27	101	102	24.2	3.5	9.7	2.8	36%	12.7%	96.1	48	24	28	32%	75%	17%	17%	17	89	24%	29%	0	1.11	8.4	116	$14
2nd Half	2	0	47	39	3.83	4.29	1.36	1.33	122	86	25.3	3.1	7.5	2.4	37%	11.5%	96.0	55	21	24	31%	76%	17%	17%	8	96	38%	38%			3.9	92	-$4
20 Proj	**12**	**0**	**174**	**170**	**4.04**	**3.52**	**1.36**	**1.25**	**108**	**98**	**23.7**	**3.0**	**8.8**	**2.9**	**36%**	**11.7%**	**95.6**	**49**	**23**	**28**	**33%**	**74%**	**16%**		**31**						**2.4**	**121**	**$7**

Gray,Sonny

Age: 30	Th: R	Role SP	Health C	LIMA Plan A
Ht: 5' 10"	Wt: 192	Type Pwr GB	PT/Exp A	Rand Var -1
			Consist A	MM 3303

Put drab 2018 behind him with a brilliant rebound as pendulum swung back hard in his favor across H%, S%, LD%. It wasn't all dumb luck, though, as evidenced by robust BPX, career-best Dom, and surging 2nd half SwK%. Still, heed xERA and xWHIP; this is a good pitcher, just maybe not 2019 good. If others want to pay that premium, let them.

Yr Tm	W	Sv	IP	K	ERA	xERA	WHIP	xWHIP	vL+	vR+	BF/G	Ctl	Dom	Cmd	Ball%	SwK	Vel	G	L	F	H%	S%	HR/F	xHR/F	GS	APC	DOM%	DIS%	Sv%	LI	RAR	BPX	R$
15 OAK	14	0	208	169	2.73	3.62	1.08	1.28	79	85	26.8	2.6	7.3	2.9	36%	10.1%	92.9	53	17	31	26%	78%	9%	10%	31	99	42%	23%			31.7	112	$26
16 OAK	5	0	117	94	5.69	4.30	1.50	1.36	103	120	23.5	3.2	7.2	2.2	38%	8.4%	92.7	54	19	27	33%	64%	17%	18%	22	89	9%	45%			-21.7	89	-$9
17 2 AL	10	0	162	153	3.55	3.85	1.21	1.29	85	93	25.1	3.2	8.5	2.7	38%	12.2%	93.0	53	20	28	28%	75%	15%	17%	27	99	37%	30%			16.2	118	$14
18 NYY	11	0	130	123	4.90	4.20	1.50	1.37	99	113	19.4	3.9	8.5	2.2	39%	10.4%	93.3	50	23	27	34%	69%	13%	14%	23	75	22%	43%	0	0.72	-12.1	86	-$4
19 CIN	11	0	175	205	2.87	3.57	1.08	1.26	81	80	22.8	3.5	10.5	3.0	39%	11.8%	93.3	51	18	31	27%	77%	13%	15%	31	94	39%	13%			35.3	135	$24
1st Half	4	0	82	91	3.94	3.72	1.24	1.25	75	101	21.4	3.5	9.9	2.8	39%	10.8%	93.3	55	17	28	30%	71%	15%	15%	16	89	25%	19%			5.8	128	$11
2nd Half	7	0	93	114	1.94	3.41	0.95	1.19	86	61	24.3	3.5	11.0	3.2	39%	12.7%	93.3	47	19	34	23%	85%	11%	14%	15	99	53%	7%			29.5	141	$36
20 Proj	**12**	**0**	**174**	**182**	**3.55**	**3.37**	**1.22**	**1.28**	**88**	**91**	**21.6**	**3.5**	**9.4**	**2.7**	**39%**	**11.3%**	**93.2**	**51**	**19**	**30**	**29%**	**74%**	**13%**		**32**						**13.0**	**120**	**$15**

Green,Chad

Age: 29	Th: R	Role RP	Health A	LIMA Plan A
Ht: 6' 3"	Wt: 210	Type Pwr FB	PT/Exp C	Rand Var +5
			Consist A	MM 5501

His 1st half luck couldn't have been worse if he had found a cursed tiki necklace on a family trip to Hawaii. Take out the bad juju, and he would have performed as well as any of the league's best RP; BPX, SwK%, expected stats confirm it's much more than a hunch. LIMA-worthy pick should be good to go in 2020—you could say we like him a bunch.

Yr Tm	W	Sv	IP	K	ERA	xERA	WHIP	xWHIP	vL+	vR+	BF/G	Ctl	Dom	Cmd	Ball%	SwK	Vel	G	L	F	H%	S%	HR/F	xHR/F	GS	APC	DOM%	DIS%	Sv%	LI	RAR	BPX	R$
15 aa	5	0	149	108	4.84	5.48	1.65				24.6	2.8	6.5	2.4							38%	70%									-16.2	73	-$13
16 NYY *	9	1	140	135	3.01	3.88	1.25	1.19	137	96	20.4	2.5	8.6	3.5	38%	12.7%	94.3	41	21	38	31%	81%	25%	23%	8	70	25%	38%	100	0.68	20.4	115	$12
17 NYY *	7	0	96	130	3.20	2.48	1.10	0.91	54	64	8.3	2.8	12.2	4.4	36%	15.9%	95.8	26	27	47	33%	71%	7%	10%	1	29	0%	0%	0	0.95	13.6	194	$11
18 NYY	8	0	76	94	2.50	3.27	1.04	1.00	88	89	4.7	1.8	11.2	6.3	32%	13.6%	96.2	31	23	46	32%	83%	10%	15%	0	20			0	1.12	15.4	187	$10
19 NYY	4	2	69	98	4.17	3.47	1.23	1.06	96	100	5.5	2.5	12.8	5.2	34%	14.1%	96.5	35	22	42	37%	71%	14%	14%	15	24	7%	40%	100	0.95	2.8	192	$3
1st Half	2	0	28	37	6.04	3.86	1.59	1.03	112	127	5.0	1.9	11.8	6.2	35%	13.6%	96.0	40	24	36	43%	67%	19%	15%	7	22	14%	29%	0	0.83	-5.3	194	-$7
2nd Half	2	2	41	61	2.88	3.36	0.98	1.01	84	76	5.9	2.9	13.5	4.7	34%	14.5%	96.8	31	21	48	30%	75%	10%	13%	8	27	0%	50%	100	1.07	8.2	190	$10
20 Proj	**5**	**0**	**73**	**95**	**3.32**	**3.01**	**1.09**	**1.02**	**89**	**86**	**5.7**	**2.4**	**11.8**	**5.0**	**35%**	**14.1%**	**96.1**	**33**	**23**	**44**	**32%**	**74%**	**12%**		**0**						**7.4**	**183**	**$6**

Greene,Shane

Age: 31	Th: R	Role RP	Health C	LIMA Plan A
Ht: 6' 4"	Wt: 197	Type Pwr	PT/Exp B	Rand Var -5
			Consist A	MM 3320

Enjoyed phenomenal run as closer in DET but stumbled badly upon joining ATL, recording only one more save the rest of the way. Skills were consistently solid across both halves, but those 1st half H% and LD% had nowhere to go but up. Improved cutter offset drop in velocity and paved the way to higher SwK%. Closer worthy, just not elite.

Yr Tm	W	Sv	IP	K	ERA	xERA	WHIP	xWHIP	vL+	vR+	BF/G	Ctl	Dom	Cmd	Ball%	SwK	Vel	G	L	F	H%	S%	HR/F	xHR/F	GS	APC	DOM%	DIS%	Sv%	LI	RAR	BPX	R$
15 DET *	5	0	119	66	6.29	5.60	1.58	1.42	140	107	20.9	3.0	5.0	1.7	34%	7.5%	91.7	44	23	33	33%	61%	14%	13%	16	74	25%	56%	0	0.70	-34.1	28	-$17
16 DET	5	2	60	59	5.82	3.87	1.33	1.29	107	80	5.1	3.3	8.8	2.7	36%	13.1%	94.0	48	21	32	33%	53%	6%	9%	3	20	0%	33%	67	1.26	-12.1	114	-$3
17 DET	4	9	67	73	2.67	4.07	1.25	1.38	100	74	4.0	4.5	9.8	2.1	37%	9.5%	95.0	47	18	35	27%	82%	10%	13%	0	15			69	1.17	14.0	94	$9
18 DET	4	32	63	65	5.12	4.12	1.37	1.21	102	116	4.2	2.7	9.2	3.4	35%	9.2%	94.3	41	21	39	33%	68%	16%	16%	0	16			84	1.21	-7.5	129	$9
19 2 TM	0	23	63	64	2.30	3.83	1.01	1.21	100	65	3.9	2.4	9.2	3.8	34%	11.7%	92.7	46	19	35	25%	85%	14%	17%	0	15			82	1.10	17.1	135	$15
1st Half	0	22	31	32	0.87	3.78	0.84	1.18	69	58	3.9	2.6	9.3	3.6	35%	11.4%	93.0	53	10	38	20%	100%	10%	15%	0	15			96	1.29	13.9	139	$24
2nd Half	0	1	32	32	3.69	3.91	1.17	1.16	135	70	3.8	2.3	9.1	4.0	34%	12.0%	92.4	41	27	33	30%	75%	18%	19%	0	14			20	0.93	3.2	132	$7
20 Proj	**2**	**10**	**65**	**66**	**3.57**	**3.52**	**1.19**	**1.23**	**106**	**81**	**4.1**	**2.9**	**9.0**	**3.1**	**35%**	**10.6%**	**93.4**	**45**	**20**	**35**	**29%**	**75%**	**14%**		**0**						**4.7**	**124**	**$6**

Greinke,Zack

Age: 36	Th: R	Role SP	Health A	LIMA Plan A
Ht: 6' 2"	Wt: 200	Type Con	PT/Exp A	Rand Var 0
			Consist A	MM 3205

Consistency, thy name is Greinke. Since 2015, only six other MLB SP have a better WHIP; two have more IP; none has more wins. At 36, some skills gradually softening: SwK%, Dom, Vel receding but still effective. Sharpened already impressive Ctl to offset lost power. Has a knack for overperforming expected stats; still a blue-chip stock.

Yr Tm	W	Sv	IP	K	ERA	xERA	WHIP	xWHIP	vL+	vR+	BF/G	Ctl	Dom	Cmd	Ball%	SwK	Vel	G	L	F	H%	S%	HR/F	xHR/F	GS	APC	DOM%	DIS%	Sv%	LI	RAR	BPX	R$
15 LA	19	0	223	200	1.66	3.14	0.84	1.12	74	68	26.3	1.6	8.1	5.0	36%	12.5%	91.8	48	19	33	24%	84%	7%	8%	32	101	56%	3%			63.3	152	$49
16 ARI	13	0	159	134	4.37	4.10	1.27	1.25	101	103	25.7	2.3	7.6	3.3	35%	10.9%	91.3	46	20	35	31%	70%	14%	15%	26	96	31%	35%			-3.5	116	$6
17 ARI	17	0	202	215	3.20	3.41	1.07	1.10	87	90	25.0	2.0	9.6	4.8	36%	12.9%	91.0	47	18	35	29%	76%	13%	15%	32	99	50%	22%			28.8	172	$29
18 ARI	15	0	208	199	3.21	3.52	1.08	1.14	88	96	25.4	1.9	8.6	4.6	35%	11.3%	89.6	45	23	32	28%	77%	15%	16%	33	97	45%	15%			24.1	147	$25
19 2 TM	18	0	209	187	2.93	3.72	0.98	1.14	80	86	24.5	1.3	8.1	6.2	35%	10.7%	90.0	45	22	33	28%	74%	11%	12%	33	94	45%	18%			40.5	145	$33
1st Half	9	0	115	99	2.90	3.73	0.94	1.09	75	89	24.4	1.2	7.7	6.6	34%	9.5%	89.7	44	23	33	26%	74%	11%	13%	18	94	56%	17%			22.8	141	$36
2nd Half	9	0	94	88	2.98	3.76	1.04	1.10	85	82	24.7	1.4	8.5	5.9	35%	12.1%	90.4	47	20	33	29%	75%	10%	12%	15	94	33%	20%			17.6	151	$31
20 Proj	**17**	**0**	**203**	**189**	**3.23**	**3.32**	**1.05**	**1.12**	**85**	**89**	**24.5**	**1.7**	**8.4**	**4.9**	**35%**	**11.5%**	**90.3**	**44**	**21**	**35**	**28%**	**74%**	**12%**		**32**						**23.0**	**145**	**$27**

Gsellman,Robert

Age: 26	Th: R	Role RP	Health D	LIMA Plan B
Ht: 6' 4"	Wt: 205	Type Con	PT/Exp C	Rand Var 0
			Consist B	MM 1100

Failed to impress in his second season in pen, which was cut short by torn right lat in August. Sharp dropoff in 2nd half SwK% really stands out: threw fewer off-speed and breaking pitches while upping his sinker usage. The added velocity is nice, but nothing else in this profile is screaming "Buy Me!" A return to rotation might make us look at 2016 again.

Yr Tm	W	Sv	IP	K	ERA	xERA	WHIP	xWHIP	vL+	vR+	BF/G	Ctl	Dom	Cmd	Ball%	SwK	Vel	G	L	F	H%	S%	HR/F	xHR/F	GS	APC	DOM%	DIS%	Sv%	LI	RAR	BPX	R$
15 aa	7	0	92	43	4.01	3.82	1.35				24.0	2.5	4.2	1.7							30%	69%									-0.5	58	-$1
16 NYM *	8	0	160	121	3.75	3.85	1.33	1.27	80	93	23.6	2.7	6.8	2.6	37%	9.8%	93.7	54	23	23	32%	72%	4%	11%	7	89	29%	14%	0	1.01	8.7	91	$6
17 NYM *	9	0	138	93	5.23	5.56	1.58	1.41	108	109	20.3	3.3	6.0	1.8	37%	7.6%	92.7	49	22	29	33%	69%	14%	12%	22	82	14%	45%	0	0.78	-14.8	40	-$7
18 NYM	6	13	80	70	4.28	4.17	1.30	1.32	98	96	5.1	3.2	7.9	2.5	35%	10.1%	94.1	49	19	32	30%	69%	11%	11%	0	19			68	1.14	-1.2	96	$5
19 NYM	2	1	64	60	4.66	4.55	1.37	1.35	108	98	5.3	3.3	8.5	2.6	37%	11.7%	95.4	44	22	34	32%	68%	11%	9%	0	21			20	1.12	-1.3	95	-$3
1st Half	1	1	44	46	5.08	4.39	1.47	1.26	115	99	5.4	3.2	9.3	2.9	37%	13.1%	95.3	45	23	32	36%	66%	10%	9%	0	21			20	1.09	-3.1	113	-$3
2nd Half	1	0	19	14	3.72	4.85	1.14	1.41	89	98	5.3	3.3	6.5	2.0	38%	8.1%	95.4	42	19	40	23%	74%	14%	8%	0	21			0	1.20	1.9	53	-$1
20 Proj	**4**	**0**	**65**	**53**	**4.37**	**4.07**	**1.33**	**1.34**	**100**	**101**	**6.3**	**3.2**	**7.3**	**2.3**	**37%**	**9.7%**	**94.5**	**47**	**20**	**33**	**30%**	**70%**	**12%**		**0**						**-1.8**	**80**	**-$2**

Guerra,Javy

Age: 34	Th: R	Role RP	Health A	LIMA Plan C
Ht: 6' 1"	Wt: 216	Type Con FB	PT/Exp D	Rand Var 0
			Consist C	MM 1100

Improved his control—backed by Ball%—but dominance has plateaued at a level of solid mediocrity. Dodged HR damage during first half in TOR despite sudden penchant for fly balls, but was unable to escape harm after moving to WAS. Still, posted a 5.00-plus xERA throughout, and in five of the last seven years. At least he has his health. *shrug emoji*

Yr Tm	W	Sv	IP	K	ERA	xERA	WHIP	xWHIP	vL+	vR+	BF/G	Ctl	Dom	Cmd	Ball%	SwK	Vel	G	L	F	H%	S%	HR/F	xHR/F	GS	APC	DOM%	DIS%	Sv%	LI	RAR	BPX	R$
15 CHW	0	0	2	0	0.00	7.14	1.80		0	200	2.3	5.4	0.0	0.0		2.8%	92.1	33	33	33	30%	100%	0%		0	12			0	0.65	0.8	-161	-$4
16 LAA *	3	12	58	48	5.30	5.57	1.80		77	118	5.4	6.2	7.4	1.2		7.5%	92.4	56	6	39	33%	72%	14%	12%	0	19			92	0.61	-8.0	46	-$3
17 MIA *	3	2	73	45	5.38	5.40	1.58		102	101	6.3	3.9	5.6	1.4		5.9%	92.3	54	18	28	31%	68%	11%	14%	0	20			40	0.99	-9.2	29	-$6
18 MIA *	4	6	54	48	3.67	3.76	1.28	1.33	117	113	5.0	2.6	8.0	3.1	33%	9.7%	93.4	45	23	32	32%	72%	11%	12%	0	18			86	0.98	3.2	111	$2
19 2 TM	3	2	68	57	4.66	5.07	1.24	1.31	102	92	5.6	2.3	7.6	3.4	30%	9.5%	92.8	33	20	47	30%	66%	10%	11%	0	21			100	0.60	-1.2	94	$0
1st Half	1	1	33	29	3.82	5.03	1.18	1.28	106	77	5.3	2.7	7.9	2.9	31%	9.4%	93.0	30	24	46	30%	68%	5%	8%	0	20			100	0.66	2.8	84	$0
2nd Half	2	1	35	28	5.45	5.27	1.30	1.21	99	108	6.0	1.8	7.3	4.0	29%	9.5%	92.6	36	16	48	30%	65%	15%	14%	0	23			100	0.54	-4.0	105	$0
20 Proj	**2**	**0**	**44**	**36**	**4.64**	**4.32**	**1.36**	**1.27**	**105**	**99**	**5.4**	**2.9**	**7.3**	**2.5**	**31%**	**9.6%**	**93.0**	**38**	**21**	**41**	**31%**	**69%**	**10%**		**0**						**-2.6**	**80**	**-$3**

ALAIN DE LEONARDIS

Guerra,Junior

Age: 35	Th: R	Role RP	Health	D	LIMA Plan B
Ht: 6' 0"	Wt: 205	Type Pwr	PT/Exp	C	Rand Var -3
			Consist	B	MM 1200

Transitioned to full-time bullpen work, which explains the bump in velocity and SwK%, but Dom actually waned. Subpar Ctl, marginal Ball% reflect his poor fastball command. Swapped out his slider for a curve that missed bats but also the plate. Very favorable H% saved his bacon. Days as SP are behind him, BPX a poor fit for closing. Pass.

Yr Tm	W	Sv	IP	K	ERA	xERA	WHIP	xWHIP	vL+	vR+	BF/G	Ctl	Dom	Cmd	Ball%	SwK	Vel	G	L	F	H%	S%	HR/F	xHR/F	GS	APC	DOM%	DIS%	Sv%	LI	RAR	BPX	R$
15 CHW *	4	7	87	83	4.63	4.59	1.49		137	147	11.1	4.4	8.6	1.9		10.6%	94.1	57	21	21	32%	71%	33%	1%	0	22			88	0.22	-7.2	74	-$2
16 MIL *	9	0	148	119	3.20	2.88	1.16	1.35	84	88	23.6	3.3	7.2	2.2	38%	11.4%	93.1	45	19	36	26%	75%	8%	12%	20	93	30%	20%			18.1	92	$13
17 MIL *	3	0	105	85	4.52	5.53	1.58	1.55	108	111	16.5	5.2	7.3	1.4	42%	11.3%	91.9	34	23	44	28%	78%	21%	14%	14	59	0%	57%	0	0.58	-2.0	26	-$5
18 MIL	6	0	141	136	4.09	4.29	1.40	1.32	109	102	19.7	3.5	8.7	2.5	37%	10.9%	93.3	43	20	37	32%	75%	13%	12%	26	74	12%	35%	0	0.78	1.1	95	$0
19 MIL	9	3	84	77	3.55	4.65	1.12	1.43	83	86	4.8	3.9	8.3	2.1	38%	11.6%	94.7	43	18	38	23%	73%	13%	13%	0	19			27	1.33	9.9	71	$9
1st Half	2	2	43	41	3.80	4.53	1.15	1.35	85	87	5.0	3.8	8.6	2.3	40%	11.7%	94.7	39	24	37	25%	70%	12%	11%	0	21			33	1.20	3.7	77	$4
2nd Half	7	1	41	36	3.29	4.75	1.10	1.41	80	84	4.5	4.0	7.9	2.0	37%	11.6%	94.8	48	12	40	21%	77%	14%	14%	0	17			20	1.46	6.1	67	$14
20 Proj	5	0	58	53	4.31	4.28	1.40	1.39	103	104	7.6	4.0	8.1	2.0	38%	11.4%	93.8	41	21	38	30%	73%	13%		0						-1.1	67	-$2

Guerrero,Tayron

Age: 29	Th: R	Role RP	Health	D	LIMA Plan D
Ht: 6' 8"	Wt: 210	Type Pwr	PT/Exp	D	Rand Var +2
			Consist	F	MM 0210

Top 5 Vel paired with Bottom 5 Ctl (min. 30 IP) yields offspring only a mother could love. Two mid-season finger injuries laid waste to his 2nd half, making bad numbers look even worse. But flamethrower's SwK% should net higher Dom; needs to throw fastball less (79%) and trust slider. When you have a trebuchet for an arm, there's always hope.

Yr Tm	W	Sv	IP	K	ERA	xERA	WHIP	xWHIP	vL+	vR+	BF/G	Ctl	Dom	Cmd	Ball%	SwK	Vel	G	L	F	H%	S%	HR/F	xHR/F	GS	APC	DOM%	DIS%	Sv%	LI	RAR	BPX	R$
15 a/a	1	14	56	53	3.25	3.11	1.34				4.8	4.8	8.5	1.8							28%	76%									4.9	100	$5
16 SD *	1	4	52	43	5.44	4.53	1.53		136	114	5.0	4.2	7.4	1.7		0.0%	95.2	50	0	50	33%	64%	0%	1%	0	22			80	0.13	-8.0	71	-$5
17 a/a	3	0	31	27	6.13	6.42	1.96				5.0	8.3	7.8	0.9							30%	72%									-6.9	23	-$8
18 MIA	1	0	58	68	5.43	4.18	1.62	1.35	131	93	4.5	4.7	10.6	2.3	39%	11.3%	98.8	45	23	32	37%	69%	15%	17%	0	19			0	0.67	-9.2	100	-$9
19 MIA	1	0	46	43	6.26	6.22	1.70	1.79	118	98	4.2	7.0	8.4	1.2	39%	13.6%	99.0	44	16	40	29%	65%	13%	16%	0	17			0	0.63	-10.0	-18	-$9
1st Half	1	0	31	32	4.35	5.77	1.52	1.70	121	74	4.1	7.0	9.3	1.3	39%	14.2%	98.9	37	18	45	27%	73%	9%	10%	0	17			0	0.79	0.6	-6	-$6
2nd Half	0	0	15	11	10.20	6.98	2.07	1.80	111	131	4.3	7.2	6.6	0.9	39%	12.4%	99.3	55	13	32	32%	52%	24%	28%	0	19			0	0.34	-10.5	-47	-$14
20 Proj	2	2	58	54	5.38	4.97	1.68	1.60	116	100	4.2	6.4	8.4	1.3	39%	12.4%	99.0	46	19	35	30%	72%	17%		0						-8.8	3	-$7

Hader,Josh

Age: 26	Th: L	Role RP	Health	A	LIMA Plan B
Ht: 6' 3"	Wt: 185	Type Pwr xFB	PT/Exp	B	Rand Var -1
			Consist	B	MM 5531

Imagine! A 5x5 closer who could be worth $30! As scary as he is already, he took another step up with bumps to velocity, Cmd and an obscene SwK%. Scarier still, that Ball% supports even better control. Unthinkable these days, but there is the real possibility of UP: 45 Sv, 150 K, which would take aim at the $35 bar.

Yr Tm	W	Sv	IP	K	ERA	xERA	WHIP	xWHIP	vL+	vR+	BF/G	Ctl	Dom	Cmd	Ball%	SwK	Vel	G	L	F	H%	S%	HR/F	xHR/F	GS	APC	DOM%	DIS%	Sv%	LI	RAR	BPX	R$
15 aa	4	1	104	104	4.07	4.06	1.36				18.1	3.2	9.0	2.8							33%	72%									-1.4	106	$0
16 a/a	3	0	126	142	4.01	3.52	1.36				21.1	3.9	10.1	2.6							34%	70%									2.7	124	$2
17 MIL *	5	0	100	112	3.90	4.12	1.29	1.17	60	82	8.7	4.6	10.1	2.2	35%	17.6%	94.3	34	14	51	26%	78%	9%	7%	0	22			0	1.14	5.6	80	$4
18 MIL	6	12	81	143	2.43	2.31	0.81	0.92	48	77	5.6	3.3	15.8	4.8	33%	19.8%	94.5	29	23	48	24%	77%	15%	14%	0	24			71	1.31	17.2	233	$21
19 MIL	3	37	76	138	2.62	2.46	0.81	0.84	82	78	4.7	2.4	16.4	6.9	31%	24.0%	95.6	22	23	55	26%	85%	21%	16%	0	19			84	1.71	17.6	252	$29
1st Half	1	20	41	77	1.77	2.29	0.61	0.77	63	58	4.8	2.7	17.0	6.4	31%	26.2%	95.3	24	15	62	16%	89%	18%	14%	0	21			95	1.83	13.7	258	$31
2nd Half	2	17	35	61	3.60	2.92	1.03	0.84	109	94	4.7	2.1	15.7	7.6	30%	21.6%	95.9	21	29	50	34%	81%	25%	18%	0	18			74	1.59	3.9	246	$27
20 Proj	4	38	80	129	3.03	2.59	0.96	0.91	75	90	5.6	3.0	14.5	4.8	32%	21.2%	95.1	26	22	52	27%	79%	18%		0						11.0	212	$27

Hamels,Cole

Age: 36	Th: L	Role SP	Health	D	LIMA Plan B
Ht: 6' 4"	Wt: 205	Type Pwr	PT/Exp	A	Rand Var 0
			Consist	B	MM 2303

Was humming along in the 1st half until oblique strain in late June trimmed five weeks off his season. After that, he was all over the place: Ball%, Ctl spiked; lost half a tick; G/L/F went haywire; BF/G sagged; H% didn't cooperate. Shoulder fatigue kept him out another two weeks in September. Still flashing skills, but also insurance card. Caveat emptor.

Yr Tm	W	Sv	IP	K	ERA	xERA	WHIP	xWHIP	vL+	vR+	BF/G	Ctl	Dom	Cmd	Ball%	SwK	Vel	G	L	F	H%	S%	HR/F	xHR/F	GS	APC	DOM%	DIS%	Sv%	LI	RAR	BPX	R$
15 2TM	13	0	212	215	3.65	3.39	1.19	1.20	89	95	27.5	2.6	9.1	3.5	34%	13.8%	92.6	48	21	31	30%	72%	12%	12%	32	104	44%	19%			8.3	142	$16
16 TEX	15	0	201	200	3.32	3.83	1.31	1.30	82	98	26.5	3.5	9.0	2.6	37%	12.8%	92.6	50	20	31	31%	79%	14%	16%	32	102	34%	25%			21.6	114	$16
17 TEX	11	0	148	105	4.20	4.61	1.20	1.41	64	101	25.6	3.2	6.4	2.0	38%	9.8%	92.0	48	19	34	26%	68%	12%	13%	24	96	25%	33%			3.0	65	$9
18 2TM	9	0	191	188	3.78	3.80	1.26	1.26	91	107	25.2	3.1	8.9	2.9	36%	12.4%	92.1	45	23	32	30%	76%	17%	18%	32	96	28%	19%			8.8	115	$10
19 CHC	7	0	142	143	3.81	4.41	1.39	1.35	92	101	22.9	3.6	9.1	2.6	37%	12.6%	91.4	47	20	33	33%	76%	13%	15%	27	89	26%	30%			12.1	101	$5
1st Half	6	0	100	97	2.98	4.04	1.20	1.27	75	93	24.2	3.2	8.8	2.8	35%	13.0%	91.6	51	18	31	29%	78%	11%	12%	17	94	29%	24%			18.8	111	$14
2nd Half	1	0	42	46	5.79	5.19	1.83	1.37	123	118	20.5	4.5	9.9	2.2	39%	11.7%	90.9	39	24	37	40%	72%	17%	21%	10	80	20%	40%			-6.6	80	-$16
20 Proj	7	0	145	142	4.07	3.88	1.41	1.32	95	106	22.6	3.5	8.8	2.5	37%	12.0%	91.7	45	21	33	32%	76%	15%		27						1.5	99	$2

Hand,Brad

Age: 30	Th: L	Role RP	Health	B	LIMA Plan A
Ht: 6' 3"	Wt: 220	Type Pwr	PT/Exp	B	Rand Var +2
			Consist	A	MM 5530

Some good things, some meh things in 2019. Overall improvements in Ball%, Ctl, SwK% pushed Cmd to elite level. H%, LD% strong candidates for regression. Tired arm cost him a chunk of September and was likely tied to decreased slider usage and 2nd half skills swoon. Swapped sinker for four seamer, as evidenced by notable shift in G/L/F. Still solid.

Yr Tm	W	Sv	IP	K	ERA	xERA	WHIP	xWHIP	vL+	vR+	BF/G	Ctl	Dom	Cmd	Ball%	SwK	Vel	G	L	F	H%	S%	HR/F	xHR/F	GS	APC	DOM%	DIS%	Sv%	LI	RAR	BPX	R$
15 MIA	4	0	93	67	5.30	4.39	1.49	1.39	70	125	10.7	3.1	6.5	2.1	40%	8.7%	92.1	46	23	30	33%	65%	10%	12%	12	41	8%	50%	0	0.60	-15.4	68	-$8
16 SD	4	1	89	111	2.92	3.34	1.11	1.20	57	94	4.4	3.6	11.2	3.1	38%	12.6%	92.8	47	17	36	28%	77%	10%	13%	0	18			14	1.30	14.0	153	$9
17 SD	3	21	79	104	2.16	2.79	0.93	1.01	78	78	4.3	2.3	11.8	5.2	36%	13.7%	93.5	46	20	34	27%	85%	15%	11%	0	17			81	1.35	21.6	210	$21
18 2TM	2	32	72	106	2.75	2.82	1.11	1.09	73	102	4.4	3.5	13.3	3.8	36%	13.7%	93.6	45	21	34	31%	81%	15%	15%	0	18			82	1.36	12.4	192	$19
19 CLE	6	34	57	84	3.30	3.46	1.24	1.08	66	102	4.0	2.8	13.2	4.7	32%	14.0%	92.7	27	31	42	38%	77%	11%	11%	0	16			87	1.31	8.6	181	$19
1st Half	4	23	35	53	2.29	3.10	0.99	0.94	65	81	3.8	2.3	13.5	5.9	31%	13.6%	92.6	20	37	43	34%	79%	6%	6%	0	14			96	1.25	9.6	195	$26
2nd Half	2	11	22	31	4.91	4.21	1.64	1.16	67	133	4.5	3.7	12.7	3.4	33%	14.4%	92.8	35	23	42	43%	75%	16%	17%	0	18			73	1.41	-1.1	155	$9
20 Proj	4	38	65	90	3.35	2.87	1.11	1.09	63	97	4.1	3.1	12.5	4.0	34%	13.6%	93.1	38	23	39	31%	75%	14%		0						6.4	180	$21

Happ,J.A.

Age: 37	Th: L	Role SP	Health	C	LIMA Plan B
Ht: 6' 5"	Wt: 205	Type	PT/Exp	A	Rand Var +3
			Consist	B	MM 2203

BPX reveals big step back skills-wise in 2019, although Ball% moved only a little, and SwK% barely at all. Recovered Vel, Dom in 2nd half at the expense of Ctl, but even if we freeze peripherals where they are, notice BF/G inch downward as age creeps up. DOM/DIS shows he never was truly dominant, or consistent. 2018 was likely his last hurrah.

Yr Tm	W	Sv	IP	K	ERA	xERA	WHIP	xWHIP	vL+	vR+	BF/G	Ctl	Dom	Cmd	Ball%	SwK	Vel	G	L	F	H%	S%	HR/F	xHR/F	GS	APC	DOM%	DIS%	Sv%	LI	RAR	BPX	R$
15 2TM	11	0	172	151	3.61	3.83	1.27	1.23	93	99	22.4	2.4	7.9	3.4	36%	8.7%	91.9	42	24	34	32%	74%	9%	9%	31	89	23%	26%	0	0.78	7.5	117	$9
16 TOR	20	0	195	163	3.18	4.13	1.17	1.29	88	91	24.9	2.8	7.5	2.7	37%	10.2%	91.6	42	22	35	27%	77%	11%	12%	32	95	31%	25%			24.2	96	$22
17 TOR	10	0	145	142	3.53	4.12	1.31	1.25	73	99	25.0	2.8	8.8	3.1	36%	10.1%	91.8	47	19	34	32%	77%	12%	11%	25	99	24%	28%			14.8	128	$10
18 2AL	17	0	178	193	3.65	3.75	1.13	1.16	67	101	23.6	2.6	9.8	3.8	36%	10.8%	92.0	40	17	42	29%	74%	13%	15%	31	98	26%	23%			11.0	143	$19
19 NYY	12	0	161	140	4.91	4.72	1.30	1.33	86	111	21.9	2.7	7.8	2.9	37%	10.7%	91.3	40	21	39	29%	69%	18%	16%	30	87	7%	43%	0	0.76	-8.0	92	$4
1st Half	7	0	84	66	5.23	4.87	1.28	1.24	108	109	22.1	2.0	7.0	3.5	36%	10.4%	90.7	43	16	41	29%	67%	18%	16%	16	84	0%	44%			-7.5	102	$3
2nd Half	5	0	77	74	4.56	4.61	1.31	1.32	63	114	21.6	3.5	8.6	2.5	38%	11.1%	91.9	36	28	36	28%	71%	18%	16%	14	90	14%	43%	0	0.74	-0.5	82	$5
20 Proj	9	0	145	138	4.38	3.83	1.29	1.25	80	108	22.4	2.8	8.5	3.1	37%	10.6%	91.7	41	21	38	30%	72%	16%		27						-4.1	112	$5

Harper,Ryne

Age: 31	Th: R	Role RP	Health	A	LIMA Plan A
Ht: 6' 3"	Wt: 215	Type Con	PT/Exp	D	Rand Var 0
			Consist	A	MM 2200

Finally appeared in first MLB game at age 30 and acquitted himself rather nicely, using a preponderance of curveballs to register above-average BPX. LI improved in 2nd half even as H%, S% turned prickly. Gotta love that 2nd half Ctl, but unless he makes friends with a Time Lord itching to get back to 1993, that Vel probably won't lead to many saves.

Yr Tm	W	Sv	IP	K	ERA	xERA	WHIP	xWHIP	vL+	vR+	BF/G	Ctl	Dom	Cmd	Ball%	SwK	Vel	G	L	F	H%	S%	HR/F	xHR/F	GS	APC	DOM%	DIS%	Sv%	LI	RAR	BPX	R$
15 aa	0	0	34	33	2.49	2.59	1.18				5.9	3.3	8.9	2.7							30%	79%									6.1	133	-$1
16 aa	4	6	68	77	3.35	3.46	1.37				6.8	3.6	10.2	2.8							35%	75%									7.1	135	$4
17 a/a	4	3	54	43	4.39	4.63	1.47				5.6	3.9	7.3	1.9							32%	72%									-0.2	64	-$1
18 a/a	1	6	65	62	6.05	4.79	1.47				7.3	1.6	8.6	5.3							40%	56%									-15.2	164	-$7
19 MIN	4	1	54	50	3.81	4.23	1.18	1.19	97	91	3.7	1.7	8.3	5.0	31%	11.8%	89.4	39	24	37	31%	72%	12%	13%	0	14			25	1.02	4.7	132	$2
1st Half	3	1	33	32	2.97	4.09	1.08	1.17	80	83	3.8	2.2	8.6	4.0	31%	11.7%	89.2	42	25	33	28%	78%	13%	8%	0	15			50	0.94	6.3	127	$5
2nd Half	1	0	21	18	5.14	4.56	1.33	1.09	122	105	3.5	0.9	7.7	9.0	31%	11.8%	89.7	34	23	43	36%	64%	11%	19%	0	13			0	1.14	-1.7	139	-$3
20 Proj	3	0	58	53	4.60	3.87	1.33	1.12	107	98	4.6	2.0	8.2	4.1	31%	11.8%	89.5	37	24	39	35%	67%	8%		0						-3.2	125	-$3

ALAIN DE LEONARDIS

Harris,Will

Age: 35	Th: R	Role RP	Health	B	LIMA Plan	A
Ht: 6' 4"	Wt: 240	Type Pwr GB	PT/Exp	D	Rand Var	-5
			Consist	A	MM	5410

The long-time LIMA stud delivered perhaps his best season yet despite a dip in Dom and jump in HR/F. An obscenely high S% drove his ERA while a reverse platoon allowed HOU to trust in all situations. He uses cutter/curveball combo to keep the ball on the ground and should continue to age gracefully.

Yr	Tm	W	Sv	IP	K	ERA	xERA	WHIP	xWHIP	vL+	vR+	BF/G	Ctl	Dom	Cmd	Ball%	SwK	Vel	G	L	F	H%	S%	HR/F	xHR/F	GS	APC	DOM%	DIS%	Sv%	LI	RAR	BPX	R$
15	HOU	5	2	71	68	1.90	3.25	0.90	1.23	63	83	4.1	2.8	8.6	3.1	38%	8.9%	91.8	51	20	30	20%	88%	15%	14%	0	17			33	1.28	18.0	130	$12
16	HOU	1	12	64	69	2.25	2.91	1.05	1.11	70	82	3.9	2.1	9.7	4.6	35%	14.0%	92.4	58	17	25	31%	80%	7%	10%	0	16			80	1.17	15.3	183	$11
17	HOU	3	2	45	52	2.98	3.05	0.97	1.00	80	84	3.8	1.4	10.3	7.4	36%	13.7%		48	16	35	28%	78%	17%	11%	0	15			50	1.33	7.7	209	$4
18	HOU	5	0	57	64	3.49	2.97	1.09	1.10	92	71	3.8	2.2	10.2	4.6	37%	14.1%	92.3	50	27	24	32%	68%	9%	15%	0	15			0	0.77	4.6	174	$3
19	HOU	4	4	60	62	1.50	3.16	0.93	1.15	65	81	3.4	2.1	9.3	4.4	38%	12.3%		55	22	24	25%	92%	17%	18%	0	14			80	1.00	22.2	157	$11
1st Half		2	0	30	26	1.19	3.33	0.96	1.16	58	78	3.4	1.8	7.7	4.3	38%	11.5%		57	23	20	27%	89%	6%	8%	0	14			0	0.94	12.4	137	$8
2nd Half		2	4	30	36	1.82	2.94	0.91	1.07	71	84	3.3	2.4	10.9	4.5	38%	13.1%		51	21	28	23%	95%	26%	27%	0	14			80	1.05	9.8	175	$14
20	**Proj**	**4**	**5**	**58**	**63**	**2.93**	**2.78**	**1.05**	**1.09**	**79**	**84**	**3.6**	**2.1**	**9.8**	**4.7**	**37%**	**13.0%**	**32.3**	**52**	**22**	**26**	**29%**	**76%**	**15%**		**0**						**8.7**	**173**	**$7**

Harvey,Hunter

Age: 25	Th: R	Role RP	Health	C	LIMA Plan	C
Ht: 6' 3"	Wt: 175	Type Pwr	PT/Exp	F	Rand Var	+5
			Consist	C	MM	2310

1-0, 1.42 ERA in 6 IP at BAL. One-time stud prospect battled various elbow and shoulder ailments including a Tommy John surgery, but found stability as RP and got an MLB call. His blazing heater is something to build on, but we have to see much more before he becomes roster-worthy. Monitor him.

Yr	Tm	W	Sv	IP	K	ERA	xERA	WHIP	xWHIP	vL+	vR+	BF/G	Ctl	Dom	Cmd	Ball%	SwK	Vel	G	L	F	H%	S%	HR/F	xHR/F	GS	APC	DOM%	DIS%	Sv%	LI	RAR	BPX	R$
15																																		
16																																		
17																																		
18	aa	1	0	33	24	6.31	5.32	1.51				15.9	2.4	6.6	2.7							35%	58%									-8.8	71	-$8
19	BAL *	4	1	84	76	6.11	6.44	1.55		90	88	11.1	3.5	8.2	2.4	35%	12.4%	98.4	45	27	27	32%	67%	33%	15%	0	20			50	1.49	-16.6	29	-$8
1st Half		2	1	61	49	6.66	7.35	1.65		0	0	18.2	3.4	7.2	2.1							33%	67%	0%		0	0					-16.2	2	-$10
2nd Half		2	0	23	28	4.64	3.97	1.26		91	86	5.1	3.8	11.0	2.9		12.4%	98.4	45	27	27	30%	68%	33%	15%	0	20			0	1.49	-0.4	102	-$1
20	**Proj**	**2**	**5**	**44**	**46**	**4.80**	**3.91**	**1.36**				**6.2**	**3.9**	**9.6**	**2.4**	**35%**	**12.4%**		**40**	**21**	**39**	**31%**	**68%**	**14%**		**0**						**-3.5**	**97**	**-$1**

Harvey,Matt

Age: 31	Th: R	Role SP	Health	F	LIMA Plan	D
Ht: 6' 4"	Wt: 220	Type	PT/Exp	C	Rand Var	+5
			Consist	D	MM	0101

3-5, 7.09 ERA in 60 IP at LAA. A solid 2018 finish (4.0 Cmd in 128 IP at CIN) offered some hope for 2019, but the skills fell apart, velo dropped, and another injury cropped up. Persistent HR issue exacerbated problems. Both xHR/F and xWHIP said it was all deserved, too. Health alone is reason enough for caution. Stay away.

Yr	Tm	W	Sv	IP	K	ERA	xERA	WHIP	xWHIP	vL+	vR+	BF/G	Ctl	Dom	Cmd	Ball%	SwK	Vel	G	L	F	H%	S%	HR/F	xHR/F	GS	APC	DOM%	DIS%	Sv%	LI	RAR	BPX	R$
15	NYM	13	0	189	188	2.71	3.25	1.02	1.11	93	77	26.0	1.8	8.9	5.1	32%	12.2%	95.9	46	18	36	29%	78%	10%	8%	29	96	55%	14%			29.2	164	$26
16	NYM	4	0	93	76	4.86	4.36	1.47	1.27	117	99	23.6	2.4	7.4	3.0	33%	10.7%	94.5	41	25	34	36%	67%	8%	10%	17	89	18%	41%			-7.6	103	-$5
17	NYM	5	0	93	67	6.70	5.59	1.69	1.54	136	105	22.7	4.6	6.5	1.4	37%	7.9%	93.8	43	23	34	31%	65%	21%	16%	18	89	0%	61%	0	0.79	-26.8	18	-$13
18	2 NL	7	0	155	131	4.94	4.25	1.30	1.23	110	106	20.7	2.1	7.6	3.5	34%	9.9%	94.0	42	20	38	31%	67%	15%	16%	28	79	25%	25%	0	0.74	-15.0	114	-$2
19	LAA *	4	0	83	62	7.52	6.17	1.62	1.62	127	109	19.3	4.1	6.7	1.6	39%	9.6%	93.2	43	27	30	32%	55%	22%	21%	12	83	8%	58%			-30.7	20	-$14
1st Half		2	0	52	37	8.68	6.58	1.64	1.47	125	111	21.2	4.0	6.4	1.6	39%	10.4%	93.4	41	28	31	31%	48%	22%	23%	10	81	10%	60%			-26.9	6	-$18
2nd Half		2	0	33	25	5.13	4.87	1.49		137	107	17.6	4.0	6.7	1.7		6.0%	92.4	50	26	24	31%	67%	22%	13%	2	93	0%	50%			-2.5	46	-$7
20	**Proj**	**4**	**0**	**87**	**68**	**5.29**	**4.54**	**1.51**	**1.38**	**119**	**102**	**20.2**	**3.8**	**7.0**	**1.9**	**36%**	**9.8%**	**94.0**	**42**	**24**	**34**	**31%**	**69%**	**16%**		**19**						**-12.2**	**52**	**-$6**

Heaney,Andrew

Age: 29	Th: L	Role SP	Health	F	LIMA Plan	D
Ht: 6' 2"	Wt: 200	Type Pwr FB	PT/Exp	C	Rand Var	+4
			Consist	D	MM	2403

Two more IL stints (elbow, shoulder) limited his season while a poor finish (7.66 ERA in September) marred his ERA. Big jump in Dom backed by a SwK surge and small velocity boost enhanced his skills profile, but a FB lean brought upon HR trouble. Health and sporadic IP cloud his outlook, but both xERA and xWHIP still believe.

Yr	Tm	W	Sv	IP	K	ERA	xERA	WHIP	xWHIP	vL+	vR+	BF/G	Ctl	Dom	Cmd	Ball%	SwK	Vel	G	L	F	H%	S%	HR/F	xHR/F	GS	APC	DOM%	DIS%	Sv%	LI	RAR	BPX	R$
15	LAA *	12	0	184	141	3.94	3.92	1.35	1.30	78	102	24.0	2.5	6.9	2.8	36%	9.0%	91.4	38	22	40	33%	71%	7%	10%	18	91	22%	28%			0.5	100	$4
16	LAA	0	0	6	7	6.00	3.11	1.17		113	115	25.0	0.0	10.5	0.0		13.8%	90.8	44	17	39	34%	60%	29%	37%	1	87	0%	0%			-1.3	251	-$4
17	LAA *	2	0	39	39	5.36	7.11	1.50		103	160	21.1	3.0	8.9	3.0		13.7%	91.9	30	22	48	31%	79%	40%	27%	5	83	0%	60%			-4.8	21	-$5
18	LAA	9	0	180	180	4.15	3.73	1.20	1.17	74	107	25.0	2.3	9.0	4.0	34%	12.1%	92.0	41	24	35	31%	70%	15%	15%	30	92	37%	13%			0.0	138	$9
19	LAA	4	0	95	118	4.91	4.05	1.29	1.18	121	98	22.7	2.8	11.1	3.9	35%	14.5%	92.5	34	23	44	33%	69%	18%	16%	18	94	17%	28%			-4.7	148	$0
1st Half		1	0	37	44	5.40	4.57	1.23	1.23	111	102	21.9	3.7	10.8	2.9	36%	14.5%	92.6	32	15	53	26%	64%	18%	16%	7	95	0%	29%			-4.0	114	-$5
2nd Half		3	0	59	74	4.60	3.83	1.33	1.07	130	94	23.3	2.3	11.4	4.9	35%	14.5%	92.5	35	27	38	36%	72%	18%	16%	11	93	27%	27%			-0.7	169	$3
20	**Proj**	**7**	**0**	**145**	**163**	**4.44**	**3.64**	**1.29**	**1.17**	**101**	**104**	**22.3**	**2.8**	**10.1**	**3.6**	**35%**	**13.4%**	**92.2**	**35**	**22**	**43**	**32%**	**72%**	**16%**		**27**						**-5.2**	**137**	**$4**

Helsley,Ryan

Age: 25	Th: R	Role RP	Health	B	LIMA Plan	C
Ht: 6' 1"	Wt: 195	Type xFB	PT/Exp	D	Rand Var	0
			Consist	C	MM	1200

2-0, 2.95 ERA in 37 IP at STL. An 83% S% at MLB buoyed the crisp ERA, but average-to-poor Dom (7.9), Ctl (3.0), and SwK (12%) didn't buy it and yielded a 5.09 xERA. If he can bring MiLB record of quality Dom and HR suppression to pair with elite heat, there could be some improvement, but for now there's little to see here.

Yr	Tm	W	Sv	IP	K	ERA	xERA	WHIP	xWHIP	vL+	vR+	BF/G	Ctl	Dom	Cmd	Ball%	SwK	Vel	G	L	F	H%	S%	HR/F	xHR/F	GS	APC	DOM%	DIS%	Sv%	LI	RAR	BPX	R$
15																																		
16																																		
17	a/a	3	0	39	37	3.48	4.35	1.44				23.5	4.3	8.7	2.0							32%	79%									4.2	82	-$2
18	a/a	5	0	69	63	4.47	3.08	1.17				23.0	3.6	8.2	2.3							26%	63%									-2.7	96	$0
19	STL *	4	1	75	65	4.20	3.96	1.34	1.36	100	95	7.6	3.8	7.8	2.0	33%	10.7%	97.8	34	21	46	29%	71%	10%	9%	0	24			50	0.65	2.8	72	$0
1st Half		1	0	35	30	5.30	3.30	1.31		103	73	8.1	4.8	7.7	1.6		16.8%	97.3	26	26	48	26%	59%	18%	12%	0	24			0	0.18	-3.5	75	-$5
2nd Half		3	1	39	34	3.21	4.55	1.37	1.30	100	102	7.2	3.0	7.9	2.6	32%	8.3%	98.0	36	19	45	32%	82%	8%	8%	0	24			50	0.84	6.3	75	$5
20	**Proj**	**3**	**0**	**51**	**45**	**4.45**	**4.49**	**1.30**	**1.42**	**83**	**85**	**11.3**	**3.8**	**8.0**	**2.1**	**36%**	**8.3%**	**98.0**	**36**	**19**	**45**	**29%**	**67%**	**8%**		**2**						**-1.9**	**65**	**-$2**

Hendricks,Kyle

Age: 30	Th: R	Role SP	Health	B	LIMA Plan	A
Ht: 6' 3"	Wt: 190	Type Con	PT/Exp	A	Rand Var	0
			Consist	A	MM	3205

He just keeps putting up solid seasons as a premium WHIP workhorse even as fantasy managers continue to fear his slow fastball. He combats mid-80s velocity with elite command and an excellent change-up. Weak Dom and average H% and S% push his xERA, but deftly limiting base runners helps him routinely beat the mark.

Yr	Tm	W	Sv	IP	K	ERA	xERA	WHIP	xWHIP	vL+	vR+	BF/G	Ctl	Dom	Cmd	Ball%	SwK	Vel	G	L	F	H%	S%	HR/F	xHR/F	GS	APC	DOM%	DIS%	Sv%	LI	RAR	BPX	R$
15	CHC	8	0	180	167	3.95	3.28	1.16	1.18	109	82	23.1	2.2	8.4	3.9	35%	8.6%	88.3	51	22	27	30%	68%	13%	11%	32	87	31%	22%			0.3	144	$9
16	CHC	16	0	190	170	2.13	3.48	0.98	1.18	84	76	24.0	2.1	8.1	3.9	35%	10.4%	87.8	48	20	31	26%	82%	9%	8%	30	93	33%	7%	0	0.76	48.2	136	$34
17	CHC	7	0	140	123	3.03	3.85	1.19	1.25	93	86	23.8	2.6	7.9	3.1	36%	8.7%	85.8	50	21	29	29%	80%	15%	12%	24	95	21%	17%			22.9	121	$13
18	CHC	14	0	199	161	3.44	3.86	1.15	1.22	91	98	24.6	2.0	7.3	3.7	34%	9.6%	86.9	47	21	32	29%	74%	12%	13%	33	92	24%	30%			17.5	118	$18
19	CHC	11	0	177	150	3.46	4.24	1.13	1.22	88	94	24.3	1.6	7.6	4.7	32%	10.5%	86.9	41	24	35	30%	73%	10%	11%	30	90	30%	27%			22.9	122	$17
1st Half		7	0	88	75	3.36	4.25	1.14	1.16	103	80	26.0	1.6	7.6	4.7	32%	9.6%	87.1	42	23	35	30%	74%	10%	14%	14	93	43%	36%			12.5	124	$18
2nd Half		4	0	89	75	3.55	4.27	1.12	1.17	74	110	22.9	1.6	7.6	4.7	31%	11.4%	86.7	41	25	35	29%	72%	11%	7%	16	87	19%	19%			10.4	122	$17
20	**Proj**	**11**	**0**	**189**	**160**	**3.36**	**3.53**	**1.14**	**1.19**	**89**	**94**	**23.3**	**1.9**	**7.6**	**4.0**	**33%**	**10.0%**	**86.8**	**45**	**23**	**33**	**29%**	**74%**	**12%**		**32**						**18.5**	**125**	**$19**

Hendriks,Liam

Age: 31	Th: R	Role RP	Health	D	LIMA Plan	B
Ht: 6' 0"	Wt: 225	Type Pwr FB	PT/Exp	C	Rand Var	-5
			Consist	B	MM	5530

From DFA to elite RP in just a year. Adding 2 mph to his fastball and slider turned him into a stud with a massive Dom boost supported by SwK gains and Ball% drop. HR suppression was predicted by 2018 xHR/F. Incredible 2nd half Ctl helped outrun H% while xERA and xWHIP back him as a top tier closer.

Yr	Tm	W	Sv	IP	K	ERA	xERA	WHIP	xWHIP	vL+	vR+	BF/G	Ctl	Dom	Cmd	Ball%	SwK	Vel	G	L	F	H%	S%	HR/F	xHR/F	GS	APC	DOM%	DIS%	Sv%	LI	RAR	BPX	R$
15	TOR	5	0	65	71	2.92	2.95	1.08	1.04	102	70	4.5	1.5	9.9	6.5	31%	11.6%	94.9	46	23	31	33%	73%	5%	8%	0	18			0	0.91	8.3	191	$5
16	OAK	0	0	65	71	3.76	3.67	1.28	1.10	82	105	5.2	1.9	9.9	5.1	32%	11.6%	94.1	40	21	39	36%	73%	8%	9%	0	20			0	0.95	3.4	170	$0
17	OAK	4	1	64	78	4.22	3.80	1.25	1.18	84	92	3.9	3.2	11.0	3.4	36%	12.9%	94.7	42	19	39	33%	68%	10%	12%	0	17			25	1.03	1.1	156	$2
18	OAK *	4	6	50	53	3.90	4.07	1.33		89	117	4.3	2.6	9.6	3.7		11.4%	94.4	40	21	39	35%	72%	11%	6%	8	18	0%	63%	86	0.64	1.6	131	$1
19	OAK	4	25	85	124	1.80	3.17	0.96	1.00	93	57	4.4	2.2	13.1	5.9	34%	17.7%	96.5	31	19	49	33%	84%	6%	7%	2	18	0%	100%	78	1.37	28.4	202	$25
1st Half		3	2	47	58	1.35	4.07	1.05	1.16	65	80	4.9	3.3	11.2	3.4	35%	13.8%	95.7	30	18	52	30%	88%	2%	4%	2	20	0%	100%	67	1.06	18.2	131	$17
2nd Half		1	23	38	66	2.35	2.43	0.86	0.72	122	27	4.0	0.9	15.5	16.5	32%	22.8%	97.4	34	21	45	37%	79%	11%	11%	0	16			79	1.68	10.2	289	$35
20	**Proj**	**4**	**27**	**65**	**86**	**3.07**	**2.93**	**1.10**	**1.01**	**96**	**74**	**4.2**	**2.2**	**11.9**	**5.3**	**34%**	**15.5%**	**95.6**	**37**	**20**	**43**	**34%**	**74%**	**8%**		**0**						**8.7**	**194**	**$17**

PAUL SPORER

Hernandez,Darwinzon

Age: 23	Th: L	Role RP	Health A	LIMA Plan F	
Ht: 6' 2"	Wt: 245	Type Pwr xGB	PT/Exp F	Rand Var +4	
			Consist F	MM 3500	

0-1, 4.45 ERA in 30 IP at BOS. Flamethrower missed bats at all 3 levels (AA/AAA/MLB), but rarely knew where it was going. A 48% H% made his MLB debut a lot worse. While strength vL offers path to a role, there's no chance at fantasy viability without sharp improvements in the control vL and vR. Monitor, but don't buy just yet.

Yr Tm	W	Sv	IP	K	ERA	xERA	WHIP	xWHIP	vL+	vR+	BF/G	Ctl	Dom	Cmd	Ball%	SwK	Vel	G	L	F	H%	S%	HR/F	xHR/F	GS	APC	DOM%	DIS%	Sv%	LI	RAR	BPX	R$
15																																	
16																																	
17																																	
18																																	
19 BOS *	2	0	88	122	6.05	4.65	1.77	1.40	51	125	8.8	7.8	12.4	1.6	42%	14.1%	95.5	45	23	32	37%	64%	5%	4%	1	23	0%	0%	0	0.61	-16.9	105	-$11
1st Half	1	0	61	71	6.84	5.26	1.88		49	142	19.0	8.2	10.5	1.3		11.8%	94.5	23	31	46	35%	62%	0%	1%	1	68	0%	0%	0	0.55	-17.4	79	-$15
2nd Half	1	0	30	51	4.00	2.84	1.40	1.33	51	119	4.1	6.3	15.2	2.4	41%	14.7%	95.8	51	21	28	37%	70%	8%	5%	0	20			0	0.62	1.9	162	-$2
20 Proj	**2**	**0**	**58**	**86**	**4.75**	**3.45**	**1.52**	**1.46**	**46**	**113**	**6.1**	**7.0**	**13.4**	**1.9**	**45%**	**14.7%**	**95.8**	**51**	**21**	**28**	**33%**	**68%**	**11%**		**0**						**-4.3**	**92**	**-$4**

Hernandez,Elieser

Age: 25	Th: R	Role SP	Health C	LIMA Plan D	
Ht: 6' 0"	Wt: 210	Type xFB	PT/Exp D	Rand Var +2	
			Consist D	MM 1203	

3-5, 5.03 ERA in 82 IP at MIA. Couldn't turn MLB 3.3 Cmd into results as longball tanked his ERA and severe FB lean says it'll continue, even if HR/F drops toward xHR/F. Trouble vL (4.0 Ctl, 2.6 HR/9) is biggest issue. Showed a glimpse of upside in final 41 IP: 4.39 ERA, 1.12 WHIP, and 4.4 Cmd. Worthy $1 flyer with healthy Dom and Cmd.

Yr Tm	W	Sv	IP	K	ERA	xERA	WHIP	xWHIP	vL+	vR+	BF/G	Ctl	Dom	Cmd	Ball%	SwK	Vel	G	L	F	H%	S%	HR/F	xHR/F	GS	APC	DOM%	DIS%	Sv%	LI	RAR	BPX	R$
15																																	
16																																	
17																																	
18 MIA	2	0	66	45	5.21	5.64	1.45	1.48	121	102	8.9	3.7	6.2	1.7	39%	8.8%	90.7	28	21	51	29%	68%	10%	12%	6	35	0%	67%	0	0.69	-8.6	20	-$7
19 MIA *	6	0	130	143	3.72	4.02	1.22	1.28	120	99	17.6	2.8	9.9	3.5	34%	11.7%	90.6	34	17	49	30%	76%	18%	12%	15	69	13%	20%	0	0.67	12.7	106	$8
1st Half	4	0	72	84	2.34	2.93	1.17	1.13	127	77	20.6	2.6	10.4	4.0	31%	14.5%	91.6	36	20	44	33%	82%	14%	8%	4	82	25%	0%	0	0.60	19.3	152	$15
2nd Half	2	0	58	59	5.43	4.99	1.29	1.26	118	110	15.8	3.1	9.2	3.0	35%	10.6%	90.2	33	16	51	27%	68%	19%	13%	11	65	9%	27%	0	0.69	-6.6	100	$0
20 Proj	**6**	**0**	**145**	**133**	**4.58**	**4.42**	**1.36**	**1.32**	**124**	**100**	**20.7**	**3.2**	**8.3**	**2.6**	**35%**	**10.8%**	**90.8**	**32**	**19**	**50**	**30%**	**74%**	**14%**		**25**						**-7.6**	**83**	**$0**

Hernandez,Felix

Age: 34	Th: R	Role SP	Health F	LIMA Plan B	
Ht: 6' 3"	Wt: 225	Type	PT/Exp B	Rand Var +5	
			Consist B	MM 1100	

A cautionary tale about excessive early career workload, but we're beating a dead horse by now. Shoulder health seems to have ended him. Mounting HR issues, sinking Dom, and sub-90s velocity have rendered him fantasy-useless. Performance vL and vR has gotten worse each of the last four years. We're now 5 years from his last good season.

Yr Tm	W	Sv	IP	K	ERA	xERA	WHIP	xWHIP	vL+	vR+	BF/G	Ctl	Dom	Cmd	Ball%	SwK	Vel	G	L	F	H%	S%	HR/F	xHR/F	GS	APC	DOM%	DIS%	Sv%	LI	RAR	BPX	R$
15 SEA	18	0	202	191	3.53	3.25	1.18	1.22	96	94	26.6	2.6	8.5	3.3	35%	11.3%	91.8	56	17	27	29%	74%	15%	12%	31	98	61%	16%			10.8	140	$18
16 SEA	11	0	153	122	3.82	4.35	1.32	1.43	100	96	26.2	3.8	7.2	1.9	37%	9.8%	90.5	50	21	29	28%	75%	15%	15%	25	98	16%	40%			7.1	64	$7
17 SEA	6	0	87	78	4.36	4.02	1.29	1.26	113	101	23.0	2.7	8.1	3.0	35%	9.9%	90.5	47	23	30	29%	74%	22%	24%	16	86	13%	31%			0.0	118	$2
18 SEA	8	0	156	125	5.55	4.57	1.40	1.38	114	108	23.6	3.4	7.2	2.1	37%	8.4%	89.3	47	19	34	30%	64%	17%	18%	28	88	11%	50%	0	0.81	-26.9	73	-$8
19 SEA	1	0	72	57	6.40	5.12	1.53	1.41	121	121	21.7	3.1	7.2	2.3	37%	8.9%	89.6	48	17	34	32%	63%	21%	20%	15	81	13%	53%			-16.8	76	-$10
1st Half	1	0	39	34	6.52	4.50	1.50	1.19	148	109	21.8	1.9	7.9	4.3	33%	9.5%	89.8	50	16	34	35%	61%	21%	16%	8	78	13%	38%			-9.6	131	-$10
2nd Half	0	0	33	23	6.27	5.90	1.58	1.57	100	140	21.6	4.6	6.3	1.4	41%	8.3%	89.4	46	19	35	28%	66%	21%	25%	7	85	14%	71%			-7.2	13	-$10
20 Proj	**2**	**0**	**58**	**47**	**5.59**	**4.48**	**1.56**	**1.37**	**119**	**121**	**22.5**	**3.7**	**7.3**	**2.0**	**37%**	**9.0%**	**89.8**	**46**	**19**	**35**	**32%**	**69%**	**18%**		**11**						**-10.3**	**64**	**-$7**

Hicks,Jordan

Age: 23	Th: R	Role RP	Health F	LIMA Plan C	
Ht: 6' 2"	Wt: 185	Type Pwr xGB	PT/Exp D	Rand Var 0	
			Consist C	MM 5310	

Strong season cut short by late-June Tommy John surgery; essentially kills 2020, too. PRO: Triple-digit velocity, SwK, GB lean, vR excellence, improved Dom. CON: Ctl (better in 2019, but Ball% is skeptical), short sample of success, modest output vL, health. A cautious dynasty buy as TJS recovery is never guaranteed.

Yr Tm	W	Sv	IP	K	ERA	xERA	WHIP	xWHIP	vL+	vR+	BF/G	Ctl	Dom	Cmd	Ball%	SwK	Vel	G	L	F	H%	S%	HR/F	xHR/F	GS	APC	DOM%	DIS%	Sv%	LI	RAR	BPX	R$
15																																	
16																																	
17																																	
18 STL	3	6	78	70	3.59	4.07	1.34	1.54	98	64	4.6	5.2	8.1	1.6	39%	10.0%	100.5	61	21	19	28%	72%	5%	6%	0	17			46	1.25	5.3	51	$2
19 STL	2	14	29	31	3.14	2.94	0.94	1.27	106	44	3.8	3.5	9.7	2.8	40%	12.1%	101.2	67	16	16	22%	68%	18%	16%	0	16			93	0.94	4.8	138	$6
1st Half	2	14	29	31	3.14	2.86	0.94	1.24	105	45	3.8	3.5	9.7	2.8	40%	12.1%	101.2	67	16	16	22%	68%	18%	16%	0	16			93	0.94	4.8	139	$6
2nd Half																																	
20 Proj	**1**	**2**	**15**	**15**	**3.32**	**2.99**	**1.10**	**1.36**	**101**	**51**	**4.0**	**4.2**	**9.1**	**2.2**	**40%**	**11.2%**	**100.9**	**65**	**18**	**17**	**24%**	**70%**	**12%**		**0**						**1.5**	**108**	**-$2**

Hill,Rich

Age: 40	Th: L	Role RP	Health F	LIMA Plan A	
Ht: 6' 5"	Wt: 221	Type Pwr	PT/Exp B	Rand Var -2	
			Consist A	MM 4401	

Perennial hot potato finally burnt fantasy managers with just 13 starts, though results remained good. A gaudy S% rate mitigated the rough HR/F, but xERA tells the real story. Eight IL stints since 2016 and turning 40 curbs the upside, but also the draft price. Only buy in leagues that allow roster flexibility to combat multiple injuries.

Yr Tm	W	Sv	IP	K	ERA	xERA	WHIP	xWHIP	vL+	vR+	BF/G	Ctl	Dom	Cmd	Ball%	SwK	Vel	G	L	F	H%	S%	HR/F	xHR/F	GS	APC	DOM%	DIS%	Sv%	LI	RAR	BPX	R$
15 BOS *	7	0	83	81	3.53	3.57	1.36		49	60	10.2	4.6	8.8	1.9		11.8%	90.2	48	16	35	29%	76%	9%	9%	4	109	50%	0%			4.4	92	$2
16 2 TM	12	0	110	129	2.12	3.18	1.00	1.13	71	73	22.0	2.7	10.5	3.9	34%	11.1%	90.2	45	19	36	29%	79%	4%	8%	20	91	40%	10%			28.2	166	$20
17 LA	12	0	136	166	3.32	3.67	1.09	1.17	112	79	22.1	3.3	11.0	3.4	33%	11.8%	89.0	37	17	46	27%	75%	13%	12%	25	89	28%	24%			17.4	151	$18
18 LA	11	0	133	150	3.66	3.62	1.12	1.16	95	96	21.9	2.8	10.2	3.7	32%	11.1%	89.3	39	21	40	28%	74%	15%	16%	24	84	29%	17%	0	0.81	8.0	144	$12
19 LA	4	0	59	72	2.45	3.36	1.13	1.15	70	99	18.6	2.8	11.0	4.0	31%	11.4%	90.3	50	18	32	29%	89%	22%	12%	13	74	15%	23%			14.8	166	$5
1st Half	4	0	53	61	2.55	3.43	1.11	1.08	75	102	21.7	2.0	10.4	5.1	30%	11.1%	90.5	49	19	33	29%	90%	23%	13%	10	86	20%	30%			12.8	173	$7
2nd Half	0	0	6	11	1.59	2.59	1.24		22	67	8.3	9.5	17.5	1.8		13.5%	88.8	67	17	17	17%	86%	0%	4%	3	37	0%	0%			2.0	111	-$9
20 Proj	**7**	**0**	**87**	**100**	**3.00**	**3.26**	**1.12**	**1.13**	**92**	**88**	**18.9**	**2.9**	**10.4**	**3.6**	**32%**	**11.4%**	**89.7**	**42**	**19**	**39**	**29%**	**80%**	**14%**		**16**						**12.3**	**149**	**$10**

Hill,Tim

Age: 30	Th: L	Role RP	Health A	LIMA Plan C	
Ht: 6' 2"	Wt: 200	Type GB	PT/Exp D	Rand Var +1	
			Consist C	MM 3210	

2-0, 3.63 ERA in 40 IP at KC. Sidearmer used a sinker/slider combo to generate a boatload of groundballs that made him particularly effective vL and passable vR. His MLB Dom was 8.9, including a sharp 9.4 mark in 2nd half when he became a bullpen mainstay. Still not much fantasy viability as pitch-to-contact soft-tosser, though.

Yr Tm	W	Sv	IP	K	ERA	xERA	WHIP	xWHIP	vL+	vR+	BF/G	Ctl	Dom	Cmd	Ball%	SwK	Vel	G	L	F	H%	S%	HR/F	xHR/F	GS	APC	DOM%	DIS%	Sv%	LI	RAR	BPX	R$
15																																	
16 aa	2	1	45	37	4.67	6.12	1.68				6.5	4.0	7.5	1.9							35%	77%									-2.7	38	-$5
17 aa	1	4	69	57	6.29	5.98	1.80				8.9	2.9	7.4	2.6							42%	62%									-16.5	90	-$11
18 KC	1	2	46	42	4.53	3.45	1.31	1.26	78	108	2.8	2.8	8.3	3.0	33%	9.0%	91.0	62	19	19	33%	66%	15%	15%	0	11			50	1.16	-2.2	132	-$3
19 KC *	3	4	71	61	3.21	3.39	1.19	1.28	61	101	3.9	2.5	7.7	3.1	35%	9.6%	90.2	57	17	26	30%	76%	15%	12%	0	14			67	1.39	11.3	101	$5
1st Half	1	3	38	27	3.15	4.39	1.35		59	161	4.5	2.8	6.3	2.2		4.2%	90.1	60	10	30	31%	81%	33%	26%	0	15			75	1.21	6.3	61	$2
2nd Half	2	1	33	34	3.27	3.17	1.00	1.13	62	87	3.4	2.2	9.3	4.3	32%	10.9%	90.2	57	18	25	28%	68%	10%	8%	0	14			50	1.43	5.0	156	$8
20 Proj	**2**	**2**	**58**	**51**	**3.98**	**3.62**	**1.34**	**1.18**	**82**	**118**	**3.9**	**2.7**	**7.8**	**2.9**	**33%**	**10.1%**	**90.5**	**54**	**18**	**28**	**32%**	**73%**	**14%**		**0**						**1.2**	**113**	**-$1**

Hirano,Yoshihisa

Age: 36	Th: R	Role RP	Health C	LIMA Plan B	
Ht: 6' 1"	Wt: 185	Type Pwr	PT/Exp B	Rand Var +3	
			Consist B	MM 2300	

A sharp 1st/2nd half split in 2018 preached caution heading into 2019. Even a nice jump in Dom couldn't spare him from the damage of higher Ctl and H%. xERA says both seasons were not that different, but the bottom line is this is a nondescript middle reliever with no real chance at saves. Pass.

Yr Tm	W	Sv	IP	K	ERA	xERA	WHIP	xWHIP	vL+	vR+	BF/G	Ctl	Dom	Cmd	Ball%	SwK	Vel	G	L	F	H%	S%	HR/F	xHR/F	GS	APC	DOM%	DIS%	Sv%	LI	RAR	BPX	R$
15 for	13	0	145	102	2.39	2.54	0.99				26.3	1.8	6.3	3.6							25%	81%									28.1	118	$22
16 for	4	0	92	80	3.05	4.57	1.29				26.9	2.8	7.8	2.8							29%	86%									12.9	71	$4
17 for	14	0	188	177	2.79	3.09	1.08				27.1	1.4	8.5	6.2							31%	77%									36.3	196	$27
18 ARI	4	3	66	59	2.44	3.81	1.09	1.31	82	87	3.5	3.1	8.0	2.6	36%	12.9%	91.4	50	16	34	25%	82%	10%	17%	0	15			43	1.44	14.0	101	$7
19 ARI	5	1	53	61	4.75	4.25	1.38	1.31	95	97	3.8	3.7	10.4	2.8	36%	14.6%	91.1	44	20	35	33%	68%	14%	15%	0	15			17	1.32	-1.6	117	-$1
1st Half	3	1	30	33	4.45	4.44	1.38	1.30	80	103	3.7	3.9	9.8	2.5	37%	13.1%	91.0	43	20	36	34%	68%	7%	15%	0	15			33	1.20	0.2	102	$0
2nd Half	2	0	23	28	5.16	3.99	1.37	1.21	115	89	3.8	3.6	11.1	3.1	35%	16.4%	91.2	46	20	34	32%	69%	24%	14%	0	16			0	1.48	-1.8	139	-$2
20 Proj	**5**	**0**	**58**	**60**	**4.05**	**3.65**	**1.30**	**1.27**	**100**	**98**	**4.6**	**3.2**	**9.3**	**2.9**	**36%**	**14.2%**	**91.2**	**45**	**19**	**36**	**31%**	**74%**	**15%**		**0**						**0.7**	**118**	**$0**

PAUL SPORER

Hoffman,Jeff

Age: 27 Th: R Role SP	Health A	LIMA Plan C	
Ht: 6' 5" Wt: 227 Type FB	PT/Exp D	Rand Var +5	
	Consist C	MM 0101	

2-6, 6.56 ERA in 70 IP at COL. Decent upticks in SwK, Dom, but to what? Hasn't missed enough bats for a while; other metrics are even worse. Ball%, Ctl are stagnant. One-time GBer was crushed by HR, RHB (1.139 OPS). H%, S% are relentless problems. Ex-1st-rounder still young, healthy enough. But next stop may be the bullpen.

Yr Tm	W	Sv	IP	K	ERA	xERA	WHIP	xWHIP	vL+	vR+	BF/G	Ctl	Dom	Cmd	Ball%	SwK	Vel	G	L	F	H%	S%	HR/F	xHR/F	GS	APC	DOM%	DIS%	Sv%	LI	RAR	BPX	R$
15 aa	2	0	48	29	4.02	3.44	1.20				21.4	2.4	5.5	2.3							28%	68%									-0.3	73	-$2
16 COL *	6	0	150	119	5.45	5.81	1.64	1.58	116	124	22.3	3.9	7.1	1.8	38%	7.0%	94.0	50	22	28	34%	69%	23%	23%	6	70	17%	83%	0	0.61	-23.4	42	-$13
17 COL *	9	0	149	118	6.03	4.87	1.48	1.40	94	129	19.4	3.6	7.1	2.0	37%	8.5%	94.4	41	18	41	32%	60%	12%	12%	16	70	31%	44%	0	0.59	-30.8	59	-$8
18 COL *	6	0	116	83	6.06	5.48	1.67		177	92	19.3	4.4	6.4	1.5		8.3%	92.8	52	35	13	34%	63%	0%	1%	1	30	0%	100%	0	0.48	-27.3	47	-$16
19 COL *	8	0	156	142	7.80	7.30	1.69	1.47	103	152	22.0	3.7	8.2	2.2	37%	9.8%	93.7	35	21	43	34%	58%	24%	21%	15	84	0%	53%			-63.4	15	-$24
1st Half	5	0	82	81	7.73	6.46	1.62	1.28	94	146	22.6	3.8	8.9	2.3	36%	9.9%	94.1	34	26	41	34%	55%	18%	22%	7	87	0%	29%			-32.4	40	-$22
2nd Half	3	0	77	61	7.64	7.89	1.72	1.55	110	160	21.8	3.5	7.2	2.0	38%	9.7%	93.4	36	18	46	33%	62%	29%	19%	8	81	0%	75%			-29.7	-10	-$26
20 Proj	**6**	**0**	**116**	**93**	**5.94**	**4.81**	**1.62**	**1.45**	**105**	**142**	**20.9**	**3.8**	**7.2**	**1.9**	**37%**	**8.9%**	**94.0**	**40**	**20**	**41**	**33%**	**67%**	**15%**		**25**						**-25.6**	**53**	**-$12**

Holder,Jonathan

Age: 27 Th: R Role RP	Health D	LIMA Plan A	
Ht: 6' 2" Wt: 235 Type Pwr FB	PT/Exp D	Rand Var +5	
	Consist A	MM 2300	

H%, S%, HR/F regression (despite nice GB% jump) were enough fuel for performance downturn. Ctl, Dom better than ever as SwK continued to climb. Nightmarish June stretch (6 games, 6 HR, 13 runs) earned a demotion; inflamed shoulder shelved him shortly thereafter. Will rebound some, Cmd still intrigues. But his is a typical bullpen story.

Yr Tm	W	Sv	IP	K	ERA	xERA	WHIP	xWHIP	vL+	vR+	BF/G	Ctl	Dom	Cmd	Ball%	SwK	Vel	G	L	F	H%	S%	HR/F	xHR/F	GS	APC	DOM%	DIS%	Sv%	LI	RAR	BPX	R$
15																																	
16 NYY *	5	16	70	86	2.80	1.92	0.88		56	116	5.4	1.5	11.1	7.4		11.1%	93.0	33	7	59	29%	71%	6%	11%	0	18			94	0.88	12.0	257	$16
17 NYY *	1	1	55	58	3.43	4.89	1.45	1.13	128	96	4.8	2.7	9.4	3.5	31%	13.2%	92.7	42	18	40	37%	80%	11%	11%	0	18			25	0.71	6.3	114	-$1
18 NYY	1	0	66	60	3.14	4.51	1.09	1.25	78	85	4.5	2.6	8.2	3.2	34%	11.0%	92.7	29	20	51	28%	72%	4%	11%	1	17	0%	0%	0	0.90	8.2	97	$2
19 NYY	5	0	41	46	6.31	4.36	1.31	1.20	102	101	5.3	2.4	10.0	4.2	33%	12.4%	92.2	38	20	43	33%	54%	15%	13%	1	20	0%	100%	0	1.00	-9.2	143	-$3
1st Half	5	0	36	40	6.81	4.75	1.43	1.19	110	107	5.2	2.8	10.1	3.6	33%	12.2%	92.2	34	21	44	35%	56%	17%	13%	0	20			0	1.07	-10.2	130	-$3
2nd Half	0	0	6	6	3.18	2.47	0.53		53	53	6.7	0.0	9.5	0.0		13.9%	92.2	64	7	29	23%	33%	0%	12%	1	24	0%	100%	0	0.30	0.9	233	-$6
20 Proj	**3**	**0**	**44**	**47**	**4.29**	**3.72**	**1.29**	**1.18**	**101**	**94**	**4.8**	**2.6**	**9.6**	**3.8**	**33%**	**12.4%**	**92.5**	**36**	**20**	**44**	**33%**	**70%**	**11%**		**0**						**-0.8**	**136**	**-$2**

Holland,Derek

Age: 33 Th: L Role RP	Health D	LIMA Plan C	
Ht: 6' 2" Wt: 213 Type Pwr	PT/Exp B	Rand Var +5	
	Consist C	MM 1200	

Coming off too-good-to-be-true 2018, RHBs began torching him again from the get-go. Early FB%, HR/F spikes and poor Ctl banished him to the bullpen after 7 starts. Just slightly more effective there; .528 OPS vL overall points to limited future utility. Next start came on season's final game: 2 IP, 4 BB, 7 runs. Free agency has been well-earned.

Yr Tm	W	Sv	IP	K	ERA	xERA	WHIP	xWHIP	vL+	vR+	BF/G	Ctl	Dom	Cmd	Ball%	SwK	Vel	G	L	F	H%	S%	HR/F	xHR/F	GS	APC	DOM%	DIS%	Sv%	LI	RAR	BPX	R$
15 TEX	4	0	59	41	4.91	4.25	1.30	1.34	102	120	24.5	2.6	6.3	2.4	39%	7.4%	92.9	42	23	35	28%	68%	17%	15%	10	91	20%	50%			-6.9	75	-$3
16 TEX	7	0	107	67	4.95	5.15	1.41	1.42	78	111	21.0	2.9	5.6	1.9	36%	8.0%	91.7	38	22	40	30%	68%	11%	12%	20	83	15%	50%	0	0.74	-10.0	45	-$3
17 CHW	7	0	135	104	6.20	5.86	1.71	1.57	95	132	21.6	5.0	6.9	1.4	40%	7.5%	91.1	38	22	40	31%	69%	18%	15%	26	85	15%	54%	0	0.69	-30.7	7	-$15
18 SF	7	0	171	169	3.57	4.17	1.29	1.31	60	111	20.2	3.5	8.9	2.5	36%	10.7%	91.6	40	24	36	30%	76%	11%	14%	30	81	27%	23%	0	0.71	12.2	95	$0
19 2 NL	2	0	84	82	6.08	5.26	1.51	1.52	70	133	7.4	4.8	8.8	1.8	37%	11.4%	92.4	41	19	40	28%	65%	21%	21%	8	29	13%	50%	0	0.72	-16.4	51	-$9
1st Half	1	0	59	62	6.07	5.19	1.52	1.44	60	139	11.6	4.9	9.4	1.9	36%	12.4%	91.8	38	19	43	29%	67%	22%	22%	7	46	14%	43%	0	0.50	-11.4	59	-$9
2nd Half	1	0	25	20	6.12	5.40	1.48	1.53	85	122	3.9	4.7	7.2	1.5	40%	9.1%	93.7	45	20	35	27%	63%	19%	20%	1	16	0%	100%	0	0.91	-5.0	29	-$8
20 Proj	**2**	**0**	**51**	**45**	**5.37**	**4.48**	**1.46**	**1.45**	**77**	**123**	**8.3**	**4.3**	**7.9**	**1.8**	**38%**	**9.8%**	**92.3**	**41**	**21**	**38**	**29%**	**68%**	**17%**		**0**						**-7.6**	**52**	**-$6**

Houser,Adrian

Age: 27 Th: R Role SP	Health A	LIMA Plan F	
Ht: 6' 4" Wt: 235 Type	PT/Exp D	Rand Var +2	
	Consist F	MM 2203	

6-7, 3.72 ERA in 111 IP at MIL. Swing-man thrived out of the pen until late June when starters were needed. Struggled as an SP until something clicked in late July; finished with a sub-4 ERA/xERA afterward. Ctl has always been reasonable; Dom, GB% took big steps forward, HR management needs attention. Role, history make him a wild card.

Yr Tm	W	Sv	IP	K	ERA	xERA	WHIP	xWHIP	vL+	vR+	BF/G	Ctl	Dom	Cmd	Ball%	SwK	Vel	G	L	F	H%	S%	HR/F	xHR/F	GS	APC	DOM%	DIS%	Sv%	LI	RAR	BPX	R$
15 MIL *	5	0	72	48	5.91	5.82	1.56		114	35	19.8	3.1	5.9	1.9		5.7%	94.5	83	17	0	33%	65%	0%		0	18			0	0.02	-17.4	28	-$9
16 aa	3	0	70	48	7.88	6.22	1.74				24.7	3.2	6.2	2.0							37%	53%									-32.0	44	-$16
17																																	
18 MIL *	2	0	94	63	5.65	6.23	1.70		63	131	15.2	3.2	6.1	1.9		10.6%	94.3	40	21	40	37%	68%	0%	5%	0	32			0	0.24	-17.4	41	-$15
19 MIL *	8	0	133	136	3.34	3.55	1.18	1.26	109	83	13.7	2.8	9.2	3.3	37%	10.4%	94.4	53	21	26	29%	76%	18%	13%	18	52	11%	39%	0	1.00	19.1	108	$12
1st Half	4	0	56	59	2.35	3.10	1.16	1.27	114	83	10.6	3.1	9.5	3.1	37%	12.0%	94.6	58	20	22	29%	84%	17%	13%	3	32	0%	67%	0	1.27	14.8	115	$11
2nd Half	4	0	78	77	4.06	3.75	1.20	1.20	107	81	17.9	2.5	8.9	3.5	37%	9.7%	94.3	52	22	27	30%	71%	19%	14%	15	70	13%	33%	0	0.75	4.3	132	$12
20 Proj	**7**	**0**	**145**	**123**	**4.33**	**3.87**	**1.40**	**1.23**	**123**	**94**	**21.1**	**3.0**	**7.6**	**2.6**	**37%**	**10.6%**	**94.5**	**49**	**22**	**29**	**32%**	**72%**	**14%**		**29**						**-3.2**	**97**	**$1**

Hudson,Dakota

Age: 25 Th: R Role RP	Health A	LIMA Plan C	
Ht: 6' 5" Wt: 215 Type xGB	PT/Exp C	Rand Var 0	
	Consist C	MM 1103	

Rookie made the most of elite GB skills and fine infield defense, aided by H%, S% support and 2nd-half SwK uptick. Needs all the help he can get with a sub-2.0 Cmd. Subpar Dom, glaring Ctl issues, shaky HR/F stack the odds against the formula working again, but he somehow keeps doing it, so there's that. Seek Ks, WHIP help elsewhere.

Yr Tm	W	Sv	IP	K	ERA	xERA	WHIP	xWHIP	vL+	vR+	BF/G	Ctl	Dom	Cmd	Ball%	SwK	Vel	G	L	F	H%	S%	HR/F	xHR/F	GS	APC	DOM%	DIS%	Sv%	LI	RAR	BPX	R$
15																																	
16																																	
17 a/a	10	0	153	78	3.75	4.31	1.45				26.1	2.9	4.6	1.6							32%	74%									11.5	54	$3
18 STL *	17	0	141	90	2.75	3.45	1.38		104	57	13.1	3.5	5.7	1.6		9.9%	96.0	61	20	19	31%	78%	0%	5%	0	17			0	1.35	24.3	81	$12
19 STL	16	1	175	136	3.35	4.74	1.41	1.55	108	90	22.9	4.4	7.0	1.6	40%	10.2%	93.7	57	22	21	28%	81%	20%	20%	32	86	16%	41%	100	0.95	24.9	45	$13
1st Half	6	1	87	62	3.40	4.57	1.51	1.47	124	84	22.8	3.9	6.4	1.6	39%	9.6%	93.7	61	20	18	31%	83%	24%	24%	16	82	19%	50%	100	1.13	11.9	53	$7
2nd Half	10	0	87	74	3.30	4.67	1.31	1.54	90	96	23.1	4.9	7.6	1.5	41%	10.8%	93.6	51	23	25	25%	79%	17%	16%	16	91	13%	31%			13.0	36	$19
20 Proj	**17**	**0**	**174**	**131**	**3.87**	**4.11**	**1.45**	**1.51**	**109**	**96**	**18.5**	**4.1**	**6.8**	**1.7**	**40%**	**10.3%**	**93.7**	**55**	**22**	**22**	**30%**	**75%**	**14%**		**34**						**6.0**	**52**	**$7**

Hudson,Daniel

Age: 33 Th: R Role RP	Health D	LIMA Plan A	
Ht: 6' 3" Wt: 225 Type Pwr FB	PT/Exp C	Rand Var -5	
	Consist A	MM 2320	

Unlikely turnabout for middling RP, but xERA said it was the same old skills. Volatile Ctl continued tightrope walk; Dom clung to relevance despite SwK plunge. As always, kept HRs from becoming an issue despite FB% spike and new ball. H%, S% helped wins and saves fuel value. Not a skill set to overpay for; role is key for 2020 free agent.

Yr Tm	W	Sv	IP	K	ERA	xERA	WHIP	xWHIP	vL+	vR+	BF/G	Ctl	Dom	Cmd	Ball%	SwK	Vel	G	L	F	H%	S%	HR/F	xHR/F	GS	APC	DOM%	DIS%	Sv%	LI	RAR	BPX	R$
15 ARI	4	4	68	71	3.86	3.78	1.32	1.26	86	105	4.5	3.3	9.4	2.8	38%	13.4%	96.1	43	22	35	32%	73%	10%	13%	1	18	0%	0%	67	1.11	0.9	121	$1
16 ARI	3	5	60	58	5.22	4.22	1.44	1.30	107	98	3.8	3.3	8.7	2.6	37%	12.3%	95.7	41	27	32	34%	64%	10%	12%	0	16			71	1.16	-7.7	102	-$2
17 PIT	2	0	62	66	4.38	4.45	1.46	1.42	106	98	3.8	4.8	9.6	2.0	39%	12.4%	95.6	43	21	36	32%	72%	12%	10%	0	16			0	0.90	-0.2	77	-$3
18 LA	3	0	46	44	4.11	4.25	1.22	1.33	72	102	4.9	3.5	8.6	2.4	35%	13.5%	95.4	37	27	36	27%	70%	13%	9%	1	18	0%	0%	0	0.95	0.2	86	-$1
19 2 TM	9	8	73	71	2.47	4.75	1.14	1.35	85	87	4.4	3.3	8.8	2.6	34%	10.6%	96.1	37	16	47	26%	84%	9%	13%	1	18	0%	100%	67	1.14	18.4	90	$13
1st Half	5	1	37	38	2.92	5.01	1.27	1.42	110	78	4.5	4.6	9.2	2.0	37%	10.5%	96.0	43	11	46	26%	83%	11%	16%	1	19	0%	100%	33	1.16	7.2	68	$8
2nd Half	4	7	36	33	2.00	4.60	1.00	1.17	60	97	4.3	2.0	8.3	4.1	31%	10.8%	96.3	32	21	48	27%	85%	6%	10%	0	16			78	1.12	11.1	114	$18
20 Proj	**4**	**12**	**65**	**64**	**4.01**	**3.91**	**1.22**	**1.31**	**84**	**95**	**4.2**	**3.5**	**8.8**	**2.6**	**35%**	**11.8%**	**95.9**	**38**	**21**	**41**	**28%**	**70%**	**10%**		**0**						**1.1**	**94**	**$6**

Hughes,Jared

Age: 34 Th: R Role RP	Health B	LIMA Plan B	
Ht: 6' 7" Wt: 240 Type Con xGB	PT/Exp C	Rand Var +3	
	Consist B	MM 3100	

GB machine was sailing along until July, when Ctl wobbled and HR began to bite a little harder. Two horrendous outings (10 runs in 1 2/3 IP) did most of the damage before Sept rebound (16 IP, 2.25 ERA, 2.8 Ctl). Subpar Dom leaves little wiggle room; historical GB-and-H% combo still provide a floor. Needs more 2018 luck to generate value.

Yr Tm	W	Sv	IP	K	ERA	xERA	WHIP	xWHIP	vL+	vR+	BF/G	Ctl	Dom	Cmd	Ball%	SwK	Vel	G	L	F	H%	S%	HR/F	xHR/F	GS	APC	DOM%	DIS%	Sv%	LI	RAR	BPX	R$
15 PIT	3	0	67	36	2.28	3.86	1.33	1.40	94	105	3.7	2.6	4.8	1.9	34%	10.0%	93.1	64	18	19	30%	84%	8%	17%	0	13			0	1.14	13.9	72	$2
16 PIT	1	1	59	34	3.03	4.62	1.42	1.48	115	102	3.8	3.3	5.2	1.5	39%	9.8%	93.0	58	16	26	30%	82%	12%	10%	0	14			33	0.72	8.5	46	-$1
17 MIL	5	1	60	48	3.02	3.73	1.22	1.40	121	85	3.6	3.6	7.2	2.0	40%	12.0%	93.5	62	19	19	27%	77%	13%	18%	0	14			25	0.92	9.9	87	$4
18 CIN	4	7	79	59	1.94	3.22	1.02	1.31	77	80	4.1	2.6	6.8	2.6	35%	12.4%	91.8	65	17	18	25%	83%	11%	17%	0	16			64	1.30	21.4	108	$12
19 2 NL	5	1	71	54	4.04	4.21	1.18	1.44	73	108	4.0	3.4	6.8	2.0	39%	10.3%	91.3	59	18	22	23%	73%	29%	20%	0	16			25	0.95	4.1	74	$3
1st Half	2	0	35	24	3.12	3.71	0.95	1.33	43	93	4.0	2.6	6.2	2.4	38%	10.0%	91.0	63	16	21	20%	72%	20%	12%	0	16			0	0.81	5.9	91	$3
2nd Half	3	1	37	30	4.91	4.51	1.39	1.46	95	122	4.0	4.2	7.4	1.8	40%	10.6%	91.5	56	21	24	25%	74%	36%	25%	0	16			33	1.06	-1.8	58	$2
20 Proj	**4**	**0**	**65**	**49**	**3.71**	**3.55**	**1.18**	**1.39**	**87**	**99**	**3.9**	**3.3**	**6.7**	**2.1**	**38%**	**11.0%**	**91.9**	**61**	**18**	**21**	**25%**	**73%**	**21%**		**0**						**3.5**	**83**	**$2**

JOCK THOMPSON

Iglesias,Raisel

Age: 30 | Th: R | Role: RP | Ht: 6' 2" | Wt: 188 | Type: Pwr FB
Health: C | PT/Exp: A | Consist: A | LIMA Plan: A | Rand Var: +2 | MM: 4530

Outperformed xERA from 2016-18, but correction finally came in 2019. Underneath that ERA slippage, featured career-best skills in second half, highlighted by suddenly-pinpoint Ctl and Vel uptick. Ball% doesn't quite buy that newfound precision, and FB% surge means HR issues likely to linger. But this profile is well-worthy of 2nd-tier closer status.

Yr Tm	W	Sv	IP	K	ERA	xERA	WHIP	xWHIP	vL+	vR+	BF/G	Ctl	Dom	Cmd	Ball%	SwK	Vel	G	L	F	H%	S%	HR/F	xHR/F	GS	APC	DOM%	DIS%	Sv%	LI	RAR	BPX	R$
15 CIN *	4	0	124	122	4.26	3.75	1.21	1.17	103	87	20.9	2.7	8.8	3.3	34%	12.5%	91.7	47	21	32	30%	68%	14%	13%	16	87	38%	25%	0	0.72	-4.6	110	$2
16 CIN	3	6	78	83	2.53	3.77	1.14	1.22	105	66	8.8	3.0	9.5	3.2	38%	12.3%	93.0	41	21	38	29%	82%	9%	8%	5	34	20%	20%	75	1.01	16.1	131	$9
17 CIN	3	28	76	92	2.49	3.38	1.11	1.17	94	61	4.9	3.2	10.9	3.4	34%	14.7%	96.4	42	25	32	30%	80%	8%	8%	0	20			93	0.99	17.5	156	$20
18 CIN	2	30	72	80	2.38	3.58	1.07	1.21	91	87	4.4	3.1	10.0	3.2	35%	15.7%	95.2	38	26	35	25%	89%	19%	18%	0	17			88	1.02	15.8	129	$19
19 CIN	3	34	67	89	4.16	3.76	1.22	1.14	105	94	4.1	2.8	12.0	4.2	35%	16.0%	95.5	30	26	44	33%	73%	17%	12%	0	17			85	1.54	2.8	160	$16
1st Half	1	14	35	46	4.41	4.48	1.47	1.27	136	83	4.6	4.4	11.9	2.7	34%	17.7%	95.1	26	31	43	35%	76%	16%	13%	0	18			88	1.57	0.4	109	$8
2nd Half	2	20	32	43	3.90	3.19	0.96	0.89	74	108	3.6	1.1	12.0	10.8	35%	14.0%	95.9	35	20	45	30%	68%	18%	11%	0	15			83	1.52	2.4	216	$25
20 Proj	**3**	**33**	**65**	**80**	**3.63**	**3.25**	**1.13**	**1.12**	**96**	**88**	**4.4**	**2.8**	**11.0**	**4.0**	**35%**	**15.1%**	**95.3**	**34**	**24**	**42**	**30%**	**74%**	**15%**		**0**						**4.2**	**156**	**$17**

Irvin,Cole

Age: 26 | Th: L | Role: SP | Ht: 6' 4" | Wt: 180 | Type: Con
Health: A | PT/Exp: D | Consist: D | LIMA Plan: D | Rand Var: +1 | MM: 1000

2-1, 5.83 ERA in 42 IP at PHI. Soft-tosser had success as command specialist in minors, but that didn't translate to the bigs in either role (SP: 5.60 ERA in 18 IP; RP: 6.00 ERA in 24 IP). Utilizes a four-pitch mix and rarely doles out free passes. Lack of velocity and movement caps ceiling, while blowup potential is unchecked.

Yr Tm	W	Sv	IP	K	ERA	xERA	WHIP	xWHIP	vL+	vR+	BF/G	Ctl	Dom	Cmd	Ball%	SwK	Vel	G	L	F	H%	S%	HR/F	xHR/F	GS	APC	DOM%	DIS%	Sv%	LI	RAR	BPX	R$
15																																	
16																																	
17 aa	5	0	84	58	4.92	4.48	1.27				26.6	2.6	6.2	2.4							28%	66%									-5.8	54	-$1
18 aaa	14	0	162	114	3.21	3.71	1.22				25.2	2.0	6.3	3.1							30%	76%									18.7	95	$14
19 PHI *	8	1	137	87	5.00	5.95	1.50	1.40	123	98	17.9	1.8	5.7	3.2	33%	10.0%	89.8	34	31	34	34%	71%	16%	16%	3	40	33%	67%	100	0.57	-8.4	52	-$4
1st Half	5	0	83	56	4.31	5.31	1.39	1.25	133	121	22.0	1.8	6.0	3.4	34%	10.6%	88.8	29	29	42	33%	74%	20%	20%	3	68	33%	67%	0	0.58	2.0	67	$0
2nd Half	3	1	53	31	6.09	6.94	1.66	1.53	106	55	14.1	1.9	5.3	2.8	32%	9.1%	91.6	44	35	21	36%	67%	0%	4%	0	23			100	0.57	-10.4	31	-$11
20 Proj	**3**	**0**	**44**	**29**	**4.96**	**4.38**	**1.44**	**1.42**	**148**	**103**	**20.0**	**2.0**	**5.9**	**3.0**	**33%**	**9.7%**	**90.5**	**38**	**29**	**33**	**33%**	**70%**	**15%**		**9**						**-4.3**	**78**	**-$5**

Jackson,Luke

Age: 28 | Th: R | Role: RP | Ht: 6' 2" | Wt: 210 | Type: Pwr GB
Health: A | PT/Exp: D | Consist: C | LIMA Plan: C | Rand Var: +5 | MM: 5510

Ascended to the closer role in late-April and lost it by the end of July. PRO: Used Vel spike to push both SwK and GB% to elite levels. CON: Ctl wavered in 2nd half; bloated H% and xHR/F speak to inconsistent command and hittability. Big SwK/Dom/GB all make him much more rosterable now even if the saves don't come back.

Yr Tm	W	Sv	IP	K	ERA	xERA	WHIP	xWHIP	vL+	vR+	BF/G	Ctl	Dom	Cmd	Ball%	SwK	Vel	G	L	F	H%	S%	HR/F	xHR/F	GS	APC	DOM%	DIS%	Sv%	LI	RAR	BPX	R$
15 TEX *	2	0	73	70	5.31	4.63	1.63		39	105	7.0	4.9	8.7	1.8		12.7%	96.1	53	16	32	35%	66%	17%	26%	0	16			0	0.14	-12.1	87	-$9
16 TEX *	1	3	58	49	6.15	7.15	1.99		187	141	6.3	6.8	7.7	1.1		5.0%	94.1	31	27	41	35%	73%	19%	10%	0	30			50	0.87	-14.0	12	-$12
17 ATL *	2	1	75	52	5.85	5.23	1.67	1.45	80	118	6.5	4.5	6.3	1.4	37%	10.7%	94.7	45	19	36	34%	64%	7%	12%	0	19			100	0.54	-13.8	49	-$10
18 ATL *	3	1	63	72	3.62	3.41	1.37	1.37	88	111	5.8	4.5	10.3	2.3	38%	11.7%	94.3	48	23	29	33%	73%	9%	11%	0	20			50	0.89	4.1	121	$0
19 ATL	9	18	73	106	3.84	2.77	1.40	1.11	72	113	4.5	3.2	13.1	4.1	36%	17.0%	96.1	60	18	22	40%	77%	26%	24%	0	18			72	1.28	6.0	204	$12
1st Half	3	13	41	57	2.85	2.47	1.22	1.06	74	94	4.6	2.9	12.5	4.4	34%	16.0%	95.9	68	14	18	36%	80%	22%	22%	0	18			68	1.53	8.4	211	$15
2nd Half	6	5	32	49	5.12	3.08	1.64	1.10	69	136	4.3	3.7	13.9	3.8	38%	18.1%	96.4	51	22	27	45%	74%	29%	26%	0	18			83	1.00	-2.4	197	$8
20 Proj	**5**	**5**	**58**	**71**	**3.68**	**3.02**	**1.29**	**1.24**	**70**	**102**	**4.9**	**3.6**	**11.0**	**3.1**	**37%**	**14.4%**	**95.3**	**52**	**20**	**27**	**33%**	**75%**	**17%**		**0**						**3.3**	**152**	**$4**

James,Josh

Age: 27 | Th: R | Role: RP | Ht: 6' 3" | Wt: 206 | Type: Pwr xFB
Health: C | PT/Exp: D | Consist: C | LIMA Plan: C | Rand Var: +5 | MM: 4501

SP prospect spent 2019 in bullpen. SwK/Dom played up to rarified levels in new role, but Ctl and FB problems kept ERA volatile. On the bright side, xHR/F, Ball%, and xERA say he deserved a better fate. Missed August with sore shoulder; returned with revamped delivery (35% Ball% in 10 Sept IP). Success as SP hinges on improving Ctl.

Yr Tm	W	Sv	IP	K	ERA	xERA	WHIP	xWHIP	vL+	vR+	BF/G	Ctl	Dom	Cmd	Ball%	SwK	Vel	G	L	F	H%	S%	HR/F	xHR/F	GS	APC	DOM%	DIS%	Sv%	LI	RAR	BPX	R$
15																																	
16																																	
17 aa	4	3	76	63	5.51	4.81	1.66				16.2	3.9	7.4	1.9							38%	64%									-10.8	90	-$7
18 HOU *	8	1	140	169	3.37	2.85	1.14		94	73	19.2	3.5	10.8	3.1		14.6%	97.1	42	15	43	29%	73%	13%	13%	3	58	33%	0%	50	0.75	13.4	136	$13
19 HOU	5	1	61	100	4.70	3.65	1.32	1.24	93	92	5.4	5.1	14.7	2.9	39%	16.6%	97.2	35	19	46	33%	69%	17%	10%	1	23	0%	0%	33	0.80	-1.4	151	$1
1st Half	3	0	41	65	4.57	3.92	1.28	1.28	91	86	5.9	5.7	14.2	2.5	40%	16.4%	97.2	34	18	48	28%	70%	18%	11%	0	26			0	0.68	-0.3	124	$2
2nd Half	2	1	20	35	4.95	3.28	1.40	1.05	95	106	4.7	4.1	15.8	3.9	38%	17.1%	97.1	36	20	43	43%	68%	16%	6%	1	19	0%	0%	50	0.99	-1.1	206	-$1
20 Proj	**5**	**0**	**73**	**100**	**3.91**	**3.21**	**1.22**	**1.15**	**86**	**93**	**7.4**	**3.7**	**12.5**	**3.4**	**39%**	**16.8%**	**97.2**	**35**	**19**	**45**	**32%**	**72%**	**13%**		**0**						**2.2**	**159**	**$4**

Jansen,Kenley

Age: 32 | Th: R | Role: RP | Ht: 6' 5" | Wt: 265 | Type: Pwr FB
Health: B | PT/Exp: A | Consist: B | LIMA Plan: B | Rand Var: +1 | MM: 5530

The pre-2018 model appears gone, as Vel/SwK/Ball% have moved in wrong direction and xHR/F shows he gets squared up much more often. This version still plays, as 2nd half downturn was mostly fluke per xHR/F, Ball%, and SwK. Set expectations around 3.50 ERA and you shouldn't be disappointed.

Yr Tm	W	Sv	IP	K	ERA	xERA	WHIP	xWHIP	vL+	vR+	BF/G	Ctl	Dom	Cmd	Ball%	SwK	Vel	G	L	F	H%	S%	HR/F	xHR/F	GS	APC	DOM%	DIS%	Sv%	LI	RAR	BPX	R$
15 LA	2	36	52	80	2.41	2.46	0.78	0.83	78	65	3.7	1.4	13.8	10.0	28%	17.6%	92.5	35	11	54	29%	77%	10%	11%	0	15			95	1.22	10.0	266	$22
16 LA	3	47	69	104	1.83	2.48	0.67	0.82	74	48	3.5	1.4	13.6	9.5	28%	18.2%	93.6	30	15	55	26%	76%	6%	7%	0	14			89	1.21	19.9	255	$33
17 LA	5	41	68	109	1.32	2.17	0.75	0.75	85	43	4.0	0.9	14.4	15.6	26%	18.6%	93.3	38	21	41	32%	89%	9%	8%	0	16			98	1.30	25.6	300	$34
18 LA	1	38	72	82	3.01	3.55	0.99	1.09	78	97	4.2	2.1	10.3	4.8	32%	13.9%	92.3	35	21	44	25%	81%	16%	13%	0	17			90	1.15	10.0	162	$21
19 LA	5	33	63	80	3.71	3.72	1.06	1.10	83	91	4.2	2.3	11.4	5.0	31%	16.3%	92.0	32	24	43	30%	71%	13%	11%	0	17			80	1.24	6.1	168	$19
1st Half	3	23	35	46	3.12	3.48	0.95	0.98	74	92	4.1	1.8	11.9	6.6	30%	16.8%	91.8	35	20	46	29%	75%	14%	14%	0	17			88	1.40	5.9	195	$24
2nd Half	2	10	28	34	4.45	4.18	1.20	1.15	93	90	4.4	2.9	10.8	3.8	31%	15.8%	92.2	30	29	41	31%	67%	13%	7%	0	18			67	1.05	0.2	137	$13
20 Proj	**3**	**35**	**58**	**76**	**3.43**	**2.93**	**1.05**	**1.01**	**88**	**87**	**4.0**	**2.0**	**11.7**	**5.8**	**30%**	**16.1%**	**92.4**	**34**	**22**	**44**	**31%**	**73%**	**13%**		**0**						**5.2**	**193**	**$19**

Jeffress,Jeremy

Age: 32 | Th: R | Role: RP | Ht: 6' 0" | Wt: 205 | Type: GB
Health: D | PT/Exp: C | Consist: D | LIMA Plan: D | Rand Var: +2 | MM: 2200

Began 2019 on IL (shoulder weakness) and landed there again in August (left hip strain) before being released by MIL on Sept 3. In between, his Vel fell sharply and SwK reverted to 2016-17 level. Restoration of GB% in 2nd half is a good sign, but Vel return not a guarantee at his age. Don't count on more than a modest rebound.

Yr Tm	W	Sv	IP	K	ERA	xERA	WHIP	xWHIP	vL+	vR+	BF/G	Ctl	Dom	Cmd	Ball%	SwK	Vel	G	L	F	H%	S%	HR/F	xHR/F	GS	APC	DOM%	DIS%	Sv%	LI	RAR	BPX	R$
15 MIL	5	0	68	67	2.65	3.08	1.26	1.24	103	87	4.0	2.9	8.9	3.0	38%	12.0%	95.4	58	24	18	32%	81%	15%	15%	0	15			0	1.15	11.0	139	$4
16 2 TM	3	27	58	42	2.33	3.64	1.26	1.34	123	65	4.1	2.8	6.5	2.3	34%	9.7%	95.1	60	24	16	30%	82%	7%	8%	0	15			96	1.08	13.3	95	$14
17 2 TM	5	0	65	51	4.68	4.74	1.64	1.53	115	110	4.8	4.7	7.0	1.5	38%	10.3%	94.5	59	17	24	32%	75%	21%	16%	1	19	0%	100%	0	0.85	-2.6	44	-$5
18 MIL	8	15	77	89	1.29	2.88	0.99	1.18	64	79	4.1	3.2	10.4	3.3	35%	14.0%	95.3	56	20	24	26%	92%	12%	14%	0	17			75	1.52	27.0	157	$21
19 MIL	3	1	52	46	5.02	4.37	1.37	1.34	99	97	4.7	2.9	8.0	2.7	35%	9.9%	93.8	48	23	28	33%	64%	11%	16%	0	18			25	0.94	-3.3	98	-$3
1st Half	2	0	31	31	4.02	4.16	1.21	1.27	80	95	4.6	3.2	8.9	2.8	37%	10.1%	93.5	42	25	33	29%	69%	11%	15%	0	20			0	1.04	1.9	104	-$1
2nd Half	1	1	21	15	6.53	4.60	1.60	1.33	124	99	4.8	2.6	6.5	2.5	32%	9.7%	94.2	56	21	23	37%	58%	13%	17%	0	17			33	0.81	-5.2	88	-$6
20 Proj	**3**	**0**	**44**	**40**	**3.83**	**3.67**	**1.34**	**1.31**	**100**	**94**	**4.4**	**3.2**	**8.2**	**2.6**	**35%**	**11.0%**	**94.5**	**51**	**21**	**28**	**32%**	**73%**	**12%**		**0**						**1.7**	**103**	**-$2**

Jimenez,Joe

Age: 25 | Th: R | Role: RP | Ht: 6' 3" | Wt: 272 | Type: Pwr xFB
Health: A | PT/Exp: D | Consist: C | LIMA Plan: C | Rand Var: +4 | MM: 3530

Assumed closer duties in August and really hit his stride in Sept (1.00 ERA, 12 K/1 BB in 9 IP). Improved Ball% implies better Ctl and the strikeouts kept coming in droves, netting out to a profile that is comfortably closer-worthy. FB tilt makes him susceptible to gopheritis, but the 2nd half line hints at ... UP: 3.50 ERA, 35 Sv.

Yr Tm	W	Sv	IP	K	ERA	xERA	WHIP	xWHIP	vL+	vR+	BF/G	Ctl	Dom	Cmd	Ball%	SwK	Vel	G	L	F	H%	S%	HR/F	xHR/F	GS	APC	DOM%	DIS%	Sv%	LI	RAR	BPX	R$
15																																	
16 a/a	3	20	36	42	2.63	1.57	0.98				3.6	3.0	10.5	3.6							27%	72%									7.0	175	$11
17 DET *	1	4	44	47	6.43	5.80	1.72		84	167	4.0	4.5	9.6	2.2		12.5%	95.3	34	23	43	39%	63%	13%	15%	0	17			67	0.55	-11.2	79	-$7
18 DET	5	3	63	78	4.31	3.76	1.20	1.16	96	83	3.9	3.2	11.2	3.5	36%	14.1%	95.6	36	19	45	33%	64%	7%	12%	0	17			43	1.08	-1.2	150	$2
19 DET	4	9	60	82	4.37	4.02	1.32	1.19	107	104	3.9	3.5	12.4	3.6	33%	15.2%	95.2	29	22	49	33%	76%	18%	16%	0	16			64	1.08	1.0	148	$4
1st Half	2	0	32	47	5.12	4.02	1.39	1.21	116	106	3.9	4.5	13.4	2.9	34%	17.0%	95.4	30	25	45	33%	70%	21%	19%	0	17			0	1.18	-2.4	137	-$2
2nd Half	2	9	28	35	3.54	4.20	1.25	1.07	100	104	3.9	2.3	11.3	5.0	31%	12.9%	94.9	29	19	52	33%	83%	16%	13%	0	15			82	0.97	3.3	162	$10
20 Proj	**4**	**26**	**65**	**82**	**3.97**	**3.53**	**1.25**	**1.14**	**104**	**97**	**3.7**	**3.3**	**11.3**	**3.4**	**34%**	**14.5%**	**95.3**	**32**	**20**	**48**	**30%**	**77%**	**17%**		**0**						**1.4**	**142**	**$13**

GREG PYRON

Junis,Jakob

Age: 27	Th: R	Role SP	Health A	LIMA Plan A	
Ht: 6' 2"	Wt: 225	Type	PT/Exp A	Rand Var +3	
			Consist A	MM 2203	

Aside from an uptick in Ball%/Ctl, his skills looked a lot like 2018. HRs continue to be his undoing. Throws four pitches, but relies heavily on slider/four-seam fastball (44%/34% usage) and the slider is his only above-average offering. Without a legit 3rd pitch or a return to dead-ball era, bullpen move may be in order.

Yr	Tm	W	Sv	IP	K	ERA	xERA	WHIP	xWHIP	vL+	vR+	BF/G	Ctl	Dom	Cmd	Ball%	SwK	Vel	G	L	F	H%	S%	HR/F	xHR/F	GS	APC	DOM%	DIS%	Sv%	LI	RAR	BPX	R$
15																																		
16	a/a	10	0	149	115	5.37	5.22	1.46				23.6	2.2	6.9	3.2							35%	65%									-21.7	81	-$6
17	KC *	12	0	169	148	4.09	4.24	1.28	1.26	104	100	21.7	2.2	7.9	3.6	36%	9.4%	91.2	40	20	40	32%	72%	12%	14%	16	76	19%	31%	0	0.88	5.6	108	$10
18	KC	9	0	177	164	4.37	4.03	1.27	1.20	107	106	25.3	2.2	8.3	3.8	35%	10.0%	91.1	42	21	37	31%	72%	16%	17%	30	95	23%	30%			-4.9	128	$4
19	KC	9	0	175	164	5.24	4.65	1.43	1.33	110	104	24.9	3.0	8.4	2.8	37%	10.0%	91.5	42	23	35	33%	68%	17%	18%	31	94	23%	29%			-15.8	99	-$3
1st Half		4	0	95	88	5.23	4.77	1.47	1.31	118	103	24.8	3.2	8.4	2.6	37%	10.5%	91.6	44	21	35	33%	69%	18%	20%	17	95	18%	24%			-8.4	93	-$5
2nd Half		5	0	81	76	5.24	4.52	1.38	1.24	101	105	25.0	2.7	8.5	3.2	37%	9.4%	91.4	40	25	34	33%	65%	15%	16%	14	94	29%	36%			-7.3	107	-$1
20	**Proj**	**10**	**0**	**174**	**158**	**4.86**	**3.89**	**1.36**	**1.24**	**108**	**104**	**23.7**	**2.5**	**8.2**	**3.2**	**36%**	**9.8%**	**91.3**	**42**	**22**	**36**	**32%**	**69%**	**15%**		**31**						**-15.3**	**113**	**$1**

Jurado,Ariel

Age: 24	Th: R	Role SP	Health A	LIMA Plan B	
Ht: 6' 1"	Wt: 180	Type Con	PT/Exp D	Rand Var +3	
			Consist B	MM 1001	

7-11, 5.81 ERA in 122 IP at TEX. Good control and GB lean are his strengths, but they aren't enough to compensate for puny SwK/Dom. Made some progress in those areas, but has several more rungs to climb before we get interested. In meantime, xHR/F says this could have been even worse, and you don't want to be around for that.

Yr	Tm	W	Sv	IP	K	ERA	xERA	WHIP	xWHIP	vL+	vR+	BF/G	Ctl	Dom	Cmd	Ball%	SwK	Vel	G	L	F	H%	S%	HR/F	xHR/F	GS	APC	DOM%	DIS%	Sv%	LI	RAR	BPX	R$
15																																		
16	aa	1	0	44	30	4.28	4.56	1.41				23.1	2.1	6.2	2.9							34%	70%									-0.5	86	-$4
17	aa	9	0	157	80	6.19	6.40	1.69				26.2	2.3	4.6	2.0							36%	64%									-35.5	28	-$17
18	TEX *	10	0	158	71	4.76	5.38	1.45	1.51	137	92	24.1	2.1	4.0	1.9	38%	4.6%	91.8	52	21	28	31%	70%	13%	17%	8	73	0%	88%	0	0.76	-12.0	26	-$6
19	TEX *	10	0	147	99	5.50	5.63	1.49	1.42	107	125	17.6	2.3	6.1	2.6	36%	7.7%	92.4	46	22	32	34%	66%	16%	20%	18	64	11%	50%	0	0.82	-18.0	48	-$6
1st Half		8	0	82	59	3.91	4.65	1.37	1.31	97	112	16.3	1.9	6.5	3.4	35%	8.2%	92.7	48	20	31	34%	74%	12%	16%	8	55	13%	25%	0	0.91	6.0	88	$5
2nd Half		2	0	65	40	7.52	5.58	1.65	1.41	117	135	19.5	2.9	5.6	1.9	37%	7.4%	92.2	44	24	32	34%	57%	19%	23%	10	74	10%	70%	0	0.72	-24.0	48	-$20
20	**Proj**	**6**	**0**	**102**	**60**	**4.90**	**4.48**	**1.52**	**1.43**	**120**	**113**	**20.8**	**2.3**	**5.3**	**2.3**	**37%**	**6.5%**	**92.2**	**48**	**22**	**30**	**33%**	**71%**	**14%**		**21**						**-9.3**	**68**	**-$6**

Kahnle,Tommy

Age: 30	Th: R	Role RP	Health C	LIMA Plan F	
Ht: 6' 1"	Wt: 235	Type Pwr	PT/Exp D	Rand Var +5	
			Consist F	MM 5500	

xERA snapped back to 2017 level, likely powered by return of (most of) 2018's lost velocity. Could have been even better, but struggled mightily in September as he battled wrist tendinitis (6 ER in 7 IP). Health and consistency grades highlight risk, but the elite SwK and GB combo makes this a closer-worthy skill set.

Yr	Tm	W	Sv	IP	K	ERA	xERA	WHIP	xWHIP	vL+	vR+	BF/G	Ctl	Dom	Cmd	Ball%	SwK	Vel	G	L	F	H%	S%	HR/F	xHR/F	GS	APC	DOM%	DIS%	Sv%	LI	RAR	BPX	R$
15	COL *	1	8	60	59	5.35	4.46	1.57	1.67	114	105	4.7	6.1	8.8	1.5	41%	13.8%	95.9	55	24	21	30%	67%	17%	12%	0	18			67	0.83	-10.3	71	-$5
16	CHW *	1	8	54	54	3.27	3.06	1.40		78	100	4.4	5.6	9.0	1.6		11.0%	96.5	49	23	28	29%	76%	10%	6%	0	17			67	0.83	6.2	106	$2
17	2 AL	2	0	62	95	2.63	2.76	1.14	0.96	98	72	3.7	2.5	13.9	5.6	33%	17.5%	97.9	40	22	38	38%	79%	8%	10%	0	15			0	1.06	13.2	241	$5
18	NYY *	4	2	50	58	6.00	5.41	1.66		90	133	4.5	5.1	10.5	2.1		15.1%	95.1	35	24	40	37%	65%	12%	15%	0	20			67	0.79	-11.3	84	-$7
19	NYY	3	0	61	88	3.67	2.83	1.06	1.07	89	79	3.4	2.9	12.9	4.4	35%	18.2%	96.5	50	21	28	30%	71%	23%	18%	0	14			0	1.03	6.3	197	$4
1st Half		2	0	32	47	3.38	2.96	1.06	1.05	86	79	3.5	3.1	13.2	4.3	35%	18.0%	96.5	54	14	32	28%	79%	25%	17%	0	14			0	0.94	4.5	203	$4
2nd Half		1	0	29	41	3.99	2.68	1.06	1.03	92	80	3.4	2.8	12.6	4.6	35%	18.5%	96.5	46	30	24	31%	64%	20%	20%	0	14			0	1.12	1.9	192	$4
20	**Proj**	**3**	**0**	**58**	**77**	**3.11**	**2.68**	**1.09**	**1.11**	**93**	**78**	**3.6**	**2.9**	**12.0**	**4.1**	**35%**	**17.3%**	**96.9**	**46**	**23**	**31**	**30%**	**76%**	**16%**		**0**						**7.4**	**186**	**$4**

Kela,Keone

Age: 27	Th: R	Role RP	Health F	LIMA Plan A	
Ht: 6' 1"	Wt: 210	Type Pwr FB	PT/Exp C	Rand Var -5	
			Consist A	MM 4520	

Right shoulder discomfort sidelined him for two months; explains the soft 1st half skills. Has now landed on the IL in three of the past four seasons, thus earning his Health grade. 2nd half ERA and HR/F are obviously unsustainable, but accompanying xERA and BPX look enough like 2017-18 to reset his baseline there. With opportunity... UP: 30 Sv

Yr	Tm	W	Sv	IP	K	ERA	xERA	WHIP	xWHIP	vL+	vR+	BF/G	Ctl	Dom	Cmd	Ball%	SwK	Vel	G	L	F	H%	S%	HR/F	xHR/F	GS	APC	DOM%	DIS%	Sv%	LI	RAR	BPX	R$
15	TEX	7	1	60	68	2.39	3.01	1.16	1.15	102	74	3.6	2.7	10.1	3.8	35%	14.2%	95.6	51	21	29	32%	82%	9%	7%	0	15			25	1.21	11.7	166	$7
16	TEX	5	0	34	45	6.09	3.57	1.38	1.27	78	119	4.3	4.5	11.9	2.6	38%	12.3%	95.7	44	22	34	32%	59%	21%	24%	0	18			0	0.84	-8.0	137	-$3
17	TEX	4	2	39	51	2.79	3.77	0.91	1.20	85	50	3.9	4.0	11.9	3.0	39%	11.4%	96.5	30	12	57	19%	74%	9%	10%	0	16			67	0.90	7.5	138	$5
18	2 TM	3	24	52	66	3.29	3.44	1.10	1.16	107	66	3.9	3.3	11.4	3.5	37%	13.2%	96.8	37	23	40	29%	73%	10%	13%	0	16			92	1.09	5.5	152	$12
19	PIT	2	1	30	33	2.12	4.10	1.01	1.28	93	72	3.7	3.3	10.0	3.0	37%	11.1%	96.3	38	20	42	24%	85%	10%	13%	0	16			20	0.99	8.7	116	$1
1st Half		1	0	12	11	4.63	5.07	1.29		154	91	3.6	3.1	8.5	2.8		9.6%	95.9	37	17	46	27%	75%	19%	22%	0	16			0	1.27	-0.2	92	-$5
2nd Half		1	1	18	22	0.50	3.55	0.83	1.19	56	56	3.8	3.5	11.0	3.1	38%	12.3%	96.6	38	23	38	22%	93%	0%	3%	0	16			100	0.78	8.9	131	$5
20	**Proj**	**5**	**14**	**58**	**73**	**3.28**	**3.28**	**1.14**	**1.19**	**95**	**82**	**3.9**	**3.6**	**11.4**	**3.1**	**38%**	**12.5%**	**96.4**	**38**	**20**	**42**	**29%**	**75%**	**12%**		**0**						**6.2**	**141**	**$10**

Keller,Brad

Age: 24	Th: R	Role SP	Health A	LIMA Plan C	
Ht: 6' 5"	Wt: 230	Type Con GB	PT/Exp B	Rand Var -1	
			Consist C	MM 1003	

Shut down for workload concerns at end of August. Before that, did a good job of keeping ball on ground and in yard, but poor Ctl and SwK/Dom left xERA and BPX lacking. Made strides toward solving Ctl in 2nd half with Ball% support, but needs a corresponding Dom leap to get us interested. Young enough for that to still happen, though.

Yr	Tm	W	Sv	IP	K	ERA	xERA	WHIP	xWHIP	vL+	vR+	BF/G	Ctl	Dom	Cmd	Ball%	SwK	Vel	G	L	F	H%	S%	HR/F	xHR/F	GS	APC	DOM%	DIS%	Sv%	LI	RAR	BPX	R$
15																																		
16																																		
17	aa	10	0	131	96	6.27	5.70	1.76				23.0	4.1	6.6	1.6							37%	63%									-30.8	56	-$15
18	KC	9	0	140	96	3.08	4.31	1.30	1.41	100	82	14.2	3.2	6.2	1.9	38%	9.3%	93.9	54	19	27	30%	77%	6%	10%	20	54	30%	25%	0	0.97	18.5	65	$8
19	KC	7	0	165	122	4.19	4.99	1.35	1.51	95	94	25.3	3.8	6.6	1.7	38%	8.6%	93.4	50	21	29	29%	70%	10%	14%	28	97	21%	36%			6.4	49	$3
1st Half		4	0	105	75	4.63	5.09	1.42	1.52	98	97	25.5	4.3	6.4	1.5	40%	8.8%	93.0	50	23	27	29%	67%	9%	16%	18	98	17%	39%			-1.6	30	$2
2nd Half		3	0	60	47	3.43	4.65	1.24	1.35	89	89	25.0	3.0	7.0	2.4	34%	8.4%	94.1	50	17	33	28%	76%	12%	10%	10	95	30%	30%			8.0	81	$6
20	**Proj**	**9**	**0**	**160**	**116**	**4.25**	**4.19**	**1.38**	**1.42**	**99**	**92**	**22.0**	**3.5**	**6.5**	**1.9**	**37%**	**8.8%**	**93.8**	**52**	**19**	**29**	**30%**	**70%**	**9%**		**26**						**-2.0**	**61**	**$2**

Keller,Mitch

Age: 24	Th: R	Role SP	Health A	LIMA Plan C	
Ht: 6' 2"	Wt: 210	Type Pwr	PT/Exp D	Rand Var +4	
			Consist C	MM 3301	

1-5, 7.13 ERA in 48 IP at PIT. Top prospect in PIT organization was greeted rudely in first taste of MLB. Most of that was due to H%/S% punishment, as evidenced by a 3.98 xERA in MLB. Ability to throw strikes and miss bats is a nice starting point, and 2nd half Ball%/SwK is even more intriguing. If things come together quickly... UP: sub-3.50 ERA

Yr	Tm	W	Sv	IP	K	ERA	xERA	WHIP	xWHIP	vL+	vR+	BF/G	Ctl	Dom	Cmd	Ball%	SwK	Vel	G	L	F	H%	S%	HR/F	xHR/F	GS	APC	DOM%	DIS%	Sv%	LI	RAR	BPX	R$
15																																		
16																																		
17	aa	2	0	35	38	4.05	2.94	1.18				23.1	3.0	9.8	3.3							31%	65%									1.3	143	-$1
18	a/a	12	0	139	111	4.10	4.02	1.38				24.3	3.4	7.2	2.1							31%	71%									0.8	81	$3
19	PIT *	8	0	153	166	5.24	5.13	1.53	1.17	130	121	22.2	3.1	9.7	3.2	34%	12.4%	95.4	39	29	32	38%	66%	13%	13%	11	85	9%	27%			-13.8	102	-$5
1st Half		6	0	83	82	4.49	4.95	1.55		101	151	22.7	3.7	8.9	2.4		11.7%	95.5	26	33	41	37%	72%	6%	9%	3	83	33%	33%			0.2	85	-$1
2nd Half		2	0	70	84	6.12	5.35	1.51	1.06	137	106	21.7	2.3	10.7	4.6	33%	12.7%	95.4	44	27	29	41%	59%	17%	15%	8	85	0%	25%			-14.0	134	-$9
20	**Proj**	**6**	**0**	**102**	**102**	**4.25**	**3.57**	**1.29**	**1.17**	**96**	**77**	**22.2**	**3.1**	**9.0**	**2.9**	**37%**	**12.7%**	**95.4**	**44**	**27**	**29**	**31%**	**69%**	**13%**		**19**						**-1.3**	**117**	**$3**

Kelley,Shawn

Age: 36	Th: R	Role RP	Health F	LIMA Plan C	
Ht: 6' 2"	Wt: 237	Type xFB	PT/Exp D	Rand Var +2	
			Consist C	MM 2310	

Worked his way back into closer role in 1st half, then missed two weeks due to right biceps soreness and struggled mightily upon return. Extreme flyball profile has always been prone to bouts of gopheritis, and that was again his undoing. Elite Cmd is well-established, but so are Health, Age, and FB%.

Yr	Tm	W	Sv	IP	K	ERA	xERA	WHIP	xWHIP	vL+	vR+	BF/G	Ctl	Dom	Cmd	Ball%	SwK	Vel	G	L	F	H%	S%	HR/F	xHR/F	GS	APC	DOM%	DIS%	Sv%	LI	RAR	BPX	R$
15	SD	2	0	51	63	2.45	3.04	1.09	1.10	92	76	3.9	2.6	11.0	4.2	35%	15.3%	91.9	43	19	38	31%	81%	9%	8%	0	15			0	0.88	9.5	177	$3
16	WAS	3	7	58	80	2.64	2.92	0.90	0.93	107	73	3.3	1.7	12.4	7.3	30%	16.4%	92.4	36	14	49	28%	81%	14%	10%	0	14			78	1.23	11.1	227	$10
17	WAS	3	4	26	25	7.27	5.77	1.54		103	149	3.7	3.8	8.7	2.3		14.4%	91.8	26	14	60	26%	68%	24%	20%	0	16			67	0.90	-9.3	68	-$4
18	2 TM	2	0	49	50	2.94	3.90	0.90	1.12	87	85	3.5	2.0	9.2	4.5	33%	11.6%	91.2	30	16	54	23%	76%	10%	10%	0	14			0	0.85	7.3	137	$3
19	TEX	5	11	47	43	4.94	4.92	1.39	1.26	147	89	4.1	2.1	8.2	3.9	32%	12.0%	92.0	29	26	45	32%	74%	18%	19%	0	15			73	1.22	-2.6	106	$3
1st Half		3	11	29	28	2.79	4.12	1.14	1.10	124	68	3.9	1.6	8.7	5.6	31%	11.3%	92.1	33	25	42	30%	86%	15%	17%	0	15			73	1.58	6.1	137	$9
2nd Half		2	0	18	15	8.35	6.45	1.80	1.34	183	112	4.3	2.9	7.4	2.5	33%	12.9%	91.8	25	26	49	35%	62%	21%	21%	0	15			0	0.76	-8.7	61	-$8
20	**Proj**	**4**	**9**	**51**	**52**	**3.91**	**3.82**	**1.24**	**1.15**	**133**	**89**	**3.7**	**2.2**	**9.2**	**4.2**	**32%**	**13.1%**	**91.8**	**31**	**21**	**48**	**30%**	**79%**	**16%**		**0**						**1.5**	**132**	**$4**

GREG PYRON

Kelly,Joe

Age: 32	Th: R	Role RP	PT/Exp C	Rand Var +5	
Ht: 6' 1"	Wt: 174	Type Pwr GB	Consist A	MM 5410	
			Health C	LIMA Plan A	

Dramatically altered pitch mix following dreadful 1st half, sharply reducing four-seam fastball and change-up usage (41% to 12%, 19% to 5%) and greatly increasing sinker and curve usage (12% to 36%, 28% to 47%). It resulted in career-best marks nearly across the board in 2nd half. Needs to carry that over, but if he does... UP: 25 Sv

Yr	Tm	W	Sv	IP	K	ERA	xERA	WHIP	xWHIP	vL+	vR+	BF/G	Ctl	Dom	Cmd	Ball%	SwK	Vel	G	L	F	H%	S%	HR/F	xHR/F	GS	APC	DOM%	DIS%	Sv%	LI	RAR	BPX	R$
15	BOS *	11	0	153	124	4.76	4.53	1.44	1.36	96	118	22.5	3.3	7.3	2.2	38%	7.9%	95.4	46	25	29	32%	68%	12%	12%	25	95	8%	40%			-15.2	73	-$3
16	BOS *	5	2	75	82	4.02	4.92	1.58	1.42	122	108	8.9	3.8	9.8	2.6	42%	10.8%	96.3	47	28	25	38%	76%	18%	20%	6	37	17%	67%	67	1.11	1.5	103	-$1
17	BOS	4	0	58	52	2.79	4.14	1.19	1.43	89	69	4.4	4.2	8.1	1.9	37%	11.2%	99.0	51	23	26	26%	77%	7%	9%	0	19			0	1.09	11.2	73	$4
18	BOS	4	2	66	68	4.39	4.02	1.36	1.38	83	98	3.9	4.4	9.3	2.1	39%	10.8%	98.1	47	25	28	31%	67%	8%	10%	0	16			29	1.05	-1.9	86	-$1
19	LA	5	1	51	62	4.56	3.36	1.38	1.28	98	91	4.1	3.9	10.9	2.8	36%	10.4%	98.0	61	22	17	34%	69%	25%	23%	0	16			17	0.87	-0.3	142	-$1
1st Half		2	0	27	32	5.93	3.83	1.72	1.31	111	112	4.8	4.3	10.5	2.5	37%	9.5%	97.7	62	19	19	40%	67%	25%	27%	0	19			0	0.60	-4.8	124	-$6
2nd Half		3	1	24	30	3.00	2.67	1.00	1.16	79	67	3.4	3.4	11.3	3.3	35%	11.7%	98.3	60	25	15	26%	73%	25%	16%	0	13			33	1.12	4.5	163	$6
20	Proj	**5**	**2**	**58**	**66**	**3.89**	**3.01**	**1.23**	**1.31**	**87**	**84**	**4.0**	**3.6**	**10.2**	**2.8**	**37%**	**10.7%**	**98.0**	**54**	**24**	**22**	**30%**	**70%**	**16%**		**0**						**1.9**	**135**	**$3**

Kelly,Merrill

Age: 31	Th: R	Role SP	PT/Exp A	Rand Var +1	
Ht: 6' 2"	Wt: 190	Type	Consist B	MM 2203	
			Health A	LIMA Plan B	

Late-bloomer returned to MLB after a four-year stint in the KBO. 2nd half ERA masks some major September gains, sparked by a mechanical tweak: 2.18 ERA, 93 mph, 53% GB and 11% SwK in 33 Sept IP. It can be foolhardy to chase September breakouts, but pay for a full-season repeat and you may end up with a tidy profit.

Yr	Tm	W	Sv	IP	K	ERA	xERA	WHIP	xWHIP	vL+	vR+	BF/G	Ctl	Dom	Cmd	Ball%	SwK	Vel	G	L	F	H%	S%	HR/F	xHR/F	GS	APC	DOM%	DIS%	Sv%	LI	RAR	BPX	R$
15	for	11	0	181	132	5.13	5.12	1.49				26.0	3.3	6.6	2.0							32%	68%									-26.0	47	-$9
16	for	9	0	200	144	4.58	4.86	1.47				27.7	3.4	6.5	1.9							32%	71%									-9.7	53	-$4
17	for	16	0	190	179	4.47	5.08	1.45				27.0	2.6	8.5	3.2							35%	73%									-2.7	93	$5
18	for	12	0	158	161	4.10	3.95	1.26				23.0	2.7	9.2	3.4							32%	70%									0.9	116	$8
19	ARI	13	0	183	158	4.42	4.69	1.31	1.34	101	101	24.3	2.8	7.8	2.8	36%	10.1%	91.9	42	22	36	30%	71%	15%	19%	32	93	22%	41%			2.0	92	$7
1st Half		7	0	99	79	4.00	4.82	1.27	1.29	95	103	24.4	2.5	7.2	2.8	36%	9.7%	91.6	40	23	37	30%	73%	13%	18%	17	93	18%	29%			6.2	86	$10
2nd Half		6	0	84	79	4.91	4.53	1.36	1.29	109	99	24.1	3.1	8.4	2.7	36%	10.5%	92.3	44	22	34	31%	69%	18%	20%	15	92	27%	53%			-4.2	98	$4
20	Proj	**13**	**0**	**174**	**158**	**4.19**	**3.89**	**1.34**	**1.29**	**104**	**101**	**24.2**	**2.8**	**8.2**	**2.9**	**36%**	**10.2%**	**92.0**	**43**	**22**	**35**	**32%**	**73%**	**14%**		**30**						**-0.9**	**105**	**$7**

Kennedy,Ian

Age: 35	Th: R	Role RP	PT/Exp B	Rand Var +1	
Ht: 6' 0"	Wt: 205	Type Pwr FB	Consist B	MM 2330	
			Health D	LIMA Plan B	

Assumed the closer role in June and never looked back. As with most converted SPs, his velocity spiked, which fueled SwK/Dom boost. Additionally, big gain in GB% helped squelch severe HR issues that had plagued him as an SP. Though xERA and xHR/F point to some pullback, it shouldn't be too drastic. But at 35, the window is small.

Yr	Tm	W	Sv	IP	K	ERA	xERA	WHIP	xWHIP	vL+	vR+	BF/G	Ctl	Dom	Cmd	Ball%	SwK	Vel	G	L	F	H%	S%	HR/F	xHR/F	GS	APC	DOM%	DIS%	Sv%	LI	RAR	BPX	R$
15	SD	9	0	168	174	4.28	3.74	1.30	1.21	116	111	23.8	2.8	9.3	3.3	36%	10.8%	91.3	38	23	39	31%	74%	17%	15%	30	97	13%	27%			-6.5	129	$4
16	KC	11	0	196	184	3.68	4.40	1.22	1.28	96	100	24.8	3.0	8.5	2.8	35%	10.1%	92.2	33	20	47	28%	77%	13%	13%	33	102	30%	27%			12.3	97	$14
17	KC	5	0	154	131	5.38	5.04	1.32	1.38	108	107	21.8	3.6	7.7	2.1	37%	9.7%	91.9	36	16	48	26%	66%	16%	16%	30	88	13%	57%			-19.3	67	-$3
18	KC	3	0	120	105	4.66	4.77	1.38	1.31	103	113	23.5	3.0	7.9	2.6	35%	8.7%	91.9	30	26	44	31%	71%	13%	16%	22	94	14%	45%			-7.6	79	-$4
19	KC	3	30	63	73	3.41	3.84	1.28	1.17	85	95	4.2	2.4	10.4	4.3	34%	11.0%	94.5	44	18	37	35%	76%	9%	13%	0	17			88	0.88	8.6	156	$15
1st Half		0	11	33	40	3.27	3.83	1.21	1.02	90	85	4.3	1.6	10.9	6.7	36%	10.7%	93.9	42	14	43	38%	74%	5%	13%	0	18			85	0.92	5.0	188	$9
2nd Half		3	19	30	33	3.56	3.95	1.35	1.24	80	108	4.1	3.3	9.8	3.0	33%	11.4%	95.0	47	22	31	33%	78%	16%	13%	0	17			90	0.84	3.5	123	$22
20	Proj	**3**	**31**	**65**	**66**	**3.68**	**3.81**	**1.32**	**1.24**	**94**	**104**	**7.0**	**2.9**	**9.1**	**3.2**	**35%**	**10.2%**	**93.2**	**39**	**21**	**40**	**32%**	**77%**	**13%**		**0**						**3.8**	**119**	**$14**

Kershaw,Clayton

Age: 32	Th: L	Role SP	PT/Exp A	Rand Var 0	
Ht: 6' 4"	Wt: 226	Type Pwr	Consist A	MM 5403	
			Health F	LIMA Plan A	

Opened 2019 on IL (shoulder inflammation). While the Vel lost in 2018 is likely gone for good, he was able to recapture the bite on his slider (25% SwK) in 2nd half, which drove the SwK/Dom rebound. Even that 2nd half was a long way from vintage, as BPX/xERA show. 2018-19 is the new baseline, and the durability concerns remain.

Yr	Tm	W	Sv	IP	K	ERA	xERA	WHIP	xWHIP	vL+	vR+	BF/G	Ctl	Dom	Cmd	Ball%	SwK	Vel	G	L	F	H%	S%	HR/F	xHR/F	GS	APC	DOM%	DIS%	Sv%	LI	RAR	BPX	R$
15	LA	16	0	233	301	2.13	2.31	0.88	0.95	76	72	27.0	1.6	11.6	7.2	32%	16.2%	93.6	50	22	28	29%	79%	10%	8%	33	103	76%	3%			52.6	231	$47
16	LA	12	0	149	172	1.69	2.43	0.72	0.89	42	72	25.9	0.7	10.4	15.6	31%	15.9%	93.1	49	20	30	26%	80%	8%	10%	21	98	76%	5%			45.9	233	$35
17	LA	18	0	175	202	2.31	2.98	0.95	1.01	97	77	25.1	1.5	10.4	6.7	31%	14.6%	92.7	48	19	33	28%	85%	16%	14%	27	93	56%	7%			44.1	206	$36
18	LA	9	0	161	155	2.73	3.35	1.04	1.11	93	86	25.0	1.6	8.6	5.3	32%	11.5%	90.9	48	23	30	29%	79%	13%	12%	26	91	35%	8%			28.2	159	$21
19	LA	16	0	178	189	3.03	3.54	1.04	1.15	84	90	24.3	2.1	9.5	4.6	33%	13.7%	90.4	48	19	33	27%	80%	19%	16%	28	92	50%	14%	0	0.77	32.5	154	$27
1st Half		7	0	92	82	3.23	3.66	1.07	1.12	76	96	25.9	1.5	8.0	5.5	33%	12.9%	90.2	51	20	29	28%	76%	17%	15%	14	95	50%	7%			14.5	146	$22
2nd Half		9	0	86	107	2.81	3.44	1.02	1.10	95	83	22.9	2.7	11.2	4.1	33%	14.5%	90.5	44	18	38	26%	84%	20%	17%	14	90	50%	21%	0	0.75	18.0	163	$32
20	Proj	**14**	**0**	**174**	**189**	**3.23**	**3.01**	**1.08**	**1.08**	**90**	**89**	**24.3**	**2.1**	**9.8**	**4.6**	**32%**	**13.6%**	**91.2**	**48**	**20**	**33**	**29%**	**76%**	**16%**		**28**						**19.8**	**166**	**$23**

Keuchel,Dallas

Age: 32	Th: L	Role SP	PT/Exp A	Rand Var +3	
Ht: 6' 3"	Wt: 205	Type Con xGB	Consist A	MM 3103	
			Health C	LIMA Plan A	

Didn't sign with ATL until June. Extreme GB% remains a strength, but there's still no second plus skill, as double-digit SwKs seem a distant memory. Low Vel puts locating pitches at a premium, making the large increase in hard contact (see xHR/F and DIS%) alarming. Heed the warning from xERA/xWHIP; expect an ERA that starts with a '4'.

Yr	Tm	W	Sv	IP	K	ERA	xERA	WHIP	xWHIP	vL+	vR+	BF/G	Ctl	Dom	Cmd	Ball%	SwK	Vel	G	L	F	H%	S%	HR/F	xHR/F	GS	APC	DOM%	DIS%	Sv%	LI	RAR	BPX	R$
15	HOU	20	0	232	216	2.48	2.80	1.02	1.15	63	85	27.6	2.0	8.4	4.2	37%	10.7%	89.6	62	19	20	28%	79%	14%	13%	33	106	42%	6%			42.3	164	$37
16	HOU	9	0	168	144	4.55	3.65	1.29	1.26	82	105	27.0	2.6	7.7	3.0	37%	9.9%	88.6	57	19	24	31%	67%	16%	16%	26	103	35%	19%			-7.5	124	$3
17	HOU	14	0	146	125	2.90	3.32	1.12	1.29	58	90	25.4	2.9	7.7	2.7	38%	11.3%	88.7	67	15	18	26%	78%	21%	16%	23	95	30%	22%			26.1	127	$19
18	HOU	12	0	205	153	3.74	4.07	1.31	1.31	97	98	25.7	2.6	6.7	2.6	38%	8.6%	89.3	54	22	24	31%	73%	11%	11%	34	97	21%	29%			10.4	97	$8
19	ATL	8	0	113	91	3.75	4.14	1.37	1.38	82	106	25.6	3.1	7.3	2.3	38%	9.4%	88.4	60	20	20	30%	78%	24%	22%	19	98	16%	47%			10.4	92	$4
1st Half		1	0	11	5	5.06	5.38	1.78		112	163	25.5	2.5	4.2	1.7		6.0%	87.7	60	15	25	34%	81%	30%	34%	2	92	0%	100%			-0.7	50	-$20
2nd Half		7	0	102	86	3.62	3.91	1.32	1.33	78	99	25.6	3.2	7.6	2.4	38%	9.8%	88.5	60	21	19	30%	77%	23%	20%	17	99	18%	41%			11.2	97	$7
20	Proj	**10**	**0**	**174**	**140**	**4.06**	**3.62**	**1.31**	**1.29**	**79**	**101**	**25.8**	**3.0**	**7.2**	**2.4**	**38%**	**10.0%**	**88.8**	**57**	**19**	**24**	**30%**	**72%**	**15%**		**28**						**2.0**	**98**	**$6**

Kikuchi,Yusei

Age: 29	Th: L	Role SP	PT/Exp A	Rand Var +3	
Ht: 6' 0"	Wt: 194	Type Con	Consist C	MM 1103	
			Health A	LIMA Plan F	

Transition from Japan to MLB fell woefully short of his mid-level SP projection. However, there is some tepid good news here: 2nd half Ball%/Ctl gains helped, and xHR/F says the level of gopheritis he suffered was a bit unfair. There's a foothold for recovery there, but not enough to make him rosterable until he finds the Dom that he left in Japan.

Yr	Tm	W	Sv	IP	K	ERA	xERA	WHIP	xWHIP	vL+	vR+	BF/G	Ctl	Dom	Cmd	Ball%	SwK	Vel	G	L	F	H%	S%	HR/F	xHR/F	GS	APC	DOM%	DIS%	Sv%	LI	RAR	BPX	R$
15																																		
16	for	12	0	143	120	3.20	3.86	1.46				27.8	5.2	7.6	1.4							29%	80%									17.4	73	$7
17	for	16	0	188	206	2.44	2.78	1.02				27.7	2.9	9.9	3.4							24%	85%									44.4	129	$33
18	for	14	0	164	145	3.82	3.70	1.15				28.3	3.1	8.0	2.6							25%	73%									6.6	79	$13
19	SEA	6	0	162	116	5.46	5.30	1.52	1.41	108	121	22.5	2.8	6.5	2.3	36%	8.9%	92.5	44	21	35	32%	70%	19%	15%	32	85	16%	50%			-18.9	69	-$9
1st Half		4	0	91	68	5.12	5.21	1.51	1.38	106	116	22.6	3.2	6.7	2.1	37%	8.7%	92.8	45	21	34	32%	72%	18%	16%	18	85	17%	39%			-7.0	64	-$7
2nd Half		2	0	70	48	5.89	5.40	1.52	1.32	111	127	22.4	2.3	6.1	2.7	35%	9.2%	92.1	43	20	37	32%	69%	20%	14%	14	85	14%	64%			-12.0	75	-$12
20	Proj	**8**	**0**	**160**	**124**	**4.61**	**4.23**	**1.36**	**1.34**	**95**	**108**	**24.5**	**3.0**	**7.0**	**2.3**	**36%**	**9.0%**	**92.4**	**44**	**20**	**36**	**29%**	**72%**	**16%**		**27**						**-9.0**	**77**	**$0**

Kimbrel,Craig

Age: 32	Th: R	Role RP	PT/Exp B	Rand Var +5	
Ht: 6' 0"	Wt: 210	Type Pwr xFB	Consist C	MM 4530	
			Health D	LIMA Plan C	

Unsigned until June; then spent time on IL in Aug/Sept with knee/elbow inflammation. So all of this slippage comes wrapped in a veil of injury, but it is also fully backed by underlying skills decay. A winter's rest followed by a normal spring training may cure a lot of this, but that is far from a guarantee. DN: 4.00+ ERA, <10 Sv

Yr	Tm	W	Sv	IP	K	ERA	xERA	WHIP	xWHIP	vL+	vR+	BF/G	Ctl	Dom	Cmd	Ball%	SwK	Vel	G	L	F	H%	S%	HR/F	xHR/F	GS	APC	DOM%	DIS%	Sv%	LI	RAR	BPX	R$
15	SD	4	39	59	87	2.58	2.61	1.04	1.07	86	72	3.9	3.3	13.2	4.0	37%	15.9%	97.3	46	20	34	30%	80%	14%	10%	0	17			91	1.49	10.1	204	$22
16	BOS	2	31	53	83	3.40	3.33	1.09	1.22	70	76	3.9	5.1	14.1	2.8	39%	15.1%	97.3	29	23	48	27%	70%	8%	12%	0	16			94	1.50	5.2	146	$16
17	BOS	5	35	69	126	1.43	1.83	0.68	0.73	76	45	3.8	1.8	16.4	9.0	32%	20.2%	98.3	37	19	44	28%	88%	13%	19%	0	17			90	1.34	24.9	314	$32
18	BOS	5	42	62	96	2.74	3.13	0.99	1.16	86	71	3.9	4.5	13.9	3.1	38%	17.6%	97.1	28	25	47	23%	78%	13%	11%	0	18			89	1.39	10.8	155	$25
19	CHC	0	13	21	30	6.53	4.56	1.60	1.35	114	159	4.2	5.2	13.1	2.5	39%	14.8%	96.2	30	20	50	30%	75%	36%	29%	0	17			81	1.29	-5.2	111	-$1
1st Half		0	1	1	1	0.00	0.00	2.00		0	407	5.0	9.0	9.0	1.0		5.0%	96.7	67	33	0	35%	100%	0%		0	20			100	1.09	0.6	-40	-$12
2nd Half		0	12	20	29	6.86	4.60	1.58	1.27	122	149	4.1	5.0	13.3	2.6	39%	15.3%	96.2	28	19	53	29%	73%	36%	29%	0	17			80	1.30	-5.7	119	$0
20	Proj	**3**	**30**	**58**	**84**	**3.73**	**3.11**	**1.15**	**1.09**	**91**	**87**	**3.8**	**4.0**	**13.1**	**3.3**	**37%**	**15.0%**	**97.2**	**32**	**21**	**47**	**29%**	**73%**	**16%**		**0**						**3.0**	**159**	**$15**

GREG PYRON

Kinley,Tyler

			Health	A	LIMA Plan	D
Age: 29	Th: R	Role: RP	PT/Exp	F	Rand Var	-3
Ht: 6' 4"	Wt: 205	Type: Pwr FB	Consist	D	MM	0300

3-1, 3.65 ERA in 49 IP at MIA. Inconsistent delivery and release point has yielded disqualifying Ctl throughout his career. Relies on a four-seam fastball/slider combo, throwing the slider a whopping 58% of the time in 2019 (19% SwK). Hitters have a difficult time squaring him up, as xHR/F attests, but absent Ctl upgrade, he's unrosterable.

Yr Tm	W	Sv	IP	K	ERA	xERA	WHIP	xWHIP	vL+	vR+	BF/G	Ctl	Dom	Cmd	Ball%	SwK	Vel	G	L	F	H%	S%	HR/F	xHR/F	GS	APC	DOM%	DIS%	Sv%	LI	RAR	BPX	R$
15																																	
16 a/a	2	6	60	53	5.70	5.01	1.67				6.1	4.6	7.9	1.7							36%	65%									-11.1	73	-$6
17 aa	1	8	26	28	6.95	7.00	2.10				4.7	6.3	9.6	1.5							43%	66%									-8.3	64	-$6
18 2 TM *	2	8	51	57	5.46	4.99	1.68		98	167	4.3	5.6	10.1	1.8		13.0%	96.6	54	11	34	37%	67%	17%	17%	0	18			80	0.33	-8.3	89	-$5
19 MIA *	3	3	67	61	3.28	3.44	1.39	1.75	101	93	4.2	6.0	8.2	1.4	38%	13.5%	95.0	38	23	40	25%	79%	9%	9%	0	17			60	0.84	10.0	73	$2
1st Half	1	1	31	36	4.53	5.04	1.72	1.61	112	114	4.5	6.6	10.7	1.6	38%	15.2%	94.9	39	25	36	35%	75%	12%	13%	0	18			50	0.43	-0.1	82	-$5
2nd Half	2	2	36	24	2.22	2.08	1.10	1.78	89	69	4.0	5.4	6.1	1.1	38%	11.6%	95.1	36	21	43	16%	84%	7%	5%	0	15			67	1.22	10.1	66	$8
20 Proj	**2**	**0**	**51**	**49**	**4.86**	**4.79**	**1.52**	**1.71**	**108**	**98**	**4.5**	**5.7**	**8.6**	**1.5**	**38%**	**13.1%**	**95.0**	**37**	**22**	**40**	**29%**	**71%**	**13%**		**0**						**-4.5**	**20**	**-$5**

Kittredge,Andrew

			Health	A	LIMA Plan	F
Age: 30	Th: R	Role: RP	PT/Exp	D	Rand Var	+2
Ht: 6' 1"	Wt: 235	Type: Pwr GB	Consist	F	MM	5400

1-0, 4.17 ERA in 50 IP at TAM. Major gains thanks to pitch mix changes. Threw more high fastballs to great effect (SwK up from 3% to 13%) and upgraded slider (37% usage/25% SwK), but addition of sinker gave him a third pitch. End result was more strikes and elite Ctl; gains in SwK and big GB tilt confirm that next step could be ... UP: 20 Sv

Yr Tm	W	Sv	IP	K	ERA	xERA	WHIP	xWHIP	vL+	vR+	BF/G	Ctl	Dom	Cmd	Ball%	SwK	Vel	G	L	F	H%	S%	HR/F	xHR/F	GS	APC	DOM%	DIS%	Sv%	LI	RAR	BPX	R$
15 a/a	2	0	75	51	4.46	4.34	1.45				8.9	3.2	6.1	1.9							32%	69%									-4.6	66	-$5
16 a/a	3	7	72	69	4.38	5.17	1.56				8.5	2.5	8.7	3.5							39%	72%									-1.7	114	-$1
17 TAM *	6	2	84	77	2.04	3.19	1.22		97	85	6.0	2.7	8.3	3.1		12.7%	94.5	47	19	35	31%	85%	13%	11%	0	16			50	0.61	23.9	127	$10
18 TAM *	9	2	84	76	5.57	5.88	1.63	1.45	101	150	7.0	3.3	8.1	2.5	36%	10.3%	93.1	50	24	25	37%	67%	21%	22%	3	19	0%	100%	67	0.77	-14.7	69	-$7
19 TAM *	3	6	88	101	3.47	3.63	1.15	1.13	120	83	5.5	1.9	10.3	5.3	32%	16.4%	95.0	50	22	28	33%	74%	18%	17%	7	22	0%	43%	86	0.56	11.2	159	$8
1st Half	2	6	44	51	2.40	2.92	1.04		33	114	5.5	1.8	10.3	5.7		15.7%	95.3	47	18	35	31%	82%	17%	11%	1	27	0%	0%	86	0.59	11.5	177	$13
2nd Half	1	0	43	50	4.57	3.38	1.27	1.09	133	77	5.5	2.1	10.4	5.0	32%	16.5%	94.9	50	23	26	35%	67%	19%	18%	6	22	0%	50%	0	0.56	-0.3	174	$3
20 Proj	**2**	**0**	**44**	**48**	**3.37**	**2.86**	**1.17**	**1.23**	**97**	**85**	**5.9**	**2.1**	**10.0**	**4.8**	**34%**	**14.0%**	**94.2**	**50**	**24**	**26**	**33%**	**75%**	**16%**		**0**						**4.2**	**175**	**$0**

Kluber,Corey

			Health	F	LIMA Plan	C
Age: 34	Th: R	Role: SP	PT/Exp	A	Rand Var	+5
Ht: 6' 4"	Wt: 215	Type: Pwr	Consist	C	MM	4305

Struggled early before suffering right ulna fracture in May; subsequent left oblique strain ended his season. H%/S%/extra walks wrecked his small sample, but velo/SwK/Dom all in typical fine form. 2017 was his high-water mark and you probably shouldn't pay for a return to 200 IP, but skills should largely be intact on a per-IP basis.

Yr Tm	W	Sv	IP	K	ERA	xERA	WHIP	xWHIP	vL+	vR+	BF/G	Ctl	Dom	Cmd	Ball%	SwK	Vel	G	L	F	H%	S%	HR/F	xHR/F	GS	APC	DOM%	DIS%	Sv%	LI	RAR	BPX	R$
15 CLE	9	0	222	245	3.49	3.07	1.05	1.07	102	77	27.7	1.8	9.9	5.4	32%	13.1%	92.8	42	22	36	30%	70%	11%	11%	32	102	47%	13%			13.0	178	$22
16 CLE	18	0	215	227	3.14	3.45	1.06	1.15	88	84	26.9	2.4	9.5	4.0	34%	13.1%	92.5	44	19	36	28%	74%	11%	11%	32	100	59%	16%			27.8	153	$29
17 CLE	18	0	204	265	2.25	2.67	0.87	0.94	76	73	26.8	1.6	11.7	7.4	32%	15.9%	92.6	45	22	33	28%	81%	13%	11%	29	102	66%	14%			52.9	229	$45
18 CLE	20	0	215	222	2.89	3.19	0.99	1.05	92	80	25.5	1.4	9.3	6.5	33%	12.4%	92.0	44	22	33	29%	77%	13%	14%	33	96	58%	9%			33.4	174	$35
19 CLE	2	0	36	38	5.80	4.94	1.65	1.36	119	102	24.0	3.8	9.6	2.5	36%	13.3%	91.6	40	23	37	39%	65%	10%	17%	7	87	29%	29%			-5.7	96	-$6
1st Half	2	0	36	38	5.80	4.95	1.65	1.31	118	104	24.0	3.8	9.6	2.5	36%	13.3%	91.6	40	23	37	39%	65%	10%	17%	7	87	29%	29%			-5.7	96	-$6
2nd Half																																	
20 Proj	**13**	**0**	**181**	**193**	**3.50**	**3.30**	**1.18**	**1.12**	**97**	**87**	**24.7**	**2.4**	**9.6**	**4.1**	**34%**	**13.7%**	**92.2**	**43**	**22**	**35**	**31%**	**74%**	**11%**		**29**						**14.5**	**149**	**$18**

Knebel,Corey

			Health	F	LIMA Plan	B
Age: 28	Th: R	Role: RP	PT/Exp	C	Rand Var	0
Ht: 6' 4"	Wt: 220	Type: Pwr	Consist	B	MM	4510

Underwent March 2019 Tommy John surgery; hopes to be ready by April 2020. Back in 2018, had made progress curbing free passes and Ball% hinted at even further gains (2.7 xCtl). Meanwhile, the strikeouts kept coming in droves. The GB% boost would be huge, if it sticks. Monitor his recovery to see which of these skills come back.

Yr Tm	W	Sv	IP	K	ERA	xERA	WHIP	xWHIP	vL+	vR+	BF/G	Ctl	Dom	Cmd	Ball%	SwK	Vel	G	L	F	H%	S%	HR/F	xHR/F	GS	APC	DOM%	DIS%	Sv%	LI	RAR	BPX	R$
15 MIL *	1	6	66	76	3.67	3.92	1.27	1.18	105	103	4.2	3.3	10.4	3.2	34%	10.5%	94.9	49	20	31	32%	76%	20%	16%	0	17			75	0.49	2.3	118	$2
16 MIL	1	2	33	38	4.68	4.13	1.47	1.33	69	124	4.1	4.4	10.5	2.4	40%	8.3%	95.2	42	21	37	35%	69%	9%	10%	0	17			50	1.00	-2.0	106	-$3
17 MIL	1	39	76	126	1.78	2.99	1.16	1.14	67	85	4.1	4.7	14.9	3.2	37%	14.7%	97.4	38	17	45	32%	89%	10%	9%	0	18			87	1.49	24.2	188	$27
18 MIL	4	16	55	88	3.58	2.43	1.08	1.04	84	99	3.9	3.6	14.3	4.0	36%	13.8%	96.9	48	21	31	31%	72%	21%	21%	0	17			84	1.21	3.9	215	$10
19																																	
1st Half																																	
2nd Half																																	
20 Proj	**2**	**5**	**51**	**71**	**3.62**	**3.04**	**1.26**	**1.18**	**77**	**105**	**4.0**	**4.1**	**12.5**	**3.1**	**37%**	**11.5%**	**96.1**	**44**	**20**	**36**	**33%**	**74%**	**13%**		**0**						**3.3**	**158**	**$2**

Kolarek,Adam

			Health	A	LIMA Plan	B
Age: 31	Th: L	Role: RP	PT/Exp	D	Rand Var	+2
Ht: 6' 3"	Wt: 215	Type: Con xGB	Consist	B	MM	3100

Extreme GB pitcher moved to LA via July 31 trade; thrived there as a lefty specialist. The minimal exposure to RH batters prompted the 2nd half gains, as opposed to any real growth. He's a solid middle reliever who should earn a fair number of Holds, but don't look for anything more.

Yr Tm	W	Sv	IP	K	ERA	xERA	WHIP	xWHIP	vL+	vR+	BF/G	Ctl	Dom	Cmd	Ball%	SwK	Vel	G	L	F	H%	S%	HR/F	xHR/F	GS	APC	DOM%	DIS%	Sv%	LI	RAR	BPX	R$
15 aa	2	1	67	49	5.51	4.38	1.51				5.7	4.0	6.6	1.7							32%	62%									-12.8	67	-$8
16 a/a	3	2	60	51	4.33	3.65	1.56				5.6	6.0	7.6	1.3							31%	70%									-1.0	87	-$3
17 TAM *	4	2	52	40	3.09	4.52	1.58		114	142	4.3	4.0	7.0	1.7		7.4%	88.1	56	22	22	35%	80%	33%	13%	0	11			40	0.75	8.1	79	-$1
18 TAM *	6	6	81	60	2.93	3.41	1.28	1.26	72	110	5.3	2.1	6.7	3.1	32%	10.3%	90.1	59	15	26	33%	76%	0%	7%	0	16			75	1.12	12.1	118	$6
19 2 TM	6	1	55	45	3.27	3.72	1.16	1.31	64	115	2.9	2.6	7.4	2.8	35%	11.6%	89.3	66	15	19	27%	77%	23%	20%	0	10			100	1.13	8.4	115	$4
1st Half	2	0	33	25	4.13	3.90	1.32	1.35	52	133	3.4	3.0	6.9	2.3	36%	9.0%	89.3	68	14	18	29%	72%	22%	22%	0	12			0	1.24	1.5	97	$0
2nd Half	4	1	22	20	2.01	3.27	0.94	1.17	77	76	2.3	2.0	8.1	4.0	33%	15.5%	89.3	63	16	21	23%	89%	23%	17%	0	8			100	1.01	6.9	144	$9
20 Proj	**6**	**0**	**58**	**47**	**3.43**	**3.41**	**1.25**	**1.25**	**70**	**110**	**3.4**	**2.8**	**7.2**	**2.5**	**33%**	**11.8%**	**89.6**	**63**	**15**	**22**	**30%**	**74%**	**12%**		**0**						**5.2**	**108**	**$2**

Kopech,Michael

			Health	F	LIMA Plan	C
Age: 24	Th: R	Role: SP	PT/Exp	D	Rand Var	0
Ht: 6' 3"	Wt: 205	Type: Pwr FB	Consist	C	MM	2401

Missed all of 2019 following Sept 2018 Tommy John surgery, but is expected to be ready for spring training. Prior to injury, he had a #1 SP ceiling, though it hinged on him doing a better job of repeating his mechanics, cutting walks and displaying more consistent quality with his secondary offerings. Future is bright, but temper 2020 expectations.

Yr Tm	W	Sv	IP	K	ERA	xERA	WHIP	xWHIP	vL+	vR+	BF/G	Ctl	Dom	Cmd	Ball%	SwK	Vel	G	L	F	H%	S%	HR/F	xHR/F	GS	APC	DOM%	DIS%	Sv%	LI	RAR	BPX	R$
15																																	
16																																	
17 a/a	9	0	134	156	3.57	2.99	1.31				22.2	4.7	10.5	2.2							31%	73%									13.1	128	$10
18 CHW *	8	0	141	166	4.45	4.18	1.40		102	177	21.3	4.1	10.6	2.6		10.5%	95.4	28	26	46	34%	70%	19%	22%	4	64	0%	0%			-5.3	109	$0
19																																	
1st Half																																	
2nd Half																																	
20 Proj	**7**	**0**	**116**	**136**	**4.09**	**3.94**	**1.37**				**21.7**	**4.3**	**10.5**	**2.4**	**38%**	**12.5%**		**33**	**22**	**44**	**33%**	**71%**	**8%**		**22**						**0.8**	**97**	**$3**

Lambert,Peter

			Health	A	LIMA Plan	D
Age: 23	Th: R	Role: SP	PT/Exp	D	Rand Var	+5
Ht: 6' 2"	Wt: 185	Type: Con	Consist	D	MM	1001

3-7, 7.25 ERA in 89 IP at COL. Finesse pitcher who relied upon good control and keeping the ball on the ground in the minors, typically posting an MiLB GB% around 50%. Thus far, only the GB% has appeared in MLB, as his Ctl soared to 3.6 in MLB. The puny SwK/Dom means lots of balls in play; that's not a viable approach anywhere these days.

Yr Tm	W	Sv	IP	K	ERA	xERA	WHIP	xWHIP	vL+	vR+	BF/G	Ctl	Dom	Cmd	Ball%	SwK	Vel	G	L	F	H%	S%	HR/F	xHR/F	GS	APC	DOM%	DIS%	Sv%	LI	RAR	BPX	R$
15																																	
16																																	
17																																	
18 a/a	10	0	150	87	4.01	4.56	1.35				24.1	1.7	5.2	3.1							32%	72%									2.7	80	$2
19 COL *	5	0	150	99	6.47	6.20	1.58	1.53	135	121	22.1	3.1	5.9	1.9	39%	7.5%	92.7	47	25	28	33%	62%	21%	14%	19	83	5%	74%			-36.4	20	-$16
1st Half	4	0	86	60	5.68	5.60	1.38	1.21	155	107	22.5	2.0	6.3	3.1	38%	8.2%	93.1	42	26	32	31%	64%	26%	12%	5	88	20%	80%			-12.4	49	-$9
2nd Half	1	0	65	39	7.52	5.95	1.84	1.58	127	125	22.1	4.5	5.4	1.2	39%	7.2%	92.6	49	25	26	35%	60%	18%	14%	14	82	0%	71%			-24.0	5	-$26
20 Proj	**5**	**0**	**116**	**72**	**5.26**	**4.48**	**1.53**	**1.43**	**125**	**107**	**22.7**	**2.7**	**5.6**	**2.0**	**38%**	**7.6%**	**92.8**	**46**	**25**	**28**	**33%**	**68%**	**15%**		**22**						**-15.9**	**58**	**-$8**

GREG PYRON

Lamet,Dinelson

Lamet,Dinelson		Health	F	LIMA Plan	A
Age: 27	Th: R Role SP	PT/Exp	D	Rand Var	+3
Ht: 6' 4"	Wt: 187 Type Pwr	Consist	A	MM	3501

3-5, 4.07 ERA in 73 IP at SD. April 2018 Tommy John surgery shelved him through 1st half of 2019. Upon return, improved already-elite SwK/Dom as well as Ball% and Ctl. Strong September (2.98 xERA, 14.3 Dom and 3.3 Ctl) and ability to handle LHH were also encouraging signs. A prime breakout candidate.

Yr Tm	W	Sv	IP	K	ERA	xERA	WHIP	xWHIP	vL+	vR+	BF/G	Ctl	Dom	Cmd	Ball%	SwK	Vel	G	L	F	H%	S%	HR/F	xHR/F	GS	APC	DOM%	DIS%	Sv%	LI	RAR	BPX	R$
15																																	
16 a/a	5	0	85	85	4.11	3.47	1.35				22.1	3.6	8.9	2.5							33%	69%									0.8	116	$1
17 SD *	10	0	153	179	4.26	3.60	1.28	1.29	115	73	21.7	4.3	10.5	2.5	38%	12.5%	95.0	37	20	43	29%	70%	15%	14%	21	92	24%	19%			1.9	109	$9
18																																	
19 SD *	4	0	88	120	4.26	3.91	1.22	1.17	98	93	20.9	3.5	12.2	3.5	36%	14.4%	96.1	36	27	36	31%	71%	20%	17%	14	88	14%	7%			2.7	121	$3
1st Half																																	
2nd Half	3	0	73	105	4.07	3.53	1.26	1.13	98	91	22.4	3.7	12.9	3.5	36%	14.4%	96.1	36	27	36	33%	74%	20%	17%	14	88	14%	7%			3.9	161	$3
20 Proj	**6**	**0**	**116**	**139**	**3.76**	**3.40**	**1.20**	**1.20**	**101**	**80**	**21.2**	**3.4**	**10.8**	**3.1**	**36%**	**13.6%**	**95.6**	**37**	**24**	**39**	**30%**	**73%**	**13%**		**22**						**5.6**	**133**	**$8**

Lauer,Eric

Lauer,Eric		Health	B	LIMA Plan	A
Age: 25	Th: L Role SP	PT/Exp	C	Rand Var	0
Ht: 6' 3"	Wt: 205 Type	Consist	A	MM	1203

Exposed in his first full season, he changed his approach in 2nd half to feature more high fastballs. While SwK/Dom jumped, so did FB% and HR/F, and xERA couldn't tell the difference. Still young enough to tinker, but one wishes there were more signs in GB% or Ctl to hang that hope on.

Yr Tm	W	Sv	IP	K	ERA	xERA	WHIP	xWHIP	vL+	vR+	BF/G	Ctl	Dom	Cmd	Ball%	SwK	Vel	G	L	F	H%	S%	HR/F	xHR/F	GS	APC	DOM%	DIS%	Sv%	LI	RAR	BPX	R$
15																																	
16																																	
17 aa	4	0	55	41	5.36	5.04	1.46				23.6	2.9	6.6	2.3							33%	65%									-6.8	61	-$5
18 SD *	8	0	134	119	4.01	4.73	1.45	1.38	115	110	21.2	3.6	8.0	2.2	37%	9.0%	91.2	38	28	35	32%	75%	13%	12%	23	88	13%	43%			2.2	73	$0
19 SD	8	0	150	138	4.45	4.81	1.40	1.35	120	95	21.7	3.1	8.3	2.7	35%	9.2%	91.9	40	22	38	33%	71%	12%	11%	29	84	10%	34%	0	0.82	1.0	92	$2
1st Half	5	0	85	66	4.22	4.77	1.34	1.30	95	99	22.8	2.5	7.0	2.8	34%	7.9%	91.6	45	20	34	32%	70%	10%	13%	16	85	13%	19%			3.0	88	$4
2nd Half	3	0	64	72	4.76	4.89	1.48	1.29	147	88	20.5	3.8	10.1	2.7	36%	10.7%	92.2	32	24	43	34%	73%	14%	9%	13	82	8%	54%	0	0.89	-2.0	98	-$1
20 Proj	**8**	**0**	**145**	**132**	**4.49**	**4.13**	**1.39**	**1.33**	**118**	**95**	**21.0**	**3.2**	**8.2**	**2.5**	**36%**	**9.3%**	**91.7**	**38**	**25**	**38**	**32%**	**71%**	**12%**		**29**						**-6.1**	**88**	**$1**

Law,Derek

Law,Derek		Health	A	LIMA Plan	C
Age: 29	Th: R Role RP	PT/Exp	D	Rand Var	+3
Ht: 6' 3"	Wt: 215 Type Pwr	Consist	C	MM	1310

Picked up a few saves in 2nd half despite ghastly control. Best assets are GB% and decent Dom, but it's not nearly enough to cover all the bad. Ctl issues are supported by Ball%; xWHIP affirms the fact he allows far too much traffic on basepaths. These skills have no business being anywhere near a fantasy roster, let alone a closer role.

Yr Tm	W	Sv	IP	K	ERA	xERA	WHIP	xWHIP	vL+	vR+	BF/G	Ctl	Dom	Cmd	Ball%	SwK	Vel	G	L	F	H%	S%	HR/F	xHR/F	GS	APC	DOM%	DIS%	Sv%	LI	RAR	BPX	R$
15 aa	0	13	26	27	6.32	6.28	1.87				4.3	3.2	9.6	3.0							46%	64%									-7.5	113	-$3
16 SF	4	1	55	50	2.13	3.24	0.96	1.11	71	82	3.5	1.5	8.2	5.6	35%	10.9%	92.9	50	22	28	28%	80%	7%	12%	0	13			50	0.90	14.0	161	$7
17 SF *	5	14	70	55	4.18	5.17	1.60	1.32	128	101	4.7	3.5	7.1	2.0	39%	10.2%	93.7	38	23	39	36%	75%	11%	12%	0	16			74	0.85	1.5	69	$3
18 SF *	2	8	56	45	5.26	3.84	1.32		89	152	5.7	2.8	7.2	2.6		11.7%	93.7	40	20	40	32%	59%	11%	7%	0	37			89	0.59	-7.6	95	-$2
19 TOR	1	5	61	67	4.90	5.04	1.66	1.56	98	115	4.9	5.9	9.9	1.7	40%	12.0%	94.1	50	20	30	34%	73%	16%	13%	4	21	0%	75%	83	0.85	-2.9	51	-$4
1st Half	0	0	26	31	6.84	4.46	1.71	1.36	87	140	5.5	4.8	10.6	2.2	38%	12.7%	93.6	54	18	28	38%	61%	18%	14%	3	24	0%	67%	0	0.67	-7.6	102	-$12
2nd Half	1	5	34	36	3.41	5.37	1.63	1.65	109	96	4.5	6.8	9.4	1.4	41%	11.4%	94.4	46	23	31	30%	83%	14%	12%	1	19	0%	100%	83	0.97	4.6	11	$1
20 Proj	**2**	**2**	**58**	**56**	**5.16**	**4.52**	**1.63**	**1.40**	**112**	**110**	**4.9**	**5.0**	**8.7**	**1.7**	**39%**	**11.2%**	**93.8**	**44**	**21**	**35**	**34%**	**71%**	**13%**		**0**						**-7.2**	**49**	**-$6**

Leake,Mike

Leake,Mike		Health	A	LIMA Plan	A
Age: 32	Th: R Role SP	PT/Exp	A	Rand Var	+2
Ht: 5' 10"	Wt: 170 Type Con	Consist	A	MM	1005

Has made a career out of limiting walks and inducing lots of GBs. That approach has yielded consistently MLB-average ratios (narrow range of BPX history) even as his SwK offers no hope for growth of feeble Dom. However, back-to-back seasons of GB% erosion and rising xHR/F threaten to upset his delicate formula. Heed the xERA warning.

Yr Tm	W	Sv	IP	K	ERA	xERA	WHIP	xWHIP	vL+	vR+	BF/G	Ctl	Dom	Cmd	Ball%	SwK	Vel	G	L	F	H%	S%	HR/F	xHR/F	GS	APC	DOM%	DIS%	Sv%	LI	RAR	BPX	R$
15 2 NL	11	0	192	119	3.70	3.95	1.16	1.34	100	89	25.9	2.3	5.6	2.4	34%	6.8%	90.9	52	22	27	26%	72%	14%	14%	30	92	27%	33%			6.1	81	$11
16 STL	9	0	177	125	4.69	3.93	1.32	1.22	103	103	25.2	1.5	6.4	4.2	34%	7.5%	90.6	54	21	25	33%	66%	14%	17%	30	89	23%	33%			-10.8	125	$1
17 2 TM	10	0	186	130	3.92	4.03	1.28	1.25	104	95	25.2	1.8	6.3	3.5	34%	8.7%	90.1	54	22	25	31%	72%	14%	14%	31	90	29%	26%			10.1	116	$9
18 SEA	10	0	186	119	4.36	4.27	1.30	1.26	100	110	25.3	1.6	5.8	3.5	32%	7.8%	88.7	49	22	29	31%	69%	13%	15%	31	90	23%	35%			-4.9	99	$2
19 2 TM	12	0	197	127	4.29	4.73	1.29	1.27	111	106	26.1	1.2	5.8	4.7	32%	8.5%	88.4	47	19	34	30%	75%	18%	18%	32	93	16%	44%			5.1	105	$7
1st Half	7	0	107	76	4.63	4.72	1.28	1.21	108	111	26.6	1.4	6.4	4.5	33%	8.1%	88.1	47	18	35	30%	72%	18%	19%	17	97	18%	35%			-1.6	110	$8
2nd Half	5	0	90	51	3.90	4.79	1.30	1.22	116	101	25.5	1.0	5.1	5.1	31%	9.0%	88.8	47	21	32	31%	79%	18%	17%	15	89	13%	53%			6.7	98	$7
20 Proj	**11**	**0**	**189**	**121**	**4.53**	**4.07**	**1.34**	**1.24**	**111**	**107**	**25.3**	**1.6**	**5.8**	**3.7**	**32%**	**8.3%**	**89.0**	**47**	**21**	**32**	**32%**	**71%**	**15%**		**31**						**-8.8**	**100**	**$2**

LeBlanc,Wade

LeBlanc,Wade		Health	D	LIMA Plan	A
Age: 35	Th: L Role RP	PT/Exp	B	Rand Var	+3
Ht: 6' 3"	Wt: 205 Type Con	Consist	A	MM	1101

Missed about a month in 1st half with an oblique strain. Logged eight starts, but spent most of the season in the bullpen, which was not a safe haven (4.57 ERA in 85 IP). When you own the slowest fastball in MLB in 2019, the margin for error is small and risk is great. Cross him off your list.

Yr Tm	W	Sv	IP	K	ERA	xERA	WHIP	xWHIP	vL+	vR+	BF/G	Ctl	Dom	Cmd	Ball%	SwK	Vel	G	L	F	H%	S%	HR/F	xHR/F	GS	APC	DOM%	DIS%	Sv%	LI	RAR	BPX	R$
15																																	
16 2 TM *	11	2	152	114	3.25	5.07	1.45	1.18	92	109	19.6	2.2	6.8	3.0	34%	9.5%	86.9	34	21	45	34%	82%	17%	16%	8	50	0%	38%	100	0.62	17.6	78	$7
17 PIT	5	1	68	54	4.50	4.20	1.19	1.26	110	89	5.7	2.3	7.1	3.2	36%	9.9%	87.3	46	23	31	28%	66%	15%	16%	0	21			33	0.71	-1.2	110	$1
18 SEA	9	0	162	130	3.72	4.40	1.18	1.25	95	100	20.7	2.2	7.2	3.3	35%	9.7%	86.3	37	20	43	28%	74%	12%	13%	27	77	11%	30%	0	0.69	8.5	98	$10
19 SEA	6	0	121	92	5.71	5.20	1.45	1.34	119	115	20.5	2.3	6.8	3.0	35%	10.0%	86.1	40	21	39	32%	67%	18%	14%	8	75	0%	50%	0	0.75	-18.0	86	-$7
1st Half	5	0	56	47	5.27	5.13	1.40	1.23	122	109	22.6	2.1	7.5	3.6	36%	9.2%	86.0	37	21	41	33%	69%	16%	16%	6	84	0%	50%	0	0.92	-5.3	103	-$3
2nd Half	1	0	65	45	6.09	5.33	1.49	1.33	117	119	18.9	2.5	6.2	2.5	34%	10.6%	86.3	42	20	38	31%	65%	20%	13%	2	69	0%	50%	0	0.62	-12.7	71	-$11
20 Proj	**6**	**0**	**102**	**78**	**4.81**	**4.23**	**1.35**	**1.27**	**110**	**109**	**14.4**	**2.3**	**6.9**	**3.0**	**35%**	**9.9%**	**86.4**	**40**	**21**	**39**	**31%**	**70%**	**15%**		**13**						**-8.3**	**93**	**-$2**

Leclerc,Jose

Leclerc,Jose		Health	B	LIMA Plan	C
Age: 26	Th: R Role RP	PT/Exp	C	Rand Var	0
Ht: 6' 0"	Wt: 190 Type Pwr xFB	Consist	C	MM	3520

Lost closer job by end of April after a run of bad outings, but regained gig in August. Chief bugaboo continues to be Ctl, and 2nd half Ball% doesn't inspire much confidence in a rebound. On the bright side, SwK/Dom remains elite and xHR/F says he hasn't been hit that hard. He'll probably get another shot at the 9th, but expect continued volatility.

Yr Tm	W	Sv	IP	K	ERA	xERA	WHIP	xWHIP	vL+	vR+	BF/G	Ctl	Dom	Cmd	Ball%	SwK	Vel	G	L	F	H%	S%	HR/F	xHR/F	GS	APC	DOM%	DIS%	Sv%	LI	RAR	BPX	R$
15 aa	6	0	103	83	6.59	5.07	1.76				18.2	6.4	7.2	1.1							32%	61%									-33.4	55	-$18
16 TEX *	2	2	81	79	3.50	3.07	1.39		145	69	6.7	5.9	8.8	1.5		12.1%	94.3	29	26	45	27%	75%	0%	3%	0	22			29	0.26	6.9	97	$1
17 TEX	2	2	46	60	3.94	4.97	1.38	1.67	91	69	4.3	7.9	11.8	1.5	44%	16.1%	95.8	40	10	50	22%	73%	8%	6%	0	18			67	0.90	2.3	22	-$1
18 TEX	2	12	58	85	1.56	3.00	0.85	1.12	61	59	3.8	3.9	13.3	3.4	38%	18.1%	95.3	32	21	47	23%	81%	2%	4%	0	16			75	1.30	18.4	165	$14
19 TEX	2	14	69	100	4.33	4.02	1.33	1.32	112	77	4.3	5.1	13.1	2.6	39%	14.1%	96.8	35	20	45	32%	69%	10%	9%	3	18	0%	67%	78	0.90	1.5	121	$6
1st Half	1	5	37	58	4.58	3.57	1.26	1.20	116	80	4.4	4.8	14.0	2.9	38%	13.3%	96.5	37	22	41	32%	67%	16%	12%	2	19	0%	50%	71	0.86	-0.3	149	$4
2nd Half	1	9	31	42	4.02	4.64	1.40	1.37	107	72	4.2	5.5	12.1	2.2	41%	15.2%	97.1	32	18	49	33%	71%	6%	5%	1	18	0%	100%	82	0.94	1.9	87	$9
20 Proj	**2**	**20**	**65**	**89**	**3.60**	**3.63**	**1.25**	**1.29**	**100**	**73**	**4.2**	**5.4**	**12.3**	**2.3**	**40%**	**15.8%**	**96.2**	**34**	**19**	**47**	**29%**	**72%**	**7%**		**0**						**4.4**	**102**	**$10**

Lester,Jon

Lester,Jon		Health	C	LIMA Plan	A
Age: 36	Th: L Role SP	PT/Exp	A	Rand Var	+3
Ht: 6' 4"	Wt: 240 Type	Consist	A	MM	2205

After outpacing xERA by a wide margin in 2018, regression took hold in 2019. Dom returned, but temper your excitement: SwK and further Vel decline both cast doubt. Full-year 2018 and 2nd half 2019 LD% show that he has been getting hit a lot harder as skills slip. Brutal 2nd half line provides a glimpse of the potential downside. Avoid.

Yr Tm	W	Sv	IP	K	ERA	xERA	WHIP	xWHIP	vL+	vR+	BF/G	Ctl	Dom	Cmd	Ball%	SwK	Vel	G	L	F	H%	S%	HR/F	xHR/F	GS	APC	DOM%	DIS%	Sv%	LI	RAR	BPX	R$
15 CHC	11	0	205	207	3.34	3.13	1.12	1.13	90	93	25.9	2.1	9.1	4.4	36%	10.7%	92.0	49	22	29	31%	72%	10%	11%	32	100	44%	16%			15.8	161	$19
16 CHC	19	0	203	197	2.44	3.42	1.02	1.17	73	85	24.9	2.3	8.7	3.8	36%	10.9%	92.1	47	20	33	26%	82%	12%	11%	32	99	50%	16%			43.7	143	$34
17 CHC	13	0	181	180	4.33	3.96	1.32	1.25	73	109	23.8	3.0	9.0	3.0	38%	11.2%	91.1	46	21	32	32%	71%	16%	12%	32	98	25%	34%			0.5	126	$9
18 CHC	18	0	182	149	3.32	4.47	1.31	1.35	120	97	23.8	3.2	7.4	2.3	38%	8.8%	91.0	38	26	36	29%	80%	12%	15%	32	98	22%	31%			18.6	73	$14
19 CHC	13	0	172	165	4.46	4.57	1.50	1.29	110	108	24.6	2.7	8.7	3.2	37%	9.2%	90.3	43	23	33	36%	74%	15%	16%	31	98	19%	35%			1.0	112	$2
1st Half	7	0	88	90	3.89	4.17	1.31	1.14	101	106	23.6	2.0	9.2	4.5	37%	9.1%	90.3	44	20	36	34%	77%	16%	19%	16	98	31%	25%			6.7	144	$9
2nd Half	6	0	84	75	5.06	5.01	1.70	1.35	121	110	25.7	3.4	8.1	2.3	38%	9.3%	90.3	43	26	31	38%	73%	13%	13%	15	99	7%	47%			-5.7	80	-$5
20 Proj	**15**	**0**	**189**	**175**	**4.54**	**4.01**	**1.45**	**1.27**	**110**	**109**	**24.2**	**3.0**	**8.3**	**2.7**	**38%**	**9.6%**	**90.8**	**43**	**22**	**36**	**34%**	**73%**	**15%**		**33**						**-9.1**	**102**	**$3**

GREG PYRON

Littell,Zack

Age: 24	Th: R	Role RP	Health	A	LIMA Plan	B
Ht: 6' 4"	Wt: 220	Type Con	PT/Exp	D	Rand Var	0
			Consist	B	MM	2200

6-0, 2.68 ERA in 37 IP at MIN. Move to bullpen seemed to suit him. In addition to Vel uptick, he narrowed his five-pitch arsenal to a four-seamer/slider combo, which pushed both SwK and Ball% in positive directions. Sticking in bullpen may be quickest path to fantasy relevance. If he starts, needs to show he can hold these gains.

Yr Tm	W	Sv	IP	K	ERA	xERA	WHIP	xWHIP	vL+	vR+	BF/G	Ctl	Dom	Cmd	Ball%	SwK	Vel	G	L	F	H%	S%	HR/F	xHR/F	GS	APC	DOM%	DIS%	Sv%	LI	RAR	BPX	R$
15																																	
16																																	
17 aa	10	0	86	70	3.38	3.68	1.32				25.3	2.8	7.3	2.6							32%	75%									10.4	102	$6
18 MIN *	6	0	149	121	5.38	5.27	1.60		141	115	20.6	3.6	7.3	2.0		8.0%	91.9	44	24	32	36%	66%	13%	13%	2	53	0%	50%	0	0.74	-22.7	67	-$13
19 MIN *	9	1	100	87	4.08	4.87	1.37	1.26	92	96	8.5	3.2	7.9	2.4	33%	13.6%	93.9	38	28	34	30%	77%	11%	16%	0	19			50	0.81	5.2	59	$4
1st Half	4	1	65	56	5.72	6.02	1.51		111	112	15.5	3.2	7.8	2.4		12.0%	93.0	34	37	29	32%	68%	10%	21%	0	32			100	0.88	-9.7	37	-$2
2nd Half	5	0	38	32	1.03	2.43	1.05	1.15	85	87	4.7	3.0	7.5	2.5	33%	14.3%	94.3	41	23	36	24%	96%	12%	14%	0	16			0	0.80	16.2	100	$13
20 Proj	**2**	**0**	**29**	**25**	**3.81**	**4.01**	**1.30**	**1.27**	**98**	**109**	**10.3**	**2.6**	**7.8**	**3.0**	**37%**	**14.3%**	**94.3**	**41**	**23**	**36**	**30%**	**78%**	**15%**		**0**						**1.2**	**103**	**-$2**

Loaisiga,Jonathan

Age: 25	Th: R	Role RP	Health	F	LIMA Plan	B
Ht: 5' 11"	Wt: 165	Type Pwr	PT/Exp	F	Rand Var	+3
			Consist	B	MM	3401

2-2, 4.55 ERA in 32 IP at NYY. Another injury-marred year, this time a shoulder strain cost him three months. Has logged just 234 total IP since turning pro in 2013, and never topped 80 IP in a season, so bullpen move may become a necessity. 2nd half SwK/Dom, Ctl, and xWHIP show upside remains intact, but health clouds all.

Yr Tm	W	Sv	IP	K	ERA	xERA	WHIP	xWHIP	vL+	vR+	BF/G	Ctl	Dom	Cmd	Ball%	SwK	Vel	G	L	F	H%	S%	HR/F	xHR/F	GS	APC	DOM%	DIS%	Sv%	LI	RAR	BPX	R$
15																																	
16																																	
17																																	
18 NYY *	5	0	60	67	5.18	5.96	1.51		108	110	14.4	2.8	10.1	3.6		13.8%	96.0	49	27	24	37%	71%	20%	20%	4	55	25%	50%	0	0.44	-7.6	91	-$5
19 NYY *	2	0	51	55	5.41	5.05	1.40	1.39	110	108	10.2	3.8	9.7	2.6	38%	14.4%	96.9	40	24	36	31%	66%	19%	13%	4	39	0%	75%	0	0.67	-5.7	67	-$5
1st Half	1	0	24	22	6.37	5.59	1.55		98	115	17.5	4.6	8.3	1.8		15.2%	96.0	39	20	41	31%	62%	12%	14%	3	67	0%	67%	0	0.63	-5.5	40	-$9
2nd Half	1	0	27	33	4.34	4.43	1.24	1.21	117	101	7.3	3.0	11.1	3.6	37%	13.6%	97.6	41	27	32	30%	73%	29%	13%	1	29	0%	100%	0	0.69	0.5	104	-$1
20 Proj	**4**	**0**	**73**	**80**	**4.54**	**3.54**	**1.31**	**1.33**	**96**	**84**	**10.9**	**3.3**	**10.0**	**3.0**	**41%**	**13.6%**	**97.6**	**41**	**27**	**32**	**31%**	**71%**	**18%**		**3**						**-3.5**	**125**	**-$1**

Lockett,Walker

Age: 26	Th: R	Role SP	Health	A	LIMA Plan	C
Ht: 6' 5"	Wt: 225	Type Con	PT/Exp	D	Rand Var	+5
			Consist	C	MM	0000

1-1, 8.34 ERA in 23 IP at NYM. Second straight year of struggling mightily in brief MLB stint. Owns track record of excellent Ctl, but GB lean hasn't shown in majors. Even with it, lack of SwK/Dom leaves far too many balls in play. His xHR/F signals the danger if he can't keep the ball on the ground. Too much risk, too little gain.

Yr Tm	W	Sv	IP	K	ERA	xERA	WHIP	xWHIP	vL+	vR+	BF/G	Ctl	Dom	Cmd	Ball%	SwK	Vel	G	L	F	H%	S%	HR/F	xHR/F	GS	APC	DOM%	DIS%	Sv%	LI	RAR	BPX	R$
15																																	
16 a/a	5	0	53	32	3.28	3.41	1.12				23.0	0.6	5.5	8.6							31%	72%									5.9	231	$3
17 aaa	5	0	55	27	4.39	5.53	1.48				23.8	1.9	4.5	2.4							33%	74%									-0.2	38	-$3
18 SD *	5	0	149	112	5.15	5.13	1.44		176	97	23.5	2.4	6.7	2.8		9.0%	92.5	54	20	26	34%	66%	29%	31%	3	73	0%	67%	0	0.58	-18.3	70	-$9
19 NYM *	4	0	82	49	5.55	6.79	1.71	1.37	132	134	18.5	1.9	5.4	2.8	32%	8.1%	92.6	42	25	33	38%	70%	23%	17%	4	41	0%	75%	0	0.69	-10.5	43	-$10
1st Half	1	0	39	17	5.71	5.77	1.47		131	134	23.9	1.9	4.0	2.1		11.7%	92.0	50	15	35	32%	64%	22%	12%	2	69	0%	100%			-5.8	18	-$11
2nd Half	3	0	45	32	5.12	7.16	1.82	1.27	132	133	16.1	1.9	6.4	3.5	30%	6.0%	93.0	38	30	32	42%	73%	24%	19%	2	33	0%	50%	0	0.64	-3.4	69	-$9
20 Proj	**2**	**0**	**44**	**27**	**5.19**	**4.58**	**1.53**	**1.40**	**106**	**110**	**20.5**	**1.9**	**5.6**	**3.0**	**33%**	**6.0%**	**93.0**	**38**	**30**	**32**	**34%**	**73%**	**17%**		**9**						**-5.6**	**76**	**-$6**

Lopez,Jorge

Age: 27	Th: R	Role RP	Health	A	LIMA Plan	A
Ht: 6' 3"	Wt: 195	Type	PT/Exp	C	Rand Var	+5
			Consist	A	MM	1101

Swingman still trying to find MLB footing. Utilized sinker-heavy mix in Aug-Sept (usage up from 21% to 37%; GB% 54%) to combat severe xHR/F-backed HR issues, but HR continued to fly and already subpar SwK/Dom crashed. Posted better skills as RP (9.2 Dom, 2.7 Ctl in 37 IP), so perhaps middle relief is best fit. Fantasy value unlikely.

Yr Tm	W	Sv	IP	K	ERA	xERA	WHIP	xWHIP	vL+	vR+	BF/G	Ctl	Dom	Cmd	Ball%	SwK	Vel	G	L	F	H%	S%	HR/F	xHR/F	GS	APC	DOM%	DIS%	Sv%	LI	RAR	BPX	R$
15 MIL *	13	0	153	128	3.22	3.56	1.32		133	112	24.4	3.6	7.5	2.1		10.2%	93.6	57	23	20	30%	77%	0%	7%	2	94	0%	50%			14.0	90	$10
16 a/a	3	0	125	98	7.20	7.26	1.96				23.8	5.3	7.0	1.3							37%	65%									-46.3	14	-$27
17 MIL *	8	7	106	89	6.60	5.37	1.62		146	135	11.7	3.8	7.6	2.0		5.7%	94.8	44	33	22	35%	59%	0%	1%	0	35			78	0.04	-29.3	64	-$8
18 2 TM *	6	5	93	65	5.64	5.21	1.51	1.46	99	114	9.4	3.3	6.3	1.9	37%	9.0%	93.7	45	23	32	33%	64%	11%	13%	7	52	29%	71%	71	0.57	-17.1	49	-$7
19 KC	4	1	124	109	6.33	4.76	1.47	1.36	129	100	14.1	3.1	7.9	2.6	38%	9.2%	94.2	46	20	34	32%	61%	21%	23%	18	53	11%	39%	50	0.78	-27.9	92	-$10
1st Half	1	0	68	67	6.12	4.54	1.48	1.29	129	105	15.8	3.3	8.9	2.7	37%	9.7%	93.7	44	23	33	33%	64%	22%	26%	10	61	10%	30%	0	0.72	-13.5	101	-$11
2nd Half	3	1	56	42	6.59	5.01	1.46	1.33	129	94	12.4	2.7	6.8	2.5	38%	8.6%	94.7	49	16	35	31%	59%	19%	20%	8	45	13%	50%	50	0.83	-14.4	81	-$9
20 Proj	**5**	**0**	**87**	**70**	**5.09**	**4.31**	**1.52**	**1.37**	**118**	**106**	**12.3**	**3.3**	**7.2**	**2.2**	**37%**	**9.1%**	**94.0**	**46**	**20**	**33**	**33%**	**71%**	**16%**		**7**						**-10.1**	**75**	**-$6**

Lopez,Pablo

Age: 24	Th: R	Role SP	Health	F	LIMA Plan	D
Ht: 6' 3"	Wt: 200	Type Con	PT/Exp	D	Rand Var	+5
			Consist	D	MM	2203

5-8, 5.09 ERA in 111 IP. Enjoyed a promising 1st half (especially if a 3 IP/10 ER outing is excluded), featuring an intriguing blend of GB%, Ctl, and Swk/Dom. Sidelined mid-June to late-Aug with a shoulder strain, clearly wasn't the same upon return. But that first-half form was an attention-grabber. If he recaptures it... UP: 3.75 ERA

Yr Tm	W	Sv	IP	K	ERA	xERA	WHIP	xWHIP	vL+	vR+	BF/G	Ctl	Dom	Cmd	Ball%	SwK	Vel	G	L	F	H%	S%	HR/F	xHR/F	GS	APC	DOM%	DIS%	Sv%	LI	RAR	BPX	R$
15																																	
16																																	
17																																	
18 MIA *	4	0	124	104	2.77	3.24	1.10	1.32	93	113	22.1	2.2	7.6	3.5	35%	11.3%	92.4	50	21	29	27%	80%	16%	19%	10	95	10%	40%			21.1	112	$11
19 MIA *	5	0	126	109	5.89	4.92	1.38	1.27	116	84	20.4	2.5	7.7	3.1	36%	10.6%	93.6	48	21	31	33%	59%	15%	17%	21	86	33%	29%			-21.7	78	-$7
1st Half	5	0	77	73	4.23	3.87	1.12	1.17	98	79	22.4	2.1	8.6	4.1	36%	11.4%	93.5	49	20	31	30%	64%	12%	15%	14	87	43%	14%			2.6	135	$5
2nd Half	0	0	50	36	8.46	7.43	1.78	1.34	153	95	19.1	3.0	6.5	2.1	36%	9.1%	93.6	45	24	31	37%	53%	20%	20%	7	83	14%	57%			-24.3	15	-$24
20 Proj	**6**	**0**	**152**	**132**	**4.25**	**3.69**	**1.31**	**1.29**	**115**	**97**	**20.6**	**2.5**	**7.8**	**3.1**	**36%**	**10.5%**	**93.1**	**48**	**22**	**30**	**31%**	**72%**	**16%**		**31**						**-1.8**	**114**	**$3**

Lopez,Reynaldo

Age: 26	Th: R	Role SP	Health	A	LIMA Plan	A
Ht: 6' 1"	Wt: 200	Type FB	PT/Exp	A	Rand Var	+1
			Consist	A	MM	1205

After a miserable 1st half, made a mechanical adjustment that sparked an uptick in Vel and much better Ball%/Ctl. Emphasis on high fastballs contributed to SwK boost that hints at further Dom upside, and xHR/F says he had enough gas to get away with that approach. Add some consistency and... UP: sub-4.00 ERA, but skills-supported this time

Yr Tm	W	Sv	IP	K	ERA	xERA	WHIP	xWHIP	vL+	vR+	BF/G	Ctl	Dom	Cmd	Ball%	SwK	Vel	G	L	F	H%	S%	HR/F	xHR/F	GS	APC	DOM%	DIS%	Sv%	LI	RAR	BPX	R$
15																																	
16 WAS *	10	0	153	151	4.51	4.46	1.40	1.43	90	121	21.6	3.5	8.9	2.5	37%	10.2%	95.8	41	23	35	33%	71%	9%	8%	6	73	17%	50%	0	0.62	-6.1	88	$1
17 CHW *	9	0	169	145	4.51	4.45	1.36	1.38	107	91	23.5	3.5	7.8	2.2	36%	9.1%	94.5	30	22	48	30%	71%	9%	9%	8	96	0%	50%			-3.3	68	$3
18 CHW	7	0	189	151	3.91	5.00	1.27	1.41	96	101	25.0	3.6	7.2	2.0	37%	9.6%	95.5	33	20	47	27%	73%	9%	12%	32	96	31%	28%			5.5	51	$6
19 CHW	10	0	184	169	5.38	5.16	1.46	1.37	114	107	24.5	3.2	8.3	2.6	36%	11.7%	95.5	35	21	44	32%	68%	14%	15%	33	96	24%	55%			-19.9	83	-$4
1st Half	4	0	93	83	6.12	5.66	1.58	1.38	124	117	24.4	3.7	8.1	2.2	37%	10.7%	94.8	33	19	48	33%	67%	16%	17%	17	99	12%	71%			-18.4	62	-$12
2nd Half	6	0	91	86	4.63	4.78	1.34	1.24	103	98	24.6	2.7	8.5	3.2	34%	12.8%	96.2	37	22	41	32%	69%	12%	12%	16	92	38%	38%			-1.4	105	$4
20 Proj	**10**	**0**	**189**	**168**	**4.39**	**4.38**	**1.38**	**1.35**	**104**	**104**	**24.3**	**3.3**	**8.0**	**2.4**	**36%**	**10.8%**	**95.5**	**35**	**21**	**44**	**31%**	**73%**	**12%**		**33**						**-5.5**	**78**	**$3**

Lopez,Yoan

Age: 27	Th: R	Role RP	Health	A	LIMA Plan	D
Ht: 6' 3"	Wt: 185	Type Con	PT/Exp	D	Rand Var	-2
			Consist	D	MM	1100

Gaudy 1st-half ERA, fueled by silly H%/S% combo, pushed him into setup role, but wheels predictably came off as H%/S% regressed. SwK/GB% also disappeared in 2nd half as slider lost effectiveness (SwK down from 22% to 11%). Tried elevating fastballs, which just led to lots of HR. Amid the noisy halves, skills are both flat and below-average.

Yr Tm	W	Sv	IP	K	ERA	xERA	WHIP	xWHIP	vL+	vR+	BF/G	Ctl	Dom	Cmd	Ball%	SwK	Vel	G	L	F	H%	S%	HR/F	xHR/F	GS	APC	DOM%	DIS%	Sv%	LI	RAR	BPX	R$
15 aa	1	0	48	28	5.92	5.08	1.62				21.3	4.6	5.2	1.1							31%	63%									-11.6	32	-$10
16 aa	4	0	62	30	8.00	7.57	1.93				21.0	5.1	4.4	0.9							33%	61%									-29.1	-30	-$16
17																																	
18 ARI *	2	12	72	81	3.48	2.68	1.12		124	87	5.2	3.5	10.1	2.8		11.6%	96.9	50	9	41	27%	71%	22%	16%	0	13			71	0.49	6.0	128	$8
19 ARI	2	1	61	42	3.41	4.67	1.14	1.38	92	100	3.5	2.5	6.2	2.5	37%	9.9%	96.3	44	26	30	24%	79%	20%	23%	0	12			25	1.10	8.2	72	$2
1st Half	1	0	32	23	1.11	3.93	0.90	1.38	39	94	3.3	3.1	6.4	2.1	38%	12.2%	96.2	53	28	19	18%	96%	18%	26%	0	12			0	0.98	13.5	69	$6
2nd Half	1	1	28	19	6.04	5.39	1.41	1.28	167	104	3.7	1.9	6.0	3.2	36%	7.6%	96.4	35	25	40	30%	66%	21%	22%	0	13			50	1.24	-5.3	77	-$3
20 Proj	**2**	**0**	**58**	**44**	**4.70**	**4.22**	**1.33**	**1.32**	**108**	**104**	**5.0**	**3.3**	**6.8**	**2.1**	**36%**	**9.3%**	**96.4**	**42**	**26**	**31**	**28%**	**70%**	**18%**		**0**						**-4.0**	**63**	**-$3**

GREG PYRON

Lorenzen,Michael

Health: D | LIMA Plan: B
Age: 28 Th: R Role: RP | PT/Exp: C | Rand Var: -2
Ht: 6' 3" Wt: 217 Type: | Consist: B | MM: 2210

Rebooted his profile with some success, ditching cutter/sinker for slider/change-up as more effective secondary offerings. GB% tilt suffered as a result, but big SwK/Dom gains more than justified the change, and 2nd half LI shows he made coaches believe too. 2nd half Ctl slip tempers optimism, but if he figures that out, UP: 25 Sv

Yr Tm	W	Sv	IP	K	ERA	xERA	WHIP	xWHIP	vL+	vR+	BF/G	Ctl	Dom	Cmd	Ball%	SwK	Vel	G	L	F	H%	S%	HR/F	xHR/F	GS	APC	DOM%	DIS%	Sv%	LI	RAR	BPX	R$
15 CIN *	8	0	156	100	4.59	5.12	1.52	1.54	138	110	20.5	3.8	5.8	1.5	40%	9.0%	94.0	41	28	31	31%	73%	16%	14%	21	74	0%	57%	0	0.69	-12.1	33	-$8
16 CIN	2	0	50	48	2.88	2.87	1.08	1.18	74	97	5.8	2.3	8.6	3.7	35%	10.1%	96.2	63	21	16	28%	78%	23%	12%	0	22			0	0.84	8.1	158	$3
17 CIN	8	2	83	80	4.45	3.97	1.35	1.34	102	86	5.2	3.7	8.7	2.4	38%	11.1%	96.4	55	20	25	31%	69%	15%	13%	0	20			29	1.00	-0.9	108	$2
18 CIN	4	1	81	54	3.11	4.59	1.38	1.49	109	89	7.6	3.8	6.0	1.6	37%	7.3%	95.1	50	25	25	29%	79%	10%	13%	3	29	0%	33%	50	0.84	10.4	39	$1
19 CIN	1	7	83	85	2.92	4.05	1.15	1.28	83	88	4.7	3.0	9.2	3.0	37%	14.6%	96.9	44	23	32	28%	79%	13%	10%	0	18			64	1.20	16.3	115	$8
1st Half	0	5	42	41	3.61	4.11	1.32	1.22	97	95	4.8	2.6	8.7	3.4	36%	12.7%	96.5	47	25	28	33%	78%	17%	16%	0	17			83	1.08	4.7	123	$4
2nd Half	1	2	41	44	2.20	3.97	0.98	1.26	69	78	4.6	3.5	9.7	2.8	38%	16.5%	97.2	41	21	38	23%	81%	8%	5%	0	19			40	1.32	11.7	107	$13
20 Proj	2	5	58	53	3.67	3.69	1.24	1.33	93	88	5.4	3.4	8.2	2.4	37%	11.9%	96.2	48	23	29	29%	73%	12%		0						3.5	94	$2

Lucchesi,Joey

Health: B | LIMA Plan: B
Age: 27 Th: L Role: SP | PT/Exp: B | Rand Var: 0
Ht: 6' 5" Wt: 204 Type: Pwr | Consist: B | MM: 2303

"Churve"-throwing southpaw had a worthy sophomore follow-up going, at least in first half. Then he lost a tick of velocity; SwK/Ctl both responded negatively. No reported injury behind that, so first half skills may still be best baseline. Career home/road ERA split: 3.22 Home/5.40 Road. For best results: leave the road starts, take the cannoli.

Yr Tm	W	Sv	IP	K	ERA	xERA	WHIP	xWHIP	vL+	vR+	BF/G	Ctl	Dom	Cmd	Ball%	SwK	Vel	G	L	F	H%	S%	HR/F	xHR/F	GS	APC	DOM%	DIS%	Sv%	LI	RAR	BPX	R$
15																																	
16																																	
17 aa	5	1	60	43	2.54	3.33	1.21				24.3	2.2	6.4	2.9							30%	81%									13.5	104	$5
18 SD	8	0	130	145	4.08	3.57	1.29	1.19	86	112	21.1	3.0	10.0	3.4	36%	11.0%	90.4	45	23	33	32%	75%	20%	20%	26	83	15%	31%			1.0	142	$4
19 SD	10	0	164	158	4.18	4.37	1.22	1.32	86	96	22.9	3.1	8.7	2.8	37%	10.9%	90.2	47	17	36	29%	70%	14%	13%	30	88	27%	33%			6.6	107	$10
1st Half	6	0	90	88	3.91	4.13	1.13	1.21	76	90	23.1	2.6	8.8	3.4	36%	11.9%	90.7	48	17	35	28%	68%	11%	13%	16	88	44%	19%			6.5	125	$14
2nd Half	4	0	74	70	4.50	4.69	1.34	1.35	95	103	22.6	3.6	8.5	2.3	38%	9.7%	89.6	46	17	37	29%	72%	17%	13%	14	89	7%	50%			0.1	86	$4
20 Proj	10	0	160	156	4.06	3.71	1.30	1.25	89	104	22.0	3.1	8.8	2.8	37%	10.8%	90.2	46	19	35	31%	74%	15%		30						1.9	113	$7

Lugo,Seth

Health: D | LIMA Plan: B
Age: 30 Th: R Role: RP | PT/Exp: B | Rand Var: 0
Ht: 6' 4" Wt: 225 Type: Pwr | Consist: B | MM: 4421

Former swingman continued shift into a more classic RP role, with terrific results. Bout of shoulder tendinitis shelved him briefly in late May, came back and was lights-out for rest of year, including late-season shot at closing. 2nd half was plenty good, but had copious H%/S% and HR/F help as well. Buy the skills, hope the role finds him again.

Yr Tm	W	Sv	IP	K	ERA	xERA	WHIP	xWHIP	vL+	vR+	BF/G	Ctl	Dom	Cmd	Ball%	SwK	Vel	G	L	F	H%	S%	HR/F	xHR/F	GS	APC	DOM%	DIS%	Sv%	LI	RAR	BPX	R$
15 a/a	8	0	136	103	4.27	4.41	1.39				23.9	2.3	6.8	2.9							34%	70%									-5.3	92	-$1
16 NYM *	8	0	137	96	4.80	5.14	1.50	1.38	91	90	15.6	2.8	6.3	2.3	36%	9.7%	92.1	43	19	38	33%	70%	10%	17%	8	57	13%	38%	0	0.65	-10.3	57	-$5
17 NYM	7	0	101	85	4.71	4.36	1.37	1.24	102	104	22.9	2.2	7.5	3.4	35%	9.2%	91.1	42	24	34	33%	68%	12%	13%	18	86	17%	33%	0	0.79	-4.4	115	$0
18 NYM	3	3	101	103	2.66	3.53	1.08	1.18	75	88	7.6	2.5	9.1	3.7	34%	10.5%	93.9	46	20	33	28%	79%	10%	12%	5	30	20%	40%	75	0.93	18.6	140	$11
19 NYM	7	6	80	104	2.70	3.10	0.90	1.01	71	77	5.1	1.8	11.7	6.5	33%	11.8%	94.4	43	18	39	28%	75%	11%	10%	0	21			55	1.34	17.8	199	$15
1st Half	3	0	40	53	3.60	3.82	1.20	1.08	98	94	5.7	2.7	11.9	4.4	34%	11.5%	94.0	38	18	44	33%	76%	13%	13%	0	23			0	1.08	4.5	172	$6
2nd Half	4	6	40	51	1.80	2.53	0.60	0.86	43	57	4.6	0.9	11.5	12.8	32%	12.1%	94.8	49	17	34	23%	73%	7%	7%	0	19			86	1.59	13.3	228	$25
20 Proj	5	12	80	88	3.09	3.04	1.04	1.09	80	86	6.8	2.0	9.9	4.9	34%	10.9%	93.6	45	19	36	29%	74%	11%		0						10.5	168	$13

Luzardo,Jesus

Health: B | LIMA Plan: A
Age: 22 Th: L Role: SP | PT/Exp: F | Rand Var: 0
Ht: 6' 0" Wt: 209 Type: | Consist: A | MM: 4301

0-0, 1.50 ERA with 2 Sv in 12 IP at OAK. Top SP prospect missed a chunk of summer with lat strain. Returned to join pen as a September call-up, was lights-out (2 ER, 3 BB/16 K). Repertoire includes fastball, curve, change, all regarded as above-average. Given missed time and minimal high-minors work, expect strict innings cap. Otherwise, all aboard.

Yr Tm	W	Sv	IP	K	ERA	xERA	WHIP	xWHIP	vL+	vR+	BF/G	Ctl	Dom	Cmd	Ball%	SwK	Vel	G	L	F	H%	S%	HR/F	xHR/F	GS	APC	DOM%	DIS%	Sv%	LI	RAR	BPX	R$
15																																	
16																																	
17																																	
18 a/a	8	0	96	89	3.47	3.34	1.19				19.3	2.2	8.3	3.8							32%	72%									8.1	133	$6
19 OAK *	1	2	43	45	2.96	2.98	1.10	1.03	27	73	13.0	2.2	9.5	4.3	39%	15.2%	96.4	42	15	42	30%	76%	9%	13%	0	29			100	0.85	8.2	144	$2
1st Half	1	0	9	8	4.36	4.22	1.28		0	0	18.7	1.9	7.7	4.1							33%	68%	0%		0	0					0.2	114	-$9
2nd Half	0	2	36	38	2.41	2.29	0.98		27	72	12.5	2.2	9.3	4.3		15.2%	96.4	42	15	42	27%	79%	9%	13%	0	29			100	0.85	9.3	152	$4
20 Proj	6	0	94	94	3.45	3.17	1.12				20.6	2.2	9.0	4.1	37%	13.3%		48	22	30	30%	72%	12%		16						8.2	148	$7

Lyles,Jordan

Health: D | LIMA Plan: D
Age: 29 Th: R Role: RP | PT/Exp: C | Rand Var: +1
Ht: 6' 5" Wt: 230 Type: Pwr | Consist: D | MM: 1203

Traded from PIT to MIL in late July. On surface it looks like MIL fixed him (ERA: 5.36 PIT, 2.45 MIL); in reality, skills were similar in both stops, and MIL just benefited from hit/strand rate regression. Skills confirm he's reached "average SP" status, which is light years better than unspeakable 2016-17. Kudos.

Yr Tm	W	Sv	IP	K	ERA	xERA	WHIP	xWHIP	vL+	vR+	BF/G	Ctl	Dom	Cmd	Ball%	SwK	Vel	G	L	F	H%	S%	HR/F	xHR/F	GS	APC	DOM%	DIS%	Sv%	LI	RAR	BPX	R$
15 COL	2	0	49	30	5.14	4.45	1.49	1.48	109	98	21.2	3.5	5.5	1.6	40%	8.5%	92.1	50	26	25	32%	63%	5%	7%	10	77	0%	30%			-7.1	39	-$6
16 COL *	8	1	103	53	6.80	6.56	1.87	1.59	122	97	10.1	4.2	4.6	1.1	39%	7.4%	92.9	51	24	25	36%	63%	8%	6%	5	24	20%	80%	25	0.98	-33.3	11	-$18
17 2 NL *	2	0	90	70	7.11	6.52	1.66	1.33	136	119	9.3	3.0	7.0	2.4	38%	9.5%	93.8	49	19	32	36%	59%	21%	16%	5	33	0%	40%	0	0.44	-30.5	38	-$15
18 2 NL	3	0	88	84	4.11	4.05	1.27	1.25	78	117	10.6	2.9	8.6	3.0	35%	10.6%	93.6	46	17	37	30%	72%	13%	15%	8	40	38%	50%	0	0.65	0.5	117	$0
19 2 NL	12	0	141	146	4.15	4.60	1.32	1.34	121	88	21.4	3.5	9.3	2.7	36%	10.7%	92.6	40	18	41	30%	75%	16%	15%	28	88	11%	29%			6.2	99	$8
1st Half	5	0	70	71	3.71	4.29	1.22	1.28	118	74	22.4	3.3	9.1	2.7	37%	10.7%	92.6	43	22	35	29%	73%	12%	14%	13	92	15%	23%			6.9	103	$8
2nd Half	7	0	71	75	4.58	4.97	1.42	1.30	125	101	20.5	3.7	9.6	2.6	36%	10.6%	92.6	38	15	47	30%	77%	18%	15%	15	84	7%	33%			-0.7	96	$7
20 Proj	8	0	131	122	4.47	4.14	1.42	1.31	113	102	13.9	3.5	8.4	2.4	36%	10.2%	93.0	42	20	39	31%	74%	15%		15						-5.1	89	$0

Lynn,Lance

Health: D | LIMA Plan: A
Age: 33 Th: R Role: SP | PT/Exp: A | Rand Var: +1
Ht: 6' 5" Wt: 280 Type: Pwr | Consist: A | MM: 3405

Lesson learned in this process: see a big G/L/F shift? Go check the pitch mix. Sure enough, de-emphasized sinker in favor of four-seamers. Results fit the expected pattern: SwK and Dom jumped, so did FB%. In this case, he got away with the FBs, and xHR/F says that wasn't just luck. Ergo, these gains should hold. Just don't pay for 200 IP of them.

Yr Tm	W	Sv	IP	K	ERA	xERA	WHIP	xWHIP	vL+	vR+	BF/G	Ctl	Dom	Cmd	Ball%	SwK	Vel	G	L	F	H%	S%	HR/F	xHR/F	GS	APC	DOM%	DIS%	Sv%	LI	RAR	BPX	R$
15 STL	12	0	175	167	3.03	3.95	1.37	1.32	111	88	24.2	3.5	8.6	2.5	39%	9.5%	91.7	44	22	34	33%	80%	8%	12%	31	98	32%	29%			20.2	98	$11
16																																	
17 STL	11	0	186	153	3.43	4.61	1.23	1.42	108	81	23.5	3.8	7.4	2.0	40%	9.4%	91.8	44	20	36	25%	78%	14%	12%	33	95	15%	42%			21.3	64	$16
18 2 AL	10	0	157	161	4.77	4.14	1.53	1.38	115	94	22.6	4.4	9.2	2.1	40%	10.7%	93.2	50	23	27	35%	69%	11%	13%	29	95	17%	34%	0	0.79	-12.0	88	-$5
19 TEX	16	0	208	246	3.67	3.86	1.22	1.17	94	88	26.5	2.5	10.6	4.2	36%	12.9%	94.2	40	21	38	34%	73%	10%	12%	33	108	45%	12%			21.4	153	$21
1st Half	10	0	108	118	4.00	3.92	1.21	1.12	97	90	26.4	2.2	9.8	4.5	37%	11.8%	93.8	42	21	37	34%	68%	8%	10%	17	106	59%	18%			6.7	151	$21
2nd Half	6	0	100	128	3.32	3.87	1.23	1.13	92	86	26.6	3.0	11.5	3.9	35%	14.1%	94.6	38	22	40	33%	77%	12%	13%	16	110	31%	6%			14.7	156	$21
20 Proj	13	0	189	205	3.80	3.46	1.26	1.25	100	87	23.6	3.1	9.8	3.2	37%	12.6%	93.4	43	22	35	32%	73%	12%		33						8.0	131	$14

Maeda,Kenta

Health: C | LIMA Plan: A
Age: 32 Th: R Role: SP | PT/Exp: A | Rand Var: 0
Ht: 6' 1" Wt: 184 Type: Pwr | Consist: A | MM: 3413

So much to like here: Vet getting better at using his arsenal, ramping up SwK without plus velocity. Ctl/Ball% remain stable; nicked up by HRs though xHR/F says that wasn't all fair. Consistent skills are undermined only by low usage. Between periodic injuries and workload management/bullpen stints, just set expectations for 140 good IP.

Yr Tm	W	Sv	IP	K	ERA	xERA	WHIP	xWHIP	vL+	vR+	BF/G	Ctl	Dom	Cmd	Ball%	SwK	Vel	G	L	F	H%	S%	HR/F	xHR/F	GS	APC	DOM%	DIS%	Sv%	LI	RAR	BPX	R$
15 for	15	0	176	170	4.32	4.37	1.27				24.8	3.2	8.7	2.7							28%	73%									-7.7	77	$7
16 LA	16	0	176	179	3.48	3.63	1.14	1.19	99	79	22.4	2.6	9.2	3.6	36%	12.2%	90.0	44	20	36	29%	73%	12%	12%	32	92	25%	19%			15.3	140	$19
17 LA	13	1	134	140	4.22	3.89	1.15	1.15	103	88	19.2	2.3	9.4	4.1	34%	12.9%	91.5	38	22	40	29%	69%	15%	11%	25	75	24%	36%	100	0.73	2.3	148	$12
18 LA	8	2	125	153	3.81	3.50	1.26	1.16	112	85	13.6	3.1	11.0	3.6	34%	14.8%	91.9	40	24	35	34%	72%	11%	13%	20	53	35%	45%	100	1.04	5.3	152	$7
19 LA	10	3	154	169	4.04	3.99	1.07	1.24	99	72	16.9	3.0	9.9	3.3	34%	15.1%	92.1	41	21	38	26%	67%	15%	10%	26	66	27%	19%	100	0.91	8.8	127	$16
1st Half	7	0	88	88	3.78	4.39	1.10	1.25	109	62	22.3	3.1	9.0	2.9	33%	14.4%	91.8	37	22	41	26%	71%	13%	9%	16	86	31%	25%			7.8	103	$18
2nd Half	3	3	66	81	4.39	3.51	1.04	1.13	84	83	12.7	2.9	11.1	3.9	35%	16.1%	92.5	46	19	35	26%	62%	18%	11%	10	50	20%	10%	100	1.02	1.0	159	$13
20 Proj	10	2	145	162	3.74	3.35	1.15	1.17	102	81	20.8	3.0	10.1	3.3	34%	14.6%	91.8	41	22	37	29%	73%	15%		28						7.4	137	$14

RAY MURPHY

Magill,Matthew

Age: 30	Th: R	Role RP	Health	C	LIMA Plan B
Ht: 6' 3"	Wt: 210	Type Pwr	PT/Exp	D	Rand Var +3
			Consist	B	MM 2320

Ditched curveball to focus on fastball/slider combo upon arriving in Seattle in late July, with excellent results. Even got one of the last rides of the year on the SEA closer carousel. It's only 25 IP, but Vel/SwK combo are the raw ingredients for another spin in 2020. UP: 25 Sv

Yr	Tm	W	Sv	IP	K	ERA	xERA	WHIP	xWHIP	vL+	vR+	BF/G	Ctl	Dom	Cmd	Ball%	SwK	Vel	G	L	F	H%	S%	HR/F	xHR/F	GS	APC	DOM%	DIS%	Sv%	LI	RAR	BPX	R$
15																																		
16	CIN *	4	1	56	49	7.22	7.26	2.00		145	146	6.3	6.0	7.8	1.3		7.3%	92.8	23	23	54	37%	66%	14%	10%	0	16			33	0.26	-21.1	19	-$13
17	aaa	6	0	96	54	4.39	6.05	1.71				22.8	3.8	5.1	1.3							34%	77%									-0.4	19	-$7
18	MIN	3	0	57	56	3.81	4.61	1.43	1.33	113	110	6.2	3.7	8.9	2.4	40%	11.8%	94.7	35	22	43	31%	81%	15%	21%	0	25			0	0.87	2.4	86	-$2
19	2 AL	5	5	51	64	4.09	4.17	1.40	1.25	111	94	4.6	3.6	11.4	3.2	35%	15.0%	95.2	38	26	36	36%	75%	14%	14%	0	18			71	0.76	2.6	136	$2
1st Half		2	0	26	31	4.50	4.40	1.42	1.29	91	108	4.9	4.2	10.7	2.6	34%	13.9%	95.4	35	31	34	35%	69%	8%	6%	0	19			0	0.56	0.0	103	-$3
2nd Half		3	5	25	33	3.65	3.98	1.38	1.12	132	79	4.3	2.9	12.0	4.1	37%	16.1%	95.1	41	22	38	36%	83%	19%	21%	0	17			71	0.95	2.6	171	$7
20	**Proj**	**5**	**15**	**58**	**61**	**3.86**	**3.77**	**1.32**	**1.25**	**109**	**94**	**5.3**	**3.2**	**9.5**	**3.0**	**37%**	**13.8%**	**95.0**	**37**	**24**	**39**	**31%**	**77%**	**15%**		**0**						**2.1**	**115**	**$7**

Mahle,Tyler

Age: 25	Th: R	Role SP	Health	C	LIMA Plan D
Ht: 6' 3"	Wt: 210	Type	PT/Exp	C	Rand Var +5
			Consist	D	MM 2203

Missed six weeks in 2nd half with hamstring, returned as a human gasoline can. Rising from the ashes, though, is a very playable skill set, as he re-discovered two foundational elements of his 2017 skills: good Ctl and a GB tilt. 2nd half upticks in Vel and SwK raise the ceiling even further. Put it all together and you get... UP: 13 Wins, 3.60 ERA

Yr	Tm	W	Sv	IP	K	ERA	xERA	WHIP	xWHIP	vL+	vR+	BF/G	Ctl	Dom	Cmd	Ball%	SwK	Vel	G	L	F	H%	S%	HR/F	xHR/F	GS	APC	DOM%	DIS%	Sv%	LI	RAR	BPX	R$
15																																		
16	aa	6	0	71	58	6.70	6.90	1.65				22.8	2.8	7.4	2.6							36%	64%									-22.0	31	-$10
17	CIN *	11	0	164	135	2.88	3.41	1.21		118	81	23.7	2.4	7.4	3.0		7.3%	92.9	52	15	33	30%	79%	0%	4%	4	92	0%	25%			30.0	111	$17
18	CIN *	9	0	143	127	4.62	5.53	1.51	1.40	135	98	22.1	4.1	8.0	2.0	35%	10.5%	92.4	39	25	36	31%	75%	18%	14%	23	90	9%	39%			-8.3	44	-$5
19	CIN	3	0	130	129	5.14	4.08	1.31	1.23	115	92	22.2	2.4	9.0	3.8	34%	10.0%	93.3	47	22	31	32%	66%	21%	17%	25	88	24%	32%			-10.1	133	-$2
1st Half		2	0	83	84	4.35	3.93	1.22	1.15	118	85	23.0	2.2	9.1	4.2	34%	9.6%	93.0	44	23	32	31%	71%	20%	17%	15	91	27%	27%			1.5	140	$2
2nd Half		1	0	47	45	6.51	4.34	1.47	1.24	111	106	21.1	2.7	8.6	3.2	33%	10.5%	94.0	51	19	30	34%	59%	23%	17%	10	84	20%	40%			-11.6	122	-$10
20	**Proj**	**9**	**0**	**160**	**146**	**4.08**	**3.79**	**1.35**	**1.28**	**114**	**92**	**21.5**	**2.7**	**8.3**	**3.0**	**34%**	**10.3%**	**93.1**	**44**	**23**	**33**	**32%**	**76%**	**18%**		**31**						**1.5**	**111**	**$5**

Manaea,Sean

Age: 28	Th: L	Role SP	Health	F	LIMA Plan C
Ht: 6' 5"	Wt: 245	Type	PT/Exp	B	Rand Var -3
			Consist	C	MM 2203

4-0, 1.21 ERA in 30 IP at OAK. Rehab from offseason shoulder surgery held him out until September; pitched brilliantly upon recall. Small-sample SwK/Dom gains appear to be fueled by heavy slider usage; can't be sure that scales over a full season. Bid to stable 2017-18 skills rather than that September 2019 flash.

Yr	Tm	W	Sv	IP	K	ERA	xERA	WHIP	xWHIP	vL+	vR+	BF/G	Ctl	Dom	Cmd	Ball%	SwK	Vel	G	L	F	H%	S%	HR/F	xHR/F	GS	APC	DOM%	DIS%	Sv%	LI	RAR	BPX	R$
15	aa	6	0	50	51	2.49	3.59	1.33				22.9	3.6	9.2	2.6							32%	84%									9.0	114	$3
16	OAK *	9	0	163	141	3.63	3.78	1.20	1.23	71	103	23.3	2.3	7.8	3.4	33%	12.3%	92.3	44	21	35	29%	74%	14%	16%	24	87	33%	29%	0	0.78	11.2	105	$11
17	OAK	12	0	159	140	4.37	4.49	1.40	1.32	79	109	23.9	3.1	7.9	2.5	35%	11.7%	91.6	44	21	35	33%	71%	11%	12%	29	93	17%	38%			-0.2	97	$4
18	OAK	12	0	161	108	3.59	4.24	1.08	1.26	86	94	24.2	1.8	6.0	3.4	32%	10.2%	90.5	44	21	35	26%	72%	12%	16%	27	88	26%	41%			11.2	95	$14
19	OAK *	7	0	58	63	2.54	2.14	0.84	1.17	74	64	21.1	2.1	9.9	4.8	35%	12.2%	89.8	41	18	41	22%	80%	11%	12%	5	89	60%	20%			14.0	153	$9
1st Half																																		
2nd Half		7	0	58	63	2.54	2.14	0.84	1.12	75	63	21.1	2.1	9.9	4.8	35%	12.2%	89.8	41	18	41	22%	80%	11%	12%	5	89	60%	20%			14.0	153	$9
20	**Proj**	**14**	**0**	**152**	**139**	**3.83**	**3.68**	**1.19**	**1.23**	**83**	**101**	**22.9**	**2.4**	**8.2**	**3.4**	**34%**	**11.6%**	**91.0**	**43**	**20**	**37**	**30%**	**72%**	**12%**		**27**						**6.0**	**119**	**$13**

Manning,Matt

Age: 22	Th: R	Role SP	Health	A	LIMA Plan F
Ht: 6' 6"	Wt: 215	Type Con	PT/Exp	F	Rand Var +1
			Consist	F	MM 3201

9th overall pick from 2016 draft spent full year in Double-A and dominated. Leverages mid-90s fastball plus curve from his big frame, predictably producing a groundball tilt. Will almost certainly get some Triple-A time to polish his change-up and prove he can hold 2nd half Ctl gains, but he will reach DET soon enough.

Yr	Tm	W	Sv	IP	K	ERA	xERA	WHIP	xWHIP	vL+	vR+	BF/G	Ctl	Dom	Cmd	Ball%	SwK	Vel	G	L	F	H%	S%	HR/F	xHR/F	GS	APC	DOM%	DIS%	Sv%	LI	RAR	BPX	R$
15																																		
16																																		
17																																		
18																																		
19	aa	11	0	135	124	3.63	2.96	1.15				22.4	2.7	8.2	3.1							29%	69%									14.6	114	$13
1st Half		6	0	88	85	3.66	3.00	1.19		0	0	23.6	3.0	8.7	2.9							30%	69%			0	0					9.2	115	$15
2nd Half		5	0	47	39	3.58	2.87	1.07		0	0	20.3	2.0	7.4	3.7							27%	68%			0	0					5.4	117	$8
20	**Proj**	**6**	**0**	**87**	**77**	**3.96**	**3.62**	**1.17**				**21.8**	**2.4**	**7.9**	**3.2**	**34%**	**11.0%**		**46**	**20**	**34**	**29%**	**70%**	**12%**		**16**						**2.0**	**116**	**$4**

Margevicius,Nick

Age: 24	Th: L	Role RP	Health	A	LIMA Plan F
Ht: 6' 5"	Wt: 220	Type Con	PT/Exp	F	Rand Var +4
			Consist	F	MM 0000

2-6, 6.79 in 57 IP at SD. Attention Chris Paddack: this is what usually happens when you ask a pitcher to skip both Double-A and Triple-A. After getting racked for 12 starts with SD, finally got sent back to Double-A for second half... until September call-up. Plan from here: an off-season of PTSD counseling, then try again in March.

Yr	Tm	W	Sv	IP	K	ERA	xERA	WHIP	xWHIP	vL+	vR+	BF/G	Ctl	Dom	Cmd	Ball%	SwK	Vel	G	L	F	H%	S%	HR/F	xHR/F	GS	APC	DOM%	DIS%	Sv%	LI	RAR	BPX	R$
15																																		
16																																		
17																																		
18																																		
19	SD *	6	0	126	86	6.04	6.42	1.54	1.42	151	105	18.9	2.3	6.2	2.6	37%	9.8%	88.3	44	25	31	33%	66%	20%	20%	12	56	8%	50%	0	0.61	-23.8	30	-$11
1st Half		3	0	66	46	5.67	6.08	1.47	1.36	151	107	19.0	2.7	6.2	2.3	37%	9.9%	88.2	43	26	31	31%	68%	21%	20%	12	74	8%	50%			-9.5	21	-$9
2nd Half		3	0	60	41	6.45	6.79	1.61		151	108	18.9	1.9	6.2	3.3		8.8%	89.7	67	17	17	36%	63%	0%	6%	0	14			0	0.23	-14.3	45	-$12
20	**Proj**	**1**	**0**	**29**	**20**	**5.55**	**4.57**	**1.57**	**1.50**	**144**	**98**	**19.0**	**2.3**	**6.2**	**2.7**	**41%**	**9.9%**	**88.2**	**42**	**24**	**34**	**34%**	**70%**	**16%**		**6**						**-5.0**	**81**	**-$6**

Marquez,German

Age: 25	Th: R	Role SP	Health	C	LIMA Plan B
Ht: 6' 1"	Wt: 225	Type	PT/Exp	A	Rand Var +5
			Consist	B	MM 3305

Lost his Coors-slaying talisman, but xERA and BPX show that this is still a very nice skill set. First half results weren't disastrous, but lost the ERA-shielding GB tilt in second half and things got out of control. Still much to like here, but as long as his home address is Coors, set ceiling expectations against that first half line.

Yr	Tm	W	Sv	IP	K	ERA	xERA	WHIP	xWHIP	vL+	vR+	BF/G	Ctl	Dom	Cmd	Ball%	SwK	Vel	G	L	F	H%	S%	HR/F	xHR/F	GS	APC	DOM%	DIS%	Sv%	LI	RAR	BPX	R$
15																																		
16	COL *	12	0	187	139	4.58	4.88	1.43		127	127	24.9	2.3	6.7	2.9		9.7%	93.3	55	30	15	34%	70%	18%	16%	3	59	0%	33%	0	0.51	-9.0	77	$0
17	COL	11	0	162	147	4.39	4.23	1.38	1.26	100	115	24.2	2.7	8.2	3.0	34%	9.6%	95.0	45	22	33	32%	73%	15%	14%	29	92	10%	34%			-0.6	116	$5
18	COL	14	0	196	230	3.77	3.22	1.20	1.13	109	83	24.8	2.6	10.6	4.0	34%	13.0%	95.2	47	23	30	32%	73%	16%	14%	33	95	36%	18%			9.3	166	$16
19	COL	12	0	174	175	4.76	3.69	1.20	1.16	104	93	25.8	1.8	9.1	5.0	33%	13.0%	95.5	49	22	29	31%	65%	20%	19%	28	93	29%	18%			-5.4	154	$9
1st Half		8	0	115	113	4.29	3.68	1.21	1.15	98	91	26.7	2.0	8.8	4.3	33%	13.6%	95.3	52	20	27	32%	68%	17%	18%	18	95	28%	11%			3.0	147	$14
2nd Half		4	0	59	62	5.68	3.69	1.18	1.05	115	98	24.1	1.4	9.5	6.9	33%	12.0%	95.8	42	26	32	31%	58%	26%	21%	10	91	30%	30%			-8.5	168	-$1
20	**Proj**	**13**	**0**	**189**	**190**	**4.47**	**3.33**	**1.26**	**1.13**	**107**	**94**	**24.2**	**2.3**	**9.1**	**4.0**	**34%**	**12.8%**	**95.4**	**46**	**23**	**31**	**32%**	**69%**	**17%**		**32**						**-7.5**	**145**	**$9**

Martin,Brett

Age: 25	Th: L	Role RP	Health	A	LIMA Plan F
Ht: 6' 4"	Wt: 190	Type GB	PT/Exp	D	Rand Var +5
			Consist	F	MM 3310

Transitioned to bullpen in mid-2018. Results so far unimpressive, but he is still consolidating the raw components of a potentially dominant skill set in that role: heavy GB tilt is a good start, Vel creeping up. 2nd half Dom gains came mostly against RHP, which will be key to getting into a higher-leverage role. One for the watch list.

Yr	Tm	W	Sv	IP	K	ERA	xERA	WHIP	xWHIP	vL+	vR+	BF/G	Ctl	Dom	Cmd	Ball%	SwK	Vel	G	L	F	H%	S%	HR/F	xHR/F	GS	APC	DOM%	DIS%	Sv%	LI	RAR	BPX	R$
15																																		
16																																		
17																																		
18	aa	2	0	89	79	9.55	8.79	2.22				15.5	3.2	8.0	2.5							48%	55%									-59.3	56	-$35
19	TEX	2	0	62	62	4.76	4.02	1.44	1.25	92	104	5.5	2.6	9.0	3.4	34%	13.7%	93.9	54	23	23	36%	69%	15%	19%	2	20	0%	100%	0	0.65	-2.0	134	-$4
1st Half		1	0	28	23	4.23	3.76	1.23	1.17	93	102	5.0	1.6	7.5	4.6	33%	13.7%	93.6	57	20	23	31%	70%	20%	20%	0	18			0	0.56	0.9	138	-$3
2nd Half		1	0	35	39	5.19	4.12	1.62	1.25	92	104	5.9	3.4	10.1	3.0	34%	13.7%	94.1	51	25	24	41%	68%	12%	18%	2	22	0%	100%	0	0.73	-2.9	131	-$4
20	**Proj**	**2**	**2**	**65**	**63**	**4.61**	**3.50**	**1.53**	**1.22**	**96**	**109**	**7.0**	**2.9**	**8.7**	**3.0**	**34%**	**13.7%**	**93.9**	**54**	**23**	**23**	**37%**	**72%**	**15%**		**0**						**-3.7**	**128**	**-$4**

RAY MURPHY

Martin,Christopher

Age: 34	Th: R	Role: RP	Health: D	LIMA Plan: F	
Ht: 6' 8"	Wt: 215	Type:	PT/Exp: D	Rand Var: +4	
			Consist: D	MM: 5410	

Mid-30s is an odd time for a Dom spike; this one comes from pitch mix adjustments. Emphasized his splitter more in 2019, as it became a wipeout pitch. Threw more sinkers (likely to play off the splitter), driving Ctl and GB gains. BPX, particularly small-sample second half level, says "yeah, that will play." Watch where this free agent lands.

Yr Tm	W	Sv	IP	K	ERA	xERA	WHIP	xWHIP	vL+	vR+	BF/G	Ctl	Dom	Cmd	Ball%	SwK	Vel	G	L	F	H%	S%	HR/F	xHR/F	GS	APC	DOM%	DIS%	Sv%	LI	RAR	BPX	R$
15 NYY *	0	3	49	37	5.16	5.47	1.67		80	123	5.0	3.3	6.8	2.0		5.9%	94.2	53	27	20	37%	69%	13%	27%	0	16			75	0.62	-7.3	66	-$8
16 for	2	0	51	54	1.54	0.86	0.70				3.4	1.5	9.6	6.2							21%	83%									16.5	231	$8
17 for	0	0	38	32	1.48	1.51	0.80				3.4	1.8	7.7	4.3							21%	89%									13.4	160	$4
18 TEX	1	0	42	37	4.54	3.75	1.22	1.10	108	96	3.8	1.1	8.0	7.4	34%	10.0%	95.2	40	27	32	34%	65%	12%	15%	0	15			0	0.90	-2.0	153	-$3
19 2 TM	1	4	56	65	3.40	2.93	1.02	0.97	77	102	3.7	0.8	10.5	13.0	29%	13.2%	95.7	50	20	30	32%	75%	20%	20%	0	15			67	0.95	7.6	213	$4
1st Half	0	3	31	32	3.48	3.29	1.06	0.99	83	112	3.9	0.9	9.3	10.7	30%	10.9%	95.9	49	21	30	29%	81%	27%	21%	0	15			75	1.10	3.9	186	$3
2nd Half	1	1	25	33	3.28	2.57	0.97	0.85	68	89	3.5	0.7	12.0	16.5	29%	15.9%	95.5	52	18	30	35%	68%	11%	18%	0	15			50	0.78	3.7	247	$6
20 Proj	**2**	**5**	**65**	**71**	**3.37**	**2.78**	**1.05**	**0.99**	**80**	**91**	**3.7**	**1.2**	**9.8**	**8.5**	**31%**	**13.4%**	**95.5**	**46**	**23**	**31**	**32%**	**73%**	**14%**		**0**						**6.3**	**196**	**$6**

Martinez,Carlos

Age: 28	Th: R	Role: SP	Health: F	LIMA Plan: D	
Ht: 6' 0"	Wt: 190	Type: Pwr	PT/Exp: A	Rand Var: -1	
			Consist: B	MM: 3303	

Shoulder weakness shut him down in spring training; eventually returned in mid-May as a reliever. Worked his way into closer role as velocity predictably ticked up in bullpen. Not much question that he could remain an effective closer, but team says they want him back in rotation. Whether he can carry that workload is a much tougher question.

Yr Tm	W	Sv	IP	K	ERA	xERA	WHIP	xWHIP	vL+	vR+	BF/G	Ctl	Dom	Cmd	Ball%	SwK	Vel	G	L	F	H%	S%	HR/F	xHR/F	GS	APC	DOM%	DIS%	Sv%	LI	RAR	BPX	R$
15 STL	14	0	180	184	3.01	3.28	1.29	1.25	104	88	24.4	3.2	9.2	2.9	35%	11.0%	95.3	54	20	25	32%	78%	11%	12%	29	92	41%	21%	0	0.82	21.2	134	$15
16 STL	16	0	195	174	3.04	3.69	1.22	1.32	99	74	26.1	3.2	8.0	2.5	35%	9.8%	95.6	56	18	26	29%	77%	11%	11%	31	98	32%	23%			27.7	108	$20
17 STL	12	0	205	217	3.64	3.64	1.22	1.23	104	82	26.8	3.1	9.5	3.1	35%	11.0%	95.6	51	19	30	30%	75%	16%	12%	32	98	41%	19%			18.1	140	$18
18 STL	8	5	119	117	3.11	4.26	1.35	1.43	94	83	15.8	4.6	8.9	2.0	36%	11.4%	93.6	49	19	32	30%	77%	5%	10%	18	60	33%	28%	100	0.97	15.2	74	$9
19 STL	4	24	48	53	3.17	3.63	1.18	1.27	86	73	4.2	3.4	9.9	2.9	35%	13.2%	95.8	56	15	28	31%	73%	6%	13%	0	16			89	1.28	8.0	132	$13
1st Half	2	2	18	18	2.55	3.22	1.02	1.23	91	68	4.9	3.1	9.2	3.0	35%	11.1%	95.9	63	14	23	26%	76%	10%	11%	0	19			50	1.23	4.3	135	-$1
2nd Half	2	22	31	35	3.52	3.81	1.27	1.24	84	76	3.9	3.5	10.3	2.9	35%	14.4%	95.6	53	16	31	34%	71%	4%	14%	0	15			96	1.30	3.7	132	$21
20 Proj	**10**	**0**	**131**	**133**	**3.54**	**3.58**	**1.28**	**1.29**	**100**	**83**	**22.9**	**3.7**	**9.1**	**2.5**	**35%**	**11.1%**	**95.2**	**50**	**19**	**31**	**30%**	**75%**	**12%**		**23**						**9.9**	**106**	**$9**

Matz,Steven

Age: 29	Th: L	Role: SP	Health: F	LIMA Plan: B	
Ht: 6' 2"	Wt: 200	Type:	PT/Exp: B	Rand Var: +2	
			Consist: B	MM: 2203	

Second straight career-high IP total, faint praise for sure. Forearm nerve injury cost him 10 days in late May, could explain first-half Vel slip. There's a lot to like in 2nd half line: Vel uptick, some overdue gains vL, cracked double-digit SwK, kept ball in park. But it's hard to count on any of this when next strain or pull is right around the corner.

Yr Tm	W	Sv	IP	K	ERA	xERA	WHIP	xWHIP	vL+	vR+	BF/G	Ctl	Dom	Cmd	Ball%	SwK	Vel	G	L	F	H%	S%	HR/F	xHR/F	GS	APC	DOM%	DIS%	Sv%	LI	RAR	BPX	R$
15 NYM *	12	0	137	122	2.13	2.75	1.12	1.22	89	91	23.5	2.7	8.0	2.9	34%	8.5%	94.3	46	21	34	28%	84%	12%	3%	6	96	17%	17%			31.1	119	$19
16 NYM	9	0	132	129	3.40	3.39	1.21	1.16	95	94	24.9	2.1	8.8	4.2	33%	10.2%	93.6	51	21	28	32%	75%	14%	10%	22	98	36%	23%			12.9	154	$10
17 NYM	2	0	67	48	6.08	4.76	1.53	1.33	101	120	22.9	2.6	6.5	2.5	36%	7.4%	93.1	47	22	31	34%	63%	17%	16%	13	90	8%	38%			-14.1	87	-$8
18 NYM	5	0	154	152	3.97	3.97	1.25	1.30	92	104	21.8	3.4	8.9	2.6	37%	9.7%	93.4	49	15	36	28%	74%	17%	13%	30	90	30%	27%			3.3	110	$5
19 NYM	11	0	160	153	4.21	4.38	1.34	1.31	106	103	21.6	2.9	8.6	2.9	36%	10.1%	93.4	47	20	33	31%	74%	17%	18%	30	84	10%	33%	0	0.80	5.8	110	$7
1st Half	5	0	80	78	4.95	4.66	1.46	1.29	130	110	22.3	3.3	8.8	2.7	35%	9.6%	92.9	46	17	36	32%	74%	21%	22%	16	88	0%	38%			-4.4	103	$0
2nd Half	6	0	80	75	3.47	4.08	1.22	1.23	78	96	20.9	2.6	8.4	3.3	36%	10.6%	94.0	48	22	30	30%	75%	13%	14%	14	80	21%	29%	0	0.80	10.2	117	$13
20 Proj	**9**	**0**	**160**	**147**	**4.04**	**3.83**	**1.33**	**1.27**	**98**	**104**	**21.4**	**3.0**	**8.3**	**2.8**	**36%**	**9.5%**	**93.5**	**46**	**19**	**35**	**31%**	**75%**	**15%**		**31**						**2.1**	**107**	**$6**

May,Dustin

Age: 22	Th: R	Role: SP	Health: A	LIMA Plan: B	
Ht: 6' 6"	Wt: 180	Type: Con GB	PT/Exp: D	Rand Var: 0	
			Consist: B	MM: 2103	

2-3, 3.63 ERA in 35 IP at LA. Tall righty made his big-league debut as a swingman, but is one of the game's top SP prospects. Combines strikeout-fueling velocity with GB-inducing plane due to his height. Raw stuff gives him a high ceiling, remarkable polish at young age suggests immediate impact.

Yr Tm	W	Sv	IP	K	ERA	xERA	WHIP	xWHIP	vL+	vR+	BF/G	Ctl	Dom	Cmd	Ball%	SwK	Vel	G	L	F	H%	S%	HR/F	xHR/F	GS	APC	DOM%	DIS%	Sv%	LI	RAR	BPX	R$
15																																	
16																																	
17																																	
18 aa	2	0	35	25	3.67	2.14	1.10				22.9	2.7	6.4	2.4							28%	63%									2.1	114	-$1
19 LA *	8	0	143	129	3.76	3.12	1.17	1.13	116	64	16.8	2.0	8.1	4.1	34%	9.2%	96.0	44	28	27	32%	67%	7%	14%	4	40	25%	0%	0	0.94	13.1	136	$10
1st Half	4	0	85	78	4.23	3.50	1.23		0	0	21.5	2.1	8.3	3.9							33%	65%	0%		0	0					2.9	127	$9
2nd Half	4	0	58	50	3.07	2.55	1.08	1.09	117	63	12.5	1.8	7.9	4.4	34%	9.2%	96.0	44	28	27	30%	71%	7%	14%	4	40	25%	0%	0	0.94	10.2	150	$12
20 Proj	**9**	**0**	**145**	**118**	**3.89**	**3.06**	**1.18**	**1.20**	**120**	**65**	**21.0**	**2.2**	**7.4**	**3.4**	**38%**	**9.2%**	**96.0**	**47**	**23**	**30**	**29%**	**71%**	**13%**		**24**						**4.6**	**114**	**$9**

May,Trevor

Age: 30	Th: R	Role: RP	Health: F	LIMA Plan: C	
Ht: 6' 5"	Wt: 240	Type: Pwr FB	PT/Exp: D	Rand Var: -3	
			Consist: C	MM: 3510	

Hung a decent first-half ERA that was smoke and mirrors, then decided to go legit: junked so-so curveball for a slider that he had fooled around with before, but suddenly turned nasty. Not only did SwK and Dom jump, but Ctl got better when he stuck to hard stuff. We had "UP: 25 Sv" in this space last year; may have just been a year early.

Yr Tm	W	Sv	IP	K	ERA	xERA	WHIP	xWHIP	vL+	vR+	BF/G	Ctl	Dom	Cmd	Ball%	SwK	Vel	G	L	F	H%	S%	HR/F	xHR/F	GS	APC	DOM%	DIS%	Sv%	LI	RAR	BPX	R$
15 MIN	8	0	115	110	4.00	3.86	1.33	1.17	104	105	10.3	2.0	8.6	4.2	34%	10.9%	92.9	39	21	40	35%	72%	8%	8%	16	39	25%	31%	0	0.87	-0.6	140	$2
16 MIN	2	0	43	60	5.27	3.57	1.31	1.14	74	119	4.3	3.6	12.7	3.5	35%	13.6%	93.9	31	26	43	35%	63%	15%	14%	0	19			0	1.18	-5.7	166	-$3
17																																	
18 MIN *	4	5	52	54	4.92	5.09	1.53		84	94	6.2	4.2	9.3	2.2		15.6%	94.1	41	22	37	34%	70%	18%	16%	1	19	0%	100%	100	1.05	-5.0	76	-$3
19 MIN	5	2	64	79	2.94	4.05	1.07	1.26	75	80	4.1	3.6	11.1	3.0	38%	13.5%	95.6	34	24	42	25%	79%	12%	14%	0	18			50	0.94	12.4	123	$7
1st Half	3	1	29	30	3.38	5.07	1.33	1.49	67	95	3.7	5.2	9.2	1.8	40%	11.4%	95.1	39	25	36	28%	76%	7%	13%	0	17			100	0.90	4.1	45	$2
2nd Half	2	1	35	49	2.57	3.39	0.86	0.98	83	66	4.5	2.3	12.6	5.4	36%	15.6%	96.1	29	23	48	23%	83%	16%	15%	0	19			33	0.98	8.3	186	$11
20 Proj	**4**	**8**	**58**	**71**	**3.42**	**3.37**	**1.18**	**1.17**	**81**	**100**	**4.6**	**3.1**	**11.0**	**3.6**	**36%**	**13.3%**	**94.7**	**33**	**24**	**43**	**31%**	**76%**	**13%**		**0**						**5.2**	**145**	**$6**

McCarthy,Kevin

Age: 28	Th: R	Role: RP	Health: A	LIMA Plan: B	
Ht: 6' 3"	Wt: 215	Type: Con xGB	PT/Exp: D	Rand Var: 0	
			Consist: B	MM: 1000	

4-2, 4.48 ERA with 1 Sv in 60 IP at KC. Sinkerball has become his calling card, which is an easy choice when there's no obvious second skill here. Both Ball% and SwK suggest that Cmd should be better than this, but low velocity and not having an answer vL indicate that it's just not hard to make contact against him. Needs a new trick.

Yr Tm	W	Sv	IP	K	ERA	xERA	WHIP	xWHIP	vL+	vR+	BF/G	Ctl	Dom	Cmd	Ball%	SwK	Vel	G	L	F	H%	S%	HR/F	xHR/F	GS	APC	DOM%	DIS%	Sv%	LI	RAR	BPX	R$
15 aa	1	0	17	7	6.89	7.12	2.05				7.7	4.1	3.8	0.9							39%	65%									-6.3	11	-$8
16 KC *	6	16	76	54	4.15	4.35	1.40		141	90	5.7	3.6	6.4	1.8		5.3%	93.7	54	25	21	30%	73%	17%	36%	0	17			70	1.04	0.4	57	$6
17 KC *	2	2	77	40	3.54	4.75	1.45	1.38	111	84	5.7	2.6	4.7	1.8	34%	9.2%	92.9	54	19	27	32%	78%	10%	11%	0	22			100	0.30	7.7	45	-$1
18 KC	5	0	72	46	3.25	3.67	1.25	1.35	112	89	4.5	2.5	5.8	2.3	35%	10.3%	91.7	64	19	16	29%	77%	19%	26%	0	16			0	1.23	8.0	90	$2
19 KC *	4	4	79	49	4.45	4.59	1.50	1.47	108	95	4.9	3.0	5.6	1.9	33%	10.2%	91.2	58	20	22	34%	69%	9%	13%	0	16			50	0.92	0.5	61	-$2
1st Half	2	4	40	20	4.44	4.64	1.56	1.59	92	109	5.5	3.2	4.5	1.4	35%	8.4%	91.0	51	24	25	34%	70%	5%	9%	0	17			100	0.95	0.3	49	-$2
2nd Half	2	0	38	29	4.46	4.16	1.43	1.33	119	88	4.5	2.8	6.8	2.4	31%	11.2%	91.2	63	18	19	34%	69%	13%	17%	0	16			0	0.90	0.2	96	-$1
20 Proj	**3**	**0**	**58**	**37**	**4.29**	**4.08**	**1.48**	**1.40**	**121**	**100**	**5.0**	**2.8**	**5.7**	**2.0**	**34%**	**10.0%**	**91.6**	**58**	**20**	**23**	**32%**	**73%**	**15%**		**0**						**-1.0**	**71**	**-$4**

McCullers,Lance

Age: 26	Th: R	Role: SP	Health: F	LIMA Plan: A	
Ht: 6' 1"	Wt: 205	Type: Pwr GB	PT/Exp: C	Rand Var: 0	
			Consist: A	MM: 4403	

Missed full season following November '18 Tommy John surgery. Declared this November that rehab is complete and he will follow a normal off-season program. Pre-injury, this was a tantalizing profile: SwK was climbing to elite levels, while GB% holding a solid floor. Durability is the open question, once and forever.

Yr Tm	W	Sv	IP	K	ERA	xERA	WHIP	xWHIP	vL+	vR+	BF/G	Ctl	Dom	Cmd	Ball%	SwK	Vel	G	L	F	H%	S%	HR/F	xHR/F	GS	APC	DOM%	DIS%	Sv%	LI	RAR	BPX	R$
15 HOU *	9	1	158	172	2.70	2.69	1.14	1.24	81	103	21.5	3.2	9.8	3.0	38%	10.1%	94.5	46	22	32	29%	79%	9%	13%	22	96	36%	18%			24.6	137	$18
16 HOU	6	0	81	106	3.22	3.24	1.54	1.33	102	98	25.1	5.0	11.8	2.4	37%	13.3%	93.8	57	22	21	38%	80%	12%	15%	14	96	21%	14%			9.7	133	$2
17 HOU	7	0	119	132	4.25	3.15	1.30	1.20	80	103	23.3	3.0	10.0	3.3	37%	12.3%	94.2	61	19	20	34%	67%	13%	15%	22	92	32%	18%			1.6	165	$5
18 HOU	10	0	128	142	3.86	3.31	1.17	1.25	78	102	21.1	3.5	10.0	2.8	37%	13.9%	94.3	55	18	27	29%	69%	13%	17%	22	84	36%	27%	0	0.91	4.6	135	$9
19																																	
1st Half																																	
2nd Half																																	
20 Proj	**9**	**0**	**131**	**145**	**3.54**	**3.28**	**1.32**	**1.27**	**86**	**100**	**22.6**	**3.9**	**10.0**	**2.6**	**37%**	**12.8%**	**94.1**	**54**	**20**	**26**	**32%**	**75%**	**12%**		**24**						**9.9**	**123**	**$8**

RAY MURPHY

McHugh,Collin

McHugh,Collin						Health	F	LIMA Plan	C
Age:	33	Th:	R	Role	RP	PT/Exp	D	Rand Var	+2
Ht:	6' 2"	Wt:	190	Type	Pwr FB	Consist	C	MM	3401

Battled right elbow soreness all year, and the result was a step back to... well, to about where he used to land. How much of that was returning to starting in 1st half, and how much was the elbow? We'll give him a mulligan and say elbow, and call for a rebound. But then, he's had problems with said elbow in two of three seasons. Risky.

Yr	Tm	W	Sv	IP	K	ERA	xERA	WHIP	xWHIP	vL+	vR+	BF/G	Ctl	Dom	Cmd	Ball%	SwK	Vel	G	L	F	H%	S%	HR/F	xHR/F	GS	APC	DOM%	DIS%	Sv%	LI	RAR	BPX	R$
15	HOU	19	0	204	171	3.89	3.90	1.28	1.25	89	106	26.8	2.3	7.6	3.2	35%	10.9%	90.4	45	20	35	32%	71%	9%	8%	32	101	41%	25%			1.8	114	$12
16	HOU	13	0	185	177	4.34	4.15	1.41	1.23	109	106	24.1	2.6	8.6	3.3	35%	11.2%	90.2	41	21	38	34%	73%	12%	10%	33	96	27%	27%			-3.4	123	$4
17	HOU *	5	0	79	71	4.07	4.61	1.43	1.24	107	94	19.8	2.9	8.1	2.8	37%	12.6%	90.2	33	22	45	34%	74%	9%	9%	12	90	25%	33%			2.8	94	$0
18	HOU	6	0	72	94	1.99	3.12	0.91	1.06	95	58	4.9	2.6	11.7	4.5	35%	13.8%	92.1	35	22	44	26%	83%	8%	12%	0	21			0	0.87	19.3	176	$12
19	HOU	4	0	75	82	4.70	4.34	1.23	1.32	85	108	9.1	3.6	9.9	2.7	37%	11.9%	90.8	38	25	38	28%	66%	16%	15%	8	37	13%	38%	0	0.55	-1.8	105	$0
1st Half		3	0	48	52	5.59	4.14	1.20	1.23	98	103	14.6	3.2	9.7	3.1	37%	12.3%	90.1	40	26	34	28%	57%	20%	17%	8	59	13%	38%	0	0.68	-6.4	117	$0
2nd Half		1	0	26	30	3.08	4.74	1.29	1.35	61	118	5.3	4.4	10.3	2.3	37%	11.2%	91.7	34	22	44	29%	81%	10%	10%	0	22			0	0.47	4.6	83	$0
20	**Proj**	**5**	**0**	**73**	**81**	**3.19**	**3.48**	**1.16**	**1.23**	**87**	**96**	**7.3**	**2.9**	**10.1**	**3.5**	**36%**	**12.2%**	**91.1**	**36**	**23**	**41**	**30%**	**77%**	**11%**		**0**						**8.6**	**134**	**$5**

McKay,Brendan

McKay,Brendan						Health	A	LIMA Plan	F
Age:	24	Th:	L	Role	SP	PT/Exp	F	Rand Var	0
Ht:	6' 2"	Wt:	212	Type	Pwr xFB	Consist	F	MM	4500

2-4, 5.14 ERA in 49 IP at TAM. Only 74 IP in high minors, so ill treatment by MLB hitters was no surprise, with struggles vR. But he showed electric flashes, and was simply dominant over his relatively short MiLB time (as 1st-half MLEs show). Patience may be needed here, but this is a skill set in which to invest—whether he hits or not.

Yr	Tm	W	Sv	IP	K	ERA	xERA	WHIP	xWHIP	vL+	vR+	BF/G	Ctl	Dom	Cmd	Ball%	SwK	Vel	G	L	F	H%	S%	HR/F	xHR/F	GS	APC	DOM%	DIS%	Sv%	LI	RAR	BPX	R$
15																																		
16																																		
17																																		
18																																		
19	TAM *	8	0	124	145	2.88	3.02	1.12	1.24	75	117	17.5	2.6	10.5	4.1	34%	10.9%	93.7	35	22	43	31%	78%	13%	13%	11	68	18%	27%	0	0.78	24.9	145	$15
1st Half		7	0	74	80	1.43	1.42	0.87		19	23	19.5	2.1	9.7	4.6		12.4%	93.7	33	27	40	25%	86%	0%	11%	1	81	0%	0%			28.2	175	$27
2nd Half		1	0	50	65	5.04	5.40	1.50	1.18	83	123	15.4	3.3	11.7	3.6	34%	10.8%	93.7	35	21	43	39%	70%	15%	14%	10	66	20%	30%	0	0.78	-3.3	109	-$3
20	**Proj**	**3**	**0**	**65**	**85**	**3.19**	**3.20**	**1.20**	**1.30**	**64**	**90**	**20.4**	**2.4**	**11.7**	**5.0**	**37%**	**10.8%**	**93.7**	**35**	**21**	**43**	**35%**	**78%**	**10%**		**13**						**7.7**	**185**	**$4**

Means,John

Means,John						Health	B	LIMA Plan	A
Age:	27	Th:	L	Role	SP	PT/Exp	C	Rand Var	-3
Ht:	6' 3"	Wt:	230	Type	Con xFB	Consist	A	MM	0003

Some saw that sparkly 1st-half ERA (and didn't see the xERA) and jumped aboard—and were treated to his usual mediocrity after. The Dom gains? SwK doesn't support them. And all those flyballs mean he's a blowup waiting to happen every time out. Lefty seems like a candidate for shift to bullpen—and no, that wouldn't help you, either.

Yr	Tm	W	Sv	IP	K	ERA	xERA	WHIP	xWHIP	vL+	vR+	BF/G	Ctl	Dom	Cmd	Ball%	SwK	Vel	G	L	F	H%	S%	HR/F	xHR/F	GS	APC	DOM%	DIS%	Sv%	LI	RAR	BPX	R$
15																																		
16	aa	4	0	96	45	5.66	5.63	1.64				23.8	2.6	4.2	1.6							35%	65%									-17.4	33	-$11
17	aa	0	0	142	107	5.17	5.07	1.60				24.2	2.0	6.8	2.6							37%	70%									-14.3	63	-$7
18	BAL *	7	0	161	106	4.88	5.53	1.49		137	171	24.0	1.9	5.9	3.1		12.1%	90.1	25	42	33	35%	69%	25%	23%	0	66			0	0.52	-14.6	70	-$9
19	BAL	12	0	155	121	3.60	5.13	1.14	1.33	73	100	20.5	2.2	7.0	3.2	37%	10.2%	91.8	31	19	50	27%	75%	10%	10%	27	86	30%	44%	0	0.88	17.3	83	$15
1st Half		7	0	76	64	2.50	4.84	1.10	1.27	76	92	18.1	2.6	7.6	2.9	39%	10.6%	91.8	37	17	47	26%	83%	8%	10%	13	82	38%	46%	0	0.98	18.7	89	$20
2nd Half		5	0	79	57	4.65	5.59	1.17	1.25	71	106	23.5	1.8	6.5	3.6	36%	9.9%	91.7	26	21	53	27%	67%	11%	10%	14	92	21%	43%			-1.4	78	$10
20	**Proj**	**10**	**0**	**160**	**115**	**4.29**	**4.57**	**1.30**	**1.26**	**82**	**113**	**21.8**	**1.9**	**6.5**	**3.4**	**37%**	**10.2%**	**91.8**	**30**	**19**	**50**	**31%**	**71%**	**8%**		**30**						**-2.8**	**85**	**$5**

Melancon,Mark

Melancon,Mark						Health	F	LIMA Plan	B
Age:	35	Th:	R	Role	RP	PT/Exp	C	Rand Var	+3
Ht:	6' 2"	Wt:	215	Type	xGB	Consist	B	MM	4220

After a wild start (for him), returned to strike-throwing ways in 2nd half. That coupled with GB spike and a small Dom/SwK rebound, and he looked like a new man—or at least the pre-injury 2015-16 version of himself. At 35, we can't just assume he'll now stay healthy, but those 2nd-half skills show he's still got the goods when he is.

Yr	Tm	W	Sv	IP	K	ERA	xERA	WHIP	xWHIP	vL+	vR+	BF/G	Ctl	Dom	Cmd	Ball%	SwK	Vel	G	L	F	H%	S%	HR/F	xHR/F	GS	APC	DOM%	DIS%	Sv%	LI	RAR	BPX	R$
15	PIT	3	51	77	62	2.23	3.00	0.93	1.17	52	95	3.8	1.6	7.3	4.4	32%	11.9%	91.5	58	20	23	26%	78%	8%	7%	0	14			96	1.35	16.4	146	$30
16	2 NL	2	47	71	65	1.64	3.01	0.90	1.10	76	64	3.6	1.5	8.2	5.4	33%	11.3%	91.8	54	21	25	26%	84%	6%	8%	0	14			92	1.04	22.4	165	$29
17	SF	1	11	30	29	4.50	3.61	1.43	1.14	95	119	4.1	1.8	8.7	4.8	36%	10.2%	92.2	53	22	26	38%	70%	13%	11%	0	16			69	1.12	-0.5	167	$1
18	SF	1	3	39	31	3.23	4.26	1.59	1.36	105	108	4.2	3.2	7.2	2.2	37%	10.4%	91.5	52	26	22	37%	80%	7%	20%	0	16			43	1.24	4.4	82	-$3
19	2 NL	5	12	67	68	3.61	3.33	1.32	1.21	89	91	4.3	2.4	9.1	3.8	36%	10.9%	92.2	62	21	17	35%	73%	12%	12%	0	16			100	0.86	7.4	151	$7
1st Half		3	0	35	33	3.89	3.89	1.64	1.36	99	111	4.6	3.9	8.6	2.2	38%	10.7%	92.0	62	21	18	38%	76%	11%	7%	0	17			0	0.83	2.6	97	-$2
2nd Half		2	12	33	35	3.31	2.65	0.98	0.98	77	70	4.0	0.8	9.6	11.7	34%	11.0%	92.6	62	22	16	32%	67%	13%	18%	0	15			100	0.89	4.8	209	$16
20	**Proj**	**3**	**25**	**65**	**61**	**3.45**	**3.08**	**1.36**	**1.19**	**92**	**97**	**4.1**	**2.3**	**8.5**	**3.7**	**36%**	**10.7%**	**92.1**	**60**	**21**	**19**	**36%**	**75%**	**11%**		**0**						**5.7**	**148**	**$11**

Mengden,Daniel

Mengden,Daniel						Health	C	LIMA Plan	B
Age:	27	Th:	R	Role	RP	PT/Exp	D	Rand Var	0
Ht:	6' 1"	Wt:	225	Type	FB	Consist	B	MM	2200

5-2, 4.83 ERA in 60 IP with OAK. Ability to miss bats sank to all-time low—and no, it wasn't great to begin with. Mix in a FB spike and Ctl/Ball% jump, and it all made for a sour cocktail. Really, there's just nothing to recommend here—especially since he shaved off that awesome handlebar 'stache in the off-season.

Yr	Tm	W	Sv	IP	K	ERA	xERA	WHIP	xWHIP	vL+	vR+	BF/G	Ctl	Dom	Cmd	Ball%	SwK	Vel	G	L	F	H%	S%	HR/F	xHR/F	GS	APC	DOM%	DIS%	Sv%	LI	RAR	BPX	R$
15																																		
16	OAK *	12	0	170	148	3.77	3.66	1.32	1.38	112	111	22.7	3.3	7.8	2.4	36%	9.5%	92.1	40	24	36	31%	72%	11%	14%	14	94	21%	36%			8.9	97	$9
17	OAK *	5	0	84	61	3.99	4.15	1.29	1.27	97	76	21.6	2.9	6.5	2.3	38%	8.9%	92.1	39	19	42	29%	73%	11%	12%	7	93	29%	57%			3.8	67	$1
18	OAK *	11	0	162	99	3.91	3.62	1.13	1.31	87	104	20.6	1.8	5.5	3.0	34%	8.3%	92.2	40	22	38	27%	69%	13%	16%	17	81	24%	35%	0	0.74	4.7	78	$10
19	OAK *	9	1	124	90	4.95	4.52	1.40	1.57	124	69	20.1	3.5	6.6	1.9	38%	6.1%	91.2	36	23	41	30%	66%	9%	11%	9	81	22%	33%	100	0.62	-6.7	53	-$1
1st Half		6	0	79	64	4.07	3.72	1.34	1.55	97	70	21.9	3.7	7.2	2.0	39%	6.7%	91.9	39	24	37	30%	70%	3%	10%	4	90	50%	25%	0	0.77	4.3	76	$4
2nd Half		3	1	47	27	6.18	5.51	1.43	1.47	141	68	18.1	2.9	5.1	1.8	38%	5.5%	90.4	34	22	44	29%	60%	14%	11%	5	73	0%	40%	100	0.50	-9.7	16	-$9
20	**Proj**	**4**	**0**	**58**	**53**	**3.21**	**3.82**	**1.13**	**1.41**	**101**	**75**	**7.2**	**2.8**	**8.2**	**2.9**	**37%**	**8.3%**	**91.6**	**38**	**22**	**40**	**26%**	**77%**	**12%**		**0**						**6.7**	**100**	**$3**

Middleton,Keynan

Middleton,Keynan						Health	F	LIMA Plan	D
Age:	26	Th:	R	Role	RP	PT/Exp	D	Rand Var	-5
Ht:	6' 3"	Wt:	215	Type	Pwr xFB	Consist	D	MM	2510

Ignore those 2019 numbers, as they were his first scuffling innings back from 2018 Tommy John surgery. Better to focus on impressive 2017 SwK and 2016-17 BPX as a measure of his upside. It would still be a lot to expect him to return to a high-leverage role right away. But past skills and willingness of club to try him in 9th means... UP: 20 Sv

Yr	Tm	W	Sv	IP	K	ERA	xERA	WHIP	xWHIP	vL+	vR+	BF/G	Ctl	Dom	Cmd	Ball%	SwK	Vel	G	L	F	H%	S%	HR/F	xHR/F	GS	APC	DOM%	DIS%	Sv%	LI	RAR	BPX	R$
15																																		
16	a/a	0	8	30	28	3.59	3.39	1.23				5.7	2.4	8.5	3.6							32%	72%									2.2	133	$1
17	LAA	6	3	58	63	3.86	4.09	1.34	1.19	97	113	3.8	2.8	9.7	3.5	35%	17.1%	96.8	38	21	41	33%	79%	16%	15%	0	15			60	0.96	3.6	139	$3
18	LAA	0	6	18	16	2.04	4.57	1.30		102	86	4.4	4.6	8.2	1.8		10.6%	96.1	33	24	42	28%	86%	5%	10%	0	19			86	1.53	4.6	39	-$1
19	LAA	0	0	8	6	1.17	7.17	1.43	2.09	33	88	3.0	8.2	7.0	0.9	43%	9.1%	94.1	30	25	45	20%	91%	0%	8%	0	13			0	0.95	3.2	-95	-$4
1st Half																																		
2nd Half		0	0	8	6	1.17	7.05	1.43		33	87	3.0	8.2	7.0	0.9		9.1%	94.1	30	25	45	20%	91%	0%	8%	0	13			0	0.95	3.2	-95	-$4
20	**Proj**	**7**	**5**	**58**	**69**	**5.17**	**3.88**	**1.57**	**1.31**	**106**	**124**	**3.6**	**3.1**	**10.7**	**3.5**	**39%**	**17.1%**	**96.8**	**38**	**21**	**41**	**38%**	**75%**	**19%**		**0**						**-7.3**	**144**	**-$2**

Mikolas,Miles

Mikolas,Miles						Health	A	LIMA Plan	A
Age:	31	Th:	R	Role	SP	PT/Exp	A	Rand Var	+1
Ht:	6' 5"	Wt:	220	Type	Con	Consist	B	MM	3105

2018 sensation turned into a 2019 pumpkin. But really, it's not far from what xERA said to expect, so it shouldn't have been a huge shock. And to be fair, he owns pretty decent skills for a SP, notably superb control. So true level probably lies somewhere in between 2018 and 2019—as our projection suggests.

Yr	Tm	W	Sv	IP	K	ERA	xERA	WHIP	xWHIP	vL+	vR+	BF/G	Ctl	Dom	Cmd	Ball%	SwK	Vel	G	L	F	H%	S%	HR/F	xHR/F	GS	APC	DOM%	DIS%	Sv%	LI	RAR	BPX	R$
15	for	13	0	145	102	2.39	2.54	0.99				26.3	1.8	6.3	3.6							25%	81%									28.1	118	$22
16	for	4	0	92	80	3.05	4.57	1.29				26.9	2.8	7.8	2.8							29%	86%									12.9	71	$4
17	for	14	0	188	177	2.79	3.09	1.08				27.1	1.4	8.5	6.2							31%	77%									36.3	196	$27
18	STL	18	0	201	146	2.83	3.73	1.07	1.18	99	70	25.3	1.3	6.5	5.0	31%	10.1%	93.9	49	22	28	29%	76%	9%	13%	32	94	38%	22%			32.8	126	$27
19	STL	9	0	184	144	4.16	4.19	1.22	1.23	103	99	23.9	1.6	7.0	4.5	34%	10.2%	93.6	47	23	30	31%	71%	16%	16%	32	90	19%	44%			7.9	119	$9
1st Half		5	0	95	69	4.34	4.29	1.25	1.22	121	91	23.3	1.6	6.5	4.1	34%	9.7%	93.5	49	23	28	30%	70%	17%	18%	17	87	12%	53%			1.9	110	$7
2nd Half		4	0	89	75	3.96	4.06	1.20	1.15	88	110	24.5	1.5	7.6	5.0	33%	10.7%	93.7	45	24	31	31%	71%	15%	14%	15	92	27%	33%			6.0	130	$11
20	**Proj**	**14**	**0**	**181**	**138**	**3.70**	**3.58**	**1.17**	**1.18**	**99**	**90**	**24.5**	**1.7**	**6.9**	**4.1**	**32%**	**10.2%**	**93.7**	**48**	**23**	**29**	**30%**	**72%**	**13%**		**34**						**10.1**	**119**	**$15**

ROD TRUESDELL

Miley,Wade

Age: 33 | Th: L | Role: SP | Ht: 6' 0" | Wt: 220 | Type:
Health: F | PT/Exp: B | Consist: B | LIMA Plan: B | Rand Var: 0 | MM: 1103

Carried a sparkly 3.06 ERA into disastrous September (16.68 Sept ERA). But monthly xERAs hovered near 4.00 or worse all year, and skills sagged even more in 2nd half, notably Ctl. Year-by-year xERA shows those skills have been consistently mediocre, at best. Odds of ERA under 4.00 for a third straight year are slim.

Yr	Tm	W	Sv	IP	K	ERA	xERA	WHIP	xWHIP	vL+	vR+	BF/G	Ctl	Dom	Cmd	Ball%	SwK	Vel	G	L	F	H%	S%	HR/F	xHR/F	GS	APC	DOM%	DIS%	Sv%	LI	RAR	BPX	R$
15	BOS	11	0	194	147	4.46	4.16	1.37	1.35	93	107	26.0	3.0	6.8	2.3	39%	8.6%	90.8	49	21	30	32%	68%	9%	10%	32	100	34%	28%			-11.9	83	-$1
16	2 AL	9	0	166	137	5.37	4.14	1.42	1.29	91	115	23.7	2.7	7.4	2.8	35%	9.2%	90.3	47	23	30	33%	65%	16%	17%	30	91	13%	37%			-24.1	103	-$6
17	BAL	8	0	157	142	5.61	4.99	1.73	1.54	88	118	22.8	5.3	8.1	1.5	42%	8.4%	91.0	50	23	27	34%	70%	19%	17%	32	95	16%	63%			-24.2	37	-$13
18	MIL *	6	0	107	71	3.33	4.02	1.33	1.42	83	90	19.3	2.7	6.0	2.2	39%	9.4%	90.8	53	24	24	31%	76%	5%	9%	16	81	19%	44%			10.8	73	$3
19	HOU	14	0	167	140	3.98	4.64	1.34	1.40	86	100	21.8	3.3	7.5	2.3	39%	9.6%	90.5	50	21	30	30%	75%	15%	12%	33	90	12%	48%			10.8	82	$9
1st Half		6	0	96	80	3.39	4.27	1.17	1.31	69	97	23.0	2.9	7.5	2.6	39%	9.8%	90.3	53	16	31	26%	78%	16%	14%	17	94	6%	47%			13.2	96	$14
2nd Half		8	0	72	60	4.77	5.04	1.58	1.40	107	103	20.6	3.8	7.5	2.0	40%	9.4%	90.7	46	26	29	34%	72%	14%	10%	16	86	19%	50%			-2.4	63	$2
20	**Proj**	**12**	**0**	**160**	**127**	**4.28**	**4.08**	**1.44**	**1.40**	**92**	**106**	**20.9**	**3.5**	**7.2**	**2.1**	**39%**	**9.3%**	**90.7**	**50**	**22**	**28**	**32%**	**73%**	**14%**		**33**						**-2.6**	**73**	**$2**

Miller,Andrew

Age: 35 | Th: L | Role: RP | Ht: 6' 7" | Wt: 205 | Type: Pwr
Health: F | PT/Exp: D | Consist: B | LIMA Plan: B | Rand Var: +4 | MM: 4520

Another troubling step backward. Skills down across the board, and got worse as the season went along. FB velocity and effectiveness both lowest since 2011 (the last season he started). No injury to blame for it this time, either. May get save opps at least early in 2020, but if these trends continue... DN: Another 4-plus ERA, <5 Sv

Yr	Tm	W	Sv	IP	K	ERA	xERA	WHIP	xWHIP	vL+	vR+	BF/G	Ctl	Dom	Cmd	Ball%	SwK	Vel	G	L	F	H%	S%	HR/F	xHR/F	GS	APC	DOM%	DIS%	Sv%	LI	RAR	BPX	R$
15	NYY	3	36	62	100	2.04	2.14	0.86	0.96	83	63	4.1	2.9	14.6	5.0	33%	18.3%	94.3	48	18	33	27%	81%	13%	13%	0	16			95	1.22	14.6	250	$24
16	2 AL	10	12	74	123	1.45	1.63	0.69	0.73	71	65	3.9	1.1	14.9	13.7	30%	17.0%	94.5	54	17	29	28%	91%	20%	16%	0	16			86	1.23	25.1	322	$25
17	CLE	4	2	63	95	1.44	2.59	0.83	1.00	64	57	4.3	3.0	13.6	4.5	32%	16.8%	94.0	40	24	36	26%	86%	7%	6%	0	17			50	1.29	22.6	218	$13
18	CLE	2	2	34	45	4.24	3.46	1.38	1.24	76	114	4.2	4.2	11.9	2.8	34%	14.1%	93.1	48	21	31	35%	70%	11%	10%	0	16			40	1.27	-0.4	145	-$2
19	STL	5	6	55	70	4.45	4.09	1.32	1.33	89	107	3.2	4.4	11.5	2.6	37%	13.2%	92.5	37	23	40	29%	74%	22%	15%	0	13			55	1.51	0.4	112	$3
1st Half		3	1	26	38	4.10	3.37	1.33	1.17	99	111	3.2	4.1	13.0	3.2	36%	13.4%	92.9	36	33	31	32%	79%	33%	26%	0	13			33	1.39	1.3	150	$1
2nd Half		2	5	28	32	4.76	4.79	1.31	1.39	77	103	3.3	4.8	10.2	2.1	38%	12.9%	92.1	38	15	46	26%	69%	15%	8%	0	13			63	1.63	-0.9	77	$4
20	**Proj**	**4**	**12**	**58**	**78**	**3.85**	**3.27**	**1.31**	**1.20**	**87**	**101**	**3.5**	**4.3**	**12.1**	**2.8**	**35%**	**14.3%**	**93.0**	**41**	**22**	**38**	**32%**	**75%**	**16%**		**0**						**2.1**	**140**	**$6**

Milone,Tommy

Age: 33 | Th: L | Role: RP | Ht: 6' 0" | Wt: 215 | Type: Con FB
Health: D | PT/Exp: D | Consist: F | LIMA Plan: F | Rand Var: +2 | MM: 1101

4-10, 4.76 ERA in 112 IP at SEA. Hit and strand rates normalized and he stayed healthy (for a change). That's about the only reason for this marginally better season. Bottom line: Now 33, and hasn't been relevant in fantasy or otherwise since 2015. (Well, I'm sure he's very relevant to his family and friends. No offense intended.)

Yr	Tm	W	Sv	IP	K	ERA	xERA	WHIP	xWHIP	vL+	vR+	BF/G	Ctl	Dom	Cmd	Ball%	SwK	Vel	G	L	F	H%	S%	HR/F	xHR/F	GS	APC	DOM%	DIS%	Sv%	LI	RAR	BPX	R$
15	MIN *	13	1	167	125	3.25	3.77	1.20	1.33	83	109	23.2	2.1	6.7	3.2	37%	8.2%	87.8	42	23	35	29%	78%	12%	13%	23	86	26%	43%	100	0.86	14.6	95	$14
16	MIN *	7	0	118	78	4.47	5.50	1.43	1.36	115	117	19.3	2.0	5.9	2.9	37%	9.1%	87.6	46	24	30	32%	75%	21%	18%	12	64	0%	67%	0	0.75	-4.1	52	-$2
17	2 NL *	2	1	68	47	7.87	9.18	1.76	1.31	88	145	14.9	2.2	6.1	2.8	36%	8.2%	88.0	36	24	40	34%	66%	22%	18%	8	51	0%	63%	100	0.60	-29.6	-37	-$15
18	WAS *	8	0	140	107	5.90	5.78	1.49		77	143	23.1	2.0	6.9	3.5		11.5%	87.1	28	22	50	35%	62%	16%	16%	4	84	25%	50%	0	0.61	-30.2	75	-$12
19	SEA *	8	0	162	127	4.71	4.73	1.23	1.25	110	98	20.5	2.0	7.1	3.5	34%	10.3%	87.1	37	18	45	29%	68%	16%	16%	6	76	17%	0%	0	0.86	-4.2	71	$4
1st Half		5	0	93	73	3.86	4.28	1.23	1.15	91	84	22.1	2.2	7.1	3.3	35%	9.8%	87.2	32	22	46	29%	74%	11%	12%	4	82	25%	0%	0	1.00	7.4	81	$9
2nd Half		3	0	69	54	5.87	4.93	1.23	1.22	123	106	19.1	1.8	7.0	3.9	34%	10.6%	87.1	39	17	44	27%	60%	19%	18%	2	73	0%	0%	0	0.78	-11.6	103	-$2
20	**Proj**	**4**	**0**	**87**	**66**	**4.97**	**4.28**	**1.38**	**1.26**	**107**	**120**	**19.6**	**2.0**	**6.8**	**3.4**	**35%**	**9.3%**	**87.5**	**38**	**21**	**41**	**31%**	**72%**	**17%**		**18**						**-8.8**	**97**	**-$4**

Minor,Mike

Age: 32 | Th: L | Role: SP | Ht: 6' 4" | Wt: 210 | Type: FB
Health: F | PT/Exp: A | Consist: A | LIMA Plan: A | Rand Var: 0 | MM: 1205

Take a gander at last two years' BPX. So what's the difference between 2018 afterthought and 2019 All-Star? A 1st-half strand rate that suppressed ERA by nearly two runs below xERA. (And remember, 2017 skills were as a reliever.) A serviceable lefty who showed he could eat innings, but he's as good a bet as any to regress in 2020.

Yr	Tm	W	Sv	IP	K	ERA	xERA	WHIP	xWHIP	vL+	vR+	BF/G	Ctl	Dom	Cmd	Ball%	SwK	Vel	G	L	F	H%	S%	HR/F	xHR/F	GS	APC	DOM%	DIS%	Sv%	LI	RAR	BPX	R$
15																																		
16	a/a	0	0	42	32	8.51	7.67	1.96				20.2	5.5	6.9	1.3							35%	59%									-22.5	-5	-$14
17	KC	6	6	78	88	2.55	3.53	1.02	1.13	56	90	4.7	2.5	10.2	4.0	34%	12.7%	94.4	42	16	41	28%	77%	6%	7%	0	18			67	1.20	17.3	162	$13
18	TEX	12	0	157	132	4.18	4.32	1.12	1.23	109	100	22.9	2.2	7.6	3.5	35%	10.1%	92.8	34	21	45	27%	68%	12%	15%	28	91	14%	43%			-0.7	103	$10
19	TEX	14	0	208	200	3.59	4.48	1.24	1.31	92	94	27.0	2.9	8.6	2.9	35%	11.9%	92.6	40	20	40	29%	77%	13%	13%	32	105	28%	25%			23.6	103	$18
1st Half		8	0	113	110	2.40	4.20	1.12	1.25	75	87	26.5	3.0	8.8	3.0	36%	12.4%	92.8	43	19	39	27%	84%	11%	13%	17	103	35%	24%			29.3	108	$29
2nd Half		6	0	96	90	4.99	4.88	1.38	1.27	106	102	27.5	2.9	8.5	2.9	35%	11.3%	92.3	37	21	41	32%	69%	15%	13%	15	107	20%	27%			-5.7	97	$6
20	**Proj**	**12**	**0**	**189**	**176**	**4.25**	**4.04**	**1.31**	**1.23**	**99**	**105**	**25.0**	**2.9**	**8.4**	**2.9**	**35%**	**11.3%**	**92.9**	**38**	**20**	**42**	**31%**	**72%**	**12%**		**30**						**-2.4**	**101**	**$8**

Minter,A.J.

Age: 26 | Th: L | Role: RP | Ht: 6' 0" | Wt: 215 | Type: Pwr
Health: B | PT/Exp: D | Consist: C | LIMA Plan: C | Rand Var: +3 | MM: 2410

3-4, 7.06 ERA with 5 Sv in 29 IP at ATL. Command issues, declining Dom, less movement on slider... all signs that barky shoulder probably bothered him all year. Owns history of superb skills, missing bats with mid-90s heat and (typically) malevolent slider. But the bum shoulder introduces some big risk.

Yr	Tm	W	Sv	IP	K	ERA	xERA	WHIP	xWHIP	vL+	vR+	BF/G	Ctl	Dom	Cmd	Ball%	SwK	Vel	G	L	F	H%	S%	HR/F	xHR/F	GS	APC	DOM%	DIS%	Sv%	LI	RAR	BPX	R$
15																																		
16	aa	1	0	19	28	3.53	2.62	1.26				4.2	3.4	13.3	3.9							40%	69%									1.5	202	-$2
17	ATL *	1	0	33	43	4.30	3.98	1.46		55	94	4.0	4.2	11.7	2.8		18.5%	95.9	38	22	41	38%	70%	8%	8%	0	16			0	0.87	0.2	137	-$4
18	ATL	4	15	61	69	3.23	3.77	1.29	1.22	72	98	4.0	3.2	10.1	3.1	36%	15.3%	96.6	37	28	35	34%	75%	5%	7%	0	16			88	1.08	7.0	127	$8
19	ATL *	5	10	54	58	5.97	6.18	1.73	1.64	95	127	4.4	4.4	9.8	2.2	37%	14.3%	96.0	37	29	34	39%	67%	10%	15%	0	16			83	1.14	-9.6	66	-$2
1st Half		2	6	32	38	5.75	5.37	1.64	1.57	91	127	4.1	5.2	10.7	2.1	39%	13.9%	95.9	37	28	35	36%	67%	11%	16%	0	16			75	1.41	-4.9	77	-$2
2nd Half		3	4	22	21	6.27	7.35	1.87		105	128	4.7	3.3	8.5	2.6		15.2%	96.2	36	30	33	42%	68%	9%	14%	0	17			100	0.52	-4.8	53	-$2
20	**Proj**	**5**	**5**	**58**	**65**	**3.98**	**3.72**	**1.43**	**1.43**	**82**	**115**	**4.1**	**3.5**	**10.0**	**2.9**	**38%**	**14.4%**	**96.2**	**37**	**28**	**35**	**35%**	**76%**	**13%**		**0**						**1.2**	**117**	**$1**

Mize,Casey

Age: 23 | Th: R | Role: SP | Ht: 6' 3" | Wt: 220 | Type: Con
Health: A | PT/Exp: F | Consist: F | LIMA Plan: F | Rand Var: 0 | MM: 1101

Top pick in 2018 draft battled 2019 shoulder issues, but finished at AA with some solid numbers, commanding an advanced four-pitch arsenal. Needs more MiLB time, but spent three years in college ball, so DET will not pamper him for too long. Solid #2/#3 level SP prospect, with rotation-anchor upside if healthy.

Yr	Tm	W	Sv	IP	K	ERA	xERA	WHIP	xWHIP	vL+	vR+	BF/G	Ctl	Dom	Cmd	Ball%	SwK	Vel	G	L	F	H%	S%	HR/F	xHR/F	GS	APC	DOM%	DIS%	Sv%	LI	RAR	BPX	R$
15																																		
16																																		
17																																		
18																																		
19	aa	6	0	80	63	4.56	4.14	1.31				22.1	2.1	7.1	3.3							33%	66%									-0.5	97	$0
1st Half		6	0	52	41	1.76	2.58	1.07		0	0	22.5	2.0	7.2	3.5							28%	86%			0	0					17.6	123	$10
2nd Half		0	0	28	22	9.71	7.01	1.77		0	0	21.6	2.4	6.9	2.9							40%	42%			0	0					-18.1	53	-$19
20	**Proj**	**3**	**0**	**73**	**57**	**4.20**	**4.07**	**1.36**				**21.2**	**2.2**	**7.0**	**3.2**	**35%**	**9.6%**		**42**	**22**	**36**	**32%**	**74%**	**13%**		**14**						**-0.4**	**101**	**-$2**

Montas,Frankie

Age: 27 | Th: R | Role: SP | Ht: 6' 2" | Wt: 245 | Type: Pwr
Health: D | PT/Exp: D | Consist: C | LIMA Plan: C | Rand Var: -2 | MM: 2303

Handed 80-game PED suspension in June (appeared once in Sept). PRO: Command growth; shiny new splitter keyed GB spike; showed durability in rotation. CON: Strand rate suppressed ERA; success came almost without warning. He'd shown most of these skills at various times, so this feels like things coming together. But can he do it again?

Yr	Tm	W	Sv	IP	K	ERA	xERA	WHIP	xWHIP	vL+	vR+	BF/G	Ctl	Dom	Cmd	Ball%	SwK	Vel	G	L	F	H%	S%	HR/F	xHR/F	GS	APC	DOM%	DIS%	Sv%	LI	RAR	BPX	R$
15	CHW *	5	0	127	117	3.85	3.47	1.41		126	79	17.9	4.3	8.3	1.9		13.3%	96.7	38	16	46	32%	71%	6%	5%	2	41	0%	50%	0	0.31	1.8	102	$0
16	a/a	0	0	16	19	2.59	3.23	1.15				9.1	1.5	10.7	7.0							36%	80%									3.2	233	-$2
17	OAK *	1	0	61	65	6.59	5.92	1.54	1.48	168	102	8.4	3.9	9.6	2.4	37%	12.1%	97.7	35	24	41	33%	62%	26%	20%	0	27			0	0.43	-16.9	56	-$9
18	OAK *	9	0	138	92	4.77	4.76	1.47	1.39	121	99	21.2	3.1	6.0	1.9	36%	9.2%	95.8	44	25	31	32%	68%	7%	15%	11	77	27%	36%	0	0.64	-10.5	58	-$5
19	OAK	9	0	96	103	2.63	3.54	1.11	1.16	85	87	24.6	2.2	9.7	4.5	35%	11.7%	96.6	49	22	29	31%	80%	11%	11%	16	93	31%	13%			22.3	155	$13
1st Half		9	0	90	97	2.70	3.49	1.12	1.11	89	83	24.7	2.1	9.7	4.6	35%	11.7%	96.6	51	21	28	32%	79%	10%	11%	15	93	33%	13%			20.0	160	$15
2nd Half		0	0	6	6	1.50	4.21	1.00		11	152	23.0	3.0	9.0	3.0		11.5%	96.5	27	33	40	22%	100%	17%	3%	1	87	0%	0%			2.2	93	-$17
20	**Proj**	**8**	**0**	**145**	**145**	**3.90**	**3.66**	**1.33**	**1.33**	**113**	**86**	**22.5**	**2.9**	**9.0**	**3.1**	**36%**	**11.3%**	**96.8**	**43**	**23**	**34**	**33%**	**74%**	**13%**		**25**						**4.5**	**120**	**$6**

ROD TRUESDELL

Montero,Rafael

Age: 29 | Th: R | Role RP | Ht: 6' 0" | Wt: 185 | Type Pwr
Health F | PT/Exp D | Consist D
LIMA Plan D | Rand Var -2 | MM 3310

2-0, 2.48 ERA in 29 IP with TEX. Former NYM prospect returned from Tommy John surgery as a reliever—and with a bang. Past strike-zone issues nowhere to be seen, as eye-popping 2019 MiLB command (31/2 K/BB in 18 IP) held up very well after call-up. Recent track record is short, clearly, but these newfound skills suggest... UP: 20 Sv

Yr Tm	W	Sv	IP	K	ERA	xERA	WHIP	xWHIP	vL+	vR+	BF/G	Ctl	Dom	Cmd	Ball%	SwK	Vel	G	L	F	H%	S%	HR/F	xHR/F	GS	APC	DOM%	DIS%	Sv%	LI	RAR	BPX	R$
15 NYM	0	0	10	13	4.50	3.62	1.40		200	66	9.2	4.5	11.7	2.6		9.9%	91.7	48	19	33	37%	64%	0%	6%	1	38	100%	0%	0	1.31	-0.7	137	-$4
16 NYM *	8	0	148	111	6.29	6.51	1.85		153	115	20.3	5.0	6.7	1.4		9.3%	92.6	36	32	32	36%	67%	22%	18%	3	43	0%	67%	0	0.54	-38.4	26	-$21
17 NYM *	5	0	148	144	4.99	5.10	1.64	1.49	107	116	16.9	4.9	8.8	1.8	38%	10.8%	93.7	48	19	32	35%	71%	11%	9%	18	65	17%	28%	0	0.71	-11.5	74	-$8
18																																	
19 TEX	2	0	29	34	2.48	3.29	0.97	1.04	48	131	5.1	1.6	10.6	6.8	36%	13.1%	95.8	40	22	38	27%	87%	19%	23%	0	21			0	0.88	7.2	181	$1
1st Half																																	
2nd Half	2	0	29	34	2.48	3.34	0.97	1.00	48	130	5.1	1.6	10.6	6.8	36%	13.1%	95.8	40	22	38	27%	87%	19%	23%	0	21			0	0.88	7.2	181	$1
20 Proj	**3**	**5**	**58**	**60**	**3.53**	**3.63**	**1.25**	**1.20**	**71**	**120**	**7.0**	**3.4**	**9.4**	**2.7**	**36%**	**13.0%**	**95.0**	**43**	**21**	**35**	**29%**	**78%**	**15%**		**0**						**4.4**	**111**	**$3**

Montgomery,Jordan

Age: 27 | Th: L | Role SP | Ht: 6' 6" | Wt: 225 | Type xFB
Health F | PT/Exp C | Consist A
LIMA Plan A | Rand Var +5 | MM 1201

Between 2018 Tommy John surgery and shoulder woes that cropped up during 2019 rehab, another lost season. Returned with some success in September; that buoys 2020 hopes, as pre-injury skills were pretty good (although not as good as 2017 hype, mind you). Could still be a useful arm, but there's plenty of rust to shake off.

Yr Tm	W	Sv	IP	K	ERA	xERA	WHIP	xWHIP	vL+	vR+	BF/G	Ctl	Dom	Cmd	Ball%	SwK	Vel	G	L	F	H%	S%	HR/F	xHR/F	GS	APC	DOM%	DIS%	Sv%	LI	RAR	BPX	R$
15																																	
16 a/a	14	0	139	113	3.02	4.25	1.46				23.9	3.2	7.3	2.3							34%	80%									20.2	90	$8
17 NYY	9	0	155	144	3.88	4.42	1.23	1.28	88	93	22.4	3.0	8.3	2.8	36%	12.4%	92.0	41	18	42	29%	73%	11%	11%	29	87	17%	28%			9.1	107	$10
18 NYY	2	0	27	23	3.62	4.67	1.35		0	105	19.3	4.0	7.6	1.9		10.4%	90.3	46	16	38	29%	76%	10%	9%	6	76	0%	17%			1.8	62	-$3
19 NYY	0	0	4	5	6.75	3.94	1.75		66	195	9.5	0.0	11.3	0.0	38%	12.2%	91.7	29	36	36	49%	67%	20%	23%	1	41	0%	0%	0	0.75	-1.1	228	-$6
1st Half																																	
2nd Half	0	0	4	5	6.75	4.05	1.75		66	192	9.5	0.0	11.3	0.0		12.2%	91.7	29	36	36	49%	67%	20%	23%	1	41	0%	0%	0	0.75	-1.1	228	-$6
20 Proj	**5**	**0**	**87**	**77**	**3.54**	**4.25**	**1.32**	**1.41**	**80**	**88**	**22.5**	**3.1**	**7.9**	**2.6**	**40%**	**12.4%**	**92.0**	**41**	**18**	**42**	**31%**	**76%**	**8%**		**16**						**6.5**	**90**	**$2**

Montgomery,Mike

Age: 31 | Th: L | Role SP | Ht: 6' 5" | Wt: 215 | Type Con GB
Health D | PT/Exp B | Consist A
LIMA Plan A | Rand Var +5 | MM 1101

The once and future Royal? Returned to original franchise in SP role with marginal late-season success. But Dom, SwK still poor, Ball% shows little hope for Ctl growth. Those 2016 skills are the clear outlier. As a lefty with good stats in the not-so-distant past, he'll keep getting chances. But skills say there's little reason for you to speculate.

Yr Tm	W	Sv	IP	K	ERA	xERA	WHIP	xWHIP	vL+	vR+	BF/G	Ctl	Dom	Cmd	Ball%	SwK	Vel	G	L	F	H%	S%	HR/F	xHR/F	GS	APC	DOM%	DIS%	Sv%	LI	RAR	BPX	R$
15 SEA *	8	0	155	112	4.33	3.95	1.34	1.46	115	102	24.0	3.1	6.5	2.1	37%	9.3%	90.9	51	20	29	30%	69%	13%	15%	16	91	19%	50%			-7.1	73	-$1
16 2 TM	4	0	100	92	2.52	3.42	1.17	1.32	77	94	8.4	3.4	8.3	2.4	39%	11.9%	93.6	58	23	19	27%	82%	16%	16%	7	31	0%	14%	0	0.75	20.6	110	$9
17 CHC	7	3	131	100	3.38	4.20	1.21	1.44	83	85	12.3	3.0	6.9	[illegible]	39%	8.9%	92.2	50	17	33	28%	74%	11%	10%	14	47	7%	29%	100	0.93	15.8	89	$11
18 CHC	5	0	124	86	3.99	4.35	1.37	1.37	92	104	14.1	2.8	6.2	2.2	36%	9.8%	91.5	52	22	27	31%	72%	10%	11%	19	51	5%	42%	0	0.69	2.4	76	-$1
19 2 TM	3	0	91	69	4.95	4.89	1.62	1.44	156	111	12.2	3.4	6.8	2.0	38%	9.5%	92.0	49	25	26	34%	75%	24%	23%	13	48	15%	54%	0	1.04	-4.9	64	-$7
1st Half	1	0	24	17	6.08	5.47	1.90	1.54	175	119	5.8	4.6	6.5	1.4	38%	9.2%	92.6	44	35	21	36%	73%	29%	28%	0	24			0	1.22	-4.6	16	-$14
2nd Half	2	0	67	52	4.54	4.60	1.51	1.34	143	108	20.8	2.9	7.0	2.4	38%	9.6%	91.7	51	21	28	33%	76%	22%	21%	13	80	15%	54%	0	0.79	-0.3	81	-$5
20 Proj	**4**	**0**	**109**	**81**	**4.43**	**4.16**	**1.48**	**1.41**	**125**	**105**	**20.6**	**3.4**	**6.7**	**2.0**	**38%**	**9.5%**	**92.0**	**51**	**23**	**26**	**32%**	**74%**	**17%**		**28**						**-3.7**	**67**	**-$4**

Moore,Matt

Age: 31 | Th: L | Role RP | Ht: 6' 3" | Wt: 210 | Type FB
Health F | PT/Exp C | Consist C
LIMA Plan C | Rand Var -5 | MM 1201

Weirdest 10-inning season ever? Skills exploded over two April starts, but in the second one, tore the meniscus in his right knee and missed rest of season. The left brain says heed the years and years (and years!) of disappointing skills. But the right brain remembers how amazing he looked in 2011! Listen to Mr. Left Hemisphere.

Yr Tm	W	Sv	IP	K	ERA	xERA	WHIP	xWHIP	vL+	vR+	BF/G	Ctl	Dom	Cmd	Ball%	SwK	Vel	G	L	F	H%	S%	HR/F	xHR/F	GS	APC	DOM%	DIS%	Sv%	LI	RAR	BPX	R$
15 TAM *	5	0	103	93	5.12	5.22	1.48	1.40	108	122	23.4	3.1	8.1	2.6	36%	9.9%	92.0	39	22	39	34%	69%	11%	14%	12	88	17%	67%			-14.7	71	-$7
16 2 TM	13	0	198	178	4.08	4.47	1.29	1.33	89	96	25.4	3.3	8.1	2.5	36%	10.9%	92.8	38	20	42	29%	72%	10%	12%	33	100	36%	33%			2.6	87	$9
17 SF	6	0	174	148	5.52	5.16	1.53	1.37	139	104	24.7	3.5	7.6	2.2	35%	9.3%	92.0	38	20	42	33%	67%	12%	16%	31	90	16%	42%	0	0.75	-25.1	72	-$9
18 TEX	3	0	102	86	6.79	5.15	1.66	1.39	119	129	12.1	3.6	7.6	2.1	35%	9.9%	92.4	38	21	41	35%	61%	14%	15%	12	46	8%	67%	0	0.68	-33.3	63	-$18
19 DET	0	0	10	9	0.00	2.77	0.40	1.04	0	30	16.5	0.9	8.1	9.0	32%	15.4%	93.0	59	9	32	14%	100%	0%	11%	2	59	50%	0%			5.6	173	-$2
1st Half	0	0	10	9	0.00	2.79	0.40		0	30	16.5	0.9	8.1	9.0		15.4%	93.0	59	9	32	14%	100%	0%	11%	2	59	50%	0%			5.6	173	-$2
2nd Half																																	
20 Proj	**4**	**0**	**87**	**76**	**5.34**	**4.43**	**1.48**	**1.37**	**109**	**110**	**18.1**	**3.4**	**7.8**	**2.3**	**35%**	**10.1%**	**92.4**	**38**	**21**	**41**	**33%**	**67%**	**12%**		**17**						**-12.8**	**76**	**-$6**

Morrow,Brandon

Age: 35 | Th: R | Role RP | Ht: 6' 3" | Wt: 205 | Type Con
Health F | PT/Exp D | Consist A
LIMA Plan A | Rand Var 0 | MM 2110

All season, they kept saying he was just a few weeks away from returning from 2018 elbow surgery—but he never did. So he now hasn't pitched since July 2018. BPX scan shows he can be effective when healthy. But over the last half-a-thousand days (plus other large chunks of career), he's been healthy for, umm... zero of them.

Yr Tm	W	Sv	IP	K	ERA	xERA	WHIP	xWHIP	vL+	vR+	BF/G	Ctl	Dom	Cmd	Ball%	SwK	Vel	G	L	F	H%	S%	HR/F	xHR/F	GS	APC	DOM%	DIS%	Sv%	LI	RAR	BPX	R$
15 SD	2	0	33	23	2.73	3.65	1.09	1.25	84	107	25.2	1.9	6.3	3.3	35%	11.0%	93.4	47	21	32	27%	79%	10%	8%	5	97	20%	20%			5.0	103	$0
16 SD *	2	2	47	26	6.63	8.26	2.06		131	90	7.2	3.3	4.9	1.5		10.3%	94.2	44	26	30	40%	70%	13%	11%	0	13			50	0.69	-14.3	-3	-$12
17 LA *	6	8	64	66	4.33	3.66	1.21	1.05	41	72	3.9	2.0	9.4	4.7	31%	16.8%	97.7	45	24	31	33%	65%	0%	6%	0	14			73	0.85	0.2	159	$5
18 CHC	0	22	31	31	1.47	3.23	1.08	1.19	59	93	3.5	2.6	9.1	3.4	35%	13.1%	97.5	52	23	25	28%	90%	10%	14%	0	14			92	1.28	10.1	141	$9
19																																	
1st Half																																	
2nd Half																																	
20 Proj	**2**	**1**	**44**	**35**	**4.05**	**3.94**	**1.45**	**1.18**	**92**	**127**	**5.3**	**2.6**	**7.3**	**2.8**	**34%**	**13.1%**	**95.9**	**48**	**23**	**29**	**34%**	**75%**	**12%**		**0**						**0.5**	**100**	**-$3**

Morton,Charlie

Age: 36 | Th: R | Role SP | Ht: 6' 5" | Wt: 215 | Type Pwr
Health D | PT/Exp A | Consist A
LIMA Plan A | Rand Var 0 | MM 5405

Less believable than Hollywood, "The Spectacular Success of Charlie Morton" continues to amaze critics. Posted best-ever season at age 35—as all pitchers do, of course!—with superb skills across the board. Yes, gravity's a powerful force, so some regression seems inevitable. And the injury risk lingers. But maybe this script is still being written.

Yr Tm	W	Sv	IP	K	ERA	xERA	WHIP	xWHIP	vL+	vR+	BF/G	Ctl	Dom	Cmd	Ball%	SwK	Vel	G	L	F	H%	S%	HR/F	xHR/F	GS	APC	DOM%	DIS%	Sv%	LI	RAR	BPX	R$
15 PIT *	11	0	149	112	4.41	4.16	1.37	1.34	123	89	24.1	2.9	6.7	2.3	35%	8.5%	92.0	57	21	21	32%	69%	15%	14%	23	87	22%	26%			-8.3	79	$0
16 PHI	1	0	17	19	4.15	3.10	1.33		101	76	17.8	4.2	9.9	2.4		12.7%	94.3	63	21	16	32%	68%	14%	10%	4	69	50%	25%			0.1	126	-$3
17 HOU	14	0	147	163	3.62	3.46	1.19	1.20	74	109	24.7	3.1	10.0	3.3	36%	11.3%	95.0	52	19	29	31%	72%	13%	11%	25	95	40%	16%			13.3	153	$15
18 HOU	15	0	167	201	3.13	3.27	1.16	1.20	95	88	23.2	3.4	10.8	3.1	36%	12.2%	95.7	47	22	30	29%	77%	15%	14%	30	90	27%	17%			21.1	146	$20
19 TAM	16	0	195	240	3.05	3.26	1.08	1.13	90	75	23.9	2.6	11.1	4.2	34%	13.4%	94.4	48	22	30	31%	74%	10%	12%	33	95	48%	15%			34.9	168	$29
1st Half	8	0	100	120	2.43	3.26	1.05	1.15	89	68	23.6	3.1	10.8	3.5	35%	13.9%	94.3	52	20	28	28%	80%	10%	11%	17	93	59%	6%			25.6	155	$32
2nd Half	8	0	95	120	3.71	3.26	1.12	1.04	90	83	24.3	2.2	11.4	5.2	33%	13.0%	94.5	45	24	32	34%	68%	11%	12%	16	97	38%	25%			9.3	184	$26
20 Proj	**15**	**0**	**181**	**211**	**3.51**	**2.98**	**1.15**	**1.16**	**92**	**86**	**23.0**	**2.9**	**10.5**	**3.6**	**35%**	**12.3%**	**94.6**	**49**	**22**	**29**	**31%**	**72%**	**12%**		**31**						**14.3**	**158**	**$21**

Munoz,Andres

Age: 21 | Th: R | Role RP | Ht: 6' 2" | Wt: 165 | Type Pwr
Health A | PT/Exp F | Consist B
LIMA Plan B | Rand Var +1 | MM 4510

1-1, 3.91 ERA with 1 Sv in 23 IP at SD. Precocious righty made quick ascent to majors and held his own. Pairing 100-mph heat (okay, fine, 99.9 mph... close enough!) with improving secondary offerings, skills were even better than stats in debut. Ctl can use some improvement, but we can call that "one skill away"... With opportunity... UP: 30 Sv

Yr Tm	W	Sv	IP	K	ERA	xERA	WHIP	xWHIP	vL+	vR+	BF/G	Ctl	Dom	Cmd	Ball%	SwK	Vel	G	L	F	H%	S%	HR/F	xHR/F	GS	APC	DOM%	DIS%	Sv%	LI	RAR	BPX	R$
15																																	
16																																	
17																																	
18 aa	2	7	19	18	1.06	1.79	1.17				3.8	4.9	8.3	1.7							25%	90%									7.2	120	$2
19 SD *	4	7	60	81	3.38	2.76	1.16	1.30	88	74	4.2	4.2	12.1	2.9	35%	15.6%	99.9	40	24	36	29%	74%	10%	16%	0	19			64	0.95	8.3	135	$7
1st Half	3	6	34	47	2.48	2.14	1.02		0	0	4.4	3.9	12.2	3.1							25%	81%	0%		0	0					8.6	143	$11
2nd Half	1	1	28	34	4.21	3.06	1.25	1.26	89	73	4.2	4.1	11.0	2.7	35%	15.6%	99.9	40	24	36	31%	66%	10%	16%	0	19			50	0.95	1.0	124	$1
20 Proj	**4**	**5**	**65**	**83**	**3.44**	**3.30**	**1.15**	**1.38**	**83**	**70**	**4.3**	**4.1**	**11.4**	**2.8**	**39%**	**15.6%**	**99.9**	**40**	**24**	**36**	**28%**	**72%**	**10%**		**0**						**5.7**	**131**	**$6**

ROD TRUESDELL

Musgrove,Joe

Age: 27	Th: R	Role SP	Health D	LIMA Plan B	
			PT/Exp B	Rand Var +1	
Ht: 6' 5"	Wt: 230	Type Con	Consist B	MM 3203	

In 2019, a .696 oOPS w/bases empty skyrocketed to .802 with men on base; that's his typical career split. (MLB average? Less than half that difference.) This deflates his strand rate and pushes up ERA more than it should given these consistently strong skills. Why does he have such trouble pitching from the stretch? Hidden gem if he can solve that.

Yr	Tm		W	Sv	IP	K	ERA	xERA	WHIP	xWHIP	vL+	vR+	BF/G	Ctl	Dom	Cmd	Ball%	SwK	Vel	G	L	F	H%	S%	HR/F	xHR/F	GS	APC	DOM%	DIS%	Sv%	LI	RAR	BPX	R$
15	aa		4	1	45	29	2.49	3.47	1.00				21.5	1.2	5.8	4.9							24%	88%									8.2	118	$4
16	HOU	*	11	0	147	131	3.63	4.01	1.20	1.22	112	97	21.9	1.6	8.0	5.0	34%	10.1%	91.7	43	21	36	32%	74%	14%	13%	10	89	30%	30%	0	0.78	10.1	143	$11
17	HOU		7	2	109	98	4.77	4.09	1.33	1.22	101	112	12.2	2.3	8.1	3.5	32%	12.4%	92.9	45	21	34	32%	69%	16%	14%	15	46	13%	53%	50	0.89	-5.6	127	$2
18	PIT	*	7	0	132	112	4.17	3.61	1.16	1.18	106	86	23.8	1.7	7.6	4.4	30%	12.2%	93.0	46	20	34	31%	66%	10%	11%	19	86	26%	11%			-0.3	133	$5
19	PIT		11	0	170	157	4.44	4.25	1.22	1.23	106	91	22.4	2.1	8.3	4.0	32%	12.2%	92.4	44	20	35	31%	66%	12%	14%	31	83	35%	26%	0	0.80	1.4	126	$9
1st Half			6	0	91	74	4.27	4.58	1.25	1.24	107	89	22.6	2.2	7.3	3.4	32%	11.4%	91.8	44	21	35	31%	67%	8%	11%	16	81	44%	31%	0	0.80	2.7	104	$9
2nd Half			5	0	80	83	4.63	3.94	1.18	1.12	104	93	22.3	1.9	9.4	4.9	32%	13.1%	93.2	45	19	36	31%	65%	16%	16%	15	86	27%	20%			-1.2	153	$9
20	**Proj**		**11**	**0**	**174**	**157**	**4.30**	**3.62**	**1.24**	**1.18**	**107**	**95**	**22.9**	**2.0**	**8.1**	**4.0**	**32%**	**12.1%**	**92.7**	**45**	**20**	**35**	**32%**	**69%**	**13%**		**31**						**-3.3**	**131**	**$8**

Nelson,Jimmy

Age: 31	Th: R	Role RP	Health F	LIMA Plan F	
			PT/Exp C	Rand Var +5	
Ht: 6' 6"	Wt: 250	Type Pwr GB	Consist F	MM 3301	

0-2, 6.95 ERA in 22 IP at MIL. After shoulder surgery cost him all of 2018, this time his elbow bothered him all season. At least the swing-and-miss returned in 2nd half, but you can bet the low GB and extreme wildness were injury related. Looked like a budding star after 2017 breakout, but don't buy in until health is affirmed.

Yr	Tm		W	Sv	IP	K	ERA	xERA	WHIP	xWHIP	vL+	vR+	BF/G	Ctl	Dom	Cmd	Ball%	SwK	Vel	G	L	F	H%	S%	HR/F	xHR/F	GS	APC	DOM%	DIS%	Sv%	LI	RAR	BPX	R$
15	MIL		11	0	177	148	4.11	3.90	1.29	1.35	120	80	25.1	3.3	7.5	2.3	36%	10.4%	93.5	51	20	29	29%	70%	12%	12%	30	93	43%	30%			-3.3	89	$5
16	MIL		8	0	179	140	4.62	4.80	1.52	1.49	106	109	25.2	4.3	7.0	1.6	37%	7.9%	93.1	49	19	31	31%	73%	15%	14%	32	93	9%	50%			-9.5	44	-$5
17	MIL		12	0	175	199	3.49	3.25	1.25	1.13	94	91	25.1	2.5	10.2	4.1	33%	12.0%	93.9	50	22	27	34%	74%	13%	12%	29	95	48%	24%			18.8	175	$16
18																																			
19	MIL	*	3	0	63	69	6.30	5.77	1.77	1.65	133	124	11.1	6.3	9.9	1.6	44%	10.0%	92.7	33	32	35	35%	66%	19%	18%	3	41	0%	67%	0	0.55	-14.0	58	-$10
1st Half			3	0	38	37	6.15	6.00	1.81		126	147	19.5	6.5	8.7	1.3		8.3%	92.1	33	35	33	33%	68%	14%	13%	3	70	0%	67%	0	0.64	-7.7	43	-$9
2nd Half			0	0	25	32	6.54	5.42	1.71		149	84	6.7	5.9	11.5	1.9		13.9%	93.8	35	24	41	37%	62%	29%	29%	0	22			0	0.50	-6.3	83	-$10
20	**Proj**		**6**	**0**	**116**	**123**	**4.29**	**3.60**	**1.39**	**1.31**	**108**	**91**	**12.5**	**4.0**	**9.6**	**2.4**	**35%**	**11.0%**	**93.5**	**50**	**21**	**29**	**32%**	**72%**	**15%**		**10**						**-2.0**	**107**	**$1**

Neris,Hector

Age: 31	Th: R	Role RP	Health A	LIMA Plan A	
			PT/Exp C	Rand Var -1	
Ht: 6' 2"	Wt: 215	Type Pwr	Consist A	MM 4531	

Threw devastating splitter more than ever, to superb effect. Resulting groundball spike meant one less HR allowed than in 2018 despite 20 more IP, and xHR/F says it should've been even fewer. Plus, his SwK remains among the best in baseball. No reason why he can't keep it up, and if team fortune and these skills align... UP: 40 Sv

Yr	Tm		W	Sv	IP	K	ERA	xERA	WHIP	xWHIP	vL+	vR+	BF/G	Ctl	Dom	Cmd	Ball%	SwK	Vel	G	L	F	H%	S%	HR/F	xHR/F	GS	APC	DOM%	DIS%	Sv%	LI	RAR	BPX	R$
15	PHI	*	3	1	78	70	4.21	5.00	1.56	1.16	106	109	5.8	4.2	8.1	1.9	38%	14.2%	93.2	39	15	46	34%	76%	15%	15%	0	21			33	0.69	-2.4	67	-$5
16	PHI		4	2	80	102	2.58	3.22	1.11	1.16	86	83	4.2	3.4	11.4	3.4	37%	15.9%	94.1	42	25	34	29%	83%	14%	13%	0	17			33	1.11	16.0	160	$9
17	PHI		4	26	75	86	3.01	4.07	1.26	1.20	95	89	4.3	3.1	10.4	3.3	33%	16.6%	94.7	33	23	44	32%	81%	10%	14%	0	17			90	1.10	12.4	136	$16
18	PHI	*	3	12	68	100	4.14	3.90	1.21	1.01	122	100	3.8	3.2	13.3	4.1	35%	19.7%	94.6	31	24	45	34%	72%	23%	21%	0	15			75	0.81	0.1	151	$6
19	PHI		3	28	68	89	2.93	3.33	1.02	1.16	78	84	4.0	3.2	11.8	3.7	36%	18.0%	94.6	45	19	36	26%	80%	18%	13%	0	17			82	1.54	13.2	163	$19
1st Half			1	16	34	46	3.18	3.38	1.06	1.08	77	85	4.1	2.9	12.2	4.2	36%	18.8%	94.4	47	14	39	30%	75%	13%	8%	0	17			89	1.52	5.6	180	$16
2nd Half			2	12	34	43	2.67	3.32	0.98	1.16	80	83	4.0	3.5	11.5	3.3	37%	17.2%	94.6	44	24	32	21%	85%	25%	20%	0	16			75	1.57	7.6	147	$22
20	**Proj**		**3**	**32**	**73**	**94**	**3.25**	**3.07**	**1.13**	**1.11**	**91**	**86**	**3.9**	**3.3**	**11.7**	**3.6**	**36%**	**17.9%**	**94.5**	**39**	**21**	**39**	**29%**	**78%**	**16%**		**0**						**8.0**	**161**	**$19**

Newcomb,Sean

Age: 27	Th: L	Role RP	Health A	LIMA Plan A	
			PT/Exp C	Rand Var -1	
Ht: 6' 5"	Wt: 255	Type Pwr	Consist A	MM 2301	

6-3, 3.16 ERA in 68 IP at ATL. Sent to bullpen after three shaky April starts, and skills improved for a while. But the plate still dances on him, as 2nd-half Ball% and Ctl show clearly, and doesn't miss enough bats to offset the walks. Lack of platoon split should help keep him out of a platoon-only role, but with so-so skills, path to value is unclear.

Yr	Tm		W	Sv	IP	K	ERA	xERA	WHIP	xWHIP	vL+	vR+	BF/G	Ctl	Dom	Cmd	Ball%	SwK	Vel	G	L	F	H%	S%	HR/F	xHR/F	GS	APC	DOM%	DIS%	Sv%	LI	RAR	BPX	R$
15	aa		2	0	36	35	3.40	2.98	1.37				21.6	6.0	8.7	1.4							26%	76%									2.5	97	-$2
16	aa		8	0	140	135	5.64	4.25	1.62				23.0	5.3	8.7	1.6							35%	63%									-25.1	93	-$10
17	ATL	*	7	0	158	172	4.13	4.44	1.57	1.45	100	107	23.1	5.3	9.8	1.8	37%	11.9%	93.7	44	23	33	34%	75%	11%	13%	19	96	11%	26%			4.4	94	$0
18	ATL		12	0	164	160	3.90	4.40	1.33	1.42	97	94	22.5	4.4	8.8	2.0	39%	10.5%	93.0	43	21	36	28%	74%	11%	11%	30	94	17%	27%	0	0.77	5.1	68	$7
19	ATL	*	8	1	91	81	3.08	3.56	1.25	1.41	89	94	6.2	3.4	8.0	2.3	37%	10.0%	94.4	49	18	34	29%	79%	12%	12%	4	21	0%	75%	33	1.06	16.0	84	$8
1st Half			4	1	60	48	2.68	3.63	1.27	1.30	98	95	8.8	2.6	7.1	2.7	36%	9.6%	93.8	45	19	36	31%	81%	7%	9%	4	27	0%	75%	100	0.98	13.5	92	$10
2nd Half			4	0	30	33	3.86	4.10	1.22	1.44	77	92	4.1	5.0	9.8	1.9	39%	10.5%	95.1	55	15	30	22%	75%	23%	19%	0	17			0	1.13	2.4	80	$4
20	**Proj**		**6**	**0**	**73**	**72**	**3.74**	**3.95**	**1.33**	**1.41**	**89**	**93**	**8.4**	**4.6**	**8.9**	**2.0**	**38%**	**10.6%**	**93.0**	**47**	**19**	**34**	**28%**	**75%**	**12%**		**0**						**3.6**	**74**	**$2**

Nola,Aaron

Age: 27	Th: R	Role SP	Health C	LIMA Plan A	
			PT/Exp A	Rand Var +2	
Ht: 6' 2"	Wt: 195	Type Pwr GB	Consist A	MM 4405	

PRO: Keeps piling up the IP; best-ever Dom rate; another sub-4.00 ERA. CON: Walks inched up; SwK didn't fully support the Dom jump; ERA spiked even more than we expected, as overall skills were worst since rookie year. Granted, they are still solid skills. But he needs that sub-3 Ctl and low-30s Ball% to be his best self.

Yr	Tm		W	Sv	IP	K	ERA	xERA	WHIP	xWHIP	vL+	vR+	BF/G	Ctl	Dom	Cmd	Ball%	SwK	Vel	G	L	F	H%	S%	HR/F	xHR/F	GS	APC	DOM%	DIS%	Sv%	LI	RAR	BPX	R$
15	PHI	*	16	0	187	151	3.10	3.58	1.17	1.21	115	87	24.1	1.8	7.2	4.1	35%	8.9%	90.5	48	20	32	30%	77%	15%	12%	13	86	31%	23%			19.9	126	$19
16	PHI		6	0	111	121	4.78	3.25	1.31	1.14	95	98	24.2	2.4	9.8	4.2	34%	10.0%	90.1	55	20	25	36%	64%	13%	12%	20	90	35%	15%			-8.1	174	$0
17	PHI		12	0	168	184	3.54	3.49	1.21	1.16	98	84	25.7	2.6	9.9	3.8	34%	11.5%	92.0	50	19	31	32%	74%	13%	12%	27	99	44%	15%			17.0	162	$16
18	PHI		17	0	212	224	2.37	3.17	0.97	1.15	76	81	25.2	2.5	9.5	3.9	33%	12.9%	92.4	51	19	30	26%	79%	11%	12%	33	97	52%	15%			46.5	154	$38
19	PHI		12	0	202	229	3.87	3.82	1.27	1.29	96	93	25.1	3.6	10.2	2.9	35%	11.5%	92.9	50	21	30	30%	74%	17%	17%	34	98	32%	26%			15.9	126	$15
1st Half			6	0	96	110	4.22	3.82	1.36	1.24	111	92	24.5	3.6	10.3	2.9	36%	10.1%	92.6	49	23	27	33%	74%	20%	19%	17	96	18%	24%			3.4	127	$9
2nd Half			6	0	106	119	3.55	3.77	1.18	1.25	85	93	25.6	3.6	10.1	2.8	34%	12.8%	93.2	50	18	32	28%	74%	15%	15%	17	100	47%	29%			12.5	124	$21
20	**Proj**		**13**	**0**	**181**	**197**	**3.58**	**3.23**	**1.21**	**1.20**	**93**	**91**	**24.6**	**3.1**	**9.8**	**3.1**	**34%**	**11.7%**	**92.4**	**50**	**20**	**30**	**30%**	**74%**	**15%**		**30**						**12.8**	**137**	**$17**

Norris,Daniel

Age: 27	Th: L	Role RP	Health F	LIMA Plan B	
			PT/Exp C	Rand Var +1	
Ht: 6' 2"	Wt: 185	Type	Consist B	MM 1201	

Prototype of a new "super opener?" Beginning August 11, started nine times, went exactly 3 IP in all nine with a 3.33 ERA and 3.9 Cmd. Unfortunately for his owners, despite better stats, it also meant he couldn't get any more wins to pair with all those losses (13 overall). Prior, another humdrum season. So either way, probably not worth your time.

Yr	Tm		W	Sv	IP	K	ERA	xERA	WHIP	xWHIP	vL+	vR+	BF/G	Ctl	Dom	Cmd	Ball%	SwK	Vel	G	L	F	H%	S%	HR/F	xHR/F	GS	APC	DOM%	DIS%	Sv%	LI	RAR	BPX	R$
15	2 AL	*	6	0	151	114	5.03	4.96	1.55	1.35	121	96	22.7	3.7	6.8	1.8	40%	9.4%	91.9	39	17	43	33%	68%	11%	10%	13	80	15%	46%			-19.9	58	-$11
16	DET	*	10	0	149	140	4.50	4.81	1.51	1.23	88	109	22.3	3.2	8.4	2.6	36%	10.8%	93.1	38	23	39	36%	71%	12%	13%	13	85	23%	31%	0	0.72	-5.7	91	-$1
17	DET		5	0	102	86	5.31	5.18	1.61	1.42	123	110	20.9	3.9	7.6	2.0	40%	9.5%	93.2	39	22	39	35%	68%	10%	14%	18	83	6%	44%	0	0.65	-12.0	59	-$8
18	DET		0	0	44	51	5.68	4.37	1.47	1.28	119	107	18.2	3.9	10.4	2.7	38%	10.8%	90.2	30	29	41	34%	65%	15%	17%	8	74	0%	25%	0	0.72	-8.4	104	-$7
19	DET		3	0	144	125	4.49	4.57	1.33	1.29	106	106	19.1	2.4	7.8	3.3	35%	10.6%	90.8	43	21	36	31%	72%	16%	17%	29	74	14%	38%	0	0.76	0.3	106	$0
1st Half			2	0	86	69	4.62	4.72	1.38	1.24	114	107	21.6	2.1	7.2	3.5	35%	9.5%	90.4	44	21	35	32%	72%	16%	18%	14	81	14%	43%	0	0.76	-1.2	104	-$1
2nd Half			1	0	59	56	4.30	4.39	1.26	1.24	94	107	16.1	2.8	8.6	3.1	35%	12.3%	91.4	40	21	39	30%	72%	16%	16%	15	65	13%	33%			1.5	108	$1
20	**Proj**		**3**	**0**	**116**	**108**	**4.91**	**4.22**	**1.46**	**1.28**	**112**	**109**	**18.6**	**3.4**	**8.4**	**2.5**	**37%**	**10.7%**	**91.3**	**38**	**23**	**39**	**33%**	**70%**	**14%**		**23**						**-10.8**	**87**	**-$5**

Nova,Ivan

Age: 33	Th: R	Role SP	Health C	LIMA Plan A	
			PT/Exp A	Rand Var +1	
Ht: 6' 5"	Wt: 250	Type Con	Consist A	MM 1005	

Third straight year of declining skills. Already paltry Dom took another step down, and couldn't make up for it anywhere else. Growing Ball% shows walk-rate climb could get worse, too. Rode fortunate S% to that 2nd-half ERA; xERA shows no real change. Regression could mean ERA dips a bit, but xERA shows... DN: 5.00+ ERA

Yr	Tm		W	Sv	IP	K	ERA	xERA	WHIP	xWHIP	vL+	vR+	BF/G	Ctl	Dom	Cmd	Ball%	SwK	Vel	G	L	F	H%	S%	HR/F	xHR/F	GS	APC	DOM%	DIS%	Sv%	LI	RAR	BPX	R$
15	NYY		6	0	94	63	5.07	4.50	1.40	1.41	123	96	24.3	3.2	6.0	1.9	37%	8.1%	93.0	49	19	32	30%	66%	13%	11%	17	90	18%	53%			-12.9	60	-$5
16	2 TM		12	1	162	127	4.17	3.74	1.25	1.19	116	98	21.4	1.6	7.1	4.5	34%	9.6%	92.6	54	19	28	32%	71%	16%	17%	26	72	31%	42%	100	0.74	0.5	139	$8
17	PIT		11	0	187	131	4.14	4.30	1.28	1.24	114	96	25.3	1.7	6.3	3.6	34%	8.7%	92.8	46	23	31	31%	73%	16%	16%	31	86	19%	29%			5.1	109	$9
18	PIT		9	0	161	114	4.19	4.38	1.28	1.27	114	99	23.6	2.0	6.4	3.3	36%	9.4%	92.9	46	20	34	30%	73%	15%	18%	29	87	17%	41%			-0.9	99	$3
19	CHW		11	0	187	114	4.72	5.06	1.45	1.40	109	112	23.7	2.3	5.5	2.4	36%	8.6%	92.4	46	24	30	32%	72%	16%	15%	34	88	15%	44%			-4.9	67	-$1
1st Half			3	0	94	62	5.92	5.06	1.56	1.34	122	119	24.4	2.4	5.9	2.5	36%	8.5%	92.2	45	24	31	34%	66%	19%	15%	17	90	18%	53%			-16.4	71	-$13
2nd Half			8	0	93	52	3.50	4.98	1.35	1.35	93	105	23.1	2.1	5.1	2.4	37%	8.6%	92.6	47	23	30	31%	78%	12%	14%	17	87	12%	35%			11.5	64	$10
20	**Proj**		**12**	**0**	**189**	**121**	**4.36**	**4.27**	**1.37**	**1.31**	**111**	**104**	**24.0**	**2.2**	**5.8**	**2.6**	**36%**	**8.8%**	**92.6**	**45**	**23**	**32**	**31%**	**73%**	**14%**		**33**						**-4.9**	**78**	**$3**

ROD TRUESDELL

Oberg,Scott

Oberg,Scott			Health	D	LIMA Plan	C
Age: 30	Th: R	Role RP	PT/Exp	D	Rand Var	-5
Ht: 6' 2"	Wt: 203	Type GB	Consist	C	MM	3210

Before another bout with blood clots in his arm, stats put him in closer mix. But BPX says he's had just one year of closer-worthy skills, and it was driven by a control rate that sticks out as an anomaly. Plus, we can't keep expecting those friendly hit and strand rates to save him again. Best to view him as an oft-injured middle-man than a plan B closer.

Yr	Tm	W	Sv	IP	K	ERA	xERA	WHIP	xWHIP	vL+	vR+	BF/G	Ctl	Dom	Cmd	Ball%	SwK	Vel	G	L	F	H%	S%	HR/F	xHR/F	GS	APC	DOM%	DIS%	Sv%	LI	RAR	BPX	R$
15	COL	3	1	58	44	5.09	4.51	1.53	1.56	107	123	4.0	4.8	6.8	1.4	41%	8.7%	95.0	54	18	28	28%	71%	21%	15%	0	16			33	1.00	-8.1	30	-$6
16	COL *	2	10	56	46	4.35	3.30	1.27		135	75	4.5	3.8	7.5	2.0		9.6%	94.5	56	11	33	28%	66%	11%	11%	0	18			83	0.63	-1.1	87	$2
17	COL	0	0	58	55	4.94	4.15	1.61	1.35	108	107	4.0	3.7	8.5	2.3	35%	12.6%	96.3	57	19	24	38%	69%	9%	8%	0	15			0	0.90	-4.2	105	-$7
18	COL *	9	3	75	67	2.38	2.63	1.03	1.12	86	73	4.2	1.7	8.1	4.7	33%	13.7%	95.3	56	25	19	28%	80%	13%	12%	0	16			38	1.28	16.3	158	$12
19	COL	6	5	56	58	2.25	3.94	1.11	1.34	86	67	4.6	3.7	9.3	2.5	35%	12.8%	94.4	49	20	31	25%	84%	12%	14%	0	18			63	1.15	15.6	103	$9
1st Half		5	3	41	44	1.33	3.58	0.93	1.26	61	69	4.4	3.5	9.7	2.8	35%	14.1%	94.3	49	21	29	21%	91%	11%	16%	0	18			50	1.30	15.9	117	$14
2nd Half		1	2	15	14	4.70	4.81	1.57	1.41	135	61	5.1	4.1	8.2	2.0	35%	9.7%	94.4	48	18	34	34%	73%	13%	11%	0	20			100	0.73	-0.4	68	-$5
20	Proj	5	2	58	54	3.49	3.57	1.29	1.31	104	80	4.4	3.4	8.4	2.5	35%	11.8%	95.0	52	21	27	30%	75%	12%		0						4.7	105	$2

Odorizzi,Jake

Odorizzi,Jake			Health	C	LIMA Plan	A
Age: 30	Th: R	Role SP	PT/Exp	A	Rand Var	-1
Ht: 6' 2"	Wt: 190	Type Pwr xFB	Consist	A	MM	2305

Another couple mph on his fastball fueled best skills of career. But before you use him near the front of your rotation, heed xERA. 2nd-half ERA moved towards it, which left him as the kind of mid-rotation arm we've come to expect. And much of 2019 value was driven by Wins, which we know are fickle. Set 4.00 ERA as baseline, and you'll be fine.

Yr	Tm	W	Sv	IP	K	ERA	xERA	WHIP	xWHIP	vL+	vR+	BF/G	Ctl	Dom	Cmd	Ball%	SwK	Vel	G	L	F	H%	S%	HR/F	xHR/F	GS	APC	DOM%	DIS%	Sv%	LI	RAR	BPX	R$
15	TAM	9	0	169	150	3.35	3.99	1.15	1.24	87	105	25.0	2.4	8.0	3.3	35%	10.6%	91.3	37	22	41	29%	75%	9%	13%	28	98	25%	11%			12.8	110	$13
16	TAM	10	0	188	166	3.69	4.33	1.19	1.26	78	111	23.4	2.6	8.0	3.1	36%	10.2%	91.6	37	19	44	28%	75%	12%	11%	33	100	21%	42%			11.5	105	$13
17	TAM	10	0	143	127	4.14	5.01	1.24	1.40	91	105	21.6	3.8	8.0	2.1	39%	11.5%	91.6	31	22	47	24%	76%	16%	12%	28	94	11%	50%			3.8	59	$8
18	MIN	7	0	164	162	4.49	4.76	1.34	1.35	104	101	22.2	3.8	8.9	2.3	39%	10.8%	91.1	28	23	49	30%	69%	9%	13%	32	96	28%	31%			-6.9	72	$0
19	MIN	15	0	159	178	3.51	4.24	1.21	1.25	100	78	21.9	3.0	10.1	3.4	36%	13.1%	92.9	35	21	44	31%	74%	9%	12%	30	93	33%	23%			19.5	123	$17
1st Half		10	0	86	94	2.73	4.28	1.07	1.18	93	67	21.3	2.8	9.9	3.5	35%	12.7%	92.9	31	19	50	28%	79%	8%	14%	16	90	38%	25%			18.7	120	$26
2nd Half		5	0	73	84	4.42	4.30	1.36	1.21	107	91	22.6	3.2	10.3	3.2	37%	13.6%	92.9	39	22	39	35%	70%	10%	9%	14	97	29%	21%			0.8	127	$7
20	Proj	13	0	189	194	3.97	3.96	1.26	1.27	99	93	21.5	3.3	9.3	2.8	37%	12.1%	92.1	33	22	45	30%	72%	10%		36						4.2	102	$13

Ohtani,Shohei

Ohtani,Shohei			Health	D	LIMA Plan	D
Age: 25	Th: R	Role SP	PT/Exp	F	Rand Var	0
Ht: 6' 4"	Wt: 210	Type Pwr FB	Consist	D	MM	3401

Recovery from Tommy John surgery delayed first full season of two-way play. Pre-injury profile shows salivating level of swinging strikes, so strikeouts are coming. Mediocre Ctl profile, high Ball% in 2018 debut, and first season back from arm surgery make control his biggest risk. Still, it's one worth taking given his ceiling.

Yr	Tm	W	Sv	IP	K	ERA	xERA	WHIP	xWHIP	vL+	vR+	BF/G	Ctl	Dom	Cmd	Ball%	SwK	Vel	G	L	F	H%	S%	HR/F	xHR/F	GS	APC	DOM%	DIS%	Sv%	LI	RAR	BPX	R$
15	for *	15	0	161	186	2.78	2.10	1.02		0	0	28.1	3.2	10.4	3.3							26%	75%	0%		0	0					23.4	153	$24
16	for *	10	0	140	165	2.32	2.07	1.08		0	0	26.0	3.6	10.6	3.0							28%	80%	0%		0	0					32.4	153	$21
17	for *	2	0	16	18	6.17	5.34	1.79		0	0	18.8	9.6	10.0	1.0							23%	70%	0%		0	0					-3.0	49	-$0
18	LAA	4	0	52	63	3.31	3.57	1.16	1.24	73	95	21.1	3.8	11.0	2.9	38%	15.5%	96.7	39	24	37	28%	76%	13%	12%	10	85	30%	40%			5.4	128	$2
19																																		
1st Half																																		
2nd Half																																		
20	Proj	10	0	116	137	3.40	3.49	1.19	1.36	67	87	25.0	3.8	10.7	2.8	42%	15.5%	96.7	39	24	37	28%	76%	12%		19						10.7	121	$11

Osuna,Roberto

Osuna,Roberto			Health	A	LIMA Plan	A
Age: 25	Th: R	Role RP	PT/Exp	B	Rand Var	-2
Ht: 6' 2"	Wt: 215	Type	Consist	A	MM	5430

Off-field issue in 2018 makes him seem riskier than he actually is. Both skills and stats tell the true story. Long track record of nifty peripherals come with backing of steadily high rate of whiffs, and they'll keep coming with that increasing FB velocity. Steadily high Sv conversion elicits faith from his real-life manager too. Keep riding.

Yr	Tm	W	Sv	IP	K	ERA	xERA	WHIP	xWHIP	vL+	vR+	BF/G	Ctl	Dom	Cmd	Ball%	SwK	Vel	G	L	F	H%	S%	HR/F	xHR/F	GS	APC	DOM%	DIS%	Sv%	LI	RAR	BPX	R$
15	TOR	1	20	70	75	2.58	3.41	0.92	1.10	88	76	4.0	2.1	9.7	4.7	35%	15.1%	95.6	34	20	46	25%	77%	9%	9%	0	16			87	1.36	11.8	156	$15
16	TOR	4	36	74	82	2.68	3.45	0.93	1.05	99	65	4.0	1.7	10.0	5.9	30%	15.7%	95.8	33	20	47	27%	78%	10%	12%	0	16			86	1.39	13.8	172	$24
17	TOR	3	39	64	83	3.38	2.65	0.86	0.92	67	69	3.8	1.3	11.7	9.2	33%	17.2%	94.6	48	18	34	31%	60%	6%	7%	0	15			80	1.36	7.8	243	$24
18	2 AL	2	21	38	32	2.37	3.50	0.97	1.08	96	62	3.9	0.9	7.6	8.0	28%	14.7%	95.2	41	25	34	30%	75%	3%	10%	0	14			95	1.10	8.3	149	$10
19	HOU	4	38	65	73	2.63	3.52	0.88	1.08	62	86	3.8	1.7	10.1	6.1	33%	17.4%	96.7	39	22	39	25%	78%	12%	11%	0	15			86	1.32	15.0	168	$25
1st Half		3	17	34	35	2.12	3.70	0.76	1.01	35	89	3.8	1.1	9.3	8.8	34%	15.0%	96.4	36	20	43	24%	78%	8%	8%	0	14			85	1.22	10.0	166	$24
2nd Half		1	21	31	38	3.19	3.43	1.00	1.07	85	82	3.9	2.3	11.0	4.8	32%	19.8%	97.0	42	23	35	27%	77%	19%	14%	0	15			88	1.44	5.0	170	$27
20	Proj	3	36	65	71	2.74	2.93	0.92	1.04	77	75	3.7	1.5	9.8	6.4	32%	16.8%	95.9	41	22	37	28%	74%	10%		0						11.3	177	$23

Ottavino,Adam

Ottavino,Adam			Health	F	LIMA Plan	D
Age: 34	Th: R	Role RP	PT/Exp	C	Rand Var	-5
Ht: 6' 5"	Wt: 220	Type Pwr	Consist	D	MM	3510

Again looked like an elite bullpen arm. "Looked" is the key word here, as both xERA and xWHIP confirm it was a mirage this time around. Volatility underscored by chronically high Ball%, so his long history of wildness isn't going away. And as that strand rate comes down, the collateral damage could come in a hurry.

Yr	Tm	W	Sv	IP	K	ERA	xERA	WHIP	xWHIP	vL+	vR+	BF/G	Ctl	Dom	Cmd	Ball%	SwK	Vel	G	L	F	H%	S%	HR/F	xHR/F	GS	APC	DOM%	DIS%	Sv%	LI	RAR	BPX	R$
15	COL	1	3	10	13	0.00	1.89	0.48		44	31	3.5	1.7	11.3	6.5		12.7%	95.7	63	5	32	16%	100%	0%	7%	0	14			100	1.05	5.0	236	$1
16	COL	1	7	27	35	2.67	2.32	0.93		106	48	3.1	2.3	11.7	5.0		11.4%	93.8	62	17	21	27%	77%	23%	13%	0	13			58	1.28	5.1	222	$4
17	COL	2	0	53	63	5.06	5.03	1.63	1.57	119	98	3.9	6.6	10.6	1.6	44%	9.6%	94.4	37	22	41	31%	72%	14%	12%	0	17			0	0.89	-4.6	34	-$6
18	COL	6	6	78	112	2.43	2.94	0.99	1.17	77	65	4.1	4.2	13.0	3.1	37%	12.7%	93.9	43	19	38	25%	78%	9%	9%	0	17			55	1.21	16.4	163	$14
19	NYY	6	2	66	88	1.90	4.26	1.31	1.41	99	75	3.9	5.4	11.9	2.2	39%	11.4%	93.9	40	19	41	30%	89%	8%	9%	0	16			22	1.13	21.3	94	$8
1st Half		3	0	37	52	1.45	4.21	1.26	1.41	103	69	4.1	6.0	12.5	2.1	41%	10.9%	94.1	38	17	45	25%	95%	12%	10%	0	17			0	1.33	14.1	86	$9
2nd Half		3	2	29	36	2.48	4.34	1.38	1.32	95	81	3.6	4.7	11.2	2.4	37%	12.1%	93.6	41	21	37	34%	82%	4%	7%	0	14			33	0.92	7.2	103	$7
20	Proj	5	2	65	87	3.75	3.45	1.29	1.32	98	81	3.8	4.9	12.0	2.4	39%	11.6%	93.9	41	20	40	30%	73%	10%		0						3.2	117	$3

Paddack,Chris

Paddack,Chris			Health	A	LIMA Plan	F
Age: 24	Th: R	Role SP	PT/Exp	D	Rand Var	-1
Ht: 6' 4"	Wt: 195	Type FB	Consist	F	MM	3303

Electric spring got him an early MLB shot, where he solidified himself as a rotation building block. Top-tier Ball% and SwK combo gives full backing to elite command. Regression of friendly H% reflected in xERA, but don't just assume that will happen, as both exit velocity and hard-hit % were well below league norms. UP: 3.00 ERA, 200 K

Yr	Tm	W	Sv	IP	K	ERA	xERA	WHIP	xWHIP	vL+	vR+	BF/G	Ctl	Dom	Cmd	Ball%	SwK	Vel	G	L	F	H%	S%	HR/F	xHR/F	GS	APC	DOM%	DIS%	Sv%	LI	RAR	BPX	R$
15																																		
16																																		
17																																		
18	aa	3	0	39	33	2.16	1.09	0.76				20.1	0.9	7.5	8.3							24%	71%									9.6	263	$4
19	SD	9	0	141	153	3.33	3.87	0.98	1.14	88	81	21.8	2.0	9.8	4.9	30%	12.3%	93.9	40	18	42	26%	75%	15%	13%	26	88	42%	19%			20.4	153	$18
1st Half		5	0	77	81	3.05	3.86	0.94	1.10	90	73	21.8	2.0	9.5	4.8	30%	11.8%	93.8	43	16	41	24%	77%	15%	14%	14	88	43%	21%			13.7	151	$21
2nd Half		4	0	64	72	3.66	4.03	1.03	1.08	85	89	21.9	2.0	10.1	5.1	31%	13.0%	94.0	37	20	43	27%	73%	15%	12%	12	87	42%	17%			6.7	157	$16
20	Proj	12	0	174	177	3.49	3.44	1.07	1.09	91	87	21.3	2.1	9.2	4.4	31%	12.5%	93.9	39	18	43	28%	74%	13%		32						14.2	145	$20

Pagan,Emilio

Pagan,Emilio			Health	A	LIMA Plan	D
Age: 29	Th: R	Role RP	PT/Exp	C	Rand Var	-5
Ht: 6' 3"	Wt: 205	Type Pwr xFB	Consist	D	MM	4530

Skilled middle-man got a sniff of saves, and man, did he run with it. Late ERA jump was fueled by a fluky hr/f. BPX confirms he got better with more leverage, which bodes well for him holding on to late-inning role. Command building blocks pristine too. Flyball tilt is his only wart, but pinpoint control diminishes the damage there. UP: 40 Sv

Yr	Tm	W	Sv	IP	K	ERA	xERA	WHIP	xWHIP	vL+	vR+	BF/G	Ctl	Dom	Cmd	Ball%	SwK	Vel	G	L	F	H%	S%	HR/F	xHR/F	GS	APC	DOM%	DIS%	Sv%	LI	RAR	BPX	R$
15																																		
16	a/a	5	10	65	71	3.05	3.78	1.32				6.6	4.1	9.8	2.4							30%	82%									9.1	100	$7
17	SEA *	4	5	82	86	3.18	2.28	0.95	1.02	109	68	5.4	1.8	9.4	5.3	31%	14.4%	93.6	22	21	57	27%	69%	9%	7%	0	21			83	1.09	11.9	188	$11
18	OAK	3	0	62	63	4.35	4.51	1.19	1.22	141	88	4.8	2.8	9.1	3.3	35%	14.5%	93.8	27	18	55	27%	72%	14%	14%	0	19			0	0.56	-1.6	110	-$1
19	TAM	4	20	70	96	2.31	3.10	0.83	0.97	94	70	4.0	1.7	12.3	7.4	30%	18.5%	95.5	34	19	47	25%	87%	16%	9%	0	16			71	1.47	18.9	206	$20
1st Half		2	4	32	40	1.14	3.31	0.82	1.06	70	58	4.1	2.6	11.4	4.4	31%	17.9%	95.3	41	20	39	23%	92%	7%	7%	0	17			57	1.28	13.2	168	$12
2nd Half		2	16	38	56	3.29	3.12	0.83	0.82	107	81	4.0	0.9	13.1	14.0	29%	19.1%	95.7	28	19	53	26%	82%	22%	11%	0	16			76	1.61	5.8	237	$27
20	Proj	4	27	65	79	3.08	3.25	0.99	1.04	111	75	4.4	2.2	10.9	5.0	32%	16.5%	94.7	29	19	52	26%	79%	14%		0						8.6	167	$18

STEPHEN NICKRAND

Palumbo,Joseph

Age: 25 Th: L Role RP	Health D	LIMA Plan F	
Ht: 6' 1" Wt: 168 Type Pwr	PT/Exp F	Rand Var +5	
	Consist F	MM 2401	

0-3, 9.18 ERA in 17 IP at TEX. Cup of coffee in majors predictably didn't go well, considering he only had 60 innings at AA at time of recall. Combine a spotty Ctl validated by bad Ball% and an xHR/F that supports continued longball problems, and you've got a flammable combination. Best to watch from afar until he makes adjustments.

Yr	Tm	W	Sv	IP	K	ERA	xERA	WHIP	xWHIP	vL+	vR+	BF/G	Ctl	Dom	Cmd	Ball%	SwK	Vel	G	L	F	H%	S%	HR/F	xHR/F	GS	APC	DOM%	DIS%	Sv%	LI	RAR	BPX	R$
15																																		
16																																		
17																																		
18																																		
19	TEX *	3	0	99	105	4.92	4.88	1.41	1.34	161	138	17.4	4.4	9.6	2.2	39%	10.2%	94.0	35	27	39	29%	71%	37%	29%	4	48	0%	75%	0	0.61	-5.1	62	-$3
1st Half		0	0	66	62	5.78	5.74	1.58		275	171	20.9	4.4	8.4	1.9		8.2%	93.5	35	26	39	32%	67%	33%	19%	2	61	0%	100%			-10.4	43	-$9
2nd Half		3	0	35	43	2.96	2.73	0.98		102	115	13.3	3.9	11.2	2.8		11.4%	94.3	35	27	38	18%	83%	40%	38%	2	42	0%	50%	0	0.55	6.6	106	$9
20	**Proj**	**4**	**0**	**80**	**89**	**4.49**	**3.87**	**1.39**				**16.4**	**4.3**	**10.0**	**2.3**	**38%**	**10.0%**		**42**	**20**	**38**	**30%**	**75%**	**19%**		**13**						**-3.3**	**95**	**-$1**

Pannone,Thomas

Age: 26 Th: L Role RP	Health A	LIMA Plan B	
Ht: 6' 0" Wt: 200 Type xFB	PT/Exp D	Rand Var +3	
	Consist B	MM 1201	

3-6, 6.16 ERA in 73 IP at TOR. Near-3 ERA at AAA got him another MLB shot, but results got worse as skills continued to lag. Step up in SwK gives hope for more, but sustaining it will be a longshot given struggles to crack 90 mph. Simply put, unproven soft-tossing flyball pitchers in these HR-happy times aren't worthy of speculation.

Yr	Tm	W	Sv	IP	K	ERA	xERA	WHIP	xWHIP	vL+	vR+	BF/G	Ctl	Dom	Cmd	Ball%	SwK	Vel	G	L	F	H%	S%	HR/F	xHR/F	GS	APC	DOM%	DIS%	Sv%	LI	RAR	BPX	R$
15																																		
16																																		
17	aa	7	0	117	94	3.85	4.36	1.27				23.9	2.4	7.2	3.1							30%	75%									7.3	84	$5
18	TOR *	4	0	90	72	5.04	5.33	1.38	1.42	109	96	19.0	2.8	7.2	2.6	37%	9.8%	88.1	35	15	50	30%	69%	10%	11%	6	58	17%	33%	0	0.52	-9.9	50	-$5
19	TOR *	6	0	108	102	5.52	4.75	1.40	1.43	90	112	10.1	3.9	8.5	2.2	36%	11.6%	89.8	33	21	46	30%	64%	13%	15%	7	34	0%	57%	0	0.65	-13.5	61	-$4
1st Half		4	0	54	56	4.72	4.60	1.40	1.45	93	112	8.5	4.1	9.3	2.3	37%	11.2%	90.6	35	18	47	31%	70%	13%	16%	2	28	0%	50%	0	0.70	-1.4	73	$0
2nd Half		2	0	54	46	6.32	4.91	1.40	1.30	87	112	12.7	3.8	7.7	2.0	35%	12.0%	88.9	31	24	45	29%	57%	13%	14%	5	44	0%	60%	0	0.58	-12.1	48	-$7
20	**Proj**	**6**	**0**	**116**	**100**	**5.19**	**4.52**	**1.37**	**1.38**	**101**	**111**	**13.9**	**3.3**	**7.8**	**2.4**	**36%**	**10.9%**	**89.0**	**33**	**19**	**48**	**30%**	**67%**	**13%**		**14**						**-14.8**	**72**	**-$3**

Parker,Blake

Age: 35 Th: R Role RP	Health A	LIMA Plan B	
Ht: 6' 3" Wt: 225 Type Pwr	PT/Exp C	Rand Var +4	
	Consist B	MM 3411	

Keeps doing just enough to find himself in saves mix. Outlook for continued auditions is marginal at best, as concurrently rising walk rate and Ball% point to more control problems. Throw in declining velocity and a soaring line-drive rate and you're left with a high-risk, middling middleman entering the latter stages of his career.

Yr	Tm	W	Sv	IP	K	ERA	xERA	WHIP	xWHIP	vL+	vR+	BF/G	Ctl	Dom	Cmd	Ball%	SwK	Vel	G	L	F	H%	S%	HR/F	xHR/F	GS	APC	DOM%	DIS%	Sv%	LI	RAR	BPX	R$
15																																		
16	2AL *	2	20	57	58	3.89	3.31	1.21		95	97	4.2	3.4	9.1	2.7		11.1%	92.2	48	13	38	29%	70%	5%	5%	0	20			91	1.26	2.1	110	$8
17	LAA	3	8	67	86	2.54	2.77	0.83	1.01	64	77	3.6	2.1	11.5	5.4	35%	14.2%	93.5	47	18	35	24%	76%	13%	15%	0	15			73	1.20	15.1	209	$13
18	LAA	2	14	66	70	3.26	3.97	1.24	1.18	106	101	4.1	2.6	9.5	3.7	37%	11.3%	92.2	34	23	43	30%	83%	15%	16%	0	17			82	0.84	7.3	131	$7
19	2TM	3	10	61	65	4.55	4.23	1.22	1.29	96	101	4.3	3.2	9.5	3.0	38%	11.5%	91.2	38	25	37	27%	71%	22%	20%	2	17	0%	50%	91	0.96	-0.3	109	$4
1st Half		0	10	29	26	4.03	4.68	1.31	1.34	91	114	4.0	3.4	8.1	2.4	37%	10.1%	91.7	47	18	35	26%	81%	23%	21%	0	16			91	1.03	1.7	85	$4
2nd Half		3	0	32	39	5.01	3.84	1.14	1.16	101	90	4.5	3.1	10.9	3.5	39%	12.8%	90.6	29	32	39	28%	61%	20%	18%	2	18	0%	50%	0	0.89	-2.0	130	$4
20	**Proj**	**3**	**2**	**73**	**80**	**4.27**	**3.63**	**1.27**	**1.18**	**101**	**101**	**4.1**	**3.1**	**9.9**	**3.1**	**37%**	**11.9%**	**91.8**	**37**	**24**	**39**	**30%**	**73%**	**17%**		**0**						**-1.1**	**124**	**$1**

Patino,Luis

Age: 20 Th: R Role SP	Health A	LIMA Plan F	
Ht: 6' 0" Wt: 192 Type	PT/Exp F	Rand Var 0	
	Consist F	MM 0200	

Top prospect dominated High-A in SD system; started two games at Double-A and didn't disappoint. Electric fastball/slider combo gives him tools of an upper-rotation arm. Lack of third pitch keeps him vulnerable against lefties, and he has yet to throw 100 innings in a professional season. Still, given age and ceiling, he's a gem in dynasty leagues.

Yr	Tm	W	Sv	IP	K	ERA	xERA	WHIP	xWHIP	vL+	vR+	BF/G	Ctl	Dom	Cmd	Ball%	SwK	Vel	G	L	F	H%	S%	HR/F	xHR/F	GS	APC	DOM%	DIS%	Sv%	LI	RAR	BPX	R$
15																																		
16																																		
17																																		
18																																		
19																																		
1st Half																																		
2nd Half																																		
20	**Proj**	**3**	**0**	**36**	**32**	**4.22**	**4.57**	**1.71**				**20.5**	**3.5**	**7.9**	**2.3**	**37%**	**11.2%**		**41**	**21**	**38**	**37%**	**80%**	**13%**		**8**						**-0.3**	**78**	**-$5**

Paxton,James

Age: 31 Th: L Role SP	Health F	LIMA Plan B	
Ht: 6' 4" Wt: 235 Type Pwr	PT/Exp A	Rand Var +1	
	Consist B	MM 4503	

Came on strong after slow start by throwing more change-ups, on which he got double the whiffs compared to a year ago. While sum of parts profiled him as 4.00 ERA pitcher, he still owns those pre-2019 xERA and Ball% skills. Even with "F" health, they're reminders that he can give you anchor-like results in stretches.

Yr	Tm	W	Sv	IP	K	ERA	xERA	WHIP	xWHIP	vL+	vR+	BF/G	Ctl	Dom	Cmd	Ball%	SwK	Vel	G	L	F	H%	S%	HR/F	xHR/F	GS	APC	DOM%	DIS%	Sv%	LI	RAR	BPX	R$
15	SEA	3	0	67	56	3.90	4.47	1.43	1.42	145	85	22.8	3.9	7.5	1.9	40%	7.4%	94.2	48	17	34	31%	76%	11%	15%	13	85	15%	38%			0.5	67	-$3
16	SEA *	10	0	172	159	4.06	4.19	1.33	1.14	99	97	23.0	2.1	8.3	4.0	34%	12.2%	96.8	48	22	30	35%	71%	8%	9%	20	98	30%	15%			2.7	127	$6
17	SEA	12	0	136	156	2.98	3.36	1.10	1.12	61	85	23.0	2.4	10.3	4.2	35%	12.8%	95.4	45	22	33	31%	74%	8%	6%	24	95	54%	21%			23.2	171	$19
18	SEA	11	0	160	208	3.76	3.16	1.10	1.05	119	86	23.0	2.4	11.7	5.0	32%	14.8%	95.4	40	19	41	31%	71%	14%	15%	28	93	32%	18%			7.7	189	$16
19	NYY	15	0	151	186	3.82	4.03	1.28	1.22	88	101	21.8	3.3	11.1	3.4	36%	14.7%	95.5	38	19	43	32%	76%	14%	13%	29	92	34%	31%			12.7	139	$14
1st Half		5	0	64	81	4.34	4.28	1.43	1.24	99	105	21.5	3.9	11.3	2.9	36%	14.4%	95.4	35	26	40	35%	73%	13%	14%	13	90	38%	31%			1.3	121	$2
2nd Half		10	0	86	105	3.44	3.94	1.17	1.13	81	97	22.1	2.8	10.9	3.9	35%	14.9%	95.5	41	14	45	30%	78%	15%	12%	16	93	31%	31%			11.3	153	$22
20	**Proj**	**15**	**0**	**174**	**209**	**3.68**	**3.29**	**1.21**	**1.14**	**94**	**94**	**21.8**	**2.9**	**10.8**	**3.7**	**35%**	**14.0%**	**95.5**	**41**	**19**	**40**	**32%**	**74%**	**13%**		**32**						**10.0**	**156**	**$17**

Peacock,Brad

Age: 32 Th: R Role RP	Health F	LIMA Plan C	
Ht: 6' 1" Wt: 210 Type Pwr FB	PT/Exp C	Rand Var 0	
	Consist C	MM 3401	

Balky shoulder got in way just as he was getting another rotation shot. While pre-2019 BPX trend was tantalizing to those prospecting for SP value, his health grade and struggles vL are reminders of why he belongs in bullpen. In that role, he's a LIMA arm worth stashing. As a SP, you'd better deal him before he gets to 100 innings.

Yr	Tm	W	Sv	IP	K	ERA	xERA	WHIP	xWHIP	vL+	vR+	BF/G	Ctl	Dom	Cmd	Ball%	SwK	Vel	G	L	F	H%	S%	HR/F	xHR/F	GS	APC	DOM%	DIS%	Sv%	LI	RAR	BPX	R$
15	HOU	0	0	5	3	5.40	5.05	1.40		160	60	22.0	3.6	5.4	1.5		5.9%	89.9	31	31	38	31%	57%	0%	1%	1	85	0%	100%			-0.9	11	-$5
16	HOU *	5	0	149	123	5.13	5.27	1.55	1.42	97	94	20.3	3.5	7.4	2.2	38%	8.5%	91.8	41	9	49	34%	69%	14%	11%	5	49	20%	60%	0	0.40	-17.3	62	-$9
17	HOU	13	0	132	161	3.00	3.70	1.19	1.24	101	68	16.1	3.9	11.0	2.8	37%	12.5%	92.1	44	19	38	30%	77%	8%	9%	21	66	24%	14%	0	0.68	22.1	138	$17
18	HOU	3	3	65	96	3.46	2.98	1.17	1.02	130	82	4.5	2.8	13.3	4.8	37%	13.6%	92.7	38	22	40	34%	78%	18%	15%	1	19	0%	100%	50	0.88	5.5	208	$4
19	HOU	7	0	92	96	4.12	4.40	1.19	1.28	120	74	16.7	3.0	9.4	3.1	37%	9.2%	92.2	39	18	43	28%	71%	14%	14%	15	66	40%	40%	0	0.74	4.3	114	$5
1st Half		6	0	85	89	4.13	4.29	1.15	1.19	119	73	20.7	2.6	9.4	3.6	37%	9.1%	92.2	39	19	42	28%	69%	13%	14%	15	81	40%	40%	0	0.74	3.9	125	$6
2nd Half		1	0	7	7	4.05	6.83	1.65		129	93	5.2	8.1	9.5	1.2		10.2%	91.9	39	6	56	20%	89%	20%	15%	0	21			0	0.71	0.4	-35	-$14
20	**Proj**	**6**	**0**	**87**	**101**	**3.75**	**3.48**	**1.23**	**1.21**	**116**	**79**	**10.9**	**3.2**	**10.4**	**3.2**	**37%**	**11.2%**	**92.2**	**41**	**18**	**41**	**31%**	**74%**	**12%**		**3**						**4.3**	**137**	**$5**

Pena,Felix

Age: 30 Th: R Role RP	Health D	LIMA Plan C	
Ht: 6' 2" Wt: 220 Type Pwr	PT/Exp D	Rand Var +3	
	Consist C	MM 2301	

Season cut short due to a torn ACL. PRO: Dominant at times vR; misses a lot of bats; Cmd vL on two-year uptick. CON: Keeps losing zip on fastball; H% and S% variability tough to pin down; old for his amount of MLB experience. Lack of pedigree, strikeout upside make him a value stock worth taking... late.

Yr	Tm	W	Sv	IP	K	ERA	xERA	WHIP	xWHIP	vL+	vR+	BF/G	Ctl	Dom	Cmd	Ball%	SwK	Vel	G	L	F	H%	S%	HR/F	xHR/F	GS	APC	DOM%	DIS%	Sv%	LI	RAR	BPX	R$
15	aa	7	0	130	116	4.58	4.18	1.41				22.0	3.6	8.0	2.2							32%	68%									-9.9	87	-$3
16	CHC *	3	4	72	79	3.87	2.82	1.17		39	70	6.1	3.3	9.8	2.9		17.3%	93.5	39	17	44	30%	67%	13%	8%	0	12			80	1.00	2.9	133	$4
17	CHC *	3	6	73	73	5.97	6.03	1.61	1.41	105	125	6.6	4.1	9.0	2.2	39%	12.4%	94.3	35	14	51	35%	67%	16%	15%	0	24			50	0.34	-14.6	53	-$6
18	LAA *	4	0	127	114	3.98	3.96	1.29	1.25	107	86	18.0	3.1	8.1	2.7	36%	11.1%	92.4	43	24	33	30%	72%	13%	11%	17	74	18%	12%	0	0.71	2.7	92	$2
19	LAA	8	0	96	101	4.58	4.21	1.18	1.29	112	75	18.5	3.2	9.4	3.0	38%	13.0%	91.5	42	22	35	27%	66%	17%	17%	7	71	0%	29%	0	0.68	-0.9	113	$4
1st Half		5	0	70	75	4.73	4.31	1.22	1.23	118	77	18.8	3.1	9.6	3.1	38%	13.8%	91.6	39	23	38	28%	68%	19%	19%	4	72	0%	50%	0	0.68	-2.0	117	$6
2nd Half		3	0	26	26	4.15	3.96	1.08	1.29	92	70	17.8	3.5	9.0	2.6	37%	10.8%	91.3	51	20	29	25%	62%	10%	10%	3	69	0%	0%	0	0.70	1.1	107	$0
20	**Proj**	**8**	**0**	**116**	**114**	**4.51**	**3.74**	**1.26**	**1.28**	**104**	**86**	**13.0**	**3.4**	**8.9**	**2.6**	**37%**	**11.8%**	**92.2**	**43**	**21**	**35**	**29%**	**67%**	**13%**		**11**						**-5.2**	**104**	**$3**

STEPHEN NICKRAND

Peralta,Freddy

Age: 24 | Th: R | Role: RP | Ht: 5' 11" | Wt: 175 | Type: Pwr xFB
Health: B | PT/Exp: D | Consist: B | LIMA Plan: B | Rand Var: +5 | MM: 2501

Torpedoed staffs with ugly 1st half as SP, then never got another rotation shot. In truth, fluky H% and S% drove early struggles and hid elite skills, which were backed by Ball% and SwK. Though skills tailed late, ended season with 20/2 K/BB over 10 IP in September. Role ambiguity, top-tier flashes of skill make him a premium profit play. UP: 200 K

Yr Tm	W	Sv	IP	K	ERA	xERA	WHIP	xWHIP	vL+	vR+	BF/G	Ctl	Dom	Cmd	Ball%	SwK	Vel	G	L	F	H%	S%	HR/F	xHR/F	GS	APC	DOM%	DIS%	Sv%	LI	RAR	BPX	R$
15																																	
16																																	
17 aa	2	1	64	81	3.36	2.80	1.29				20.1	4.8	11.4	2.4							31%	74%									7.9	142	$2
18 MIL *	12	0	139	173	3.72	2.61	1.18	1.32	118	55	19.2	4.2	11.2	2.6	38%	11.5%	90.8	31	18	52	29%	69%	9%	12%	14	86	29%	14%	0	0.75	7.4	138	$12
19 MIL	7	1	85	115	5.29	4.28	1.46	1.25	90	114	9.8	3.9	12.2	3.1	35%	13.9%	93.6	32	24	44	37%	68%	15%	15%	8	41	25%	38%	50	0.88	-8.3	134	-$1
1st Half	3	0	58	70	5.12	4.30	1.40	1.12	98	111	16.2	2.5	10.9	4.4	33%	12.9%	92.7	33	27	41	37%	69%	16%	17%	8	65	25%	38%	0	0.84	-4.4	152	-$1
2nd Half	4	1	27	45	5.67	4.47	1.59	1.39	64	123	5.3	7.0	15.0	2.1	37%	15.8%	95.5	30	18	52	37%	67%	14%	10%	0	24			50	0.91	-3.9	97	-$1
20 Proj	**11**	**0**	**123**	**162**	**4.25**	**3.64**	**1.34**	**1.30**	**97**	**100**	**10.0**	**4.4**	**11.9**	**2.7**	**37%**	**13.5%**	**92.9**	**34**	**20**	**46**	**32%**	**73%**	**13%**		**0**						**-1.5**	**122**	**$6**

Perdomo,Luis

Age: 27 | Th: R | Role: RP | Ht: 6' 2" | Wt: 185 | Type: Con GB
Health: C | PT/Exp: C | Consist: B | LIMA Plan: B | Rand Var: 0 | MM: 2101

2-4, 4.00 ERA in 72 IP at SD. Best skills of career didn't even net a sub-4 ERA. As a SP, lack of third pitch prevents his good raw stuff from generating whiffs. Move to bullpen kept him around plate more but didn't move SwK needle much. End result is a pitcher that doesn't know how to use his tools, making him free agent fodder.

Yr Tm	W	Sv	IP	K	ERA	xERA	WHIP	xWHIP	vL+	vR+	BF/G	Ctl	Dom	Cmd	Ball%	SwK	Vel	G	L	F	H%	S%	HR/F	xHR/F	GS	APC	DOM%	DIS%	Sv%	LI	RAR	BPX	R$
15																																	
16 SD	9	0	147	105	5.71	4.20	1.59	1.35	117	114	18.9	2.8	6.4	2.3	36%	8.9%	93.6	59	20	21	35%	67%	22%	22%	20	68	10%	40%	0	0.65	-27.4	91	-$12
17 SD	8	0	164	118	4.67	4.32	1.51	1.43	107	103	24.7	3.6	6.5	1.8	38%	9.4%	94.2	62	17	21	32%	70%	16%	18%	29	88	0%	48%			-6.4	72	-$3
18 SD *	7	0	120	90	4.99	5.27	1.52	1.46	135	109	20.8	3.1	6.7	2.1	39%	7.8%	93.3	43	29	28	34%	69%	10%	12%	10	69	10%	30%	0	0.65	-12.4	56	-$7
19 SD *	4	1	87	68	3.96	4.24	1.31	1.31	103	81	6.2	2.3	7.1	3.1	32%	8.9%	94.2	53	20	28	32%	72%	10%	13%	1	22	0%	0%	25	0.83	5.8	88	$1
1st Half	1	0	31	25	2.32	4.16	1.03	1.22	98	71	6.2	2.0	7.3	3.6	34%	7.9%	94.2	48	19	33	26%	83%	10%	16%	1	22	0%	0%	0	0.74	8.3	111	$4
2nd Half	1	0	41	30	5.27	4.25	1.34	1.30	107	88	6.4	2.4	6.6	2.7	31%	9.7%	94.2	55	20	24	32%	60%	10%	10%	0	22			0	0.91	-3.9	95	$0
20 Proj	**3**	**0**	**73**	**54**	**4.56**	**3.89**	**1.37**	**1.35**	**112**	**91**	**9.8**	**2.7**	**6.7**	**2.5**	**35%**	**8.7%**	**93.9**	**52**	**22**	**26**	**32%**	**68%**	**13%**		**0**						**-3.6**	**89**	**-$3**

Perez,Martin

Age: 29 | Th: L | Role: SP | Ht: 6' 0" | Wt: 200 | Type: Con
Health: F | PT/Exp: A | Consist: A | LIMA Plan: A | Rand Var: +1 | MM: 1103

New club refined delivery and got more velocity out of arm, which helped him resurrect his career... for two months. Uptick in whiffs ended up being offset by continued shaky control, leaving him pretty much the same pitcher we've been used to (see xERA). Ugly DOM/DIS% seals it. Let others hope for something more.

Yr Tm	W	Sv	IP	K	ERA	xERA	WHIP	xWHIP	vL+	vR+	BF/G	Ctl	Dom	Cmd	Ball%	SwK	Vel	G	L	F	H%	S%	HR/F	xHR/F	GS	APC	DOM%	DIS%	Sv%	LI	RAR	BPX	R$
15 TEX *	3	0	104	68	4.73	4.69	1.49	1.39	74	110	22.5	2.3	5.9	2.5	35%	8.2%	91.8	60	18	22	35%	67%	5%	13%	14	87	21%	50%			-9.9	79	-$8
16 TEX	10	0	199	103	4.39	4.92	1.41	1.52	73	107	25.9	3.4	4.7	1.4	36%	8.3%	92.7	53	20	26	29%	70%	10%	15%	33	93	12%	40%			-5.0	26	-$1
17 TEX	13	0	185	115	4.82	4.95	1.54	1.43	88	115	25.3	3.1	5.6	1.8	38%	7.5%	93.1	47	25	28	33%	71%	13%	14%	32	97	9%	66%			-10.5	52	-$4
18 TEX	2	0	85	52	6.22	5.32	1.78	1.51	102	135	18.0	3.8	5.5	1.4	38%	7.5%	92.7	51	20	29	35%	68%	18%	17%	15	64	0%	73%	0	0.83	-21.8	29	-$17
19 MIN	10	0	165	135	5.12	5.01	1.52	1.45	77	112	23.0	3.6	7.3	2.0	35%	10.3%	94.1	48	23	29	33%	69%	15%	12%	29	87	21%	55%	0	0.73	-12.5	65	-$5
1st Half	7	0	89	82	4.15	4.58	1.36	1.38	80	94	22.6	3.8	8.3	2.2	36%	11.0%	94.3	47	24	30	31%	70%	9%	11%	14	88	36%	43%	0	0.68	3.9	77	$5
2nd Half	3	0	76	53	6.25	5.38	1.70	1.43	74	131	23.5	3.4	6.2	1.8	34%	9.4%	93.8	49	22	29	34%	68%	21%	12%	15	85	7%	67%			-16.4	52	-$16
20 Proj	**8**	**0**	**174**	**129**	**5.03**	**4.51**	**1.61**	**1.44**	**85**	**121**	**21.6**	**3.5**	**6.7**	**1.9**	**36%**	**8.9%**	**93.4**	**48**	**22**	**30**	**34%**	**72%**	**15%**		**36**						**-18.8**	**58**	**-$10**

Peters,Dillon

Age: 27 | Th: L | Role: SP | Ht: 5' 11" | Wt: 190 | Type: Con
Health: A | PT/Exp: D | Consist: D | LIMA Plan: D | Rand Var: +3 | MM: 0000

4-4, 5.38 ERA in 72 IP at LAA. Thrust into rotation work due to injuries, and boy, was it ugly. Any hope dashed by growing struggles vR. Worse, as a lefty, he has an equal number of strikeouts as walks vs LHB in his career. Even if he gets another shot, you don't want him anywhere near your roster.

Yr Tm	W	Sv	IP	K	ERA	xERA	WHIP	xWHIP	vL+	vR+	BF/G	Ctl	Dom	Cmd	Ball%	SwK	Vel	G	L	F	H%	S%	HR/F	xHR/F	GS	APC	DOM%	DIS%	Sv%	LI	RAR	BPX	R$
15																																	
16 aa	3	0	23	14	2.47	3.03	1.07				22.1	1.7	5.4	3.3							26%	81%									4.8	99	$0
17 MIA *	7	0	77	60	3.74	3.65	1.37	1.58	137	94	21.5	3.7	7.1	1.9	40%	10.4%	91.4	63	16	21	31%	72%	16%	19%	6	87	17%	50%			5.8	87	$2
18 MIA *	8	0	132	86	6.75	6.82	1.76		109	125	23.3	3.1	5.9	1.9		7.5%	90.9	44	27	30	37%	63%	14%	12%	5	72	0%	80%	0	0.68	-42.2	27	-$23
19 LAA *	8	0	129	99	5.76	6.63	1.60	1.44	94	135	19.0	3.0	6.9	2.3	36%	9.3%	91.1	40	22	38	34%	70%	20%	16%	12	75	17%	67%	0	0.68	-19.9	25	-$10
1st Half	3	0	55	44	4.62	5.47	1.51		140	122	16.9	2.4	7.2	3.0		8.4%	91.9	41	11	48	36%	72%	23%	25%	0	39			0	0.24	-0.8	72	-$7
2nd Half	5	0	74	55	6.59	7.49	1.67	1.40	81	134	20.9	3.4	6.7	2.0	36%	9.5%	90.9	40	23	37	33%	68%	19%	15%	12	86	17%	67%	0	0.82	-19.1	-6	-$12
20 Proj	**3**	**0**	**44**	**32**	**5.40**	**4.64**	**1.63**	**1.47**	**110**	**128**	**20.8**	**3.2**	**6.6**	**2.1**	**38%**	**9.8%**	**91.1**	**44**	**21**	**35**	**35%**	**71%**	**15%**		**9**						**-6.7**	**63**	**-$7**

Petit,Yusmeiro

Age: 35 | Th: R | Role: RP | Ht: 6' 1" | Wt: 255 | Type: Con xFB
Health: A | PT/Exp: C | Consist: A | LIMA Plan: A | Rand Var: -4 | MM: 3201

Without a prominent role or flashy stuff, he always seems be available, yet he keeps on producing. Credit nasty change-up and curveball. Sure, that H% won't repeat, but an 83rd-percentile exit velocity drove that more than luck. If you can get him late or for a single-digit bid, he's a reliable LIMA arm worthy of your investment.

Yr Tm	W	Sv	IP	K	ERA	xERA	WHIP	xWHIP	vL+	vR+	BF/G	Ctl	Dom	Cmd	Ball%	SwK	Vel	G	L	F	H%	S%	HR/F	xHR/F	GS	APC	DOM%	DIS%	Sv%	LI	RAR	BPX	R$
15 SF	1	1	76	59	3.67	4.34	1.18	1.22	114	96	7.5	1.8	7.0	3.9	33%	10.1%	88.5	33	21	46	29%	75%	10%	8%	1	27	0%	100%	100	0.84	2.7	106	$1
16 WAS	3	1	62	49	4.50	4.51	1.32	1.26	125	95	7.4	2.2	7.1	3.3	33%	9.0%	88.6	42	17	41	30%	73%	15%	12%	1	27	0%	0%	50	0.82	-2.4	106	-$2
17 LAA	5	4	91	101	2.76	3.64	0.95	1.06	85	70	5.9	1.8	10.0	5.6	33%	11.2%	89.6	33	18	49	28%	76%	8%	9%	1	22	100%	0%	80	0.92	18.0	171	$14
18 OAK	7	0	93	76	3.00	4.15	1.01	1.19	83	95	5.0	1.7	7.4	4.2	32%	9.4%	89.3	36	20	44	25%	78%	11%	15%	0	18			0	1.06	13.2	114	$10
19 OAK	5	0	83	71	2.71	4.16	0.81	1.14	89	68	3.9	1.1	7.7	7.1	34%	12.1%	89.2	30	21	49	22%	75%	10%	12%	0	14			0	1.36	18.4	128	$12
1st Half	2	0	46	38	2.53	4.63	0.86	1.11	80	90	4.2	1.2	7.4	6.3	33%	11.2%	89.2	25	21	55	23%	82%	10%	12%	0	16			0	1.34	11.3	113	$11
2nd Half	3	0	37	33	2.95	3.79	0.74	1.05	105	43	3.4	1.0	8.1	8.3	35%	13.3%	89.2	37	21	42	21%	65%	10%	11%	0	13			0	1.37	7.1	146	$13
20 Proj	**5**	**0**	**80**	**70**	**3.19**	**3.55**	**0.91**	**1.12**	**92**	**74**	**4.4**	**1.4**	**7.9**	**5.6**	**33%**	**11.2%**	**89.2**	**34**	**20**	**46**	**24%**	**71%**	**10%**		**0**						**9.5**	**133**	**$9**

Pineda,Michael

Age: 31 | Th: R | Role: SP | Ht: 6' 7" | Wt: 280 | Type:
Health: F | PT/Exp: C | Consist: A | LIMA Plan: A | Rand Var: 0 | MM: 3303

Return from Tommy John surgery got better as season went along. Credit skill or PED? Elite command sub-indicators still drive sub-4 ERA potential, and upside for more exists if he can find his GB tilt again. But Sept suspension puts all of it in doubt and will delay 2020 start. Steadily rising xERA and declining BPX support skepticism even if he's clean.

Yr Tm	W	Sv	IP	K	ERA	xERA	WHIP	xWHIP	vL+	vR+	BF/G	Ctl	Dom	Cmd	Ball%	SwK	Vel	G	L	F	H%	S%	HR/F	xHR/F	GS	APC	DOM%	DIS%	Sv%	LI	RAR	BPX	R$
15 NYY	12	0	161	156	4.37	3.21	1.23	1.07	102	107	24.7	1.2	8.7	7.4	32%	12.4%	92.8	48	22	30	34%	68%	15%	13%	27	94	30%	37%			-8.1	180	$6
16 NYY	6	0	176	207	4.82	3.45	1.35	1.15	109	105	23.6	2.7	10.6	3.9	35%	14.6%	94.1	46	22	33	35%	68%	17%	18%	32	94	9%	25%			-13.6	168	$1
17 NYY	8	0	96	92	4.39	3.77	1.29	1.16	101	105	24.1	2.0	8.6	4.4	34%	12.7%	93.9	51	19	31	32%	74%	22%	16%	17	91	35%	29%			-0.4	157	$3
18																																	
19 MIN	11	0	146	140	4.01	4.24	1.16	1.18	88	102	23.1	1.7	8.6	5.0	32%	12.9%	92.6	36	23	41	30%	71%	13%	14%	26	88	27%	19%			9.0	134	$12
1st Half	5	0	87	75	4.78	4.57	1.19	1.15	90	110	22.4	1.6	7.8	5.0	32%	12.5%	92.5	36	22	42	30%	65%	14%	16%	16	85	31%	31%			-2.9	122	$8
2nd Half	6	0	59	65	2.88	3.91	1.11	1.09	85	91	24.2	2.0	9.9	5.0	33%	13.5%	92.6	36	26	38	31%	81%	13%	10%	10	91	20%	0%			11.9	151	$16
20 Proj	**10**	**0**	**131**	**129**	**4.21**	**3.60**	**1.26**	**1.13**	**99**	**107**	**23.2**	**2.1**	**8.9**	**4.3**	**33%**	**13.2%**	**93.1**	**39**	**22**	**38**	**32%**	**73%**	**16%**		**23**						**-1.0**	**141**	**$6**

Pivetta,Nick

Age: 27 | Th: R | Role: RP | Ht: 6' 5" | Wt: 220 | Type: Pwr
Health: A | PT/Exp: C | Consist: C | LIMA Plan: C | Rand Var: +4 | MM: 2301

4-6, 5.38 ERA in 94 IP at PHI. Just when he looked on the cusp of a breakout, it all imploded. While fastball stayed strong, he lost feel for his off-speed pitches and couldn't throw anything over plate. On bright side, surging BPX heading into 2019 gives hope for rebound, and it could come fast if he can find feel of his soft stuff again. Bid a buck.

Yr Tm	W	Sv	IP	K	ERA	xERA	WHIP	xWHIP	vL+	vR+	BF/G	Ctl	Dom	Cmd	Ball%	SwK	Vel	G	L	F	H%	S%	HR/F	xHR/F	GS	APC	DOM%	DIS%	Sv%	LI	RAR	BPX	R$
15 aa	2	0	43	28	8.13	7.25	1.92				20.5	5.6	5.8	1.0							33%	60%									-22.3	-10	-$14
16 a/a	12	0	149	121	3.90	3.94	1.33				22.9	3.1	7.4	2.4							31%	73%									5.4	85	$7
17 PHI *	13	0	165	172	5.21	4.90	1.41	1.32	93	133	22.5	3.2	9.4	2.9	37%	9.3%	94.4	44	20	36	34%	67%	18%	14%	26	94	12%	31%			-17.3	90	$1
18 PHI	7	0	164	188	4.77	3.51	1.30	1.16	107	99	21.0	2.8	10.3	3.7	34%	12.5%	94.8	47	19	35	34%	67%	16%	15%	32	86	31%	38%	0	0.80	-12.6	156	$1
19 PHI *	9	1	135	138	4.89	4.85	1.43	1.40	114	116	14.7	4.1	9.2	2.2	37%	10.7%	94.6	43	25	32	31%	70%	22%	21%	13	54	15%	46%	100	0.78	-6.3	66	$0
1st Half	8	0	93	90	5.05	5.02	1.42	1.30	114	133	24.7	3.8	8.7	2.3	36%	10.6%	94.0	40	27	32	31%	69%	25%	23%	10	95	20%	50%			-6.2	61	$3
2nd Half	1	1	42	48	4.54	4.47	1.45	1.43	113	97	7.7	5.0	10.3	2.1	39%	11.0%	95.3	48	22	30	31%	72%	19%	15%	3	34	0%	33%	100	0.79	-0.2	80	-$6
20 Proj	**5**	**0**	**73**	**73**	**4.44**	**3.81**	**1.36**	**1.29**	**100**	**100**	**14.0**	**3.9**	**9.1**	**2.4**	**37%**	**11.2%**	**94.7**	**45**	**21**	**33**	**30%**	**72%**	**17%**		**9**						**-2.6**	**96**	**-$1**

STEPHEN NICKRAND

Plesac,Zach

Age:	25	Th:	R	Role	SP	Health	A	LIMA Plan	A
						PT/Exp	D	Rand Var	0
Ht:	6' 3"	Wt:	220	Type	Con	Consist	A	MM	1101

8-6, 3.81 ERA in 116 IP at CLE. Unheralded prospect with familiar surname delivered surprising value in debut. Problem is, MLB xERA came in at 5.00, and that ugly xWHIP provided no validation for his actual mark. And league-average SwK, Ball% don't give his skills much growth potential. View him as one of many end-rotation options.

Yr	Tm	W	Sv	IP	K	ERA	xERA	WHIP	xWHIP	vL+	vR+	BF/G	Ctl	Dom	Cmd	Ball%	SwK	Vel	G	L	F	H%	S%	HR/F	xHR/F	GS	APC	DOM%	DIS%	Sv%	LI	RAR	BPX	R$
15																																		
16																																		
17																																		
18	aa	3	0	22	18	3.35	3.74	1.26				22.4	1.8	7.3	4.1							33%	74%									2.2	131	-$2
19	CLE *	12	0	181	142	3.27	3.37	1.13	1.43	90	105	23.1	2.5	7.1	2.8	35%	9.9%	94.0	39	22	39	27%	76%	15%	14%	21	90	19%	29%			27.6	85	$19
1st Half		7	0	100	78	2.65	2.91	1.02	1.36	94	109	24.1	2.0	7.0	3.6	35%	9.9%	94.4	40	18	42	25%	80%	18%	18%	7	96	29%	14%			23.0	106	$26
2nd Half		5	0	80	63	4.05	3.95	1.27	1.38	88	103	21.9	3.2	7.1	2.2	35%	9.9%	93.7	39	25	36	28%	72%	12%	12%	14	87	14%	36%			4.5	68	$11
20	**Proj**	**8**	**0**	**116**	**91**	**4.35**	**4.26**	**1.29**	**1.37**	**95**	**111**	**23.4**	**2.9**	**7.0**	**2.4**	**35%**	**9.9%**	**94.0**	**39**	**22**	**39**	**29%**	**71%**	**13%**		**20**						**-2.8**	**75**	**$2**

Plutko,Adam

Age:	28	Th:	R	Role	SP	Health	A	LIMA Plan	F
						PT/Exp	D	Rand Var	+2
Ht:	6' 3"	Wt:	215	Type	Con xFB	Consist	F	MM	0001

7-5, 4.86 ERA in 109 IP at CLE. Acted as rotation filler in second extended MLB look. Chances of a third audition slim due to lack of swing-and-miss stuff, flyball tilt, and ugly DOM/DIS%. In fact, it all came crashing down in September (6.49 ERA, 1.75 WHIP). There are much better end-game dart throws out there.

Yr	Tm	W	Sv	IP	K	ERA	xERA	WHIP	xWHIP	vL+	vR+	BF/G	Ctl	Dom	Cmd	Ball%	SwK	Vel	G	L	F	H%	S%	HR/F	xHR/F	GS	APC	DOM%	DIS%	Sv%	LI	RAR	BPX	R$
15	aa	9	0	116	72	4.05	3.97	1.25				24.9	1.9	5.6	2.9							30%	70%									-1.2	81	$3
16	CLE *	9	0	165	98	5.30	5.13	1.52		45	177	23.9	3.0	5.3	1.8		3.8%	90.9	23	15	62	33%	66%	13%	11%	0	40			0	0.10	-22.7	42	-$9
17	aaa	7	0	136	74	8.43	7.99	1.92				26.8	4.1	4.9	1.2							35%	58%									-68.2	-28	-$32
18	CLE *	11	1	163	123	3.71	3.75	1.11	1.32	143	99	20.6	2.3	6.8	3.0	35%	9.1%	91.1	27	16	57	25%	74%	15%	15%	12	75	17%	42%	100	0.55	8.8	76	$13
19	CLE *	8	0	127	90	5.52	5.31	1.37	1.36	108	104	21.2	2.2	6.4	2.9	34%	8.8%	91.1	31	23	46	31%	64%	14%	11%	20	85	10%	45%	0	0.70	-15.9	52	-$4
1st Half		4	0	54	38	6.50	5.88	1.39	1.16	97	123	20.5	1.5	6.4	4.4	32%	9.2%	91.0	32	24	44	33%	57%	19%	13%	6	83	0%	33%	0	0.62	-13.2	73	-$9
2nd Half		4	0	73	52	4.81	5.67	1.36	1.35	114	95	22.4	2.7	6.4	2.4	36%	8.6%	91.2	31	23	46	30%	69%	11%	11%	14	87	14%	50%			-2.7	56	$0
20	**Proj**	**6**	**0**	**102**	**70**	**5.14**	**4.89**	**1.39**	**1.29**	**120**	**102**	**22.2**	**2.5**	**6.2**	**2.4**	**34%**	**9.0%**	**91.1**	**29**	**21**	**50**	**30%**	**68%**	**11%**		**19**						**-12.4**	**57**	**-$4**

Poche,Colin

Age:	26	Th:	L	Role	RP	Health	A	LIMA Plan	F
						PT/Exp	F	Rand Var	+5
Ht:	6' 3"	Wt:	235	Type	Pwr xFB	Consist	F	MM	3500

5-5, 4.70 ERA in 52 IP at TAM. Three reasons why there's something good here despite mediocre MLB debut... 1) Electric early (193 BPV in Jun, 224 BPV in Jul) before fading late; 2) filthy SwK, strong Ball% support 1st half Cmd; 3) punished by fluky H% and S%. As an xFB pitcher, there's blowup risk. But with opportunity, could be in saves mix.

Yr	Tm	W	Sv	IP	K	ERA	xERA	WHIP	xWHIP	vL+	vR+	BF/G	Ctl	Dom	Cmd	Ball%	SwK	Vel	G	L	F	H%	S%	HR/F	xHR/F	GS	APC	DOM%	DIS%	Sv%	LI	RAR	BPX	R$
15																																		
16																																		
17																																		
18	a/a	6	2	66	96	1.02	1.23	0.89				6.1	2.7	13.1	4.9							29%	91%									25.5	221	$15
19	TAM *	7	2	80	113	5.71	4.14	1.25	1.15	82	89	4.6	3.2	12.7	3.9	33%	17.6%	93.0	18	19	62	34%	57%	13%	11%	0	17			29	1.63	-11.8	132	$1
1st Half		3	0	40	58	6.36	4.77	1.38		72	59	5.3	2.4	12.9	5.5		22.6%	92.7	12	27	62	42%	54%	6%	4%	0	16			0	1.70	-9.3	169	-$4
2nd Half		4	2	39	55	5.03	4.27	1.12	1.19	85	98	4.1	4.1	12.6	3.1	34%	16.2%	93.1	20	17	63	24%	61%	15%	13%	0	18			33	1.60	-2.6	124	$6
20	**Proj**	**5**	**0**	**51**	**73**	**4.11**	**3.46**	**1.10**	**1.31**	**72**	**87**	**5.0**	**3.1**	**12.9**	**4.1**	**37%**	**16.2%**	**93.1**	**20**	**17**	**63**	**31%**	**65%**	**8%**		**0**						**0.2**	**167**	**$2**

Pomeranz,Drew

Age:	31	Th:	L	Role	RP	Health	D	LIMA Plan	F
						PT/Exp	B	Rand Var	+5
Ht:	6' 6"	Wt:	240	Type	Pwr	Consist	F	MM	3401

Starter or reliever? You decide... SP: 5.97 ERA, 1.66 WHIP, 2.4 Cmd. RP: 1.88 ERA, 0.84 WHIP, 6.3 Cmd. That transition happened in 2nd half, and explosion in skills out of 'pen came with backing of elite SwK and Ball%. As long as they don't get all excited now and send him back to rotation, there's something interesting here... UP: 20 Sv

Yr	Tm	W	Sv	IP	K	ERA	xERA	WHIP	xWHIP	vL+	vR+	BF/G	Ctl	Dom	Cmd	Ball%	SwK	Vel	G	L	F	H%	S%	HR/F	xHR/F	GS	APC	DOM%	DIS%	Sv%	LI	RAR	BPX	R$
15	OAK	5	3	86	82	3.66	3.84	1.19	1.30	60	106	6.7	3.2	8.6	2.6	37%	11.6%	91.5	43	21	36	28%	71%	9%	11%	9	27	22%	33%	50	1.27	3.2	105	$5
16	2 TM	11	0	171	186	3.32	3.71	1.18	1.25	87	90	22.7	3.4	9.8	2.9	37%	11.7%	90.3	46	17	37	28%	77%	14%	13%	30	92	30%	27%	0	0.83	18.3	128	$16
17	BOS	17	0	174	174	3.32	4.22	1.35	1.31	103	94	23.1	3.6	9.0	2.5	38%	10.3%	91.3	43	22	35	32%	79%	11%	13%	32	96	19%	22%			22.3	104	$16
18	BOS *	3	0	101	77	6.35	6.70	1.76	1.56	96	132	14.5	5.6	6.9	1.2	39%	7.5%	89.3	37	24	39	31%	69%	13%	16%	11	56	0%	64%	0	0.63	-27.5	5	-$18
19	2 NL	2	2	104	137	4.85	3.97	1.43	1.25	88	115	9.9	3.8	11.9	3.1	36%	11.6%	92.7	39	23	38	35%	73%	21%	18%	18	43	11%	39%	100	0.99	-4.4	139	-$2
1st Half		2	0	63	77	6.25	4.68	1.72	1.30	102	130	19.9	4.3	10.9	2.6	38%	9.7%	91.9	37	27	36	39%	69%	23%	17%	15	85	13%	40%			-13.6	106	-$9
2nd Half		0	2	41	60	2.66	3.01	0.98	1.03	64	88	5.0	3.1	13.3	4.3	33%	15.3%	93.8	44	14	43	27%	82%	18%	19%	3	22	0%	33%	100	1.11	9.3	193	$9
20	**Proj**	**3**	**0**	**73**	**82**	**3.87**	**3.63**	**1.29**	**1.28**	**80**	**105**	**7.0**	**3.7**	**10.2**	**2.8**	**37%**	**10.9%**	**91.6**	**41**	**21**	**39**	**30%**	**76%**	**16%**		**0**						**2.6**	**117**	**$1**

Ponce de Leon,Daniel

Age:	28	Th:	R	Role	RP	Health	A	LIMA Plan	B
						PT/Exp	D	Rand Var	0
Ht:	6' 3"	Wt:	200	Type	Pwr	Consist	B	MM	1200

1-2, 3.70 ERA in 49 IP at STL. Unproven swingman with shaky control offers little hope for anything more in spite of ability to miss bats. High volume of balls makes control improvement unlikely. Without it, little hope to stick as SP. And control out of bullpen (7 BB in 14 IP) wasn't any better in a small sample. We need to see more. And better.

Yr	Tm	W	Sv	IP	K	ERA	xERA	WHIP	xWHIP	vL+	vR+	BF/G	Ctl	Dom	Cmd	Ball%	SwK	Vel	G	L	F	H%	S%	HR/F	xHR/F	GS	APC	DOM%	DIS%	Sv%	LI	RAR	BPX	R$
15																																		
16	aa	9	0	151	97	4.47	4.01	1.40				23.6	3.5	5.8	1.7							30%	68%									-5.1	62	-$1
17	aaa	2	0	29	19	2.74	3.32	1.30				19.9	4.2	6.0	1.4							26%	81%									5.8	67	-$2
18	STL *	9	1	130	117	2.64	3.04	1.29	1.34	62	102	17.8	4.4	8.1	1.8	36%	13.3%	93.4	34	24	41	28%	80%	6%	11%	4	53	0%	0%	100	0.78	24.2	98	$11
19	STL *	9	0	134	118	3.63	3.78	1.37	1.47	69	101	19.3	4.8	7.9	1.7	37%	12.0%	93.4	45	16	39	27%	76%	13%	13%	8	66	25%	50%	0	0.74	14.5	70	$6
1st Half		4	0	76	61	4.26	4.50	1.47	1.30	54	91	21.9	4.9	7.2	1.5	37%	12.2%	93.6	47	9	44	28%	74%	15%	14%	3	86	33%	0%	0	0.61	2.3	50	$2
2nd Half		5	0	57	57	2.79	2.81	1.23	1.51	76	109	16.6	4.6	8.9	1.9	37%	11.8%	93.3	44	21	35	26%	79%	11%	13%	5	58	20%	80%	0	0.80	12.1	97	$12
20	**Proj**	**4**	**0**	**58**	**50**	**3.91**	**4.44**	**1.33**	**1.39**	**71**	**106**	**18.8**	**4.4**	**7.8**	**1.8**	**37%**	**12.5%**	**93.4**	**41**	**19**	**40**	**28%**	**71%**	**7%**		**11**						**1.7**	**46**	**$0**

Porcello,Rick

Age:	31	Th:	R	Role	SP	Health	A	LIMA Plan	C
						PT/Exp	A	Rand Var	+2
Ht:	6' 5"	Wt:	205	Type	Con	Consist	C	MM	2203

It'd be easy to blame this blowup on a bad S%, but the problems ran deeper. As swinging-strike rate continues to wane, room for error is becoming razor thin. Whiff rates on sinker and change are in two-year declines, so we can't assume return to above-par BPX. His speculative value to you lies at the back of your rotation.

Yr	Tm	W	Sv	IP	K	ERA	xERA	WHIP	xWHIP	vL+	vR+	BF/G	Ctl	Dom	Cmd	Ball%	SwK	Vel	G	L	F	H%	S%	HR/F	xHR/F	GS	APC	DOM%	DIS%	Sv%	LI	RAR	BPX	R$
15	BOS	9	0	172	149	4.92	3.77	1.36	1.20	112	106	26.3	2.0	7.8	3.9	35%	9.0%	91.0	46	22	33	34%	67%	14%	14%	28	98	43%	32%			-20.3	132	-$4
16	BOS	22	0	223	189	3.15	3.72	1.01	1.12	81	92	27.0	1.3	7.6	5.9	33%	8.7%	90.2	43	19	38	28%	73%	9%	13%	33	103	55%	9%			28.7	147	$32
17	BOS	11	0	203	181	4.65	4.49	1.40	1.21	113	108	26.8	2.1	8.0	3.8	33%	9.9%	91.1	39	21	40	34%	73%	15%	14%	33	103	30%	24%			-7.3	125	$3
18	BOS	17	0	191	190	4.28	3.76	1.18	1.17	99	94	24.5	2.3	8.9	4.0	34%	9.1%	90.4	44	20	36	30%	68%	14%	14%	33	94	27%	24%			-3.1	140	$13
19	BOS	14	0	174	143	5.52	5.12	1.39	1.32	109	106	24.0	2.3	7.4	3.2	33%	8.4%	90.5	38	20	41	32%	64%	13%	15%	32	93	16%	41%			-21.9	94	-$2
1st Half		5	0	94	76	5.07	5.31	1.40	1.33	104	101	24.4	2.9	7.3	2.5	34%	8.2%	90.7	40	19	41	32%	66%	10%	16%	17	92	24%	41%			-6.6	78	-$3
2nd Half		9	0	80	67	6.05	5.01	1.38	1.19	114	112	23.5	1.7	7.5	4.5	32%	8.7%	90.2	36	22	42	33%	61%	16%	15%	15	93	7%	40%			-15.3	114	$0
20	**Proj**	**13**	**0**	**160**	**140**	**4.83**	**3.91**	**1.32**	**1.21**	**107**	**103**	**23.6**	**2.1**	**7.9**	**3.7**	**33%**	**8.9%**	**90.5**	**40**	**21**	**39**	**32%**	**68%**	**14%**		**28**						**-13.4**	**119**	**$4**

Pressly,Ryan

Age:	31	Th:	R	Role	RP	Health	D	LIMA Plan	B
						PT/Exp	C	Rand Var	+1
Ht:	6' 3"	Wt:	210	Type	Pwr	Consist	B	MM	5510

Good-turned-great reliever, and it's legit. Skills have surged with higher leverage use. Filthy SwK%, Ball% put yet another Cmd uptick on horizon, and GB lean limits blowup potential. Fluky liner off knee caused IP dip, so no worries there. While others speculate on sexier names, you'll draft skills and hope for opportunity. With it... UP: 30 Sv

Yr	Tm	W	Sv	IP	K	ERA	xERA	WHIP	xWHIP	vL+	vR+	BF/G	Ctl	Dom	Cmd	Ball%	SwK	Vel	G	L	F	H%	S%	HR/F	xHR/F	GS	APC	DOM%	DIS%	Sv%	LI	RAR	BPX	R$
15	MIN	3	0	28	22	2.93	4.39	1.41		93	88	4.4	3.9	7.2	1.8		9.4%	94.2	47	20	33	33%	77%	0%	4%	0	16			0	0.93	3.5	58	-$2
16	MIN	6	1	75	67	3.70	4.36	1.35	1.27	89	105	4.6	2.7	8.0	2.9	35%	11.8%	95.1	39	24	36	33%	76%	10%	14%	0	17			17	1.19	4.5	103	$2
17	MIN	2	0	61	61	4.70	3.71	1.16	1.22	108	84	4.4	2.8	9.0	3.2	34%	12.9%	95.8	51	17	33	27%	64%	19%	15%	0	16			0	0.94	-2.6	138	-$1
18	2 AL	2	2	71	101	2.54	2.69	1.11	1.04	70	92	3.8	2.8	12.8	4.6	33%	18.0%	95.8	52	17	32	34%	81%	12%	14%	0	14			25	1.16	14.1	213	$7
19	HOU	2	3	54	72	2.32	2.58	0.90	1.01	48	96	3.8	2.0	11.9	6.0	31%	18.0%	95.6	51	28	21	28%	81%	22%	21%	0	15			38	1.25	14.7	207	$8
1st Half		1	3	37	41	1.47	2.63	0.74	0.95	44	89	3.8	1.0	10.1	10.3	29%	16.3%	95.7	53	25	22	23%	91%	20%	18%	0	15			43	1.28	13.7	202	$11
2nd Half		1	0	18	31	4.08	2.37	1.25	1.04	56	108	3.9	4.1	15.8	3.9	35%	21.1%	95.4	46	34	20	39%	70%	29%	29%	0	16			0	1.19	0.9	216	$0
20	**Proj**	**3**	**2**	**65**	**88**	**2.95**	**2.54**	**1.11**	**1.07**	**67**	**97**	**3.8**	**2.8**	**12.1**	**4.3**	**33%**	**17.4%**	**95.6**	**49**	**25**	**27**	**32%**	**78%**	**18%**		**0**						**9.7**	**194**	**$6**

STEPHEN NICKRAND

Price,David

Age: 34	Th: L	Role SP	Health F	LIMA Plan A	
Ht: 6' 5"	Wt: 215	Type Pwr	PT/Exp B	Rand Var +4	
			Consist A	MM 3403	

Wrist injury resulted in Sept surgery and likely contributed to late fade. Healthy version hurt by H% more than own doing, as skills were even better than prior levels. He's offsetting declining velocity by developing curve into strikeout pitch, in tandem with already strong change-up. There's profit here now...as long as you use 150 IP as baseline.

Yr	Tm	W	Sv	IP	K	ERA	xERA	WHIP	xWHIP	vL+	vR+	BF/G	Ctl	Dom	Cmd	Ball%	SwK	Vel	G	L	F	H%	S%	HR/F	xHR/F	GS	APC	DOM%	DIS%	Sv%	LI	RAR	BPX	R$
15	2 AL	18	0	220	225	2.45	3.36	1.08	1.12	90	86	27.8	1.9	9.2	4.8	31%	12.3%	94.2	40	23	36	30%	80%	8%	10%	32	106	63%	9%			41.1	157	$33
16	BOS	17	0	230	228	3.99	3.60	1.20	1.14	102	97	27.2	2.0	8.9	4.6	32%	12.1%	92.9	44	22	34	32%	71%	14%	14%	35	103	40%	23%			5.6	154	$17
17	BOS	6	0	75	76	3.38	4.14	1.19	1.23	65	94	19.8	2.9	9.2	3.2	35%	12.8%	94.3	40	22	39	30%	75%	10%	13%	11	78	27%	36%	0	0.85	9.1	126	$5
18	BOS	16	0	176	177	3.58	3.83	1.14	1.19	92	97	24.1	2.6	9.1	3.5	35%	10.2%	92.7	40	21	39	28%	74%	13%	15%	30	91	43%	27%			12.4	129	$18
19	BOS	7	0	107	128	4.28	3.86	1.31	1.18	88	104	20.8	2.7	10.7	4.0	34%	11.8%	92.0	41	24	35	35%	71%	14%	16%	22	85	23%	23%			3.0	152	$4
1st Half		5	0	72	82	3.36	3.53	1.12	1.06	59	94	20.9	1.9	10.2	5.5	34%	13.0%	92.0	44	22	34	33%	73%	11%	16%	14	83	29%	21%			10.2	170	$10
2nd Half		2	0	35	46	6.17	4.65	1.71	1.27	122	124	20.8	4.4	11.8	2.7	35%	9.8%	92.0	35	27	39	40%	69%	21%	16%	8	88	13%	25%			-7.2	117	-$10
20	**Proj**	**11**	**0**	**145**	**163**	**3.75**	**3.37**	**1.20**	**1.19**	**88**	**97**	**22.8**	**2.8**	**10.1**	**3.6**	**34%**	**11.1%**	**92.7**	**39**	**23**	**37**	**30%**	**75%**	**16%**		**26**						**7.2**	**142**	**$12**

Pruitt,Austin

Age: 30	Th: R	Role RP	Health A	LIMA Plan F	
Ht: 5' 10"	Wt: 185	Type Con GB	PT/Exp D	Rand Var +4	
			Consist F	MM 2100	

3-0, 4.40 ERA in 47 IP at TAM. In age of strikeouts-or-bust, pitchers like this struggle to find a niche. Contact-oriented approach leaves him in hands of defense, and when he's not hitting his spots, he gets hammered (see .937 oOPS vR). And don't be drawn in by SwK spike, as it still falls below average level of a reliever. Next.

Yr	Tm	W	Sv	IP	K	ERA	xERA	WHIP	xWHIP	vL+	vR+	BF/G	Ctl	Dom	Cmd	Ball%	SwK	Vel	G	L	F	H%	S%	HR/F	xHR/F	GS	APC	DOM%	DIS%	Sv%	LI	RAR	BPX	R$
15	aa	10	0	160	100	3.76	4.16	1.44				26.2	2.2	5.6	2.5							35%	72%									4.1	91	$0
16	aaa	8	0	163	120	5.47	6.04	1.54				25.3	1.8	6.7	3.8							36%	68%									-25.6	78	-$11
17	TAM *	7	2	108	92	4.96	4.90	1.40	1.28	93	125	11.6	2.0	7.7	3.8	34%	10.1%	91.6	48	21	32	35%	67%	13%	13%	8	44	25%	13%	67	0.61	-8.0	105	$0
18	TAM *	5	5	111	80	4.40	3.51	1.18	1.32	94	101	12.0	2.0	6.5	3.3	33%	9.7%	91.9	48	18	33	29%	63%	9%	10%	0	45			83	0.53	-3.4	104	$4
19	TAM *	6	0	96	78	5.88	6.43	1.60	1.29	79	125	13.3	2.4	7.3	3.0	33%	11.4%	91.9	52	20	28	36%	67%	18%	14%	2	51	50%	0%	0	0.72	-16.3	52	-$9
1st Half		4	0	51	38	6.87	7.02	1.79	1.43	91	138	13.0	3.0	6.8	2.3	34%	11.7%	92.2	60	17	23	39%	63%	18%	9%	0	36			0	0.69	-14.8	36	-$14
2nd Half		2	0	48	40	4.54	5.33	1.32	1.16	75	118	14.1	1.8	7.6	4.3	33%	11.3%	91.8	48	22	30	32%	73%	19%	16%	2	63	50%	0%	0	0.73	-0.2	85	-$3
20	**Proj**	**2**	**0**	**44**	**34**	**4.83**	**3.85**	**1.40**	**1.29**	**93**	**126**	**13.5**	**2.1**	**7.0**	**3.3**	**34%**	**10.6%**	**91.9**	**51**	**19**	**30**	**33%**	**69%**	**15%**		**5**						**-3.7**	**113**	**-$4**

Puk,A.J.

Age: 25	Th: L	Role SP	Health C	LIMA Plan A	
Ht: 6' 7"	Wt: 238	Type Pwr	PT/Exp F	Rand Var 0	
			Consist A	MM 3401	

2-0, 3.18 ERA in 11 IP at OAK. Handled carefully in first season after Tommy John surgery, this premium prospect is expected to transition back into starting role. Add to his electric fastball/slider combo an ability to produce grounders, and floor is higher than that of many prospects. If he can master a third pitch, he'll blossom in a hurry.

Yr	Tm	W	Sv	IP	K	ERA	xERA	WHIP	xWHIP	vL+	vR+	BF/G	Ctl	Dom	Cmd	Ball%	SwK	Vel	G	L	F	H%	S%	HR/F	xHR/F	GS	APC	DOM%	DIS%	Sv%	LI	RAR	BPX	R$
15																																		
16																																		
17	aa	2	0	64	71	4.95	4.00	1.40				21.2	3.3	10.0	3.0							30%	64%									4.7	137	$4
18																																		
19	OAK *	6	0	31	37	4.64	4.50	1.27	1.33	117	73	5.1	3.2	10.6	3.3	36%	14.4%	97.1	48	10	41	30%	70%	8%	1%	0	20			0	1.00	-0.5	95	-$1
1st Half		0	0	2	3	5.55	7.42	2.22		0	0	10.6	4.5	14.1	3.2							58%	72%	0%		0	0					-0.3	142	-$15
2nd Half		6	0	29	34	4.60	4.32	1.20		118	72	4.9	3.1	10.3	3.3		14.4%	97.1	48	10	41	28%	70%	8%	1%	0	20			0	1.00	-0.3	92	$0
20	**Proj**	**8**	**0**	**87**	**94**	**3.90**	**3.50**	**1.25**				**21.1**	**3.5**	**9.7**	**2.8**	**36%**	**14.0%**		**45**	**21**	**34**	**30%**	**73%**	**15%**		**17**						**2.7**	**119**	**$5**

Quantrill,Cal

Age: 25	Th: R	Role SP	Health A	LIMA Plan C	
Ht: 6' 3"	Wt: 208	Type Con	PT/Exp D	Rand Var +3	
			Consist C	MM 1101	

6-8, 5.16 ERA in 103 IP at SD. MLB debut saw flashes of promise (see 1st half SwK), but sum of toolbox underwhelmed. Out of four-pitch mix, only slider generated whiffs, which drove SwK down as year went along. And solid control not validated by Ball%, so walks could inch up, too. DOM/DIS% cements his high-risk profile.

Yr	Tm	W	Sv	IP	K	ERA	xERA	WHIP	xWHIP	vL+	vR+	BF/G	Ctl	Dom	Cmd	Ball%	SwK	Vel	G	L	F	H%	S%	HR/F	xHR/F	GS	APC	DOM%	DIS%	Sv%	LI	RAR	BPX	R$
15																																		
16																																		
17	aa	1	0	42	29	5.51	7.11	1.88				24.9	3.5	6.1	1.7							39%	73%									-6.0	26	-$9
18	a/a	9	0	148	106	5.16	5.50	1.55				23.1	2.5	6.5	2.6							36%	68%									-18.4	67	-$10
19	SD *	10	0	140	116	4.95	4.44	1.33	1.30	112	78	19.4	2.5	7.5	2.9	37%	10.4%	94.5	44	21	35	32%	65%	14%	14%	18	77	11%	44%	0	0.83	-7.7	80	$2
1st Half		6	0	74	59	4.53	4.43	1.38	1.30	131	67	18.3	2.9	7.2	2.5	39%	12.5%	94.8	50	19	31	32%	69%	15%	16%	6	65	0%	33%	0	0.91	-0.2	75	$3
2nd Half		4	0	66	57	5.43	4.71	1.27	1.23	101	83	21.8	2.2	7.7	3.6	36%	9.1%	94.3	40	23	37	31%	59%	13%	13%	12	87	17%	50%	0	0.77	-7.5	107	$0
20	**Proj**	**7**	**0**	**116**	**89**	**4.93**	**4.26**	**1.48**	**1.26**	**126**	**87**	**21.6**	**2.6**	**6.9**	**2.7**	**37%**	**10.5%**	**94.5**	**44**	**21**	**35**	**34%**	**70%**	**13%**		**23**						**-11.2**	**88**	**-$4**

Quintana,Jose

Age: 31	Th: L	Role SP	Health A	LIMA Plan A	
Ht: 6' 1"	Wt: 220	Type	PT/Exp A	Rand Var +2	
			Consist A	MM 2203	

R$ (heading south) and xERA (heading north) are the columns to look at here. That combination shows his prior near-3 ERA baseline's a thing of the past. Then add a Ball% that shows he's playing with fire to his dwindling Dom, and you're left with a risky innings-eater whose sole value comes from the fickleness of wins.

Yr	Tm	W	Sv	IP	K	ERA	xERA	WHIP	xWHIP	vL+	vR+	BF/G	Ctl	Dom	Cmd	Ball%	SwK	Vel	G	L	F	H%	S%	HR/F	xHR/F	GS	APC	DOM%	DIS%	Sv%	LI	RAR	BPX	R$
15	CHW	9	0	206	177	3.36	3.60	1.27	1.19	91	104	26.9	1.9	7.7	4.0	35%	9.5%	91.6	47	23	30	33%	75%	9%	10%	32	105	38%	16%			15.4	134	$11
16	CHW	13	0	208	181	3.20	3.98	1.16	1.21	88	95	26.2	2.2	7.8	3.6	37%	8.1%	92.1	40	21	39	30%	76%	10%	7%	32	103	47%	19%			25.3	119	$21
17	2 TM	11	0	189	207	4.15	3.71	1.22	1.19	77	99	24.7	2.9	9.9	3.4	38%	8.9%	92.1	45	21	34	31%	69%	13%	12%	32	99	31%	22%			4.8	147	$13
18	CHC	13	0	174	158	4.03	4.28	1.32	1.35	95	104	23.1	3.5	8.2	2.3	38%	8.3%	91.6	43	22	34	29%	74%	15%	15%	32	91	28%	34%			2.6	84	$7
19	CHC	13	0	171	152	4.68	4.49	1.39	1.29	82	107	23.3	2.4	8.0	3.3	38%	8.7%	91.4	44	25	31	34%	68%	12%	13%	31	88	23%	45%	0	0.80	-3.8	110	$4
1st Half		5	0	94	78	4.21	4.66	1.37	1.30	92	104	23.8	2.8	7.5	2.7	37%	9.3%	91.4	45	23	32	32%	73%	13%	13%	16	90	25%	50%	0	0.80	3.4	90	$4
2nd Half		8	0	77	74	5.26	4.26	1.40	1.17	66	111	22.7	2.0	8.6	4.4	38%	8.0%	91.4	44	26	30	37%	63%	11%	13%	15	86	20%	40%			-7.2	135	$4
20	**Proj**	**12**	**0**	**174**	**160**	**4.38**	**3.78**	**1.35**	**1.25**	**85**	**108**	**23.0**	**2.8**	**8.3**	**3.0**	**38%**	**8.5%**	**91.6**	**44**	**23**	**33**	**32%**	**71%**	**14%**		**32**						**-4.9**	**111**	**$5**

Rainey,Tanner

Age: 27	Th: R	Role RP	Health A	LIMA Plan A	
Ht: 6' 2"	Wt: 235	Type Pwr GB	PT/Exp F	Rand Var +5	
			Consist A	MM 2500	

2-3, 3.91 ERA in 48 IP at WAS. Just looking at pure stuff, he'd be an intriguing dollar play given ability to both pump out whiffs and grounders. Problem is, he's got no idea how to throw it over the plate—and it's been a career-long issue. That bugaboo will keep him relegated to low-leverage work. Tuck away the upside, but monitor from afar.

Yr	Tm	W	Sv	IP	K	ERA	xERA	WHIP	xWHIP	vL+	vR+	BF/G	Ctl	Dom	Cmd	Ball%	SwK	Vel	G	L	F	H%	S%	HR/F	xHR/F	GS	APC	DOM%	DIS%	Sv%	LI	RAR	BPX	R$
15																																		
16																																		
17	aa	1	4	17	23	2.68	4.27	1.47				5.2	7.3	12.1	1.7							24%	92%									3.5	85	-$1
18	CIN *	7	3	58	60	6.06	4.42	1.65		215	183	5.0	7.9	9.3	1.2		12.2%	97.8	31	23	46	27%	64%	33%	21%	0	24			50	0.41	-13.7	72	-$6
19	WAS *	4	2	66	99	4.20	4.06	1.54	1.49	124	70	4.3	6.9	13.4	1.9	40%	17.7%	97.8	53	18	29	33%	75%	21%	22%	0	17			22	0.71	2.5	113	-$1
1st Half		3	2	35	50	5.14	4.59	1.61	1.46	153	67	4.4	6.6	12.8	1.9	40%	19.2%	97.5	49	19	32	35%	70%	25%	24%	0	18			22	0.97	-2.7	102	-$2
2nd Half		1	0	31	49	3.16	3.50	1.47	1.45	112	73	4.1	7.2	14.1	2.0	39%	16.8%	97.9	55	17	28	31%	81%	19%	19%	0	17			0	0.55	5.2	101	$0
20	**Proj**	**5**	**0**	**58**	**76**	**4.35**	**3.93**	**1.58**	**1.46**	**134**	**75**	**4.5**	**7.4**	**11.9**	**1.6**	**40%**	**17.8%**	**97.8**	**53**	**18**	**30**	**30%**	**75%**	**17%**		**0**						**-1.4**	**52**	**-$3**

Ramirez,Nick

Age: 30	Th: L	Role RP	Health A	LIMA Plan C	
Ht: 6' 3"	Wt: 240	Type	PT/Exp D	Rand Var 0	
			Consist C	MM 0000	

5-4, 4.07 ERA in 80 IP at DET. Upper-quartile SwK not congruent with a fastball that only occasionally cracks 90 mph. Credit one of the better change-ups in MLB for that anomaly. But it also means hitters have to chase the pitch, as high Ball% shows. That's a poor recipe for sustained success, and at age 30, his time is running out.

Yr	Tm	W	Sv	IP	K	ERA	xERA	WHIP	xWHIP	vL+	vR+	BF/G	Ctl	Dom	Cmd	Ball%	SwK	Vel	G	L	F	H%	S%	HR/F	xHR/F	GS	APC	DOM%	DIS%	Sv%	LI	RAR	BPX	R$
15																																		
16																																		
17	a/a	7	3	79	43	1.88	3.45	1.26				6.6	3.1	4.9	1.6							27%	89%									24.3	59	$9
18	a/a	11	1	71	39	5.07	5.23	1.65				8.2	4.9	4.9	1.0							31%	70%									-8.1	27	-$5
19	DET *	6	0	104	95	3.96	4.83	1.44	1.43	85	107	8.7	3.6	8.3	2.3	39%	13.1%	89.8	46	20	34	32%	77%	14%	17%	0	29			0	0.91	7.0	68	$1
1st Half		4	0	57	53	3.86	5.19	1.44	1.33	78	105	12.9	3.0	8.3	2.8	38%	12.8%	89.5	42	17	40	34%	79%	15%	18%	0	40			0	0.58	4.6	71	$2
2nd Half		2	0	46	42	4.08	4.73	1.45	1.43	88	109	6.3	4.3	8.2	1.9	40%	13.3%	89.9	49	22	29	31%	74%	13%	15%	0	24			0	1.06	2.4	64	-$1
20	**Proj**	**5**	**0**	**58**	**42**	**4.53**	**4.63**	**1.49**	**1.39**	**92**	**116**	**7.7**	**4.1**	**6.6**	**1.6**	**39%**	**13.1%**	**89.7**	**46**	**20**	**33**	**30%**	**73%**	**14%**		**0**						**-2.7**	**38**	**-$3**

STEPHEN NICKRAND

Ramirez,Noe

Age: 30	Th: R	Role RP	Health B	LIMA Plan A
Ht: 6' 3"	Wt: 205	Type Pwr	PT/Exp D	Rand Var +1
			Consist A	MM 3401

PRO: Keeps refining control; steady BPX improvement each year; sinker/change-up combo makes up for lack of velocity. CON: Steady Ball% caps further Ctl reduction; LI reflects lack of trust from skippers; xERA validates recent 4.00 ERA baseline. In the end, he's only worth your time as a $1 LIMA reliever in very deep leagues.

Yr Tm	W	Sv	IP	K	ERA	xERA	WHIP	xWHIP	vL+	vR+	BF/G	Ctl	Dom	Cmd	Ball%	SwK	Vel	G	L	F	H%	S%	HR/F	xHR/F	GS	APC	DOM%	DIS%	Sv%	LI	RAR	BPX	R$
15 BOS *	4	3	56	43	3.63	4.36	1.52		73	122	5.1	4.5	7.0	1.5		12.4%	89.8	41	18	41	32%	77%	19%	20%	0	15			75	1.02	2.3	66	-$1
16 BOS *	2	7	57	56	3.88	5.97	1.66		117	151	5.8	3.5	8.8	2.5		12.4%	89.7	36	22	42	38%	81%	27%	25%	0	16			88	0.59	2.1	70	-$1
17 2AL *	3	5	66	62	3.36	3.43	1.17		156	47	5.4	3.1	8.5	2.7		15.0%	89.8	47	17	37	27%	77%	18%	26%	0	18			83	0.90	8.2	99	$5
18 LAA	7	1	83	95	4.54	3.70	1.26	1.21	108	102	5.1	3.2	10.3	3.2	36%	11.7%	90.1	43	19	38	30%	70%	18%	16%	1	20	0%	100%	25	0.72	-4.0	136	$1
19 LAA	5	0	68	79	3.99	3.88	1.17	1.18	89	95	5.5	2.7	10.5	4.0	34%	13.9%	89.2	39	21	41	31%	70%	13%	11%	7	22	0%	57%	0	0.67	4.3	146	$3
1st Half	3	0	42	51	3.24	3.94	1.06	1.12	75	99	6.0	2.8	11.0	3.9	34%	14.3%	89.2	34	20	46	26%	81%	17%	14%	3	25	0%	33%	0	0.42	6.5	147	$6
2nd Half	2	0	26	28	5.19	3.91	1.35	1.15	119	89	4.9	2.4	9.7	4.0	34%	13.2%	89.1	45	22	33	37%	59%	4%	7%	4	19	0%	75%	0	0.97	-2.2	144	-$2
20 Proj	**5**	**0**	**73**	**78**	**4.22**	**3.55**	**1.26**	**1.17**	**102**	**96**	**5.1**	**3.0**	**9.7**	**3.3**	**35%**	**12.9%**	**89.5**	**42**	**20**	**38**	**32%**	**70%**	**12%**		**0**						**-0.6**	**132**	**$1**

Ray,Robbie

Age: 28	Th: L	Role SP	Health D	LIMA Plan A
Ht: 6' 2"	Wt: 195	Type Pwr	PT/Exp A	Rand Var +4
			Consist A	MM 3503

Hard to find a guy with better stuff, as evident by long history of impactful SwK. But he gets in trouble when he doesn't generate whiffs: reference LD% and chronically high Ball%. And xHR/F confirms said solid contact is prone to leaving the yard, which keeps 4+ ERA in play. Declining velocity puts a ribbon on a potentially combustible package.

Yr Tm	W	Sv	IP	K	ERA	xERA	WHIP	xWHIP	vL+	vR+	BF/G	Ctl	Dom	Cmd	Ball%	SwK	Vel	G	L	F	H%	S%	HR/F	xHR/F	GS	APC	DOM%	DIS%	Sv%	LI	RAR	BPX	R$
15 ARI *	7	0	169	166	3.55	3.86	1.42	1.33	99	103	22.5	3.9	8.8	2.3	37%	9.4%	93.3	44	22	35	34%	75%	7%	9%	23	98	22%	26%			8.6	104	$3
16 ARI	8	0	174	218	4.90	3.62	1.47	1.22	93	109	24.3	3.7	11.3	3.1	36%	11.9%	94.1	46	22	33	37%	69%	15%	16%	32	99	22%	19%			-15.4	152	-$2
17 ARI	15	0	162	218	2.89	3.47	1.15	1.19	82	88	23.8	3.9	12.1	3.1	37%	14.7%	94.3	40	19	40	28%	82%	16%	13%	28	97	43%	25%			29.4	156	$24
18 ARI	6	0	124	165	3.93	3.75	1.35	1.33	62	109	21.9	5.1	12.0	2.4	38%	13.2%	93.7	39	22	39	30%	76%	17%	14%	24	95	17%	25%			3.3	110	$3
19 ARI	12	0	174	235	4.34	3.90	1.34	1.28	85	108	22.6	4.3	12.1	2.8	37%	14.1%	92.4	37	26	37	32%	74%	20%	20%	33	93	18%	12%			3.6	127	$9
1st Half	5	0	99	129	4.10	4.00	1.36	1.27	81	106	23.5	4.5	11.8	2.6	38%	14.1%	92.5	40	24	37	32%	74%	16%	19%	18	97	28%	11%			4.9	119	$9
2nd Half	7	0	76	106	4.64	3.77	1.32	1.20	90	110	21.6	4.2	12.6	3.0	36%	14.2%	92.3	33	29	37	31%	73%	25%	21%	15	88	7%	13%			-1.2	137	$9
20 Proj	**12**	**0**	**174**	**231**	**4.26**	**3.38**	**1.32**	**1.25**	**81**	**105**	**21.9**	**4.4**	**12.0**	**2.7**	**37%**	**13.6%**	**93.1**	**38**	**24**	**38**	**31%**	**73%**	**18%**		**33**						**-2.3**	**130**	**$9**

Reid-Foley,Sean

Age: 24	Th: R	Role RP	Health A	LIMA Plan F
Ht: 6' 3"	Wt: 220	Type Pwr FB	PT/Exp D	Rand Var +5
			Consist F	MM 0301

2-4, 4.26 ERA in 32 IP at TOR. Solid prospect couldn't stick at MLB level due to extreme wildness, both at AAA and in bigs. On plus side, control was much better in minors during few seasons prior, and good raw stuff gives hope for SwK rebound. Still, with these warts, you simply can't roster him without a bench spot.

Yr Tm	W	Sv	IP	K	ERA	xERA	WHIP	xWHIP	vL+	vR+	BF/G	Ctl	Dom	Cmd	Ball%	SwK	Vel	G	L	F	H%	S%	HR/F	xHR/F	GS	APC	DOM%	DIS%	Sv%	LI	RAR	BPX	R$
15																																	
16																																	
17 aa	10	0	133	106	6.49	6.67	1.70				22.2	3.7	7.2	1.9							35%	66%									-34.8	25	-$15
18 TOR *	14	0	165	168	4.38	4.03	1.38	1.43	102	118	22.3	4.0	9.2	2.3	39%	12.4%	93.8	37	26	37	32%	70%	19%	17%	7	91	29%	43%			-4.8	95	$4
19 TOR *	5	0	121	115	7.48	6.15	1.81	1.69	114	103	19.3	6.7	8.6	1.3	38%	10.0%	92.6	42	15	42	32%	60%	12%	11%	6	68	0%	67%	0	0.62	-44.3	35	-$21
1st Half	3	0	78	72	7.47	5.59	1.75		132	99	21.1	6.9	8.3	1.2		10.6%	93.1	42	16	42	30%	58%	15%	12%	2	54	0%	50%	0	0.50	-28.6	41	-$22
2nd Half	2	0	42	43	7.51	7.20	1.92	1.63	107	103	16.7	6.3	9.2	1.4	37%	9.8%	92.4	43	15	43	36%	64%	10%	11%	4	75	0%	75%	0	0.67	-15.7	24	-$19
20 Proj	**7**	**0**	**116**	**112**	**5.85**	**4.79**	**1.66**	**1.55**	**110**	**119**	**19.9**	**5.2**	**8.7**	**1.7**	**38%**	**10.8%**	**93.0**	**40**	**19**	**40**	**33%**	**68%**	**14%**		**26**						**-24.3**	**38**	**-$11**

Reyes,Alex

Age: 25	Th: R	Role RP	Health F	LIMA Plan F
Ht: 6' 3"	Wt: 175	Type Pwr FB	PT/Exp F	Rand Var +5
			Consist F	MM 1401

0-1, 15.00 ERA in 3 IP at STL. Once the top pitching prospect in the game, he's not any closer to relevancy. Finger, pectoral ailments plagued him this time. But even when he pitched, he still couldn't find the plate. Has never been able to throw strikes as SP and clearly doesn't have durability for that role anyway. Maybe one day, again? But not now.

Yr Tm	W	Sv	IP	K	ERA	xERA	WHIP	xWHIP	vL+	vR+	BF/G	Ctl	Dom	Cmd	Ball%	SwK	Vel	G	L	F	H%	S%	HR/F	xHR/F	GS	APC	DOM%	DIS%	Sv%	LI	RAR	BPX	R$
15 aa	3	0	35	48	3.24	1.87	1.13				17.1	4.4	12.4	2.8							30%	70%									3.1	172	$1
16 STL *	6	1	111	129	3.84	3.57	1.39	1.36	91	69	18.0	4.3	10.4	2.4	38%	11.9%	96.5	43	15	41	34%	72%	2%	4%	5	66	20%	0%	100	0.95	4.8	123	$4
17																																	
18 STL *	2	0	20	23	0.00	-0.83	0.55		86	92	22.7	2.6	10.3	4.0		4.1%	94.8	40	20	40	13%	100%	0%	1%	1	73	0%	0%			10.4	211	$3
19 STL *	1	0	31	31	9.49	7.08	2.05		38	192	10.8	8.7	9.1	1.0	51%	5.6%	96.8	30	20	50	33%	54%	20%	12%	0	18			0	1.00	-19.1	23	-$13
1st Half	1	0	31	31	9.49	7.08	2.05		37	195	10.8	8.7	9.1	1.0		5.6%	96.8	30	20	50	33%	54%	20%	12%	0	18			0	1.00	-19.1	23	-$13
2nd Half																																	
20 Proj	**6**	**0**	**94**	**104**	**5.17**	**4.37**	**1.49**	**1.49**	**97**	**94**	**14.0**	**6.6**	**10.0**	**1.8**	**42%**	**11.9%**	**96.6**	**42**	**18**	**40**	**30%**	**67%**	**11%**		**12**						**-11.8**	**56**	**-$4**

Richards,Garrett

Age: 32	Th: R	Role SP	Health F	LIMA Plan B
Ht: 6' 3"	Wt: 210	Type Pwr GB	PT/Exp D	Rand Var +5
			Consist B	MM 3301

Recovery from Tommy John surgery (July 2018) extended into another year, giving him fewer IP in past four seasons than most SP tally in one. Proven ability to miss bats and keep ball on ground keeps ceiling high, but high Ball% adds another layer of risk on top of poor durability. Don't view him as anything more than a late-round dart throw.

Yr Tm	W	Sv	IP	K	ERA	xERA	WHIP	xWHIP	vL+	vR+	BF/G	Ctl	Dom	Cmd	Ball%	SwK	Vel	G	L	F	H%	S%	HR/F	xHR/F	GS	APC	DOM%	DIS%	Sv%	LI	RAR	BPX	R$
15 LAA	15	0	207	176	3.65	3.75	1.24	1.35	86	100	27.0	3.3	7.6	2.3	36%	11.5%	95.5	55	17	28	28%	73%	12%	14%	32	102	34%	31%			8.1	97	$13
16 LAA	1	0	35	34	2.34	4.03	1.33	1.35	66	117	24.7	3.9	8.8	2.3	38%	11.2%	95.6	46	25	29	31%	84%	7%	15%	6	103	33%	0%			7.9	92	$0
17 LAA	0	0	28	27	2.28	3.35	0.90		68	64	18.0	2.3	8.8	3.9		12.6%	95.8	54	17	29	25%	75%	5%	11%	6	71	17%	17%			7.1	154	$0
18 LAA	5	0	76	87	3.66	3.70	1.28	1.30	89	101	20.3	4.0	10.3	2.6	39%	11.9%	95.9	49	19	31	29%	77%	17%	18%	16	82	13%	44%			4.7	119	$2
19 SD	0	0	9	11	8.31	4.86	1.85	1.52	92	226	13.7	6.2	11.4	1.8	39%	10.2%	95.1	43	26	30	37%	57%	29%	33%	3	52	0%	67%			-4.1	64	-$7
1st Half																																	
2nd Half	0	0	9	11	8.31	4.79	1.85		93	223	13.7	6.2	11.4	1.8		10.2%	95.1	43	26	30	37%	57%	29%	33%	3	52	0%	67%			-4.1	64	-$7
20 Proj	**5**	**0**	**87**	**86**	**4.05**	**3.63**	**1.31**	**1.33**	**83**	**105**	**23.2**	**3.7**	**8.9**	**2.4**	**38%**	**11.6%**	**95.7**	**51**	**20**	**29**	**30%**	**71%**	**13%**		**16**						**1.1**	**101**	**$2**

Richards,Trevor

Age: 27	Th: R	Role SP	Health A	LIMA Plan B
Ht: 6' 2"	Wt: 190	Type Pwr FB	PT/Exp C	Rand Var 0
			Consist B	MM 1301

After struggling to throw strikes as starter, stuff played up in shorter stints after trade to TAM. But tools aren't good enough to be a difference maker in bullpen. And as a flyball pitcher with only two pitches, he'll continue to underwhelm as a SP even if he can replicate good MiLB control. There are better speculations out there.

Yr Tm	W	Sv	IP	K	ERA	xERA	WHIP	xWHIP	vL+	vR+	BF/G	Ctl	Dom	Cmd	Ball%	SwK	Vel	G	L	F	H%	S%	HR/F	xHR/F	GS	APC	DOM%	DIS%	Sv%	LI	RAR	BPX	R$
15																																	
16																																	
17 aa	5	0	75	66	3.94	4.09	1.37				22.5	2.4	7.9	3.3							35%	71%									3.9	119	$1
18 MIA *	7	0	166	161	3.92	3.99	1.29	1.33	91	116	22.1	3.1	8.7	2.8	38%	11.2%	90.8	36	25	39	31%	73%	11%	13%	25	89	32%	32%			4.6	97	$5
19 2 TM	6	0	135	127	4.06	5.03	1.35	1.42	100	99	19.3	3.7	8.4	2.3	36%	12.3%	90.9	35	22	43	30%	74%	12%	12%	23	76	22%	30%	0	0.78	7.5	70	$4
1st Half	3	0	94	83	4.02	5.15	1.30	1.40	101	94	23.5	3.8	7.9	2.1	36%	12.1%	91.0	36	21	44	28%	73%	11%	11%	17	92	24%	24%			5.6	58	$6
2nd Half	3	0	41	44	4.14	4.81	1.48	1.28	99	112	13.9	3.5	9.6	2.8	36%	12.9%	90.7	34	25	41	34%	78%	14%	13%	6	55	17%	50%	0	0.82	1.9	98	-$1
20 Proj	**5**	**0**	**87**	**84**	**4.23**	**4.09**	**1.36**	**1.33**	**95**	**107**	**22.1**	**3.3**	**8.7**	**2.7**	**37%**	**12.0%**	**90.8**	**35**	**24**	**41**	**32%**	**72%**	**11%**		**16**						**-0.8**	**93**	**$0**

Roark,Tanner

Age: 33	Th: R	Role SP	Health A	LIMA Plan A
Ht: 6' 2"	Wt: 240	Type	PT/Exp A	Rand Var +2
			Consist A	MM 1203

When you do what he did in 2016, there's always someone that will bid on a repeat. It ain't coming, though. Good 1st-half stretch driven by friendly HR/F; as that regressed late, ERA more closely aligned with xERA. Speaking of that metric, its three-year trend could make the next step an even uglier one. DN: 5.00 ERA

Yr Tm	W	Sv	IP	K	ERA	xERA	WHIP	xWHIP	vL+	vR+	BF/G	Ctl	Dom	Cmd	Ball%	SwK	Vel	G	L	F	H%	S%	HR/F	xHR/F	GS	APC	DOM%	DIS%	Sv%	LI	RAR	BPX	R$
15 WAS	4	1	111	70	4.38	4.17	1.31	1.32	119	100	11.7	2.1	5.7	2.7	36%	7.5%	92.8	48	22	31	30%	71%	15%	16%	12	45	17%	50%	50	0.90	-5.7	85	-$2
16 WAS	16	0	210	172	2.83	4.00	1.17	1.34	84	88	25.1	3.1	7.4	2.4	38%	9.3%	92.1	49	20	31	27%	79%	9%	12%	33	99	36%	18%	0	0.81	35.3	89	$24
17 WAS	13	0	181	166	4.67	4.21	1.33	1.31	111	84	24.3	3.2	8.2	2.6	37%	10.4%	92.2	48	20	32	31%	68%	14%	12%	30	101	23%	30%	0	0.76	-6.9	106	$6
18 WAS	9	0	180	146	4.34	4.35	1.28	1.28	105	100	24.5	2.5	7.3	2.9	37%	8.9%	91.5	41	22	38	30%	70%	12%	13%	30	95	30%	40%	0	0.83	-4.3	95	$3
19 2 TM	10	0	165	158	4.35	4.62	1.40	1.30	115	99	23.3	2.8	8.6	3.1	38%	9.0%	92.1	36	27	37	33%	74%	15%	15%	31	97	16%	32%			3.1	102	$4
1st Half	5	0	86	87	3.36	4.43	1.31	1.25	115	74	23.1	3.0	9.1	3.0	38%	9.6%	92.2	36	29	35	33%	76%	8%	12%	16	95	13%	25%			12.1	105	$10
2nd Half	5	0	80	71	5.42	4.87	1.49	1.25	115	127	23.5	2.5	8.0	3.2	38%	8.4%	91.9	36	26	38	33%	72%	22%	18%	15	98	20%	40%			-9.0	100	-$2
20 Proj	**10**	**0**	**174**	**152**	**4.60**	**4.10**	**1.37**	**1.27**	**111**	**100**	**22.1**	**2.8**	**7.8**	**2.8**	**38%**	**9.1%**	**92.0**	**38**	**24**	**38**	**31%**	**71%**	**14%**		**33**						**-9.6**	**94**	**$2**

STEPHEN NICKRAND

Robertson,David

Age: 35 Th: R Role RP	Health F	LIMA Plan F	Lost year to elbow injury that eventually required Tommy John surgery in August, so he could miss the whole season. Elite skills pre-2019 are reflected in BPX history, and although age is against him, resumed dominance is plausible. If he pitches in 2020, watch to see if Dom, Ctl return, and if so, keep him on your radar for 2021.
Ht: 5' 11" Wt: 195 Type Pwr	PT/Exp C	Rand Var -1	
	Consist F	MM 5500	

Yr	Tm	W	Sv	IP	K	ERA	xERA	WHIP	xWHIP	vL+	vR+	BF/G	Ctl	Dom	Cmd	Ball%	SwK	Vel	G	L	F	H%	S%	HR/F	xHR/F	GS	APC	DOM%	DIS%	Sv%	LI	RAR	BPX	R$
15	CHW	6	34	63	86	3.41	2.60	0.93	0.96	63	92	4.2	1.8	12.2	6.6	32%	14.3%	92.2	36	30	34	30%	67%	14%	15%	0	16			83	1.35	4.3	219	$21
16	CHW	5	37	62	75	3.47	3.94	1.36	1.34	83	103	4.3	4.6	10.8	2.3	37%	13.0%	91.8	45	14	40	32%	77%	10%	11%	0	17			84	1.44	5.6	111	$17
17	2 AL	9	14	68	98	1.84	2.71	0.85	1.04	58	71	4.3	3.0	12.9	4.3	35%	17.3%	91.6	47	16	37	23%	85%	12%	11%	0	17			88	1.19	21.2	211	$21
18	NYY	8	5	70	91	3.23	3.20	1.03	1.15	85	80	4.1	3.4	11.8	3.5	38%	13.9%	92.3	45	17	37	27%	72%	12%	16%	0	17			56	1.20	7.9	166	$10
19	PHI	0	0	7	6	5.40	7.54	2.10	1.92	75	174	4.7	8.1	8.1	1.0	42%	11.0%	91.7	33	24	43	35%	77%	11%	11%	0	19			0	1.24	-0.7	-67	-$6
1st Half		0	0	7	6	5.40	7.45	2.10		75	176	4.7	8.1	8.1	1.0		11.0%	91.7	33	24	43	35%	77%	11%	11%	0	19			0	1.24	-0.7	-67	-$6
2nd Half																																		
20	**Proj**	**1**	**0**	**15**	**19**	**3.06**	**2.99**	**1.10**	**1.16**	**75**	**87**	**4.1**	**3.5**	**11.7**	**3.3**	**36%**	**14.3%**	**92.0**	**44**	**18**	**38**	**29%**	**76%**	**12%**		**0**						**1.9**	**159**	**-$2**

Robles,Hansel

Age: 29 Th: R Role RP	Health B	LIMA Plan B	Previously unremarkable middle reliever seized closer role on strength of change-up that earns plentiful whiffs vL/vR alike. xERA, xWHIP gaps tell us good fortune was involved, so expect some regression. Improved Ctl, velocity uptick, and plenty of swinging strikes add up to set of saves-worthy skills. Not a bad choice for a second closer.
Ht: 6' 0" Wt: 220 Type Pwr FB	PT/Exp C	Rand Var -3	
	Consist B	MM 2330	

Yr	Tm	W	Sv	IP	K	ERA	xERA	WHIP	xWHIP	vL+	vR+	BF/G	Ctl	Dom	Cmd	Ball%	SwK	Vel	G	L	F	H%	S%	HR/F	xHR/F	GS	APC	DOM%	DIS%	Sv%	LI	RAR	BPX	R$
15	NYM	4	0	54	61	3.67	3.64	1.02	1.19	77	101	3.8	3.0	10.2	3.4	35%	13.1%	95.7	33	18	49	24%	70%	12%	9%	0	16			0	1.02	2.0	135	$3
16	NYM	6	1	78	85	3.48	4.31	1.35	1.34	79	107	4.9	4.2	9.8	2.4	36%	11.6%	95.2	30	29	41	32%	77%	8%	10%	0	20			33	1.07	6.8	86	$3
17	NYM *	7	4	80	78	5.39	5.31	1.54	1.40	94	104	5.4	5.0	8.8	1.7	39%	9.4%	94.9	34	22	44	30%	70%	15%	15%	0	21			50	1.11	-10.2	49	-$3
18	2 TM	2	2	56	59	3.70	4.39	1.39	1.34	118	98	4.6	4.0	9.5	2.4	38%	11.4%	96.0	35	24	41	31%	80%	14%	13%	0	18			67	0.99	3.1	87	-$1
19	LAA	5	23	73	75	2.48	3.84	1.02	1.16	77	81	4.0	2.0	9.3	4.7	34%	12.5%	97.1	39	21	40	29%	79%	8%	10%	1	16	0%	0%	85	1.12	18.2	142	$19
1st Half		3	11	38	38	3.11	4.28	1.12	1.12	97	75	3.9	1.9	9.1	4.8	35%	10.3%	96.9	37	18	45	31%	74%	6%	9%	1	17	0%	0%	85	0.89	6.5	138	$15
2nd Half		2	12	35	37	1.80	3.48	0.91	1.10	56	88	4.1	2.1	9.5	4.6	32%	15.4%	97.5	42	24	35	25%	86%	10%	12%	0	16			86	1.41	11.7	148	$23
20	**Proj**	**4**	**28**	**65**	**68**	**3.25**	**3.70**	**1.19**	**1.23**	**89**	**94**	**4.3**	**3.1**	**9.4**	**3.0**	**35%**	**12.0%**	**96.4**	**37**	**22**	**41**	**29%**	**78%**	**11%**		**0**						**7.2**	**114**	**$16**

Rodney,Fernando

Age: 43 Th: R Role RP	Health B	LIMA Plan B	The wheels that had been wobbling for years finally fell off in 1st half as Ctl tanked, leading to DFA in May. After catching on with Nationals, velocity and SwK bounced back for a 2nd half not unlike 2018. Though he may vulture some saves thanks to his track record, BPX says he's unlikely to keep high-leverage role, even if given the chance.
Ht: 5' 11" Wt: 240 Type Pwr	PT/Exp B	Rand Var +4	
	Consist B	MM 2310	

Yr	Tm	W	Sv	IP	K	ERA	xERA	WHIP	xWHIP	vL+	vR+	BF/G	Ctl	Dom	Cmd	Ball%	SwK	Vel	G	L	F	H%	S%	HR/F	xHR/F	GS	APC	DOM%	DIS%	Sv%	LI	RAR	BPX	R$
15	2 TM	7	16	63	58	4.74	4.05	1.40	1.41	116	102	4.1	4.2	8.3	2.0	39%	10.2%	94.7	51	18	31	30%	70%	16%	10%	0	16			70	1.22	-6.0	79	$4
16	2 NL	2	25	65	74	3.44	3.66	1.39	1.42	99	83	4.2	5.1	10.2	2.0	40%	13.0%	94.4	55	22	23	31%	77%	14%	11%	0	17			89	1.13	6.0	94	$10
17	ARI	5	39	55	65	4.23	3.63	1.19	1.30	88	67	3.8	4.2	10.6	2.5	39%	12.6%	94.6	52	16	32	29%	63%	7%	10%	0	16			87	1.28	0.9	127	$19
18	2 AL	4	25	64	70	3.36	4.17	1.46	1.37	78	116	4.2	4.5	9.8	2.2	39%	11.5%	94.2	44	24	32	33%	80%	12%	12%	0	17			78	1.21	6.3	89	$10
19	2 TM	0	2	48	49	5.66	4.79	1.62	1.53	103	99	3.8	5.3	9.3	1.8	38%	11.6%	93.9	50	22	29	34%	65%	13%	14%	0	16			33	0.87	-6.8	56	-$7
1st Half		0	1	16	17	8.27	5.30	2.02	1.68	118	116	4.0	7.2	9.4	1.3	41%	9.8%	93.2	54	20	26	38%	58%	17%	17%	0	17			50	0.60	-7.6	8	-$13
2nd Half		0	1	31	32	4.31	4.43	1.40	1.38	95	89	3.7	4.3	9.2	2.1	37%	12.5%	94.2	47	23	30	32%	71%	12%	12%	0	16			25	1.01	0.8	81	-$4
20	**Proj**	**1**	**1**	**36**	**39**	**4.83**	**3.93**	**1.51**	**1.43**	**96**	**99**	**3.9**	**4.9**	**9.6**	**1.9**	**39%**	**11.6%**	**94.1**	**49**	**21**	**30**	**33%**	**69%**	**12%**		**0**						**-3.0**	**76**	**-$4**

Rodon,Carlos

Age: 27 Th: L Role SP	Health F	LIMA Plan B	Before undergoing TJ surgery in May, showed intriguing Dom/SwK spike that didn't manifest on surface, due to H% and S% bad luck. Even with added Ks, Ctl improvement remains elusive key to unlocking long-dormant #2 SP potential. Might return in late 2020, but with uncertainty of recovery, wait-and-see rather than draft-and-stash.
Ht: 6' 3" Wt: 235 Type Pwr	PT/Exp C	Rand Var +5	
	Consist B	MM 2400	

Yr	Tm	W	Sv	IP	K	ERA	xERA	WHIP	xWHIP	vL+	vR+	BF/G	Ctl	Dom	Cmd	Ball%	SwK	Vel	G	L	F	H%	S%	HR/F	xHR/F	GS	APC	DOM%	DIS%	Sv%	LI	RAR	BPX	R$
15	CHW	9	0	139	139	3.75	4.00	1.44	1.42	72	113	23.3	4.6	9.0	2.0	39%	10.6%	93.4	47	23	30	32%	75%	10%	12%	23	94	26%	26%	0	0.87	3.7	75	$2
16	CHW	9	0	165	168	4.04	3.96	1.39	1.24	83	109	25.5	2.9	9.2	3.1	37%	10.5%	93.4	44	21	35	34%	75%	14%	10%	28	100	18%	25%			3.1	128	$4
17	CHW	2	0	69	76	4.15	4.07	1.37	1.32	99	105	24.8	4.0	9.9	2.5	39%	10.9%	93.1	44	22	34	30%	76%	19%	13%	12	98	33%	25%			1.7	109	-$1
18	CHW	6	0	121	90	4.18	4.99	1.26	1.50	118	91	25.6	4.1	6.7	1.6	40%	9.4%	93.0	41	16	43	25%	70%	10%	10%	20	98	30%	30%			-0.4	33	$2
19	CHW	3	0	35	46	5.19	4.24	1.44	1.31	49	101	22.6	4.4	11.9	2.7	38%	12.6%	91.5	43	19	38	36%	65%	11%	13%	7	99	29%	14%			-2.9	127	-$4
1st Half		3	0	35	46	5.19	4.26	1.44	1.26	49	102	22.6	4.4	11.9	2.7	38%	12.6%	91.5	43	19	38	36%	65%	11%	13%	7	99	29%	14%			-2.9	127	-$4
2nd Half																																		
20	**Proj**	**3**	**0**	**44**	**47**	**4.41**	**3.95**	**1.40**	**1.34**	**88**	**102**	**23.3**	**4.3**	**9.7**	**2.3**	**39%**	**11.1%**	**92.7**	**42**	**21**	**38**	**31%**	**72%**	**13%**		**8**						**-1.4**	**90**	**-$3**

Rodriguez,Dereck

Age: 28 Th: R Role RP	Health A	LIMA Plan F	6-11, 5.64 in 99 IP at SF. As predicted, regressed big-time as H%, S%, and HR/F luck normalized, and suffered significant pullback of Dom and Ctl. Throws five pitches, but none earns more than 13% SwK. Doesn't possess any skill that is average, let alone plus, making him a poor bet to contribute to MLB rotation or your fantasy roster.
Ht: 6' 1" Wt: 215 Type Con	PT/Exp D	Rand Var +2	
	Consist F	MM 1101	

Yr	Tm	W	Sv	IP	K	ERA	xERA	WHIP	xWHIP	vL+	vR+	BF/G	Ctl	Dom	Cmd	Ball%	SwK	Vel	G	L	F	H%	S%	HR/F	xHR/F	GS	APC	DOM%	DIS%	Sv%	LI	RAR	BPX	R$
15																																		
16																																		
17	aa	5	0	75	48	5.86	6.23	1.68				22.6	3.6	5.7	1.6							34%	68%									-14.0	21	-$9
18	SF *	10	0	169	131	3.06	3.53	1.18	1.33	96	88	22.6	2.5	7.0	2.8	36%	9.4%	91.4	39	23	37	28%	78%	7%	7%	19	89	32%	21%	0	0.81	22.9	90	$15
19	SF *	9	0	130	92	5.38	5.43	1.44	1.46	110	109	16.3	3.3	6.4	2.0	38%	8.9%	90.6	44	23	34	30%	68%	19%	16%	16	60	25%	50%	0	0.68	-14.0	30	-$4
1st Half		4	0	66	41	5.07	5.25	1.48	1.49	107	106	14.8	3.8	5.6	1.5	39%	8.6%	90.8	45	23	32	29%	70%	17%	18%	8	57	13%	38%	0	0.47	-4.6	21	-$6
2nd Half		5	0	65	52	5.69	5.61	1.41	1.31	114	114	18.2	2.7	7.2	2.6	37%	9.3%	90.3	41	22	36	31%	65%	22%	14%	8	64	38%	63%	0	1.00	-9.4	42	-$3
20	**Proj**	**6**	**0**	**102**	**74**	**4.95**	**4.40**	**1.40**	**1.36**	**109**	**107**	**19.2**	**3.0**	**6.6**	**2.2**	**37%**	**9.1%**	**90.9**	**42**	**23**	**36**	**30%**	**69%**	**14%**		**21**						**-10.0**	**66**	**-$3**

Rodriguez,Eduardo

Age: 27 Th: L Role SP	Health D	LIMA Plan A	Finally stayed healthy and delivered season owners had been waiting for. Succeeded with solid Dom and so-so Ctl, primarily by inducing plenty of ground balls, and relied on change-up (27% SwK) and sinker (70% GB) to neutralize platoon advantage vR. Skills-wise, a repeat is well within reach... if he can again defy his Health grade.
Ht: 6' 2" Wt: 220 Type Pwr	PT/Exp A	Rand Var 0	
	Consist A	MM 3305	

Yr	Tm	W	Sv	IP	K	ERA	xERA	WHIP	xWHIP	vL+	vR+	BF/G	Ctl	Dom	Cmd	Ball%	SwK	Vel	G	L	F	H%	S%	HR/F	xHR/F	GS	APC	DOM%	DIS%	Sv%	LI	RAR	BPX	R$
15	BOS *	14	0	170	136	3.92	3.95	1.30	1.31	113	93	24.1	2.4	7.2	3.1	36%	8.5%	94.0	43	24	33	32%	71%	10%	11%	21	96	33%	33%			0.9	100	$7
16	BOS *	3	0	145	120	4.75	4.51	1.31	1.32	96	100	22.2	3.0	7.4	2.5	38%	11.2%	93.5	32	22	46	29%	69%	11%	11%	20	93	30%	35%			-10.0	65	-$2
17	BOS	6	0	137	150	4.19	4.21	1.28	1.24	107	97	23.3	3.3	9.8	3.0	36%	11.9%	93.3	35	22	43	31%	71%	12%	13%	24	98	17%	21%	0	0.77	2.8	122	$6
18	BOS	13	0	130	146	3.82	3.93	1.26	1.21	94	95	20.5	3.1	10.1	3.2	37%	11.5%	93.3	39	20	41	32%	74%	11%	14%	23	86	30%	26%	0	0.81	5.3	132	$9
19	BOS	19	0	203	213	3.81	4.11	1.33	1.30	103	93	25.3	3.3	9.4	2.8	37%	12.1%	93.1	48	19	33	32%	75%	13%	15%	34	103	29%	21%			17.5	116	$17
1st Half		8	0	98	102	4.79	4.23	1.36	1.22	120	99	24.6	2.9	9.4	3.3	37%	11.9%	92.8	44	22	35	33%	69%	15%	18%	17	100	18%	18%			-3.4	124	$7
2nd Half		11	0	106	111	2.90	3.97	1.30	1.30	84	88	25.9	3.7	9.5	2.5	38%	12.3%	93.3	53	17	30	31%	80%	11%	11%	17	106	41%	24%			21.0	109	$25
20	**Proj**	**15**	**0**	**189**	**198**	**3.89**	**3.62**	**1.27**	**1.25**	**99**	**93**	**22.7**	**3.2**	**9.5**	**2.9**	**37%**	**11.7%**	**93.2**	**43**	**20**	**37**	**31%**	**73%**	**13%**		**34**						**6.1**	**120**	**$14**

Rodriguez,Jefry

Age: 26 Th: R Role SP	Health F	LIMA Plan A	1-5, 4.63 in 47 IP at CLE. Despite some prospect love during his ascent, has not come close to harnessing potential. And while 2nd half move to bullpen looked good on the surface, don't buy it: Dom, Cmd are off-the-charts bad, and formerly-heavy fastball lost 2 mph. Still a work in progress, but there's not much here unless he starts missing bats.
Ht: 6' 6" Wt: 232 Type	PT/Exp D	Rand Var +1	
	Consist A	MM 0100	

Yr	Tm	W	Sv	IP	K	ERA	xERA	WHIP	xWHIP	vL+	vR+	BF/G	Ctl	Dom	Cmd	Ball%	SwK	Vel	G	L	F	H%	S%	HR/F	xHR/F	GS	APC	DOM%	DIS%	Sv%	LI	RAR	BPX	R$
15																																		
16																																		
17																																		
18	WAS *	10	0	154	121	4.86	4.53	1.51	1.76	123	95	20.2	4.8	7.1	1.5	41%	8.7%	95.4	42	17	41	30%	69%	13%	15%	8	65	0%	50%	0	0.77	-13.4	58	-$6
19	CLE *	2	0	75	48	4.79	4.21	1.40	1.55	108	98	18.7	4.1	5.8	1.4	39%	8.3%	93.5	49	20	31	28%	67%	11%	14%	8	78	0%	25%	0	0.64	-2.7	45	-$4
1st Half		2	0	61	43	5.24	4.44	1.45	1.47	108	99	23.6	4.2	6.4	1.5	38%	8.3%	93.5	49	20	30	30%	65%	12%	16%	8	92	0%	25%			-5.5	50	-$5
2nd Half		0	0	14	5	2.45	2.95	1.14		97	101	9.5	3.5	3.1	0.9		8.0%	92.9	40	20	40	21%	83%	0%	2%	0	25			0	0.01	3.6	27	-$4
20	**Proj**	**3**	**0**	**58**	**43**	**4.74**	**4.71**	**1.47**	**1.59**	**110**	**96**	**22.1**	**4.4**	**6.6**	**1.5**	**39%**	**8.5%**	**94.3**	**46**	**19**	**35**	**30%**	**69%**	**9%**		**8**						**-4.2**	**28**	**-$5**

ARIK FLORIMONTE

Rodriguez,Richard

Age: 30 Th: R Role RP	Health B	PT/Exp D	Consist D
Ht: 6' 4" Wt: 230 Type Pwr xFB	LIMA Plan D	Rand Var -2	MM 2300

Couldn't repeat 2018 breakout as SwK, Dom, and Ctl all sagged, and also got hurt by unfortunate HR/F. 2nd half skill rebound is encouraging, as it was backed by Ball%, SwK, and velocity resurgence. While bad version is not roster-worthy, good version could earn high-leverage role, making him an intriguing late pick in very deep leagues.

Yr Tm	W	Sv	IP	K	ERA	xERA	WHIP	xWHIP	vL+	vR+	BF/G	Ctl	Dom	Cmd	Ball%	SwK	Vel	G	L	F	H%	S%	HR/F	xHR/F	GS	APC	DOM%	DIS%	Sv%	LI	RAR	BPX	R$
15 a/a	7	0	84	59	3.68	4.16	1.27				7.4	2.7	6.3	2.4							28%	76%									2.9	63	$2
16 aaa	6	2	82	67	3.83	4.35	1.45				7.3	3.5	7.4	2.1							33%	75%									3.6	79	$1
17 BAL *	4	10	76	68	4.30	5.04	1.46		29	269	6.9	3.0	8.0	2.7		6.7%	93.8	46	13	42	34%	74%	40%	36%	0	24			83	0.27	0.5	77	$3
18 PIT	4	0	69	88	2.47	3.30	1.07	1.06	60	102	4.4	2.5	11.4	4.6	33%	14.5%	92.9	38	15	48	32%	80%	7%	10%	0	18			0	0.81	14.4	178	$7
19 PIT	4	1	65	63	3.72	4.85	1.35	1.34	119	85	4.0	3.2	8.7	2.7	35%	11.3%	93.2	42	15	43	30%	82%	17%	12%	0	16			20	0.97	6.3	99	$1
1st Half	2	1	36	30	4.04	5.60	1.51	1.47	140	85	4.1	4.3	7.6	1.8	36%	10.7%	92.9	41	17	41	28%	84%	20%	13%	0	17			25	1.07	2.1	44	-$1
2nd Half	2	0	30	33	3.34	4.17	1.15	1.08	94	85	3.8	1.8	10.0	5.5	33%	12.1%	93.6	42	13	45	31%	79%	13%	10%	0	15			0	0.85	4.3	165	$4
20 Proj	4	0	65	67	3.99	3.87	1.31	1.17	101	100	4.4	2.8	9.3	3.3	34%	12.6%	93.2	38	17	45	32%	76%	13%		0						1.3	124	$0

Rogers,Taylor

Age: 29 Th: L Role RP	Health A	PT/Exp C	Consist B
Ht: 6' 3" Wt: 190 Type Pwr	LIMA Plan B	Rand Var 0	MM 5430

Consolidated prior year improvements and took them up a notch, with shrinking Ball% translating to elite Ctl, and GB% returning to career-high level. Dom spiked, but given merely average SwK, he could see regression in Ks in 2020. BPX, xERA, xWHIP all agree: this is an elite skill set, but the window may have closed on getting him at a non-elite price.

Yr Tm	W	Sv	IP	K	ERA	xERA	WHIP	xWHIP	vL+	vR+	BF/G	Ctl	Dom	Cmd	Ball%	SwK	Vel	G	L	F	H%	S%	HR/F	xHR/F	GS	APC	DOM%	DIS%	Sv%	LI	RAR	BPX	R$
15 aaa	11	0	174	98	5.56	5.58	1.65				27.8	2.4	5.1	2.1							37%	65%									-34.3	55	-$18
16 MIN *	3	0	79	75	4.61	4.97	1.48	1.16	74	111	5.3	2.6	8.5	3.3	36%	8.1%	92.6	51	20	28	37%	71%	14%	13%	0	18			0	0.84	-4.1	104	-$4
17 MIN	7	0	56	49	3.07	4.31	1.31	1.35	74	104	3.4	3.4	7.9	2.3	35%	9.0%	93.2	45	24	31	30%	81%	12%	15%	0	13			0	1.23	8.8	89	$3
18 MIN	1	2	68	75	2.63	2.98	0.95	1.09	58	90	3.6	2.1	9.9	4.7	33%	11.6%	93.4	45	26	30	28%	73%	6%	11%	0	14			50	1.04	12.8	166	$7
19 MIN	2	30	69	90	2.61	2.82	1.00	0.98	88	82	4.6	1.4	11.7	8.2	31%	11.3%	94.8	51	18	31	32%	80%	15%	16%	0	18			83	1.50	16.1	220	$21
1st Half	2	10	36	44	1.98	3.22	1.05	1.01	82	87	4.8	1.7	10.9	6.3	31%	10.5%	94.4	48	20	33	32%	88%	13%	14%	0	18			77	1.39	11.3	191	$16
2nd Half	0	20	33	46	3.31	2.46	0.95	0.86	96	77	4.4	1.1	12.7	11.5	31%	12.2%	95.2	54	16	30	33%	70%	18%	17%	0	18			87	1.61	4.8	251	$26
20 Proj	2	34	58	66	2.86	2.82	1.09	1.05	78	93	4.2	2.0	10.3	5.2	32%	10.8%	94.0	49	21	30	31%	79%	14%		0						9.2	183	$18

Romo,Sergio

Age: 37 Th: R Role RP	Health D	PT/Exp C	Consist A
Ht: 5' 11" Wt: 185 Type Pwr FB	LIMA Plan A	Rand Var -1	MM 2310

Season totals show solid year, but it was a tale of two halves—Ctl, Dom tanked in 1st half, then he bounced back to post elite BPX in 2nd. Avoids fastballs (<25%) and instead relies heavily on slider vR and slider/change-up mix vL, driving high SwK rate. He'll remain good as long as these pitches do; 1st half cautions what happens when they falter.

Yr Tm	W	Sv	IP	K	ERA	xERA	WHIP	xWHIP	vL+	vR+	BF/G	Ctl	Dom	Cmd	Ball%	SwK	Vel	G	L	F	H%	S%	HR/F	xHR/F	GS	APC	DOM%	DIS%	Sv%	LI	RAR	BPX	R$
15 SF	0	2	57	71	2.98	2.70	1.06	0.99	128	66	3.3	1.6	11.1	7.1	32%	17.3%	87.5	45	23	32	35%	72%	7%	7%	0	13			50	1.26	6.9	216	$3
16 SF	1	4	31	33	2.64	3.50	1.08	1.10	107	92	2.9	2.1	9.7	4.7	35%	14.9%	85.8	38	14	47	28%	86%	14%	16%	0	12			100	1.27	5.9	160	$2
17 2 TM	3	0	56	59	3.56	3.99	1.10	1.23	97	86	4.1	3.1	9.5	3.1	37%	15.2%	86.1	37	20	43	25%	75%	15%	12%	0	17			0	0.88	5.5	125	$3
18 TAM	3	25	67	75	4.14	3.90	1.26	1.17	97	101	3.9	2.7	10.0	3.8	37%	13.9%	86.3	36	20	44	32%	73%	14%	14%	5	15	0%	40%	76	1.29	0.0	141	$10
19 2 TM	2	20	60	60	3.43	4.47	1.11	1.26	86	86	3.8	2.5	9.0	3.5	34%	14.6%	86.4	36	19	45	28%	73%	9%	11%	0	15			87	1.05	8.0	116	$11
1st Half	1	15	31	25	4.35	5.53	1.29	1.43	99	89	4.2	3.8	7.3	1.9	33%	13.1%	86.4	38	16	46	27%	69%	9%	13%	0	15			94	1.04	0.6	48	$10
2nd Half	1	5	29	35	2.45	3.62	0.92	0.97	72	82	3.5	1.2	10.7	8.8	34%	16.0%	86.3	34	22	43	30%	79%	9%	9%	0	15			71	1.07	7.4	188	$13
20 Proj	2	7	58	61	3.92	3.72	1.24	1.16	101	99	3.7	2.7	9.5	3.5	35%	14.8%	86.3	37	20	44	30%	75%	14%		0						1.6	128	$3

Rondon,Hector

Age: 32 Th: R Role RP	Health A	PT/Exp C	Consist B
Ht: 6' 3" Wt: 230 Type	LIMA Plan B	Rand Var 0	MM 2200

On the surface, a solid ERA and WHIP; xERA and xWHIP tell a different story. Dom and SwK dropped below average as his slider lost 7 points of SwK both vL and vR. Without any other weapons, only H% luck kept his year from being a disaster. Velocity and GB rate remain strong, but unless Ks come back, he's roster filler.

Yr Tm	W	Sv	IP	K	ERA	xERA	WHIP	xWHIP	vL+	vR+	BF/G	Ctl	Dom	Cmd	Ball%	SwK	Vel	G	L	F	H%	S%	HR/F	xHR/F	GS	APC	DOM%	DIS%	Sv%	LI	RAR	BPX	R$
15 CHC	6	30	70	69	1.67	3.04	1.00	1.13	88	71	3.9	1.9	8.9	4.6	34%	11.2%	96.4	52	20	27	28%	86%	8%	8%	0	15			88	1.51	19.8	164	$23
16 CHC	2	18	51	58	3.53	2.95	0.98	1.00	101	78	3.7	1.4	10.2	7.3	33%	11.2%	96.0	46	20	34	28%	71%	18%	13%	0	15			78	1.09	4.2	202	$10
17 CHC	4	0	57	69	4.24	3.46	1.22	1.17	107	92	3.9	3.1	10.8	3.5	35%	12.2%	96.4	48	17	35	30%	72%	20%	16%	0	16			0	0.72	0.8	164	$1
18 HOU	2	15	59	67	3.20	3.60	1.32	1.20	97	95	4.0	3.1	10.2	3.4	35%	13.6%	97.2	46	22	33	35%	77%	8%	10%	0	16			68	1.19	6.9	145	$6
19 HOU	3	0	61	48	3.71	4.69	1.25	1.39	105	97	4.1	3.0	7.1	2.4	37%	10.1%	96.7	50	16	34	27%	77%	16%	13%	1	16	0%	100%	0	0.99	6.0	83	$0
1st Half	3	0	31	26	2.90	4.89	1.35	1.44	68	118	4.0	4.1	7.5	1.9	37%	10.4%	96.5	51	13	36	29%	82%	9%	8%	0	16			0	1.13	6.1	60	$2
2nd Half	0	0	30	22	4.55	4.46	1.15	1.23	140	76	4.3	1.8	6.7	3.7	37%	9.6%	97.0	49	19	32	25%	70%	23%	18%	1	16	0%	100%	0	0.82	-0.2	107	-$1
20 Proj	3	0	58	54	4.26	3.85	1.33	1.24	100	95	4.0	3.1	8.3	2.7	36%	11.4%	96.8	46	19	35	31%	71%	12%		0						-0.8	104	-$2

Ross,Joe

Age: 27 Th: R Role SP	Health F	PT/Exp D	Consist C
Ht: 6' 4" Wt: 220 Type Con	LIMA Plan C	Rand Var +2	MM 1101

4-4, 5.48 in 61 IP at WAS. Bounced between AAA and majors in return from 2017 Tommy John surgery, and couldn't reestablish plus Ctl, nor convert average SwK into Ks. He'll need both just to get back to "passable," and then still lacks a solution vL (.864 career oOPS). Has time for growth, but you don't need to invest until he shows some.

Yr Tm	W	Sv	IP	K	ERA	xERA	WHIP	xWHIP	vL+	vR+	BF/G	Ctl	Dom	Cmd	Ball%	SwK	Vel	G	L	F	H%	S%	HR/F	xHR/F	GS	APC	DOM%	DIS%	Sv%	LI	RAR	BPX	R$
15 WAS *	10	0	153	127	3.45	3.09	1.15	1.23	111	65	20.2	2.4	7.5	3.1	35%	12.1%	93.4	50	16	34	29%	72%	10%	14%	13	72	38%	15%	0	0.71	9.6	115	$11
16 WAS	7	0	105	93	3.43	3.96	1.30	1.24	112	83	23.5	2.5	8.0	3.2	36%	11.5%	92.7	43	27	30	33%	76%	10%	11%	19	90	26%	32%			9.9	116	$5
17 WAS *	7	0	101	86	5.34	6.05	1.54	1.23	122	109	24.5	2.5	7.7	3.0	34%	10.5%	91.4	38	25	38	35%	70%	19%	14%	13	93	31%	46%			-12.3	62	-$5
18 WAS *	2	0	34	15	4.80	4.53	1.31		101	143	23.6	2.2	4.0	1.8		9.2%	93.1	36	22	42	29%	66%	13%	14%	3	83	0%	33%			-2.7	33	-$5
19 WAS *	6	0	104	82	5.38	5.59	1.66	1.53	119	102	13.3	3.6	7.1	2.0	39%	10.5%	94.1	44	24	31	37%	68%	11%	17%	9	42	0%	33%	0	0.81	-11.3	59	-$8
1st Half	2	0	37	26	7.12	6.96	1.81		252	111	7.7	3.2	6.3	1.9		11.2%	93.9	47	19	34	38%	61%	17%	27%	0	18			0	0.82	-11.8	29	-$17
2nd Half	4	0	67	57	4.44	4.85	1.58	1.44	104	95	22.8	3.8	7.6	2.0	39%	10.3%	94.1	43	26	30	36%	71%	9%	13%	9	84	0%	33%	0	0.79	0.6	75	-$4
20 Proj	7	0	116	89	4.92	4.23	1.44	1.30	119	96	21.5	2.9	6.9	2.4	36%	11.0%	93.0	43	25	32	32%	68%	13%		20						-11.0	77	-$3

Ryan,Kyle

Age: 28 Th: L Role RP	Health A	PT/Exp D	Consist F
Ht: 6' 5" Wt: 215 Type Pwr xGB	LIMA Plan F	Rand Var 0	MM 2200

Every so often he emerges from obscurity to deliver an adequate season. Superb ground ball rate provides ERA floor, but poor Dom and Ctl means it comes with inflated WHIP. While Cmd ratio vL (2.7) is passable, he doesn't have a pitch to get whiffs vR, so unless he finds a new trick, he's a situational reliever and not fantasy relevant.

Yr Tm	W	Sv	IP	K	ERA	xERA	WHIP	xWHIP	vL+	vR+	BF/G	Ctl	Dom	Cmd	Ball%	SwK	Vel	G	L	F	H%	S%	HR/F	xHR/F	GS	APC	DOM%	DIS%	Sv%	LI	RAR	BPX	R$
15 DET *	6	0	159	80	4.79	5.04	1.56	1.49	112	111	21.2	3.1	4.5	1.5	37%	7.9%	88.1	48	22	30	33%	69%	16%	11%	6	56	0%	50%	0	1.07	-16.3	38	-$12
16 DET	4	0	56	35	3.07	4.05	1.13	1.35	85	87	4.0	2.4	5.7	2.3	36%	9.1%	89.3	56	18	26	27%	72%	4%	13%	0	15			0	0.64	7.7	84	$3
17 DET *	3	0	51	31	7.40	8.54	2.35		145	132	4.7	6.8	5.5	0.8		7.4%	90.5	52	29	19	40%	69%	0%	3%	0	15			0	1.49	-19.1	-4	-$17
18 aaa	1	0	66	47	3.44	3.82	1.17				12.0	2.7	6.5	2.4							26%	77%									5.8	65	$0
19 CHC	4	0	61	58	3.54	4.25	1.38	1.45	75	99	3.6	4.3	8.6	2.0	38%	9.9%	89.6	58	17	25	30%	76%	12%	11%	0	14			0	1.09	7.3	81	$0
1st Half	2	0	30	31	3.56	3.77	1.35	1.27	86	94	3.4	3.3	9.2	2.8	38%	10.1%	89.4	57	21	21	33%	76%	16%	12%	0	14			0	1.12	3.5	123	$0
2nd Half	2	0	31	27	3.52	4.60	1.40	1.57	64	103	3.7	5.3	7.9	1.5	39%	9.7%	89.7	59	12	28	28%	76%	9%	11%	0	15			0	1.07	3.7	41	$1
20 Proj	3	0	51	45	4.13	3.94	1.47	1.42	91	110	4.8	4.2	8.0	1.9	37%	9.3%	89.3	56	17	27	32%	74%	13%		0						0.2	75	-$3

Ryu,Hyun-Jin

Age: 33 Th: L Role SP	Health F	PT/Exp B	Consist B
Ht: 6' 3" Wt: 255 Type Con	LIMA Plan A	Rand Var -2	MM 4203

Rode H%, S% to otherworldy 1st half ERA, then saw 2nd half fade, possibly from fatigue as IP doubled. But make no mistake, his skills are elite. What he lacks in Ks, he recoups with superb Ctl and GB tilt, and among his five effective pitches, change-up excels both vL and vR (19% SwK, .290 oSLG). Excellent rotation stabilizer after aces are gone.

Yr Tm	W	Sv	IP	K	ERA	xERA	WHIP	xWHIP	vL+	vR+	BF/G	Ctl	Dom	Cmd	Ball%	SwK	Vel	G	L	F	H%	S%	HR/F	xHR/F	GS	APC	DOM%	DIS%	Sv%	LI	RAR	BPX	R$
15																																	
16 LA	0	0	5	4	11.57	5.53	2.14		108	169	24.0	3.9	7.7	2.0		11.2%	89.8	41	24	35	43%	44%	17%	13%	1	89	0%	100%			-4.2	64	-$6
17 LA	5	1	127	116	3.77	4.25	1.37	1.31	127	99	21.6	3.2	8.2	2.6	37%	11.4%	90.3	45	23	32	31%	79%	19%	16%	24	85	13%	33%	100	0.76	9.3	102	$4
18 LA	7	0	82	89	1.97	3.19	1.01	1.06	98	83	21.6	1.6	9.7	5.9	34%	12.3%	90.2	46	19	35	29%	88%	12%	13%	15	83	40%	20%			22.2	178	$13
19 LA	14	0	183	163	2.32	3.50	1.01	1.13	71	87	24.9	1.2	8.0	6.8	34%	11.8%	90.6	50	24	25	29%	82%	13%	12%	29	93	45%	7%			49.3	153	$31
1st Half	9	0	103	94	1.83	3.25	0.90	1.01	64	86	24.6	0.6	8.2	13.4	33%	12.2%	90.4	49	24	26	28%	87%	13%	12%	16	93	44%	13%			33.9	173	$39
2nd Half	5	0	80	69	2.94	3.77	1.14	1.19	83	88	25.3	1.9	7.8	4.1	34%	11.4%	90.8	52	24	24	30%	77%	13%	11%	13	94	46%	0%			15.4	129	$20
20 Proj	13	0	174	159	3.12	3.19	1.08	1.12	92	88	22.5	1.6	8.2	5.0	34%	11.8%	90.4	48	22	30	29%	76%	13%		30						22.1	149	$21

ARIK FLORIMONTE

Sabathia,CC

Age: 39 | Th: L | Role: | Ht: 6' 6" | Wt: 300 | Type:
Health: F | PT/Exp: B | Consist: A | LIMA Plan: | Rand Var: | MM:

Injuries caught up to him in the end, but for all the workload/conditioning concerns early in his career, he tossed 200+ IP every year from ages 26-32. 3,707 career IP in regular + postseason, and he threw until there was nothing left. When asked what he loved most: "50,000 people in the Bronx, and [EXPLETIVE] don't start until I'm ready."

Yr	Tm	W	Sv	IP	K	ERA	xERA	WHIP	xWHIP	vL+	vR+	BF/G	Ctl	Dom	Cmd	Ball%	SwK	Vel	G	L	F	H%	S%	HR/F	xHR/F	GS	APC	DOM%	DIS%	Sv%	LI	RAR	BPX	R$
15	NYY	6	0	167	137	4.73	4.08	1.42	1.30	71	122	25.0	2.7	7.4	2.7	35%	9.4%	90.1	46	22	32	32%	71%	17%	10%	29	93	17%	41%			-15.9	100	-$6
16	NYY	9	0	180	152	3.91	4.22	1.32	1.35	90	99	25.6	3.3	7.6	2.3	36%	10.2%	90.0	50	17	33	30%	74%	13%	12%	30	97	23%	33%			6.3	92	$7
17	NYY	14	0	149	120	3.69	4.20	1.27	1.34	90	98	23.1	3.0	7.3	2.4	36%	9.3%	90.9	50	22	28	28%	76%	17%	12%	27	87	22%	37%			12.2	93	$12
18	NYY	9	0	153	140	3.65	4.23	1.31	1.29	86	102	22.9	3.0	8.2	2.7	34%	11.3%	90.3	44	20	35	31%	76%	12%	11%	29	86	31%	31%			9.5	103	$6
19	NYY	5	0	107	107	4.95	4.73	1.41	1.34	95	117	20.3	3.3	9.0	2.7	36%	11.6%	89.2	40	20	40	30%	74%	21%	13%	22	75	5%	45%	0	0.80	-5.8	99	-$2
1st Half		5	0	69	66	4.04	4.87	1.36	1.31	63	123	22.7	3.4	8.6	2.5	35%	11.0%	88.9	40	19	42	29%	80%	18%	13%	13	84	0%	38%			3.9	88	$3
2nd Half		0	0	38	41	6.57	4.57	1.49	1.23	146	109	17.3	3.1	9.6	3.2	37%	12.8%	89.7	40	22	38	32%	64%	28%	13%	9	63	11%	56%	0	0.82	-9.8	119	-$12
20	Proj																																	

Sadler,Casey

Age: 29 | Th: R | Role: RP | Ht: 6' 3" | Wt: 205 | Type: Con GB
Health: A | PT/Exp: D | Consist: C | LIMA Plan: C | Rand Var: -3 | MM: 1000

4-0, 2.14 ERA in 46 IP at LA/TAM. How lucky can one guy be? S% kept ERA low, Ball% didn't support improved Ctl, and he vultured his way into four MLB wins. When regression takes all that away, RAR, R$ will likely return to negative ways, and he can once again be safely ignored. Like the fella once said, ain't that a kick in the head?

Yr	Tm	W	Sv	IP	K	ERA	xERA	WHIP	xWHIP	vL+	vR+	BF/G	Ctl	Dom	Cmd	Ball%	SwK	Vel	G	L	F	H%	S%	HR/F	xHR/F	GS	APC	DOM%	DIS%	Sv%	LI	RAR	BPX	R$
15	PIT *	7	0	86	42	5.49	4.68	1.40		0	121	25.9	2.9	4.4	1.5		7.8%	90.7	42	33	25	29%	62%	33%	37%	1	77	0%	0%			-16.3	29	-$6
16																																		
17	a/a	3	0	67	39	6.66	6.36	1.70				15.1	1.6	5.2	3.3							39%	60%									-18.9	73	-$12
18	PIT *	6	1	81	48	4.61	6.09	1.73		204	82	12.8	3.5	5.3	1.5		7.0%	92.1	68	16	16	36%	75%	0%	25%	0	43			100	0.42	-4.7	32	-$8
19	2 TM *	5	3	87	71	2.89	4.20	1.23	1.39	94	82	7.6	2.0	7.4	3.7	37%	9.6%	93.5	52	18	30	30%	83%	12%	10%	1	21	0%	100%	60	0.45	17.2	96	$7
1st Half		1	1	54	44	2.69	4.04	1.17	1.37	89	77	10.7	1.7	7.5	4.4	39%	9.3%	93.2	54	18	28	30%	85%	12%	11%	0	31			50	0.29	12.0	111	$7
2nd Half		4	2	33	27	3.22	4.47	1.33	1.33	98	86	5.3	2.5	7.3	3.0	36%	9.9%	93.8	50	19	31	32%	81%	12%	10%	1	17	0%	100%	67	0.51	5.2	80	$7
20	**Proj**	**3**	**0**	**44**	**30**	**4.84**	**4.36**	**1.53**	**1.34**	**123**	**107**	**9.4**	**3.1**	**6.2**	**2.0**	**37%**	**9.6%**	**93.5**	**52**	**18**	**30**	**33%**	**71%**	**14%**		**0**						**-3.7**	**67**	**-$5**

Salazar,Danny

Age: 30 | Th: R | Role: RP | Ht: 6' 0" | Wt: 195 | Type: Pwr
Health: F | PT/Exp: D | Consist: D | LIMA Plan: D | Rand Var: +4 | MM: 2300

0-1, 4.50 ERA in 4 IP at CLE. Skills were so bad in 2019 (how bad were they?) that it's as if he hasn't pitched since 2017... (rimshot). Ended year by cutting rehab assignment short, leaving us with unanswered questions about health and how much talent remains in his injury-ravaged arm. Speculate if you must, but only with the end-gamiest of flyers.

Yr	Tm	W	Sv	IP	K	ERA	xERA	WHIP	xWHIP	vL+	vR+	BF/G	Ctl	Dom	Cmd	Ball%	SwK	Vel	G	L	F	H%	S%	HR/F	xHR/F	GS	APC	DOM%	DIS%	Sv%	LI	RAR	BPX	R$
15	CLE	14	0	185	195	3.45	3.44	1.13	1.17	99	89	25.2	2.6	9.5	3.7	35%	12.2%	94.8	44	19	37	29%	74%	12%	14%	30	102	33%	17%			11.6	147	$18
16	CLE	11	0	137	161	3.87	3.75	1.34	1.29	85	103	23.4	4.1	10.6	2.6	37%	11.5%	94.7	48	17	35	32%	74%	13%	14%	25	96	36%	28%			5.5	124	$8
17	CLE	5	0	103	145	4.28	3.38	1.34	1.16	103	91	19.1	3.8	12.7	3.3	35%	16.8%	95.1	39	25	36	35%	72%	16%	16%	10	70	26%	10%	0	0.07	1.0	170	$0
18																																		
19	CLE *	0	0	21	15	4.15	5.28	1.59		66	224	11.7	5.5	6.5	1.2	45%	4.5%	86.3	42	8	50	28%	79%	33%	36%	1	66	0%	100%			0.9	26	-$5
1st Half																																		
2nd Half		0	0	21	15	4.15	5.28	1.59		66	220	11.7	5.5	6.5	1.2		4.6%	86.3	42	8	50	28%	79%	33%	36%	1	66	0%	100%			0.9	26	-$5
20	**Proj**	**2**	**0**	**44**	**46**	**4.00**	**3.91**	**1.39**	**1.20**	**101**	**97**	**17.1**	**4.3**	**9.6**	**2.2**	**36%**	**13.7%**	**94.9**	**43**	**21**	**36**	**31%**	**75%**	**13%**		**8**						**0.8**	**90**	**-$2**

Sale,Chris

Age: 31 | Th: L | Role: SP | Ht: 6' 6" | Wt: 180 | Type: Pwr
Health: D | PT/Exp: A | Consist: B | LIMA Plan: B | Rand Var: +5 | MM: 5503

Elbow inflammation was treated with PRP injection rather than surgery, so Health grade must be heeded. Bloated ERA could still leave him undervalued but xERA tells the truth. Skills remain elite, even as HR/F turned against him in 2nd half. Risk means you can't build your staff around him; instead, look to acquire at a price that matches his last name.

Yr	Tm	W	Sv	IP	K	ERA	xERA	WHIP	xWHIP	vL+	vR+	BF/G	Ctl	Dom	Cmd	Ball%	SwK	Vel	G	L	F	H%	S%	HR/F	xHR/F	GS	APC	DOM%	DIS%	Sv%	LI	RAR	BPX	R$
15	CHW	13	0	209	274	3.41	2.74	1.09	0.98	84	93	27.5	1.8	11.8	6.5	32%	15.0%	94.5	43	22	35	34%	73%	13%	10%	31	107	65%	10%			14.3	220	$23
16	CHW	17	0	227	233	3.34	3.42	1.04	1.09	79	90	28.3	1.8	9.3	5.2	33%	11.7%	92.8	41	21	38	29%	73%	12%	11%	32	107	66%	13%			23.9	163	$29
17	BOS	17	0	214	308	2.90	2.79	0.97	0.92	70	83	26.6	1.8	12.9	7.2	32%	15.5%	94.4	39	20	41	32%	76%	12%	12%	32	107	69%	3%			38.6	241	$40
18	BOS	12	0	158	237	2.11	2.35	0.86	0.90	58	77	22.9	1.9	13.5	7.0	32%	16.4%	94.7	44	20	36	30%	79%	9%	14%	27	94	63%	11%			39.8	245	$34
19	BOS	6	0	147	218	4.40	2.94	1.09	1.00	88	94	24.5	2.3	13.3	5.9	33%	14.6%	93.2	43	21	36	33%	65%	20%	18%	25	99	32%	16%			2.0	218	$12
1st Half		3	0	101	148	3.82	3.00	1.03	0.95	86	88	24.5	2.1	13.1	6.2	33%	14.8%	93.0	43	19	38	33%	67%	15%	15%	17	98	29%	12%			8.6	218	$17
2nd Half		3	0	46	70	5.67	2.95	1.22	0.98	90	107	24.4	2.5	13.7	5.4	35%	14.2%	93.5	42	26	32	35%	60%	31%	24%	8	100	38%	25%			-6.6	216	-$1
20	**Proj**	**11**	**0**	**160**	**230**	**3.26**	**2.48**	**1.03**	**0.95**	**76**	**89**	**23.3**	**2.2**	**13.0**	**5.8**	**33%**	**15.0%**	**93.8**	**42**	**21**	**37**	**32%**	**74%**	**16%**		**26**						**17.6**	**223**	**$23**

Samardzija,Jeff

Age: 35 | Th: R | Role: SP | Ht: 6' 5" | Wt: 240 | Type: Con FB
Health: F | PT/Exp: B | Consist: C | LIMA Plan: C | Rand Var: -2 | MM: 1103

Would be nice to believe narrative that once-successful pitcher rediscovered himself in 2nd half, but xERA, BPX put the lie to that notion. Reality is we should be concerned about continued Dom/SwK loss, and fact that Ctl bump wasn't backed by return to pre-2018 Ball% levels. If FB% spikes again as in 2018, 1st half of 2019... DN: 5.00 ERA

Yr	Tm	W	Sv	IP	K	ERA	xERA	WHIP	xWHIP	vL+	vR+	BF/G	Ctl	Dom	Cmd	Ball%	SwK	Vel	G	L	F	H%	S%	HR/F	xHR/F	GS	APC	DOM%	DIS%	Sv%	LI	RAR	BPX	R$
15	CHW	11	0	214	163	4.96	4.25	1.29	1.26	115	97	28.4	2.1	6.9	3.3	33%	10.3%	94.2	39	21	40	31%	64%	11%	11%	32	104	28%	28%			-26.4	101	-$2
16	SF	12	0	203	167	3.81	4.00	1.20	1.26	106	87	25.9	2.4	7.4	3.1	34%	9.8%	94.3	46	20	34	29%	72%	12%	14%	32	100	28%	34%			9.6	110	$14
17	SF	9	0	208	205	4.42	3.67	1.14	1.08	102	94	26.5	1.4	8.9	6.4	33%	10.5%	94.3	41	22	36	31%	65%	14%	14%	32	102	41%	16%			-1.6	170	$14
18	SF *	1	0	66	45	6.01	5.41	1.53	1.65	125	98	19.0	4.2	6.2	1.5	40%	8.4%	92.3	30	24	47	30%	63%	9%	16%	10	81	0%	50%			-15.0	28	-$11
19	SF	11	0	181	140	3.52	4.86	1.11	1.35	99	84	23.1	2.4	6.9	2.9	36%	9.2%	91.9	36	22	41	25%	75%	13%	15%	32	94	22%	28%			22.0	80	$18
1st Half		4	0	84	72	4.52	5.10	1.29	1.29	105	97	22.6	2.8	7.7	2.8	36%	9.6%	91.7	35	22	43	29%	70%	13%	13%	16	91	6%	25%			-0.1	84	$5
2nd Half		7	0	98	68	2.67	4.71	0.95	1.28	94	73	23.7	2.1	6.3	3.0	36%	8.8%	92.1	38	23	40	21%	81%	12%	16%	16	97	38%	31%			22.1	78	$29
20	**Proj**	**8**	**0**	**174**	**136**	**4.31**	**4.22**	**1.22**	**1.34**	**107**	**90**	**22.1**	**2.7**	**7.0**	**2.6**	**36%**	**9.2%**	**92.6**	**36**	**22**	**41**	**27%**	**69%**	**12%**		**32**						**-3.5**	**79**	**$7**

Sampson,Adrian

Age: 28 | Th: R | Role: SP | Ht: 6' 2" | Wt: 210 | Type: Con FB
Health: D | PT/Exp: C | Consist: B | LIMA Plan: B | Rand Var: +5 | MM: 0001

Had one great month (3.65 ERA, 9.2 Dom, 5.4 Cmd in June) as he threw slider more often, but it didn't last. And while improvements in Dom, SwK are encouraging, he's still not even league average in either. 1st half xERA represents his MLB skill peak thus far. Don't expect more than that. UPDATE: Signed with KBO

Yr	Tm	W	Sv	IP	K	ERA	xERA	WHIP	xWHIP	vL+	vR+	BF/G	Ctl	Dom	Cmd	Ball%	SwK	Vel	G	L	F	H%	S%	HR/F	xHR/F	GS	APC	DOM%	DIS%	Sv%	LI	RAR	BPX	R$
15	aaa	10	0	163	106	4.38	4.61	1.43				24.7	1.8	5.9	3.3							35%	69%									-8.3	97	-$3
16	SEA *	7	0	85	54	4.05	4.55	1.36		203	136	25.4	1.4	5.7	4.1		3.5%	91.1	33	39	28	34%	72%	40%	37%	1	85	0%	100%			1.5	108	$1
17																																		
18	TEX *	8	0	151	79	4.89	5.85	1.52		99	136	17.3	1.9	4.7	2.5		8.3%	91.1	36	22	42	34%	71%	19%	21%	4	68	0%	50%	0	0.66	-13.9	39	-$9
19	TEX	6	0	125	101	5.89	5.23	1.53	1.35	105	137	16.1	2.6	7.3	2.8	36%	10.2%	92.5	40	19	40	33%	67%	17%	18%	15	59	13%	53%	0	0.79	-21.4	86	-$9
1st Half		6	0	89	73	4.16	4.87	1.36	1.23	98	119	21.1	2.0	7.4	3.7	34%	10.4%	92.5	38	22	40	33%	75%	13%	17%	11	77	18%	45%	0	0.71	3.8	103	-$1
2nd Half		0	0	37	28	10.06	6.26	1.94	1.45	122	172	10.8	3.9	6.9	1.8	38%	9.8%	92.5	44	14	41	35%	53%	25%	21%	4	39	0%	75%	0	0.88	-25.1	44	-$29
20	Proj																																	

Sanchez,Aaron

Age: 28 | Th: R | Role: SP | Ht: 6' 4" | Wt: 210 | Type: Pwr
Health: F | PT/Exp: C | Consist: B | LIMA Plan: B | Rand Var: +3 | MM: 1100

September shoulder surgery will keep him out 'til at least mid-season, possibly all of 2020. That sours the outlook for an already-shaky skill set, where even 2nd half Ctl, Cmd shift is questionable since Ball% remained subpar. There have been 250 IL days since his only good year—between Health grade and R$, maybe we should take a hint.

Yr	Tm	W	Sv	IP	K	ERA	xERA	WHIP	xWHIP	vL+	vR+	BF/G	Ctl	Dom	Cmd	Ball%	SwK	Vel	G	L	F	H%	S%	HR/F	xHR/F	GS	APC	DOM%	DIS%	Sv%	LI	RAR	BPX	R$
15	TOR	7	0	92	61	3.22	4.08	1.28	1.56	121	61	9.3	4.3	5.9	1.4	41%	7.2%	94.9	61	18	22	25%	78%	16%	12%	11	35	0%	45%	0	1.08	8.5	36	$4
16	TOR	15	0	192	161	3.00	3.77	1.17	1.31	89	81	26.3	3.0	7.5	2.6	37%	8.6%	94.7	54	20	25	28%	77%	11%	16%	30	97	43%	17%			28.2	105	$21
17	TOR	1	0	36	24	4.25	5.70	1.72	1.62	87	129	20.9	5.0	6.0	1.2	41%	6.2%	94.9	48	24	29	32%	80%	17%	17%	8	77	13%	75%			0.5	-1	-$6
18	TOR	4	0	105	86	4.89	4.98	1.56	1.55	120	92	23.7	5.0	7.4	1.5	41%	9.8%	93.7	49	19	32	31%	70%	11%	16%	20	90	10%	55%			-9.5	29	-$8
19	2 AL	5	0	131	115	5.89	5.27	1.62	1.53	112	108	22.4	4.7	7.9	1.7	38%	9.2%	93.6	47	23	30	33%	66%	16%	15%	27	85	4%	48%			-22.5	45	-$12
1st Half		3	0	87	72	6.31	5.49	1.77	1.58	106	121	22.8	5.4	7.4	1.4	39%	9.2%	94.0	50	23	27	34%	66%	17%	18%	18	85	0%	50%			-19.4	18	-$16
2nd Half		2	0	44	43	5.08	4.68	1.33	1.29	122	83	21.7	3.2	8.7	2.7	38%	9.1%	92.9	40	23	37	31%	65%	15%	11%	9	87	11%	44%			-3.1	96	-$4
20	**Proj**	**2**	**0**	**44**	**36**	**4.95**	**4.42**	**1.52**	**1.48**	**112**	**100**	**20.4**	**4.4**	**7.5**	**1.7**	**39%**	**8.7%**	**93.8**	**47**	**22**	**31**	**31%**	**70%**	**15%**		**9**						**-4.3**	**48**	**-$5**

BRANDON KRUSE

Sanchez,Anibal

Sanchez,Anibal			Health	D	LIMA Plan	F
Age: 36	Th: R	Role: SP	PT/Exp	B	Rand Var	-1
Ht: 6' 0"	Wt: 205	Type	Consist	F	MM	2203

Reports of his rebirth have been greatly exaggerated, mostly by H% and S%. His 2018 skills were at least rosterable though; the 2019 package, not so much. There's certainly middle ground to be found, especially since steady SwK suggests Dom will rebound, but another year of double-digit value is probably asking too much.

Yr Tm	W	Sv	IP	K	ERA	xERA	WHIP	xWHIP	vL+	vR+	BF/G	Ctl	Dom	Cmd	Ball%	SwK	Vel	G	L	F	H%	S%	HR/F	xHR/F	GS	APC	DOM%	DIS%	Sv%	LI	RAR	BPX	R$
15 DET	10	0	157	138	4.99	4.11	1.28	1.28	93	122	26.4	2.8	7.9	2.8	37%	9.8%	91.9	40	21	39	29%	66%	16%	10%	25	101	40%	24%			-19.9	101	-$1
16 DET	7	0	153	135	5.87	4.59	1.46	1.32	105	121	19.1	3.1	7.9	2.5	36%	9.5%	91.1	40	19	41	32%	64%	16%	12%	26	74	12%	38%	0	0.84	-31.8	91	-$10
17 DET *	3	0	121	118	6.53	7.05	1.64	1.21	109	134	16.9	2.6	8.8	3.3	37%	10.2%	90.8	36	25	40	37%	66%	19%	15%	17	66	12%	35%	0	0.58	-32.4	55	-$15
18 ATL	7	0	137	135	2.83	3.75	1.08	1.22	78	96	22.1	2.8	8.9	3.2	36%	10.9%	90.7	45	18	37	27%	79%	11%	12%	24	85	38%	29%	0	0.75	22.2	125	$15
19 WAS	11	0	166	134	3.85	5.14	1.27	1.41	98	90	23.7	3.1	7.3	2.3	36%	10.4%	90.5	38	23	39	28%	74%	11%	11%	30	90	20%	37%			13.4	67	$10
1st Half	4	0	78	73	3.82	5.00	1.33	1.33	110	85	22.7	3.5	8.5	2.4	37%	10.1%	90.1	35	27	39	30%	76%	12%	10%	15	87	7%	40%			6.5	78	$6
2nd Half	7	0	88	61	3.87	5.29	1.22	1.38	89	95	24.8	2.9	6.2	2.2	35%	10.7%	90.8	41	20	40	27%	72%	10%	12%	15	92	33%	33%			6.9	58	$14
20 Proj	**9**	**0**	**160**	**144**	**4.16**	**3.98**	**1.29**	**1.30**	**95**	**102**	**21.1**	**2.9**	**8.1**	**2.8**	**36%**	**10.4%**	**90.7**	**40**	**21**	**39**	**30%**	**72%**	**13%**		**31**						**-0.2**	**97**	**$6**

Sanchez,Sixto

Sanchez,Sixto			Health	A	LIMA Plan	F
Age: 21	Th: R	Role: SP	PT/Exp	F	Rand Var	0
Ht: 6' 0"	Wt: 185	Type: Con	Consist	F	MM	2101

One of game's top pitching prospects held his own in first AA exposure, though strikeouts faded down the stretch. Both two- and four-seamer can touch 100 mph, and he's owned excellent Ctl rates every step of the way so far through minors. 2019's 114 IP was career high, so workload still a concern, but seems like 2020 call-up to MIA is in play.

Yr Tm	W	Sv	IP	K	ERA	xERA	WHIP	xWHIP	vL+	vR+	BF/G	Ctl	Dom	Cmd	Ball%	SwK	Vel	G	L	F	H%	S%	HR/F	xHR/F	GS	APC	DOM%	DIS%	Sv%	LI	RAR	BPX	R$
15																																	
16																																	
17																																	
18																																	
19 aa	8	0	103	85	3.90	3.89	1.29				23.5	1.9	7.5	4.0							34%	70%									7.8	121	$4
1st Half	3	0	52	48	4.26	4.80	1.48		0	0	24.8	1.8	8.2	4.7							39%	70%			0	0					1.6	138	-$1
2nd Half	5	0	51	38	3.53	2.97	1.10		0	0	22.2	2.0	6.7	3.3							28%	69%			0	0					6.2	107	$10
20 Proj	**5**	**0**	**73**	**59**	**3.97**	**3.77**	**1.29**				**21.8**	**2.2**	**7.3**	**3.3**	**37%**	**10.0%**		**48**	**20**	**32**	**31%**	**74%**	**14%**		**12**						**1.6**	**113**	**$1**

Sandoval,Patrick

Sandoval,Patrick			Health	A	LIMA Plan	F
Age: 23	Th: L	Role: RP	PT/Exp	F	Rand Var	+5
Ht: 6' 3"	Wt: 190	Type: Pwr	Consist	F	MM	1301

0-4, 5.03 ERA in 39 IP at LAA. Control has been spotty in minors; that issue carried over to majors, and damage was exacerbated by H%, S% and HR/F. But thanks to GB-heavy approach, MLB xERA was more acceptable (4.20), and Dom history, small-sample SwK lend him some deep league appeal. Could be worth a speculative flyer.

Yr Tm	W	Sv	IP	K	ERA	xERA	WHIP	xWHIP	vL+	vR+	BF/G	Ctl	Dom	Cmd	Ball%	SwK	Vel	G	L	F	H%	S%	HR/F	xHR/F	GS	APC	DOM%	DIS%	Sv%	LI	RAR	BPX	R$
15																																	
16																																	
17																																	
18 aa	1	0	21	24	1.58	1.49	1.02				20.4	3.3	10.1	3.0							28%	83%									6.7	163	-$1
19 LAA *	4	0	120	127	5.70	5.61	1.67	1.41	135	89	18.0	4.5	9.5	2.1	40%	13.7%	93.0	47	26	27	37%	67%	21%	17%	9	71	11%	56%	0	0.72	-17.8	71	-$11
1st Half	3	0	57	61	6.22	6.46	1.86		0	0	17.8	4.3	9.7	2.3							43%	66%	0%		0	0					-12.1	76	-$14
2nd Half	1	0	63	65	5.24	4.84	1.49	1.36	136	88	18.2	4.6	9.3	2.0	40%	13.7%	93.0	47	26	27	32%	68%	21%	17%	9	71	11%	56%	0	0.72	-5.7	68	-$8
20 Proj	**4**	**0**	**116**	**121**	**4.84**	**4.13**	**1.57**	**1.50**	**136**	**92**	**17.8**	**4.4**	**9.4**	**2.2**	**44%**	**13.7%**	**93.0**	**45**	**23**	**33**	**35%**	**71%**	**12%**		**22**						**-9.8**	**85**	**-$6**

Scherzer,Max

Scherzer,Max			Health	D	LIMA Plan	A
Age: 35	Th: R	Role: SP	PT/Exp	A	Rand Var	+2
Ht: 6' 3"	Wt: 215	Type: Pwr FB	Consist	A	MM	5503

While 2nd half was cut short by shoulder inflammation and back strain, skills didn't skip a beat—ERA got trashed by H%, HR/F. Had hit the IL only once in prior nine seasons, but at his age, we can't assume return to 200+ IP is a given. Still every bit the ace, just probably not the first pitcher you take off the board this time around.

Yr Tm	W	Sv	IP	K	ERA	xERA	WHIP	xWHIP	vL+	vR+	BF/G	Ctl	Dom	Cmd	Ball%	SwK	Vel	G	L	F	H%	S%	HR/F	xHR/F	GS	APC	DOM%	DIS%	Sv%	LI	RAR	BPX	R$
15 WAS	14	0	229	276	2.79	3.00	0.92	0.97	90	76	27.2	1.3	10.9	8.1	29%	16.1%	94.2	36	19	45	29%	76%	11%	10%	33	102	58%	9%			32.9	207	$37
16 WAS	20	0	228	284	2.96	3.33	0.97	1.05	103	65	26.5	2.2	11.2	5.1	32%	15.9%	94.3	33	19	48	27%	77%	12%	11%	34	105	65%	12%			34.7	182	$38
17 WAS	16	0	201	268	2.51	3.13	0.90	1.03	91	57	25.2	2.5	12.0	4.9	32%	16.3%	94.1	37	17	47	26%	79%	11%	9%	31	100	65%	3%			45.7	198	$41
18 WAS	18	0	221	300	2.53	3.01	0.91	0.98	83	76	26.2	2.1	12.2	5.9	31%	16.7%	94.4	34	18	48	28%	78%	10%	11%	33	106	67%	6%			44.1	203	$44
19 WAS	11	0	172	243	2.92	2.97	1.03	0.97	100	70	25.7	1.7	12.7	7.4	31%	17.1%	94.9	41	21	38	34%	76%	12%	11%	27	103	52%	7%			33.6	219	$27
1st Half	8	0	122	170	2.43	2.99	1.00	0.93	88	76	27.2	1.6	12.5	7.7	31%	17.5%	95.0	42	20	38	34%	79%	8%	12%	18	107	72%	6%			31.4	220	$36
2nd Half	3	0	50	73	4.14	3.16	1.10	0.95	122	55	22.7	2.0	13.1	6.6	32%	16.2%	94.7	37	24	40	34%	70%	19%	10%	9	94	11%	11%			2.3	216	$3
20 Proj	**12**	**0**	**174**	**240**	**3.08**	**2.70**	**1.01**	**0.97**	**102**	**68**	**24.1**	**2.0**	**12.4**	**6.3**	**31%**	**16.6%**	**94.6**	**37**	**20**	**43**	**32%**	**75%**	**13%**		**28**						**23.1**	**212**	**$27**

Senzatela,Antonio

Senzatela,Antonio			Health	C	LIMA Plan	D
Age: 25	Th: R	Role: SP	PT/Exp	C	Rand Var	+5
Ht: 6' 1"	Wt: 246	Type: Con	Consist	D	MM	0001

11-11, 6.71 ERA in 124 IP at COL. Control faltered, Dom cratered, and thin air of Coors is not kind to skill weakness. 2nd half line is so bleak it reads like the opening chapter of a dystopian sci-fi novel. GB% remains a strength, and he's still young enough to bounce back, but his road ERA was a full run WORSE than Coors... help!

Yr Tm	W	Sv	IP	K	ERA	xERA	WHIP	xWHIP	vL+	vR+	BF/G	Ctl	Dom	Cmd	Ball%	SwK	Vel	G	L	F	H%	S%	HR/F	xHR/F	GS	APC	DOM%	DIS%	Sv%	LI	RAR	BPX	R$
15																																	
16 aa	4	0	35	22	2.79	3.45	1.29				20.3	2.6	5.6	2.1							30%	79%									6.0	83	$0
17 COL	10	0	135	102	4.68	4.36	1.30	1.37	99	104	15.7	3.1	6.8	2.2	38%	7.3%	94.3	50	22	28	28%	67%	16%	12%	20	62	10%	50%	0	0.64	-5.3	79	$3
18 COL *	9	0	130	102	3.77	3.88	1.30	1.35	95	114	17.2	2.9	7.1	2.4	38%	8.8%	93.7	46	21	33	30%	73%	11%	12%	13	66	15%	38%	0	0.73	6.1	85	$5
19 COL *	12	0	160	85	6.61	6.66	1.74	1.58	124	113	22.8	3.8	4.8	1.3	40%	7.7%	93.7	54	22	24	34%	64%	18%	19%	25	89	8%	68%			-41.5	2	-$19
1st Half	7	0	89	50	4.67	5.57	1.61	1.58	122	99	23.2	4.0	5.1	1.3	41%	6.9%	93.8	52	24	24	31%	74%	18%	18%	15	95	13%	60%			-1.8	19	-$9
2nd Half	5	0	71	35	9.04	8.02	1.91	1.47	126	138	22.3	3.4	4.5	1.3	37%	9.1%	93.3	57	20	23	36%	53%	19%	20%	10	82	0%	80%			-39.6	-19	-$32
20 Proj	**7**	**0**	**102**	**64**	**5.56**	**4.66**	**1.60**	**1.44**	**112**	**118**	**21.9**	**3.5**	**5.7**	**1.6**	**38%**	**8.3%**	**93.7**	**49**	**22**	**28**	**33%**	**67%**	**14%**		**21**						**-17.7**	**42**	**-$9**

Severino,Luis

Severino,Luis			Health	F	LIMA Plan	A
Age: 26	Th: R	Role: SP	PT/Exp	B	Rand Var	-5
Ht: 6' 2"	Wt: 215	Type: Pwr	Consist	A	MM	4403

Spring training shoulder injury begat lat strain, lat strain begat June rehab setback. Strikeouts were there in mid-Sept return, but sample is too small to be meaningful, so we're left hoping young stud can resume march toward acedom. Health risk means you can't target at 2017-18 values, but even diminished version of these skills is worth owning.

Yr Tm	W	Sv	IP	K	ERA	xERA	WHIP	xWHIP	vL+	vR+	BF/G	Ctl	Dom	Cmd	Ball%	SwK	Vel	G	L	F	H%	S%	HR/F	xHR/F	GS	APC	DOM%	DIS%	Sv%	LI	RAR	BPX	R$
15 NYY *	14	0	162	143	3.07	2.97	1.16	1.31	97	99	21.5	2.8	8.0	2.9	36%	10.0%	95.4	50	20	30	29%	75%	17%	16%	11	93	9%	27%			17.7	115	$17
16 NYY *	11	0	148	135	5.25	4.75	1.43	1.30	101	119	18.0	2.7	8.2	3.1	38%	9.5%	96.1	45	24	31	35%	64%	16%	15%	11	58	9%	64%	0	0.70	-19.4	95	-$4
17 NYY	14	0	193	230	2.98	3.11	1.04	1.09	88	74	25.3	2.4	10.7	4.5	33%	13.4%	97.6	51	19	31	29%	76%	14%	12%	31	99	65%	13%			32.9	189	$30
18 NYY	19	0	191	220	3.39	3.28	1.14	1.09	94	90	24.4	2.2	10.3	4.8	33%	12.8%	97.6	41	26	33	33%	74%	11%	15%	32	99	41%	9%			18.0	169	$23
19 NYY	1	0	12	17	1.50	3.55	1.00	1.26	61	53	16.0	4.5	12.8	2.8	34%	11.4%	96.1	42	13	46	26%	83%	0%	4%	3	73	33%	0%			4.4	139	-$2
1st Half																																	
2nd Half	1	0	12	17	1.50	3.59	1.00		62	52	16.0	4.5	12.8	2.8		11.4%	96.1	42	13	46	26%	83%	0%	4%	3	73	33%	0%			4.4	139	-$2
20 Proj	**13**	**0**	**160**	**175**	**3.52**	**3.24**	**1.23**	**1.20**	**92**	**93**	**22.5**	**2.8**	**9.9**	**3.6**	**35%**	**11.3%**	**96.7**	**46**	**23**	**31**	**32%**	**74%**	**12%**		**29**						**12.3**	**146**	**$15**

Shafer,Justin

Shafer,Justin			Health	A	LIMA Plan	D
Age: 27	Th: R	Role: RP	PT/Exp	D	Rand Var	0
Ht: 6' 2"	Wt: 195	Type: Pwr FB	Consist	D	MM	0110

2-1, 3.86 ERA in 39 IP at TOR. Rode an 82% strand rate to success in majors; MLB xERA was 5.87, as walk rate jumped from 2.4 at AAA to 5.7 at TOR. SwK suggests he might further improve emerging Dom, but Ctl looks to be an ongoing issue, and one made worse by high FB%. Simply too many negatives here to make him of interest.

Yr Tm	W	Sv	IP	K	ERA	xERA	WHIP	xWHIP	vL+	vR+	BF/G	Ctl	Dom	Cmd	Ball%	SwK	Vel	G	L	F	H%	S%	HR/F	xHR/F	GS	APC	DOM%	DIS%	Sv%	LI	RAR	BPX	R$
15																																	
16																																	
17 a/a	5	1	62	43	4.89	4.80	1.50				6.9	4.4	6.2	1.4							29%	70%									-4.1	39	-$3
18 TOR *	5	16	66	41	1.74	3.13	1.31		70	115	5.1	4.2	5.6	1.3		6.2%	92.8	45	21	34	27%	88%	10%	10%	0	24			94	0.64	19.4	70	$11
19 TOR *	2	8	72	66	4.26	5.32	1.57	1.62	126	103	5.4	4.3	8.3	1.9	39%	12.7%	94.3	32	26	42	34%	77%	12%	11%	0	22			89	0.66	2.1	57	-$1
1st Half	0	7	39	34	2.36	3.94	1.29		122	108	5.9	3.5	7.9	2.3		12.2%	94.2	19	33	48	29%	88%	15%	20%	0	27			88	0.74	10.2	76	$5
2nd Half	2	1	33	32	6.47	6.91	1.89	1.48	127	101	5.1	5.2	8.7	1.7	38%	12.9%	94.3	36	24	40	38%	68%	11%	8%	0	20			100	0.65	-8.1	39	-$7
20 Proj	**3**	**2**	**58**	**49**	**4.55**	**4.87**	**1.51**	**1.63**	**122**	**95**	**5.4**	**4.4**	**7.6**	**1.7**	**42%**	**11.5%**	**94.3**	**36**	**24**	**40**	**30%**	**75%**	**13%**		**0**						**-2.9**	**37**	**-$3**

BRANDON KRUSE

Shaw,Bryan

Age: 32	Th: R	Role RP	PT/Exp	C	Rand Var +4
Ht: 6' 1"	Wt: 232	Type Pwr GB	Consist	B	MM 2200
			Health	B	LIMA Plan B

Once-reliable setup man has been "shanked" since arriving in Coors. Is there any chance for redemption? Hope might be a dangerous thing. While S% misfortune contributed to struggles, he's also pitched in by losing strike zone, a bit of Dom, and some of GB tilt. Contract may thwart escape from thin air, too, so best to just leave him be.

Yr	Tm	W	Sv	IP	K	ERA	xERA	WHIP	xWHIP	vL+	vR+	BF/G	Ctl	Dom	Cmd	Ball%	SwK	Vel	G	L	F	H%	S%	HR/F	xHR/F	GS	APC	DOM%	DIS%	Sv%	LI	RAR	BPX	R$
15	CLE	3	2	64	54	2.95	3.81	1.22	1.28	92	99	3.6	2.7	7.6	2.8	35%	10.7%		46	24	31	29%	81%	14%	17%	0	14			33	1.21	8.0	105	$3
16	CLE	2	1	67	69	3.24	3.59	1.26	1.31	103	87	3.7	3.8	9.3	2.5	38%	12.1%		54	19	27	29%	79%	17%	14%	0	15			25	1.13	7.8	116	$2
17	CLE	4	3	77	73	3.52	3.43	1.21	1.22	78	94	3.9	2.6	8.6	3.3	35%	12.5%	95.0	56	22	22	32%	72%	11%	8%	0	15			50	1.07	7.9	142	$5
18	COL	4	0	55	54	5.93	4.65	1.79	1.43	106	137	4.2	4.6	8.9	1.9	40%	12.1%	94.5	49	21	30	38%	70%	17%	18%	0	17			0	0.87	-12.0	72	-$10
19	COL	3	1	72	58	5.38	4.85	1.36	1.45	81	126	4.4	3.6	7.3	2.0	40%	11.2%	93.0	49	20	31	28%	64%	18%	15%	0	17			17	0.85	-7.7	65	-$4
1st Half		2	0	47	35	3.83	4.66	1.23	1.37	88	105	4.6	3.1	6.7	2.2	40%	11.4%		49	21	30	27%	73%	14%	17%	0	17			0	0.78	3.9	70	-$1
2nd Half		1	1	25	23	8.28	5.05	1.60	1.47	68	167	4.2	4.7	8.3	1.8	40%	10.9%	93.0	49	19	32	31%	50%	25%	10%	0	17			33	0.97	-11.6	55	-$10
20	**Proj**	**3**	**0**	**58**	**53**	**4.79**	**4.01**	**1.48**	**1.38**	**85**	**126**	**4.1**	**3.9**	**8.2**	**2.1**	**39%**	**11.6%**	**65.8**	**50**	**21**	**29**	**32%**	**71%**	**16%**		**0**						**-4.6**	**81**	**-$4**

Sheffield,Justus

Age: 24	Th: L	Role SP	PT/Exp	D	Rand Var +3
Ht: 6' 0"	Wt: 200	Type Pwr xGB	Consist	F	MM 2203
			Health	A	LIMA Plan F

0-1, 5.50 ERA in 36 IP at SEA. Control woes bumped him back to AA from AAA, but improvement there (2.19 ERA, 85/18 K/BB in 78 IP) earned him first MLB starts late in year. DOM/DIS gives a sense how those went, largely due to command struggles resurfacing. SwK, GB% offer hint of good things to come, but there's still work to be done.

Yr	Tm	W	Sv	IP	K	ERA	xERA	WHIP	xWHIP	vL+	vR+	BF/G	Ctl	Dom	Cmd	Ball%	SwK	Vel	G	L	F	H%	S%	HR/F	xHR/F	GS	APC	DOM%	DIS%	Sv%	LI	RAR	BPX	R$
15																																		
16																																		
17	aa	7	0	93	73	4.43	6.43	1.61				24.3	3.4	7.0	2.1							33%	81%									-0.8	23	-$3
18	NYY *	7	0	119	108	3.33	3.25	1.31		96	233	17.5	4.2	8.2	2.0		1.8%	94.4	55	18	27	29%	75%	33%	28%	0	19			0	0.14	12.0	98	$6
19	SEA *	7	0	169	155	5.20	5.30	1.56	1.44	109	120	22.5	4.2	8.3	2.0	38%	13.1%	92.8	52	18	30	34%	69%	16%	15%	7	84	0%	43%	0	0.73	-14.5	57	-$7
1st Half		3	0	78	67	6.67	6.33	1.77		184	83	21.0	5.8	7.7	1.3		9.3%	92.6	57	0	43	32%	65%	33%	30%	0	75			0	0.58	-20.9	23	-$19
2nd Half		4	0	91	88	3.94	4.42	1.39	1.33	97	120	23.9	2.8	8.7	3.1	37%	13.6%	92.9	52	19	29	35%	73%	14%	14%	7	85	0%	43%			6.3	100	$3
20	**Proj**	**7**	**0**	**131**	**121**	**4.36**	**3.99**	**1.46**	**1.46**	**83**	**99**	**20.8**	**4.0**	**8.4**	**2.1**	**41%**	**13.5%**	**92.9**	**52**	**19**	**29**	**32%**	**73%**	**13%**		**27**						**-3.3**	**85**	**-$1**

Shoemaker,Matthew

Age: 33	Th: R	Role SP	PT/Exp	D	Rand Var -5
Ht: 6' 2"	Wt: 225	Type	Consist	B	MM 2201
			Health	F	LIMA Plan B

Oft-sidelined hurler was off to fortunate start before yet another devastating injury, this time ACL. Was already throwing bullpens by mid-Oct, so should be set to give it another go this spring. In small 2019 sample, SwK looked good, GB% intriguing, so it wasn't all smoke and mirrors. There are worse lottery tickets; just have a backup ready.

Yr	Tm	W	Sv	IP	K	ERA	xERA	WHIP	xWHIP	vL+	vR+	BF/G	Ctl	Dom	Cmd	Ball%	SwK	Vel	G	L	F	H%	S%	HR/F	xHR/F	GS	APC	DOM%	DIS%	Sv%	LI	RAR	BPX	R$
15	LAA	7	0	135	116	4.46	4.12	1.26	1.24	100	112	22.8	2.3	7.7	3.3	37%	9.6%	90.2	39	18	42	29%	71%	14%	12%	24	84	38%	42%	0	0.76	-8.2	111	$1
16	LAA	9	0	160	143	3.88	3.91	1.23	1.15	96	102	24.7	1.7	8.0	4.8	33%	13.4%	91.5	40	24	36	32%	71%	10%	15%	27	92	26%	30%			6.1	139	$9
17	LAA	6	0	78	69	4.52	4.69	1.30	1.33	105	106	23.3	3.2	8.0	2.5	36%	11.8%	91.5	38	15	47	28%	72%	15%	15%	14	90	21%	36%			-1.5	87	$1
18	LAA	2	0	31	33	4.94	3.72	1.26	1.21	83	106	18.6	2.9	9.6	3.3	36%	13.0%	91.3	44	22	34	32%	61%	10%	19%	7	71	0%	29%			-3.0	134	-$4
19	TOR	3	0	29	24	1.57	4.06	0.87	1.34	82	66	21.6	2.8	7.5	2.7	35%	13.9%	90.5	51	12	36	19%	91%	11%	22%	5	84	40%	60%			10.4	96	$2
1st Half		3	0	29	24	1.57	4.07	0.87	1.29	82	67	21.6	2.8	7.5	2.7	35%	13.9%	90.5	51	12	36	19%	91%	11%	22%	5	84	40%	60%			10.4	97	$2
2nd Half																																		
20	**Proj**	**6**	**0**	**73**	**66**	**3.74**	**3.82**	**1.22**	**1.26**	**99**	**99**	**21.7**	**2.7**	**8.2**	**3.0**	**35%**	**12.6%**	**91.0**	**44**	**17**	**39**	**29%**	**75%**	**13%**		**14**						**3.7**	**109**	**$3**

Sims,Lucas

Age: 26	Th: R	Role RP	PT/Exp	D	Rand Var +3
Ht: 6' 2"	Wt: 225	Type Pwr xFB	Consist	A	MM 1400
			Health	A	LIMA Plan A

2-1, 4.60 ERA in 43 IP at CIN. Used primarily out of bullpen, he ratcheted velocity up another notch, and SwK, Dom followed. Otherwise, skills not crying out for higher-leverage work or another rotation shot. Control remains a problem, and FB% headed in wrong direction, perpetuating HR issues. Time is still on his side, but for now it's a "no."

Yr	Tm	W	Sv	IP	K	ERA	xERA	WHIP	xWHIP	vL+	vR+	BF/G	Ctl	Dom	Cmd	Ball%	SwK	Vel	G	L	F	H%	S%	HR/F	xHR/F	GS	APC	DOM%	DIS%	Sv%	LI	RAR	BPX	R$
15	aa	4	0	48	51	3.89	2.47	1.31				21.9	5.6	9.7	1.7							28%	68%									0.4	124	-$1
16	a/a	7	0	141	144	5.88	5.27	1.74				23.0	6.5	9.2	1.4							33%	67%									-29.5	65	-$15
17	ATL *	10	0	173	161	5.01	4.78	1.37	1.42	121	112	21.3	3.2	8.4	2.6	37%	8.9%	91.8	38	23	39	31%	68%	13%	12%	10	70	10%	60%	0	0.74	-14.0	74	$1
18	2 NL *	4	0	118	114	4.42	4.88	1.47		112	115	17.4	4.2	8.7	2.1		11.5%	92.5	37	22	41	32%	74%	16%	13%	0	35			0	0.52	-3.9	69	-$4
19	CIN *	7	0	122	145	5.56	4.80	1.44	1.26	88	99	13.0	4.4	10.7	2.4	37%	15.6%	93.6	25	19	57	33%	65%	15%	11%	4	31	25%	50%	0	0.66	-15.9	82	-$4
1st Half		5	0	74	83	6.79	5.87	1.61		44	161	22.0	4.2	10.0	2.4		19.0%	93.2	18	29	53	36%	60%	11%	3%	1	100	100%	0%			-20.9	66	-$8
2nd Half		2	0	48	62	3.65	3.13	1.17	1.27	101	89	7.6	4.7	11.7	2.5	38%	15.1%	93.6	26	16	58	25%	75%	15%	13%	3	28	0%	67%	0	0.66	5.0	109	$4
20	**Proj**	**3**	**0**	**58**	**64**	**4.78**	**4.31**	**1.40**	**1.33**	**112**	**100**	**13.7**	**4.4**	**9.9**	**2.3**	**38%**	**12.7%**	**92.9**	**31**	**19**	**50**	**31%**	**69%**	**11%**		**7**						**-4.5**	**79**	**-$3**

Smeltzer,Devin

Age: 24	Th: L	Role RP	PT/Exp	D	Rand Var 0
Ht: 6' 3"	Wt: 195	Type Con FB	Consist	B	MM 1101
			Health	A	LIMA Plan B

2-2, 3.86 ERA in 49 IP at MIN. Unheralded rookie shuttled between AAA/majors, rotation/bullpen, and showed some promise. Perhaps unsurprisingly, finesse arsenal did not generate swings and misses at same rate as in minors, but Ctl is legit. For 2020, might remain on rotation fringes, but has time to develop into a little something more.

Yr	Tm	W	Sv	IP	K	ERA	xERA	WHIP	xWHIP	vL+	vR+	BF/G	Ctl	Dom	Cmd	Ball%	SwK	Vel	G	L	F	H%	S%	HR/F	xHR/F	GS	APC	DOM%	DIS%	Sv%	LI	RAR	BPX	R$
15																																		
16																																		
17																																		
18	aa	5	4	97	68	5.45	5.45	1.51				12.7	1.9	6.3	3.3							36%	64%									-15.6	80	-$7
19	MIN *	6	1	154	123	3.81	4.59	1.26	1.32	114	101	20.3	2.1	7.2	3.4	33%	9.7%	89.1	39	22	40	30%	77%	14%	16%	6	67	17%	17%	100	0.64	13.3	77	$8
1st Half		3	0	89	72	2.61	3.53	1.10		64	120	23.1	1.7	7.4	4.2		9.9%	88.9	41	15	44	28%	84%	27%	25%	2	76	50%	0%			20.7	113	$15
2nd Half		3	1	68	50	5.23	5.72	1.43	1.26	137	95	18.0	2.5	6.6	2.7	34%	9.6%	89.2	38	24	39	31%	69%	9%	12%	4	65	0%	25%	100	0.61	-6.1	40	-$2
20	**Proj**	**4**	**0**	**87**	**64**	**4.65**	**4.38**	**1.37**	**1.39**	**128**	**94**	**16.1**	**2.1**	**6.7**	**3.2**	**37%**	**9.6%**	**89.2**	**38**	**24**	**39**	**32%**	**70%**	**11%**		**14**						**-5.4**	**91**	**-$3**

Smith,Caleb

Age: 28	Th: L	Role SP	PT/Exp	C	Rand Var 0
Ht: 6' 2"	Wt: 205	Type Pwr xFB	Consist	A	MM 1303
			Health	F	LIMA Plan A

Through 12 GS, seemed to be making quantum leap, then hip got inflamed, and he wasn't same guy after IL stint. Gave back Ctl gains, Dom crashed, and RHB hit him hard, all issues for extreme fly-baller ever at risk of HR spikes. Fatigue may have been cause, as this was career-high IP total; off-season rest may put him back on upward trajectory.

Yr	Tm	W	Sv	IP	K	ERA	xERA	WHIP	xWHIP	vL+	vR+	BF/G	Ctl	Dom	Cmd	Ball%	SwK	Vel	G	L	F	H%	S%	HR/F	xHR/F	GS	APC	DOM%	DIS%	Sv%	LI	RAR	BPX	R$
15	a/a	10	0	135	81	4.75	4.91	1.59				22.9	4.1	5.4	1.3							32%	70%									-13.2	42	-$8
16	aa	3	3	64	58	5.76	5.82	1.69				10.6	3.2	8.2	2.6							39%	66%									-12.3	80	-$7
17	NYY *	9	0	119	101	4.22	4.60	1.40		118	113	18.0	3.4	7.6	2.2		13.5%	94.0	28	29	43	31%	74%	16%	15%	2	38	0%	100%	0	0.35	2.1	67	$2
18	MIA	5	0	77	88	4.19	4.29	1.24	1.28	98	96	20.4	3.8	10.2	2.7	37%	12.3%	92.8	28	21	51	29%	70%	10%	14%	16	87	19%	25%			-0.4	100	$1
19	MIA	10	0	153	168	4.52	4.80	1.23	1.33	82	106	23.1	3.5	9.9	2.8	35%	13.4%	91.6	26	21	52	26%	72%	16%	16%	28	95	25%	36%			-0.3	94	$8
1st Half		3	0	66	82	3.41	3.84	1.02	1.10	94	91	21.7	2.7	11.2	4.1	33%	15.9%	92.2	29	23	48	25%	78%	18%	19%	12	92	33%	17%			8.9	147	$11
2nd Half		7	0	87	86	5.36	5.72	1.39	1.39	73	116	24.1	4.1	8.9	2.2	37%	11.7%	91.3	24	20	55	28%	68%	14%	14%	16	97	19%	50%			-9.2	55	$6
20	**Proj**	**11**	**0**	**160**	**170**	**4.16**	**4.11**	**1.28**	**1.27**	**93**	**105**	**21.5**	**3.4**	**9.6**	**2.8**	**36%**	**12.9%**	**92.1**	**27**	**21**	**52**	**29%**	**74%**	**12%**		**30**						**-0.1**	**99**	**$8**

Smith,Joe

Age: 36	Th: R	Role RP	PT/Exp	D	Rand Var -5
Ht: 6' 2"	Wt: 205	Type	Consist	B	MM 4300
			Health	F	LIMA Plan B

Didn't debut until mid-July (Achilles surgery), but then was as good as ever, right? In reality, H%, S% did most of heavy lifting, as Dom slipped, issues vL crept in. Usage suggests HOU realized graceful slide toward retirement is underway, so past smattering of saves likely gone for good. Maybe has one more sub-4 ERA in him, but that's about it.

Yr	Tm	W	Sv	IP	K	ERA	xERA	WHIP	xWHIP	vL+	vR+	BF/G	Ctl	Dom	Cmd	Ball%	SwK	Vel	G	L	F	H%	S%	HR/F	xHR/F	GS	APC	DOM%	DIS%	Sv%	LI	RAR	BPX	R$
15	LAA	5	5	65	57	3.58	3.49	1.27	1.26	108	83	3.9	2.6	7.9	3.0	33%	8.2%	88.3	52	23	25	32%	72%	9%	12%	0	14			56	1.29	3.1	120	$3
16	2 TM	2	6	52	40	3.46	4.05	1.25	1.36	99	97	4.0	3.1	6.9	2.2	34%	9.0%	88.3	50	23	27	27%	79%	20%	18%	0	15			67	0.90	4.7	81	$2
17	2 AL	3	1	54	71	3.33	2.65	1.04	0.96	93	74	3.6	1.7	11.8	7.1	30%	12.0%	88.9	50	21	29	34%	69%	11%	9%	0	14			50	1.22	6.8	235	$4
18	HOU	5	0	46	46	3.74	3.54	1.01	1.17	88	90	3.2	2.4	9.1	3.8	31%	10.3%	87.8	44	18	38	25%	69%	16%	14%	0	12			0	0.93	2.3	140	$2
19	HOU	1	0	25	22	1.80	3.73	0.96	1.20	101	59	3.4	1.8	7.9	4.4	31%	9.6%	88.0	49	20	30	26%	86%	10%	10%	0	12			0	0.65	8.3	132	$0
1st Half																																		
2nd Half		1	0	25	22	1.80	3.73	0.96	1.16	101	58	3.4	1.8	7.9	4.4	31%	9.6%	88.0	49	20	30	26%	86%	10%	10%	0	12			0	0.65	8.3	132	$0
20	**Proj**	**4**	**0**	**58**	**58**	**3.47**	**3.17**	**1.11**	**1.15**	**101**	**80**	**3.5**	**2.2**	**9.0**	**4.2**	**31%**	**10.1%**	**88.3**	**49**	**21**	**31**	**30%**	**72%**	**12%**		**0**						**4.9**	**149**	**$3**

KRISTOPHER OLSON

Smith,Will

Age: 30 Th: L Role RP	Health F	LIMA Plan A	
Ht: 6' 5" Wt: 248 Type Pwr	PT/Exp C	Rand Var 0	
	Consist A	MM 5530	

All told, a steady season holding down closer role from wire to wire, though there were minor warning flags in 2nd half, including 7 HR allowed—all hit by RHB—which xHR/F says were legit. Did battle some back soreness, so perhaps that contributed. But even in "bad" half, skills were good enough, setting up another year of saves ahead.

Yr Tm	W	Sv	IP	K	ERA	xERA	WHIP	xWHIP	vL+	vR+	BF/G	Ctl	Dom	Cmd	Ball%	SwK	Vel	G	L	F	H%	S%	HR/F	xHR/F	GS	APC	DOM%	DIS%	Sv%	LI	RAR	BPX	R$
15 MIL	7	0	63	91	2.70	2.88	1.20	1.10	108	77	3.5	3.4	12.9	3.8	35%	15.6%	93.2	46	15	39	35%	80%	9%	10%	0	14			0	1.15	9.9	196	$6
16 2 NL	2	0	40	48	3.35	3.78	1.21	1.27	85	88	3.2	4.0	10.7	2.7	37%	12.0%	91.9	35	25	40	30%	74%	8%	7%	0	12			0	1.58	4.2	116	$0
17																																	
18 SF	2	14	53	71	2.55	2.95	0.98	1.04	60	81	3.9	2.5	12.1	4.7	31%	15.1%	92.7	42	20	38	30%	76%	7%	9%	0	15			78	1.44	10.5	194	$10
19 SF	6	34	65	96	2.76	2.92	1.03	1.05	52	95	4.1	2.9	13.2	4.6	34%	15.8%	92.7	42	22	36	29%	82%	20%	16%	0	17			89	1.58	14.1	196	$24
1st Half	1	21	33	51	2.16	2.40	0.81	0.90	63	68	3.6	2.2	13.8	6.4	33%	16.0%	92.8	42	28	31	27%	79%	15%	9%	0	16			100	1.29	9.6	228	$24
2nd Half	5	13	32	45	3.38	3.55	1.25	1.14	42	121	4.6	3.7	12.7	3.5	35%	15.7%	92.5	42	18	40	31%	85%	24%	21%	0	18			76	1.91	4.5	163	$23
20 Proj	**5**	**33**	**65**	**90**	**3.13**	**2.83**	**1.13**	**1.08**	**69**	**96**	**3.8**	**3.1**	**12.5**	**4.0**	**34%**	**15.0%**	**92.6**	**41**	**21**	**37**	**32%**	**77%**	**14%**		**0**						**8.2**	**184**	**$20**

Smyly,Drew

Age: 31 Th: L Role SP	Health F	LIMA Plan F	
Ht: 6' 3" Wt: 190 Type Pwr xFB	PT/Exp D	Rand Var +5	
	Consist F	MM 1301	

Looked to be at end of line when TEX, MIL released him, but 2nd half skills with PHI finally hinted he may have a bit left in the tank, two-plus years after Tommy John surgery. HR issues linger, but velocity uptick brought back SwK, and he also induced a few more ground balls. May never get back to his heyday, but could be a useful innings eater.

Yr Tm	W	Sv	IP	K	ERA	xERA	WHIP	xWHIP	vL+	vR+	BF/G	Ctl	Dom	Cmd	Ball%	SwK	Vel	G	L	F	H%	S%	HR/F	xHR/F	GS	APC	DOM%	DIS%	Sv%	LI	RAR	BPX	R$
15 TAM	5	0	67	77	3.11	3.53	1.17	1.15	70	106	22.9	2.7	10.4	3.9	34%	12.0%	90.3	37	19	44	30%	82%	14%	17%	12	95	25%	33%			7.0	154	$4
16 TAM	7	0	175	167	4.88	4.44	1.27	1.22	98	105	24.6	2.5	8.6	3.4	35%	11.1%	90.2	31	19	49	30%	67%	13%	11%	30	96	27%	33%			-14.9	113	$2
17																																	
18																																	
19 2 TM	4	1	114	120	6.24	5.27	1.59	1.44	142	116	20.6	4.3	9.5	2.2	38%	11.0%	91.2	33	22	45	32%	68%	21%	20%	21	85	19%	48%	100	0.73	-24.3	70	-$11
1st Half	1	1	51	52	8.42	6.62	1.91	1.56	164	129	19.3	6.0	9.1	1.5	40%	9.6%	90.7	27	23	50	33%	63%	23%	20%	9	81	0%	67%	100	0.69	-24.8	9	-$23
2nd Half	3	0	63	68	4.45	4.30	1.32	1.21	121	104	21.9	3.0	9.8	3.2	37%	12.4%	91.8	39	21	40	31%	74%	19%	20%	12	90	33%	33%			0.4	122	-$1
20 Proj	**5**	**0**	**123**	**128**	**4.46**	**4.07**	**1.37**	**1.28**	**113**	**108**	**21.5**	**3.2**	**9.3**	**2.9**	**37%**	**11.2%**	**90.8**	**34**	**21**	**46**	**31%**	**75%**	**16%**		**24**						**-4.7**	**106**	**$0**

Snell,Blake

Age: 27 Th: L Role SP	Health D	LIMA Plan B	
Ht: 6' 4" Wt: 215 Type Pwr FB	PT/Exp B	Rand Var +5	
	Consist B	MM 4505	

Cy Young encore didn't go as planned. Made quick return from April toe injury, but then HR/F, H%, and S% conspired to sink results before elbow injury arose in mid-July, shelving him for two months. Through all the drama, skills remained mostly intact; indeed, SwK, Dom took steps forward. To bounce back big-time, all he needs is health.

Yr Tm	W	Sv	IP	K	ERA	xERA	WHIP	xWHIP	vL+	vR+	BF/G	Ctl	Dom	Cmd	Ball%	SwK	Vel	G	L	F	H%	S%	HR/F	xHR/F	GS	APC	DOM%	DIS%	Sv%	LI	RAR	BPX	R$
15 a/a	12	0	113	119	1.97	2.49	1.12				21.2	3.3	9.4	2.8							28%	85%									27.8	133	$18
16 TAM *	9	0	152	176	3.77	4.57	1.61	1.44	89	102	21.7	4.9	10.4	2.1	40%	11.5%	93.5	37	27	36	38%	77%	6%	7%	19	90	26%	37%			7.9	107	$1
17 TAM *	10	0	173	171	3.95	4.31	1.40	1.41	65	100	23.6	3.9	8.9	2.2	40%	11.0%	94.3	44	18	38	31%	75%	11%	11%	24	95	17%	29%			8.7	86	$7
18 TAM	21	0	181	221	1.89	3.16	0.97	1.16	56	82	22.6	3.2	11.0	3.5	38%	15.3%	95.8	45	19	36	25%	86%	11%	14%	31	94	55%	19%			50.3	156	$39
19 TAM	6	0	107	147	4.29	3.47	1.27	1.16	118	89	19.2	3.4	12.4	3.7	36%	18.2%	95.6	39	25	36	35%	70%	15%	11%	23	82	26%	48%			2.8	162	$5
1st Half	5	0	85	117	4.87	3.28	1.28	1.09	109	94	20.6	3.1	12.4	4.0	35%	18.8%	95.7	43	25	32	36%	65%	18%	14%	17	86	29%	41%			-3.8	175	$7
2nd Half	1	0	22	30	2.05	4.30	1.23	1.25	150	70	15.0	4.5	12.3	2.7	38%	16.6%	95.4	24	22	53	30%	88%	8%	5%	6	73	17%	67%			6.7	111	-$3
20 Proj	**13**	**0**	**181**	**236**	**3.19**	**3.28**	**1.21**	**1.24**	**100**	**86**	**22.0**	**3.8**	**11.7**	**3.1**	**38%**	**15.3%**	**95.2**	**37**	**22**	**41**	**31%**	**77%**	**11%**		**31**						**21.5**	**144**	**$21**

Soria,Joakim

Age: 36 Th: R Role RP	Health C	LIMA Plan A	
Ht: 6' 3" Wt: 200 Type Pwr	PT/Exp C	Rand Var +2	
	Consist A	MM 4410	

Another year's worth of elite Cmd, but LI says he's fading from late-inning mix. Maybe it's because we're two years removed from comforting ground ball rates, a shift that led to second-highest total of HR allowed in 2019. Yet we know one guy who kept getting save opps with worse skills (rhymes with "Hernando Godney"), so never say never.

Yr Tm	W	Sv	IP	K	ERA	xERA	WHIP	xWHIP	vL+	vR+	BF/G	Ctl	Dom	Cmd	Ball%	SwK	Vel	G	L	F	H%	S%	HR/F	xHR/F	GS	APC	DOM%	DIS%	Sv%	LI	RAR	BPX	R$
15 2 TM	3	24	68	64	2.53	3.54	1.09	1.21	99	75	3.8	2.5	8.5	3.4	33%	10.3%	92.2	42	23	35	27%	83%	13%	8%	0	16			80	1.35	12.0	125	$15
16 KC	5	1	67	68	4.05	3.96	1.46	1.31	91	127	4.2	3.6	9.2	2.5	36%	12.1%	92.7	50	20	30	33%	77%	18%	22%	0	17			13	1.25	1.1	113	$0
17 KC	4	1	56	64	3.70	3.24	1.23	1.20	90	71	3.9	3.2	10.3	3.2	37%	13.5%	92.9	55	22	23	34%	68%	3%	13%	0	17			13	1.14	4.6	158	$2
18 2 TM	3	16	61	75	3.12	3.48	1.14	1.08	96	76	3.9	2.4	11.1	4.7	34%	15.0%	92.4	36	23	41	34%	74%	6%	8%	0	16			76	1.13	7.7	173	$10
19 OAK	2	1	69	79	4.30	3.81	1.03	1.18	89	72	3.9	2.6	10.3	4.0	34%	13.4%	92.7	38	23	39	27%	61%	13%	14%	1	16	0%	100%	17	0.92	1.7	143	$3
1st Half	1	0	38	40	4.74	3.93	1.08	1.18	85	76	4.2	2.6	9.5	3.6	34%	12.2%	92.7	42	22	36	29%	55%	8%	11%	1	17	0%	100%	0	0.91	-1.1	131	$0
2nd Half	1	1	31	39	3.77	3.76	0.97	1.09	94	69	3.6	2.6	11.3	4.3	34%	15.0%	92.7	32	24	44	24%	71%	18%	17%	0	15			25	0.93	2.8	156	$6
20 Proj	**3**	**2**	**58**	**68**	**3.74**	**3.17**	**1.10**	**1.14**	**92**	**75**	**3.7**	**2.7**	**10.5**	**3.9**	**35%**	**13.8%**	**92.6**	**40**	**23**	**38**	**30%**	**69%**	**12%**		**0**						**2.9**	**154**	**$3**

Soroka,Michael

Age: 22 Th: R Role SP	Health F	LIMA Plan B	
Ht: 6' 5" Wt: 225 Type Con GB	PT/Exp C	Rand Var -2	
	Consist B	MM 3105	

Finally got shoulder strains behind him, and results were stunning, if a bit over his head. Still, there's plenty to like here, starting with Ctl and GB%, though the latter did leak a bit in 2nd half. Given SwK, a few more strikeouts also within reach, especially as he refines arsenal. If you bid to low-3s ERA and health holds, he shouldn't disappoint.

Yr Tm	W	Sv	IP	K	ERA	xERA	WHIP	xWHIP	vL+	vR+	BF/G	Ctl	Dom	Cmd	Ball%	SwK	Vel	G	L	F	H%	S%	HR/F	xHR/F	GS	APC	DOM%	DIS%	Sv%	LI	RAR	BPX	R$
15																																	
16																																	
17 aa	11	0	154	117	3.75	3.80	1.28				24.2	2.2	6.8	3.1							32%	72%									11.4	106	$10
18 ATL *	4	0	53	48	2.91	3.15	1.23		86	120	21.3	2.1	8.2	3.8		10.6%	92.6	44	32	24	34%	75%	5%	13%	5	81	20%	40%			8.1	146	$2
19 ATL	13	0	175	142	2.68	3.92	1.11	1.27	99	72	24.2	2.1	7.3	3.5	35%	10.7%	92.5	51	23	25	28%	79%	11%	12%	29	88	34%	17%			39.3	113	$23
1st Half	9	0	85	67	2.13	3.63	0.98	1.22	80	68	24.3	2.0	7.1	3.5	33%	10.6%	92.7	57	21	22	26%	80%	8%	10%	14	87	50%	14%			24.9	119	$30
2nd Half	4	0	90	75	3.20	4.08	1.23	1.23	114	76	24.1	2.2	7.5	3.4	36%	10.7%	92.3	46	26	29	31%	78%	14%	14%	15	90	20%	20%			14.5	108	$17
20 Proj	**13**	**0**	**181**	**153**	**3.21**	**3.42**	**1.19**	**1.23**	**108**	**77**	**22.9**	**2.2**	**7.6**	**3.5**	**35%**	**10.7%**	**92.5**	**50**	**24**	**26**	**30%**	**76%**	**12%**		**32**						**21.0**	**122**	**$18**

Sparkman,Glenn

Age: 28 Th: R Role RP	Health D	LIMA Plan B	
Ht: 6' 2" Wt: 210 Type Con	PT/Exp C	Rand Var +3	
	Consist B	MM 0003	

After firing PQS-5 on 5/1 and joining rotation permanently by month's end, spent rest of year proving what a grave mistake that was. Simply doesn't miss bats, yields too many LD and FB, and, after some initial success vR, was an equal opportunity OPS booster in 2nd half. Name notwithstanding, if you're looking for a spark, he's not your man.

Yr Tm	W	Sv	IP	K	ERA	xERA	WHIP	xWHIP	vL+	vR+	BF/G	Ctl	Dom	Cmd	Ball%	SwK	Vel	G	L	F	H%	S%	HR/F	xHR/F	GS	APC	DOM%	DIS%	Sv%	LI	RAR	BPX	R$
15 aa	2	0	20	17	4.34	3.79	1.42				21.2	4.0	7.8	1.9							32%	69%									-0.9	92	-$4
16 aa	0	0	18	16	6.79	7.07	1.85				20.6	2.8	8.2	2.9							42%	64%									-5.7	68	-$7
17 TOR *	2	1	28	12	5.77	6.46	1.78		232	271	11.7	3.4	3.9	1.1		3.6%	94.0	20	40	40	35%	69%	0%	0%	0	28			100	0.70	-4.9	4	-$7
18 KC *	8	0	142	84	4.66	5.45	1.51	1.44	108	117	18.6	1.8	5.3	3.0	37%	10.1%	93.9	47	23	30	35%	70%	8%	9%	3	45	0%	67%	0	0.89	-9.0	69	-$7
19 KC	4	0	136	81	6.02	5.88	1.51	1.47	118	115	19.5	2.7	5.4	2.0	37%	7.6%	93.5	37	24	40	31%	65%	16%	15%	23	73	9%	70%	0	0.74	-25.4	42	-$12
1st Half	2	0	55	30	4.07	5.57	1.28	1.38	113	88	15.9	2.3	4.9	2.1	36%	6.9%	93.8	38	25	37	27%	75%	14%	14%	7	60	14%	57%	0	0.67	3.0	47	-$3
2nd Half	2	0	81	51	7.36	6.10	1.66	1.42	121	133	23.0	3.0	5.7	1.9	37%	8.1%	93.3	36	23	41	33%	60%	17%	16%	16	86	6%	75%			-28.4	38	-$18
20 Proj	**5**	**0**	**131**	**78**	**5.45**	**4.70**	**1.50**	**1.42**	**115**	**117**	**18.8**	**2.3**	**5.3**	**2.3**	**37%**	**8.7%**	**93.6**	**41**	**23**	**36**	**33%**	**67%**	**14%**		**26**						**-20.9**	**60**	**-$9**

Stammen,Craig

Age: 36 Th: R Role RP	Health D	LIMA Plan B	
Ht: 6' 4" Wt: 230 Type Con	PT/Exp C	Rand Var 0	
	Consist B	MM 4211	

No one who rostered him is asking for refund after 35 saves-plus-holds, but he also made clear that 2018 was a career year. SwK dipped dramatically despite added velocity; HR/F regression arrived right on cue. He's still got nifty GB%, record of success close-and-late. But wherever he lands, save chances likely to go to more electric arm.

Yr Tm	W	Sv	IP	K	ERA	xERA	WHIP	xWHIP	vL+	vR+	BF/G	Ctl	Dom	Cmd	Ball%	SwK	Vel	G	L	F	H%	S%	HR/F	xHR/F	GS	APC	DOM%	DIS%	Sv%	LI	RAR	BPX	R$
15 WAS	0	0	4	3	0.00	5.18	1.25		69	76	3.4	6.8	6.8	1.0		12.3%	91.6	55	9	36	19%	100%	0%	0%	0	13			0	1.63	2.0	-33	-$4
16 a/a	0	0	24	13	5.19	6.88	1.71				5.5	2.3	4.9	2.1							36%	74%									-3.0	13	-$6
17 SD	2	0	80	74	3.14	3.92	1.20	1.30	106	80	5.5	3.1	8.3	2.6	36%	11.8%	91.5	52	17	31	27%	81%	17%	16%	0	21			0	1.18	12.1	114	$4
18 SD	8	0	79	88	2.73	3.05	1.04	1.07	90	73	4.3	1.9	10.0	5.2	32%	14.4%	91.7	49	21	30	32%	73%	5%	9%	0	16			0	1.33	13.8	179	$10
19 SD	8	4	82	73	3.29	3.94	1.16	1.19	80	109	4.5	1.6	8.0	4.9	35%	9.4%	92.8	51	19	30	30%	79%	18%	13%	0	16			31	1.36	12.3	140	$9
1st Half	5	4	43	33	4.22	4.26	1.27	1.19	83	126	4.7	1.5	7.0	4.7	34%	9.5%	92.4	53	18	28	30%	76%	23%	14%	0	17			40	1.57	1.5	127	$7
2nd Half	3	0	39	40	2.29	3.60	1.04	1.10	76	89	4.2	1.8	9.2	5.0	37%	9.4%	93.2	48	21	32	29%	84%	12%	12%	0	16			0	1.14	10.8	154	$10
20 Proj	**6**	**2**	**73**	**67**	**3.58**	**3.29**	**1.14**	**1.14**	**88**	**92**	**4.4**	**2.0**	**8.3**	**4.1**	**34%**	**9.9%**	**92.3**	**50**	**20**	**30**	**30%**	**72%**	**13%**		**0**						**5.1**	**141**	**$6**

KRISTOPHER OLSON

Stanek,Ryne

Age: 28	Th: R	Role RP	PT/Exp	D	Rand Var 0
Ht: 6' 4"	Wt: 225	Type Pwr xFB	Consist	B	MM 2410
			Health	B	LIMA Plan B

Converted just 1 of 5 save chances after mid-season trade to MIA, with Ctl unravelling and favorable HR/F reversing course in 2nd half. Was July hip injury the culprit? Quite possibly, but elevated FB% will continue to invite HR risk, while Ball% history adds layer of skepticism. Strikeout upside still enticing though, so don't entirely dismiss just yet.

Yr	Tm		W	Sv	IP	K	ERA	xERA	WHIP	xWHIP	vL+	vR+	BF/G	Ctl	Dom	Cmd	Ball%	SwK	Vel	G	L	F	H%	S%	HR/F	xHR/F	GS	APC	DOM%	DIS%	Sv%	LI	RAR	BPX	R$
15	aa		4	1	62	35	4.75	4.45	1.47				16.5	4.5	5.1	1.1							27%	70%									-6.0	32	-$5
16	a/a		4	3	103	95	5.68	4.66	1.55				13.2	4.6	8.4	1.8							33%	63%									-18.9	74	-$8
17	TAM	*	3	8	65	79	2.99	3.90	1.39		81	172	4.7	4.2	10.9	2.6		15.6%	98.2	35	22	43	34%	82%	26%	18%	0	20			89	0.82	10.9	121	$5
18	TAM		2	0	66	81	2.98	3.79	1.09	1.22	70	95	4.5	3.7	11.0	3.0	38%	16.3%	98.0	33	15	52	26%	78%	10%	13%	29	18	3%	48%	0	0.89	9.5	127	$4
19	2 TM		0	1	77	89	3.97	4.75	1.30	1.41	94	90	5.2	4.6	10.4	2.3	39%	15.7%	97.6	32	23	46	28%	74%	12%	15%	27	21	0%	19%	20	0.96	5.0	81	$0
1st Half			0	0	46	50	2.76	4.47	1.14	1.27	85	76	5.5	3.5	9.9	2.8	38%	16.4%	97.6	35	19	46	28%	78%	6%	11%	23	21	0%	22%	0	0.77	9.8	103	$3
2nd Half			0	1	31	39	5.74	5.24	1.53	1.48	106	108	4.9	6.0	11.2	1.9	41%	14.8%	97.6	28	28	45	28%	70%	22%	20%	4	20	0%	0%	20	1.18	-4.8	48	-$5
20	**Proj**		**1**	**2**	**65**	**76**	**3.59**	**3.90**	**1.27**	**1.32**	**89**	**98**	**5.0**	**4.1**	**10.5**	**2.6**	**39%**	**15.7%**	**97.8**	**31**	**20**	**48**	**29%**	**77%**	**12%**		**0**						**4.5**	**101**	**$1**

Stephenson,Robert

Age: 27	Th: R	Role RP	PT/Exp	D	Rand Var -1
Ht: 6' 3"	Wt: 215	Type Pwr FB	Consist	A	MM 3500
			Health	D	LIMA Plan A

Former first-round pick handled transition to bullpen with aplomb. Leaned heavily on ridiculous slider (56% usage, 27% SwK) while adding almost two ticks of velocity, sending SwK/Dom soaring alongside nice gains in the BB dept. Rising LI suggests he's gaining the confidence of management, which could mean... UP: 25 Sv

Yr	Tm		W	Sv	IP	K	ERA	xERA	WHIP	xWHIP	vL+	vR+	BF/G	Ctl	Dom	Cmd	Ball%	SwK	Vel	G	L	F	H%	S%	HR/F	xHR/F	GS	APC	DOM%	DIS%	Sv%	LI	RAR	BPX	R$
15	a/a		8	0	134	128	4.84	4.05	1.46				22.9	5.0	8.6	1.7							30%	68%									-14.5	82	-$4
16	CIN	*	10	0	174	137	5.97	5.54	1.60	1.50	130	112	24.0	5.0	7.1	1.4	39%	9.6%	93.2	34	24	41	30%	66%	19%	13%	8	90	0%	63%			-38.1	28	-$14
17	CIN	*	6	1	125	125	4.73	4.74	1.44	1.53	104	111	16.1	4.8	9.0	1.9	40%	13.3%	93.7	38	22	41	29%	73%	13%	14%	11	59	0%	36%	100	0.63	-5.7	62	-$1
18	CIN	*	11	0	125	124	4.27	4.45	1.46		163	126	22.2	5.4	8.9	1.7		11.3%	93.2	33	28	40	28%	75%	13%	16%	3	62	0%	67%	0	0.57	-1.8	67	$1
19	CIN		3	0	65	81	3.76	3.97	1.04	1.22	100	72	4.6	3.3	11.3	3.4	34%	19.6%	95.0	32	22	46	25%	69%	13%	8%	0	18			0	0.96	6.0	134	$4
1st Half			2	0	30	40	3.30	3.78	1.07	1.16	92	74	4.9	3.6	12.0	3.3	34%	21.2%	94.5	33	27	40	29%	70%	7%	7%	0	18			0	0.67	4.5	141	$3
2nd Half			1	0	35	41	4.15	4.25	1.01	1.17	106	70	4.3	3.1	10.6	3.4	35%	18.2%	95.3	31	18	51	22%	68%	16%	8%	0	18			0	1.19	1.5	127	$4
20	**Proj**		**4**	**0**	**65**	**78**	**3.81**	**3.59**	**1.20**	**1.35**	**101**	**87**	**7.3**	**3.8**	**10.8**	**2.8**	**37%**	**15.5%**	**94.3**	**34**	**22**	**44**	**28%**	**74%**	**14%**		**0**						**2.7**	**119**	**$2**

Strahm,Matt

Age: 28	Th: L	Role RP	PT/Exp	D	Rand Var +2
Ht: 6' 3"	Wt: 185	Type Pwr FB	Consist	D	MM 3401
			Health	F	LIMA Plan D

Draft season helium appeared justified through May (3.21 ERA), only to come crashing down (28 ER in 24 IP) before July move to pen. In relief, regained lost velocity, SwK/Dom returned, and already-solid Ctl/Ball% reached new heights. Viable late-round option, even if durability and past performance question whether value will come as SP.

Yr	Tm		W	Sv	IP	K	ERA	xERA	WHIP	xWHIP	vL+	vR+	BF/G	Ctl	Dom	Cmd	Ball%	SwK	Vel	G	L	F	H%	S%	HR/F	xHR/F	GS	APC	DOM%	DIS%	Sv%	LI	RAR	BPX	R$
15																																			
16	KC	*	5	0	124	114	4.49	5.24	1.48		87	56	12.4	2.7	8.3	3.1		13.4%	93.8	47	24	29	35%	73%	0%	8%	0	21			0	1.66	-4.6	00	-$3
17	KC		2	0	36	37	5.45	5.01	1.50	1.53	96	107	6.4	5.7	9.6	1.7	39%	10.5%	93.6	37	19	44	28%	67%	15%	11%	3	27	0%	33%	0	0.81	-4.7	40	-$5
18	SD	*	4	0	76	86	2.27	2.67	1.07	1.19	106	66	6.0	3.0	10.2	3.4	34%	12.8%	93.5	35	21	44	28%	84%	9%	15%	5	24	20%	40%	0	0.91	17.8	139	$9
19	SD		6	0	115	118	4.71	4.19	1.25	1.16	106	105	10.6	1.7	9.3	5.4	30%	11.1%	91.5	37	23	41	33%	69%	16%	17%	16	39	13%	25%	0	0.90	-2.9	147	$2
1st Half			3	0	75	71	4.94	4.58	1.23	1.16	137	99	22.6	1.9	8.6	4.4	32%	10.4%	90.9	35	21	43	30%	67%	17%	18%	14	83	14%	29%			-4.0	126	$3
2nd Half			3	0	40	47	4.28	3.69	1.28	1.01	68	119	5.3	1.4	10.6	7.8	27%	12.5%	92.8	39	25	36	37%	71%	15%	15%	2	19	0%	0%	0	0.96	1.1	187	$2
20	**Proj**		**4**	**0**	**73**	**80**	**3.72**	**3.35**	**1.16**	**1.18**	**96**	**97**	**6.9**	**2.0**	**9.9**	**4.9**	**32%**	**11.9%**	**92.8**	**37**	**22**	**41**	**31%**	**74%**	**14%**		**0**						**3.8**	**159**	**$3**

Strasburg,Stephen

Age: 31	Th: R	Role SP	PT/Exp	A	Rand Var +2
Ht: 6' 5"	Wt: 235	Type Pwr	Consist	A	MM 5505
			Health	D	LIMA Plan A

Elite season from one of the best, setting career-highs in W, K while avoiding IL for first time since 2014. GB% spike fueled by trade-off of 4-seamers for more sinkers and curveballs, and top-shelf SwK eases concerns about fading velocity. BPX history of consistency a thing of beauty, but his value proposition always hinges on health.

Yr	Tm		W	Sv	IP	K	ERA	xERA	WHIP	xWHIP	vL+	vR+	BF/G	Ctl	Dom	Cmd	Ball%	SwK	Vel	G	L	F	H%	S%	HR/F	xHR/F	GS	APC	DOM%	DIS%	Sv%	LI	RAR	BPX	R$
15	WAS		11	0	127	155	3.46	2.94	1.11	1.03	79	104	22.7	1.8	11.0	6.0	33%	11.6%	95.4	42	23	34	33%	72%	12%	11%	23	89	39%	22%			7.8	200	$13
16	WAS		15	0	148	183	3.60	3.30	1.10	1.10	83	90	24.9	2.7	11.2	4.2	34%	11.9%	94.9	40	21	39	31%	70%	11%	11%	24	99	58%	13%			10.8	174	$17
17	WAS		15	0	175	204	2.52	3.25	1.02	1.10	76	80	25.0	2.4	10.5	4.3	33%	13.4%	95.6	47	19	34	29%	78%	9%	11%	28	98	46%	11%			39.9	178	$31
18	WAS		10	0	130	156	3.74	3.32	1.20	1.12	99	97	24.7	2.6	10.8	4.1	36%	12.5%	94.5	44	22	34	32%	74%	16%	18%	22	98	36%	5%			6.6	167	$10
19	WAS		18	0	209	251	3.32	3.19	1.04	1.12	77	86	25.5	2.4	10.8	4.5	35%	13.9%	93.9	51	20	29	29%	73%	16%	14%	33	103	52%	9%			30.7	173	$31
1st Half			9	0	109	124	3.88	3.34	1.07	1.10	73	95	26.0	2.2	10.2	4.6	35%	14.4%	93.5	51	19	30	30%	67%	16%	14%	17	101	59%	12%			8.4	167	$27
2nd Half			9	0	100	127	2.70	3.01	1.00	1.07	81	75	24.9	2.6	11.4	4.4	35%	13.5%	94.3	51	22	27	28%	79%	17%	13%	16	105	44%	6%			22.3	179	$36
20	**Proj**		**16**	**0**	**189**	**227**	**3.25**	**2.79**	**1.09**	**1.09**	**84**	**89**	**24.0**	**2.5**	**10.9**	**4.4**	**34%**	**13.2%**	**94.5**	**49**	**20**	**30**	**30%**	**75%**	**15%**		**31**						**20.9**	**179**	**$26**

Stratton,Chris

Age: 29	Th: R	Role RP	PT/Exp	C	Rand Var +4
Ht: 6' 2"	Wt: 211	Type	Consist	B	MM 1201
			Health	D	LIMA Plan B

Next in long line of failed SP prospects to become dominant bullpen weapon? Maybe not. Bothered by side discomfort for much of the year, he did show nice 2nd half skills growth upon move to pen, with a couple extra ticks of velocity aiding SwK boost. Nonetheless, his road to fantasy relevance is a long one.

Yr	Tm		W	Sv	IP	K	ERA	xERA	WHIP	xWHIP	vL+	vR+	BF/G	Ctl	Dom	Cmd	Ball%	SwK	Vel	G	L	F	H%	S%	HR/F	xHR/F	GS	APC	DOM%	DIS%	Sv%	LI	RAR	BPX	R$
15	a/a		5	0	148	92	4.80	4.06	1.46				24.4	4.0	5.6	1.4							30%	66%									-15.3	59	-$8
16	SF	*	13	0	136	89	4.63	4.35	1.48		93	116	20.8	3.1	5.9	1.9		7.7%	91.3	41	16	44	33%	67%	7%	4%	0	24			0	0.31	-7.4	71	-$1
17	SF	*	8	1	138	107	5.32	5.65	1.65	1.45	107	91	22.0	3.4	7.0	2.0	38%	9.3%	91.6	43	28	29	36%	69%	10%	11%	10	80	20%	30%	50	0.68	-16.3	59	-$9
18	SF	*	13	0	169	130	4.85	4.90	1.45	1.39	114	103	22.5	3.3	6.9	2.1	36%	9.0%	91.1	43	25	32	32%	69%	13%	17%	26	88	23%	38%	0	0.80	-14.6	59	-$3
19	2 TM		1	0	76	69	5.57	5.19	1.66	1.44	117	115	9.8	3.9	8.2	2.1	37%	10.8%	92.2	40	26	34	36%	70%	16%	13%	5	39	0%	60%	0	0.53	-9.9	65	-$9
1st Half			1	0	41	31	7.52	6.07	1.94	1.51	133	129	14.9	4.4	6.9	1.6	38%	8.4%	91.1	38	27	35	38%	63%	16%	14%	5	58	0%	60%	0	0.46	-15.1	22	-$16
2nd Half			0	0	35	38	3.31	4.19	1.33	1.25	98	97	6.8	3.3	9.7	2.9	35%	13.8%	93.4	42	25	32	32%	81%	16%	12%	0	27			0	0.57	5.2	115	-$2
20	**Proj**		**3**	**0**	**87**	**79**	**4.36**	**4.08**	**1.43**	**1.38**	**106**	**101**	**7.4**	**3.6**	**8.1**	**2.3**	**37%**	**11.3%**	**91.8**	**42**	**26**	**32**	**32%**	**73%**	**14%**		**0**						**-2.3**	**80**	**-$2**

Strickland,Hunter

Age: 31	Th: R	Role RP	PT/Exp	D	Rand Var +1
Ht: 6' 3"	Wt: 225	Type FB	Consist	A	MM 1110
			Health	F	LIMA Plan A

Poised to claim SEA closer role before lat strain shelved him for nearly four months, only to get traded not long after return. On the field, recovered some lost velocity and threw more strikes, with SwK pointing to better Dom ahead. Three-year xERA/xWHIP trend paints scary picture though, making it safe to remove "potential closer" tag for now.

Yr	Tm		W	Sv	IP	K	ERA	xERA	WHIP	xWHIP	vL+	vR+	BF/G	Ctl	Dom	Cmd	Ball%	SwK	Vel	G	L	F	H%	S%	HR/F	xHR/F	GS	APC	DOM%	DIS%	Sv%	LI	RAR	BPX	R$
15	SF	*	4	5	73	70	2.28	1.63	0.87	1.10	70	79	3.8	1.6	8.6	5.3	30%	15.2%	96.9	40	20	40	25%	76%	8%	11%	0	13			71	1.28	15.1	196	$12
16	SF		3	3	61	57	3.10	3.72	1.13	1.25	101	70	3.5	2.8	8.4	3.0	36%	12.0%	96.8	47	22	30	29%	74%	8%	12%	0	14			38	1.29	8.2	120	$5
17	SF		4	1	61	58	2.64	4.97	1.43	1.42	116	79	3.9	4.3	8.5	2.0	36%	11.4%	95.7	39	17	44	32%	83%	5%	13%	0	14			33	1.37	13.0	66	$2
18	SF		3	14	45	37	3.97	5.11	1.41	1.46	86	123	4.1	4.2	7.3	1.8	38%	11.4%	94.9	38	22	40	29%	75%	9%	13%	0	16			78	1.07	1.0	41	$3
19	2 TM		2	2	24	18	5.55	5.52	1.23	1.43	170	63	3.8	3.0	6.7	2.3	36%	12.0%	95.9	33	20	47	24%	63%	17%	16%	0	14			67	1.09	-3.1	55	-$3
1st Half			0	2	2	3	11.57	3.97	0.86		275	0	3.3	0.0	11.6	0.0		17.7%	95.4	17	17	67	22%	0%	25%	25%	0	11			67	1.60	-2.0	221	-$8
2nd Half			2	0	22	15	4.91	5.79	1.27	1.43	158	68	3.8	3.3	6.1	1.9	36%	11.5%	95.9	34	20	46	24%	70%	16%	15%	0	14			0	1.03	-1.1	38	-$3
20	**Proj**		**4**	**5**	**58**	**49**	**4.56**	**4.41**	**1.38**	**1.37**	**129**	**91**	**3.8**	**3.5**	**7.6**	**2.2**	**36%**	**11.9%**	**95.9**	**39**	**20**	**41**	**30%**	**71%**	**13%**		**0**						**-2.9**	**68**	**$0**

Stripling,Ross

Age: 30	Th: R	Role RP	PT/Exp	C	Rand Var +1
Ht: 6' 2"	Wt: 220	Type	Consist	A	MM 4301
			Health	D	LIMA Plan A

Lack of steady rotation spot and July neck/back issues kept unsung righty from following up on 2018 breakthrough. Nice GB lean with Ball% and Ctl that speak to continued stinginess with free passes. Meanwhile, velocity/SwK slippage coupled with mounting durability concerns temper enthusiasm. Roster for ratios, cross fingers for more.

Yr	Tm		W	Sv	IP	K	ERA	xERA	WHIP	xWHIP	vL+	vR+	BF/G	Ctl	Dom	Cmd	Ball%	SwK	Vel	G	L	F	H%	S%	HR/F	xHR/F	GS	APC	DOM%	DIS%	Sv%	LI	RAR	BPX	R$
15	aa		3	0	67	44	5.20	4.91	1.42				22.0	2.6	5.9	2.3							32%	65%									-10.3	54	-$6
16	LA	*	5	0	117	87	4.06	4.09	1.30	1.33	89	103	17.8	2.5	6.7	2.7	37%	8.4%	90.5	51	20	29	31%	71%	11%	12%	14	72	14%	50%	0	0.99	1.9	84	$2
17	LA		3	2	74	74	3.75	3.57	1.18	1.17	73	108	6.2	2.3	9.0	3.9	35%	12.0%	92.9	49	22	29	30%	73%	17%	13%	2	24	50%	0%	40	0.86	5.5	152	$4
18	LA		8	0	122	136	3.02	3.24	1.19	1.05	90	110	15.2	1.6	10.0	6.2	33%	11.7%	91.7	45	22	33	34%	82%	16%	13%	21	61	29%	19%	0	0.83	16.9	184	$11
19	LA		4	0	91	93	3.47	3.65	1.15	1.16	93	92	11.6	2.0	9.2	4.7	34%	10.6%	90.5	50	19	31	31%	74%	14%	14%	15	45	13%	27%	0	0.73	11.5	153	$6
1st Half			3	0	53	52	3.08	4.02	1.20	1.24	93	91	10.4	2.9	8.9	3.1	35%	11.1%	90.6	49	20	31	30%	78%	11%	16%	7	41	29%	14%	0	0.74	9.3	118	$7
2nd Half			1	0	38	41	4.03	3.20	1.08	0.97	94	94	13.7	0.7	9.7	13.7	33%	9.9%	90.5	52	18	30	33%	69%	19%	13%	8	53	0%	38%	0	0.70	2.2	202	$4
20	**Proj**		**7**	**0**	**109**	**111**	**3.61**	**3.11**	**1.17**	**1.11**	**90**	**102**	**11.3**	**1.8**	**9.2**	**5.1**	**34%**	**10.8%**	**91.2**	**49**	**20**	**31**	**32%**	**74%**	**16%**		**10**						**7.3**	**165**	**$8**

BRIAN SLACK

Stroman,Marcus

Age: 29	Th: R	Role SP	Health	D	LIMA Plan	A
Ht: 5' 7"	Wt: 180	Type xGB	PT/Exp	A	Rand Var	-1
			Consist	A	MM	3205

Proved 2018 shoulder injury was behind him as he topped 30 starts for third time in four years. Relied less on sinker while throwing more cutters (25% usage, 10% SwK), helping explain GB% drop and corresponding SwK/Dom boost. Gradual xERA/Ball% slippage suggests it won't all be sunshine and daffodils ahead though. Don't go overboard.

Yr	Tm	W	Sv	IP	K	ERA	xERA	WHIP	xWHIP	vL+	vR+	BF/G	Ctl	Dom	Cmd	Ball%	SwK	Vel	G	L	F	H%	S%	HR/F	xHR/F	GS	APC	DOM%	DIS%	Sv%	LI	RAR	BPX	R$
15	TOR	4	0	27	18	1.67	3.13	0.96		71	91	25.8	2.0	6.0	3.0		7.5%	92.0	64	18	18	24%	88%	14%	9%	4	93	75%	25%			7.6	114	$2
16	TOR	9	0	204	166	4.37	3.55	1.29	1.26	100	95	26.7	2.4	7.3	3.1	36%	9.6%	92.4	60	20	20	31%	68%	17%	17%	32	97	34%	31%			-4.5	125	$5
17	TOR	13	0	201	164	3.09	3.65	1.31	1.30	86	104	25.3	2.8	7.3	2.6	37%	10.2%	93.3	62	18	20	31%	80%	18%	17%	33	95	39%	27%			31.4	117	$17
18	TOR	4	0	102	77	5.54	4.02	1.48	1.37	102	108	23.6	3.2	6.8	2.1	38%	9.3%	92.4	62	18	20	33%	62%	14%	19%	19	90	16%	42%			-17.6	88	-$9
19	2 TM	10	0	184	159	3.22	4.20	1.31	1.33	102	82	24.2	2.8	7.8	2.7	38%	10.6%	92.5	54	20	26	31%	78%	13%	12%	32	95	25%	28%			29.2	104	$14
1st Half		5	0	105	81	3.18	4.26	1.26	1.32	101	79	24.2	2.8	7.0	2.5	38%	10.3%	92.7	57	16	27	30%	78%	12%	12%	18	96	22%	33%			17.1	94	$15
2nd Half		5	0	80	78	3.28	3.99	1.37	1.25	103	87	24.2	2.9	8.8	3.0	39%	11.1%	92.3	49	26	25	34%	79%	14%	11%	14	95	29%	21%			12.1	116	$12
20	**Proj**	**9**	**0**	**181**	**160**	**3.95**	**3.48**	**1.33**	**1.30**	**97**	**91**	**23.9**	**3.1**	**8.0**	**2.5**	**38%**	**10.8%**	**92.6**	**57**	**20**	**23**	**31%**	**72%**	**15%**		**32**						**4.4**	**108**	**$7**

Strop,Pedro

Age: 35	Th: R	Role RP	Health	D	LIMA Plan	A
Ht: 6' 1"	Wt: 220	Type Pwr GB	PT/Exp	C	Rand Var	+5
			Consist	A	MM	3410

Double-digit saves for second consecutive year barely enough to net positive R$ return. Ill-timed hamstring issue cost him most of May, and neck issues may have lingered in 2nd half, but can't overlook fades in velocity, Ctl, SwK, and surge in HR/F. At his age, and absent clear path to saves, it's hard to bet on resurgence. Let someone else chase it.

Yr	Tm	W	Sv	IP	K	ERA	xERA	WHIP	xWHIP	vL+	vR+	BF/G	Ctl	Dom	Cmd	Ball%	SwK	Vel	G	L	F	H%	S%	HR/F	xHR/F	GS	APC	DOM%	DIS%	Sv%	LI	RAR	BPX	R$
15	CHC	2	3	68	81	2.91	2.98	1.00	1.24	88	67	3.6	3.8	10.7	2.8	38%	17.0%	95.1	51	20	29	23%	73%	11%	7%	0	14			60	1.30	8.8	141	$7
16	CHC	2	0	47	60	2.85	2.58	0.89	1.10	82	64	3.5	2.9	11.4	4.0	36%	16.5%	94.9	58	16	25	24%	71%	15%	15%	0	14			0	0.98	7.8	195	$4
17	CHC	5	0	60	65	2.83	3.58	1.18	1.31	66	95	3.6	3.9	9.7	2.5	40%	15.8%	96.1	59	11	30	28%	78%	9%	8%	0	15			0	1.09	11.3	128	$5
18	CHC	6	13	60	57	2.26	3.78	0.99	1.28	88	66	4.0	3.2	8.6	2.7	35%	16.6%	95.1	46	18	36	23%	80%	7%	12%	0	15			76	1.31	13.9	107	$13
19	CHC	2	10	42	49	4.97	3.87	1.27	1.35	90	104	3.6	4.3	10.6	2.5	38%	13.8%	93.6	53	16	31	28%	64%	19%	21%	0	15			63	0.93	-2.4	114	$2
1st Half		1	9	19	20	4.34	3.38	0.96	1.24	83	87	3.3	3.4	9.6	2.9	38%	17.2%	93.9	59	11	30	20%	60%	23%	31%	0	14			82	0.99	0.4	130	$5
2nd Half		1	1	23	29	5.48	4.20	1.52	1.36	96	113	3.8	5.1	11.3	2.2	38%	11.4%	93.4	48	20	32	35%	66%	16%	15%	0	15			20	0.89	-2.8	102	-$1
20	**Proj**	**4**	**2**	**58**	**65**	**4.10**	**3.49**	**1.27**	**1.29**	**93**	**96**	**3.6**	**4.1**	**10.0**	**2.5**	**37%**	**13.5%**	**94.5**	**50**	**16**	**34**	**30%**	**70%**	**12%**		**0**						**0.4**	**114**	**$1**

Suarez,Jose

Age: 22	Th: L	Role RP	Health	A	LIMA Plan	D
Ht: 5' 10"	Wt: 225	Type Pwr xFB	PT/Exp	D	Rand Var	+4
			Consist	D	MM	1201

2-6, 7.11 ERA in 81 IP at LAA. MLB debut could have gone... um... better. Nice step forward in minors last year raised hopes despite shaky Ctl as he's risen up ranks. Change-up (27% usage, 18% SwK) profiles as above-average, and xHR/F says he was a tad unlucky. Still, needs big improvement vR if he's going to stick. Patience required.

Yr	Tm	W	Sv	IP	K	ERA	xERA	WHIP	xWHIP	vL+	vR+	BF/G	Ctl	Dom	Cmd	Ball%	SwK	Vel	G	L	F	H%	S%	HR/F	xHR/F	GS	APC	DOM%	DIS%	Sv%	LI	RAR	BPX	R$
15																																		
16																																		
17																																		
18	a/a	3	0	110	113	4.00	3.99	1.41				19.4	3.0	9.2	3.0							36%	70%									2.0	123	-$2
19	LAA *	4	0	114	100	5.93	5.82	1.49	1.44	87	140	18.9	3.7	7.9	2.1	38%	11.2%	91.8	35	22	43	30%	66%	21%	14%	15	78	7%	60%	0	0.81	-20.0	33	-$9
1st Half		4	0	50	44	3.88	4.00	1.28	1.39	117	121	20.5	3.9	7.9	2.0	40%	13.0%	91.7	27	18	55	26%	75%	18%	11%	4	87	0%	50%			3.9	62	$2
2nd Half		0	0	64	56	7.53	7.24	1.67	1.37	70	143	17.9	3.6	7.8	2.2	38%	10.6%	91.8	38	23	39	34%	60%	23%	16%	11	76	9%	64%	0	0.82	-23.9	11	-$17
20	**Proj**	**4**	**0**	**116**	**109**	**5.24**	**4.44**	**1.47**	**1.38**	**82**	**115**	**19.1**	**3.5**	**8.4**	**2.4**	**38%**	**11.5%**	**91.7**	**34**	**21**	**45**	**33%**	**67%**	**12%**		**24**						**-15.6**	**80**	**-$6**

Suarez,Ranger

Age: 24	Th: L	Role RP	Health	A	LIMA Plan	C
Ht: 6' 1"	Wt: 180	Type Con xGB	PT/Exp	D	Rand Var	+1
			Consist	C	MM	2101

6-1, 3.14 ERA in 49 IP at PHI. Impressed after late-June call-up with sub-3.00 ERA, working exclusively out of bullpen. Generates plenty of GB with good command of 4-pitch mix, but scouting reports, early SwK returns agree that his K ceiling is fairly low, and encouraging gains vR tempered by worsening Ball%. Current path to value murky.

Yr	Tm	W	Sv	IP	K	ERA	xERA	WHIP	xWHIP	vL+	vR+	BF/G	Ctl	Dom	Cmd	Ball%	SwK	Vel	G	L	F	H%	S%	HR/F	xHR/F	GS	APC	DOM%	DIS%	Sv%	LI	RAR	BPX	R$
15																																		
16																																		
17																																		
18	PHI *	7	0	140	87	3.46	4.00	1.35		78	157	23.4	2.6	5.6	2.1		8.0%	91.8	51	18	31	31%	75%	19%	17%	3	56	0%	67%	0	0.58	12.0	72	$3
19	PHI *	8	0	87	70	4.69	5.37	1.40	1.26	75	110	8.3	2.3	7.3	3.2	38%	10.0%	92.4	55	22	22	32%	72%	18%	17%	0	21			0	1.00	-2.0	64	$0
1st Half		2	0	45	38	6.38	6.78	1.55		82	148	19.8	2.4	7.6	3.2		15.3%	92.1	35	39	26	34%	65%	33%	28%	0	41			0	0.29	-10.5	39	-$8
2nd Half		6	0	41	32	2.83	3.85	1.23	1.25	74	100	5.0	2.2	7.0	3.2	39%	8.9%	92.5	59	19	22	30%	81%	15%	14%	0	19			0	1.06	8.5	113	$9
20	**Proj**	**6**	**0**	**73**	**56**	**3.97**	**3.75**	**1.42**	**1.38**	**77**	**106**	**10.2**	**2.9**	**6.9**	**2.4**	**43%**	**8.9%**	**92.5**	**59**	**19**	**22**	**32%**	**75%**	**16%**		**1**						**1.6**	**96**	**$0**

Suero,Wander

Age: 28	Th: R	Role RP	Health	A	LIMA Plan	A
Ht: 6' 4"	Wt: 211	Type Pwr	PT/Exp	D	Rand Var	+2
			Consist	A	MM	3400

Solid middle relief contributor with ERA slightly inflated due to unfortunate S%. Workload may have taken toll, as SwK (12%) and cutter velocity (93 mph) tailed off in September. Previous MiLB closing experience and lack of platoon splits can't hurt chances of working into higher-leverage role. Worth keeping an eye on if he does.

Yr	Tm	W	Sv	IP	K	ERA	xERA	WHIP	xWHIP	vL+	vR+	BF/G	Ctl	Dom	Cmd	Ball%	SwK	Vel	G	L	F	H%	S%	HR/F	xHR/F	GS	APC	DOM%	DIS%	Sv%	LI	RAR	BPX	R$
15	aa	1	0	34	24	8.14	7.04	1.92				9.5	4.0	6.2	1.6							39%	57%									-17.5	27	-$13
16	aa	3	4	55	39	3.38	5.05	1.63				6.3	3.8	6.3	1.7							35%	80%									5.5	60	-$1
17	a/a	3	20	65	52	2.38	3.50	1.30				5.0	2.9	7.1	2.5							31%	83%									15.9	100	$12
18	WAS *	5	1	65	59	4.03	3.83	1.29	1.24	97	102	4.9	2.7	8.3	3.0	35%	11.0%	92.1	34	23	42	32%	70%	7%	13%	0	20			50	0.82	1.0	109	$0
19	WAS	6	1	71	81	4.54	3.89	1.26	1.26	87	90	3.8	3.3	10.2	3.1	35%	13.8%	95.0	41	27	32	33%	64%	8%	13%	0	16			14	1.01	-0.3	125	$2
1st Half		1	1	35	47	5.35	3.62	1.27	1.11	98	94	4.1	3.1	12.0	3.9	34%	14.5%	95.0	36	28	35	36%	59%	13%	17%	0	17			33	1.02	-3.7	161	-$3
2nd Half		5	0	36	34	3.75	4.16	1.25	1.33	78	85	3.6	3.5	8.5	2.4	37%	13.1%		45	26	29	31%	68%	4%	9%	0	15			0	1.01	3.4	89	$6
20	**Proj**	**5**	**0**	**58**	**63**	**3.98**	**3.59**	**1.29**	**1.24**	**93**	**103**	**4.4**	**3.2**	**9.8**	**3.1**	**35%**	**12.6%**	**60.6**	**38**	**26**	**36**	**33%**	**71%**	**11%**		**0**						**1.2**	**123**	**$0**

Suter,Brent

Age: 30	Th: L	Role RP	Health	F	LIMA Plan	F
Ht: 6' 5"	Wt: 195	Type Con	PT/Exp	D	Rand Var	-5
			Consist	F	MM	2101

4-0, 0.49 ERA in 18 IP at MIL. September return from Tommy John surgery went swimmingly while working multi-inning stints out of bullpen. Elite Ctl remains calling card, and return of GB% could help keep ERA down. Nonetheless, durability and role uncertainty raise profile risk, which already had little margin for error given soft-tossing ways.

Yr	Tm	W	Sv	IP	K	ERA	xERA	WHIP	xWHIP	vL+	vR+	BF/G	Ctl	Dom	Cmd	Ball%	SwK	Vel	G	L	F	H%	S%	HR/F	xHR/F	GS	APC	DOM%	DIS%	Sv%	LI	RAR	BPX	R$
15	a/a	8	0	118	66	3.04	4.32	1.46				19.5	3.3	5.0	1.5							32%	80%									13.4	53	$2
16	MIL *	8	2	132	74	3.94	5.07	1.49		142	81	14.2	1.3	5.1	3.8		9.2%	83.8	43	19	37	36%	74%	12%	6%	2	25	0%	100%	100	0.75	4.1	98	$0
17	MIL *	6	0	118	93	3.94	4.68	1.38	1.28	72	102	15.5	2.3	7.1	3.1	32%	9.4%	85.8	45	24	31	33%	75%	10%	9%	14	58	21%	43%	0	0.67	6.1	88	$2
18	MIL	8	0	101	84	4.44	4.19	1.19	1.19	93	108	21.2	1.7	7.5	4.4	34%	10.4%	86.7	33	29	38	29%	69%	16%	15%	18	82	22%	22%	0	0.83	-3.6	115	$3
19	MIL *	4	0	35	31	0.26	0.07	0.59	1.06	85	48	7.8	1.2	8.0	6.6	31%	14.2%	87.5	52	15	33	18%	100%	6%	7%	0	26			0	0.84	18.1	224	$7
1st Half																																		
2nd Half		4	0	35	31	0.26	0.07	0.59	1.02	86	47	7.8	1.2	8.0	6.6	31%	14.2%	87.5	52	15	33	18%	100%	6%	7%	0	26			0	0.84	18.1	225	$7
20	**Proj**	**8**	**0**	**102**	**78**	**4.09**	**3.82**	**1.25**	**1.16**	**102**	**106**	**13.4**	**1.8**	**6.9**	**3.8**	**32%**	**11.1%**	**86.6**	**45**	**22**	**34**	**31%**	**72%**	**14%**		**10**						**0.7**	**113**	**$4**

Swanson,Erik

Age: 26	Th: R	Role RP	Health	A	LIMA Plan	F
Ht: 6' 3"	Wt: 235	Type FB	PT/Exp	D	Rand Var	+5
			Consist	F	MM	2310

1-5, 5.74 ERA in 58 IP at SEA. Rocky audition in rotation (26 ER, 29 IP) led to early season demotion. Worked in bullpen upon July return, which scouting reports suggested could be long-term home given fastball/slider dependency. Even though 2nd half MLB work (including 4.0 Cmd) bodes well for real-life future, fantasy appeal is quite limited.

Yr	Tm	W	Sv	IP	K	ERA	xERA	WHIP	xWHIP	vL+	vR+	BF/G	Ctl	Dom	Cmd	Ball%	SwK	Vel	G	L	F	H%	S%	HR/F	xHR/F	GS	APC	DOM%	DIS%	Sv%	LI	RAR	BPX	R$
15																																		
16																																		
17																																		
18	a/a	8	0	117	110	3.44	3.67	1.18				21.3	2.5	8.4	3.4							29%	75%									10.2	111	$8
19	SEA *	1	2	83	75	5.85	5.78	1.35	1.23	121	95	9.4	2.6	8.2	3.1	35%	10.0%	92.7	38	20	42	29%	65%	23%	20%	8	36	0%	63%	100	0.57	-13.7	46	-$6
1st Half		1	0	49	39	6.97	7.37	1.55	1.20	116	129	15.4	2.0	7.1	3.5	34%	9.3%	92.5	32	25	42	33%	62%	23%	23%	6	75	0%	67%	0	0.75	-15.0	27	-$11
2nd Half		0	2	34	36	4.21	3.47	1.07	1.14	131	62	5.7	3.5	9.7	2.8	36%	10.8%	93.0	47	12	41	21%	70%	22%	13%	2	22	0%	50%	100	0.50	1.2	83	$2
20	**Proj**	**2**	**1**	**58**	**57**	**4.14**	**3.85**	**1.31**	**1.16**	**126**	**91**	**10.8**	**2.7**	**8.8**	**3.3**	**35%**	**10.2%**	**92.8**	**41**	**17**	**41**	**31%**	**76%**	**17%**		**2**						**0.1**	**121**	**-$1**

BRIAN SLACK

Syndergaard,Noah

		Health	D	LIMA Plan	B
Age: 27	Th: R Role SP	PT/Exp	B	Rand Var	+1
Ht: 6' 6"	Wt: 240 Type	Consist	B	MM	4303

New career high in IP; unfortunately, ERA reached new "heights," too, but xERA consoles that the spike shouldn't have been so severe. Control is fine, and wrong-way movement in fly balls, SwK turned around a bit in 2nd half. May never crack 200 IP, but no reason he can't bring ERA back down under 4, perhaps by fair amount.

Yr	Tm	W	Sv	IP	K	ERA	xERA	WHIP	xWHIP	vL+	vR+	BF/G	Ctl	Dom	Cmd	Ball%	SwK	Vel	G	L	F	H%	S%	HR/F	xHR/F	GS	APC	DOM%	DIS%	Sv%	LI	RAR	BPX	R$
15	NYM *	12	0	180	195	2.99	2.87	1.03	1.07	95	85	23.8	1.9	9.8	5.1	35%	13.0%	97.1	46	20	34	29%	76%	14%	12%	24	99	42%	17%			21.5	173	$23
16	NYM	14	0	184	218	2.60	2.90	1.15	1.07	97	79	24.0	2.1	10.7	5.1	32%	14.7%	98.0	51	22	27	34%	79%	9%	10%	30	95	50%	10%	0	0.78	36.1	195	$25
17	NYM	1	0	30	34	2.97	2.75	1.05	0.97	65	89	17.7	0.9	10.1	11.3	33%	14.2%	98.3	58	19	24	36%	69%	0%	11%	7	66	43%	29%			5.2	232	$0
18	NYM	13	0	154	155	3.03	3.43	1.21	1.17	90	90	25.8	2.3	9.0	4.0	34%	14.0%	97.4	49	24	27	33%	76%	8%	7%	25	96	36%	16%			21.3	148	$16
19	NYM	10	0	198	202	4.28	3.89	1.23	1.20	99	91	25.8	2.3	9.2	4.0	32%	12.9%	97.7	48	20	32	32%	68%	13%	12%	32	97	41%	16%			5.5	142	$11
1st Half		5	0	101	98	4.56	4.14	1.24	1.20	85	104	26.2	2.4	8.8	3.6	33%	12.3%	97.7	47	18	35	32%	65%	12%	10%	16	101	31%	19%			-0.7	128	$8
2nd Half		5	0	97	104	3.99	3.65	1.23	1.12	113	78	25.4	2.1	9.6	4.5	32%	13.4%	97.7	49	22	29	33%	71%	15%	14%	16	93	50%	13%			6.2	157	$14
20	**Proj**	**11**	**0**	**160**	**167**	**3.59**	**3.12**	**1.20**	**1.12**	**95**	**91**	**23.2**	**2.0**	**9.4**	**4.7**	**33%**	**13.5%**	**97.7**	**48**	**22**	**30**	**33%**	**73%**	**13%**		**28**						**11.0**	**162**	**$14**

Taillon,Jameson

		Health	F	LIMA Plan	B
Age: 28	Th: R Role SP	PT/Exp	B	Rand Var	+1
Ht: 6' 5"	Wt: 230 Type Con	Consist	B	MM	3200

After seven starts, hit IL on May 1 with elbow pain, then finally succumbed to second Tommy John surgery in mid-August. Delay means he'll likely miss all of 2020, so he's only relevant in keeper leagues, where improving SwK, strong ground ball rate make him a decent $1 end-game stash for those with an eye on 2021.

Yr	Tm	W	Sv	IP	K	ERA	xERA	WHIP	xWHIP	vL+	vR+	BF/G	Ctl	Dom	Cmd	Ball%	SwK	Vel	G	L	F	H%	S%	HR/F	xHR/F	GS	APC	DOM%	DIS%	Sv%	LI	RAR	BPX	R$
15																																		
16	PIT *	9	0	166	133	3.25	3.21	1.09	1.16	99	92	23.1	1.3	7.2	5.5	34%	8.8%	94.3	52	20	27	30%	73%	15%	13%	18	86	11%	28%			19.3	165	$16
17	PIT	8	0	134	125	4.44	4.15	1.48	1.29	110	102	23.5	3.1	8.4	2.7	36%	9.1%	95.3	47	25	28	36%	71%	10%	10%	25	93	16%	32%			-1.4	112	$0
18	PIT	14	0	191	179	3.20	3.66	1.18	1.18	101	86	24.5	2.2	8.4	3.9	34%	11.0%	95.2	46	22	31	31%	77%	12%	12%	32	93	25%	16%			22.3	135	$19
19	PIT	2	0	37	30	4.10	4.21	1.13	1.26	88	93	22.6	1.9	7.2	3.8	31%	12.1%	94.8	50	23	27	28%	66%	13%	17%	7	79	14%	29%			1.9	116	-$1
1st Half		2	0	37	30	4.10	4.17	1.13	1.22	88	94	22.6	1.9	7.2	3.8	31%	12.1%	94.8	50	23	27	28%	66%	13%	17%	7	79	14%	29%			1.9	115	-$1
2nd Half																																		
20	**Proj**	**1**	**0**	**15**	**13**	**3.91**	**3.51**	**1.25**	**1.23**	**99**	**94**	**22.6**	**2.3**	**7.9**	**3.4**	**34%**	**10.3%**	**95.0**	**49**	**23**	**28**	**32%**	**71%**	**12%**		**3**						**0.4**	**123**	**-$4**

Tanaka,Masahiro

		Health	C	LIMA Plan	B
Age: 31	Th: R Role SP	PT/Exp	A	Rand Var	+1
Ht: 6' 3"	Wt: 215 Type Con	Consist	B	MM	3203

Drop in SwK, rise in vL+ tied to lost effectiveness of splitter (K% fell from 23% to 12%), which he attributed to "new" baseball. Tinkered with grip for much of year—unclear if he ever solved issue, though he did post 13% SwK in Sept. Should be okay after October elbow bone spur surgery, so main question might be whether he can "get a grip."

Yr	Tm	W	Sv	IP	K	ERA	xERA	WHIP	xWHIP	vL+	vR+	BF/G	Ctl	Dom	Cmd	Ball%	SwK	Vel	G	L	F	H%	S%	HR/F	xHR/F	GS	APC	DOM%	DIS%	Sv%	LI	RAR	BPX	R$
15	NYY	12	0	154	139	3.51	3.34	0.99	1.13	96	92	25.4	1.6	8.1	5.1	33%	11.7%	91.8	47	19	34	25%	73%	17%	18%	24	95	50%	21%			8.6	153	$17
16	NYY	14	0	200	165	3.07	3.68	1.08	1.17	89	87	26.0	1.6	7.4	4.6	33%	11.4%	90.6	48	21	31	28%	76%	12%	11%	31	95	35%	16%			27.7	138	$24
17	NYY	13	0	178	194	4.74	3.51	1.24	1.11	99	107	25.1	2.1	9.8	4.7	33%	15.5%	92.2	49	18	33	32%	68%	21%	18%	30	94	30%	23%			-8.5	177	$9
18	NYY	12	0	156	159	3.75	3.43	1.13	1.13	89	106	23.5	2.0	9.2	4.5	33%	14.4%	91.7	47	20	33	29%	74%	18%	17%	27	89	37%	33%			7.7	156	$14
19	NYY	11	0	182	149	4.45	4.38	1.24	1.27	110	89	23.7	2.0	7.4	3.7	33%	11.1%	91.5	48	20	33	30%	69%	15%	15%	31	87	26%	39%	0	0.74	1.2	115	$8
1st Half		5	0	99	85	3.74	4.19	1.18	1.21	108	82	23.8	2.1	7.8	3.7	33%	11.4%	91.4	47	20	32	29%	74%	15%	14%	17	86	29%	35%			9.3	118	$12
2nd Half		6	0	83	64	5.29	4.62	1.32	1.23	113	98	23.6	1.8	6.9	3.8	32%	10.8%	91.5	48	19	33	32%	64%	15%	15%	14	89	21%	43%	0	0.75	-8.1	110	$3
20	**Proj**	**12**	**0**	**174**	**157**	**4.05**	**3.50**	**1.21**	**1.17**	**103**	**97**	**23.4**	**2.0**	**8.1**	**4.0**	**33%**	**12.6%**	**91.6**	**48**	**19**	**33**	**30%**	**73%**	**17%**		**30**						**2.1**	**134**	**$11**

Tate,Dillon

		Health	A	LIMA Plan	B
Age: 26	Th: R Role RP	PT/Exp	D	Rand Var	+5
Ht: 6' 2"	Wt: 195 Type Con xGB	Consist	B	MM	1000

0-2, 6.43 ERA in 21 IP at BAL. Rough time in MLB, but held his own as reliever, even logging 7 saves in minors, though SwK doesn't scream closer potential. Still, like the guy he was traded for, Zack Britton, seems to have some talent for inducing ground balls. That might be his only plus skill, however. Pass.

Yr	Tm	W	Sv	IP	K	ERA	xERA	WHIP	xWHIP	vL+	vR+	BF/G	Ctl	Dom	Cmd	Ball%	SwK	Vel	G	L	F	H%	S%	HR/F	xHR/F	GS	APC	DOM%	DIS%	Sv%	LI	RAR	BPX	R$
15																																		
16																																		
17	aa	1	0	25	15	4.65	5.78	1.55				27.3	3.6	5.3	1.5							30%	76%									-0.9	12	-$5
18	aa	7	0	124	77	4.80	4.26	1.33				23.4	2.5	5.6	2.3							31%	64%									-9.9	65	-$3
19	BAL *	4	7	65	49	4.82	4.10	1.24	1.40	100	96	7.2	2.7	6.8	2.5	38%	8.3%	93.7	59	14	27	28%	64%	19%	14%	0	22			88	1.03	-2.5	64	$2
1st Half		1	2	26	20	5.48	5.64	1.40		0	0	9.1	2.4	7.1	3.0							31%	67%	0%		0	0					-3.1	50	-$6
2nd Half		3	5	39	29	4.66	3.36	1.18	1.36	100	94	6.3	3.1	6.6	2.1	38%	8.3%	93.7	59	14	27	26%	62%	19%	14%	0	22			83	1.03	-0.7	70	$7
20	**Proj**	**3**	**0**	**44**	**28**	**4.91**	**4.12**	**1.34**	**1.50**	**97**	**97**	**10.2**	**3.0**	**5.9**	**1.9**	**41%**	**8.3%**	**93.7**	**59**	**14**	**27**	**29%**	**66%**	**14%**		**0**						**-4.0**	**70**	**-$4**

Taylor,Josh

		Health	A	LIMA Plan	D
Age: 27	Th: L Role RP	PT/Exp	D	Rand Var	0
Ht: 6' 5"	Wt: 225 Type Pwr GB	Consist	D	MM	3410

2-2, 3.04 ERA in 47 IP at BOS. It's taken a while, but big-bodied converted starter seems to finally be reining in control while retaining ability to miss bats, with late-sinking fastball capable of inducing plenty of ground balls, too. May never throw enough strikes to be a serious saves candidate, but he's on his way to being solidly useful.

Yr	Tm	W	Sv	IP	K	ERA	xERA	WHIP	xWHIP	vL+	vR+	BF/G	Ctl	Dom	Cmd	Ball%	SwK	Vel	G	L	F	H%	S%	HR/F	xHR/F	GS	APC	DOM%	DIS%	Sv%	LI	RAR	BPX	R$
15																																		
16	aa	3	0	55	39	7.16	6.48	1.82				23.0	3.2	6.4	2.0							39%	59%									-20.0	47	-$12
17	aa	4	1	97	75	6.98	7.01	2.00				14.2	4.6	7.0	1.5							40%	64%									-31.4	41	-$20
18	a/a	2	8	39	31	4.78	6.01	1.88				5.4	4.4	7.2	1.6							40%	73%									-3.1	67	-$5
19	BOS *	3	3	71	87	3.27	3.67	1.28	1.15	74	94	4.1	3.5	10.9	3.1	38%	15.6%	94.9	44	21	35	33%	78%	13%	12%	1	16	0%	100%	60	1.00	10.9	119	$4
1st Half		1	3	37	44	4.40	4.66	1.50		125	98	5.0	3.9	10.7	2.7		16.1%	94.9	36	24	39	37%	72%	8%	7%	0	21			75	1.02	0.5	104	$0
2nd Half		2	0	35	43	2.08	3.31	1.04	1.14	55	91	3.4	3.1	11.2	3.6	37%	15.3%	94.8	48	20	33	27%	88%	15%	14%	1	15	0%	100%	0	0.99	10.4	155	$9
20	**Proj**	**3**	**5**	**65**	**72**	**3.93**	**3.60**	**1.37**	**1.25**	**67**	**108**	**5.2**	**3.6**	**9.9**	**2.8**	**41%**	**15.3%**	**94.8**	**48**	**20**	**33**	**34%**	**74%**	**12%**		**0**						**1.8**	**124**	**$1**

Teheran,Julio

		Health	B	LIMA Plan	A
Age: 29	Th: R Role SP	PT/Exp	A	Rand Var	-1
Ht: 6' 2"	Wt: 205 Type Pwr FB	Consist	A	MM	1205

Has a history of outpitching xERA, but this was a bit ridiculous. Yields plenty of fly balls, and xHR/F shows he was lucky a few more didn't clear fence, while walks have been issue for two years, with no relief in sight via Ball%. Indeed, was initially left off playoff roster after September correction (6.56 ERA). No surprise if that carries into 2020.

Yr	Tm	W	Sv	IP	K	ERA	xERA	WHIP	xWHIP	vL+	vR+	BF/G	Ctl	Dom	Cmd	Ball%	SwK	Vel	G	L	F	H%	S%	HR/F	xHR/F	GS	APC	DOM%	DIS%	Sv%	LI	RAR	BPX	R$
15	ATL	11	0	201	171	4.04	4.15	1.31	1.35	123	82	25.5	3.3	7.7	2.3	37%	11.2%	91.2	40	24	36	29%	73%	13%	11%	33	99	36%	27%			-1.9	81	$6
16	ATL	7	0	188	167	3.21	3.95	1.05	1.18	102	77	25.3	2.0	8.0	4.1	35%	10.9%	90.9	39	19	42	27%	74%	10%	13%	30	99	43%	23%			22.8	128	$20
17	ATL	11	0	188	151	4.49	4.93	1.37	1.39	104	102	25.4	3.4	7.2	2.1	35%	9.7%	91.4	40	20	40	29%	72%	14%	11%	32	96	19%	34%			-3.1	66	$4
18	ATL	9	0	176	162	3.94	4.52	1.17	1.44	99	87	23.4	4.3	8.3	1.9	39%	11.8%	89.8	38	20	42	22%	72%	13%	14%	31	90	29%	35%			4.4	57	$10
19	ATL	10	0	175	162	3.81	5.07	1.32	1.48	92	97	22.8	4.3	8.3	2.0	38%	9.7%	89.7	39	21	40	28%	75%	11%	13%	33	92	21%	24%			14.9	56	$10
1st Half		5	0	95	85	3.99	5.24	1.37	1.48	94	98	23.1	4.7	8.1	1.7	39%	10.4%	89.9	40	22	38	28%	74%	11%	14%	18	93	11%	28%			6.0	41	$8
2nd Half		5	0	80	77	3.60	4.87	1.26	1.36	88	97	22.6	3.8	8.7	2.3	37%	8.8%	89.4	38	19	43	27%	77%	12%	12%	15	90	33%	20%			8.9	74	$12
20	**Proj**	**10**	**0**	**181**	**164**	**4.15**	**4.28**	**1.31**	**1.40**	**101**	**98**	**23.0**	**3.9**	**8.2**	**2.1**	**37%**	**10.2%**	**90.1**	**39**	**20**	**41**	**28%**	**73%**	**13%**		**32**						**0.0**	**66**	**$7**

Tepera,Ryan

		Health	F	LIMA Plan	B
Age: 32	Th: R Role RP	PT/Exp	C	Rand Var	0
Ht: 6' 1"	Wt: 195 Type	Consist	B	MM	1210

Created intrigue with strong 1st half in 2018, but elbow woes have derailed him since. Lost more than three months in 2019, and after September return, while results were a little better, velocity was still down, as were SwK, Dom. Not exactly a spring chicken, so between health and AWOL skills, he may have tough time renewing our interest.

Yr	Tm	W	Sv	IP	K	ERA	xERA	WHIP	xWHIP	vL+	vR+	BF/G	Ctl	Dom	Cmd	Ball%	SwK	Vel	G	L	F	H%	S%	HR/F	xHR/F	GS	APC	DOM%	DIS%	Sv%	LI	RAR	BPX	R$
15	TOR *	3	4	67	51	2.45	2.69	1.00	1.24	78	105	4.8	2.9	6.8	2.3	34%	9.9%	95.0	45	16	38	21%	85%	22%	15%	0	15			80	0.50	12.5	81	$8
16	TOR *	1	18	64	54	3.92	4.32	1.46		92	82	4.8	4.0	7.6	1.9		13.8%	95.2	58	15	26	32%	75%	7%	5%	0	15			95	0.67	2.1	75	$4
17	TOR	7	2	78	81	3.59	4.03	1.13	1.29	95	79	4.4	3.6	9.4	2.6	38%	13.5%	95.0	42	18	41	27%	70%	9%	9%	0	17			50	1.00	7.3	110	$7
18	TOR	5	7	65	68	3.62	3.79	1.22	1.26	110	97	3.9	3.3	9.5	2.8	38%	14.3%	94.9	44	17	39	29%	76%	14%	14%	0	15			47	1.29	4.2	118	$5
19	TOR	0	0	22	14	4.98	5.40	1.29	1.51	145	86	4.0	3.3	5.8	1.8	38%	12.9%	93.7	41	24	35	24%	70%	21%	20%	1	15	0%	100%	0	0.97	-1.3	37	-$5
1st Half		0	0	11	9	6.55	6.23	1.64		177	98	4.3	4.9	7.4	1.5		16.0%	93.7	34	23	43	27%	71%	27%	25%	0	16			0	0.88	-2.8	13	-$8
2nd Half		0	0	11	5	3.38	4.47	0.94		106	71	3.6	1.7	4.2	2.5		9.2%	93.6	48	24	27	22%	67%	11%	12%	1	14	0%	100%	0	1.06	1.5	62	-$2
20	**Proj**	**3**	**5**	**58**	**51**	**4.02**	**4.14**	**1.32**	**1.26**	**103**	**105**	**4.4**	**3.5**	**8.0**	**2.2**	**36%**	**12.5%**	**95.0**	**43**	**19**	**38**	**29%**	**75%**	**14%**		**0**						**1.0**	**78**	**$1**

KRISTOPHER OLSON

Thornton,Trent

Age: 26 | Th: R | Role: SP | Ht: 6' 0" | Wt: 195 | Type: Con FB | Health: A | PT/Exp: C | Consist: C | LIMA Plan: C | Rand Var: 0 | MM: 1103

Results may not have warranted full season of starts, but it's not like TOR had many better ideas. Did shake off early control woes, which didn't jibe with minor league history. But he's simply very hittable, yielding lots of havoc-wreaking line drives, fly balls. MLEs further dim hopes there's a next level he can get to, so seek upside elsewhere.

Yr Tm	W	Sv	IP	K	ERA	xERA	WHIP	xWHIP	vL+	vR+	BF/G	Ctl	Dom	Cmd	Ball%	SwK	Vel	G	L	F	H%	S%	HR/F	xHR/F	GS	APC	DOM%	DIS%	Sv%	LI	RAR	BPX	R$
15																																	
16 aa	3	0	46	31	2.87	3.97	1.17				26.2	1.0	6.1	6.3							30%	81%									7.5	161	$1
17 a/a	9	0	131	88	5.59	5.54	1.52				22.8	1.5	6.0	4.1							37%	64%									-19.9	100	-$7
18 aaa	9	0	125	100	4.39	3.92	1.24				21.2	2.0	7.2	3.5							31%	66%									-3.7	106	$3
19 TOR	6	0	154	149	4.84	5.03	1.41	1.39	102	102	21.2	3.6	8.7	2.4	39%	10.3%	92.9	32	27	40	32%	69%	13%	12%	29	86	21%	41%	0	0.77	-6.4	77	-$1
1st Half	2	0	86	91	4.60	4.94	1.45	1.36	109	96	22.2	4.2	9.5	2.3	41%	10.7%	93.3	30	30	39	32%	72%	14%	13%	17	92	24%	35%			-1.1	73	-$2
2nd Half	4	0	68	58	5.14	5.18	1.35	1.30	94	110	20.0	2.8	7.6	2.8	37%	9.8%	92.3	35	24	42	31%	65%	12%	10%	12	80	17%	50%	0	0.72	-5.3	82	$0
20 Proj	7	0	131	109	4.70	4.22	1.35	1.32	100	105	21.1	2.5	7.5	3.0	38%	10.1%	92.7	33	26	41	32%	68%	11%		26						-8.8	90	$0

Tomlin,Josh

Age: 35 | Th: R | Role: RP | Ht: 6' 1" | Wt: 190 | Type: Con FB | Health: D | PT/Exp: C | Consist: B | LIMA Plan: B | Rand Var: 0 | MM: 1001

"Cousin" Lily once said, "I always wanted to be somebody, but now I realize I should have been more specific." He'd have rather been flame-throwing ace, not soft-tossing control artist using hit, strand rate help to cling to low-leverage bullpen role. Rotation chances, fantasy relevance appear over. And that's the truth. Thbpbpthbt!

Yr Tm	W	Sv	IP	K	ERA	xERA	WHIP	xWHIP	vL+	vR+	BF/G	Ctl	Dom	Cmd	Ball%	SwK	Vel	G	L	F	H%	S%	HR/F	xHR/F	GS	APC	DOM%	DIS%	Sv%	LI	RAR	BPX	R$
15 CLE *	8	0	90	71	3.79	4.11	1.08	1.08	62	118	23.3	1.0	7.1	6.8	32%	9.7%	88.4	38	16	46	28%	74%	15%	16%	10	95	50%	10%			1.9	162	$6
16 CLE	13	0	174	118	4.40	4.22	1.19	1.18	93	115	24.2	1.0	6.1	5.9	32%	7.8%	87.7	44	21	35	29%	71%	18%	16%	29	87	17%	28%	0	0.74	-4.4	123	$8
17 CLE	10	0	141	109	4.98	4.18	1.28	1.12	109	107	22.5	0.9	7.0	7.8	32%	8.9%	87.7	40	23	37	33%	65%	14%	15%	26	80	23%	31%			-10.8	143	$2
18 CLE	2	0	70	46	6.14	5.33	1.48	1.26	154	112	10.0	1.5	5.9	3.8	34%	9.1%	87.8	31	24	45	31%	71%	21%	19%	9	37	0%	78%	0	0.55	-17.3	85	-$10
19 ATL	2	2	79	51	3.74	4.88	1.12	1.23	96	101	6.3	0.8	5.8	7.3	33%	9.4%	89.3	33	24	43	28%	75%	13%	12%	1	22	0%	0%	50	0.69	7.5	102	$3
1st Half	1	1	46	31	3.94	4.69	0.99	1.14	94	91	6.4	0.8	6.1	7.8	32%	11.0%	89.6	35	21	43	25%	69%	15%	13%	0	22			33	0.75	3.2	111	$4
2nd Half	1	1	34	20	3.48	5.31	1.31	1.20	100	111	6.1	0.8	5.3	6.7	34%	7.4%	88.8	31	27	42	32%	79%	10%	12%	1	22	0%	0%	100	0.60	4.3	91	$2
20 Proj	3	0	73	46	4.77	4.48	1.33	1.18	117	112	8.5	1.3	5.8	4.5	33%	8.9%	88.5	33	23	44	31%	72%	15%		0						-5.6	92	-$3

Toussaint,Touki

Age: 24 | Th: R | Role: SP | Ht: 6' 3" | Wt: 185 | Type: Pwr GB | Health: A | PT/Exp: D | Consist: F | LIMA Plan: F | Rand Var: +5 | MM: 1301

4-0, 5.62 ERA in 42 IP at ATL. Another example that development isn't always a straight line. After dominating minors, holding own in majors in 2018, he simply couldn't find the plate in 2019, and LHB crushed him when he did. Young and talented enough to right the ship, but you may want to see proof that's occurring before you risk rostering.

Yr Tm	W	Sv	IP	K	ERA	xERA	WHIP	xWHIP	vL+	vR+	BF/G	Ctl	Dom	Cmd	Ball%	SwK	Vel	G	L	F	H%	S%	HR/F	xHR/F	GS	APC	DOM%	DIS%	Sv%	LI	RAR	BPX	R$
15																																	
16																																	
17 aa	3	0	40	40	4.42	4.27	1.54				24.7	5.6	9.1	1.6							32%	72%									-0.3	85	-$3
18 ATL *	11	0	166	171	3.14	2.99	1.25		70	98	21.8	3.9	9.3	2.4		9.9%	93.2	48	28	24	30%	75%	6%	14%	5	68	20%	0%	0	0.67	20.8	117	$14
19 ATL *	5	0	83	81	7.49	6.61	1.93	1.55	159	78	11.6	5.9	8.8	1.5	42%	12.3%	93.5	44	17	39	38%	61%	11%	12%	1	33	0%	100%	0	1.24	-30.6	47	-$17
1st Half	5	0	51	45	5.80	5.77	1.70	1.38	163	68	10.1	4.6	7.9	1.7	41%	13.0%	93.3	46	15	40	35%	67%	10%	10%	1	33	0%	100%	0	1.32	-8.2	50	-$11
2nd Half	0	0	32	37	10.23	7.97	2.30		123	138	14.7	8.1	10.4	1.3		8.9%	94.5	33	33	33	43%	54%	20%	27%	0	31			0	0.83	-22.4	45	-$27
20 Proj	4	0	73	75	4.49	4.45	1.56	1.51	163	65	20.2	5.0	9.3	1.9	45%	13.0%	93.3	46	15	40	33%	75%	11%		13						-3.0	66	-$4

Treinen,Blake

Age: 32 | Th: R | Role: RP | Ht: 6' 5" | Wt: 225 | Type: Pwr | Health: B | PT/Exp: B | Consist: D | LIMA Plan: D | Rand Var: +1 | MM: 2310

To be sure, injuries (elbow, shoulder, back) were big reason he was one of year's biggest duds; it's also an open question whether 2018 levels were one-shot deal. Ground ball rate steadily declining, control went haywire in 2019, but was never special before 2018. Could he close again? Sure, but there are impediments—health is just the first.

Yr Tm	W	Sv	IP	K	ERA	xERA	WHIP	xWHIP	vL+	vR+	BF/G	Ctl	Dom	Cmd	Ball%	SwK	Vel	G	L	F	H%	S%	HR/F	xHR/F	GS	APC	DOM%	DIS%	Sv%	LI	RAR	BPX	R$
15 WAS	2	0	68	65	3.86	3.25	1.39	1.40	128	69	4.7	4.3	8.6	2.0	36%	11.2%	96.3	62	23	15	32%	72%	15%	16%	0	17			0	0.93	0.9	96	-$2
16 WAS	4	1	67	63	2.28	3.32	1.22	1.40	100	82	3.6	4.2	8.5	2.0	39%	10.9%	95.4	66	14	20	27%	84%	15%	13%	0	14			33	1.23	15.8	100	$6
17 2 TM	3	16	76	74	3.93	3.58	1.39	1.25	116	84	4.5	3.0	8.8	3.0	36%	13.5%	97.2	58	19	23	35%	73%	12%	14%	0	17			76	1.30	4.0	137	$7
18 OAK	9	38	80	100	0.78	2.63	0.83	1.06	63	52	4.6	2.4	11.2	4.8	32%	18.6%	97.4	52	24	24	26%	92%	4%	7%	0	17			88	1.60	33.3	194	$36
19 OAK	6	16	59	59	4.91	5.33	1.62	1.59	104	103	4.7	5.7	9.1	1.6	37%	12.6%	96.7	43	24	33	32%	73%	16%	16%	0	18			76	1.40	-2.9	33	$3
1st Half	2	16	35	36	4.08	4.98	1.53	1.50	95	96	5.2	5.3	9.2	1.7	38%	13.2%	97.1	43	23	34	32%	75%	9%	14%	0	19			89	1.72	1.9	46	$8
2nd Half	4	0	23	23	6.17	5.70	1.76	1.60	118	110	4.1	6.2	8.9	1.4	36%	11.8%	96.3	42	25	32	31%	71%	26%	20%	0	16			0	1.04	-4.8	15	-$3
20 Proj	7	8	65	69	3.76	3.67	1.38	1.37	99	88	4.3	4.4	9.5	2.2	35%	13.0%	96.8	40	23	28	30%	76%	16%		0						3.2	92	$5

Trivino,Lou

Age: 28 | Th: R | Role: RP | Ht: 6' 5" | Wt: 240 | Type: Pwr | Health: A | PT/Exp: D | Consist: B | LIMA Plan: B | Rand Var: 0 | MM: 2300

Cruised through mid-April (16/1 K/BB, 2 ER in 12.2 IP), then hurt thumb. Did it affect him rest of year? Whatever the cause, control got shakier, SwK tanked, and he became easier to hit, despite little change in Ball%, velocity. Chance that health can bring back solid setup man skills may be worth a small bet.

Yr Tm	W	Sv	IP	K	ERA	xERA	WHIP	xWHIP	vL+	vR+	BF/G	Ctl	Dom	Cmd	Ball%	SwK	Vel	G	L	F	H%	S%	HR/F	xHR/F	GS	APC	DOM%	DIS%	Sv%	LI	RAR	BPX	R$
15																																	
16 aa	1	1	18	10	2.98	3.18	1.26				6.2	3.4	4.8	1.4							27%	77%									2.7	60	-$2
17 a/a	8	5	68	52	3.57	3.54	1.38				6.0	2.7	6.8	2.5							34%	71%									6.7	112	$4
18 OAK	8	4	74	82	2.92	3.53	1.14	1.28	88	79	4.3	3.8	10.0	2.6	36%	14.9%	97.6	47	23	31	26%	79%	14%	13%	1	16	0%	0%	44	1.18	11.2	118	$9
19 OAK	4	0	60	57	5.25	5.22	1.53	1.51	105	102	4.4	4.7	8.6	1.8	37%	12.7%	97.5	45	16	39	32%	67%	10%	8%	0	16			0	1.08	-5.5	56	-$5
1st Half	3	0	38	38	4.74	5.21	1.53	1.42	123	79	4.4	4.5	9.0	2.0	37%	13.5%	97.5	40	18	43	34%	69%	7%	5%	0	17			0	1.12	-1.1	64	-$3
2nd Half	1	0	22	19	6.14	5.19	1.55	1.52	71	138	4.3	4.9	7.8	1.6	37%	11.1%	97.5	54	12	34	29%	63%	18%	16%	0	15			0	1.02	-4.4	43	-$7
20 Proj	5	0	58	60	4.03	3.75	1.34	1.40	91	99	4.4	3.8	9.3	2.4	37%	13.2%	97.5	47	18	35	31%	72%	11%		0						0.8	103	$0

Tuivailala,Sam

Age: 27 | Th: R | Role: RP | Ht: 6' 3" | Wt: 225 | Type: Pwr FB | Health: F | PT/Exp: D | Consist: B | LIMA Plan: B | Rand Var: -5 | MM: 1300

Returned in mid-July after Achilles surgery kept him off MLB mound for nearly a year. Results seem promising, but closer look shows how much hit rate, HR/F helped. Regression of latter would be big issue if he can't regain ground ball tilt, and control a cause for concern, too. While further distance from injury may help, no reason to rush in.

Yr Tm	W	Sv	IP	K	ERA	xERA	WHIP	xWHIP	vL+	vR+	BF/G	Ctl	Dom	Cmd	Ball%	SwK	Vel	G	L	F	H%	S%	HR/F	xHR/F	GS	APC	DOM%	DIS%	Sv%	LI	RAR	BPX	R$
15 STL *	3	17	60	58	2.08	2.92	1.30		96	109	4.3	5.1	8.8	1.7		12.1%	96.4	49	19	32	27%	87%	17%	17%	0	19			100	1.05	13.9	101	$10
16 STL *	3	17	56	64	5.96	4.91	1.67		101	106	4.6	4.5	10.4	2.3		5.7%	95.8	44	25	31	40%	62%	0%	2%	0	18			74	0.10	-12.1	111	-$1
17 STL *	4	6	64	50	2.23	2.69	1.02	1.26	92	80	4.4	2.0	7.1	3.6	33%	10.0%	95.4	49	20	32	26%	84%	10%	13%	0	17			100	0.43	16.7	123	$10
18 2 TM	4	0	37	30	3.41	4.30	1.43	1.32	144	74	4.6	2.9	7.3	2.5	35%	10.4%	95.2	49	24	27	34%	78%	9%	11%	0	18			0	0.77	3.4	92	-$2
19 SEA	1	0	23	27	2.35	4.51	1.04	1.37	81	66	4.1	4.3	10.6	2.5	39%	11.3%	93.5	33	13	54	24%	78%	3%	7%	2	17	0%	0%	0	0.87	6.1	93	-$1
1st Half																																	
2nd Half	1	0	23	27	2.35	4.58	1.04	1.31	82	65	4.1	4.3	10.6	2.5	39%	11.3%	93.5	33	13	54	24%	78%	3%	7%	2	17	0%	0%	0	0.87	6.1	93	-$1
20 Proj	3	0	51	50	3.59	4.08	1.28	1.29	116	81	4.3	3.9	8.8	2.3	36%	10.5%	94.7	39	18	42	28%	76%	11%		0						3.5	81	$0

Turnbull,Spencer

Age: 27 | Th: R | Role: SP | Ht: 6' 3" | Wt: 215 | Type: Pwr | Health: C | PT/Exp: C | Consist: B | LIMA Plan: B | Rand Var: +1 | MM: 2203

On-the-job training involved taking plenty of lumps (17 losses). Looks like wheels came off in 2nd half, but skills didn't change; indeed, biggest difference was actually slight uptick in SwK, Dom. Has a knack for inducing ground balls, and if he could pair that with better Ctl, we might have something, even if that something isn't particularly special.

Yr Tm	W	Sv	IP	K	ERA	xERA	WHIP	xWHIP	vL+	vR+	BF/G	Ctl	Dom	Cmd	Ball%	SwK	Vel	G	L	F	H%	S%	HR/F	xHR/F	GS	APC	DOM%	DIS%	Sv%	LI	RAR	BPX	R$
15																																	
16																																	
17 aa	0	0	20	17	8.04	5.60	1.74				23.2	3.8	7.7	2.0							39%	50%									-9.2	77	-$8
18 DET *	5	0	131	110	5.76	4.43	1.50		89	94	22.6	3.6	7.5	2.1		9.9%	94.1	46	28	26	35%	59%	8%	15%	3	71	0%	33%	0	0.89	-25.9	87	-$12
19 DET	3	0	148	146	4.61	4.48	1.44	1.36	107	95	21.9	3.6	8.9	2.5	39%	11.1%	93.8	48	19	32	34%	69%	10%	14%	30	89	7%	33%			-1.9	97	-$2
1st Half	3	0	90	84	3.31	4.47	1.34	1.32	108	83	22.9	3.4	8.4	2.5	38%	10.9%	93.8	49	18	33	32%	78%	9%	14%	17	92	6%	29%			13.2	95	$6
2nd Half	0	0	59	62	6.60	4.44	1.59	1.32	105	113	20.5	3.8	9.5	2.5	39%	11.5%	93.8	47	22	31	37%	57%	11%	14%	13	85	8%	38%			-15.1	101	-$14
20 Proj	4	0	160	150	4.44	3.93	1.43	1.32	105	103	23.3	3.6	8.5	2.3	39%	11.3%	93.8	48	20	32	33%	72%	13%		29						-5.6	92	-$2

KRISTOPHER OLSON

Urena,Jose

Age: 28	Th: R	Role SP	Health	F	LIMA Plan	B
Ht: 6' 2"	Wt: 200	Type Con	PT/Exp	A	Rand Var	+2
			Consist	B	MM	1011

Prior to back injury that cost him 3 months, poor Dom and so-so Ctl justified lousy ERA/WHIP. Amazingly, he closed upon return, but don't let tiny Sept sample fool you. Sinker-heavy approach induces GB and limits HR, but tepid Ball% and SwK, no plus pitch to lean on, gives little hope for success in rotation or pen. Observe from a safe distance.

Yr Tm	W	Sv	IP	K	ERA	xERA	WHIP	xWHIP	vL+	vR+	BF/G	Ctl	Dom	Cmd	Ball%	SwK	Vel	G	L	F	H%	S%	HR/F	xHR/F	GS	APC	DOM%	DIS%	Sv%	LI	RAR	BPX	R$
15 MIA *	7	0	129	61	4.32	4.75	1.52	1.57	120	110	18.1	3.2	4.3	1.4	39%	8.5%	93.8	48	20	32	32%	72%	7%	11%	9	50	0%	56%	0	0.59	-5.7	37	-$6
16 MIA *	7	1	132	92	5.33	4.63	1.45	1.40	117	99	14.1	3.5	6.3	1.8	39%	9.0%	94.9	48	22	30	31%	64%	13%	12%	12	51	8%	50%	33	0.90	-18.6	53	-$6
17 MIA	14	0	170	113	3.82	5.07	1.27	1.45	100	97	21.3	3.4	6.0	1.8	39%	8.5%	95.5	43	19	38	26%	76%	13%	14%	28	85	7%	46%	0	0.73	11.3	45	$11
18 MIA	9	0	174	130	3.98	4.12	1.18	1.32	100	89	23.0	2.6	6.7	2.5	38%	9.2%	95.8	50	18	32	27%	69%	12%	12%	31	90	16%	26%			3.6	90	$8
19 MIA	4	3	85	62	5.21	4.83	1.48	1.39	120	98	15.4	2.8	6.6	2.4	37%	10.1%	95.9	50	21	29	33%	68%	16%	16%	13	57	8%	38%	60	1.03	-7.3	78	-$4
1st Half	4	0	75	51	4.70	4.82	1.45	1.36	115	100	24.8	2.8	6.1	2.2	37%	9.1%	95.7	51	21	28	32%	70%	15%	14%	13	91	8%	38%			-1.8	70	-$3
2nd Half	0	3	10	11	9.00	4.52	1.70		157	90	4.3	2.7	9.9	3.7		16.4%	97.4	45	21	33	39%	50%	27%	23%	0	17			60	1.33	-5.5	140	-$10
20 Proj	**4**	**5**	**73**	**53**	**4.64**	**4.18**	**1.39**	**1.40**	**114**	**102**	**20.3**	**2.8**	**6.5**	**2.3**	**38%**	**9.3%**	**95.3**	**48**	**20**	**32**	**31%**	**71%**	**15%**		**15**						**-4.4**	**78**	**-$1**

Urias,Julio

Age: 23	Th: L	Role RP	Health	F	LIMA Plan	F
Ht: 6' 0"	Wt: 225	Type Pwr	PT/Exp	D	Rand Var	-4
			Consist	F	MM	2301

In first full season back from shoulder surgery, former top prospect excelled as starter, middle reliever, and opener. Rise in FB% hurt his xERA, but underneath not only did his velocity recover to prior heights, strong SwK rate also suggests more Ks could come. If they do, this post-hype sleeper should be above-average in any role.

Yr Tm	W	Sv	IP	K	ERA	xERA	WHIP	xWHIP	vL+	vR+	BF/G	Ctl	Dom	Cmd	Ball%	SwK	Vel	G	L	F	H%	S%	HR/F	xHR/F	GS	APC	DOM%	DIS%	Sv%	LI	RAR	BPX	R$
15 a/a	3	0	73	72	4.04	3.14	1.19				19.4	2.2	9.0	4.0							33%	65%									-0.7	153	$0
16 LA *	10	0	122	128	2.69	3.24	1.24	1.28	100	99	17.1	2.8	9.5	3.4	37%	10.7%	92.6	44	27	30	33%	80%	8%	9%	15	79	13%	33%	0	0.73	22.5	140	$13
17 LA *	3	0	55	39	3.91	2.97	1.31		178	77	20.5	4.4	6.5	1.5		9.2%	93.1	40	28	32	27%	69%	4%	5%	5	82	20%	40%			3.0	84	-$1
18 LA	0	0	4	7	0.00	1.18	0.25		0	28	4.3	0.0	15.8	0.0		22.4%	93.1	50	17	33	19%	0%	0%	1%	0	19			0	0.00	2.0	359	-$3
19 LA	4	4	80	85	2.49	4.12	1.08	1.27	89	76	8.8	3.1	9.6	3.1	36%	14.4%	95.2	39	22	39	27%	81%	9%	9%	8	36	38%	25%	80	0.96	19.9	117	$10
1st Half	4	3	50	51	2.50	4.13	0.97	1.22	93	67	10.7	2.9	9.1	3.2	35%	14.1%	95.2	40	22	39	24%	80%	10%	11%	5	43	60%	40%	75	0.88	12.4	114	$15
2nd Half	0	1	29	34	2.45	4.14	1.26	1.22	81	91	6.8	3.4	10.4	3.1	36%	14.8%	95.2	37	23	40	33%	83%	7%	5%	3	29	0%	0%	100	1.04	7.4	122	$3
20 Proj	**6**	**0**	**102**	**103**	**3.66**	**3.67**	**1.21**	**1.24**	**98**	**90**	**11.0**	**3.3**	**9.1**	**2.7**	**36%**	**12.9%**	**94.1**	**41**	**22**	**37**	**28%**	**74%**	**14%**		**4**						**6.1**	**108**	**$6**

Urquidy,Jose

Age: 25	Th: R	Role RP	Health	A	LIMA Plan	F
Ht: 6' 0"	Wt: 180	Type xFB	PT/Exp	F	Rand Var	+4
			Consist	F	MM	2301

2-1, 3.95 in 41 IP at HOU. Blew through AA/AAA on the back of Dom breakout to earn July call-up, but Ks haven't shown up in bigs yet. All four pitches worked vL, supporting the reverse platoon split he carried through minors. Scouts love his command, and slider has been effective vR (19% SwK), making him an intriguing arm to take a flyer on.

Yr Tm	W	Sv	IP	K	ERA	xERA	WHIP	xWHIP	vL+	vR+	BF/G	Ctl	Dom	Cmd	Ball%	SwK	Vel	G	L	F	H%	S%	HR/F	xHR/F	GS	APC	DOM%	DIS%	Sv%	LI	RAR	BPX	R$
15																																	
16																																	
17																																	
18																																	
19 HOU *	9	0	144	153	5.20	4.76	1.26	1.16	70	110	20.2	1.8	9.6	5.3	36%	12.3%	93.3	37	18	45	33%	63%	12%	14%	7	77	29%	29%	0	0.93	-12.4	130	$3
1st Half	5	0	78	88	4.27	3.51	1.12		0	0	20.6	1.8	10.1	5.6							32%	65%	0%		0	0					2.3	165	$8
2nd Half	4	0	68	65	6.10	5.94	1.37	1.10	70	108	20.4	1.8	8.6	4.9	36%	12.3%	93.3	37	18	45	33%	62%	12%	14%	7	77	29%	29%	0	0.93	-13.4	93	-$4
20 Proj	**5**	**0**	**87**	**89**	**4.11**	**3.64**	**1.18**	**1.21**	**73**	**112**	**20.0**	**1.8**	**9.2**	**5.2**	**40%**	**12.3%**	**93.3**	**35**	**22**	**43**	**30%**	**74%**	**15%**		**17**						**0.5**	**151**	**$3**

Valdez,Framber

Age: 26	Th: L	Role RP	Health	A	LIMA Plan	D
Ht: 5' 11"	Wt: 170	Type Pwr xGB	PT/Exp	D	Rand Var	+5
			Consist	D	MM	3301

4-7, 5.86 in 71 IP at HOU. Boasts elite ability to induce GB, but still not enough to counter poor Ctl. He needs a weapon to address platoon splits, and while scouts don't love his change-up, it has flashed promise vR in tiny sample (23% SwK in 48 thrown). If he can match 3.1 Cmd ratio from minors, GB% could make him viable #4 starter.

Yr Tm	W	Sv	IP	K	ERA	xERA	WHIP	xWHIP	vL+	vR+	BF/G	Ctl	Dom	Cmd	Ball%	SwK	Vel	G	L	F	H%	S%	HR/F	xHR/F	GS	APC	DOM%	DIS%	Sv%	LI	RAR	BPX	R$
15																																	
16																																	
17 aa	5	0	49	46	7.38	6.75	1.93				19.4	4.3	8.5	2.0							42%	61%									-18.3	64	-$11
18 HOU *	10	1	142	140	3.95	3.83	1.35	1.62	58	91	19.8	3.5	8.8	2.5	44%	8.5%	92.0	70	13	16	32%	71%	20%	16%	5	79	0%	20%	50	0.93	3.5	104	$5
19 HOU *	9	1	116	124	5.05	4.31	1.47	1.57	87	112	13.8	4.8	9.6	2.0	40%	10.8%	93.0	62	21	17	32%	67%	26%	19%	8	45	25%	50%	100	0.46	-7.7	83	-$1
1st Half	3	1	49	46	4.41	3.70	1.28	1.37	71	104	9.6	3.5	8.4	2.4	37%	11.0%	92.8	59	21	20	30%	67%	19%	17%	4	38	50%	50%	100	0.44	0.6	88	-$1
2nd Half	6	0	66	78	5.52	4.77	1.60	1.82	112	124	19.6	5.8	10.6	1.8	43%	10.5%	93.3	67	22	12	34%	66%	44%	23%	4	61	0%	50%	0	0.50	-8.3	83	-$1
20 Proj	**7**	**0**	**87**	**89**	**4.60**	**3.46**	**1.52**	**1.63**	**82**	**110**	**16.5**	**4.5**	**9.2**	**2.0**	**42%**	**9.8%**	**92.6**	**60**	**22**	**18**	**34%**	**71%**	**19%**		**15**						**-4.8**	**95**	**-$2**

Vargas,Jason

Age: 37	Th: L	Role SP	Health	F	LIMA Plan	B
Ht: 6' 0"	Wt: 215	Type FB	PT/Exp	A	Rand Var	0
			Consist	B	MM	1101

Missed three weeks in May, traded to PHI at the deadline. Perhaps Phillies were fooled by 1st half ERA; you shouldn't be, as he was aided by lucky H% and HR/F. Relied heavily on change-up (19% SwK), but even so, Dom remained poor all year. Subpar G/F ratio plus Ctl slide is a recipe for disaster, making him a high-risk, low-reward pick.

Yr Tm	W	Sv	IP	K	ERA	xERA	WHIP	xWHIP	vL+	vR+	BF/G	Ctl	Dom	Cmd	Ball%	SwK	Vel	G	L	F	H%	S%	HR/F	xHR/F	GS	APC	DOM%	DIS%	Sv%	LI	RAR	BPX	R$
15 KC	5	0	43	27	3.98	4.71	1.35	1.37	111	100	20.3	2.5	5.7	2.3	38%	8.0%	87.7	41	19	40	30%	74%	9%	13%	9	76	0%	22%			-0.1	63	-$2
16 KC *	0	0	28	25	5.78	6.29	1.42		181	59	17.0	1.3	7.9	5.9		10.5%	86.3	36	15	48	34%	67%	6%	6%	3	70	33%	0%			-5.5	112	-$6
17 KC	18	0	180	134	4.16	4.86	1.33	1.36	112	101	23.6	2.9	6.7	2.3	37%	10.1%	85.6	40	19	40	29%	74%	12%	11%	32	91	22%	41%			4.4	73	$10
18 NYM	7	0	92	84	5.77	4.44	1.41	1.29	99	118	20.2	2.9	8.2	2.8	37%	11.2%	86.4	39	21	39	32%	63%	17%	15%	20	78	20%	55%			-18.4	99	-$6
19 2 NL	7	0	150	124	4.51	5.36	1.36	1.48	101	100	21.6	3.8	7.5	2.0	39%	10.1%	84.3	39	19	42	29%	70%	11%	13%	29	84	17%	48%	0	0.73	-0.1	53	$1
1st Half	3	0	66	57	3.66	5.13	1.28	1.40	87	97	20.1	3.8	7.7	2.0	38%	8.9%	85.0	41	18	41	27%	75%	10%	15%	13	77	23%	54%	0	0.70	6.9	61	$3
2nd Half	4	0	83	67	5.18	5.57	1.43	1.43	115	102	22.9	3.8	7.2	1.9	40%	11.1%	83.6	37	20	43	30%	67%	12%	12%	16	89	13%	44%			-7.0	47	$0
20 Proj	**8**	**0**	**116**	**95**	**4.91**	**4.52**	**1.43**	**1.37**	**109**	**112**	**21.1**	**3.5**	**7.3**	**2.1**	**38%**	**10.2%**	**85.3**	**39**	**20**	**41**	**30%**	**71%**	**15%**		**23**						**-10.8**	**64**	**-$2**

Vazquez,Felipe

Age: 28	Th: L	Role RP	Health	A	LIMA Plan	A
Ht: 6' 2"	Wt: 225	Type Pwr	PT/Exp	B	Rand Var	-5
			Consist	A	MM	5500

Name a stat, and it agrees he was an elite closer, right up until he was arrested and charged in multiple states. Could face years of jail time and/or deportation, plus supplemental discipline by MLB (which doesn't require a conviction). Most likely won't pitch in 2020—or maybe ever—but if by some twist of fate he does, he should be elite again.

Yr Tm	W	Sv	IP	K	ERA	xERA	WHIP	xWHIP	vL+	vR+	BF/G	Ctl	Dom	Cmd	Ball%	SwK	Vel	G	L	F	H%	S%	HR/F	xHR/F	GS	APC	DOM%	DIS%	Sv%	LI	RAR	BPX	R$
15 WAS	2	2	48	43	2.79	3.41	0.95	1.18	67	85	3.9	2.0	8.0	3.9	32%	11.8%	95.4	45	21	33	26%	70%	5%	13%	0	16			67	1.10	7.0	133	$4
16 2 NL	1	1	77	92	4.09	3.46	1.29	1.25	104	85	4.4	3.9	10.8	2.8	35%	15.0%	95.8	48	22	30	32%	70%	12%	16%	0	17			25	1.04	0.9	137	$0
17 PIT	5	21	75	88	1.67	3.00	0.89	1.10	34	77	4.1	2.4	10.5	4.4	32%	16.1%	98.5	53	19	28	26%	84%	8%	10%	0	16			91	1.21	25.0	187	$23
18 PIT	4	37	70	89	2.70	3.31	1.24	1.14	62	93	4.2	3.1	11.4	3.7	33%	15.1%	98.1	43	25	32	35%	80%	7%	9%	0	17			88	1.28	12.5	165	$20
19 PIT	5	28	60	90	1.65	2.66	0.93	0.94	85	74	4.2	2.0	13.5	6.9	31%	14.4%	98.5	42	21	37	32%	88%	11%	14%	0	17			90	1.21	21.1	229	$23
1st Half	2	19	35	55	1.80	2.84	1.03	0.93	115	73	4.5	2.3	14.1	6.1	32%	14.6%	98.1	39	25	36	35%	88%	11%	15%	0	18			95	1.28	11.7	228	$24
2nd Half	3	9	25	35	1.44	2.53	0.80	0.86	50	75	3.8	1.4	12.6	8.8	29%	14.1%	98.9	47	16	37	28%	89%	11%	12%	0	16			82	1.11	9.5	232	$21
20 Proj	**0**	**0**	**15**	**19**	**2.06**	**2.58**	**1.00**	**1.02**	**65**	**81**	**4.0**	**2.3**	**12.0**	**5.2**	**32%**	**14.7%**	**98.2**	**45**	**21**	**34**	**31%**	**83%**	**9%**		**0**						**3.7**	**203**	**-$3**

Velasquez,Vincent

Age: 28	Th: R	Role RP	Health	F	LIMA Plan	B
Ht: 6' 3"	Wt: 205	Type Pwr FB	PT/Exp	B	Rand Var	+3
			Consist	B	MM	2303

Split time between SP/RP in yet another season where results lagged behind skills. With strong Dom and decent Ctl, problem is fly balls, and home park hasn't helped (+25% HR). Leans heavily on fastball, which yields 13% SwK but few GB, while underused slider and curve get both. Could still turn it around, but it's safer to wait and see.

Yr Tm	W	Sv	IP	K	ERA	xERA	WHIP	xWHIP	vL+	vR+	BF/G	Ctl	Dom	Cmd	Ball%	SwK	Vel	G	L	F	H%	S%	HR/F	xHR/F	GS	APC	DOM%	DIS%	Sv%	LI	RAR	BPX	R$
15 HOU *	5	0	89	97	3.54	3.01	1.20	1.27	88	114	12.7	3.4	9.9	2.9	36%	10.7%	94.6	31	22	47	30%	72%	7%	11%	7	51	14%	0%	0	0.64	4.6	129	$4
16 PHI	8	0	131	152	4.12	3.81	1.33	1.19	106	102	23.0	3.1	10.4	3.4	36%	12.0%	93.7	35	24	41	33%	75%	15%	14%	24	92	17%	13%			1.1	140	$5
17 PHI	2	0	72	68	5.13	4.65	1.50	1.41	116	112	21.0	4.3	8.5	2.0	35%	9.6%	93.9	43	23	35	30%	72%	21%	17%	15	85	7%	40%			-6.8	71	-$5
18 PHI	9	0	147	161	4.85	4.08	1.34	1.28	122	85	20.3	3.6	9.9	2.7	36%	12.2%	93.8	38	21	41	33%	65%	10%	9%	30	80	27%	30%	0	0.83	-12.6	111	$0
19 PHI	7	0	117	130	4.91	4.59	1.39	1.29	109	112	15.6	3.3	10.0	3.0	36%	11.8%	94.1	34	22	44	32%	72%	18%	16%	23	64	4%	35%	0	0.85	-5.8	112	$0
1st Half	2	0	51	60	4.73	4.72	1.42	1.29	106	115	11.8	4.0	10.5	2.6	38%	11.9%	94.6	37	17	47	31%	75%	19%	16%	9	49	0%	44%	0	0.90	-1.4	104	-$4
2nd Half	5	0	66	70	5.05	4.58	1.36	1.20	111	109	20.9	2.7	9.5	3.5	35%	11.8%	93.8	33	25	42	33%	70%	18%	17%	14	85	7%	29%			-4.4	119	$3
20 Proj	**7**	**0**	**131**	**139**	**4.82**	**4.03**	**1.40**	**1.27**	**112**	**105**	**17.1**	**3.6**	**9.6**	**2.6**	**36%**	**11.5%**	**94.0**	**35**	**22**	**43**	**32%**	**71%**	**15%**		**23**						**-10.8**	**101**	**-$1**

ARIK FLORIMONTE

VerHagen,Drew

Age: 29	Th: R	Role RP	Health	D	LIMA Plan F
Ht: 6' 6"	Wt: 230	Type Con	PT/Exp	D	Rand Var +5
			Consist	F	MM 1101

4-3, 5.90 in 58 IP at DET. Working mainly in middle relief—likely his ceiling—pedestrian SwK, Dom, Ctl returned, and only his nice GB% survived. Results in majors could have been better (4.66 xERA) if not for H%/S%/HR misfortune trifecta. Though his slider can get whiffs, it's also a liability both vL and vR (.656 SLG). No reason to watch this space.

Yr Tm	W	Sv	IP	K	ERA	xERA	WHIP	xWHIP	vL+	vR+	BF/G	Ctl	Dom	Cmd	Ball%	SwK	Vel	G	L	F	H%	S%	HR/F	xHR/F	GS	APC	DOM%	DIS%	Sv%	LI	RAR	BPX	R$
15 DET *	5	3	61	33	3.27	3.43	1.38		95	69	6.4	4.1	4.9	1.2		6.4%	93.9	75	16	9	28%	76%	14%	18%	0	20			60	0.99	5.2	60	$1
16 DET	1	0	19	10	7.11	5.20	1.84		151	120	4.7	3.3	4.7	1.4		6.4%	94.4	60	14	26	36%	63%	16%	13%	0	18			0	0.66	-6.8	40	-$7
17 DET *	7	0	132	77	6.98	7.02	1.88	1.30	144	123	14.4	4.1	5.3	1.3	38%	9.6%	94.0	50	15	34	36%	64%	26%	23%	2	22	0%	100%	0	0.92	-42.5	7	-$23
18 DET *	5	0	91	90	3.79	2.67	1.12	1.28	102	81	7.0	3.1	9.0	2.9	39%	12.7%	94.1	48	11	41	28%	66%	9%	10%	1	22	0%	100%	0	0.78	4.0	126	$5
19 DET *	8	0	111	87	6.25	6.57	1.73	1.41	118	116	15.3	3.1	7.1	2.3	36%	9.6%	93.2	51	19	29	38%	65%	17%	17%	4	43	0%	50%	0	0.80	-23.9	45	-$12
1st Half	4	0	44	31	6.04	6.14	1.79		127	170	11.3	4.0	6.4	1.6		8.8%	93.1	45	30	25	37%	66%	20%	18%	0	14			0	0.86	-8.3	43	-$12
2nd Half	4	0	67	56	6.39	6.86	1.69	1.23	117	107	20.1	2.5	7.5	3.0	34%	9.8%	93.2	52	18	30	38%	65%	17%	17%	4	67	0%	50%	0	0.76	-15.5	51	-$12
20 Proj	**7**	**0**	**102**	**79**	**5.03**	**4.31**	**1.46**	**1.27**	**117**	**101**	**10.6**	**3.3**	**7.0**	**2.1**	**37%**	**10.5%**	**93.7**	**48**	**17**	**34**	**32%**	**67%**	**11%**		**2**						**-11.1**	**72**	**-$4**

Verlander,Justin

Age: 37	Th: R	Role SP	Health	B	LIMA Plan B
Ht: 6' 5"	Wt: 225	Type Pwr xFB	PT/Exp	A	Rand Var -2
			Consist	B	MM 5505

Nearly a carbon copy of 2018, at an age when pitchers are typically retiring. Held Dom and Ctl gains, and recovered GB rate, which was timely because HR/F luck of years past finally ran out. BPX, Ball%, SwK%, and durability all confirm he's one of the few true aces. All good careers end eventually, but there are zero red flags in this profile.

Yr Tm	W	Sv	IP	K	ERA	xERA	WHIP	xWHIP	vL+	vR+	BF/G	Ctl	Dom	Cmd	Ball%	SwK	Vel	G	L	F	H%	S%	HR/F	xHR/F	GS	APC	DOM%	DIS%	Sv%	LI	RAR	BPX	R$
15 DET	5	0	133	113	3.38	4.03	1.09	1.22	85	92	26.8	2.2	7.6	3.5	35%	10.2%	92.8	35	20	46	28%	72%	7%	5%	20	108	40%	30%			9.7	110	$9
16 DET	16	0	228	254	3.04	3.63	1.00	1.11	82	90	26.6	2.3	10.0	4.5	33%	12.8%	93.5	34	19	48	27%	76%	11%	11%	34	108	62%	9%			32.2	157	$33
17 2 AL	15	0	206	219	3.36	4.15	1.17	1.24	94	83	25.7	3.1	9.6	3.0	34%	11.0%	95.2	33	24	43	28%	77%	11%	12%	33	107	55%	15%			25.3	118	$24
18 HOU	16	0	214	290	2.52	3.05	0.90	0.93	80	86	24.5	1.6	12.2	7.8	31%	15.3%	95.1	29	20	51	29%	81%	11%	9%	34	101	62%	3%			42.9	212	$42
19 HOU	21	0	223	300	2.58	3.09	0.80	0.98	74	80	24.9	1.7	12.1	7.1	32%	16.8%	94.7	36	19	45	23%	80%	16%	14%	34	101	59%	6%			52.9	203	$50
1st Half	10	0	120	147	2.86	3.54	0.79	1.01	71	85	25.4	2.0	11.1	5.7	32%	16.5%	94.7	35	19	46	19%	79%	18%	16%	18	103	67%	11%			24.3	174	$48
2nd Half	11	0	103	153	2.26	2.78	0.81	0.84	77	73	24.3	1.4	13.3	9.6	32%	17.2%	94.7	37	19	44	28%	82%	14%	12%	16	100	50%	0%			28.6	237	$52
20 Proj	**17**	**0**	**203**	**261**	**2.97**	**2.90**	**0.95**	**0.99**	**82**	**85**	**24.3**	**2.0**	**11.6**	**5.7**	**32%**	**15.0%**	**94.7**	**34**	**20**	**46**	**27%**	**77%**	**14%**		**32**						**29.5**	**190**	**$36**

Vizcaino,Arodys

Age: 29	Th: R	Role RP	Health	F	LIMA Plan B
Ht: 6' 0"	Wt: 245	Type Pwr	PT/Exp	D	Rand Var -5
			Consist	B	MM 2410

Underwent labrum surgery in April, missed whole year—typical recovery timeline could have him ready for spring training. Dom has lagged behind SwK, and BPX, xERA history are more representative of his skill. Unfortunately, labrum surgery has poor odds of return to prior performance levels, making him a risky bet, especially in high-leverage role.

Yr Tm	W	Sv	IP	K	ERA	xERA	WHIP	xWHIP	vL+	vR+	BF/G	Ctl	Dom	Cmd	Ball%	SwK	Vel	G	L	F	H%	S%	HR/F	xHR/F	GS	APC	DOM%	DIS%	Sv%	LI	RAR	BPX	R$
15 ATL	3	9	34	37	1.60	3.66	1.19	1.26	80	90	3.9	3.5	9.9	2.8	36%	12.1%	97.7	35	28	37	31%	87%	3%	12%	0	15			90	1.12	9.8	116	$6
16 ATL	1	10	39	50	4.42	4.09	1.63	1.45	82	102	4.2	6.1	11.6	1.9	39%	14.3%	97.4	54	16	30	37%	73%	10%	8%	0	17			71	1.15	-1.1	93	$0
17 ATL	5	14	57	64	2.83	4.02	1.10	1.23	99	71	3.8	3.3	10.0	3.0	34%	15.3%	97.8	39	16	45	26%	80%	10%	12%	0	14			82	1.28	10.8	131	$11
18 ATL	2	16	38	40	2.11	4.11	1.17	1.29	98	82	4.1	3.5	9.4	2.7	36%	14.5%	97.6	32	27	42	28%	88%	10%	13%	0	16			89	1.06	9.6	97	$8
19 ATL	1	1	4	6	2.25	5.10	1.50		162	100	4.3	6.8	13.5	2.0	35%	13.2%	96.0	13	13	75	27%	100%	17%	18%	0	17			50	0.80	1.1	56	-$4
1st Half	1	1	4	6	2.25	5.21	1.50		161	101	4.3	6.8	13.5	2.0		13.2%	96.0	13	13	75	27%	100%	17%	18%	0	17			50	0.80	1.1	56	-$4
2nd Half																																	
20 Proj	**2**	**2**	**36**	**42**	**3.98**	**3.71**	**1.32**	**1.33**	**94**	**94**	**3.9**	**4.4**	**10.4**	**2.4**	**37%**	**13.5%**	**97.6**	**41**	**21**	**38**	**29%**	**75%**	**15%**		**0**						**0.8**	**102**	**-$1**

Voth,Austin

Age: 28	Th: R	Role SP	Health	C	LIMA Plan C
Ht: 6' 2"	Wt: 201	Type Con xFB	PT/Exp	D	Rand Var +2
			Consist	C	MM 1101

2-1, 3.30 in 44 IP at WAS. Fringy prospect missed six weeks with arm fatigue, but showed improved Dom and Ctl. Relies primarily on four-seamer, but three secondary pitches get 20% SwK and fewer FB, giving him potential weapons vL and vR. Worth keeping tabs on in very deep leagues, in case a pitch-mix change unlocks something more.

Yr Tm	W	Sv	IP	K	ERA	xERA	WHIP	xWHIP	vL+	vR+	BF/G	Ctl	Dom	Cmd	Ball%	SwK	Vel	G	L	F	H%	S%	HR/F	xHR/F	GS	APC	DOM%	DIS%	Sv%	LI	RAR	BPX	R$
15 aa	6	0	157	123	3.66	3.59	1.27				23.0	2.4	7.0	2.9							31%	72%									5.8	105	$5
16 aaa	7	0	157	110	4.65	4.84	1.54				25.4	3.7	6.3	1.7							33%	71%									-8.9	56	-$6
17 a/a	4	0	121	70	7.57	7.66	1.92				24.9	3.8	5.2	1.4							37%	62%									-47.8	-6	-$26
18 WAS *	7	0	140	103	6.04	5.50	1.53		100	114	21.7	3.2	6.6	2.1		7.9%	91.4	43	14	43	33%	62%	19%	8%	2	54	0%	50%	0	0.44	-32.5	48	-$14
19 WAS *	6	0	118	105	5.11	5.04	1.43	1.25	101	79	20.9	2.5	8.0	3.3	36%	13.0%	92.8	35	24	42	35%	66%	11%	11%	8	76	25%	13%	0	0.74	-8.8	85	-$3
1st Half	3	0	72	63	5.27	5.76	1.53		90	109	22.5	2.2	7.8	3.5		13.0%	93.5	43	13	43	37%	68%	15%	14%	2	81	0%	50%			-6.9	82	-$7
2nd Half	3	0	45	43	3.86	3.01	1.11	1.23	104	67	17.9	2.6	8.4	3.2	36%	13.0%	92.6	31	28	41	28%	67%	9%	10%	6	75	33%	0%	0	0.73	3.6	111	$3
20 Proj	**5**	**0**	**102**	**84**	**4.97**	**4.48**	**1.34**	**1.35**	**131**	**92**	**20.7**	**2.8**	**7.4**	**2.6**	**39%**	**13.0%**	**92.6**	**34**	**22**	**44**	**30%**	**68%**	**12%**		**20**						**-10.2**	**80**	**-$2**

Wacha,Michael

Age: 29	Th: R	Role SP	Health	F	LIMA Plan B
Ht: 6' 6"	Wt: 215	Type	PT/Exp	B	Rand Var +3
			Consist	B	MM 1103

Though he lost only two weeks to injury (including shoulder in late Sept), IP totals sagged due to short outings and relief work. Despite kid gloves, Ctl/Dom couldn't rebound, and this time surface numbers matched. Owns solid GB%, but he's a threat to ratios and injury/workload history negates any value as an accumulator. BPX sums it up: avoid.

Yr Tm	W	Sv	IP	K	ERA	xERA	WHIP	xWHIP	vL+	vR+	BF/G	Ctl	Dom	Cmd	Ball%	SwK	Vel	G	L	F	H%	S%	HR/F	xHR/F	GS	APC	DOM%	DIS%	Sv%	LI	RAR	BPX	R$
15 STL	17	0	181	153	3.38	3.91	1.21	1.30	85	101	25.4	2.9	7.6	2.6	34%	10.3%	94.2	46	22	32	29%	76%	11%	11%	30	98	23%	23%			13.1	99	$16
16 STL	7	0	138	114	5.09	4.33	1.48	1.32	99	116	22.4	2.9	7.4	2.5	36%	8.7%	93.2	47	24	30	34%	67%	12%	13%	24	86	25%	33%	0	0.72	-15.3	95	-$6
17 STL	12	0	166	158	4.13	4.01	1.36	1.27	96	101	23.4	3.0	8.6	2.9	35%	10.0%	95.1	48	21	31	33%	72%	12%	12%	30	90	27%	30%			4.7	120	$8
18 STL	8	0	84	71	3.20	4.31	1.23	1.41	80	99	23.7	3.8	7.6	2.0	39%	10.2%	93.5	43	29	27	26%	78%	14%	18%	15	95	40%	33%			9.9	62	$5
19 STL	6	0	127	104	4.76	5.06	1.56	1.48	107	120	19.4	3.9	7.4	1.9	38%	10.1%	93.1	48	22	30	32%	76%	22%	23%	24	76	8%	58%	0	0.80	-4.0	58	-$5
1st Half	5	0	73	62	5.30	5.21	1.60	1.49	92	135	21.7	4.6	7.6	1.7	39%	9.2%	92.6	46	22	31	31%	73%	23%	23%	13	83	0%	46%	0	0.79	-7.2	42	-$5
2nd Half	1	0	54	42	4.02	4.71	1.51	1.35	124	100	16.9	3.0	7.0	2.3	35%	11.2%	93.6	50	22	28	33%	80%	21%	23%	11	68	18%	73%	0	0.80	3.2	80	-$5
20 Proj	**8**	**0**	**131**	**110**	**4.52**	**4.11**	**1.43**	**1.38**	**96**	**105**	**20.3**	**3.7**	**7.6**	**2.0**	**37%**	**10.2%**	**93.6**	**47**	**24**	**29**	**31%**	**71%**	**14%**		**27**						**-6.0**	**70**	**-$1**

Waguespack,Jacob

Age: 26	Th: R	Role SP	Health	C	LIMA Plan A
Ht: 6' 6"	Wt: 235	Type GB	PT/Exp	D	Rand Var 0
			Consist	A	MM 0103

5-5, 4.38 in 78 IP at TOR. Non-prospect had some initial success not backed by skills, and regressed in September. Safe to ignore the reverse platoon split, it was H% driven. Has induced 48% ground balls over all levels, a skill that hasn't shown up in MLB yet; he'll need it to provide any kind of floor. But it won't be enough to make him rosterable.

Yr Tm	W	Sv	IP	K	ERA	xERA	WHIP	xWHIP	vL+	vR+	BF/G	Ctl	Dom	Cmd	Ball%	SwK	Vel	G	L	F	H%	S%	HR/F	xHR/F	GS	APC	DOM%	DIS%	Sv%	LI	RAR	BPX	R$
15																																	
16																																	
17 aa	3	0	37	30	4.52	4.99	1.63				23.5	4.0	7.3	1.8							36%	72%									-0.7	73	-$5
18 a/a	6	1	124	90	6.38	5.81	1.73				20.2	3.6	6.5	1.8							37%	61%									-34.3	56	-$19
19 TOR *	7	0	132	104	5.52	5.67	1.55	1.43	86	114	20.6	3.9	7.1	1.8	37%	9.7%	91.6	40	22	38	32%	68%	13%	15%	13	83	15%	54%	0	0.76	-16.6	34	-$8
1st Half	2	0	58	48	6.98	6.98	1.79		59	101	20.7	4.4	7.5	1.7		17.3%	92.9	38	25	38	36%	64%	0%	4%	0	75			0	0.70	-17.7	20	-$19
2nd Half	5	0	74	56	4.38	5.26	1.35	1.41	88	113	21.2	3.4	6.8	2.0	37%	9.2%	91.6	40	22	38	28%	73%	14%	15%	13	84	15%	54%	0	0.77	1.2	54	$1
20 Proj	**9**	**0**	**160**	**120**	**5.51**	**4.75**	**1.63**	**1.55**	**93**	**122**	**24.5**	**3.9**	**6.8**	**1.7**	**41%**	**9.2%**	**91.6**	**46**	**22**	**32**	**34%**	**69%**	**13%**		**29**						**-26.8**	**46**	**-$12**

Wainwright,Adam

Age: 38	Th: R	Role SP	Health	F	LIMA Plan B
Ht: 6' 7"	Wt: 235	Type	PT/Exp	B	Rand Var +1
			Consist	B	MM 2203

Rebounded with competent full season after injury-plagued years. Value results from accumulating, however; not only are Dom and Ctl subpar, but Ball% and SwK% are consistent with even weaker skills. Solid GB rate sets a performance floor, but struggles vL are worrisome. With injury history, he's high-risk to repeat, and without upside.

Yr Tm	W	Sv	IP	K	ERA	xERA	WHIP	xWHIP	vL+	vR+	BF/G	Ctl	Dom	Cmd	Ball%	SwK	Vel	G	L	F	H%	S%	HR/F	xHR/F	GS	APC	DOM%	DIS%	Sv%	LI	RAR	BPX	R$
15 STL	2	0	28	20	1.61	3.35	1.04		91	76	15.9	1.3	6.4	5.0		8.4%	89.6	51	26	23	30%	83%	0%	7%	4	55	25%	0%	0	0.51	8.1	131	$1
16 STL	13	0	199	161	4.62	4.23	1.40	1.30	114	101	25.7	2.7	7.3	2.7	37%	8.6%	90.3	44	25	31	33%	69%	12%	13%	33	97	27%	33%			-10.6	96	$1
17 STL	12	0	123	96	5.11	4.64	1.50	1.38	109	104	22.8	3.3	7.0	2.1	37%	7.8%	89.7	47	25	28	33%	67%	13%	11%	23	90	30%	39%	0	0.74	-11.4	75	-$2
18 STL *	4	0	59	54	3.03	3.94	1.34	1.36	102	105	19.0	3.4	8.2	2.4	39%	9.3%	89.3	49	18	33	32%	80%	13%	14%	8	92	25%	38%			8.2	94	$1
19 STL	14	0	172	153	4.19	4.53	1.43	1.38	116	94	24.0	3.4	8.0	2.4	38%	8.0%	89.9	49	22	29	32%	74%	15%	15%	31	93	16%	39%			6.6	88	$6
1st Half	5	0	83	76	4.35	4.31	1.38	1.35	130	88	23.6	3.6	8.3	2.3	39%	7.8%	89.9	51	21	28	31%	72%	17%	17%	15	90	20%	47%			1.5	88	$3
2nd Half	9	0	89	77	4.04	4.64	1.47	1.32	106	99	24.4	3.1	7.8	2.5	36%	8.1%	90.0	47	23	30	34%	76%	13%	14%	16	96	13%	31%			5.1	88	$9
20 Proj	**11**	**0**	**138**	**120**	**4.40**	**4.02**	**1.43**	**1.34**	**109**	**99**	**22.3**	**3.3**	**7.8**	**2.4**	**38%**	**8.4%**	**89.8**	**47**	**21**	**32**	**33%**	**72%**	**12%**		**26**						**-4.2**	**89**	**$2**

ARIK FLORIMONTE

Walden,Marcus

Age: 31 Th: R Role RP	Health A	LIMA Plan F
Ht: 6' 0" Wt: 195 Type Pwr GB	PT/Exp D	Rand Var 0
	Consist F	MM 2211

After brief 15 IP debut in 2018, late bloomer's electric start soon landed him in BOS saves mix. Ctl/Ball% fell off quickly though, and Dom reverted closer to MiLB track record. GB% emerged as most repeatable skill. Can't bank on another Win-driven R$, leaving only a narrow path to returning value. And not one you want to travel with him.

Yr	Tm	W	Sv	IP	K	ERA	xERA	WHIP	xWHIP	vL+	vR+	BF/G	Ctl	Dom	Cmd	Ball%	SwK	Vel	G	L	F	H%	S%	HR/F	xHR/F	GS	APC	DOM%	DIS%	Sv%	LI	RAR	BPX	R$
15																																		
16	a/a	1	6	56	29	3.64	3.75	1.40				5.7	3.0	4.6	1.6							31%	72%									3.8	64	$0
17	aaa	10	0	106	62	6.71	6.15	1.86				17.0	4.0	5.3	1.3							38%	62%									-30.6	39	-$16
18	BOS *	0	3	49	31	6.59	7.36	2.08		83	99	9.2	4.4	5.7	1.3		12.2%	94.0	59	22	20	41%	67%	0%	10%	0	27			75	0.22	-14.7	33	-$15
19	BOS	9	2	78	76	3.81	4.10	1.19	1.37	80	89	4.7	3.7	8.8	2.4	37%	13.6%	94.2	54	19	27	28%	69%	10%	10%	0	18			33	1.08	6.7	98	$7
1st Half		6	1	44	50	3.48	3.33	1.11	1.12	82	94	5.3	2.5	10.2	4.2	34%	14.9%	94.2	52	22	26	30%	73%	17%	14%	0	21			25	1.13	5.6	161	$10
2nd Half		3	1	34	26	4.24	5.09	1.29	1.63	77	83	4.1	5.3	6.9	1.3	40%	12.1%	94.1	56	15	29	25%	65%	4%	6%	0	16			50	1.03	1.1	16	$2
20	Proj	5	2	73	65	4.25	3.89	1.39	1.42	97	104	5.8	4.1	8.0	2.0	38%	13.2%	94.1	54	18	28	30%	71%	12%		0						-0.9	76	$0

Walker,Taijuan

Age: 27 Th: R Role SP	Health F	LIMA Plan A
Ht: 6' 4" Wt: 235 Type	PT/Exp D	Rand Var +5
	Consist A	MM 1201

Former top prospect lost last two years to Tommy John surgery and subsequent shoulder procedure. Prime bounceback candidate? Not so fast. Prior to injury, Cmd was in midst of troubling decline, and SwK erosion didn't point to impending Dom surge. Rising GB% and pedigree provide hope, while xERA/xWHIP remind us health isn't the only concern.

Yr	Tm	W	Sv	IP	K	ERA	xERA	WHIP	xWHIP	vL+	vR+	BF/G	Ctl	Dom	Cmd	Ball%	SwK	Vel	G	L	F	H%	S%	HR/F	xHR/F	GS	APC	DOM%	DIS%	Sv%	LI	RAR	BPX	R$
15	SEA	11	0	170	157	4.56	3.78	1.20	1.19	98	101	24.3	2.1	8.3	3.9	34%	10.6%	94.3	39	22	39	30%	66%	13%	14%	29	91	34%	34%			-12.6	131	$5
16	SEA *	9	0	149	124	4.21	4.46	1.26	1.24	98	110	21.7	2.7	7.5	2.8	35%	10.3%	93.9	44	18	38	28%	74%	18%	16%	25	92	28%	40%			-0.5	67	$5
17	ARI	9	0	157	146	3.49	4.30	1.33	1.33	96	100	24.4	3.5	8.4	2.4	37%	9.3%	93.8	49	18	33	31%	77%	11%	13%	28	98	18%	32%			16.9	100	$10
18	ARI	0	0	13	9	3.46	4.79	1.54		132	73	18.7	3.5	6.2	1.8		6.7%	93.7	43	28	30	34%	79%	8%	20%	3	75	0%	67%			1.1	46	-$5
19	ARI	0	0	1	1	0.00	4.51	1.00		0	201	4.0	0.0	9.0	0.0	27%	13.3%	93.3	33	0	67	35%	0%	0%	10%	1	15	0%	100%			0.6	188	-$5
1st Half																																		
2nd Half		0	0	1	1	0.00	4.79	1.00		0	198	4.0	0.0	9.0	0.0		13.3%	93.3	33	0	67	35%	0%	0%	10%	1	15	0%	100%			0.6	189	-$5
20	Proj	7	0	116	105	4.26	4.04	1.34	1.25	99	104	23.5	3.4	8.1	2.4	36%	10.0%	94.0	44	20	37	30%	73%	14%		21						-1.5	88	$2

Weaver,Luke

Age: 26 Th: R Role SP	Health F	LIMA Plan C
Ht: 6' 2" Wt: 170 Type	PT/Exp C	Rand Var -1
	Consist C	MM 3303

Season derailed by May elbow injury, but not before rekindled excitement about long-term outlook. Off-season work on curveball and ramped-up cutter usage boosted once-lagging SwK, putting K contribution back in play. Ctl outpaced mediocre Ball% though, and ERA/xERA gap says minor brake tap in order. Still, with health, a lot to like here.

Yr	Tm	W	Sv	IP	K	ERA	xERA	WHIP	xWHIP	vL+	vR+	BF/G	Ctl	Dom	Cmd	Ball%	SwK	Vel	G	L	F	H%	S%	HR/F	xHR/F	GS	APC	DOM%	DIS%	Sv%	LI	RAR	BPX	R$
15																																		
16	STL *	8	0	119	120	2.80	3.60	1.20	1.16	139	104	21.8	1.8	9.0	5.0	37%	10.3%	91.9	31	37	33	33%	80%	21%	17%	8	76	13%	38%	0	0.71	20.4	103	$12
17	STL *	17	0	138	132	3.47	3.47	1.23	1.11	70	107	20.0	2.4	8.6	3.6	34%	9.9%	93.2	49	24	27	32%	73%	16%	15%	10	80	40%	30%	0	0.64	15.2	135	$15
18	STL	7	0	136	121	4.95	4.64	1.50	1.36	115	101	20.3	3.6	8.0	2.2	36%	10.1%	93.7	42	22	36	33%	70%	13%	14%	25	80	16%	40%	0	0.69	-13.5	78	-$7
19	ARI	4	0	64	69	2.94	3.78	1.07	1.14	80	91	21.7	2.0	9.7	4.9	36%	11.8%	93.9	41	22	38	30%	76%	9%	13%	12	88	42%	25%			12.4	152	$5
1st Half		4	0	62	68	3.03	3.83	1.11	1.10	83	94	23.1	2.0	9.8	4.9	36%	12.0%	93.9	41	22	38	31%	76%	10%	14%	11	94	45%	27%			11.3	154	$6
2nd Half		0	0	2	1	0.00	3.54	0.00		0	0	6.0	0.0	4.5	0.0		0.0%	95.0	40	20	40	0%	0%	0%	1%	1	19	0%	0%			1.1	108	-$12
20	Proj	14	0	174	172	3.63	3.52	1.24	1.17	89	94	20.8	2.4	8.9	3.7	36%	10.6%	93.3	43	23	35	32%	73%	10%		30						11.1	133	$15

Webb,Jacob

Age: 26 Th: R Role RP	Health D	LIMA Plan B
Ht: 6' 1" Wt: 200 Type xFB	PT/Exp F	Rand Var -5
	Consist B	MM 1200

Not a bad debut for unheralded rookie, who enjoyed gifts from H%/S% gods to post pristine surface stats in small sample. Impressive SwK points to better Dom ahead, but bigger question marks revolve around how/when he returns from August elbow surgery. xERA/xWHIP, lack of track record say you don't need to wait around to find out.

Yr	Tm	W	Sv	IP	K	ERA	xERA	WHIP	xWHIP	vL+	vR+	BF/G	Ctl	Dom	Cmd	Ball%	SwK	Vel	G	L	F	H%	S%	HR/F	xHR/F	GS	APC	DOM%	DIS%	Sv%	LI	RAR	BPX	R$
15																																		
16																																		
17	aa	3	0	24	23	3.84	4.05	1.60				6.6	6.2	8.5	1.4							31%	76%									1.5	87	-$3
18	a/a	3	18	57	55	3.95	3.54	1.18				4.5	3.7	8.7	2.4							25%	72%									1.4	85	$7
19	ATL	4	2	32	28	1.39	4.87	1.11	1.41	65	100	3.6	3.3	7.8	2.3	35%	13.2%	95.1	38	17	45	24%	97%	10%	9%	0	15			50	0.86	12.4	72	$3
1st Half		4	2	29	25	1.23	4.99	1.06	1.36	51	106	3.6	3.4	7.7	2.3	35%	12.0%	95.0	35	16	48	22%	100%	11%	10%	0	15			50	0.92	11.9	66	$5
2nd Half		0	0	3	3	3.00	4.00	1.67		194	66	3.8	3.0	9.0	3.0		24.1%	95.7	60	20	20	42%	80%	0%	0%	0	14			0	0.40	0.6	130	-$9
20	Proj	3	0	29	26	4.17	4.43	1.28	1.50	59	128	4.1	3.2	8.0	2.5	39%	12.0%	95.0	35	16	48	27%	77%	14%		0						-0.1	82	-$2

Webb,Logan

Age: 23 Th: R Role SP	Health A	LIMA Plan A
Ht: 6' 2" Wt: 220 Type GB	PT/Exp F	Rand Var +3
	Consist A	MM 1103

2-3, 5.22 ERA in 40 IP at SF. Team's top pitching prospect sandwiched sparkling AA run around 80-game PED suspension, then had mixed results in late-season debut. MLB xERA (4.21), nice GB% offset by so-so Ball% and merely average strikeout profile. With bullpen and more MiLB time both in range of outcomes, best to wait before buying in.

Yr	Tm	W	Sv	IP	K	ERA	xERA	WHIP	xWHIP	vL+	vR+	BF/G	Ctl	Dom	Cmd	Ball%	SwK	Vel	G	L	F	H%	S%	HR/F	xHR/F	GS	APC	DOM%	DIS%	Sv%	LI	RAR	BPX	R$
15																																		
16																																		
17																																		
18	aa	1	0	32	22	4.38	4.61	1.40				22.7	3.1	6.3	2.0							31%	71%									-0.9	58	-$5
19	SF *	3	0	89	82	3.82	4.65	1.45	1.34	92	123	22.3	2.7	8.3	3.0	38%	9.8%	92.9	49	28	23	36%	75%	18%	19%	8	85	13%	38%			7.5	97	-$1
1st Half		1	0	27	26	2.98	4.23	1.43		0	0	23.0	2.6	8.6	3.2							37%	79%	0%		0	0					5.1	115	-$4
2nd Half		2	0	62	56	4.32	5.01	1.50	1.30	92	121	22.2	2.8	8.2	2.9	38%	9.8%	92.9	49	28	23	36%	73%	18%	19%	8	85	13%	38%			1.4	87	$0
20	Proj	4	0	131	108	4.41	4.10	1.48	1.43	84	112	22.8	3.2	7.5	2.3	42%	9.8%	92.9	47	25	28	34%	71%	10%		25						-4.2	84	-$3

Webb,Tyler

Age: 29 Th: L Role RP	Health A	LIMA Plan D
Ht: 6' 5" Wt: 230 Type	PT/Exp D	Rand Var -4
	Consist D	MM 1200

Big-bodied lefty saw LI rise as season wore on, using 4-pitch mix to make up for underwhelming velocity. Good news ends there though, as extremely low H% masked otherwise unimpressive skills. Don't try to envision this turning into something greater. After all, a flute with no holes is not a flute—and a donut with no hole... is a Danish.

Yr	Tm	W	Sv	IP	K	ERA	xERA	WHIP	xWHIP	vL+	vR+	BF/G	Ctl	Dom	Cmd	Ball%	SwK	Vel	G	L	F	H%	S%	HR/F	xHR/F	GS	APC	DOM%	DIS%	Sv%	LI	RAR	BPX	R$
15	aaa	2	2	38	34	3.93	6.12	1.65				6.8	2.9	8.0	2.8							38%	81%									0.1	68	-$4
16	aaa	4	1	73	66	5.27	5.26	1.57				8.9	3.3	8.2	2.5							37%	67%									-9.7	81	-$6
17	2 TM *	4	1	58	59	4.99	5.78	1.50		135	114	5.3	2.4	9.1	3.9		8.7%	91.2	43	35	22	37%	72%	40%	14%	0	17			14	1.03	-4.5	98	-$3
18	2 NL *	1	0	64	51	3.16	3.49	1.25		101	128	5.0	3.1	7.3	2.4		11.0%	89.8	33	22	44	29%	77%	11%	14%	0	16			0	0.73	7.8	90	$0
19	STL	2	1	55	48	3.76	4.71	1.02	1.45	68	91	3.4	3.8	7.9	2.1	38%	10.6%	89.9	41	20	39	20%	67%	12%	11%	0	14			100	0.74	5.0	64	$2
1st Half		0	1	28	24	3.90	5.13	1.19	1.53	67	107	3.5	4.9	7.8	1.6	39%	11.2%	89.6	41	21	38	22%	70%	11%	9%	0	14			100	0.54	2.1	30	-$1
2nd Half		2	0	27	24	3.62	4.30	0.84	1.26	69	73	3.3	2.6	7.9	3.0	36%	9.9%	90.3	41	19	40	17%	63%	14%	12%	0	14			0	0.95	3.0	98	$6
20	Proj	2	0	44	38	4.27	4.10	1.31	1.37	92	115	4.2	3.2	7.9	2.5	37%	10.4%	90.0	41	20	39	30%	70%	11%		0						-0.7	87	-$3

Wheeler,Zack

Age: 30 Th: R Role SP	Health D	LIMA Plan B
Ht: 6' 4" Wt: 195 Type	PT/Exp A	Rand Var 0
	Consist B	MM 3305

Dramatic mid-season turnaround? xERA/BPX say 1st half skills actually a tad better, with HR/S% pendulum swinging back in favorable direction for final months. Worked deep into games (+6 IP in 23 of 31 GS) and another 180+ IP season adds feather to durability cap, while SwK/Dom confirm respectable K profile. A good bet for more of the same.

Yr	Tm	W	Sv	IP	K	ERA	xERA	WHIP	xWHIP	vL+	vR+	BF/G	Ctl	Dom	Cmd	Ball%	SwK	Vel	G	L	F	H%	S%	HR/F	xHR/F	GS	APC	DOM%	DIS%	Sv%	LI	RAR	BPX	R$
15																																		
16																																		
17	NYM	3	0	86	81	5.21	4.55	1.59	1.40	114	109	22.7	4.2	8.4	2.0	37%	9.7%	94.6	47	23	30	34%	71%	19%	17%	17	92	18%	47%			-9.1	77	-$7
18	NYM	12	0	182	179	3.31	3.73	1.12	1.22	93	77	25.7	2.7	8.8	3.3	34%	11.3%	95.9	44	20	35	29%	72%	8%	10%	29	99	45%	28%			18.9	124	$19
19	NYM	11	0	195	195	3.96	4.20	1.26	1.22	102	85	26.7	2.3	9.0	3.9	33%	11.0%	96.7	43	21	35	33%	71%	11%	12%	31	102	45%	19%			13.1	131	$13
1st Half		6	0	108	115	4.51	4.11	1.26	1.18	95	92	26.9	2.6	9.6	3.7	33%	11.0%	96.9	44	21	35	32%	68%	14%	15%	17	104	41%	12%			-0.1	137	$12
2nd Half		5	0	88	80	3.29	4.36	1.25	1.18	111	77	26.4	2.0	8.2	4.2	33%	11.1%	96.5	42	22	36	33%	76%	7%	9%	14	100	50%	29%			13.2	125	$14
20	Proj	13	0	181	176	3.83	3.61	1.26	1.23	102	85	24.8	2.7	8.7	3.3	34%	10.9%	96.1	44	21	35	32%	72%	11%		30						7.2	123	$13

BRIAN SLACK

Whitley,Forrest

Age: 22	Th: R	Role SP	Health A	LIMA Plan F	
Ht: 6' 7"	Wt: 195	Type Pwr	PT/Exp F	Rand Var +5	
			Consist F	MM 3401	

Considered game's top pitching prospect entering year, struggled mightily at AAA before shoulder fatigue shelved him for two months—marking second straight injury-stunted season. Reworked mechanics aimed to relieve stress on shoulder give hope he can deliver on sky-high potential by mid-season, if not sooner. Spring will be telling.

Yr Tm	W	Sv	IP	K	ERA	xERA	WHIP	xWHIP	vL+	vR+	BF/G	Ctl	Dom	Cmd	Ball%	SwK	Vel	G	L	F	H%	S%	HR/F	xHR/F	GS	APC	DOM%	DIS%	Sv%	LI	RAR	BPX	R$
15																																	
16																																	
17																																	
18 aa	0	0	27	30	4.48	2.21	1.03				13.1	3.6	9.9	2.8							24%	56%									-1.1	130	-$3
19 a/a	2	0	49	57	10.53	7.62	1.93				16.7	6.2	10.4	1.7							37%	45%									-36.7	25	-$18
1st Half	0	0	25	26	12.87	9.69	2.08		0	0	15.4	5.1	9.2	1.8							39%	38%			0	0					-25.9	-22	-$25
2nd Half	2	0	24	32	6.39	4.44	1.65		0	0	18.0	7.1	11.8	1.7							33%	60%			0	0					-5.6	96	-$10
20 Proj	**7**	**0**	**94**	**109**	**4.08**	**3.50**	**1.25**				**21.3**	**3.4**	**10.4**	**3.1**	**35%**	**13.0%**	**95.0**	**41**	**19**	**40**	**30%**	**74%**	**17%**		**16**						**0.8**	**132**	**$4**

Wick,Rowan

Age: 27	Th: R	Role RP	Health A	LIMA Plan B	
Ht: 6' 3"	Wt: 235	Type Pwr xGB	PT/Exp D	Rand Var -4	
			Consist B	MM 2310	

2-0, 2.43 ERA with 2 Sv in 33 IP at CHC. Converted catcher emerged as high-leverage weapon, converting all 8 saves chances across AAA/MLB. Good foundation with effective fastball (65% usage, 14% SwK), plus curveball to help generate loads of GB. Ctl still biggest concern, but Ball% not beyond hope. Small investment could pay dividends.

Yr Tm	W	Sv	IP	K	ERA	xERA	WHIP	xWHIP	vL+	vR+	BF/G	Ctl	Dom	Cmd	Ball%	SwK	Vel	G	L	F	H%	S%	HR/F	xHR/F	GS	APC	DOM%	DIS%	Sv%	LI	RAR	BPX	R$
15																																	
16 aa	0	0	20	16	5.23	3.90	1.59				4.1	6.6	7.3	1.1							28%	66%									-2.5	72	-$5
17 a/a	2	6	38	26	4.58	4.49	1.52				5.5	4.5	6.2	1.4							30%	71%									-1.0	53	-$2
18 SD *	4	14	65	59	3.38	3.61	1.38		99	158	4.6	4.5	8.2	1.8		11.3%	94.6	39	14	46	30%	76%	8%	13%	0	13			88	0.76	6.1	90	$6
19 CHC *	3	8	68	69	2.44	2.72	1.18	1.41	84	59	4.7	3.5	9.1	2.6	36%	12.1%	95.9	54	15	31	29%	81%	0%	12%	0	19			100	0.98	17.4	116	$9
1st Half	0	4	34	32	2.78	4.13	1.34		16	142	5.9	3.2	8.6	2.6		15.6%	95.1	58	8	33	32%	84%	0%	26%	0	24			100	0.19	7.3	89	$2
2nd Half	3	4	37	37	1.97	1.05	0.95	1.36	95	41	4.1	3.5	9.1	2.6	35%	11.4%	96.0	53	16	30	24%	77%	0%	10%	0	18			100	1.09	11.4	142	$15
20 Proj	**3**	**2**	**58**	**56**	**3.32**	**3.71**	**1.29**	**1.50**	**121**	**56**	**4.8**	**3.7**	**8.7**	**2.3**	**39%**	**11.4%**	**96.0**	**53**	**16**	**30**	**30%**	**77%**	**10%**		**0**						**5.9**	**100**	**$2**

Williams,Trevor

Age: 28	Th: R	Role SP	Health C	LIMA Plan A	
Ht: 6' 3"	Wt: 230	Type Con	PT/Exp A	Rand Var +1	
			Consist A	MM 1103	

Ratios pullback not completely unexpected given 2018 xERA/xWHIP, and this year's uncooperative H%/S% were compounded by rising FB%, HR/F. Notable 1st half gains in Ctl/Ball% and Dom/SwK make one wonder if perhaps May/June side strain lingered in 2nd half. Still, track record of mediocrity only growing longer. Set expectations low.

Yr Tm	W	Sv	IP	K	ERA	xERA	WHIP	xWHIP	vL+	vR+	BF/G	Ctl	Dom	Cmd	Ball%	SwK	Vel	G	L	F	H%	S%	HR/F	xHR/F	GS	APC	DOM%	DIS%	Sv%	LI	RAR	BPX	R$
15 a/a	7	0	131	84	4.79	5.13	1.60				23.2	3.1	5.8	1.9							35%	70%									-13.4	59	-$10
16 PIT *	10	0	123	70	4.10	5.03	1.54		184	121	19.9	2.8	5.1	1.8		9.8%	92.8	45	25	30	34%	74%	31%	25%	1	32	0%	100%	0	0.70	1.4	48	-$2
17 PIT	7	0	150	117	4.07	4.47	1.31	1.36	98	93	20.7	3.1	7.0	2.3	36%	8.9%	92.1	48	21	31	30%	70%	10%	10%	25	78	16%	24%	0	0.75	5.3	82	$5
18 PIT	14	0	171	126	3.11	4.51	1.18	1.36	87	95	22.6	2.9	6.6	2.3	36%	8.4%	90.5	41	22	37	27%	76%	8%	11%	31	88	16%	32%			21.9	69	$17
19 PIT	7	0	146	113	5.38	5.23	1.41	1.38	125	104	24.5	2.7	7.0	2.6	35%	10.8%	91.3	37	23	40	31%	66%	15%	14%	26	90	19%	31%			-15.6	73	-$5
1st Half	2	0	66	53	4.25	4.57	1.19	1.16	101	99	25.0	1.4	7.3	5.3	31%	11.1%	91.4	37	25	38	31%	67%	10%	12%	11	92	27%	9%			2.1	119	$0
2nd Half	5	0	80	60	6.30	5.86	1.60	1.46	143	108	24.1	3.8	6.8	1.8	38%	10.5%	91.2	37	22	42	31%	66%	18%	15%	15	88	13%	47%			-17.7	36	-$8
20 Proj	**9**	**0**	**174**	**130**	**4.57**	**4.38**	**1.37**	**1.35**	**111**	**102**	**22.4**	**2.9**	**6.7**	**2.3**	**36%**	**9.7%**	**91.1**	**40**	**22**	**38**	**30%**	**70%**	**12%**		**32**						**-9.1**	**70**	**$1**

Wilson,Bryse

Age: 22	Th: R	Role SP	Health A	LIMA Plan A	
Ht: 6' 1"	Wt: 225	Type Con FB	PT/Exp D	Rand Var +3	
			Consist A	MM 1200	

1-1, 7.20 ERA in 20 IP at ATL. Named to Opening Day rotation only to get demoted after first start. Mid-season recall not much better, as HR paired with lack of punchouts to wreak havoc on ERA. Better GB% and workable 3-pitch mix in minors, and still has youth on his side. Just doesn't look ready to provide profit for fantasy owners in 2020.

Yr Tm	W	Sv	IP	K	ERA	xERA	WHIP	xWHIP	vL+	vR+	BF/G	Ctl	Dom	Cmd	Ball%	SwK	Vel	G	L	F	H%	S%	HR/F	xHR/F	GS	APC	DOM%	DIS%	Sv%	LI	RAR	BPX	R$
15																																	
16																																	
17																																	
18 ATL *	7	0	106	107	5.35	4.73	1.44		118	124	19.7	2.9	9.1	3.2		15.6%	95.0	29	48	24	36%	63%	0%	16%	1	45	0%	0%	0	0.35	-15.7	107	-$6
19 ATL *	11	0	141	116	4.77	5.14	1.44	1.57	149	130	22.2	2.3	7.4	3.2	34%	9.0%	94.7	31	26	43	35%	69%	18%	17%	4	59	0%	50%	0	0.58	-4.6	79	$0
1st Half	4	0	88	77	5.14	5.39	1.45		155	119	22.0	2.2	7.9	3.6		11.9%	94.4	38	27	35	35%	67%	22%	22%	2	56	0%	50%	0	0.58	-6.9	86	-$2
2nd Half	7	0	56	39	3.99	4.41	1.37		144	138	23.3	2.4	6.3	2.6		6.4%	94.9	26	26	49	32%	73%	16%	14%	2	63	0%	50%	0	0.59	3.6	72	$4
20 Proj	**6**	**0**	**68**	**60**	**4.68**	**4.30**	**1.44**				**21.5**	**2.7**	**7.8**	**2.9**	**34%**	**9.3%**		**35**	**23**	**42**	**33%**	**73%**	**14%**		**11**						**-3.8**	**93**	**-$3**

Wilson,Justin

Age: 32	Th: L	Role RP	Health D	LIMA Plan A	
Ht: 6' 2"	Wt: 205	Type Pwr	PT/Exp C	Rand Var -4	
			Consist A	MM 3510	

Missed most of May/June with elbow issue, then returned with sparkling 2nd half ERA while racking up a few saves. GB% a throwback to 2016 ways, while Ctl metrics continue to cause unease. Even though high-LI history points to possible closer fill-in, handedness and eventual S% correction say it could be short-lived.

Yr Tm	W	Sv	IP	K	ERA	xERA	WHIP	xWHIP	vL+	vR+	BF/G	Ctl	Dom	Cmd	Ball%	SwK	Vel	G	L	F	H%	S%	HR/F	xHR/F	GS	APC	DOM%	DIS%	Sv%	LI	RAR	BPX	R$
15 NYY	5	0	61	66	3.10	3.17	1.13	1.20	86	83	3.3	3.0	9.7	3.3	34%	12.8%	95.1	44	27	29	30%	73%	7%	11%	0	14			0	1.26	6.5	140	$4
16 DET	4	1	59	65	4.14	3.37	1.33	1.16	105	91	3.8	2.6	10.0	3.8	35%	12.9%	95.1	55	15	30	35%	71%	12%	12%	0	15			17	1.25	0.3	169	$0
17 2 TM	4	13	58	80	3.41	4.02	1.29	1.35	93	81	3.8	5.4	12.4	2.3	39%	12.9%	96.0	37	18	44	30%	76%	9%	7%	0	17			81	1.21	6.8	110	$8
18 CHC	4	0	55	69	3.46	4.20	1.43	1.40	88	99	3.3	5.4	11.4	2.1	35%	12.2%	94.7	35	24	40	32%	78%	9%	11%	0	15			0	1.21	4.7	82	-$1
19 NYM	4	4	39	44	2.54	3.99	1.33	1.38	83	92	3.7	4.4	10.2	2.3	37%	12.1%	95.1	51	21	28	31%	85%	15%	9%	0	15			80	1.23	9.5	102	$3
1st Half	1	1	9	9	4.82	4.40	1.39		65	132	4.2	3.9	8.7	2.3		10.2%	95.0	52	16	32	29%	73%	25%	9%	0	18			100	1.29	-0.4	90	-$8
2nd Half	3	3	30	35	1.82	3.79	1.31	1.33	90	79	3.5	4.6	10.6	2.3	37%	12.8%	95.1	51	23	26	31%	89%	11%	9%	0	15			75	1.22	9.8	106	$6
20 Proj	**5**	**4**	**58**	**71**	**3.64**	**3.48**	**1.32**	**1.31**	**93**	**87**	**3.5**	**4.5**	**11.0**	**2.5**	**36%**	**12.7%**	**95.2**	**44**	**21**	**34**	**31%**	**75%**	**12%**		**0**						**3.6**	**114**	**$3**

Wingenter,Trey

Age: 26	Th: R	Role RP	Health B	LIMA Plan C	
Ht: 6' 7"	Wt: 200	Type Pwr	PT/Exp D	Rand Var +5	
			Consist C	MM 3500	

Between a couple trips to minors and May IL stint (shoulder), big right-hander used fastball/slider combo to generate top-shelf SwK/Dom. Control issues still the main obstacle, although Ball% took a step forward in small-sample 2nd half. Aberrant S% should return to normal, putting another sub-4.00 ERA in play—with room for more.

Yr Tm	W	Sv	IP	K	ERA	xERA	WHIP	xWHIP	vL+	vR+	BF/G	Ctl	Dom	Cmd	Ball%	SwK	Vel	G	L	F	H%	S%	HR/F	xHR/F	GS	APC	DOM%	DIS%	Sv%	LI	RAR	BPX	R$
15																																	
16																																	
17 aa	2	20	48	53	3.42	3.94	1.28				4.0	3.8	10.0	2.7							29%	80%									5.5	100	$9
18 SD *	3	4	64	72	3.48	2.89	1.20		96	84	4.2	4.7	10.1	2.2		17.1%	97.5	36	21	43	25%	74%	17%	15%	0	15			67	1.00	5.3	109	$3
19 SD	1	1	51	72	5.65	3.91	1.22	1.32	63	106	4.3	4.9	12.7	2.6	37%	16.1%	95.9	36	24	40	29%	53%	11%	12%	1	18	0%	0%	25	1.06	-7.2	119	-$3
1st Half	0	1	30	43	3.56	3.75	1.09	1.28	53	103	4.1	5.0	12.8	2.5	39%	15.6%	96.1	39	19	42	23%	70%	12%	11%	0	18			33	1.03	3.5	120	$0
2nd Half	1	0	21	29	8.71	4.13	1.40	1.27	77	110	4.5	4.8	12.6	2.6	34%	16.8%	95.6	32	30	38	35%	33%	11%	13%	1	18	0%	0%	0	1.09	-10.7	118	-$7
20 Proj	**2**	**0**	**58**	**73**	**3.98**	**3.57**	**1.25**	**1.27**	**69**	**110**	**4.1**	**4.6**	**11.4**	**2.5**	**36%**	**16.3%**	**95.8**	**35**	**26**	**40**	**29%**	**71%**	**11%**		**0**						**1.2**	**106**	**$0**

Wisler,Matt

Age: 27	Th: R	Role RP	Health A	LIMA Plan B	
Ht: 6' 3"	Wt: 215	Type Pwr FB	PT/Exp D	Rand Var +5	
			Consist B	MM 2300	

A few years removed from mild prospect buzz, converted SP found home in SEA bullpen at year's end. SwK took major step forward and Dom followed suit, thanks to extreme reliance on slider (70% usage, 18% SwK). xHR/F suggests HR/F will drop—and with S% help, could emerge as decent option in Holds leagues. Forgotten, but not gone.

Yr Tm	W	Sv	IP	K	ERA	xERA	WHIP	xWHIP	vL+	vR+	BF/G	Ctl	Dom	Cmd	Ball%	SwK	Vel	G	L	F	H%	S%	HR/F	xHR/F	GS	APC	DOM%	DIS%	Sv%	LI	RAR	BPX	R$
15 ATL *	11	0	174	116	5.00	4.95	1.46	1.44	135	94	23.3	2.8	6.0	2.1	36%	8.5%	93.3	34	23	43	32%	68%	10%	15%	19	89	11%	53%	0	0.74	-22.2	53	-$8
16 ATL *	9	1	183	134	4.97	4.69	1.34	1.35	104	101	24.6	2.7	6.6	2.5	37%	9.4%	92.8	40	21	38	30%	67%	14%	13%	26	90	12%	35%	100	0.83	-17.7	58	-$1
17 ATL *	7	0	126	77	5.61	5.65	1.61	1.46	148	114	14.7	2.5	5.5	2.2	37%	9.7%	92.6	32	19	49	36%	65%	9%	13%	1	28	0%	100%	0	0.25	-19.4	50	-$10
18 2 NL *	6	0	131	102	4.79	5.31	1.45	1.19	107	109	14.4	1.8	7.0	3.9	35%	10.7%	92.3	33	21	47	36%	69%	14%	15%	3	34	33%	33%	0	0.54	-10.3	99	-$6
19 2 TM	3	0	51	63	5.61	4.07	1.40	1.19	122	101	5.1	2.8	11.0	3.9	34%	15.1%	92.8	36	25	38	36%	65%	18%	13%	8	21	0%	38%	0	0.90	-7.0	149	-$4
1st Half	2	0	29	34	5.28	4.06	1.52	1.19	135	95	6.1	3.1	10.6	3.4	34%	15.6%	92.9	43	25	31	38%	69%	19%	15%	0	25			0	0.95	-2.8	139	-$5
2nd Half	1	0	22	29	6.04	4.18	1.25	1.07	100	108	4.1	2.4	11.7	4.8	35%	14.4%	92.8	27	25	48	33%	57%	17%	11%	8	18	0%	38%	0	0.86	-4.2	163	-$4
20 Proj	**3**	**0**	**58**	**61**	**4.64**	**3.86**	**1.35**	**1.22**	**115**	**102**	**7.1**	**2.6**	**9.4**	**3.6**	**35%**	**13.0%**	**92.7**	**33**	**23**	**44**	**34%**	**70%**	**13%**		**0**						**-3.5**	**127**	**-$2**

BRIAN SLACK

Wittgren,Nick

Age: 29	Th: R	Role RP	Health D	LIMA Plan B	
Ht: 6' 2"	Wt: 216	Type	PT/Exp D	Rand Var -4	
			Consist B	MM 2310	

Saves upside? PRO: LI shows he's close to opportunity; career-best Dom; 1st half xERA, BPX say he's very closer-worthy. CON: 2nd half xERA, BPX disagree, and huge Cmd drop a concern; declining SwK; vL+ collapse in 2nd half; big gap between full-season ERA, xERA. VERDICT: Too much skill inconsistency to place your trust in him.

Yr Tm	W	Sv	IP	K	ERA	xERA	WHIP	xWHIP	vL+	vR+	BF/G	Ctl	Dom	Cmd	Ball%	SwK	Vel	G	L	F	H%	S%	HR/F	xHR/F	GS	APC	DOM%	DIS%	Sv%	LI	RAR	BPX	R$
15 a/a	1	20	64	54	3.75	3.89	1.21				4.9	1.2	7.7	6.4							33%	71%									1.7	185	$7
16 MIA	4	0	52	42	3.14	4.16	1.16	1.20	84	98	4.4	1.7	7.3	4.2	33%	6.8%	92.2	39	21	40	30%	78%	10%	11%	0	18			0	1.01	6.7	121	$2
17 MIA	3	0	42	43	4.68	4.43	1.39	1.22	121	97	4.8	2.8	9.1	3.3	36%	11.7%	92.4	33	24	43	35%	69%	9%	10%	0	20			0	0.74	-1.7	121	-$3
18 MIA *	2	2	66	59	4.74	5.08	1.51	1.40	82	92	4.8	3.2	8.0	2.5	36%	10.0%	92.1	46	17	37	35%	70%	3%	11%	0	19			33	0.65	-4.8	78	-$5
19 CLE	5	4	58	60	2.81	4.01	1.08	1.20	101	83	4.2	2.3	9.4	4.0	35%	9.7%	92.3	38	23	39	27%	85%	17%	18%	0	18			67	1.08	12.1	132	$7
1st Half	3	1	30	35	3.26	3.39	1.05	1.01	91	84	4.4	1.5	10.4	7.0	33%	9.9%	92.2	38	30	33	32%	72%	12%	16%	0	20			33	1.14	4.6	177	$6
2nd Half	2	3	27	25	2.30	4.83	1.10	1.32	116	83	4.0	3.3	8.2	2.5	36%	9.6%	92.6	39	16	45	20%	100%	21%	19%	0	16			100	1.03	7.4	83	$8
20 Proj	**4**	**2**	**65**	**63**	**3.86**	**3.78**	**1.24**	**1.25**	**104**	**95**	**4.4**	**2.7**	**8.7**	**3.3**	**35%**	**9.8%**	**92.3**	**40**	**21**	**40**	**30%**	**75%**	**14%**		**0**						**2.3**	**117**	**$2**

Wojciechowski,Asher

Age: 31	Th: R	Role SP	Health A	LIMA Plan D	
Ht: 6' 4"	Wt: 235	Type xFB	PT/Exp D	Rand Var 0	
			Consist D	MM 0101	

4-8, 4.92 ERA in 82 IP at BAL. Today's game is hard enough if you can't keep Dom above 9.0 or FB% below 50%; the fact that he can't seem to do either makes him unrosterable. SwK growth, 2nd half Dom bump open up possibility more strikeouts will come, but with career 5.26 xERA, there isn't much worth chasing here. At least he has his Health.

Yr Tm	W	Sv	IP	K	ERA	xERA	WHIP	xWHIP	vL+	vR+	BF/G	Ctl	Dom	Cmd	Ball%	SwK	Vel	G	L	F	H%	S%	HR/F	xHR/F	GS	APC	DOM%	DIS%	Sv%	LI	RAR	BPX	R$
15 HOU *	8	0	132	86	5.68	5.92	1.67		155	98	23.7	3.3	5.9	1.8		6.4%	91.0	20	31	49	35%	67%	7%	7%	3	62	0%	67%	0	0.52	-27.8	37	-$15
16 a/a	5	0	86	49	6.64	7.38	1.99				20.6	4.5	5.2	1.1							37%	68%									-25.9	2	-$18
17 CIN *	6	0	93	91	5.32	5.24	1.42	1.22	130	111	11.9	2.8	8.8	3.2	35%	10.9%	92.7	29	20	51	33%	67%	15%	12%	8	44	13%	38%	0	0.60	-11.0	83	-$3
18 aaa	5	0	120	95	6.30	7.05	1.57				21.1	3.4	7.1	2.1							31%	68%									-31.9	3	-$15
19 BAL *	12	0	169	140	5.10	5.75	1.41	1.34	116	99	22.3	3.5	7.5	2.1	37%	12.1%	91.6	30	19	51	28%	73%	14%	15%	16	86	25%	50%	0	0.72	-12.4	24	-$1
1st Half	8	0	86	60	5.28	6.56	1.51		0	0	24.9	4.0	6.3	1.6							26%	77%	0%		0	0					-8.2	-13	-$2
2nd Half	4	0	82	80	4.92	5.23	1.31	1.27	117	98	21.2	3.1	8.7	2.9	37%	12.1%	91.6	30	19	51	29%	69%	14%	15%	16	86	25%	50%	0	0.72	-4.2	90	$1
20 Proj	**6**	**0**	**102**	**85**	**5.53**	**4.86**	**1.48**	**1.25**	**132**	**112**	**20.2**	**3.4**	**7.5**	**2.2**	**36%**	**11.7%**	**92.0**	**30**	**19**	**51**	**31%**	**70%**	**15%**		**16**						**-17.2**	**60**	**-$6**

Wood,Alex

Age: 29	Th: L	Role SP	Health F	LIMA Plan B	
Ht: 6' 4"	Wt: 215	Type	PT/Exp B	Rand Var +5	
			Consist B	MM 3301	

Back problems kept him out until July, flared up again in September. It hurt effectiveness of sinker and slider, causing GB% to slide and xHR/F to explode. Other skills weren't far off from 2018, so rebound seems like reasonable expectation. But projecting how many innings he'll thow is a crapshoot. Almost have to treat him like one-half an SP slot.

Yr Tm	W	Sv	IP	K	ERA	xERA	WHIP	xWHIP	vL+	vR+	BF/G	Ctl	Dom	Cmd	Ball%	SwK	Vel	G	L	F	H%	S%	HR/F	xHR/F	GS	APC	DOM%	DIS%	Sv%	LI	RAR	BPX	R$
15 2 NL	12	0	190	139	3.84	4.01	1.36	1.35	71	111	25.0	2.8	6.6	2.4	36%	8.5%	89.1	49	23	28	32%	73%	9%	11%	32	91	28%	22%			2.8	84	$5
16 LA	1	0	60	66	3.73	3.32	1.26	1.20	105	85	18.2	3.0	9.8	3.3	35%	10.2%	90.6	53	20	27	33%	72%	12%	14%	10	70	30%	20%	0	0.60	3.4	152	$0
17 LA	16	0	152	151	2.72	3.36	1.06	1.16	80	85	22.7	2.2	8.9	4.0	33%	12.4%	91.8	53	20	27	28%	79%	14%	12%	25	84	44%	24%	0	0.78	30.8	157	$25
18 LA	9	0	152	135	3.68	3.77	1.21	1.23	81	97	19.3	2.4	8.0	3.4	34%	11.3%	89.9	49	22	29	31%	72%	11%	11%	27	74	19%	26%	0	0.81	8.8	123	$9
19 CIN	1	0	36	30	5.80	4.65	1.40	1.30	120	124	21.9	2.3	7.6	3.3	36%	11.4%	90.0	38	28	34	30%	69%	30%	22%	7	84	14%	43%			-5.7	99	-$6
1st Half																																	
2nd Half	1	0	36	30	5.80	4.65	1.40	1.24	121	123	21.9	2.3	7.6	3.3	36%	11.4%	90.0	38	28	34	30%	69%	30%	22%	7	84	14%	43%			-5.7	99	-$6
20 Proj	**6**	**0**	**116**	**111**	**4.02**	**3.58**	**1.28**	**1.22**	**93**	**102**	**20.6**	**2.4**	**8.6**	**3.5**	**35%**	**11.2%**	**90.4**	**43**	**23**	**33**	**32%**	**73%**	**15%**		**23**						**1.8**	**127**	**$4**

Wood,Hunter

Age: 26	Th: R	Role RP	Health B	LIMA Plan D	
Ht: 6' 1"	Wt: 175	Type	PT/Exp D	Rand Var -5	
			Consist D	MM 2200	

Is he the GB-leaning power pitcher of 2018, or FB-heavy control artist of 2019? xERA shows one is clearly preferable to the other, though anyone looking solely at S%-aided 2019 ERA might get wrong impression. Ball% trend suggests Ctl gains are genuine, but minor league Dom, batted ball data was just as wishy-washy. Shrug and move on.

Yr Tm	W	Sv	IP	K	ERA	xERA	WHIP	xWHIP	vL+	vR+	BF/G	Ctl	Dom	Cmd	Ball%	SwK	Vel	G	L	F	H%	S%	HR/F	xHR/F	GS	APC	DOM%	DIS%	Sv%	LI	RAR	BPX	R$
15																																	
16 aa	6	0	49	43	3.97	3.48	1.26				20.1	3.8	7.9	2.1							27%	71%									1.3	85	$1
17 TAM *	7	0	124	99	6.02	5.57	1.58		0	0	17.0	3.5	7.2	2.1		0.0%	90.0	0	0	100	34%	63%	0%		0	5			0	0.11	-25.4	54	-$10
18 TAM *	3	3	83	96	3.79	3.56	1.23	1.34	98	103	6.3	3.1	10.4	3.3	39%	13.5%	94.4	44	24	32	32%	72%	11%	10%	8	24	13%	75%	100	0.77	3.7	129	$3
19 2 AL	1	1	45	39	2.98	5.05	1.28	1.31	85	103	5.4	2.4	7.7	3.3	34%	12.8%	93.6	32	23	45	31%	84%	11%	8%	2	21	0%	50%	100	0.57	8.5	93	$0
1st Half	1	1	24	20	2.25	5.03	1.17	1.24	73	96	6.7	2.3	7.5	3.3	33%	14.1%	93.1	30	24	46	30%	85%	6%	7%	2	26	0%	50%	100	0.69	6.7	89	$1
2nd Half	0	0	21	19	3.80	5.21	1.41	1.26	97	111	4.5	2.5	8.0	3.2	36%	11.4%	94.2	35	22	43	32%	84%	17%	9%	0	18			0	0.47	1.9	97	-$2
20 Proj	**2**	**0**	**51**	**47**	**3.85**	**4.01**	**1.33**	**1.29**	**90**	**102**	**6.5**	**2.9**	**8.4**	**2.9**	**36%**	**12.9%**	**94.0**	**37**	**23**	**39**	**31%**	**76%**	**13%**		**0**						**1.9**	**101**	**-$2**

Woodruff,Brandon

Age: 27	Th: R	Role SP	Health D	LIMA Plan B	
Ht: 6' 4"	Wt: 215	Type Pwr GB	PT/Exp C	Rand Var +1	
			Consist B	MM 4405	

Oblique injury shortened 2nd half, prevented breakout from reaching full potential. But look at the skills: career-best Ctl backed by Ball% growth, rising velocity/SwK led to career-best Dom, xWHIP supports career-best WHIP. Still a work-in-progress vL, though 35% hit rate inflated results there a bit. If health cooperates in 2020, he's a near-ace.

Yr Tm	W	Sv	IP	K	ERA	xERA	WHIP	xWHIP	vL+	vR+	BF/G	Ctl	Dom	Cmd	Ball%	SwK	Vel	G	L	F	H%	S%	HR/F	xHR/F	GS	APC	DOM%	DIS%	Sv%	LI	RAR	BPX	R$
15																																	
16 aa	10	0	114	107	4.52	3.53	1.29				23.4	2.7	8.5	3.2							33%	64%									-4.6	125	$3
17 MIL *	8	0	118	91	4.66	4.62	1.40	1.36	115	77	20.8	2.9	6.9	2.4	34%	9.4%	94.3	47	19	34	32%	69%	11%	8%	8	90	38%	63%			-4.3	72	$0
18 MIL *	6	1	114	103	3.95	4.11	1.34	1.19	85	92	13.2	3.5	8.1	2.3	36%	11.1%	95.3	53	18	29	31%	73%	12%	16%	4	39	0%	50%	100	0.51	2.7	84	$2
19 MIL	11	0	122	143	3.62	3.42	1.14	1.12	100	74	22.4	2.2	10.6	4.8	33%	12.4%	96.3	45	23	32	33%	71%	12%	12%	22	90	32%	9%			13.2	167	$13
1st Half	10	0	102	120	3.79	3.47	1.14	1.08	100	75	24.3	2.2	10.6	4.8	33%	12.4%	96.1	43	24	33	33%	69%	12%	12%	17	96	35%	6%			9.0	166	$17
2nd Half	1	0	20	23	2.75	3.24	1.17	1.09	99	71	16.0	2.3	10.5	4.6	33%	12.3%	96.8	54	19	27	33%	81%	14%	10%	5	68	20%	20%			4.3	174	-$10
20 Proj	**14**	**0**	**181**	**200**	**3.46**	**3.05**	**1.18**	**1.16**	**97**	**80**	**22.1**	**2.5**	**9.9**	**4.0**	**34%**	**11.4%**	**95.8**	**50**	**20**	**30**	**32%**	**74%**	**13%**		**30**						**15.3**	**162**	**$19**

Workman,Brandon

Age: 31	Th: R	Role RP	Health F	LIMA Plan A	
Ht: 6' 5"	Wt: 235	Type Pwr	PT/Exp D	Rand Var -5	
			Consist A	MM 4520	

Outlasted all other members of BOS closer committee by ramping up GB% and strikeouts, thanks to career-best velocity, SwK. Of course, also got major assist from H%/S% combo, and technically HR/F, though xHR/F says he really was that stingy. But Ctl problems could undo it all, and that makes any pursuit of these saves a risky endeavor.

Yr Tm	W	Sv	IP	K	ERA	xERA	WHIP	xWHIP	vL+	vR+	BF/G	Ctl	Dom	Cmd	Ball%	SwK	Vel	G	L	F	H%	S%	HR/F	xHR/F	GS	APC	DOM%	DIS%	Sv%	LI	RAR	BPX	R$
15																																	
16																																	
17 BOS *	5	2	69	62	2.96	3.81	1.29	1.22	120	97	5.5	3.6	8.2	2.2	35%	10.8%	92.3	43	19	38	28%	82%	17%	14%	0	18			50	0.76	11.9	84	$5
18 BOS *	8	1	71	61	4.61	3.96	1.21	1.35	92	101	4.8	2.8	7.7	2.8	39%	10.8%	91.3	45	18	38	28%	66%	14%	15%	0	15			50	0.96	-4.0	83	$1
19 BOS	10	16	72	104	1.88	3.29	1.03	1.36	61	54	3.9	5.7	13.1	2.3	40%	13.3%	92.9	51	20	29	22%	81%	3%	5%	0	17			73	1.40	23.2	121	$21
1st Half	7	3	37	53	1.70	3.51	1.03	1.42	65	48	3.7	6.3	12.9	2.0	40%	13.2%	92.6	50	18	32	18%	84%	5%	8%	0	16			50	1.43	12.8	97	$16
2nd Half	3	13	35	51	2.08	2.95	1.04	1.24	58	61	4.2	4.9	13.2	2.7	40%	13.4%	93.2	52	22	25	27%	78%	0%	1%	0	18			81	1.36	10.4	148	$23
20 Proj	**7**	**24**	**65**	**81**	**3.05**	**3.15**	**1.13**	**1.31**	**78**	**80**	**4.4**	**4.3**	**11.2**	**2.6**	**39%**	**12.1%**	**92.3**	**48**	**19**	**33**	**27%**	**75%**	**10%**		**0**						**8.9**	**128**	**$17**

Wright,Kyle

Age: 24	Th: R	Role SP	Health A	LIMA Plan C	
Ht: 6' 4"	Wt: 200	Type	PT/Exp D	Rand Var +5	
			Consist C	MM 1100	

0-3, 8.69 ERA in 19 IP at ATL. Oof. Not what anyone wanted from former 1st-round pick with A-list caliber stuff. Second year that walk problems turned nightmarish in majors (5.9 Ctl), and has yet to figure out how to turn velocity into strikeouts. GB lean is a good start, but seems destined for another year on the "A-Rod 10-Step Path to Stardom."

Yr Tm	W	Sv	IP	K	ERA	xERA	WHIP	xWHIP	vL+	vR+	BF/G	Ctl	Dom	Cmd	Ball%	SwK	Vel	G	L	F	H%	S%	HR/F	xHR/F	GS	APC	DOM%	DIS%	Sv%	LI	RAR	BPX	R$
15																																	
16																																	
17																																	
18 ATL *	8	0	146	116	4.33	3.98	1.37		178	65	19.8	3.5	7.2	2.1		10.2%	94.0	41	18	41	31%	69%	29%	20%	0	32			0	0.21	-3.3	79	$0
19 ATL *	11	0	133	112	5.98	5.46	1.54	1.66	134	123	20.7	3.4	7.6	2.3	43%	9.4%	94.6	42	27	32	34%	63%	21%	23%	4	50	0%	75%	0	0.46	-24.1	56	-$7
1st Half	5	0	72	55	7.20	5.77	1.54		146	114	20.9	3.6	6.9	1.9		7.6%	94.4	45	19	36	32%	55%	27%	25%	3	79	0%	67%			-23.9	32	-$13
2nd Half	6	0	61	57	4.54	5.11	1.54		98	140	20.4	3.1	8.5	2.8		13.3%	95.3	33	44	22	37%	72%	0%	17%	1	28	0%	100%	0	0.24	-0.2	86	-$1
20 Proj	**3**	**0**	**36**	**29**	**4.89**	**4.25**	**1.47**				**20.3**	**3.4**	**7.3**	**2.2**	**39%**	**9.9%**		**47**	**20**	**33**	**32%**	**70%**	**13%**		**8**						**-3.3**	**75**	**-$4**

BRANDON KRUSE

Yacabonis,Jimmy

Yacabonis,Jimmy		Health	A	LIMA Plan	F
Age: 28	Th: R Role RP	PT/Exp	D	Rand Var	+2
Ht: 6' 3"	Wt: 205 Type Pwr FB	Consist	F	MM	0100

1-2, 6.80 ERA in 41 IP at BAL. As xERA and BPX trends show, he keeps finding new ways to get worse. This time around, it was more walks and fly balls, with each skill reaching career-worst levels. We like to say that around age 26, players go from prospect to suspect; at this point, we might have enough evidence to convict.

Yr Tm	W	Sv	IP	K	ERA	xERA	WHIP	xWHIP	vL+	vR+	BF/G	Ctl	Dom	Cmd	Ball%	SwK	Vel	G	L	F	H%	S%	HR/F	xHR/F	GS	APC	DOM%	DIS%	Sv%	LI	RAR	BPX	R$
15																																	
16 aa	2	6	44	40	2.50	3.15	1.25				5.3	3.2	8.1	2.5							31%	81%									9.2	112	$4
17 BAL *	6	11	82	49	2.47	2.39	1.26		85	104	6.1	5.2	5.3	1.0		5.9%	95.4	49	13	38	23%	80%	8%	6%	0	24			79	0.43	19.1	76	$11
18 BAL *	3	0	116	81	5.77	4.95	1.48	1.45	128	104	15.1	4.2	6.3	1.5	39%	10.5%	93.5	42	18	40	29%	63%	17%	13%	7	56	0%	43%	0	0.65	-23.2	38	-$12
19 BAL *	3	2	65	50	6.43	7.03	1.90	1.65	122	129	6.7	5.6	6.9	1.2	42%	9.1%	93.6	36	22	43	35%	69%	16%	18%	4	27	0%	50%	67	0.62	-15.4	13	-$11
1st Half	2	2	45	32	6.02	6.33	1.72	1.48	116	117	7.2	5.1	6.5	1.3	41%	7.7%	93.9	37	17	46	32%	69%	16%	20%	2	27	0%	50%	67	0.86	-8.3	13	-$10
2nd Half	1	0	20	17	7.34	8.56	2.31	1.74	131	148	5.8	6.7	7.6	1.1	42%	10.9%	93.4	33	29	37	42%	69%	16%	12%	2	26	0%	50%	0	0.34	-7.1	15	-$14
20 Proj	**2**	**0**	**44**	**33**	**5.51**	**5.42**	**1.72**	**1.56**	**115**	**113**	**7.1**	**5.1**	**6.7**	**1.3**	**41%**	**10.0%**	**93.5**	**38**	**22**	**41**	**33%**	**69%**	**9%**		**0**						**-7.3**	**-2**	**-$8**

Yamamoto,Jordan

Yamamoto,Jordan		Health	B	LIMA Plan	D
Age: 24	Th: R Role SP	PT/Exp	D	Rand Var	+3
Ht: 6' 0"	Wt: 185 Type Pwr FB	Consist	D	MM	1203

4-5, 4.46 ERA in 78 IP at MIA. Luck bought him 1.59 ERA over first 6 MLB starts, but regression set in quickly as Ctl, FB% caught up with him. Throws five different pitches, though none are considered plus, and with no above-average skills in sight (apart from tiny 2018 sample), there's no cause for expecting growth. A back-end starter, at best.

Yr Tm	W	Sv	IP	K	ERA	xERA	WHIP	xWHIP	vL+	vR+	BF/G	Ctl	Dom	Cmd	Ball%	SwK	Vel	G	L	F	H%	S%	HR/F	xHR/F	GS	APC	DOM%	DIS%	Sv%	LI	RAR	BPX	R$
15																																	
16																																	
17																																	
18 aa	1	0	17	20	2.42	2.32	1.02				21.7	2.1	10.7	5.1							31%	78%									3.6	193	-$2
19 MIA *	7	0	145	137	4.98	3.98	1.31	1.41	76	94	22.1	4.1	8.5	2.1	38%	9.7%	91.5	36	21	43	28%	64%	13%	10%	15	92	20%	33%			-8.6	72	$1
1st Half	6	0	89	78	4.56	3.86	1.35	1.45	50	57	23.2	4.2	7.8	1.9	39%	9.5%	91.0	34	17	49	29%	67%	0%	6%	4	92	50%	0%			-0.6	73	$4
2nd Half	1	0	56	59	5.66	4.61	1.24	1.32	83	110	21.5	3.9	9.5	2.5	37%	9.8%	91.7	36	23	41	26%	59%	18%	12%	11	92	9%	45%			-7.9	89	-$5
20 Proj	**6**	**0**	**160**	**151**	**4.93**	**4.41**	**1.39**	**1.37**	**96**	**117**	**22.1**	**4.1**	**8.5**	**2.1**	**38%**	**9.7%**	**91.4**	**35**	**20**	**44**	**29%**	**68%**	**13%**		**30**						**-15.3**	**65**	**-$2**

Yarbrough,Ryan

Yarbrough,Ryan		Health	A	LIMA Plan	C
Age: 28	Th: L Role SP	PT/Exp	C	Rand Var	+4
Ht: 6' 5"	Wt: 210 Type Con	Consist	C	MM	2203

11-6, 4.13 ERA in 141 IP at TAM. Rode Ball% growth to career-best Ctl and traditional starter usage over final two months. If SwK increase paves the way for similar bump in Dom, he could emerge as very appealing option in 2020. Added GB tilt, found success vR (7.9 Cmd), doubled BPX—there's a lot to like, and maybe... UP: sub-3.50 ERA

Yr Tm	W	Sv	IP	K	ERA	xERA	WHIP	xWHIP	vL+	vR+	BF/G	Ctl	Dom	Cmd	Ball%	SwK	Vel	G	L	F	H%	S%	HR/F	xHR/F	GS	APC	DOM%	DIS%	Sv%	LI	RAR	BPX	R$
15																																	
16 aa	12	0	128	84	3.75	3.79	1.30				21.1	2.3	5.9	2.6							31%	71%									6.9	86	$6
17 aaa	13	0	157	131	4.87	5.38	1.47				25.9	2.6	7.5	2.9							34%	71%									-10.0	72	$0
18 TAM	16	0	147	128	3.91	4.40	1.29	1.32	89	106	16.5	3.1	7.8	2.6	35%	9.2%	89.4	38	25	37	30%	73%	11%	12%	6	63	0%	50%	0	1.21	4.4	86	$9
19 TAM *	13	0	168	146	4.25	3.11	1.04	1.18	93	84	19.6	1.3	7.8	6.2	33%	10.6%	88.2	44	20	36	29%	61%	10%	10%	14	73	50%	29%	0	0.90	5.2	171	$16
1st Half	9	0	81	68	4.15	2.78	1.01	1.18	105	82	18.3	1.4	7.6	5.6	34%	10.0%	88.2	44	23	33	28%	59%	10%	11%	4	67	50%	0%	0	0.99	3.6	160	$18
2nd Half	4	0	86	77	4.36	3.42	1.07	1.09	82	85	21.0	1.1	8.0	7.0	32%	11.0%	88.1	44	18	38	30%	61%	10%	9%	10	79	50%	40%	0	0.82	1.6	184	$13
20 Proj	**14**	**0**	**160**	**136**	**3.94**	**3.81**	**1.22**	**1.20**	**97**	**100**	**20.9**	**2.1**	**7.7**	**3.7**	**34%**	**10.0%**	**88.6**	**40**	**22**	**37**	**31%**	**71%**	**10%**		**31**						**4.2**	**115**	**$11**

Yates,Kirby

Yates,Kirby		Health	B	LIMA Plan	A
Age: 33	Th: R Role RP	PT/Exp	B	Rand Var	-5
Ht: 5' 10"	Wt: 210 Type Pwr	Consist	A	MM	5530

xERA, Cmd, LI, and BPX all track his evolution from disaster to lights-out closer, with 2019 second half line suggesting he's not done improving. High Sv total and fact that tiny ERA got help from S%, HR/F will make value repeat difficult, though not impossible. Age becoming a consideration as well. But even if skills regress a little, he'll still be elite.

Yr Tm	W	Sv	IP	K	ERA	xERA	WHIP	xWHIP	vL+	vR+	BF/G	Ctl	Dom	Cmd	Ball%	SwK	Vel	G	L	F	H%	S%	HR/F	xHR/F	GS	APC	DOM%	DIS%	Sv%	LI	RAR	BPX	R$
15 TAM *	2	6	46	48	7.56	7.83	1.72		172	118	4.8	4.0	9.4	2.3		10.3%	92.4	25	22	52	34%	64%	30%	22%	0	20			86	0.43	-20.3	4	-$9
16 NYY *	2	4	58	64	4.46	4.18	1.45	1.28	79	113	4.5	4.1	10.0	2.4	37%	12.3%	93.2	44	23	34	35%	70%	14%	10%	0	20			57	0.61	-1.9	108	-$1
17 2 TM	4	1	57	88	3.97	3.24	1.11	1.01	111	80	3.7	3.0	14.0	4.6	33%	18.0%	94.0	29	15	56	31%	75%	18%	15%	0	16			25	0.85	2.7	213	$4
18 SD	5	12	63	90	2.14	2.68	0.92	0.99	91	58	3.8	2.4	12.9	5.3	34%	17.1%	94.0	43	20	37	29%	83%	12%	17%	0	16			92	1.37	15.6	215	$15
19 SD	0	41	61	101	1.19	2.26	0.89	0.87	75	60	4.1	1.9	15.0	7.8	34%	16.2%	93.5	48	17	35	36%	88%	5%	9%	0	17			93	1.60	24.8	265	$28
1st Half	0	27	35	56	1.27	2.49	0.85	0.89	79	48	3.9	2.3	14.3	6.2	33%	16.9%	93.3	46	15	39	31%	86%	4%	9%	0	15			96	1.59	14.1	239	$31
2nd Half	0	14	25	45	1.07	2.07	0.95	0.77	70	77	4.3	1.4	16.0	11.3	34%	15.4%	93.7	50	20	30	42%	91%	6%	7%	0	19			88	1.62	10.7	303	$24
20 Proj	**2**	**36**	**58**	**90**	**2.31**	**2.30**	**1.01**	**0.94**	**85**	**74**	**3.8**	**2.4**	**13.9**	**5.9**	**34%**	**16.1%**	**93.7**	**44**	**19**	**38**	**34%**	**82%**	**12%**		**0**						**13.2**	**240**	**$22**

Ynoa,Gabriel

Ynoa,Gabriel		Health	F	LIMA Plan	A
Age: 27	Th: R Role RP	PT/Exp	D	Rand Var	+3
Ht: 6' 2"	Wt: 205 Type Con FB	Consist	A	MM	0000

1-10, 5.61 ERA in 110 IP at BAL. After shoulder issue, shin splits limited him to 7 AA IP in 2018, returned to mound with more lackluster results. GB%, Ctl provide decent skill base, but ongoing lack of Dom undermines everything—even with growth, R$ shows he'd have uphill climb just to get to $0. His zen goal: achieve a state of nothingness.

Yr Tm	W	Sv	IP	K	ERA	xERA	WHIP	xWHIP	vL+	vR+	BF/G	Ctl	Dom	Cmd	Ball%	SwK	Vel	G	L	F	H%	S%	HR/F	xHR/F	GS	APC	DOM%	DIS%	Sv%	LI	RAR	BPX	R$
15 aa	9	0	152	72	4.46	4.45	1.34				25.4	1.8	4.3	2.4							31%	68%									-9.3	55	-$2
16 NYM *	13	0	173	87	4.01	4.50	1.42		102	101	20.9	2.4	4.5	1.9		10.8%	93.5	49	26	25	32%	73%	0%	8%	3	32	33%	67%	0	0.60	3.9	51	$2
17 BAL *	8	0	141	88	6.39	6.06	1.66	1.26	128	88	21.1	2.3	5.6	2.4	36%	10.2%	94.3	38	14	48	37%	61%	9%	15%	4	60	0%	50%	0	0.66	-35.4	54	-$16
18																																	
19 BAL *	2	0	128	77	5.66	5.87	1.36	1.39	117	111	13.7	2.3	5.4	2.4	35%	9.5%	93.5	47	15	38	28%	66%	20%	18%	13	50	0%	69%	0	0.74	-18.2	13	-$8
1st Half	1	0	68	44	6.16	5.94	1.47	1.40	103	131	15.3	3.1	5.9	1.9	38%	9.0%	93.1	46	16	39	29%	63%	18%	19%	7	58	0%	71%	0	0.55	-13.8	11	-$11
2nd Half	1	0	60	33	5.10	5.16	1.25	1.27	132	96	12.6	1.4	5.0	3.7	33%	10.0%	94.0	47	15	37	26%	71%	22%	18%	6	45	0%	67%	0	0.89	-4.4	85	-$4
20 Proj	**2**	**0**	**58**	**32**	**5.39**	**5.02**	**1.58**	**1.30**	**133**	**113**	**17.2**	**2.3**	**5.0**	**2.2**	**35%**	**9.8%**	**93.9**	**43**	**15**	**42**	**34%**	**70%**	**12%**		**11**						**-8.9**	**57**	**-$8**

Young,Alex

Young,Alex		Health	A	LIMA Plan	A
Age: 26	Th: L Role SP	PT/Exp	D	Rand Var	+1
Ht: 6' 2"	Wt: 205 Type Con GB	Consist	A	MM	1103

7-5, 3.56 ERA in 83 IP at ARI. Promising debut was helped by low H%, high S% in 2nd half; MLB xERA was nearly a run higher (4.53). Strikeouts have been improving, and he finished strong—9.3 Dom, 14% SwK in September—but velocity likely puts a cap on upside, and RHB hit 11 of his 14 HR allowed. Good chance he's overvalued this spring.

Yr Tm	W	Sv	IP	K	ERA	xERA	WHIP	xWHIP	vL+	vR+	BF/G	Ctl	Dom	Cmd	Ball%	SwK	Vel	G	L	F	H%	S%	HR/F	xHR/F	GS	APC	DOM%	DIS%	Sv%	LI	RAR	BPX	R$
15																																	
16																																	
17 aa	9	0	137	85	5.13	5.27	1.60				22.4	4.1	5.6	1.4							32%	69%									-13.0	34	-$7
18 a/a	10	0	132	88	5.41	5.29	1.52				19.8	2.6	6.0	2.3							35%	65%									-20.6	60	-$9
19 ARI *	11	0	140	121	4.46	4.66	1.40	1.35	74	103	15.9	3.4	7.8	2.3	36%	12.9%	89.3	48	17	35	31%	72%	16%	17%	15	78	13%	47%	0	0.76	0.8	66	$3
1st Half	5	0	61	55	5.46	5.43	1.63		187	32	13.0	3.8	8.1	2.1		10.8%	89.5	31	15	54	37%	67%	14%	15%	1	74	0%	0%			-7.2	67	-$7
2nd Half	6	0	78	66	3.68	4.54	1.21	1.32	66	106	20.6	3.0	7.6	2.5	36%	13.0%	89.3	49	17	34	27%	77%	17%	17%	14	78	14%	50%	0	0.76	8.0	91	$11
20 Proj	**10**	**0**	**131**	**101**	**4.57**	**4.36**	**1.46**	**1.45**	**71**	**117**	**20.8**	**3.2**	**7.0**	**2.2**	**39%**	**13.0%**	**89.3**	**49**	**17**	**34**	**31%**	**74%**	**15%**		**27**						**-6.7**	**76**	**-$1**

Zimmermann,Jordan

Zimmermann,Jordan		Health	F	LIMA Plan	B
Age: 34	Th: R Role SP	PT/Exp	B	Rand Var	+5
Ht: 6' 2"	Wt: 225 Type Con FB	Consist	B	MM	0001

Hit the IL in April with a sprained UCL, and odds are it affected him all year. Fallout was career worsts in ERA, velocity, R$; second-worst xERA, WHIP, and RAR. Sure, skills did get better in 2nd half, so we can't rule out some rebound, but to what? 2018 levels? Going by R$, that possibility is only worth a buck. Is it really worth the risk?

Yr Tm	W	Sv	IP	K	ERA	xERA	WHIP	xWHIP	vL+	vR+	BF/G	Ctl	Dom	Cmd	Ball%	SwK	Vel	G	L	F	H%	S%	HR/F	xHR/F	GS	APC	DOM%	DIS%	Sv%	LI	RAR	BPX	R$
15 WAS	13	0	202	164	3.66	3.82	1.20	1.19	107	87	25.2	1.7	7.3	4.2	32%	8.9%	93.0	42	22	36	31%	74%	11%	11%	33	94	27%	18%			7.5	125	$13
16 DET *	9	0	126	74	4.41	4.88	1.39	1.33	100	118	22.1	2.2	5.3	2.4	33%	8.0%	91.8	43	18	39	31%	72%	10%	14%	18	90	17%	39%	0	0.73	-3.3	51	-$1
17 DET	8	0	160	103	6.08	5.46	1.55	1.36	120	118	24.6	2.5	5.8	2.3	34%	8.4%	92.2	33	25	42	33%	64%	13%	13%	29	91	10%	48%			-33.9	58	-$13
18 DET	7	0	131	111	4.52	4.41	1.26	1.19	110	111	22.2	1.8	7.6	4.3	33%	9.5%	91.2	35	22	43	30%	72%	16%	15%	25	83	12%	28%			-6.0	117	$1
19 DET	1	0	112	82	6.91	5.07	1.52	1.32	130	102	21.9	2.0	6.6	3.3	35%	8.9%	90.5	42	24	34	35%	56%	15%	18%	23	81	13%	52%			-33.2	92	-$15
1st Half	0	0	45	31	5.36	5.50	1.39	1.39	115	92	21.8	3.0	6.2	2.1	36%	8.8%	90.3	40	20	40	30%	63%	10%	13%	9	79	22%	44%			-4.8	52	-$11
2nd Half	1	0	67	51	7.97	4.78	1.61	1.19	139	108	22.0	1.4	6.9	5.1	34%	8.9%	90.6	43	27	29	38%	51%	19%	23%	14	82	7%	57%			-28.4	119	-$18
20 Proj	**4**	**0**	**116**	**82**	**4.98**	**4.56**	**1.46**	**1.26**	**122**	**107**	**21.9**	**2.2**	**6.4**	**2.9**	**34%**	**8.9%**	**91.1**	**36**	**22**	**42**	**33%**	**71%**	**13%**		**23**						**-11.8**	**81**	**-$6**

BRANDON KRUSE

THE NEXT TIER (*=includes MLEs)   Pitchers

The preceding section provided player boxes and analysis for 427 pitchers. As we know, far more than 427 pitchers will play in the major leagues in 2020. Many of those additional pitchers are covered in the minor league section, but that still leaves a gap: established major leaguers who don't play enough, or well enough, to merit a player box.

This section looks to fill that gap. Here, you will find "The Next Tier" of pitchers who are mostly past their growth years, but who are likely to see some playing time in 2020. We are including their 2018-19 statlines here for reference for you to do your own analysis. This way, if Clay Buchholz is rumored to be pushing for a rotation spot at some point in 2020, a quick check here would confirm that … he's still Clay Buchholz. Or if David Hernandez sneaks into a more prominent bullpen role in 2020, this chart shows that he has some scattered elements of high skill in his past that indicate some consolidation would not be unheard of.

Pitcher	T	Yr	Age	W	Sv	IP	K	ERA	xERA	WHIP	vL+	vR+	Ctl	Dom	Cmd	SwK	Ball%	G/L/F	H%	S%	BPX
Albers, Matt	R	18	35	3	1	34	32	7.34	4.37	1.66	147	122	3.1	8.4	2.7	10.8	37	46/22/33	35	62	104
		19	36	8	4	60	57	5.13	4.59	1.37	128	83	4.4	8.6	2.0	9.9	39	51/20/30	29	65	72
Allen, Cody	R	18	29	4	27	67	80	4.70	4.37	1.36	111	94	4.4	10.7	2.4	13.3	38	30/19/51	30	70	94
		19	30	0	4	23	29	6.26	7.06	1.91	137	131	7.8	11.3	1.5	10.2	42	20/15/65	29	80	-10
Alvarez, Jose	L	18	29	6	1	63	59	2.71	3.98	1.16	84	85	3.1	8.4	2.7	11.1	34	45/20/35	29	77	103
		19	30	3	1	59	51	3.36	4.40	1.42	87	113	2.7	7.8	2.8	11.5	33	49/24/27	33	82	101
Avilan, Luis	L	18	28	2	2	45	51	3.77	4.08	1.37	89	100	3.6	10.1	2.8	10.8	40	36/25/39	35	73	115
		19	29	4	0	32	30	5.06	4.62	1.47	49	138	3.9	8.4	2.1	11.7	42	47/24/29	32	69	77
Bleier, Richard	L	18	31	3	0	33	15	1.93	4.07	1.22	87	96	1.1	4.1	3.8	8.8	33	59/18/23	32	83	94
		19	32	3	4	55	30	5.37	4.32	1.32	73	132	1.3	4.9	3.8	8.3	32	60/20/20	32	60	99
Blevins, Jerry	L	18	34	3	1	43	41	4.85	5.31	1.36	109	93	4.6	8.6	1.9	9.4	41	22/21/57	27	67	35
		19	35	1	1	32	37	3.90	4.83	1.27	72	109	4.5	10.3	2.3	11.1	37	29/26/45	27	75	79
Boxberger, Brad	R	18	30	3	32	53	71	4.39	3.90	1.43	117	89	5.4	12.0	2.2	11.2	36	46/16/38	31	75	108
		19*	31	2	2	43	42	5.88	5.73	1.73	87	112	5.7	8.7	1.5	12.1	38	39/21/39	34	68	50
Brach, Brad	R	18	32	2	12	63	60	3.59	4.54	1.60	116	95	4.0	8.6	2.1	13.0	37	46/24/30	36	79	81
		19	33	5	0	54	60	5.47	4.91	1.62	151	76	5.1	9.9	1.9	12.5	37	39/26/35	36	65	62
Brasier, Ryan	R	18*	30	4	13	75	57	1.92	2.42	1.04	90	43	2.0	6.9	3.4	16.5	31	40/20/40	27	83	128
		19	31	2	7	56	61	4.85	4.71	1.29	115	80	3.4	9.9	2.9	16.0	34	32/21/47	30	67	104
Buchholz, Clay	R	18*	33	8	0	128	95	2.30	3.01	1.11	76	94	2.5	6.7	2.7	10.0	32	43/21/37	27	83	96
		19	34	2	0	59	39	6.56	5.22	1.49	123	119	2.4	5.9	2.4	9.7	34	45/18/37	32	60	70
Buchter, Ryan	L	18	31	6	0	39	41	2.75	4.48	1.19	69	115	3.4	9.4	2.7	11.6	37	25/21/53	29	81	91
		19	32	1	0	45	50	2.98	5.07	1.43	97	119	4.6	9.9	2.2	12.0	38	25/29/46	30	88	64
Diekman, Jake	L	18	31	1	2	53	66	4.73	3.98	1.50	122	85	5.2	11.1	2.1	11.8	40	48/20/32	35	68	98
		19	32	1	0	61	81	4.72	4.06	1.44	89	89	5.8	12.0	2.1	15.7	37	47/27/26	34	66	92
Fry, Jace	L	18	24	2	4	51	70	4.38	3.11	1.11	56	94	3.5	12.3	3.5	15.2	37	45/21/34	31	60	172
		19	25	3	0	55	68	4.75	4.53	1.58	82	107	7.0	11.1	1.6	14.2	44	57/19/24	30	73	49
Garcia, Luis	R	18	31	3	1	46	51	6.07	3.68	1.46	106	106	3.5	10.0	2.8	14.8	38	48/24/27	36	57	127
		19	32	2	1	62	57	4.35	5.10	1.52	106	106	4.8	8.3	1.7	13.1	40	47/20/33	29	79	49
Godley, Zachary	R	18	28	15	0	178	185	4.74	4.01	1.45	101	100	4.1	9.3	2.3	12.0	38	49/23/28	34	68	98
		19	29	4	2	92	70	5.97	5.48	1.50	112	106	4.1	6.8	1.7	10.5	38	43/21/36	30	62	36
Gonzalez, Alex	R	19*	27	6	0	150	102	6.40	6.48	1.70	114	95	4.3	6.1	1.4	8.5	40	43/25/32	33	66	11
Grace, Matt	L	18	29	1	0	60	48	2.87	3.92	1.14	86	89	2.0	7.2	3.7	8.3	33	48/20/31	29	78	119
		19	30	1	0	47	35	6.36	4.62	1.52	109	131	1.9	6.8	3.5	8.9	35	49/23/28	34	63	105
Gregerson, Luke	R	18	34	0	0	13	12	7.11	4.10	1.58	90	133	4.3	8.5	2.0	13.0	41	55/24/21	34	56	82
		19	35	0	0	6	2	7.94	5.83	2.12	104	140	1.6	3.2	2.0	4.8	38	50/29/21	44	58	46
Hale, David	R	18*	30	3	0	71	41	5.76	6.54	1.71	160	89	3.2	5.2	1.6	11.1	36	42/21/38	35	69	16
		19*	31	6	2	72	45	4.22	4.94	1.47	96	93	2.4	5.7	2.4	8.3	35	50/21/29	34	72	60
Hardy, Blaine	L	18*	31	7	1	113	90	3.08	3.12	1.11	94	96	2.1	7.2	3.3	9.1	34	42/16/42	28	75	112
		19	32	1	0	44	29	4.47	4.97	1.15	137	82	2.6	5.9	2.2	10.3	35	49/15/36	23	71	67
Hellickson, Jeremy	R	18	31	5	0	91	65	3.45	4.05	1.07	89	98	2.0	6.4	3.3	8.8	34	46/21/33	26	72	99
		19	32	2	0	39	30	6.23	6.23	1.72	140	101	4.6	6.9	1.5	6.1	39	39/21/40	32	69	19
Hernandez, David	R	18	33	5	0	64	65	2.53	3.82	0.98	94	82	2.4	9.1	3.8	12.2	34	33/21/46	26	79	128
		19	34	2	2	43	53	8.02	4.81	1.71	147	102	4.2	11.2	2.7	15.4	33	28/31/41	41	53	102
Herrera, Kelvin	R	18	28	2	17	44	38	2.44	4.28	1.20	95	95	2.0	7.7	3.8	13.2	33	36/21/43	30	87	113
		19	29	3	1	51	53	6.14	5.10	1.62	103	112	4.0	9.3	2.3	12.3	35	36/26/38	36	64	79
Hess, David	R	18*	24	6	0	151	109	4.66	5.03	1.40	115	111	3.5	6.5	1.9	8.7	37	35/19/47	29	72	39
		19*	25	4	1	122	104	6.59	6.83	1.53	106	138	3.2	7.7	2.4	8.9	38	33/22/46	31	65	14
Holland, Greg	R	18	32	2	3	46	47	4.66	5.13	1.62	91	99	6.2	9.1	1.5	13.8	39	40/25/35	33	70	17
		19	33	1	17	36	41	4.54	4.81	1.37	83	98	6.1	10.3	1.7	12.5	39	45/16/38	25	70	50

THE NEXT TIER (*=includes MLEs)

Pitcher	T	Yr	Age	W	Sv	IP	K	ERA	xERA	WHIP	vL+	vR+	Ctl	Dom	Cmd	SwK	Ball%	G/L/F	H%	S%	BPX
Jackson, Edwin	R	18*	34	10	0	164	113	3.94	4.26	1.39	97	91	3.9	6.2	1.6	9.2	39	36/24/40	29	74	53
		19*	35	4	0	90	63	9.66	9.26	2.01	139	152	4.6	6.3	1.4	10.3	40	42/20/37	35	56	-42
Kintzler, Brandon	R	18	33	3	2	61	43	4.60	4.52	1.47	119	101	3.3	6.4	2.0	7.4	36	50/22/28	33	69	63
		19	34	3	1	57	48	2.68	3.84	1.04	69	94	2.1	7.6	3.7	8.3	36	55/16/29	27	78	124
Leone, Dominic	R	18	26	1	0	24	26	4.50	4.18	1.46	115	85	3.0	9.8	3.3	15.2	35	30/34/37	37	72	118
		19*	27	2	1	74	77	4.61	4.41	1.37	105	111	4.5	9.4	2.1	14.7	38	36/23/41	28	71	69
Liriano, Francisco	L	18	34	5	0	134	110	4.58	4.80	1.50	71	113	4.9	7.4	1.5	10.2	42	48/22/30	29	73	31
		19	35	5	0	70	63	3.47	4.87	1.36	89	96	4.5	8.1	1.8	14.0	38	50/16/34	28	78	57
McFarland, T.J.	L	18	29	2	1	72	42	2.00	3.82	1.19	54	104	2.8	5.3	1.9	8.1	39	68/15/17	27	85	76
		19	30	0	0	56	35	4.82	4.80	1.63	102	122	3.2	5.6	1.8	10.3	38	61/21/18	35	72	58
McGee, Jake	L	18	31	2	1	51	47	6.49	4.48	1.46	130	116	2.8	8.2	2.9	10.6	35	40/21/39	33	58	104
		19	32	0	0	41	35	4.35	5.10	1.40	92	139	2.4	7.6	3.2	9.1	36	36/19/46	31	81	94
Miller, Shelby	R	18	27	0	0	16	19	10.69	4.38	2.00	113	176	4.5	10.7	2.4	8.8	38	49/20/31	42	48	113
		19*	28	2	0	66	45	7.62	6.51	1.91	102	133	6.4	6.2	1.0	7.8	39	41/20/39	33	60	16
Morgan, Adam	L	18	28	0	1	49	50	3.83	3.94	1.44	92	101	4.0	9.1	2.3	12.5	35	54/17/29	33	76	101
		19	29	3	0	30	29	3.94	4.28	1.01	60	100	3.0	8.8	2.9	15.8	33	41/18/41	23	65	104
Morin, Michael	R	18*	27	5	3	59	48	4.69	4.29	1.39	86	171	2.3	7.4	3.3	13.8	35	27/45/27	35	65	109
		19	28	1	1	51	26	4.62	5.23	1.11	76	98	1.8	4.6	2.6	11.5	32	40/23/37	25	60	58
Moronta, Reyes	R	18	25	5	1	65	79	2.49	3.89	1.09	84	61	5.1	10.9	2.1	14.5	39	42/16/42	22	79	90
		19	26	3	0	57	70	2.86	4.66	1.31	82	79	5.2	11.1	2.1	12.3	39	37/18/45	29	80	80
Neshek, Pat	R	18	37	3	5	24	15	2.59	4.93	1.15	125	75	1.8	5.5	3.0	10.8	28	38/16/46	28	81	76
		19	38	0	3	18	9	5.00	5.63	1.39	126	105	1.0	4.5	4.5	8.9	30	42/18/40	30	75	81
Nicasio, Juan	R	18	31	1	1	42	53	6.00	3.41	1.38	104	120	1.1	11.4	10.6	11.8	32	36/21/43	42	58	218
		19	32	2	1	47	45	4.75	4.78	1.65	108	106	4.0	8.6	2.1	9.7	36	46/28/26	37	72	76
Osich, Josh	L	18*	29	0	0	58	41	6.23	6.92	1.97	177	126	4.1	6.3	1.6	13.7	39	45/29/26	41	67	44
		19	30	4	0	68	61	4.66	4.19	1.14	73	119	2.0	8.1	4.1	13.0	35	42/21/37	27	68	122
Otero, Dan	R	18	33	2	1	59	43	5.22	3.40	1.26	137	99	0.8	6.6	8.6	8.7	32	59/22/19	32	65	155
		19*	34	0	0	46	23	4.38	6.02	1.32	92	130	1.1	4.4	4.1	6.3	34	53/20/27	29	78	41
Peralta, Wily	R	18*	29	1	15	69	63	4.91	5.59	1.77	95	108	6.1	8.2	1.3	10.1	41	46/19/35	34	74	55
		19	30	2	2	40	24	5.80	5.86	1.59	135	97	4.2	5.4	1.3	8.8	40	45/21/34	30	67	5
Perez, Oliver	L	18	36	1	0	32	43	1.39	2.53	0.74	68	44	1.9	12.0	6.1	15.8	31	41/24/35	25	83	209
		19	37	2	1	41	48	3.98	3.77	1.23	81	117	2.7	10.6	4.0	13.8	31	44/21/35	33	71	154
Phelps, David	R	19	32	2	1	34	36	3.41	4.88	1.40	121	88	4.5	9.4	2.1	8.0	39	40/17/43	30	81	74
Richard, Clayton	L	18	34	7	0	159	108	5.33	4.27	1.38	92	109	3.4	6.1	1.8	8.9	37	57/22/22	29	63	61
		19	35	1	0	45	22	5.96	5.49	1.57	82	126	3.6	4.4	1.2	6.3	37	56/21/24	29	66	18
Roe, Chaz	R	18	31	1	1	50	53	3.58	3.36	1.01	111	78	2.9	9.5	3.3	11.4	36	48/19/33	25	69	137
		19	32	1	1	51	65	4.06	4.47	1.57	91	93	5.5	11.5	2.1	10.1	38	45/20/35	37	74	89
Ross, Tyson	R	18	31	8	0	150	122	4.15	4.33	1.30	117	77	3.7	7.3	2.0	9.1	38	46/26/28	28	71	64
		19	32	1	0	35	25	6.11	5.58	1.67	96	131	4.6	6.4	1.4	7.2	37	51/22/27	31	67	22
Santiago, Hector	L	18	30	6	2	102	103	4.41	5.26	1.58	111	110	5.3	9.1	1.7	8.8	38	33/17/50	32	77	36
		19*	31	5	0	114	94	6.26	7.08	1.77	133	122	4.6	7.4	1.6	11.7	38	32/22/46	34	70	10
Sipp, Tony	L	18	34	3	0	39	42	1.86	3.56	1.03	77	83	3.0	9.8	3.2	14.0	36	41/18/40	28	82	130
		19	35	1	0	21	18	4.71	5.34	1.33	88	80	3.9	7.7	2.0	12.9	39	38/22/41	30	63	55
Steckenrider, Drew	R	18	27	4	5	65	74	3.90	4.03	1.27	112	74	3.8	10.3	2.7	11.5	34	34/24/42	31	72	110
		19	28	0	0	14	14	6.28	5.10	0.98	78	122	3.1	8.8	2.8	9.3	38	32/3/66	10	50	91
Straily, Dan	R	18	29	5	0	122	99	4.12	4.89	1.30	115	91	3.8	7.3	1.9	10.4	37	32/26/42	26	74	44
		19*	30	7	0	115	86	6.99	7.41	1.64	128	172	3.2	6.7	2.1	7.9	40	28/21/51	32	64	-4
Swarzak, Anthony	R	18	32	0	4	26	31	6.15	4.41	1.59	145	100	4.8	10.6	2.2	9.2	36	30/28/42	34	67	80
		19	33	3	4	53	52	4.56	4.94	1.48	122	95	4.6	8.8	1.9	12.2	40	46/20/35	29	78	64
Tillman, Chris	R	18*	30	1	0	51	20	10.56	10.12	2.46	166	139	6.1	3.6	0.6	5.4	43	42/25/33	40	57	-48
Triggs, Andrew	R	18	29	3	0	41	43	5.23	4.18	1.33	100	101	3.9	9.4	2.4	10.0	41	47/16/37	29	65	101
Velazquez, Hector	R	18	29	7	0	85	53	3.18	4.62	1.45	112	100	2.8	5.6	2.0	8.4	36	50/22/28	33	80	63
		19*	30	1	1	73	59	5.30	5.14	1.56	108	108	5.0	7.2	1.4	10.3	40	39/22/40	30	69	39
Volstad, Chris	R	18	31	1	0	47	29	6.27	4.61	1.63	144	116	2.3	5.5	2.4	5.4	36	55/18/26	35	65	81
Warren, Adam	R	18	30	3	0	52	52	3.14	4.33	1.32	101	91	3.5	9.1	2.6	11.0	40	38/23/40	31	81	98
		19	31	4	0	29	25	5.34	5.01	1.40	69	148	3.8	7.8	2.1	10.3	42	43/20/37	25	74	66
Watson, Tony	L	18	33	4	0	66	72	2.59	3.22	1.03	79	85	1.9	9.8	5.1	13.7	31	43/23/34	30	77	168
		19	34	2	0	54	41	4.17	4.71	1.26	121	91	2.0	6.8	3.4	13.4	32	44/20/36	30	73	99
Weber, Ryan	R	18*	27	9	1	121	67	3.77	5.35	1.52	73	119	2.1	5.0	2.4	4.1	34	52/19/29	35	77	56
		19*	28	3	0	119	74	6.25	6.62	1.72	129	81	2.8	5.6	2.0	6.4	34	49/23/29	37	65	28

5-Year Injury Log

The following chart details the injured list stints for all players during the past five years. Use this as a supplement to our health grades in the player profile boxes as well as the "Risk Management" charts that start on page 260. It's also where to turn when in May you want to check whether, say, Trevor Cahill's elbow injury should be concerning (answer: Yes, very).

For each injury, the number of days the player missed during the season is listed. A few IL stints are for fewer than 15 days (or fewer than 10 days in 2017, 2018 and 2019); these are cases when a player was placed on the IL prior to Opening Day (only in-season time lost is listed).

Abbreviations:

Lt, L = left
Rt, R = right
fx = fractured
R/C = rotator cuff
str = strained
surg = surgery
TJS = Tommy John surgery (ulnar collateral ligament reconstruction)
x 2 = two occurrences of the same injury
x 3 = three occurrences of the same injury

Throughout the spring and all season long, BaseballHQ.com has comprehensive injury coverage.

FIVE-YEAR INJURY LOG — Hitters

Batter	Yr	Days	Injury
Abreu, Jose	18	20	Surg to repair ABD muscle
Acuna, Ronald	18	32	L knee & ACL strain
Adams, Matt	15	105	Strained R quad
	16	22	L should inflammation
	18	15	Fractured L index finger
	19	18	L shoulder strain
Adduci, James	17	54	Strained R oblique muscle
Adrianza, Ehire	16	109	Fractured L foot
	17	48	R oblique muscle; ab muscle
	18	11	Strained L hamstring
	19	11	Strained ab muscle
Ahmed, Nick	16	72	R hip impingement
	17	95	Fractured R hand
Alberto, Hanser	17	182	Tightness R shoulder
	18	11	R hamstring strain
Alfaro, Jorge	19	8	Concussion
Almonte, Abraham	17	66	Strained R biceps; L hammy
Alonso, Yonder	15	46	Low back strain; bruised R shoulder
Altherr, Aaron	16	117	Repair torn tendon L wrist
	17	43	Strained R hamstring x 2
Altuve, Jose	18	24	R knee discomfort
	19	39	Strained L hamstring
Anderson, Brian	19	38	Fx L finger
Anderson, Tim	19	34	Sprained R ankle
Andrus, Elvis	18	67	Fractured R elbow
	19	11	Strained R hamstring
Andujar, Miguel	19	175	Surg repair torn labrum R shoulder
Arroyo, Christian	18	30	Strained L oblique
	19	109	Strained R forearm
Astudillo, Willians	19	82	Strained R hamstring
Austin, Tyler	17	107	Fx L ankle; strained R ham
Avila, Alex	15	55	Loose bodies L knee
	16	66	Strained R hamstring x 2
	18	11	Strained R hamstring
	19	51	Strained L calf
Bader, Harrison	19	11	Strained R hamstring
Baez, Javier	16	12	Bruised L thumb
Barnes, Austin	19	11	Strained L groin
Barnhart, Tucker	19	32	Strained L oblique
Barrera, Luis	19	22	R shoulder surgery
Bautista, Jose	16	53	Sprnd L knee; L big toe
Beaty, Matt	19	11	Strained L hip flexor
Beckham, Gordon	16	56	Strained L hamstring x2

FIVE-YEAR INJURY LOG — Hitters

Batter	Yr	Days	Injury
Beckham, Tim	15	25	R hamstring strain
	17	10	Sprained L ankle
	18	62	Strained L groin
Bell, Josh	18	12	Strained L oblique
Bellinger, Cody	17	10	Sprained R ankle
Belt, Brandon	17	57	Concussion
	18	35	Appendectomy; hyperexnd R knee
Beltre, Adrian	15	21	Sprained L thumb
	17	68	Tight R calf; L hammy
	18	31	Strained L hamstring
Bemboom, Anthony	19	61	Sprained L knee
Benintendi, Andrew	16	20	Sprnd L knee
Berti, Jon	19	72	Strained L oblique
Betts, Mookie	15	13	Concussion
	18	11	Pulled abdominal muscle
Bird, Gregory	16	183	Rec fr surg.-torn labrum R should
	17	116	Bruised R ankle
	18	59	R ankle surgery
	19	168	Torn plantar fascia L foot
Bishop, Braden	19	89	Lacerated spleen
Blackmon, Charlie	16	15	Turf toe on L foot
	19	12	Strained R calf
Blanco, Gregor	15	9	Concussion
	16	24	R should impingement
Blandino, Alex	18	73	Torn ACL - R knee
Bogaerts, Xander	18	19	Stress fracture L ankle
Bour, Justin	16	62	Sprnd R ankle
	17	55	BruisedL ankle; strained R oblique
	18	11	Strained L oblique
Bourjos, Peter	16	15	Sprnd R should
	17	10	Elbow injury
Bradley, Jackie	17	20	Sprained R knee; L thumb
Brantley, Michael	16	164	R shldr fatigue; rec R shldr surg
	17	61	Sprained R ankle x2
	18	9	Recovery R ankle surgery
Brantly, Rob	15	45	Avulsion fracture, L thumb
Braun, Ryan	17	42	Strained L calf x 2
	18	22	Mid-back tightness
Brinson, Lewis	18	60	L hip inflammation
Brito, Socrates	16	42	Fractured toe R foot
	17	74	Dislocated L ring finger
Bruce, Jay	18	66	Sore R hip
	19	47	Strained R oblique muscle

FIVE-YEAR INJURY LOG — Hitters

Batter	Yr	Days	Injury
Bryant,Kris	18	54	L shoulder inflammation x 2
Buxton,Byron	15	45	Sprained L thumb
	17	17	Strained L groin
	18	57	Fractured great L toe; migraines
	19	73	Concus;L shldr sublux;bruise R wrist
Cabrera,Asdrubal	15	16	Strained R hamstring
	16	17	Strained patella tendon L knee
	17	21	Sprained L thumb x 2
Cabrera,Miguel	15	41	L calf strain
	17	10	Strained R groin
	18	140	R ham. strn; Rup L biceps tendon
Cain,Lorenzo	16	30	Strained L hamstring
	18	13	L groin strain
Calhoun,Kole	18	17	R oblique strain
Calhoun,Willie	19	27	Strained L quadriceps
Camargo,Johan	17	27	Bruised R knee
	18	21	Strained R oblique
	19	18	Fx shin R lower leg
Candelario,Jeimer	18	12	L wrist tendinitis
	19	71	Sprained L thumb; L shldr inflam
Canha,Mark	16	146	Strained back
	19	16	Sprain R wrist
Cano,Robinson	17	12	Stralned R quadriceps
	18	93	Fractured R hand
	19	52	Strained L quadriceps
Caratini,Victor	19	35	Fx hamate bone L hand
Carpenter,Matt	16	29	Strained R oblique muscle
	19	33	Bruised R foot
Casali,Curt	15	40	Strained L hamstring
	19	40	Sprained R knee
Castellanos,Nick	16	51	Fractured L hand
Castillo,Welington	17	24	Tendinitis R should; testicular inj
	18	11	R shoulder inflammation
	19	37	Concussion; strained L oblique
Castro,Jason	15	19	Strained R quad
	17	11	Concussion
	18	149	Torn meniscus - R knee
Castro,Starlin	17	52	Strained R ham x2
Cervelli,Francisco	16	38	Fractured L hand
	17	59	Concuss x2; L wrist inflam; L quad
	18	30	Concussion
	19	90	Concussion
Cespedes,Yoenis	16	15	Strained R quadriceps
	17	79	Strained L ham; strained R ham
	18	136	Strained R hip; heel calcifications
	19	187	Recovery from L and R heel injuries
Chapman,Matt	17	11	L knee cellulitis
	18	18	R hand soreness
Chavis,Michael	19	49	Sprained AC joint L shoulder
Chirinos,Robinson	15	37	L shoulder strain
	16	60	Fractured R forearm
Chisenhall,Lonnie	16	17	R forearm injury
	17	73	Sprnd R shldr; concussion; R calf
	18	150	Strained R calf
	19	187	Fx R index finger
Choi,Ji-Man	19	11	Sprained L ankle
Choo,Shin-Soo	16	124	Strnd R calf/L ham/back; FX L 4arm
Conforto,Michael	17	48	Bruised L hand; Disloc L shoulder
	18	8	Recovery from L shoulder surgery
	19	10	Concussion
Contreras,Willson	17	32	Strained R hamstring
	19	42	Strn R foot; strained R hamstring

FIVE-YEAR INJURY LOG — Hitters

Batter	Yr	Days	Injury
Cooper,Garrett	17	46	L hamstring tendinitis
	18	163	R wrist contusion
	19	42	Strained L calf
Cordero,Franchy	18	140	L abductor strain; bone spur R elb
	19	176	Sprained R elb; stress reax R elbow
Cordoba,Allen	18	95	Concussion
Correa,Carlos	17	47	Torn ligament L thumb
	18	43	Lower back soreness
	19	87	Fx ribs; lower back strain
Cowart,Kaleb	18	13	Sprained L ankle
Cozart,Zack	15	116	R knee surgery
	16	7	Sore R knee
	17	21	Strained R quad; L quad
	18	109	Sprained L ankle
	19	141	Strained neck; L shoulder inflam
Cozens,Dylan	18	16	Strained L quadriceps
Crawford,Brandon	17	12	Strained R groin
Crawford,J.P.	18	91	Strained R elbow
	19	17	Sprained L ankle
Cron,C.J.	16	42	Fractured L hand
	17	15	Bruised L foot
	19	25	R thumb inflammation
Cruz,Nelson	18	12	Sprained R ankle
Cuevas,Noel	19	42	Strained L quadriceps
Culberson,Charlie	15	67	Lumbar disc inflammation
	19	13	Fx R cheekbone
Cuthbert,Cheslor	17	41	Sprained L wrist
	18	136	Lower back strain
Dahl,David	17	108	Stress reaction ribcage
	18	123	Fractured R foot
	19	10	Strained abdominal
d'Arnaud,Travis	15	88	Hyperextended L elbow; fx R hand
	16	56	Strained R rotator cuff
	17	19	Bone bruise R wrist
	18	174	TJS
	19	11	TJS
Davidson,Matthew	16	94	Fractured R foot
	17	18	Bruised R wrist
	18	8	Back spasms
Davis,Chris	17	29	Strained R oblique
	19	10	L hip flexor inflammation
Davis,Jonathan	19	28	Sprained R ankle
Davis,Khris	15	37	Torn meniscus, R knee
	18	9	Strained R groin
	19	11	L hip contusion
Davis,Rajai	17	10	Strained L hamstring
	18	11	Medical condition
Daza,Yonathan	19	28	Strained L shoulder
DeJong,Paul	18	50	Fractured L hand
Delmonico,Nicky	17	11	Sprained R wrist
	18	63	Fractured R hand
Descalso,Daniel	16	40	Fractured L hand
	19	40	Sprained L ankle
DeShields,Delino	15	20	Strained L hamstring
	18	48	Fx R fing; concussion; Fx L hamate
Desmond,Ian	17	72	Fx L hand; strained R calf x 2
Devers,Rafael	18	40	L should. inflam; strained L ham.
Diaz,Aledmys	16	40	Fractured R thumb
	18	25	Sprained L ankle
	19	67	Dizziness; strained L hamstring
Diaz,Elias	16	128	Disc R elbow, cellulitis L knee
	19	25	Viral infection
Diaz,Yandy	19	91	Strained R ham; bruised L foot

FIVE-YEAR INJURY LOG — Hitters

Batter	Yr	Days	Injury
Dickerson,Alex	17	182	Herniated disc
	18	187	TJS
	19	28	Strn R oblique muscle; strn R wrist
Dickerson,Corey	15	98	Non-displaced rib fx; fasciitis L ft x2
	18	8	Strained L hamstring
	19	80	Strained R shoulder; Fx L foot
Dietrich,Derek	16	11	Bruised R knee
	19	20	L shoulder inflammation
Donaldson,Josh	17	42	Strained R calf
	18	125	R shoulder inflam; tight L calf x 2
Dozier,Hunter	17	60	Strained L oblique
	19	22	Bruised chest
Drury,Brandon	18	94	Migraines; fractured L hand
Duda,Lucas	15	16	Lower back strain
	16	117	Stress fracture lower back
	17	21	Hyperextended L elbow
	18	41	Plantar fasciitis - R Foot
	19	49	Strained lumbar spine
Duffy,Matt	16	78	Recovering from surg. on L Achilles
	17	182	Recovery surgery L Achilles
	18	11	Strained R hamstring
	19	118	Tightness L hamstring
Duggar,Steven	18	34	Torn labrum - L shoulder
	19	67	Strn low back;sprn AC joint L shldr
Dyson,Jarrod	16	16	Strained R oblique muscle
	17	13	Strained R groin
	18	89	Strained R groin
Eaton,Adam	17	155	Torn ACL L knee
	18	60	Bone bruise - L ankle
Ellis,A.J.	15	15	R knee inflammation
Ellsbury,Jacoby	15	49	R knee sprain
	17	33	Concussion
	18	187	R oblique strain
	19	187	R plant fasciitis; recovery hip surg
Encarnacion,Edwin	18	11	L biceps inflammation
	19	32	Fx R wrist
Escobar,Alcides	15	7	Concussion & L cheek contusion
Escobar,Eduardo	16	16	Strnd L groin
Estrada,Thairo	19	22	Strained R hamstring
Evans,Phillip	18	61	Fractured L tibia
Farmer,Kyle	19	27	Strained L oblique; concussion
Federowicz,Tim	15	128	Torn meniscus, R knee
Fisher,Derek	18	15	Gastrointestinal discomfort
Flaherty,Ryan	15	30	Strained R groin x2
	17	88	Strained R shoulder
Flores,Wilmer	16	17	Strained L hamstring
	17	12	Infection R knee
	18	19	Lower back soreness
	19	59	Fx R foot
Florimon,Pedro	17	26	Dislocated/sprained R ankle
	18	95	R foot fracture
Flowers,Tyler	16	33	Fractured L hand
	17	10	Bruised L wrist
	18	29	L oblique strain
Forsythe,Logan	16	27	Fractured L scapula
	17	34	Fractured R big toe
	18	31	R shoulder inflammation
Fowler,Dexter	16	32	Strained R hamstring
	17	25	Spur R heel; L forearm
	18	59	Fractured L foot
Fowler,Dustin	17	93	Ruptured patella tendon R knee
Franco,Maikel	15	48	Fractured L wrist

FIVE-YEAR INJURY LOG — Hitters

Batter	Yr	Days	Injury
Franklin,Nick	15	42	Strained L oblique
	16	7	Concussion
	18	146	Strained R quad
Frazier,Adam	17	29	Strained L ham x 2
Frazier,Clint	17	33	Strained L oblique
	18	113	Concussion
	19	12	Sprained L ankle
Frazier,Todd	18	54	Strnd L hammy; strnd L rib cage
	19	26	Strained L oblique
Freeman,Freddie	15	47	Strained R oblique; bruised R wrist
	17	47	Fractured L wrist
Freese,David	15	40	Fractured R index finger
	17	13	Strained R hamstring
	19	56	Strained L hamstring
Gallagher,Cameron	19	25	Strained L oblique
Gallo,Joey	17	7	Concussion
	19	92	Strained L oblique
Garcia,Avisail	16	14	Sprnd R knee
	17	13	Sprained R thumb
	18	72	Strained R hamstring x 2
	19	11	Strained R oblique muscle
Garcia,Leury	17	70	Sprained L finger; R thumb
	18	75	Strn L hamstring x 2; spr. L knee
Garcia,Luis	19	13	Strained lower back
Gardner,Brett	19	12	L knee inflammation
Garver,Mitch	19	19	High ankle sprain L ankle
Gattis,Evan	16	11	Rec fr surg. to repair sports hernia
	17	30	Concussion; R wrist
Gennett,Scooter	15	14	L hand laceration
	16	14	Strained R oblique muscle
	19	93	Strained R groin
Gentry,Craig	16	90	Strained R lumbar spine
	17	10	Fractured R finger
	18	52	Fractured L rib
Goins,Ryan	16	30	Tightness R forearm
Gomes,Yan	15	47	R knee sprain
	16	77	Separated R should
Gomez,Carlos	15	15	R hamstring strain
	16	15	Bruised L rib cage
	17	42	Strained R ham; cyst R shoulder
	18	11	R groin strain
Gonzalez,Carlos	17	11	Strained R shoulder
	18	9	R hamstring strain
Gonzalez,Erik	19	105	Fx L clavicle
Gonzalez,Marwin	19	11	Strained R hamstring
Goodrum,Niko	19	38	Strained L groin
Goodwin,Brian	17	40	Strained L groin
	18	109	L wrist contusion; groin strain
	19	14	Bruised R wrist
Gordon,Alex	15	54	Strained L groin
	16	33	Fractured R wrist
	18	15	L hip labral tear
Gordon,Dee	15	11	Dislocated L thumb
	18	10	Fractured R great toe
	19	41	Strained L quad; bruised R wrist
Gosselin,Phil	15	105	Avulsion fracture, L thumb
Grandal,Yasmani	15	7	Concussion
	16	9	Sore R forearm
Graterol,Juan	19	44	Concussion
Green,Zach	19	24	L hip impingement
Gregorius,Didi	17	26	Strained R shoulder
	18	18	Bruised L heel
	19	72	TJS
Greiner,Grayson	19	70	Strained lower back

FIVE-YEAR INJURY LOG — Hitters

Batter	Yr	Days	Injury
Grichuk,Randal	15	47	R elbow strain
	17	11	Strained lower back
	18	32	R knee sprain
Grossman,Robbie	17	18	Fractured L thumb
	18	14	Strained R hamstring
Gurriel,Lourdes	18	32	Concussion; sprained L knee/ankle
	19	43	Appendectomy; strained L quad
Gurriel,Yulieski	18	11	Recov hamate surgery, L hand
Gutierrez,Kelvin	19	19	Fx toe R foot
Guyer,Brandon	16	23	Strained L hamstring
	17	43	L wrist injury
	18	23	L cervical strain
Guzman,Ronald	18	8	Concussion
	19	32	Strained R hamstring
Gyorko,Jedd	17	16	Strained R hamstring
	18	29	Ham strain; R shoulder impinge
	19	81	Strained back; strained L calf
Hamilton,Billy	16	25	Strained L oblique; concussion
	17	12	Fractured L thumb
Hanigan,Ryan	15	61	Fractured knuckle, R hand
	16	58	L ankle tendinitis; neck strain
	17	16	Strained L groin
Haniger,Mitch	17	66	Strained R oblique; face laceration
	19	116	Ruptured testicle
Hanson,Alen	18	20	L hamstring strain
Harper,Bryce	17	44	Hyperextended L knee
Harrison,Josh	15	46	Torn L thumb ligaments
	16	7	Strained R groin
	17	28	Fractured metacarpal L hand
	18	35	Fractured metacarpal - L hand
	19	91	Strn L ham tendon; L shldr inflam
Haseley,Adam	19	23	Strained L groin
Hays,Austin	18	8	Sprained R ankle
Healy,Ryon	18	18	Sprained R ankle
	19	133	Lower back inflammation
Hechavarria,Adeiny	17	59	Strained IL oblique; L ham
	18	30	Strained R hamstring
Hedges,Austin	17	12	Concussion
Heineman,Scott	19	98	Recovery from surgery L shoulder
Heisey,Chris	17	54	Ruptured R biceps; strained L groin
Hermosillo,Michael	19	187	Abdominal muscle injury
Hernandez,Cesar	15	21	Dislocated L thumb
	17	36	Strained L oblique
Hernandez,Enrique	16	32	L ribcage inflammation
	19	23	Sprained L hand
Hernandez,Gorkys	15	11	L shoulder discomfort
Hernandez,Marco	17	150	L shoulder subluxation
	18	187	Recovery from L shoulder surgery
	19	29	Recovery from L shoulder surgery
Hernandez,Teoscar	17	18	Bruised L knee
Herrera,Dilson	15	26	Fractured R middle finger
Herrera,Odubel	17	17	Strained L hamstring
	19	16	Strained R hamstring
Herrmann,Chris	16	51	Strained R hamstring; fx L wrist
	18	20	R oblique strain
	19	97	R knee surgery
Heyward,Jason	17	24	Sprn R finger; lacerated R hand
	18	28	Concussion; R hamstring tightness
Hicks,Aaron	15	34	Strained L ham; R forearm
	16	15	Strained R hamstring
	17	68	Strained R oblique; L oblique
	18	14	R intercostal muscle strain
	19	105	Strained L lower back
Hicks,John	18	55	Strained R groin

FIVE-YEAR INJURY LOG — Hitters

Batter	Yr	Days	Injury
Hill,Aaron	17	32	Strained R forearm
Hiura,Keston	19	12	Strained L hamstring
Holaday,Bryan	16	26	Bruised L thumb
Holliday,Matt	15	85	Strained R quad x 2
	16	52	Fractured L thumb
	17	42	Viral infection
Holt,Brock	16	42	Concussion
	17	86	Vertigo
	18	12	Strained L hamstring
	19	52	Scratched cornea R eye
Hoskins,Rhys	18	10	Facial injury
Hundley,Nick	15	24	Cervical strain
	16	37	Strained L oblique; concussion
	19	46	Back spasms
Iannetta,Chris	17	7	Concussion
	19	19	Strained R lat muscle
Iglesias,Jose	16	15	Strained L hamstring
	17	7	Concussion
	18	33	Lower abdominal strain
Inciarte,Ender	15	31	Strained R hamstring
	16	26	Strained L hamstring
	19	109	Strn lumbar region; str. R hammy
Jackson,Alex	19	26	Sprained L knee
Jackson,Austin	15	22	Sprained R ankle
	16	115	Torn meniscus L knee
	17	52	Hyperextended L big toe; L quad
Jankowski,Travis	17	102	Bone bruise R foot
	19	117	Fx L wrist
Jay,Jon	15	79	Bone bruise, L wrist + tendon
	16	70	Fractured R forearm
	19	121	Sore L shoulder
Jimenez,Eloy	19	36	Bruise uln nerve R elb;R ankle sprn
Jones,JaCoby	17	15	Lacerated lip
	18	15	R hamstring strain
	19	82	Sprn R shldr; strn back; Fx L wrist
Joseph,Caleb	16	30	Testicular injury
Joyce,Matt	15	35	Concussion
	18	74	Lumbar strain x 2
Judge,Aaron	16	19	Strained R oblique
	18	50	Chip fracture, R wrist
	19	62	Strained L oblique
Kang,Jung Ho	15	14	Torn L meniscus, fx L tibia
	16	49	Sore L should; recov L knee surg.
	19	26	Strained L oblique
Kelly,Carson	18	10	R hamstring strain
Kemp,Matt	17	31	Strained R hamstring x 2
	19	12	Fx L rib
Kendrick,Howie	15	56	Strained L hamstring
	16	9	Strained L calf
	17	62	Strained R Ab; L ham
	18	135	Torn R Achilles
	19	20	Strained L hamstring
Kieboom,Spencer	19	23	R elbow inflammation
Kiermaier,Kevin	16	54	Fractured L hand
	17	70	Fractured R hip
	18	65	Torn ligament R rhumb
	19	11	Sprained L thumb
Kiner-Falefa,Isiah	19	44	Sprained ligament R middle finger
Kingery,Scott	19	30	Strained R hamstring
Kinsler,Ian	17	10	Strained L hamstring
	18	27	L adductor strain; strained L ham.
	19	49	Herniated cervical disc low region

FIVE-YEAR INJURY LOG — Hitters

Batter	Yr	Days	Injury
Kipnis, Jason	15	15	R shoulder inflammation
	17	72	R shoulder inflam; R ham x2
	19	19	Strained R calf
Knapp, Andrew	17	37	Fractured R hand
Kratz, Erik	15	36	Plantar fasciitis, L foot
	19	9	Strained L hamstring
La Stella, Tommy	15	119	Strained R oblique
	16	27	Strained R hamstring
	19	87	Fx tibia L leg
Lagares, Juan	16	66	Torn lig L thumb; sprnd L thumb
	17	66	Strained L oblique; L thumb
	18	137	L toe surgery
Lamb, Jake	15	46	Stress reaction, L foot
	18	113	Sprained L AC joint
	19	83	Strained L quad
Laureano, Ramon	19	38	R lower leg stress reaction
LeMahieu, D.J.	18	40	Strained R ham; L thumb; L oblique
Lin, Tzu-Wei	19	150	Sprained L knee
Lindor, Francisco	19	24	Strained R calf
Longoria, Evan	18	42	Fractured L hand
	19	21	Plantar fasciitis L foot
Lopes, Timmy	19	12	Concussion
Lowe, Brandon	19	83	Bone bruise R shin
Lowrie, Jed	15	93	Torn ligament, R thumb
	16	74	Bunion on L foot; bruised R shin
	19	164	Sprained L knee capsule
Lucroy, Jonathan	15	41	Broken L toe
	19	23	Concussion
Luplow, Jordan	19	28	Strained R hamstring
Mahtook, Mikie	16	46	Fractured L hand
Maile, Luke	17	59	Inflam R knee
	19	53	L oblique strain
Margot, Manuel	17	31	Strained R calf
	18	11	Bruised ribs
Marisnick, Jake	15	16	Strained L hamstring
	17	7	Concussion
	18	22	L groin discomfort
Markakis, Nick	19	49	Fractured L wrist
Marrero, Deven	18	39	Strained L oblique
Marte, Jefry	17	23	Fractured L foot
	18	24	L wrist sprain
Marte, Ketel	16	32	Sprnd L thumb; mono
Marte, Starling	18	9	Strained R oblique
	19	11	Bruised abdominal wall
Martin, Jason	19	28	Dislocated L shoulder
Martin, Leonys	16	14	Strained L hamstring
	18	83	Strnd L ham x2; bacterial infection
Martin, Russell	17	45	Nerve irritation L shldr; L oblique
	19	18	Lower back inflam
Martinez, J.D.	16	48	Fractured R elbow
	17	42	Sprained ligament R foot
Martinez, Jose	17	22	Strained L groin
	19	21	Sprained AC joint R shoulder
Martinez, Victor	15	31	L knee inflammation
	17	47	Irregular heartbeat x2
Martini, Nick	19	62	Sprained R knee
Mathis, Jeff	15	53	Fractured R ring finger
	17	38	Fractured R hand
Mauer, Joe	17	10	strained lower back
	18	27	Concussion
Maybin, Cameron	16	60	Sprnd L thumb; fractured L wrist
	17	27	Strained L oblique; MCL R knee
	19	35	Strained L calf

FIVE-YEAR INJURY LOG — Hitters

Batter	Yr	Days	Injury
Mazara, Nomar	18	28	Sprained R thumb
	19	13	Strained L oblique
McCann, Brian	17	17	Concussion; sore R knee
	18	72	Strained R knee
	19	23	L knee spasm; L ham strain
McCann, James	16	21	Sprnd R ankle
	17	14	Laceration on L hand
McCutchen, Andrew	19	119	Torn ACL L knee
McKinney, Billy	18	55	L AC shoulder sprain
McMahon, Ryan	19	13	Sprained L elbow
McNeil, Jeff	19	29	Strained L ham; Fx R wrist
Meadows, Austin	19	20	Sprained R thumb
Mejia, Francisco	19	41	Strn R oblique muscle; sore L knee
Mercer, Jordy	15	34	Lower leg contusion
	18	14	Strained L calf
	19	73	Strained R quad
Mesoraco, Devin	15	133	L hip strain
	16	154	Torn labrum L should
	17	86	Rec surg R hip;sprn L Shld;Fx R foot
Middlebrooks, Will	16	36	Strained R lower leg
Miller, Brad	17	44	Strained L ab; L groin
	18	12	Groin strain
	19	12	Strained R hip flexor
Molina, Yadier	18	31	Pelvic injury
	19	48	Strained tendon R thumb
Moncada, Yoan	17	11	Bone bruise R shin
	18	10	Tight L hamstring
	19	23	Strained R hamstring
Mondesi, Adalberto	18	33	R shoulder impingement syndrome
	19	61	Strained R groin
Montero, Miguel	15	21	Sprained L thumb
	17	12	Strained groin
Moore, Dylan	19	12	Bruised R wrist
Morales, Kendrys	18	11	Strained R hamstring
	19	110	Strained L calf
Moran, Colin	17	56	Facial fractures
Moreland, Mitch	15	14	L elbow surgery
	19	59	Strained R quad
Morrison, Logan	16	34	Strained R forearm,strained L wrist
	18	63	L hip impingement
Moss, Brandon	16	28	Sprnd L ankle
Motter, Taylor	18	22	Concussion
Moustakas, Mike	16	146	Torn ACL R knee; FX L thumb
Muncy, Max	19	16	Fx R wrist
Munoz, Yairo	18	12	Sprained R wrist
Murphy, Daniel	15	25	Strained L quad
	18	76	Surgery R knee
	19	25	Fractured L index finger
Murphy, Tom	17	74	Fractured R forearm
Myers, Wil	15	104	Bone spurs, L wrist + tend
	18	81	Nerve irrit; bone bruise L Ft; L obliq
Naquin, Tyler	18	101	R hip strain; strained L ham.
	19	53	Torn ACL R knee; strained L calf
Nava, Daniel	15	54	Strained L thumb
	16	51	Strained L groin; tend. L kneecap
Negron, Kris	15	21	Torn labrum Lt shdlr
	19	11	Stiff neck
Newman, Kevin	19	24	Lacerated R middle finger
Nido, Tomas	19	9	Concussion
Nimmo, Brandon	17	64	Strained R ham; collapsed lung
	18	9	Bruised L index finger
	19	132	Stiff neck

FIVE-YEAR INJURY LOG — Hitters

Batter	Yr	Days	Injury
Nunez,Eduardo	15	12	L oblique strain
	17	21	Strained hamstring
	19	17	Strained lower back
Nunez,Renato	18	19	Strained L hamstring
O'Brien,Peter	19	143	Bruised L rib
Odor,Rougned	18	32	Strained L hamstring
	19	14	Sprained R knee
Ohtani,Shohei	18	26	Sprained UCL, R elbow
	19	41	Recovery from TJS
Olson,Matt	19	41	R hand surgery
O'Neill,Tyler	18	22	Inflammation groin area
	19	41	Ulnar nerve subluxation R elbow
Osuna,Jose	19	37	Strained neck
Owings,Christopher	16	42	Plantar fasciitis L foot
	17	62	Fractured R middle finger
Ozuna,Marcell	18	11	R shoulder inflammation
	19	94	Fx middle finger on R hand
Panik,Joe	15	54	Lower back discomfort + inflam
	16	29	Concussion
	17	10	Concussion
	18	59	Sprnd L thumb; L groin strain
Parra,Gerardo	16	53	Sprnd L ankle
	17	30	Strained R quadriceps
Pearce,Steven	15	33	L oblique strain
	16	43	Strnd R ham, strnd flexor R elbow
	17	32	Strained R calf
	18	50	L oblique strain
	19	129	Strained lower back; L calf muscle
Pederson,Joc	16	18	Sprnd AC joint R should
	17	32	Strained R groin; concussion
Pedroia,Dustin	15	67	R hamstring strain x2
	17	45	Sprained L wrist; L knee inflam
	18	180	L knee surgery (meniscus)
	19	178	Recovery from L knee surgery
Pence,Hunter	15	112	L oblique; Fx L forearm; sore L wrist
	16	58	Strained R hamstring
	17	20	Strained L hamstring
	18	44	Sprained R thumb
	19	68	Strained R groin; strained low back
Peralta,David	16	118	R wrist inflam; lower back strain
	19	70	R shoulder AC joint inflammation
Peralta,Jhonny	16	80	Strained + torn ligament L thumb
	17	29	Upper respiratory ailment
Perez,Carlos	18	31	Sprained R ankle
Perez,Michael	18	32	L hamstring strain
	19	34	Strained R oblique
Perez,Roberto	16	78	Fractured R thumb
Perez,Salvador	17	16	Strained R intercostal
	18	27	Sprained R MCL
	19	187	Recovery from TJS
Pham,Tommy	15	63	L quadriceps strain
	16	43	Strained L oblique
	18	14	Fractured R foot
Phegley,Josh	17	44	Concussion; L oblique
	18	24	Fractured R hand
	19	17	L thumb contusion
Pillar,Kevin	16	15	Sprnd L thumb
	18	20	Sprained R shoulder
Pina,Manny	18	22	R calf strain; L biceps strain
	19	17	Strained R hamstring
Pinder,Chad	17	37	Strained L hamstring
	18	20	Hyperext. L knee; L elb laceration
Pirela,Jose	15	32	Concussion
	19	90	Strained L oblique

FIVE-YEAR INJURY LOG — Hitters

Batter	Yr	Days	Injury
Piscotty,Stephen	17	32	Strained R ham; R groin
	19	68	Sprained R knee; R ankle
Plawecki,Kevin	18	46	Hairline fracture - L hand
Polanco,Gregory	17	45	Strained L ham x 3
	18	14	Surgery to stabilize L shoulder
	19	127	L shoulder inflammation
Pollock,A.J.	16	146	Fractured R elbow; strained L groin
	17	50	Strained R groin
	18	49	Fractured L thumb
	19	74	R elbow inflammation
Pompey,Dalton	17	182	Concussion
	19	118	Concussion
Posey,Buster	17	7	Concussion
	18	37	R hip surgery
	19	20	Concussion; strained R hamstring
Powell,Boog	18	117	Sprained R knee
Prado,Martin	15	29	R shoulder sprain
	17	136	Strained R ham x 2; R knee
	18	118	Recovery from R knee surgery
	19	35	Strained R hamstring
Profar,Jurickson	15	183	Recovery from shoulder surgery
Puello,Cesar	15	182	Stress fracture lower back
	19	57	Strained L hip flexor
Puig,Yasiel	15	79	Strained R hamstring
	16	18	Strained L hamstring
	18	31	L hip pointer; strained R oblique
Pujols,Albert	18	44	L knee surgery
Quinn,Roman	19	181	Strn R groin; Strn R oblique muscle
Ramirez,Hanley	15	30	R shoulder inflammation
Ramirez,Jose	19	31	Fx hamate bone R hand
Ramos,Wilson	17	85	Surg R knee to repair torn ACL
	18	29	Strained L hamstring
Rasmus,Colby	16	23	Ear infection
	17	51	Recov surgery on hip; hip tend
	18	76	L hip flexor strain
Realmuto,Jacob	18	20	Lower back bruise
Reddick,Josh	15	8	Strained R oblique
	16	39	Fractured L thumb
	17	7	Concussion
	18	15	Leg infection
Reed,Michael	18	30	Strained lower back
Rendon,Anthony	15	89	Strained L quad; Sprain L knee
	18	13	L toe contusion
	19	11	Bruised L elbow
Renfroe,Hunter	17	10	Strained neck
	18	38	R elbow inflammation
Rengifo,Luis	19	13	Fx hamate bone L hand
Reyes,Jose	15	27	Cracked L rib
	16	14	Strained L intercostal
	17	10	Strained L oblique
Reynolds,Mark	16	19	Recovering from L wrist surg.
Rickard,Joey	16	73	R thumb ligament injury
	17	19	Sprnd L pinky fing & middle fing
Riddle,J.T.	17	68	L biceps tendinitis
	18	36	Recovery from L shoulder surgery
	19	75	Strained R forearm
Riley,Austin	19	33	Torn LCL R knee
Rivera,Rene	18	88	R knee inflammation
Rivera,T.J.	17	65	Partially torn UCL R elbow
	18	187	TJS
Rizzo,Anthony	18	9	Lower back tightness
Robertson,Daniel	17	35	Neck spasms
	18	71	Sprnd L thumb; strnd L hamstring
	19	39	Recov R knee surgery (meniscus)

FIVE-YEAR INJURY LOG — Hitters

Batter	Yr	Days	Injury
Robinson, Drew	18	16	Sore L hip
Robinson, Shane	16	48	Strained R hip flexor; R ankle
Rodgers, Brendan	19	98	R shoulder impingement
Rodriguez, Sean	17	106	Recovery from L shoulder surgery
	18	42	Strained R quad; strained L abdom
	19	15	Strained R abdominal muscle
Rojas, Miguel	17	70	Fractured R thumb
	19	26	Strained R hamstring
Rosario, Eddie	16	1	Fractured L thumb
	19	19	Sprained L ankle
Rua, Ryan	15	69	Sprained R ankle
	18	45	Back spasms
Russell, Addison	17	44	Strained R foot
	18	11	Sprained L middle finger
	19	8	Concussion
Rutledge, Josh	16	108	Patellar tendinitis L knee
	17	127	Strained L ham: concussion
Saladino, Tyler	17	48	Back spasms
	18	37	Sprained L ankle
Sanchez, Gary	17	27	Strained R biceps
	18	65	R groin strain
	19	32	Strained L groin
Sanchez, Hector	15	27	Strained L hamstring
	17	57	Concussion; bruised R foot
Sandoval, Pablo	16	173	Strained L should
	17	59	Sprained R knee; ear infection
	18	63	R hamstring strain
	19	50	R elbow inflammation
Sano, Miguel	16	30	Strained L hamstring
	17	39	Stress reaction L shin
	18	24	Strained L hamstring
	19	49	Laceration on R heel
Santana, Daniel	16	69	Sprnd AC joint L should; strain ham.
	17	54	Bacterial infection; strained L quad
Santana, Domingo	16	85	Sore R elbow; sore R should
	19	30	Inflammation R elbow
Santander, Anthony	17	136	R elbow inflammation
Sardinas, Luis	18	67	Lower back strain
Schebler, Scott	17	17	Strained L shoulder
	18	51	R ulnar nerve bruise; sprn R A/C
Schoop, Jonathan	15	78	R knee sprain
	18	25	R oblique strain
Schwarber, Kyle	16	178	Torn ligaments L knee
Seager, Corey	18	154	UCL strain - R elbow
	19	29	Strained L hamstring
Seager, Kyle	19	58	Recovery from surgery L hand
Segura, Jean	15	15	Fractured R pinky finger
	17	33	Strained R ham; high R ankle sprain
	19	11	Strained L hamstring
Semien, Marcus	17	81	Bruised R wrist
Shaw, Travis	19	21	Strained R wrist
Shuck, J.B.	15	15	Strained L hamstring
Simmons, Andrelton	16	36	Torn ligament L thumb
	18	11	Grade 2 R ankle sprain
	19	60	Sprained L ankle
Slater, Austin	17	59	Strained R groin
Smith Jr., Dwight	19	38	Concussion; strained L calf
Smith, Dominic	19	62	Stress reaction L foot
Smith, Kevan	16	26	Back inj (sacroiliac joint dysfunct)
	18	24	Sprained L ankle
	19	55	Concuss; sprn L hand; back spasms
Smith, Mallex	16	87	Fractured L thumb
	17	13	Strained R hamstring
	18	10	Viral infection

FIVE-YEAR INJURY LOG — Hitters

Batter	Yr	Days	Injury
Smoak, Justin	19	11	Strained L quadriceps
Smolinski, Jake	17	153	Recovery surgery R shoulder
	18	58	R arm nerve irritation
Sogard, Eric	16	183	Cervical strain
	17	16	Strained L ankle
Solano, Jhonatan	18	175	Bone spurs R elbow
Solarte, Yangervis	16	41	Strained R hamstring
	17	37	Strained L oblique muscle
	18	29	Strained R oblique
Soler, Jorge	15	56	L oblique; Sprain L ankle
	16	59	Strained L hamstring
	17	34	Strained L oblique
	18	107	Fractured L toe
Soto, Geovany	16	121	L knee inf; R knee inf.; torn menisc
	17	154	R elbow inflam
Soto, Juan	19	11	Back spasms
Souza, Steven	15	54	Fractured L hand; cut finger
	16	28	Brsd/strnd L hip, recov surg. L hip
	18	81	Strained R pectoral muscle
	19	186	Recovery from torn ACL, PCL & LCL
Spangenberg, Cory	15	45	L knee contusion
	16	166	Strained L quadriceps
Springer, George	15	70	Fx R wrist; concussion
	17	12	L quadriceps injury
	18	12	Sprained L thumb
	19	31	Strained L hamstring
Stanton, Giancarlo	15	100	L wrist hamate fracture
	16	23	Strained L groin
	19	164	Sprained PCL R knee
Starling, Bubba	17	36	Strained R oblique
	18	30	Sprained R UCL
Stassi, Max	16	37	Surg. to repair fractured L wrist
	17	10	L hand inflammation
	19	27	Sore L knee
Stevenson, Andrew	19	16	Back spasms
Stewart, Christin	19	45	Concussion; strained R quad
Stewart, D.J.	19	50	Concussion; sprained R ankle
Story, Trevor	16	62	Torn ligament L thumb
	17	12	Strained L shoulder
	19	13	Sprained R thumb
Stubbs, Drew	16	79	Sprnd L little toe
Suarez, Eugenio	18	18	Fractured R thumb
Sucre, Jesus	16	127	Fractured fibula leg
Susac, Andrew	15	58	Sprained R wrist
	17	28	strained trap x 2
Swanson, Dansby	18	16	L wrist inflammation
	19	34	Bruised R heel
Swihart, Blake	15	17	Sprained L foot
	16	120	Sprnd L ankle
	18	12	Strained R hamstring
	19	68	Strained R oblique
Tapia, Raimel	19	11	Bruised L hand
Tatis Jr., Fernando	19	86	Strn L ham; stress reax low back
Tauchman, Mike	19	22	Strained L calf
Taylor, Chris	15	14	Fractured R wrist
	19	37	Fx L forearm
Taylor, Michael	17	37	Strained R oblique muscle
	19	12	Sprained L knee
Tejada, Ruben	16	16	strnd L quadriceps
Thames, Eric	18	58	Strained R hamstring
Thomas, Lane	19	34	Fx R wrist
Tilson, Charlie	16	61	Torn L hamstring
	17	182	Stress reaction R foot
Tocci, Carlos	18	41	Bruised L hip

FIVE-YEAR INJURY LOG — Hitters

Batter	Yr	Days	Injury
Toles,Andrew	17	144	Torn ACL R knee
Tomas,Yasmany	17	117	R groin tendinitis
Tomlinson,Kelby	16	31	Sprnd L thumb
Torres,Gleyber	18	22	Strained R hip
Travis,Devon	15	101	L shoulder strain; inflam
	16	52	Recovering from surg. on L should
	17	117	Bone bruise R knee
	19	187	Recov meniscus surgery L knee
Trout,Mike	17	46	Torn ligament L thumb
	18	15	R wrist inflammation
Trumbo,Mark	17	10	Strained ribcage
	18	77	Strained R quad muscle
	19	160	Recovery R knee surgery 2018
Tulowitzki,Troy	16	21	Strained R quadriceps
	17	98	Strained R ham; sprained R ankle
	18	187	R heel bone spurs
	19	180	Strained L calf
Turner,Justin	15	13	R thigh skin infection
	17	21	Strained R hamstring
	18	59	Recover fr fx L wrist; groin strain
Turner,Trea	17	71	Strained R ham; fractured R wrist
	19	45	Fx R index finger
Upton,Justin	18	10	L index finger laceration
	19	82	Turf toe L foot
Urshela,Giovanny	18	37	Strained R hamstring
	19	11	Tightness L groin
Utley,Chase	15	44	R ankle inflammation
	18	55	Sprained L thumb; L wrist inflam.
Valbuena,Luis	16	66	Strained R hamstring
	17	31	Strained R hamstring
Van Slyke,Scott	15	15	L mid-back inflammation
	16	107	R wrist injury; lower back strain
Vazquez,Christian	15	189	R elbow sprain
	16	12	Recovering from TJS
	18	56	R fifth finger fx
Verdugo,Alex	19	56	Strained R oblique muscle
Villanueva,Christian	16	183	Fractured fibula R leg
	18	40	Fractured R middle finger
Villar,Jonathan	17	17	Strained lower back
	18	19	Sprained R thumb
Vogt,Stephen	17	31	Sprained L knee
	18	187	R shoulder strain
Voit,Luke	19	45	Strained ab muscle; sports hernia
Votto,Joey	18	14	R lower leg contusion
	19	13	Lower back strain
Wade,LaMonte	19	57	Dislocated R thumb
Walker,Christian	18	3	Sinus bone fracture
Walker,Neil	16	27	Herniated disk lower back
	17	44	Strained L hamstring
	19	12	Sprained R index finger
Wallach,Chad	19	132	Concussion
Wendle,Joe	17	28	Strained R shoulder
	19	98	Strained L hamstring; Fx L wrist
White,Tyler	19	49	Strained R trapezius muscle
Wieters,Matt	15	61	Recovery from R elbow surgery
	18	70	Strained L oblique; strained L ham
Wilkerson,Steve	18	50	L oblique strain
Williams,Justin	19	187	Fx second metacarpal R hand
Williams,Mason	15	106	R shoulder inflammation
	16	106	Recovering from surg. on R should
Williamson,Mac	16	36	Strnd L should; strained R quad
	17	22	Strained L quadriceps
	18	28	Concussion
Wilson,Bobby	18	36	Sprained R ankle

FIVE-YEAR INJURY LOG — Hitters

Batter	Yr	Days	Injury
Winker,Jesse	17	19	Strained L hip flexor
	18	68	R shoulder subluxation
	19	43	Strained cervical spine
Wolters,Tony	16	12	Concussion
	17	13	Concussion
Wong,Kolten	17	37	Strained L elbow; R triceps
	18	21	L knee inflammation
Wynns,Austin	19	21	Strained L oblique
Yelich,Christian	15	33	Rt knee contusion; low back strain
	18	10	Strained R oblique
Young,Chris	16	76	Strained R hamstring; R forearm
	18	90	Strained L hamstring
Zagunis,Mark	18	28	R shoulder inflammation
Zimmer,Bradley	18	18	L rib contusion
	19	156	Recovery from surgery (July 2018)
Zimmerman,Ryan	15	47	Plantar fasciitis, L foot
	16	33	Bruised L wrist; strained L ribcage
	18	71	Strained R oblique
	19	106	Plantar fasciitis R foot
Zobrist,Ben	15	30	Medial meniscus tear, L knee
	17	15	L wrist inflammation
	18	8	Back tightness
Zunino,Mike	18	39	Strained L oblique
	19	22	Strained L quadriceps

FIVE-YEAR INJURY LOG — Pitchers

Pitchers	Yr	Days	Injury
Adams, Austin	19	60	Strained R shoulder
Adleman, Timothy	16	74	Strnd L oblique
Albers, Matt	15	84	Broken finger, R hand
	18	63	R shoulder strain
Alcantara, Sandy	18	35	R axillary/armpit infection
Alcantara, Victor	19	23	Wisdom tooth; bruise R mid fing
Alexander, Scott	17	29	Strained R hamstring
	19	115	L forearm inflam
Allen, Cody	19	12	Strained lower back
Almonte, Miguel	17	40	R rotator cuff inflam
Altavilla, Dan	18	95	R AC joint inflam; R UCL sprain
	19	58	Strained R forearm
Alvarado, Jose	19	75	Strained R oblique muscle
Alvarez, Dario	17	10	Strained L elbow
Alvarez, Henderson	15	169	R shoulder inflammation x2
	16	184	Rec fr surg. on R should
Anderson, Brett	16	163	Rec fr back surg. - bulging disc
	17	80	Strained lower back
	18	68	Strained L shoulder
Anderson, Chase	15	19	R triceps inflammation
	17	52	Strained L oblique muscle
	18	9	Food poisoning
	19	17	Lacerated R middle finger
Anderson, Cody	15	18	L oblique strain
	17	182	Surg on R elbow
	18	187	TJS
	19	81	Surgery flexor tendon R arm
Anderson, Justin	19	30	Strained trap upper R back
Anderson, Shaun	19	17	Blister on R middle finger
Anderson, Tyler	16	36	Strnd R oblique muscle
	17	99	L knee inflammation x2
	19	148	Recovery from L knee surgery
Andriese, Matt	17	87	Strnd groin; stress reaction R hip
	19	23	L foot contusion
Arano, Victor	18	18	Strained R rotator cuff
	19	165	R elbow inflammation
Araujo, Pedro	18	113	Sprained UCL - R elbow
Archer, Chris	18	35	L abdominal strain
	19	60	R thumb inflammation
Armstrong, Shawn	19	27	Strained R forearm
Arrieta, Jake	19	48	Bone spur R elbow
Avilan, Luis	17	15	L triceps soreness
	19	60	Sore L elbow
Axford, John	17	45	Strained R shoulder
	18	35	Fractured R fibula
Baez, Pedro	15	43	R pectoral strain
	17	12	Bruised R wrist
	18	42	R biceps tendinitis
Bailey, Homer	15	174	Torn UCL, R elbow; TJS surg
	16	116	Rec fr TJS
	17	86	Bone spurs R elbow
	18	53	R knee inflammation
Banda, Anthony	19	180	TJS
Banuelos, Manny	15	35	L elbow inflammation
	16	51	Rec fr surg. L elbow spur
	19	86	Strained L shoulder
Barbato, Johnny	18	43	Strained R forearm
Bard, Luke	19	12	Bruised R triceps
Barnes, Danny	17	10	R shoulder impingement
	18	41	L knee tendinitis
Barnes, Jacob	16	37	Sore R elbow
Barnes, Matt	17	10	Strained lower back

FIVE-YEAR INJURY LOG — Pitchers

Pitchers	Yr	Days	Injury
Barnette, Tony	17	16	Sprained R ring finger
	18	115	Low back strain; R shldr inflam
	19	88	R shoulder inflammation
Barraclough, Kyle	17	20	R shoulder impingement
	18	15	Lower back stiffness
	19	25	R radial nerve irritation
Barrett, Aaron	15	86	R elbow sprain; R biceps
	16	183	Rec fr TJS
Barrett, Jake	17	41	Stiffness R shoulder
	19	131	R elbow inflammation
Bass, Anthony	18	34	Viral illness; R mid-thoracic strain
Bassitt, Chris	16	157	Torn ligament R elbow
	17	115	Recovery from TJS
	19	19	R lower leg contusion
Bauer, Trevor	18	39	Stress fracture, R fibula
Baumann, Buddy	16	89	Strnd lower back
	17	112	Strained L shoulder
Bautista, Gerson	19	70	Strained R pectoral muscle
Beato, Pedro	17	18	Strained L hamstring
Bedrosian, Cam	16	55	Flexor tendinitis R finger
	17	56	Strained R groin
	19	33	Strained R forearm
Belisle, Matt	15	74	R elbow inflammation
	16	48	Strnd R calf
	18	26	R knee chondromalacia
Benoit, Joaquin	16	22	R should inflammation
	17	20	Sprained FT knee; L knee Inflam
	18	187	Strained R forearm
Bergen, Travis	19	81	Strained L shoulder
Bergman, Christian	15	32	R shoulder fatigue
	16	50	Strnd L oblique
Betances, Dellin	19	184	R shldr impinge; torn Achilles ten
Bettis, Chad	15	36	R elbow inflammation
	17	131	Testicular cancer
	18	36	R middle finger blister
	19	48	L hip impingement
Biagini, Joe	18	11	Strained L oblique
Biddle, Jesse	16	183	Rec fr TJS
	19	96	L shoulder fatigue
Black, Ray	16	30	Bone spur R elbow
Blackburn, Clayton	18	187	TJS
Blackburn, Paul	17	37	Bruised R forearm
	18	157	Strained R forearm
Blazek, Michael	15	52	Fractured R hand
	16	36	Strnd R forearm; R elbow imping
Bleier, Richard	18	109	Torn upper lat; L shoulder surg
	19	36	L shoulder tendinitis
Blevins, Jerry	15	167	Fractured L forearm
Borucki, Ryan	19	182	Surg remove bone spur R elbow
Boshers, Jeffrey	16	22	L elbow inflammation
Bowman, Matthew	18	45	Blisters pitching hand
Boxberger, Brad	16	116	Strnd L oblique; recov. core surg.
	17	89	Strained R flexor
Boyer, Blaine	15	12	R elbow inflammation
	17	26	Strained R elbow; strained neck
	18	75	R lower back strain
Bracho, Silvino	19	186	Recovery from TJS
Bradford, Chasen	19	135	R shoulder inflam; strn R forearm
Bradley, Archie	15	98	R shoulder tend; facial bruise
Brault, Steven	19	32	Strained L shoulder
Brennan, Brandon	19	73	Inflammation R shoulder
Brewer, Colten	18	37	Strained L oblique

FIVE-YEAR INJURY LOG — Pitchers

Pitchers	Yr	Days	Injury
Brice,Austin	17	59	Ulnar neuritis R elb; R lat strain
	18	11	Mid-back strain
	19	79	Gastroenteritis
Britton,Zach	17	76	Strained L forearm x2
	18	75	Ruptured R Achilles
Brooks,Aaron	16	183	Bruised hip
Buchter,Ryan	18	60	Strained L shoulder
Buehler,Walker	18	32	R rib microfracture
Bumgarner,Madison	17	85	Bruised ribs, sprained L shoulder
	18	69	Fractured L hand
Bundy,Dylan	15	11	Strained R shoulder
	18	11	L ankle sprain
	19	11	R knee tendinitis
Burdi,Nick	18	157	TJS
	19	161	Sore R elbow
Burnes,Corbin	19	17	R shoulder irritation
Burr,Ryan	19	141	R shldr AC joint inflam; str R elbow
Bush,Matt	17	21	Sprained MCL R knee
	18	109	Strained R elbow
Butler,Eddie	18	96	R groin strain
Cabrera,Mauricio	17	35	Strained R elbow
Cahill,Trevor	16	32	Patellar tendinitis R knee
	17	85	Strn back; R shldr; R Shldr impinge
	18	37	R elbow impingement
	19	21	R elbow inflammation
Caminero,Arquimedes	16	17	Strnd L quadriceps
Canning,Griffin	19	55	Inflammation R elbow
Capps,Carter	15	63	R elbow strain
	16	183	Rec fr TJS
	17	92	Recovery from TJS; blood clots
	18	78	Recovery from TJS
Carle,Shane	18	25	R shoulder inflammation
Carpenter,Ryan	18	56	Strained R oblique
Carrasco,Carlos	15	13	R shoulder inflammation
	16	38	Strnd L hamstring
	18	20	R elbow contusion
	19	89	Leukemia
Cashner,Andrew	16	37	Strnd R hamstring; str neck
	17	25	Tendinitis R biceps; L oblique
	18	21	Lower back strain; strained neck
Casilla,Santiago	18	14	R shoulder strain
Castillo,Diego	19	19	R shoulder inflam/impingement
Castillo,Jose	18	22	R hamstring strain
	19	187	Torn L finger tendon
Castro,Miguel	16	26	R should inflammation
Cecil,Brett	16	46	Strnd L triceps
	18	62	Strained L shoulder; R foot inflam
	19	186	Carpal tunnel syndrome L hand
Cedeno,Xavier	17	153	Tightness L forearm
	19	177	L wrist inflammation
Cessa,Luis	17	47	Ribcage injury
	18	64	L oblique strain
Chacin,Jhoulys	19	84	Strained lower back; oblique
Chafin,Andrew	16	62	L should tendinitis
Chapman,Aroldis	17	35	L rotator cuff injury
	18	29	L knee tendinitis
Chargois,J.T.	17	26	R elbow surg
	18	35	Nerve irritation neck
Chatwood,Tyler	16	33	Tightness upper back x 2
	17	10	Strained R calf
	18	12	L hip tightness
Chavez,Jesse	15	19	Fractured rib
	19	49	Strained R groin

FIVE-YEAR INJURY LOG — Pitchers

Pitchers	Yr	Days	Injury
Chen,Wei-Yin	16	57	Sprnd L elbow
	17	122	L arm fatigue
	18	31	Inflamed L elbow
Chirinos,Yonny	18	35	R forearm strain
	19	48	R middle finger inflammation
Cingrani,Tony	15	37	Strained L shoulder
	17	47	Strained R oblique
	18	114	Strained rotator cuff L shoulder
	19	187	L shoulder impingement
Cishek,Steve	16	15	Torn labrum L hip
	19	10	L hip inflammation
Clarke,Taylor	19	17	Lower L back inflammation
Claudio,Alexander	16	148	R should stiffness
	18	7	Sprained L ankle
Clevinger,Mike	19	81	Strn R upper back; sprained R ankle
Cobb,Alex	15	183	R forearm tendinitis; TJS
	16	149	Rec fr TJS
	17	15	Turf toe R big toe
	19	176	Strn R groin; R hip impinge surg
Cole,A.J.	18	13	L neck strain
	19	52	R shoulder impingement
Cole,Gerrit	16	66	R elbow inflam; R triceps strain
Cole,Taylor	17	10	Fractured R toe
	19	12	Strained R shoulder
Coleman,Louis	16	29	R should fatigue
Collins,Tim	15	183	L elbow surg
	16	183	Rec fr TJS
Colome,Alex	15	34	Pneumonia
	16	16	R biceps tendinitis
Colon,Bartolo	17	22	Strained L oblique
	18	9	Lower back strain
Conley,Adam	16	43	L middle finger tendinitis
Cook,Ryan	16	183	Strnd back muscle
Corbin,Patrick	15	91	Recovery from L elbow surg
Cotton,Jharel	17	24	Blister on R thumb
	18	187	Recovery from TJS
	19	187	Recovery from TJS
Covey,Dylan	17	80	Strained L oblique
	19	53	Inflammation R shoulder
Crick,Kyle	19	30	Tight R triceps; surg R index fing
Cruz,Rhiner	18	86	R groin strain
Cueto,Johnny	17	48	Blisters on R hand
	18	133	Spr R ankle; R elbow inflam x 3; TJS
	19	167	TJS
Darvish,Yu	15	183	R elbow surg
	16	88	Rec fr TJS; R should strain
	17	10	Lower back tightness
	18	138	Viral infection; R triceps tendinitis
Davies,Zach	18	106	R rotator cuff inflammation
	19	57	Back spasms
Davis,Austin	18	17	Lower back tightness
Davis,Rookie	17	14	Bruised R forearm
	18	152	Recovery - R hip surg
	19	66	Blister on R middle finger
Davis,Wade	16	48	Strnd flexor R forearm
	19	17	Strained L oblique
Dayton,Grant	17	90	Strained L intercostal; stiff neck x 2
	18	187	TJS
	19	67	Fractured R big toe
De La Rosa,Jorge	15	15	Strained L groin
	16	27	Strnd L groin
	18	13	R Achilles bursitis
De Leon,Jose	18	187	TJS
	19	98	TJS

FIVE-YEAR INJURY LOG — Pitchers

Pitchers	Yr	Days	Injury
deGrom,Jacob	18	8	Hyperextended R elbow
	19	11	Sore R elbow
Delgado,Randall	15	68	Sprained R ankle
	17	77	R elbow inflammation
	18	100	Strained L oblique
DeSclafani,Anthony	16	68	Strnd oblique muscle
	17	182	Sprained UCL R elbow
	18	69	L oblique strain
Despaigne,Odrisamer	17	10	Strained L oblique muscle
	18	32	R forearm strain
Devenski,Chris	18	27	L hamstring tightness
Diaz,Jairo	16	183	Rec fr TJS
	17	48	Recovery surg R elbow
Diaz,Jose	17	17	R arm fatigue
Diaz,Miguel	17	67	Strained R forearm
	19	162	Recov R knee surgery (meniscus)
Diekman,Jake	16	16	Lacerated L index finger
	17	156	Colitis
Dominguez,Seranthon	19	117	Torn UCL R elbow
Doolittle,Sean	15	136	L shoulder strain; torn rotator cuff
	16	64	Strnd L should
	17	38	Strained L shoulder
	18	60	L toe inflammation
	19	15	Tendonitis R knee
Dowdy,Kyle	19	55	R elbow impingement
Duensing,Brian	15	15	R intercostal strain
	16	75	Surg. on L elbow
	17	12	Lower back spasms
	18	46	L shoulder fatigue x 2
Duffy,Danny	15	30	L biceps tendinitis
	17	57	Strained L oblique; L elbow imping
	18	11	L shoulder impingement
	19	59	L shoulder impinge; strn L ham
Duke,Zach	17	114	Surg on L elbow
	19	12	Strained R calf
Dull,Ryan	17	68	Strained R knee
	18	17	Strained R shoulder
Dunn,Michael	16	58	Strnd L forearm
	17	10	Back spasms
	18	107	L shoulder surg; L rhomboid strain
	19	8	Strained L groin
Duplantier,Jon	19	38	R shoulder inflammation
Dyson,Sam	17	11	Bruised R hand
	19	10	R biceps tendinitis
Edgin,Josh	16	37	Rec fr TJS
Edwards,C.J.	18	38	R shoulder fatigue
	19	89	Strained R shoulder
Eflin,Zach	16	55	Patellar tendinopathy both knees
	17	50	Rec surg pat tend both knees; R shldr
	18	9	Blister - R middle finger
	19	11	Tightness lower back
Eickhoff,Jerad	17	50	Strnd upper back; nerve irrit R hand
	18	159	R lat strain
	19	106	R biceps tendinitis
Elias,Roenis	17	138	R intercostal injury
	18	20	Strained L triceps
	19	27	Strained R hamstring
Eovaldi,Nathan	16	52	R elbow tendon injury
	17	183	Rec. Tommy John surg
	18	63	Loose bodies R elbow
	19	92	R elbow surg remove loose bodies
Erlin,Robbie	16	165	Strnd L elbow
	17	182	TJS L elbow
Estevez,Carlos	18	109	Strained L oblique

FIVE-YEAR INJURY LOG — Pitchers

Pitchers	Yr	Days	Injury
Estrada,Marco	16	24	Back strain
	18	18	Strained L glute
	19	126	Lumbar strain
Familia,Jeurys	17	106	Blood clot R shoulder
	18	10	Sore R shoulder
	19	27	Bennett lesion R shoulder
Faria,Jake	17	26	Strained L abdominal
	18	71	Strained L oblique
Farquhar,Danny	18	164	Brain aneurysm
Farrell,Luke	19	150	Fractured jaw
Fedde,Erick	17	27	Strained flexor R forearm
	18	62	R shoulder inflammation
Feliz,Michael	17	38	R shoulder injury
	18	14	R shoulder inflammation
Feliz,Neftali	15	38	Axillary abscess on R side
	17	13	Ulnar nerve palsy R arm
Ferguson,Caleb	19	19	Strained L oblique
Fernandez,Julian	18	187	TJS
	19	187	Recovery from TJS
Ferrell,Riley	19	187	Biceps tendinitis
Fields,Josh	17	10	Strained lower back
	18	64	R shoulder inflammation
Fiers,Michael	18	11	R lumbar strain
Finnegan,Brandon	17	168	Strained L trapezius; torn R labrum
	18	17	Strained L biceps
Fister,Doug	15	34	R forearm tightness
	18	130	Strained R hip; R knee strain
Floro,Dylan	19	25	Neck inflam; strn L intercostal lig
Flynn,Brian	17	123	Strained L groin
	19	59	Sprained UCL pitching elbow
Foltynewicz,Mike	15	13	Costochondritis
	16	26	Sore R elbow
	18	10	R triceps tightness
	19	31	Bone spur R elbow
Font,Wilmer	18	94	R lat strain
Freeland,Kyle	17	10	Strained L groin
	19	40	Blister L middle finger
Freeman,Sam	18	21	L shoulder inflammation
Fried,Max	18	43	Blister L index finger; L groin strain
	19	12	Blister on L index finger
Fry,Jace	19	11	Sore L shoulder
Fulmer,Carson	19	30	Strained R hamstring
Fulmer,Michael	17	11	Ulnar neuritis R elbow
	18	47	Strn L oblique; torn meniscs R knee
	19	187	Recovery from TJS
Gallardo,Yovani	16	56	R biceps tendinitis
Gant,John	16	54	Strnd L oblique
	17	47	Strained R groin
Garcia,Jaime	15	75	L groin strain; recov L shldr surg
	18	32	L shoulder fatigue
Garcia,Jarlin	17	10	Strained L biceps
	18	12	R ankle contusion
Garcia,Luis	18	36	Strained R wrist
Garcia,Yimi	16	163	Sore R biceps
	18	49	R forearm inflammation
Gardewine,Nick	18	38	R forearm strain
Garrett,Amir	17	10	R hip inflammation
	18	13	Strained L Achilles
	19	17	Strained lat L shoulder
Gausman,Kevin	15	43	R shoulder tendinitis
	16	22	R should tendinitis
	19	50	R foot plant fasc;tendinitis R shldr
Gearrin,Cory	16	43	Strnd R should
German,Domingo	19	26	Strained L hip flexor

FIVE-YEAR INJURY LOG — Pitchers

Pitchers	Yr	Days	Injury
Gibson,Kyle	16	45	Sore/strnd R should
	19	10	Ulcerative colitis
Giles,Ken	19	9	Inflammation R elbow
Giolito,Lucas	19	32	Strn L hammy; strn R muscle
Glasnow,Tyler	16	35	Sore R should
	19	121	Strained R forearm
Glover,Koda	17	128	L hip imping; lower back strain
	18	116	Tendinitis - R shoulder
	19	187	Flexor mass strain R forearm
Goeddel,Erik	15	81	Strained R elbow
	18	57	R lat inflammation
Gohara,Luiz	18	49	Spr L ankle; L shoulder soreness
Gomez,Jeanmar	17	16	R elbow impingement
Gonzales,Marco	18	16	Cervical neck muscle strain
Gonzalez,Chi Chi	17	182	TJS July 2017
Gonzalez,Gio	19	50	L arm fatigue
Gonzalez,Miguel	15	45	R shoulder tend; R groin strain
	16	25	Strnd R groin
	17	26	A/C joint inflamR shoulder
	18	162	R/C inflammation - R shoulder
Gonzalez,Rayan	18	187	TJS
Goody,Nick	18	152	R elbow inflammation
Gossett,Daniel	18	119	TJS
	19	187	Recovery from TJS
Gott,Trevor	19	47	Strained R elbow
Grace,Matt	18	46	Strained L groin
Graveman,Kendall	15	100	Strained L oblique
	17	76	Strained R shoulder x2
	18	31	TJS
	19	187	Recovery from TJS
Graves,Brett	18	79	Strained L oblique
Gray,Jon	16	20	Strnd abdominal muscle
	17	77	Stress fracture L foot
	19	41	Fractured L foot
Gray,Sonny	16	55	Strnd R forearm; R trap.
	17	30	Strained lat muscle R shoulder
Green,Chad	16	26	Strnd tendon R forearm
Greene,Shane	16	37	Blister on R middle finger
	18	12	R shoulder strain
Gregerson,Luke	16	17	Strnd L oblique
	18	142	R shldr impinge x 2; torn meniscs
	19	38	R shoulder impingement
Greinke,Zack	16	37	Strnd L oblique
Griffin,A.J.	15	172	R shoulder strain
	16	48	R should stiffness
	17	81	Gout L ankle; L intercoastal
Grimm,Justin	15	26	R forearm inflammation
	17	14	Infection R index finger
	18	61	Back stiffness; R shoulder impinge
Grosser,Alec	16	58	Back strain
Gsellman,Robert	17	48	Strained L hamstring
	19	48	Strained R tightness
Guerra,Javy	15	16	R shoulder inflammation
Guerra,Junior	16	25	R elbow inflammation
	17	63	Strained R calf; bruised R shin
	18	11	R forearm tightness
Guerrero,Tayron	18	27	Strained L lumbar spine
	19	44	Blister R middle finger
Guerrieri,Taylor	17	26	Strained R elbow
Gustave,Jandel	17	164	Tightness R forearm
	18	187	TJS

FIVE-YEAR INJURY LOG — Pitchers

Pitchers	Yr	Days	Injury
Hahn,Jesse	15	86	R forearm strain
	16	27	Strnd R should
	17	10	Strained R triceps
	18	187	Sprained R UCL
	19	160	Recovery from TJS
Hale,David	15	61	Groin strain
	19	60	Strained lumbar spine
Haley,Justin	17	71	R biceps tendinitis; R shoulder
Hamels,Cole	17	54	Strained R oblique
	19	35	Strained L oblique
Hamilton,Ian	19	8	R shoulder inflammation
Hancock,Justin	18	98	R shoulder inflammation
Hanhold,Eric	18	7	Strnd L oblique; R shoulder inflam
Happ,J.A.	17	42	L elbow inflammation
	18	8	Viral infection
Hardy,Blaine	16	16	L should impingement
	18	15	L elbow tendinitis
	19	73	Strained L flexor tendon
Harris,Will	17	41	R shoulder inflam x2
Harvey,Matt	16	90	Thoracic outlet synd, R should
	17	79	Stress fracture R scapula
	19	50	Upper back strain
Hatcher,Chris	15	58	L oblique strain
	16	75	Strnd L oblique
	17	51	R shoulder inflammation
Heaney,Andrew	16	180	Strnd L flexor
	17	130	Recovery surg UCL L elbow
	18	16	L elbow inflammation
	19	83	L elbow inflam; L shoulder inflam
Hearn,Taylor	19	158	Tightness L elbow
Heller,Ben	18	183	Bone spurs - R elbow
	19	167	TJS
Hellickson,Jeremy	15	22	Strained L hamstring
	18	52	Spr R wrist; strained R hamstring
	19	104	R shoulder strain
Helsley,Ryan	19	21	R shoulder impingement
Hembree,Heath	15	37	R shoulder soreness
	19	74	Strained R elbow extensor
Hendricks,Kyle	17	46	R hand tendinitis
	19	17	R shoulder inflammation
Hendriks,Liam	16	40	Strnd R triceps
	18	53	R groin strain
Hernandez,David	15	64	Recovery from R elbow surg
	18	30	R shoulder inflammation
	19	13	R shoulder fatigue
Hernandez,Elieser	18	55	Finger blister; dental surg
Hernandez,Felix	16	49	Strnd R calf
	17	98	R shoulder bursitis; R biceps tend
	18	12	Lower back stiffness
	19	105	Strained R shoulder
Herrera,Kelvin	18	50	Strnd E R/C joint; ligamnt surg L foot
	19	25	Strained R oblique muscle
Herrera,Ronald	18	187	R labrum inflammation
Hicks,Jordan	19	98	Torn UCL R elbow
Hill,Rich	16	58	Blister L finger; L groin
	17	39	Blister L middle finger x 2
	18	52	Blisters L hand x 2
	19	117	Strn L forearm; sprained L knee
Hinojosa,Dalier	16	64	Bruised R hand
Hirano,Yoshihisa	19	23	R elbow inflammation
Holder,Jonathan	19	52	R shoulder inflammation
Holland,Derek	15	130	Subscapular strain R shoulder
	16	62	L should inflammation
	19	22	Bruise L wrist; bruise L index fing

FIVE-YEAR INJURY LOG — Pitchers

Pitchers	Yr	Days	Injury
Holland,Greg	15	18	R pectoral strain
	18	25	R hip impingement
Holmes,Clay	19	31	R triceps inflammation
Honeywell,Brent	18	187	TJS
Hoover,J.J.	17	23	R shoulder inflammation
House,T.J.	15	20	L shoulder inflammation
Hoyt,James	18	10	Strained L oblique
Hudson,Daniel	18	49	R forearm tightness
Hughes,Jared	16	27	Strnd L lat back
Hughes,Phil	15	32	Lower back inflammation
	16	115	L knee injury
	17	112	R biceps tendon inflam; TOS surg
	18	40	Strnd L oblique; R rhomboid strain
Hunter,Tommy	16	39	Back strain; core muscle surg.
	17	32	Strained R calf
	18	25	Strained R hamstring
	19	172	R forearm surgery
Iglesias,Raisel	15	36	Strained L oblique
	16	51	R should impingement
	18	8	Strained L biceps
Jackson,Edwin	16	31	Strnd R triceps
	19	27	Lower back strain
Jackson,Luke	16	10	Stress reaction lower back
	17	13	Strained R shoulder
James,Josh	19	41	Inflammation R shoulder
Jansen,Kenley	15	40	L foot surg
	18	11	Irregular heartbeat
Jeffress,Jeremy	17	12	strained lower back
	19	57	R shoulder inflammation
Jennings,Dan	15	24	Neck inflammation
Jewell,Jake	18	96	Fractured R fibula
Johnson,Brian	17	21	L shoulder impingement
	18	8	L hip inflammation
	19	108	L elbow inflam; undisclosed issue
Johnson,Jim	16	24	Strnd R groin
	18	38	Lumbar strain
Jones,Nate	15	131	Recovery from R elbow surg
	17	150	R elbow neuritis
	18	90	Strained pronator muscle - R arm
	19	157	Recovery from surgery R shoulder
Jones,Zach	16	80	Sore R should
	18	30	Sore R shoulder
Junis,Jake	18	14	Lower back inflammation
Kahnle,Tommy	18	39	R shoulder tendinitis
Karns,Nate	16	65	Strnd lower back
	17	130	Nerve Irritation R elbow
	18	187	R elbow inflammation
	19	175	Strained R forearm
Kela,Keone	16	85	R elbow impingement
	17	60	Sore R shoulder x2
	19	79	Shoulder and elbow inflammation
Kelley,Shawn	15	14	Strained L calf
	17	72	Str low back;R Trap;bone chip R elb
	18	14	Ulnar nerve irritation, R arm
	19	33	Bacterial infection
Kelly,Joe	15	8	R biceps tightness
	16	32	R should impingement
	17	21	Strained L hamstring
Kennedy,Brett	19	187	Strained R shoulder
Kennedy,Ian	15	15	Strained L hamstring
	17	16	Strained R hamstring
	18	68	Strained L oblique

FIVE-YEAR INJURY LOG — Pitchers

Pitchers	Yr	Days	Injury
Kershaw,Clayton	16	47	Herniated disc lower back
	17	39	Strained lower back
	18	49	L biceps tendinitis; low back strain
	19	19	L shoulder inflammation
Keuchel,Dallas	17	61	Pinched nerve neck; strained neck
Kimbrel,Craig	16	23	Torn meniscus L knee
	19	30	R knee inflam; R elbow inflam
Kintzler,Brandon	15	75	L knee tendinitis
	18	16	Flexor muscle strain - R arm
	19	10	R pectoral muscle inflammation
Kluber,Corey	17	29	strained lower back
	19	151	Fractured ulna R forearm
Knebel,Corey	16	67	Strnd L oblique
	18	34	L hamstring strain
	19	187	Recovery from TJS
Koehler,Tom	17	28	R shoulder bursitis
	18	187	Strained anterior cuff - R shoulder
Kontos,George	16	28	Strnd flexor R elbow
	17	16	Strained R groin
Kopech,Michael	18	24	TJS
	19	187	Recovery from TJS
Krol,Ian	17	28	Strained L oblique muscle
Kuhl,Chad	18	95	Strained R forearm
	19	187	TJS
Lamb,John	16	30	Rec fr back surg.
	18	97	L elbow surg
Lamet,Dinelson	18	187	Recovery from TJS
	19	99	Recovery from TJS
Lauer,Eric	18	32	L forearm strain
Law,Derek	16	17	Strnd R elbow
Leake,Mike	15	15	Strained L hamstring
	16	9	Shingles
LeBlanc,Wade	17	14	Strained L quadriceps
	19	35	Strained R oblique
Leclerc,Jose	17	25	Bruised R index finger
Leiter,Mark	18	49	Strained R forearm
Leone,Dominic	18	114	R upper arm nerve irritation
Lester,Jon	17	15	L shoulder fatigue
	19	17	Strained L hamstring
Lewicki,Artie	18	48	TJS
Liberatore,Adam	16	16	L elbow inflammation
	17	137	Strnd L groin; L forearm tightness
Lincecum,Tim	15	95	R forearm contusion
	18	69	blister pitching hand
Lindblom,Josh	17	35	L side injury
Lindgren,Jacob	18	187	TJS
Liriano,Francisco	17	22	L shoulder Inflammation
	18	25	Strained R hamstring
Lively,Ben	18	14	Strained lower back
Loaisiga,Jonathan	19	93	Strained R shoulder
Logan,Boone	15	18	L elbow inflammation
	16	19	L should inflammation
	17	72	Strained lat muscle
	18	43	Strained L triceps
Lopez,Pablo	18	31	R shoulder strain
	19	69	Strained R shoulder
Lopez,Reynaldo	17	13	Strained back
Lorenzen,Michael	16	80	Sprnd UCL R elbow
	18	56	R shoulder strain
Loup,Aaron	16	55	Sore L elbow
	18	34	Strained L forearm
	19	176	Strained L elbow
Lucas,Josh	19	19	Inflammation/strain R shoulder
Lucchesi,Joey	18	37	R hip strain

FIVE-YEAR INJURY LOG — Pitchers

Pitchers	Yr	Days	Injury
Luciano,Elvis	19	92	Sprained R elbow
Luebke,Cory	15	183	Strained L elbow
	16	31	Tightness R hamstring
Lugo,Seth	17	82	Part torn UCL R elb; R shldr imping
	19	12	R shoulder tendinitis
Lyles,Jordan	15	126	Sprained L big toe
	18	36	R elbow inflammation
	19	29	Strained L ham; strained L oblique
Lynn,Lance	15	13	Strained R forearm
	16	183	Rec fr TJS
Lyons,Tyler	16	62	Stress reaction R knee
	17	42	Rec surg R knee; R intercostal
	18	52	Mid-back strain; sprained L elbow
Maddox,Austin	18	187	R shoulder strain
Madson,Ryan	17	15	Sprained R finger
	18	26	Strnd R pec; lumbar nerve irrit
Maeda,Kenta	17	14	Hamstring tightness
	18	15	R hip strain
	19	10	Bruised L adductor muscle
Magill,Matt	19	30	R shoulder tendinitis
Mahle,Tyler	19	32	Strained L hamstring
Manaea,Sean	16	15	Strnd pronator L forearm
	17	15	Strained L shoulder
	18	37	L shoulder impingement
	19	158	R shoulder surgery rehab
Marinez,Jhan	18	29	Strained R hamstring
Marquez,German	19	39	R arm inflammation
Marshall,Evan	15	27	Fractured skull
	17	88	Strained R hamstring
	18	50	R elbow inflammation
Martes,Francis	19	45	recovery from TJS
Martin,Chris	15	22	R elbow tendinitis
	18	54	R forearm irrit;str R calf;str L groin
Martinez,Carlos	15	9	R shoulder strain
	18	59	R lat strain; R oblique strain
	19	51	Strained R shoulder cuff
Maton,Phil	18	40	R lat strain
Matz,Steven	15	53	Partially torn L lat muscle
	16	42	Tightness L should
	17	109	L elbow inflam; Ulnar nerve irrit
	18	14	L flexor pronator strain
	19	10	Sore L elbow
Maurer,Brandon	15	55	R shoulder inflammation
May,Trevor	16	75	Strnd lower back x 2
	17	182	TJS R elbow
	18	71	TJS
Mayers,Mike	18	17	R shoulder inflammation
	19	99	Strained lat R shoulder
Mayza,Tim	19	26	Ulnar neuritis L 4arm; TJS
McAllister,Zach	16	22	R hip injury
McCarthy,Brandon	15	161	Torn UCL,R elbow
	16	173	Rec fr TJS
	17	79	Sore L shld;R knee tend;blst R hand
	18	96	R knee tendinitis
McCullers,Lance	16	103	Sore R elbow; R should
	17	49	Sore lower back x2
	18	51	R elbow discomfort
	19	187	Recovery from TJS
McFarland,T.J.	16	57	L knee inflammation
	17	11	Bruised L ankle
	18	12	L neck strain
	19	34	Inflammation L shoulder

FIVE-YEAR INJURY LOG — Pitchers

Pitchers	Yr	Days	Injury
McGee,Jake	15	86	Torn L knee menisc; rec R elb surg
	16	21	L knee inflammation
	17	10	Strained mid-back
	19	46	Sprained L knee
McHugh,Collin	17	114	Hypertrophy R arm
	19	66	R elbow pain
Means,John	19	26	Strained L biceps; strained L shldr
Medlen,Kris	15	112	Recovery from R elbow surg
	16	144	R rotator cuff inflammation
Mejia,Adalberto	17	36	Brachialis strain L arm
	18	53	Strained L wrist
	19	62	Strained R calf
Melancon,Mark	17	56	R elbow tendinitis x 2
	18	65	R elbow flexor strain
Mella,Keury	18	28	L oblique strain
Mendez,Yohander	19	152	Sprained UCL R elbow
Mengden,Daniel	17	48	Fractured R foot
	18	18	L shoulder impingement
Merritt,Ryan	18	107	Sprained L knee x 2
Meyer,Alex	17	77	Back spasms; R shoulder inflam
	18	187	Recovery from R shoulder surg
Middleton,Keynan	18	151	R elbow inflammation
	19	153	Recovery from TJS
Miley,Wade	16	12	Inflammation L should
	17	10	Medical
	18	101	Strained R oblique x 2
Miller,Andrew	15	27	L flexor forearm muscle strain
	17	39	Patella tendinitis R knee x2
	18	99	L shldr; R knee inflam x2; str L ham
Miller,Justin	16	59	Strnd L oblique
	19	88	Low back strain; strn AC R shldr
Miller,Shelby	16	24	Sprnd R index finger
	17	160	R elbow inflammation
	18	169	Recovery from TJS - R elbow
Milner,Hoby	19	20	Bruised cervical nerve
Milone,Tommy	15	13	Strained L elbow
	16	28	L biceps tendinitis
	17	87	Sprained L knee
	18	14	L shoulder soreness
Minaya,Juan	17	24	Strained R Ab
Minor,Mike	15	185	L rotator cuff inflammation
	16	183	Rec fr surg. on L should
Minter,A.J.	19	26	L shoulder inflammation x2
Mitchell,Bryan	15	10	Concussion,nasal fracture
	16	143	Surg. to repair fractured L big toe
	18	74	R elbow impingement
Montas,Frankie	16	113	Rec fr rib re-section surg.
Montero,Rafael	15	158	R rotator cuff inflammation
	18	187	TJS
Montgomery,Jordan	18	151	TJS
	19	172	TJS
Montgomery,Mike	18	14	L shoulder inflammation
	19	33	Inflammation L shoulder
Moore,Matt	15	88	Recovery from L elbow surg
	18	12	R knee soreness
	19	178	Recovery meniscus surgery R knee
Morejon,Adrian	19	55	L shoulder impingement
Morgan,Adam	18	11	Back strain
	19	85	Strained L forearm
Morin,Michael	15	38	L oblique strain
	17	36	Stiff neck
Moronta,Reyes	19	27	Torn labrum R shoulder

FIVE-YEAR INJURY LOG — Pitchers

Pitchers	Yr	Days	Injury
Morrow,Brandon	15	153	R shoulder inflammation
	18	83	R biceps inflam; low back tightness
	19	187	Debride surg R elbow (Nov. 2018)
Morton,Charlie	15	51	Hip injury
	16	162	Strnd L hamstring
	17	40	Strained R lat muscle
	18	11	R shoulder discomfort
Moscot,Jon	16	38	Strnd R intercostal; L should inflam
Moya,Gabriel	19	28	L shoulder tendinitis
Moylan,Peter	18	76	Strained R forearm
Mujica,Edward	15	28	Fractured R thumb
Mujica,Jose	18	29	R forearm strain
Musgrave,Harrison	18	11	R hip flexor strain
	19	75	Strained flexor L elbow
Musgrove,Joe	17	13	R shoulder injury
	18	62	Strnd R shldr; infected R index fing
Nelson,Jimmy	15	13	Head contusion
	17	17	strained rotator cuff R shoulder
	18	187	Recovery from R rotator cuff surg
	19	126	Labrum surg R shldr; effusion R elb
Neshek,Pat	18	94	R shoulder strain
	19	126	Strn R shdlr; strained L hamstring
Neverauskas,Dovydas	19	20	Strained L oblique
Newberry,Jake	19	19	R shoulder inflammation
Newcomb,Sean	19	7	Concussion
Nicasio,Juan	15	11	L abdominal strain
	18	71	R knee effusion
	19	45	Strn L groin; tendinitis R/C R shldr
Nicolino,Justin	17	18	Bruised L index finger
Nix,Jacob	19	187	Strained R elbow
Nola,Aaron	16	61	Strnd R elbow
	17	27	Strained lower back
Nolasco,Ricky	15	144	R ankle impinge.; R elbow inflam
Norris,Bud	15	20	Bronchitis
	16	15	Strnd mid-back
	17	21	R knee inflam x2
Norris,Daniel	15	27	R oblique strain
	16	52	Strnd R oblique muscle; lower back
	17	57	Strained L groin
	18	125	L groin strain
Nova,Ivan	15	81	Recovery from R elbow surg
	18	14	Sprained R ring finger
Nuno,Vidal	18	60	Strained R hamstring
Oaks,Trevor	19	187	Surgery R hip (labrum)
Oberg,Scott	16	42	Axillary artery thrombosis R arm
	18	18	Back strain
	19	45	Blood clot R arm
O'Day,Darren	16	87	Strnd R rotator cuff; R hamstring
	17	14	Strained R shoulder
	18	129	Hyperext R elbow; str L hamstring
	19	162	Strained R forearm
Odorizzi,Jake	15	32	Strained L oblique
	17	30	Strained L ham; lower back
	19	11	Blister R index finger
O'Flaherty,Eric	15	31	L shoulder strain
	16	78	L elbow neuritis; strnd R knee
	17	53	Strnd low back; L rotatr cuff tend
O'Grady,Chris	17	42	Strained R oblique
	18	166	Sprained L shoulder
Oh,Seung-Hwan	19	46	Strained L abdominal
Ohtani,Shohei	18	26	Sprained UCL, R elbow
Olson,Tyler	15	24	R knee contusion
	18	25	Strained L lat muscle
	19	60	Shingles

FIVE-YEAR INJURY LOG — Pitchers

Pitchers	Yr	Days	Injury
O'Rourke,Ryan	17	182	Strained L elbow/forearm
Osich,Josh	16	35	Strnd L forearm
	18	14	Strained R hip
Osuna,Roberto	17	10	Cervical spasms
Otero,Dan	19	94	R shoulder inflammation
Ottavino,Adam	15	161	R triceps inflammation
	16	138	Rec fr TJS
	17	10	R shoulder inflammation
	18	18	L oblique strain
Paulino,David	17	44	R arm inflam; bone spurs R elbow
Paxton,James	15	107	Strained tendon L middle finger
	16	16	Bruised L elbow
	17	61	Strained L forearm; L pec muscle
	18	36	Low back inflam; L forearm bruise
	19	26	L knee inflammation
Peacock,Brad	15	184	L intercostal strain; rec R hip surg
	19	78	Sore R shoulder
Pena,Felix	19	58	Torn ACL R knee
Peralta,Freddy	19	17	Sore AC joint R shoulder
Peralta,Wandy	19	28	Strained R hip flexor
Peralta,Wily	15	63	Strained L oblique
	17	32	Strained R calf
Perdomo,Luis	17	12	R shoulder inflammation
	18	38	R shoulder strain
Perez,Martin	15	109	Recovery from L elbow surg
	17	10	Fractured R thumb
	18	84	R elbow discomfort
Petricka,Jacob	15	15	Strained R forearm
	16	151	R hip impingement
	17	115	Strained R lat; R elbow x2
Phelps,David	15	49	Stress fracture,R forearm
	16	33	Strnd L oblique
	17	54	R elbow imping x2
	18	187	TJS
	19	82	Recovery from TJS
Pineda,Michael	15	27	Strained R forearm
	17	79	Torn UCL R elbow
	18	187	TJS
	19	25	R knee tendinitis; strn R triceps
Pomeranz,Drew	15	14	Sprained L AC joint
	17	12	Strained flexor L forearm
	18	73	L forearm strain; L biceps tendinitis
	19	11	Strained L Lat
Poppen,Sean	19	30	R elbow contusion
Porcello,Rick	15	24	Strained R triceps
Poyner,Bobby	18	11	Strained L hamstring
Pressly,Ryan	15	91	R lat strain
	19	41	Sore R knee
Price,David	17	106	Strained L elbow; L elbow inflam
	19	46	TFCC cyst L wrist; L elb tendinitis
Ramirez,Erasmo	18	129	R shldr/lat strn; R teres major strn
Ramirez,J.C.	17	41	Strained R forearm
	18	177	R elbow surg
	19	125	Recovery from TJS
Ramirez,Jose	18	167	R shoulder inflammation
Ramirez,Neil	15	113	L ab soreness; R shoulder inflam
	18	11	Lower back spasms
Ramirez,Noe	19	19	Viral infection
Ramirez,Yefry	19	11	Strained R calf
Ramos,A.J.	16	16	Fractured R middle finger
	18	127	R shoulder surg
Ramos,Edubray	18	33	R shldr imping; R pat tend; fing blst
	19	94	Stiff R shldr; R shldr impingement

FIVE-YEAR INJURY LOG — Pitchers

Pitchers	Yr	Days	Injury
Ravin,Josh	15	34	L hernia
	16	140	Fx L forearm; R triceps strain
	17	47	Strained R groin
	18	19	Viral infection
Ray,Robbie	17	26	Concussion
	18	59	Strained R oblique
	19	10	Lower R back spasms
Rea,Colin	16	63	R elbow injury
	18	85	TJS
Reed,Addison	18	20	R triceps tightness
	19	50	Sprained L thumb
Reed,Cody	16	18	Back spasms
Reyes,Alex	17	182	Surg on R elbow
	18	187	Recovery from TJS; back surg
Rhame,Jacob	19	58	Ulnar nerve transp surg R elb
Richard,Clayton	16	24	Blister on L middle finger
	18	35	L knee inflammation
	19	104	Stress reaction R knee
Richards,Garrett	15	15	Recovery from L knee surg
	16	150	Torn UCL R elbow
	17	151	Strained R biceps
	18	103	Strained L hamstring; TJS
	19	1/3	Recovery from TJS
Robertson,David	19	169	Strained R shoulder
Robles,Hansel	18	29	Sprained R knee
Rodgers,Brady	17	29	TJS
	18	107	TJS
Rodon,Carlos	16	22	Sprnd L wrist
	17	95	Bursitis L biceps; L shoulder inflam
	18	73	Surg on L shoulder
	19	152	L elbow inflammation
Rodriguez,Dereck	18	8	Strained R hamstring
Rodriguez,Eduardo	16	59	Dislocated R kneecap
	17	45	R knee subluxation
	18	90	Recov fr R knee surg.; spr. R ankle
Rodriguez,Jefry	19	98	Strained R shoulder
Rodriguez,Ricardo	18	62	R biceps tendinitis
Rodriguez,Richard	18	11	R shoulder discomfort
	19	11	R shoulder inflammation
Roe,Chaz	15	22	R shoulder injury
	17	85	Strained R lat muscle
	18	38	R groin strain
	19	9	Strained R flexor
Rogers,Josh	19	96	Sprained L elbow
Romero,Enny	16	15	Strnd back
	17	28	Strained L forearm
	18	65	L shoulder impingement
Romo,Sergio	16	81	Strnd flexor tendon R elbow
	17	10	Sprained L ankle
Rondon,Bruce	15	71	R biceps tendinitis
Rondon,Hector	18	18	Strnd R triceps
Rosenthal,Trevor	16	51	R rotator cuff inflammation
	17	56	Strained R lat; R elbow irritation
	19	44	Viral infection
Ross,Joe	16	77	R should inflammation
	17	79	TJS
	18	160	TJS
Ross,Robbie	17	132	Flu; L elbow inflam
Ross,Tyson	16	178	R should inflammation
	17	94	Rec surg TOS; blister index finger
	19	142	Ulnar neuritis R elbow
Rosscup,Zachary	15	58	L shoulder inflammation
	16	183	L should inflammation
	18	131	Blister L middle finger; L calf strain

FIVE-YEAR INJURY LOG — Pitchers

Pitchers	Yr	Days	Injury
Rucinski,Drew	18	33	R groin strain
Rumbelow,Nick	16	31	Rec fr TJS
Rusin,Chris	16	43	Strnd L should
	17	10	Strained R oblique muscle
	18	27	R intercostal strn; L plant fasciitis
	19	65	Strained lower back
Ryu,Hyun-Jin	15	183	L shoulder inflammation
	16	171	L elbow tendinitis; L should surg.
	17	30	Bruised L hip; bruised L foot
	18	105	L groin strain
	19	23	Strained L groin; neck stiffness
Sabathia,C.C.	15	16	R knee inflammation
	16	15	Strnd L groin
	17	29	Strained L ham; R knee inflam
	18	25	R knee inflammation; R hip strain
	19	56	R knee inflam; rec heart procedure
Sadler,Casey	15	34	R elbow discomfort
Sadzeck,Connor	19	119	R elbow inflammation
Salazar,Danny	16	15	R elbow inflammation
	17	60	Sore R shoulder; R elbow inflam
	18	187	R shldr surg, bursa repair/cleanup
	19	186	Rec surg R shoulder; strn R groin
Sale,Chris	15	7	Fractured R foot
	18	38	Inflamed L shoulder x 2
	19	44	L elbow inflammation
Samardzija,Jeff	18	141	Strnd R pec muscle; R shldr tight
Sampson,Adrian	16	101	Strnd R flexor mass
	19	14	Lower back spasms
Sanchez,Aaron	15	40	R lat strain
	17	146	Laceration/blister R middle fing x2
	18	64	R index finger contusion
	19	41	Stained R pectoral muscle
Sanchez,Anibal	15	46	R rotator cuff inflammation
	17	14	Strained L hamstring
	18	42	R hamstring strain
	19	13	Strained L hamstring
Santana,Dennis	18	116	Strained R rotator cuff
Santana,Edgar	19	187	TJS
Santana,Ervin	16	16	Strnd lower back
	18	163	Surg on R middle finger
Santiago,Hector	17	107	Strained L shoulder
Saupold,Warwick	16	46	Strnd R groin
Sborz,Josh	19	11	Sore lower back
Scahill,Rob	15	67	R forearm tightness
Scheppers,Tanner	15	29	L knee inflam; R ankle sprain
	16	159	Torn cartilage L knee
	17	13	Sore L abdominal muscle
Scherzer,Max	17	10	Neck inflammation
	19	42	Inflamed bursa sac back/shoulder
Schugel,A.J.	18	150	R shoulder discomfort
Senzatela,Antonio	18	24	Finger blister; R shoulder inflam
	19	19	Infected blister on R heel
Severino,Luis	16	16	Strnd R triceps
	19	174	Inflammation R/C R shoulder
Shackelford,Kevin	18	27	R forearm strain
Shaw,Bryan	18	18	R calf strain
Sherriff,Ryan	18	27	R big toe fracture
Shields,James	17	58	Strained R lat muscle
Shipley,Braden	18	11	R elbow inflammation
Shoemaker,Matt	16	28	Fractured skull,hematoma
	17	106	Strained R forearm
	18	154	R forearm strain
	19	163	Torn ACL L knee
Shreve,Chasen	16	24	Sprnd AC joint L should

FIVE-YEAR INJURY LOG — Pitchers

Pitchers	Yr	Days	Injury
Simmons,Shae	16	128	Rec fr TJS
	17	154	Strained flexor R forearm
Sipp,Tony	17	32	Sore L calf
	18	9	Strained R oblique
	19	14	Strained L oblique
Skoglund,Eric	18	102	Sprained L UCL
Slegers,Aaron	18	75	R shoulder inflammation
Smith,Burch	15	180	R elbow surg
Smith,Caleb	17	15	Viral infection
	18	99	L lat surg
	19	30	L hip inflammation
Smith,Carson	16	167	Tommy John surg.
	17	157	Recovery from TJS
	18	140	Surg R should repaired dislocation
Smith,Drew	19	187	TJS
Smith,Joe	16	39	Strnd L hamstring
	17	33	R shoulder inflammation
	18	24	R elbow soreness
	19	107	Recovery surgery L Achilles
Smith,Will	16	60	Torn LCL R knee
	17	182	Surg on L elbow
	18	34	TJS
	19	11	Concussion
Smoker,Josh	17	36	Strained L shoulder
Smyly,Drew	15	118	L shoulder soreness x2
	17	182	Strained flexor L arm
	18	187	Recovery from L elbow surg
	19	16	Tightness L arm
Snell,Blake	18	13	L shoulder fatigue
	19	69	Fx R big toe; loose bodies L elbow
Sobotka,Chad	19	27	Strained L ab muscle
Solis,Sammy	15	20	L shoulder inflammation
	16	59	L should inflam; sore R knee
	17	73	L elbow inflammation
Soria,Joakim	17	29	Strained L oblique
	18	15	R thigh strain
Soroka,Michael	18	130	R shoulder strain
Sparkman,Glenn	17	88	Fractured R thumb
Springs,Jeffrey	19	77	L biceps tendinitis
Stammen,Craig	15	173	Torn R flexor tendon
Stanek,Ryne	19	17	Bruised R hip
Steckenrider,Drew	19	147	R elbow inflammation
Stephens,Jackson	18	37	Torn lateral meniscus, R knee
Stephenson,Robert	17	10	Bruised R shoulder
	18	33	R shoulder tendinitis
	19	17	Strained cervical spine
Stewart,Brock	17	66	R shoulder tendinitis
	18	30	R oblique strain
Stock,Robert	19	77	Inflammation R biceps
Strahm,Matthew	17	92	Torn patellar tendon L knee
	18	40	Torn L patellar tendon
	19	9	Strained L rib ligament
Straily,Dan	18	33	R forearm inflammation
Strasburg,Stephen	15	58	L oblique; neck strain
	16	33	Sore R elbow; strnd upper back
	17	23	R elbow nerve impingement
	18	71	R shoulder inflammation
Stratton,Chris	17	10	Dislocated/sprained R ankle
	19	45	Inflammation R ribcage

FIVE-YEAR INJURY LOG — Pitchers

Pitchers	Yr	Days	Injury
Strickland,Hunter	18	61	Fractured R hand
	19	121	Strained R lat muscle
Stripling,Ross	18	35	Low back inflam; R big toe inflam.
	19	39	R biceps tendinitis
Stroman,Marcus	15	159	Torn ACL,L knee
	18	60	R shldr fatigue; fing blisters
Strop,Pedro	16	43	Torn meniscus L knee
	19	36	Strn L hamstring; neck tightness
Stumpf,Daniel	18	34	L ulnar nerve irritation
	19	15	Strained L elbow
Suter,Brent	17	19	strained L rotator cuff
	18	80	Torn UCL - TJS
	19	158	Recovery from TJS
Swarzak,Anthony	16	26	Strnd R rotator cuff
	18	100	Strained L oblique; R shldr inflam
	19	20	R shoulder inflammation
Syndergaard,Noah	17	145	Torn R lat muscle
	18	57	Strained R index finger; viral infect
	19	15	Strained R hamstring
Taillon,Jameson	16	15	R should fatigue
	17	37	Ttesticular cancer
	19	150	Strained flexor R elbow
Tanaka,Masahiro	15	35	Strained R forearm
	17	10	R shoulder inflam
	18	32	Strained R and L hamstrings
Tarpley,Stephen	19	33	L shoulder impingement
Taylor,Ben	17	35	Strained L intercostal muscle
Tazawa,Junichi	16	18	R should impingement
	17	36	Rib cage inflammation
Teheran,Julio	16	17	Strnd R lat muscle
	18	12	R thumb contusion
Tepera,Ryan	18	16	R elbow inflammation
	19	126	R elbow inflammation
Thornburg,Tyler	17	182	R shoulder impingement
	18	98	recovery from R shoulder surg
	19	49	R hip impingement
Thornton,Matt	16	50	Tendinitis L Achilles
Thornton,Trent	19	11	Inflammation R elbow
Tillman,Chris	16	18	Bursitis R should
	17	35	Bursitis R shoulder
	18	71	Lower back strain
Tomlin,Josh	15	117	R shoulder surg
	17	32	Strained L hamstring
	18	45	Strained R hamstring
Treinen,Blake	19	12	Strained R shoulder
Triggs,Andrew	16	14	Bruised L shin
	17	113	Strained L hip
	18	137	Blood clot, L calf
Tropeano,Nicholas	16	96	Torn lig R elbow; strnd R should
	17	182	Surg on R elbow to repair UCL
	18	105	R shoulder inflammation
	19	63	Strained R shoulder
Tuivailala,Sam	18	77	L knee strain; strained R Achilles
	19	110	Surgery on R Achilles
Turley,Nik	18	96	Sprained L elbow
Turnbull,Spencer	19	34	Strn upper back; R shoulder fatigue
Turner,Jacob	15	183	Strained flexor tendon,R elbow
Urena,Jose	15	28	L knee contusion
	18	13	R shoulder impingement
	19	86	Strained L lower back
Urias,Julio	18	150	Recovery from L shoulder surg
Valdez,Cesar	17	54	R shoulder impingement
Valdez,Jose	18	133	R elbow inflammation

FIVE-YEAR INJURY LOG — Pitchers

Pitchers	Yr	Days	Injury
Vargas,Jason	15	131	Torn lig.,L elbow; L flexor strain x2
	16	166	Rec fr surg. on L elbow
	18	65	Fractured R hand; strained calf
	19	20	Strained L hamstring
Vazquez,Felipe	15	29	Gastrointestinal bleeding
Velasquez,Vincent	16	17	Strnd R biceps
	17	99	Strnd flexr R elbow;R index fing str
	18	11	Bruised R forearm
	19	18	Strained R forearm
Velazquez,Hector	18	11	Lower back strain
	19	31	Strained lower back
Venditte,Patrick	15	51	Strained R shoulder
Venters,Jonny	18	31	Strained R hamstring
	19	111	Strained L shoulder
VerHagen,Drew	16	108	Thoracic outlet syndrome R should
	18	20	Fractured nose
	19	11	Strained R forearm
Verlander,Justin	15	66	Strained R triceps
Vincent,Nick	16	39	Strnd mid-back
	18	27	Strained R groin
	19	62	Strained R pectoral muscle
Vizcaino,Arodys	16	67	R should inflam; strnd R oblique
	17	14	Strained R index finger
	18	73	R shoulder inflammation
	19	173	Surgery to repair torn labrum
Volquez,Edinson	17	96	Blister R thumb; L knee tendinitis
	19	150	Sprained R elbow
Voth,Austin	19	43	Sprained AC joint R shoulder
Wacha,Michael	16	36	R should inflammation
	18	103	L oblique strain
	19	11	Patellar tendinitis L knee
Waguespack,Jacob	19	36	Strained R shoulder
Wahl,Bobby	17	130	Strained R shoulder
	18	46	Strained R hamstring
	19	187	Torn ACL R knee
Wainwright,Adam	15	162	Torn L Achilles
	17	44	Tight mid-back; R elbow imping
	18	150	R elbow inflam x 2; str L hamstring
	19	10	Strained L hamstring
Walker,Taijuan	16	31	R foot tendinitis
	17	24	Blister on R index finger
	18	170	R elbow surg
	19	186	Recovery from TJS
Wang,Chien-Ming	16	171	R biceps tendinitis
Warren,Adam	17	46	Strnd trapezius; low back strain x2
	18	45	Strained back
	19	114	Strained R forearm
Watson,Tony	19	16	Fx L wrist
Weaver,Luke	19	118	Tightness R forearm
Webb,Jacob	19	65	R elbow impingement
Weber,Ryan	17	122	Strained R biceps
Webster,Allen	19	143	Radial nerve inflammation R arm
Whalen,Rob	16	40	R should fatigue
	17	27	Strained calf
Wheeler,Zack	15	183	Torn ligament,R elbow
	16	183	Rec fr TJS
	17	83	R biceps tend; stress react R arm
	19	15	R shoulder fatigue
Whitley,Chase	15	143	Sprained R elbow
	16	162	Rec fr TJS
	18	20	R heel infection
Williams,Austen	19	165	Strained L hamstring
Williams,Taylor	18	11	R elbow soreness
Williams,Trevor	19	34	Strained R side

FIVE-YEAR INJURY LOG — Pitchers

Pitchers	Yr	Days	Injury
Wilson,Alex	16	14	Sore R should
	18	32	Strained L plantar fascia
Wilson,Justin	19	67	Sore R elbow
Wingenter,Trey	19	15	Strained R shoulder
Winkler,Daniel	15	158	Recovery from R elbow surg
	16	175	Fractured R elbow
	17	141	Recovery surg fractured R elbow
Withrow,Chris	16	24	R elbow inflammation
Wittgren,Nick	17	65	Strained R elbow
	18	21	Bruised middle finger - R hand
Wood,Alex	16	112	Sore L tricep/elb; Debride L elb
	17	24	SC joint inflam L shoulder x 2
	18	11	L wrist inflammation
	19	123	Lower back strain
Wood,Blake	18	162	TJS
Wood,Hunter	19	17	R shoulder inflammation
Woodruff,Brandon	17	41	Strained R hamstring
	19	58	Strained L oblique
Workman,Brandon	15	175	R elbow soreness
	16	183	Rec fr TJS
Wright,Steven	15	51	Concussion
	16	15	Bursitis R should
	17	153	Surg on L knee
	18	68	Recovery from L knee surg
	19	78	Bruised R big toe
Yamamoto,Jordan	19	25	Strained R forearm
Yates,Kirby	15	41	R pectoral strain
	18	12	R ankle tendinitis
Ynoa,Gabriel	17	16	Strained R hamstring
	18	187	Stress reaction R shin
Zastryzny,Rob	18	13	Back spasms
Ziegler,Brad	17	37	Strained R back
Zimmermann,Jordan	16	60	Strnd R lat; neck
	18	40	R shoulder impingement
	19	68	Sprained UCL R elbow

Top 75 Impact Prospects for 2020

by Chris Blessing

Let's be honest, you've come to this part of the Forecaster to grab a sneak peek at the rookies you'll be spending most of your FAAB on this year. As in past years, in the following pages you'll find skills and narrative profiles of the 75 rookie-eligible prospects most likely to have an impact in 2020.

Below, each prospect is listed in alphabetical order with his own narrative capsule included. Consider it a primer on his strengths and weaknesses that attempt to balance raw skill, readiness for the majors and likelihood of 2020 playing time.

We've also ranked the Top 40 prospects in terms of projected 2020 Rotisserie value mostly from our figures elsewhere in the book. Those are listed, along with projected 2020 Mayberry scores, on page 227. Beyond those 40 prospects, we provide 35 more, presented in alphabetical order, who could see time in the majors in 2020, but whose raw skill might be less polished or a step below the others in terms of potential 2020 impact. Those also have projected 2020 Mayberry scores. Keep in mind, this is just a pre-season snapshot. Prospects develop at different paces and making that one adjustment or finding opportunity when one doesn't seem to exist can make all the difference.

For even more detail, including profiles of over 900 prospects, statistics and our overall HQ100 top prospect list, see our sister publication, the *2020 Minor League Baseball Analyst*—as well as the weekly scouting reports and minor league information at BaseballHQ.com. Happy Prospecting!

Jo Adell (OF, LAA) is a toolsy prospect with bat speed and power potential. He missed time with a leg injury suffered in spring training 2018. Split between three levels, Adell slashed .289/.359/.475 with 10 HR and 7 SB. He will need to improve his plate discipline to reach his projection of an all-star caliber OF.

Logan Allen (LHP, CLE) was traded at the deadline in a three-team deal from San Diego. Allen is a 4-pitch pitcher who primarily relies on commanding a low-90s fastball and changing speeds with a plus change-up. When his command is off, like last season, he struggles. He could be in line for starts throughout the summer.

Ian Anderson (RHP, ATL) showed improved control and command throughout the summer in Double-A before those issues reappeared in Triple-A. A three-pitch pitcher, Anderson throws from an over-the-top arm slot, which causes low spin rate pitches to play up. He's likely a mid-rotation starter at projection.

Randy Arozarena (OF, STL) is a high-contact, aggressive hitter who made his MLB debut last season. He is a hit-over-power prospect with a quick, compact swing but can be overly aggressive. He is a plus runner and can steal 15-plus SB but will struggle with efficiency.

Seth Beer (1B, ARI) is a 1B/DH-only prospect who the Diamondbacks acquired in the Zack Greinke deal. He is a booming power hitter (26 HR in 450 High-A/Double-A AB) with advanced plate skills. Beer sprays the ball well for a slugger and shows power to all fields. Beer may be a second half MLB addition.

Alec Bohm (1B/3B, PHI) made it to Double-A in his first full pro season. Bohm is a power-hitting corner infielder with some question marks about his long-term defensive position. There's 30-plus HR potential in Bohm's swing and he should maintain a high average, too.

Bobby Bradley (1B, CLE) struggled during a brief MLB debut. Bradley is a Three True Outcomes hitter with double-plus raw power, which plays to the pull side. He controls the strike zone well, working pitchers and getting in favorable counts. His lumbering swing may struggle against higher velocities.

Vidal Brujan (2B/SS, TAM) is a switch-hitting athlete who could eventually develop into a super utility player. Brujan is a patient hitter who battles at the plate. His hit tool is better from the left side than his right. There's minimal power in his body. Brujan's double-plus speed should help him on the base paths.

Dylan Carlson (OF, STL) blossomed into a force in 2019, living up to his 1st-round pedigree. A cerebral hitter, Carlson improved his hit and power output without compromising his plate discipline. Carlson's intangibles may play his profile up to a plus-level performer.

Willi Castro (SS, DET) is a defense-over-offense middle infielder who made his MLB debut last season. A switch-hitter, Castro is likely a below-average hitter with minimal pop but he has 10-15 SB potential. Given opportunity, Castro could be a streaming option during stretches in 2020.

Jazz Chisholm (SS, MIA) was acquired by the Marlins in the Zac Gallen deal last July. Chisholm is an athletic, left-handed hitting SS who maxes out his swing to generate loft, which has caused his hit tool to back up. There's 20/20 potential waiting to be tapped into, even if the hit tool is below average.

Zack Collins (C/DH, CHW) struggled in his MLB debut last season after producing in Triple-A. Collins is a Three True Outcomes hitter when things are going right. When they aren't, he struggles to make consistent hard contact. Collins has limited position versatility and likely will end up as a DH.

Bobby Dalbec (3B, BOS) is a prospect with two double-plus tools, his throwing arm and his raw power. Known for majestic HR, Dalbec struggled in 2019 making consistent hard contact but still hit 27 HR and cut down his strikeout rate. With a streaky profile, Dalbec could be a streaming option for power.

Lewin Diaz (1B, MIA) is a power-hitting 1B who slimmed down, making offensive strides in 2019. Acquired mid-season from Minnesota, Diaz got to his barrel more, which increased both his average and power production. Diaz is a solid defensive 1B and should stick at the position.

Yusniel Diaz (OF, BAL) had an okay season in Double-A last season. Still, Diaz is searching for power in his swing to wash away

any "tweener" profile talk. In Baltimore, there is greater opportunity for Diaz to receive regular playing time. He could help by providing owners a solid average and some power.

Mauricio Dubon (SS, SF) was acquired in the Drew Pomeranz deal in July with Milwaukee. Dubon played well with the Giants, slashing .279/.312/.442 and has always hit for average. However, Dubon's SB ability has backed up and he should only be viewed as a 10-20 SB threat.

Justin Dunn (RHP, SEA) is a college closer-turned-starter who could eventually become an MLB late-inning reliever. Dunn had a solid MLB debut last season but struggled with overall command. He's a three-pitch pitcher, relying mostly on his fastball/slider combination, both of which are out pitches.

Jon Duplantier (RHP, ARI) was on the Triple-A shuttle during his MLB debut, mostly working as RP. He throws five pitches, including a four-seam fastball and a sinking fastball. His secondary pitches are all average-or-better offerings. Duplantier's injury history and command may push him to RP role.

Alex Faedo (RHP, DET) is a solid, back-of-the-rotation ceiling prospect who has been stung by the home run ball. He sits low 90s with an underwhelming fastball and must live in the bottom half of the zone. His best pitch is a plus slider. Faedo throws strikes and is a workable option if he pitches to his strengths.

Wander Franco (SS, TAM) is the best prospect in baseball. The 19-year-old could be knocking on Tampa's door by mid-season. Franco dominated A-Ball levels with a .327/.398/.487 slash. Plus-plus hit and plus power tools make him a potential superstar player. Franco could move off SS as he bulks up.

Deivi Garcia (RHP, NYY) is a high-strikeout machine who continues to struggle with walks despite a solid, athletic delivery. He's got three pitches and really spins his curveball, his primary out pitch. A shorter-stature pitcher, some believe Garcia makes his impact as a RP in 2020.

Logan Gilbert (RHP, SEA) is a big, athletic hurler who rapidly moved from Single-A to Double-A in his pro debut. Gilbert does well to command a low-90s fastball and can reach up to 97 MPH. His curveball and slider are both possibly plus offerings at maturity. Gilbert could hit the ground running with a mid-season promotion.

Andres Gimenez (SS, NYM) is a left-handed-hitting middle infielder who has found additional athleticism in recent seasons. His hit tool regressed this season, and it will likely be average at maturity. Gimenez gets the most out of his above-average run tool, using instincts to be a 20-plus SB threat.

Tony Gonsolin (RHP, LA) pitched effectively during his MLB debut. Gonsolin mixes a 4-pitch average-or-better arsenal very well. He works everything off a low-to-mid-90s 4-seam fastball he commands for strikes. Gonsolin will find his way into the Dodgers carousel of starting pitchers this season.

MacKenzie Gore (LHP, SD) is one of the top pitching prospects in baseball. Gore's delivery is picture perfect, using plus extension and creating angles with his arm slot, playing up an above-average-to-plus repertoire of pitches. His best secondary pitch is a change-up with late fade and great deception.

Brusdar Graterol (RHP, MIN) made his MLB debut last season pitching out of the Twins pen. He sits high-90s with his sinking fastball and has a future double-plus slider. The change-up is improving, and he could become a mid-rotation SP—or a dominant, late-inning reliever.

Monte Harrison (OF, MIA) struggled to stay on the field last season in Triple-A. He showed improvement by making harder contact. This is a plus toolshed; it's a question of whether the baseball skills will catch up. Harrison should have opportunity in Miami's OF and could provide immediate SB and HR help.

Ke'Bryan Hayes (3B, PIT) is a better real-life prospect than a fantasy one. A lot of Hayes' value is tied to his defensive skill. However, offensively, he should be at least an average-regular at 3B, hitting for a high average, 12-18 HR and stealing 10 or more bases. Hayes should see regular playing time this season.

Austin Hays (OF, BAL) made it back to the big leagues last season and should be a regular in Baltimore's Opening Day OF. Hays has potentially double-plus game power in his profile. His bat-to-ball skills are solid. However, Hays struggles with aggressiveness, hurting his batting average potential.

Nico Hoerner (SS, CHC) is a line-drive hitting machine who spent time on the IL last season due to a wrist injury. There's .300 hitter potential here, with double-digit SBs and defensive versatility. His HR power is likely below average. However, Hoerner should be a doubles machine with his gap-to-gap approach.

Brent Honeywell (RHP, TAM) hasn't pitched since 2017 due to several arm injuries. When healthy, Honeywell mixes five average-or-better offerings. While his screwball steals headlines, his best secondary pitch is a double-plus change-up. Hopefully, Honeywell can get back to where he was.

Nolan Jones (3B, CLE) erased question marks about his defensive position by improving dramatically at 3B. Jones continues to improve his hit tool. While there will always be some swing-and-miss concerns and low batting average risk, the power should play plus to double-plus like other fantasy 3B.

Jarred Kelenic (OF, SEA) made it to Double-A during his full-season debut last season. Likely a fixture in CF for the Mariners in the future, Kelenic tinkered with his hand placement and saw immediate results reaching for and controlling his barrel in his swing. Kelenic is an MLB option as the season wears on.

Mitch Keller (RHP, PIT) was up and down in his MLB debut. The good news: his curveball was dominant and played like a double-plus offering. Keller's fastball, despite an encouraging a spin rate, struggled mightily to avoid barrels. Effectiveness in the rotation is only possible if he can corral bats against his fastball.

Carter Kieboom (SS, WAS) had a forgettable MLB debut, but his outstanding plate skills and discipline push his hit tool to plus. While over-the-fence power may be average, his biggest offensive attribute may be his ability to find gaps. Versatile defensively, Kieboom could play several infield spots this season.

Top 75 Impact Prospects for 2020

Mayberry scores are explained in the Encyclopedia, and here reflect 2020 only, not a player's long-term impact. Batters are dark shaded; pitchers are lighter shaded.

RANK/BATTER/POS, TM	POWER	SPEED	BATAVG
RANK/PITCHER/POS, TM	**ERA**	**DOM**	**SAVES**
1 Gavin Lux (2B/SS, LA)	3	1	3
2 Nick Solak (2B/OF, TEX)	3	1	3
3 Nick Madrigal (2B, CHW)	1	4	3
4 Jo Adell (OF, LAA)	4	2	3
5 Mauricio Dubon (SS, SF)	1	3	3
6 Luis Robert (OF, CHW)	3	3	2
7 Austin Hays (OF, BAL)	3	1	2
8 Carter Kieboom (SS, WAS)	2	1	3
9 Willi Castro (SS, DET)	1	3	2
10 Dustin May (RHP, LA)	3	3	0
11 Brendan Rodgers (IF, COL)	3	2	2
12 Kyle Lewis (OF, SEA)	3	1	2
13 Alec Bohm (3B, PHI)	3	1	3
14 Sean Murphy (C, OAK)	2	1	2
15 Jesus Luzardo (LHP, OAK)	3	3	0
16 Dylan Carlson (OF, STL)	2	2	3
17 Cristian Pache (OF, ATL)	2	2	3
18 Nico Hoerner (SS, CHC)	2	2	3
19 Abraham Toro (IF, HOU)	3	1	2
20 Bobby Dalbec (3B, BOS)	4	1	1
21 Jarred Kelenic (OF, SEA)	2	3	3
22 Tony Gonsolin (RHP, LA)	2	2	0
23 A.J. Puk (LHP, OAK)	1	3	1
24 Jake Rogers (C, DET)	2	1	1
25 Yusniel Diaz (OF, BAL)	1	1	3
26 Brendan McKay (LHP, TAM)	2	2	0
27 Forrest Whitley (RHP, HOU)	2	3	0
28 Matt Manning (RHP, DET)	2	3	0
29 Michael Kopech (RHP, CHW)	2	3	0
30 Zack Collins (C/1B, CHW)	2	0	1
31 Mitch Keller (RHP, PIT)	2	2	0
32 Isaac Paredes (SS/3B, DET)	1	3	2
33 Ryan Mountcastle (1B, BAL)	2	1	2
34 Sixto Sanchez (RHP, MIA)	1	2	0
35 Brusdar Graterol (RHP, MIN)	1	2	1
36 MacKenzie Gore (LHP, SD)	1	2	0
37 Casey Mize (RHP, DET)	1	2	0
38 Nolan Jones (3B, CLE)	2	0	1
39 Randy Arozarena (OF, STL)	1	2	2
40 Kyle Wright (RHP, ATL)	1	2	0

THE NEXT 35

BATTER/POS, TM	POWER	SPEED	BATAVG
PITCHER/POS, TM	**ERA**	**DOM**	**SAVES**
Ian Anderson (RHP, ATL)	1	2	0
Logan Allen (LHP, SD)	2	1	0
Seth Beer (1B, ARI)	2	0	2
Bobby Bradley (1B, CLE)	2	0	1
Vidal Brujan (2B, TAM)	0	2	2
Jazz Chisholm (SS, MIA)	2	1	1
Lewin Diaz (1B, MIA)	2	0	1
Justin Dunn (RHP, SEA)	2	1	0
Jon Duplantier (RHP, ARI)	1	1	1
Alex Faedo (RHP, DET)	1	1	0
Wander Franco (SS, TAM)	1	1	4
Delvi Garcia (RHP, NYY)	1	2	0
Logan Gilbert (RHP, SEA)	1	2	0
Andres Gimenez (SS, NYM)	1	2	2
Monte Harrison (OF, MIA)	2	2	1
Ke'Bryan Hayes (3B, PIT)	2	2	2
Brent Honeywell (RHP, TAM)	1	2	0
Alex Kirilloff (OF, MIN)	2	1	2
Andrew Knizner (C, STL)	1	0	2
Jackson Kowar (RHP, KC)	1	2	0
Trevor Larnach (OF, MIN)	2	1	2
Royce Lewis (SS, MIN)	2	2	2
Brandon Marsh (OF, LAA)	1	1	2
Jorge Mateo (2B/SS, OAK)	1	3	2
Adrian Morejon (LHP, SD)	1	2	0
Kyle Muller (LHP, ATL)	1	2	0
Nate Pearson (RHP, TOR)	1	3	0
Keibert Ruiz (C, LA)	1	1	2
Jesus Sanchez (OF, MIA)	1	1	2
Justus Sheffield (LHP, SEA)	1	2	0
Brady Singer (RHP, KC)	1	2	0
Daulton Varsho (C/OF, ARI)	1	2	2
Drew Waters (OF, ATL)	1	2	2
Evan White (1B, SEA)	2	1	2
Bryse Wilson (RHP, ATL)	1	2	0

Alex Kirilloff (OF, MIN) struggled with a wrist injury last season, but people close to the organization aren't worried about him. A student of hitting, he will aim to return to his 2018 form, when his above-average power and plus hit tool emerged. Kirilloff could help down the stretch.

Andrew Knizner (C, STL) made his MLB debut last season after a solid Triple-A campaign. He has a quick bat and average HR potential. He's a bat-to-ball guy who limits swings-and-misses but does battle with over-aggressiveness. Knizner could see opportunity if age ever catches up to Yadier Molina.

Michael Kopech (RHP, CHW) missed all of 2019 recovering from elbow surgery before reappearing in instructional league. When healthy, he features a high-velocity fastball and power slider as his primary workhorse pitches. He also features a change-up. If healthy, Kopech should compete for a regular SP role.

Jackson Kowar (RHP, KC) is mostly known as a fastball/change-up pitcher but has been developing a solid curveball of late. Kowar has an extremely good feel of his change-up, a true out pitch. He commands his mid-90s fastball well enough and uses both a two-seam and four seam fastball effectively. Opportunity exists for Kowar to debut in 2020.

Trevor Larnach (OF, MIN) had a solid season split between High-A and Double-A. Larnach is a power hitter with a spray approach who could also maintain a high batting average throughout his career. Limited to the corners defensively, he could be a sneaky second half performer.

Kyle Lewis (OF, SEA) is a power-hitting OF who has dealt with a series of knee injuries, which has washed away some of his athleticism. He had a solid debut, surprising some after lackluster MiLB numbers. Lewis has a big power bat with lighting-quick hands. He's likely regulated to the corner OF.

Royce Lewis (SS, MIN) battled injuries early, struggling for first time in his career. Lewis began tapping into above-average raw power to go with elite athleticism and versatility. Lewis has a long trigger and some length in his swing, which could cause struggles with his hit tool against RHP. Lewis could help late.

Gavin Lux (2B/SS, LA) emerged as a Top 5 prospect, eventually making his MLB debut in September, playing 2B for LA. Lux controls the barrel extremely well. He didn't compromise his spray approach as he began tapping into more power. Lux could be a regular contributor this season.

Jesus Luzardo (LHP, OAK) made his MLB debut working out of the A's pen late in the year as he missed most of the season rehabbing from elbow surgery. It's a rare command/control profile with plus-stuff. Best pitches are Luzardo's late dropping sinker and power curveball. He should compete for rotation spot this spring.

Nick Madrigal (2B, CHW) has two double-plus tools, an 80-grade contact tool and a 70-grade defensive profile at 2B. His contact rate doesn't include many hard hits. An inside-out swing limits his power, which is below average at best. Madrigal's SB ability will carry the profile as he debuts.

Matt Manning (RHP, DET) had his best developmental year in 2019, improving his delivery and becoming a better bet to start in MLB. He is a 3-pitch pitcher with a plus fastball and 11-5 curveball. Manning's change-up continues to come along and could be ready for meaningful MLB innings by mid-season.

Brandon Marsh (OF, LAA) is a hit-over-power OF who comes with some tweener risk due to a lack of carrying tool. Marsh is a gap-to-gap hitter, who shoots line drives into holes when he is going well. There is above-average raw power in his frame, but swing trajectory plays it down to below-average HR power.

Jorge Mateo (2B/SS, OAK) has struggled to take the next step in his career, but finally performed in the upper minors. Mateo's athletic skill and versatility push his profile. His ability to swipe bases with a solid OBP gives him a chance to be a solid fantasy performer. Mateo could fit a super-utility role.

Dustin May (RHP, LA) made his MLB debut last season, mostly in relief. Tall, May dominates hitters with two double-plus offerings, a mid-90s fastball and a hard slider. Lacking a good enough feel for a change-up, he has developed a cutter to neutralize LHH. May should be in the Dodgers merry-go-round of pitchers this season.

Brendan McKay (LHP/DH, TAM) is a two-way player who struggled in his MLB debut last season. A better pitcher than hitter, McKay projects as a mid-rotation SP with an assortment of solid pitches. Offensively, McKay will need to find his raw power in games to make his two-way profile attractive.

Casey Mize (RHP, DET) had glimpses of greatness sprinkled in with some injury setbacks in 2019. He features four average-or-better pitches. Mize's best offering is a throwback to the 80s, a double-plus splitter he can add and subtract to while commanding it well. Mize should find MLB innings by June.

Adrian Morejon (LHP, SD) was overmatched in his MLB debut. Morejon is a three-pitch pitcher with mid-rotation upside whose lack of fastball command was cause for his struggles. An athletic performer, command issues should be resolved over time. Morejon's change-up is potentially plus and his slurve is solid.

Ryan Mountcastle (1B, BAL) continues to establish himself as a quality prospect. He's potentially a plus-hitter and his power is coming along nicely after some swing trajectory adjustments. There's potential for a .280 average and 30-plus HR. Mountcastle is ready to make his MLB debut soon.

Kyle Muller (LHP, ATL) is a poster child of remaking himself after working at a pitching lab (Driveline). His best pitch is a fastball, which sits mid-90s with good angles thrown from a bigger frame. His curveball and change-up are both average offerings. Muller struggles with control and ideally looks more like a late-inning RP.

Sean Murphy (C, OAK) is a top catching prospect who made his MLB debut last season, seeing success in a 20-game sample. Murphy has solid plate skills and has the bat speed to get to velocity. He also has above-average HR potential. Murphy is ready defensively and could be the starter sooner than later.

Cristian Pache (OF, ATL) is a potential Gold Glove CF who continues to make strides offensively. He developed some patience and tapped into more power, increasing the probability he'll have an impact in fantasy, despite diminishing returns on the bases. Defense may carry Pache to a regular role in 2020.

Isaac Paredes (SS/3B, DET) is a natural hitter, though his future position remains in question. He's not agile enough for shortstop, but lacks the thump of a classic third baseman. Paredes has incredible plate skills and makes tons of contact, but there are hard-hit rate concerns about his below average raw power.

Nate Pearson (RHP, TOR) has electric stuff. The Blue Jays managed Pearson's workload early to keep him healthy and his stuff kept getting better. He has a near elite fastball and his slider is double-plus too. The change-up is improving. Toronto will manage Pearson's workload, but he should still see action in big leagues.

A.J. Puk (LHP, OAK) is recovered from elbow surgery and emerged late to make his MLB debut last season. Puk is a hard thrower with excellent running action on his fastball. His slider is plus as well. There's reliever risk in Puk's profile. However, he should be a source for strikeouts in 2020, regardless of role.

Luis Robert (OF, CHW) is an athletic physical specimen. The RHH Robert has lighting-quick hands, allowing his bat to find barrels. He also has plus-plus raw power, which plays in games, and he's a plus runner with SB ability. There are some questions about his current below-average pitch recognition, but he should have value in 2020.

Brendan Rodgers (IF, COL) made his MLB debut but ended up tearing the labrum in his right shoulder and was lost for the season. Rodgers, who struggled to curb his aggressiveness, still has above-average regular potential. With health and opportunity, Rodgers could be a starting player in 2020.

Jake Rogers (C, DET) is a defensive-minded catcher who struggled with his below-average hit tool in his MLB debut. However, he offers fantasy owners power at a position traditionally weak offensively. Rogers' glove will dictate playing time this season.

Keibert Ruiz (C, LA) is a contact-oriented catcher still learning plate discipline and how to tap into power. His high contact-rate reminds scouts of a young Yadier Molina. However, because of poor discipline, Ruiz misses the barrel, resulting in soft contact. Defense will dictate his playing time.

Jesus Sanchez (OF, MIA) has double-plus bat speed and is slowly developing discipline at the plate. With a high-ball swing trajectory, Sanchez is tailor-made for today's pitching trend of throwing up in the zone. He has a plus hit tool and average power potential. He could find opportunity in the Marlins OF this season.

Sixto Sanchez (RHP, MIA) is a three-pitch pitcher known for his command of a power pitcher's arsenal. He hits high 90s with both his 2-seam and 4-seam fastball. His slider is a tightly shaped, two-plane power pitch while his change-up features solid arm-side fading action. Sanchez could compete for SP role by mid-season.

Justus Sheffield (LHP, SEA) is still clinging to prospect eligibility after a 2nd MLB cup of coffee. He is a three-pitch pitcher who struggles commanding a mid-90s fastball. Sheffield's best pitch is his plus slider and his change-up is a solid offering too. If command doesn't improve, Sheffield is likely ticketed for RP role.

Brady Singer (RHP, KC) made it to Double-A in his first full season of pro ball. A bulldog on the mound, Singer dominates RHHs with a fastball/slider mix. Questions remain whether he'll refine his change-up enough to keep LHHs honest. 2020 is a big development year for Singer. He could see big league action in the 2nd half.

Nick Solak (2B/OF, TEX) was acquired by the Rangers in a mid-season trade with the Rays. He hit 27 HR split between Triple-A and the big leagues. Solak is a plus hitter who works counts and sprays the ball around the field. He is likely a DH long term and should be a regular in the Rangers lineup this season.

Abraham Toro (IF, HOU) received a late 2019 call-up after dominating the upper minors. A switch-hitter, Toro is a plus-hitter with average or better power potential. His swing is ready from the left side but needs refinement from the right. Defensively, he's passable at 3B but will likely end up at 1B.

Daulton Varsho (C/OF, ARI) is an athletic, 2nd generation prospect who has struggled defensively sticking at catcher. Varsho improved his contact and barrel rate while also being a threat to steal bases. Catching eligibility may make him a must grab rookie given his skill set at the position.

Drew Waters (OF, ATL) is a switch-hitter who battles aggressiveness at the plate. With a plus hit tool from the left side, Waters controls the barrel well and serves line drives to all fields despite an unorthodox swing. He's limited from the right side. Power should be average at projection and is an SB threat.

Evan White (1B, SEA) enjoyed an offensive breakout in his Double-A debut. Always known for his exceptional defense at 1B, he finally cashed in on some of his above-average power potential while also maintaining his solid hitting profile. White could debut sometime in the 2nd half of the season.

Forrest Whitley (RHP, HOU) has a monster arsenal of pitches. He struggled with injury and ineffectiveness before dominating this fall. Whitley is a 5-pitch pitcher who utilizes angles in his delivery to play up his stuff. He has several out pitches and could find his way into the rotation by mid-season.

Bryse Wilson (RHP, ATL) is a 4-pitch pitcher who has struggled commanding his fastball as a big leaguer. Wilson relies heavily on his fastball, accounting for 70% of his pitches, mostly of the 4-seam variety. He attacks hitters and is very competitive. If he doesn't win a job as a SP, stuff would play up in RP role.

Kyle Wright (RHP, ATL) has struggled with fastball command in MLB. Wright features top-of-the-rotation stuff. Evaluators believe it is just a matter of time before it plays in the majors. He could battle for a rotation spot out of spring camp and could be a source of strike outs if he discovers fastball command.

Top International Players for 2020 and Beyond

Since the 2008 edition, the *Baseball Forecaster* has profiled a handful of Japanese prospects who may make the jump to Major League Baseball in the coming years. This provides owners in deep keeper leagues the chance to get the jump on talent before it arrives in the States. As more MLB teams now draw regularly from the international player pool, we've expanded our coverage to include both Korean players as well as top Caribbean talent. With each, we list a "possible," "probable" or "definite" MLB ETA—but for most of these, you'll need to be patient.

Japanese and Korean Players *(by Tom Mulhall)*

2019 was not a banner year for rookie Japanese players. But perhaps the struggles of Yusei Kikuchi may mean that your competitors will overlook newcomers. With Shogo Akiyama and Yoshitomo Tsutsugo, this could finally be the season we see the most impactful hitter from Japan since Hideki Matsui.

Shogo Akiyama (OF, Seibu Lions) is just the sixth player with a 200-hit season and is the only player since the "deader" ball was introduced in 2011. He has consistently produced in all five categories but is not a true power hitter. At age 32, his speed is diminishing but he might still be capable of leading off. A six-time Gold Glove winner, he never seems to have an injury. While the Lions reportedly will offer him a huge multi-year contract to stay, Akiyama has filed for international free agency. It seems likely that he will pursue his dream and sign with a MLB team.
Probable ETA: 2020

Ryosuke Kikuchi (SS, Hiroshima Toyo Carp) is almost certain to try out the MLB in 2020. At age 33, time is fast running out for the multiple Gold Glove winner. A slick defender and durable player, Kikuchi just doesn't offer enough offense to justify a fantasy selection. He projects as a decent utility player in MLB.
Probable ETA: 2020

Seong-Beom Na (OF, NC Dinos) is considered the top MLB prospect in Korea. (His name is sometimes rendered as Sung-Bum Na.) The lefty has a solid batting eye and raw power, along with a little speed. He is eligible to be posted after the 2019 season and signed with Scott Boras to make that happen. But he sustained a serious leg injury in the spring and had only 4 HR in 93 AB in 2019. That may push his arrival back a year, as MLB teams will want to see if he fully recovers.
Probable ETA: 2021

Takahiro Norimoto (RHP, Rakuten Golden Eagles) has battled injuries that have probably cost him a chance to sign with a MLB team. The diminutive pitcher possesses an excellent fastball that sits in the low to mid 90s, coupled with a forkball and slider. This team does have a history of posting its stars early, as with Tanaka and Iwakuma. However, injury concerns led him to accept the security of a seven-year contract from the Golden Eagles which, at a minimum, pushes off his posting for several years.
Possible ETA: 2022

Chen Po-Yu (RHP, Taiwan) is considered to be the best pitching prospect out of Taiwan in a long time. Major League scouts regard him as a complete package, and at age 17, he has lots of room for improvement. Chen has an easy delivery with good mechanics. His fastball sits in the low 90s, with a solid slider and curveball. A long-term prospect, watch to see if he signs with a MLB team.
Possible ETA: 2022

Hayato Sakamoto (SS, Yomuri Giants) hit a career high 40 HR in 2019. While the power increase was something of a surprise, he did hit 31 in 2010 and 23 in 2016. Sakamoto holds the NPB on-base record by reaching the bases in 35 straight games. Considered by many to be the best offensive shortstop in the Giants legendary history, he is also a plus defender. His ownership is almost certain to keep the 31 year-old under tight control for as long as possible.
Possible ETA: 2021

Kodai Senga (RHP, SoftBank Hawks) is a 27 year old pitcher who badly wants to play in the MLB. Unfortunately, his team rarely posts a player early and Senga may have to wait for international free agency. That will not happen until sometime in 2022, but there are rumors they may make an exception for him. Senga is major league ready, with a 98 mph fastball and an excellent forkball/splitter. He ended the 2019 season with 227 strikeouts in 180.1 innings and a 2.79 ERA. Senga is a top pitching target for MLB teams among Japanese players.
Possible ETA: 2021

Tomoyuki Sugano (RHP, Yomiuri Giants) has command of up to seven pitches, the best being a slider and curveball, which complement a fastball in the mid-90s. The two-time Sawamura Award winner plays for the Yomiuri Giants, so the odds of him coming to the MLB seem remote since they rarely post players early. However, Sugano has recently voiced a desire to pitch in the majors and should reach international free agency in 2021. Of all the pitchers in Japan, he could have the biggest impact.
Possible ETA: 2021

Seiya Suzuki (OF, Hiroshima Carp) is a hard-working and hard-hitting player who incorporates western-style techniques into his workouts. Averaging 28 HR over the past four seasons, he also has some speed (25 SB in 2019, a career high) and has twice won a Gold Glove. He has an excellent batting eye, with an OBP of .438 and .453 in the past two seasons. Suzuki has dreams of playing MLB and is well worth a stash on your farm club.
Possible ETA: 2021

Yoshitomo Tsutsugo (OF, Yokohama DeNA BayStar) is a multiple All-Star and power hitter in Japan who has finally achieved his wish to be posted for play in MLB. Tsutsugo is a poor defender and may not be able to handle the outfield in MLB so a move to 1B or a DH position may be required. While not an elite hitter, his potential power, durability and .382 lifetime OBP make him worth a gamble, but realize that's what he is.
Definite ETA: 2020

Tetsuto Yamada (2B/SS, Tokyo Yakult Swallows) has gone 30/30 in four of the past five years, and this season successfully stole 38 consecutive bases before getting caught. Possibly the best

all-round offensive player in Japan, the 28-year old Yamada is now reaching his prime years. His team could post him early as they did Kaz Ishii and Nori Aoki, but there are questions about his desire to play outside of Japan. If he does, Yamada could easily be a top MLB middle infielder.

Possible ETA: 2021

Yuki Yanagita (OF, SoftBank Hawks) is another power-speed combination who has gone 30/30. He bounced back from elbow surgery in 2015 but missed games again in 2019. Along with Yamada and Suzuki, he would have the biggest impact as a position player, possibly even as a five category contributor. While he plays for a financially solid team with little incentive to post him early, Yanagita is nearing free agency and there are rumors he will be posted after the 2020 season.

Probable ETA: 2021

Notes: See the main article about Japan and Korea in the Encyclopedia of Fanalytics regarding style of play and the posting systems. The Sawamura Award is roughly equivalent to the Cy Young Award but is not given every year.

Caribbean Players *(by Chris Blessing)*

The following players were signed by MLB teams in the international signing period that began last July 2. These players are all of interest to those playing in dynasty league formats, who might be able to draft these players for the first time this spring.

Jasson Dominguez (OF, NYY) is the top prospect of this year's July 2nd Caribbean class. The 16-year-old switch hitter from the Dominican Republic signed for $5.1 million with the Yankees. Because there weren't any recent showcases leading up to this year's free agent period, there wasn't much new information about Dominguez released until he played at New York's Dominican complex in the fall. He's built like a football running back at 5'10", 200 lbs and has the speed, athleticism and strength to be a force in baseball. Scouts have comped his body type and tool shed to Yasiel Puig, Bo Jackson and even Mickey Mantle. Dominguez has plus-or-better tools across the board. His speed, defensive ability and power potential all could be plus-plus tools at maturity. It's suspected he'll make his stateside and professional debut on one of the Yankees Gulf Coast League teams in 2020.

Possible ETA: 2024

Robert Puason (SS, OAK) is the second best prospect in this year's Caribbean class and the top-rated infielder. Puason had verbally agreed to sign with the Braves as a 14-year-old. However, the contract was considered null and void due to Atlanta's violation of international scouting rules. The 17-year-old switch-hitter from the Dominican Republic signed with the Athletics for $5.1 million. Puason is a quick-twitch athlete with a good defensive profile, and likely to stick at SS for the long term. He has a natural knack for finding the barrel, but the crudeness of his swing will need to be refined for him to reach his potential. There's power in Puason's swing and his 6'3" frame should be primed to add solid muscle too. Scouts are betting on his athleticism to push the profile. He could make his stateside debut next season.

Possible ETA: 2024

Erick Pena (OF, KC) is a 16-year-old Dominican prospect who the Royals signed for $3.9 million. A left-handed hitter, Pena's athletic ability and overall tool profile has been compared to former Royals OF Carlos Beltran by other outlets. A must-see attraction during Royals instructs this fall in Arizona, Pena's quick whipping bat was on full display. While there is some noise in his set-up and he hits in parts, Pena has lightning quick hands and is able to utilize solid leverage to get under balls with a line-drive oriented upper-cut swing. There's a lot of refinement needed to make his swing workable. However, there's plenty of time for the refinement needed to be a MLB player. He's long and lean with a good body to add weight too. Currently, Pena plays CF and could move off the position as he adds mass, but has the arm to play RF.

Possible ETA: 2025

Bayron Lora (OF, TEX) is a power prospect signed by the Rangers for $3.9 million out of the Dominican Republic. Lora has a maturing body and looks the part of a budding power hitter with plus-plus raw power in his swing and frame. He has above-average bat speed with a very easy setup, getting to the pitch effortlessly out in front of the plate. The ball carries well off his bat, producing backspin and loft. A right-handed hitter, there's 40-plus HR power in the bat. Lora has a very strong arm and should slot in as RF in his professional debut. He's got fringe-average speed and will likely be a below average runner by the time he debuts. Think power first bat with some hitting skills, ala Nelson Cruz.

Possible ETA: 2025

Luis Rodriguez (OF, LA) is a solid all-around prospect. Signed by the Dodgers for $2.7 million out of Venezuela, the 17-year-old right-handed hitter has quick hands and wrists and is developing barrel control, even though the symmetry of his body during his swing is very uneven. There's plus raw-power in his frame and should be at least an average power tool at maturity. Rodriguez has a solid body to build strength on. His 6'2' frame could ideally hold 200 pounds as he enters the big leagues. He's a solid defender with good baseball instincts throughout. While he lacks plus speed, Rodriguez could end up in CF due to his plus first step and solid route running skills.

Possible ETA: 2025

Ronnier Quintero (C, CHC) is a Venezuelan catching prospect known for his plus-plus raw power potential. Signed for $2.9 million by the Cubs, the 17-year-old left-handed hitter does well to stay under control in the batter's box. He does a nice job getting his barrel out in front of the plate, resulting in hard contact. An upper-cut oriented swing, combined with solid leverage derived from powerful base, should help him reach a plus-power outcome, which has been missing amongst catchers in the international market since Gary Sanchez signed in 2009. Quintero has a strong arm behind the plate and solid athleticism, boding well for his defensive development. Listed 6'0", 175, Quintero has room to grow but may lose some athleticism behind the dish and on the bases as he matures into his frame.

Possible ETA: 2025

MAJOR LEAGUE EQUIVALENTS

In his 1985 *Baseball Abstract*, Bill James introduced the concept of major league equivalencies. His assertion was that, with the proper adjustments, a minor leaguer's statistics could be converted to an equivalent major league level performance with a great deal of accuracy.

Because of wide variations in the level of play among different minor leagues, it is difficult to get a true reading on a player's potential. For instance, a .300 batting average achieved in the high-offense Pacific Coast League is not nearly as much of an accomplishment as a similar level in the Eastern League. MLEs normalize these types of variances, for all statistical categories.

The actual MLEs are not projections. They represent how a player's previous performance might look at the major league level. However, the MLE stat line can be used in forecasting future performance in just the same way as a major league stat line would.

The model we use contains a few variations to James' version and updates all of the minor league and ballpark factors. In addition, we designed a module to convert pitching statistics, which is something James did not originally do.

Players are listed if they spent at least part of 2018 or 2019 in Triple-A or Double-A and had at least 100 AB or 30 IP within those two levels (players who split a season at both levels are indicated as a/a). Major league and Single-A (and lower) stats are excluded. Each player is listed in the organization with which they finished the season. Some players over age 30 with major-league experience have been omitted for space.

These charts also provide the unique perspective of looking at two years' worth of data. These are only short-term trends, for sure. But even here we can find small indications of players improving their skills, or struggling, as they rise through more difficult levels of competition. Since players—especially those with any modicum of talent —are promoted rapidly through major league systems, a two-year scan is often all we get to spot any trends. Five-year trends do appear in the *Minor League Baseball Analyst*.

Used correctly, MLEs are excellent indicators of potential. But, just like we cannot take traditional major league statistics at face value, the same goes for MLEs. The underlying measures of base skill—contact rates, pitching command ratios, BPV, etc.—are far more accurate in evaluating future talent than raw home runs, batting averages or ERAs. This chart format focuses more on those underlying gauges.

Here are some things to look for as you scan these charts:

Target players who...
- had a full season's worth of playing time in AA and then another full year in AAA
- had consistent playing time from one year to the next
- improved their base skills as they were promoted

Raise the warning flag for players who...
- were stuck at the same level both years, or regressed
- displayed marked changes in playing time from one year to the next
- showed large drops in BPIs from one year to the next

BATTER	yr	b	age	pos	lvl	org	ab	hr	sb	ba	bb%	ct%	px	sx	bpv
Abreu, Osvaldo	18	R	24	SS	aa	WAS	360	6	3	160	7	69	76	74	-25
Abreu, Willie	19	L	24	RF	aa	COL	159	2	5	223	10	69	87	128	-3
Acuna, Ronald	18	R	21	LF	aaa	ATL	90	1	4	195	9	71	35	73	-48
Adames, Cristhian	18	B	27	3B	aaa	MIA	449	5	5	215	6	81	45	81	-1
	19	B	28	3B	aaa	SF	184	5	1	221	10	74	56	119	-8
Adams, Lane	18	R	29	CF	aaa	ATL	175	0	8	130	6	51	50	133	-100
	19	R	30	LF	a/a	ATL	310	9	8	192	8	53	150	139	-12
Adams, Riley	19	R	23	C	aa	TOR	287	11	3	252	10	61	155	140	23
Adell, Jo	18	R	19	CF	aa	LAA	63	2	2	225	8	63	146	109	20
	19	R	20	RF	a/a	LAA	280	7	6	257	8	67	141	116	29
Aguilar, Angel	19	R	24	3B	aa	NYY	143	3	2	197	4	63	115	131	-5
Ahmed, Mike	18	R	26	3B	a/a	LA	234	4	1	199	6	59	83	71	-62
	19	R	27	3B	aa	SEA	215	4	6	203	7	56	109	138	-33
Alberto, Hanser	18	R	26	SS	aaa	TEX	361	5	0	280	2	91	52	44	25
Alcantara, Arismer	19	B	28	2B	a/a	NYM	403	12	17	227	8	64	119	212	29
Alcantara, Sergio	18	B	22	SS	aa	DET	441	1	7	252	7	78	41	84	-14
	19	B	23	SS	aa	DET	324	2	7	237	12	77	39	80	-20
Alemais, Stephen	18	R	23	2B	aa	PIT	402	1	13	254	8	82	39	101	8
	19	R	24	SS	aa	PIT	45	0	2	250	2	79	0	82	-51
Alford, Anthony	18	R	24	CF	aaa	TOR	375	4	15	222	6	67	79	104	-22
	19	R	25	RF	aaa	TOR	282	6	18	232	8	62	119	178	11
Allday, Forrestt	18	L	27	RF	a/a	SD	433	3	8	213	8	76	47	95	-12
Allemand, Blake	18	B	26	2B	aa	MIL	305	6	2	230	8	76	62	52	-13
	19	B	27	2B	a/a	MIL	120	5	0	193	9	73	130	80	32
Allen, Austin	18	L	24	C	aa	SD	451	17	0	254	6	75	113	20	11
	19	L	25	C	aaa	SD	270	13	0	262	5	75	167	48	61
Allen, Greg	18	B	25	CF	aaa	CLE	171	2	9	265	8	71	83	90	-7
	19	B	26	CF	aaa	CLE	198	4	8	232	7	74	87	170	30
Almonte, Abraham	19	B	30	CF	aaa	ARI	319	9	7	188	10	71	137	163	58
Alonso, Peter	18	R	24	1B	a/a	NYM	478	25	0	229	11	68	142	30	17
Altmann, Josh	19	R	25	LF	aa	TEX	162	4	1	210	5	71	124	73	17
Alvarez, Alexander	19	R	23	C	aa	MIL	139	1	0	244	10	64	87	30	-50
Alvarez, Eddy	18	B	28	2B	aaa	CHW	308	6	4	201	10	67	107	95	5
	19	B	29	3B	a/a	MIA	238	9	10	262	10	71	143	158	61
Alvarez, Eliezer	18	B	24	LF	aa	TEX	408	10	20	205	8	67	90	159	6
	19	B	25	CF	aa	TEX	352	8	11	219	11	63	103	128	-13
Alvarez, Mandy	18	R	24	3B	aa	NYY	359	11	2	233	6	85	92	77	49
	19	R	25	3B	a/a	NYY	448	10	3	236	6	81	92	55	26
Alvarez, Yordan	18	L	21	LF	a/a	HOU	335	17	5	261	9	70	136	66	28
	19	L	22	LF	aaa	HOU	213	17	1	292	12	73	210	54	91
Amaral, Beau	18	L	27	RF	aa	SEA	384	2	8	200	6	72	45	96	-32
Amaya, Gioskar	19	R	27	3B	aa	CHC	269	2	1	213	5	69	80	87	-23
Amburgey, Trey	18	R	24	LF	aa	NYY	481	16	10	231	4	74	93	101	11
	19	R	25	RF	aaa	NYY	470	20	5	236	5	72	135	115	43
Andreoli, John	18	R	28	RF	aaa	SEA	327	2	14	222	11	65	64	119	-28
	19	R	29	LF	aaa	SEA	408	11	8	187	13	53	132	136	-24
Antequera, Jose	19	R	24	2B	a/a	PHI	100	0	1	209	5	75	17	39	-63
Aplin, Andrew	18	L	27	CF	a/a	SEA	287	4	1	196	9	75	68	49	-10
	19	L	28	CF	aaa	ARI	78	1	1	145	7	70	36	82	-55
Aquino, Aristides	18	R	24	RF	aa	CIN	404	18	3	216	7	68	123	55	3
	19	R	25	RF	aaa	CIN	294	25	4	268	6	67	217	106	85
Arauz, Jonathan	19	S	21	2B	aa	HOU	108	3	1	225	8	81	79	129	39
Arcia, Francisco	18	L	29	C	a/a	LAA	160	2	1	201	4	78	35	76	-28
	19	L	30	C	a/a	NYY	231	1	0	159	3	76	32	32	-49
Arenado, Jonah	18	R	23	3B	aa	SF	340	4	1	179	5	77	62	38	-21
	19	R	24	3B	aa	SF	378	3	2	230	6	77	60	70	-10
Arozarena, Randy	18	R	23	LF	a/a	STL	358	9	20	237	7	74	83	104	10
	19	R	24	CF	a/a	STL	343	12	14	299	8	77	127	135	62
Arraez, Luis	18	L	21	2B	aa	MIN	178	2	2	277	6	91	35	55	20
	19	L	22	2B	a/a	MIN	212	0	4	331	9	93	41	82	42
Arroyo, Christian	18	R	23	3B	aaa	TAM	170	2	2	207	4	78	66	62	-6
	19	R	24	3B	aaa	TAM	121	6	1	270	8	74	162	107	71
Arteaga, Humbert	18	R	24	3B	aaa	KC	414	4	2	259	4	81	53	42	-13
	19	R	25	SS	aaa	KC	284	3	8	255	3	86	48	104	27
Ascanio, Rayder	19	R	23	SS	aa	STL	267	5	3	240	5	78	84	70	13
Asche, Cody	18	L	28	3B	aaa	NYM	328	6	0	153	6	63	81	63	-48
	19	L	29	LF	aa	BOS	72	1	2	179	15	54	81	74	-81
Astudillo, Willians	18	R	27	C	aaa	MIN	286	10	6	242	3	94	83	69	72
	19	R	28	C	a/a	MIN	95	6	1	348	2	97	94	76	98
Asuaje, Carlos	18	L	27	2B	aaa	SD	175	1	0	241	6	81	60	91	13
	19	L	28	2B	aaa	ARI	159	3	1	173	7	75	71	122	6
Avans, Drew	19	L	23	LF	aa	LA	220	6	15	263	7	67	90	151	-1
Avelino, Abiatal	18	R	23	SS	a/a	SF	477	10	21	249	5	76	66	139	12
	19	R	24	SS	aaa	SF	473	8	13	249	4	80	85	190	57
Aviles Jr., Luis	18	R	23	SS	aa	MIL	207	4	13	238	9	72	91	90	9
	19	R	24	SS	aa	MIL	300	2	28	248	10	67	75	151	-13
Azocar, Jose	19	R	23	RF	aa	DET	504	10	10	276	4	73	84	149	14
Baez, Jeffrey	18	R	25	RF	aa	CHC	256	6	13	228	9	64	96	120	-11
	19	R	26	RF	aa	ARI	359	13	9	212	7	66	125	100	5
Baker, Chris	19	R	25	3B	aa	SD	104	2	1	164	10	60	53	90	-77
Balaguert , Yasiel	18	R	25	1B	aa	CHC	449	7	1	198	5	79	62	45	-9
Baldoquin, Robert	18	R	24	SS	aa	LAA	193	1	3	235	5	72	42	70	-43
	19	R	25	3B	aa	LAA	272	2	2	202	6	70	54	72	-43
Bandy, Jett	18	R	28	C	aaa	MIL	192	6	2	219	3	78	96	43	11
	19	R	29	C	aaa	TEX	242	9	0	182	4	65	109	34	-30
Banks, Nick	19	L	25	RF	aa	WAS	156	1	6	269	8	70	99	164	24
Bannon, Rylan	18	R	22	2B	aa	BAL	98	2	0	177	15	74	72	31	-5
	19	R	23	3B	a/a	BAL	470	10	7	239	8	80	95	107	43

BATTER	yr	b	age	pos	lvl	org	ab	hr	sb	ba	bb%	ct%	px	sx	bpv
Barnes, Barrett	19	R	28	RF	aa	NYM	311	10	4	187	12	60	125	53	-27
Barnum, Keon	18	L	25	1B	aa	CHW	272	14	0	182	3	59	135	28	-40
Baron, Steven	18	R	28	C	aaa	STL	136	0	0	166	4	71	27	25	-79
	19	R	29	C	aaa	PIT	133	1	0	142	7	65	42	70	-71
Barrera, Luis	18	L	23	CF	aa	OAK	131	0	10	295	5	85	65	160	52
	19	L	24	CF	aa	OAK	224	3	8	294	4	76	106	165	50
Barrera, Tres	19	R	25	C	aa	WAS	357	8	1	233	8	78	96	44	17
Barreto, Franklin	18	R	22	2B	aaa	OAK	282	14	4	231	10	60	156	90	13
	19	R	23	2B	aaa	OAK	373	14	12	258	8	66	167	223	78
Basabe, Luis	19	B	23	CF	aa	CHW	256	3	9	234	10	63	81	129	-30
Batten, Matthew	18	R	23	2B	a/a	SD	187	1	8	219	12	65	46	96	-51
	19	R	24	2B	a/a	SD	359	4	6	252	6	72	79	125	3
Bauers, Jake	18	L	23	1B	aaa	TAM	197	4	9	247	9	72	91	83	6
	19	L	24	LF	aaa	CLE	89	3	7	224	12	67	137	94	23
Beaty, Matt	18	L	25	1B	aaa	LA	101	1	0	231	8	80	81	27	10
	19	L	26	3B	aaa	LA	121	2	0	244	5	88	70	67	39
Beck, Preston	18	L	28	1B	aa	TEX	442	10	0	215	6	75	74	45	-14
	19	L	29	RF	a/a	TEX	422	8	2	215	8	73	93	111	15
Bednar, Brandon	18	R	26	2B	aa	COL	272	6	1	253	4	79	80	58	6
Beer, Seth	19	L	23	1B	aa	ARI	322	16	0	258	9	72	136	42	24
Bell, Brantley	19	R	25	2B	aa	CIN	359	6	9	216	7	79	72	84	11
Beltre, Michael	19	S	24	RF	aa	CIN	231	3	3	213	10	71	57	116	-22
Bemboom, Anthoi	18	L	28	C	aaa	COL	211	3	0	181	8	73	58	17	-38
	19	L	29	C	aaa	LAA	104	2	0	185	5	75	65	81	-10
Benedetti, Carmei	18	L	24	LF	aa	HOU	271	7	10	246	11	66	109	106	5
	19	L	25	LF	aa	HOU	73	0	1	141	9	47	52	140	-112
Bernard, Wynton	18	R	28	CF	a/a	CHC	252	2	18	192	5	75	55	141	-4
	19	R	29	LF	a/a	CHC	126	1	6	228	9	75	99	168	45
Berti, Jon	18	R	28	3B	a/a	TOR	345	6	22	249	8	78	71	151	33
	19	R	29	3B	aaa	MIA	62	3	4	226	16	77	89	109	31
Betts, Jordan	18	R	27	1B	a/a	BOS	332	8	0	205	5	66	85	20	-50
Bichette, Bo	18	R	20	SS	aa	TOR	539	10	28	281	7	81	104	140	65
	19	R	21	SS	aaa	TOR	222	7	13	265	7	77	134	163	77
Bichette, Dante	19	R	27	2B	aa	WAS	256	2	3	266	6	83	64	144	37
Biggio, Cavan	18	L	23	2B	aa	TOR	449	22	17	233	16	64	150	114	45
	19	L	24	2B	aaa	TOR	138	5	4	285	17	77	123	113	60
Bird, Corey	19	L	24	CF	aa	MIA	298	3	16	216	7	81	39	157	15
Birk, Ryne	18	L	24	2B	aa	HOU	412	1	11	190	8	76	34	116	-18
Bishop, Braden	18	R	25	CF	aa	SEA	345	6	4	238	8	76	70	78	1
	19	R	26	CF	aaa	SEA	185	6	1	217	8	70	125	52	9
Blanco, Dairon	19	R	26	CF	aa	KC	427	5	28	239	7	64	112	200	20
Blandino, Alex	19	R	27	2B	aaa	CIN	239	4	1	207	12	61	100	68	-39
Blankenhorn, Trav	19	L	23	2B	aa	MIN	388	17	10	266	4	75	126	148	55
Blash, Jabari	18	R	29	RF	aaa	LAA	287	17	3	221	9	52	194	63	0
Bohm, Alec	19	R	23	3B	aa	PHI	238	14	2	252	10	82	136	80	73
Bolt, Skye	18	B	24	CF	aa	OAK	285	7	8	220	7	71	102	119	15
	19	B	25	RF	aaa	OAK	305	8	5	224	8	64	124	147	13
Bonifacio, Jorge	18	R	25	RF	aaa	KC	51	0	0	350	10	74	100	87	22
	19	R	26	LF	aaa	KC	451	13	4	183	6	69	103	138	14
Booker, Joel	18	R	25	LF	aa	CHW	267	2	11	236	7	66	58	119	-37
	19	R	26	LF	a/a	CHW	351	4	16	209	5	69	54	143	-24
Borenstein, Zacha	18	L	28	LF	aaa	NYM	484	14	2	174	9	51	132	58	-54
	19	L	29	RF	aaa	CHC	41	1	0	192	4	45	51	38	-158
Bossart, Austin	18	R	25	C	aa	PHI	176	6	0	228	4	74	80	26	-23
	19	R	26	C	aa	NYM	260	6	2	167	12	70	89	76	-9
Bostick, Christoph	18	R	25	CF	aaa	MIA	362	3	6	244	6	72	71	79	-18
	19	R	26	2B	aaa	BAL	392	9	3	212	6	71	96	112	7
Boswell, Bret	19	L	25	2B	aa	COL	365	16	5	222	8	65	154	50	12
Bousfield, Auston	18	R	25	CF	a/a	SD	313	1	5	196	9	73	61	92	-13
Boyd, B.J.	18	L	25	LF	aaa	OAK	391	2	5	231	5	79	42	75	-15
Bradley, Bobby	18	L	22	1B	a/a	CLE	483	23	1	212	9	67	142	60	20
	19	L	23	1B	aaa	CLE	402	28	0	244	9	58	228	34	40
Brantly, Rob	18	L	29	C	aaa	CLE	229	1	0	169	2	73	47	27	-54
Brentz, Bryce	18	R	30	RF	aaa	NYM	193	8	1	180	6	53	167	52	-27
	19	R	30	LF	aaa	BOS	310	13	0	177	8	52	174	38	-27
Brigman, Bryson	18	R	23	2B	aa	MIA	42	1	2	273	4	84	59	31	1
	19	R	24	SS	aa	MIA	312	2	2	236	11	78	62	62	-5
Brinson, Lewis	18	R	24	CF	a/a	MIA	50	1	1	153	5	75	51	66	-29
	19	R	25	CF	aaa	MIA	296	12	14	230	9	60	157	206	43
Brito, Socrates	18	L	26	RF	aaa	ARI	428	9	9	239	6	70	101	107	6
	19	L	27	LF	aaa	TOR	394	13	9	243	5	71	143	167	59
Brockmeyer, Cael	18	R	27	C	a/a	LA	224	3	2	241	6	64	73	57	-57
	19	R	28	1B	aa	BAL	28	0	1	87	6	67	32	139	-55
Brodey, Quinn	19	L	24	CF	aa	NYM	247	5	5	224	8	71	95	66	-7
Brooks, Trenton	19	L	24	RF	aa	CLE	241	8	1	260	7	83	145	101	90
Brosseau, Michae	18	R	24	3B	aa	TAM	370	10	9	226	6	76	96	106	27
	19	R	25	3B	aaa	TAM	270	12	2	255	9	74	149	87	54
Brown, Seth	18	L	26	1B	aa	OAK	502	10	4	233	6	67	101	84	-11
	19	L	27	1B	aaa	OAK	451	25	6	237	6	65	183	191	78
Broxton, Keon	18	R	28	CF	aaa	MIL	299	7	16	189	6	49	112	126	-64
Brugman, Jaycob	18	L	26	LF	a/a	BAL	264	7	4	209	7	68	81	106	-16
	19	L	27	DH	aaa	SEA	301	17	0	216	7	62	187	41	22
Brujan, Vidal	19	S	21	2B	aa	TAM	207	3	22	256	9	81	77	202	61
Bruno, Stephen	18	R	28	2B	aaa	CHC	271	2	3	184	4	79	42	50	-25
Brusa, Gio	19	B	26	1B	a/a	SF	301	8	3	190	9	60	131	89	-14
Burch, Luke	19	L	25	LF	aa	DET	130	0	5	298	5	60	36	97	-91
Burcham, Scott	18	R	25	SS	aa	COL	175	2	5	241	7	69	62	61	-40
	19	R	26	SS	aa	COL	220	3	5	199	10	69	89	88	-14

BATTER	yr	b	age	pos	lvl	org	ab	hr	sb	ba	bb%	ct%	px	sx	bpv
Burks, Charcer	18	R	23	LF	aa	CHC	437	5	12	207	11	68	60	114	-22
	19	R	24	LF	a/a	CHC	387	2	14	219	10	70	62	180	-1
Burns, Andrew	19	R	29	3B	aaa	TOR	411	14	5	224	9	75	103	78	19
Burns, Billy	18	B	29	CF	aaa	KC	376	3	7	201	5	83	28	76	-11
	19	B	30	CF	aaa	NYY	267	2	10	198	7	80	54	160	25
Burt, D.J.	19	R	24	LF	aa	KC	257	2	23	210	9	72	53	146	-10
Calabuig, Chase	19	L	24	LF	aa	OAK	403	3	6	250	12	72	56	115	-19
Caldwell, Bruce	18	L	27	2B	a/a	NYY	426	9	1	213	9	65	96	43	-29
	19	L	28	SS	aa	MIL	313	9	2	196	10	64	112	51	-26
Calhoun, Willie	18	L	24	LF	aaa	TEX	432	7	3	259	5	88	71	61	40
	19	L	25	LF	aaa	TEX	138	6	1	258	15	81	119	30	44
Calica, Andrew	18	L	24	CF	aa	CLE	421	5	22	257	10	73	66	109	-3
	19	L	25	DH	aa	CLE	25	0	0	184	13	59	86	157	-30
Calixte, Orlando	18	R	26	SS	aaa	SF	400	6	10	213	5	71	59	106	-24
	19	R	27	3B	aaa	SEA	97	1	2	215	5	68	45	66	-61
Call, Alex	18	R	24	RF	aa	CHW	236	7	2	219	9	63	123	67	-7
	19	R	25	CF	aa	CLE	293	5	4	190	6	64	90	117	-23
Cameron, Daz	18	R	21	CF	a/a	DET	257	4	12	259	8	73	103	142	36
	19	R	22	CF	aaa	DET	448	12	15	204	11	65	122	182	28
Cancel, Gabriel	19	R	23	2B	aa	KC	464	15	13	232	6	67	135	131	29
Candelario, Jeimer	19	B	26	3B	aaa	DET	153	7	0	281	10	74	157	130	76
Canelo, Malquin	18	R	24	SS	aa	PHI	470	8	18	212	6	72	58	123	-15
	19	R	25	SS	aaa	PHI	423	2	6	218	5	60	78	100	-55
Capel, Conner	19	L	22	LF	a/a	STL	371	9	8	222	5	74	85	103	7
Capra, Vinny	19	R	23	2B	aa	TOR	388	3	14	224	7	77	67	147	19
Cardona, Jose	18	R	24	CF	a/a	TEX	365	6	10	221	6	80	45	70	-8
Carlson, Dylan	19	B	21	CF	a/a	STL	489	21	17	265	9	75	139	180	78
Caro, Roberto	19	B	26	RF	aa	CHC	376	2	27	213	12	70	56	172	-10
Carpio, Luis	19	R	22	2B	aa	NYM	243	3	2	245	10	77	75	40	-4
Carrizales, Omar	18	L	23	CF	aa	COL	279	6	9	221	6	72	93	111	11
	19	L	24	LF	a/a	NYY	44	0	0	139	9	74	35	95	-32
Casteel, Ryan	19	R	28	1B	aa	ATL	411	19	0	236	9	66	151	66	17
Castellano, Angelo	19	R	24	1B	aa	KC	217	4	5	201	8	72	77	96	-9
Castillo, Ali	18	R	29	3B	aa	SF	329	1	5	205	5	87	45	93	23
	19	R	30	2B	a/a	PHI	466	7	4	252	5	81	71	98	22
Castillo, Ivan	19	B	24	2B	aa	SD	432	6	13	277	4	85	86	162	68
Castillo, Rusney	18	R	31	CF	aaa	BOS	474	4	9	268	4	80	60	58	-5
	19	R	32	RF	aaa	BOS	460	12	4	229	4	83	87	50	29
Castro, Daniel	18	R	26	SS	aaa	COL	251	2	1	254	3	89	53	55	24
	19	R	27	SS	aaa	SEA	280	2	2	178	4	87	32	69	5
Castro, Harold	18	L	25	3B	a/a	DET	351	2	4	232	2	79	34	55	-36
	19	L	26	2B	aaa	DET	122	3	1	286	6	76	91	104	20
Castro, Willi	18	B	21	SS	a/a	DET	497	8	16	250	6	77	80	120	19
	19	B	22	SS	aaa	DET	465	10	15	290	6	76	114	196	65
Cave, Jake	18	L	26	RF	aaa	MIN	216	5	3	241	9	71	78	72	-10
	19	L	27	CF	aaa	MIN	196	6	4	302	6	70	156	182	72
Cecchini, Gavin	18	R	25	2B	aaa	NYM	109	1	1	222	4	83	82	66	27
	19	R	26	2B	a/a	NYM	145	2	3	200	8	70	56	62	-43
Centeno, Juan	18	L	29	C	aaa	TEX	205	1	0	183	5	80	39	41	-25
	19	L	30	C	aaa	BOS	266	3	1	205	6	79	66	59	-2
Cervenka, Martin	18	R	26	C	aa	BAL	337	11	1	210	6	78	94	30	9
	19	R	27	C	a/a	BAL	203	3	2	200	7	62	53	49	-83
Cesar, Randy	18	R	23	3B	aa	HOU	446	9	3	269	7	72	83	59	-13
	19	R	24	3B	a/a	MIN	191	3	0	226	10	62	110	45	-35
Chang, Yu-Cheng	18	R	23	SS	aaa	CLE	457	10	3	236	7	65	105	58	-20
	19	R	24	2B	aaa	CLE	253	8	3	229	8	70	118	126	27
Chatham, C.J.	19	R	25	SS	a/a	BOS	436	4	6	278	4	78	87	105	25
Chavez, Alberti	18	R	23	SS	aa	CIN	60	0	0	196	3	79	0	37	-64
	19	R	24	SS	a/a	CIN	179	1	1	201	7	71	42	103	-39
Chavez, Santiago	18	R	23	C	aa	OAK	91	0	0	182	2	80	73	58	2
	19	R	24	C	aa	MIA	248	1	0	164	7	62	31	46	-99
Chavis, Michael	18	R	23	3B	a/a	BOS	155	6	2	279	7	68	134	72	16
	19	R	24	2B	aaa	BOS	70	6	0	236	8	68	220	28	68
Chester, Carl	19	R	24	LF	aa	TAM	121	2	5	241	4	70	99	172	23
Chinea, Chris	18	R	24	1B	aa	STL	299	10	0	192	4	73	82	31	-24
	19	R	25	1B	a/a	STL	294	7	0	235	4	68	99	45	-25
Chisholm, Jasrado	19	L	21	SS	aa	MIA	396	21	18	220	13	61	170	190	64
Chu, Li-Jen	18	R	24	C	a/a	CLE	58	2	0	219	4	75	73	12	-28
	19	R	25	C	aa	CLE	210	5	0	212	6	64	109	32	-36
Ciuffo, Nick	18	L	23	C	aaa	TAM	221	4	0	232	5	67	75	30	-50
	19	L	24	C	aaa	CIN	143	3	1	207	8	64	120	103	-2
Clare, Chris	19	R	25	2B	a/a	BAL	103	1	1	149	9	71	49	90	-36
Clark, Ledarious	19	R	26	CF	aa	TEX	110	5	2	185	5	63	117	96	-13
Clement, Ernie	18	R	22	SS	aa	CLE	65	0	1	238	4	89	68	103	49
	19	R	23	SS	a/a	CLE	405	1	15	254	6	91	40	125	45
Coats, Jason	18	R	28	LF	aaa	TAM	397	11	2	196	4	70	104	89	-1
	19	R	29	LF	aaa	TAM	336	13	4	190	4	61	125	74	-20
Cole, Hunter	18	R	26	RF	a/a	TEX	378	12	1	255	8	67	95	50	-23
	19	R	27	RF	aaa	TEX	104	4	0	258	8	63	140	99	8
Collier, Zach	18	L	28	RF	aa	WAS	307	4	4	170	9	62	86	97	-35
	19	L	29	CF	aa	WAS	23	1	0	186	13	73	99	116	23
Collins, Zack	18	L	23	C	aa	CHW	418	15	5	218	19	58	134	69	-2
	19	L	24	C	aaa	CHW	294	16	0	243	14	61	185	68	28
Colon, Christian	18	R	29	2B	aaa	NYM	319	3	7	200	7	84	54	69	15
	19	R	30	3B	aaa	CIN	497	8	18	238	8	84	82	86	42
Contreras, Mark	19	L	24	LF	aa	MIN	281	9	8	197	7	64	125	148	14
Contreras, William	19	R	22	C	aa	ATL	191	3	0	253	8	79	74	65	6
Corcino, Edgar	18	B	26	RF	a/a	MIN	296	6	2	230	6	78	83	91	20

BATTER	yr	b	age	pos	lvl	org	ab	hr	sb	ba	bb%	ct%	px	sx	bpv
Cordell, Ryan	18	R	26	CF	a/a	CHW	188	4	6	208	5	70	77	98	-17
	19	R	27	RF	aaa	CHW	51	1	1	219	5	58	150	157	12
Cordero, Andretty	19	R	22	1B	aa	TEX	500	16	2	271	5	80	92	58	24
Costello, Ryan	19	L	23	3B	aa	MIN	129	6	0	230	14	63	166	110	34
Coulter, Clint	18	R	25	RF	a/a	MIL	265	10	1	218	5	64	122	85	-9
Court, Ryan	18	R	30	SS	aaa	CHC	386	7	3	195	9	50	99	55	-84
Cowan, Jordan	19	L	24	2B	aa	SEA	440	2	17	246	11	78	34	105	-16
Cowart, Kaleb	18	B	26	SS	aaa	LAA	258	4	5	210	4	75	76	96	-2
	19	B	27	3B	a/a	LAA	326	7	2	214	6	75	81	91	3
Cozens, Dylan	18	L	24	RF	aaa	PHI	297	19	7	218	11	51	215	91	27
	19	L	25	RF	aaa	TAM	85	5	4	148	17	39	279	199	58
Craig, Will	18	R	24	1B	aa	PIT	480	16	5	219	7	71	110	86	13
	19	R	25	1B	aaa	PIT	494	17	2	214	7	67	115	48	-13
Crawford, J.P.	18	L	23	SS	aaa	PHI	58	1	1	231	7	66	71	90	-37
Crawford, Rashad	18	L	25	CF	a/a	NYY	202	2	7	200	7	69	54	93	-38
	19	L	26	CF	aa	NYY	401	7	18	230	8	70	63	109	-26
Cribbs, Galli	18	L	26	SS	aa	ARI	308	2	5	178	7	58	69	124	-58
	19	L	27	2B	aa	ARI	245	2	2	186	8	54	95	145	-53
Cron, Kevin	18	R	25	3B	aaa	ARI	392	12	1	235	5	69	108	39	-13
	19	R	26	1B	aaa	ARI	305	22	1	251	11	69	195	66	66
Cronenworth, Jake	18	L	24	SS	a/a	TAM	443	3	18	219	8	80	49	140	19
	19	L	25	SS	aaa	TAM	344	8	10	283	10	78	107	167	61
Cronin, Joe	18	R	24	2B	aa	MIN	26	0	0	100	10	54	0	42	-147
	19	R	25	2B	aa	MIN	231	4	8	175	13	63	78	196	-12
Crook, Narciso	18	R	23	LF	aa	CIN	161	2	3	261	9	71	54	87	-27
	19	R	24	LF	a/a	CIN	346	10	9	254	6	65	145	176	42
Cruz, Oneil	19	L	21	SS	aa	PIT	119	1	3	269	11	70	114	151	32
Cuevas, Noel	18	R	27	RF	aaa	COL	160	3	2	273	6	84	85	80	40
	19	R	28	CF	aaa	COL	205	3	2	225	7	74	91	123	17
Cumana, Grenny	19	R	24	RF	a/a	PHI	186	2	1	266	3	86	55	99	27
Cumberland, Brett	18	S	23	C	aa	BAL	60	2	0	145	6	70	66	25	-47
Curletta, Joey	18	R	24	1B	aa	SEA	465	19	1	242	12	66	113	28	-8
	19	R	25	1B	a/a	BOS	422	11	3	199	10	61	117	81	-24
Cuthbert, Cheslor	19	R	27	1B	aaa	KC	197	5	0	254	6	72	130	66	26
Daal, Calten	19	R	26	2B	aa	CIN	279	0	4	263	3	77	31	117	-22
Dalbec, Bobby	18	R	23	3B	aa	BOS	111	4	0	240	4	56	176	56	-9
	19	R	24	3B	a/a	BOS	472	22	5	224	11	68	140	84	27
Davidson, Austin	18	L	25	LF	aa	WAS	267	8	1	247	9	80	95	61	35
	19	L	26	1B	aa	WAS	213	4	0	206	11	73	102	52	5
Davidson, Matthew	19	R	28	1B	aaa	TEX	469	24	1	214	6	62	157	47	0
Davis, Brendon	19	R	22	LF	aa	TEX	346	3	0	204	11	67	64	57	-49
Davis, Dylan	18	R	25	LF	a/a	SF	438	8	3	192	5	69	84	73	-22
	19	R	26	LF	aa	SF	31	0	0	147	23	35	195	26	-76
Davis, J.D.	18	R	25	3B	aaa	HOU	333	12	2	273	7	75	112	62	23
Davis, Jaylin	18	R	24	RF	aa	MIN	240	5	4	243	6	69	90	83	-15
	19	R	25	RF	a/a	SF	468	25	9	265	11	67	166	113	47
Davis, Jonathan	18	R	26	CF	a/a	TOR	490	8	21	248	7	78	79	141	33
	19	R	27	CF	aaa	TOR	294	8	10	225	10	66	129	182	38
Davis, Taylor	18	R	29	C	aaa	CHC	356	3	0	208	7	79	43	20	-25
	19	R	30	C	aaa	CHC	204	4	0	183	10	76	45	27	-36
Dawson, Ronnie	18	L	23	CF	aa	HOU	114	6	5	264	4	67	139	120	25
	19	L	24	CF	a/a	HOU	426	13	10	172	8	59	125	123	-15
Daza, Yonathan	18	R	24	CF	aa	COL	219	3	3	289	2	89	86	82	55
	19	R	25	CF	aaa	COL	387	8	8	316	4	85	102	107	65
De Goti, Alex	18	R	24	SS	a/a	HOU	452	10	5	238	5	79	79	68	12
	19	R	25	2B	aaa	HOU	481	10	3	217	7	73	90	89	5
De La Cruz, Bryan	19	R	23	LF	aa	HOU	269	4	6	256	7	75	81	168	28
De La Cruz, Michael	18	B	25	C	aaa	TOR	43	0	0	174	10	56	154	74	-7
	19	B	26	C	aaa	TOR	162	4	1	238	11	76	105	54	21
De La Guerra, Ch	18	L	26	2B	a/a	BOS	389	12	5	212	6	66	94	89	-20
	19	L	27	SS	aaa	BOS	226	10	1	251	7	67	163	74	36
De La Trinidad, Er	19	L	23	LF	aa	MIN	122	2	0	196	11	72	52	58	-37
De Leon, Michael	18	B	21	SS	aa	TEX	503	3	1	248	3	86	40	37	-5
	19	B	22	SS	aa	TEX	477	3	3	261	6	87	41	58	10
Dean, Austin	18	R	25	LF	a/a	MIA	397	9	2	292	8	83	73	77	31
	19	R	26	1B	aaa	MIA	252	14	3	282	9	75	161	97	72
DeCarlo, Joe	18	R	25	C	aa	SEA	207	6	0	206	8	69	113	47	-3
	19	R	26	C	aa	SEA	171	1	0	146	10	54	42	57	-118
Deglan, Kellin	19	L	27	C	a/a	NYY	249	8	1	216	6	62	122	85	-18
Deichmann, Greg	19	L	24	RF	aa	OAK	301	9	16	194	9	62	106	169	-4
Delay, Jason	19	R	24	C	aa	PIT	231	7	1	219	5	71	114	86	12
DeLuzio, Ben	18	R	24	CF	aa	ARI	263	1	27	229	7	69	58	158	-14
	19	R	25	CF	a/a	ARI	374	3	13	247	8	70	90	170	17
Demeritte, Travis	18	R	24	LF	aa	ATL	428	15	5	204	10	64	123	108	9
	19	R	25	LF	aaa	ATL	339	16	3	250	11	65	184	112	54
Dewees, Donnie	18	L	25	CF	a/a	KC	507	6	12	228	5	80	64	119	18
	19	L	26	LF	aaa	CHC	368	12	5	215	8	81	104	132	59
Diaz, Edwin	18	R	23	3B	aa	OAK	103	1	1	141	6	66	59	33	-64
	19	R	24	3B	a/a	OAK	471	10	2	202	8	63	144	152	25
Diaz, Francisco	18	B	28	C	a/a	NYY	161	1	0	241	10	72	39	45	-46
	19	B	29	C	aa	NYY	39	0	0	210	17	68	0	46	-97
Diaz, Isan	18	L	22	2B	a/a	MIA	431	10	12	205	12	64	101	117	-2
	19	L	23	2B	aaa	MIA	377	21	5	270	11	71	159	136	68
Diaz, Lewin	19	L	23	1B	aa	MIA	241	14	0	240	8	77	186	69	90
Diaz, Yandy	18	R	27	3B	aaa	CLE	348	2	1	249	13	74	66	33	-12
Diaz, Yusniel	18	R	22	RF	aa	BAL	354	9	9	253	11	80	75	87	30
	19	R	23	RF	aa	BAL	286	11	0	243	9	75	134	102	53
Dickerson, Alex	19	L	29	DH	aaa	SF	114	3	0	261	10	78	86	85	20

BATTER	yr	b	age	pos	lvl	org	ab	hr	sb	ba	bb%	ct%	px	sx	bpv
Didder, Ray-Patric	18	R	24	SS	aa	ATL	131	1	8	253	9	69	64	128	-14
	19	R	25	SS	aa	ATL	340	4	29	196	13	62	77	158	-29
Difo, Wilmer	19	R	27	SS	aaa	WAS	233	3	9	244	7	73	81	165	20
Dini, Nick	18	R	25	C	a/a	KC	319	8	5	217	3	76	74	81	-5
	19	R	26	C	aaa	KC	186	9	5	244	8	82	123	87	65
Dixon, Brandon	18	R	26	2B	aaa	CIN	179	5	7	295	5	63	151	109	18
	19	R	27	1B	aaa	DET	46	1	0	146	0	60	38	127	-80
Donahue, Christiar	19	L	24	2B	aa	CHC	331	3	8	193	7	75	60	134	0
Dorow, Ryan	19	R	24	3B	aa	TEX	183	4	3	210	9	62	86	155	-22
Dosch, Drew	18	L	26	3B	aaa	BAL	355	6	1	236	7	64	90	46	-42
Downs, Jerry	19	L	26	1B	aa	BOS	153	2	0	164	7	59	100	27	-65
Drake, Blake	18	R	25	RF	aa	STL	289	4	4	193	5	70	74	56	-32
Duarte, Osvaldo	19	R	23	SS	aa	HOU	458	11	19	211	5	64	94	187	-2
Dubon, Mauricio	18	R	24	SS	aaa	MIL	108	3	4	283	1	79	109	119	43
	19	R	25	SS	aaa	SF	503	13	8	257	4	85	83	88	42
Duenez, Samir	18	L	22	1B	aa	KC	287	8	4	264	9	75	103	92	31
	19	L	23	1B	a/a	CIN	389	8	0	194	7	74	72	55	-19
Duggar, Steven	18	L	25	CF	aaa	SF	316	2	8	222	8	62	100	119	-20
	19	L	26	CF	aaa	SF	83	2	2	284	14	70	122	148	40
Dunand, Joe	18	R	23	SS	aa	MIA	217	6	0	183	6	63	100	38	-43
	19	R	24	SS	aa	MIA	462	5	2	228	8	71	74	82	-17
Duran, Jarren	19	L	23	CF	aa	BOS	320	1	25	247	6	73	59	207	12
Duvall, Adam	19	R	31	LF	aaa	ATL	369	23	1	208	9	71	167	127	69
Eaves, Kody	18	L	25	3B	a/a	DET	329	3	3	173	9	71	64	86	-20
	19	L	26	2B	a/a	DET	430	14	3	217	7	66	136	161	32
Edman, Tommy	18	S	23	SS	a/a	STL	518	5	23	263	6	81	50	119	15
	19	R	24	2B	aaa	STL	197	5	7	261	5	81	103	209	82
Ellis, Drew	19	R	24	3B	aa	ARI	379	13	0	217	14	68	124	32	-1
Engel, Adam	19	R	28	CF	aaa	CHW	248	7	9	213	6	68	109	186	27
English, Tanner	18	R	25	CF	aa	MIN	299	3	10	191	5	64	85	144	-21
	19	R	26	CF	a/a	MIN	152	2	7	144	6	55	63	202	-58
Erceg, Lucas	18	L	23	3B	aa	MIL	463	13	3	236	7	80	78	58	17
	19	L	24	3B	aaa	MIL	357	12	1	187	8	67	114	78	-5
Ervin, Phillip	18	R	26	LF	aaa	CIN	173	4	8	245	8	73	107	120	31
	19	R	27	CF	aaa	CIN	145	5	5	245	10	70	123	117	29
Espinal, Edwin	18	R	24	1B	aaa	DET	335	5	0	219	9	79	41	24	-23
Espinal, Santiago	18	R	24	2B	aa	TOR	147	1	2	261	7	83	64	84	27
	19	R	25	2B	a/a	TOR	471	6	10	262	7	82	73	66	21
Esposito, Nathan	18	R	25	C	aa	KC	45	0	1	136	3	63	44	87	-77
Estevez, Omar	19	R	21	2B	aa	LA	299	6	0	272	8	74	112	25	8
Estrada, Thairo	18	R	22	SS	aaa	NYY	33	0	0	135	0	73	23	14	-82
	19	R	23	SS	aaa	NYY	241	7	2	236	5	77	116	126	49
Evans, Phillip	18	R	26	3B	aaa	NYM	219	8	2	188	6	76	84	61	2
	19	R	27	3B	aaa	CHC	466	13	1	236	9	81	100	75	40
Fairchild, Stuart	19	R	23	CF	aa	CIN	153	4	3	257	10	83	114	113	70
Fargas, Johneshw	19	R	25	CF	aa	SF	413	4	46	231	7	75	52	195	13
Farmer, Kyle	18	R	28	3B	aaa	LA	288	5	1	225	4	78	84	50	3
Featherston, Tayl	18	R	29	2B	a/a	CIN	315	6	7	156	6	51	76	117	-85
	19	R	30	SS	a/a	KC	406	11	4	192	4	48	134	131	-51
Feliz, Anderson	18	B	26	3B	a/a	BAL	438	8	15	231	7	70	67	104	-22
	19	B	27	3B	a/a	BAL	272	3	4	202	8	64	92	72	-34
Ferguson, Drew	19	R	27	CF	aaa	HOU	402	7	17	212	10	67	84	174	2
Fermin, Freddy	19	R	24	C	aa	KC	107	2	0	232	2	77	66	39	-18
Fernandez, Vince	19	L	24	LF	aa	COL	230	16	1	269	11	62	251	133	105
Fernandez, Xavier	18	R	23	C	aa	KC	119	2	2	304	6	85	91	106	58
	19	R	24	C	a/a	KC	183	5	1	223	7	81	75	50	12
Ficociello, Dominic	18	B	26	1B	aa	DET	366	6	7	227	8	64	72	74	-46
Field, Johnny	18	R	26	LF	aaa	MIN	89	1	2	231	8	77	66	73	2
	19	R	27	RF	aaa	CHC	278	6	5	195	6	63	134	148	18
Fields, Roemon	18	L	28	CF	aaa	TOR	328	2	20	200	7	71	41	118	-34
	19	L	29	CF	aaa	TOR	299	2	12	207	7	78	38	138	-2
Filia, Eric	18	L	26	RF	aa	SEA	296	2	1	224	10	87	38	54	19
	19	L	27	RF	aaa	SEA	121	1	0	257	13	84	92	53	41
Fisher, Derek	18	L	25	CF	aaa	HOU	239	7	7	196	10	58	106	101	-33
	19	L	26	CF	aaa	HOU	224	10	5	221	11	63	128	102	-1
Fisher, Jameson	18	L	25	LF	aa	CHW	315	6	3	192	11	58	77	62	-63
Fleming, Billy	18	R	26	2B	a/a	NYY	259	6	2	245	6	75	88	56	2
	19	R	27	1B	a/a	MIA	187	4	0	231	10	63	93	56	-42
Fletcher, David	18	R	24	SS	aaa	LAA	254	4	4	273	4	90	82	110	67
Flete, Bryant	18	L	25	3B	a/a	CHW	284	2	3	216	10	68	51	73	-45
Flores, Jecksson	18	R	25	2B	aa	KC	459	5	21	278	5	83	72	118	35
	19	R	26	SS	aaa	KC	410	5	12	206	7	79	52	104	2
Flores, Ramon	18	L	26	LF	aaa	BOS	195	2	2	196	9	76	53	52	-19
	19	L	27	LF	aaa	MIN	107	2	2	263	14	76	78	103	13
Flores, Rudy	18	L	28	1B	aa	ARI	438	11	1	223	9	65	100	57	-24
Fontana, Nolan	18	L	27	SS	aaa	LAA	145	2	2	166	13	67	83	95	-10
	19	L	28	2B	aaa	TEX	108	2	0	133	12	57	85	41	-77
Forbes, TiQuan	19	R	23	3B	aa	CHW	392	3	4	230	10	70	68	98	-22
Ford, Mike	18	L	26	1B	aaa	NYY	367	14	1	215	7	77	95	35	12
	19	L	27	1B	aaa	NYY	294	20	0	252	11	77	164	34	65
Fowler, Dustin	18	L	24	CF	aaa	OAK	229	3	10	302	3	80	94	147	47
	19	L	25	CF	aaa	OAK	556	17	8	230	5	70	107	163	25
Fox, Lucius	18	B	21	SS	aa	TAM	104	1	5	201	6	78	40	123	-3
	19	B	22	SS	a/a	TAM	407	3	35	205	12	71	70	220	22
Fraley, Jake	19	L	24	CF	a/a	SEA	382	16	18	262	7	72	150	177	75
France, Ty	18	R	24	3B	a/a	SD	509	16	2	223	6	80	88	58	21
	19	R	25	3B	aaa	SD	296	17	1	322	7	79	170	99	95
Franco, Carlos	18	L	27	1B	aaa	ATL	437	12	1	206	6	58	105	41	-56

BATTER	yr	b	age	pos	lvl	org	ab	hr	sb	ba	bb%	ct%	px	sx	bpv
Franklin, Nick	18	B	27	RF	aa	MIL	59	2	3	251	14	86	77	75	56
	19	B	28	2B	aaa	LAA	260	4	3	169	8	70	82	87	-13
Frazier, Clint	18	R	24	CF	aaa	NYY	190	10	3	276	9	68	155	107	50
	19	R	25	LF	a/a	NYY	250	8	2	216	6	74	123	86	32
Freeman, Ronnie	18	R	27	C	a/a	SF	232	2	0	204	5	74	37	27	-53
	19	R	28	C	aaa	SF	122	3	0	235	8	71	75	87	-16
Freitas, David	18	R	29	C	aaa	SEA	146	3	0	267	8	75	89	31	-3
	19	R	30	C	aaa	MIL	328	9	0	293	9	77	98	27	10
Friedl Jr., T.J.	18	L	23	LF	aa	CIN	261	2	16	251	9	76	49	137	2
	19	L	24	RF	aa	CIN	226	5	11	216	10	74	99	200	50
Fuentes, Josh	18	R	25	3B	aaa	COL	551	10	2	281	2	80	91	88	24
	19	R	26	3B	aaa	COL	402	12	1	213	4	67	118	92	2
Fuentes, Reymon	18	L	27	CF	aaa	ARI	302	3	6	193	6	74	50	105	-20
Gale, Rocky	18	R	30	C	aaa	LA	295	3	1	211	3	78	48	41	-32
	19	R	31	C	a/a	TAM	176	1	1	213	4	73	46	94	-30
Gallagher, Camer	18	R	26	C	aaa	KC	268	3	1	224	7	84	49	34	0
Galloway, Isaac	18	R	29	RF	aaa	MIA	324	6	15	199	5	70	83	146	1
	19	R	30	LF	aaa	MIA	103	5	2	169	1	49	184	167	2
Gamache, Dan	18	L	28	2B	aa	WAS	413	4	1	222	9	68	59	32	-51
	19	L	29	1B	aa	OAK	144	0	0	154	10	71	37	34	-63
Gamboa, Arquime	19	S	22	SS	aa	PHI	356	3	19	177	13	64	62	169	-26
Garcia, Anthony	18	R	26	DH	aaa	OAK	480	18	1	209	9	74	108	45	17
	19	R	27	LF	aaa	SF	183	4	1	231	9	70	78	37	-32
Garcia, Aramis	18	R	25	C	a/a	SF	339	7	0	192	5	70	71	50	-37
	19	R	26	C	aaa	SF	332	10	0	224	7	60	139	84	-10
Garcia, Jose Adol	18	R	25	RF	aaa	STL	406	16	7	213	2	72	114	110	20
	19	R	26	RF	aaa	STL	491	23	10	205	3	62	150	178	34
Garcia, Luis	19	L	19	SS	aa	WAS	525	4	11	268	3	84	58	159	40
Garcia, Robel	19	B	26	3B	a/a	CHC	338	22	3	246	10	58	208	102	45
Garcia, Wilson	19	B	25	1B	aa	CLE	257	9	0	250	5	85	131	35	66
Garlick, Kyle	18	R	26	RF	a/a	LA	402	16	1	209	3	58	133	68	-32
	19	R	27	RF	aaa	LA	271	16	1	247	6	60	225	97	63
Garrett, Stone	19	R	24	LF	aa	MIA	412	13	16	228	4	66	126	191	34
Gatewood, Jacob	18	R	23	1B	aa	MIL	352	19	2	234	7	64	154	60	14
	19	R	24	3B	aa	MIL	353	14	3	185	7	56	138	147	-10
George, Jordan	18	B	26	DH	aa	PIT	342	4	0	223	9	84	39	31	-3
	19	B	27	1B	aa	KC	91	0	2	240	16	75	51	25	-35
Gerber, Mike	18	L	26	CF	aaa	DET	287	11	2	186	6	60	127	79	-21
	19	L	27	CF	aaa	SF	464	16	4	250	6	64	163	103	29
Gettys, Michael	18	R	23	CF	aa	SD	430	12	14	204	6	58	114	110	-30
	19	R	24	CF	aaa	SD	507	20	9	205	4	62	146	160	24
Giambrone, Trent	18	R	25	2B	aa	CHC	398	14	21	218	9	74	97	109	28
	19	R	26	2B	aaa	CHC	431	18	13	203	7	64	146	107	19
Gibbons, Zach	18	R	25	LF	aa	LAA	395	3	5	222	8	82	53	91	17
Gibson, Cam	18	L	24	LF	aa	DET	152	3	5	223	9	70	87	129	7
	19	L	25	LF	aa	DET	400	8	23	220	9	73	103	183	42
Gillaspie, Casey	18	B	25	1B	aaa	CHW	255	3	0	184	7	58	88	17	-78
Gilliam, Isiah	19	S	23	RF	aa	NYY	161	9	0	172	7	59	168	35	-7
Gimenez, Andres	18	L	20	SS	aa	NYM	137	0	9	250	5	82	52	120	20
	19	L	21	SS	aa	NYM	432	9	28	235	5	74	94	181	36
Gittens, Chris	18	R	24	1B	aa	NYY	183	6	0	176	11	60	103	26	-47
	19	R	25	1B	aa	NYY	398	23	0	256	14	60	169	42	4
Glendinning, Robb	19	R	24	3B	aa	PIT	184	4	3	245	11	62	101	105	-24
Godoy, Jose	18	L	24	C	aa	STL	31	0	0	190	4	89	20	28	-8
	19	L	25	C	a/a	STL	239	5	0	233	7	78	91	39	10
Goeddel, Tyler	18	R	26	LF	a/a	LA	237	3	3	175	6	72	51	95	-27
	19	R	27	CF	aa	WAS	197	1	1	186	9	58	73	112	-60
Goetzman, Granc	18	R	26	RF	aa	STL	172	2	2	197	3	74	82	108	0
	19	R	27	RF	aa	HOU	306	13	1	187	8	64	129	51	-10
Gomez, Jose	19	R	23	2B	aa	PHI	292	3	4	233	6	71	61	110	-22
Gomez, Miguel	18	B	26	2B	a/a	SF	423	4	1	241	2	82	62	61	2
Gonzalez, Alfredo	18	R	26	C	a/a	CHW	213	2	2	206	7	64	47	47	-75
	19	R	27	C	a/a	CHW	208	2	0	191	11	69	62	50	-44
Gonzalez, Benji	18	B	28	SS	aaa	WAS	312	2	7	198	7	74	49	85	-24
	19	B	29	SS	aaa	WAS	48	0	0	143	6	71	51	69	-41
Gonzalez, Luis	19	L	24	CF	aa	CHW	473	9	16	231	9	79	73	145	30
	18	R	24	SS	aa	CIN	391	3	4	216	4	79	43	74	-18
Gonzalez, Luis	19	R	25	2B	a/a	CIN	84	0	0	263	7	77	83	151	32
Gonzalez, Yariel	19	S	25	3B	a/a	STL	237	10	2	220	6	81	104	46	33
Goodwin, Brian	18	L	28	LF	a/a	KC	55	2	1	176	8	70	121	69	16
Gordon, Nick	18	L	23	SS	a/a	MIN	544	6	17	230	5	79	58	122	10
	19	L	24	SS	aaa	MIN	292	3	12	271	5	76	120	175	63
Gore, Jordan	18	S	24	SS	aa	MIN	136	1	1	222	8	77	63	113	9
	19	S	25	SS	aa	MIN	304	3	2	186	7	71	52	55	-47
Gore, Terrance	18	R	27	LF	aaa	CHC	176	0	14	152	7	66	17	163	-55
	19	R	28	CF	aaa	NYY	55	0	2	127	14	62	63	167	-36
Goris, Diego	18	R	28	3B	aaa	SD	325	4	2	195	3	69	67	64	-42
Granite, Zack	18	L	26	CF	aaa	MIN	237	0	8	188	7	87	23	85	8
	19	L	27	LF	aaa	TEX	504	2	17	243	4	90	43	140	47
Graterol, Juan	18	R	29	C	aaa	MIN	206	0	0	252	2	92	32	32	11
	19	R	30	C	aaa	CIN	209	2	0	196	5	88	41	57	16
Gray, Tristan	19	L	23	1B	aa	TAM	418	15	2	209	12	75	110	101	33
Green, Zach	18	R	24	3B	a/a	PHI	402	18	1	243	7	62	165	64	14
	19	R	25	3B	aaa	SF	252	16	1	233	11	55	248	83	57
Greiner, Grayson	18	R	26	C	aaa	DET	158	3	0	233	10	70	83	32	-21
	19	R	27	C	aaa	DET	48	2	0	211	6	62	93	72	-44
Grisham, Trent	18	L	22	RF	aa	MIL	335	7	10	225	15	72	67	92	0
	19	L	23	CF	a/a	MIL	370	25	11	282	14	78	179	161	120

BATTER	yr	b	age	pos	lvl	org	ab	hr	sb	ba	bb%	ct%	px	sx	bpv
Grotjohn, Ryan	19	L	24	CF	aa	ARI	227	3	3	221	9	68	94	179	15
Grullon, Deivy	18	R	22	C	aa	PHI	326	18	0	244	4	71	127	17	3
	19	R	23	C	aaa	PHI	407	19	1	249	8	61	159	42	-1
Grzelakowski, Tay	19	L	26	1B	aa	MIN	196	1	1	165	10	71	58	106	-25
Guerra, Javier	18	L	23	SS	aaa	SD	430	9	1	182	4	56	98	99	-59
Guerrero Jr., Vlad	18	R	19	3B	a/a	TOR	600	32	5	669	9	89	133	53	98
	19	R	20	3B	aaa	TOR	30	3	1	359	11	93	158	71	134
Guerrero, Gabriel	18	R	25	RF	a/a	CIN	502	17	3	256	5	71	100	78	-2
	19	R	26	RF	a/a	MIA	359	9	5	221	2	66	102	119	-9
Guillorme, Luis	18	L	24	SS	aaa	NYM	247	2	1	236	8	81	54	63	2
	19	L	25	2B	aaa	NYM	228	6	3	254	12	77	82	47	4
Guillotte, Andrew	18	R	25	LF	a/a	TOR	342	2	8	220	9	76	51	85	-8
	19	R	26	SS	aaa	TOR	82	0	2	138	4	61	40	175	-62
Gurriel, Lourdes	18	R	25	SS	a/a	TOR	206	6	3	270	3	77	90	74	9
	19	R	26	2B	aaa	TOR	123	3	0	244	2	78	138	60	52
Gurwitz, Zane	19	R	25	3B	aa	LAA	103	1	3	178	9	66	57	83	-51
Gushue, Taylor	18	B	25	C	a/a	WAS	343	8	0	185	8	69	90	43	-21
	19	B	26	C	aaa	WAS	263	8	0	260	5	71	123	50	11
Gutierrez, Kelvin	18	R	24	3B	aa	KC	472	8	16	247	6	75	63	128	3
	19	R	25	3B	aaa	KC	286	6	9	244	8	72	75	143	5
Guzman, Ronald	19	L	25	1B	a/a	TEX	135	5	0	268	9	72	132	50	22
Haase, Eric	18	R	26	C	aaa	CLE	433	15	2	203	5	61	125	66	-22
	19	R	27	C	aaa	CLE	350	22	1	191	9	52	210	120	25
Hager, Jake	18	R	25	SS	a/a	MIL	335	9	6	241	7	78	100	76	32
	19	R	26	1B	aaa	MIL	327	9	4	198	6	60	114	114	-21
Haggerty, Sam	18	B	24	3B	a/a	CLE	297	3	21	219	14	69	95	136	22
	19	B	25	2B	a/a	NYM	289	3	20	226	12	63	77	213	-7
Haley, Jim	19	R	24	3B	aa	TAM	133	7	8	261	4	80	139	236	112
Hall, Darick	18	L	23	1B	aa	PHI	295	13	1	194	5	69	102	54	-16
	19	L	24	1B	aa	PHI	456	20	4	213	10	65	173	104	45
Hamilton, Caleb	19	R	24	C	a/a	MIN	335	6	6	206	9	69	93	117	-3
Hampson, Garrett	18	R	24	2B	a/a	COL	444	8	25	282	8	82	76	139	48
	19	R	25	2B	aaa	COL	109	1	4	230	3	75	105	141	37
Hannemann, Jacol	18	L	27	CF	aaa	CHC	375	4	15	187	5	73	50	114	-23
	19	L	28	RF	aaa	CHC	117	4	6	201	9	77	108	148	53
Hanson, Alen	18	B	26	2B	aaa	SF	62	2	4	327	8	86	99	138	83
	19	B	27	2B	aaa	TOR	166	2	5	158	4	72	48	147	-17
Happ, Ian	19	B	25	CF	aaa	CHC	359	12	7	209	13	64	126	126	10
Harris, Trey	19	R	23	RF	aa	ATL	146	2	1	283	3	76	90	136	30
Harrison, Monte	18	R	23	CF	aa	MIA	521	15	24	209	7	53	109	133	-44
	19	R	24	CF	aaa	MIA	215	7	18	239	9	61	114	215	14
Haseley, Adam	18	L	22	CF	aa	PHI	136	5	0	282	9	84	74	32	23
	19	L	23	CF	a/a	PHI	233	9	4	248	9	75	129	117	54
Hayes, KeBryan	18	R	21	3B	aa	PIT	437	6	10	275	10	80	86	110	44
	19	R	22	3B	aaa	PIT	427	8	10	245	8	78	100	145	48
Hays, Austin	18	R	23	RF	aa	BAL	273	10	4	209	3	77	89	83	11
	19	R	24	CF	a/a	BAL	296	11	8	226	4	73	132	133	51
Heath, Nick	18	L	25	CF	aa	KC	105	0	8	230	9	65	55	172	-24
	19	L	26	CF	a/a	KC	408	6	47	222	10	60	91	221	-5
Heidt, Gunnar	18	R	26	1B	a/a	TOR	347	5	6	210	7	66	86	80	-27
	19	R	27	1B	a/a	TOR	75	1	6	116	6	39	109	192	-87
Heim, Jonah	18	B	23	C	aa	OAK	137	1	0	157	5	83	28	42	-22
	19	B	24	C	a/a	OAK	287	7	0	270	9	82	99	36	33
Heineman, Scott	18	R	26	CF	a/a	TEX	447	9	13	262	6	75	72	89	-1
	19	R	27	RF	aaa	TEX	159	6	3	286	7	67	120	138	19
Heineman, Tyler	18	B	27	C	a/a	MIL	243	3	3	202	10	82	49	49	4
	19	B	28	C	aaa	MIA	244	9	3	270	7	82	121	147	81
Hendrix, Jeff	18	L	25	CF	aa	NYY	308	1	7	168	11	57	31	74	-101
	19	L	26	CF	aa	NYY	80	0	2	174	6	58	27	89	-109
Hermosillo, Michae	18	R	23	CF	aaa	LAA	273	8	6	209	6	63	101	102	-24
	19	R	24	CF	aaa	LAA	259	10	4	188	6	60	123	126	-13
Hernandez, Elier	18	R	24	RF	a/a	KC	484	2	8	256	4	76	63	74	-14
	19	R	25	LF	aaa	KC	396	7	6	207	5	67	71	108	-30
Hernandez, Jan	18	R	23	RF	aa	PHI	350	12	5	228	6	60	108	84	-35
	19	R	24	RF	aaa	PHI	232	10	2	216	8	48	201	89	-8
Hernandez, Marco	19	L	27	2B	aaa	BOS	137	1	2	251	3	73	105	96	17
Hernandez, Oscar	18	R	25	C	aaa	BOS	151	1	1	191	7	73	50	48	-36
	19	R	26	C	a/a	BOS	172	5	0	174	6	72	111	67	7
Hernandez, Ramoı	19	R	23	1B	aa	ARI	309	10	0	226	4	73	107	118	26
Hernandez, Yonny	19	S	21	2B	aa	TEX	170	0	15	283	15	85	39	188	46
Herrera, Carlos	19	L	23	2B	aa	COL	162	1	2	222	5	72	110	149	32
Herrera, Dilson	18	R	24	2B	aaa	CIN	185	6	0	263	8	68	103	22	-19
	19	R	25	2B	aaa	NYM	407	19	10	203	8	62	166	116	29
Herrera, Rosell	18	B	26	CF	aaa	KC	126	3	4	236	6	80	120	134	71
	19	B	27	3B	aaa	MIA	165	4	2	253	7	76	97	93	23
Herum, Marty	18	R	27	3B	aa	ARI	280	3	1	245	5	80	55	45	-10
	19	R	28	3B	a/a	ARI	139	3	0	171	6	62	92	33	-56
Heyward, Jacob	19	R	24	LF	a/a	SF	388	8	9	188	16	58	106	62	-48
Higashioka, Kyle	18	R	28	C	aaa	NYY	188	4	1	162	6	71	79	56	-22
	19	R	29	C	aaa	NYY	241	16	0	222	7	72	163	36	42
Higgins, P.J.	18	R	25	C	aa	CHC	145	1	1	204	7	79	38	62	-21
	19	R	26	C	a/a	CHC	385	8	4	244	8	76	82	88	8
Hill, Derek	19	R	24	CF	aa	DET	470	13	20	231	7	67	112	200	31
Hill, Logan	18	R	25	LF	aa	PIT	391	13	1	196	8	62	99	49	-39
	19	R	26	DH	a/a	PIT	456	11	1	218	7	67	121	90	7
Hilliard, Sam	18	L	24	RF	aa	COL	435	8	18	247	7	64	89	105	-25
	19	L	25	RF	aaa	COL	500	25	14	227	7	64	176	191	67

BATTER	yr	b	age	pos	lvl	org	ab	hr	sb	ba	bb%	ct%	px	sx	bpv
Hinojosa, C.J.	19	R	25	2B	aa	MIL	415	9	3	268	9	83	86	72	37
Hiura, Keston	18	R	22	2B	aa	MIL	279	6	10	264	7	78	92	105	34
	19	R	23	2B	aaa	MIL	213	16	5	292	8	65	229	117	93
Hodges, Jesse	18	R	24	3B	aa	CHC	307	3	1	175	6	65	67	48	-59
	19	R	25	3B	aa	CHC	119	2	0	183	5	68	80	100	-23
Hoerner, Nico	19	R	22	SS	aa	CHC	268	3	7	275	7	88	76	155	71
Holder, Kyle	18	L	24	SS	aa	NYY	117	1	0	220	6	85	39	49	0
	19	L	25	SS	aa	NYY	412	9	6	236	8	82	87	119	46
Hood, Destin	18	R	28	RF	a/a	TEX	378	11	3	180	5	62	92	73	-45
Houchins, Zach	18	R	26	3B	a/a	LAA	277	10	1	203	4	70	93	55	-19
	19	R	27	1B	a/a	SF	381	7	2	194	4	70	92	87	-10
Howard, Ryan	18	R	24	SS	aa	SF	422	3	8	244	7	85	69	89	40
	19	R	25	SS	a/a	SF	462	5	6	201	6	80	51	106	4
Hudson, Joe	18	R	27	C	a/a	LAA	167	3	0	225	7	70	73	34	-37
	19	R	28	C	aaa	STL	197	7	0	173	6	58	107	72	-50
Hummel, Cooper	19	S	25	LF	aa	MIL	342	18	4	241	16	67	147	137	43
Hurst, Scott	19	L	23	RF	aa	STL	141	1	1	168	9	65	76	82	-41
Ibanez, Andy	18	R	25	3B	aaa	TEX	463	9	1	244	6	82	61	30	0
	19	R	26	3B	aaa	TEX	467	15	5	255	8	78	109	83	37
Ice, Logan	18	S	23	C	aa	CLE	48	0	0	235	8	59	103	95	-34
	19	S	24	C	aa	CLE	239	4	0	170	12	66	53	56	-61
India, Jonathan	19	R	23	3B	aa	CIN	111	3	4	252	16	73	74	114	3
Isabel, Ibandel	19	R	24	1B	aa	CIN	334	25	0	225	7	46	270	77	37
Jackson, Alex	18	R	23	C	a/a	ATL	333	7	0	185	7	61	116	66	-27
	19	R	24	C	aaa	ATL	306	22	1	201	5	58	200	82	27
Jackson, Bralin	18	R	25	RF	aa	PIT	206	2	4	185	4	66	53	85	-58
	19	R	26	LF	aa	PIT	272	0	6	233	5	71	54	146	-17
Jackson, Drew	18	R	25	2B	aa	LA	342	11	16	205	8	68	104	102	3
	19	R	26	2B	aaa	LA	273	4	6	164	7	59	74	107	-59
Jackson, Jhalan	18	R	25	RF	aa	NYY	346	16	6	182	8	50	163	100	-19
	19	R	26	RF	aa	NYY	45	2	0	175	4	58	186	154	40
Jagielo, Eric	18	L	26	1B	aa	MIA	399	8	1	160	6	58	86	37	-72
James, Mac	18	R	25	C	a/a	TAM	167	0	1	161	10	81	12	40	-33
	19	R	26	C	aaa	TAM	203	3	1	180	10	68	50	47	-61
Jankowski, Travis	18	L	27	CF	aaa	SD	80	1	3	280	8	66	52	71	-54
	19	L	28	CF	aaa	SD	160	0	4	233	8	75	34	85	-36
Jansen, Danny	18	R	23	C	aaa	TOR	298	11	4	260	11	82	109	74	63
Jenista, Greyson	19	L	23	LF	aa	ATL	222	5	2	244	11	65	72	60	-50
Jimenez, Eloy	18	R	22	LF	a/a	CHW	416	21	0	315	7	81	128	50	59
	19	R	23	LF	aaa	CHW	22	1	0	280	0	74	108	47	5
Joe, Connor	18	R	26	1B	a/a	LA	364	12	2	243	10	70	116	69	17
	19	R	27	1B	aaa	LA	360	10	1	235	11	72	115	67	14
Johnson Jr., Danie	18	L	23	RF	aa	WAS	356	5	17	240	5	72	79	146	8
	19	L	24	RF	a/a	CLE	483	17	10	269	8	73	145	131	60
Johnson, Bryce	19	S	24	RF	aa	SF	210	2	8	229	10	72	94	122	13
Johnson, Shermaı	18	L	28	3B	a/a	LAA	215	3	2	186	8	62	80	112	-37
	19	L	29	2B	aaa	CIN	203	3	3	193	12	64	80	97	-35
Jones, Hunter	18	R	27	CF	a/a	WAS	386	4	10	252	8	77	50	102	-4
	19	R	28	CF	a/a	WAS	159	2	4	140	7	62	56	97	-66
Jones, Jahmai	18	R	21	2B	aa	LAA	184	2	10	223	10	70	77	161	10
	19	R	22	2B	aa	LAA	482	5	8	218	9	75	65	103	-2
Jones, Mylz	18	R	24	3B	aa	COL	404	9	8	236	3	76	78	99	3
	19	R	25	RF	a/a	COL	339	8	13	210	5	75	90	133	26
Jones, Nolan	19	L	21	3B	aa	CLE	178	8	2	252	14	63	171	147	49
Jones, Ryder	18	L	24	3B	aaa	SF	441	6	1	227	5	72	69	71	-23
Jones, Taylor	18	R	25	1B	a/a	HOU	452	14	2	232	9	67	113	54	-3
	19	R	26	1B	aaa	HOU	447	15	0	225	9	69	115	46	-5
Jones, Travis	19	R	24	1B	aa	KC	195	2	14	243	9	67	75	153	-10
Joseph, Corban	18	L	30	2B	aa	BAL	459	12	5	236	7	88	72	67	46
	19	L	31	2B	aaa	OAK	383	8	0	284	6	84	106	88	60
Joseph, Tommy	18	R	27	1B	a/a	TEX	345	16	0	237	6	72	124	18	8
	19	R	28	1B	aa	BOS	50	0	0	230	3	61	72	77	-66
Justus, Connor	18	R	24	SS	aa	LAA	247	0	1	146	12	62	35	61	-80
	19	R	25	SS	aa	LAA	347	2	6	161	9	69	57	91	-37
Kaczmarski, Kevii	18	L	26	CF	aaa	NYM	160	0	2	223	6	65	45	76	-67
	19	L	27	RF	aa	NYM	137	2	4	202	12	64	68	52	-58
Karaviotis, Mark	19	R	24	LF	aa	ARI	112	1	0	157	7	65	35	54	-83
Katoh, Gosuke	18	L	24	1B	aa	NYY	433	5	9	201	11	67	75	83	-21
	19	L	25	2B	a/a	NYY	359	10	9	235	11	65	95	98	-21
Keller, Alec	18	L	26	LF	aa	WAS	223	2	1	287	5	84	53	69	11
	19	L	27	RF	aaa	WAS	381	2	7	245	4	80	50	151	19
Kelley, Christian	18	R	25	C	aa	PIT	311	6	0	203	6	77	65	48	-11
	19	R	26	C	aaa	PIT	252	4	0	150	6	65	69	73	-52
Kelly, Carson	18	R	24	C	aaa	STL	294	5	0	229	11	82	59	31	7
Kelly, Dalton	18	L	24	1B	aa	TAM	417	4	18	195	11	71	64	125	-3
	19	L	25	1B	a/a	TAM	420	8	10	242	12	66	86	104	-20
Kelly, Juan	18	B	24	1B	aa	TOR	290	11	2	199	10	66	115	37	-10
Kemmer, Jon	18	L	28	DH	aaa	MIN	410	14	4	209	8	64	124	100	4
	19	L	29	RF	aaa	LA	119	4	0	187	8	58	116	71	-40
Kerrigan, Jimmy	18	R	24	CF	a/a	MIN	205	6	0	207	5	64	85	33	-57
	19	R	25	CF	a/a	MIN	347	13	13	196	4	69	116	129	18
Kieboom, Carter	18	R	21	SS	aa	WAS	248	4	3	247	7	75	83	77	4
	19	R	22	SS	aaa	WAS	412	13	4	274	11	73	115	111	34
Kieboom, Spenceı	18	R	27	C	aaa	WAS	84	1	0	211	9	86	44	19	4
	19	R	28	C	aa	WAS	168	1	0	172	8	75	46	30	-40
Kirilloff, Alex	19	L	22	RF	aa	MIN	375	8	7	276	7	79	88	100	29
Kirtley, Zach	19	R	23	1B	aa	STL	187	4	2	203	8	68	109	87	-3
Knapp, Aaron	19	L	25	LF	a/a	SEA	305	2	12	173	10	58	48	164	-65

BATTER	yr	b	age	pos	lvl	org	ab	hr	sb	ba	bb%	ct%	px	sx	bpv
Knight, Nash	18	S	26	3B	aa	TOR	31	1	0	137	5	81	36	30	-25
	19	S	27	3B	a/a	TOR	361	6	3	216	11	70	96	58	-10
Knizner, Andrew	18	R	23	C	a/a	STL	335	5	0	273	6	84	58	23	3
	19	R	24	C	aaa	STL	246	9	2	235	7	83	88	80	40
Kohlwey, Taylor	18	L	24	RF	aa	SD	204	5	3	232	9	67	88	100	-10
	19	L	25	LF	a/a	SD	226	3	5	230	10	70	74	137	-5
Kowalczyk, Alex	19	R	26	C	aa	TEX	176	3	1	231	4	63	58	56	-73
Kramer, Kevin	18	L	25	2B	aaa	PIT	476	11	10	266	6	70	102	91	2
	19	L	26	2B	aaa	PIT	393	7	3	221	8	66	115	62	-11
Kranson, Mitchell	18	L	24	3B	aa	MIN	187	2	0	231	10	79	58	29	-8
	19	L	25	DH	aa	MIN	120	4	0	197	7	82	61	55	8
Krieger, Tyler	18	B	24	LF	aa	CLE	468	4	16	255	6	79	57	102	7
	19	B	25	3B	a/a	CLE	207	3	8	188	8	71	68	136	-7
Krizan, Jason	18	L	29	2B	aaa	DET	368	6	3	204	9	78	67	80	10
	19	L	30	1B	a/a	NYM	386	11	1	210	9	84	98	63	49
Kruger, Jack	18	R	24	C	aa	LAA	174	3	2	267	2	79	73	77	4
	19	R	25	C	aa	LAA	346	3	2	210	6	77	48	60	-24
La O, Luis	18	R	27	2B	aa	TEX	286	2	4	245	4	82	38	71	-11
Lago, Alay	18	R	27	2B	aa	ATL	295	2	4	213	2	86	41	86	11
Landon, Logan	18	R	25	RF	a/a	LA	72	1	1	147	1	56	62	87	-97
	19	R	26	CF	a/a	LA	222	4	2	177	7	65	72	86	-42
Larnach, Trevor	19	L	22	RF	aa	MIN	156	7	0	286	12	67	112	48	-14
Lartique, Henri	19	S	24	C	aa	PHI	242	7	3	124	12	57	88	89	-58
Laureano, Ramon	18	R	24	RF	aaa	OAK	246	10	9	256	9	68	117	103	17
LaValley, Gavin	18	R	24	1B	aa	CIN	393	12	2	187	9	65	87	39	-41
	19	R	25	3B	aa	CIN	394	10	2	227	10	66	107	96	-7
Law, Adam	18	R	28	2B	a/a	SEA	383	2	5	196	5	70	57	72	-42
Leblanc, Charles	19	R	23	3B	aa	TEX	479	7	3	263	8	76	63	115	1
Leblebijian, Jason	18	R	27	3B	aaa	TOR	282	8	5	189	9	59	88	80	-48
Lee, Braxton	18	L	25	RF	a/a	MIA	289	1	6	190	9	77	37	89	-15
	19	L	26	CF	a/a	NYM	384	2	8	224	8	67	64	99	-37
Lee, Khalil	18	L	20	CF	aa	KC	102	2	2	231	8	72	72	64	-10
	19	L	21	RF	aa	KC	470	7	49	259	12	67	89	189	9
Leon, Julian Franc	19	R	23	C	aa	LAA	213	5	0	164	14	54	117	40	-64
Leonard, Patrick	18	R	26	3B	aaa	CHW	430	9	2	200	8	59	108	58	-43
	19	R	27	1B	aa	MIL	355	10	9	277	10	63	135	153	22
Lester, Josh	18	L	24	1B	aa	DET	464	17	1	229	10	73	103	64	13
	19	L	25	1B	a/a	DET	466	17	0	203	8	70	127	63	13
Lewis, Kyle	18	R	23	CF	aa	SEA	132	3	1	190	10	72	88	49	-7
	19	R	24	LF	aa	SEA	457	11	3	245	11	61	117	102	-15
Lewis, Royce	19	R	20	SS	aa	MIN	134	2	6	233	7	75	102	154	41
Leyba, Domingo	18	B	23	2B	aa	ARI	320	4	4	239	8	84	58	80	25
	19	B	24	SS	aaa	ARI	457	11	0	237	4	80	104	89	42
Liberato, Luis	19	L	24	CF	a/a	SEA	198	2	3	210	6	71	66	130	-13
Liddi, Alex	18	R	30	1B	aa	KC	393	15	3	196	4	61	123	82	-24
Lien, Connor	18	R	24	CF	aa	ATL	268	6	7	182	7	54	122	88	-44
	19	R	25	CF	a/a	ATL	213	9	5	192	11	41	241	176	25
Lin, Tzu-Wei	18	L	24	SS	aaa	BOS	277	4	3	293	6	75	93	66	11
	19	L	25	SS	aaa	BOS	224	3	5	224	7	72	81	115	-1
Lipka, Matthew	18	R	26	CF	aa	SF	304	3	17	207	10	78	55	143	21
	19	R	27	CF	a/a	NYY	294	4	15	218	5	69	82	157	1
Liriano, Rymer	18	R	27	LF	aaa	MIL	352	13	7	193	7	55	114	85	-45
	19	R	28	RF	aaa	NYM	201	7	5	159	13	42	173	101	-48
Listi, Austin	18	R	25	DH	aa	PHI	217	7	0	234	9	71	87	14	-24
	19	R	26	1B	a/a	PHI	468	17	1	213	9	72	113	56	8
Locastro, Tim	18	R	26	CF	aaa	LA	301	3	13	227	6	79	71	132	26
	19	R	27	CF	aaa	ARI	123	5	5	225	5	76	142	228	97
Lockhart, Daniel	18	L	26	3B	aa	ATL	356	5	8	203	9	68	70	116	-18
	19	L	27	3B	aa	ATL	250	5	3	218	7	75	73	73	-5
Long, Shed	18	L	23	2B	aa	CIN	452	11	16	239	10	69	92	119	8
	19	L	24	2B	aaa	SEA	226	7	1	227	6	65	101	122	-9
Longhi, Nick	18	R	23	LF	a/a	CIN	266	2	1	220	5	72	55	45	-42
	19	R	24	1B	aaa	CIN	389	11	0	255	6	69	133	80	18
Longo, Mitch	19	L	24	LF	aa	CLE	327	5	10	234	8	75	85	164	32
Lopes, Christian	18	R	26	2B	aaa	TEX	429	9	11	220	11	80	69	81	24
	19	R	27	2B	a/a	TEX	446	10	11	229	10	73	102	99	20
Lopes, Tim	18	R	24	2B	aaa	TOR	354	2	15	256	6	82	56	107	19
	19	R	25	2B	aaa	SEA	374	7	19	244	7	76	102	126	36
Lopez, Deiner	18	B	24	2B	a/a	BOS	183	2	2	214	3	71	99	95	-1
	19	B	25	SS	a/a	BOS	112	1	3	150	3	57	87	82	-65
Lopez, Irving	19	L	24	2B	a/a	STL	362	8	1	226	6	76	93	135	32
Lopez, Jack	18	R	26	2B	aaa	KC	395	5	11	212	3	69	52	112	-40
	19	R	27	3B	aaa	ATL	359	9	7	229	4	70	87	125	0
Lopez, Nicky	18	L	23	SS	a/a	KC	504	7	12	281	9	89	48	104	45
	19	L	24	SS	aaa	KC	116	2	7	311	12	95	69	148	96
Lovullo, Nick	18	R	25	2B	aa	BOS	187	1	1	179	8	77	50	62	-16
	19	R	26	3B	a/a	BOS	108	1	1	166	6	64	26	58	-94
Lowe, Brandon	18	L	24	2B	a/a	TAM	380	18	7	258	11	68	150	80	40
Lowe, Josh	19	L	21	CF	aa	TAM	448	17	29	241	12	67	136	184	48
Lowe, Nathaniel	18	L	23	1B	a/a	TAM	288	14	1	278	11	77	121	56	45
	19	L	24	1B	aaa	TAM	329	13	1	246	15	70	136	62	25
Lugo, Dawel	18	R	23	2B	aaa	DET	509	3	11	251	2	86	49	101	20
	19	R	24	3B	aaa	DET	282	4	5	305	4	80	103	169	65
Lukes, Nathan	18	L	24	RF	aa	TAM	435	5	8	240	6	74	72	95	-3
	19	L	25	CF	aaa	TAM	260	3	6	184	7	74	56	132	-7
Lund, Brennon	18	L	24	CF	aa	LAA	401	7	18	230	8	71	77	133	2
	19	L	25	CF	aaa	LAA	352	5	4	214	6	68	98	120	-1
Lundquist, Brock	19	L	23	LF	aa	TOR	370	6	7	227	9	70	98	130	10

BATTER	yr	b	age	pos	lvl	org	ab	hr	sb	ba	bb%	ct%	px	sx	bpv
Luplow, Jordan	18	R	25	LF	aaa	PIT	314	6	5	245	9	77	93	85	28
	19	R	26	LF	aaa	CLE	45	2	2	271	15	64	145	94	16
Lux, Gavin	18	L	21	SS	aa	LA	105	3	2	287	9	79	79	79	21
	19	L	22	SS	a/a	LA	458	22	8	314	10	75	146	150	75
Machado, Dixon	18	R	26	SS	aaa	DET	147	1	3	195	9	79	33	69	-18
	19	R	27	SS	aaa	CHC	329	13	0	217	12	71	125	46	14
Machin, Vimael	18	L	25	2B	aa	CHC	250	4	2	190	12	75	59	58	-9
	19	L	26	SS	a/a	CHC	447	6	7	257	12	84	71	97	37
Maddox, Will	18	L	26	2B	aa	DET	398	3	5	256	4	81	51	96	3
	19	L	27	3B	aa	SF	130	1	4	171	6	76	38	130	-13
Madrigal, Nick	19	R	22	2B	a/a	CHW	282	2	16	314	8	96	59	166	95
Madris, Bligh	19	L	23	RF	aa	PIT	457	7	3	250	8	77	86	73	13
Maggi, Drew	18	R	29	2B	aaa	CLE	232	1	8	219	6	69	50	93	-41
	19	R	30	3B	a/a	MIN	427	8	8	210	10	70	93	147	13
Mahan, Riley	19	L	23	2B	aa	MIA	207	6	0	213	4	67	116	95	2
Mahtook, Mikie	18	R	29	CF	aaa	DET	283	9	5	209	6	66	108	115	-2
	19	R	30	RF	aaa	DET	354	16	11	208	10	64	142	113	16
Marabell, Connor	18	L	24	RF	a/a	CLE	462	11	4	251	4	82	91	82	37
	19	L	25	RF	a/a	CLE	485	8	7	239	5	87	69	95	43
Marin, Adrian	18	R	24	SS	a/a	BAL	340	0	5	193	6	77	25	71	-37
Maris, Peter	18	L	25	3B	aa	TAM	153	5	4	209	10	69	108	95	13
	19	L	26	3B	a/a	SF	170	1	2	165	5	75	55	146	-2
Mariscal, Chris	18	R	25	2B	aa	SEA	444	6	4	219	8	64	60	78	-54
	19	R	26	3B	a/a	SEA	323	10	2	191	7	66	96	79	-21
Marlette, Tyler	18	R	25	1B	aa	ATL	423	10	4	219	9	72	77	70	-10
Marmolejos, Jose	18	L	25	1B	aaa	WAS	493	7	0	235	6	78	60	28	-19
	19	L	26	1B	a/a	WAS	391	15	1	274	6	74	141	85	47
Marrero, Deven	18	R	28	3B	aaa	ARI	66	1	0	161	6	62	71	71	-62
	19	R	29	SS	aaa	MIA	383	11	8	190	8	67	94	144	-1
Mars, Danny	18	B	24	RF	aa	BOS	411	2	14	231	7	74	57	109	-7
Marsh, Brandon	19	L	22	CF	aa	LAA	360	7	17	281	11	72	98	125	18
Marte, Hamlet	19	R	25	C	aa	SF	187	2	2	173	7	61	66	74	-75
Marte, Luis	18	R	25	SS	a/a	ATL	431	4	8	237	2	79	51	83	-13
	19	R	26	SS	aaa	ATL	312	4	4	223	4	72	57	99	-26
Martin, Jason	18	L	23	CF	a/a	PIT	468	10	10	246	7	74	78	108	8
	19	L	24	CF	aaa	PIT	370	6	7	231	6	77	99	135	39
Martinez, Carlos	18	R	23	C	aa	ATL	137	1	0	233	6	87	46	30	9
	19	R	24	C	aa	ATL	187	2	3	195	6	81	37	67	-13
Martinez, Eddy	18	R	23	RF	aa	CHC	411	10	4	198	6	76	84	83	9
	19	R	24	RF	aa	CHC	141	3	0	195	10	76	58	52	-18
Martinez, Jose	18	B	22	SS	aa	STL	60	0	1	174	8	64	44	38	-77
	19	B	23	3B	a/a	STL	169	3	2	234	10	75	78	70	0
Martini, Nick	18	L	28	1B	aaa	OAK	276	4	4	237	12	70	64	82	-19
	19	L	29	LF	aaa	OAK	274	5	0	251	11	76	85	59	4
Marzilli, Evan	18	L	27	CF	a/a	ARI	161	1	3	181	9	60	66	106	-53
	19	L	28	CF	a/a	ARI	57	1	0	93	13	36	67	67	-164
Mastrobuoni, Miles	18	L	23	LF	aa	TAM	43	0	1	226	9	81	0	48	-42
	19	L	24	LF	a/a	TAM	392	3	13	261	9	74	51	155	-3
Mateo, Jorge	18	R	23	SS	aaa	OAK	470	2	20	209	5	68	70	141	-18
	19	R	24	SS	aaa	OAK	532	13	18	249	4	69	125	192	45
Matheny, Tate	18	R	24	CF	aa	BOS	398	1	9	230	7	66	63	98	-41
	19	R	25	RF	a/a	BOS	341	6	10	217	4	64	97	110	-20
Mathias, Mark	18	R	24	2B	aa	CLE	397	7	9	215	11	74	87	104	20
	19	R	25	2B	aaa	CLE	412	10	10	240	9	75	115	130	44
Mathisen, Wyatt	18	R	25	1B	a/a	PIT	268	8	2	224	9	72	95	68	6
	19	R	26	3B	aaa	ARI	283	13	1	212	8	64	158	111	29
Matijevic, J.J.	19	L	24	1B	aa	HOU	281	8	7	216	8	60	145	148	15
May, Jacob	18	B	26	CF	aaa	CHW	314	2	12	210	5	72	57	83	-31
Mayfield, Jack	18	R	28	2B	aaa	HOU	433	11	3	198	5	73	87	58	-11
	19	R	29	SS	aaa	HOU	380	17	4	207	6	73	130	109	40
Mazeika, Patrick	18	L	25	C	aa	NYM	295	7	0	188	10	86	57	18	15
	19	L	26	C	aa	NYM	413	14	1	209	8	74	115	79	23
McBroom, Ryan	18	R	26	1B	a/a	NYY	461	14	1	258	5	65	98	41	-35
	19	R	27	1B	aaa	NYY	413	22	1	261	10	70	158	57	39
McCarthy, Joe	18	L	24	LF	aaa	TAM	160	7	3	233	12	68	142	89	37
	19	L	25	RF	aaa	SF	227	4	1	156	11	58	99	136	-31
McCormick, Chas	18	R	23	RF	aa	HOU	250	2	11	253	8	86	40	95	21
	19	R	24	LF	a/a	HOU	368	11	12	228	12	80	72	161	43
McCoy, Mason	19	R	24	SS	aa	BAL	429	2	9	242	7	79	44	179	17
McDonald, Mickey	19	S	24	CF	aa	OAK	156	0	3	216	7	65	41	66	-73
McDowell, Max	18	R	24	C	aa	MIL	102	1	3	208	12	80	45	68	2
	19	R	25	C	aa	MIL	258	4	2	205	12	74	84	81	4
McElroy Jr., C.J.	18	R	25	CF	a/a	CIN	268	3	15	203	4	75	45	124	-15
	19	R	26	CF	aa	SF	53	0	5	175	9	70	40	197	-14
McGuire, Reese	18	L	23	C	aaa	TOR	322	6	3	218	8	74	60	61	-18
	19	L	24	C	aaa	TOR	243	4	3	225	8	80	77	112	28
McKay, Brendan	19	L	24	DH	a/a	TAM	145	4	1	174	9	59	93	65	-57
McKenna, Ryan	18	R	21	CF	aa	BAL	213	3	3	213	9	72	54	94	-18
	19	R	22	CF	aa	BAL	488	9	23	218	10	74	90	186	40
McKinney, Billy	18	L	24	RF	a/a	TOR	294	13	1	203	8	72	129	88	35
	19	L	25	LF	aaa	TOR	129	3	1	245	12	78	124	118	62
McKinstry, Zach	18	L	23	3B	aa	LA	83	2	0	162	3	71	55	47	-48
	19	L	24	2B	a/a	LA	430	15	6	259	7	75	120	110	42
McNeil, Jeff	18	L	26	2B	a/a	NYM	339	13	4	268	7	84	106	103	69
Meadows, Austin	18	L	23	CF	aaa	TAM	261	10	10	268	5	83	117	101	70
Medrano, Kevin	18	L	28	2B	a/a	ARI	396	2	7	252	5	75	72	104	1
Mejia, Alex	18	R	27	1B	aaa	STL	322	3	4	220	4	80	22	68	-32

BATTER	yr	b	age	pos	lvl	org	ab	hr	sb	ba	bb%	ct%	px	sx	bpv
Mejia, Erick	19	B	25	SS	aaa	KC	495	5	14	232	7	77	66	172	24
Mejia, Francisco	18	B	23	C	aaa	SD	427	9	0	242	4	77	85	38	-1
Mejias-Brean, Setl	18	R	27	3B	a/a	SEA	476	7	4	205	8	74	55	67	-21
	19	R	28	SS	aaa	SD	411	6	3	236	5	76	64	93	-6
Melendez, Manuel	19	L	22	CF	aa	COL	500	7	18	277	4	89	67	142	62
Mendick, Danny	18	R	25	SS	aa	CHW	453	13	18	220	10	77	86	79	22
	19	R	26	2B	aaa	CHW	477	14	14	229	9	75	94	93	19
Mendoza, Evan	18	R	22	3B	aa	STL	366	4	1	223	6	77	43	46	-29
	19	R	23	3B	a/a	STL	222	1	4	222	6	77	43	108	-11
Mendoza, Yonatha	18	B	24	SS	aa	SEA	333	0	4	223	10	83	20	77	-8
	19	B	25	SS	aa	CIN	30	0	0	206	8	76	60	67	-15
Meneses, Joey	18	R	26	1B	aaa	PHI	492	20	0	263	6	72	108	30	-2
Mercado, Oscar	18	R	24	CF	aaa	CLE	485	6	29	251	7	80	64	112	21
	19	R	25	CF	aaa	CLE	119	3	11	262	10	69	142	172	57
Mercedes, Yermin	19	R	26	C	a/a	CHW	334	20	2	274	9	76	152	57	55
Merrell, Kevin	19	L	24	SS	aa	KC	455	2	19	228	5	75	63	195	22
Mesa, Victor Victc	19	R	23	CF	aa	MIA	107	0	3	171	3	84	16	114	-7
Metzler, Ryan	18	R	25	2B	a/a	COL	313	6	10	209	7	68	79	68	-28
	19	R	26	2B	a/a	COL	102	1	1	166	7	61	51	17	-95
Michael, Levi	18	R	27	SS	a/a	NYM	396	7	9	232	6	69	87	93	-13
	19	R	28	2B	a/a	SF	380	7	6	199	6	68	84	185	6
Michalczewski, Tr	18	B	23	2B	aa	CHW	451	6	4	234	5	67	86	92	-22
	19	B	24	3B	a/a	CHW	234	5	1	189	10	57	104	34	-66
Mieses, Johan	18	R	23	RF	aa	STL	219	6	0	174	4	69	81	47	-35
	19	R	24	RF	a/a	STL	386	17	5	199	7	72	108	101	18
Milian, J.C.	18	R	22	3B	a/a	MIA	24	0	1	185	10	82	0	83	-27
	19	R	23	3B	a/a	MIA	279	4	1	251	7	80	72	33	1
Miller, Anderson	18	L	24	LF	aa	KC	432	10	8	228	6	79	81	89	21
	19	L	25	LF	aa	KC	307	4	9	226	5	69	62	140	-19
Miller, Bradley	18	L	29	SS	aaa	MIL	27	1	1	132	6	57	47	65	-102
Miller, Brian	18	L	23	LF	aa	MIA	262	0	18	235	6	83	26	116	1
	19	L	24	LF	aa	MIA	449	2	23	251	8	80	64	176	37
Miller, Ian	18	L	26	CF	aaa	SEA	422	1	24	210	7	74	37	120	-24
	19	L	27	CF	aaa	MIN	450	9	27	225	8	77	100	188	57
Miller, Jalen	19	R	23	2B	aa	SF	491	9	27	207	9	77	73	147	25
Miller, Michael	18	R	29	SS	aaa	BOS	320	3	8	241	7	80	42	66	-11
	19	R	30	SS	aaa	MIN	279	2	3	200	7	80	46	56	-15
Miller, Owen	19	R	23	SS	aa	SD	507	10	4	261	7	81	83	91	32
Miller, Sean	18	R	24	SS	a/a	MIN	183	1	1	177	5	74	29	56	-52
	19	R	25	SS	aa	BAL	54	0	0	82	2	60	0	124	-114
Milone, Thomas	18	L	23	CF	aa	TAM	365	3	8	227	5	68	64	124	-29
	19	L	24	RF	aa	TAM	84	1	6	193	12	74	51	102	-19
Mineo, Alberto	19	L	25	C	aa	TOR	300	5	1	205	8	62	76	85	-51
Miroglio, Dominic	18	R	23	C	aa	ARI	78	0	0	206	1	83	46	59	-9
	19	R	24	C	aa	ARI	146	2	0	216	10	80	67	40	2
Monasterio, Andru	19	R	22	2B	aa	CLE	249	1	5	213	8	76	31	52	-43
Mondou, Nate	18	L	23	3B	aa	OAK	165	0	2	222	8	83	30	41	-14
	19	L	24	2B	aa	OAK	427	4	6	221	10	75	55	99	-10
Moniak, Mickey	19	L	21	CF	aa	PHI	465	11	14	241	6	73	126	199	66
Montero, Elehuris	19	R	21	3B	aa	STL	224	6	0	170	5	65	88	47	-42
Montgomery, Troy	18	L	24	CF	aa	DET	209	1	7	222	11	69	49	121	-25
	19	L	25	LF	aa	DET	53	1	0	139	12	67	73	71	-35
Mooney, Peter	18	L	28	SS	a/a	MIA	252	4	2	221	8	82	48	56	0
	19	L	29	2B	aaa	COL	306	3	4	204	7	79	87	112	30
Moore, Dylan	18	R	26	3B	a/a	MIL	408	11	17	250	6	80	106	137	59
	19	R	27	SS	aaa	SEA	29	0	1	131	7	87	0	84	-15
Moorman, Chuck	18	R	24	C	aa	TEX	157	2	0	171	9	58	83	37	-70
	19	R	25	C	a/a	TEX	63	3	0	200	7	67	110	4	-29
Mora, Angelo	18	B	25	2B	a/a	LA	314	6	4	223	5	76	73	76	-4
	19	B	26	3B	a/a	LA	295	3	5	217	5	72	67	126	-10
Mora, John	18	L	25	CF	aa	NYM	351	4	3	191	8	70	66	89	-23
Morales, Jonathan	18	R	23	C	a/a	ATL	188	1	0	244	5	83	38	40	-13
	19	R	24	C	a/a	ATL	275	2	0	225	8	81	52	43	-9
Morgan, Gareth	19	R	23	RF	aa	LAA	107	1	1	187	7	43	74	23	-151
Morgan, Josh	18	R	23	C	aa	TEX	294	2	1	212	7	82	50	45	-1
Moroff, Max	18	B	25	SS	aaa	PIT	247	6	4	188	12	69	92	94	4
	19	B	26	SS	aaa	CLE	108	3	1	184	16	63	101	55	-32
Morozowski, Jasoı	18	R	24	RF	aa	ARI	281	4	3	171	6	66	68	77	-44
Mountcastle, Ryar	18	R	21	3B	aa	BAL	394	11	2	267	5	79	81	77	15
	19	R	22	1B	aaa	BAL	520	22	2	281	4	73	134	72	34
Mullins II, Cedric	18	B	24	CF	a/a	BAL	443	10	16	252	6	83	85	141	58
	19	B	25	CF	a/a	BAL	467	9	27	201	8	80	64	160	34
Mundell, Brian	18	R	24	1B	aa	COL	441	6	1	247	9	82	65	33	9
	19	R	25	LF	aaa	COL	390	8	1	289	7	76	117	106	43
Murphy, John	19	R	28	C	aaa	ATL	171	7	0	185	6	67	121	86	3
Murphy, Sean	18	R	24	C	a/a	OAK	265	6	2	248	7	79	110	101	52
	19	R	25	C	aaa	OAK	120	7	0	256	9	70	164	104	55
Myers, Connor	18	R	24	CF	aa	CHC	129	1	3	200	7	63	34	106	-75
	19	R	25	CF	aa	CHC	338	3	14	238	5	63	102	192	2
Navarreto, Brian	18	R	24	C	aa	MIN	357	3	0	217	3	83	50	32	-12
	19	R	25	C	aa	NYY	160	6	0	158	4	78	87	12	-3
Navarro, Reynaldo	18	B	29	2B	a/a	NYY	274	10	1	182	4	82	73	24	4
Nay, Mitch	18	R	25	3B	aa	CIN	221	5	2	230	11	77	71	56	5
	19	R	26	1B	a/a	CIN	353	15	1	243	8	74	145	105	57
Naylor, Josh	18	L	21	LF	aa	SD	501	14	4	274	10	85	72	48	33
	19	L	22	RF	aaa	SD	223	7	1	265	8	85	117	101	78
Neslony, Tyler	18	L	24	RF	aa	ATL	451	4	8	224	6	74	61	81	-18
	19	L	25	RF	aa	ATL	192	5	4	281	10	76	108	176	56

BATTER	yr	b	age	pos	lvl	org	ab	hr	sb	ba	bb%	ct%	px	sx	bpv
Netzer, Brett	19	L	23	2B	aa	BOS	454	7	3	242	8	71	91	71	-10
Neuse, Sheldon	18	R	24	3B	aaa	OAK	499	4	3	228	5	62	69	74	-64
	19	R	25	3B	aaa	OAK	498	19	2	265	8	69	138	91	26
Nevin, Tyler	19	R	22	1B	aa	COL	466	14	6	271	12	81	114	111	65
Newman, Kevin	18	R	25	SS	aaa	PIT	437	3	22	258	5	87	57	114	41
	19	R	26	SS	aaa	PIT	30	0	0	199	12	74	60	70	-22
Ngoepe, Gift	18	R	28	SS	aaa	TOR	131	2	2	141	13	43	74	86	-117
	19	R	29	2B	a/a	PIT	152	4	2	160	9	45	145	87	-65
Nichting, T.J.	19	S	24	LF	aa	BAL	352	6	6	232	4	78	75	133	25
Nido, Tomas	18	R	24	C	a/a	NYM	232	3	0	218	3	80	81	36	5
	19	R	25	C	aaa	NYM	38	0	0	239	2	58	28	36	-125
Nogowski, John	18	R	25	1B	aa	STL	298	8	0	256	9	92	55	19	37
	19	R	26	1B	aaa	STL	380	11	1	241	12	83	88	64	39
Nola, Austin	18	R	29	C	aaa	MIA	226	1	1	212	8	75	56	45	-23
	19	R	30	C	aaa	SEA	196	5	3	240	9	72	104	99	14
Nolan, Nate	19	R	25	C	a/a	CHW	165	4	0	157	6	51	123	83	-61
Noll, Jake	18	R	24	3B	aa	WAS	237	2	3	246	5	82	41	81	-5
	19	R	25	3B	aaa	WAS	456	8	4	242	4	77	74	81	4
Noonan, Nick	18	L	29	SS	a/a	TEX	285	3	1	210	4	70	61	78	-38
Norwood, John	18	R	26	RF	aa	MIA	396	5	11	199	8	63	66	85	-50
Nottingham, Jacol	18	R	23	C	aaa	MIL	178	7	1	235	5	62	136	85	-7
	19	R	24	C	aaa	MIL	290	4	5	197	7	62	106	102	-25
Numata, Chace	18	B	26	C	aa	NYY	128	0	1	150	4	77	37	58	-35
	19	B	27	C	a/a	DET	254	3	0	212	5	79	69	115	16
Nunez, Dom	18	L	23	C	aa	COL	324	8	6	212	10	77	67	47	-1
	19	L	24	C	aaa	COL	213	12	1	214	10	65	189	100	56
Nunez, Jhon	18	B	24	C	aa	BOS	232	1	3	218	6	79	42	89	-11
	19	B	25	C	aa	BOS	211	4	4	263	5	80	87	98	31
O'Brien, Peter	18	R	28	1B	a/a	MIA	356	21	1	166	11	53	163	36	-23
	19	R	29	1B	aaa	MIA	255	12	0	168	10	47	170	50	-48
O'Grady, Brian	19	L	27	1B	aaa	CIN	429	24	16	238	9	60	201	117	49
O'Hearn, Ryan	18	L	25	1B	aaa	KC	353	8	2	201	9	69	92	58	-12
	19	L	26	1B	aaa	KC	129	6	0	245	9	72	162	75	55
O'Neill, Tyler	18	R	23	LF	aaa	STL	238	19	2	270	9	68	175	95	61
	19	R	24	LF	a/a	STL	175	10	2	215	6	62	155	95	12
Ockimey, Josh	18	L	23	1B	a/a	BOS	404	16	1	229	12	61	136	46	-7
	19	L	24	1B	aaa	BOS	377	20	0	188	15	60	177	75	23
Odom, Joseph	18	R	26	C	a/a	SEA	287	4	0	188	6	64	73	21	-66
	19	R	27	C	a/a	SEA	345	5	1	191	7	60	82	27	-72
O'Grady, Brian	18	L	26	LF	a/a	CIN	322	12	7	239	9	70	127	113	35
OKeefe, Brian	19	R	26	C	aa	STL	301	10	1	190	8	73	83	40	-17
Okey, Chris	18	R	24	C	aa	CIN	263	5	2	176	5	69	72	46	-42
	19	R	25	C	a/a	CIN	182	6	0	186	8	57	133	89	-25
Oliva, Jared	19	R	24	CF	aa	PIT	447	5	32	262	8	75	85	204	43
Olivares, Edward	19	R	23	RF	aa	SD	488	14	30	254	7	78	98	158	51
ONeill, Michael	19	R	27	LF	a/a	CIN	340	4	12	236	6	64	60	135	-44
O'Neill, Michael	18	R	26	CF	a/a	TEX	462	9	23	214	7	69	83	113	-9
Orf, Nate	18	R	28	2B	aaa	MIL	399	4	13	223	7	77	64	104	5
	19	R	29	RF	aaa	MIL	405	8	7	208	10	76	75	116	14
Orozco, Rodrigo	19	B	24	LF	a/a	SD	369	3	13	230	8	78	57	136	10
Ortega, Rafael	18	L	27	LF	aaa	MIA	280	1	9	222	11	86	48	144	50
	19	L	28	CF	aaa	ATL	431	15	11	234	9	73	136	130	56
Ortiz, Danny	18	L	28	LF	aaa	PHI	392	12	0	186	4	67	94	27	-41
Osuna, Jose	18	R	26	3B	aaa	PIT	302	7	4	269	7	80	91	53	27
	19	R	27	RF	aaa	PIT	71	1	2	224	9	64	153	166	42
Overstreet, Kyle	18	R	25	1B	aa	SD	470	7	2	233	5	81	57	44	-4
	19	R	26	1B	aa	SD	367	5	1	218	6	74	56	68	-25
Owen, Hunter	19	R	26	3B	a/a	PIT	357	15	1	226	6	62	152	89	9
Owings, Christoph	18	R	27	2B	aaa	ARI	91	1	1	210	1	77	49	109	-19
	19	R	28	SS	aaa	BOS	163	8	5	277	6	64	176	58	26
Pabst, Arden	18	R	23	C	a/a	PIT	60	2	0	192	6	71	70	43	-30
	19	R	24	C	aa	PIT	250	3	0	181	4	69	81	93	-21
Pache, Cristian	18	R	20	CF	aa	ATL	104	1	0	256	4	72	49	66	-41
	19	R	21	CF	a/a	ATL	487	11	8	273	8	74	131	138	57
Padlo, Kevin	19	R	23	3B	a/a	TAM	351	18	11	236	15	61	206	121	64
Paez, Michael	19	R	25	2B	aa	NYM	311	3	0	191	8	78	52	53	-19
Palacios, Jermain	18	R	22	SS	aa	TAM	164	1	3	168	5	71	47	84	-40
	19	R	23	2B	aa	TAM	123	2	8	181	10	75	55	170	9
Palacios, Joshua	19	L	24	CF	aa	TOR	286	7	14	255	13	73	114	146	43
Palka, Daniel	18	L	27	RF	aaa	CHW	63	2	1	234	11	58	121	52	-29
	19	L	28	RF	aaa	CHW	395	21	1	207	11	65	156	79	23
Palmeiro, Preston	19	L	24	1B	aa	BAL	350	5	2	214	6	74	79	109	3
Panas, Connor	18	L	25	RF	aa	TOR	370	7	3	206	5	74	71	69	-13
	19	L	26	1B	aaa	SD	30	2	0	203	6	72	165	55	49
Pantoja, Alexis	18	B	22	3B	aa	CLE	79	0	0	182	3	69	25	41	-83
	19	L	23	2B	aa	CLE	416	2	6	248	6	81	44	83	-2
Papi, Mike	18	L	26	RF	aaa	CLE	243	5	1	214	13	63	111	52	-18
	19	L	27	RF	a/a	CLE	267	0	0	175	8	67	57	39	-62
Paredes, Isaac	18	R	19	3B	aa	DET	131	3	1	311	11	83	82	42	36
	19	R	20	3B	aa	DET	478	13	5	286	10	87	86	86	59
Park, Hoy Jun	19	L	23	2B	aa	NYY	416	3	18	252	11	76	66	157	18
Parker, Jarrett	19	L	30	RF	aaa	LAA	346	15	1	183	10	51	163	67	-29
Patterson, Jordan	18	L	26	1B	aaa	COL	413	17	4	224	6	65	125	75	-2
	19	L	27	1B	aaa	TOR	359	13	2	200	5	57	149	146	4
Paul, Chris	18	R	26	3B	aa	MIN	338	5	1	215	4	75	72	69	-12
Payton, Mark	18	L	27	LF	aaa	NYY	197	5	2	214	12	69	74	63	-18
	19	L	28	LF	aaa	OAK	395	20	5	262	7	76	154	114	73

BATTER	yr	b	age	pos	lvl	org	ab	hr	sb	ba	bb%	ct%	px	sx	bpv
Pena,Roberto	19	R	27	C	a/a	LAA	200	5	1	197	9	75	90	60	4
Pentecost,Max	18	R	25	C	aa	TOR	344	8	1	224	3	71	87	62	-20
Pereda,Jhonny	19	R	23	C	aa	CHC	344	2	2	227	12	83	49	41	-3
Perez,Alex	18	L	26	2B	a/a	MIN	286	0	2	216	10	74	32	69	-35
Perez,Arvicent	18	R	24	C	aa	DET	39	0	0	226	0	78	19	23	-65
	19	R	25	DH	aa	COL	186	2	3	259	1	81	55	36	-11
Perez,Brallan	19	R	23	2B	aa	OAK	268	1	4	230	8	80	32	80	-16
Perez,Carlos	18	R	28	C	a/a	TEX	95	4	0	249	7	79	97	14	11
	19	R	29	C	a/a	BAL	374	11	0	192	4	82	90	28	19
Perez,Michael	18	L	26	C	aaa	ARI	218	3	0	211	5	77	52	44	-23
	19	L	27	C	aaa	TAM	184	9	0	195	11	65	138	8	-13
Perkins,Blake	19	S	23	LF	aa	KC	110	2	4	209	7	71	66	152	-2
Perkins,Cameron	18	R	28	1B	aaa	SEA	362	7	6	197	5	75	79	86	2
	19	R	29	RF	aaa	LA	294	6	5	210	5	78	93	105	30
Persico,Luke	19	R	24	LF	aa	OAK	136	2	1	230	7	69	82	163	2
Peter,Jake	18	L	25	2B	aaa	LA	329	5	3	200	6	66	61	85	-49
	19	L	26	2B	aaa	LA	261	5	1	156	12	59	105	105	-34
Peters,DJ	18	R	23	CF	aa	LA	491	22	1	201	6	55	146	62	-29
	19	R	24	CF	a/a	LA	457	19	2	213	9	57	146	86	-14
Peterson,Cole	19	L	24	SS	a/a	DET	151	0	3	202	2	77	37	128	-14
Peterson,D.J.	18	R	26	3B	aaa	CIN	422	14	2	235	4	66	114	42	-20
	19	R	27	3B	aaa	CHW	130	5	1	147	6	64	107	88	-20
Peterson,Dustin	18	R	24	LF	aaa	ATL	406	9	2	237	5	74	81	49	-14
	19	R	25	1B	aaa	DET	301	9	1	253	4	71	97	34	-15
Peterson,Jace	19	L	29	3B	aaa	BAL	326	7	9	242	9	79	101	149	54
Peterson,Kort	18	L	24	RF	aa	KC	166	5	5	206	5	60	129	135	-3
	19	L	25	RF	aa	KC	294	6	3	205	4	66	95	143	-5
Peterson,Shane	18	L	30	LF	aaa	SD	426	6	1	205	5	64	85	59	-45
	19	L	31	RF	aaa	LA	278	7	3	178	5	59	111	150	-20
Phillips,Brett	18	L	24	RF	aaa	MIL	258	4	7	195	8	57	98	137	-33
	19	L	25	RF	aaa	KC	333	12	16	207	14	61	147	222	42
Pill,Tyler	19	L	29	RF	aaa	TEX	103	1	0	104	7	75	47	43	-35
Pinero,Danny	19	R	25	3B	a/a	DET	408	13	4	213	9	71	125	85	23
Pinto,Rene	19	R	23	C	aa	TAM	260	5	1	215	8	70	92	35	-23
Pirela,Jose	19	R	30	RF	aaa	PHI	342	17	1	253	5	70	150	105	41
Pizzano,Dario	18	L	27	DH	aa	SEA	400	8	2	230	8	82	65	51	15
	19	L	28	LF	aa	NYM	115	3	0	186	12	86	46	76	17
Plaia,Colton	18	R	28	C	aaa	NYM	196	5	0	179	7	58	113	46	-47
	19	R	29	C	aaa	NYM	125	1	0	111	4	48	69	26	-132
Polo,Tito	18	R	24	CF	aa	CHW	163	1	14	223	7	76	51	160	8
	19	R	25	CF	aaa	SEA	38	0	1	210	4	87	72	61	35
Pompey,Dalton	18	B	26	RF	a/a	TOR	160	3	7	219	8	68	80	92	-16
Pope,Brett	19	L	23	SS	aa	PIT	282	2	7	242	8	78	64	108	11
Potts,Hudson	18	R	20	3B	aa	SD	78	2	1	142	10	55	45	31	-112
	19	R	21	3B	aa	SD	409	13	3	209	7	67	125	101	10
Powell,Boog	18	L	25	RF	aaa	OAK	147	0	4	188	11	72	11	61	-61
	19	L	26	CF	aaa	SD	340	5	9	223	10	67	96	141	0
Profar,Juremi	18	R	22	3B	aa	TEX	349	8	1	216	6	86	57	29	12
	19	R	23	1B	a/a	TEX	434	9	0	249	7	83	84	38	23
Puello,Cesar	18	R	27	LF	aaa	SF	294	3	4	245	8	72	53	84	-27
	19	R	28	CF	aaa	MIA	149	5	2	219	11	66	109	73	-10
Querecuto,Juniel	18	B	26	3B	a/a	ARI	419	1	12	268	5	84	43	96	9
	19	B	27	SS	aaa	ARI	386	5	4	216	2	78	70	122	13
Quiroz,Esteban	18	L	26	2B	aa	BOS	87	5	1	256	10	75	134	53	44
	19	L	27	2B	aaa	SD	306	11	2	203	10	67	143	75	19
Rabago,Chris	18	R	25	C	aa	NYY	230	4	7	169	8	69	82	107	-10
	19	R	26	C	a/a	COL	199	3	6	199	10	71	85	53	-16
Rademacher,Bijar	18	L	27	RF	aaa	CHC	342	1	1	198	7	76	34	26	-44
Raleigh,Cal	19	S	23	C	aa	SEA	145	7	0	217	9	63	147	33	-6
Raley,Luke	18	L	24	1B	aa	MIN	484	16	3	244	5	69	101	111	3
	19	L	25	RF	aaa	MIN	126	6	3	267	4	63	148	135	20
Ramirez,Harold	18	R	24	RF	aa	TOR	463	9	13	292	5	79	94	81	26
	19	R	25	LF	aaa	MIA	110	3	1	305	5	80	142	117	78
Ramirez,Tyler	18	L	23	LF	aa	OAK	512	7	4	253	9	68	91	78	-11
	19	L	24	LF	a/a	OAK	396	6	4	195	12	64	87	123	-23
Ramos,Henry	18	B	26	CF	aaa	LA	357	7	6	242	6	76	82	82	9
	19	B	27	RF	aaa	SF	335	7	2	217	5	74	94	73	4
Ramos,Roberto	18	L	24	1B	aa	COL	199	13	2	216	9	61	169	31	9
	19	L	25	1B	aaa	COL	431	21	0	264	8	64	168	22	10
Randolph,Corneliu	18	L	21	LF	aa	PHI	410	4	2	213	9	74	50	45	-29
	19	L	22	LF	aa	PHI	348	10	8	234	9	67	114	143	15
Ravelo,Rangel	18	R	26	1B	aaa	STL	347	9	0	253	8	83	75	45	26
	19	R	27	1B	aaa	STL	334	8	0	240	7	78	90	56	14
Ray,Corey	18	L	24	CF	aa	MIL	532	26	33	227	9	63	164	155	49
	19	L	25	CF	a/a	MIL	247	6	5	177	8	51	125	76	-59
Read,Raudy	18	R	25	C	a/a	WAS	197	2	0	244	5	78	66	40	-12
	19	R	26	C	aaa	WAS	306	15	1	227	4	77	132	103	58
Reed,A.J.	18	L	25	1B	aaa	HOU	462	20	0	201	8	67	118	42	-7
	19	L	26	1B	aaa	CHW	231	10	0	177	8	56	159	52	-20
Reed,Buddy	18	S	23	CF	aa	SD	179	1	15	158	5	61	46	130	-69
	19	S	24	CF	aa	SD	381	11	19	200	9	63	106	135	-8
Reed,Michael	18	R	26	CF	a/a	ATL	333	9	8	298	13	66	118	73	6
	19	R	27	LF	aaa	SF	53	1	1	184	9	53	119	92	-50
Refsnyder,Rob	18	R	27	RF	aaa	TAM	184	3	0	230	7	68	70	41	-43
	19	R	28	RF	aaa	CIN	302	9	0	257	8	62	135	68	-8
Rei,Austin	18	R	25	C	aa	BOS	265	5	1	219	9	70	81	55	-19
	19	R	26	C	aa	BOS	83	1	0	146	6	61	95	18	-61

BATTER	yr	b	age	pos	lvl	org	ab	hr	sb	ba	bb%	ct%	px	sx	bpv
Reinheimer,Jack	19	R	27	SS	aaa	BAL	342	3	9	197	8	74	54	112	-15
Reks,Zach	18	L	25	DH	aa	LA	260	2	4	236	8	66	62	65	-47
	19	L	26	LF	a/a	LA	444	22	2	241	9	64	150	92	18
Renda,Tony	18	R	27	2B	a/a	BOS	267	4	8	277	5	81	76	97	26
	19	R	28	3B	aaa	BOS	20	1	0	173	4	83	142	79	79
Rengifo,Luis	18	S	21	SS	a/a	LAA	341	4	14	246	9	82	68	147	49
	19	R	22	SS	aaa	LAA	110	4	2	220	6	75	90	81	9
Reyes,Alfredo	18	R	25	2B	a/a	PIT	118	1	9	211	7	60	45	110	-74
	19	R	26	SS	a/a	PIT	166	1	6	164	9	58	65	128	-63
Reyes,Pablo	18	R	25	LF	a/a	PIT	401	6	13	245	6	79	71	103	17
	19	R	26	LF	aaa	PIT	175	7	4	242	6	76	148	54	50
Reyes,Victor	19	B	25	RF	aaa	DET	289	9	8	270	4	81	105	128	58
Reynolds,Bryan	18	B	23	CF	aa	PIT	331	6	3	275	10	76	76	79	12
	19	B	24	CF	aaa	PIT	49	4	2	327	11	75	173	137	94
Reynolds,Matt	18	R	28	SS	aaa	WAS	309	3	2	219	9	71	101	86	9
	19	R	29	SS	aaa	WAS	376	11	6	229	10	68	130	122	27
Rice,Ian	18	R	25	C	aa	CHC	272	7	1	216	14	64	99	41	-22
	19	R	26	DH	a/a	CHC	223	2	0	174	10	66	62	46	-58
Rickard,Joey	18	R	27	CF	aaa	BAL	153	2	2	229	12	79	78	84	28
	19	R	28	LF	aaa	SF	236	6	1	262	8	78	119	119	55
Riddle,J.T.	18	L	27	SS	a/a	MIA	88	2	2	276	7	77	75	98	14
	19	L	28	SS	aaa	MIA	121	3	2	189	4	79	107	184	69
Rifaela,Ademar	18	L	24	LF	aa	BAL	359	6	1	224	6	71	75	47	-30
	19	L	25	LF	a/a	BAL	345	9	1	215	6	67	110	118	5
Rijo,Wendell	18	R	23	2B	aa	NYY	255	4	3	188	10	79	60	64	3
	19	R	24	2B	a/a	NYY	324	12	3	224	7	72	127	95	30
Riley,Austin	18	R	21	3B	a/a	ATL	390	16	1	280	7	67	144	65	17
	19	R	22	3B	aaa	ATL	174	12	0	272	9	76	193	74	96
Rincon,Carlos	19	R	22	RF	aa	LA	254	9	1	202	6	64	123	57	-16
Rios,Edwin	18	L	24	3B	aaa	LA	309	8	0	260	5	58	130	32	-41
	19	L	25	3B	aaa	LA	393	22	1	220	0	53	212	82	20
Ripken,Ryan	19	L	26	1B	aa	BAL	103	1	0	246	3	74	64	59	-25
Ritchie,Jamie	18	R	25	C	a/a	HOU	242	2	2	241	9	72	68	58	-21
	19	R	26	C	aaa	HOU	252	3	1	206	10	72	86	82	-3
Rivas,Raul	19	B	23	2B	a/a	PHI	155	0	3	190	6	68	48	155	-32
Rivas,Webster	18	R	28	C	aa	SD	217	3	1	222	4	73	48	45	-47
	19	R	29	C	a/a	SD	231	4	1	212	8	75	72	88	-4
Rivera,Emmanue	19	R	23	3B	aa	KC	496	6	5	245	4	84	55	117	25
Rivera,Jeremy	18	B	23	SS	aa	BOS	496	4	9	240	4	82	38	76	-10
	19	B	24	SS	aa	BOS	339	5	11	226	5	78	64	130	14
Rivera,Laz	19	R	25	SS	aa	CHW	424	2	9	225	4	78	54	94	-6
Rivera,Yadiel	19	R	27	SS	aaa	MIA	300	10	12	239	2	67	104	122	-2
Roache,Victor	18	R	27	LF	a/a	STL	433	12	3	171	7	61	77	63	-61
Robert,Luis	19	R	22	CF	a/a	CHW	428	23	25	288	5	72	172	225	103
Robertson,Daniel	18	R	33	CF	a/a	ARI	355	5	9	189	7	78	62	83	1
	19	R	25	SS	aaa	TAM	104	2	1	218	11	71	35	44	-61
Robertson,Krame	19	R	25	SS	a/a	STL	373	8	11	193	12	74	74	108	4
Robinson,Chuckie	19	R	25	C	aa	HOU	374	6	8	186	5	63	81	104	-39
Robinson,Drew	18	L	26	CF	a/a	TEX	219	8	4	255	9	54	182	113	14
	19	L	27	CF	aaa	STL	189	4	7	211	12	55	101	132	-43
Robinson,Errol	18	R	24	SS	aa	LA	433	7	13	205	6	72	54	77	-33
	19	R	25	SS	a/a	LA	346	4	7	219	8	73	57	69	-30
Robson,Jake	18	L	24	CF	a/a	DET	482	9	15	266	10	69	93	107	3
	19	L	25	LF	aaa	DET	409	8	21	237	9	65	99	154	-2
Rodgers,Brendan	18	R	22	SS	a/a	COL	426	14	9	250	5	78	102	84	32
	19	R	23	2B	aaa	COL	143	7	0	315	6	80	145	100	78
Rodriguez,Aderlin	18	R	27	1B	aa	BAL	483	17	1	229	4	77	83	48	-2
	19	R	28	1B	aaa	SD	265	11	0	238	3	78	143	64	56
Rodriguez,Alfredc	18	R	24	SS	aa	CIN	26	0	0	170	6	69	0	59	-92
	19	R	25	SS	a/a	CIN	486	1	14	235	5	81	44	113	6
Rodriguez,David	18	R	22	C	aa	TAM	252	3	2	206	7	73	64	56	-23
	19	R	23	C	aa	TAM	262	6	4	209	10	70	94	159	18
Rodriguez,Jonath	18	R	29	1B	aaa	MIA	287	9	1	186	11	57	108	52	-43
Rodriguez,Jorma	18	R	22	2B	aa	CLE	24	0	0	326	7	82	104	59	45
Rodriguez,Luigi	18	L	26	RF	aa	SF	380	9	12	230	8	63	89	119	-23
Rodriguez,Nellie	18	R	24	1B	a/a	CLE	346	12	0	208	8	54	139	26	-45
	19	R	25	1B	aa	CLE	277	11	0	184	9	51	166	44	-34
Rodriguez,Ronny	18	R	26	3B	aaa	DET	260	8	8	300	3	80	114	128	57
	19	R	27	2B	aaa	DET	172	9	4	274	3	73	152	187	79
Rogers,Jake	18	R	23	C	aa	DET	352	14	6	197	9	66	111	95	2
	19	R	24	C	a/a	DET	252	13	0	232	11	67	162	122	48
Rojas,Jose	18	L	25	1B	a/a	LAA	381	12	7	231	6	72	100	92	10
	19	L	26	2B	aaa	LAA	515	21	2	219	6	68	145	93	29
Rojas,Josh	18	L	24	LF	aa	HOU	390	6	23	222	11	78	75	124	32
	19	L	25	2B	a/a	ARI	416	16	24	281	9	80	139	188	103
Roman,Mitch	18	R	23	2B	aa	CHW	95	0	3	213	3	54	35	89	-123
	19	R	24	2B	aa	CHW	121	1	1	154	11	65	51	130	-44
Romanski,Jake	19	R	29	C	a/a	BOS	110	0	0	178	2	70	45	80	-50
Rondon,Jose	18	R	24	SS	aaa	CHW	313	16	4	219	4	70	132	89	21
	19	R	25	SS	aaa	BAL	73	2	1	182	10	66	93	58	-29
Rooker,Brent	18	R	24	1B	aa	MIN	503	18	5	224	8	67	121	85	10
	19	R	25	LF	aaa	MIN	228	11	2	248	11	53	214	71	20
Rortvedt,Ben	19	L	22	C	aa	MIN	197	5	0	232	10	73	84	28	-17
Rosa,Garabez	18	R	29	1B	aaa	BAL	481	9	1	222	2	69	64	51	-50
Rosario,Wilin	19	R	30	DH	aaa	MIN	413	15	1	241	4	77	108	74	27
Rose,Matt	18	R	24	1B	aa	CHW	426	16	0	167	7	61	110	22	-46
Ruiz,Keibert	18	S	20	C	aa	LA	377	10	0	240	5	90	58	24	27
	19	R	21	C	a/a	LA	314	5	0	236	7	92	45	47	32

BATTER	yr	b	age	pos	lvl	org	ab	hr	sb	ba	bb%	ct%	px	sx	bpv
Ruiz, Rio	18	L	24	3B	aaa	ATL	498	7	2	238	6	80	63	71	4
	19	L	25	3B	a/a	BAL	22	1	0	199	4	80	64	-19	-24
Russell, Michael	18	R	25	3B	a/a	TAM	301	2	7	211	5	71	56	114	-24
Ruta, Ben	18	L	24	LF	aa	NYY	121	0	10	278	7	76	54	120	0
	19	L	25	LF	aa	NYY	442	8	22	232	9	78	86	156	41
Rutherford, Blake	19	L	22	RF	aa	CHW	438	7	9	258	8	71	77	142	0
Saez, Jorge	18	R	28	C	aa	NYY	152	5	2	195	9	66	73	48	-46
	19	R	29	C	aa	NYY	112	4	0	134	11	59	115	54	-41
Sagdal, Ian	19	L	26	3B	aa	WAS	447	7	1	247	8	77	95	91	27
Saladino, Tyler	18	R	29	SS	aaa	MIL	130	2	6	190	9	72	57	135	-8
	19	R	30	SS	aaa	MIL	265	12	5	220	9	66	158	125	44
Salazar, Alejandro	18	R	22	2B	a/a	ATL	193	0	4	283	4	82	40	85	-6
	19	R	23	2B	aa	ATL	408	2	11	206	4	71	40	119	-35
Salcedo, Erick	18	B	25	SS	aa	BAL	432	0	1	184	5	86	32	66	0
	19	B	26	SS	a/a	LAA	328	2	3	159	4	83	46	91	6
Salters, Daniel	18	L	25	C	a/a	CLE	251	4	1	213	5	69	64	28	-53
	19	L	26	C	aa	CLE	20	1	0	90	8	77	75	-19	-24
Sanchez, Adrian	18	R	28	SS	aaa	WAS	269	3	8	193	4	81	58	84	7
	19	R	29	2B	aa	WAS	256	5	9	270	6	81	94	121	49
Sanchez, Ali	19	R	22	C	a/a	NYM	326	1	1	234	7	78	49	52	-20
Sanchez, Jesus	18	L	21	RF	aa	TAM	98	1	1	191	9	76	76	65	3
	19	L	22	RF	a/a	MIA	415	12	5	245	9	74	86	100	8
Sanchez, Tony	18	R	30	C	aaa	TEX	225	5	0	232	5	69	80	35	-39
	19	R	31	C	aa	TEX	228	3	0	210	5	71	71	45	-32
Sandoval, Brandor	18	R	23	RF	aa	LAA	247	2	13	242	8	70	41	89	-42
	19	R	24	LF	aa	LAA	268	2	8	254	5	72	44	108	-33
Sanger, Brendon	18	L	25	RF	aa	LAA	304	6	3	199	12	72	60	44	-25
	19	L	26	RF	aa	LAA	355	11	3	176	10	60	108	82	-35
Santana, Cristian	19	R	22	3B	aa	LA	399	9	0	282	2	76	95	53	5
Santana, Daniel	18	B	28	CF	aaa	ATL	322	12	9	214	3	70	118	122	18
	19	B	29	SS	aaa	TEX	35	0	1	278	7	65	133	119	17
Santander, Anthor	18	B	24	RF	a/a	BAL	253	6	3	213	4	82	71	86	21
	19	B	25	RF	aaa	BAL	193	4	2	216	5	78	95	85	25
Sardinas, Luis	18	B	25	SS	aaa	BAL	231	4	2	230	3	80	67	47	-3
	19	B	26	SS	a/a	WAS	227	1	1	202	7	81	44	54	-12
Sawyer, Wynston	18	R	27	C	a/a	MIN	101	2	0	219	11	76	46	35	-25
	19	R	28	C	aaa	MIN	154	2	0	216	5	63	127	69	-15
Scavuzzo, Jacob	18	R	24	LF	a/a	LA	392	20	9	217	5	68	141	88	22
	19	R	25	RF	aaa	CHW	188	13	2	208	5	58	197	133	43
Schales, Brian	18	R	22	3B	aa	MIA	422	8	3	230	11	71	87	64	-2
	19	R	23	3B	a/a	MIN	148	5	0	177	11	48	190	96	-14
Schebler, Scott	18	L	28	RF	a/a	CIN	52	1	0	155	9	76	51	20	-29
	19	L	29	CF	aaa	CIN	194	4	0	173	5	65	72	31	-61
Schrock, Max	18	L	24	2B	aaa	STL	417	3	8	212	4	90	42	63	24
	19	L	25	3B	aaa	STL	265	1	9	230	9	79	71	129	25
Schulz, Nick	18	R	27	RF	a/a	SD	289	5	3	158	9	57	67	47	-84
Schwindel, Frank	18	R	26	DH	aaa	KC	510	16	2	243	5	84	100	40	40
	19	R	27	1B	a/a	DET	354	13	0	229	5	81	102	50	32
Scivicque, Kade	18	R	25	C	a/a	DET	151	2	0	214	5	81	59	6	-15
	19	R	26	C	a/a	DET	254	8	0	262	4	77	125	56	37
Sedio, Chad	18	L	24	LF	aa	DET	165	2	1	226	6	70	63	74	-34
	19	L	25	2B	a/a	DET	145	4	0	222	3	72	139	127	47
Segovia, Joantgel	19	R	23	RF	aa	MIL	255	2	7	243	6	84	68	86	27
Selsky, Steve	18	R	29	1B	aaa	CIN	268	8	1	210	7	62	108	55	-34
Senzel, Nick	18	R	23	2B	aaa	CIN	171	5	7	280	9	74	114	99	36
	19	R	24	CF	aaa	CIN	35	1	0	230	7	56	97	93	-58
Serven, Brian	19	R	24	C	aa	COL	242	10	1	210	8	74	125	69	32
Sever, Joe	18	R	28	3B	a/a	CLE	488	5	7	215	6	78	66	70	0
Seymour, Anferne	18	B	23	RF	aa	MIA	51	1	3	222	9	80	78	82	27
	19	B	24	RF	aa	MIA	276	1	18	247	7	66	65	166	-22
Sharpe, Chris	19	R	23	LF	aa	PIT	231	10	2	206	7	70	149	152	56
Shaver, Colton	19	R	24	3B	aa	HOU	188	13	0	199	14	56	202	88	27
Shaw, Chris	18	L	25	LF	aaa	SF	394	14	0	204	4	57	127	53	-46
	19	L	26	LF	a/a	SF	442	19	2	251	7	71	147	110	47
Shaw, Travis	19	L	29	3B	aaa	MIL	133	9	2	221	16	64	161	48	15
Sheets, Gavin	19	L	23	1B	aa	CHW	464	17	3	256	10	76	99	79	22
Short, Zack	18	R	23	SS	aa	CHC	436	15	7	205	14	66	121	83	16
	19	R	24	SS	a/a	CHC	197	5	2	203	12	62	134	131	8
Siddall, Brett	18	L	24	DH	aa	OAK	253	1	2	176	6	72	47	68	-39
Sierra, Anibal	18	R	24	SS	aa	HOU	221	2	3	179	5	65	62	90	-52
	19	R	25	SS	a/a	HOU	376	5	2	171	6	61	60	37	-86
Sierra, Magneuris	18	L	22	CF	aaa	MIA	346	2	12	231	3	76	43	133	-12
	19	L	23	CF	a/a	MIA	517	6	32	255	5	81	65	222	54
Silviano, John	18	L	24	1B	aa	MIA	54	2	0	142	10	49	119	89	-60
	19	L	25	1B	aa	MIA	205	4	0	138	9	55	98	44	-74
Siri, Jose	18	R	23	CF	aa	CIN	253	11	12	211	8	59	147	151	18
	19	R	24	CF	a/a	CIN	468	10	22	214	7	58	103	140	-30
Sisco, Chance	18	L	23	C	aaa	BAL	128	3	0	221	10	70	68	41	-32
	19	L	24	C	aaa	BAL	168	8	0	252	9	71	142	53	27
Slater, Austin	18	R	26	RF	aaa	SF	195	3	6	276	7	76	117	103	43
	19	R	27	1B	aaa	SF	240	8	4	250	13	66	132	81	8
Smith, Dominic	18	L	23	1B	aaa	NYM	337	4	2	202	6	73	64	64	-22
Smith, Dwight	18	L	26	LF	aaa	TOR	310	5	7	238	10	80	86	75	36
	19	L	27	LF	aaa	BAL	45	2	0	254	5	79	118	65	42
Smith, Kevin	19	R	23	SS	aa	TOR	430	18	11	205	6	62	159	120	25
Smith, Pavin	19	L	23	1B	aa	ARI	440	11	2	282	11	85	109	136	84
Smith, Will	18	R	23	C	a/a	LA	352	15	4	200	8	64	126	69	-5
	19	R	24	C	aaa	LA	224	15	1	223	11	74	163	99	72
Smolinski, Jacob	18	R	29	CF	aaa	OAK	126	7	1	212	9	58	132	50	-26
	19	R	30	RF	aaa	TAM	248	8	6	204	8	68	129	133	30
Snyder, Matt	19	L	29	1B	aaa	MIA	148	4	1	210	7	66	106	37	-26
Solak, Nick	18	R	23	2B	aa	TAM	478	16	18	250	11	73	85	112	15
	19	R	24	2B	aaa	TEX	419	21	4	256	8	73	135	89	39
Sosa, Edmundo	18	R	22	SS	a/a	STL	452	9	5	238	4	78	81	69	5
	19	R	23	SS	aaa	STL	453	13	2	254	3	77	90	106	21
Soto, Elliot	18	R	29	SS	aaa	COL	238	1	1	224	6	79	45	86	-7
	19	R	30	SS	aaa	COL	410	6	5	240	6	73	93	143	22
Spanberger, Chad	19	L	24	RF	aa	TOR	431	12	4	227	8	70	129	71	19
Spangenberg, Cor	18	L	27	3B	aaa	SD	88	2	2	262	4	56	157	112	-5
	19	L	28	LF	aaa	MIL	424	10	19	244	7	59	133	191	11
Sparks, Taylor	18	R	25	3B	a/a	CIN	407	12	4	180	7	47	145	110	-46
Sportman, J.P.	18	R	26	2B	a/a	OAK	435	10	14	226	4	75	88	94	10
Stallings, Jacob	18	R	29	C	aaa	PIT	256	2	1	222	4	75	74	59	-11
	19	R	30	C	aaa	PIT	51	1	0	217	5	78	182	95	100
Stamets, Eric	18	R	27	2B	aaa	CLE	238	4	4	169	5	69	68	77	-36
	19	R	28	SS	aaa	CLE	295	5	10	202	7	66	77	189	-7
Stankiewicz, Drew	18	L	25	2B	aa	PHI	156	2	1	162	8	64	72	64	-48
Starling, Bubba	18	R	26	CF	aaa	KC	35	0	1	219	10	80	43	58	-5
	19	R	27	CF	aaa	KC	261	5	6	254	5	73	75	116	1
Stassi, Brock	18	L	29	1B	aaa	SF	177	1	0	204	11	69	75	29	-30
	19	L	30	1B	a/a	SF	86	1	0	242	10	75	74	22	-18
Stephen, Josh	19	L	22	LF	aa	PHI	362	12	6	256	9	65	169	140	53
Stephenson, Tyler	19	R	23	C	aa	CIN	312	6	0	266	10	78	91	71	19
Stevenson, Andre	18	L	24	CF	aaa	WAS	293	5	10	212	8	72	59	91	-21
	19	L	25	CF	a/a	WAS	386	6	11	281	5	70	96	183	25
Stewart, Christin	18	L	25	LF	aaa	DET	444	20	0	236	11	73	114	50	24
	19	L	26	LF	aaa	DET	83	3	1	250	15	66	103	54	-20
Stewart, D.J.	18	L	25	RF	aaa	BAL	421	11	9	205	9	73	86	87	7
	19	L	26	LF	a/a	BAL	243	11	4	248	12	75	151	111	70
Stokes Jr., Troy	18	R	22	LF	aa	MIL	467	19	18	228	11	66	133	142	38
	19	R	23	LF	aaa	MIL	322	7	11	203	10	69	109	107	10
Straw, Myles	18	R	24	CF	a/a	HOU	516	1	55	244	10	77	32	150	0
	19	R	25	CF	aaa	HOU	277	1	13	255	7	78	40	152	2
Stubbs, Garrett	18	L	25	C	aaa	HOU	297	3	4	244	7	78	66	115	17
	19	L	26	C	aaa	HOU	204	5	8	183	7	77	78	111	17
Sturgeon, Cole	18	L	27	RF	a/a	BOS	364	7	10	230	6	74	64	81	-13
	19	L	28	LF	aaa	BOS	343	7	5	237	5	71	94	100	0
Suiter, Jerrick	18	R	25	RF	aaa	PIT	191	1	5	172	8	58	86	97	-52
	19	R	26	1B	aa	PIT	408	3	2	212	5	79	44	57	-20
Sullivan, Brett	18	L	24	C	aa	TAM	421	6	14	230	6	84	54	101	26
	19	L	25	LF	aa	TAM	364	9	20	250	8	84	102	194	90
Sweeney, Darnell	18	B	27	2B	aaa	TOR	292	8	5	205	8	55	121	116	-32
	19	B	28	LF	a/a	PIT	140	3	2	179	5	52	124	107	-49
Swihart, Blake	19	B	27	RF	aaa	ARI	106	3	0	138	8	65	88	128	-20
Szczur, Matthew	18	R	29	CF	aaa	SD	38	0	0	231	6	75	64	63	-14
Taijeron, Travis	18	R	29	RF	aaa	LA	280	8	1	206	7	49	137	60	-61
	19	R	30	1B	aaa	NYM	371	17	4	169	11	40	235	134	3
Tanielu, Nick	18	R	26	3B	a/a	HOU	392	7	2	232	5	85	61	56	16
	19	R	27	3B	aaa	HOU	454	13	1	221	6	76	115	68	28
Tapia, Raimel	18	L	24	CF	aaa	COL	434	8	13	264	5	79	97	141	47
Tatis Jr., Fernanc	18	R	19	SS	aa	SD	353	14	14	274	8	67	136	145	39
Tauchman, Mike	18	L	28	CF	aaa	COL	403	13	7	259	8	80	101	93	46
	19	L	29	CF	aaa	NYY	95	2	3	211	11	78	121	202	86
Tavarez, Aneury	18	L	26	RF	aaa	BOS	394	6	7	205	6	71	72	89	-20
	19	L	27	RF	aa	BOS	73	0	2	175	8	72	55	139	-12
Taveras, Leody	19	B	21	CF	aa	TEX	264	3	10	273	8	77	82	157	36
Taylor, Beau	18	L	28	C	aaa	OAK	302	2	1	198	10	64	62	81	-46
	19	L	29	C	aaa	TOR	223	6	0	202	15	57	145	91	-14
Taylor, Chuck	18	B	25	LF	aa	SEA	502	2	2	250	9	81	44	55	-6
	19	B	26	LF	a/a	WAS	393	10	1	198	8	71	90	62	-11
Taylor, Kevin	18	L	27	LF	aa	NYM	437	1	2	207	5	84	34	63	-5
Taylor, Logan	18	R	25	3B	a/a	SEA	230	5	0	228	7	63	80	35	-57
	19	R	26	3B	aa	SEA	387	7	4	189	6	59	82	89	-61
Taylor, Michael	19	R	28	CF	aa	WAS	218	8	9	217	9	62	164	150	38
Taylor, Tyrone	18	R	24	CF	aaa	MIL	446	14	8	228	4	80	92	114	39
	19	R	25	RF	aaa	MIL	334	11	4	220	0	70	120	96	15
Telis, Tomas	18	B	27	C	aaa	MIA	282	3	2	248	5	87	34	74	9
	19	B	28	C	aaa	MIN	306	6	0	275	4	87	85	83	53
Tellez, Rowdy	18	L	23	1B	aaa	TOR	393	11	6	254	8	80	89	50	23
	19	L	24	1B	aaa	TOR	93	6	0	336	11	70	222	47	86
Tendler, Luke	18	L	27	LF	aa	BOS	374	10	1	229	6	71	86	24	-27
	19	L	28	LF	aa	BOS	413	9	3	207	7	69	100	62	-11
Tenerowicz, Robb	19	R	24	1B	aa	TAM	255	4	7	194	8	72	62	95	-22
Thaiss, Matt	18	L	23	1B	a/a	LAA	525	12	6	233	6	77	87	91	19
	19	L	24	3B	aaa	LAA	310	10	1	212	11	75	99	89	21
Theroux, Collin	19	R	25	C	a/a	OAK	324	9	0	149	10	33	195	55	-82
Thomas, Cody	19	L	25	RF	aa	LA	474	20	4	207	7	65	132	140	19
Thomas, Dillon	19	L	27	RF	aa	MIL	449	13	21	245	8	65	135	181	36
Thomas, Lane	18	R	23	CF	a/a	STL	515	20	13	228	7	71	105	105	17
	19	R	24	CF	aaa	STL	265	7	9	228	8	66	123	128	15
Thompson, David	18	R	25	3B	aaa	NYM	66	1	1	193	4	63	78	78	-54
	19	R	26	1B	a/a	NYM	405	7	11	179	7	69	86	146	2
Thompson, Trayc	18	R	27	RF	aaa	CHW	160	3	2	171	7	56	113	71	-49
	19	R	28	LF	aaa	CLE	334	18	6	181	7	51	187	131	6
Thompson-Williar	19	L	24	CF	aa	SEA	432	12	15	218	7	59	136	172	10

BATTER	yr	b	age	pos	lvl	org	ab	hr	sb	ba	bb%	ct%	px	sx	bpv
Tilson, Charlie	19	L	27	LF	aaa	CHW	236	2	3	231	6	77	64	110	5
Tobias, Josh	18	B	26	3B	aa	BOS	123	1	1	196	4	71	37	44	-65
	19	B	27	2B	a/a	BOS	215	3	2	266	7	72	105	50	2
Tocci, Carlos	18	R	23	CF	a/a	TEX	50	0	2	237	9	79	45	120	7
	19	R	24	CF	aaa	TEX	328	3	3	215	6	79	39	53	-25
Toerner, Justin	19	L	23	RF	aa	STL	166	6	8	186	12	64	99	118	-13
Toffey, William	18	L	23	3B	aa	NYM	134	3	2	217	16	69	114	53	17
	19	L	24	3B	aa	NYM	269	5	5	195	15	61	113	114	-15
Tolbert, L.T.	19	L	23	2B	aa	ARI	106	1	0	242	4	81	47	97	1
Toles, Andrew	18	L	26	LF	aaa	LA	258	5	2	250	3	73	84	73	-8
Tolman, Mitchell	19	L	25	2B	a/a	PIT	434	5	8	229	9	73	72	141	5
Tom, Kaai	19	L	25	RF	a/a	CLE	479	20	4	263	10	70	150	136	56
Tom, Ka'ai	18	L	24	CF	aa	CLE	421	10	11	226	8	73	88	94	10
Tomas, Yasmany	18	R	28	LF	aaa	ARI	355	7	1	186	2	63	91	72	-47
	19	R	29	1B	aaa	ARI	405	16	1	214	3	65	133	103	7
Tomscha, Damek	18	R	27	3B	a/a	PHI	427	14	1	220	5	78	74	40	-4
	19	R	28	1B	a/a	CHW	346	10	2	196	6	67	103	63	-19
Toro-Hernandez, A	18	S	22	3B	aa	HOU	178	2	3	211	8	72	96	83	7
	19	S	23	3B	a/a	HOU	442	14	3	280	9	79	115	116	55
Torrens, Luis	19	R	23	C	aa	SD	350	12	1	270	9	79	117	61	42
Torres, Ramon	18	B	25	2B	aaa	KC	370	4	5	200	5	82	61	85	15
	19	B	26	SS	a/a	CHW	224	4	0	213	3	80	91	125	39
Torreyes, Ronald	18	R	26	2B	aaa	NYY	97	0	0	206	5	86	19	25	-19
	19	R	27	SS	aaa	MIN	308	9	2	217	3	87	71	106	49
Tovar, Wilfredo	18	R	27	SS	aaa	STL	360	3	8	239	4	86	40	66	7
	19	R	28	SS	aaa	LAA	327	3	2	228	3	82	54	91	8
Trahan, Blake	18	R	25	SS	aaa	CIN	444	2	5	210	8	72	38	63	-44
	19	R	26	SS	aaa	CIN	354	4	2	193	5	71	65	77	-31
Trammell, Taylor	19	L	22	LF	aa	SD	436	8	17	214	12	70	70	149	-3
Travis, Sam	18	R	25	1B	aaa	BOS	361	6	1	238	6	73	61	27	-37
	19	R	26	LF	aaa	BOS	236	5	4	246	9	71	108	109	15
Trejo, Alan	19	R	23	SS	aa	COL	437	16	5	255	5	76	115	55	25
Trevino, Jose	18	R	26	C	aa	TEX	104	2	0	201	5	83	47	43	-3
	19	R	27	C	aaa	TEX	146	1	1	186	4	78	72	68	1
Triunfel, Alberto	18	R	24	SS	aaa	LAA	117	3	1	210	3	69	81	80	-26
	19	R	25	2B	aa	STL	212	0	1	159	5	68	53	56	-58
Tromp, Chad	18	R	23	C	a/a	CIN	259	2	2	233	8	82	50	51	0
	19	R	24	C	aaa	CIN	77	6	0	262	11	62	221	115	73
Tromp, Jiandido	18	R	25	RF	a/a	PHI	304	3	3	187	8	65	62	88	-45
Tucker, Cole	18	B	22	SS	aa	PIT	517	4	30	240	8	79	53	135	17
	19	B	23	SS	aaa	PIT	310	6	9	237	9	75	91	168	37
Tucker, Kyle	18	L	21	RF	aaa	HOU	407	19	15	284	8	77	120	109	53
	19	L	22	RF	aaa	HOU	463	25	22	223	9	72	151	159	69
Twine, Justin	18	R	23	2B	aa	MIA	112	3	4	360	2	76	84	98	8
	19	R	24	2B	aa	MIA	359	1	6	227	7	71	49	138	-22
Unroe, Riley	18	B	23	2B	a/a	LAA	364	3	8	188	9	68	40	75	-52
	19	B	24	3B	a/a	ATL	311	5	9	253	9	75	75	120	9
Urena, Jhoan	18	B	24	RF	aa	NYM	421	11	2	219	7	69	85	45	-28
	19	B	25	1B	aa	LAA	468	9	2	229	9	65	116	80	-9
Urena, Richard	18	B	22	SS	aaa	TOR	250	4	2	208	4	80	72	91	14
	19	B	23	SS	aaa	TOR	369	5	3	255	5	75	82	114	11
Urias, Luis	18	R	21	2B	aaa	SD	450	6	1	252	10	73	81	83	1
	19	R	22	SS	aaa	SD	295	13	5	266	8	77	137	142	72
Urias, Ramon	18	R	24	2B	a/a	STL	311	9	1	254	5	79	108	40	27
	19	R	25	2B	a/a	STL	324	7	3	223	9	74	99	84	16
Valentin, Jesmuel	18	B	24	2B	aaa	PHI	129	2	2	209	11	75	56	81	-6
	19	B	25	SS	aa	BAL	403	7	9	227	9	74	89	102	12
Valenzuela, Luis	18	L	25	SS	aa	ATL	369	2	4	254	3	80	56	82	-4
	19	L	26	3B	aa	CHW	302	3	2	180	4	74	64	116	-7
Valera, Breyvic	18	B	26	2B	aaa	BAL	341	8	6	224	8	89	61	83	46
	19	B	27	SS	aaa	NYY	379	12	7	250	9	86	89	68	48
Valerio, Adrian	19	B	22	SS	aa	PIT	106	0	1	196	5	72	38	174	-17
Van Gansen, Pete	18	L	24	2B	aa	SD	336	3	0	221	9	83	48	38	0
	19	L	25	SS	a/a	SD	280	9	0	204	6	72	100	84	5
Van Horn, Brandon	19	R	26	SS	a/a	SF	150	1	0	185	4	64	54	67	-68
VanMeter, Josh	18	L	23	2B	a/a	CIN	428	11	8	235	9	76	114	96	43
	19	L	24	2B	aaa	CIN	181	13	7	318	10	76	199	133	117
Vargas, Ildemaro	18	B	27	SS	aaa	ARI	537	4	6	230	3	89	50	93	33
	19	B	28	SS	aaa	ARI	124	1	1	306	5	95	71	116	83
Vargas, Kennys	18	B	28	1B	aaa	MIN	463	18	0	205	9	66	109	7	-25
Varsho, Daulton	19	L	23	C	aa	ARI	396	16	20	289	9	83	132	215	116
Vazquez, Luis	19	R	20	SS	a/a	CHC	111	1	4	210	4	76	41	147	-9
Velazquez, Andrew	18	B	24	SS	a/a	TAM	458	11	26	222	6	65	90	160	-6
	19	B	25	CF	aaa	CLE	174	3	2	235	4	74	110	118	33
Verdugo, Alex	18	L	22	CF	aaa	LA	343	8	6	294	7	85	72	58	30
Vertigan, Brett	18	L	28	LF	a/a	OAK	364	0	7	198	8	74	44	96	-22
Vielma, Engelb	18	B	24	SS	aaa	BAL	38	0	0	162	8	74	57	74	-17
Vigil, Rodrigo	18	R	25	C	aa	MIA	286	4	1	205	3	85	47	39	-4
	19	R	26	C	a/a	MIA	156	1	3	166	5	77	25	80	-34
Viloria, Meibrys	19	L	22	C	aa	KC	220	1	2	256	9	72	66	61	-28
Vincej, Zach	18	R	27	SS	aaa	SEA	385	4	5	194	6	79	45	77	-12
	19	R	28	3B	aaa	BAL	366	6	0	212	5	79	70	32	-7
Vinicio, Jose	18	R	25	SS	a/a	ARI	275	2	7	183	3	69	53	122	-35
Vizcaino, Vance	19	L	25	LF	aa	COL	304	7	30	272	9	68	119	206	43
Vogelbach, Daniel	18	L	26	1B	aaa	SEA	297	15	0	235	16	75	116	20	33
Voit, Luke	18	R	27	1B	a/a	NYY	269	10	0	252	9	74	109	43	19
Vosler, Jason	18	L	25	3B	a/a	CHC	471	18	1	212	8	63	126	53	-12
	19	L	26	3B	aaa	SD	375	12	0	224	7	67	115	94	2

BATTER	yr	b	age	pos	lvl	org	ab	hr	sb	ba	bb%	ct%	px	sx	bpv
Wade, LaMonte	18	L	24	LF	a/a	MIN	424	9	8	234	11	81	57	87	20
	19	L	25	RF	a/a	MIN	285	4	6	221	15	80	73	121	32
Wade, Tyler	18	L	24	SS	aaa	NYY	364	4	9	223	8	74	60	93	-10
	19	L	25	SS	aaa	NYY	301	4	10	252	6	70	86	161	11
Wagner, Brandon	18	L	23	1B	aa	NYY	130	1	1	236	16	67	66	37	-35
	19	L	24	1B	a/a	NYY	396	8	1	159	9	58	81	96	-62
Walding, Mitch	18	L	26	3B	aaa	PHI	388	17	2	224	13	53	150	67	-21
	19	L	27	3B	aaa	PHI	282	9	1	165	14	40	165	93	-64
Walker, Christian	18	R	27	1B	aaa	ARI	324	10	1	219	5	66	117	82	-5
Walker, Jared	19	L	23	1B	aa	LA	321	12	4	194	12	53	125	100	-41
Wall, Forrest	18	L	23	CF	aa	TOR	299	6	15	217	8	68	83	131	-4
	19	L	24	CF	a/a	TOR	462	10	12	251	9	71	116	153	35
Walls, Taylor	19	S	23	SS	aa	TAM	211	5	14	252	11	72	142	206	79
Walsh, Jared	18	L	25	1B	a/a	LAA	327	11	1	221	7	62	131	46	-19
	19	L	26	1B	aaa	LAA	382	24	0	247	9	62	203	45	38
Walton, Donnie	18	L	24	2B	aa	SEA	208	1	2	200	8	81	55	71	4
	19	L	25	SS	aa	SEA	480	11	10	275	11	82	78	97	36
Ward, Drew	18	L	24	1B	a/a	WAS	374	11	1	221	12	66	102	71	-8
	19	L	25	3B	a/a	WAS	296	14	1	243	5	54	205	86	16
Ward, Taylor	18	R	25	3B	a/a	LAA	375	10	13	283	11	69	97	76	1
	19	R	26	LF	aaa	LAA	421	18	7	230	10	70	145	87	36
Warmoth, Logan	19	R	24	2B	aa	TOR	220	0	11	193	8	63	76	189	-17
Waters, Drew	19	S	21	LF	a/a	ATL	527	6	16	306	7	68	124	192	41
Way, Bo	18	L	27	CF	a/a	LAA	234	0	5	239	6	80	36	68	-18
	19	L	28	CF	a/a	LAA	361	5	5	192	6	77	71	92	3
Weeks, Drew	18	R	25	LF	a/a	COL	289	8	3	228	6	72	91	98	5
	19	R	26	LF	aaa	COL	395	14	4	243	5	79	121	129	63
Weiss, Erich	18	L	27	1B	aaa	PIT	219	4	1	190	5	71	76	91	-15
	19	L	28	1B	aaa	KC	130	4	1	209	5	66	116	105	0
Welker, Colton	19	R	22	3B	aa	COL	353	11	2	272	8	81	122	76	59
Westbrook, Jamie	18	R	23	LF	a/a	ARI	431	12	3	245	4	81	83	84	25
	19	R	24	LF	a/a	ARI	448	12	1	236	8	79	91	70	23
White, Eli	18	R	24	2B	aa	OAK	504	6	14	266	9	74	80	118	15
	19	R	25	SS	aaa	TEX	438	11	10	221	7	65	106	153	5
White, Evan	19	R	23	1B	aa	SEA	365	18	2	281	7	71	132	125	42
White, Mikey	18	R	25	3B	aa	OAK	225	4	0	180	8	59	62	22	-90
	19	R	26	1B	a/a	OAK	399	8	2	216	7	69	100	66	-12
White, Tyler	18	R	28	2B	aaa	HOU	255	9	1	248	10	80	96	40	32
Whitefield, Aaron	19	R	23	CF	aa	MIN	102	0	5	132	3	62	35	204	-53
Wiel, Zander	18	R	25	1B	a/a	MIN	437	8	7	265	7	76	82	80	10
	19	R	26	1B	aaa	MIN	469	19	2	221	6	62	190	148	55
Williams, Christian	19	L	25	1B	aa	TOR	281	4	1	214	5	55	112	115	-44
Williams, Justin	18	L	23	RF	aaa	STL	425	8	3	218	5	75	67	45	-22
	19	L	24	RF	a/a	STL	159	6	1	255	9	67	111	65	-10
Williams, Luke	19	R	23	2B	aa	PHI	441	11	27	219	9	70	118	187	46
Williams, Mason	18	L	27	CF	aaa	CIN	318	5	4	231	7	78	71	89	10
	19	L	28	RF	aaa	BAL	442	14	3	245	7	76	82	52	0
Williams, Nick	19	L	26	LF	aaa	PHI	190	8	1	263	5	65	170	117	44
Williamson, Mac	18	R	28	RF	aaa	SF	182	7	1	199	8	69	97	63	-9
	19	R	29	RF	aaa	SEA	90	6	1	276	9	59	202	69	32
Wilson, Jacob	18	R	28	3B	a/a	WAS	377	5	1	226	7	75	75	37	-10
	19	R	29	3B	aaa	WAS	197	10	1	241	9	72	148	83	46
Wilson, Marcus	19	R	23	RF	aa	BOS	240	9	8	221	11	59	177	154	38
Wilson, Weston	18	R	24	3B	aa	MIL	46	1	1	221	6	83	46	59	-1
	19	R	25	3B	aa	MIL	445	21	12	224	12	71	135	159	57
Wisdom, Patrick	18	R	27	3B	aaa	STL	371	10	8	231	8	64	105	89	-17
	19	R	28	3B	aaa	TEX	396	22	5	194	8	63	153	72	9
Wiseman, Rhett	19	L	25	RF	aa	WAS	335	14	6	201	9	59	161	103	9
Witte, Jantzen	18	R	28	3B	a/a	BOS	381	9	4	229	7	67	101	82	-10
	19	R	29	3B	a/a	BOS	413	7	6	230	6	74	79	64	-10
Wong, Connor	19	R	23	C	aa	LA	149	8	2	323	6	62	191	67	34
Wong, Kean	18	L	23	2B	aaa	TAM	451	8	6	250	7	71	73	87	-15
	19	L	24	2B	aaa	TAM	453	8	5	265	7	70	101	150	20
Wood, Eric	18	R	26	RF	aaa	PIT	283	8	4	223	5	68	122	91	10
	19	R	27	RF	aaa	PIT	227	6	1	204	7	65	105	44	-29
Woodrow, Danny	18	L	23	RF	aa	DET	342	3	16	285	7	78	48	106	-2
	19	L	24	LF	aaa	DET	376	1	20	250	8	75	47	197	9
Wren, Kyle	18	L	27	LF	aaa	BOS	262	2	8	235	8	71	65	91	-18
	19	L	28	CF	aaa	CIN	50	0	1	181	10	61	60	147	-49
Wrenn, Stephen	18	R	24	RF	aa	HOU	472	8	39	219	7	67	79	153	-7
	19	R	25	RF	a/a	HOU	390	6	19	204	8	66	100	199	16
Wynns, Austin	18	R	28	C	aaa	BAL	139	3	0	189	6	68	63	35	-55
	19	R	29	C	a/a	BAL	214	2	0	211	9	78	42	46	-27
Yahn, Willy	19	R	24	3B	aa	BAL	112	0	1	200	2	78	67	87	1
Yastrzemski, Mike	18	L	28	LF	a/a	BAL	428	8	6	198	8	71	85	89	-4
	19	L	29	CF	aaa	SF	136	7	1	243	11	67	186	137	71
Young, Andy	18	R	24	2B	aa	STL	135	6	0	270	4	78	90	44	7
	19	R	25	2B	a/a	ARI	462	20	2	227	6	70	142	139	47
Young, Chesny	18	R	26	2B	aaa	CHC	271	0	3	214	4	76	23	71	-45
Young, Jared	19	L	24	1B	aa	CHC	455	4	4	217	6	74	63	90	-13
Zagunis, Mark	18	R	25	RF	aaa	CHC	371	5	8	224	13	68	60	75	-30
	19	R	26	RF	aaa	CHC	255	5	5	251	7	57	164	106	2
Zammarelli III, Ni	19	L	25	DH	aa	SEA	347	9	2	211	8	63	101	102	-24
Zavala, Seby	18	R	25	C	a/a	CHW	380	12	0	224	7	66	104	29	-28
	19	R	26	C	aaa	CHW	297	16	1	182	6	53	185	66	-9
Zehner, Zack	18	R	26	LF	a/a	NYY	418	13	2	230	7	64	117	78	-12
	19	R	27	LF	a/a	NYY	363	11	2	190	8	63	107	105	-20
Zimmerman, Jord	19	R	25	3B	aa	LAA	125	2	2	239	6	72	107	103	17

PITCHER	yr	t	age	lvl	org	ip	era	whip	bf/g	ctl	dom	cmd	hr/9	h%	s%	bpv
Abbott,Cory	19	R	24	aa	CHC	148	4.26	1.36	23.9	3.6	8.4	2.3	1.2	30	62	70
Abreu,Albert	19	R	24	aa	NYY	98	5.83	1.91	20.2	5.5	7.0	1.3	1.2	36	64	-4
Abreu,Bryan Enri	19	R	22	aa	HOU	78	6.98	1.61	17.3	6.0	10.2	1.7	0.9	33	49	41
Acevedo,Doming	18	R	24	aa	NYY	66	3.88	1.28	19.4	3.0	6.0	2.0	0.6	29	70	65
	19	R	25	a/a	NYY	53	5.60	1.27	6.8	2.6	7.5	2.8	2.6	26	36	82
Adams,Chance	18	R	24	aaa	NYY	113	6.24	1.63	18.6	4.9	7.6	1.5	1.8	31	65	25
	19	R	25	aaa	NYY	83	5.66	1.60	20.4	4.4	7.1	1.6	1.6	31	56	26
Adams,Spencer	18	R	22	a/a	CHW	161	4.73	1.55	25.2	3.4	4.7	1.4	1.4	31	74	12
Adcock,Brett	18	L	23	aa	HOU	40	4.25	1.55	19.5	5.0	5.4	1.1	0.5	30	72	41
	19	L	24	aa	HOU	88	10.06	1.92	18.2	5.7	7.5	1.3	1.8	35	35	-2
Adon,Melvin	19	R	25	a/a	SF	56	6.48	1.89	5.5	6.1	9.8	1.6	0.5	40	61	30
Agrazal,Dario	18	R	24	aa	PIT	87	4.93	1.40	24.5	1.4	4.3	3.1	1.0	33	66	54
	19	R	25	a/a	PIT	89	6.24	1.45	23.7	1.4	5.9	4.3	1.3	35	47	87
Aguilar,Miguel	19	L	28	aa	ARI	31	3.25	1.15	4.8	1.5	7.2	4.9	0.4	32	67	107
Akin,Keegan	18	L	23	aa	BAL	139	3.68	1.32	23.1	3.7	7.5	2.1	1.2	28	77	59
	19	L	24	aaa	BAL	113	5.66	1.68	20.3	5.0	8.4	1.7	0.9	35	60	34
Alcala,Jorge	18	R	23	aa	MIN	62	5.14	1.60	19.6	4.5	7.0	1.6	0.8	33	68	49
	19	R	24	a/a	MIN	113	7.34	1.67	16.4	3.4	7.5	2.2	1.2	37	47	62
Alcantara,Raul	18	R	26	aaa	OAK	84	6.55	1.61	11.6	1.6	4.4	2.8	1.1	36	59	40
Alcantara,Sandy	18	R	23	aaa	MIA	117	4.33	1.34	25.7	2.9	5.8	2.0	0.7	30	68	57
Alcantara,Victor	18	R	25	aaa	DET	52	3.93	1.42	7.6	1.3	6.3	4.7	0.7	36	73	110
Alexander,Jason	18	R	25	a/a	LAA	71	4.56	1.41	20.2	2.3	4.9	2.2	0.9	32	69	44
	19	R	26	a/a	LAA	102	7.50	1.89	20.9	3.3	6.9	2.1	1.0	41	53	53
Alexander,Tyler	18	L	24	a/a	DET	140	5.94	1.78	24.8	1.5	4.9	3.2	1.3	39	68	41
	19	L	28	a/a	OAK	102	7.63	1.73	16.0	4.1	7.4	1.8	2.5	33	42	40
Alexander,Tyler	19	L	25	aaa	DET	99	6.99	1.67	22.2	2.2	7.6	3.4	2.1	38	46	95
Allard,Kolby	18	L	21	aaa	ATL	113	3.16	1.29	24.4	2.5	6.1	2.4	0.5	31	76	75
	19	L	22	aaa	TEX	115	4.61	1.53	23.8	3.0	6.9	2.3	1.3	34	63	60
Allen,Logan	18	L	21	a/a	SD	150	2.62	1.09	23.5	2.8	8.0	2.9	0.6	27	78	102
	19	L	22	aaa	CLE	80	7.39	1.79	20.5	4.0	7.9	2.0	1.9	37	48	52
Allie,Stetson	18	R	27	a/a	LA	24	4.78	1.24	4.1	5.9	7.7	1.3	1.2	19	64	58
	19	R	28	a/a	LA	39	11.09	2.22	4.8	9.0	8.9	1.0	2.5	34	37	-63
Almeida,Adrian	18	L	23	aa	LAA	50	5.21	1.72	6.9	9.2	8.4	0.9	0.6	25	69	65
Almonte,Yency	18	R	24	aaa	COL	45	6.26	1.43	10.7	2.8	5.3	1.9	1.8	29	60	14
	19	R	25	aaa	COL	30	4.74	1.97	4.8	7.9	7.4	0.9	0.7	34	72	-61
Altavilla,Dan	19	R	27	a/a	SEA	31	5.86	1.24	4.5	4.6	11.8	2.6	0.4	32	46	107
Alvarado,Cristian	19	R	25	aa	BAL	75	3.79	1.14	7.4	2.5	6.6	2.7	1.2	26	59	71
Alvarez,Daniel	19	R	23	a/a	NYY	61	2.80	1.19	5.2	3.6	9.5	2.6	0.8	29	72	92
Alvarez,Hendersc	19	R	29	aaa	WAS	53	7.76	2.02	10.7	3.4	4.7	1.4	3.1	36	48	10
Alvarez,R.J.	18	R	27	aaa	TEX	44	4.95	1.63	4.4	4.3	6.8	1.6	0.5	35	69	55
	19	R	28	aaa	MIA	55	6.50	1.69	5.0	5.3	8.1	1.5	2.3	31	50	20
Alzolay,Adbert	18	R	23	aaa	CHC	41	5.06	1.47	22.1	2.8	5.0	1.8	0.9	32	66	37
	19	R	24	aaa	CHC	66	5.57	1.47	18.9	4.6	10.3	2.2	1.6	32	52	79
Anderson,Drew	18	R	24	aaa	PHI	106	4.80	1.32	23.1	2.6	6.2	2.4	1.5	29	68	44
	19	R	25	aaa	PHI	49	6.80	1.71	20.2	5.1	6.3	1.2	2.0	30	49	-6
Anderson,Ian	18	R	20	aa	ATL	20	2.87	1.24	20.4	3.9	9.5	2.4	0.0	31	74	118
	19	R	21	a/a	ATL	137	4.77	1.45	22.5	4.5	9.6	2.1	1.0	32	60	70
Anderson,Jack	19	R	25	aa	SEA	54	2.33	1.64	5.9	3.1	7.2	2.3	0.2	38	84	63
Anderson,Nick	18	R	28	aaa	MIN	60	5.26	1.52	6.7	3.4	9.7	2.8	1.8	35	71	62
Anderson,Shaun	18	R	24	a/a	SF	142	4.17	1.35	23.7	2.1	6.7	3.2	0.8	33	70	83
	19	R	25	aaa	SF	39	4.65	1.46	20.9	3.2	7.5	2.4	0.7	34	63	67
Anderson,Tanner	18	R	25	aaa	PIT	62	3.17	1.49	6.9	2.2	5.6	2.5	0.3	35	78	71
	19	R	26	aaa	OAK	96	7.19	1.93	21.7	3.9	4.4	1.1	2.0	35	53	-9
Andrews,Clayton	19	L	23	aa	MIL	32	4.10	1.34	7.9	5.0	8.1	1.6	1.3	25	62	29
Angulo,Argenis	18	R	24	aa	CLE	53	7.07	2.00	5.5	5.5	9.0	1.6	0.9	41	64	51
	19	R	25	a/a	CLE	64	4.79	1.53	5.8	6.1	10.0	1.6	1.3	29	62	34
Antone,Tejay	19	R	26	a/a	CIN	149	5.47	1.74	25.2	3.7	6.7	1.8	0.9	37	63	39
Aquino,Jayson	18	L	26	a/a	BAL	59	6.51	1.79	22.7	4.3	4.7	1.1	0.2	36	60	37
Araujo,Pedro	19	R	26	a/a	BAL	51	6.90	1.55	8.0	4.7	6.6	1.4	3.0	25	37	11
Arauz,Harold	18	R	23	a/a	PHI	142	5.44	1.57	24.0	2.8	7.0	2.5	1.4	35	68	45
	19	R	24	a/a	STL	87	7.77	1.92	21.8	3.7	4.3	1.2	1.8	36	50	-4
Archer,Tristan	18	R	28	a/a	MIL	78	5.58	1.54	6.6	3.2	6.0	1.9	1.1	33	65	39
	19	R	29	aaa	CIN	30	7.88	2.21	7.5	4.1	5.7	1.4	2.2	41	55	10
Armenteros,Roge	18	R	24	aaa	HOU	118	3.66	1.31	22.1	3.3	8.6	2.6	1.1	31	76	79
	19	R	25	aaa	HOU	85	5.51	1.59	19.7	3.3	7.4	2.3	1.6	34	57	63
Aro,Jonathan	18	R	28	aaa	SD	44	3.97	1.43	4.9	3.9	5.7	1.5	0.6	30	72	50
	19	R	29	a/a	ATL	65	5.77	1.62	9.3	1.5	4.0	2.6	0.6	37	59	49
Arredondo,Edgar	18	R	21	aa	TEX	45	6.11	1.53	21.8	2.1	4.6	2.1	1.0	34	60	35
	19	R	22	aa	TEX	102	6.06	1.75	23.3	2.8	5.5	1.9	1.4	37	58	40
Asher,Alec	18	R	27	aaa	MIL	101	6.38	1.72	20.9	3.2	3.5	1.1	1.2	34	64	-1
Atkinson,Ryan	18	R	25	aa	ARI	109	5.96	1.64	16.8	5.1	8.2	1.6	1.2	33	65	48
	19	R	26	a/a	ARI	55	8.40	2.12	6.8	5.9	8.5	1.4	0.9	42	54	11
Bachar,Lake	18	R	23	aa	SD	87	6.72	1.75	19.9	4.0	5.5	1.4	1.6	34	64	5
	19	R	24	aa	SD	128	5.05	1.62	23.7	4.4	7.3	1.7	1.4	33	62	31
Baez,Joan	19	R	25	a/a	WAS	65	4.30	1.56	6.21	4.8	5.6	1.2	1.0	29	67	-10
Baez,Sandy	18	R	25	aa	DET	105	7.31	1.80	14.7	4.2	5.7	1.4	2.0	34	62	-5
Bahr,Jason	19	R	24	aa	TEX	64	4.93	1.34	22.2	4.2	7.6	1.8	0.4	30	58	42
Bailey,Brandon	18	R	24	aa	HOU	26	4.88	1.32	21.7	3.2	6.6	2.1	2.1	26	72	24
	19	R	25	aa	HOU	94	4.87	1.50	18.5	4.5	8.1	1.8	1.6	30	59	43
Baker,Bryan	19	R	25	a/a	TOR	54	4.58	1.58	4.85	6.7	9.6	1.4	0.7	30	66	10
Baldonado,Albert	18	L	25	aaa	CHC	59	5.62	1.84	7.44	5.9	8.2	1.4	0.8	37	70	50
Ball,Matt	18	R	23	aa	LAA	20	6.76	1.63	22.5	3.1	5.0	1.6	0.0	36	54	56
	19	R	24	a/a	LAA	80	5.12	1.62	16.2	4.5	8.3	1.8	1.3	34	61	46
Ball,Trey	18	L	24	aa	BOS	66	9.52	2.15	9.67	3.6	6.1	1.7	1.7	42	56	1
Banks,Tanner	18	L	27	aa	CHW	61	3.97	1.59	26.9	2.7	5.2	1.9	1.1	34	78	31
	19	L	28	a/a	CHW	128	6.05	1.62	19	1.8	4.8	2.7	1.2	36	55	57
Bannister,Nathan	18	R	25	a/a	SEA	143	7.10	1.80	24.5	3.1	4.7	1.5	1.5	36	62	1
Banuelos,Manuel	18	L	27	aaa	LA	110	4.38	1.56	15.6	3.4	8.2	2.4	0.9	36	73	69

PITCHER	yr	t	age	lvl	org	ip	era	whip	bf/g	ctl	dom	cmd	hr/9	h%	s%	bpv
Baragar,Caleb	19	L	25	a/a	SF	125	5.11	1.30	22.4	3.6	6.5	1.8	1.0	27	52	37
Barker,Luke	19	R	27	a/a	MIL	61	1.92	0.80	5.5	2.6	7.8	3.0	0.6	19	71	89
Barlow,Joe	19	R	24	a/a	TEX	34	6.74	1.93	5.1	8.0	10.3	1.3	0.7	37	60	-12
Barlow,Scott	18	R	26	a/a	KC	51	7.46	1.83	17.0	4.0	7.4	1.9	1.7	38	61	21
Barnes,Charlie	19	L	24	a/a	MIN	95	5.74	1.80	24.4	3.6	6.8	1.9	0.6	39	63	44
Barrett,Jake	18	R	27	aaa	ARI	54	2.72	1.24	5.2	4.6	8.7	1.9	0.4	27	78	93
Barria,Jaime	18	R	22	aaa	LAA	18	3.09	1.31	14.9	2.1	8.4	4.0	0.8	34	79	110
	19	R	23	aaa	LAA	49	8.43	1.65	21.9	1.6	7.0	4.3	2.6	37	31	100
Bashlor,Tyler	18	R	25	aa	NYM	24	3.08	1.21	4.8	4.8	9.4	2.0	0.8	25	77	91
	19	R	26	aaa	NYM	37	4.26	1.38	4.7	3.9	7.5	1.9	0.8	30	63	48
Bass,Blake	19	R	26	aa	TEX	72	7.36	1.73	9.6	4.5	6.9	1.5	0.6	36	51	20
Battenfield,Blake	19	R	25	aa	CHW	97	6.89	1.77	23.5	2.7	5.3	2.0	1.8	36	51	42
Baumann,Michae	19	R	24	aa	BAL	70	3.26	1.14	21.3	3.0	6.7	2.2	0.3	27	67	58
Bautista,Gerson	18	R	23	a/a	NYM	51	4.90	1.68	6.2	3.0	10.5	3.5	0.5	44	70	113
Bautista,Wendol	19	R	26	a/a	CIN	48	8.62	2.28	14.4	2.8	6.8	2.4	1.3	47	55	63
Baxendale,D.J.	18	R	28	aaa	MIN	68	5.90	2.00	10.3	3.0	5.9	2.0	1.0	42	71	28
	19	R	29	aaa	MIN	50	9.25	2.05	9.1	5.8	6.7	1.2	2.4	35	42	-18
Bazardo,Eduard	19	R	24	aa	BOS	33	4.01	1.48	6.8	3.9	7.7	2.0	0.7	33	68	51
Beasley,Jeremy	18	R	23	aa	LAA	45	3.03	1.15	17.9	2.8	6.4	2.3	0.7	26	76	74
	19	R	24	a/a	LAA	125	4.76	1.51	20.9	3.4	7.0	2.1	1.1	33	62	52
Beck,Landon	18	R	26	a/a	STL	65	4.62	1.51	6.6	3.2	6.1	1.9	1.0	33	71	45
Beckwith,Andrew	19	R	24	aa	KC	37	7.93	2.02	6.9	4.1	5.5	1.3	0.6	41	55	7
Bednar,David	19	R	25	aa	SD	58	3.87	1.38	5.5	3.1	10.7	3.5	0.7	37	67	128
Beede,Tyler	18	R	25	aaa	SF	74	7.46	1.95	10.7	6.6	7.4	1.1	1.0	36	61	34
	19	R	26	aaa	SF	36	2.89	1.24	21.0	3.8	9.5	2.5	0.7	29	72	86
Beeks,Jalen	18	L	25	aaa	BOS	88	4.28	1.36	23.0	2.8	9.4	3.3	1.3	33	73	87
Beggs,Dustin	18	R	25	aa	MIA	25	1.75	1.14	24.8	3.0	6.9	2.3	0.4	27	86	88
	19	R	26	a/a	MIA	85	6.84	1.86	25.0	3.7	5.1	1.4	1.8	36	54	9
Belisario,Johan	19	R	26	a/a	MIL	90	6.92	1.64	16.1	3.2	5.9	1.8	1.6	34	47	38
Bell,Chadwick	18	L	29	aaa	ATL	58	7.85	1.87	8.5	3.0	6.3	2.1	1.6	39	59	19
Bellatti,Andrew	19	R	28	aa	NYY	32	7.59	1.70	6.9	2.7	5.8	2.1	1.8	35	44	48
Bencomo,Omar	18	R	29	a/a	MIN	133	5.20	1.54	20.7	1.5	5.5	3.6	1.6	35	71	49
Benjamin,Wes	18	L	25	aa	TEX	81	4.85	1.50	23.4	2.9	6.3	2.1	1.3	33	71	40
	19	L	26	aaa	TEX	136	6.89	1.80	23.3	3.9	5.7	1.5	1.9	35	52	17
Bergman,Christia	18	R	30	aaa	SEA	143	6.45	1.81	25.5	2.8	5.5	2.0	1.1	38	65	26
Bettinger,Alec	19	R	24	aa	MIL	147	5.68	1.41	23.9	2.6	8.2	3.2	1.3	34	50	96
Bieber,Shane	18	R	23	a/a	CLE	81	1.90	0.92	23.4	0.8	7.2	8.7	0.5	28	83	218
Bielak,Brandon	18	R	22	aa	HOU	62	2.88	1.32	23.4	3.2	7.2	2.3	0.7	31	80	74
	19	R	23	a/a	HOU	123	5.22	1.35	22.3	3.8	7.5	2.0	1.1	29	53	52
Binford,Christian	18	R	26	aa	DET	78	6.19	1.80	19.0	1.1	5.0	4.4	1.4	40	68	61
Bird,Kyle	18	L	25	a/a	TAM	78	2.91	1.27	7.5	4.2	8.6	2.0	0.8	28	80	82
	19	L	26	aaa	TEX	36	3.43	1.63	5.6	4.1	7.4	1.8	1.2	34	74	40
Bivens,Blake	18	R	23	aa	TAM	23	7.02	1.71	17.5	4.7	5.2	1.1	1.7	31	61	0
	19	R	24	aa	TAM	57	5.58	1.96	10.1	6.9	4.5	0.7	1.0	32	67	-87
Blach,Ty	19	L	29	aaa	BAL	97	8.73	2.17	25.5	2.9	4.7	1.6	1.8	42	51	25
Black,Ray	18	R	28	a/a	SF	37	3.00	0.98	3.9	3.1	12.1	3.9	0.4	28	69	159
	19	R	29	aaa	MIL	30	5.34	1.39	4.4	5.0	10.3	2.0	1.5	29	52	67
Blackburn,Paul	19	R	26	aaa	OAK	134	5.14	1.43	23.8	2.3	4.9	2.1	1.2	31	56	43
Blackwood,Nolan	18	R	23	aa	DET	61	5.21	1.61	6.0	2.9	6.6	2.3	0.9	36	68	54
	19	R	24	a/a	DET	70	3.66	1.45	6.8	4.1	6.5	1.6	0.7	30	70	24
Blazek,Michael	19	R	30	aaa	WAS	40	7.69	1.86	5.5	4.0	6.9	1.7	2.5	36	46	34
Blewett,Scott	18	R	22	aa	KC	149	5.91	1.60	25.4	3.0	5.1	1.7	0.7	34	62	37
	19	R	23	a/a	KC	108	9.15	2.00	22.7	4.7	6.1	1.3	2.3	37	42	2
Bolanos,Ronald	19	R	23	aa	SD	78	5.21	1.47	22.4	3.6	8.5	2.3	0.9	34	58	73
Bollinger,Ryan	18	L	27	a/a	NYY	113	5.42	1.51	24.5	3.0	6.1	2.0	0.8	34	64	50
Bolton,Cody	19	R	21	aa	PIT	40	8.29	1.57	19.5	3.9	6.3	1.6	1.6	31	34	25
Bonnell,Bryan	18	R	25	aa	SEA	49	3.79	1.51	6.6	2.3	5.9	2.6	1.2	34	79	47
	19	R	26	a/a	WAS	64	4.66	1.35	7.0	2.2	6.8	3.1	1.6	31	56	82
Borucki,Ryan	18	L	24	aaa	TOR	77	4.45	1.39	24.9	3.5	5.6	1.6	0.9	29	69	43
Bostick,Akeem	18	R	23	a/a	HOU	98	4.01	1.36	18.6	3.2	8.2	2.6	0.8	33	72	83
	19	R	24	aaa	HOU	81	8.17	1.87	18.1	4.6	6.8	1.5	2.2	35	44	17
Bourque,James	18	R	25	aa	WAS	21	1.09	1.32	5.9	6.3	8.2	1.3	0.0	25	91	95
Bowman,Matthew	18	R	27	aaa	STL	23	5.17	1.56	5.6	3.2	8.9	2.8	0.8	38	67	83
	19	R	28	aaa	CIN	39	2.96	1.50	5.8	5.0	6.5	1.3	0.3	30	78	0
Boyle,Michael	19	L	25	aa	LA	55	3.99	1.52	6.0	4.7	7.7	1.6	1.7	29	60	28
Boyles,Ty	19	L	24	aa	CIN	66	5.98	1.80	6.5	5.2	7.7	1.5	1.7	34	59	15
Bracewell,Ben	18	R	28	a/a	OAK	150	4.25	1.40	25.3	1.9	5.6	3.0	0.8	33	71	67
	19	R	29	a/a	OAK	76	4.03	1.82	8.2	5.5	6.5	1.2	0.5	35	74	-13
Brady,Sean	18	L	24	a/a	CLE	148	6.05	1.68	23.8	3.7	5.0	1.4	1.4	33	66	11
	19	L	25	a/a	PIT	163	5.96	1.65	27.0	3.2	4.2	1.3	1.1	33	57	9
Bragg,Sam	18	R	25	a/a	OAK	75	4.62	1.66	9.9	3.1	4.6	1.5	0.6	35	72	31
Bray,Adam	19	R	26	a/a	MIN	93	3.76	1.38	11.2	2.9	6.3	2.2	0.6	32	68	53
Braymer,Ben	19	L	25	a/a	WAS	139	6.14	1.66	24	3.9	6.1	1.6	2.1	32	53	22
Brennan,Brandon	18	R	27	a/a	CHW	76	4.48	1.34	7.21	3.3	7.5	2.2	0.7	31	67	76
Brentz,Jake	19	L	25	a/a	KC	54	5.47	1.79	6.09	5.1	7.7	1.5	0.9	36	64	20
Brickhouse,Bryar	19	R	27	a/a	KC	30	9.40	1.75	6.6	8.1	5.1	0.6	2.0	22	31	-108
Bridwell,Parker	18	R	27	aaa	LAA	28	8.50	2.23	23.6	2.7	4.8	1.8	1.2	44	61	6
	19	R	28	aaa	LAA	90	7.87	2.04	19.9	4.3	6.1	1.4	1.8	39	53	12
Brigham,Jeff	18	R	26	a/a	MIA	91	3.02	1.31	23.5	2.3	7.1	3.1	0.8	32	80	84
Brill,Matt	19	R	25	aa	ARI	34	9.12	2.00	5.15	6.2	6.8	1.1	0.3	38	48	-29
Brogdon,Connor	19	R	24	a/a	PHI	58	3.49	1.05	5.51	3.0	11.3	3.7	1.6	25	56	138
Brooks,Aaron	18	R	28	aaa	MIL	100	3.70	1.45	16.4	2.6	5.2	2.0	0.8	32	76	46
Brooks,Craig	18	R	26	a/a	CHC	53	4.26	1.51	5.61	6.2	8.5	1.4	0.6	29	72	72
	19	R	27	a/a	CHC	60	5.40	1.67	6.59	6.8	10.9	1.6	2.7	28	56	31
Broom,Robert	19	R	23	aa	CLE	38	1.37	1.04	5.89	3.7	7.0	1.9	0.6	21	84	43
Broussard,Joe	18	R	27	aaa	LA	67	3.68	1.43	5	2.9	7.5	2.6	0.6	34	75	80
Brown,Aaron	18	L	26	aa	PHI	24	5.86	1.80	6.16	9.1	5.3	0.6	0.5	25	66	42
	19	L	27	aa	PHI	66	5.51	1.77	6.73	5.5	9.1	1.7	1.2	36	62	33

PITCHER	yr	t	age	lvl	org	ip	era	whip	bf/g	ctl	dom	cmd	hr/9	h%	s%	bpv
Brown,Daniel	19	L	24	aa	MIL	48	5.29	1.72	6.22	7.0	7.4	1.1	0.9	30	64	-39
Brown,Zack	18	R	24	aa	MIL	127	3.52	1.27	23.7	2.9	6.9	2.4	0.8	30	75	72
	19	R	25	aaa	MIL	118	6.69	1.91	22.4	5.0	6.2	1.2	1.4	36	58	-5
Broyles,Shane	18	R	27	aaa	COL	55	6.90	1.91	6.2	4.8	7.5	1.6	1.2	38	64	31
Brubaker,Jonatha	18	R	25	a/a	PIT	154	3.51	1.47	23.6	2.7	6.0	2.2	0.5	34	76	64
Bugg,Parker	19	R	25	a/a	MIA	61	8.01	1.52	6.5	4.6	9.0	2.0	2.1	30	31	57
Bukauskas,J.B.	19	R	23	aa	ARI	94	7.74	1.93	20.3	6.4	8.7	1.4	1.0	37	53	2
Burke,Brock	18	L	22	aa	TAM	56	2.28	1.03	24	2.2	10.3	4.6	0.3	31	78	161
	19	L	23	a/a	TEX	54	5.04	1.37	20.6	3.1	8.1	2.6	0.6	33	57	80
Burnes,Corbin	18	R	24	aaa	MIL	80	5.14	1.47	18.1	3.3	7.7	2.4	0.8	34	65	70
Burr,Ryan	18	R	24	a/a	CHW	52	3.18	1.32	5.84	4.8	7.5	1.6	0.7	27	78	69
Burrows,Beau	18	R	22	aa	DET	134	5.06	1.50	22.3	3.8	7.1	1.9	0.9	33	67	54
	19	R	23	a/a	DET	71	7.06	1.72	20.2	4.5	6.6	1.5	2.0	32	48	14
Cabrera,Edward	19	R	21	aa	MIA	40	3.78	1.26	20.5	3.3	8.5	2.6	1.7	27	61	82
Cabrera,Genesis	18	L	22	a/a	STL	141	4.41	1.33	21.7	4.2	8.0	1.9	0.8	29	68	72
	19	L	23	aaa	STL	99	6.82	1.60	21.9	3.4	8.0	2.4	1.8	34	46	70
Cabrera,Mauricio	19	R	26	aa	CHW	48	7.13	2.63	6.38	10.4	10.3	1.0	0.6	46	69	-78
Cabrera,Yordy	19	R	29	aa	LA	62	5.82	1.80	7.56	4.0	5.8	1.5	0.4	38	63	16
Camarena,Daniel	18	L	26	a/a	SF	127	6.20	1.79	23.5	3.9	5.6	1.5	0.8	37	65	30
	19	L	27	aaa	NYY	104	8.11	1.75	26.4	2.1	6.4	3.0	2.6	37	38	75
Campbell,Paul	19	R	24	aa	TAM	87	4.67	1.33	22.6	2.3	5.7	2.4	0.8	31	58	57
Canning,Griffin	18	R	22	a/a	LAA	106	4.02	1.29	19	3.1	8.4	2.7	0.6	32	69	93
Carasiti,Matt	19	R	28	aaa	SEA	44	4.11	1.50	6.15	3.9	6.5	1.7	0.9	32	67	30
Carle,Shane	19	R	28	aaa	TEX	40	7.38	2.14	7.35	4.4	5.7	1.3	0.6	42	60	2
Carlton,Drew	19	R	24	aa	DET	68	2.20	1.21	6.23	2.6	6.8	2.6	0.6	29	79	70
Carpenter,Ryan	18	L	28	aaa	DET	77	7.63	2.02	26.7	2.9	6.2	2.1	1.3	42	63	23
	19	L	29	aaa	DET	77	7.91	1.77	25.2	3.5	6.3	1.8	1.8	36	44	36
Carpenter,Tyler	19	R	27	a/a	LAA	61	4.76	1.46	18.8	2.8	5.0	1.8	1.5	30	59	33
Carter,Will	18	R	25	aa	NYY	31	8.01	2.16	22.2	7.4	4.8	0.6	0.4	36	60	20
	19	R	26	a/a	NYY	69	7.21	1.93	8.65	6.2	4.5	0.7	0.9	33	56	-69
Casimiro,Ranfi	18	R	26	a/a	PHI	88	4.48	1.61	11.9	4.4	6.3	1.4	1.3	32	76	27
Castano,Daniel	19	L	25	aa	MIA	86	5.53	1.54	20.8	2.0	6.3	3.1	0.3	38	59	76
Castellani,Ryan	18	R	22	aa	COL	135	7.76	1.81	24.1	5.2	4.9	1.0	1.4	32	57	1
	19	R	23	aaa	COL	44	8.84	1.99	21.2	5.9	7.7	1.3	3.1	34	40	-3
Castillo,Jesus	18	R	23	aa	LAA	99	6.20	1.47	20.2	2.8	4.7	1.7	0.7	32	56	38
	19	R	24	aa	LAA	101	3.64	1.51	11.5	2.6	6.0	2.4	0.5	35	72	57
Castro,Anthony	19	R	24	aa	DET	103	6.59	1.65	17.1	6.3	8.1	1.3	1.1	30	52	-6
Cease,Dylan	18	R	23	aa	CHW	53	2.33	1.16	21.1	4.2	11.5	2.8	0.7	29	83	122
	19	R	24	aaa	CHW	69	5.30	1.72	20.9	4.2	8.1	1.9	0.6	38	64	51
Cederlind,Blake	19	R	23	a/a	PIT	53	3.19	1.32	6.49	3.3	6.5	2.0	0.4	30	72	47
Cervenka,Hunter	18	L	28	a/a	DET	35	2.59	1.20	5.27	2.9	6.5	2.2	0.7	27	81	73
	19	L	29	aaa	BAL	56	3.66	1.45	5.34	5.1	7.8	1.5	0.4	30	71	20
Cesar,Joel	19	R	23	aa	PIT	39	5.37	1.58	6.14	3.1	6.8	2.2	1.4	34	58	57
Chargois,J.T.	18	R	28	aaa	LA	15	2.20	1.53	5.94	4.3	4.2	1.0	0.0	31	84	46
	19	R	29	aaa	LA	34	3.16	1.45	5.41	4.3	7.4	1.7	0.9	30	74	35
Cheshire,Jonatha	19	R	25	a/a	MIN	35	2.88	1.40	7.44	2.6	5.1	2.0	0.3	32	77	40
Chiang,Shao-Chir	18	R	25	a/a	CLE	138	5.27	1.41	23.4	1.7	4.9	2.8	1.1	33	64	51
	19	R	26	aaa	CLE	131	7.08	1.89	23.7	4.4	7.0	1.6	1.7	37	54	24
Civale,Aaron	18	R	23	aa	CLE	107	5.27	1.53	22.2	1.9	5.5	2.9	1.3	35	68	47
	19	R	24	a/a	CLE	74	3.21	1.30	23.6	2.0	7.0	3.5	1.1	32	70	90
Clark,Bailey	19	R	25	aa	CHC	44	5.39	1.79	6.15	6.0	6.3	1.0	0.8	33	65	-31
Clark,Brian	18	L	25	aa	CHW	63	6.74	1.65	6.88	3.5	7.8	2.2	1.0	37	59	56
Clark,Ryan	18	R	25	a/a	LAA	61	6.26	1.61	6.19	4.3	8.0	1.9	1.3	34	63	45
	19	R	26	a/a	LAA	53	3.82	1.28	6.64	2.6	9.1	3.5	1.2	32	63	112
Clarke,Taylor	18	R	25	aaa	ARI	152	3.72	1.27	23	2.4	6.0	2.5	0.5	31	71	75
	19	R	26	aaa	ARI	38	6.21	1.58	21	3.9	5.2	1.3	1.2	31	52	7
Clarkin,Ian	18	L	23	aa	CHW	70	6.69	1.79	18	4.4	3.9	0.9	1.2	33	63	-2
Clase,Emmanuel	19	R	21	aa	TEX	39	4.66	1.31	4.91	2.1	7.5	3.6	0.3	34	59	97
Clay,Sam	18	L	25	aa	MIN	52	7.52	1.98	7.34	6.5	8.3	1.3	0.2	39	58	64
	19	L	26	a/a	MIN	72	4.47	1.70	7.27	4.0	7.0	1.8	0.0	38	71	37
Cleavinger,Garrel	19	L	25	aa	PHI	53	4.91	1.46	6.7	6.3	12.1	1.9	0.5	32	61	64
Clifton,Trevor	18	R	23	a/a	CHC	128	3.97	1.36	20.6	3.8	6.0	1.6	0.6	29	71	56
	19	R	24	aaa	CHC	99	6.62	1.74	18.8	5.0	6.3	1.3	2.1	31	51	-2
Cloney,J.C.	19	L	25	aa	KC	101	5.42	1.68	20.7	2.6	5.7	2.2	1.4	36	61	49
Cole,Taylor	18	R	29	aaa	LAA	56	5.43	1.57	7.25	4.2	7.9	1.9	0.9	34	66	58
Coley,Austin	18	R	26	a/a	PIT	52	8.58	2.07	18.2	3.9	3.9	1.0	1.2	39	58	-9
Colina,Edwar	19	R	22	a/a	MIN	37	5.13	1.41	17.5	4.3	8.4	2.0	0.3	32	59	53
Collado,Willy	19	R	21	aa	HOU	38	2.98	1.42	8.95	1.8	7.6	4.3	0.6	37	75	107
Comer,Kevin	18	R	26	aaa	DET	56	5.61	1.71	5.28	3.6	7.0	1.9	1.1	37	68	42
Condra-Bogan,Ja	19	R	25	aa	WAS	63	5.57	1.30	6.85	1.8	5.8	3.2	1.3	31	47	73
Conlon,P.J.	18	L	25	aaa	NYM	114	6.12	1.66	22.2	2.9	5.4	1.9	1.3	35	65	23
Connolly,Michael	18	R	27	a/a	SF	100	6.85	1.77	15.9	3.6	4.8	1.3	1.1	35	61	15
Coonrod,Sam	19	R	27	aaa	SF	33	8.97	2.16	5	5.4	8.9	1.6	1.1	44	51	31
Copping,Corey	18	R	24	a/a	TOR	69	3.11	1.44	6.55	4.9	8.4	1.7	0.5	31	79	79
	19	R	25	a/a	TOR	52	7.98	1.98	7.16	5.6	6.9	1.2	2.3	35	49	-9
Corcino,Daniel	18	R	28	a/a	LA	113	3.99	1.33	16.8	3.4	6.8	2.0	0.9	30	72	62
	19	R	29	aaa	LA	120	5.85	1.66	22.4	4.7	6.0	1.3	2.1	30	55	-1
Cordero,Jimmy	18	R	27	aaa	WAS	46	2.77	1.76	5.14	4.9	8.0	1.6	0.0	39	82	77
	19	R	28	a/a	CHW	37	3.86	1.61	6.14	4.2	6.4	1.5	1.0	33	71	20
Cortes,Nestor	18	L	24	a/a	NYY	117	4.80	1.37	20.5	3.2	6.4	2.0	1.4	29	69	41
	19	L	25	aaa	NYY	41	4.63	1.13	23.3	2.6	7.5	2.9	0.9	27	50	83
Coshow,Cale	18	R	26	aaa	NYY	57	6.65	1.74	6.86	4.9	8.4	1.7	2.0	34	66	21
Coulombe,Daniel	18	L	29	aaa	OAK	29	3.30	1.56	5.55	2.1	6.3	3.1	1.0	36	83	62
	19	L	30	aaa	NYY	37	6.35	1.94	5.69	4.9	11.0	2.2	3.2	39	55	83
Covey,Dylan	18	R	27	aaa	CHW	40	2.96	1.43	24.4	3.8	6.3	1.6	0.9	30	83	48
	19	R	28	aaa	CHW	51	3.69	1.66	17.6	1.7	6.4	3.6	1.3	38	73	85
Cozart,Logan	18	R	25	aa	COL	70	3.29	1.28	5.33	2.4	6.1	2.5	1.2	29	79	57
	19	R	26	a/a	COL	56	4.96	1.71	5.92	3.5	6.3	1.8	2.0	34	63	38
Crawford,Leo	19	L	22	aa	LA	31	2.96	1.39	21.8	2.0	7.1	3.6	0.7	35	75	93
Creasy,Jason	19	R	27	a/a	ATL	62	6.94	1.74	5.79	3.4	6.7	2.0	1.8	36	50	46
Crismatt,Nabil	18	R	24	a/a	NYM	146	5.01	1.51	23.5	3.4	7.4	2.2	0.9	34	68	61
	19	R	25	a/a	SEA	133	5.67	1.39	20.8	2.3	9.0	3.9	1.7	34	48	118
Crowe,Wil	18	R	24	aa	WAS	27	7.53	1.97	26	5.5	4.1	0.7	1.5	33	63	-16
	19	R	25	a/a	WAS	150	6.33	1.60	25.5	3.1	6.3	2.0	1.1	35	52	48
Cruz,Jesus	19	R	24	a/a	STL	64	6.95	1.65	5.54	6.4	10.1	1.6	1.2	32	49	28
Cuevas,William	18	R	28	aaa	BOS	136	5.39	1.57	26	3.0	5.9	2.0	1.6	33	69	24
Culbreth,Ty	19	L	25	aa	COL	81	7.48	1.98	21.6	3.2	4.5	1.4	2.0	38	53	13
Curry,Parker	18	R	25	aa	LA	22	7.16	1.85	20.7	3.4	4.0	1.2	2.9	33	69	-51
	19	R	26	aa	LA	98	5.11	1.38	17.1	2.0	6.6	3.4	1.7	32	52	85
Curtiss,John	18	R	25	aaa	MIN	56	4.07	1.58	6.49	5.6	7.7	1.4	0.7	31	75	59
	19	R	26	aaa	PHI	35	9.07	2.02	7.74	5.9	9.5	1.6	2.9	37	41	29
Custodio,Claudio	19	R	29	aa	ATL	80	4.95	1.54	11.3	3.4	5.5	1.6	0.4	34	63	24
Custred,Matt	18	R	25	a/a	LAA	56	4.56	1.52	6.42	5.8	7.6	1.3	0.3	30	68	71
Cutura,Andro	19	R	26	a/a	MIN	50	7.26	1.93	15.8	2.9	4.9	1.7	0.7	40	56	29
Cyr,Tyler	19	R	26	a/a	SF	51	2.76	1.37	5.64	4.6	8.1	1.7	0.2	30	77	39
Danish,Tyler	18	R	24	aaa	CHW	73	3.66	1.43	9.42	3.7	5.6	1.5	0.9	29	77	40
Darnell,Logan	18	L	29	a/a	WAS	123	6.85	1.86	22.2	2.5	4.6	1.9	1.5	38	65	7
Davidson,Tucker	19	L	23	a/a	ATL	131	3.12	1.50	22.6	4.0	7.6	1.9	0.4	34	76	46
Davis,Austin	18	L	25	a/a	PHI	39	3.39	1.18	5.59	2.4	9.8	4.1	0.9	32	74	125
	19	L	26	aaa	PHI	53	3.32	1.44	6.12	4.3	9.1	2.1	0.4	34	74	67
Davis,Rookie	18	R	25	aa	CIN	16	7.59	1.52	11.7	1.9	5.1	2.7	2.3	32	53	12
	19	R	26	aaa	PIT	54	7.28	1.85	19.5	4.0	5.1	1.3	1.7	35	51	1
Davis,Tyler	18	R	25	aa	TEX	80	8.59	2.20	13	3.2	4.9	1.5	1.2	43	60	3
De Horta,Adrian	19	R	24	a/a	LAA	50	5.86	1.49	13.5	5.7	10.6	1.9	2.2	27	48	56
De Jong,Chase	18	R	25	a/a	MIN	162	4.96	1.54	25.3	2.8	5.4	2.0	1.0	34	69	38
	19	R	26	aaa	MIN	46	13.19	2.61	19.3	5.6	4.6	0.8	4.0	40	33	-52
De La Cruz,Jass	19	R	22	aa	ATL	87	6.30	1.57	22.5	4.4	6.4	1.5	1.0	32	52	15
De La Cruz,Osca	18	R	23	aa	CHC	78	6.56	1.57	21.5	3.8	7.1	1.9	1.1	34	58	47
	19	R	24	aa	CHC	82	5.81	1.41	11.2	3.7	8.0	2.2	1.1	31	50	63
De Leon,Jose	19	R	27	aaa	TAM	52	4.18	1.66	13.4	5.2	10.3	2.0	0.8	35	66	63
De Los Santos,E	18	R	23	aaa	PHI	128	3.20	1.29	24	3.1	6.9	2.2	1.0	29	80	61
	19	R	24	aaa	PHI	94	5.17	1.36	20.7	3.4	7.0	2.1	1.8	28	50	53
De Paula,Rafael	18	R	27	a/a	CIN	60	4.58	1.60	6.35	5.2	8.7	1.7	1.9	31	78	33
	19	R	28	a/a	ATL	43	6.49	1.92	5.84	6.3	7.8	1.2	1.2	36	60	-13
DeCaster,Ethan	19	R	25	a/a	DET	57	3.67	1.32	6.75	2.1	6.9	3.3	0.6	33	67	86
DeGraaf,Josh	18	R	25	a/a	TOR	86	5.95	1.68	19.4	2.9	6.6	2.3	1.7	36	68	28
DeJuneas,Tomm	19	R	24	aa	HOU	31	11.90	2.56	7.27	10.7	9.1	0.8	2.0	39	43	-109
Delaplane,Sam	19	R	24	aa	SEA	37	0.74	0.74	5.27	2.5	12.3	4.9	0.7	21	88	171
DeMasi,Dominic	18	R	25	a/a	CLE	88	9.26	1.87	12.5	3.0	5.1	1.7	1.6	38	50	5
Dennis,Matt	19	R	24	aa	COL	82	5.72	1.85	27.3	2.8	5.1	1.8	2.1	37	61	33
Derby,Bubba	18	R	24	aaa	MIL	119	4.54	1.53	16.7	3.5	6.1	1.7	0.7	33	71	50
	19	R	25	aaa	MIL	116	5.81	1.60	19	3.9	6.7	1.7	1.8	32	54	34
Diaz,Miguel	18	R	24	a/a	SD	79	3.62	1.40	13.9	4.8	7.8	1.6	0.7	29	75	69
	19	R	25	a/a	SD	33	4.04	1.31	13.8	2.8	8.7	3.1	2.6	27	56	99
Diaz,Yennsy	19	R	23	aa	TOR	145	5.51	1.50	24.1	3.6	6.1	1.7	1.0	32	56	29
Dibrell,Tony	19	R	24	aa	NYM	40	12.73	2.19	22.4	5.3	7.2	1.4	2.8	39	25	6
Diehl,Phillip	18	L	24	aa	NYY	28	1.74	1.21	8.13	3.8	7.8	2.0	0.9	26	92	73
	19	L	25	a/a	COL	60	7.01	1.57	5.28	3.0	7.4	2.5	3.3	30	35	70
Dillon,Justin	18	R	25	a/a	TOR	74	6.58	1.53	17.9	3.2	4.0	1.3	1.2	31	57	11
	19	R	26	a/a	TOR	57	5.23	1.57	19.2	3.2	5.3	1.7	1.1	33	60	27
Diplan,Marcos	18	R	22	aa	MIL	57	6.43	1.91	22.5	6.1	7.9	1.3	1.3	36	68	29
	19	R	23	aa	MIN	70	6.71	1.70	8.35	6.2	7.8	1.3	1.2	31	52	-9
Dobnak,Randy	19	R	24	a/a	MIN	114	3.26	1.17	22.8	2.1	6.1	3.0	0.6	29	67	72
Dobzanski,Bryan	19	R	24	a/a	STL	38	4.57	1.65	6.33	4.7	8.2	1.8	1.5	34	66	40
Donatella,Justin	18	R	24	aa	ARI	130	4.22	1.38	20.2	3.4	5.9	1.8	0.6	30	70	56
	19	R	25	a/a	ARI	87	7.26	1.90	15.8	3.9	5.7	1.5	1.4	38	54	16
Donato,Chad	19	R	24	aa	HOU	53	5.24	1.38	20.3	2.9	8.6	3.0	1.6	32	52	96
Dopico,Danny	19	R	26	aa	CHW	64	4.00	1.41	6.31	5.8	8.4	1.4	0.0	29	68	12
Dowdy,Kyle	18	R	25	a/a	CLE	126	6.95	1.77	19.3	4.0	6.9	1.7	1.1	37	61	36
	19	R	26	a/a	CLE	43	5.16	1.75	12.3	5.1	6.5	1.3	0.6	35	66	-4
Dragmire,Brady	18	R	25	a/a	WAS	151	5.97	1.59	24.7	2.2	4.7	2.1	1.2	35	63	29
Duffey,Tyler	18	R	28	aaa	MIN	59	4.62	1.54	8.31	3.7	7.1	1.9	1.1	33	73	47
Dugger,Robert	18	R	23	aa	MIA	110	4.39	1.36	25.6	3.0	7.6	2.5	1.0	32	70	69
	19	R	24	a/a	MIA	126	7.31	1.66	24.6	3.0	7.3	2.4	1.5	36	46	67
Dull,Ryan	18	R	29	aaa	OAK	28	4.72	1.57	5.34	2.9	8.4	2.9	1.8	36	76	52
	19	R	30	aaa	NYY	50	7.18	1.62	6.19	3.2	7.6	2.4	2.3	34	41	68
Duncan,Frank	18	R	26	aa	COL	90	7.86	1.83	18.2	3.0	2.8	0.9	1.7	34	58	-28
Dunn,Justin	18	R	23	aa	NYM	91	4.67	1.45	26	3.7	9.0	2.4	0.7	35	68	86
	19	R	24	aa	SEA	133	5.34	1.50	23	3.0	9.3	3.1	1.2	36	56	103
Dunning,Dane	18	R	24	aa	CHW	62	3.87	1.58	24.8	3.8	8.6	2.2	0.0	38	73	95
Duno,Angel	19	R	25	aa	OAK	46	8.33	1.56	6.94	1.7	7.0	4.2	1.5	37	33	99
Dunshee,Parker	18	R	23	aa	OAK	82	2.25	0.97	26	1.5	7.4	5.0	0.5	27	79	144
	19	R	24	a/a	OAK	130	5.32	1.38	21	3.4	7.1	2.1	1.6	29	51	55
Duplantier,Jon	18	R	24	aa	ARI	67	3.27	1.34	19.9	3.9	7.6	1.9	0.5	30	76	76
	19	R	25	aaa	ARI	38	4.98	1.55	12.8	6.3	8.4	1.3	0.2	31	64	0
Duran,Jhoan	19	R	21	aa	MIN	37	6.68	1.37	22.1	2.3	8.5	3.7	0.6	36	43	109
DuRapau,Montan	18	R	26	a/a	PIT	32	6.42	1.40	7.15	3.0	8.2	2.7	1.9	31	57	51
	19	R	27	aaa	PIT	47	2.85	0.90	4.74	3.0	8.2	2.7	0.7	21	62	84
Duval,Max	18	R	27	aa	MIA	88	9.10	1.95	17.5	3.4	6.2	1.8	2.5	38	56	-17
Dykxhoorn,Brock	18	R	24	a/a	HOU	129	4.34	1.23	21	2.6	7.3	2.8	1.0	29	67	76
Dziedzic,Jonathai	18	L	27	aaa	KC	140	5.24	1.61	24.8	3.0	4.6	1.5	0.8	34	67	30
	19	L	28	aaa	KC	59	6.70	1.99	11.4	5.4	3.9	0.7	2.1	33	58	-58
Eades,Ryan	18	R	27	a/a	MIN	77	5.04	1.67	9.61	2.9	7.7	2.7	0.8	39	70	70
	19	R	28	aaa	BAL	53	6.91	1.82	7.95	3.2	8.0	2.5	1.5	40	53	75
Eastman,Colton	19	R	23	aa	PHI	34	3.84	1.25	23.2	3.3	7.1	2.1	1.1	27	62	55

PITCHER	yr	t	age	lvl	org	ip	era	whip	bf/g	ctl	dom	cmd	hr/9	h%	s%	bpv
Ecker, Mark	19	R	24	aa	DET	33	8.62	2.32	7.73	6.3	6.9	1.1	1.9	41	54	-28
Effross, Scott	18	R	25	aa	CHC	64	7.78	1.94	6.94	3.1	6.8	2.2	1.2	41	60	34
	19	R	26	aa	CHC	35	8.41	1.77	9.52	2.8	3.5	1.2	1.0	36	44	5
Elledge, Seth	18	R	22	aa	STL	18	4.14	1.06	5.44	2.7	8.4	3.1	1.3	24	66	88
	19	R	23	a/a	STL	69	4.95	1.47	6.32	4.0	8.1	2.0	0.8	33	60	54
Ellis, Chris	18	R	26	a/a	STL	134	4.50	1.30	17.8	2.5	6.5	2.6	0.9	31	66	70
	19	R	27	aaa	STL	79	9.03	2.14	9.8	5.6	7.1	1.3	1.6	40	49	-5
Emanuel, Kent	18	L	26	aaa	HOU	85	5.61	1.66	12.3	2.6	7.3	2.8	1.0	39	67	62
	19	L	27	aaa	HOU	103	4.64	1.38	15.5	2.1	5.6	2.7	0.9	32	60	62
Enns, Dietrich	18	L	27	a/a	MIN	131	6.51	1.73	23.9	3.3	5.5	1.7	1.1	36	63	24
	19	L	28	aaa	SD	137	7.38	1.97	23.4	3.8	5.2	1.4	2.3	37	52	8
Eppler, Tyler	18	R	25	aaa	PIT	153	4.37	1.50	23.6	2.4	5.5	2.3	0.8	34	72	51
Erwin, Tyler	19	L	25	a/a	BAL	45	4.22	1.59	5.4	3.2	5.6	1.7	0.3	35	70	32
Erwin, Zack	19	L	25	aa	OAK	60	4.18	1.72	7.02	2.4	8.2	3.4	1.0	41	71	102
Escobar, Luis	18	R	22	aa	PIT	37	5.26	1.48	22.9	5.1	5.1	1.0	1.0	26	66	27
	19	R	23	aaa	PIT	55	5.10	1.75	10.5	5.4	7.7	1.4	1.2	34	65	9
Eshelman, Tom	18	R	24	aaa	PHI	141	7.31	1.93	24.8	3.0	5.8	1.9	1.7	39	64	7
	19	R	25	a/a	BAL	95	6.02	1.62	24.9	1.9	5.7	3.1	1.6	36	54	71
Espinal, Raynel	18	R	27	aaa	NYY	67	4.30	1.50	7.07	4.0	10.1	2.5	0.8	36	72	91
	19	R	28	aaa	NYY	75	5.75	1.58	18.3	3.0	7.3	2.4	1.7	34	54	67
Espinal, Yoel	18	R	26	aa	TAM	56	2.47	1.19	5.63	5.0	9.5	1.9	0.9	23	84	88
	19	R	27	a/a	TEX	51	8.07	1.86	7.49	7.8	7.1	0.9	1.5	29	47	-64
Estevez, Wirkin	18	R	26	aa	WAS	52	5.69	1.57	20.8	3.2	5.6	1.8	1.3	33	66	28
Eubank, Luke	18	R	24	a/a	CLE	57	4.44	1.56	5.57	4.0	7.4	1.9	0.8	34	72	59
Evans, Demarcus	19	R	23	aa	TEX	39	1.37	1.11	5.14	5.9	11.2	1.9	0.7	20	85	60
Eveld, Tommy	19	R	26	a/a	MIA	50	7.58	1.54	5.2	3.6	8.6	2.4	2.6	31	32	77
Faedo, Alex	18	R	23	aa	DET	60	6.24	1.43	21.3	3.4	7.2	2.1	2.6	28	65	10
	19	R	24	aa	DET	116	5.86	1.41	22.3	2.1	8.3	3.9	1.8	34	46	109
Fagalde, Alex	19	R	25	aa	STL	67	5.66	1.47	24	3.2	5.5	1.7	1.6	30	51	30
Fairbanks, Peter	19	R	26	a/a	TAM	32	6.88	1.34	4.61	2.5	12.9	5.1	1.3	40	36	181
Falter, Bailey	19	L	22	aa	PHI	78	4.94	1.44	23.8	1.8	6.5	3.7	1.4	34	57	87
Faria, Jake	18	R	25	aaa	TAM	30	5.74	1.46	18.4	4.1	7.1	1.7	1.7	29	65	31
	19	R	26	aaa	MIL	68	4.59	1.57	10.3	4.3	8.9	2.1	1.4	34	64	62
Farrell, Luke	18	R	27	aaa	CHC	55	4.32	1.43	19.5	5.0	7.7	1.5	0.7	29	70	65
Faulkner, Andrew	18	L	26	aaa	BAL	58	6.73	1.86	5.9	5.0	6.2	1.2	1.3	35	65	16
Fedde, Erick	19	R	26	a/a	WAS	36	7.22	1.58	22.7	2.5	7.3	3.0	2.3	34	39	83
Fedde, Erick	18	R	25	a/a	WAS	72	5.61	1.70	23.3	2.7	7.4	2.8	0.5	40	65	78
Feigl, Brady	18	L	28	a/a	TEX	60	2.12	1.37	6.01	2.7	4.1	1.5	0.0	31	83	56
Feltman, Durbin	19	R	22	aa	BOS	52	7.35	1.62	5.38	5.6	7.8	1.4	1.7	29	43	7
Fernandez, Jose	18	L	25	a/a	TOR	62	3.93	1.47	6.06	4.9	7.6	1.5	1.2	28	78	46
	19	L	26	a/a	DET	62	7.52	1.90	7.73	3.7	4.7	1.3	1.8	36	51	3
Fernandez, Junior	18	R	21	aa	STL	21	5.33	1.64	5.85	6.2	6.2	1.0	0.4	30	66	52
	19	R	22	a/a	STL	54	1.74	1.11	5.91	3.5	9.7	2.8	0.0	29	83	99
Fernandez, Pedro	18	R	24	a/a	KC	68	4.20	1.55	9.32	3.6	5.2	1.5	0.4	33	72	46
Ferrell, Justin	18	R	24	aa	HOU	48	4.36	1.43	7.56	4.1	9.1	2.2	0.9	33	71	77
	19	R	25	a/a	HOU	35	9.32	2.03	7.79	7.6	5.9	0.8	1.2	32	45	-82
Ferrell, Riley	18	R	25	a/a	HOU	53	5.00	1.66	5.54	5.6	9.3	1.6	0.9	34	71	64
Festa, Matthew	18	R	25	aa	SEA	49	3.35	1.46	4.77	2.3	10.5	4.6	1.2	39	82	117
	19	R	26	aaa	SEA	32	2.85	1.27	5.72	4.0	7.7	1.9	0.9	27	73	49
Feyereisen, J.P.	18	R	25	aaa	NYY	60	4.60	1.61	7.18	4.1	7.3	1.8	1.1	34	74	47
	19	R	26	aaa	NYY	62	3.14	1.28	6.36	4.9	10.9	2.2	1.2	27	70	81
File, Dylan	19	R	23	aa	MIL	82	4.45	1.42	24.9	1.9	7.0	3.6	0.0	35	63	91
Fillmyer, Heath	18	R	24	aaa	KC	68	7.13	1.85	24.5	3.8	5.0	1.3	0.7	37	60	25
	19	R	25	aaa	KC	50	6.09	1.67	11.8	4.9	7.2	1.5	1.4	32	55	16
Finnegan, Brandoı	18	L	25	aaa	CIN	69	9.02	2.23	12.5	5.7	6.2	1.1	1.7	40	60	-8
Finnegan, Kyle	18	R	27	a/a	OAK	44	5.13	1.54	5.67	3.9	7.0	1.8	0.4	34	65	65
	19	R	28	a/a	OAK	52	2.98	1.36	5.19	3.6	9.4	2.6	0.6	33	74	90
Fishman, Jake	19	L	24	aa	TOR	64	5.09	1.55	6.69	2.8	8.6	3.0	0.8	38	62	96
Fisk, Conor	18	R	26	a/a	TOR	74	3.03	1.45	7.72	3.1	5.9	1.9	0.6	32	81	56
	19	R	27	aaa	TOR	97	7.26	1.77	13.9	3.3	6.6	2.0	2.4	35	46	50
Flaa, Jay	18	R	26	aa	BAL	65	3.35	1.09	6.2	4.0	7.1	1.8	1.2	20	75	63
	19	R	27	a/a	BAL	71	6.50	1.78	8.17	4.6	6.8	1.5	1.5	35	55	15
Fleming, Josh	19	L	23	a/a	TAM	150	4.53	1.38	25.3	1.7	5.8	3.4	1.0	33	60	75
Flexen, Chris	18	R	24	aaa	NYM	92	4.03	1.51	22.1	2.8	6.5	2.3	0.9	34	75	57
	19	R	25	aaa	NYM	80	5.35	1.66	13.8	2.5	8.8	3.6	1.3	40	61	110
Flores Jr., Bernar	18	L	23	aa	CHW	79	3.75	1.43	25.8	1.8	4.7	2.6	0.8	33	75	54
	19	L	24	aa	CHW	79	5.01	1.44	22.4	1.9	6.7	3.5	1.7	33	56	87
Flores, Jose	18	R	29	a/a	SF	60	8.68	2.14	15	4.8	4.9	1.0	1.0	40	58	4
Flynn, Brian	19	L	29	aaa	KC	44	6.21	1.84	18.7	4.2	6.2	1.5	1.6	36	59	16
Foley, Jordan	18	R	25	aa	NYY	67	4.10	1.81	8.39	5.2	7.4	1.4	1.2	35	81	33
	19	R	26	aa	COL	59	8.55	2.19	7.05	5.3	7.5	1.4	1.4	42	53	9
Foltynewicz, Mike	19	R	28	aaa	ATL	52	5.52	1.63	23.2	3.4	5.8	1.7	0.2	36	62	31
Fossas, Aaron	19	R	27	aa	CIN	47	9.48	1.87	7.91	3.4	5.7	1.6	1.1	38	40	27
Foster, Matt	18	R	23	aa	CHW	32	5.79	1.76	6.11	4.1	7.4	1.8	1.1	37	68	39
	19	R	24	a/a	CHW	66	4.19	1.24	6.26	3.0	8.6	2.8	1.6	28	57	91
Francis, Bowden	19	R	23	aa	MIL	130	6.40	1.58	22.9	4.0	8.7	2.2	1.5	34	50	67
Franco, Daniel	18	R	26	a/a	ATL	136	5.09	1.54	20.5	3.1	6.8	2.2	1.2	34	69	45
	19	R	27	aaa	SF	113	7.89	1.90	20.5	3.2	5.9	1.9	1.9	38	48	39
Frare, Caleb	18	L	25	a/a	CHW	60	1.00	1.07	5.47	3.7	9.6	2.6	0.2	27	91	123
Freeland, Kyle	19	L	26	aaa	COL	31	9.65	2.02	25.2	4.7	6.1	1.3	1.3	39	43	0
French, Parker	18	R	25	aa	COL	60	12.01	2.56	11.9	7.4	3.2	0.4	1.6	39	51	-40
Fried, Max	18	L	24	a/a	ATL	79	5.02	1.50	22.8	3.9	8.1	2.1	0.5	34	65	76
Friedrichs, Kyle	18	R	26	a/a	OAK	84	6.58	1.63	23.5	2.6	5.1	1.9	1.4	34	61	18
	19	R	27	aa	OAK	114	4.71	1.67	25.6	2.7	5.0	1.8	0.5	37	68	34
Fuentes, Steven	19	R	22	aa	WAS	65	3.85	1.47	18.6	2.3	7.5	3.3	0.2	38	70	92
Fulmer, Carson	18	R	25	aaa	CHW	69	6.59	1.87	13	5.9	6.7	1.2	1.6	33	67	11
	19	R	26	aaa	CHW	34	5.95	1.75	6.48	5.8	11.0	1.9	0.6	39	61	59
Funkhouser, Kyle	18	R	24	a/a	DET	99	5.22	1.71	23.7	4.7	6.9	1.5	1.1	34	71	35
Funkhouser, Kyle	19	R	25	a/a	DET	89	9.53	2.07	19.9	6.3	7.4	1.2	0.7	39	47	-19
Gage, Matt	18	L	25	a/a	NYM	103	5.37	1.78	23.7	2.3	5.8	2.6	0.6	40	69	57
Gagnon, Drew	18	R	28	a/a	NYM	165	4.84	1.36	24.7	2.5	7.3	2.9	1.2	32	67	67
	19	R	29	aaa	NYM	90	3.07	1.34	25	1.9	5.6	2.9	1.4	30	71	66
Gallen, Zac	18	R	23	aaa	MIA	134	4.08	1.59	23.6	3.2	7.9	2.5	0.9	37	76	66
	19	R	24	aaa	MIA	92	2.30	0.83	24	1.8	9.2	5.2	1.0	22	64	135
Garabito, Gerson	19	R	24	aa	KC	141	5.34	1.80	25.1	4.3	5.8	1.4	1.0	36	65	7
Garcia, Bryan	19	R	24	a/a	DET	38	4.04	1.29	4.61	3.6	7.7	2.2	1.6	27	60	61
Garcia, Deivi	19	R	20	a/a	NYY	95	5.37	1.46	18.5	4.4	11.2	2.5	1.2	35	55	101
Garcia, Edgar	18	R	22	a/a	PHI	67	4.01	1.21	5.22	3.6	8.7	2.5	1.2	27	71	77
Garcia, Elniery	18	L	24	a/a	STL	64	6.69	1.99	12.9	4.2	5.2	1.3	1.1	39	67	10
Garcia, Jarlin	18	L	25	aaa	MIA	50	5.48	1.61	22.2	2.6	4.9	1.9	0.9	35	66	34
Garcia, Jason	18	R	26	aa	COL	20	13.74	2.69	7.42	8.0	5.7	0.7	2.0	42	47	-35
	19	R	27	aa	TAM	51	7.42	2.07	25	4.4	5.0	1.1	0.7	40	59	-11
Garcia, Julian	19	R	24	aa	PHI	30	8.06	1.87	23.6	3.2	6.8	2.1	0.8	41	50	54
Garcia, Rico	18	R	24	aa	COL	67	3.38	1.38	25.6	3.1	6.4	2.1	1.6	29	83	36
	19	R	25	a/a	COL	130	5.82	1.58	22	3.9	7.4	1.9	1.7	32	53	45
Garcia, Rony	19	R	22	aa	NYY	106	5.86	1.45	22.6	3.5	7.7	2.2	1.7	31	48	63
Garcia, Yeudy	18	R	26	aa	PIT	54	6.77	1.86	6.84	5.8	8.7	1.5	0.6	38	62	62
	19	R	27	aa	PIT	62	9.69	2.36	9.73	6.0	5.8	1.0	0.8	42	53	-40
Garrett, Reed	18	R	25	a/a	TEX	63	2.64	1.41	5.25	3.2	6.8	2.1	0.5	33	83	70
	19	R	26	aaa	TEX	41	6.05	1.93	5.74	4.6	6.7	1.5	1.1	38	63	14
Garton, Ryan	18	R	29	aaa	SEA	44	3.87	1.38	5.3	5.4	6.8	1.3	0.5	26	71	65
	19	R	30	aaa	SEA	66	4.84	1.58	7.45	4.5	8.1	1.8	1.4	32	62	42
Garza, Ralph	18	R	24	a/a	HOU	68	3.82	1.37	8.16	4.1	8.2	2.0	0.4	31	71	85
	19	R	25	aaa	HOU	78	4.67	1.20	7.47	3.3	7.6	2.3	1.1	27	52	68
Gatto, Joe	18	R	23	aa	LAA	78	7.13	1.74	22.3	4.2	4.9	1.2	1.1	34	59	14
	19	R	24	aa	LAA	55	6.46	1.98	8.26	5.1	7.9	1.6	0.4	41	63	23
Gavin, Grant	18	R	23	aa	KC	31	4.04	1.59	6.51	5.0	7.2	1.4	1.2	31	78	38
	19	R	24	aa	KC	53	5.05	1.55	5.66	4.7	9.9	2.1	1.2	34	60	69
German, Angel	19	R	23	aa	PIT	52	6.32	1.47	5.72	6.0	6.8	1.1	1.7	23	45	-22
Gibaut, Ian	18	R	25	aaa	TAM	56	2.68	1.16	4.64	3.6	10.3	2.9	0.5	29	78	118
Gibbons, Michael	19	R	26	aa	NYM	38	7.36	1.87	22.3	5.0	7.9	1.6	2.2	36	50	26
Gilbert, Logan	19	R	22	aa	SEA	50	4.20	1.19	22.3	3.0	9.1	3.1	0.5	31	59	102
Gilbert, Tyler	18	L	25	a/a	PHI	72	3.82	1.10	5.92	2.0	7.3	3.7	1.1	28	69	97
	19	L	26	aaa	PHI	49	3.36	1.25	5.56	2.7	7.1	2.6	0.9	29	67	73
Gilliam, Ryley	19	R	23	a/a	NYM	30	8.69	1.88	6.48	5.0	10.5	2.1	1.3	42	44	74
Gillies, Darin	18	R	26	a/a	SEA	64	6.13	1.45	6.69	3.7	8.0	2.2	1.4	31	59	52
	19	R	27	a/a	SEA	63	8.26	1.84	7.37	3.7	8.6	2.3	2.1	39	43	73
Gilmartin, Sean	18	L	28	aaa	BAL	62	6.13	1.65	8.98	3.1	4.8	1.6	1.5	33	65	9
	19	L	29	aaa	BAL	66	5.32	1.46	8.83	3.6	7.3	2.0	1.4	31	55	52
Ginkel, Kevin	18	R	24	aa	ARI	44	1.98	0.90	4.84	1.9	10.1	5.3	0.6	27	82	170
	19	R	25	a/a	ARI	36	2.02	0.98	4.77	3.4	12.3	3.7	1.0	25	74	149
Gohara, Luiz	18	L	22	a/a	ATL	60	5.76	1.42	19.7	2.6	7.5	2.9	1.5	33	62	58
Gold, Brandon	19	R	25	aa	COL	144	6.32	1.84	25.8	1.7	5.5	3.2	1.7	40	58	71
Gomber, Austin	18	L	25	aaa	STL	69	3.89	1.37	24.1	2.6	7.9	3.1	1.2	33	75	76
	19	L	26	a/a	STL	50	3.41	1.40	19.2	3.2	7.6	2.4	1.0	32	71	69
Gomez, Ofreidy	19	R	24	a/a	KC	131	5.49	1.67	21.1	4.2	6.6	1.5	1.0	34	61	22
Gonsalves, Steph	18	L	24	a/a	MIN	122	3.67	1.33	22	5.1	7.1	1.4	0.7	25	74	62
Gonsolin, Tony	18	R	24	aa	LA	45	2.58	1.10	19.7	2.9	8.3	2.8	0.6	27	79	103
	19	R	25	aaa	LA	42	4.69	1.56	14.2	4.2	8.8	2.1	0.9	35	64	64
Gonzalez, Alex	19	R	27	aaa	COL	87	7.20	1.87	25.5	3.9	5.8	1.5	1.8	36	52	17
Gonzalez, Brian	18	L	23	aa	BAL	93	6.37	1.74	23.6	3.8	0.3	1.7	1.6	35	66	15
	19	L	24	aa	BAL	43	5.87	1.24	9.76	2.5	5.9	2.3	2.5	24	32	55
Gonzalez, Harol	18	R	23	a/a	NYM	58	7.28	1.81	26.9	2.8	4.2	1.5	1.4	36	60	1
	19	R	24	a/a	NYM	139	3.87	1.26	22.7	2.3	6.3	2.8	1.5	28	61	70
Gonzalez, Luis	18	L	26	a/a	BAL	72	4.05	1.40	7.25	3.5	8.2	2.3	0.8	32	72	76
	19	L	27	a/a	BAL	49	9.40	2.02	6.26	3.6	9.1	2.6	2.4	43	40	86
Gonzalez, Meranc	18	R	23	aa	MIA	73	5.04	1.51	22.6	4.1	5.0	1.2	0.8	30	67	31
	19	R	24	aa	STL	42	8.00	2.26	6.3	6.7	6.8	1.0	1.2	40	58	-40
Gonzalez, Nelson	18	R	28	aaa	COL	47	6.82	1.76	10.8	3.4	6.2	1.8	2.4	34	67	-8
	19	R	29	aaa	COL	50	7.54	1.98	12.7	5.5	5.1	0.9	2.9	32	50	-40
Gonzalez, Victor	19	L	24	a/a	LA	63	3.06	1.45	8.98	2.5	6.9	2.8	1.1	34	74	75
Gorman III, John	18	R	26	aa	OAK	66	3.31	1.23	6.38	2.1	5.0	2.4	1.0	28	77	53
	19	R	27	aa	OAK	58	6.44	1.76	6.2	3.3	8.7	2.6	1.3	40	56	85
Gorst, Matthew	18	R	24	a/a	BOS	42	2.60	1.12	8.35	2.2	4.3	1.9	0.8	25	80	51
	19	R	25	a/a	BOS	64	5.88	1.55	7.03	4.6	5.8	1.3	1.1	30	54	-1
Goudeau, Ashton	18	R	26	a/a	SEA	90	7.15	1.84	14.5	3.5	5.5	1.6	1.2	37	61	16
	19	R	27	aa	COL	79	3.79	1.33	20.5	1.8	7.6	4.3	0.8	34	66	107
Graham, Josh	18	R	25	aa	ATL	41	9.21	2.09	6.32	7.1	7.2	1.0	1.1	37	54	23
	19	R	26	aa	ATL	52	6.17	1.57	6.03	3.9	6.0	1.6	1.6	31	51	23
Graterol, Brusdar	19	R	21	a/a	MIN	60	2.54	1.10	14.8	3.6	7.3	2.0	0.5	24	73	53
Graves, Brett	19	R	26	a/a	MIA	63	3.87	1.40	5.92	5.2	8.4	1.6	1.0	27	66	28
Gray, Josiah	19	R	22	aa	LA	40	3.45	1.23	18.1	2.4	8.1	3.4	0.0	33	69	99
Green, Josh	19	R	24	aa	ARI	49	6.22	1.79	28.3	1.7	4.8	2.8	0.5	40	60	59
Green, Nick	18	R	23	aa	NYY	18	4.64	1.22	24.4	3.7	3.9	1.0	1.4	21	66	14
	19	R	24	aa	NYY	70	9.57	2.09	23	4.9	5.5	1.1	0.6	40	48	-16
Greene, Conner	18	R	23	a/a	STL	90	4.33	1.57	9.92	5.9	5.7	1.0	0.3	29	71	52
	19	R	24	a/a	KC	113	6.58	1.73	17.8	4.6	6.1	1.3	1.1	34	55	4
Grey, Connor	19	R	25	a/a	ARI	48	5.67	1.84	13.2	4.5	5.2	1.2	1.3	35	63	-9
Griep, Nate	18	R	25	aa	MIL	58	4.85	1.77	5.24	6.2	6.8	1.1	0.9	32	74	36
	19	R	26	a/a	MIL	59	2.57	1.25	5.5	5.0	7.1	1.4	0.2	25	77	10
Griffin, Foster	18	L	23	aa	KC	154	6.42	1.77	25.3	2.4	5.6	2.3	1.2	38	65	32
	19	L	24	aaa	KC	132	6.13	1.66	23.7	4.4	6.1	1.4	1.3	32	55	7
Griggs, Scott	18	R	27	aa	COL	57	5.48	1.73	5.29	4.3	7.3	1.7	1.5	35	72	28
	19	R	28	aa	COL	46	7.39	1.75	4.68	4.7	6.3	1.3	1.8	32	47	4
Grills, Evan	18	L	26	aa	COL	86	5.97	1.61	23.9	2.0	6.3	3.1	1.3	37	65	55
	19	L	27	aaa	COL	44	6.48	1.89	14.9	3.2	5.0	1.5	0.7	39	60	21

PITCHER	yr	t	age	lvl	org	ip	era	whip	bf/g	ctl	dom	cmd	hr/9	h%	s%	bpv
Grimes, Matthew	18	R	27	a/a	BAL	88	4.87	1.67	11.3	3.9	5.0	1.3	1.1	33	73	19
Grotz, Zac	19	R	26	a/a	SEA	61	3.11	1.21	8.8	1.9	8.8	4.5	0.7	33	69	125
Guduan, Reymin	18	L	26	aaa	HOU	56	3.77	1.43	5.55	4.8	10.7	2.2	0.8	33	75	94
Guerrero, Jordan	18	L	24	a/a	CHW	131	6.24	1.77	23.1	3.6	7.0	2.0	0.9	38	64	46
	19	L	25	a/a	MIA	85	9.53	2.44	16.5	6.1	6.8	1.1	2.5	42	51	-25
Guerrieri, Taylor	18	R	26	aaa	TOR	58	7.25	1.94	12	3.8	5.0	1.3	1.6	37	64	-5
	19	R	27	aaa	TEX	37	4.36	1.66	7.23	4.1	7.1	1.7	0.3	36	70	34
Guilbeau, Taylor	19	L	26	a/a	SEA	50	3.55	1.36	5.39	3.4	8.2	2.5	0.2	34	71	75
Guillen, Alexander	19	R	24	aa	COL	78	2.60	1.22	8.55	3.0	8.2	2.8	0.8	30	75	86
Gunkel, Joe	18	R	27	aaa	MIA	66	3.68	1.27	12.3	1.0	5.3	5.1	0.8	32	73	111
	19	R	28	aaa	MIA	89	5.31	1.54	20.5	1.8	4.7	2.7	1.3	34	58	55
Gutierrez, Alfred	18	R	23	a/a	DET	35	10.45	2.33	22.5	4.0	6.7	1.7	1.9	45	55	-6
	19	R	24	aa	SF	124	6.17	1.81	21.3	5.0	7.1	1.4	0.8	36	60	10
Gutierrez, Vladimi	18	R	23	aa	CIN	147	5.78	1.41	23.1	2.5	7.7	3.1	1.4	33	61	66
	19	R	24	aaa	CIN	137	7.90	1.66	22.7	3.5	6.8	1.9	2.2	33	38	46
Guzman, Jorge	19	R	23	aa	MIA	140	5.49	1.50	24.2	5.3	7.0	1.3	1.1	28	56	0
Hackimer, Tom	19	R	25	aa	MIN	42	4.73	1.44	6.64	4.6	8.2	1.8	0.3	32	63	40
Haley, Justin	18	R	27	aaa	BOS	115	5.86	1.81	24.2	3.0	6.3	2.1	1.1	39	68	36
Hall, Matt	18	L	25	a/a	DET	115	2.88	1.28	12.8	3.8	8.2	2.2	0.2	31	76	97
	19	L	26	aaa	DET	88	7.31	1.87	16.5	3.4	8.2	2.4	2.1	40	50	73
Halstead, Ryan	18	R	26	a/a	SF	62	3.76	1.43	7.58	2.5	6.3	2.5	1.1	33	78	53
	19	R	27	a/a	SF	71	4.58	1.38	8.83	2.9	5.3	1.8	0.4	31	62	34
Hamilton, Ian	18	R	23	a/a	CHW	53	2.18	1.18	4.95	2.9	9.1	3.1	0.4	31	83	116
Hammer, J. D.	19	R	25	a/a	PHI	38	7.84	1.70	5.77	4.7	8.5	1.8	1.5	35	43	43
Hanhold, Eric	18	R	25	a/a	NYM	45	4.78	1.47	6.24	3.2	8.7	2.7	0.4	37	66	97
	19	R	26	a/a	NYM	66	4.96	1.73	6.29	3.9	6.1	1.6	1.0	36	66	22
Hansen, Alec	18	R	24	aa	CHW	37	8.81	2.30	21.2	11.6	7.2	0.6	1.0	31	60	29
	19	R	25	aa	CHW	41	8.12	2.43	7.21	9.3	8.2	0.9	1.6	39	60	-86
Harper, Ryne	18	R	29	a/a	MIN	65	6.05	1.47	7.34	1.6	8.6	5.3	0.4	40	56	142
Harris, Jon	18	R	25	a/a	TOR	149	6.22	1.62	24.5	2.1	5.2	2.5	1.6	35	65	23
Harrison, Jordan	18	L	26	a/a	TAM	58	2.01	1.34	4.84	5.0	6.8	1.4	0.4	27	86	71
	19	L	27	a/a	ATL	56	4.85	1.73	6.75	4.6	6.7	1.5	0.7	36	68	16
Hart, Kyle	18	L	26	aa	BOS	140	4.68	1.61	25.9	3.3	4.0	1.5	0.9	33	72	28
	19	L	27	a/a	BOS	158	5.25	1.49	25.3	3.4	6.0	1.7	0.8	32	58	33
Hartlieb, Geoff	18	R	25	aa	PIT	59	3.91	1.56	5.51	3.9	6.7	1.7	0.5	34	75	59
	19	R	26	aaa	PIT	41	3.19	1.34	6.6	3.6	8.4	2.3	0.0	33	74	72
Hartman, Ryan	18	L	24	aa	HOU	122	3.43	1.25	19.9	2.0	8.8	4.5	1.0	33	76	118
	19	L	25	aaa	HOU	117	6.66	1.71	21.3	3.5	7.4	2.1	2.2	35	49	58
Harvey, Hunter	18	R	24	aa	BAL	33	6.31	1.51	15.9	2.4	6.6	2.7	0.9	35	58	61
	19	R	25	a/a	BAL	77	6.50	1.58	13.1	3.3	7.6	2.3	2.4	33	45	66
Hatch, Thomas	18	R	24	aa	CHC	145	4.89	1.51	24.2	4.1	6.0	1.4	1.2	30	70	32
	19	R	25	aa	TOR	136	6.23	1.59	22.2	3.0	6.8	2.3	1.7	34	51	60
Hauschild, Mike	18	R	28	aaa	TOR	120	7.22	1.98	25.1	4.1	5.8	1.4	1.0	39	63	19
	19	R	29	aaa	STL	38	10.26	2.23	19.3	6.4	4.0	0.6	1.3	36	45	-85
Hearn, Taylor	18	L	24	aa	TEX	129	4.67	1.40	22.7	3.7	7.9	2.1	1.0	31	68	66
Hedges, Zach	18	R	26	a/a	CHC	90	4.13	1.36	10.5	2.0	4.6	2.3	0.9	31	72	46
Helsley, Ryan	18	R	24	a/a	STL	69	4.47	1.17	23	3.6	8.2	2.3	0.9	26	63	83
	19	R	25	aaa	STL	38	5.40	1.42	9.5	4.7	7.7	1.6	0.7	29	55	29
Helton, Bret	18	R	25	aa	PIT	61	7.76	1.89	8.23	5.9	5.2	0.9	1.3	33	59	4
Hennigan, Jonatha	19	L	25	aa	PHI	47	6.08	1.99	7.31	5.9	6.7	1.1	0.5	38	65	-20
Hentges, Sam	19	L	23	aa	CLE	130	7.32	1.99	24.1	5.0	7.4	1.5	1.0	40	57	16
Henzman, Lincoln	19	R	24	aa	CHW	80	8.36	1.82	24.8	2.3	4.2	1.8	0.8	39	46	32
Herb, Tyler	18	R	26	aaa	SF	72	5.65	1.71	25.1	3.4	5.8	1.7	0.9	36	67	35
	19	R	27	a/a	BAL	134	7.89	1.99	24.9	4.3	5.5	1.3	2.2	36	50	-1
Herget, Jimmy	18	R	25	aaa	CIN	61	4.42	1.56	5.36	3.4	8.0	2.4	1.0	36	73	65
	19	R	26	aaa	CIN	60	3.87	1.55	5.48	6.2	8.6	1.4	1.4	27	69	5
Herget, Kevin	18	R	27	aaa	STL	140	5.47	1.56	21.9	2.2	5.9	2.6	1.4	35	68	40
Hernandez, Ariel	18	R	26	a/a	MIL	58	3.47	1.58	6.12	6.5	6.7	1.0	0.2	29	77	65
Hernandez, Arnalc	18	R	22	a/a	KC	76	4.47	1.30	24.2	2.9	5.1	1.8	1.1	28	68	39
	19	R	23	a/a	KC	130	7.00	1.89	23.6	3.7	4.8	1.3	1.9	36	54	4
Hernandez, Darwi	19	L	23	a/a	BOS	58	6.89	1.78	15.7	7.8	10.0	1.3	0.8	33	55	-12
Hernandez, Eliese	19	R	24	aaa	MIA	48	1.47	1.20	21.4	2.8	10.8	3.9	0.0	35	86	137
Hernandez, Jakob	19	L	23	aa	PHI	71	2.18	1.13	5.99	3.6	8.3	2.3	0.7	26	77	70
Hernandez, Jonatl	18	R	22	aa	TEX	64	6.33	1.68	24	5.5	6.7	1.2	1.0	32	62	35
	19	R	23	aa	TEX	96	7.70	1.80	20.1	4.2	7.2	1.7	1.5	37	48	36
Herrera, Ronald	19	R	24	a/a	TEX	83	10.01	1.87	18.6	2.5	5.2	2.1	3.0	36	28	44
Herrmann, Max	19	L	26	a/a	LAA	74	4.80	1.70	21.1	4.6	4.1	0.9	0.1	33	68	-32
Herrmann, Spenc	18	L	25	aa	SEA	66	5.96	1.76	10.5	4.0	6.4	1.6	0.5	38	64	49
Hess, David	18	R	25	aaa	BAL	47	4.18	1.45	22.4	4.0	6.6	1.7	0.8	31	72	54
	19	R	26	aaa	BAL	42	5.65	1.49	14	2.8	7.7	2.8	1.8	33	51	83
Hessler, Keith	18	L	29	aaa	COL	54	6.91	2.20	6.48	6.4	6.6	1.0	1.9	38	72	-11
Heuer, Codi	19	R	23	aa	CHW	30	2.67	1.32	5.67	2.3	5.7	2.5	0.0	33	78	59
Higgins, Tyler	18	R	27	aaa	SEA	35	3.43	1.38	5.25	2.5	8.0	3.2	1.1	34	80	80
	19	R	28	a/a	SD	56	5.72	1.30	6.11	2.3	7.6	3.3	2.3	28	39	93
Hightower, Scoote	18	R	25	aa	PIT	38	3.03	1.21	14	2.3	5.8	2.6	0.3	30	74	85
	19	R	26	aa	PIT	44	9.20	1.89	20.8	2.9	3.3	1.1	2.2	35	38	-1
Hill, Taylor	18	R	29	a/a	SF	78	7.57	1.89	18.5	2.5	4.4	1.7	1.5	38	61	-1
Hill, Tim	19	L	29	aaa	KC	31	2.67	1.29	4.75	2.0	6.2	3.2	0.6	32	76	77
Hoekstra, Kurt	19	R	26	a/a	ATL	30	2.33	1.75	9.86	4.8	6.7	1.4	0.8	35	84	8
Hofacket, Adam	18	R	24	a/a	LAA	37	8.85	2.05	6.96	3.8	4.1	1.1	1.0	39	55	0
	19	R	25	a/a	LAA	67	2.82	1.44	7.96	2.8	7.3	2.6	0.4	35	77	73
Hoffman, Jeff	18	R	25	aaa	COL	107	5.79	1.60	22.6	4.1	6.5	1.6	0.9	33	64	43
	19	R	26	aaa	COL	86	8.80	1.78	23.3	3.2	7.7	2.4	2.3	37	36	70
Holder, Heath	19	R	27	a/a	COL	101	4.11	1.39	13.7	2.9	6.9	2.4	1.2	31	64	64
Holman, David	18	R	28	aaa	COL	72	6.67	1.81	16.7	3.6	3.2	0.9	1.9	33	67	-30
	19	R	29	aaa	COL	36	12.00	2.41	13.5	4.9	3.2	0.6	2.2	40	39	-58
Holmberg, David	18	L	27	aaa	COL	107	6.48	1.86	22.7	2.7	4.0	1.5	1.8	36	68	-14

PITCHER	yr	t	age	lvl	org	ip	era	whip	bf/g	ctl	dom	cmd	hr/9	h%	s%	bpv
Holmes, Ben	19	L	28	a/a	LA	61	6.90	1.93	20.7	4.5	7.3	1.6	2.2	37	55	29
Holmes, Clay	18	R	25	aaa	PIT	96	4.10	1.59	19.2	3.9	7.4	1.9	0.4	36	73	69
Holmes, Grant	19	R	23	a/a	OAK	89	3.73	1.30	16	2.8	6.9	2.5	1.0	30	65	67
Horacek, Mitch	18	L	27	aa	COL	62	3.43	1.64	5.43	4.8	7.9	1.7	0.7	35	80	61
	19	L	28	a/a	COL	49	9.45	2.40	5.58	5.9	7.4	1.3	1.6	44	53	-7
Houck, Tanner	19	R	23	a/a	BOS	109	5.50	1.63	14.7	4.0	7.2	1.8	0.7	36	61	41
Houser, Adrian	18	R	25	a/a	MIL	80	6.05	1.74	17.4	2.9	6.2	2.1	1.2	38	67	33
Houston, Zac	18	R	24	a/a	DET	56	2.15	1.09	4.76	4.3	10.2	2.4	0.6	24	83	113
	19	R	25	a/a	DET	59	6.41	1.59	6.53	4.7	8.1	1.7	0.2	35	54	37
Howard, Brian	18	R	23	aa	OAK	68	3.93	1.40	23.9	2.9	6.9	2.4	0.9	32	74	64
	19	R	24	a/a	OAK	145	5.22	1.66	24.1	3.0	6.9	2.3	0.7	38	63	62
Howard, Sam	18	L	25	aaa	COL	96	6.02	1.66	20.5	3.3	5.7	1.7	1.4	34	66	20
	19	L	26	aaa	COL	52	4.38	1.57	5.45	4.1	8.1	2.0	1.0	34	67	53
Howard, Spencer	19	R	23	aa	PHI	32	2.96	1.05	20.8	2.7	9.5	3.6	0.8	27	66	118
Hu, Chih-Wei	18	R	25	aaa	TAM	103	5.93	1.62	19.1	2.6	6.8	2.6	1.4	36	65	46
	19	R	26	a/a	CHC	76	9.49	2.09	16.3	4.7	5.9	1.3	3.3	36	39	-2
Huang, Wei-Chieh	18	R	25	aa	TEX	47	5.24	1.46	10.6	3.3	8.6	2.6	1.5	33	68	61
	19	R	26	a/a	TEX	42	6.88	1.69	7.93	6.7	9.1	1.4	2.0	28	48	0
Hudson, Dakota	18	R	24	aaa	STL	113	2.77	1.39	25.1	2.9	5.6	1.9	0.1	32	78	72
Huffman, Chris	18	R	26	a/a	SD	100	6.47	1.81	17.2	4.0	4.4	1.1	1.2	35	65	5
Hurlbut, David	18	L	29	aaa	TEX	85	8.04	2.16	23.5	3.1	4.7	1.5	1.8	41	65	-18
Hursh, Jason	18	R	27	a/a	ATL	68	5.13	1.89	6.04	5.4	5.9	1.1	0.0	37	70	51
	19	R	28	aa	ATL	47	6.45	1.74	6.3	3.7	4.6	1.2	0.3	36	58	-1
Hutchison, Drew	18	R	28	aaa	LA	42	2.62	1.42	19.8	2.8	6.6	2.3	0.2	34	81	81
	19	R	29	aaa	LAA	132	5.29	1.62	23.5	3.7	6.9	1.9	1.4	34	60	42
Irvin, Cole	18	L	24	aaa	PHI	162	3.21	1.22	25.2	2.0	6.3	3.1	0.8	30	76	83
	19	L	25	aaa	PHI	95	4.64	1.54	24.4	1.4	5.3	3.9	1.5	35	62	76
Isaacs, Dusty	18	R	27	a/a	TOR	60	7.23	1.90	6.43	6.3	7.4	1.2	1.5	34	63	18
	19	R	28	aaa	TOR	27	8.21	1.63	7.09	2.7	9.1	3.4	1.3	39	38	109
Istler, Andrew	18	R	26	a/a	LA	64	2.57	1.02	7.95	2.0	6.0	3.0	0.1	27	73	105
Ivey, Tyler	19	R	23	aa	HOU	46	2.25	1.15	16.6	3.4	10.3	3.0	1.3	27	75	110
Jackson, Zach	18	R	24	aa	TOR	62	3.21	1.44	6.14	7.8	8.0	1.1	0.3	22	77	89
	19	R	25	aaa	TOR	68	5.41	1.57	6.49	4.9	7.3	1.5	1.7	30	57	18
James, Joshua	18	R	25	a/a	HOU	117	3.58	1.18	20.4	3.7	10.7	2.9	0.7	30	71	115
Jankins, Thomas	18	R	23	a/a	MIL	136	4.98	1.38	23.8	2.5	5.7	2.3	1.0	31	65	50
	19	R	24	a/a	MIL	136	5.65	1.59	24	2.5	5.6	2.3	1.5	34	56	52
Javier, Cristian	19	R	22	a/a	HOU	85	2.47	1.00	17.1	4.6	12.1	2.6	0.7	22	70	112
Jax, Griffin	19	R	25	a/a	MIN	128	4.06	1.40	23.5	2.1	5.3	2.5	0.6	33	66	56
Jay, Tyler	18	L	24	aa	MIN	61	5.15	1.77	7.39	3.0	5.8	1.9	1.2	37	73	27
	19	L	25	aa	CIN	62	5.27	2.00	8.57	5.2	7.5	1.4	0.4	41	70	13
Jaye, Myles	18	R	27	aaa	CLE	72	8.82	1.99	20.4	3.6	3.4	0.9	2.2	35	58	-44
Jefferies, Daulton	19	R	24	aa	OAK	64	4.76	1.31	12.6	1.0	8.4	8.1	1.1	36	55	141
Jensen, Chris	18	R	28	a/a	TEX	91	8.67	2.33	16.8	5.4	4.3	0.8	1.7	40	64	-30
Jerez, Williams	18	L	26	aaa	LAA	57	4.22	1.45	6.42	3.7	9.4	2.6	0.8	35	72	87
	19	L	27	aaa	SF	56	5.09	1.35	4.97	2.9	7.5	2.6	1.0	32	55	75
Jester, Jason	18	R	27	aa	SD	61	5.60	1.65	6.83	2.1	6.5	3.1	0.3	40	64	83
Jewell, Jake	18	R	25	a/a	LAA	38	3.38	1.60	6.46	4.3	6.9	1.6	0.7	34	81	51
	19	R	26	aaa	LAA	39	4.76	1.53	5.02	3.7	7.6	2.1	0.7	35	64	56
Jimenez, Dany	19	R	26	aa	TOR	35	2.82	1.25	5.74	3.6	9.3	2.6	1.5	28	71	89
Jimenez, Dedgar	18	L	22	a/a	BOS	144	5.63	1.45	23.7	3.5	6.3	1.8	1.3	30	63	37
	19	L	23	a/a	BOS	96	6.22	1.65	13.9	5.0	6.2	1.2	1.2	31	54	-5
Jimenez, Eduardo	19	R	24	a/a	DET	59	4.11	1.24	5.59	3.1	6.3	2.0	1.2	26	59	47
Jimenez, Francisc	18	R	24	aaa	BAL	22	6.00	1.55	8.79	3.5	4.9	1.4	0.5	33	59	39
	19	R	25	a/a	BAL	64	4.84	1.50	9.24	2.8	7.3	2.6	1.8	33	59	75
Jiminian, Johendi	18	R	26	aa	SEA	71	4.24	1.60	19.7	4.2	5.5	1.3	1.2	31	77	23
	19	R	27	a/a	CIN	100	6.42	1.94	16.4	4.2	5.5	1.3	1.2	38	61	4
Johnson, Chase	18	R	26	aa	SF	59	5.00	1.48	14.1	3.5	4.5	1.3	0.4	31	65	40
	19	R	27	a/a	SF	79	6.94	2.04	10.7	5.4	6.1	1.1	0.6	39	61	-20
Johnson, Jordan	18	R	25	a/a	SF	138	4.69	1.60	23.5	4.2	6.0	1.4	0.3	34	69	54
	19	R	26	aa	CIN	40	9.60	2.14	22.2	7.7	7.3	1.0	1.0	37	47	-56
Johnson, Michael	18	L	27	a/a	LA	68	5.72	1.66	7.1	3.5	5.0	1.4	1.4	33	68	11
Johnstone, Conno	18	R	24	a/a	ATL	40	4.66	1.61	14.8	3.4	5.0	1.5	1.9	31	78	-1
	19	R	25	a/a	ATL	94	6.27	1.83	12.5	2.9	4.3	1.5	0.6	38	60	17
Jokisch, Eric	18	L	29	aaa	OAK	150	5.36	1.76	26.5	3.1	5.3	1.7	0.8	37	70	32
Jones, Connor	18	R	24	a/a	STL	112	4.53	1.71	19.6	5.0	5.3	1.1	0.4	33	72	40
	19	R	25	a/a	STL	51	5.46	1.95	5.67	6.2	7.0	1.1	0.9	36	67	-24
Jones, Damon	19	L	25	a/a	PHI	56	5.57	1.44	19.9	6.0	8.9	1.5	0.8	27	54	16
Jones, James	19	L	31	a/a	TEX	66	3.92	1.49	6.36	5.1	6.8	1.3	1.2	28	68	1
Jurado, Ariel	18	R	22	aa	TEX	103	4.15	1.40	27.2	1.6	4.2	2.6	1.3	31	75	37
	19	R	23	aaa	TEX	24	3.94	1.45	25.9	0.8	6.6	8.6	0.4	39	69	117
Kalish, Jake	18	L	27	a/a	KC	129	5.20	1.56	17.2	1.6	6.5	4.0	0.7	38	66	92
	19	L	28	a/a	KC	129	6.77	1.63	21.3	2.1	5.2	2.5	2.1	34	46	55
Kaminsky, Rob	18	L	24	aa	CLE	27	4.16	1.76	5.39	6.7	6.1	0.9	0.9	30	78	32
	19	L	25	a/a	CLE	58	4.83	1.48	5.98	3.9	7.6	2.0	1.0	32	61	51
Kaprielian, James	19	R	25	a/a	OAK	33	2.03	1.11	16.3	2.2	7.0	3.1	0.6	28	79	84
Kasowski, Marsha	19	R	24	aa	LA	30	3.19	1.23	4.52	4.9	11.6	2.4	0.4	30	70	96
Kay, Anthony	19	L	24	a/a	TOR	135	4.15	1.49	22.4	4.1	7.4	1.8	1.0	32	66	42
Keel, Jerry	18	L	25	a/a	SD	150	5.10	1.49	23.1	2.4	5.4	2.2	0.9	33	67	45
	19	L	26	aaa	SD	152	7.11	1.90	24.8	3.5	5.3	1.5	1.5	38	55	18
Keller, Brian	18	R	24	aa	NYY	125	5.09	1.51	24.6	2.9	6.9	2.4	1.3	34	69	47
	19	R	25	a/a	NYY	72	5.27	1.42	25.5	2.6	5.9	2.3	0.7	33	56	54
Keller, Kyle	18	R	25	a/a	MIA	37	4.34	1.38	5.39	5.1	11.2	2.2	0.5	33	68	109
	19	R	26	a/a	MIA	57	6.43	1.48	6.29	3.9	9.8	2.5	1.5	34	46	88
Keller, Mitch	18	R	22	a/a	PIT	139	4.10	1.38	24.3	3.4	7.2	2.1	0.7	31	71	70
	19	R	23	aaa	PIT	105	4.38	1.39	23.3	3.1	8.6	2.8	0.8	34	63	90
Kelley, Trevor	18	R	25	a/a	BOS	57	3.94	1.56	6.11	3.7	5.6	1.5	0.4	33	74	51
	19	R	26	aaa	BOS	66	2.52	1.35	5.3	3.1	6.6	2.1	1.4	29	77	52
Kelly, Casey	18	R	29	aaa	SF	136	5.50	1.67	25.4	2.6	5.5	2.1	1.1	36	68	33

PITCHER	yr	t	age	lvl	org	ip	era	whip	bf/g	ctl	dom	cmd	hr/9	h%	s%	bpv
Kelly, Michael	18	R	26	a/a	BAL	68	10.98	2.47	11.6	11.0	6.3	0.6	1.4	34	54	3
Kelly, Zack	19	R	24	aa	LAA	76	5.16	1.67	17.1	3.8	8.3	2.2	0.8	38	64	65
Kennedy, Brett	18	R	24	aaa	SD	90	2.67	1.13	22.2	2.0	6.8	3.3	0.5	29	78	102
Kent, Matt	18	L	26	a/a	BOS	150	5.19	1.55	23.5	2.4	6.0	2.5	1.0	35	67	52
	19	L	27	a/a	BOS	153	7.65	1.91	25.8	3.6	4.4	1.2	0.9	38	53	-1
Keselica, Sean	18	L	25	aa	PIT	59	6.26	1.57	6.49	7.0	5.9	0.8	0.7	25	59	43
	19	L	26	a/a	PIT	61	5.29	1.97	8.11	6.6	6.5	1.0	0.7	35	69	-43
Kiekhefer, Dean	18	L	29	a/a	OAK	61	4.25	1.50	5.91	1.3	5.4	4.2	0.7	37	72	91
Kilome, Franklyn	18	R	23	aa	NYM	140	4.71	1.45	23	4.0	7.0	1.8	0.6	31	67	62
King, Michael	18	R	23	a/a	NYY	121	2.33	1.01	25.7	1.5	6.9	4.6	0.7	27	81	125
	19	R	24	a/a	NYY	39	7.40	1.44	24	2.0	6.9	3.5	1.2	35	37	88
Kingham, Nick	18	R	27	a/a	PIT	68	5.00	1.45	22.4	2.5	6.2	2.5	0.8	34	65	63
Kingham, Nolan	19	R	23	aa	ATL	37	6.10	1.48	26.7	2.8	5.0	1.8	1.7	30	47	32
Kinley, Jeff	18	L	26	a/a	MIA	61	3.77	1.22	6.03	4.1	6.3	1.5	0.8	24	70	60
	19	L	27	a/a	MIA	46	8.08	2.05	6.83	4.4	8.1	1.8	1.2	42	53	44
Kittredge, Andrew	18	R	28	aaa	TAM	46	3.75	1.45	9.35	2.7	9.1	3.4	0.7	37	75	101
	19	R	29	aaa	TAM	38	2.56	1.00	5.4	1.7	10.1	6.1	0.8	30	69	156
Klonowski, Alex	18	R	26	a/a	LAA	108	5.32	1.56	22.5	2.6	6.1	2.4	0.9	35	66	54
	19	R	27	aaa	LAA	63	10.03	2.22	19.9	3.6	3.5	1.0	2.1	40	44	-15
Koch, Matt	18	R	28	aaa	ARI	55	5.79	1.53	21.8	1.9	3.8	2.0	1.5	33	65	13
	19	R	29	aaa	ARI	100	7.71	1.86	22.3	2.8	5.4	1.9	1.7	38	48	39
Koerner, Brody	18	R	25	a/a	NYY	65	6.20	1.57	13.6	2.7	4.7	1.7	0.6	34	59	39
	19	R	26	a/a	NYY	140	6.69	1.86	24.3	3.8	5.6	1.5	1.6	37	56	17
Kopech, Michael	18	R	22	aaa	CHW	127	4.39	1.39	22.3	4.4	10.7	2.4	0.7	33	69	100
Kowar, Jackson	19	R	23	aa	KC	75	4.83	1.51	25	2.8	7.7	2.8	1.1	35	61	82
Krauth, Ben	19	L	25	a/a	CLE	57	6.51	1.82	7.57	6.3	6.8	1.1	1.9	31	55	-30
Krehbiel, Joey	18	R	26	aaa	ARI	58	3.94	1.29	4.97	3.6	8.7	2.4	1.1	29	73	78
	19	R	27	aaa	ARI	65	7.59	1.91	6.04	6.1	7.1	1.2	1.9	33	50	-19
Kremer, Dean	18	R	22	aa	BAL	53	2.46	1.21	23.8	3.3	9.1	2.8	0.6	30	82	105
	19	R	23	a/a	BAL	106	5.06	1.49	24.1	2.9	7.5	2.6	1.1	34	59	74
Kriske, Brooks	19	R	25	aa	NYY	50	3.54	1.29	5.73	4.7	9.4	2.0	0.8	27	67	60
Krol, Ian	18	L	27	aaa	NYM	57	2.61	1.64	5.92	4.0	7.4	1.8	0.5	36	85	63
	19	L	28	aaa	MIN	46	7.62	2.12	4.94	5.0	8.5	1.7	0.8	44	58	35
Krook, Matt	18	L	24	aa	TAM	74	5.25	1.60	8.85	6.3	10.1	1.6	0.4	34	65	89
	19	L	25	aa	TAM	50	6.50	1.89	7.37	6.6	8.0	1.2	0.7	36	60	-17
Kruczynski, Evan	18	L	23	aa	STL	41	2.57	0.94	25.8	2.0	6.0	2.9	0.2	24	71	106
	19	L	24	a/a	STL	149	7.25	1.74	24.3	4.0	7.2	1.8	1.3	36	50	39
Kubat, Kyle	19	L	27	a/a	CHW	105	5.87	1.54	22.9	2.3	4.8	2.1	1.1	34	54	41
Kuhnel, Joel	19	R	24	a/a	CIN	55	2.84	1.19	5.4	2.9	7.2	2.5	1.3	26	70	68
Kuntz, Brad	18	L	26	aa	MIL	55	5.22	1.91	7.25	5.0	8.1	1.6	1.2	39	75	35
Kurcz, Aaron	19	R	29	aa	MIL	31	3.75	1.39	5.03	2.3	7.3	3.1	2.1	31	64	86
Ladwig, A.J.	18	R	26	a/a	DET	135	6.60	1.67	24.3	1.8	5.0	2.7	1.5	36	63	27
Lail, Brady	18	R	25	a/a	NYY	65	7.12	1.85	8.25	5.5	7.5	1.4	1.6	35	63	20
	19	R	26	a/a	NYY	48	4.80	1.32	7.99	3.2	9.6	3.0	1.1	33	56	105
Lakins, Travis	18	R	24	a/a	BOS	55	3.11	1.20	6.15	3.1	7.5	2.4	0.6	28	75	87
	19	R	25	aaa	BOS	45	6.41	1.84	5.24	4.9	6.6	1.3	1.0	36	59	4
Lamb, John	18	L	28	aaa	LAA	51	3.34	1.34	16.4	2.5	7.4	3.0	1.1	32	80	73
Lambert, Jimmy	18	R	24	aa	CHW	25	4.04	1.28	20.5	2.5	9.2	3.7	1.0	33	71	107
	19	R	25	aa	CHW	60	6.96	1.89	25.8	4.7	8.8	1.9	2.5	37	52	50
Lambert, Peter	18	R	21	a/a	COL	150	4.01	1.35	24.1	1.7	5.2	3.1	0.8	32	72	69
	19	R	22	aaa	COL	61	5.32	1.35	23.2	2.2	6.2	2.8	1.6	30	50	69
Lane, Trevor	18	L	24	aa	NYY	21	5.22	1.83	8.93	2.8	7.6	2.7	0.6	42	71	69
	19	L	25	a/a	NYY	74	2.73	1.14	6.83	3.5	7.1	2.0	0.7	25	71	50
Lange, Alex	19	R	24	aa	DET	56	5.56	1.67	15.8	4.8	5.5	1.1	0.9	32	61	-12
LaRue, Carson	19	R	23	a/a	HOU	109	7.13	1.60	21	3.3	6.1	1.9	1.6	33	44	39
Latcham, Will	19	R	23	aa	STL	42	8.36	2.01	6.58	4.2	5.5	1.3	2.0	37	48	3
Lau, Adam	18	R	24	aa	BOS	58	5.11	1.66	7.24	4.4	7.3	1.7	1.5	33	73	29
	19	R	25	a/a	BOS	63	5.15	1.63	7.04	5.3	7.8	1.5	1.1	32	62	16
Lawrence, Justin	19	R	25	a/a	COL	39	11.37	2.32	5.32	7.4	5.6	0.8	1.3	38	42	-80
Lawson, Brandon	18	R	24	aa	TAM	43	5.15	1.85	14.4	3.7	6.0	1.6	0.9	38	73	30
	19	R	25	aa	SF	129	5.74	1.85	25.1	3.9	4.6	1.2	0.7	37	64	-4
Leal, Erick	19	R	24	aa	CHC	54	8.11	1.92	23.3	4.4	7.4	1.7	1.1	40	50	33
LeBlanc, Randy	18	R	26	aa	MIN	51	2.75	1.48	24.5	2.4	5.4	2.2	0.4	34	82	62
Lee, Andrew	19	R	26	aa	WAS	40	3.93	1.42	15.5	4.5	5.3	1.2	1.0	27	67	-8
Lee, Chris	18	L	26	a/a	BAL	29	8.06	2.68	10.6	5.7	5.3	0.9	0.0	48	67	22
	19	L	27	a/a	BAL	49	7.86	2.00	12.5	4.8	6.8	1.4	2.2	37	50	10
Lee, Dylan	18	L	24	a/a	MIA	31	2.04	1.03	5.43	3.0	9.3	3.1	0.0	28	78	137
	19	L	25	a/a	MIA	60	4.19	1.50	5.79	3.6	6.9	1.9	1.3	32	66	44
Lee, Zach	18	R	27	a/a	TAM	147	4.78	1.62	25.1	2.4	5.3	2.3	0.7	36	71	48
	19	R	28	a/a	NYM	124	7.09	1.87	24.3	2.8	5.8	2.1	1.0	40	55	47
Leftwich, Luke	18	R	24	aa	PHI	64	4.20	1.37	6.11	3.5	8.8	2.5	0.5	33	69	94
	19	R	25	a/a	PHI	44	6.53	1.50	6.82	4.3	10.5	2.4	2.1	32	42	90
Leibrandt, Brandon	18	L	26	aaa	PHI	52	1.81	1.02	10	1.9	4.6	2.4	0.2	25	82	82
Lemoine, Jake	19	R	26	a/a	TEX	56	6.07	1.89	6.02	4.1	6.2	1.5	1.1	38	62	19
Lenik, Kevin	18	R	27	aaa	KC	50	6.49	1.68	6.64	4.9	6.9	1.4	0.8	34	60	45
	19	R	28	a/a	BOS	34	6.12	1.53	6.19	6.2	7.4	1.2	1.4	26	51	-16
Leone, Dominic	19	R	28	aaa	STL	33	3.48	1.21	5.81	4.0	8.5	2.1	0.9	26	65	61
Lewicki, Artie	18	R	26	aaa	DET	63	6.62	1.61	23.3	2.6	6.0	2.3	1.0	36	58	47
Lewis, Sam	18	R	27	aa	ARI	46	7.61	1.68	14.8	3.7	6.1	1.7	0.8	35	53	39
	19	R	28	aa	ARI	49	3.84	1.41	13	4.4	6.9	1.6	0.5	29	68	23
Leyer, Robinson	18	R	25	aa	CIN	59	3.55	1.44	5.99	4.8	8.3	1.7	0.8	30	78	67
	19	R	26	a/a	BOS	55	6.51	1.95	7.12	6.4	8.5	1.3	0.6	38	61	-1
Lillis-White, Connor	18	L	26	a/a	LAA	74	3.80	1.37	6.78	3.8	9.6	2.6	0.8	33	74	93
Liranzo, Jesus	18	R	23	a/a	PIT	57	4.73	1.37	5.82	5.4	8.4	1.6	1.2	25	68	61
	19	R	24	a/a	PIT	59	6.91	1.69	6.33	5.7	6.6	1.2	1.3	30	50	-17
Littell, Zack	18	R	23	a/a	MIN	129	5.25	1.57	23.6	3.4	7.4	2.2	0.7	36	66	66
	19	R	24	aaa	MIN	63	4.91	1.49	13.6	3.8	7.9	2.1	1.9	30	57	57
Lively, Ben	19	R	27	aaa	ARI	73	4.42	1.56	13.3	3.6	7.2	2.0	1.5	33	65	49
Llovera, Mauricio	19	R	23	aa	PHI	66	5.96	1.54	20.6	4.0	8.8	2.2	1.3	34	53	67
Lloyd, Kyle	18	R	28	aaa	SD	48	5.84	1.61	14.3	3.6	6.1	1.7	0.9	34	64	41
	19	R	29	a/a	SD	115	5.23	1.67	18.5	3.1	5.9	1.9	1.7	35	61	41
Lockett, Walker	18	R	24	aaa	SD	134	4.65	1.37	24.4	2.0	6.7	3.3	1.0	33	68	77
	19	R	25	aaa	NYM	59	4.48	1.70	24.2	1.8	5.1	2.9	0.8	39	69	62
Logue, Zach	19	L	23	a/a	TOR	105	5.71	1.54	22.9	3.3	6.0	1.8	1.6	32	53	37
Long, Jaron	18	R	27	a/a	WAS	130	5.24	1.69	21.8	2.2	4.1	1.9	0.8	37	69	29
Long, Lucas	18	R	26	a/a	BAL	112	7.39	1.79	15.7	2.3	4.4	1.9	1.3	37	59	11
Long, Nolan	18	R	24	aa	LA	37	5.20	1.19	6.21	3.8	8.2	2.2	0.5	27	54	93
	19	R	25	aa	LA	63	3.11	1.40	6.64	5.8	9.6	1.7	1.3	26	72	34
Lopez, Edua	18	R	23	aa	TAM	59	5.15	1.53	21.4	4.5	5.1	1.2	0.5	30	65	42
Lopez, Jose	18	R	25	aaa	CIN	141	5.85	1.55	23.7	2.9	6.2	2.2	1.6	33	66	30
	19	R	26	aaa	CIN	50	9.33	2.19	22.8	5.4	6.7	1.2	3.2	37	44	-7
Lopez, Pablo	18	R	22	a/a	MIA	65	1.55	0.95	20.6	1.6	8.0	4.9	0.8	26	90	140
	19	R	23	a/a	MIA	15	11.80	2.41	15.8	4.6	8.1	1.8	2.1	47	40	40
Lopez, Yoan	18	R	25	aa	ARI	63	3.54	1.15	5.58	3.9	9.9	2.5	0.6	28	70	110
Lovelady, Richard	18	L	23	aaa	KC	73	3.03	1.13	6.28	2.6	7.2	2.8	0.4	28	73	99
	19	L	24	aaa	KC	27	3.54	1.37	4.73	2.4	7.7	3.3	0.3	35	70	93
Lovvorn, Zach	18	R	24	a/a	KC	145	6.54	1.67	24.1	3.1	4.1	1.3	0.9	34	60	16
	19	R	25	a/a	KC	89	10.13	2.29	15.7	5.6	5.6	1.0	2.1	40	45	-32
Lowther, Zac	19	L	23	aa	BAL	148	3.53	1.31	23.5	4.2	7.7	1.8	0.6	28	68	44
Lugo, Luis	18	L	24	aa	KC	25	5.06	1.65	14.1	4.1	6.0	1.5	1.1	33	71	29
	19	L	25	aa	CHC	61	4.95	1.67	21.1	4.3	8.0	1.8	1.3	35	64	45
Luzardo, Jesus	18	L	21	a/a	OAK	96	3.47	1.19	19.3	2.2	8.3	3.8	0.6	32	72	116
	19	L	22	aaa	OAK	31	3.52	1.26	18.1	2.2	8.5	3.9	0.8	33	67	112
Machado, Andres	18	R	25	a/a	KC	83	7.18	1.97	10.7	4.4	6.1	1.4	1.0	39	63	21
	19	R	26	aaa	KC	76	3.51	1.42	7.35	4.1	5.9	1.4	1.5	27	69	12
Mader, Michael	18	L	24	a/a	ATL	104	4.70	1.70	15.7	4.6	6.0	1.3	0.6	34	72	41
Madero, Luis	19	R	22	aa	LAA	91	7.36	1.80	21.1	2.5	6.5	2.6	1.4	39	50	67
Magliaro, Marc	18	R	28	aa	COL	50	6.94	1.75	6.37	3.4	6.5	1.9	1.7	36	63	18
Magnifico, Damien	18	R	27	aaa	PIT	72	4.43	1.68	7.74	5.9	6.0	1.0	0.1	32	71	55
	19	R	28	a/a	ARI	55	4.47	1.84	5.16	4.9	8.3	1.7	0.2	40	73	35
Mahle, Greg	18	L	25	a/a	LAA	63	4.99	1.34	6.11	3.3	6.7	2.1	0.9	30	63	61
	19	L	26	a/a	LAA	89	4.92	1.68	20.1	2.7	5.3	2.0	1.6	35	64	41
Mahoney, Kolton	18	R	26	a/a	MIA	95	5.55	1.74	14.4	2.7	5.5	2.0	1.1	37	69	31
	19	R	27	a/a	MIA	111	4.98	1.59	15.9	3.7	6.9	1.9	0.7	35	63	42
Manning, Matt	19	R	21	aa	DET	135	3.63	1.15	22.4	2.7	8.2	3.1	0.6	29	63	95
Mantiply, Joe	19	L	28	a/a	NYY	41	5.87	1.45	7.04	1.6	5.5	3.6	1.6	33	49	76
Mapes, Tyler	18	R	27	aa	WAS	44	5.49	1.68	24.8	2.7	5.3	2.0	0.8	37	67	40
	19	R	28	aa	WAS	134	8.28	2.07	26.2	3.6	5.4	1.5	1.5	41	52	19
Maples, Dillon	18	R	26	aaa	CHC	40	3.16	1.68	4.41	9.3	13.3	1.4	0.2	32	80	121
	19	R	27	aaa	CHC	43	5.14	1.60	5	8.8	12.9	1.5	0.3	30	64	13
Margevicius, Nick	19	L	23	aa	SD	69	5.42	1.48	24.7	1.8	5.8	3.3	2.0	33	52	74
Mark, Tyler	19	R	25	aa	ARI	31	9.56	2.40	7.77	10.3	7.6	0.7	1.5	36	52	-121
Markel, Parker	19	R	29	a/a	PIT	44	2.48	1.19	5.74	6.5	10.9	1.7	0.8	19	75	41
Markey, Brad	18	R	26	a/a	CHC	58	5.44	1.52	7.65	2.4	5.8	2.4	2.1	32	71	15
	19	R	27	a/a	CIN	93	8.81	1.84	16.1	3.1	4.9	1.6	2.4	35	38	23
Marte, Yunior	18	R	23	aa	KC	81	3.65	1.37	7.9	3.3	7.3	2.2	0.8	31	75	69
	19	R	24	a/a	KC	61	4.57	1.54	5.79	4.2	8.5	2.0	0.8	34	65	57
Martin, Brett	18	L	23	aa	TEX	89	9.55	2.22	15.5	3.2	8.0	2.5	0.9	48	55	49
Martin, Cody	18	R	29	aaa	NYM	82	7.04	1.82	22.5	4.4	5.9	1.3	1.8	34	64	0
Martin, Corbin	18	R	23	aa	HOU	103	3.76	1.24	19.9	2.5	7.2	2.9	0.7	30	71	86
	19	R	24	aaa	HOU	38	3.48	1.44	18.1	4.2	9.0	2.1	0.5	34	72	66
Martin, Jarret	18	L	29	a/a	OAK	51	5.10	1.86	5.99	6.8	7.4	1.1	0.4	35	71	54
Martin, Kyle	18	R	27	aaa	BOS	52	5.13	1.65	7.76	5.6	7.4	1.3	0.5	33	68	60
Martinez, Emerson	19	R	24	aa	TEX	59	6.49	1.88	18.6	3.6	5.4	1.5	1.1	38	59	18
Martinez, Henry	18	R	24	a/a	CLE	45	6.15	1.62	4.78	2.8	7.6	2.7	0.2	39	59	86
	19	R	25	a/a	CLE	61	6.07	1.67	5.85	4.9	5.7	1.2	0.8	32	57	-10
Martinez, Juan	18	L	26	a/a	CIN	31	7.51	1.93	7.39	4.6	7.8	1.7	1.2	40	61	35
	19	L	27	a/a	CIN	51	7.79	1.95	6.77	4.4	5.5	1.3	2.3	35	49	-2
Martinez, Luis	19	R	24	aa	CHW	62	6.38	1.59	7.02	4.1	9.0	2.2	1.1	36	52	70
Martinez, Seth	19	R	25	aa	OAK	30	1.58	1.18	7.55	2.9	8.0	2.8	0.0	31	85	84
Marvel, James	18	R	25	aa	PIT	33	3.85	1.36	27.6	2.6	4.7	1.8	0.3	31	70	57
	19	R	26	a/a	PIT	165	4.13	1.34	24.6	2.9	5.7	2.0	0.7	30	64	43
Marzi, Anthony	18	L	26	aa	MIN	82	7.17	1.85	17.4	3.5	5.5	1.6	1.1	38	61	21
Mata, Bryan	10	R	20	aa	BOS	55	6.73	1.62	22.3	4.0	8.3	2.1	1.2	35	50	60
Maton, Phil	19	R	26	aaa	CLE	30	3.70	1.30	5.64	3.4	11.2	3.3	1.2	34	65	127
Mattson, Isaac	19	R	24	a/a	LAA	55	3.01	1.10	7.48	2.9	11.0	3.8	0.5	31	68	138
May, Dustin	18	R	21	aa	LA	35	3.67	1.10	22.9	2.7	6.4	2.4	0.0	28	63	99
	19	R	22	a/a	LA	108	3.80	1.19	21.7	2.2	8.1	3.6	0.4	32	63	103
Mazza, Chris	18	R	29	a/a	SEA	50	3.27	1.36	16.1	2.8	5.5	1.9	1.5	28	84	29
McCanna, Kevin	19	R	25	a/a	ARI	87	2.53	1.22	11.4	3.0	7.9	2.6	0.3	30	76	78
McCasland, Jake	18	R	27	aa	SF	107	6.20	1.83	15.6	4.0	4.9	1.2	0.6	37	65	27
McCaughan, Darren	19	R	23	a/a	SEA	146	5.34	1.41	23.8	1.3	6.8	5.1	1.7	34	51	105
McClain, Reggie	19	R	27	a/a	SEA	58	3.55	1.19	10.2	3.8	6.8	1.8	0.6	25	65	37
McClelland, Jackson	19	R	25	a/a	TOR	58	5.38	1.61	5.99	5.5	7.0	1.3	1.2	30	59	-5
McCreery, Adam	18	L	25	a/a	ATL	112	4.67	1.79	6.18	6.1	9.1	1.5	0.2	38	72	79
	19	L	26	a/a	LAA	46	3.98	1.72	6	5.6	7.9	1.4	0.9	34	73	8
McCurry, Brendan	18	R	26	aaa	HOU	64	3.73	1.34	5.8	2.2	8.2	3.7	0.7	35	73	105
	19	R	27	aaa	HOU	56	5.04	1.44	6.46	3.9	8.6	2.2	1.6	31	56	69
McGarry, Seth	18	R	24	aa	PHI	69	4.50	1.55	6.72	5.4	7.4	1.4	0.9	30	72	50
	19	R	25	a/a	PHI	62	6.14	1.77	11.9	4.2	7.0	1.7	1.7	35	57	31
McGeorge, Austin	18	R	24	aa	NYM	26	9.16	2.24	5.98	2.9	8.0	2.8	1.8	47	60	27
	19	R	25	aa	NYM	33	5.15	1.89	11.1	4.4	6.3	1.4	1.7	36	66	13
McGough, Scott	18	R	29	aaa	COL	72	7.14	1.89	7.9	3.1	7.1	2.3	2.1	39	66	11
McGowan, Kevin	18	R	27	a/a	NYM	84	4.99	1.63	11.3	3.8	6.6	1.7	1.2	34	72	34
	19	R	28	a/a	WAS	64	6.71	1.69	24.1	4.4	5.3	1.2	1.9	31	50	-4

PITCHER	yr	t	age	lvl	org	ip	era	whip	bf/g	ctl	dom	cmd	hr/9	h%	s%	bpv
McGowin,Kyle	18	R	27	a/a	WAS	132	3.66	1.09	24.6	2.1	7.2	3.4	0.9	27	69	97
	19	R	28	a/a	WAS	95	4.78	1.45	23.9	2.8	7.5	2.6	1.3	33	59	76
McGrath,Daniel	18	L	24	aa	BOS	90	4.57	1.58	12	3.8	6.3	1.7	0.4	35	70	57
	19	L	25	a/a	BOS	124	2.83	1.31	17.7	3.9	6.6	1.7	0.5	28	75	32
McGrath,Kyle	18	L	26	aaa	SD	53	2.80	1.20	4.96	2.9	5.8	2.0	0.9	26	81	56
	19	L	27	a/a	SD	64	9.13	1.89	11.6	3.0	4.6	1.5	2.4	36	37	20
McGuire,Deck	18	R	29	aaa	LAA	58	4.29	1.38	16.3	4.2	5.9	1.4	0.9	27	70	44
McKay,Brendan	19	L	24	a/a	TAM	75	1.41	0.94	18.8	2.3	10.6	4.6	0.4	28	82	146
McKay,David	18	R	23	a/a	SEA	53	2.70	1.15	5.87	3.5	10.7	3.0	0.5	30	78	124
	19	R	24	aaa	DET	47	6.42	1.49	6.57	6.2	11.7	1.9	1.0	32	49	62
McKee,Colin	19	R	25	a/a	HOU	64	3.12	1.35	6.67	6.6	9.5	1.4	1.4	21	71	11
McKenzie,Tristor	18	R	21	aa	CLE	92	3.49	1.13	22.8	2.9	7.4	2.6	1.0	26	73	80
McRae,Alex	18	R	25	aaa	PIT	117	5.80	1.80	20.8	4.0	6.3	1.6	0.7	37	67	39
	19	R	26	aaa	PIT	115	6.86	1.80	24.2	3.7	6.1	1.6	1.8	36	52	27
McWilliams,Sam	18	R	23	aa	TAM	101	6.02	1.67	23.9	3.6	7.4	2.1	1.2	36	65	44
	19	R	24	a/a	TAM	133	5.30	1.76	23.5	3.4	6.4	1.9	0.8	38	65	41
Means,John	18	L	25	a/a	BAL	158	4.70	1.48	24.3	1.9	5.8	3.0	1.1	35	70	59
Medeiros,Kodi	18	L	22	aa	CHW	139	4.79	1.58	22.7	4.8	8.1	1.7	1.1	32	72	52
	19	L	23	aa	CHW	83	7.58	1.91	14	6.1	7.1	1.2	1.7	34	51	-20
Medina,Adonis	19	R	23	aa	PHI	107	6.46	1.57	21.4	3.6	6.2	1.7	1.3	32	50	31
Megill,Trevor	18	R	25	aa	SD	17	3.98	1.56	6.77	3.9	3.9	1.0	1.2	30	78	8
	19	R	26	a/a	SD	58	4.74	1.61	7.17	3.4	9.6	2.8	0.8	40	65	99
Meisinger,Ryan	18	R	24	a/a	BAL	48	3.71	1.37	6.33	2.9	8.2	2.8	1.1	33	77	75
	19	R	25	aaa	STL	35	3.72	1.49	7.19	2.6	8.6	3.3	1.3	36	69	103
Meisner,Casey	18	R	23	aa	STL	40	3.85	1.17	22.8	2.9	6.2	2.1	0.6	27	67	71
	19	R	24	a/a	SF	43	9.07	1.81	20.1	3.0	4.4	1.5	2.6	34	34	17
Mejia,Adalberto	18	L	25	aaa	MIN	64	4.82	1.47	18.4	3.2	6.9	2.2	0.6	34	67	67
Mekkes,Dakota	18	R	24	a/a	CHC	55	1.37	1.31	5.57	5.0	9.6	1.9	0.4	29	91	100
	19	R	25	aaa	CHC	50	6.80	1.83	5.42	6.8	8.9	1.3	1.3	34	55	-6
Mella,Keury	18	R	25	a/a	CIN	108	4.01	1.41	21.8	3.4	7.0	2.1	1.0	31	74	57
	19	R	26	aaa	CIN	144	6.81	1.85	24.9	4.0	5.4	1.3	1.9	35	54	6
Mendez,Roman	18	R	28	aa	WAS	54	5.04	1.52	5.33	3.7	7.4	2.0	1.7	32	72	34
Mendez,Yohande	18	L	23	a/a	TEX	92	6.46	1.66	22.9	3.6	6.6	1.8	2.2	33	67	4
	19	L	24	a/a	TEX	16	3.73	1.16	7.17	5.0	9.3	1.9	1.5	20	58	51
Mendoza,Hector	18	R	24	a/a	STL	62	5.44	1.36	5.32	3.0	5.4	1.4	1.2	26	62	30
Menez,Conner	18	L	23	a/a	SF	85	4.71	1.47	21.5	4.0	9.1	2.3	0.1	36	65	101
	19	L	24	a/a	SF	123	5.08	1.42	22.7	4.0	9.1	2.3	1.3	32	56	75
Mengden,Daniel	18	R	25	aaa	OAK	46	3.58	1.16	20.4	1.4	5.3	3.8	0.4	30	68	102
	19	R	26	aaa	OAK	64	5.06	1.36	20.6	2.9	6.8	2.4	1.1	31	54	63
Merritt,Ryan	18	L	26	aaa	CLE	72	5.08	1.47	20.6	0.3	5.2	18.3	1.6	36	70	357
	19	L	27	aaa	TAM	78	9.12	2.17	14.4	3.0	6.0	2.0	2.5	42	46	47
Meyer,Ben	18	R	25	aaa	MIA	65	4.86	1.49	18.8	2.7	5.6	2.1	0.5	34	67	56
	19	R	26	a/a	COL	83	10.52	2.08	19.4	5.8	6.9	1.2	3.4	34	31	-13
Milbrath,Jordan	18	R	27	a/a	CLE	65	5.54	1.79	6.99	4.7	6.5	1.4	0.2	37	66	56
	19	R	28	a/a	MIA	67	5.91	1.72	8.47	4.3	7.4	1.7	1.4	35	58	36
Milburn,Matt	19	R	26	aa	OAK	152	6.59	1.75	26.8	2.4	4.0	1.7	1.2	36	55	26
Miller,Evan	19	R	24	a/a	SD	33	6.11	1.61	6.41	3.8	7.8	2.0	1.0	35	54	55
Miller,Tyson	19	R	24	a/a	CHC	138	5.81	1.53	23.1	3.1	6.6	2.1	1.5	33	53	53
Mills,Alec	18	R	27	aaa	CHC	126	5.74	1.51	23.7	3.2	6.0	1.9	0.8	33	61	49
	19	R	28	aaa	CHC	104	7.12	1.80	25.3	3.1	6.3	2.0	1.8	37	51	48
Mills,Jordan	18	L	26	aa	WAS	21	2.79	1.12	5.57	3.2	6.7	2.1	0.0	27	72	96
	19	L	27	a/a	WAS	55	6.47	1.81	5.67	4.6	9.0	2.0	0.9	40	58	56
Mills,McKenzie	18	L	23	aa	MIA	18	8.64	1.59	20.1	2.0	3.4	1.7	1.5	33	44	2
	19	L	24	aa	MIA	84	8.66	1.90	14.2	4.1	6.6	1.6	2.0	37	43	27
Mills,Wyatt	19	R	24	aa	SEA	54	6.31	1.40	5.58	3.3	9.5	2.9	0.5	36	48	102
Milner,Hoby	18	L	27	aaa	TAM	42	3.71	1.50	4.56	4.0	8.5	2.1	0.8	34	77	74
	19	L	28	aaa	TAM	63	3.96	1.18	5.06	2.1	10.1	4.8	1.1	33	58	143
Minch,Jordan	18	L	25	aa	CHC	42	5.06	1.64	6.97	5.0	4.5	0.9	1.5	28	73	-1
	19	L	26	a/a	CHC	59	6.20	1.62	5.85	4.6	6.4	1.4	1.3	31	53	8
Misiewicz,Anthon	18	L	24	aa	SEA	98	6.57	1.87	21.9	2.7	7.3	2.7	1.4	41	67	41
	19	L	25	a/a	SEA	134	5.80	1.47	22.2	2.5	7.1	2.8	1.4	34	51	78
Mitchell,Bryan	19	R	28	aaa	SD	44	10.37	2.40	17.7	5.9	5.2	0.9	1.7	41	48	-48
Mize,Casey	19	R	22	aa	DET	80	4.56	1.31	22.1	2.1	7.1	3.3	0.8	33	59	87
Moats,Dalton	18	L	23	aa	TAM	63	6.37	1.52	6.69	4.2	8.2	2.0	1.8	31	62	37
	19	L	24	aa	TAM	66	4.62	1.55	6.88	3.7	7.3	2.0	1.3	33	63	51
Molina,Marcos	18	R	23	a/a	NYM	83	6.80	1.81	24.1	3.5	6.0	1.7	1.4	37	64	17
	19	R	24	aa	BAL	86	6.03	1.59	25.3	3.1	4.9	1.6	2.1	31	51	21
Moll,Sam	18	L	26	aaa	TOR	20	6.94	1.81	6.24	2.5	6.7	2.6	0.6	41	59	63
	19	L	27	a/a	SF	51	3.32	1.63	5.57	4.7	7.2	1.5	0.2	35	77	21
Montas,Frankie	18	R	25	aaa	OAK	73	5.56	1.48	21	3.2	6.0	1.8	0.9	32	62	46
Moore,Andrew	18	R	24	a/a	TAM	134	4.76	1.46	22.1	3.0	5.8	2.0	1.5	31	72	28
	19	R	25	a/a	SEA	103	10.14	1.85	20.1	3.0	5.7	1.9	2.6	36	28	40
Morales,Andrew	18	R	25	a/a	STL	65	4.68	1.40	5.61	3.9	8.1	2.1	0.9	31	68	68
Morales,Osmer	18	R	26	aaa	LAA	102	6.17	1.80	19.6	4.5	6.7	1.5	1.2	36	67	25
Moran,Jovani	19	L	22	aa	MIN	35	6.75	1.64	7.83	6.3	10.8	1.7	1.0	34	51	43
Morejon,Adrian	19	L	20	aa	SD	36	5.09	1.32	9.31	3.7	9.7	2.6	0.8	32	54	91
Morgan,Elijah	19	R	23	a/a	CLE	107	5.28	1.56	23.4	3.2	7.5	2.3	1.3	35	59	67
Morimando,Shaw	18	L	26	aaa	TOR	45	8.20	2.16	25	2.7	3.5	1.3	1.5	41	63	-23
	19	L	27	aaa	TOR	71	8.46	1.96	21.2	4.7	7.5	1.6	2.1	37	45	25
Morin,Michael	18	R	27	aaa	SEA	55	4.54	1.36	5.64	2.3	6.9	3.1	0.5	34	66	88
Morrison,Preston	18	R	25	a/a	CHC	63	5.61	1.38	7.37	2.6	6.3	2.4	1.4	30	62	44
Moseley,Ryan	19	R	25	aa	LA	51	4.33	1.54	7.4	3.7	6.1	1.7	0.9	32	67	29
Moss,Benton	18	R	25	aa	TAM	102	3.44	1.23	23	2.0	5.6	2.8	1.3	28	78	56
Moss,Scott	19	L	25	a/a	CLE	132	4.17	1.56	22.3	5.4	8.8	1.6	0.7	32	69	29
Moya,Gabriel	18	L	23	aaa	MIN	44	2.62	1.37	7.13	2.6	8.4	3.2	0.5	35	82	100
	19	L	24	a/a	MIN	48	7.18	1.78	6.56	4.3	8.3	2.0	1.9	37	49	53
Muckenhirn,Zach	18	L	23	aa	BAL	27	6.44	1.73	6.14	5.9	7.4	1.3	0.4	34	60	59
	19	L	24	a/a	BAL	59	5.13	1.48	6.23	4.5	8.9	2.0	0.8	33	59	56

PITCHER	yr	t	age	lvl	org	ip	era	whip	bf/g	ctl	dom	cmd	hr/9	h%	s%	bpv
Muller,Kyle	18	L	21	aa	ATL	29	4.06	1.10	22.7	1.8	7.2	4.0	1.1	28	67	100
	19	L	22	aa	ATL	113	5.11	1.64	23	6.2	8.1	1.3	0.6	32	64	-4
Munoz,Andres	18	R	19	aa	SD	19	1.06	1.17	3.79	4.9	8.3	1.7	0.0	25	90	105
	19	R	20	a/a	SD	37	3.06	1.16	4.23	4.1	12.4	3.0	0.9	30	68	130
Murphy,Patrick	19	R	24	aa	TOR	84	7.13	1.53	20.3	3.3	7.6	2.3	1.0	35	44	67
Murray,Joey	19	R	23	aa	TOR	45	5.01	1.49	21.6	4.0	8.8	2.2	1.1	33	59	69
Naile,James	18	R	25	a/a	OAK	152	5.43	1.62	26	2.5	4.0	1.6	0.8	34	66	24
	19	R	26	a/a	OAK	142	6.86	1.86	24.6	3.4	4.6	1.4	1.1	37	56	11
Naughton,Packy	19	L	23	aa	CIN	107	4.85	1.50	24.4	2.4	6.1	2.5	0.9	35	62	63
Navas,Carlos	18	R	26	aa	CIN	74	4.41	1.42	8.06	2.2	8.8	4.0	1.0	37	71	102
	19	R	27	a/a	SF	86	4.86	1.39	10.4	2.7	6.6	2.5	1.2	31	57	64
Navilhon,Joe	18	R	25	aa	DET	37	5.12	1.55	6.74	2.3	8.7	3.7	1.8	37	73	70
	19	R	26	a/a	DET	50	6.92	1.55	7.57	2.6	7.8	3.0	1.7	35	43	88
Neidert,Nick	18	R	22	aa	MIA	154	3.67	1.22	24	1.8	7.9	4.4	1.0	32	73	113
	19	R	23	aaa	MIA	41	6.45	1.86	21.3	5.1	6.9	1.4	0.9	37	59	6
Nelson,Jimmy	19	R	30	aaa	MIL	41	5.95	1.69	11.6	6.0	9.4	1.6	1.1	34	58	27
Nelson,Kyle	19	L	23	a/a	CLE	38	3.88	1.21	4.5	3.6	10.4	2.9	1.5	28	59	108
Nelson,Nick	19	R	24	a/a	NYY	86	3.80	1.49	21.8	4.8	9.4	2.0	0.9	33	70	58
Neverauskas,Dov	18	R	25	aaa	PIT	47	3.02	1.44	6.08	5.9	8.7	1.5	0.4	28	79	83
	19	R	26	aaa	PIT	52	6.67	1.69	6.52	4.2	9.7	2.3	1.6	38	51	80
Newberry,Jake	18	R	24	a/a	KC	51	2.01	1.26	5.1	2.5	7.5	2.9	0.6	32	87	94
	19	R	25	aaa	KC	28	4.67	1.74	5.81	4.7	7.6	1.6	1.0	36	68	28
Newsome,Ljay	19	R	23	a/a	SEA	57	3.69	1.08	22.4	1.3	6.3	4.8	0.9	28	58	96
Nicolino,Justin	18	L	27	aaa	CIN	135	6.37	1.82	25.1	2.7	4.6	1.7	1.2	38	66	13
	19	L	28	aaa	CHW	136	7.95	1.78	26.1	3.0	5.0	1.7	3.0	33	39	28
Nittoli,Vinny	19	R	29	a/a	TOR	62	8.47	1.71	8.3	3.0	6.4	2.1	1.5	37	39	53
Nix,Jacob	18	R	22	a/a	SD	60	1.89	0.92	22.5	1.3	5.8	4.6	0.4	25	81	131
Nogosek,Stepher	18	R	23	aa	NYM	20	9.13	1.96	5.97	9.6	8.2	0.9	1.4	28	52	34
	19	R	24	a/a	NYM	51	1.37	1.11	5.74	4.7	7.7	1.6	0.2	22	86	29
Northcraft,Aaron	19	R	29	a/a	SEA	41	2.46	1.08	5.37	3.3	6.5	1.9	0.6	23	73	44
Norwood,James	18	R	25	a/a	CHC	53	2.90	1.29	5.49	4.4	7.8	1.8	0.6	27	79	70
	19	R	26	aaa	CHC	59	5.47	1.44	5.61	5.4	9.8	1.8	1.6	28	52	49
Oaks,Trevor	18	R	25	aaa	KC	129	4.11	1.58	25.8	3.2	3.8	1.2	0.4	33	73	32
Oberholtzer,Brett	18	L	29	aaa	COL	134	7.41	1.95	26.7	3.3	4.3	1.3	2.2	37	66	-29
O'Brien,Riley	19	R	24	aa	TAM	70	5.44	1.47	21.5	4.2	8.0	1.9	0.6	33	57	50
Ogando,Emilio	18	L	25	aa	KC	119	6.27	1.96	21.9	5.8	5.6	1.0	1.8	34	72	-9
	19	L	26	a/a	KC	74	6.86	1.58	8.83	3.1	7.3	2.4	0.5	37	50	66
Okert,Steven	18	L	27	aaa	SF	33	4.79	1.52	4.37	2.2	9.1	4.1	0.7	40	68	114
	19	L	28	aaa	SF	59	6.98	1.74	5.4	3.1	8.5	2.7	2.2	38	48	87
Olczak,Jon	18	R	25	aa	MIL	57	2.12	1.19	5.45	3.3	7.8	2.4	0.2	29	82	100
	19	R	26	a/a	MIL	50	5.57	1.72	6.53	2.9	7.0	2.5	1.2	38	61	67
O'Reilly,Mike	18	R	24	a/a	STL	79	5.92	1.52	18.1	3.0	4.4	1.5	1.4	31	63	11
Ort,Kaleb	18	R	26	aa	NYY	33	3.10	1.66	6.72	6.8	9.3	1.4	0.0	33	79	91
	19	R	27	a/a	NYY	48	4.92	1.72	6.62	5.9	10.4	1.8	0.5	38	67	47
Ortiz,Luis	18	R	23	a/a	BAL	101	4.44	1.37	19.3	2.3	6.3	2.7	1.2	32	71	57
	19	R	24	aaa	BAL	67	7.60	1.81	22.2	4.3	5.1	1.2	2.3	32	46	-6
Ortiz,Willy	19	R	24	aa	TOR	54	8.82	1.78	15.5	4.5	6.1	1.3	1.6	34	39	5
Oswalt,Corey	18	R	25	aaa	NYM	53	5.54	1.49	20.8	3.2	7.4	2.3	1.3	33	65	52
	19	R	26	aaa	NYM	88	3.57	1.33	22.9	1.6	6.7	4.1	1.0	33	68	95
Ott,Travis	18	L	23	a/a	TAM	72	4.26	1.38	6.89	4.0	10.1	2.5	0.8	33	70	94
Ouellette,William	19	R	26	a/a	TOR	57	5.57	1.51	9.93	1.8	4.1	2.3	1.1	34	55	44
Overton,Dillon	18	L	27	a/a	SD	96	3.27	1.23	17	2.3	4.7	2.0	1.1	27	78	40
	19	L	28	aaa	SD	116	5.98	1.69	20.9	2.5	6.0	2.4	1.8	36	55	59
Oviedo,Johan	19	R	21	aa	STL	113	6.73	1.74	22.4	4.9	8.7	1.8	0.7	38	55	43
Palumbo,Joseph	19	L	25	a/a	TEX	82	4.06	1.34	20.1	4.4	9.2	2.1	1.3	28	62	66
Pannone,Thomas	18	L	24	a/a	TOR	47	5.82	1.54	25.7	2.4	8.1	3.3	2.1	35	68	49
	19	L	25	aaa	TOR	35	4.17	1.35	18.4	4.2	8.5	2.0	1.3	28	62	59
Paredes,Enoli	19	R	24	aa	HOU	50	5.55	1.22	16.8	4.3	10.5	2.5	0.2	30	48	92
Parke,John	19	L	24	aa	CHW	77	3.90	1.43	23.4	2.4	4.3	1.8	0.9	31	68	31
Parkinson,David	19	L	24	aa	PHI	119	5.53	1.46	23.2	3.2	7.8	2.5	1.0	34	54	73
Parsons,Tommy	19	R	24	a/a	STL	89	6.62	1.45	25.4	1.5	6.8	4.5	3.0	32	34	100
Parsons,Wes	18	R	26	a/a	ATL	118	3.72	1.39	20.7	2.8	6.2	2.2	0.8	32	75	61
	19	R	27	aaa	ATL	58	3.95	1.70	9.75	3.6	6.4	1.8	0.2	38	74	34
Patterson,Jacob	19	L	24	aa	STL	59	6.86	1.63	5.16	2.8	9.6	3.5	2.2	38	45	117
Paulino,David	19	R	25	aaa	TOR	30	4.46	1.63	19.2	3.5	6.5	1.8	0.7	36	68	40
Paulino,Felix	18	R	23	aa	CHW	40	8.30	1.93	23.9	5.0	4.5	0.9	1.5	34	57	-10
	19	R	24	aa	CHW	35	5.86	1.76	26.7	3.8	6.6	1.7	1.9	35	58	34
Paulson,Jake	18	R	26	aa	CLE	116	4.39	1.49	25	2.9	5.6	1.9	1.0	32	73	39
	19	R	27	a/a	CLE	133	5.72	1.80	22	3.3	4.2	1.3	0.8	36	63	4
Payamps,Joel	18	R	24	a/a	ARI	117	3.99	1.19	15.1	2.0	7.8	3.9	0.7	31	67	113
	19	R	25	a/a	ARI	80	4.46	1.40	22.6	2.1	6.2	2.9	0.9	33	62	73
Payano,Pedro	18	R	24	aa	TEX	120	7.32	1.67	21.6	4.1	5.2	1.3	1.4	32	57	11
	19	R	25	a/a	TEX	86	6.59	1.66	20.3	5.5	7.6	1.4	1.5	31	51	6
Pazos,James	19	L	28	aaa	COL	52	10.00	2.42	5.93	5.6	5.7	1.0	1.7	42	50	-29
Peacock,Matt	19	R	25	aa	ARI	116	4.44	1.53	24	4.0	5.0	1.3	0.5	31	66	2
Pearce,Matt	18	R	24	aa	STL	54	5.81	1.54	23.6	1.7	6.2	3.6	1.3	36	64	65
Pearson,Nate	19	R	23	a/a	TOR	82	3.65	1.11	17	2.8	7.8	2.8	0.8	26	60	82
Pelaez,Ivan	19	L	25	aa	TAM	57	6.15	1.60	7.01	1.8	4.4	2.4	1.4	35	53	49
Pelham,C.D.	18	L	23	aa	TEX	19	8.08	2.02	3.83	6.8	7.4	1.1	0.6	38	57	43
	19	L	24	a/a	TEX	35	14.68	2.93	4.85	11.4	7.5	0.7	2.0	42	40	-154
Pena,Luis	18	R	23	a/a	LAA	107	5.03	1.42	19.8	4.4	7.3	1.7	1.2	28	67	48
	19	R	24	a/a	LAA	47	4.96	1.32	8.17	3.9	8.5	2.2	1.7	27	52	65
Pena,Richelson	18	R	25	a/a	TEX	119	4.40	1.57	23.8	1.8	5.4	3.0	1.1	36	75	51
	19	R	26	a/a	TEX	73	8.25	1.55	16	2.3	5.6	2.4	1.5	34	34	57
Peoples,Michael	18	R	27	a/a	CLE	45	7.44	1.67	20.3	3.0	6.4	2.1	1.1	37	54	41
	19	R	28	aaa	CLE	146	5.66	1.66	26.2	2.1	5.7	2.7	1.4	37	58	64
Peralta,Freddy	18	R	22	aaa	MIL	61	3.03	1.24	19	3.7	11.3	3.0	0.1	34	74	137
Perdomo,Angel	19	L	25	a/a	MIL	70	5.87	1.68	6.72	6.6	11.5	1.7	1.4	34	57	47

PITCHER	yr	t	age	lvl	org	ip	era	whip	bf/g	ctl	dom	cmd	hr/9	h%	s%	bpv
Perdomo, Luis	18	R	25	aaa	SD	75	3.76	1.30	23.8	2.4	6.1	2.6	1.3	29	76	53
	19	R	26	aaa	SD	15	3.79	1.82	6.33	2.4	8.0	3.4	1.6	42	74	98
Perez, Cionel	18	L	22	a/a	HOU	75	2.18	1.19	15.1	3.1	9.3	3.0	0.4	31	82	117
	19	L	23	aaa	HOU	47	5.95	1.74	16.5	4.4	7.1	1.6	1.2	35	59	26
Perez, Hector	18	R	22	aa	TOR	43	4.43	1.37	18.1	5.1	8.9	1.8	0.2	30	65	94
	19	R	23	aa	TOR	122	6.77	1.97	22.5	5.5	7.3	1.3	0.9	39	60	2
Perez, Williams	18	R	27	a/a	SEA	99	3.05	1.30	24	1.6	6.7	4.3	0.6	34	78	109
	19	R	28	aa	STL	68	7.58	1.91	24.8	4.1	6.9	1.7	1.6	39	52	32
Perrin, Jon	18	R	25	a/a	KC	70	4.83	1.49	9.18	4.2	6.5	1.5	0.7	31	68	52
Peters, Dillon	18	L	26	aaa	MIA	104	6.64	1.76	25.1	2.7	5.9	2.2	1.3	38	63	30
	19	L	27	aaa	LAA	57	6.24	1.68	19.7	2.6	6.9	2.7	1.7	37	54	72
Peterson, David	18	R	28	aaa	ATL	25	7.65	2.11	7.31	3.4	2.7	0.8	0.4	40	61	-2
	19	L	24	aa	NYM	116	5.96	1.65	21.6	3.2	8.2	2.6	0.9	39	57	80
Peterson, Tim	18	R	27	aaa	NYM	40	3.27	1.02	4.83	2.2	9.9	4.5	0.8	29	70	141
	19	R	28	aaa	NYM	55	3.85	1.23	5.43	2.4	7.1	3.0	1.3	29	61	81
Pfeifer, Philip	18	L	26	a/a	ATL	57	7.44	1.79	6.77	6.6	6.4	1.0	0.4	32	55	48
	19	L	27	a/a	ATL	42	3.76	1.59	13.3	4.8	8.0	1.7	0.9	33	72	31
Phillips, Alex	19	R	25	aa	MIN	33	6.43	1.63	6.68	4.0	6.5	1.6	1.5	33	51	26
Phillips, Evan	18	R	24	aaa	BAL	52	3.01	1.15	5.31	3.2	10.0	3.2	0.5	30	74	124
	19	R	25	aaa	BAL	41	4.57	1.44	6.51	3.9	7.6	1.9	0.5	32	63	49
Phillips, Tyler	19	R	22	aa	TEX	94	6.86	1.51	22.6	2.2	5.9	2.7	2.0	32	41	65
Pierpont, Matt	18	R	27	aa	COL	60	3.08	1.44	4.65	3.9	8.4	2.2	0.7	33	81	78
	19	R	28	aaa	COL	34	3.19	1.73	6.19	4.0	6.3	1.6	1.6	34	77	24
Pill, Tyler	18	R	28	a/a	LA	83	6.35	1.85	16.9	2.8	4.8	1.7	1.3	38	67	10
Pinales, Erasmo	18	R	24	aa	HOU	57	6.50	1.61	6.68	5.0	9.5	1.9	1.0	35	59	68
	19	R	25	aa	HOU	18	6.00	2.22	7.57	6.9	12.8	1.9	3.5	43	64	63
Pineyro, Ivan	18	R	27	a/a	LAA	124	7.55	1.71	21.6	2.3	6.3	2.7	1.2	38	55	46
Pinto, Ricardo	18	R	24	aaa	CHW	55	7.10	1.89	9.61	3.9	5.3	1.4	1.4	37	63	6
	19	R	25	a/a	TAM	126	5.51	1.61	20	4.2	6.7	1.6	1.7	31	57	25
Pivetta, Nick	19	R	26	aaa	PHI	41	3.76	1.23	18.5	5.1	10.7	2.1	0.5	27	64	74
Plesac, Zach	18	R	23	aa	CLE	22	3.35	1.26	22.4	1.8	7.3	4.1	0.5	33	74	114
	19	R	24	a/a	CLE	65	2.31	0.96	24.7	1.4	7.4	5.4	0.4	28	72	114
Plutko, Adam	18	R	27	aaa	CLE	86	2.32	0.92	23	1.9	6.6	3.4	0.7	23	78	106
	19	R	28	aaa	CLE	17	9.76	1.89	20.3	2.5	6.4	2.6	0.7	42	40	66
Poche, Colin	18	L	24	a/a	TAM	66	1.02	0.89	6.12	2.7	13.1	4.9	0.3	29	91	192
	19	L	25	aaa	TAM	28	7.55	1.70	6.35	3.1	13.1	4.3	1.4	47	46	171
Ponce, Cody	18	R	24	aa	MIL	95	6.37	1.59	14.4	3.6	7.1	2.0	1.4	34	61	37
	19	R	25	a/a	PIT	65	5.60	1.39	8.09	3.1	7.6	2.5	1.0	32	51	71
Poncedeleon, Dan	18	R	26	aaa	STL	97	2.61	1.35	21.3	4.7	7.9	1.7	0.4	29	81	81
	19	R	27	aaa	STL	85	3.59	1.42	22.6	4.7	6.9	1.5	0.8	28	70	15
Poppen, Sean	18	R	24	aa	MIN	94	4.79	1.41	22.1	2.7	6.1	2.2	1.2	31	69	45
	19	R	25	a/a	MIN	91	5.56	1.69	20.6	4.8	8.4	1.7	0.5	37	62	39
Poteet, Cody	18	R	24	aa	MIA	121	6.19	1.64	24.6	3.4	6.2	1.8	1.1	35	63	35
	19	R	25	a/a	MIA	137	5.23	1.53	26	2.9	5.0	1.7	1.3	32	58	30
Pounders, Brooks	18	R	28	aaa	COL	31	4.43	1.49	5.14	3.2	7.5	2.3	1.1	34	73	58
	19	R	29	aaa	NYM	57	5.69	1.49	5.72	3.6	8.1	2.2	1.5	32	52	67
Povse, Max	18	R	25	a/a	SEA	100	6.28	1.67	25	4.3	8.0	1.8	0.8	36	61	59
Powers, Alex	18	R	26	aa	CIN	43	3.21	1.18	4.42	2.6	9.4	3.6	0.9	31	76	112
	19	R	27	a/a	CIN	50	2.31	1.32	5.18	3.8	9.8	2.5	0.8	32	79	90
Poyner, Bobby	18	L	26	a/a	BOS	44	4.36	1.56	5.67	2.5	5.7	2.3	1.0	35	74	44
	19	L	27	aaa	BOS	58	5.41	1.59	5.96	4.7	8.2	1.7	1.8	31	57	39
Quantrill, Cal	18	R	23	a/a	SD	148	5.16	1.55	23.1	2.5	6.5	2.6	0.9	36	68	59
	19	R	24	aaa	SD	37	4.40	1.39	22.4	2.8	6.5	2.4	0.6	33	63	61
Quiala, Yoanys	18	R	24	aa	HOU	58	7.60	1.72	20.3	3.5	5.7	1.6	1.0	36	54	31
	19	R	25	a/a	SF	105	8.72	1.96	23.9	3.7	6.7	1.8	2.0	39	44	37
Quijada, Jose	18	L	23	a/a	MIA	65	3.32	1.08	5.79	4.0	9.6	2.4	0.4	25	69	115
	19	L	24	aaa	MIA	30	5.46	1.51	5.93	3.8	8.8	2.3	1.6	33	55	72
Radke, Travis	18	L	25	a/a	SD	17	2.32	0.96	10.9	1.5	3.4	2.2	0.0	24	73	79
	19	L	26	a/a	SD	60	3.36	1.68	6.01	3.3	7.7	2.3	0.3	39	77	67
Rainey, Tanner	18	R	26	aaa	CIN	51	3.54	1.38	4.87	6.9	9.4	1.4	0.5	24	74	90
	19	R	27	aaa	WAS	18	4.99	1.79	5.19	6.4	12.4	2.0	0.6	42	68	70
Ramirez, Emmanı	18	R	24	a/a	SD	28	2.82	1.23	22.7	2.5	8.7	3.5	0.6	32	79	111
	19	R	25	a/a	SD	132	6.99	1.62	21.8	3.5	6.3	1.8	1.9	33	45	38
Ramirez, Erasmo	18	R	28	a/a	SEA	24	2.83	1.06	15.7	1.2	6.8	5.5	0.4	30	74	150
	19	R	29	aaa	BOS	126	7.17	1.77	21.4	3.6	4.9	1.4	1.7	34	50	9
Ramirez, Roel	18	R	23	aa	STL	52	3.88	1.33	6.01	3.5	8.0	2.3	0.8	31	72	77
	19	R	24	a/a	STL	76	5.74	1.56	7.75	3.5	8.2	2.3	0.7	36	57	70
Ramirez, Williams	18	R	26	aa	MIN	54	7.40	1.93	6.57	6.0	9.8	1.6	0.8	40	60	62
Ramirez, Yefry	18	R	25	aaa	BAL	72	5.31	1.41	21.8	3.0	7.1	2.3	1.2	32	64	56
	19	R	26	aaa	PIT	63	5.51	1.72	15	6.0	9.0	1.5	1.1	34	62	19
Ramirez, Yohan	19	R	24	aa	HOU	63	6.91	1.78	17.1	8.3	10.7	1.3	1.0	31	54	-14
Rasmussen, Drew	19	R	24	aa	MIL	61	5.87	1.67	12.5	5.2	9.7	1.9	0.9	36	58	53
Rea, Colin	18	R	28	a/a	SD	76	6.79	1.93	20.1	4.5	6.4	1.4	1.7	37	68	4
	19	R	29	aaa	CHC	148	5.64	1.78	26.2	4.4	5.4	1.2	1.3	34	62	-4
Reed, Cody	18	L	25	aaa	CIN	107	5.05	1.56	26.1	2.8	7.4	2.6	1.4	35	71	50
	19	L	26	aaa	CIN	22	3.31	1.15	4.91	3.7	8.5	2.3	0.6	27	66	71
Reed, Jake	18	R	26	aaa	MIN	49	2.79	1.41	6.95	4.4	7.0	1.6	0.3	31	80	74
	19	R	27	aaa	MIN	75	8.12	1.83	7.75	4.8	8.4	1.8	1.1	38	47	40
Reeves, James	18	L	25	a/a	NYY	59	3.71	1.33	7.47	5.7	9.0	1.6	0.9	25	74	77
	19	L	26	aa	NYY	56	2.55	1.25	8.46	4.0	8.0	2.0	1.0	27	75	55
Reid-Foley, Sean	18	R	23	a/a	TOR	131	4.20	1.34	22.7	3.6	8.6	2.4	0.6	32	69	88
	19	R	24	aaa	TOR	89	8.63	1.85	20.8	7.0	8.8	1.3	1.6	33	43	-12
Reininger, Zac	18	R	25	aaa	DET	52	3.69	1.47	6.04	3.1	7.1	2.3	0.7	34	76	69
	19	R	26	aaa	DET	58	5.66	1.92	8.35	4.4	6.0	1.4	1.4	37	64	8
Reyes, Arturo	18	R	26	aaa	STL	35	7.51	2.05	7.46	4.4	7.0	1.6	1.3	41	64	20
	19	R	27	a/a	TAM	137	6.13	1.64	21.8	3.6	6.0	1.7	1.7	33	53	30
Reyes, Denyi	19	R	23	aa	BOS	152	5.99	1.44	24.9	2.3	5.6	2.4	1.0	33	50	56
Reyes, Gerardo	18	R	25	aa	SD	39	3.76	1.44	5.36	4.1	9.4	2.3	0.3	35	72	100
Reyes, Gerardo	19	R	26	aaa	SD	46	3.70	1.37	5.68	3.9	9.4	2.4	1.4	31	66	82
Reyes, Jesus	18	R	25	a/a	CIN	79	5.47	1.66	9.34	4.5	5.9	1.3	1.1	32	68	28
	19	R	26	aaa	CIN	77	6.85	2.04	8.7	7.3	6.3	0.9	1.8	33	59	-65
Reyes, Luis	18	R	24	aa	WAS	65	6.45	1.73	24.7	4.6	4.1	0.9	1.4	31	65	-5
Rhoades, Jeremy	18	R	25	a/a	LAA	80	2.70	1.23	6.02	2.1	6.5	3.0	0.7	30	81	85
	19	R	26	aaa	LAA	59	6.61	1.63	6.1	5.0	9.1	1.8	1.6	33	49	47
Rios, Yacksel	18	R	25	aaa	PHI	24	4.78	1.66	4.93	6.8	8.2	1.2	1.0	29	73	52
	19	R	26	aaa	PIT	50	7.64	1.99	6.03	5.2	6.8	1.3	1.2	38	54	1
Rivero, Alexis	18	R	24	a/a	PHI	48	4.06	1.48	7.94	4.6	5.9	1.3	1.4	27	78	25
	19	R	25	a/a	PHI	30	6.86	1.62	8.97	4.1	4.9	1.2	2.3	28	44	-5
Roach, Donn	18	R	29	aaa	CHW	95	3.68	1.58	26.1	2.4	4.4	1.9	0.4	35	76	45
	19	R	30	aaa	CHW	80	10.48	2.45	23.4	3.3	4.5	1.4	2.3	44	47	10
Robinson, Duncan	18	R	25	a/a	CHC	143	3.79	1.44	23.5	1.7	6.1	3.6	0.6	36	74	86
	19	R	26	aaa	CHC	24	5.95	1.66	21.7	3.8	3.2	0.9	0.4	33	59	-26
Robinson, Jared	19	R	25	a/a	CLE	48	4.78	1.54	8.08	6.0	9.4	1.6	1.2	29	62	26
Robles, Domingo	19	L	21	aa	PIT	103	5.69	1.57	25.1	2.0	5.7	2.9	1.4	35	55	67
Rodriguez, Dereck	18	R	26	aaa	SF	51	3.61	1.29	23.3	1.9	7.4	3.9	1.6	31	80	79
	19	R	27	aaa	SF	31	4.57	1.40	22	3.2	6.1	1.9	1.2	30	60	42
Rodriguez, Jefry	18	R	25	a/a	WAS	102	4.42	1.50	23.2	4.0	7.2	1.8	0.6	33	71	62
	19	R	26	a/a	CLE	28	5.06	1.28	16.6	4.1	4.8	1.2	0.9	24	52	-6
Rodriguez, Joely	18	L	27	aaa	BAL	50	6.42	1.69	6.85	3.7	7.0	1.9	0.3	38	59	67
Rodriguez, Jose	18	R	23	aa	LAA	116	7.64	1.82	23.4	3.2	7.0	2.2	0.9	40	56	48
	19	R	24	a/a	LAA	63	6.96	1.70	12.4	3.9	8.3	2.1	1.4	37	50	61
Rodriguez, Paco	18	L	27	aa	MIN	26	5.52	1.63	6.12	6.0	4.9	0.8	0.0	30	62	51
	19	L	28	a/a	SD	49	4.07	1.40	7.41	1.8	5.9	3.3	1.0	34	65	76
Roeder, Joshua	19	R	27	a/a	MIA	65	5.72	1.72	15.6	4.3	5.3	1.2	1.7	32	58	-3
Roegner, Camero	18	L	25	a/a	MIL	24	6.80	1.98	16.7	4.2	5.2	1.2	2.3	36	71	-26
	19	L	26	aa	MIL	76	7.79	1.97	21.4	4.9	7.1	1.4	1.0	39	54	12
Rogers, Blake	19	R	25	aa	SD	65	7.26	1.89	7.66	4.1	7.2	1.8	0.9	40	55	38
Rogers, Josh	18	L	24	aaa	BAL	141	4.70	1.53	25.6	2.5	5.2	2.1	1.4	33	73	28
	19	L	25	aaa	BAL	55	10.48	2.05	24.4	1.7	4.3	2.5	3.5	39	30	48
Rogers, Tyler	18	R	28	aaa	SF	69	2.35	1.19	5.45	3.1	5.9	1.9	0.4	27	81	72
	19	R	29	aaa	SF	62	5.82	1.78	5.82	4.7	5.8	1.2	0.9	35	61	-5
Romano, Jordan	18	R	25	a/a	TOR	143	5.55	1.44	23.5	3.1	6.5	2.1	1.2	32	63	47
	19	R	26	aaa	TOR	39	7.34	1.60	7.22	3.6	9.7	2.7	2.3	35	39	96
Romano, Sal	19	R	26	aaa	CIN	70	5.78	1.73	7.41	3.8	8.2	2.1	1.1	38	60	62
Romero, Fernand	18	R	24	aaa	MIN	92	5.14	1.56	25.3	3.4	5.4	1.6	0.7	33	67	42
	19	R	25	aaa	MIN	59	5.74	1.65	7.56	4.8	7.6	1.6	1.3	33	57	25
Romero, JoJo	18	L	22	aa	PHI	108	4.14	1.35	25	3.3	7.5	2.3	1.2	30	73	61
	19	L	23	a/a	PHI	114	6.97	1.70	21.6	3.8	6.5	1.7	1.2	35	51	33
Romero, Miguel	18	R	24	aa	OAK	30	7.01	1.73	6.2	3.5	8.0	2.3	1.2	38	59	51
	19	R	25	aaa	OAK	74	4.55	1.50	7.13	4.4	8.0	1.8	1.3	31	63	43
Rondon, Angel	19	R	22	aa	STL	115	3.85	1.33	23.9	3.2	7.4	2.3	0.9	31	65	66
Rondon, Manuel	19	L	24	aa	CHC	35	6.27	1.99	7.32	6.8	4.3	0.6	0.3	34	64	-90
Rosa, Adonis	18	R	24	a/a	NYY	35	5.07	1.42	25.1	1.9	4.1	2.1	1.4	31	68	21
	19	R	25	a/a	NYY	104	5.50	1.61	18.4	3.2	6.2	2.0	1.4	34	58	45
Rosario, Randy	18	L	24	aaa	CHC	24	0.84	0.86	5.94	2.3	4.6	2.0	0.4	20	94	78
	19	L	25	aaa	CHC	39	3.89	1.83	5.89	3.6	5.8	1.6	1.3	37	74	25
Roseboom, David	18	L	26	a/a	NYM	56	3.73	1.34	5.46	3.9	8.6	2.2	1.1	30	76	73
Rosenberg, Kenny	19	L	24	a/a	TAM	139	4.49	1.53	23.3	4.1	6.4	1.6	0.8	32	65	22
Ross, Joe	18	R	25	a/a	WAS	18	4.57	1.32	25.1	2.1	4.0	1.9	0.6	30	65	45
	19	R	26	aaa	WAS	40	5.22	1.64	22.3	1.9	5.7	3.1	0.5	39	63	71
Russo, Ramon	19	R	23	a/a	PHI	125	5.39	1.42	22.2	3.4	7.5	2.2	1.9	30	51	62
Roth, Michael	18	L	28	aaa	TEX	102	5.94	1.99	23.4	4.0	4.0	1.0	1.4	37	72	-12
Rowley, Chris	18	R	28	aaa	TEX	144	4.55	1.72	27.3	4.3	4.4	1.0	1.0	33	76	10
	19	R	29	aaa	SD	17	11.86	2.43	18	5.0	4.3	0.8	2.5	40	39	-41
Rucker, Michael	18	R	24	aa	CHC	134	4.77	1.31	21.3	2.8	6.6	2.3	1.3	29	67	51
	19	R	25	a/a	CHC	81	5.66	1.59	9.95	3.2	8.4	2.6	1.4	37	56	83
Ruiz, Norge	18	R	24	a/a	OAK	135	5.75	1.62	25	2.5	4.7	1.9	1.0	35	65	28
	19	R	25	a/a	OAK	72	7.74	1.96	9.12	3.0	5.4	1.8	1.8	39	51	36
Rumbelow, Nick	18	R	27	a/a	SEA	21	2.11	1.27	5.78	3.7	9.0	2.5	0.5	31	85	99
	19	R	28	aaa	NYM	33	9.20	2.40	7.23	5.2	6.1	1.2	1.9	43	53	-12
Russ, Addison	19	R	25	aa	PHI	58	3.42	1.40	4.46	3.4	10.8	3.2	1.1	36	70	120
Ryan, Kyle	18	L	27	aaa	CHC	66	3.44	1.17	12	2.7	6.5	2.4	1.3	26	77	57
Ryan, Ryder	18	R	23	aa	NYM	34	4.45	1.17	5.26	2.7	8.3	3.1	1.3	28	66	82
	19	R	24	aa	NYM	45	4.26	1.49	7.79	5.1	6.9	1.4	0.5	30	67	5
Ryan, Zac	18	R	24	aa	LAA	33	7.00	1.92	7.87	5.8	7.1	1.2	0.3	38	61	51
	19	R	25	a/a	LAA	56	4.07	1.37	6.22	5.5	9.2	1.7	0.7	28	65	37
Sadler, Casey	18	R	28	aaa	PIT	77	4.41	1.67	12.8	3.4	5.3	1.6	0.9	35	75	29
	19	R	29	aaa	LA	40	3.76	1.31	12.8	1.4	9.0	6.6	1.5	35	63	143
Salinas, Jhonleider	19	R	24	aa	TAM	30	3.82	1.69	5.88	5.7	10.2	1.8	0.7	36	74	46
Sammons, Bryan	19	L	24	aa	MIN	82	6.01	1.53	21	4.4	7.6	1.7	1.6	30	51	35
Sampson, Adrian	18	R	27	aaa	TEX	128	5.00	1.57	17.1	2.0	4.5	2.3	1.1	35	70	33
Sanabria, Carlos	19	R	22	aa	HOU	55	4.39	1.51	6.44	6.4	10.2	1.6	0.9	30	66	30
Sanchez, Mario	19	R	25	a/a	WAS	130	5.04	1.34	20.1	1.7	6.6	3.9	1.7	31	51	91
Sanchez, Miguel	18	R	24	a/a	MIL	43	3.02	1.27	7.33	3.4	11.5	3.4	0.8	34	79	124
	19	R	25	aaa	MIL	60	5.09	1.47	6.44	3.5	7.8	2.2	0.9	34	59	63
Sanchez, Ricardo	18	L	21	aa	ATL	59	5.17	1.70	20.6	3.6	5.8	1.6	0.5	36	69	44
	19	L	22	aa	SEA	146	6.48	1.64	24.1	2.6	7.5	2.9	0.8	39	53	84
Sanchez, Sixto	19	R	21	aa	MIA	103	3.90	1.29	23.5	1.9	7.5	4.0	0.5	34	65	102
Sanders, Phoenix	19	R	24	a/a	TAM	63	2.42	1.29	5.78	4.0	8.4	2.1	0.8	29	78	61
Sandoval, Patrick	18	L	22	aa	LAA	21	1.58	1.02	20.4	3.3	10.1	3.0	0.0	28	83	141
	19	L	23	a/a	LAA	81	6.03	1.81	18.8	4.5	9.4	2.1	0.9	40	61	65
Sanmartin, Reiver	19	L	23	aa	CIN	58	5.84	1.60	21.4	2.9	7.5	2.6	1.3	36	56	74
Santana, Dennis	18	R	22	a/a	LA	51	2.59	1.03	19.7	2.5	10.1	4.0	0.5	29	76	143
	19	R	23	aaa	LA	94	7.25	1.77	16	4.5	8.7	1.9	1.5	37	50	51
Santiago, Andres	18	R	29	a/a	ATL	108	6.50	1.72	18.9	3.5	4.8	1.3	1.4	34	64	5
	19	R	30	a/a	ATL	55	9.11	2.33	15	6.1	3.6	0.6	1.9	37	52	-83

PITCHER	yr	t	age	lvl	org	ip	era	whip	bf/g	ctl	dom	cmd	hr/9	h%	s%	bpv
Santillan, Tony	18	R	21	aa	CIN	63	4.54	1.46	24.6	2.4	7.8	3.3	1.4	35	74	68
	19	R	22	aa	CIN	103	6.32	1.84	22.9	5.1	7.4	1.4	0.9	37	60	12
Santos, Antonio	19	R	23	aa	COL	47	8.10	1.62	26.2	2.3	6.7	2.9	1.0	38	40	77
Santos, Luis	18	R	27	aaa	TOR	44	3.83	1.56	9.69	3.1	6.3	2.1	0.5	35	76	59
	19	R	28	aaa	TAM	65	6.41	1.74	9.28	4.4	8.2	1.9	1.6	36	54	46
Santos, Ramon	18	R	24	aa	STL	58	5.91	1.70	7.73	3.8	5.8	1.5	0.9	35	65	33
Saucedo, Tayler	18	L	25	aa	TOR	64	6.70	1.78	26.9	2.7	4.3	1.6	1.5	36	64	-1
	19	L	26	a/a	TOR	85	5.30	1.82	11	4.3	5.8	1.3	0.9	36	66	5
Saupold, Warwick	18	R	28	aaa	DET	54	7.33	1.86	16.9	3.3	5.2	1.6	1.4	37	61	8
Sborz, Josh	18	R	25	a/a	LA	54	4.29	1.38	4.93	3.1	9.8	3.1	0.2	37	66	121
	19	R	26	aaa	LA	50	5.25	1.55	4.75	2.4	9.9	4.1	0.4	42	61	132
Scheetz, Kit	18	L	24	aa	HOU	40	3.48	1.38	6.73	1.9	8.1	4.4	0.6	37	75	120
	19	L	25	a/a	HOU	53	6.64	1.72	7.77	3.6	8.8	2.4	1.7	38	52	79
Schlitter, Craig	18	R	26	a/a	COL	53	6.44	1.70	9.63	4.0	5.3	1.3	2.5	31	69	-22
Scholtens, Jesse	18	R	24	a/a	SD	137	4.54	1.33	21	2.2	6.6	3.0	0.6	33	65	86
	19	R	25	aa	SD	125	7.09	1.77	23.9	3.2	7.5	2.4	1.2	39	52	67
Schreiber, John	18	R	24	aa	DET	58	3.20	1.32	4.9	3.1	7.3	2.4	0.4	32	75	86
	19	R	25	a/a	DET	67	3.32	1.22	5.12	3.5	8.6	2.4	0.9	28	67	77
Schryver, Hunter	19	L	24	a/a	CHW	65	5.16	1.65	7.14	4.2	7.3	1.7	0.7	35	64	35
Schultz, Jaime	18	R	27	aaa	TAM	36	7.69	2.26	5.71	6.4	11.8	1.9	1.5	48	67	50
	19	R	28	aaa	LA	49	6.65	1.81	4.85	4.9	8.8	1.8	0.6	39	58	43
Scioneaux, Tate	18	R	26	aa	PIT	61	6.39	1.78	6.53	3.0	7.8	2.6	1.7	39	67	38
	19	R	27	aa	COL	41	11.35	2.02	6.03	3.2	8.7	2.8	3.2	41	24	89
Scott, Adam	19	L	24	aa	CLE	76	5.78	1.50	23.5	2.9	7.3	2.5	1.5	34	52	71
Scott, Tanner	19	L	25	aaa	BAL	46	3.61	1.24	6.25	3.1	8.8	2.8	0.5	32	66	93
Scott, Tayler	18	R	26	aaa	TEX	62	4.18	1.66	6.33	4.1	5.8	1.4	0.7	34	76	38
	19	R	27	aaa	BAL	51	5.90	1.52	6.71	4.3	9.0	2.1	0.9	34	54	66
Scrubb, Andre	19	R	24	aa	HOU	66	3.99	1.65	7.21	5.0	8.7	1.7	0.6	36	72	39
Seabold, Connor	18	R	22	aa	PHI	60	5.29	1.30	22.6	2.7	8.7	3.2	1.7	30	64	71
	19	R	23	aa	PHI	40	2.98	1.32	23.7	2.4	7.3	3.1	0.6	33	74	85
Seddon, Joel	18	R	26	aa	OAK	118	5.86	1.66	18.9	3.0	4.8	1.6	1.5	34	67	9
Sedlock, Cody	19	R	24	aa	BAL	34	5.22	1.76	17.3	5.9	7.2	1.2	1.1	33	65	-11
Self, Derek	18	R	28	a/a	WAS	60	4.01	1.34	5.68	1.2	4.8	4.1	1.0	32	72	80
	19	R	29	aaa	WAS	76	7.56	1.84	7.41	2.1	4.8	2.3	2.2	38	48	48
Semple, Shawn	19	R	24	a/a	NYY	40	8.15	1.06	23.9	5.4	6.8	1.3	2.1	35	47	-5
Sendelbach, Logan	18	R	24	aa	PIT	70	5.34	1.76	9.17	5.5	4.9	0.9	0.8	32	70	19
Senzatela, Antonio	18	R	23	aaa	COL	39	2.36	1.13	19.4	2.8	7.7	2.8	0.3	29	79	106
	19	R	24	aaa	COL	35	6.24	1.71	22.7	2.5	2.4	1.0	2.0	32	53	-7
Sewald, Paul	19	R	29	aaa	NYM	51	4.48	1.76	5.7	3.0	7.2	2.4	1.2	39	69	65
Shafer, Justin	18	R	26	a/a	TOR	57	1.53	1.28	4.99	3.7	6.1	1.6	0.2	28	88	73
	19	R	27	aaa	TOR	32	4.77	1.46	5.74	2.5	7.6	3.0	1.1	35	60	87
Shaffer, Brian	19	R	23	aa	TAM	72	3.29	1.26	11.8	2.9	7.8	2.7	0.0	33	71	80
Sharp, Sterling	18	R	23	aa	WAS	70	5.22	1.57	23.7	3.4	5.0	1.5	0.9	33	67	31
	19	R	24	aa	WAS	51	5.91	1.74	26	2.8	6.6	2.3	0.3	40	62	61
Shaw, Joe	18	R	25	aa	NYM	66	7.52	1.82	25.5	4.2	5.6	1.3	1.3	35	59	13
	19	R	26	a/a	NYM	42	5.23	1.74	9.11	4.5	8.0	1.8	1.0	37	64	40
Shawaryn, Michael	18	R	24	a/a	BOS	152	4.58	1.32	24.3	2.4	6.3	2.7	0.9	31	66	67
	19	R	25	aaa	BOS	91	6.19	1.63	15.6	5.2	5.9	1.1	1.6	29	53	-16
Sheffield, Jordan	19	R	24	aa	LA	39	4.59	1.64	5.15	7.5	9.3	1.2	0.9	29	67	-16
Sheffield, Justus	18	L	22	a/a	NYY	116	3.18	1.28	19	4.0	8.4	2.1	0.4	29	75	91
	19	L	23	a/a	SEA	133	5.12	1.52	23.1	4.1	8.0	1.9	1.2	32	59	51
Sheller, Walker	18	R	23	aa	KC	51	4.46	1.41	6.17	2.5	3.9	1.5	0.9	30	70	26
Shepherd, Chandler	18	R	26	aaa	BOS	131	5.87	1.74	24	2.7	5.7	2.1	1.2	38	68	30
	19	R	27	aaa	BAL	102	7.95	1.98	22.2	3.8	6.9	1.8	2.1	39	49	39
Sherfy, Jimmie	18	R	27	aaa	ARI	45	1.54	1.16	4.72	3.8	9.0	2.4	0.2	28	87	113
	19	R	28	aaa	ARI	35	3.68	1.63	4.45	5.4	9.5	1.7	0.5	35	74	42
Shew, Anthony	18	R	25	aa	STL	114	5.01	1.54	26.2	2.5	6.0	2.5	1.0	35	69	51
	19	R	26	a/a	STL	69	5.11	1.69	20.8	3.5	7.1	2.0	1.1	37	64	51
Shipley, Braden	18	R	26	aaa	ARI	75	5.42	1.75	11.4	4.0	5.5	1.4	1.2	35	71	17
	19	R	27	aaa	ARI	96	5.89	1.64	14.3	3.4	6.3	1.9	1.6	34	55	40
Shore, Logan	18	R	24	aa	OAK	70	6.29	1.65	24.2	2.4	5.1	2.1	0.9	36	61	38
	19	R	25	aa	DET	97	5.30	1.70	19.1	4.1	4.2	1.0	1.1	32	63	-17
Short, Wyatt	18	L	24	aa	CHC	30	4.26	1.46	5.83	2.6	7.0	2.6	1.4	33	76	51
	19	L	25	a/a	CHC	60	3.91	1.54	6.11	4.4	8.0	1.8	0.6	34	71	42
Shreve, Chasen	19	L	29	aaa	STL	60	4.54	1.44	5.01	4.3	7.4	1.7	1.0	30	62	37
Simms, John	18	R	26	aaa	WAS	64	5.06	1.72	12.1	4.3	6.3	1.4	1.4	34	74	19
Simpson, William	18	R	27	aa	SF	30	2.01	2.00	5	9.6	8.6	0.9	0.0	33	89	76
	19	R	28	aa	SF	30	3.96	1.42	5.55	6.8	9.1	1.3	0.4	26	68	-1
Sims, Lucas	18	R	24	aaa	CIN	102	3.95	1.42	21.6	3.7	8.7	2.4	1.2	32	76	66
	19	R	25	aaa	CIN	79	6.08	1.59	21.8	4.6	10.0	2.2	1.4	35	53	73
Singer, Brady	19	R	23	aa	KC	92	4.75	1.46	24.7	2.8	6.8	2.5	0.9	34	61	66
Singer, Jeff	18	L	25	a/a	PHI	39	5.06	1.37	5.31	5.5	7.4	1.3	0.6	26	62	68
	19	L	26	aa	PHI	63	3.22	1.19	6.03	3.5	8.9	2.5	0.6	28	68	82
Siri, Dalbert	19	R	24	a/a	CLE	49	3.82	1.60	4.73	5.9	7.9	1.3	0.7	31	72	0
Skoglund, Eric	18	L	26	a/a	KC	18	5.28	1.50	19.5	1.1	3.8	3.6	1.6	33	69	38
	19	L	27	a/a	KC	73	8.32	1.93	26.7	2.7	4.5	1.7	1.7	38	47	26
Skubal, Tarik	19	L	23	aa	DET	43	3.09	1.19	19.2	4.1	13.9	3.4	0.6	35	70	158
Slack, Ryne	18	L	26	aa	TEX	50	9.27	2.04	7.17	5.5	5.4	1.0	1.9	35	55	-16
Slania, Dan	18	R	26	aa	SF	71	3.16	1.21	6.1	2.9	6.9	2.4	0.9	28	77	73
Slegers, Aaron	18	R	26	aaa	MIN	86	5.74	1.57	25.2	2.3	4.6	2.0	1.8	33	68	8
	19	R	27	aaa	TAM	113	6.50	1.71	19.7	2.5	5.2	2.1	2.0	35	52	45
Smeltzer, Devin	18	L	23	aa	MIN	97	5.45	1.51	12.7	1.9	6.3	3.3	1.0	36	64	70
	19	L	24	a/a	MIN	105	3.78	1.26	21.4	2.1	7.2	3.5	1.5	30	61	93
Smith, Burch	19	R	29	aaa	SF	93	3.61	1.49	22.3	5.2	7.2	1.4	0.7	29	72	9
Smith, Kevin	19	L	22	aa	NYM	32	4.59	1.45	22.8	4.5	7.1	1.6	0.3	31	64	24
Smith, Riley	19	R	24	a/a	ARI	136	4.99	1.52	23.7	2.4	6.0	2.5	1.3	34	60	60
Snead, Kirby	18	L	24	aa	TOR	44	5.56	1.83	5.71	5.4	6.7	1.2	0.7	36	69	39
	19	L	25	a/a	TOR	64	4.87	1.49	5.54	3.0	7.7	2.6	1.3	34	60	77
Sneed, Cy	18	R	26	aaa	HOU	127	3.91	1.43	20.7	3.5	6.5	1.8	0.4	32	72	66
	19	R	27	aaa	HOU	83	4.97	1.33	18.2	2.7	6.1	2.2	1.6	28	52	54
Solbach, Markus	19	R	28	aa	LA	42	3.74	1.39	22.1	1.9	6.5	3.4	0.3	35	69	83
Sopko, Andrew	18	R	24	aa	LA	54	4.12	1.56	16.9	2.0	6.8	3.4	1.5	36	79	58
	19	R	25	a/a	TOR	91	7.42	1.65	21.5	4.0	5.4	1.4	2.2	30	41	8
Sosebee, David	18	R	25	a/a	NYY	39	4.37	1.72	7.43	4.1	8.6	2.1	1.7	37	80	39
	19	R	26	a/a	NYY	54	4.71	1.58	7.24	3.8	8.8	2.3	1.4	35	63	74
Sotillet, Andres	19	R	22	aa	KC	76	4.51	1.49	9.65	3.7	6.2	1.7	0.8	32	64	31
Soto, Gregory	19	L	24	a/a	DET	38	7.04	1.64	18.9	4.3	7.9	1.8	1.2	34	48	44
Sparkman, Glenn	18	R	26	a/a	KC	103	4.74	1.47	24.6	1.1	5.0	4.4	1.0	35	69	84
Speer, David	18	L	26	aa	CLE	62	5.06	1.59	5.95	2.2	5.7	2.6	0.2	38	66	72
	19	L	27	a/a	CLE	58	2.99	1.40	7.44	3.5	5.3	1.5	1.1	28	74	19
Speier, James	18	R	23	aa	KC	61	4.47	1.75	6.06	2.9	5.8	2.0	0.5	39	74	51
	19	R	24	a/a	KC	63	5.71	1.60	5.94	3.9	8.4	2.1	1.8	34	55	62
Spitzbarth, Shea	18	R	24	a/a	LA	68	4.63	1.26	6.96	3.2	9.6	3.0	1.5	30	68	84
	19	R	25	a/a	LA	66	4.97	1.41	5.37	3.3	10.0	3.0	1.1	35	57	108
Springs, Jeffrey	18	L	26	a/a	TEX	58	5.45	1.48	7.59	3.4	11.7	3.4	0.4	41	61	129
Spurlin, Tyler	19	R	28	aa	MIL	31	3.13	1.32	5.88	4.2	7.0	1.7	0.5	28	73	31
St. John, Locke	18	L	25	aa	TEX	17	5.79	1.72	7.02	4.9	7.1	1.5	2.0	32	72	8
	19	L	26	a/a	TEX	52	5.78	1.51	5.83	4.8	8.5	1.8	1.4	30	53	41
Stallings, Jesse	19	R	25	aa	CIN	33	8.40	1.71	4.99	1.3	4.5	3.5	0.8	39	43	64
Stankiewicz, Teddy	18	R	25	a/a	BOS	151	6.87	1.66	26	2.7	5.4	2.0	1.7	34	61	12
	19	R	26	aaa	BOS	131	5.48	1.69	24.6	2.9	5.6	1.9	2.2	34	58	40
Stapler, Cole	19	R	25	aa	ARI	49	4.16	1.45	19	2.4	5.8	2.4	1.0	33	66	57
Stashak, Cody	18	R	24	aa	MIN	57	3.35	1.21	6.58	2.1	8.7	4.2	0.7	33	74	122
	19	R	25	a/a	MIN	54	4.45	1.24	6.66	1.7	9.8	5.9	1.1	35	56	149
Staumont, Josh	18	R	25	aaa	KC	75	4.45	1.68	8.24	6.5	9.7	1.5	0.5	34	73	79
	19	R	26	aaa	KC	52	3.85	1.47	6.99	6.8	9.8	1.4	0.7	27	69	12
Steele, Justin	19	L	24	aa	CHC	40	7.70	1.99	17.6	5.2	7.8	1.5	0.9	40	55	19
Stephan, Trevor	18	R	23	aa	NYY	84	5.99	1.52	21.5	3.3	8.4	2.5	0.8	36	60	78
	19	R	24	aa	NYY	47	7.13	1.92	18.6	5.2	9.1	1.8	0.8	41	57	43
Stephens, Jackson	18	R	24	aaa	CIN	44	6.81	1.64	12.3	3.5	6.1	1.7	1.0	35	58	35
	19	R	25	aaa	CIN	84	6.86	1.87	8.38	4.5	7.4	1.7	0.9	39	57	30
Stephens, Jordan	18	R	26	a/a	CHW	148	5.76	1.71	24	3.8	6.9	1.8	1.0	37	67	42
	19	R	27	a/a	CLE	90	10.54	2.15	18.7	3.9	6.4	1.6	2.8	40	37	27
Stephenson, Robert	18	R	25	aaa	CIN	113	3.75	1.35	23.6	5.0	9.0	1.8	1.2	27	77	65
Stevens, Tyler	18	R	22	a/a	LAA	49	6.97	1.80	6.89	3.3	10.6	3.2	1.0	45	61	88
	19	R	23	a/a	MIA	57	4.01	1.22	6.42	3.1	7.9	2.5	1.1	28	59	76
Stewart, Brock	18	R	27	aaa	LA	97	3.54	1.32	21.2	2.7	5.9	2.2	0.7	30	75	62
	19	R	28	aaa	TOR	85	10.61	2.31	23	5.3	5.9	1.1	3.1	39	40	-18
Stewart, Kohl	18	R	24	a/a	MIN	110	5.95	1.76	24	2.8	6.6	2.3	0.7	40	65	55
	19	R	25	aaa	MIN	91	6.94	1.76	20.8	4.7	6.3	1.3	1.2	34	52	3
Stinnett, Jake	18	R	26	aa	CHC	52	6.52	1.76	5.69	4.3	7.8	1.8	1.7	36	66	26
	19	R	27	aa	CHC	58	7.81	1.80	8.96	5.3	7.9	1.5	1.3	36	48	17
Stout, Eric	18	L	25	aaa	KC	55	6.08	1.79	6.67	2.2	5.7	2.5	0.9	40	66	46
	19	L	26	a/a	CIN	63	8.36	2.08	14.7	6.1	6.5	1.1	3.0	34	47	-31
Strahan, Wyatt	18	R	25	aa	CIN	120	8.72	2.00	21.4	4.4	5.2	1.2	1.5	37	56	-5
	19	R	26	aa	CIN	56	10.76	2.13	7.96	5.1	5.9	1.2	1.4	40	40	-13
Stull, Cody	18	L	26	aa	OAK	43	6.38	1.96	7.34	3.6	6.5	1.8	0.2	42	65	54
	19	L	27	a/a	OAK	47	3.71	1.44	5.94	3.5	5.8	1.6	0.2	32	71	27
Suarez, Albert	18	R	29	aaa	ARI	64	4.96	1.81	9.58	4.6	5.3	1.2	0.9	35	74	20
Suarez, Andrew	18	L	26	aaa	SF	18	1.07	1.00	23.2	3.4	6.3	1.8	0.0	23	88	95
	19	L	27	aaa	SF	88	7.56	2.02	23.7	3.8	4.4	1.2	1.1	39	56	-3
Suarez, Jose	18	L	20	a/a	LAA	110	4.00	1.41	19.4	3.0	9.2	3.0	0.4	36	70	107
	19	L	21	aaa	LAA	33	3.03	1.13	18.7	4.0	7.5	1.9	0.7	24	68	46
Suarez, Ranger	18	L	23	a/a	PHI	125	3.22	1.30	24.6	2.5	5.4	2.1	0.3	31	75	69
	19	L	24	aaa	PHI	38	6.67	1.50	23.5	2.4	6.7	2.8	2.3	32	41	74
Sulser, Beau	19	R	25	aa	PIT	96	4.14	1.59	12.8	3.4	4.7	1.4	0.5	33	70	10
Sulser, Cole	18	R	28	a/a	CLE	62	5.52	1.51	5.74	2.9	10.4	3.5	0.8	40	63	109
	19	R	29	aaa	TAM	66	4.44	1.43	5.73	3.8	9.5	2.5	0.6	35	64	85
Supak, Trey	18	R	22	aa	MIL	88	3.87	1.36	23	3.1	6.7	2.2	0.6	32	72	71
	19	R	23	a/a	MIL	154	4.73	1.20	23	2.0	6.0	3.0	0.9	29	52	72
Swanson, Erik	18	R	25	a/a	NYY	117	3.44	1.18	21.3	2.5	8.4	3.4	1.1	29	75	96
	19	R	26	aaa	SEA	25	6.09	1.77	11.5	4.4	8.4	1.9	1.9	36	57	50
Swarmer, Matt	18	R	25	aa	CHC	78	5.02	1.30	21.5	1.8	7.1	3.9	1.1	33	63	91
	19	R	26	aaa	CHC	152	7.50	1.82	26.1	3.0	6.4	2.2	2.5	36	46	54
Szkutnik, Trent	18	L	25	aa	DET	46	4.35	1.58	5.99	3.7	7.7	2.1	0.9	35	74	58
	19	L	26	a/a	DET	69	6.58	1.85	7.51	4.8	6.7	1.4	1.3	36	57	8
Takahashi, Rodrigo	18	R	21	aa	ARI	73	5.43	1.26	21.3	2.4	8.3	3.4	1.4	30	60	82
	19	R	22	aa	ARI	120	5.20	1.46	23.4	3.2	6.7	2.1	1.1	32	57	52
Tapia, Domingo	18	R	27	a/a	CIN	65	5.03	1.69	6.11	4.6	5.0	1.1	0.8	32	71	26
	19	R	28	aaa	BOS	66	7.71	2.07	7.34	5.0	5.2	1.0	1.4	38	55	-23
Tarpley, Stephen	18	L	25	a/a	NYY	71	2.58	1.12	7.8	3.6	7.4	2.0	0.5	25	79	86
	19	L	26	aaa	NYY	33	3.80	1.35	7.7	3.9	7.4	1.9	1.1	29	66	46
Tate, Dillon	18	R	24	aa	BAL	124	4.80	1.33	23.4	2.5	5.6	2.3	0.8	31	64	57
	19	R	25	a/a	BAL	44	4.05	1.22	8.51	2.2	5.9	2.7	1.3	28	58	65
Taveras, Jose	18	R	25	aa	PHI	21	6.49	1.80	16.3	4.4	6.1	1.4	2.0	34	68	-3
	19	R	26	a/a	PHI	58	6.91	1.66	15.3	3.0	4.7	1.6	1.7	33	48	21
Taylor, Ben	18	R	26	aaa	CLE	58	3.36	1.09	4.93	1.6	8.6	5.5	1.0	30	73	144
	19	R	27	aaa	ARI	56	5.62	1.75	5.56	4.1	8.7	2.1	2.1	36	59	63
Taylor, Blake	19	L	24	a/a	NYM	40	2.33	1.07	8.22	2.9	8.8	3.1	0.5	27	74	99
Taylor, Corey	18	R	25	a/a	NYM	67	3.21	1.52	6.48	2.3	6.3	2.8	0.2	37	78	81
	19	R	26	aaa	NYM	19	2.96	1.67	8.53	3.5	5.9	1.7	0.0	37	80	29
Taylor, Cory	18	R	25	aa	SF	56	4.94	1.65	22.9	4.6	4.0	0.9	1.2	30	73	3
Taylor, Curtis	18	R	23	aa	TAM	62	2.80	1.05	8.03	3.8	9.5	2.5	0.9	23	78	100
	19	R	24	aa	TAM	19	3.97	1.21	5.17	2.6	6.5	2.5	0.0	30	64	64
Tenuta, Matt	18	L	25	a/a	SEA	60	3.56	1.54	6.9	3.6	7.9	2.2	0.2	37	75	87
	19	L	26	a/a	SEA	60	4.93	1.44	6.12	3.1	7.2	2.3	1.5	32	57	64

PITCHER	yr	t	age	lvl	org	ip	era	whip	bf/g	ctl	dom	cmd	hr/9	h%	s%	bpv
Terrero,Franco	18	R	23	aa	KC	65	6.63	1.95	7.07	5.5	7.0	1.3	1.6	36	68	12
	19	R	24	aa	KC	45	7.07	2.08	5.14	5.3	7.7	1.4	1.2	41	60	12
Tetreault,Jacksoı	19	R	23	aa	WAS	87	6.95	1.95	23.1	4.6	5.5	1.2	1.2	37	58	-7
Thompson,Cory	19	R	25	aa	CIN	37	5.77	1.90	5.31	3.9	5.6	1.4	2.7	35	60	14
Thompson,Jake	18	R	24	aaa	MIL	53	4.32	1.46	6.89	4.6	7.9	1.7	0.9	30	72	62
Thompson,Keega	18	R	23	aa	CHC	62	5.15	1.62	21.2	3.3	6.6	2.0	0.5	37	67	61
Thompson,Zach	18	R	25	aa	CHW	40	1.93	1.42	8.08	4.7	7.5	1.6	0.9	29	92	57
	19	R	26	a/a	CHW	77	7.16	1.74	7.82	3.1	8.0	2.6	2.4	37	46	78
Thornton,Trent	18	R	25	aaa	HOU	125	4.39	1.24	21.2	2.0	7.2	3.5	0.9	31	66	92
Thorpe,Lewis	18	L	23	a/a	MIN	131	4.62	1.43	21.5	2.6	8.8	3.5	1.4	35	72	82
	19	L	24	aaa	MIN	97	6.00	1.42	20.6	2.5	9.0	3.6	1.5	35	47	113
Tice,Ty	19	R	23	a/a	TOR	59	3.16	1.42	5.46	4.7	8.2	1.7	0.4	31	75	39
Tinoco,Jesus	18	R	23	aa	COL	141	6.94	1.64	24.2	2.7	6.7	2.5	2.1	35	62	19
	19	R	24	aaa	COL	34	4.39	1.60	5.19	4.7	4.8	1.0	1.2	29	67	-22
Tols,Josh	18	L	29	aa	PHI	33	4.21	1.11	5.64	5.5	8.9	1.6	1.1	17	65	81
Torres,Joshua	18	R	24	a/a	NYM	55	2.99	1.40	5.82	3.3	9.5	2.8	0.7	35	81	96
	19	R	25	aa	NYM	29	10.82	2.05	8.31	2.8	7.7	2.7	3.2	41	29	80
Torres-Costa,Qu	18	L	24	a/a	MIL	55	1.57	1.03	4.93	4.2	9.0	2.2	0.0	24	83	121
Torrez,Daury	18	R	25	a/a	CHC	77	5.16	1.62	10.4	2.8	4.8	1.7	0.9	35	69	30
Toussaint,Touki	19	R	23	aaa	ATL	41	9.39	2.18	20.6	6.3	8.0	1.3	1.2	41	49	-8
Toussaint,Touki	18	R	22	a/a	ATL	137	2.95	1.23	23.1	3.4	9.1	2.7	0.5	31	77	105
Tropeano,Nichola	19	R	29	aaa	LAA	81	5.81	1.63	21.3	3.4	7.1	2.1	1.3	35	56	53
Tseng,Jen-Ho	18	R	24	aaa	CHC	137	7.03	1.63	23.5	3.0	6.3	2.1	1.4	35	57	33
Tully,Tanner	19	L	25	a/a	CLE	146	6.22	1.71	25.5	2.0	4.4	2.2	0.9	37	57	43
Turley,Josh	18	L	28	a/a	DET	70	7.10	1.95	24	7.3	5.2	0.7	0.3	33	61	34
Turnbull,Spencer	18	R	26	a/a	DET	114	5.72	1.54	23.7	3.8	7.4	2.0	0.4	35	60	72
Turner,Colton	18	L	27	a/a	CHW	66	3.05	1.22	7.23	3.2	7.1	2.2	0.9	27	79	69
	19	L	28	aaa	CHW	95	7.04	1.75	11.7	3.6	7.5	2.1	1.8	37	49	56
Turner,Jacob	18	R	27	aaa	DET	104	5.92	1.76	18.3	3.7	4.8	1.3	1.2	35	68	11
Uceta,Adonis	18	R	24	aa	NYM	26	4.76	1.56	7.15	4.3	8.2	1.9	0.7	35	70	68
	19	R	25	a/a	NYM	59	2.83	1.31	6.43	3.2	7.4	2.3	0.7	31	74	66
Uceta,Edwin	19	R	21	aa	LA	73	4.06	1.43	19.4	3.9	8.3	2.1	0.7	32	66	62
Underwood Jr.,Dı	18	R	24	aaa	CHC	120	5.07	1.51	19.2	2.8	6.5	2.3	0.6	35	66	65
	19	R	25	aaa	CHC	83	6.49	1.78	11.6	4.9	8.3	1.7	1.0	37	57	35
Unsworth,Dylan	18	R	26	a/a	LAA	104	6.39	1.66	19.4	2.0	5.1	2.5	1.5	36	64	26
Urquidy,Jose	19	R	24	a/a	HOU	103	5.70	1.32	21.3	1.9	9.9	5.1	1.8	35	44	144
Valdez,Bryan	19	L	25	aa	ARI	49	6.07	1.73	20.3	3.0	3.2	1.1	1.5	33	57	-6
Valdez,Dauris	19	R	24	aa	SD	56	5.36	1.65	5.83	5.0	9.0	1.8	1.9	32	58	44
Valdez,Framber	18	L	25	a/a	HOU	105	4.57	1.38	20.1	2.7	9.0	3.4	0.6	36	67	105
	19	L	26	aaa	HOU	45	3.77	1.15	17.9	3.5	11.2	3.2	0.7	30	61	124
Valdez,Gabriel	19	R	24	a/a	HOU	35	5.92	1.49	12.6	5.1	6.3	1.2	2.8	23	45	-7
Valdez,Jose	18	R	28	aaa	SF	50	5.48	1.75	6.19	6.5	7.9	1.2	0.5	34	67	61
Valdez,Phillips	18	R	27	a/a	WAS	137	3.71	1.50	19.1	3.4	5.2	1.6	0.8	32	77	37
	19	R	28	aaa	TEX	80	6.33	1.89	14.5	4.7	5.3	1.1	1.4	35	59	-12
Vargas,Cesar	18	R	27	a/a	WAS	99	7.39	2.06	24.2	4.6	5.0	1.1	1.5	38	65	-8
Vargas,Emilio	18	R	22	aa	ARI	37	4.53	1.15	24.6	1.9	6.3	3.3	1.4	27	65	69
	19	R	23	aa	ARI	87	5.37	1.37	21.5	2.7	6.1	2.2	1.3	30	51	54
Varner,Seth	18	L	26	aa	CIN	120	4.71	1.40	20.3	2.7	6.1	2.3	2.0	29	74	24
Vasquez,Andrew	18	L	25	a/a	MIN	38	1.62	1.08	7.1	2.0	13.2	6.5	0.3	38	86	214
	19	L	26	a/a	MIN	36	7.87	2.18	6.24	9.6	8.7	0.9	0.3	37	59	-85
Vasquez,Kelvin	18	R	25	a/a	ATL	50	7.14	1.72	7.58	5.7	5.9	1.0	0.9	31	57	31
Vasquez,Pedro	18	R	23	aa	PIT	64	6.23	1.56	21.6	2.6	5.3	2.1	1.4	33	62	27
	19	R	24	a/a	PIT	133	4.18	1.34	21.3	2.5	5.5	2.2	0.7	31	60	51
Vera,Eduardo	18	R	24	aa	PIT	97	4.55	1.26	23.3	2.2	5.1	2.3	1.1	28	67	47
	19	R	25	a/a	WAS	135	9.10	1.83	24.2	2.7	4.9	1.8	1.8	37	38	32
VerHagen,Drew	18	R	28	aaa	DET	34	2.40	1.06	13.3	3.1	9.8	3.1	0.0	29	75	139
	19	R	29	aaa	DET	53	6.64	1.87	22.6	2.6	6.2	2.4	1.2	40	57	60
Verrett,Logan	19	R	29	aa	OAK	35	5.59	1.29	20.6	1.2	6.3	5.2	1.3	32	46	99
Vest,Will	19	R	24	a/a	DET	35	6.55	1.77	7.03	3.0	5.7	1.9	1.7	36	54	39
Vieaux,Cam	18	L	25	aa	PIT	89	4.54	1.28	24.4	1.8	5.7	3.1	1.1	30	67	66
	19	L	26	a/a	PIT	141	4.93	1.54	23.7	4.2	5.9	1.4	1.6	29	60	10
Villines,Stephen	19	R	24	a/a	NYM	61	3.45	1.51	6.45	3.5	6.9	2.0	0.8	34	73	49
Vines,Jace	18	R	24	aa	KC	43	8.06	1.81	22.2	3.3	4.7	1.4	1.1	37	54	12
	19	R	25	aa	KC	51	7.92	2.14	23	4.2	5.6	1.3	1.1	41	56	4
Viza,Tyler	18	R	24	a/a	PHI	85	3.56	1.39	15	2.8	7.1	2.5	0.6	33	75	76
	19	R	25	a/a	PHI	76	9.43	2.09	18.7	2.9	7.0	2.4	2.8	42	41	66
Vizcaino,Raffi	19	R	24	aa	SF	40	6.39	1.73	6.86	5.8	6.7	1.1	0.6	33	64	-19
Vizcaya,Anthony	19	R	26	aa	MIN	46	1.18	1.43	7.52	4.6	7.0	1.6	0.5	30	90	27
Voelker,Paul	18	R	26	aaa	DET	68	4.62	1.47	6.79	3.6	5.9	1.6	1.2	30	72	32
Voth,Austin	18	R	26	aaa	WAS	127	5.98	1.54	23.1	3.1	6.5	2.1	1.2	34	62	43
	19	R	27	a/a	WAS	74	6.17	1.64	22.1	2.3	7.4	3.2	1.3	38	54	89
Waddell,Brandon	18	L	24	a/a	PIT	138	4.30	1.51	21.4	3.7	5.4	1.5	0.5	32	71	47
	19	L	25	a/a	PIT	98	8.75	1.94	13	5.0	8.0	1.6	1.2	39	46	26
Wade,Konner	19	R	28	a/a	BOS	101	4.13	1.51	24.3	1.7	4.3	2.6	0.6	35	68	50
Wagner,Tyler	18	R	27	a/a	TEX	104	6.59	1.90	19.6	3.6	3.8	1.1	1.5	36	67	-13
Waguespack,Jac	18	R	25	a/a	TOR	124	6.38	1.73	20.2	3.6	6.5	1.8	0.6	37	61	49
	19	R	26	aaa	TOR	54	7.16	1.85	21.1	4.6	6.9	1.5	1.9	35	52	17
Walker,Jeremy	19	R	24	a/a	ATL	84	4.15	1.31	10.9	1.3	7.1	5.4	0.4	36	64	111
Walker,Matt	18	R	24	aa	SEA	62	4.33	1.46	6.81	3.3	7.1	2.2	0.8	33	71	63
Walsh,Connor	18	R	26	aa	CHW	30	14.81	2.74	8.85	6.7	10.0	1.5	2.6	50	45	-14
	19	R	27	a/a	CHW	63	7.12	1.93	6.82	6.0	7.3	1.2	1.0	36	56	-12
Walter,Corey	18	R	26	aa	OAK	76	7.50	1.82	13.6	3.3	3.6	1.1	0.7	36	57	10
Wantz,Andrew	19	R	24	aa	LAA	48	9.72	2.12	18.2	5.4	8.6	1.6	3.1	39	39	27
Warner,Austin	18	L	24	a/a	STL	68	5.27	1.80	24.2	3.8	5.2	1.4	1.3	35	73	11
	19	L	25	a/a	STL	143	5.69	1.67	24.7	3.5	7.2	2.0	1.7	35	57	52
Warren,Art	18	R	25	aa	SEA	17	1.91	1.54	5.36	7.6	9.8	1.3	0.0	28	86	102
	19	R	26	aa	SEA	33	2.58	1.42	4.85	4.2	9.3	2.2	0.4	33	79	70

PITCHER	yr	t	age	lvl	org	ip	era	whip	bf/g	ctl	dom	cmd	hr/9	h%	s%	bpv
Watkins,Spenser	19	R	27	a/a	DET	121	9.92	1.98	24.3	3.2	5.9	1.8	2.6	38	35	37
Webb,Jacob	18	R	25	a/a	ATL	57	3.95	1.18	4.51	3.7	8.7	2.4	1.3	25	72	73
Webb,Logan	18	R	22	aa	SF	32	4.39	1.40	22.7	3.1	6.3	2.0	1.0	31	71	51
	19	R	23	a/a	SF	49	2.69	1.45	23.3	2.4	8.2	3.5	0.4	37	79	102
Weber,Ryan	18	R	28	aaa	TAM	116	3.71	1.53	20.2	2.0	5.1	2.5	0.8	35	78	51
	19	R	29	aaa	BOS	78	6.85	1.90	23	3.4	5.2	1.5	1.4	38	56	21
Weems,Jordan	18	R	26	a/a	BOS	47	5.68	1.89	6.18	5.4	6.8	1.2	0.9	36	70	31
	19	R	27	a/a	BOS	57	6.43	1.93	6.63	5.9	8.2	1.4	0.4	39	62	5
Weickel,Walker	19	R	26	aa	TEX	72	5.77	1.58	7.37	4.5	5.9	1.3	1.2	31	56	3
Weigel,Patrick	19	R	25	a/a	ATL	81	4.07	1.39	12.2	5.2	6.3	1.2	1.3	24	64	-9
Weiman,Blake	19	L	24	a/a	PIT	33	3.71	1.12	5.47	2.4	7.4	3.1	1.3	26	58	87
Weir,T.J.	18	R	27	a/a	SD	73	3.30	1.29	6.84	3.4	6.2	1.8	0.5	29	75	67
	19	R	28	aa	SD	42	8.39	2.59	25.3	6.3	7.1	1.1	0.3	48	64	-23
Weiss,Zack	18	R	26	a/a	CIN	20	7.30	2.19	6.33	9.6	7.3	0.8	1.8	32	69	3
	19	R	27	a/a	MIN	30	9.57	2.19	9.53	5.2	6.8	1.3	2.0	40	46	0
Wells,Alex	19	L	22	aa	BAL	138	3.97	1.26	23.5	1.7	5.7	3.4	0.8	31	62	76
Wendelken,Jeffre	18	R	25	a/a	OAK	50	3.46	1.34	6.33	3.6	10.7	3.0	0.9	34	77	104
	19	R	26	aaa	OAK	40	6.44	1.87	6.29	4.4	7.6	1.8	1.8	38	57	38
Wentz,Joey	19	L	22	aa	DET	130	6.02	1.46	22.3	3.6	7.9	2.2	1.5	31	48	62
Whalen,Rob	18	R	24	a/a	SEA	106	6.12	1.77	22.1	3.4	7.4	2.2	0.5	40	64	62
White,Mitchell	18	R	24	aa	LA	106	4.84	1.47	20.7	2.6	6.3	2.4	1.0	34	69	54
	19	R	25	a/a	LA	95	6.09	1.45	17.7	2.9	8.2	2.9	1.7	33	46	88
Whitehouse,Matt	18	L	27	a/a	CLE	86	5.69	1.89	11.6	5.6	6.2	1.1	1.0	35	71	25
	19	L	28	a/a	COL	82	7.91	1.99	12.3	5.1	7.1	1.4	1.3	39	52	9
Whitley,Forrest	18	R	21	aa	HOU	27	4.48	1.03	13.1	3.6	9.9	2.8	0.8	24	56	113
	19	R	22	a/a	HOU	49	10.53	1.93	16.7	6.2	10.4	1.7	2.3	37	30	37
Whitley,Kodi	19	R	24	a/a	STL	65	2.01	1.19	5.57	2.3	8.2	3.5	0.4	32	80	102
Whitlock,Garrett	19	R	23	aa	NYY	71	4.12	1.53	22.1	2.5	6.2	2.5	0.7	35	69	61
Wick,Rowan	18	R	26	a/a	SD	56	2.92	1.34	4.78	5.0	8.3	1.7	0.5	28	79	82
	19	R	27	aaa	CHC	35	2.45	1.21	5.23	2.7	8.8	3.3	0.9	31	75	104
Widener,Taylor	18	R	24	aa	ARI	138	3.34	1.16	21.1	2.9	9.5	3.3	0.8	30	74	111
	19	R	25	aaa	ARI	101	7.66	1.76	20.1	3.4	7.8	2.3	1.7	38	46	65
Wiles,Collin	18	R	24	aa	TEX	22	7.60	1.74	25.4	2.3	8.5	3.7	2.6	39	62	38
	19	R	25	aa	TEX	31	8.59	1.69	15.5	3.2	5.0	1.6	2.2	33	34	22
Williams,Austen	18	R	26	a/a	WAS	70	1.55	0.98	8.35	2.4	9.0	3.8	0.0	28	82	148
Williams,Devin	19	R	25	a/a	MIL	59	2.94	1.33	7.24	5.1	10.4	2.1	0.6	30	74	68
Williams,Garrett	18	L	24	aa	SF	83	7.48	2.13	12.5	6.9	6.5	1.0	0.6	38	63	31
	19	L	25	aa	SF	110	5.59	1.72	17.2	5.9	7.0	1.2	0.6	33	63	-14
Williams,Ronnie	19	R	23	aa	STL	34	5.19	1.70	6.15	5.5	7.9	1.4	1.7	32	62	12
Williams,Taylor	19	R	28	aaa	MIL	54	3.54	1.34	4.89	3.8	7.4	1.9	1.6	27	66	48
Wilson,Bryse	18	R	21	a/a	ATL	99	5.27	1.40	20.9	2.5	9.2	3.6	0.9	36	63	102
	19	R	22	aaa	ATL	121	4.37	1.38	24.2	1.9	7.4	3.8	1.0	35	62	99
Wilson,Steven	19	R	25	aaa	SD	35	4.24	1.42	5.93	5.5	8.7	1.6	1.1	27	64	26
Wilson,Tommy	19	R	23	aa	NYM	69	6.91	1.45	22.7	2.6	7.0	2.7	1.8	32	39	74
Windle,Tom	18	L	26	aaa	PHI	54	5.47	1.67	4.85	5.1	7.2	1.4	1.3	32	70	32
	19	L	27	aaa	PHI	52	5.17	1.64	5.55	5.9	7.2	1.2	0.4	32	64	-11
Winkelman,Alex	18	L	24	aa	HOU	79	3.96	1.73	11.3	6.8	7.7	1.1	0.4	32	77	61
Winkler,Daniel	19	R	29	aaa	SF	32	3.86	1.73	4.89	7.5	5.9	0.8	0.6	28	74	-78
Wisler,Matthew	18	R	26	aaa	CIN	91	5.01	1.55	19	1.9	6.9	3.7	0.8	38	68	86
Wojciechowski,As	18	R	30	aaa	CHW	120	6.30	1.57	21.1	3.4	7.1	2.1	2.7	31	68	2
	19	R	31	aaa	CLE	86	5.28	1.51	24.9	4.0	6.3	1.6	2.8	26	51	24
Woodford,Jake	18	R	22	a/a	STL	145	5.22	1.56	22.7	3.5	5.3	1.5	1.0	32	68	29
	19	R	23	aaa	STL	153	4.75	1.38	24.8	4.2	6.4	1.5	1.3	27	57	19
Woodruff,Brando	18	R	25	aaa	MIL	72	4.15	1.44	18.1	3.8	7.0	1.8	1.0	31	74	52
Wotherspoon,Ma	18	R	27	aaa	BAL	94	6.57	1.79	11.1	4.2	7.6	1.8	1.8	36	66	22
	19	R	28	aaa	DET	71	7.82	1.77	9.06	4.0	6.9	1.7	1.9	35	44	34
Wright,Daniel	18	R	27	aa	CIN	152	5.92	1.55	23.7	2.5	5.0	2.0	2.1	31	68	2
Wright,Kyle	18	R	23	a/a	ATL	140	4.32	1.35	21.7	3.2	7.1	2.2	0.6	31	68	74
	19	R	24	aaa	ATL	113	5.51	1.48	23.2	2.9	7.5	2.6	1.2	34	55	74
Wright,Mike	19	R	29	aaa	SEA	58	6.39	1.62	17.2	2.9	6.8	2.4	0.7	37	54	62
Wynkoop,Jack	18	L	25	aa	COL	82	9.76	2.21	25.9	2.1	3.1	1.5	1.8	42	56	-32
	19	L	26	aa	COL	149	6.46	1.71	28.1	1.7	4.5	2.6	2.0	36	52	53
Yacabonis,Jimmy	18	R	26	aaa	BAL	76	5.96	1.50	15.6	4.2	5.7	1.3	1.0	30	60	34
	19	R	27	aaa	BAL	24	5.79	2.03	6.85	6.2	6.2	1.0	0.9	37	67	-37
Yamamoto,Jorda	18	R	22	aa	MIA	17	2.42	1.02	21.7	2.1	10.7	5.1	0.5	31	78	168
	19	R	23	aa	MIA	66	5.61	1.50	23.8	4.0	7.4	1.9	1.2	32	54	45
Yardley,Eric	18	R	28	a/a	SD	63	4.76	1.56	5.78	2.9	4.1	1.4	0.6	33	69	30
	19	R	29	aaa	SD	65	3.11	1.32	6.28	2.1	5.3	2.6	0.4	32	73	58
Ynoa,Huascar	19	R	21	a/a	ATL	89	7.31	1.80	18	4.2	8.1	1.9	2.0	37	49	51
Young,Alex	18	L	25	a/a	ARI	132	5.41	1.52	19.8	2.6	6.0	2.3	0.9	35	65	52
	19	L	26	aaa	ARI	56	5.79	1.70	12.7	4.0	8.1	2.0	0.8	38	60	55
Young,Danny	18	L	24	aa	TOR	58	5.22	1.65	6.51	3.1	6.1	2.0	0.5	37	67	50
	19	L	25	a/a	TOR	51	3.81	1.59	5.96	5.1	6.0	1.2	0.7	31	72	-12
Ysla,Luis	18	L	26	a/a	BAL	96	6.80	1.93	13.9	5.9	7.3	1.2	1.4	36	66	19
	19	L	27	aaa	BAL	87	8.36	2.07	19.4	6.2	6.4	1.0	1.8	36	50	-35
Zambrano,Jesus	19	R	23	aa	OAK	46	1.49	1.34	6.87	2.6	5.3	2.0	0.2	32	87	43
Zamora,Daniel	18	L	25	aa	NYM	53	3.97	1.12	5.25	2.9	9.8	3.4	0.5	30	64	125
	19	L	26	aaa	NYM	30	5.25	1.30	4.26	2.2	9.0	4.0	0.3	36	54	120
Zanghi,Joseph	18	R	24	a/a	NYM	31	5.58	1.41	6.94	3.1	6.4	2.1	0.5	32	58	66
	19	R	25	a/a	NYM	66	3.42	1.45	7.89	4.7	6.5	1.4	0.3	30	73	7
Zastryzny,Rob	18	L	26	aaa	CHC	56	4.54	1.52	7.36	4.8	6.4	1.3	0.9	30	71	43
	19	L	27	a/a	LA	115	6.94	1.82	23.3	3.1	6.4	2.1	1.6	38	53	50
Zeuch,T.J.	18	R	23	aa	TOR	120	3.92	1.45	24.4	2.4	5.1	2.1	0.6	33	73	53
	19	R	24	aaa	TOR	78	4.92	1.53	26.1	3.9	3.7	1.0	0.8	29	62	-21
Zimmer,Kyle	19	R	28	aaa	KC	54	5.61	1.75	6.67	6.1	6.4	1.0	1.1	31	62	-32
Zimmermann,Brı	18	L	23	aa	BAL	50	4.50	1.63	20.2	4.6	6.2	1.4	1.0	32	74	33
	19	L	24	a/a	BAL	142	4.11	1.51	24.7	3.5	6.8	1.9	0.9	33	68	46

LEADERBOARDS

This section provides rankings of projected skills indicators for 2020. Rather than take shots in the dark predicting league leaders in the exact number of home runs, or stolen bases, or strikeouts, the Forecaster's Leaderboards focus on the component elements of each skill.

For batters, we've ranked the top players in terms of pure power, speed, and batting average skill, breaking each down in a number of different ways. For pitchers, we rank some of the key base skills, differentiating between starters and relievers, and provide a few interesting cuts that might uncover some late round sleepers. Plus, some potential gainers/faders lists in several categories.

These are clearly not exhaustive lists of sorts and filters—drop us a note if you see something we should consider for next year's book. Also, the database at BaseballHQ.com allows you to construct your own custom sorts and filters. Finally, remember that these are just tools. Some players will appear on multiple lists—even mutually exclusive lists—so you have to assess what makes most sense and make decisions for your specific application.

Power

Top PX, 400+ AB: Top power skills among projected full-time players.

Top PX, –300 AB: Top power skills among projected part-time players; possible end-game options are here.

Position Scarcity: See which positions have deepest power options.

Top PX, ct% over 75%: Top power skills among the top contact hitters. Best pure power options here.

Top PX, ct% under 70%: Top power skills among the worst contact hitters; free-swingers who might be prone to streakiness and lower BAs.

Top PX, FB% over 40%: Top power skills among the most extreme fly ball hitters. Most likely to convert their power into home runs.

Top PX, FB% under 35%: Top power skills among those with lesser fly ball tendencies. There may be more downside to their home run potential.

Speed

Top Spd, 400+ AB: Top speed skills among projected full-time players.

Top Spd, -300 AB: Top speed skills among projected part-time players; possible end-game options here.

Position Scarcity: See which positions have deepest speed options.

Top Spd, OB% .330 and above: Top speed skills among those who get on base most often. Best opportunities for stolen bases here.

Top Spd, OB% under .300: Top speed skills among those who have trouble getting on base; worth watching if they can improve OB%.

Top Spd, SBO% over 20%: Top speed skills among those who get the green light most often. Most likely to convert their speed into stolen bases.

Top Spd, SBO% under 15%: Top speed skills among those who are currently not running; sleeper SBs here if given more opportunities.

Batting Average

Top ct%, 400+ AB: Top contact skills among projected full-time players. Contact is strongly correlated to higher BAs.

Top ct%, -300 AB: Top contact skills among projected part-time players; possible end-gamers here.

Low ct%, 400+ AB: The poorest contact skills among projected full-time players. Potential BA killers.

Top ct%, bb% over 9%: Top contact skills among the most patient hitters. Best batting average upside here.

Top ct%, bb% under 6%: Top contact skills among the least patient hitters; free-swingers who might be prone to streakiness or lower BAs.

Top ct%, GB% over 50%: Top contact skills among the most extreme ground ball hitters. A ground ball has a higher chance of becoming a hit than a non-HR fly ball so there may be some batting average upside here.

Top ct%, GB% under 40%: Top contact skills from those with lesser ground ball tendencies. These players make contact but hit more fly balls, which tend to convert to hits at a lower rate than GB.

Potential Gainers and Faders

These charts look to identify upcoming changes in performance by highlighting 2019 results that were in conflict with their corresponding skill indicators. Use these as a check on recency bias, as players here could compile stats in the upcoming season that look every different than the one just completed. Additional details are provided on the page in which the charts appear.

Pitching Skills

Top Command: Leaders in projected K/BB rates.

Top Control: Leaders in fewest projected walks allowed.

Top Dominance: Leaders in projected strikeout rate.

Top Ground Ball Rate: GB pitchers tend to have lower ERAs (and higher WHIP) than fly ball pitchers.

Top Fly Ball Rate: FB pitchers tend to have higher ERAs (and lower WHIP) than ground ball pitchers.

High GB, Low Dom: GB pitchers tend to have lower K rates, but these are the most extreme examples.

High GB, High Dom: The best at dominating hitters and keeping the ball down. These are the pitchers who keep runners off the bases and batted balls in the park, a skills combination that is the most valuable a pitcher can own.

Lowest xERA: Leaders in projected skills-based ERA.

Top BPV: Two lists of top skilled pitchers. For starters, those projected to be rotation regulars (180+ IP) and fringe starters with skill (<150 IP). For relievers, those projected to be frontline closers (10+ saves) and high-skilled bullpen fillers (<9 saves).

Risk Management

These lists include players who've accumulated the most days on the disabled list over the past five years (Grade "F" in Health) and whose performance was the most consistent over the past three years. Also listed are the most reliable batters and pitchers overall, with a focus on positional and skills reliability. As a reminder, reliability in this context is not tied to skill level; it is a gauge of which players manage to accumulate playing time and post consistent output from year to year, whether that output is good or bad.

Daily Fantasy Indicators

Players splits, teams and park factors designed to give you an edge in DFS.

BATTER SKILLS RANKING - Power

TOP PX, 400+ AB

NAME	POS	PX
Gallo,Joey	7 8	215
Sano,Miguel	5	185
Trout,Mike	8	170
Judge,Aaron	9	164
Thames,Eric	3	162
Alvarez,Yordan	0	160
Alonso,Peter	3	160
Yelich,Christian	9	157
Hernandez,Teoscar	7 8	155
Schwarber,Kyle	7	154
Sanchez,Gary	2	154
Olson,Matt	3	152
Bellinger,Cody	3 8 9	150
Stanton,Giancarlo	7	149
Chapman,Matt	5	148
Martinez,J.D.	0 9	148
Muncy,Max	3 4 5	147
Cruz,Nelson	0	145
Harper,Bryce	9	145
Story,Trevor	6	142
Renfroe,Hunter	7 9	142
Donaldson,Josh	5	140
Hoskins,Rhys	3	140
Tatis Jr.,Fernando	6	139
Voit,Luke	0 3	138
Soler,Jorge	0 9	137
Aquino,Aristides	9	137
Tellez,Rowdy	0 3	136
Hiura,Keston	4	136
Grichuk,Randal	8 9	136
Soto,Juan	7	136
Reyes,Franmil	0 9	135
Acuna,Ronald	7 8 9	135
Suarez,Eugenio	5	135
Davis,Khris	0	135
Encarnacion,Edwin	0 3	135
Upton,Justin	7	134
Laureano,Ramon	8	134
Baez,Javier	6	134
Freeman,Freddie	3	134

TOP PX, 300 or fewer AB

NAME	POS	PX
Cordero,Franchy	8	145
Happ,Ian	7	138
Duvall,Adam	7	136
Walsh,Jared	3	136
Murphy,Tom	2	136
Adams,Matt	3	132
Cespedes,Yoenis	0	131
Luplow,Jordan	7 9	130
Barreto,Franklin	4	129
Cave,Jake	8 9	125
Tauchman,Mike	7	125
O Hearn,Ryan	3	125
Fraley,Jake	8	125
Thaiss,Matt	5	125
Miller,Brad	5	124
Bird,Gregory	3	122
Zunino,Mike	2	121
Dalbec,Bobby	0	120
Hicks,Aaron	8	118
Beckham,Tim	6	116
Brown,Seth	7	116
Marisnick,Jake	8	116
Carlson,Dylan	7	116

POSITIONAL SCARCITY

NAME	POS	PX
Alvarez,Yordan	DH	160
Martinez,J.D.	2	148
Cruz,Nelson	3	145
Ohtani,Shohei	4	140
Voit,Luke	5	138
Soler,Jorge	6	137
Sanchez,Gary	CA	154
Garver,Mitch	2	144
Murphy,Tom	3	136
Contreras,Willson	4	127
Chirinos,Robinson	5	126
Smith,Will	6	125
Zunino,Mike	7	121
Grandal,Yasmani	8	119
Thames,Eric	1B	162
Alonso,Peter	2	160
Olson,Matt	3	152
Bellinger,Cody	4	150
Muncy,Max	5	147
Hoskins,Rhys	6	140
Voit,Luke	7	138
Tellez,Rowdy	8	136
Walsh,Jared	9	136
Encarnacion,Edwin	10	135
Muncy,Max	2B	147
Lowe,Brandon	2	144
Hiura,Keston	3	136
Odor,Rougned	4	130
Barreto,Franklin	5	129
Chavis,Michael	6	123
Biggio,Cavan	7	123
McMahon,Ryan	8	120
Sano,Miguel	3B	185
Chapman,Matt	2	148
Muncy,Max	3	147
Donaldson,Josh	4	140
Suarez,Eugenio	5	135
Bryant,Kris	6	131
Rendon,Anthony	7	129
Carpenter,Matt	8	129
Devers,Rafael	9	128
Dozier,Hunter	10	127
Story,Trevor	SS	142
Tatis Jr.,Fernando	2	139
Baez,Javier	3	134
Correa,Carlos	4	130
Bichette,Bo	5	127
Bregman,Alex	6	118
Torres,Gleyber	7	118
DeJong,Paul	8	117
Gallo,Joey	OF	215
Trout,Mike	2	170
Judge,Aaron	3	164
Yelich,Christian	4	157
Hernandez,Teoscar	5	155
Schwarber,Kyle	6	154
Bellinger,Cody	7	150
Stanton,Giancarlo	8	149
Martinez,J.D.	9	148
Cordero,Franchy	10	145
Harper,Bryce	11	145
Renfroe,Hunter	12	142
Happ,Ian	13	138
Soler,Jorge	14	137
Aquino,Aristides	15	137
Duvall,Adam	16	136

TOP PX, ct% over 75%

NAME	ct%	PX
Yelich,Christian	76	157
Bellinger,Cody	76	150
Soto,Juan	76	136
Encarnacion,Edwin	75	135
Freeman,Freddie	78	134
Jimenez,Eloy	76	130
Luplow,Jordan	76	130
Meadows,Austin	78	130
Rendon,Anthony	84	129
Devers,Rafael	78	128
Bichette,Bo	78	127
Castellanos,Nick	76	126
Springer,George	77	126
Betts,Mookie	84	126
Tauchman,Mike	78	125
Arenado,Nolan	82	124
Moreland,Mitch	75	123
Bell,Josh	79	120
Braun,Ryan	78	120
Ramirez,Jose	86	120
Bruce,Jay	75	120
Dickerson,Corey	78	120
Blackmon,Charlie	81	118
Gurriel,Lourdes	76	118
Bregman,Alex	85	118
Bogaerts,Xander	80	117
Moustakas,Mike	83	115
Abreu,Jose	78	115
Mancini,Trey	75	114
Ford,Mike	79	112
Turner,Justin	83	112
Kepler,Max	81	111
Osuna,Jose	79	111
Healy,Ryon	77	110
Anderson,Brian	75	110
Seager,Corey	80	109
Escobar,Eduardo	79	108
Realmuto,J.T.	79	108
Lindor,Francisco	84	107
Mazara,Nomar	75	107

TOP PX, ct% under 70%

NAME	ct%	PX
Gallo,Joey	56	215
Sano,Miguel	58	185
Judge,Aaron	63	164
Thames,Eric	66	162
Alonso,Peter	69	160
Hernandez,Teoscar	66	155
Schwarber,Kyle	69	154
Sanchez,Gary	70	154
Stanton,Giancarlo	67	149
Muncy,Max	69	147
Cordero,Franchy	63	145
Lowe,Brandon	65	144
Story,Trevor	69	142
Renfroe,Hunter	70	142
Tatis Jr.,Fernando	67	139
Happ,Ian	65	138
Soler,Jorge	69	137
Aquino,Aristides	68	137
Duvall,Adam	70	136
Lewis,Kyle	66	136
Walsh,Jared	61	136
Murphy,Tom	64	136
Reyes,Franmil	69	135

TOP PX, FB% over 40%

NAME	FB%	PX
Gallo,Joey	49	215
Sano,Miguel	42	185
Trout,Mike	46	170
Thames,Eric	46	162
Alonso,Peter	41	160
Hernandez,Teoscar	44	155
Schwarber,Kyle	42	154
Sanchez,Gary	43	154
Olson,Matt	44	152
Bellinger,Cody	43	150
Chapman,Matt	45	148
Muncy,Max	41	147
Garver,Mitch	44	144
Story,Trevor	43	142
Renfroe,Hunter	47	142
Hoskins,Rhys	50	140
Aquino,Aristides	45	137
Duvall,Adam	48	136
Grichuk,Randal	43	136
Murphy,Tom	44	136
Suarez,Eugenio	41	135
Davis,Khris	42	135
Encarnacion,Edwin	47	135
Upton,Justin	43	134
Adams,Matt	45	132
Bryant,Kris	43	131
Riley,Austin	48	131
Cespedes,Yoenis	46	131
Odor,Rougned	45	130
Luplow,Jordan	42	130
Meadows,Austin	42	130
Barreto,Franklin	48	129
Rendon,Anthony	44	129
Carpenter,Matt	43	129
Pederson,Joc	41	127
Dozier,Hunter	41	127
Chirinos,Robinson	42	126
Goodwin,Brian	41	126
Betts,Mookie	44	126
Smith,Will	48	125

TOP PX, FB% under 35%

NAME	FB%	PX
Yelich,Christian	34	157
Martinez,J.D.	35	148
Cordero,Franchy	31	145
Ohtani,Shohei	28	140
Tatis Jr.,Fernando	30	139
Lewis,Kyle	35	136
Hiura,Keston	33	136
Reyes,Franmil	32	135
Baez,Javier	32	134
Freeman,Freddie	35	134
Jimenez,Eloy	34	130
Bichette,Bo	34	127
Contreras,Willson	33	127
Dahl,David	34	126
Springer,George	35	126
Cave,Jake	25	125
Tauchman,Mike	33	125
Santana,Domingo	32	124
McMahon,Ryan	29	120
Braun,Ryan	30	120
Alfaro,Jorge	28	117
Myers,Wil	35	117
Adell,Jo	30	115

BATTER SKILLS RANKING - Speed

TOP Spd, 400+ AB

NAME	POS	Spd
Tatis Jr.,Fernando	6	174
Smith,Mallex	8 9	173
Gordon,Dee	4	169
Turner,Trea	6	168
Mondesi,Adalberto	6	157
Rosario,Amed	6	157
Eaton,Adam	9	151
Marte,Ketel	4 8	147
Hernandez,Cesar	4	145
Bader,Harrison	8	142
Urias,Luis	4 6	142
Robles,Victor	8	141
Marte,Starling	8	141
Buxton,Byron	8	141
Acuna,Ronald	7 8 9	141
Merrifield,Whit	4 9	140
Newman,Kevin	4 6	139
Moncada,Yoan	5	138
Albies,Ozzie	4	138
Lux,Gavin	4	135
Lopez,Nicky	4 6	134
Garcia,Leury	7 8 9	134
Dozier,Hunter	5 9	133
Baez,Javier	6	132
Story,Trevor	6	132
Bichette,Bo	6	131
Dubon,Mauricio	4	131
Solak,Nick	5	131
Altuve,Jose	4	130
Anderson,Tim	6	130
Reynolds,Bryan	7 8 9	130
Senzel,Nick	8	130
Betts,Mookie	9	129
Crawford,J.P.	6	129
Inciarte,Ender	8	127
Adames,Willy	6	127
Kingery,Scott	5 8	126
Bellinger,Cody	3 8 9	126
Blackmon,Charlie	9	125
Arcia,Orlando	6	125

TOP Spd, 300 or fewer AB

NAME	POS	Spd
Hamilton,Billy	8	165
Quinn,Roman	8	163
Phillips,Brett	8	162
Cordero,Franchy	8	155
Locastro,Tim	7 8 9	149
Straw,Myles	6	149
Dyson,Jarrod	8 9	148
Pache,Cristian	0	146
Engel,Adam	8	142
Allen,Greg	7	139
Brinson,Lewis	8	136
Cordell,Ryan	9	136
Martin,Richie	6	136
Duggar,Steven	8 9	135
Gonzalez,Erik	6	133
Culberson,Charlie	7	132
Fowler,Dustin	0	132
Vargas,Ildemaro	4	131
Tucker,Cole	6	130
Adrianza,Ehire	3 5 6	129
Munoz,Yairo	5	129
Marisnick,Jake	8	128
Lagares,Juan	8	126

POSITIONAL SCARCITY

NAME	POS	Spd
Ohtani,Shohei	DH	131
Diaz,Yusniel	2	124
Pham,Thomas	3	118
Meadows,Austin	4	113
Pence,Hunter	5	109
Garcia,Avisail	6	106
Mejia,Francisco	CA	118
Realmuto,J.T.	2	116
Wolters,Tony	3	116
Barnes,Austin	4	115
Kiner-Falefa,Isiah	5	114
Alfaro,Jorge	6	110
Greiner,Grayson	7	107
Contreras,Willson	8	105
Adrianza,Ehire	1B	129
Bellinger,Cody	2	126
Santana,Daniel	3	122
Dixon,Brandon	4	119
LeMahieu,DJ	5	110
Mancini,Trey	6	110
Diaz,Aledmys	7	109
Nola,Austin	8	108
Lamb,Jacob	9	108
Goldschmidt,Paul	10	106
Gordon,Dee	2B	169
Hampson,Garrett	2	158
Madrigal,Nick	3	150
Marte,Ketel	4	147
Hernandez,Cesar	5	145
Urias,Luis	6	142
Edman,Tommy	7	142
Merrifield,Whit	8	140
Berti,Jon	3B	149
Edman,Tommy	2	142
Moncada,Yoan	3	138
Dozier,Hunter	4	133
Solak,Nick	5	131
Adrianza,Ehire	6	129
Munoz,Yairo	7	129
Kingery,Scott	8	126
Bryant,Kris	9	121
Toro,Abraham	10	117
Tatis Jr.,Fernando	SS	174
Turner,Trea	2	168
Mondesi,Adalberto	3	157
Rosario,Amed	4	157
Berti,Jon	5	149
Straw,Myles	6	149
Urias,Luis	7	142
Newman,Kevin	8	139
Sierra,Magneuris	OF	184
Smith,Mallex	2	173
Hamilton,Billy	3	165
Quinn,Roman	4	163
Phillips,Brett	5	162
Hampson,Garrett	6	158
Robert,Luis	7	158
Cordero,Franchy	8	155
Margot,Manuel	9	155
Eaton,Adam	10	151
Locastro,Tim	11	149
Berti,Jon	12	149
Dyson,Jarrod	13	148
Marte,Ketel	14	147
Pache,Cristian	15	146
Tapia,Raimel	16	142

TOP Spd, .330+ OBP

NAME	OBP	Spd
Tatis Jr.,Fernando	350	174
Turner,Trea	347	168
Eaton,Adam	376	151
Madrigal,Nick	343	150
Locastro,Tim	340	149
Berti,Jon	333	149
Marte,Ketel	356	147
Hernandez,Cesar	346	145
Urias,Luis	348	142
Robles,Victor	340	141
Marte,Starling	342	141
Acuna,Ronald	354	141
Merrifield,Whit	346	140
Moncada,Yoan	338	138
Albies,Ozzie	340	138
Taylor,Chris	332	135
Lux,Gavin	342	135
Story,Trevor	348	132
Ohtani,Shohei	347	131
Gardner,Brett	335	131
Solak,Nick	347	131
Altuve,Jose	370	130
Reynolds,Bryan	362	130
Betts,Mookie	392	129
Inciarte,Ender	342	127
Bellinger,Cody	378	126
Carlson,Dylan	336	126
Blackmon,Charlie	365	125
Slater,Austin	340	125
Semien,Marcus	349	124
Diaz,Yusniel	332	124
Jimenez,Eloy	334	123
Frazier,Adam	335	123
Dahl,David	333	122
Bryant,Kris	380	121
Cain,Lorenzo	350	121
Garcia,Greg	348	121
McNeil,Jeff	368	120
Hiura,Keston	344	119
Canha,Mark	355	119

TOP Spd, OBP under .300

NAME	OBP	Spd
Sierra,Magneuris	281	184
Hamilton,Billy	291	165
Phillips,Brett	299	162
Robert,Luis	276	158
Mondesi,Adalberto	288	157
Cordero,Franchy	297	155
Engel,Adam	292	142
Demeritte,Travis	299	142
Buxton,Byron	293	141
Kiermaier,Kevin	291	140
Brinson,Lewis	271	136
Cordell,Ryan	263	136
Martin,Richie	289	136
Gonzalez,Erik	274	133
Culberson,Charlie	286	132
Fowler,Dustin	282	132
Dubon,Mauricio	294	131
Almora,Albert	288	129
Castro,Harold	283	128
Marisnick,Jake	292	128
Lagares,Juan	291	126
Kingery,Scott	296	126
Arcia,Orlando	288	125

TOP Spd, SBO% over 20%

NAME	SBO%	Spd
Sierra,Magneuris	22%	184
Tatis Jr.,Fernando	23%	174
Smith,Mallex	42%	173
Gordon,Dee	31%	169
Turner,Trea	32%	168
Hamilton,Billy	38%	165
Quinn,Roman	40%	163
Hampson,Garrett	25%	158
Robert,Luis	32%	158
Mondesi,Adalberto	49%	157
Rosario,Amed	22%	157
Margot,Manuel	23%	155
Madrigal,Nick	33%	150
Locastro,Tim	31%	149
Berti,Jon	29%	149
Straw,Myles	32%	149
Dyson,Jarrod	33%	148
Engel,Adam	22%	142
Edman,Tommy	20%	142
Robles,Victor	32%	141
Marte,Starling	26%	141
DeShields Jr.,Delino	29%	141
Buxton,Byron	30%	141
Acuna,Ronald	25%	141
Kiermaier,Kevin	24%	140
Allen,Greg	30%	139
Martin,Richie	24%	136
Bichette,Bo	29%	131
Dubon,Mauricio	22%	131
Munoz,Yairo	20%	129
Marisnick,Jake	24%	128
Broxton,Keon	34%	124
Villar,Jonathan	28%	124
Zimmer,Bradley	24%	123
Moore,Dylan	34%	123
Reyes,Victor	21%	123
Santana,Daniel	26%	122
Andrus,Elvis	20%	122
Mercado,Oscar	29%	119
Peraza,Jose	21%	119

TOP Spd, SBO% under 15%

NAME	SBO%	Spd
Cordero,Franchy	13%	155
Eaton,Adam	11%	151
Marte,Ketel	9%	147
Pache,Cristian	11%	146
Hernandez,Cesar	9%	145
Urias,Luis	4%	142
Demeritte,Travis	8%	142
Sanchez,Yolmer	10%	140
Moncada,Yoan	13%	138
Albies,Ozzie	15%	138
Taylor,Chris	14%	135
Lux,Gavin	11%	135
Lopez,Nicky	10%	134
Dozier,Hunter	5%	133
Rodgers,Brendan	7%	132
Culberson,Charlie	7%	132
Gardner,Brett	11%	131
Solak,Nick	10%	131
Vargas,Ildemaro	11%	131
Altuve,Jose	8%	130
Reynolds,Bryan	5%	130
Adrianza,Ehire	4%	129
Betts,Mookie	15%	129

BATTER SKILLS RANKING - Batting Average

TOP ct%, 400+ AB

NAME	ct%	BA
Arraez,Luis	91	308
Simmons,Andrelton	91	279
Alberto,Hanser	90	276
Lopez,Nicky	89	262
Fletcher,David	88	281
Brantley,Michael	88	308
Gurriel,Yulieski	88	292
Iglesias,Jose	87	277
Rojas,Miguel	87	274
Segura,Jean	87	290
Newman,Kevin	87	280
La Stella,Tommy	86	273
Pujols,Albert	86	246
Ramirez,Jose	86	282
Molina,Yadier	86	271
McNeil,Jeff	86	303
Frazier,Adam	86	275
Markakis,Nick	85	292
Murphy,Daniel	85	291
Gordon,Dee	85	270
Marte,Ketel	85	292
Gregorius,Didi	85	251
Reddick,Josh	85	268
LeMahieu,DJ	85	309
Posey,Buster	85	261
Andujar,Miguel	85	282
Bregman,Alex	85	298
Altuve,Jose	84	310
Andrus,Elvis	84	276
Betts,Mookie	84	309
Calhoun,Willie	84	265
Cano,Robinson	84	272
Lindor,Francisco	84	282
Rizzo,Anthony	84	291
Pillar,Kevin	84	260
Profar,Jurickson	84	253
Rendon,Anthony	84	303
Inciarte,Ender	84	267
Ramos,Wilson	84	287
Verdugo,Alex	83	291
Turner,Justin	83	298
Winker,Jesse	83	289
Guerrero Jr.,Vladimir	83	296
Wong,Kolten	83	270
Dubon,Mauricio	83	267
Moustakas,Mike	83	262
Arenado,Nolan	82	298
Albies,Ozzie	82	285
Rosario,Eddie	82	279
Merrifield,Whit	82	298
Santana,Carlos	82	260
Cain,Lorenzo	82	282
Semien,Marcus	82	275
Heyward,Jason	82	256
Urshela,Giovanny	82	274
Marte,Starling	81	291
Polanco,Jorge	81	272
Castro,Starlin	81	276
Blackmon,Charlie	81	307
Eaton,Adam	81	288
Kepler,Max	81	255
Machado,Manny	81	267
Naylor,Josh	81	265
Seager,Corey	80	278
Bogaerts,Xander	80	295
Vazquez,Christian	80	261

LOW ct%, 400+ AB

NAME	ct%	BA
Gallo,Joey	56	242
Sano,Miguel	58	247
Santana,Domingo	60	246
Alfaro,Jorge	63	246
Judge,Aaron	63	275
Riley,Austin	65	249
Thames,Eric	66	247
Hernandez,Teoscar	66	239
Myers,Wil	66	248
Upton,Justin	66	242
Dozier,Hunter	67	248
Biggio,Cavan	67	241
Chavis,Michael	67	241
Diaz,Isan	67	223
Nimmo,Brandon	67	243
Tatis Jr.,Fernando	67	287
Stanton,Giancarlo	67	260
Aquino,Aristides	68	240
Bader,Harrison	68	235
Mondesi,Adalberto	68	255
McMahon,Ryan	68	261
Moncada,Yoan	68	270
Alonso,Peter	69	255
Muncy,Max	69	253
Reyes,Franmil	69	257
Schwarber,Kyle	69	254
Goodrum,Niko	69	249
Soler,Jorge	69	258
Story,Trevor	69	282
Suarez,Eugenio	70	274
Davis,Khris	70	241
Renfroe,Hunter	70	243
Vogelbach,Daniel	70	231
Sanchez,Gary	70	245
Voit,Luke	70	260
Walker,Christian	70	244

TOP ct%, 300 or fewer AB

NAME	ct%	BA
Astudillo,Willians	96	286
Vargas,Ildemaro	91	281
Panik,Joe	90	260
Cabrera,Melky	88	275
Suzuki,Kurt	87	266
Bohm,Alec	85	279
Beaty,Matt	85	251
Kemp,Anthony	83	230
Lugo,Dawel	83	267
Lucroy,Jonathan	82	244
Diaz,Elias	82	245
Dyson,Jarrod	81	223
Trevino,Jose	81	212
Kiner-Falefa,Isiah	81	246
Mullins II,Cedric	81	243
Kelenic,Jarred	80	228
Parra,Gerardo	80	265
McGuire,Reese	80	247
Wendle,Joe	80	247
Martinez,Jose	79	281
Ford,Mike	79	262
Locastro,Tim	79	239
Straw,Myles	79	258
Grossman,Robert	79	255
Reyes,Pablo	79	248
Dickerson,Alex	79	268
Adrianza,Ehire	79	259

TOP ct%, bb% over 9%

NAME	bb%	ct%
Arraez,Luis	9	91
Ramirez,Jose	10	86
Markakis,Nick	9	85
Bregman,Alex	15	85
Betts,Mookie	12	84
Rizzo,Anthony	12	84
Profar,Jurickson	10	84
Rendon,Anthony	12	84
Inciarte,Ender	10	84
Turner,Justin	10	83
Winker,Jesse	12	83
Guerrero Jr.,Vladimir	9	83
Arenado,Nolan	10	82
Sogard,Eric	9	82
Santana,Carlos	15	82
Semien,Marcus	10	82
Heyward,Jason	10	82
Dyson,Jarrod	10	81
Eaton,Adam	11	81
Jansen,Danny	9	81
Kepler,Max	10	81
Machado,Manny	9	81
Naylor,Josh	9	81
Lowrie,Jed	10	80
Bogaerts,Xander	10	80
Hernandez,Cesar	9	80
Tsutsugo,Yoshitomo	12	79
Narvaez,Omar	10	79
Wolters,Tony	10	79
Ford,Mike	11	79
Cabrera,Asdrubal	10	79
Straw,Myles	10	79
Grossman,Robert	13	79
Votto,Joey	14	79
Bell,Josh	12	79
Freeman,Freddie	12	78
Benintendi,Andrew	10	78
Diaz,Yandy	11	78
Cabrera,Miguel	10	78
Gardner,Brett	10	78

TOP ct%, bb% under 6%

NAME	bb%	ct%
Astudillo,Willians	3	96
Vargas,Ildemaro	4	91
Alberto,Hanser	3	90
Gurriel,Yulieski	5	88
Cabrera,Melky	5	88
Flores,Wilmer	6	88
Iglesias,Jose	4	87
Rojas,Miguel	5	87
Segura,Jean	5	87
Newman,Kevin	6	87
Peraza,Jose	4	86
Molina,Yadier	6	86
Gordon,Dee	4	85
Gregorius,Didi	5	85
Andujar,Miguel	5	85
Andrus,Elvis	6	84
Pillar,Kevin	4	84
Lugo,Dawel	3	83
Dubon,Mauricio	4	83
Rosario,Eddie	4	82
Edman,Tommy	5	82
Almora,Albert	5	82
Urshela,Giovanny	5	82

TOP ct%, GB% over 50%

NAME	GB%	ct%
Simmons,Andrelton	52	91
Madrigal,Nick	53	91
Lopez,Nicky	55	89
Iglesias,Jose	51	87
Segura,Jean	53	87
Newman,Kevin	52	87
Gordon,Dee	56	85
LeMahieu,DJ	51	85
Andrus,Elvis	50	84
Ramos,Wilson	58	84
Kendrick,Howie	51	83
Duffy,Matt	52	82
Almora,Albert	50	82
Marte,Starling	50	81
Kiner-Falefa,Isiah	50	81
Naylor,Josh	52	81
Ramirez,Harold	57	80
Peralta,David	52	79
Sierra,Magneuris	57	79
Castro,Harold	52	79
Munoz,Yairo	56	79
Arcia,Orlando	53	78
Diaz,Yandy	50	78
Haseley,Adam	57	78
Tucker,Cole	50	77
Holt,Brock	51	77
Caratini,Victor	53	76
Hosmer,Eric	57	76
Kiermaier,Kevin	51	76
Garcia,Greg	52	75
Garcia,Leury	53	75
Smith,Mallex	52	75
Mancini,Trey	50	75
Pham,Thomas	51	75
Berti,Jon	54	75
Travis,Sam	56	75
Contreras,Willson	51	74
Cooper,Garrett	52	74
Nido,Tomas	54	74
Solak,Nick	51	74

TOP ct%, GB% under 40%

NAME	GB%	ct%
Arraez,Luis	40	91
Flores,Wilmer	36	88
Suzuki,Kurt	35	87
Peraza,Jose	39	86
Ramirez,Jose	35	86
Murphy,Daniel	38	85
Gregorius,Didi	39	85
Reddick,Josh	38	85
Bregman,Alex	33	85
Betts,Mookie	32	84
Calhoun,Willie	38	84
Rendon,Anthony	34	84
Turner,Justin	32	83
Moustakas,Mike	36	83
Arenado,Nolan	36	82
Sogard,Eric	35	82
Albies,Ozzie	38	82
Rosario,Eddie	37	82
Merrifield,Whit	38	82
Semien,Marcus	39	82
Polanco,Jorge	33	81
Blackmon,Charlie	40	81
Jansen,Danny	35	81

POTENTIAL SKILLS GAINERS AND FADERS - Batters

Power Gainers
Batters whose 2019 Power Index (PX) fell significantly short of their underlying power skill (xPX). If they show the same xPX skill in 2020, they are good candidates for more power output.

Power Faders
Batters whose 2019 Power Index (PX) noticeably outpaced their underlying power skill (xPX). If they show the same xPX skill in 2020, they are good candidates for less power output.

BA Gainers
Batters who had strong Hard Contact Index levels in 2019, but lower hit rates (h%). Since base hits come most often on hard contact, if these batters can make hard contact at the same strong rate again in 2020, they may get better results in terms of hit rate, resulting in a batting average improvement.

BA Faders
Batters who had weak Hard Contact Index levels in 2019, but higher hit rates (h%). Since base hits come most often on hard contact, if these batters only make hard contact at the same weak rate again in 2020, they may get worse results in terms of hit rate, resulting in a batting average decline.

PX GAINERS

NAME	PX	xPX
Lamb,Jacob	92	170
Bader,Harrison	97	141
Belt,Brandon	96	139
Carpenter,Matt	99	138
Cabrera,Asdrubal	98	134
Forsythe,Logan	82	134
Polanco,Jorge	98	132
VanMeter,Josh	96	132
Fowler,Dexter	99	129
Davis,Khristopher	90	126
Longoria,Evan	97	123
Beckham,Gordon	97	122
Zimmerman,Ryan	87	118
Votto,Joey	87	116
Kemp,Anthony	80	110
Kipnis,Jason	86	108
Molina,Yadier	68	108
Gordon,Alex	71	107
Aguilar,Jesus	83	106
Crawford,Brandon	70	106
Diaz,Isan	77	106
La Stella,Tommy	80	104
Descalso,Daniel	50	102
Shaw,Travis	72	101
Walker,Neil	77	100

PX FADERS

NAME	PX	xPX
Aquino,Aristides	168	110
Miller,Bradley	161	107
Freese,David	161	105
Luplow,Jordan	152	110
Bichette,Bo	150	97
Buxton,Byron	149	92
Baez,Javier	146	108
Moreland,Mitch	135	101
Guzman,Ronald	131	92
Tauchman,Mike	130	93
Smith,Dominic	130	89
Desmond,Ian	127	94
Devers,Rafael	127	93
Gardner,Brett	126	80
Altuve,Jose	119	85
Long,Shed	114	64
Gurriel,Yulieski	114	79
Marisnick,Jake	109	66
Villar,Jonathan	101	70
Robles,Victor	95	57
Heredia,Guillermo	89	54
Kiermaier,Kevin	88	59
Bauers,Jake	87	65

BA GAINERS

NAME	h%	HctX
Lamb,Jacob	24	129
Ozuna,Marcell	26	127
Kelly,Carson	27	126
Morales,Kendrys	22	121
Wieters,Matt	23	120
Kepler,Max	25	119
Pederson,Joc	25	118
Ramirez,Jose	26	118
Chapman,Matt	27	117
Moustakas,Mike	25	117
Calhoun,Willie	26	117
Pujols,Albert	24	116
Jansen,Danny	23	114
Panik,Joe	26	114
McCann,Brian	27	112
Hoskins,Rhys	27	111
Dean,Austin	27	111
Davis,Khristopher	27	111
Bruce,Jay	20	110
Smoak,Justin	22	110
Pillar,Kevin	27	110
Profar,Jurickson	22	109
Smith,Will	27	107
DeJong,Paul	26	107
Hernandez,Enrique	27	107
Renfroe,Hunter	25	106
Granderson,Curtis	22	106
Encarnacion,Edwin	24	104
Odor,Rougned	25	104
Calhoun,Kole	27	104
Suzuki,Kurt	25	104
Hechavarria,Adeiny	27	103
Maldonado,Martin	25	103
Kipnis,Jason	27	103
Prado,Martin	27	103
Seager,Kyle	25	102
O Hearn,Ryan	23	102

BA FADERS

NAME	h%	HctX
Engel,Adam	34	64
Villar,Jonathan	34	73
Chavis,Michael	35	74
Garcia,Leury	36	75
Demeritte,Travis	34	76
Freeman,Michael	40	77
DeShields Jr.,Delino	34	77
Tapia,Raimel	34	79
Frazier,Clint	34	83
Bichette,Bo	37	84
Tauchman,Mike	34	85
Murphy,Tom	34	87
Bote,David	34	87
Anderson,Tim	40	87
Gamel,Benjamin	35	87
Dahl,David	39	89
Mondesi,Adalberto	36	89
Moran,Colin	35	89
Goodwin,Brian	34	90
Taylor,Chris	35	90
Voit,Luke	35	90
Berti,Jon	36	90
Baez,Javier	35	91
Maybin,Cameron	37	91
Haseley,Adam	34	91
Lowe,Brandon	38	92
Santana,Domingo	35	92
Rosario,Amed	34	92
Dixon,Brandon	34	93
Goodrum,Niko	34	93
Holt,Brock	37	93
Gallo,Joey	37	95
Moncada,Yoan	41	95
McCann,James	36	95
Lowe,Nathaniel	35	96
Ervin,Phillip	34	96
Tatis Jr.,Fernando	42	97

POTENTIAL SKILLS GAINERS AND FADERS - Pitchers

Dom Gainers

From a pitcher's swinging-strike rate (SwK), we can establish a typical range in which we would expect to find their Dom (k/9). The pitchers on this list posted a 2019 Dom that was in the bottom of that expected range based on their SwK. The names above the break line are in the bottom 10% of that range, and are the strongest candidates for Dom gains. The names below the break line are in the bottom 25%, and are also good candidates for strikeout gains.

Dom Faders

From a pitcher's swinging-strike rate (SwK), we can establish a typical range in which we would expect to find their Dom (k/9). The pitchers on this list posted a 2019 Dom that was in the top of that expected range based on their SwK. The names above the break line are in the top 10% of that range, and are the strongest candidates for a Dom fade. The names below the break line are in the top 25%, and are also good candidates for a Dom fade.

Ctl Gainers

From a pitcher's Ball%, we can establish a typical range in which we would expect to find their Ctl (bb/9). These pitchers posted a 2019 Ctl that was in the bottom of that expected range based on their Ball%. The names above the break line are in the bottom 10% of that range, and are the strongest candidates for Ctl gains. The names below the break line are in the bottom 25%, and are also good candidates for Ctl gains.

Ctl Faders

From a pitcher's Ball%, we can establish a typical range in which we would expect to find their Ctl (bb/9). These pitchers posted a 2019 Ctl that was in the top 10% of that expected range based on their Ball%, making them the strongest candidates for a Ctl fade. The names below the break line are in the bottom 25%, and are also good candidates for a Ctl fade.

DOM GAINERS

NAME	SwK	K/9
Young,Alex	13	7.7
Petit,Yusmeiro	12	7.7
Alcantara,Sandy	11	6.9
Shaw,Bryan	11	7.3
Tanaka,Masahiro	11	7.4
Williams,Trevor	11	7.0
Soroka,Mike	11	7.3
Yarbrough,Ryan	11	7.5
Godley,Zack	10	6.8
Sanchez,Anibal	10	7.3
Hughes,Jared	10	6.8
Means,John	10	7.0
Mikolas,Miles	10	7.0
Hudson,Dakota	10	7.0
Urena,Jose	10	6.6
Walden,Marcus	14	8.8
Cessa,Luis	13	8.3
Ramirez,Nick	13	8.4
Pineda,Michael	13	8.6
Richards,Trevor	12	8.5
Musgrove,Joe	12	8.3
Wojciechowski,Asher	12	8.8
Castro,Miguel	12	8.7
Gaviglio,Sam	12	8.3
Bumgarner,Madison	12	8.8
Ryu,Hyun-Jin	12	8.1
Chirinos,Yonny	11	7.7
Happ,J.A.	11	7.8
Lopez,Pablo	11	7.7
Stroman,Marcus	11	7.8
Norris,Daniel	11	7.8
Hendricks,Kyle	11	7.6
Clarke,Taylor	10	7.3
Perez,Martin	10	7.4
Sampson,Adrian	10	7.3
Cahill,Trevor	10	7.1

DOM FADERS

NAME	SwK	K/9
Chavez,Jesse	7	8.3
Chacin,Jhoulys	8	8.8
Peacock,Brad	9	9.5
Bassitt,Chris	9	8.8
Yamamoto,Jordan	10	9.4
Bradley,Archie	11	11.0
Andriese,Matt	11	10.1
Pomeranz,Drew	12	11.9
Price,David	12	10.8
Lugo,Seth	12	11.7
Gray,Sonny	12	10.5
Arrieta,Jake	8	7.3
Wainwright,Adam	8	8.0
Quintana,Jose	9	8.0
Roark,Tanner	9	8.6
Lauer,Eric	9	8.3
Lester,Jon	9	8.7
Teheran,Julio	10	8.4
Houser,Adrian	10	9.5
DeSclafani,Anthony	10	9.0
Stripling,Ross	11	9.3
Lyles,Jordan	11	9.3
Smyly,Drew	11	9.5
Cease,Dylan	11	10.0
Nola,Aaron	11	10.2
Montas,Frankie	12	9.7
Velasquez,Vince	12	10.0
Buttrey,Ty	12	10.5
Woodruff,Brandon	12	10.6
Bauer,Trevor	13	10.7
Buehler,Walker	13	10.6
Lynn,Lance	13	10.6

CTL GAINERS

NAME	Ball%	BB/9
Gausman,Kevin	33	2.8
Brebbia,John	33	3.4
Hudson,Daniel	34	3.3
Maeda,Kenta	34	3.0
Giolito,Lucas	34	2.9
Anderson,Chase	35	3.2
Plesac,Zach	35	3.1
Alcantara,Sandy	35	3.7
Andriese,Matt	35	3.5
Smith,Caleb	35	3.5
Font,Wilmer	35	3.1
Nola,Aaron	35	3.6
Perez,Martin	35	3.7
Bassitt,Chris	35	2.9
Peralta,Freddy	35	3.9
Minor,Mike	35	2.9
Bailey,Homer	35	2.9
Gallen,Zac	35	4.1
Lauer,Eric	35	3.1
Bundy,Dylan	35	3.2
Suero,Wander	35	3.3
Eflin,Zach	34	2.6
Morton,Charlie	34	2.6
Darvish,Yu	34	2.8
Price,David	34	2.7
Hernandez,Elieser	34	2.9
Estevez,Carlos	34	2.9
Foltynewicz,Mike	35	2.8
Williams,Trevor	35	2.7
Buttrey,Ty	35	2.9
Heaney,Andrew	35	2.8

CTL FADERS

NAME	Ball%	BB/9
Stammen,Craig	35	1.6
Greinke,Zack	35	1.3
Mikolas,Miles	34	1.6
Petit,Yusmeiro	34	1.1
Ryu,Hyun-Jin	34	1.2
Bieber,Shane	34	1.7
Yarbrough,Ryan	33	1.3
Tomlin,Josh	33	0.8
Gonzalez,Gio	42	3.8
Quintana,Jose	38	2.4
Means,John	37	2.2
Chirinos,Yonny	35	1.9
Robles,Hansel	34	2.0
Milone,Tommy	34	1.9
Stripling,Ross	34	2.0
Leake,Mike	32	1.2

PITCHER SKILLS RANKINGS - Starting Pitchers

Top Command (k/bb)

NAME	Cmd
Scherzer,Max	6.3
Bieber,Shane	6.1
Sale,Chris	5.8
Verlander,Justin	5.7
deGrom,Jacob	5.4
Cole,Gerrit	5.3
Urquidy,Jose	5.2
Ryu,Hyun-Jin	5.0
Greinke,Zack	4.9
Syndergaard,Noah	4.7
Kershaw,Clayton	4.6
Buehler,Walker	4.5
Paddack,Chris	4.4
Strasburg,Stephen	4.4
Pineda,Michael	4.3
Glasnow,Tyler	4.1
Luzardo,Jesus	4.1
Kluber,Corey	4.1
Mikolas,Miles	4.1
Bumgarner,Madison	4.0
Woodruff,Brandon	4.0
Marquez,German	4.0
Hendricks,Kyle	4.0
Musgrove,Joe	4.0
Chirinos,Yonny	4.0
Tanaka,Masahiro	4.0
McKay,Brendan	3.9
Darvish,Yu	3.8
Boyd,Matt	3.8
Paxton,James	3.7
Leake,Mike	3.7

Top Control (bb/9)

NAME	Ctl
Leake,Mike	1.6
Agrazal,Dario	1.6
Ryu,Hyun-Jin	1.6
Bieber,Shane	1.7
Mikolas,Miles	1.7
Greinke,Zack	1.7
Urquidy,Jose	1.8
Chirinos,Yonny	1.9
Lockett,Walker	1.9
Hendricks,Kyle	1.9
Dobnak,Randy	1.9
Scherzer,Max	2.0
Milone,Tommy	2.0
Irvin,Cole	2.0
Verlander,Justin	2.0
Syndergaard,Noah	2.0
Musgrove,Joe	2.0
deGrom,Jacob	2.0
Tanaka,Masahiro	2.0
Pineda,Michael	2.1
Paddack,Chris	2.1
Smeltzer,Devin	2.1
Bumgarner,Madison	2.1
Yarbrough,Ryan	2.1
Kershaw,Clayton	2.1
Porcello,Rick	2.1
May,Dustin	2.2
Soroka,Michael	2.2
Mize,Casey	2.2
Zimmermann,Jordan	2.2
Means,John	2.2

Top Dominance (k/9)

NAME	Dom
Sale,Chris	13.0
Scherzer,Max	12.4
Cole,Gerrit	12.2
Ray,Robbie	12.0
Snell,Blake	11.7
Verlander,Justin	11.6
Clevinger,Mike	11.3
Darvish,Yu	11.2
Giolito,Lucas	11.0
deGrom,Jacob	10.9
McKay,Brendan	10.9
Strasburg,Stephen	10.9
Archer,Chris	10.8
Paxton,James	10.8
Lamet,Dinelson	10.8
Ohtani,Shohei	10.7
Bauer,Trevor	10.6
Kopech,Michael	10.5
Buehler,Walker	10.5
Boyd,Matt	10.5
Morton,Charlie	10.5
Castillo,Luis	10.5
Whitley,Forrest	10.4
Hill,Rich	10.4
Bieber,Shane	10.2
Corbin,Patrick	10.2
Flaherty,Jack	10.1
Price,David	10.1
Heaney,Andrew	10.1
Maeda,Kenta	10.1
McCullers,Lance	10.0

Top Ground Ball Rate

NAME	GB
Valdez,Framber	60
Keuchel,Dallas	57
Stroman,Marcus	57
Hudson,Dakota	55
McCullers,Lance	54
Anderson,Brett	54
Fried,Max	52
Castillo,Luis	52
Sheffield,Justus	52
Keller,Brad	52
Montgomery,Mike	51
Dobnak,Randy	51
Gray,Sonny	51
Richards,Garrett	51
Gibson,Kyle	50
Woodruff,Brandon	50
Soroka,Michael	50
Arrieta,Jake	50
Nola,Aaron	50
Martinez,Carlos	50
Miley,Wade	50
Corbin,Patrick	50
Gray,Jonathan	49
Strasburg,Stephen	49
Senzatela,Antonio	49
Houser,Adrian	49
Young,Alex	49
Morton,Charlie	49
Fedde,Erick	49
Taillon,Jameson	49
Jurado,Ariel	48

Top Fly Ball Rate

NAME	FB
Smith,Caleb	52
Wojciechowski,Asher	51
Means,John	50
Plutko,Adam	50
Hernandez,Elieser	50
Verlander,Justin	46
Boyd,Matt	46
Smyly,Drew	46
Suarez,Jose	45
Odorizzi,Jake	45
Barria,Jaime	45
Kopech,Michael	44
Lopez,Reynaldo	44
Yamamoto,Jordan	44
Alzolay,Adbert	44
Voth,Austin	44
Anderson,Chase	44
Gonsolin,Tony	44
McKay,Brendan	43
Heaney,Andrew	43
Urquidy,Jose	43
Scherzer,Max	43
Velasquez,Vincent	43
Paddack,Chris	43
Minor,Mike	42
Bundy,Dylan	42
Gore,MacKenzie	42
Wilson,Bryse	42
Ynoa,Gabriel	42
Duffy,Danny	42
Zimmermann,Jordan	42

High GB, Low Dom

NAME	GB	Dom
Keuchel,Dallas	57	7.2
Hudson,Dakota	55	6.8
Anderson,Brett	54	5.0
Keller,Brad	52	6.5
Montgomery,Mike	51	6.7
Dobnak,Randy	51	6.2
Soroka,Michael	50	7.6
Arrieta,Jake	50	7.2
Miley,Wade	50	7.2
Senzatela,Antonio	49	5.7
Houser,Adrian	49	7.6
Young,Alex	49	7.0
Fedde,Erick	49	6.3
Jurado,Ariel	48	5.3
Freeland,Kyle	48	6.6
Sanchez,Sixto	48	7.3
Mikolas,Miles	48	6.9
Urena,Jose	48	6.5
Perez,Martin	48	6.7
Sanchez,Aaron	47	7.5
May,Dustin	47	7.4
Wright,Kyle	47	7.3
Webb,Logan	47	7.5
Leake,Mike	47	5.8
Wacha,Michael	47	7.6
Rodriguez,Jefry	46	6.6
Lambert,Peter	46	5.6
Cueto,Johnny	46	7.5
Agrazal,Dario	46	5.0
Cashner,Andrew	46	6.2
Waguespack,Jacob	46	6.8

High GB, High Dom

NAME	GB	Dom
Valdez,Framber	60	9.2
McCullers,Lance	54	10.0
Fried,Max	52	9.2
Castillo,Luis	52	10.5
Gray,Sonny	51	9.4
Woodruff,Brandon	50	9.9
Nola,Aaron	50	9.8
Martinez,Carlos	50	9.1
Corbin,Patrick	50	10.2
Strasburg,Stephen	49	10.9
Morton,Charlie	49	10.5
Syndergaard,Noah	48	9.4
Glasnow,Tyler	48	10.0
Kershaw,Clayton	48	9.8
Marquez,German	46	9.1
Buehler,Walker	46	10.5
Severino,Luis	46	9.9
Cease,Dylan	46	9.3
Toussaint,Touki	46	9.3
deGrom,Jacob	45	10.9
Puk,A.J.	45	9.7
Sandoval,Patrick	45	9.4
Keller,Mitch	44	9.0
Bieber,Shane	44	10.2
Rodriguez,Eduardo	43	9.5
Lynn,Lance	43	9.8
Salazar,Danny	43	9.6
Kluber,Corey	43	9.6
Montas,Frankie	43	9.0
Sale,Chris	42	13.0
Hill,Rich	42	10.4

Lowest xERA

NAME	xERA
Sale,Chris	2.48
Cole,Gerrit	2.67
Scherzer,Max	2.70
deGrom,Jacob	2.74
Strasburg,Stephen	2.79
Verlander,Justin	2.90
Buehler,Walker	2.93
Morton,Charlie	2.98
Castillo,Luis	2.99
Bieber,Shane	3.00
Kershaw,Clayton	3.01
Glasnow,Tyler	3.03
Woodruff,Brandon	3.05
Darvish,Yu	3.08
Corbin,Patrick	3.10
Clevinger,Mike	3.10
Syndergaard,Noah	3.12
Luzardo,Jesus	3.17
Flaherty,Jack	3.18
Giolito,Lucas	3.18
Ryu,Hyun-Jin	3.19
Nola,Aaron	3.23
Severino,Luis	3.24
Hill,Rich	3.26
Snell,Blake	3.28
McCullers,Lance	3.28
Paxton,James	3.29
Kluber,Corey	3.30
Fried,Max	3.32
Greinke,Zack	3.32
Marquez,German	3.33

Top BPV, 160+ IP

NAME	BPV
Scherzer,Max	185
Cole,Gerrit	176
Verlander,Justin	166
deGrom,Jacob	165
Bieber,Shane	160
Strasburg,Stephen	156
Buehler,Walker	150
Kershaw,Clayton	144
Darvish,Yu	143
Woodruff,Brandon	141
Morton,Charlie	138
Castillo,Luis	137
Giolito,Lucas	136
Paxton,James	135
Corbin,Patrick	134
Clevinger,Mike	133
Kluber,Corey	130
Ryu,Hyun-Jin	129
Flaherty,Jack	127
Marquez,German	127
Boyd,Matt	126
Paddack,Chris	126
Greinke,Zack	126
Snell,Blake	125
Bauer,Trevor	121
Nola,Aaron	120
Tanaka,Masahiro	116
Weaver,Luke	116
Lynn,Lance	114
Musgrove,Joe	114
Bumgarner,Madison	113

Top BPV, <120 IP

NAME	BPV
Glasnow,Tyler	140
McKay,Brendan	135
Urquidy,Jose	131
Hill,Rich	130
Luzardo,Jesus	128
Lamet,Dinelson	116
Whitley,Forrest	115
Wood,Alex	111
Taillon,Jameson	107
Ohtani,Shohei	106
Puk,A.J.	104
Keller,Mitch	102
Manning,Matt	101
Sanchez,Sixto	98
Shoemaker,Matthew	95
Cessa,Luis	92
Dobnak,Randy	89
Burke,Brock	89
Mize,Casey	88
Richards,Garrett	88
Milone,Tommy	85
Fulmer,Michael	84
Kopech,Michael	84
Gore,MacKenzie	84
Palumbo,Joseph	83
Valdez,Framber	83
Richards,Trevor	81
Wilson,Bryse	81
Bassitt,Chris	80
Smeltzer,Devin	79
Montgomery,Jordan	79

PITCHER SKILLS RANKINGS - Relief Pitchers

Top Command (k/bb)

NAME	Cmd
Martin,Christopher	8.5
Osuna,Roberto	6.4
Yates,Kirby	5.9
Jansen,Kenley	5.8
Petit,Yusmeiro	5.6
Hendriks,Liam	5.3
Rogers,Taylor	5.2
Vazquez,Felipe	5.2
Stripling,Ross	5.1
Pagan,Emilio	5.0
Green,Chad	5.0
Gallegos,Giovanny	4.9
Lugo,Seth	4.9
Anderson,Nick	4.9
Strahm,Matt	4.9
Hader,Josh	4.8
Kittredge,Andrew	4.8
Giles,Ken	4.7
Harris,Will	4.7
Doolittle,Sean	4.6
Tomlin,Josh	4.5
Carrasco,Carlos	4.5
Diaz,Edwin	4.5
Garcia,Yimi	4.3
Pressly,Ryan	4.3
Smith,Joe	4.2
Kelley,Shawn	4.2
Stammen,Craig	4.1
Kahnle,Tommy	4.1
Poche,Colin	4.1
Harper,Ryne	4.1

Top Control (bb/9)

NAME	Ctl
Martin,Christopher	1.2
Tomlin,Josh	1.3
Petit,Yusmeiro	1.4
Osuna,Roberto	1.5
Stripling,Ross	1.8
Suter,Brent	1.8
Rogers,Taylor	2.0
Stammen,Craig	2.0
Lugo,Seth	2.0
Harper,Ryne	2.0
Strahm,Matt	2.0
Jansen,Kenley	2.0
Garcia,Yimi	2.1
Kittredge,Andrew	2.1
Harris,Will	2.1
Pruitt,Austin	2.1
Gallegos,Giovanny	2.1
Doolittle,Sean	2.2
Smith,Joe	2.2
Pagan,Emilio	2.2
Clase,Emmanuel	2.2
Kelley,Shawn	2.2
Hendriks,Liam	2.2
Melancon,Mark	2.3
Erlin,Robert	2.3
LeBlanc,Wade	2.3
Vazquez,Felipe	2.3
Carrasco,Carlos	2.3
Yates,Kirby	2.4
Green,Chad	2.4
Gaviglio,Sam	2.4

Top Dominance (k/9)

NAME	Dom
Hader,Josh	14.5
Diaz,Edwin	14.5
Chapman,Aroldis	14.3
Betances,Dellin	14.0
Yates,Kirby	13.9
Barnes,Matt	13.6
Hernandez,Darwinzon	13.4
Kimbrel,Craig	13.1
Anderson,Nick	13.0
Poche,Colin	12.9
Knebel,Corey	12.5
Hand,Brad	12.5
James,Josh	12.5
Smith,Will	12.5
Leclerc,Jose	12.3
Giles,Ken	12.2
Miller,Andrew	12.1
Adams,Austin L	12.1
Pressly,Ryan	12.1
Kahnle,Tommy	12.0
Ottavino,Adam	12.0
Vazquez,Felipe	12.0
Hendriks,Liam	11.9
Rainey,Tanner	11.9
Peralta,Freddy	11.9
Green,Chad	11.8
Robertson,David	11.7
Neris,Hector	11.7
Jansen,Kenley	11.7
Munoz,Andres	11.4
Feliz,Michael	11.4

Top Ground Ball Rate

NAME	GB
Britton,Zach	75
Bummer,Aaron	68
Hicks,Jordan	65
Kolarek,Adam	63
Hughes,Jared	61
Clase,Emmanuel	61
Tate,Dillon	59
Suarez,Ranger	59
McCarthy,Kevin	58
Melancon,Mark	58
Dyson,Sam	58
Fry,Paul	56
Claudio,Alex	56
Ryan,Kyle	56
Brennan,Brandon	55
Dominguez,Seranthony	55
Kelly,Joe	54
Walden,Marcus	54
Cimber,Adam	54
Hill,Tim	54
Martin,Brett	54
Chatwood,Tyler	53
Wick,Rowan	53
Floro,Dylan	53
Castillo,Diego	53
Adams,Austin L	53
Rainey,Tanner	53
Jackson,Luke	52
Familia,Jeurys	52
Perdomo,Luis	52
Oberg,Scott	52

Top Fly Ball Rate

NAME	FB
Poche,Colin	63
Clippard,Tyler	56
Garcia,Yimi	55
Goody,Nick	54
Doolittle,Sean	53
Hader,Josh	52
Pagan,Emilio	52
Brebbia,John	51
Sims,Lucas	50
Stanek,Ryne	48
Webb,Jacob	48
Gallegos,Giovanny	48
Jimenez,Joe	48
Pannone,Thomas	48
Kelley,Shawn	48
Cole,A.J.	47
Cortes,Nestor	47
Leclerc,Jose	47
Kimbrel,Craig	47
Petit,Yusmeiro	46
Peralta,Freddy	46
Baez,Pedro	46
Devenski,Christopher	45
Helsley,Ryan	45
James,Josh	45
Rodriguez,Richard	45
Armstrong,Shawn	45
Tomlin,Josh	44
Font,Wilmer	44
Green,Chad	44
Holder,Jonathan	44

High GB, Low Dom

NAME	GB	Dom
Kolarek,Adam	63	7.2
Hughes,Jared	61	6.7
Tate,Dillon	59	5.9
Suarez,Ranger	59	6.9
McCarthy,Kevin	58	5.7
Dyson,Sam	58	7.5
Claudio,Alex	56	6.1
Cimber,Adam	54	6.5
Floro,Dylan	53	7.7
Perdomo,Luis	52	6.7
Bettis,Chad	52	6.0
Sadler,Casey	52	6.2
Pruitt,Austin	51	7.0
Alcantara,Victor	50	5.9
Brice,Austin	50	7.6
Castro,Miguel	49	7.4
Morrow,Brandon	48	7.3
VerHagen,Drew	48	7.0
Gaviglio,Sam	48	7.5
Gsellman,Robert	47	7.3
Biagini,Joe	46	7.3
Ramirez,Nick	46	6.6
Lopez,Jorge	46	7.2
Gant,John	45	7.6
Suter,Brent	45	6.9
Garcia,Jarlin	44	6.5
Erlin,Robert	44	7.2
Lopez,Yoan	42	6.8
LeBlanc,Wade	40	6.9
Conley,Adam	40	7.1
Elias,Roenis	39	7.7

High GB, High Dom

NAME	GB	Dom
Hicks,Jordan	65	9.1
Dominguez,Seranthony	55	10.4
Kelly,Joe	54	10.2
Chatwood,Tyler	53	9.5
Castillo,Diego	53	10.4
Adams,Austin L	53	12.1
Rainey,Tanner	53	11.9
Jackson,Luke	52	11.0
Familia,Jeurys	52	9.8
Harris,Will	52	9.8
Hernandez,Darwinzon	51	13.4
Kittredge,Andrew	50	10.0
Strop,Pedro	50	10.0
Nelson,Jimmy	50	9.6
Treinen,Blake	49	9.5
Rodney,Fernando	49	9.6
Stripling,Ross	49	9.2
Drake,Oliver	49	10.5
Rogers,Taylor	49	10.3
Pressly,Ryan	49	12.1
Buttrey,Ty	48	10.1
Chafin,Andrew	48	10.6
Workman,Brandon	48	11.2
Alvarado,Jose	48	10.9
Barnes,Matt	48	13.6
Taylor,Josh	48	9.9
Trivino,Lou	47	9.3
Andriese,Matt	47	9.0
Garrett,Amir	47	10.6
Bradley,Archie	47	9.5
Martin,Christopher	46	9.8

Lowest xERA

NAME	xERA
Yates,Kirby	2.30
Pressly,Ryan	2.54
Diaz,Edwin	2.56
Vazquez,Felipe	2.58
Chapman,Aroldis	2.59
Hader,Josh	2.59
Betances,Dellin	2.65
Kahnle,Tommy	2.68
Giles,Ken	2.78
Harris,Will	2.78
Martin,Christopher	2.78
Rogers,Taylor	2.82
Barnes,Matt	2.82
Smith,Will	2.83
Kittredge,Andrew	2.86
Anderson,Nick	2.86
Hand,Brad	2.87
Osuna,Roberto	2.93
Hendriks,Liam	2.93
Jansen,Kenley	2.93
Hicks,Jordan	2.99
Robertson,David	2.99
Adams,Austin L	3.00
Kelly,Joe	3.01
Green,Chad	3.01
Jackson,Luke	3.02
Castillo,Diego	3.02
Knebel,Corey	3.04
Lugo,Seth	3.04
Neris,Hector	3.07
Carrasco,Carlos	3.09

Top BPV, 10+ Saves

NAME	BPV
Yates,Kirby	209
Diaz,Edwin	192
Hader,Josh	184
Giles,Ken	170
Hendriks,Liam	169
Jansen,Kenley	168
Smith,Will	160
Rogers,Taylor	159
Hand,Brad	157
Chapman,Aroldis	155
Osuna,Roberto	154
Lugo,Seth	146
Pagan,Emilio	145
Neris,Hector	140
Kimbrel,Craig	138
Iglesias,Raisel	136
Doolittle,Sean	128
Melancon,Mark	127
Jimenez,Joe	123
Kela,Keone	122
Miller,Andrew	122
Workman,Brandon	111
Givens,Mychal	111
Greene,Shane	108
Kennedy,Ian	103
Magill,Matthew	100
Bradley,Archie	100
Robles,Hansel	99
Colome,Alex	94
Leclerc,Jose	89
Hudson,Daniel	82

Top BPV, <10 Saves

NAME	BPV
Vazquez,Felipe	176
Martin,Christopher	170
Pressly,Ryan	169
Anderson,Nick	168
Kahnle,Tommy	162
Green,Chad	160
Betances,Dellin	153
Kittredge,Andrew	152
Harris,Will	150
Carrasco,Carlos	146
Poche,Colin	145
Stripling,Ross	144
Barnes,Matt	139
Robertson,David	139
James,Josh	139
Strahm,Matt	139
Knebel,Corey	138
Castillo,Diego	137
Ginkel,Kevin	136
Soria,Joakim	134
Duffey,Tyler	132
Smith,Joe	130
Buttrey,Ty	126
May,Trevor	126
Drake,Oliver	126
Middleton,Keynan	126
Stammen,Craig	123
Gausman,Kevin	123
Chafin,Andrew	123
Clase,Emmanuel	119
Peacock,Brad	119

RISK MANAGEMENT

GRADE "F" in HEALTH

Pitchers		Batters
Anderson,Brett	Middleton,Keynan	Andujar,Miguel
Archer,Chris	Miley,Wade	Bird,Gregory
Bailey,Homer	Miller,Andrew	Buxton,Byron
Bassitt,Chris	Minor,Mike	Cabrera,Miguel
Betances,Dellin	Montero,Rafael	Cano,Robinson
Bettis,Chad	Montgomery,Jordan	Castro,Jason
Brice,Austin	Moore,Matt	Cespedes,Yoenis
Britton,Zach	Morrow,Brandon	Cooper,Garrett
Cahill,Trevor	Nelson,Jimmy	Cordero,Franchy
Carrasco,Carlos	Norris,Daniel	Correa,Carlos
Chacin,Jhoulys	Ottavino,Adam	Cuthbert,Cheslor
Chen,Wei-Yin	Paxton,James	D Arnaud,Travis
Cobb,Alex	Peacock,Brad	Dahl,David
Covey,Dylan	Perez,Martin	Dickerson,Alex
Cueto,Johnny	Pineda,Michael	Duffy,Matt
Darvish,Yu	Price,David	Eaton,Adam
Davies,Zachary	Reyes,Alex	Goodwin,Brian
DeSclafani,Anthony	Richards,Garrett	Haniger,Mitch
Diaz,Jairo	Robertson,David	Healy,Ryon
Dominguez,Seranthony	Rodon,Carlos	Hicks,Aaron
Doolittle,Sean	Rodriguez,Jefry	Holt,Brock
Duffy,Danny	Ross,Joe	Inciarte,Ender
Eickhoff,Jerad	Ryu,Hyun-Jin	Kendrick,Howie
Elias,Roenis	Sabathia,CC	Kiermaier,Kevin
Eovaldi,Nathan	Salazar,Danny	La Stella,Tommy
Erlin,Robert	Samardzija,Jeff	Lagares,Juan
Familia,Jeurys	Sanchez,Aaron	Lamb,Jacob
Fulmer,Michael	Severino,Luis	Lowrie,Jed
Garcia,Yimi	Shoemaker,Matthew	McCutchen,Andrew
Glasnow,Tyler	Smith,Caleb	Naquin,Tyler
Goody,Nick	Smith,Joe	Nimmo,Brandon
Gray,Jonathan	Smith,Will	Pence,Hunter
Harvey,Matt	Smyly,Drew	Peralta,David
Heaney,Andrew	Soroka,Michael	Perez,Salvador
Hernandez,Felix	Strahm,Matt	Polanco,Gregory
Hicks,Jordan	Strickland,Hunter	Pollock,A.J.
Hill,Rich	Suter,Brent	Quinn,Roman
Kela,Keone	Taillon,Jameson	Sandoval,Pablo
Kelley,Shawn	Tepera,Ryan	Seager,Corey
Kershaw,Clayton	Tuivailala,Sam	Souza,Steven
Kluber,Corey	Urena,Jose	Stanton,Giancarlo
Knebel,Corey	Urias,Julio	Vogt,Stephen
Kopech,Michael	Vargas,Jason	Zimmer,Bradley
Lamet,Dinelson	Velasquez,Vincent	Zimmerman,Ryan
Loaisiga,Jonathan	Vizcaino,Arodys	
Lopez,Pablo	Wacha,Michael	
Manaea,Sean	Wainwright,Adam	
Martinez,Carlos	Walker,Taijuan	
Matz,Steven	Weaver,Luke	
May,Trevor	Wood,Alex	
McCullers,Lance	Workman,Brandon	
McHugh,Collin	Ynoa,Gabriel	
Melancon,Mark	Zimmermann,Jordan	

Highest Reliability Grades-Health/Experience/Consistency (Min. Grade BBB)

CA	POS	Rel
Grandal,Yasmani	23	ABA
Realmuto,J.T.	2	AAB

1B/DH	POS	Rel
Abreu,Jose	03	AAB
Bauers,Jake	037	ABB
Cron,C.J.	3	BBB
Encarnacion,Edwin	03	BAB
Freeman,Freddie	3	BAB
Grandal,Yasmani	23	ABA
Gurriel,Yulieski	35	ABB
Nunez,Renato	03	ABB
Olson,Matt	3	BBB
Pujols,Albert	03	BAA
Rizzo,Anthony	3	BAA

2B	POS	Rel
Albies,Ozzie	4	AAA
Cabrera,Asdrubal	45	BBA
Castro,Starlin	45	BAB
Escobar,Eduardo	45	AAB
Fletcher,David	456	ABB
Frazier,Adam	4	ABA
Galvis,Freddy	46	AAA
Gordon,Dee	4	BAB
Hernandez,Cesar	4	AAB
Merrifield,Whit	49	AAB
Odor,Rougned	4	BAB
Taylor,Chris	467	BBB
Villar,Jonathan	46	AAB

SS	POS	Rel
Adames,Willy	6	ABA
Arcia,Orlando	6	ABB
Baez,Javier	6	AAB
Bogaerts,Xander	6	AAB
Crawford,Brandon	6	AAB
DeJong,Paul	6	BBB
Fletcher,David	456	ABB
Galvis,Freddy	46	AAA
Iglesias,Jose	6	BBA
Lindor,Francisco	6	AAA
Polanco,Jorge	6	ABA
Rosario,Amed	6	AAA
Segura,Jean	6	BAB
Semien,Marcus	6	BAB
Swanson,Dansby	6	BBA
Taylor,Chris	467	BBB
Villar,Jonathan	46	AAB

3B	POS	Rel
Anderson,Brian	59	BBA
Arenado,Nolan	5	AAA
Cabrera,Asdrubal	45	BBA
Castro,Starlin	45	BAB
Escobar,Eduardo	45	AAB
Fletcher,David	456	ABB
Gurriel,Yulieski	35	ABB
Lugo,Dawel	5	ABB
Rendon,Anthony	5	BAA
Suarez,Eugenio	5	AAB

OF	POS	Rel
Acuna,Ronald	789	ABA
Anderson,Brian	59	BBA
Bauers,Jake	037	ABB
Bradley,Jackie	8	ABA
Braun,Ryan	7	BBB
Calhoun,Kole	9	AAB
Demeritte,Travis	9	ABA
Desmond,Ian	78	BBA
Gardner,Brett	78	AAB
Gordon,Alex	7	BAB
Grichuk,Randal	89	BBB
Grossman,Robert	79	ABB
Hamilton,Billy	8	ABB
Heyward,Jason	89	BBA
Margot,Manuel	8	ABA
Marte,Starling	8	ABA
Mazara,Nomar	9	BBA
McBroom,Ryan	9	ABB
Mercado,Oscar	78	ABA
Merrifield,Whit	49	AAB
Pham,Thomas	07	BAB
Pillar,Kevin	89	AAA
Puig,Yasiel	9	BBB
Rosario,Eddie	7	AAA
Taylor,Chris	467	BBB
VanMeter,Josh	7	ABB

SP		Rel
Berrios,Jose		AAA
Bieber,Shane		ABA
Boyd,Matt		AAB
Buehler,Walker		BBB
Bundy,Dylan		BAA
Castillo,Luis		AAA
Cole,Gerrit		BAB
deGrom,Jacob		AAB
Fiers,Mike		BAA
Flaherty,Jack		ABB
Greinke,Zack		AAA
Hendricks,Kyle		BAA
Junis,Jakob		AAA
Kelly,Merrill		AAB
Leake,Mike		AAA
Lopez,Reynaldo		AAA
Lucchesi,Joey		BBB
Mikolas,Miles		AAB
Quintana,Jose		AAA
Roark,Tanner		AAA
Teheran,Julio		BAA
Verlander,Justin		BAB

RP		Rel
Colome,Alex		BBB
Giles,Ken		ABA
Hader,Josh		ABB
Hand,Brad		BBA
Jansen,Kenley		BAB
Osuna,Roberto		ABA
Rodney,Fernando		BBB
Vazquez,Felipe		ABA
Yates,Kirby		BBA

RISK MANAGEMENT

GRADE "A" in CONSISTENCY

Pitchers (min 100 IP)	Batters (min 400 AB)
Anderson,Chase	Acuna,Ronald
Archer,Chris	Adames,Willy
Arrieta,Jake	Ahmed,Nick
Berrios,Jose	Albies,Ozzie
Bieber,Shane	Alfaro,Jorge
Bumgarner,Madison	Anderson,Brian
Bundy,Dylan	Arenado,Nolan
Canning,Griffin	Bichette,Bo
Carrasco,Carlos	Biggio,Cavan
Cashner,Andrew	Bradley,Jackie
Castillo,Luis	Brantley,Michael
Chirinos,Yonny	Cabrera,Asdrubal
Clevinger,Mike	Crawford,J.P.
Davies,Zachary	Desmond,Ian
Duffy,Danny	Dickerson,Corey
Fiers,Mike	Frazier,Adam
German,Domingo	Garcia,Leury
Gonzalez,Gio	Grandal,Yasmani
Gray,Jonathan	Heyward,Jason
Gray,Sonny	Iglesias,Jose
Greinke,Zack	Kipnis,Jason
Hendricks,Kyle	Lindor,Francisco
Junis,Jakob	Marte,Starling
Kershaw,Clayton	Mazara,Nomar
Keuchel,Dallas	Mercado,Oscar
Lamet,Dinelson	Molina,Yadier
Lauer,Eric	Moreland,Mitch
Leake,Mike	Myers,Wil
LeBlanc,Wade	Narvaez,Omar
Lester,Jon	Pillar,Kevin
Lopez,Reynaldo	Polanco,Jorge
Lynn,Lance	Pujols,Albert
Maeda,Kenta	Rendon,Anthony
McCullers,Lance	Renfroe,Hunter
Means,John	Rizzo,Anthony
Minor,Mike	Rosario,Amed
Montgomery,Mike	Rosario,Eddie
Morton,Charlie	Schwarber,Kyle
Nola,Aaron	Solak,Nick
Nova,Ivan	Swanson,Dansby
Odorizzi,Jake	Torres,Gleyber
Perez,Martin	
Pineda,Michael	
Plesac,Zach	
Price,David	
Quintana,Jose	
Ray,Robbie	
Roark,Tanner	
Rodriguez,Eduardo	
Scherzer,Max	
Severino,Luis	
Smith,Caleb	
Strasburg,Stephen	
Stripling,Ross	
Stroman,Marcus	
Teheran,Julio	
Waguespack,Jacob	
Walker,Taijuan	
Webb,Logan	
Williams,Trevor	
Young,Alex	

TOP COMBINATION OF SKILLS AND RELIABILITY
Maximum of one "C" in Reliability Grade

BATTING POWER (Min. 400 AB)

PX 100+	PX	Rel
Trout,Mike	170	BAC
Thames,Eric	162	BCB
Hernandez,Teoscar	155	ACB
Schwarber,Kyle	154	CBA
Olson,Matt	152	BBB
Chapman,Matt	148	AAC
Martinez,J.D.	148	BAC
Story,Trevor	142	BAC
Renfroe,Hunter	142	BCA
Hoskins,Rhys	140	AAC
Tellez,Rowdy	136	ACB
Grichuk,Randal	136	BBB
Reyes,Franmil	135	ABC
Acuna,Ronald	135	ABA
Suarez,Eugenio	135	AAB
Davis,Khris	135	BAC
Encarnacion,Edwin	135	BAB
Baez,Javier	134	AAB
Freeman,Freddie	134	BAB
Bryant,Kris	131	BAC
Odor,Rougned	130	BAB
Goldschmidt,Paul	129	AAC
Rendon,Anthony	129	BAA
Conforto,Michael	129	BAC
Pederson,Joc	127	ACB
Castellanos,Nick	126	AAC
Cron,C.J.	126	BBB
Arenado,Nolan	124	AAA
Moreland,Mitch	123	CBA
Moncada,Yoan	122	BBC
Bell,Josh	120	CAB
Braun,Ryan	120	BBB
Grandal,Yasmani	119	ABA
Blackmon,Charlie	118	AAC
Bregman,Alex	118	AAC
Torres,Gleyber	118	ACA
DeJong,Paul	117	BBB
Alfaro,Jorge	117	ACA
Myers,Wil	117	CBA
Bogaerts,Xander	117	AAB
Vogelbach,Daniel	116	ACB
Moustakas,Mike	115	CAB
Abreu,Jose	115	AAB
Nunez,Renato	115	ABB
Goodrum,Niko	112	BCB
Bradley,Jackie	112	ABA
Turner,Justin	112	CBB
Kepler,Max	111	CAB
Calhoun,Kole	111	AAB
Anderson,Brian	110	BBA
Escobar,Eduardo	108	AAB
Realmuto,J.T.	108	AAB
Lindor,Francisco	107	AAA
Mazara,Nomar	107	BBA
Rosario,Eddie	107	AAA
Belt,Brandon	106	CBB
Ozuna,Marcell	106	BAC
Santana,Carlos	105	AAC
Seager,Kyle	105	CBB
Rizzo,Anthony	104	BAA
Puig,Yasiel	104	BBB
Pham,Thomas	103	BAB
Desmond,Ian	103	BBA
Adames,Willy	103	ABA
Choo,Shin-Soo	102	CAB
Albies,Ozzie	102	AAA

RUNNER SPEED (Min. 400 AB)

Spd 100+	SX	Rel
Gordon,Dee	169	BAB
Turner,Trea	168	CAB
Rosario,Amed	157	AAA
Marte,Ketel	147	ABC
Hernandez,Cesar	145	AAB
Bader,Harrison	142	ACB
Urias,Luis	142	ACB
Marte,Starling	141	ABA
Acuna,Ronald	141	ABA
Merrifield,Whit	140	AAB
Newman,Kevin	139	CBB
Moncada,Yoan	138	BBC
Albies,Ozzie	138	AAA
Baez,Javier	132	AAB
Story,Trevor	132	BAC
Dubon,Mauricio	131	ACB
Solak,Nick	131	ACA
Altuve,Jose	130	BAC
Anderson,Tim	130	BBC
Adames,Willy	127	ABA
Blackmon,Charlie	125	AAC
Arcia,Orlando	125	ABB
Hernandez,Teoscar	124	ACB
Semien,Marcus	124	BAB
Villar,Jonathan	124	AAB
Frazier,Adam	123	ABA
Ahmed,Nick	122	CBA
Bryant,Kris	121	BAC
Goodrum,Niko	121	BCB
Cain,Lorenzo	121	BAC
Swanson,Dansby	120	BBA
Mercado,Oscar	119	ABA
Segura,Jean	119	BAB
Castellanos,Nick	118	AAC
Desmond,Ian	118	BBA
Pham,Thomas	118	BAB
Fletcher,David	117	ABB
Realmuto,J.T.	116	AAB
Polanco,Jorge	114	ABA
Grichuk,Randal	113	BBB
Myers,Wil	112	CBA
Wong,Kolten	111	BBC
Trout,Mike	111	BAC
Alfaro,Jorge	110	ACA
LeMahieu,DJ	110	BAC
Bregman,Alex	109	AAC
Reddick,Josh	109	BBC
Simmons,Andrelton	108	CAB
Anderson,Brian	108	BBA
Heyward,Jason	108	BBA
Longoria,Evan	107	CAB
Goldschmidt,Paul	106	AAC
Iglesias,Jose	106	BBA
Lindor,Francisco	105	AAA
Escobar,Eduardo	103	AAB
Arenado,Nolan	103	AAA
Thames,Eric	101	BCB
Rojas,Miguel	101	CBB
Bogaerts,Xander	101	AAB
Martinez,J.D.	101	BAC
Chapman,Matt	101	AAC
Bradley,Jackie	101	ABA
Castro,Starlin	100	BAB
Pillar,Kevin	100	AAA

OVERALL PITCHING SKILL

BPV over 80	BPV	Rel
Yates,Kirby	209	BBA
Diaz,Edwin	192	AAC
Hader,Josh	184	ABB
Vazquez,Felipe	176	ABA
Cole,Gerrit	176	BAB
Giles,Ken	170	ABA
Jansen,Kenley	168	BAB
Verlander,Justin	166	BAB
deGrom,Jacob	165	AAB
Bieber,Shane	160	ABA
Green,Chad	160	ACA
Rogers,Taylor	159	ACB
Hand,Brad	157	BBA
Osuna,Roberto	154	ABA
Buehler,Walker	150	BBB
Neris,Hector	140	ACA
Barnes,Matt	139	ACA
Castillo,Luis	137	AAA
Iglesias,Raisel	136	CAA
Corbin,Patrick	134	BAC
Flaherty,Jack	127	ABB
Marquez,German	127	CAB
Boyd,Matt	126	AAB
Greinke,Zack	126	AAA
Bauer,Trevor	121	CAB
Nola,Aaron	120	CAA
Maeda,Kenta	119	CAA
German,Domingo	118	BCA
Tanaka,Masahiro	116	CAB
Petit,Yusmeiro	116	ACA
Devenski,Christopher	112	BCB
Givens,Mychal	111	ACA
Hendricks,Kyle	109	BAA
Greene,Shane	108	CBA
Parker,Blake	108	ACB
Berrios,Jose	107	AAA
Clippard,Tyler	106	ACA
Gray,Sonny	104	CAA
Mikolas,Miles	104	AAB
Porcello,Rick	103	AAC
Hirano,Yoshihisa	103	CBB
Fried,Max	103	BCB
Bradley,Archie	100	BCA
Robles,Hansel	99	BCB
Lucchesi,Joey	98	BBB
Junis,Jakob	98	AAA
Gaviglio,Sam	97	ACB
Happ,J.A.	97	CAB
Quintana,Jose	96	AAA
Colome,Alex	94	BBB
Gibson,Kyle	93	CAB
Bundy,Dylan	93	BAA
Kelly,Merrill	91	AAB
Rondon,Hector	91	ACB
Odorizzi,Jake	89	CAA
Lester,Jon	89	CAA
Leake,Mike	87	AAA
Keuchel,Dallas	85	CAA
Roark,Tanner	81	AAA
Richards,Trevor	81	ACB

DAILY FANTASY INDICATORS

Top OPS v LHP, 2018-2019

Hitter	OPS
Martinez,J.D.	1190
Arenado,Nolan	1116
Bryant,Kris	1090
Bregman,Alex	1073
Castellanos,Nick	1061
Cruz,Nelson	1058
Judge,Aaron	1039
Stanton,Giancarlo	1038
Suarez,Eugenio	1008
Story,Trevor	1002
Betts,Mookie	1001
Rendon,Anthony	995
Trout,Mike	990
Machado,Manny	989
Albies,Ozzie	988
Marte,Ketel	983
LeMahieu,DJ	980
Turner,Justin	979
Abreu,Jose	973
Cron,C.J.	971
Goldschmidt,Paul	964
Yelich,Christian	959
Baez,Javier	947
Acuna,Ronald	945
Gallo,Joey	942
Reyes,Franmil	939
Ramos,Wilson	932
Gurriel,Lourdes	928
Garver,Mitch	925
Soler,Jorge	924
Cabrera,Miguel	918
Pham,Thomas	917
Desmond,Ian	910
Santana,Carlos	907
Torres,Gleyber	907
Voit,Luke	903
Harper,Bryce	902
Altuve,Jose	902
Braun,Ryan	901
Contreras,Willson	900
Haniger,Mitch	897

600+ PA, 2018-2019

Top OPS v RHP, 2018-2019

Hitter	OPS
Trout,Mike	1121
Yelich,Christian	1091
Betts,Mookie	989
Soto,Juan	977
Bellinger,Cody	972
Rendon,Anthony	950
Ohtani,Shohei	947
Freeman,Freddie	944
Muncy,Max	941
Rizzo,Anthony	931
Bogaerts,Xander	928
Bregman,Alex	927
McNeil,Jeff	925
Martinez,J.D.	924
Ramirez,Jose	917
Blackmon,Charlie	912
Brantley,Michael	908
Pederson,Joc	908
Peralta,David	905
Meadows,Austin	903
Devers,Rafael	899
Bell,Josh	894
Voit,Luke	894
Cruz,Nelson	891
Choo,Shin-Soo	889
Olson,Matt	887
Dahl,David	886
Soler,Jorge	885
Winker,Jesse	885
Acuna,Ronald	883
Choi,Ji-Man	882
Story,Trevor	882
Schwarber,Kyle	881
Arenado,Nolan	880
Donaldson,Josh	880
Suarez,Eugenio	878
Harper,Bryce	877
Polanco,Jorge	877
Judge,Aaron	875
Springer,George	873
Dickerson,Corey	867

Top L-R Splits, 2018-2019

Hitter	OPS vL-vR
Bryant,Kris	273
Martinez,J.D.	266
Castellanos,Nick	256
Albies,Ozzie	248
Cron,C.J.	244
Stanton,Giancarlo	241
Desmond,Ian	240
Arenado,Nolan	237
LeMahieu,DJ	220
Abreu,Jose	202
Cabrera,Miguel	191
Machado,Manny	185
Perez,Roberto	180
Ramos,Wilson	173
Cruz,Nelson	167
Ahmed,Nick	164
Judge,Aaron	164
Gomes,Yan	161
Gurriel,Lourdes	160

Top R-L Splits, 2018-2019

Hitter	OPS vR-vL
Pederson,Joc	404
Shaw,Travis	301
Winker,Jesse	297
Vogelbach,Daniel	282
Upton,Justin	281
Choi,Ji-Man	277
Hosmer,Eric	246
Martin,Leonys	235
Choo,Shin-Soo	232
Guzman,Ronald	224
Ohtani,Shohei	222
Peralta,David	208
Bour,Justin	207
Happ,Ian	203
Devers,Rafael	201
Adames,Willy	198
Brantley,Michael	195
Thames,Eric	191
Rizzo,Anthony	189

Best Parks - LH HR

Ballpark	Factor
LAA	25%
CHW	23%
COL	23%
PHI	22%
NYY	19%
CIN	16%
TEX	15%
BAL	13%
WAS	12%
LAD	12%

Worst Parks - LH HR

Ballpark	Factor
SF	-41%
BOS	-21%
MIA	-20%
SD	-19%
KC	-16%
OAK	-15%
CHC	-12%

Best Parks - RH HR

Ballpark	Factor
PHI	26%
BAL	23%
COL	19%
CIN	16%
WAS	15%
HOU	14%
TOR	13%
CHW	7%
TEX	7%

Worst Parks-RH HR

Ballpark	Factor
SF	-26%
MIA	-25%
PIT	-21%
KC	-20%
STL	-19%
ARI	-11%
OAK	-10%
ATL	-10%

Best Parks - Runs

Ballpark	Factor
COL	34%
TEX	27%
WAS	10%

Worst Parks - Runs

Ballpark	Factor
NYM	-17%
SF	-12%
MIA	-12%
STL	-9%
SD	-9%
SEA	-9%
LAD	-9%

Best Parks - Ks

Ballpark	Factor
CIN	11%
SEA	11%
NYM	9%
MIL	7%
PHI	7%
TAM	7%

Worst Parks - Ks

Ballpark	Factor
COL	-11%
TEX	-10%
KC	-10%
DET	-10%

Best Parks - BB

Ballpark	Factor
SD	9%
TEX	8%

Worst Parks - BB

Ballpark	Factor
LAD	-13%
DET	-7%

Note: for Runs, the best parks for hitters are also the worst for pitchers and vice versa

Consistent High-PQS SP

Pitcher	QC*
Verlander,Justin	94
Glasnow,Tyler	84
deGrom,Jacob	80
Scherzer,Max	76
Clevinger,Michael	74
Strasburg,Stephen	68
Ryu,Hyun-Jin	62
Bieber,Shane	60
Kershaw,Clayton	44
Lynn,Lance	42
Morton,Charlie	36
Cole,Gerrit	36
Giolito,Lucas	36
Flaherty,Jack	36
Bauer,Trevor	34
Buehler,Walker	34
Woodruff,Brandon	28
Gray,Sonny	26
Gallen,Zac	26
Greinke,Zack	18

Consistent Low-PQS SP

Pitcher	QC*
Richard,Clayton	(320)
Jackson,Edwin	(308)
Detwiler,Ross	(300)
Gonzalez,Alex	(300)
Ynoa,Gabriel	(276)
Buchholz,Clay	(268)
Fedde,Erick	(268)
Covey,Dylan	(268)
Sparkman,Glenn	(262)
Senzatela,Antonio	(256)
Barria,Jaime	(248)
Brooks,Aaron	(246)
Cahill,Trevor	(238)
Peters,Dillon	(234)
Suarez,Jose	(226)
Freeland,Kyle	(218)
Eovaldi,Nathan	(216)
Harvey,Matt	(216)

10+ Games Started, 2019
*Quality-Consistency score

Most DOMinant SP

Pitcher	DOM
deGrom,Jacob	66%
Verlander,Justin	59%
Glasnow,Tyler	58%
Clevinger,Michael	57%
Strasburg,Stephen	52%
Scherzer,Max	52%
Yarbrough,Ryan	50%
Kershaw,Clayton	50%
Morton,Charlie	48%
Bieber,Shane	48%
Bauer,Trevor	47%
Wheeler,Zack	45%
Greinke,Zack	45%
Lynn,Lance	45%
Ryu,Hyun-Jin	45%
Buehler,Walker	43%
Carrasco,Carlos	42%
Weaver,Luke	42%
Paddack,Chris	42%
Cole,Gerrit	42%

Most DISastrous SP

Pitcher	DIS
Richard,Clayton	80%
Jackson,Edwin	77%
Detwiler,Ross	75%
Gonzalez,Alex	75%
Sparkman,Glenn	70%
Ynoa,Gabriel	69%
Senzatela,Antonio	68%
Peters,Dillon	67%
Brooks,Aaron	67%
Buchholz,Clay	67%
Fedde,Erick	67%
Covey,Dylan	67%
Cahill,Trevor	64%
Barria,Jaime	62%
Suarez,Jose	60%
Freeland,Kyle	59%
Eovaldi,Nathan	58%
Harvey,Matt	58%

Universal Draft Grid

Most publications and websites provide cheat sheets with ranked player lists for different fantasy draft formats. The biggest problem with these tools is that they perpetuate the myth that players can be ranked in a linear fashion.

Since rankings are based on highly variable projections, it is foolhardy to draw conclusions that a $24 player is better than a $23 player is better than a $22 player. Yes, a first round pick is better than a 10th round pick, but within most rounds, all players are pretty much interchangeable commodities.

But typical cheat sheets don't reflect that reality. Auction sheets rank players by dollar value. Snake draft sheets rank players within round, accounting for position and categorical scarcity. But just as ADPs have a ridiculously low success rate, these cheat sheets are similarly flawed.

We have a tool at BaseballHQ.com called the Rotisserie Grid. It is a chart—that can be customized to your league parameters—which organizes players into pockets of skill, by position. It is one of the most popular tools on the site. One of the best features of this grid is that its design provides immediate insight into position scarcity.

So in the *Forecaster*, we have transitioned to this format as a sort of Universal Draft Grid.

How to use the chart

Across the top of the grid, players are sorted by position. First and third base, and second and shortstop are presented side-by-side for easy reference when considering corner and middle infielders, respectively.

The vertical axis separates each group of players into tiers based on potential fantasy impact. At the top are the Elite players; at the bottom are the Fringe players.

Auction leagues: The tiers in the grid represent rough break-points for dollar values. Elite players could be considered those that are purchased for $30 and up. Each subsequent tier is a step down of approximately $5.

Snake drafters: Tiers can be used to rank players similarly, though most tiers will encompass more than one round. Any focus on position scarcity will bump some players up a bit. In recent years, Catcher has been the only position to exhibit any real positional scarcity effect. As such, one might opt to draft J.T. Realmuto (from the Stars tier) before the Gold level Marcus Semien.

To build the best foundation, try to stay balanced in the first 10 rounds of your draft: 2 MI, 2 CI, 3 OF, and 3 SP (likely one closer) is a foundation target that will set you up for maximum flexibility in the mid- and end-games.

The **players** are listed at the position where they both qualify and provide the most fantasy value. Additional position eligibility (20 games) is listed in parentheses. Listings in bold are players with high reliability grades (minimum "B" across the board).

Each player is presented with his 7-character Mayberry score. The first four digits (all on a 0-5 scale) represent skill: power, speed, batting average and playing time for batters; ERA, dominance, saves potential and playing time for pitchers. The last three alpha characters are the reliability grade (A-F): health, experience and consistency.

Within each tier, players are sorted by the first character of their Mayberry score. This means that batters are sorted by power; pitchers by ERA potential. If you need to prospect for the best skill sets among players in a given tier, target those with 4s and 5s in whatever skill you need.

CAVEATS and DISCLAIMERS

The placement of players in tiers does not represent average draft positions (ADP) or average auction values (AAV). It represents where each player's true value may lie. It is the variance between this true value and the ADP/AAV market values—or better, the value that your league-mates place on each player—where you will find your potential for profit or loss.

That means ***you cannot take this chart right into your draft with you***. You have to compare these rankings with your ADPs and AAVs, and build your draft list from there. In other words, if we project Ozzie Albies as a "Elite" level pick but you know the other owners (or your ADPs) see him as a third-rounder, you can probably wait to pick him up in round two. If you are in an auction league with owners who overvalue young players and Fernando Tatis Jr. (projected at $27) gets bid past $30, you will likely take a loss should you decide to chase the bidding, especially given the depth of shortstops in 2020.

Finally, this chart is intended as a preliminary look based on current factors. For Draft Day, you will need to make your own adjustments based upon many different criteria that will impact the world between now and then. Daily updates appear online at BaseballHQ.com. A free projections update is available in March at **http://www.baseballhq.com/bf2020**

Simulation League Cheat Sheet   Using Runs Above Replacement creates a more real-world ranking of player value, which serves simulation gamers well. Batters and pitchers are integrated, and value break-points are delineated.

Universal Draft Grid

TIER	FIRST BASE	THIRD BASE	SECOND BASE	SHORTSTOP
Elite	Bellinger,Cody (O) (4455 AAF) **Freeman,Freddie (4255 BAB)**	Ramirez,Jose (4355 BAD) **Arenado,Nolan (4255 AAA)** Devers,Rafael (4145 BBD) **Rendon,Anthony (4255 BAA)**	**Albies,Ozzie (3545 AAA)** **Merrifield,Whit (O) (2545 AAB)**	Story,Trevor (4525 BAC) **Lindor,Francisco (3355 AAA)** Bregman,Alex (3) (3355 AAC) Mondesi,Adalberto (3515 CDB) Turner,Trea (2545 CAB) **Villar,Jonathan (2) (2525 AAB)**
Gold	Goldschmidt,Paul (4235 AAC)	**Suarez,Eugenio (4225 AAB)** Bryant,Kris (O) (4335 BAC) Moncada,Yoan (4425 BBC)	Hiura,Keston (4335 AFF) Altuve,Jose (3455 BAC) Marte,Ketel (O) (3555 ABC) McNeil,Jeff (O) (2355 ACD) LeMahieu,DJ (31) (1255 BAC)	Bichette,Bo (4555 ADA) **Baez,Javier (4445 AAB)** Tatis Jr.,Fernando (4535 CDD) **Bogaerts,Xander (3255 AAB)** **Semien,Marcus (3345 BAB)** Anderson,Tim (2535 BBC) **Rosario,Amed (1535 AAA)** Andrus,Elvis (1445 CAC)
Stars	Alonso,Peter (4135 ACD) **Olson,Matt (4235 BBB)** Hoskins,Rhys (4225 AAC) Bell,Josh (4045 CAB) **Rizzo,Anthony (3155 BAA)** Mancini,Trey (O) (3245 AAD) **Abreu,Jose (3145 AAB)** Santana,Carlos (3245 AAC) Santana,Daniel (O) (3525 CDC) Votto,Joey (2245 BAF)	Chapman,Matt (4135 AAC) Turner,Justin (3255 CBB) **Gurriel,Yulieski (1) (2255 ABB)** Guerrero Jr.,Vladimir (2045 ADF)	Muncy,Max (31) (4135 ACF) Moustakas,Mike (3) (3145 CAB)	Correa,Carlos (4345 FCF) Machado,Manny (3) (3235 AAF) Torres,Gleyber (2) (3235 ACA) Seager,Corey (3255 FCB) **Polanco,Jorge (2245 ABA)** **Segura,Jean (1455 BAB)** Simmons,Andrelton (1345 CAB)
Regulars	Thames,Eric (5325 BCB) **Encarnacion,Edwin (4135 BAB)** Tellez,Rowdy (4045 ACB) **Cron,C.J. (4035 BBB)** Pederson,Joc (4135 ACB) Cooper,Garrett (O) (3045 FDF) **Nunez,Renato (3225 ABB)** Murphy,Daniel (2155 DBD) Hosmer,Eric (2135 AAD)	Sano,Miguel (5015 DCF) Donaldson,Josh (4245 DBC) Kingery,Scott (O) (3515 BBD) **Anderson,Brian (O) (3235 BBA)** Davis,J.D. (O) (3345 ACC) Seager,Kyle (3035 CBB) Solak,Nick (2425 ACA) Longoria,Evan (2335 CAB)	Biggio,Cavan (4305 ADA) McMahon,Ryan (3) (4225 ACF) **Escobar,Eduardo (3) (3235 AAB)** Edman,Tommy (3) (2543 ACB) **Castro,Starlin (3) (2235 BAB)** Profar,Jurickson (2345 BBD) Lux,Gavin (2325 AFC) Dubon,Mauricio (2355 ACB) Kendrick,Howie (1) (2253 FDC) Wong,Kolten (1435 BBC) **Hernandez,Cesar (1535 AAB)** **Frazier,Adam (1255 ABA)** **Gordon,Dee (0545 BAB)** Arraez,Luis (O) (0255 AFD) Madrigal,Nick (1553 AFF)	**Adames,Willy (3325 ABA)** **DeJong,Paul (3225 BBB)** Goodrum,Niko (2O) (3425 BCB) Gregorius,Didi (2235 DDC) **Swanson,Dansby (2325 BBA)** Newman,Kevin (2) (1445 CBB) Berti,Jon (3O) (1543 CDB) **Fletcher,David (23) (0345 ABB)**
Mid-Level	Moreland,Mitch (4145 CBA) Voit,Luke (4035 BCC) Choi,Ji-Man (4133 ACA) Walker,Christian (4325 CCD) Belt,Brandon (3225 CBB) Smith,Dominic (O) (3033 CCF) Zimmerman,Ryan (3133 FCD) Aguilar,Jesus (3023 ACD) Vogelbach,Daniel (3015 ACD) Lowe,Nate (3133 AFD) Osuna,Jose (O) (3143 BDA) **Pujols,Albert (2135 BAA)** Cabrera,Miguel (2035 FCF)	Dozier,Hunter (O) (4215 BCC) Carpenter,Matt (4225 BAF) Lamb,Jacob (1) (3223 FCD) Diaz,Yandy (1) (2135 DCB) Gonzalez,Marwin (1O) (2133 ABD) Urshela,Giovanny (2043 BDD) Duffy,Matt (1333 FFD)	**Odor,Rougned (4225 BAB)** Chavis,Michael (1) (4115 BDB) Lowe,Brandon (4423 CDC) Dozier,Brian (3223 AAC) Hampson,Garrett (O) (2513 AFD) Gennett,Scooter (2225 DCF) Cano,Robinson (2045 FBD) **Cabrera,Asdrubal (3) (2235 BBA)** Kipnis,Jason (2225 CCA) Flores,Wilmer (2143 CCB) Diaz,Aledmys (1) (2233 DDB) La Stella,Tommy (3) (1055 FFC) Alberto,Hanser (3) (1245 DDB)	Taylor,Chris (2O) (3523 BBB) Rodriguez,Ronny (2) (3323 ACA) Kieboom,Carter (3313 AFB) Ahmed,Nick (2345 CBA) **Iglesias,Jose (1255 BBA)** Rojas,Miguel (1245 CBB) Peraza,Jose (2O) (1433 ABD) **Arcia,Orlando (1325 ABB)** Crawford,J.P. (1415 CDA) Lopez,Nicky (2) (0335 ACD)
Bench	Cron,Kevin (4043 ACC) Adams,Matt (4123 CDC) O Hearn,Ryan (4123 ACA) Dixon,Brandon (O) (3313 ACB) Ford,Mike (3041 ACF) Smoak,Justin (3023 AAC) Guzman,Ronald (3133 BCA) **Bauers,Jake (O) (2223 ABB)** Beaty,Matt (O) (2251 ADC)	Miller,Brad (4213 BDB) Healy,Ryon (3033 FCB) Shaw,Travis (3203 ABD) Candelario,Jeimer (1) (2223 CBB) Moran,Colin (2035 BCA) Franco,Maikel (2333 ABD) Bohm,Alec (2231 AFF) Frazier,Todd (2113 CBB) Drury,Brandon (2023 CCB) Gyorko,Jedd (1213 DDD) Munoz,Yairo (1431 ADA) Walker,Neil (1) (1233 CCC) Ruiz,Rio (1013 ACA) Dalbec,Bobby (3201 AFA)	Barreto,Franklin (4301 ACB) Schoop,Jonathan (3023 BBC) Dietrich,Derek (1) (3113 ACB) Brosseau,Michael (3111 AFC) Pinder,Chad (O) (3023 BDB) France,Ty (3) (3031 ACC) Hernandez,Enrique (O) (2323 BCC) Bote,David (3) (2313 ACB) Diaz,Isan (2205 ADB) Neuse,Sheldon (2103 ADF) Rodgers,Brendan (1323 DDA) Rengifo,Luis (1323 ADB) Wendle,Joe (3) (1433 DCF) Vargas,Ildemaro (1451 ACC) Sogard,Eric (1333 DDF) Sanchez,Yolmer (1313 CAB) Kemp,Anthony (O) (1321 ACC) Castro,Harold (O) (0333 ACC) Panik,Joe (0341 CBC) Lowrie,Jed (1223 FBF)	Beckham,Tim (3213 CCC) Moore,Dylan (O) (3411 ACD) **Galvis,Freddy (2) (2323 AAA)** Camargo,Johan (2233 BDC) Russell,Addison (2) (2313 BCA) Castro,Willi (1413 ADA) Urias,Luis (2) (1325 ACB) **Crawford,Brandon (1135 ABC)** Tucker,Cole (1533 ACB) Perez,Hernan (2) (1313 ACA) Martin,Richie (1521 ACD) Straw,Myles (0511 ADB)
Fringe	Bird,Gregory (4021 FFC) Walsh,Jared (4301 ADB) Davis,Chris (3103 BBC) Nola,Austin (2311 ADB) Alonso,Yonder (2031 ABD) Travis,Sam (1201 ADB)	Thaiss,Matt (4131 ACB) Sandoval,Pablo (1) (3031 FDB) Toro,Abraham (2231 AFC) **Lugo,Dawel (1341 ABB)** Cuthbert,Cheslor (1) (1001 FFB) Forsythe,Logan (1) (1303 CCA)	Farmer,Kyle (2121 ADB) Long,Shed (2311 CDA) Holt,Brock (1223 FDD) Garcia,Greg (1221 CDB)	Mercer,Jordy (2133 CCA) Adrianza,Ehire (31) (1221 DDA) Gonzalez,Erik (1511 DFC)

Universal Draft Grid

Elite

TIER	CATCHER	DH	OUTFIELD	
Elite			Trout,Mike (5455 BAC)	Blackmon,Charlie (3255 AAC)
			Yelich,Christian (4455 AAF)	**Pham,Thomas (3445 BAB)**
			Betts,Mookie (4555 AAF)	**Marte,Starling (2555 ABA)**
			Acuna,Ronald (4535 ABA)	
			Harper,Bryce (4345 AAD)	
			Martinez,J.D. (4355 BAC)	

Gold

TIER	CATCHER	DH	OUTFIELD	
Gold		Alvarez,Yordan (5145 ADF)	Meadows,Austin (4445 ACC)	Robles,Victor (2535 ADC)
		Cruz,Nelson (4045 AAD)	Springer,George (4345 CAD)	Smith,Mallex (1525 BBD)
			Soto,Juan (4455 CCB)	**Mercado,Oscar (1525 ABA)**
			Laureano,Ramon (4435 BCC)	
			Jimenez,Eloy (4045 BDD)	
			Castellanos,Nick (4145 AAC)	
			Rosario,Eddie (3245 AAA)	
			Puig,Yasiel (3335 BBB)	

Stars

TIER	CATCHER	DH	OUTFIELD	
Stars	Realmuto,J.T. (3445 AAB)	Andujar,Miguel (3155 FDF)	Judge,Aaron (5125 DBC)	Ozuna,Marcell (3245 BAC)
			Gallo,Joey (5115 DBC)	Choo,Shin-Soo (3335 CAB)
			Conforto,Michael (4235 BAC)	Brantley,Michael (2255 CBA)
			Soler,Jorge (4225 DCC)	Reynolds,Bryan (2345 ADC)
			Braun,Ryan (4353 BBB)	Cain,Lorenzo (1445 BAC)
			Dahl,David (4335 FFC)	Eaton,Adam (1535 FCB)
			Stanton,Giancarlo (4125 FBC)	Inciarte,Ender (1445 FBB)
			Reyes,Franmil (4035 ABC)	
			Schwarber,Kyle (4135 CBA)	
			Benintendi,Andrew (3435 AAD)	

Regulars

TIER	CATCHER	DH	OUTFIELD	
Regulars	Contreras,Willson (4245 BBD)	Davis,Khris (4225 BAC)	**Grichuk,Randal (4325 BBB)**	**Bradley,Jackie (3325 ABA)**
	Sanchez,Gary (4035 DCD)	Ohtani,Shohei (4543 CDD)	Upton,Justin (4115 DBC)	Adell,Jo (3433 AFA)
	Garver,Mitch (4133 ADD)		Buxton,Byron (4525 FDD)	**Desmond,Ian (3335 BBA)**
	Grandal,Yasmani (1) (3125 ABA)		Dickerson,Corey (4255 DBA)	Tsutsugo,Yoshitomo (3043 AAC)
	Ramos,Wilson (1135 CCD)		Hernandez,Teoscar (4325 ACB)	**Pillar,Kevin (2345 AAA)**
	Molina,Yadier (1245 CBA)		Santana,Domingo (4305 CBC)	Garcia,Avisail (2225 CBC)
	Perez,Salvador (3125 FDC)		Canha,Mark (4235 CCC)	Peralta,David (2345 FBD)
			Nimmo,Brandon (4425 FCF)	Winker,Jesse (2055 DCC)
			Aquino,Aristides (4215 ACD)	Senzel,Nick (2425 DDF)
			Haniger,Mitch (4235 FCD)	Grisham,Trent (2315 ADF)
			Myers,Wil (3415 CBA)	Verdugo,Alex (2155 BCA)
			McCutchen,Andrew (3235 FBB)	Bader,Harrison (2505 ACB)
			Pollock,A.J. (3443 FCA)	Piscotty,Stephen (2135 CCD)
			Mazara,Nomar (3235 BBA)	Tucker,Kyle (2313 ADC)
			Calhoun,Willie (3245 ACC)	Arozarena,Randy (2423 ADC)
			Kepler,Max (3135 CAB)	**VanMeter,Josh (2323 ABB)**
			Gurriel,Lourdes (3235 CDB)	Markakis,Nick (1255 CAC)

Mid-Level

TIER	CATCHER	DH	OUTFIELD	
Mid-Level	Smith,Will (4313 AFD)	Cespedes,Yoenis (4233 FFC)	Yastrzemski,Mike (4225 ACC)	Hays,Austin (2333 ADD)
	Chirinos,Robinson (4213 BCB)		Riley,Austin (4105 BDC)	Maybin,Cameron (2323 CCB)
	Kelly,Carson (3035 ADC)		Renfroe,Hunter (4325 BCA)	Naylor,Josh (2035 ACC)
	Alfaro,Jorge (3215 ACA)		Luplow,Jordan (4233 ADD)	**Heyward,Jason (1335 BBA)**
	Mejia,Francisco (3133 BDC)		Goodwin,Brian (4313 FDB)	Tapia,Raimel (1543 ACC)
	Suzuki,Kurt (2043 ADB)		Fraley,Jake (4321 AFF)	Reddick,Josh (1335 BBC)
	McCann,James (2123 ACD)		Robert,Luis (3513 AFF)	Garcia,Leury (1533 DCA)
	Narvaez,Omar (1035 ACA)		**Calhoun,Kole (3125 AAB)**	DeShields Jr.,Delino (1503 BCC)
	Vazquez,Christian (1235 CCF)		O'Neill,Tyler (3303 BCD)	Ramirez,Harold (1243 ABC)
	Posey,Buster (1245 CBD)		Polanco,Gregory (3323 FCD)	Reyes,Victor (1433 ACD)
			Jones,JaCoby (3413 DCA)	Rojas,Josh (1433 ADC)
			Gardner,Brett (2523 AAB)	**Margot,Manuel (1523 ABA)**
			Dean,Austin (2135 ADB)	Locastro,Tim (1513 ADA)
			Fowler,Dexter (2325 CBF)	**Gordon,Alex (1135 BAB)**
			Santander,Anthony (2225 CDF)	Dyson,Jarrod (0523 DCB)
			Kiermaier,Kevin (2533 FCB)	

Bench

TIER	CATCHER	DH	OUTFIELD	
Bench	Murphy,Tom (4211 BFD)	Pence,Hunter (2423 FCF)	Tauchman,Mike (4251 ADB)	Naquin,Tyler (2231 FFB)
	Perez,Roberto (3103 BDD)	Diaz,Yusniel (2121 ADB)	Lewis,Kyle (4313 AFC)	**McBroom,Ryan (2023 ABB)**
	Gomes,Yan (3313 BCB)		Bruce,Jay (4023 CCC)	Stewart,Christin (2213 BCB)
	Murphy,Sean (3133 CFC)		Frazier,Clint (4313 DDD)	Slater,Austin (2323 BDA)
	Vogt,Stephen (3133 FFA)		Cordero,Franchy (4521 FFB)	Duggar,Steven (2313 DFA)
	Rogers,Jake (2203 AFA)		Cave,Jake (4333 ACB)	Kelenic,Jarred (2521 AFF)
	Castro,Jason (3203 FDF)		Happ,Ian (4313 ACB)	Engel,Adam (2501 ACA)
	Jansen,Danny (2133 ADD)		Duvall,Adam (4223 ABC)	Stewart,D.J. (2103 CCB)
	Caratini,Victor (1) (2233 BDD)		Dickerson,Alex (3533 FFF)	Culberson,Charlie (2211 BDF)
	D'Arnaud,Travis (1) (2023 FDB)		Marisnick,Jake (3501 ADB)	Jones,Adam (1223 CAB)
	Stallings,Jacob (2023 AFC)		Hicks,Aaron (3221 FCB)	Quinn,Roman (1501 FFC)
	Wieters,Matt (2021 CDB)		**Demeritte,Travis (3403 ABA)**	Haseley,Adam (1233 AFC)
	Romine,Austin (2121 ADB)		Phillips,Brett (3503 ACD)	Allen,Greg (1511 ADB)
	Flowers,Tyler (2003 BDB)		Brown,Seth (3311 ADA)	Almora,Albert (1343 ACC)
	Hicks,John (1) (2103 BDC)		Carlson,Dylan (3431 AFF)	Cabrera,Melky (1153 ACA)
	McGuire,Reese (2333 AFC)		Zimmer,Bradley (3501 FFC)	**Grossman,Robert (1223 ABB)**
	Astudillo,Willians (1051 CFA)		Ervin,Phillip (2323 ADA)	Parra,Gerardo (1241 BCC)
	Barnhart,Tucker (1125 BCB)		Herrera,Odubel (2323 ACC)	Gamel,Ben (1323 ACB)
	Kiner-Falefa,Isiah (3) (1321 BCB)		Martinez,Jose (2443 BCD)	Sierra,Magneuris (0533 ACC)
			Reyes,Pablo (2323 ACA)	**Hamilton,Billy (0501 ABB)**
			Fisher,Derek (2303 ADB)	Mullins II,Cedric (0411 ACC)

Fringe

TIER	CATCHER	DH	OUTFIELD	
Fringe	McCann,Brian (0000 DDD)	Collins,Zack (3403 ADC)	McKinney,Billy (3221 BCB)	
	Zunino,Mike (4003 BCD)		Broxton,Keon (3501 ADC)	
	Sisco,Chance (3103 ADC)		Granderson,Curtis (3111 ACC)	
	Hedges,Austin (2203 ADD)		Smith,Dwight (2223 BDA)	
	Severino,Pedro (2123 ADB)		Wilkerson,Steve (2103 BFB)	
	Maldonado,Martin (2011 ACA)		Cordell,Ryan (2401 AFB)	
	Diaz,Elias (1013 CDF)		Brinson,Lewis (1403 BCC)	
	Phegley,Joshua (1011 DFA)		Starling,Bubba (1201 BFA)	
	Barnes,Austin (1301 ADF)		Lagares,Juan (1411 FFF)	
	Lucroy,Jonathan (1331 BCB)		Fowler,Dustin (2411 BCC)	
	Trevino,Jose (1221 ADA)		Pache,Cristian (2223 AFC)	
	Greiner,Grayson (1001 CDB)		Souza,Steven (3313 FDD)	
	Nido,Tomas (1001 AFB)			
	Wolters,Tony (0223 CDB)			

Universal Draft Grid

TIER	STARTING PITCHERS				RELIEF PITCHERS			
Elite	Cole,Gerrit	(5505 BAB)	Verlander,Justin	(5505 BAB)				
	deGrom,Jacob	(5505 AAB)						
Gold	**Buehler,Walker**	**(5405 BBB)**	**Flaherty,Jack**	**(4405 ABB)**	Hader,Josh	(5531 ABB)		
	Scherzer,Max	(5503 DAA)	**Greinke,Zack**	**(3205 AAA)**				
	Strasburg,Stephen	(5505 DAA)						
Stars	**Bieber,Shane**	**(5405 ABA)**	Clevinger,Mike	(4505 DBA)	Chapman,Aroldis	(5530 DBB)		
	Kershaw,Clayton	(5403 FAA)	Giolito,Lucas	(4505 CBC)	**Hand,Brad**	**(5530 BBA)**		
	Morton,Charlie	(5405 DAA)	Ryu,Hyun-Jin	(4203 FBB)	Osuna,Roberto	(5430 ABA)		
	Sale,Chris	(5503 DAB)	Snell,Blake	(4505 DBB)	**Yates,Kirby**	**(5530 BBA)**		
Regulars	**Castillo,Luis**	**(5405 AAA)**	Bumgarner,Madison	(3205 DAA)	Diaz,Edwin	(5530 AAC)	Iglesias,Raisel	(4530 CAA)
	Corbin,Patrick	(4405 BAC)	Gray,Sonny	(3303 CAA)	**Giles,Ken**	**(5530 ABA)**	Kimbrel,Craig	(4530 DBC)
	Darvish,Yu	(4505 FBB)	**Hendricks,Kyle**	**(3205 BAA)**	Hendriks,Liam	(5530 DCB)	Neris,Hector	(4531 ACA)
	Kluber,Corey	(4305 FAC)	**Mikolas,Miles**	**(3105 CAA)**	**Jansen,Kenley**	**(5530 BAB)**	Pagan,Emilio	(4530 ACD)
	Nola,Aaron	(4405 CAA)	Paddack,Chris	(3303 ADF)	Rogers,Taylor	(5430 ACB)	Workman,Brandon	(4520 FDA)
	Paxton,James	(4503 FAB)	Soroka,Michael	(3105 FCB)	Smith,Will	(5530 FCA)	Bradley,Archie	(3331 BCA)
	Woodruff,Brandon	(4405 DCB)			Carrasco,Carlos	(4403 FAA)	Robles,Hansel	(2330 BCB)
Mid-Level	Glasnow,Tyler	(5401 FCB)	Rodriguez,Eduardo	(3305 DAA)	Gallegos,Giovanny	(4411 ADB)		
	Severino,Luis	(4403 FBA)	Tanaka,Masahiro	(3203 CAB)	Lugo,Seth	(4421 DBB)		
	Syndergaard,Noah	(4303 DBB)	Weaver,Luke	(3303 FCC)	Melancon,Mark	(4220 FCB)		
	Bauer,Trevor	(3405 CAB)	Wheeler,Zack	(3305 DAB)	Doolittle,Sean	(3430 FBC)		
	Fried,Max	(3305 BCB)	**Berrios,Jose**	**(2305 AAA)**	Givens,Mychal	(3520 ACA)		
	Lynn,Lance	(3405 DAA)	Gallen,Zac	(2203 ADD)	Jimenez,Joe	(3530 ADC)		
	Maeda,Kenta	(3413 CAA)	Manaea,Sean	(2203 FBC)	Leclerc,Jose	(3520 BCC)		
	Ohtani,Shohei	(3401 DFD)	Odorizzi,Jake	(2305 CAA)	**Colome,Alex**	**(2330 BBB)**		
	Price,David	(3403 FAB)	Yarbrough,Ryan	(2203 ACC)	Kennedy,Ian	(2330 DBB)		
Bench	Hill,Rich	(4401 FBA)	Happ,I.A.	(2203 CAB)	Anderson,Nick	(5510 ADF)		
	Luzardo,Jesus	(4301 BFA)	**Kelly,Merrill**	**(2203 AAB)**	Castillo,Diego	(5410 BDC)		
	McCullers,Lance	(4403 FCA)	**Lucchesi,Joey**	**(2303 BBB)**	Green,Chad	(5501 ACA)		
	Boyd,Matt	**(3403 AAB)**	Mahle,Tyler	(2203 CCD)	Harris,Will	(5410 BDA)		
	German,Domingo	(3403 BCA)	Matz,Steven	(2203 FBB)	Martin,Christopher	(5410 DDD)		
	Gray,Jonathan	(3303 FAA)	May,Dustin	(2103 ADB)	Pressly,Ryan	(5510 DCB)		
	Keuchel,Dallas	(3103 CAA)	Montas,Frankie	(2303 DDC)	Kela,Keone	(4520 FCA)		
	Lamet,Dinelson	(3501 FDA)	**Quintana,Jose**	**(2203 AAA)**	Miller,Andrew	(4520 FDB)		
	Marquez,German	(3305 CAB)	Sanchez,Anibal	(2203 DBF)	Munoz,Andres	(4510 AFB)		
	Martinez,Carlos	(3303 FAB)	Anderson,Chase	(1203 DAA)	Stammen,Craig	(4211 DCB)		
	Musgrove,Joe	(3203 DBB)	**Fiers,Mike**	**(1103 BAA)**	Stripling,Ross	(4301 DCA)		
	Pineda,Michael	(3303 FCA)	Gonsolin,Tony	(1201 AFC)	Greene,Shane	(3320 CBA)		
	Ray,Robbie	(3503 DAA)	Hudson,Dakota	(1103 ACC)	May,Trevor	(3510 FDC)		
	Stroman,Marcus	(3205 DAA)	Minor,Mike	(1205 FAA)	Petit,Yusmeiro	(3201 ACA)		
	Chirinos,Yonny	(2103 DCA)	Samardzija,Jeff	(1103 FBC)	Hudson,Daniel	(2320 DCA)		
	Cueto,Johnny	(2103 FCB)	Smith,Caleb	(1303 FCA)	Magill,Matthew	(2320 CDB)		
	DeSclafani,Anthony	(2203 FCC)	**Teheran,Julio**	**(1205 BAA)**	Peralta,Freddy	(2501 BDB)		
	Foltynewicz,Mike	(2203 DBB)			Urias,Julio	(2301 FDF)		
Fringe	Archer,Chris	(3503 FAA)	Eflin,Zach	(1103 DCC)	Barnes,Matt	(5510 ACA)	Ramirez,Noe	(3401 BDA)
	Keller,Mitch	(3301 ADC)	Gonzales,Marco	(1103 ABC)	Betances,Dellin	(5510 FDD)	Stephenson,Robert	(3500 DDA)
	Manning,Matt	(3201 AFF)	Keller,Brad	(1003 ABC)	Jackson,Luke	(5510 ADC)	Strahm,Matt	(3401 FDD)
	McKay,Brendan	(3501 AFF)	Kikuchi,Yusei	(1103 AAC)	Kahnle,Tommy	(5500 CDF)	Strop,Pedro	(3410 DCA)
	Puk,A.J.	(3401 CFA)	Lauer,Eric	(1203 BCA)	Kelly,Joe	(5410 CCA)	Suero,Wander	(3400 ADA)
	Richards,Garrett	(3301 FDB)	**Leake,Mike**	**(1005 AAA)**	Kittredge,Andrew	(5400 ADF)	Taylor,Josh	(3410 ADD)
	Whitley,Forrest	(3401 AFF)	**Lopez,Reynaldo**	**(1205 DAA)**	Britton,Zach	(4210 FCA)	Wilson,Justin	(3510 DCA)
	Wood,Alex	(3301 FBB)	Miley,Wade	(1103 FBB)	Bummer,Aaron	(4201 ADA)	Wingenter,Trey	(3500 BDC)
	Arrieta,Jake	(2103 DAA)	Montgomery,Jordan	(1201 FCA)	Buttrey,Ty	(4410 ADD)	Baez,Pedro	(2300 DCA)
	Bundy,Dylan	**(2303 BAA)**	Nova,Ivan	(1005 CAA)	Chafin,Andrew	(4400 BDA)	Brebbia,John	(2401 ADB)
	Burke,Brock	(2201 AFF)	Plesac,Zach	(1101 ADA)	Clase,Emmanuel	(4210 AFF)	Cishek,Steve	(2210 BCB)
	Canning,Griffin	(2301 DDA)	**Roark,Tanner**	**(1203 AAA)**	Dominguez,Seranthony	(4410 FFF)	Clippard,Tyler	(2400 ACA)
	Dobnak,Randy	(2001 AFF)	Smyly,Drew	(1301 FDF)	Duffey,Tyler	(4401 ADD)	Devenski,Christopher	(2300 BCB)
	Fulmer,Michael	(2101 FCA)	Thornton,Trent	(1103 ACC)	James,Josh	(4501 CDC)	Diaz,Jairo	(2220 FFF)
	Gibson,Kyle	(2305 CAB)	Walker,Taijuan	(1201 FDA)	Knebel,Corey	(4510 FCB)	Estevez,Carlos	(2310 DDF)
	Gonzalez,Gio	(2203 DBA)	Williams,Trevor	(1103 CAA)	Smith,Joe	(4300 FDB)	Hirano,Yoshihisa	(2300 CBB)
	Hamels,Cole	(2303 DAB)	Means,John	(0003 BCA)	Soria,Joakim	(4410 CCA)	Kelley,Shawn	(2310 FDC)
	Heaney,Andrew	(2403 FCD)			Alvarado,Jose	(3510 DDC)	Lorenzen,Michael	(2210 DCB)
	Houser,Adrian	(2203 ADF)			Feliz,Michael	(3510 CDA)	Minter,A.J.	(2410 BDC)
	Junis,Jakob	**(2203 AAA)**			Fernandez,Junior	(3410 AFF)	Newcomb,Sean	(2301 ACA)
	Kopech,Michael	(2401 FDC)			Gausman,Kevin	(3410 DAA)	Pena,Felix	(2301 DDC)
	Lester,Jon	(2205 CAA)			Hughes,Jared	(3100 BCB)	Rodriguez,Richard	(2300 BDD)
	Lopez,Pablo	(2203 FDD)			Kolarek,Adam	(3100 ADB)	Romo,Sergio	(2310 DCA)
	Porcello,Rick	(2203 AAC)			McHugh,Collin	(3401 FDC)	Stanek,Ryne	(2410 BDB)
	Sanchez,Sixto	(2101 AFF)			Middleton,Keynan	(3510 FDD)	Suter,Brent	(2101 FDF)
	Shoemaker,Matthew	(2201 FDB)			Montero,Rafael	(3310 FDD)	Treinen,Blake	(2310 BBD)
	Urquidy,Jose	(2301 AFF)			Nelson,Jimmy	(3301 FCF)	Walden,Marcus	(2211 ADF)
	Wainwright,Adam	(2203 FBB)			Oberg,Scott	(3210 DDC)	Wick,Rowan	(2310 ADB)
	Alcantara,Sandy	(1105 BBC)			Ottavino,Adam	(3510 FCD)	Wittgren,Nick	(2310 DDB)
	Cease,Dylan	(1303 ADF)			Parker,Blake	(3411 ACB)	Gant,John	(1211 CCC)
	Civale,Aaron	(1101 ADF)			Peacock,Brad	(3401 FCC)	Lyles,Jordan	(1203 DCD)
	Davies,Zachary	(1003 FBA)			Poche,Colin	(3500 AFF)	Tepera,Ryan	(1210 FCB)
	Duffy,Danny	(1203 FAA)			Pomeranz,Drew	(3401 DBF)	Tuivailala,Sam	(1300 FDB)

Universal Draft Grid

TIER	STARTING PITCHERS				RELIEF PITCHERS			
Below Fringe	Taillon,Jameson	(3200 FBB)	Rodriguez,Dereck	(1101 ADF)	Adams,Austin L	(5500 ADF)	Ryan,Kyle	(2200 ADF)
	Valdez,Framber	(3301 ADD)	Ross,Joe	(1101 FDC)	Hicks,Jordan	(5310 FDC)	Shaw,Bryan	(2200 BCB)
	Beede,Tyler	(2303 ADB)	Sanchez,Aaron	(1100 FCB)	Robertson,David	(5500 FCF)	Suarez,Ranger	(2101 ADC)
	Cessa,Luis	(2201 DDC)	Sandoval,Patrick	(1301 AFF)	Vazquez,Felipe	**(5500 ABA)**	Swanson,Erik	(2310 ADF)
	Eovaldi,Nathan	(2303 FDC)	Smeltzer,Devin	(1101 ADB)	Drake,Oliver	(4400 ADA)	Trivino,Lou	(2300 ADB)
	Palumbo,Joseph	(2401 DFF)	Suarez,Jose	(1201 ADD)	Ginkel,Kevin	(4500 AFA)	Vizcaino,Arodys	(2410 FDB)
	Rodon,Carlos	(2400 FCB)	Toussaint,Touki	(1301 ADF)	Chatwood,Tyler	(3301 BBD)	Wisler,Matt	(2300 ADB)
	Salazar,Danny	(2300 FDD)	Urena,Jose	(1011 FAB)	Dyson,Sam	(3110 BCC)	Wood,Hunter	(2200 BDD)
	Sheffield,Justus	(2203 ADF)	Vargas,Jason	(1101 FAB)	Hernandez,Darwinzon	(3500 AFF)	Anderson,Justin	(1400 CDD)
	Turnbull,Spencer	(2203 CCB)	Voth,Austin	(1101 CDC)	Hill,Tim	(3210 ADC)	Armstrong,Shawn	(1310 BDF)
	Velasquez,Vincent	(2303 FBB)	Wacha,Michael	(1103 FBB)	Loaisiga,Jonathan	(3401 FFB)	Bettis,Chad	(1001 FCB)
	Agrazal,Dario	(1001 ADA)	Webb,Logan	(1103 AFA)	Martin,Brett	(3310 ADF)	Biagini,Joe	(1100 ADD)
	Allard,Kolby	(1101 ADB)	Wilson,Bryse	(1200 ADA)	Andriese,Matt	(2300 DCA)	Brennan,Brandon	(1210 DDC)
	Anderson,Brett	(1001 FCC)	Wright,Kyle	(1100 ADC)	Barlow,Scott	(2300 ADF)	Brice,Austin	(1100 FDA)
	Anderson,Shaun	(1110 BDB)	Yamamoto,Jordan	(1203 BDD)	Bass,Anthony	(2210 CDF)	Castro,Miguel	(1111 ACC)
	Bailey,Homer	(1103 FBD)	Young,Alex	(1103 ADA)	Bedrosian,Cam	(2300 DCA)	Chavez,Jesse	(1201 DBB)
	Bassitt,Chris	(1201 FCB)	Allen,Logan	(0100 ADF)	Brewer,Colten	(2300 BDD)	Chen,Wei-Yin	(1100 FCA)
	Beeks,Jalen	(1201 ACA)	Alzolay,Adbert	(0201 AFC)	Burnes,Corbin	(2301 BDF)	Claudio,Alex	(1000 DCB)
	Brault,Steven	(1201 CCB)	Barria,Jaime	(0101 ADC)	Cimber,Adam	(2000 ADB)	Cole,A.J.	(1300 DDC)
	Cahill,Trevor	(1201 FCD)	Blach,Ty	(0000 ABF)	Erlin,Robert	(2100 FDF)	Cole,Taylor	(1200 BDF)
	Chacin,Jhoulys	(1201 FAA)	Brooks,Aaron	(0001 DCD)	Familia,Jeurys	(2410 FCC)	Crick,Kyle	(1400 CDB)
	Cobb,Alex	(1001 FBB)	Cabrera,Genesis	(0200 ADF)	Ferguson,Caleb	(2400 BDD)	Davis,Wade	(1400 DBC)
	Covey,Dylan	(1003 FDD)	Cashner,Andrew	(0003 DAA)	Floro,Dylan	(2200 BDD)	Elias,Roenis	(1200 FDF)
	Dunn,Justin	(1301 ADB)	Clarke,Taylor	(0001 BDC)	Font,Wilmer	(2300 DCB)	Farmer,Buck	(1201 ACB)
	Fedde,Erick	(1001 DDA)	Dugger,Robert	(0100 ADD)	Fry,Paul	(2310 ADD)	Garcia,Jarlin	(1010 BDB)
	Freeland,Kyle	(1103 DBD)	Eickhoff,Jerad	(0100 FDB)	Garcia,Yimi	(2300 FDD)	Gsellman,Robert	(1100 DCB)
	Gore,MacKenzie	(1301 AFF)	Harvey,Matt	(0101 FCD)	Garrett,Amir	(2400 CDD)	Guerra,Javy	(1100 ADC)
	Hernandez,Elieser	(1203 CDD)	Hoffman,Jeff	(0101 ADC)	Gaviglio,Sam	(2101 ACB)	Guerra,Junior	(1200 DCB)
	Hernandez,Felix	(1100 FBB)	Lockett,Walker	(0000 ADC)	Gott,Trevor	(2300 DDC)	Helsley,Ryan	(1200 BDC)
	Irvin,Cole	(1000 ADD)	Margevicius,Nick	(0000 AFF)	Graterol,Brusdar	(2300 AFF)	Holland,Derek	(1200 DBC)
	Jurado,Ariel	(1001 ADB)	Patino,Luis	(0200 AFF)	Harper,Ryne	(2200 ADA)	Law,Derek	(1310 ADC)
	Lambert,Peter	(1001 ADD)	Peters,Dillon	(0000 ADD)	Harvey,Hunter	(2310 CFC)	LeBlanc,Wade	(1101 DBA)
	Mengden,Daniel	(1000 CDB)	Plutko,Adam	(0001 ADF)	Holder,Jonathan	(2300 DDA)	Lopez,Jorge	(1101 ACA)
	Milone,Tommy	(1101 DDF)	Reid-Foley,Sean	(0301 ADF)	Jeffress,Jeremy	(2200 DCD)	Lopez,Yoan	(1100 ADD)
	Mize,Casey	(1101 AFF)	Rodriguez,Jefry	(0100 FDA)	Littell,Zack	(2200 ADB)	McCarthy,Kevin	(1000 ADB)
	Montgomery,Mike	(1101 DBA)	Sampson,Adrian	(0001 DCB)	Morrow,Brandon	(2110 FDA)	Pannone,Thomas	(1201 ADB)
	Moore,Matt	(1201 FCC)	Senzatela,Antonio	(0001 CCD)	Perdomo,Luis	(2101 CCB)	Reyes,Alex	(1401 FFF)
	Norris,Daniel	(1201 FCB)	Sparkman,Glenn	(0003 DCB)	Pivetta,Nick	(2301 ACC)	Sadler,Casey	(1000 ADC)
	Perez,Martin	(1103 FAA)	Waguespack,Jacob	(0103 CDA)	Pruitt,Austin	(2100 ADF)	Sims,Lucas	(1400 ADA)
	Ponce de Leon,Daniel	(1200 ADB)	Wojciechowski,Asher	(0101 ADD)	Rainey,Tanner	(2500 AFA)	Stratton,Chris	(1201 DCB)
	Quantrill,Cal	(1101 ADC)	Ynoa,Gabriel	(0000 FDA)	Rodney,Fernando	**(2310 BBB)**	Strickland,Hunter	(1110 FDA)
	Richards,Trevor	(1301 ACB)	Zimmermann,Jordan	(0001 FBB)	Rondon,Hector	(2200 ACB)	Tate,Dillon	(1000 ADB)

SIMULATION LEAGUE DRAFT   TOP 500+

NAME	POS	RAR
Trout,Mike	8	82.4
Yelich,Christian	9	74.1
Betts,Mookie	9	59.9
Freeman,Freddie	3	52.7
Bellinger,Cody	389	51.9
Bregman,Alex	56	50.7
Soto,Juan	7	50.1
Martinez,J.D.	9	49.0
Rendon,Anthony	5	48.4
Arenado,Nolan	5	45.9
Springer,George	89	43.1
Altuve,Jose	4	42.9
Bogaerts,Xander	6	42.7
Harper,Bryce	9	42.4
Acuna,Ronald	789	41.1
Blackmon,Charlie	9	39.9
Gallo,Joey	78	39.8
Marte,Ketel	48	38.6
Judge,Aaron	9	37.5
Story,Trevor	6	36.5
Cruz,Nelson	0	36.2
Alvarez,Yordan	0	35.8
Contreras,Willson	2	34.7
Rizzo,Anthony	3	34.1
deGrom,Jacob	P	33.9
Lindor,Francisco	6	33.9
Goldschmidt,Paul	3	33.8
Ramirez,Jose	5	33.7
Devers,Rafael	5	33.5
Cole,Gerrit	P	32.9
Laureano,Ramon	8	32.5
Albies,Ozzie	4	32.3
LeMahieu,DJ	345	32.3
Realmuto,J.T.	2	32.2
Bryant,Kris	579	32.1
Turner,Justin	5	32.1
Muncy,Max	345	31.0
Tatis Jr.,Fernando	6	30.8
Turner,Trea	6	30.8
Brantley,Michael	7	29.8
Verlander,Justin	P	29.5
Suarez,Eugenio	5	29.1
Jimenez,Eloy	7	29.1
Garver,Mitch	2	29.0
Correa,Carlos	6	29.0
Grandal,Yasmani	23	28.8
Donaldson,Josh	5	28.3
Merrifield,Whit	49	27.7
Bell,Josh	3	27.4
Semien,Marcus	6	27.4
Marte,Starling	8	27.3
Sanchez,Gary	2	27.3
Guerrero Jr.,Vladimir	5	27.0
Torres,Gleyber	46	26.8
McNeil,Jeff	479	26.8
Hiura,Keston	4	26.8
Alonso,Peter	3	26.6
Castellanos,Nick	9	26.3
Chapman,Matt	5	26.2
Schwarber,Kyle	7	26.0
Olson,Matt	3	25.9
Dahl,David	789	25.6
Santana,Carlos	3	25.3

NAME	POS	RAR
Baez,Javier	6	25.1
Flaherty,Jack	P	24.8
Ramos,Wilson	2	24.8
Hoskins,Rhys	3	24.5
Meadows,Austin	79	24.5
Seager,Corey	6	24.1
Bichette,Bo	6	23.8
Buehler,Walker	P	23.6
Conforto,Michael	89	23.5
Scherzer,Max	P	23.1
Greinke,Zack	P	23.0
Winker,Jesse	78	23.0
Reynolds,Bryan	789	22.7
Votto,Joey	3	22.1
Pham,Thomas	7	22.1
Ryu,Hyun-Jin	P	22.1
Kelly,Carson	2	21.7
Snell,Blake	P	21.5
Biggio,Cavan	4	21.2
Soroka,Michael	P	21.0
Bieber,Shane	P	21.0
Mancini,Trey	39	21.0
Strasburg,Stephen	P	20.9
Canha,Mark	89	20.7
Stanton,Giancarlo	7	20.5
Clevinger,Mike	P	20.4
Encarnacion,Edwin	3	20.4
Nimmo,Brandon	78	20.4
Abreu,Jose	3	20.0
Kershaw,Clayton	P	19.8
Verdugo,Alex	789	19.7
Arraez,Luis	47	19.0
Narvaez,Omar	2	18.7
Sano,Miguel	5	18.5
Hendricks,Kyle	P	18.5
Soler,Jorge	9	18.2
Benintendi,Andrew	7	18.1
McCutchen,Andrew	7	17.7
Sale,Chris	P	17.6
Braun,Ryan	7	17.4
Ohtani,Shohei	0	17.0
Dickerson,Corey	7	16.9
Grisham,Trent	8	16.9
Polanco,Jorge	6	16.5
Voit,Luke	3	16.4
Gallen,Zac	P	16.3
Hernandez,Teoscar	78	16.2
Machado,Manny	56	16.2
Moustakas,Mike	45	16.1
Reyes,Franmil	9	16.1
Cain,Lorenzo	8	16.0
Corbin,Patrick	P	16.0
McMahon,Ryan	45	15.8
Molina,Yadier	2	15.8
Choi,Ji-Man	3	15.5
Thames,Eric	3	15.4
Smith,Will	2	15.4
Woodruff,Brandon	P	15.3
Eaton,Adam	9	15.3
Kendrick,Howie	34	15.1
Moncada,Yoan	5	15.0
Pollock,A.J.	8	15.0
Tsutsugo,Yoshitomo	7	14.9

NAME	POS	RAR
Gurriel,Yulieski	35	14.8
Ozuna,Marcell	7	14.5
Kluber,Corey	P	14.5
Rosario,Eddie	7	14.3
Morton,Charlie	P	14.3
Paddack,Chris	P	14.2
Murphy,Daniel	3	14.1
Anderson,Tim	6	13.9
Chirinos,Robinson	2	13.8
Peralta,David	7	13.8
Andujar,Miguel	0	13.4
Davis,J.D.	57	13.3
La Stella,Tommy	45	13.2
Yates,Kirby	P	13.2
Castillo,Luis	P	13.2
Gallegos,Giovanny	P	13.1
Robles,Victor	8	13.0
Mejia,Francisco	2	13.0
Gray,Sonny	P	13.0
Nola,Aaron	P	12.8
Cespedes,Yoenis	0	12.8
Markakis,Nick	9	12.7
Giolito,Lucas	P	12.7
Glasnow,Tyler	P	12.6
Calhoun,Willie	7	12.5
Caratini,Victor	23	12.4
Severino,Luis	P	12.3
Hill,Rich	P	12.3
Profar,Jurickson	4	12.2
Tellez,Rowdy	3	12.2
Lux,Gavin	4	12.2
Puig,Yasiel	9	12.0
Cano,Robinson	4	12.0
Vazquez,Christian	2	11.9
Choo,Shin-Soo	79	11.9
Kepler,Max	89	11.8
Luplow,Jordan	79	11.7
Suzuki,Kurt	2	11.7
Murphy,Sean	2	11.5
Chapman,Aroldis	P	11.5
Jansen,Danny	2	11.4
Osuna,Roberto	P	11.3
Inciarte,Ender	8	11.3
Weaver,Luke	P	11.1
Posey,Buster	2	11.1
Hader,Josh	P	11.0
Syndergaard,Noah	P	11.0
Segura,Jean	6	10.9
DeJong,Paul	6	10.8
Ohtani,Shohei	P	10.7
Adames,Willy	6	10.7
Anderson,Brian	59	10.7
Flores,Wilmer	4	10.6
Lugo,Seth	P	10.5
Escobar,Eduardo	45	10.5
Carpenter,Matt	5	10.4
Cooper,Garrett	39	10.3
D Arnaud,Travis	23	10.3
Mikolas,Miles	P	10.1
Paxton,James	P	10.0
Hernandez,Cesar	4	10.0
Senzel,Nick	8	9.9
McCullers,Lance	P	9.9

NAME	POS	RAR
Martinez,Carlos	P	9.9
Pederson,Joc	379	9.8
Moreland,Mitch	3	9.7
Pressly,Ryan	P	9.7
Castro,Starlin	45	9.6
Giles,Ken	P	9.6
Bummer,Aaron	P	9.5
Petit,Yusmeiro	P	9.5
Gardner,Brett	78	9.4
Rogers,Taylor	P	9.2
Martinez,Jose	9	9.2
Darvish,Yu	P	9.2
Rosario,Amed	6	9.1
McCann,James	2	9.1
Lowe,Nate	3	9.0
Wong,Kolten	4	9.0
Carrasco,Carlos	P	9.0
Barnhart,Tucker	2	9.0
Haniger,Mitch	89	9.0
Bradley,Archie	P	8.9
Alfaro,Jorge	2	8.9
Workman,Brandon	P	8.9
Lowe,Brandon	4	8.9
Villar,Jonathan	46	8.8
Hendriks,Liam	P	8.7
Harris,Will	P	8.7
Vogt,Stephen	2	8.7
Castillo,Diego	P	8.6
Pagan,Emilio	P	8.6
Dozier,Brian	4	8.5
Diaz,Yandy	35	8.5
Berrios,Jose	P	8.4
Betances,Dellin	P	8.3
Upton,Justin	7	8.2
Smith,Will	P	8.2
Hicks,Aaron	8	8.2
McGuire,Reese	2	8.2
Luzardo,Jesus	P	8.2
Lynn,Lance	P	8.0
Neris,Hector	P	8.0
Adell,Jo	7	8.0
Perez,Roberto	2	7.8
Bumgarner,Madison	P	7.7
Kieboom,Carter	6	7.6
Murphy,Tom	2	7.6
Davis,Khris	0	7.5
Frazier,Adam	4	7.5
Renfroe,Hunter	79	7.5
Tauchman,Mike	7	7.5
Green,Chad	P	7.4
Kahnle,Tommy	P	7.4
Maeda,Kenta	P	7.4
Edman,Tommy	45	7.4
Andrus,Elvis	6	7.4
Zimmerman,Ryan	3	7.3
Stripling,Ross	P	7.3
Ford,Mike	3	7.3
Robles,Hansel	P	7.2
Wheeler,Zack	P	7.2
Desmond,Ian	78	7.2
Swanson,Dansby	6	7.2
Buxton,Byron	8	7.2
Price,David	P	7.2

SIMULATION LEAGUE DRAFT   TOP 500+

NAME	POS	RAR	NAME	POS	RAR	NAME	POS	RAR	NAME	POS	RAR
Aguilar,Jesus	3	7.0	Cabrera,Asdrubal	45	4.4	Gray,Jonathan	P	2.4	German,Domingo	P	1.0
Mazara,Nomar	9	7.0	Montero,Rafael	P	4.4	Odor,Rougned	4	2.4	Quinn,Roman	8	1.0
Goodrum,Niko	467	6.5	Leclerc,Jose	P	4.4	Haseley,Adam	78	2.4	Barreto,Franklin	4	1.0
Camargo,Johan	6	6.5	Stroman,Marcus	P	4.4	Wittgren,Nick	P	2.3	Beckham,Tim	6	1.0
Montgomery,Jordan	P	6.5	Fraley,Jake	8	4.4	Dean,Austin	7	2.3	Tepera,Ryan	P	1.0
Castro,Jason	2	6.5	Barnes,Matt	P	4.4	Lucroy,Jonathan	2	2.2	Bedrosian,Cam	P	0.9
Hand,Brad	P	6.4	Dobnak,Randy	P	4.4	James,Josh	P	2.2	Lamb,Jacob	35	0.9
Martin,Christopher	P	6.3	Peacock,Brad	P	4.3	Matz,Steven	P	2.1	Kipnis,Jason	4	0.9
Gomes,Yan	2	6.3	Odorizzi,Jake	P	4.2	Miller,Andrew	P	2.1	Graterol,Brusdar	P	0.9
Anderson,Nick	P	6.3	Yarbrough,Ryan	P	4.2	Tanaka,Masahiro	P	2.1	Polanco,Gregory	9	0.9
Kela,Keone	P	6.2	Kittredge,Andrew	P	4.2	Magill,Matthew	P	2.1	Goodwin,Brian	78	0.9
Astudillo,Williams	2	6.2	Iglesias,Raisel	P	4.2	Manning,Matt	P	2.0	Trivino,Lou	P	0.8
Taylor,Chris	467	6.2	Garcia,Avisail	9	4.1	Keuchel,Dallas	P	2.0	Kopech,Michael	P	0.8
Belt,Brandon	3	6.2	McHugh,Collin	P	4.1	Robertson,David	P	1.9	Ramirez,Harold	789	0.8
Walker,Christian	3	6.1	VanMeter,Josh	7	4.0	Wood,Hunter	P	1.9	Berti,Jon	568	0.8
Urias,Julio	P	6.1	Bauer,Trevor	P	4.0	Kelly,Joe	P	1.9	Whitley,Forrest	P	0.8
Hampson,Garrett	48	6.1	Smith,Dominic	37	4.0	Lucchesi,Joey	P	1.9	Salazar,Danny	P	0.8
Rodriguez,Eduardo	P	6.1	Vargas,Ildemaro	4	3.9	Wood,Alex	P	1.8	Fulmer,Michael	P	0.8
Flowers,Tyler	2	6.0	Grichuk,Randal	89	3.9	Taylor,Josh	P	1.8	Ahmed,Nick	6	0.8
Hudson,Dakota	P	6.0	Strahm,Matt	P	3.8	Smoak,Justin	3	1.8	Vizcaino,Arodys	P	0.8
Clase,Emmanuel	P	6.0	Gonsolin,Tony	P	3.8	Gurriel,Lourdes	7	1.7	Ferguson,Caleb	P	0.7
Manaea,Sean	P	6.0	Kennedy,Ian	P	3.8	Givens,Mychal	P	1.7	Suter,Brent	P	0.7
Wick,Rowan	P	5.9	Vazquez,Felipe	P	3.7	Ponce de Leon,Daniel	P	1.7	Hirano,Yoshihisa	P	0.7
McKay,Brendan	P	5.8	Gonzalez,Marwin	359	3.7	Jeffress,Jeremy	P	1.7	Frazier,Clint	9	0.7
Carlson,Dylan	7	5.8	Pillar,Kevin	89	3.7	Cueto,Johnny	P	1.7	Rogers,Jake	2	0.6
Munoz,Andres	P	5.7	Ginkel,Kevin	P	3.7	Newman,Kevin	46	1.7	Fowler,Dexter	89	0.6
Gennett,Scooter	4	5.7	Shoemaker,Matthew	P	3.7	Suarez,Ranger	P	1.6	Familia,Jeurys	P	0.6
Wieters,Matt	2	5.7	Newcomb,Sean	P	3.6	Romo,Sergio	P	1.6	Heyward,Jason	89	0.5
Melancon,Mark	P	5.7	Wilson,Justin	P	3.6	Brosseau,Michael	4	1.6	Morrow,Brandon	P	0.5
Lamet,Dinelson	P	5.6	Myers,Wil	78	3.6	Aquino,Aristides	9	1.6	Alonso,Yonder	3	0.5
Fernandez,Junior	P	5.6	Duffey,Tyler	P	3.6	Floro,Dylan	P	1.6	O Neill,Tyler	7	0.5
Cordero,Franchy	8	5.5	Hughes,Jared	P	3.5	Reddick,Josh	79	1.6	Smith,Mallex	89	0.5
Diaz,Edwin	P	5.5	Tuivailala,Sam	P	3.5	Sanchez,Sixto	P	1.6	Cron,Kevin	3	0.5
Britton,Zach	P	5.4	Lorenzen,Michael	P	3.5	Bass,Anthony	P	1.6	Diaz,Jairo	P	0.5
Hernandez,Enrique	48	5.4	Dietrich,Derek	34	3.5	Solak,Nick	5	1.5	Healy,Ryon	5	0.5
Simmons,Andrelton	6	5.4	Santana,Domingo	79	3.4	Kelley,Shawn	P	1.5	Urquidy,Jose	P	0.5
Mercado,Oscar	78	5.3	Buttrey,Ty	P	3.4	Hamels,Cole	P	1.5	Barnes,Austin	2	0.4
Cishek,Steve	P	5.3	Jackson,Luke	P	3.3	Mahle,Tyler	P	1.5	Taillon,Jameson	P	0.4
Bradley,Jackie	8	5.2	Knebel,Corey	P	3.3	Dyson,Sam	P	1.5	Strop,Pedro	P	0.4
May,Trevor	P	5.2	Ottavino,Adam	P	3.2	Clippard,Tyler	P	1.5	Slater,Austin	9	0.3
Kolarek,Adam	P	5.2	Sisco,Chance	2	3.2	Hicks,Jordan	P	1.5	Pence,Hunter	0	0.3
Schoop,Jonathan	4	5.2	Treinen,Blake	P	3.2	Civale,Aaron	P	1.5	Garcia,Yimi	P	0.3
Cave,Jake	89	5.2	Riley,Austin	7	3.1	Chirinos,Yonny	P	1.5	Gausman,Kevin	P	0.3
Jansen,Kenley	P	5.2	Dozier,Hunter	59	3.1	Hays,Austin	8	1.5	Gonzalez,Gio	P	0.2
Dickerson,Alex	7	5.1	Kimbrel,Craig	P	3.0	Jimenez,Joe	P	1.4	Poche,Colin	P	0.2
Stammen,Craig	P	5.1	Dominguez,Seranthony	P	2.9	Foltynewicz,Mike	P	1.4	Miller,Brad	5	0.2
Cron,C.J.	3	5.0	Baez,Pedro	P	2.9	Feliz,Michael	P	1.4	Osuna,Jose	39	0.2
Bohm,Alec	5	4.9	Soria,Joakim	P	2.9	Rodriguez,Richard	P	1.3	Arozarena,Randy	9	0.2
Smith,Joe	P	4.9	Romine,Austin	2	2.9	Yastrzemski,Mike	79	1.3	Rojas,Miguel	6	0.2
Fried,Max	P	4.8	Doolittle,Sean	P	2.9	Reyes,Victor	78	1.3	Gregorius,Didi	6	0.2
Happ,Ian	7	4.8	Stallings,Jacob	2	2.8	Wingenter,Trey	P	1.2	Estevez,Carlos	P	0.2
Kingery,Scott	58	4.8	Mondesi,Adalberto	6	2.8	Herrera,Odubel	8	1.2	Ryan,Kyle	P	0.2
Brebbia,John	P	4.7	Naylor,Josh	79	2.8	Hill,Tim	P	1.2	Kiner-Falefa,Isiah	25	0.1
Oberg,Scott	P	4.7	Stephenson,Robert	P	2.7	Littell,Zack	P	1.2	Chatwood,Tyler	P	0.1
Vogelbach,Daniel	3	4.7	Tapia,Raimel	7	2.7	Suero,Wander	P	1.2	Margot,Manuel	8	0.1
Greene,Shane	P	4.7	Urshela,Giovanny	5	2.7	Minter,A.J.	P	1.2	Swanson,Erik	P	0.1
Alvarado,Jose	P	4.7	Middleton,Keynan	P	2.7	Maybin,Cameron	79	1.2	Jones,JaCoby	8	0.1
May,Dustin	P	4.6	Puk,A.J.	P	2.7	Seager,Kyle	5	1.1	Diaz,Elias	2	0.0
Colome,Alex	P	4.6	Severino,Pedro	2	2.6	Richards,Garrett	P	1.1	Hicks,John	23	0.0
Stanek,Ryne	P	4.5	Holt,Brock	4	2.5	Hudson,Daniel	P	1.1	Marisnick,Jake	8	0.0
Chafin,Andrew	P	4.5	Pomeranz,Drew	P	2.5	France,Ty	45	1.1	Urias,Luis	46	0.0
Montas,Frankie	P	4.5	Longoria,Evan	5	2.4	Bader,Harrison	8	1.1			
Cabrera,Miguel	3	4.4	Adams,Austin L	P	2.4	Duvall,Adam	7	1.0			

Spring Training just got better.

Introducing...

Join us in St. Petersburg, Florida from **February 28 through March 1, 2020** for two and a half days filled with baseball chatter and events, all aimed at preparing you for the 2020 season!

Modeled after our wildly popular First Pitch Arizona event, First Pitch Florida will feature:

- Interactive sessions on topics like player analysis, breakout picks and injury warning signs
- Gaming strategies for auctions and drafts, including current ADP feedback
- Live drafts where you can complete against your peers
- Tickets to two spring training games—with a group of the friendliest, most passionate fantasy baseball fans around—just like you!

In addition, First Pitch Florida welcomes the granddaddy of expert leagues, USA TODAY's League of Alternative Baseball Reality (LABR)! Attendees will be able to take in both 12-team AL and 12-team NL auctions live and we'll break 'em down afterwards!

Details about specific panels, speakers, program schedule, Grapefruit League games and more will be updated throughout the next several months at the link below. Register NOW!

www.baseballhq.com/first-pitch-florida

*Save the date: **First Pitch Arizona** in Phoenix at the Arizona Fall League • October 8-11, 2020*

Get Forecaster Insights
Every Single Day.

The **Baseball Forecaster** provides the core concepts in player evaluation and gaming strategy. You can maintain that edge all season long.

From spring training to the season's last pitch, **BaseballHQ.com** covers all aspects of what's happening on and off the field—all with the most powerful fantasy slant on the Internet:

- Nationally-renowned baseball analysts.
- MLB news analysis; including anticipating the **next** move.
- Dedicated columns on starting pitching, relievers, batters, and our popular Fact or Fluke? player profiles.
- Minor-league coverage beyond just scouting and lists.
- FAAB targets, starting pitcher reports, strategy articles, daily game resources, call-up profiles and more!

Plus, **BaseballHQ.com** gets personal, with customizable tools and valuable resources:

- Team Stat Tracker and Power Search tools
- Custom Draft Guide for YOUR league's parameters
- Sortable and downloadable stats and projection files
- Subscriber forums, the friendliest on the baseball Internet

Visit **www.baseballhq.com/subscribe**
to lock down your path to a 2020 championship!

Full Season subscription **$89**
(prorated at the time of order; auto-renews each October)

Draft Prep subscription **$39**
(complete access from January through April 30, 2020)

Please read our Terms of service at www.baseballhq.com/terms.html

Baseball Forecaster & BaseballHQ.com:
Your season-long championship lineup.

2020 CHEATER'S BOOKMARK

BATTING STATISTICS

Abbrv	Term	Formula / Desc.	BAD UNDER	'19 LG AVG AL	'19 LG AVG NL	BEST OVER
Avg	Batting Average	h/ab	235	254	259	280
xBA	Expected Batting Average	See glossary		253	259	
OB	On Base Average	(h+bb)/(ab+bb)	290	319	326	350
Slg	Slugging Average	total bases/ab	370	440	446	500
OPS	On Base plus Slugging	OB+Slg	660	759	772	850
bb%	Walk Rate	bb/(ab+bb)	6%	9%	9%	10%
ct%	Contact Rate	(ab-k) / ab	73%	74%	75%	83%
Eye	Batting Eye	bb/k	0.30	0.37	0.40	0.50
PX	Power Index	Normalized power skills	80	100	100	120
Spd	Speed Score	Normalized speed skills	80	100	100	120
SBO	Stolen Base Opportunity %	(sb+cs)/(singles+bb)		8%	7%	
G/F	Groundball/Flyball Ratio	gb / fb		1.2	1.2	
G	Ground Ball Per Cent	gb / balls in play		42%	43%	
L	Line Drive Per Cent	ld / balls in play		21%	22%	
F	Fly Ball Per Cent	fb / balls in play		36%	35%	
BPV	Base Performance Value	See glossary	20	27	32	55
PRO	Percentage Ratio Outcome	See glossary	-37%	-18%	-18%	-17%
RC/G	Runs Created per Game	See glossary	3.00	5.22	4.49	6.00
RAR	Runs Above Replacement	See glossary	0.0			10.0

Batting statistics do not include pitchers' batting statistics

PITCHING STATISTICS

Abbrv	Term	Formula / Desc.	BAD OVER	'19 LG AVG AL	'19 LG AVG NL	BEST UNDER
ERA	Earned Run Average	er*9/ip	5.00	4.62	4.39	3.10
xERA	Expected ERA	See glossary		3.94	3.82	
WHIP	Baserunners per Inning	(h+bb)/ip	1.45	1.35	1.32	1.15
BF/G	Batters Faced per Game		28.0			
PC	Pitch Counts per Start		120	84	89	
OBA	Opposition Batting Avg	Opp. h/ab	270	255	250	220
OOB	Opposition On Base Avg	Opp. (h+bb)/(ab+bb)	340	319	316	285
BABIP	BatAvg on balls in play	(h-hr)/(BatFaced-(bb+hbp+sac))+h-k-hr		298	295	
Ctl	Control Rate	bb*9/ip		3.3	3.3	2.5
Ball%	Ball Percentage	balls/total pitches	38%	36%	36%	34%
hr/9	Homerun Rate	hr*9/ip		1.4	1.4	1.2
hr/f	Homerun per Fly ball	hr/fb		15%	15%	
S%	Strand Rate	(h+bb-er)/(h+bb-hr)		70%	71%	
DIS%	PQS Disaster Rate	% GS that are PQS 0/1		39%	33%	15%

Abbrv	Term	Formula / Desc.	BAD UNDER	'19 LG AVG AL	'19 LG AVG NL	BEST OVER
RAR	Runs Above Replacement	See glossary	-0.0			+10
Dom	Dominance Rate	k*9/ip		8.8	8.9	10.5
Cmd	Command Ratio	k/bb		2.7	2.7	3.5
G/F	Groundball/Flyball Ratio	gb / fb		1.16	1.24	
SwK	Swinging Strike Percentage	swinging strikes/pitches		11.5%	11.7%	13.0%
FpK	First Pitch Strike Percentage	first pitch strikes/batters		61%	61%	64%
BPV	Base Performance Value	See glossary	50	90	93	100
PRO	Percentage Ratio Outcome	See glossary	7%	18%	18%	27%
DOM%	PQS Dominance Rate	% GS that are PQS 4/5		19%	22%	50%
Sv%	Saves Conversion Rate	(saves / save opps)		64%	63%	80%
REff%	Relief Effectiveness Rate	See glossary		66%	66%	80%

NOTES